THE PERIMETER

To my parents, Susan and John, for showing me the path.

HUTCHINSON HEINEMANN

UK | USA | Canada | Ireland | Australia
India | New Zealand | South Africa

Hutchinson Heinemann is part of the Penguin Random House group of companies whose addresses can be found at global.penguinrandomhouse.com

Penguin Random House UK,
One Embassy Gardens, 8 Viaduct Gardens, London SW11 7BW

penguin.co.uk
global.penguinrandomhouse.com

Penguin Random House UK

First published 2025
001

Designed by Clare Skeats

Map illustrations by BARNEBY *design & art direction*

Printed and bound in China by C&C Offset Printing Co., Ltd

The authorised representative in the EEA is Penguin Random House Ireland, Morrison Chambers, 32 Nassau Street, Dublin D02 YH68

A CIP catalogue record for this book is available from the British Library

ISBN: 978–1–529–15445–0

THE PERIMETER

A Photographic Journey around the Coast of Britain

QUINTIN LAKE

HUTCHINSON
HEINEMANN

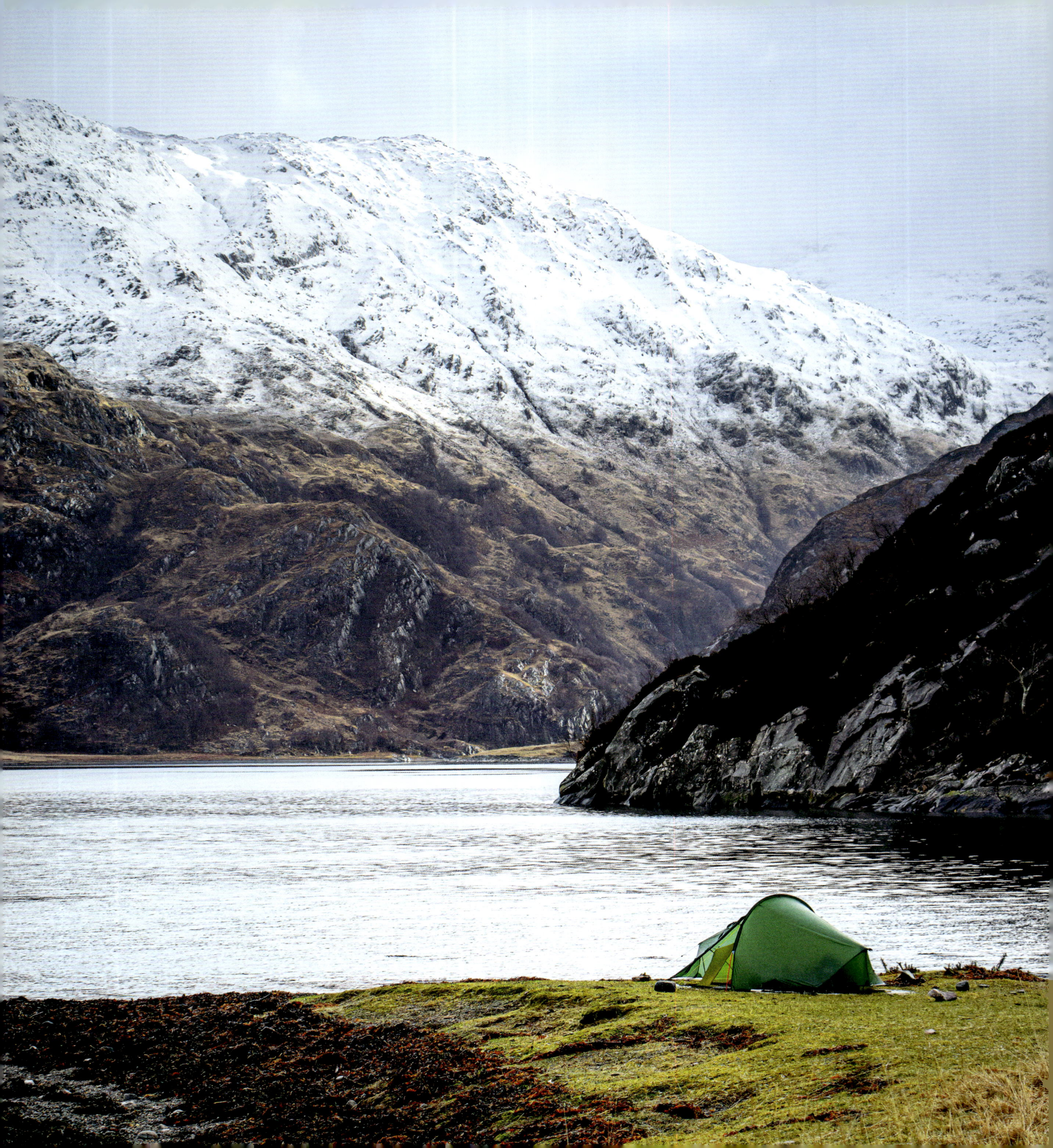

CONTENTS

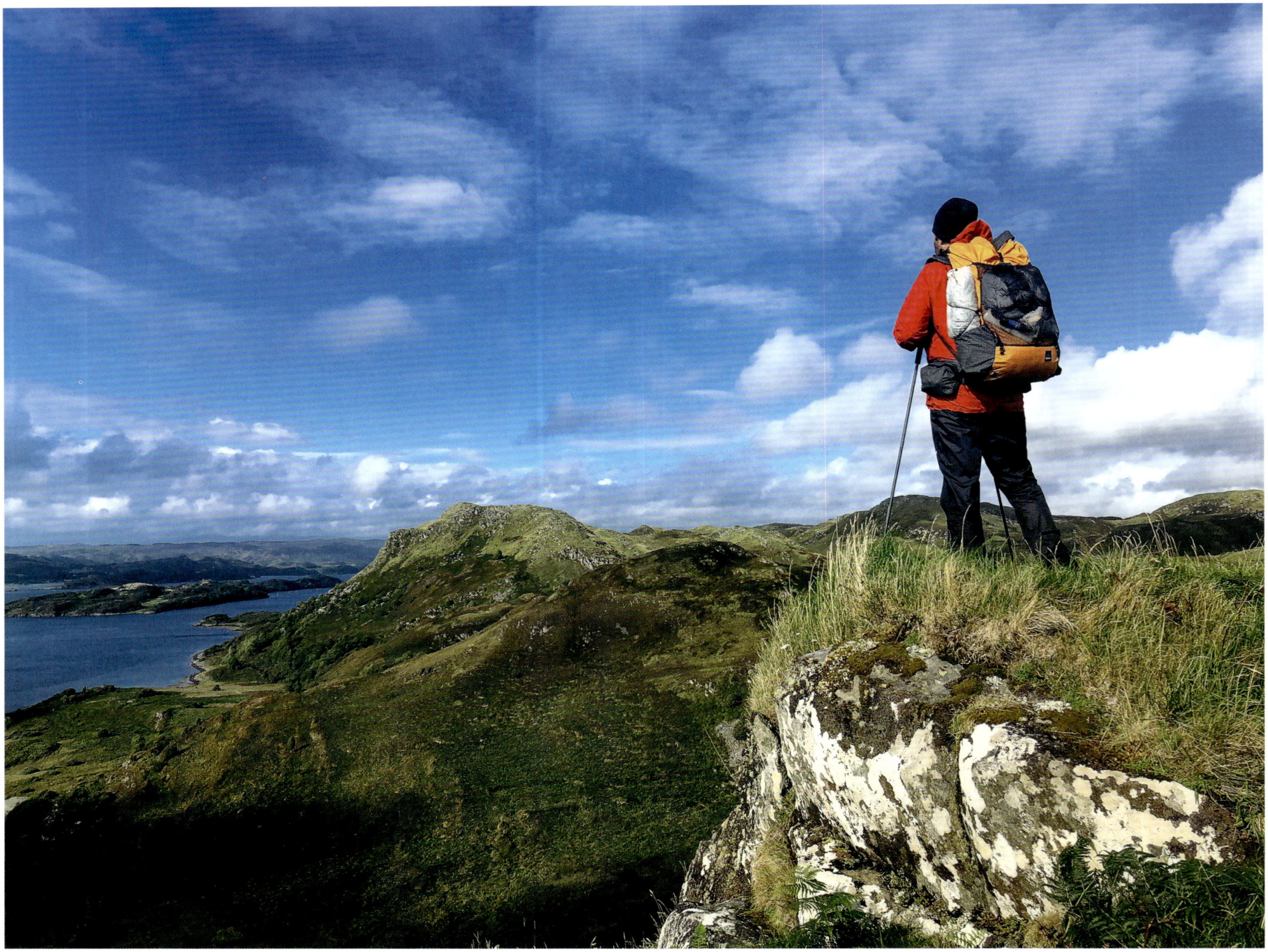
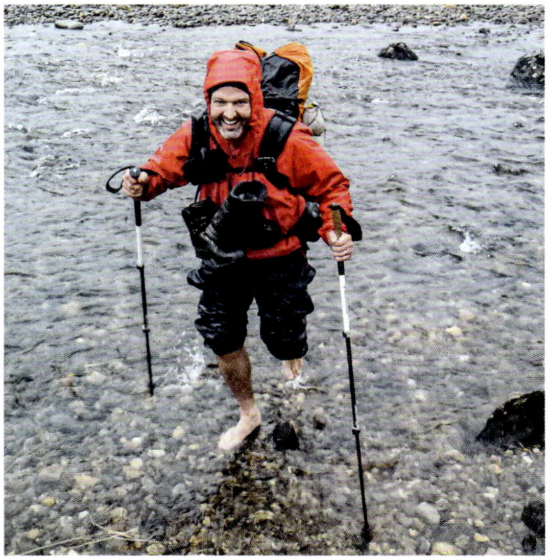
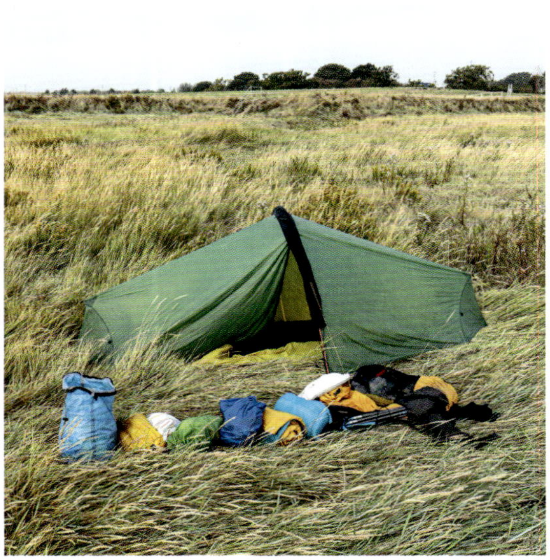
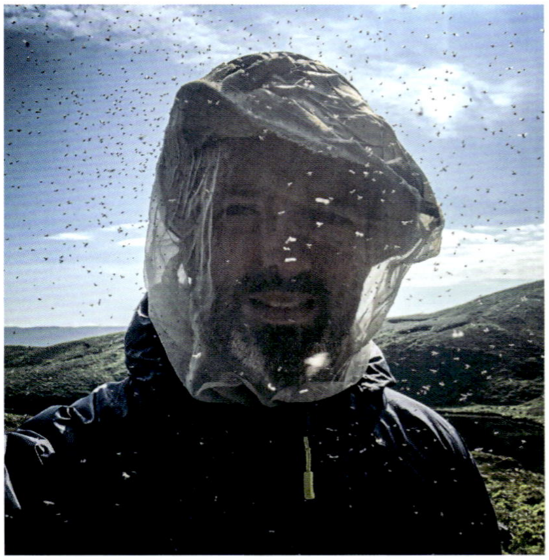

INTRODUCTION

'Travelers, there is no path; paths are made by walking.'
– ANTONIO MACHADO

Previous:

Camp at Runival by Loch Hourn, Knoydart, Scotland

Opposite, from top left:

Day 235: Contemplating which route to take through the wild landscape between Crinan and Ardfern, Scotland. Deer make the only paths through here. August 2018

Day 272: Fording the River Carnach into Knoydart as the bridge had washed away, Scotland. March, 2019

Day 451: Packing up the camping kit for the last time on the journey at Stanford-le-Hope Marshes, Essex, England. September 2020

Day 214: Swarmed by midges at camp by the Kyles of Bute, Scotland. The biggest difficulty is trying to eat in these conditions. June 2018

Long-distance walking has been a part of my life since I was ten, when my mum decided we should walk 480 kilometres from John o'Groats to Glasgow over the summer holidays. Despite never having done it before, walking every day immediately felt natural and I was thrilled by the adventure of being immersed in nature and enduring. After a long day by Loch Lomond, we spent the night sitting on the path under a silver survival blanket as we had no torch to reach our destination. Crouched beneath the crinkly cover, surrounded by the sounds of unseen animals in the pitch-black woodland, I wasn't fearful – I was happy.

By the time I was twenty, I'd learnt the art of backpacking and had walked from Land's End back to John o'Groats, a journey of 1,677 kilometres that I undertook alone in the winter, sleeping in a bivvy bag. In the following years, I would travel further afield. As a photographer, my job involved capturing new landscapes, from the Arctic ice cap to the jungles of Borneo. Drawn to the wild and exotic corners of the world, I would come to visit over seventy countries. Still, every year I returned to Britain, where I found myself combining backpacking and photography – my two favourite pursuits. And it turned out there was as much beauty and inspiration to be found in the British countryside as there was abroad. Gradually, I started taking on ever-more challenges, from walking the Southern Upland Way to the Cambrian Way, and producing photo series of each of my adventures. That is, until I contracted meningitis, which left me barely able to walk down the street without needing rest.

The idea to walk the entirety of Britain's coast was born in 2014 as I slowly recovered. Being on bed rest, I craved the outdoors, and as soon as I got well enough, I planned a walk along the Thames, from its trickling source at Kemble in Gloucestershire to the Houses of Parliament in Westminster. Then, I walked along Britain's longest river, the Severn, from the source to the sea. It was the first time I'd traversed a coastal area with my camera in hand and I was captivated by the stark contrast between nuclear power stations and pylons sat against a backdrop of vast expanses of tidal sands. I grew hungry to discover more of the coast, to capture this inspiring in-between world that was neither land nor sea. Why not walk the whole thing?

A few weeks later, I registered a home for the project at theperimeter.uk. I was determined to trek the coast of the British mainland as a means to producing a body of photographic work that would get under the surface of the landscape. I wanted to understand better the island nation that I call home and to share with others my discoveries along the way.

So, over the course of 454 days within the next five years, I walked 11,000 kilometres around the mainland coast of Britain in one-week to two-month sections. Armed with hiking and photography gear that weighed anywhere from 10 kilos in the summer to 24 kilos in the winter, I put one foot after the other, following paths along the coast and detouring inland only where necessary or to ascend the highest summits of England, Wales and Scotland (Scafell Pike, Snowdon / Yr Wyddfa and Ben Nevis). In Scotland, where there were often no footpaths at all, I forged my own way, clambering over rocks and backtracking repeatedly when the ground got too steep or the vegetation too dense.

With my camping gear, power banks, food and camera, I was fully self-sufficient and walked an average of 25 kilometres a day, sleeping in a tent to stay connected to the landscape. Most days ended with a litany of aches and pains as I refused any form of vehicle or mechanised assistance. But gradually, I began to adapt and accept the things beyond my control – like sore muscles, blisters, and bruising from backpack straps. In the Knoydart Peninsula on the west coast of Scotland, each evening I poured water out of my boots and peeled off wet clothes before curling up in a sleeping bag in the sanctuary of my tent. Later, when I developed overuse injuries that would take weeks to recover from, it was my curiosity about the people, landscape and history of what lay ahead that kept me going.

Over the course of five years of walking and three years of editing, I took 179,222 images, subsequently culled to 12,000 favourites, of which over 1,300 have been curated for this book. True to my experience, the finished project is organised by fifty-three chapters based on historic counties in the order that I walked them, starting in London from the steps of St Paul's Cathedral on Friday 17 April 2015 and travelling clockwise. To capture the geographic scale of the coast, the length of each chapter varies depending on the distance I covered, so there is more content from longer counties like South Argyllshire, which has a coastline of 857 kilometres, and less from smaller counties like Midlothian, which has a coastline of 36 kilometres. Counties with two non-contiguous coastlines, such as Devon, are separated into South and North, and each has its own chapter.

Overall, the counties are grouped into five national sections – South England, Wales, North-West England, Scotland and East England – and a map is provided for orientation at the start of each. Throughout Wales and Scotland, historic county boundaries and naming conventions have been used as these regions are more similarly sized in contrast to modern counties (which can be highly fragmented in urban areas and cover enormous regions in less populated areas). For readers who'd like more detail on how I chose which conventions to follow, please see page 9.

Walking is the best technique I know to open the heart and mind, and photography is how I express myself. Each photograph in this collection is more than a visual record; it is a moment of compositional harmony, a sense of place, and a story. The accompanying text I hope provides a fuller sense of my journey. When I first started blogging, I naively felt I could communicate everything I wanted to say with photography. Quickly, I realised there were only so many novel experiences that could be expressed through images, so in addition to the photos, each chapter contains stories from my journal: about the people I met and the injuries I overcame, the difficulties of wild camping and the oddities that brought a smile to my face. To this day, a toaster mounted on the top of a fence post in Suffolk still leaves me scratching my head.

The built-up areas of Britain consist of only 6 per cent of the total country, and as I walked away from London, the sense of the urban was sloughed off in a single day. Walking across the rolling grass above the chalk cliffs of the Seven Sisters in East Sussex felt like flying over the sea, and by the time I got to the coast in Devon, dramatic cliffs became the norm; in Cornwall the coast path is so vertiginous it often involves hundreds of metres of daily ascent.

Soon, distinct themes began to emerge. Infrastructure captured my attention first – pylons, chemical works, bridges and factories often appeared bizarrely out of place against the natural backdrop of the coastline, creating a striking contrast. The Welsh coast path was consistently fascinating – plumes of steam rising from the Port Talbot steelworks were as jaw-dropping as the stunning Worms Head on the Gower Peninsula. At Barmouth, the rail bridge runs like a zip across the landscape, with Cadair Idris and the surrounding mountains behind – the natural and the man-made in perfect harmony.

Then there were the challenges of coastal photography – navigating harsh weather, capturing fleeting light, and conveying the essence of an ever-changing seascape. Bad weather was captivating: the sky would turn an inky black, or a fleeting glimmer of light would illuminate a subject against a grey backdrop, creating dramatic and compelling images. As I approached Eilean Donan Castle from Loch Duich, the intervals of rain and golden sunlight were so rapid that I could create images that appeared to be from opposing seasons separated by a few seconds.

Almost half my journey – some 200 days – took place in Scotland, and this was a completely distinct experience, as the right to wild-camp and walk anywhere gave me a sense of belonging that I never felt in England. Physically, the walking in Scotland was far more challenging: the lack of paths meant that crossing the mountainous landscape required more initiative.

Britain is a small island with a vast coastline. What follows is a chronicle of my adventures along its perimeter, from my battle with midges to stress fractures, to discovering the differences between a Welsh oggie and a Cornish pasty and clambering up cliffs to escape a rising tide. So join me in exploring Britain as you've never seen it before, for five years and across all four seasons, through heatwaves and a pandemic, from charming seaside towns such as Tenby in Pembrokeshire to the desert landscape of Dungeness in Kent, the (now vanished) steelworks of Teesside and the beautiful desolation of Scotland's Cape Wrath.

A CONFECTION OF COUNTIES

When planning my journey, I needed to subdivide it into manageable chunks as the overall distance was too vast to contemplate. It seemed obvious to break it down into counties until I discovered that modern counties cover enormous areas on the one hand – such as Highland, which would take months to walk around – in contrast to the highly fragmented metropolitan counties, such as Liverpool, which can be walked through in hours. It soon became apparent that historic counties were far more geographically comparable in size and often better approximating geological and cultural divisions. But even here, confusion still abounds as many historic county boundaries have shifted in border and nomenclature over the ages.

The county divisions I chose weren't just of academic interest; they influenced how I perceived the island of Britain, both when walking and creating the photographs and subsequently when curating a set of pictures that form a visual poem to represent the specificity of each county. The historic counties gave me a hook on which to hang a collection of images and observations. On the ground, I discovered they often accurately mark a difference to their neighbouring county, be that cultural or geographical.

As a result, the map I created for the project is a confection of counties – the Ceremonial Counties of England, the Preserved Counties of Wales, and the Shires of Scotland – a combination that, to the best of my ability, represents the history and geography of each country. To make things even easier, I occasionally merged counties for clarity, as outlined below.

For England, I used the Ceremonial Counties in use from 1974 to 1996, which in many cases follow the historic counties of England that were established for administration by the Normans, often based on earlier kingdoms and shires created by the Angles, Saxons, Jutes, Celts and others. I merged West and East Sussex into Sussex for Chapter 3 and removed Cleveland, as it only existed as a county between 1974 and 1996. Chapter 16 – Merseyside – contains a few kilometres of Chester, mainly along the River Dee.

For Wales, I used the Preserved Counties (Welsh: *siroedd cadwedig*) that were utilised for local government and other purposes between 1974 and 1996 rather than the Historic Counties that preceded them, as the latter contained anglicised naming conventions. I merged Mid, South and West Glamorgan into Glamorgan for Chapter 12.

For Scotland, I used the Shires of Scotland, which were established in the Middle Ages and used as administrative divisions until 1975. An unfortunate downside of this choice is the prevalence of the anglicised 'shire' in many of the Scottish counties, and for this I apologise to my Scottish readers.

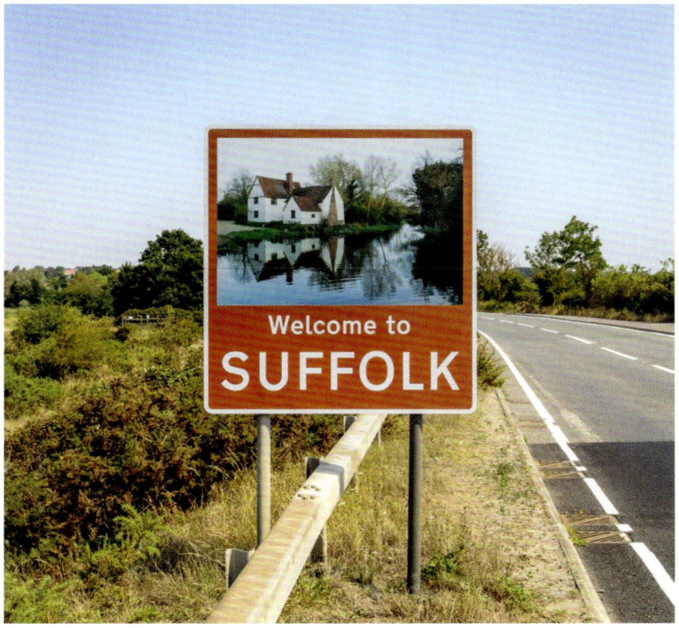

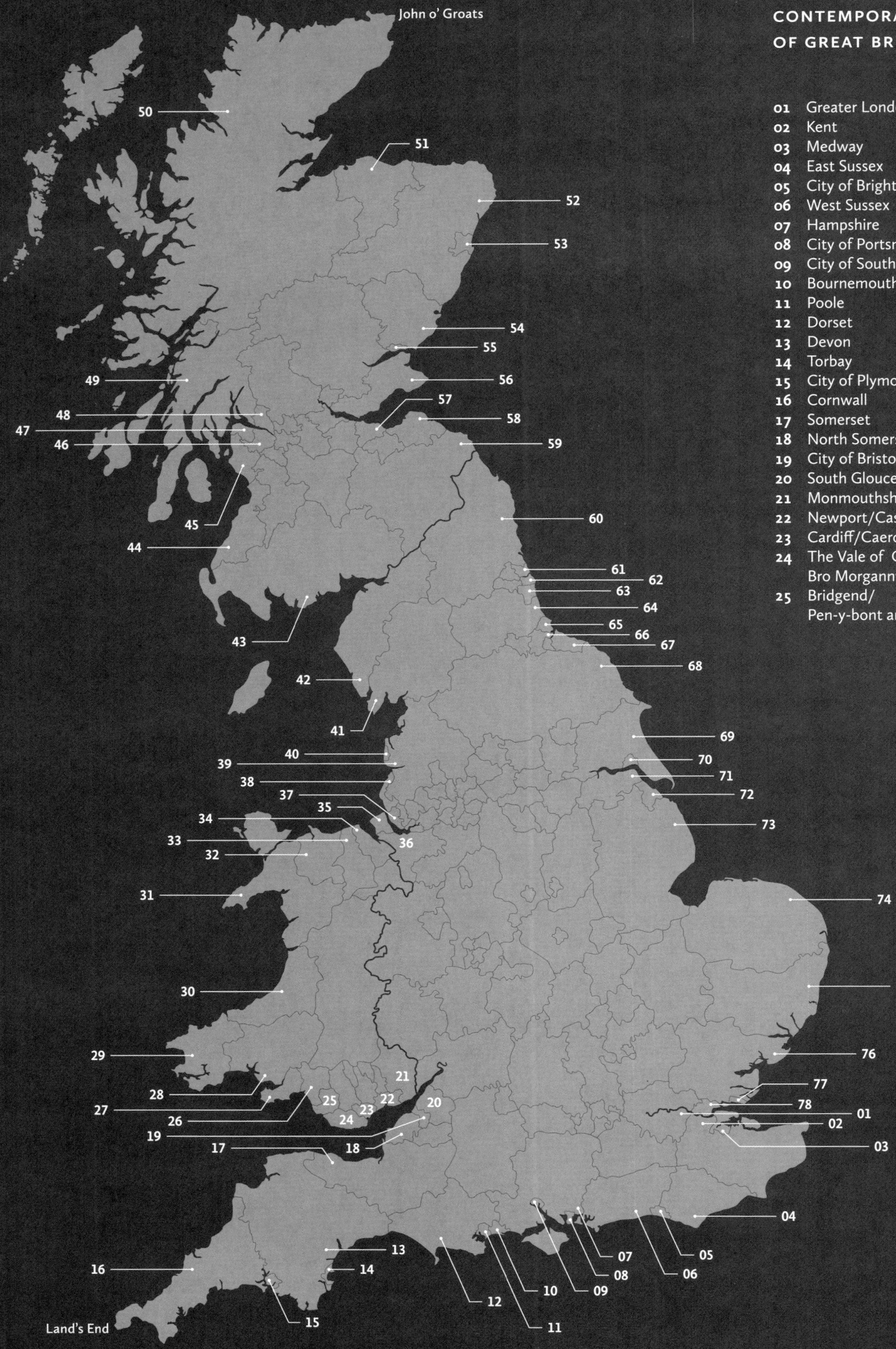

CONTEMPORARY ADMINISTRATIVE COUNTIES OF GREAT BRITAIN

01 Greater London Authority
02 Kent
03 Medway
04 East Sussex
05 City of Brighton and Hove
06 West Sussex
07 Hampshire
08 City of Portsmouth
09 City of Southampton
10 Bournemouth
11 Poole
12 Dorset
13 Devon
14 Torbay
15 City of Plymouth
16 Cornwall
17 Somerset
18 North Somerset
19 City of Bristol
20 South Gloucestershire
21 Monmouthshire/Sir Fynwy
22 Newport/Casnewydd
23 Cardiff/Caerdydd
24 The Vale of Glamorgan/ Bro Morgannwg
25 Bridgend/ Pen-y-bont ar Ogwr
26 Neath Port Talbot/ Castell-nedd Port Talbot
27 Swansea/Abertawe
28 Carmarthenshire/ Sir Gaerfyrddin
29 Pembrokeshire/Sir Benfro
30 Ceredigion/Sir Ceredigion
31 Gwynedd
32 Conwy
33 Denbighshire/ Sir Ddinbych
34 Flintshire/Sir Y Fflint
35 Wirral
36 Cheshire West and Chester
37 Liverpool
38 Sefton
39 Lancashire
40 Blackpool
41 Westmorland and Furness
42 Cumberland
43 Dumfries and Galloway
44 South Ayrshire
45 North Ayrshire
46 Renfrewshire
47 Inverclyde
48 West Dunbartonshire
49 Argyll and Bute
50 Highland
51 Moray
52 Aberdeenshire
53 Aberdeen City
54 Angus
55 Dundee City
56 Fife
57 City of Edinburgh
58 East Lothian
59 Scottish Borders
60 Northumberland
61 North Tyneside
62 South Tyneside
63 Sunderland
64 County Durham
65 Hartlepool
66 Stockton-on-Tees
67 Redcar and Cleveland
68 North Yorkshire
69 East Riding of Yorkshire
70 City of Kingston upon Hull
71 North Lincolnshire
72 North East Lincolnshire
73 Lincolnshire
74 Norfolk
75 Suffolk
76 Essex
77 Southend-on-Sea
78 Thurrock

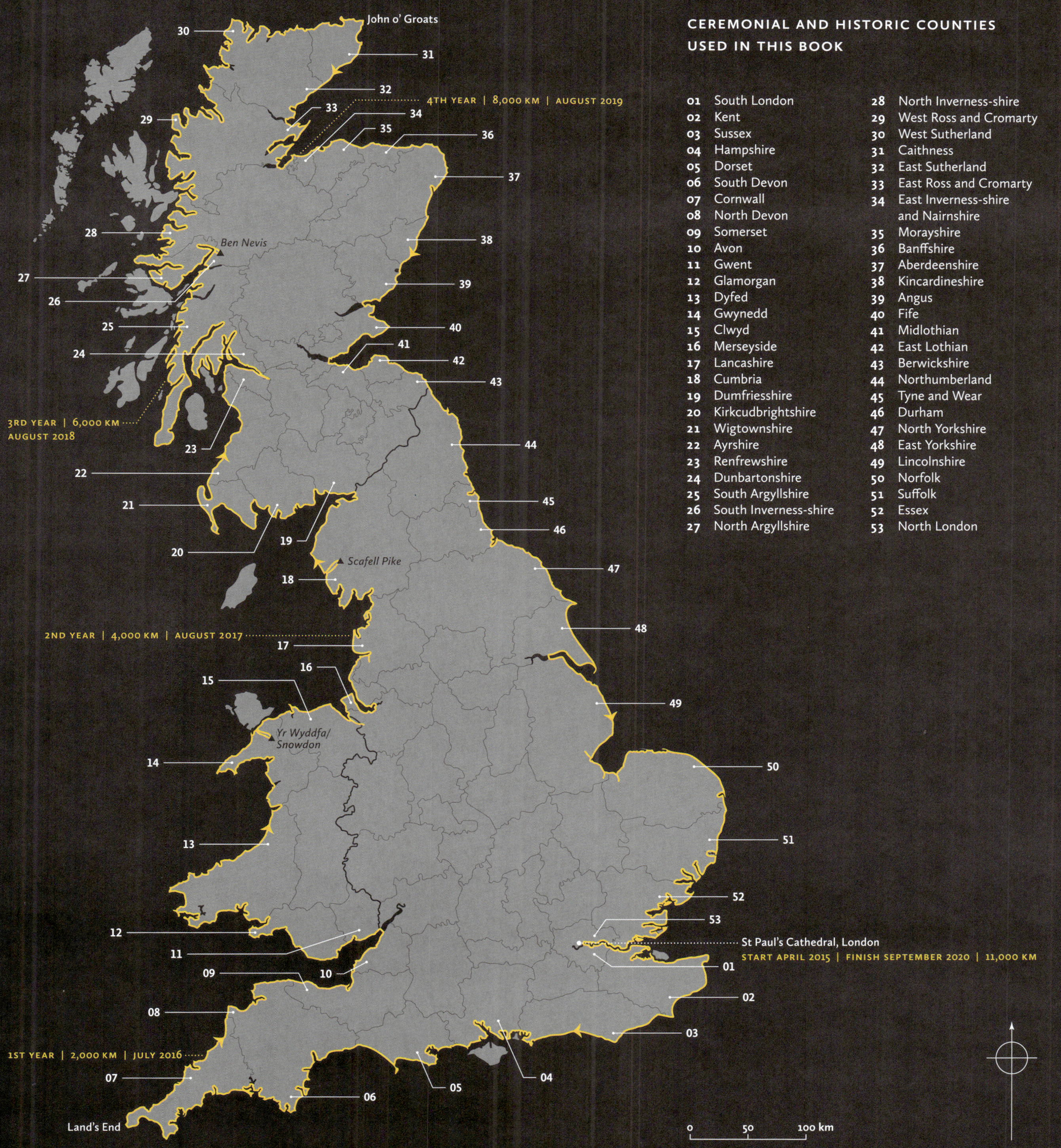
CEREMONIAL AND HISTORIC COUNTIES USED IN THIS BOOK
01 South London
02 Kent
03 Sussex
04 Hampshire
05 Dorset
06 South Devon
07 Cornwall
08 North Devon
09 Somerset
10 Avon
11 Gwent
12 Glamorgan
13 Dyfed
14 Gwynedd
15 Clwyd
16 Merseyside
17 Lancashire
18 Cumbria
19 Dumfriesshire
20 Kirkcudbrightshire
21 Wigtownshire
22 Ayrshire
23 Renfrewshire
24 Dunbartonshire
25 South Argyllshire
26 South Inverness-shire
27 North Argyllshire
28 North Inverness-shire
29 West Ross and Cromarty
30 West Sutherland
31 Caithness
32 East Sutherland
33 East Ross and Cromarty
34 East Inverness-shire and Nairnshire
35 Morayshire
36 Banffshire
37 Aberdeenshire
38 Kincardineshire
39 Angus
40 Fife
41 Midlothian
42 East Lothian
43 Berwickshire
44 Northumberland
45 Tyne and Wear
46 Durham
47 North Yorkshire
48 East Yorkshire
49 Lincolnshire
50 Norfolk
51 Suffolk
52 Essex
53 North London
John o' Groats
4TH YEAR | 8,000 KM | AUGUST 2019
Ben Nevis
3RD YEAR | 6,000 KM
AUGUST 2018
Scafell Pike
2ND YEAR | 4,000 KM | AUGUST 2017
Yr Wyddfa/
Snowdon
St Paul's Cathedral, London
START APRIL 2015 | FINISH SEPTEMBER 2020 | 11,000 KM
1ST YEAR | 2,000 KM | JULY 2016
Land's End
0 50 100 km

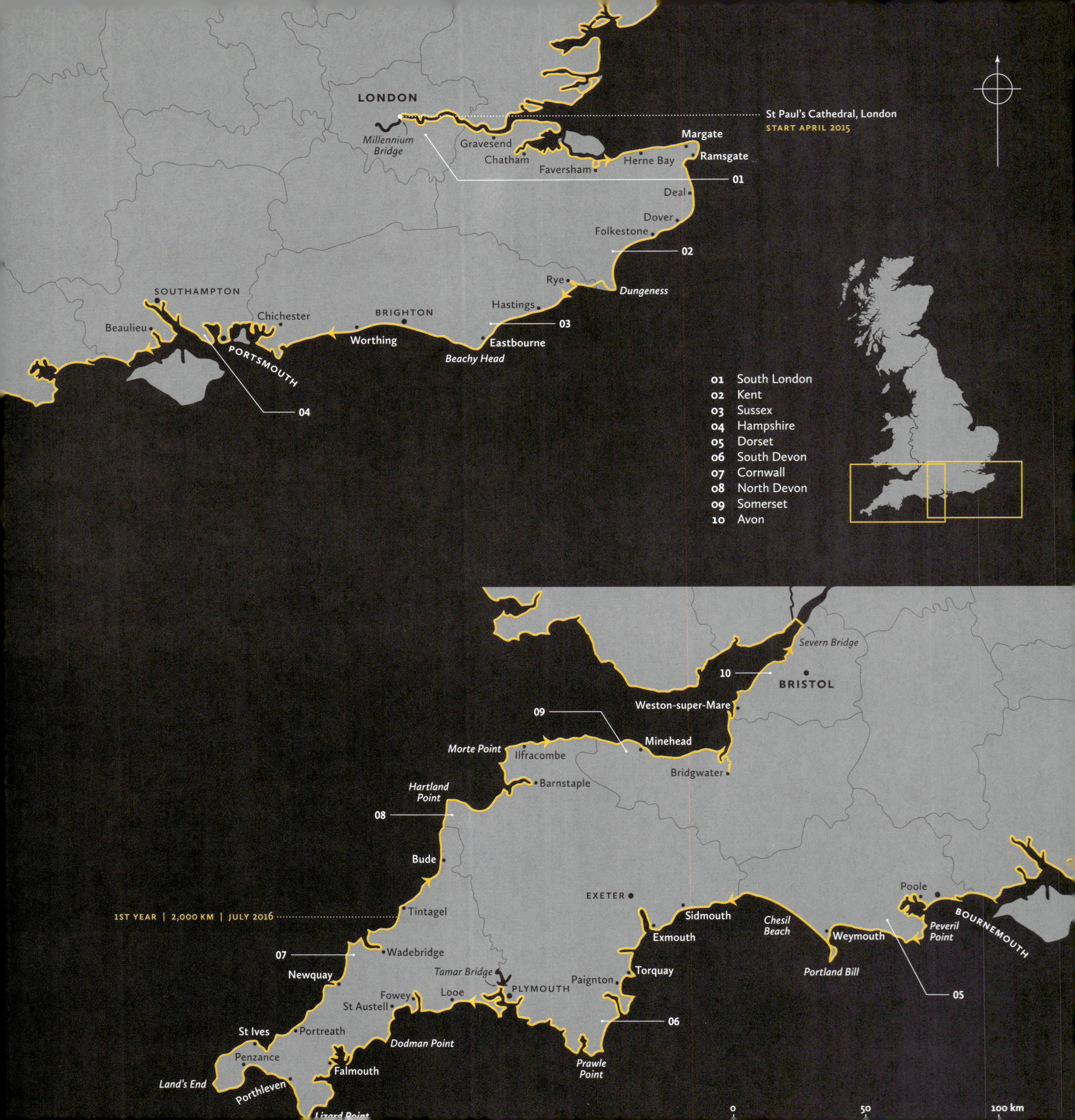

LONDON
St Paul's Cathedral, London
START APRIL 2015
Millennium Bridge
Gravesend
Chatham
Faversham
Herne Bay
Margate
Ramsgate
01
Deal
Dover
Folkestone
02
Rye
Dungeness
Hastings
03
Eastbourne
Beachy Head
BRIGHTON
Worthing
Chichester
SOUTHAMPTON
Beaulieu
PORTSMOUTH
04
01 South London
02 Kent
03 Sussex
04 Hampshire
05 Dorset
06 South Devon
07 Cornwall
08 North Devon
09 Somerset
10 Avon
Severn Bridge
10
BRISTOL
Weston-super-Mare
09
Minehead
Morte Point
Ilfracombe
Bridgwater
Barnstaple
Hartland Point
08
Bude
1ST YEAR | 2,000 KM | JULY 2016
Tintagel
07
Wadebridge
Newquay
Tamar Bridge
PLYMOUTH
Fowey
Looe
St Austell
St Ives
Portreath
Penzance
Dodman Point
Falmouth
Land's End
Porthleven
Lizard Point
Prawle Point
06
Paignton
Torquay
EXETER
Exmouth
Sidmouth
Chesil Beach
Weymouth
Portland Bill
Poole
Peveril Point
BOURNEMOUTH
05
0
50
100 km

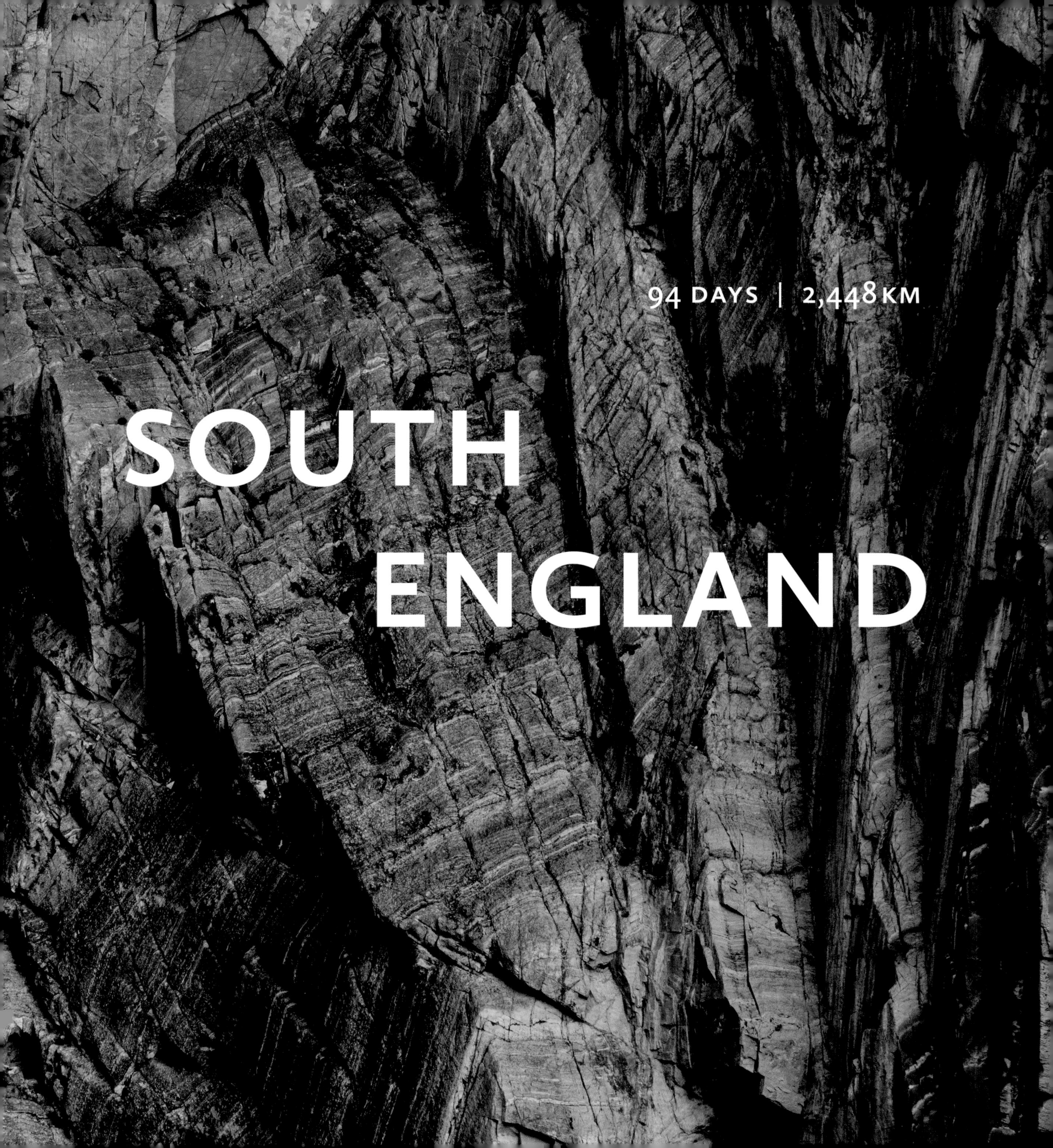

94 DAYS | 2,448 KM

SOUTH ENGLAND

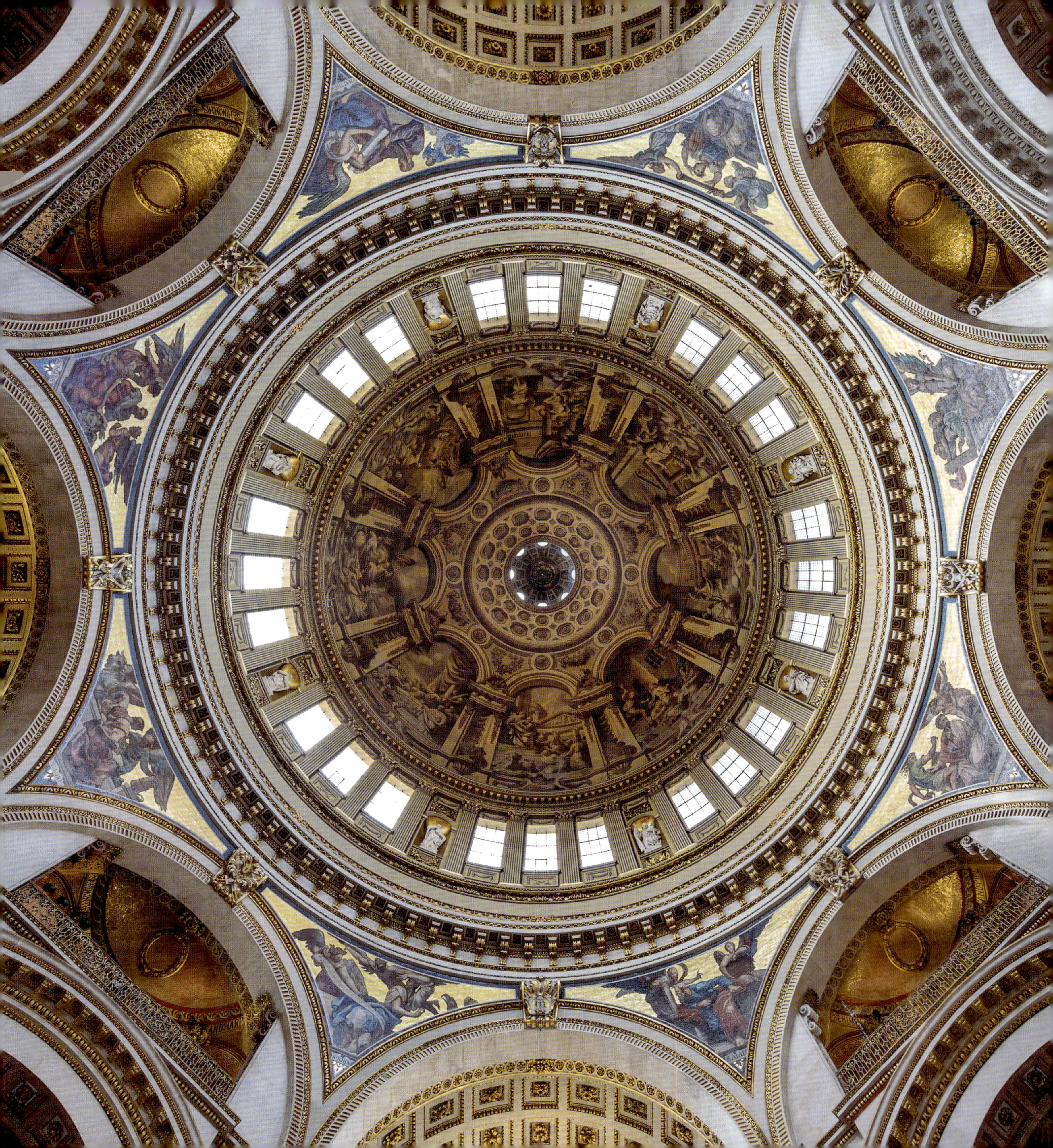

01 SOUTH LONDON

APRIL 2015

DAY 001–002 | 00000–00040KM | 40KM

The journey starts on my knees under the dome of St Paul's Cathedral, not in prayer exactly but in adjusting the tripod to be as close to the ground as possible. The space below the dome is so vast I can only capture its enormity by using a 14mm lens and splaying the tripod legs out so wide that the back of the camera rests just above the compass design on the floor. It ends up standing at the very centre of the transept crossing, circling which is written architect Christopher Wren's laconic epitaph: *If you would seek his monument, look around you*.

Two weeks ago, I decided I would try to walk and photograph the coastline of mainland Britain. Having picked London to start and end the walk, I debated where exactly to begin. Tower Bridge is the closest overwater pedestrian crossing on the Thames to the sea. Still, I wanted to start further into the heart of London, somewhere that represents the capital's spirit, history and culture. Where better than St Paul's Cathedral, an architectural marvel and miraculous survivor of the Blitz? Once, the dome was even the tallest building in London and could be seen throughout the entire city. So I wrote to the cathedral authorities explaining that I wanted to start my walk under the dome and asked if I could gain access to the building when it wasn't in use.

Once the photo is taken, I descend the cathedral steps to cross the Millennium Bridge towards Tate Modern, blending in with dozens of other camera-wielding, backpack-wearing travellers, who are far outnumbered by the faster-walking Londoners going about their business. I walk for a few hours along the Thames towards Greenwich Naval College, and dutifully queue to place my left foot in the Western Hemisphere and my right in the Eastern at the prime meridian, the starting point for measuring distance both east and west around Earth and the centre of world time. It's a lingering echo of the British Empire's reach that the prime meridian has been in Greenwich since the nineteenth century, and when I discover it was once located in St Paul's, I realise that the decision to start my journey there may not have been so original after all.

I leave and head east. Soon, the curated South Bank of London gives way to remnants of derelict industry, which in turn are replaced by housing developments. Between Greenwich and Woolwich, much of the path is a viewless corridor winding its way through building sites with occasional property adverts depicting preternaturally attractive and carefree couples drinking champagne in their riverside apartments.

By the second day of walking, it feels like I'm in a different London altogether – one that's about utility and not appearances. The riverside east of Thamesmead is almost entirely infrastructural and accentuated by the hum of machinery, the clang of steel and the occasional siren. Despite being within Greater London, I am the only one walking here on the concrete flood defences that double as a path. As I look out across the water, I spot the gigantic steel guillotine of the Barking Creek tidal barrier and the scrap and container yards in Dagenham; close to hand are Crossness Pumping Station, London bus depots and Tesco distribution centres. By a waste energy plant, scraps of plastic bags caught on razor-wire fences flutter in the wind haphazardly.

Ahead, the Dartford Crossing spans the Thames like the gateway into Kent. London was my home for ten years, so it is thrilling and surprising to learn I can walk away from it entirely in just two days.

Previous:

Butter Hole, Cornwall

Opposite:

St Paul's Cathedral, interior of the dome showing James Thornhill's 1714–17 painting depicting eight scenes from the life of St Paul while continuing an illusion of the real architectural features

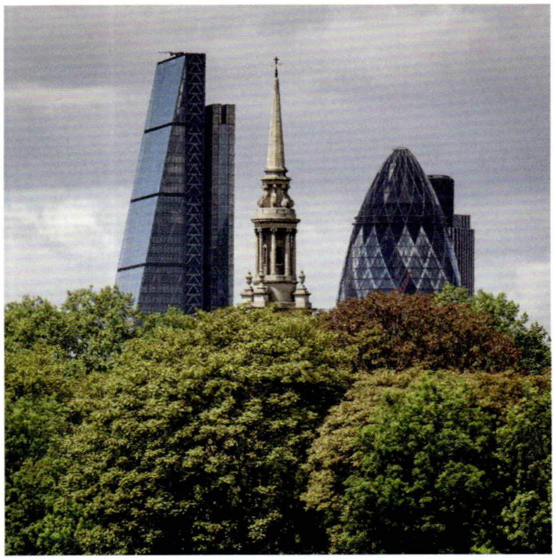

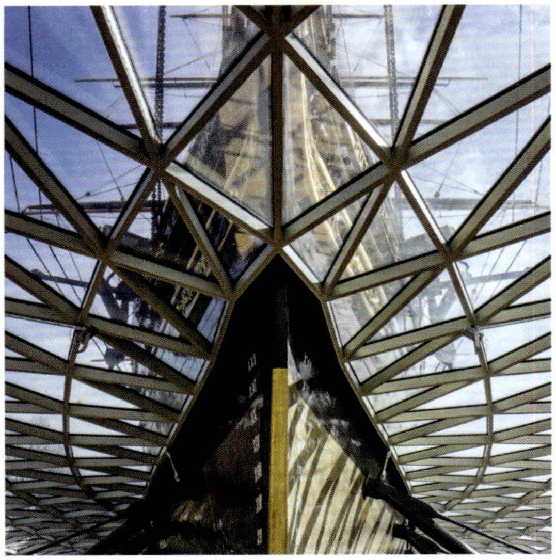

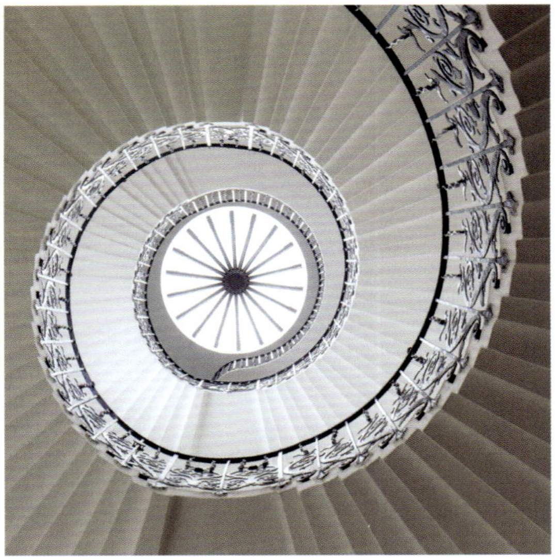

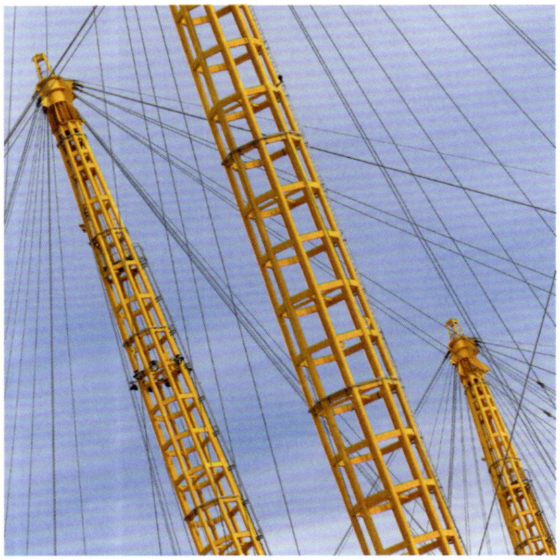

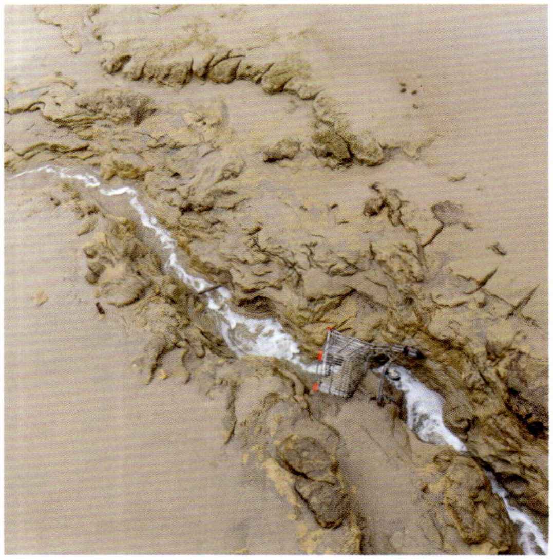

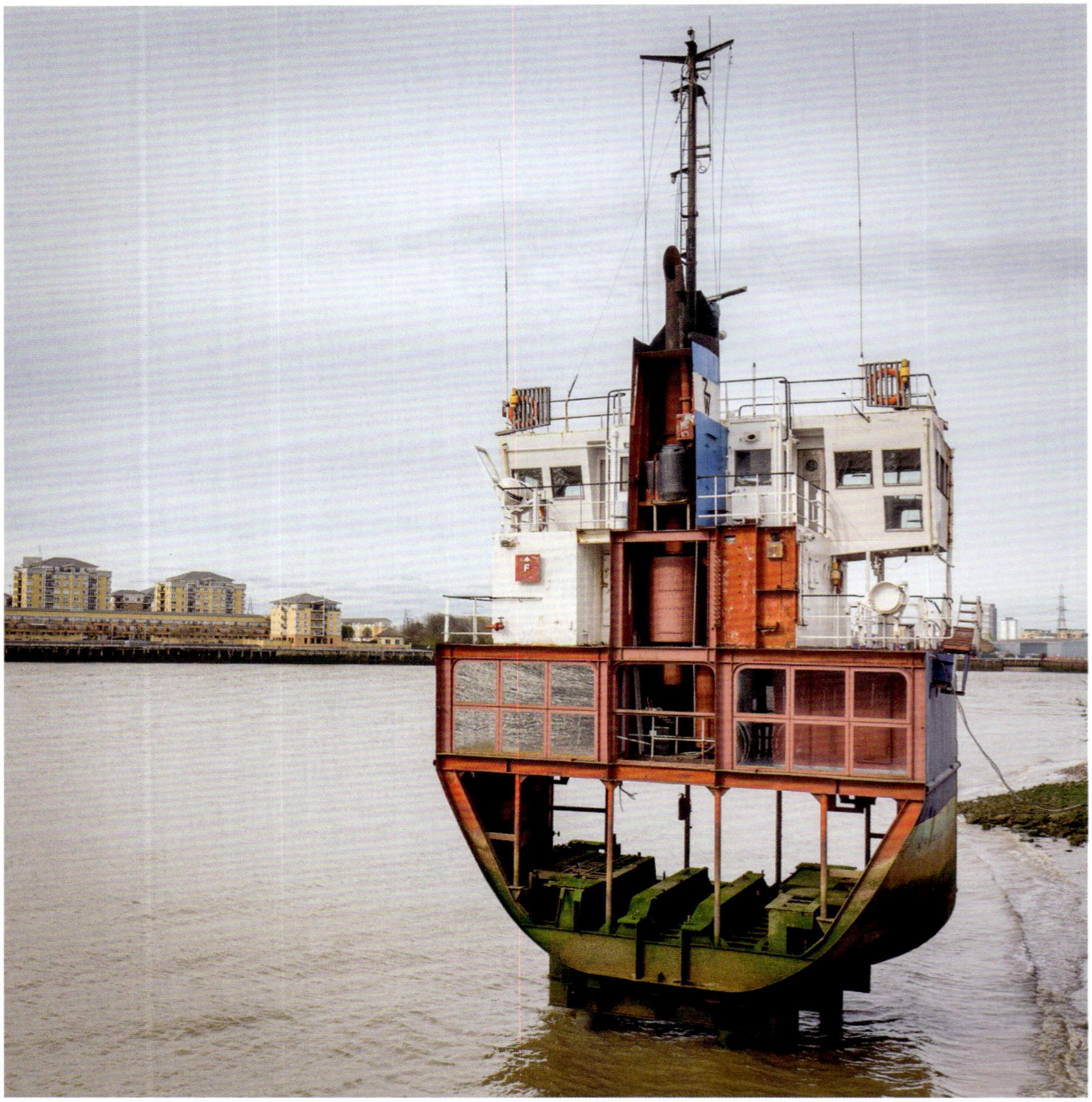

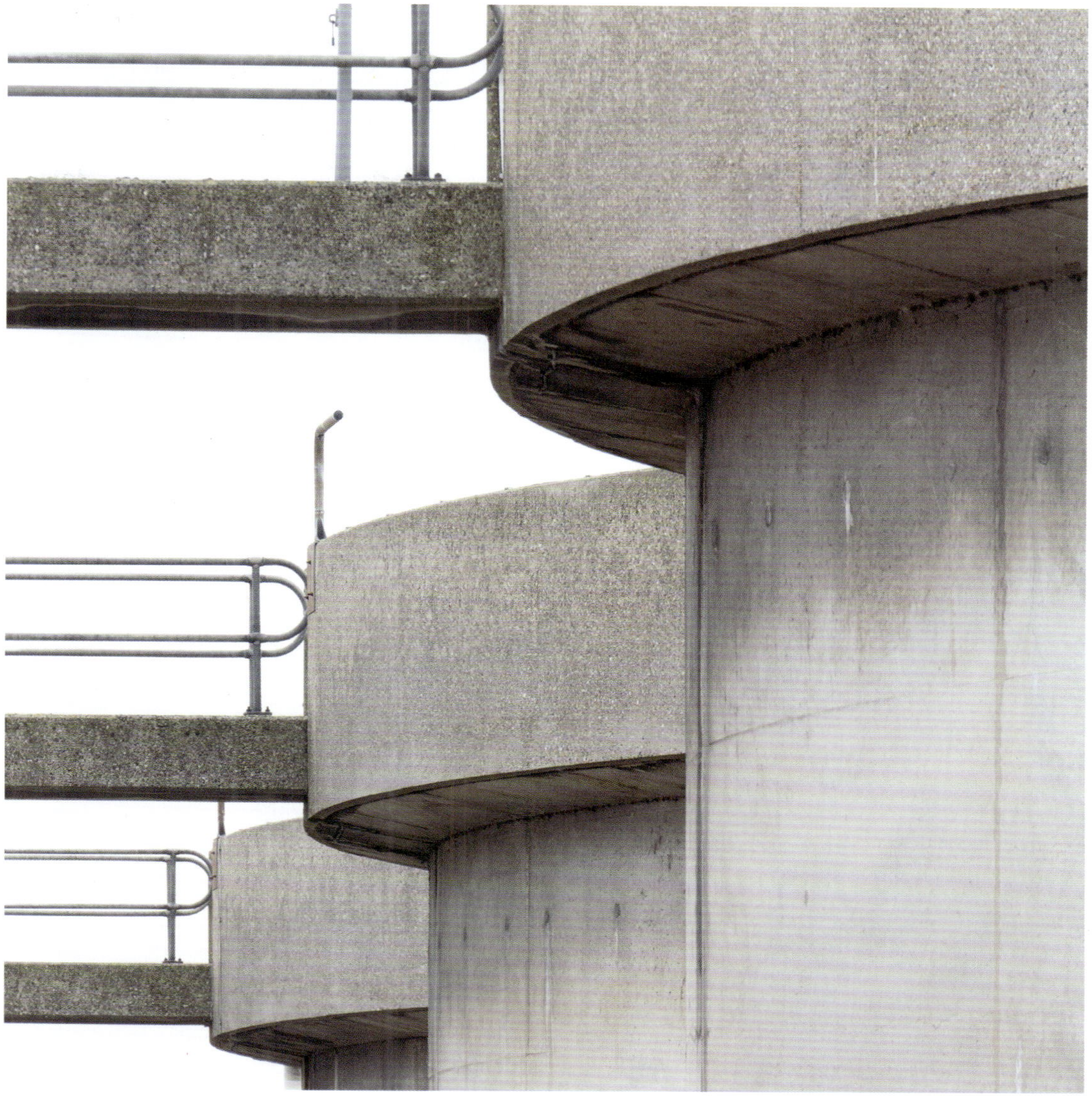

Opposite, clockwise from top left:

The Cheesegrater, St Paul's Shadwell and the Gherkin from Rotherhithe

The *Cutty Sark*, one of the last tea clippers and one of the fastest, floating on a 2012 structure by Grimshaw Architects

The Tulip Stairs, the first geometric self-supporting spiral staircase in Britain. Designed by Inigo Jones in 1635 for the Queen's House, Greenwich

Slice of Reality, a sculpture sitting in the tidal Thames by Richard Wilson, 2000

Adrift trolley, River Thames, Greenwich

Three of the twelve 100-metre-high support towers of the O2 Arena, formerly the Millennium Dome, by Richard Rogers Architects. There is one for each month of the year, or each hour of the clock face, representing the role played by Greenwich Mean Time

From top left:

Crossness Sewage Treatment Works, serving 2 million Londoners

Riverside Resource Recovery facility in Belvedere, London. A waste-to-energy plant

Crossness Pumping Station, designed by engineer Joseph Bazalgette and architect Charles Henry Driver in 1865

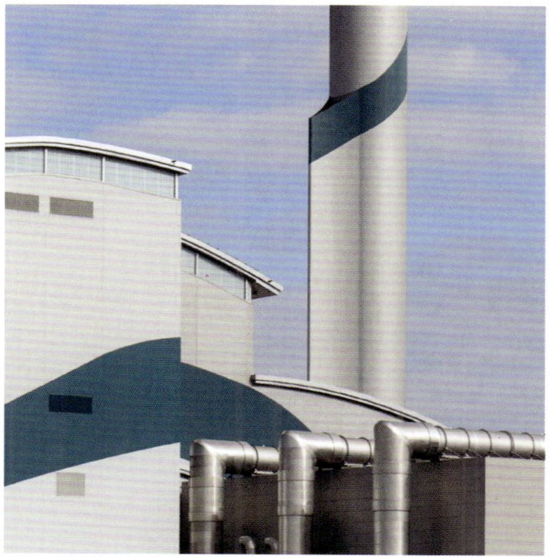

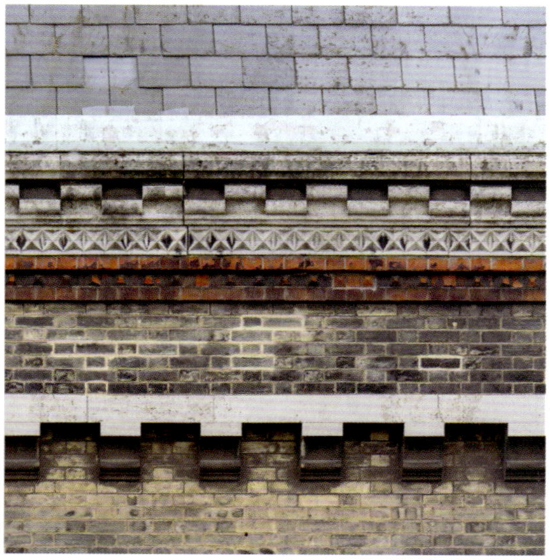

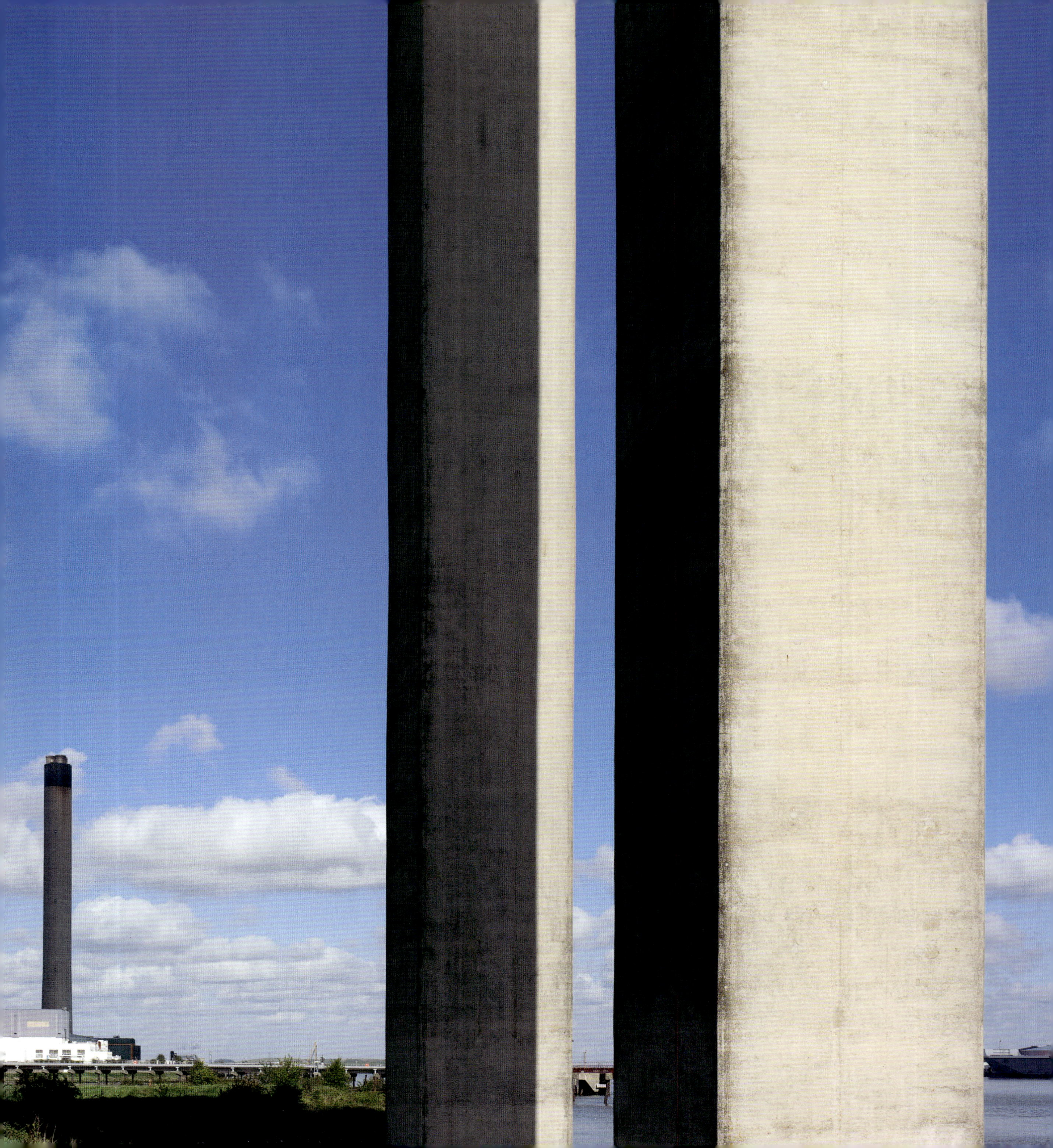

02 KENT

MAY–JUNE 2015

DAY 003–014 | 00040–00361KM | 321KM

London fades into Kent as I meander across the Isle of Grain, an other-worldly marshland of big skies, gas storage depots and obscure military installations where the Thames Estuary fans out to the open sea. Apart from a pair of shire horses, once again, I am the only one walking here, in these flat marshes, and it's easy to get lost in my thoughts when there's only the distant clunking activity of London Gateway port for company. As I'm trying to pick a route through the grid of drainage ditches at Cliffe Marshes, I notice 'The Saxon Shore Way' marked on the map running far inland, showing where the Kent coastline used to sit before the effects of uplift and sedimentation. Seeing the movement of container ships up the Thames reminds me that Kent has always been a place of arrivals and departures and was one of the first regions to be settled by Germanic tribes following the withdrawal of the Romans.

I wait patiently for the tide to fall to explore 'No. 1 The Thames', a Martello tower that guarded the mouth of the River Medway and the vital dockyards at Chatham in Napoleonic times. To reach the sturdy round structure on foot is a journey in itself and I squelch through the muddy causeway at shallow tide where access is via a dilapidated ladder tied wonkily to a rusty piece of steel. The vaulted interior has an intact shell-lifting device and enormous gun mountings with metal stairs leading to the observation tower added in the Second World War. I hurry back to shore before the tide rises and cuts me off, feeling a sense of awe at the history and wonder of this place. The next day I reach the Swale, the river that separates the mainland from the Isle of Sheppey, where the mudflats start to show some brown. It's a riot of colour after all the grey mud of the Medway. Whitstable appears on the horizon like a proper seaside town and the gateway to the sea after the ambiguities of the Thames Estuary. Further along, Faversham is also alluring, with perfectly proportioned white-painted clapperboard and handsome brick houses. A winding creek leads me to a hawthorn tree by the sea wall that overlooks the Isle of Sheppey, where I pull out my Jetboil to make a brew and eat a Chelsea bun fresh from the bakery at Faversham.

It takes three days of walking for me to reach the brilliant-white chalk cliffs by the English Channel, where a slight drop in the terrain suddenly reveals the Port of Dover far below. From above, I marvel at the perpetual stream of cars and trucks heading to and fro, lining up in allocated rows until the ferry arrives before the process repeats. There seems to be so much that could go wrong with the constant flow of people and goods, but they work in harmony. Even up on the clifftops, I can hear tannoy announcements blaring in French and English: 'Unattended luggage will be removed.' A few minutes later, I pass the sinister-looking Immigration Removal Centre. I suppose everything isn't so harmonious after all.

It's cloudless up above as I follow the chalk drama of Shakespeare Cliff and the high-level coast path to the Battle of Britain Memorial, where a statue of a lone pilot stares up to the heavens. Behind the statue is inscribed: *Behind each name a story lies / Of bravery in summer skies*.

Two days later, a desolate 10-kilometre detour around the mangled wrecks of military vehicles at Lydd Ranges gives way to the uplifting expanse of Camber Sands sparkling in the sun at low tide. The beach is busy. Most are wearing bikinis or surf shorts. Reggae plays. 'Sun must be good for business?' I ask in a cafe. 'It's the only time we get any, to be honest, mate.'

Opposite:

Below the Dartford Crossing with Tilbury Power Station (demolished 2016–19)

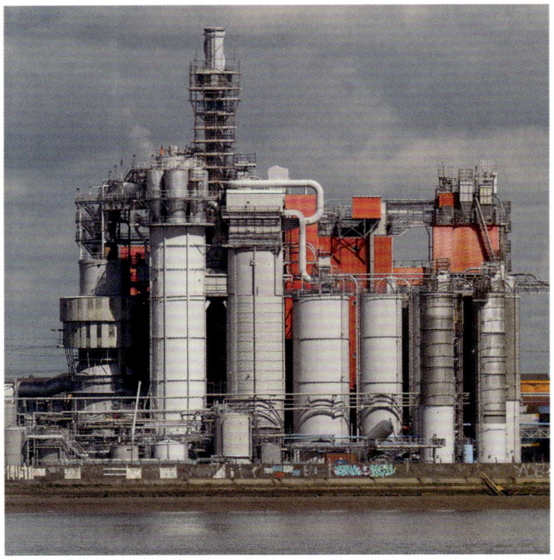
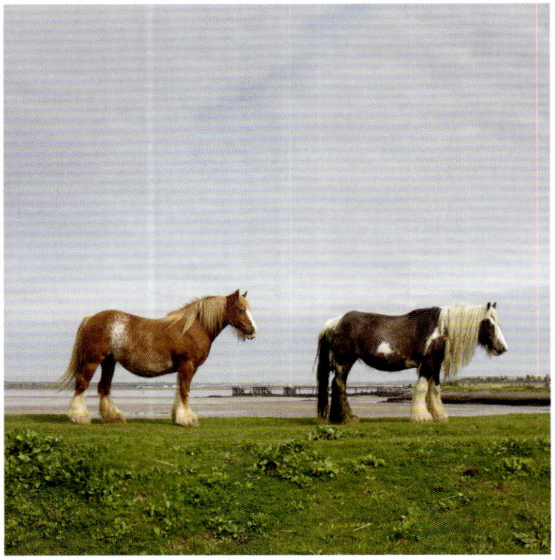
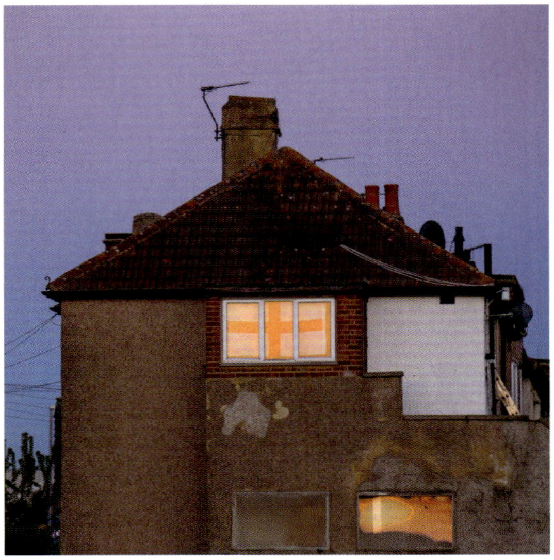
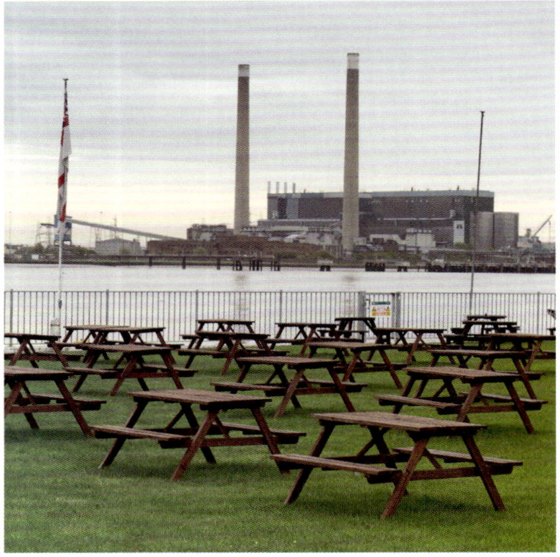
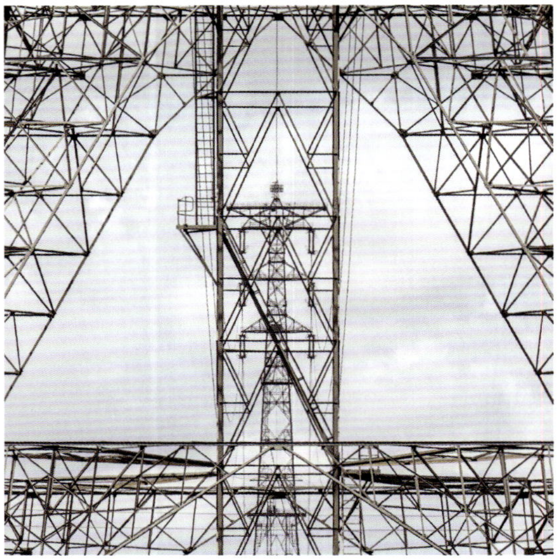
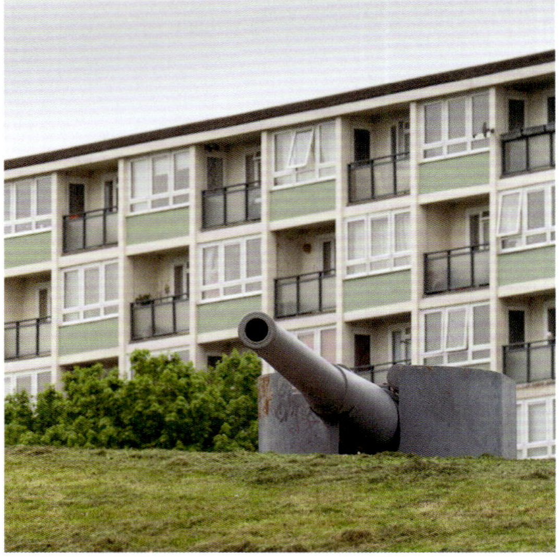
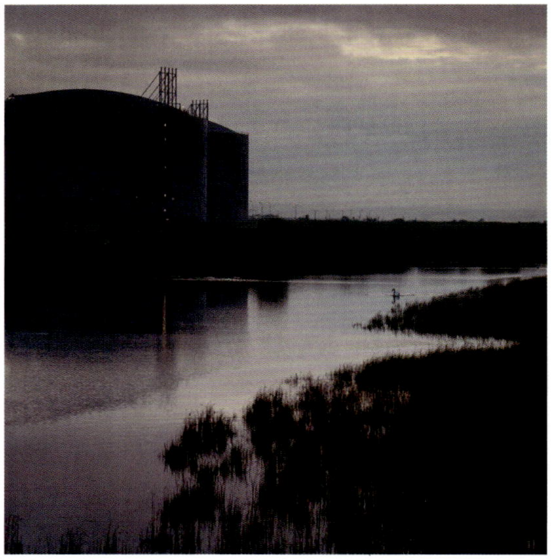
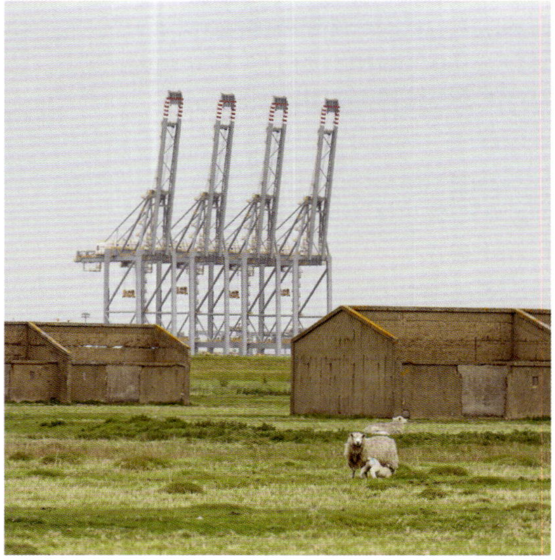
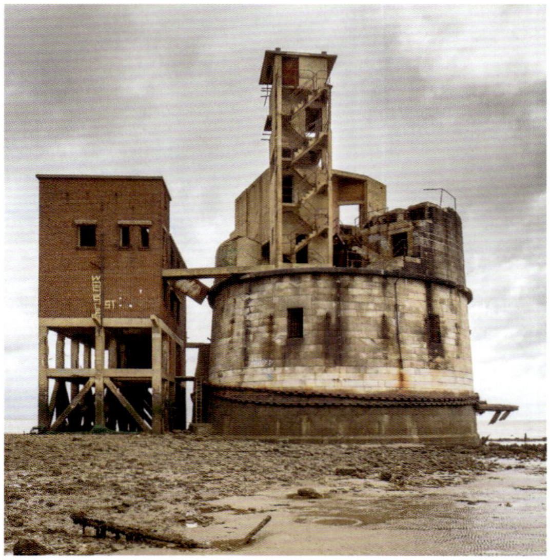

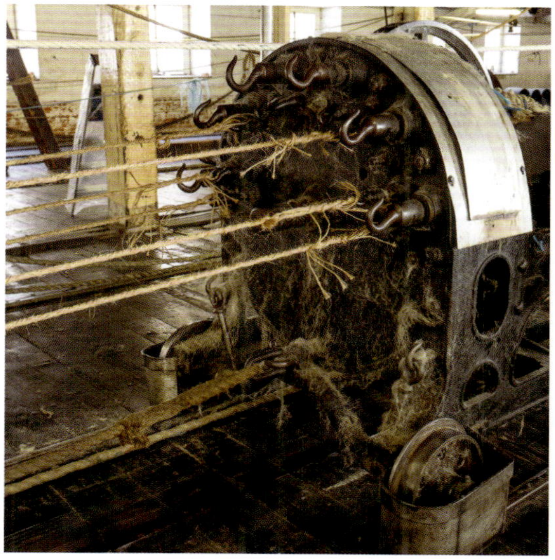

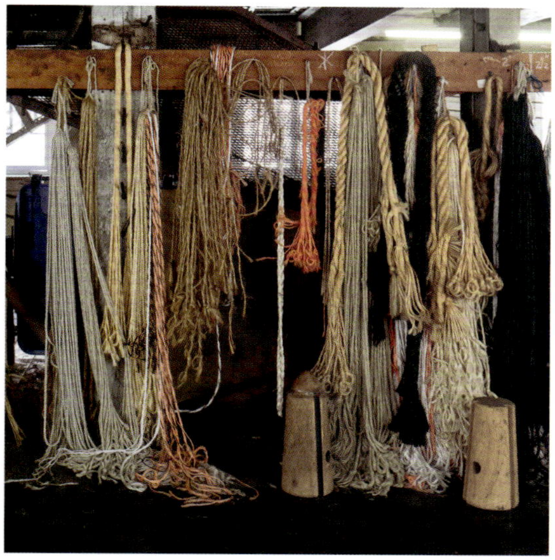

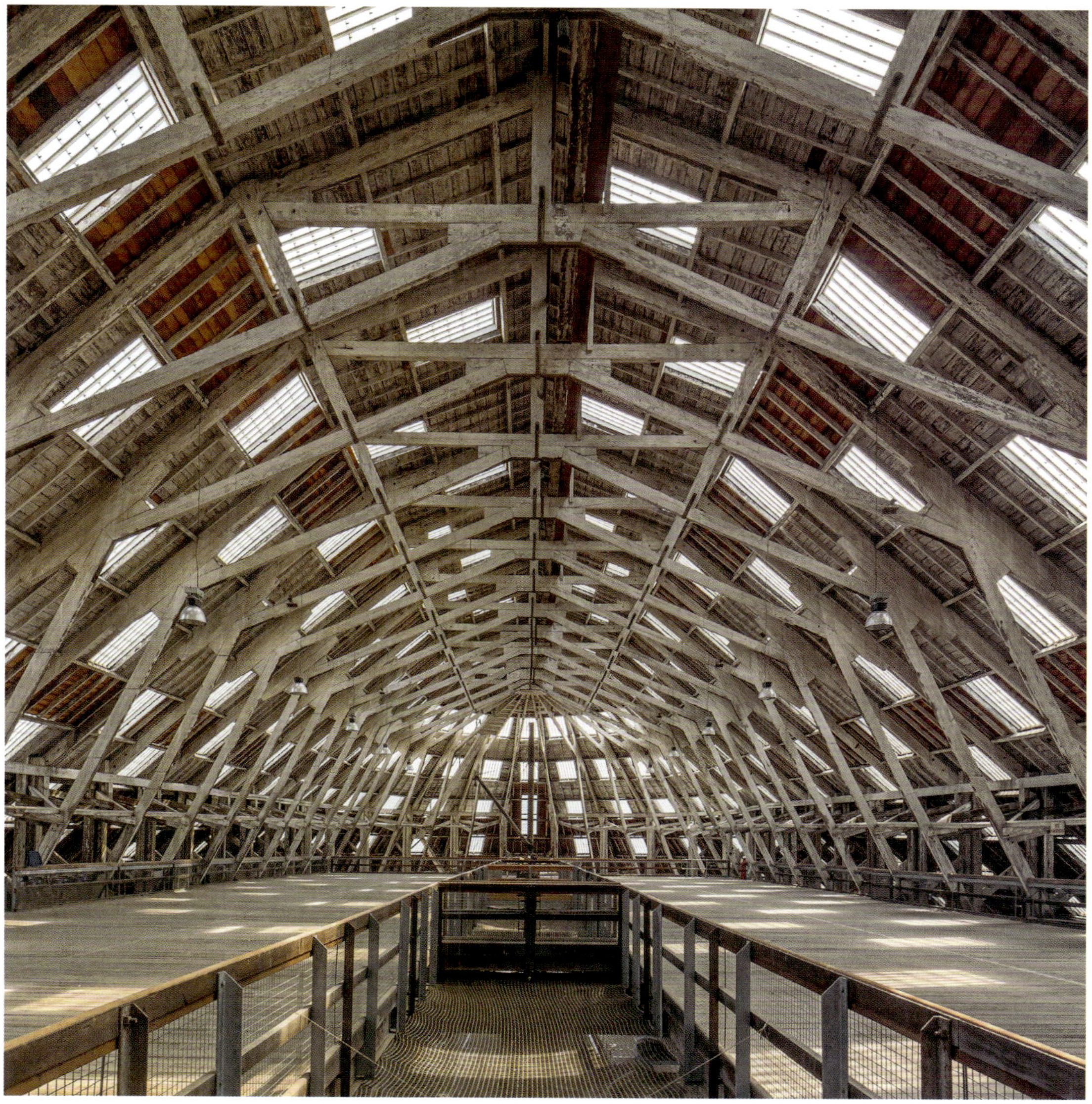

Opposite, from top left:

Procter & Gamble soap-making works, Thurrock

A horse of a different colour: by the Thames, Hoo Peninsula

The first house I passed in Kent

From centre left:

The Clarendon Royal Hotel garden, and Tilbury Power Station (demolished 2016–19)

Thames Grid Crossing, tallest pylon in the UK at 190 metres. The Kent tower frames the Essex tower, Swanscombe

Neighbourhood Watch: New Tavern Fort, Gravesend

From bottom left:

Liquefied natural gas plant, Isle of Grain

Cliffe explosives works, Hoo Peninsula, with London Gateway Port

Grain Tower Battery, built to protect the important dockyards at Sheerness and Chatham in 1855 due to a perceived French naval threat during a period of tension in the 1850s. In the First World War the tower found an additional purpose as one end of a boom defence stretching across the Medway to Sheerness. The massive iron chain from the boom is still present, wrapped around the base of the tower. In the Second World War, more changes were made, including the directing tower and barracks block at the rear

From top left:

Rope strands prior to twisting, the Ropewalk, the Historic Dockyard Chatham

Samples in the Ropewalk, the Victorian ropery where rope has been made at Chatham Dockyard for over 400 years, rigging vessels that include Nelson's *Victory*

No. 3 slip, the Historic Dockyard Chatham. One of Europe's widest span structures when constructed in 1838

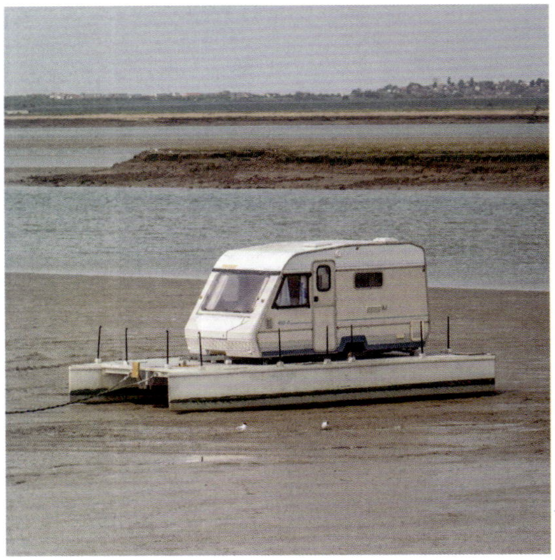

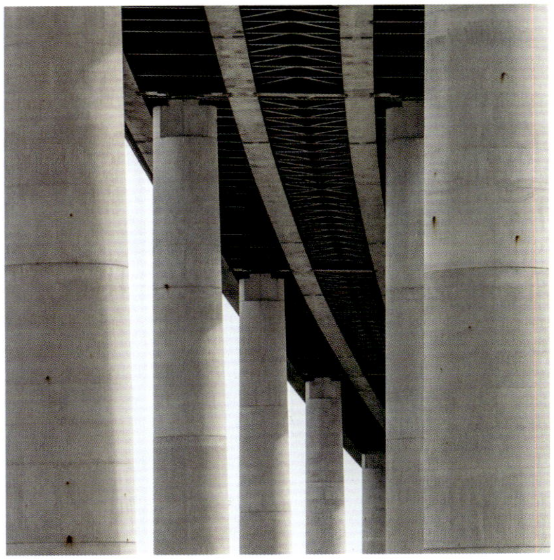

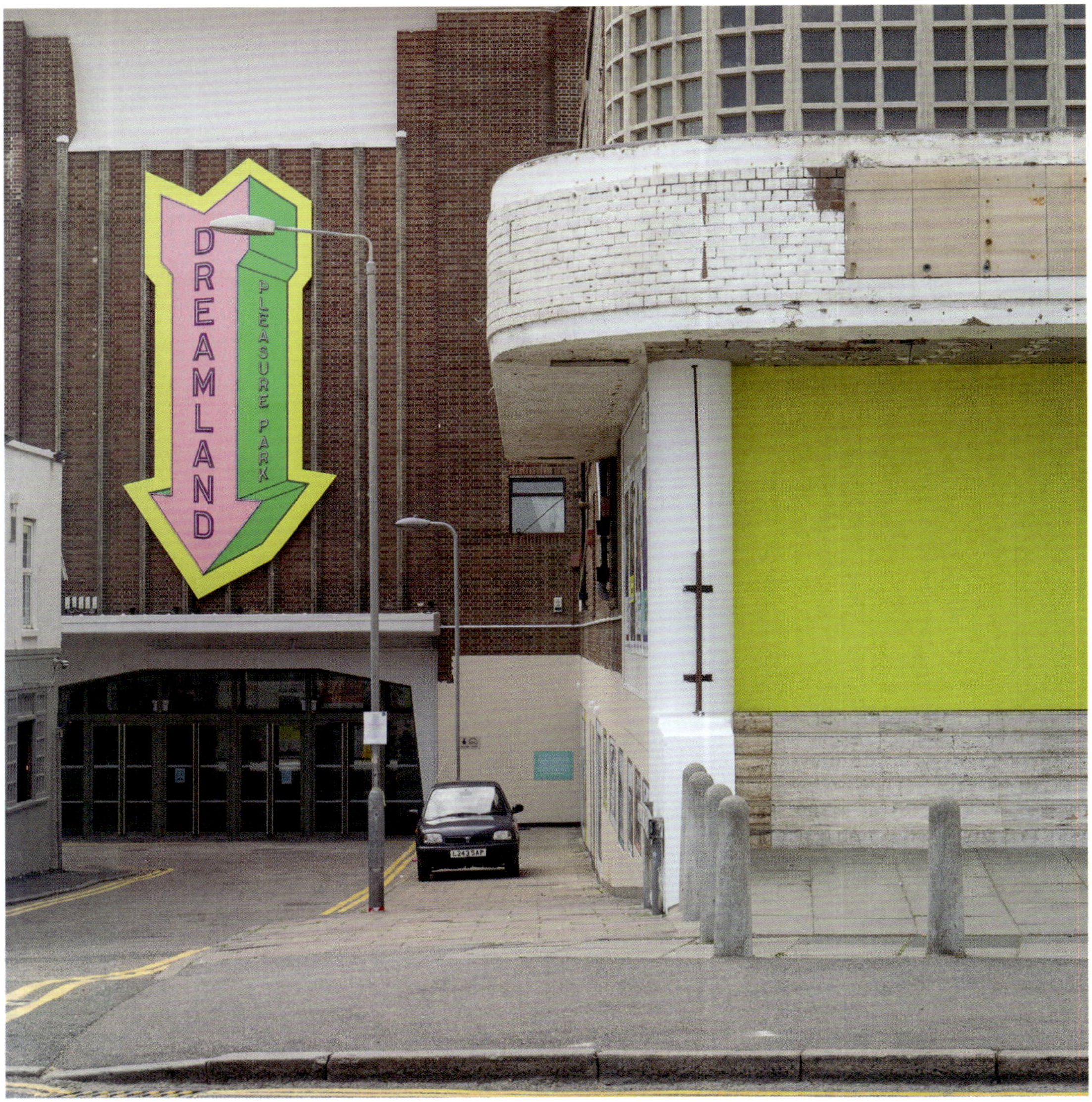

From top left:

One way to make a houseboat: Swale

Kingsferry Bridge, which connects the Isle of Sheppey to mainland Kent

Dreamland, Margate

Opposite, clockwise from top left:

Walpole Bay Tidal Pool, Margate

We Will See How Everything Reverberates, a sculpture by Carlos Amorales, 2012. Turner Contemporary, Margate

An open book (with Red Sands Sea Forts), Whitstable

White Ness chalk arch at Kingsgate Bay

Brick sandwich: Sandwich

Pinks, Whitstable

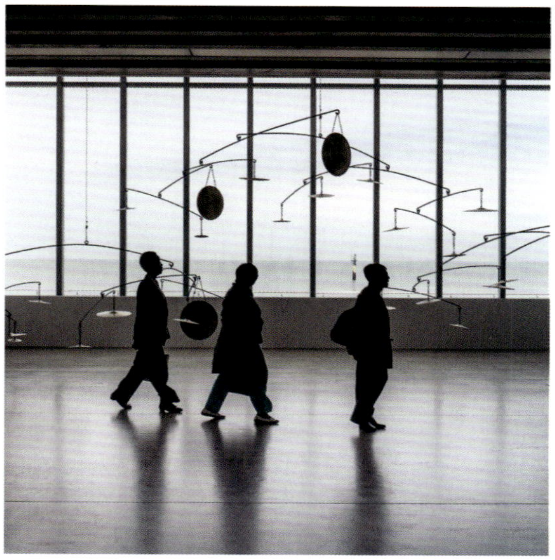
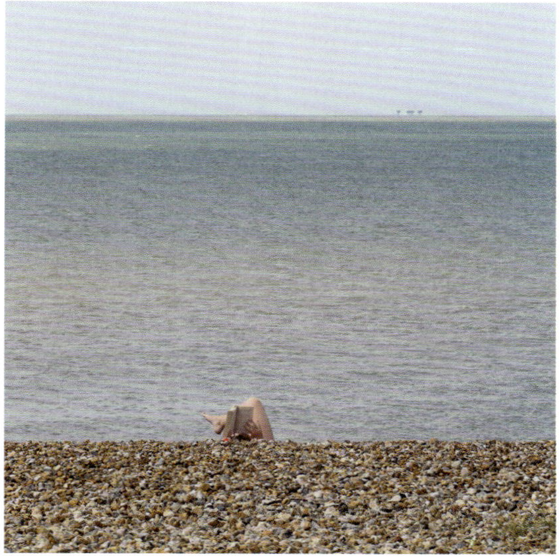
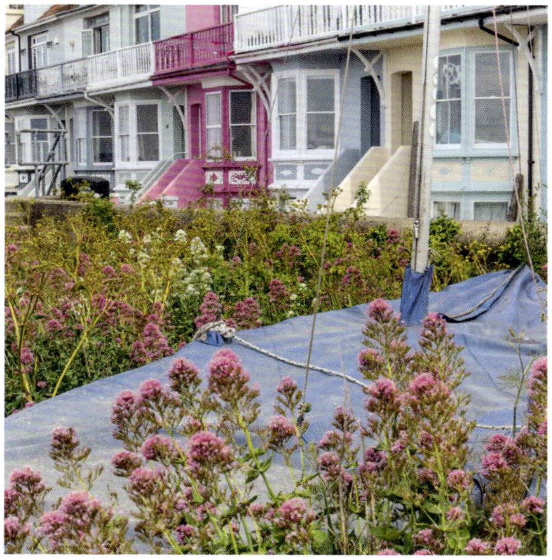
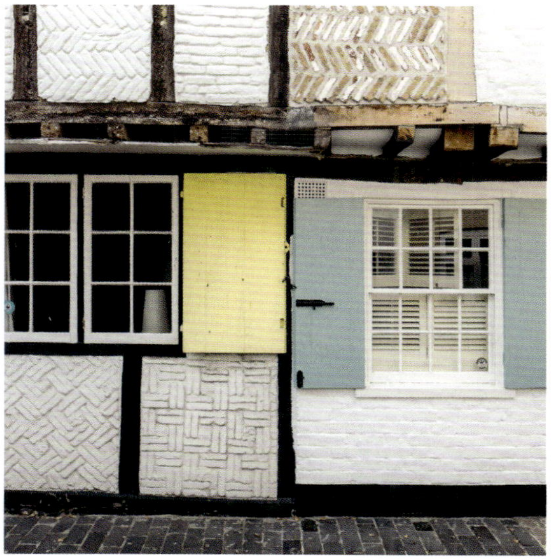
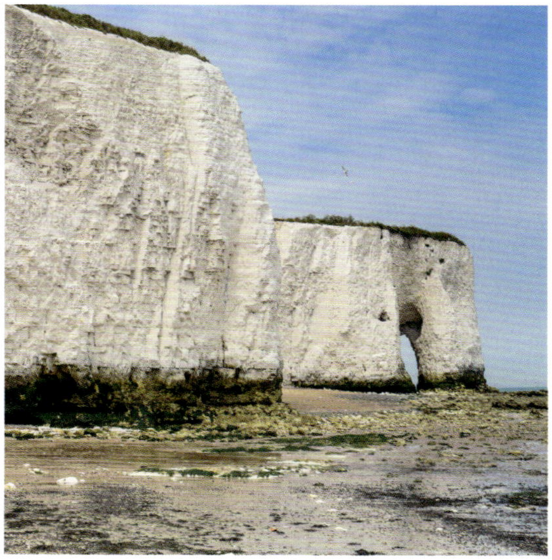

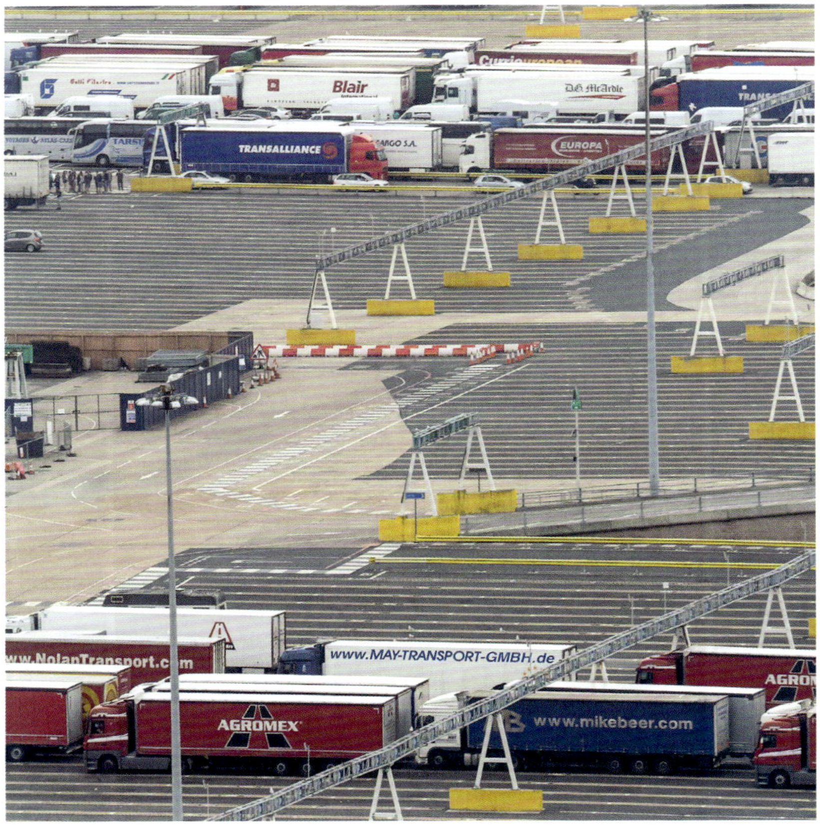
TRANSALLIANCE
EUROPA
Blair
www.MAY-TRANSPORT-GMBH.de
AGROMEX
www.mikebeer.com

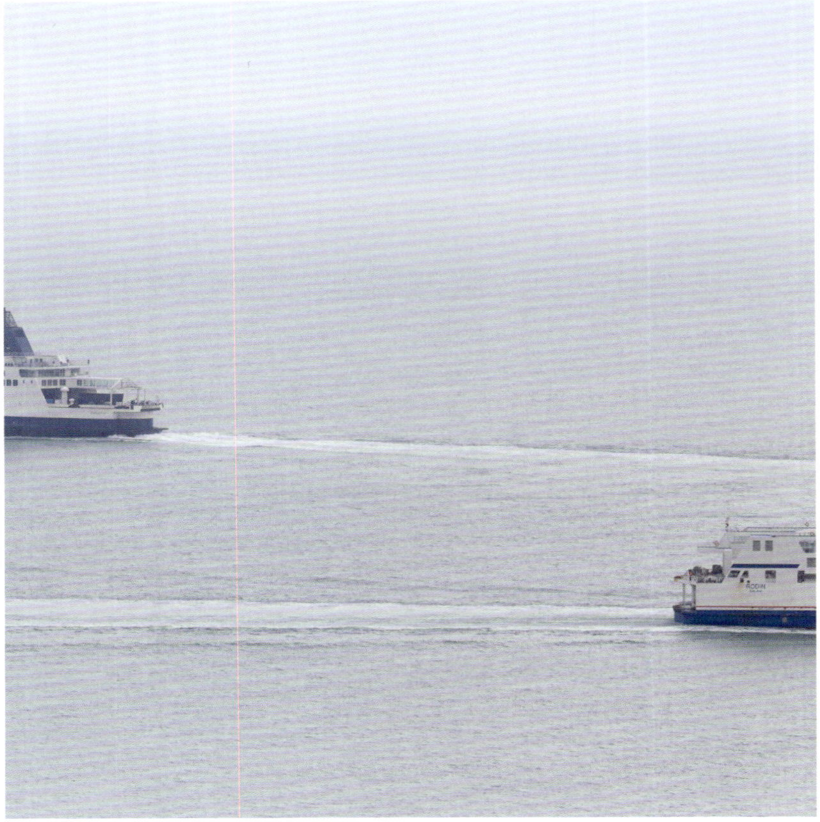

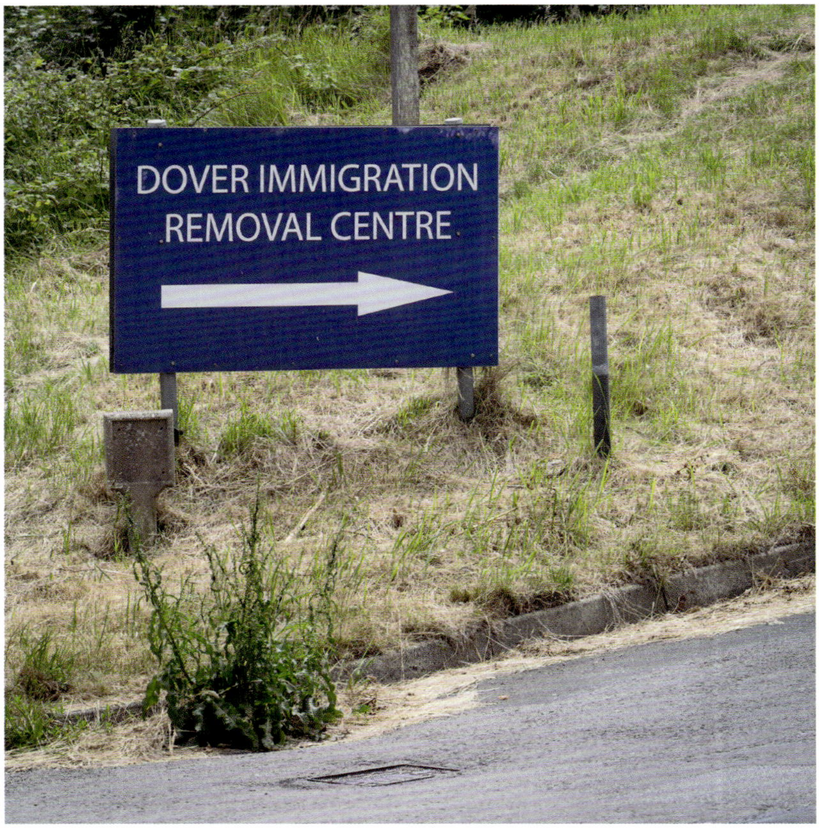
DOVER IMMIGRATION
REMOVAL CENTRE

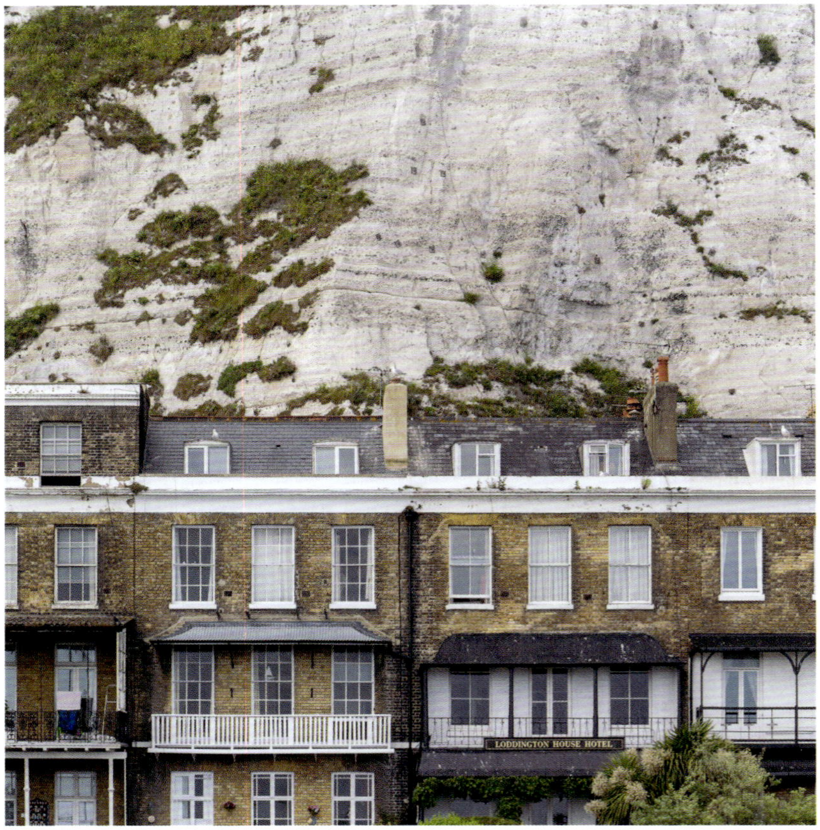
LODDINGTON HOUSE HOTEL

Opposite, from top left:

Trucks waiting to leave the Port of Dover

Like ships that pass: Calais–Dover ferries *Pride of Kent* and *Rodin*

From bottom left:

Dover Immigration Removal Centre, located in the historic citadel of the Western Heights fortifications in Dover (closed in 2015)

White cliffs below Dover Castle

From top left:

Abbot's Cliff acoustic mirror, between Folkestone and Dover, a precursor to radar that was used as a listening device for detecting Zeppelins and planes in the First World War

Channel Tunnel ventilation facility on Samphire Hoe, an area of land created by using 4.9 million cubic metres of chalk marl from the Channel Tunnel excavations, Dover

From centre left:

Reactor building, Dungeness. A nuclear power station that ceased generation in 2006

Shipping marker, Dungeness. Prior to GPS, fishing-boat crews would align this structure with a similar T-shaped one further along the shore to get their bearings

From bottom left:

Prospect Cottage, Derek Jarman's house, Dungeness

Camber Sands, Sussex

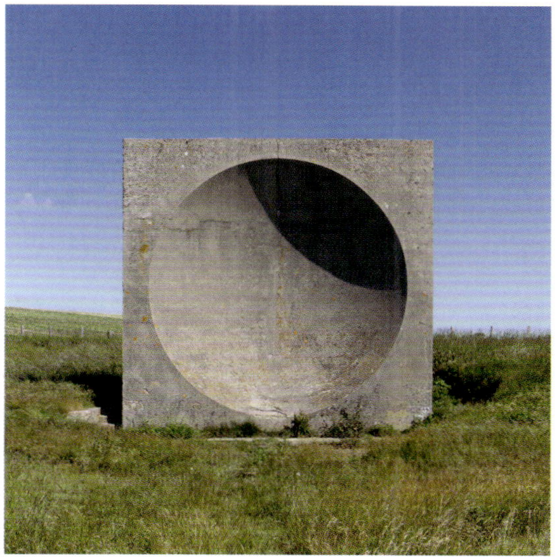

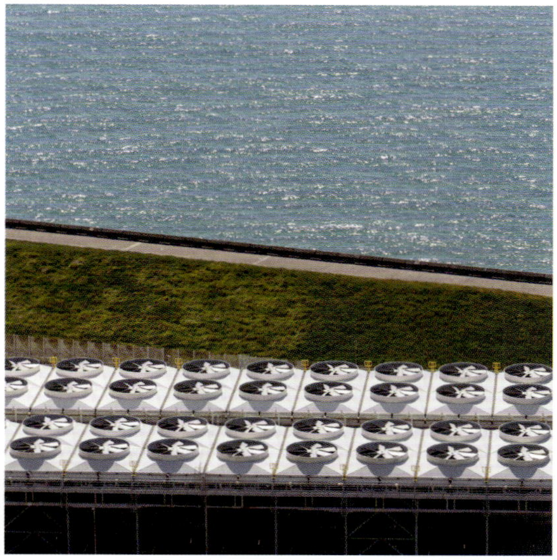

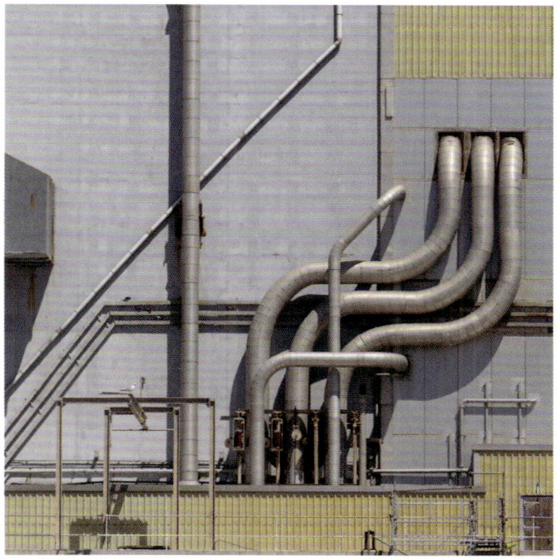

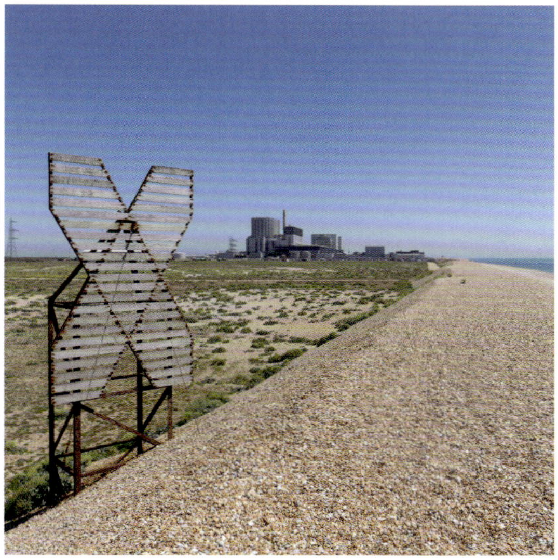

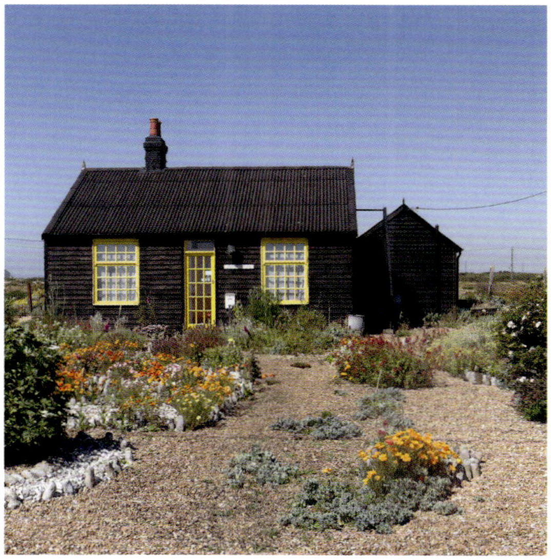

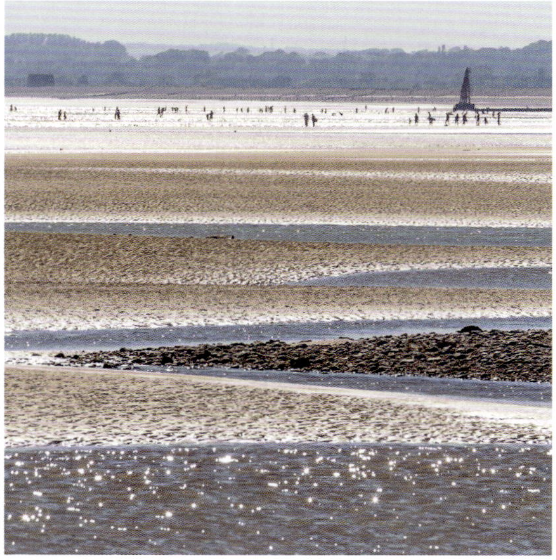

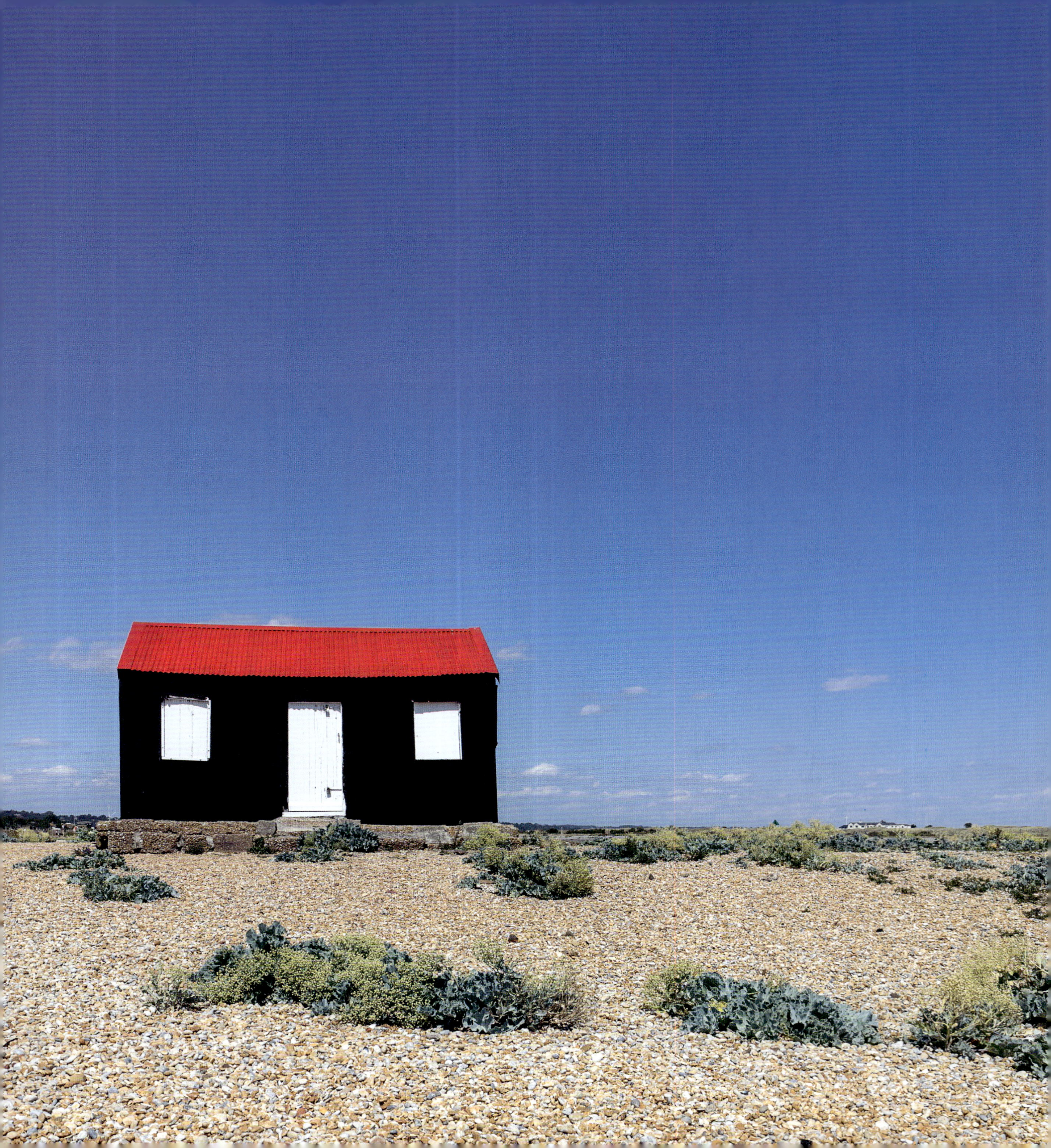

03 SUSSEX

AUGUST 2015

DAY 015–022 | 00361–00580KM | 219KM

Arriving in Rye on a sunny summer's day comes with a health warning for the family walking along the medieval cobbled streets next to me. 'Mum, stay off the vodkas this time – remember when we went to Birmingham and booked that nice Italian restaurant, and you were too pissed to go?' The whole family laughs. I'm waiting patiently for a good shot of the timber-framed Mermaid Pub in front of which a man is photographing his wife, charmed by its having been a sailors' haunt when Rye was once an important trading port before the retreating sea left the town high and dry. The winding streets here are steeped in history, and once I've had my fill of antique shops, I leave the port without a sea to follow a silted-up channel back to the coast, excited to be heading west along the foot of England.

The next day in Hastings, I am making my way between the extraordinary tall, thin wooden sheds known as net shops when I hear screeches along the shore as stout fishing boats, each surrounded by a cloud of gulls, are winched very slowly up the inclining shingle by a steel cable on greased timbers that are pulled from the stern and replaced at the bow by yellow-clad fishermen. As I walk along the seafront, I see preparations are afoot in a nearby car park for an anachronistic beauty parade: a dozen girls in salmon-pink dresses sashed with 'DOVER' curtsy before a portly man with a large camera.

That evening, Eastbourne glides into view, its pier given a rosy halo by the setting sun. At the B&B, everything aches, and I'm in bed as soon as the camera batteries are charging. From the promenade early the next morning, I spot two swimmers far out at sea, steadily crawling towards the towering white cliffs of Beachy Head. Within half an hour, I'm following the cliff edge above a sheer 150-metre drop to the wave-washed rocks beneath. The rolling grass, lack of fences and shimmering ultramarine sea so far below make me feel free, weightless, like I'm flying above the ocean. Perhaps because of this illusion, tragedy punctuates the landscape in the form of a Samaritans sign a few metres back from the edge, a last attempt to remind potential jumpers that somebody out there will listen. Later, I discover that more people choose to end their lives here at Beachy Head than anywhere else in the UK.

On my fourth day in Sussex, I realise I'm getting close to Brighton when I walk on to a naturist beach by accident. Soon, I see Brighton Pier etched against the overcast sky, and the sea mist makes my hands and camera sticky. Next morning, homeless people cohabit on the park benches with displaced revellers. The seagulls squawk above the brightly painted, padlocked and shuttered shops, and everyone I pass who is not horizontal carries an object telegraphing their originality: a guitar, a zigzag poncho, a neck tattoo, a longboard or a long beard.

Later, in Littlehampton, the rain falls so relentlessly that the geese stand with their bills tucked under their wings. Walking along the sand strip at the waves' edge, I am happy in this milky void. Sky, land and sea – everything is water.

With the downpour, it's tough-going for the next four days, and at Medmerry I seek shelter in a dilapidated marsh barn of flint and brick. I ignore the *No Entry* sign in order to get out of the deluge and make a brew. Munching my provisions while sitting on a sack of seed in an ancient grain barn makes me sense a connection to the foot travellers of the past. Buying a data bolt-on for my iPhone to keep in touch with the rest of the world, less so. I drink my tea as the rain sloughs off the barn roof through the fingers of the burnt-out door.

Opposite:

Beach hut with red roof, Rye Harbour

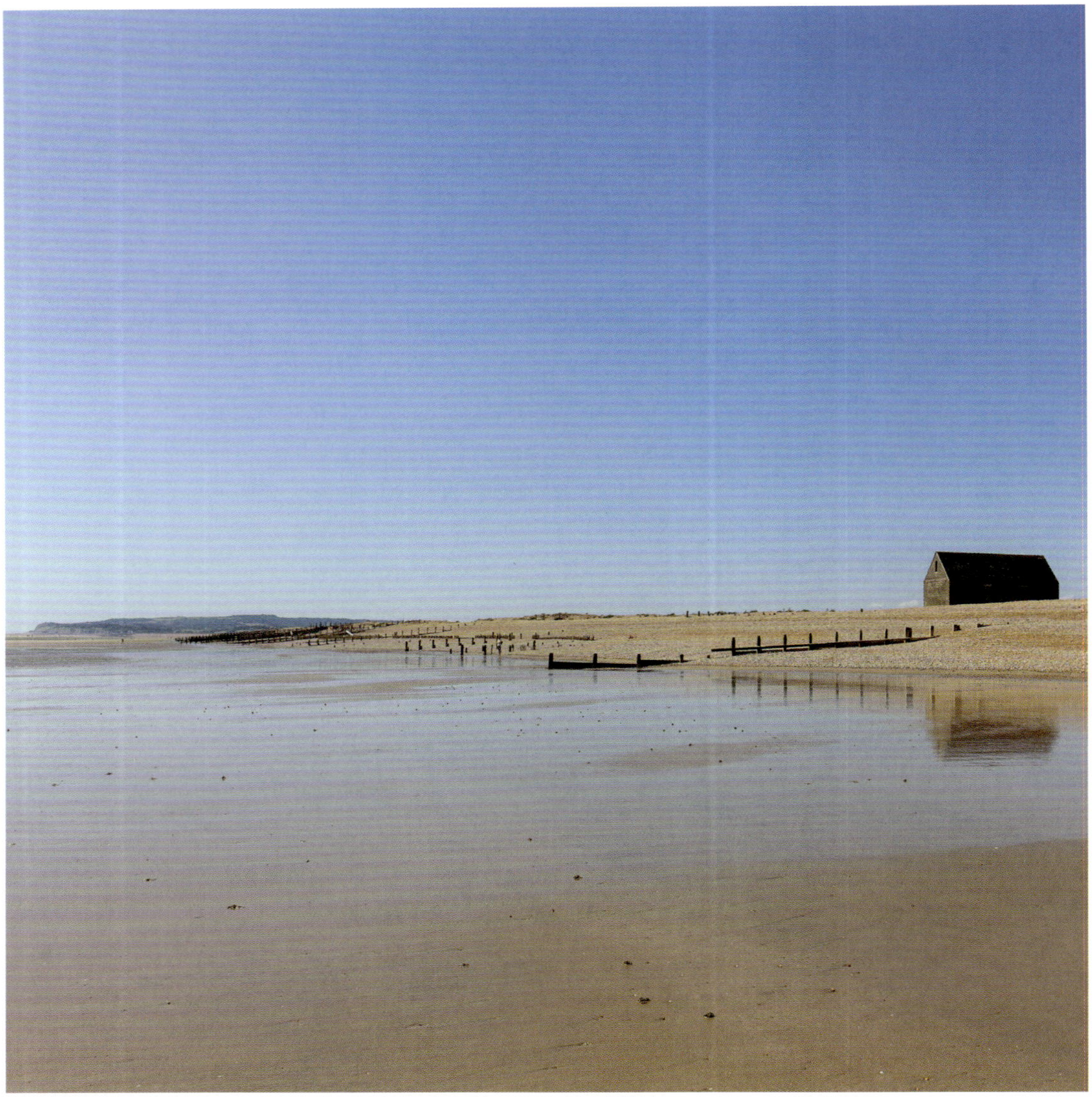
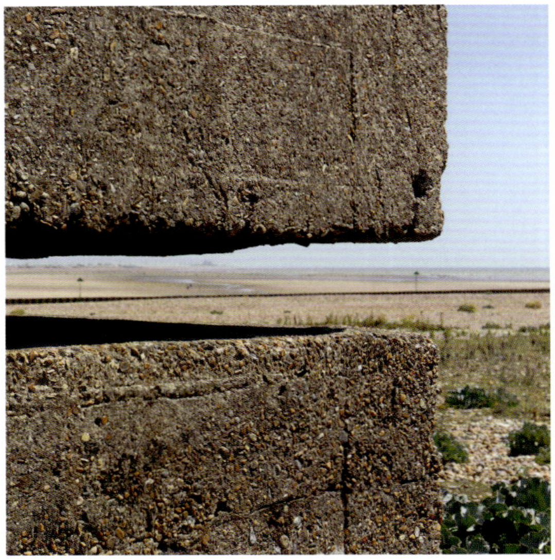
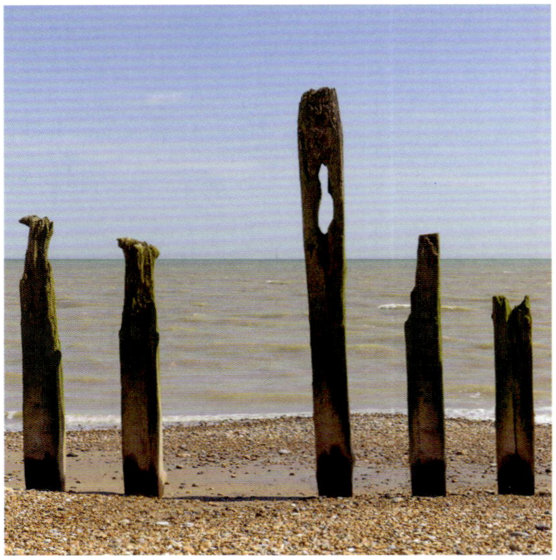
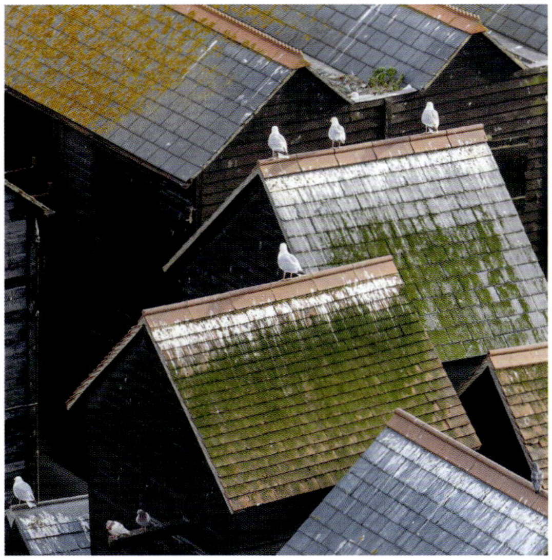
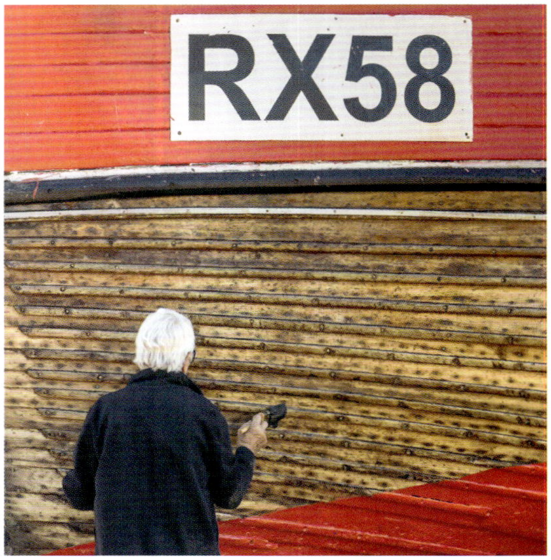
RX58
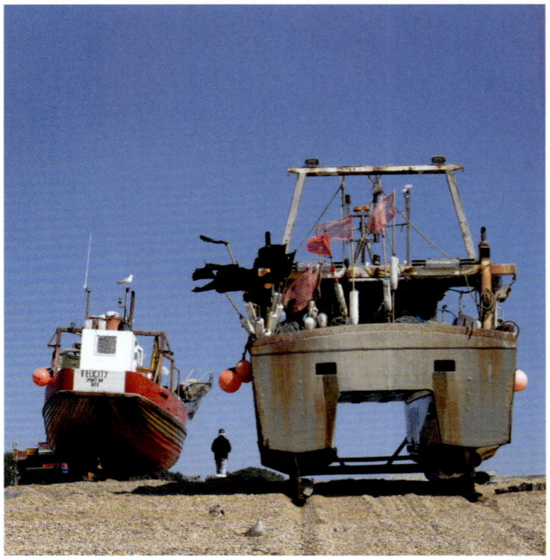

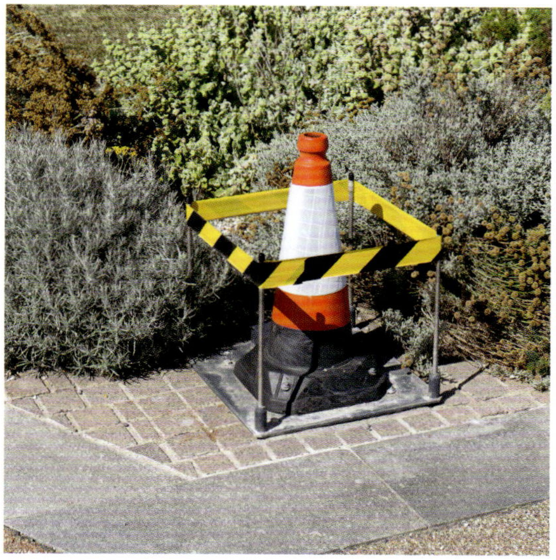

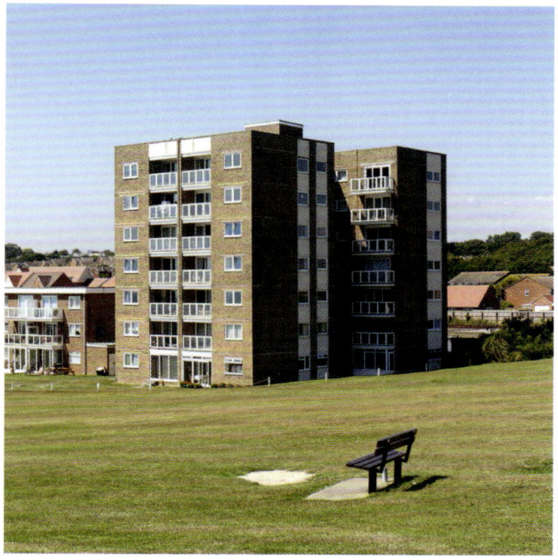

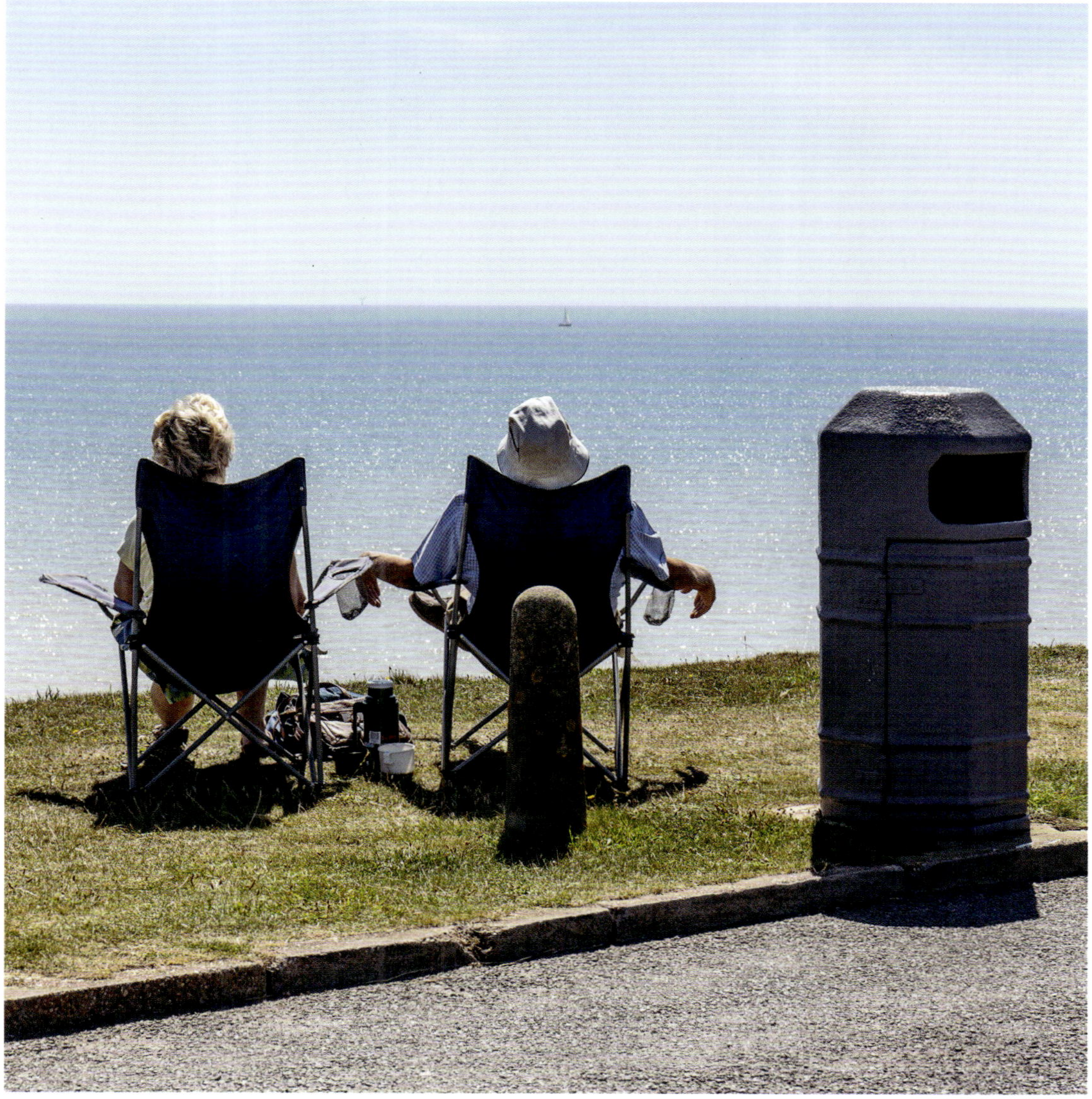

Opposite, clockwise from top left:

Mary Stanford Lifeboat House, Winchelsea Beach. On 15 November 1928, while attempting a rescue in gale-force winds, the whole of the seventeen-man crew of the *Mary Stanford* lifeboat were drowned, practically the entire male fishing population of the village of Rye Harbour

Line of fire: Rye Harbour pillbox

Broken breakwater, Cliff End

Fishing boats, The Stade, Hastings

RX58 having her hull varnished, The Stade, Hastings

Net shops, Hastings. Tall black wooden huts which were built to provide a weatherproof store for fishing gear

From top left:

Belt and braces: Bexhill-on-Sea

Wallington Towers, Bexhill-on-Sea

Just the three of us: Bexhill-on-Sea

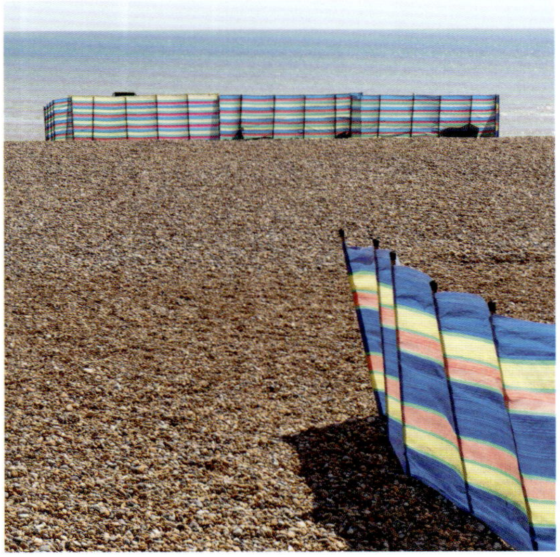

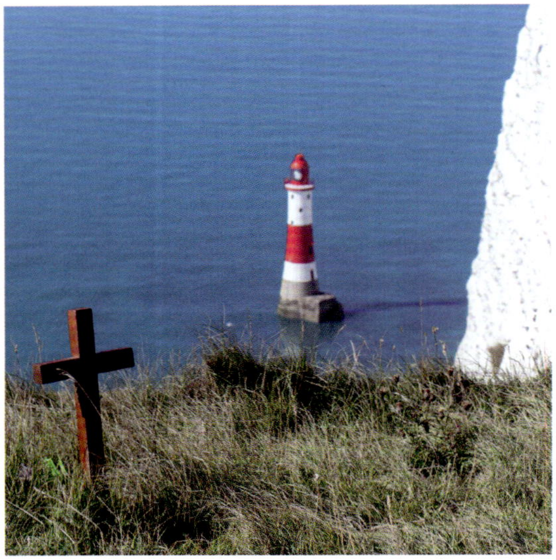

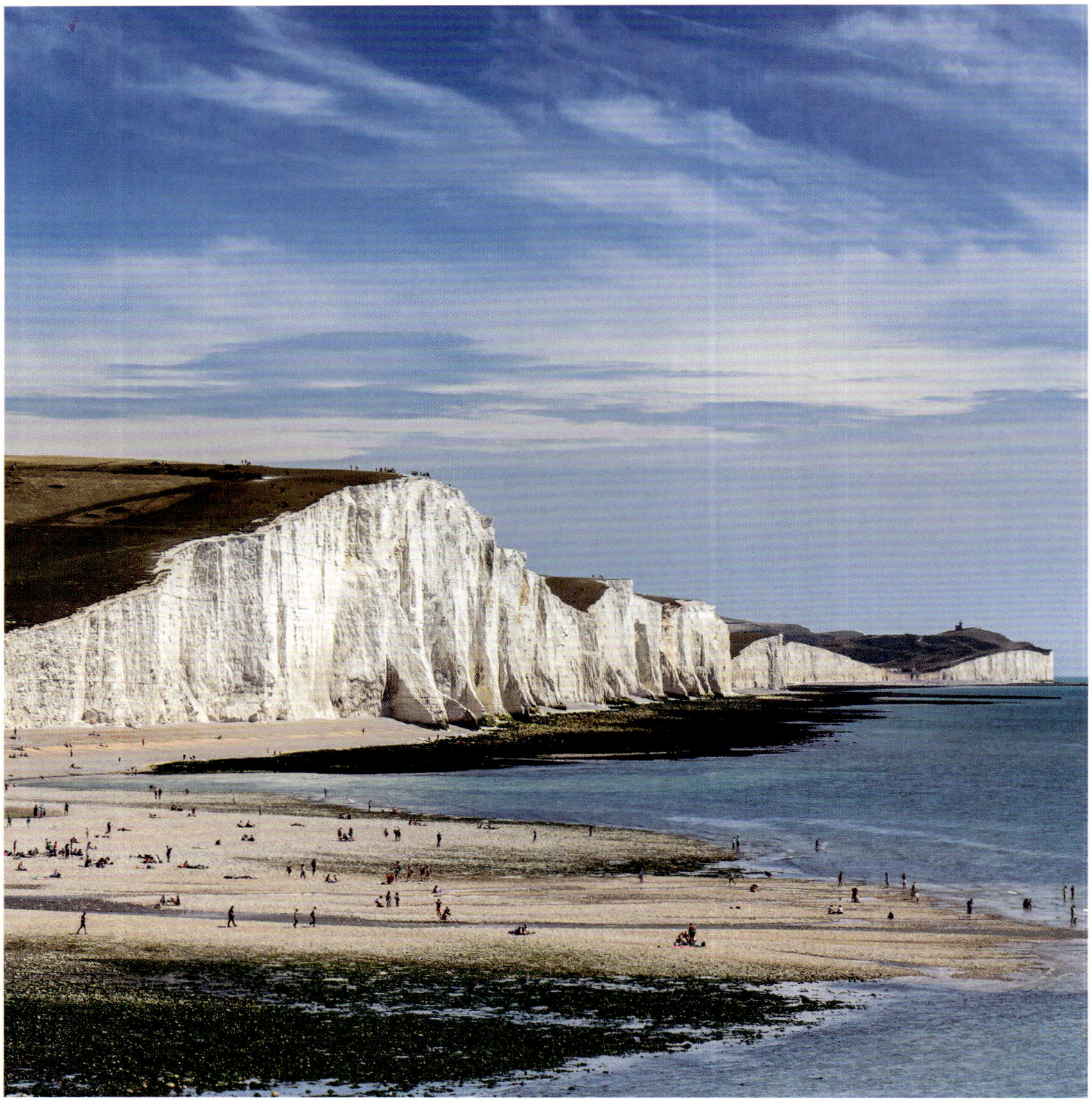

From top left:

Marking territory: Bexhill-on-Sea

Jumpers' memorial, Beachy Head. About twenty-three people die each year by jumping from the cliffs. In 2010, it was the third most common suicide spot in the world

Cuckmere Haven and the Seven Sisters from Seaford Head

Opposite, clockwise from top left:

Drinks on the shore, Ferring

West Pier, Brighton. The pier closed to the public in 1975 and deteriorated over time. Major sections fell into the sea during storms in late 2002, and two separate fires, both thought to be arson, in March and May 2003 destroyed most of the remaining structure

Larry Lobster, Brighton

'99', Brighton

Helter-skelter, Brighton Palace Pier

Above the beach huts, Rottingdean

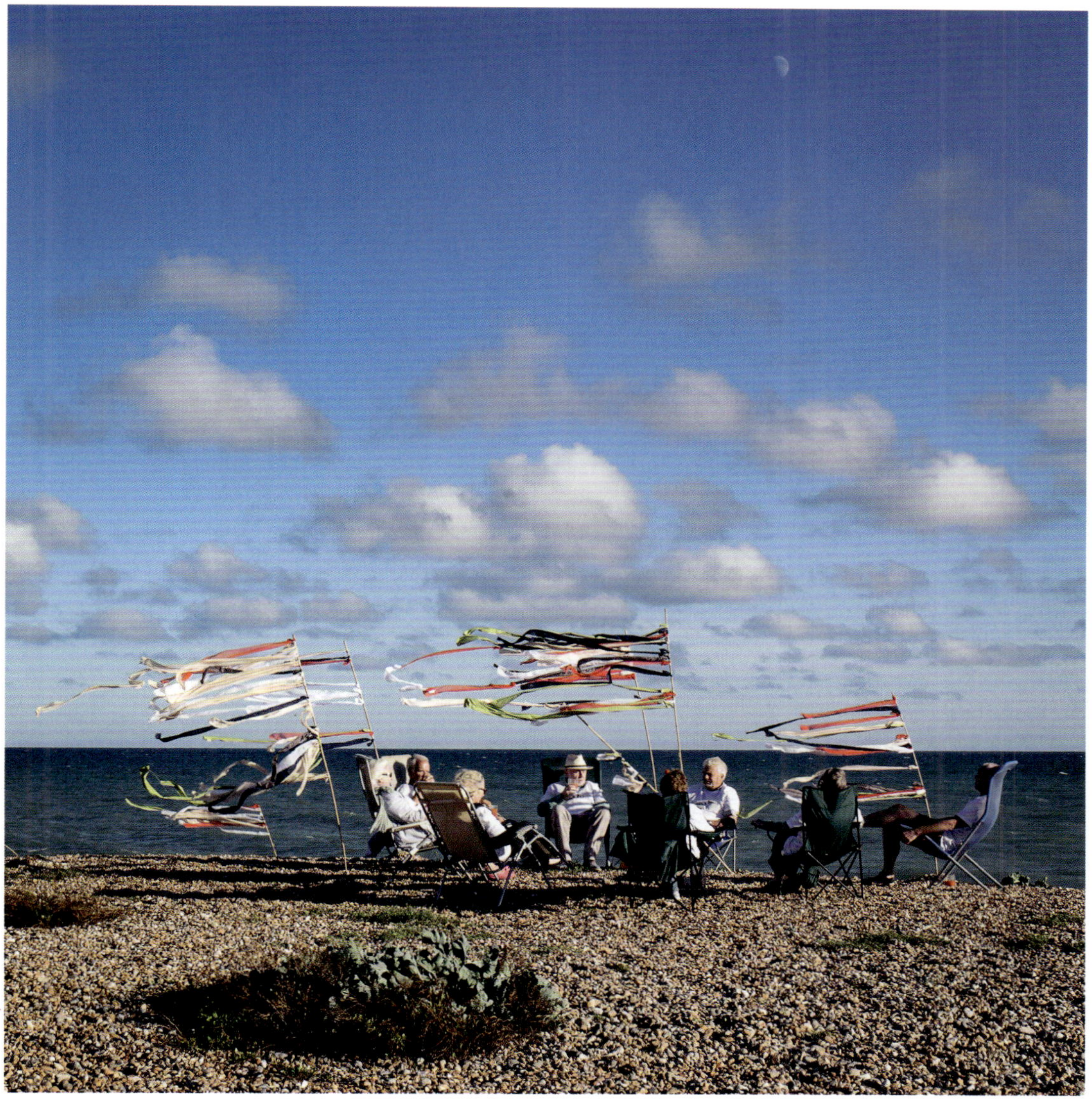

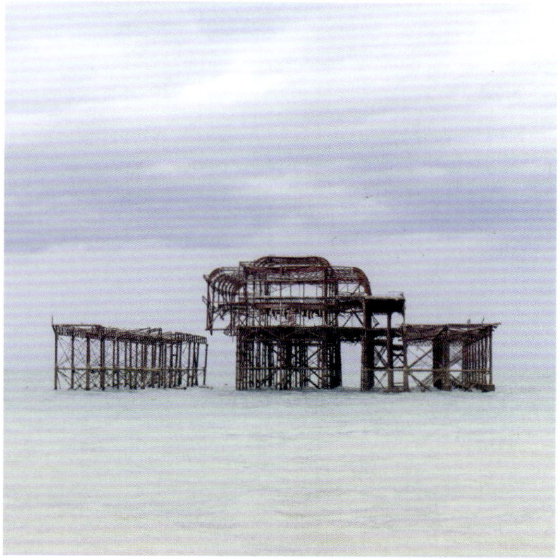

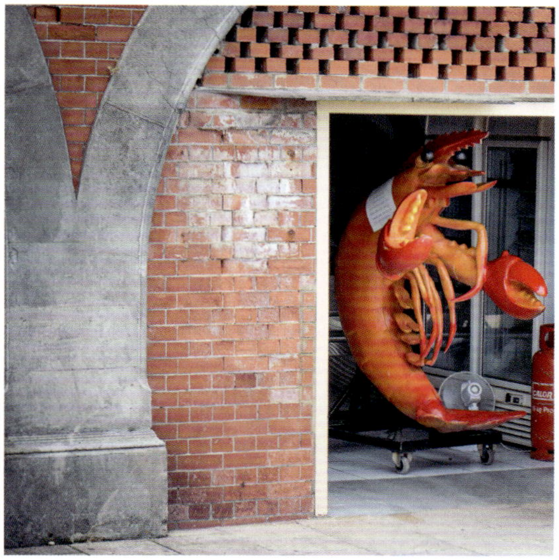

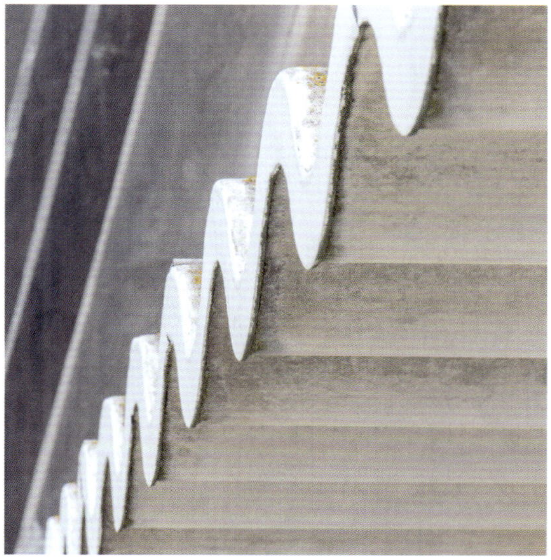

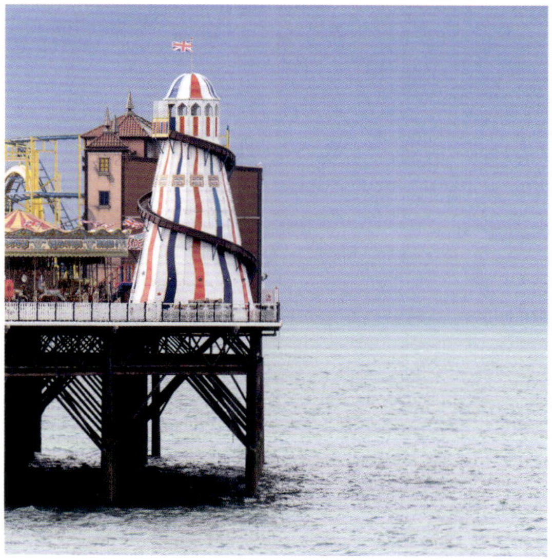

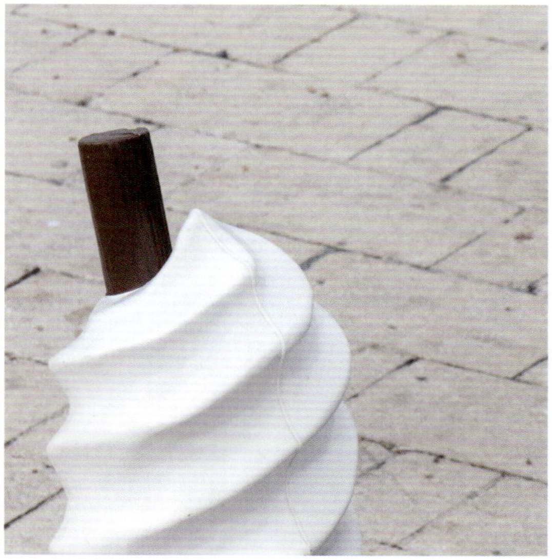

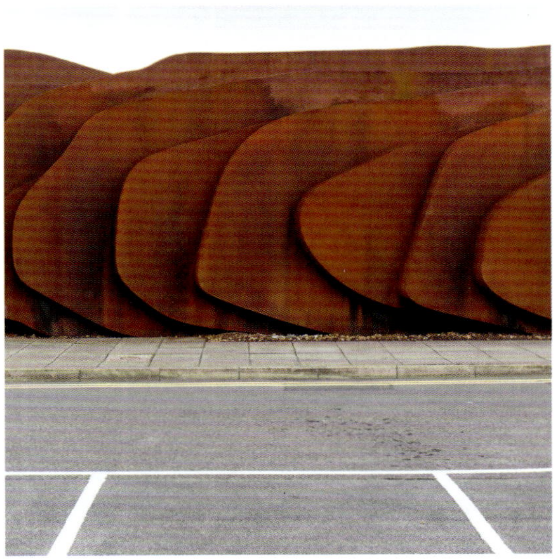

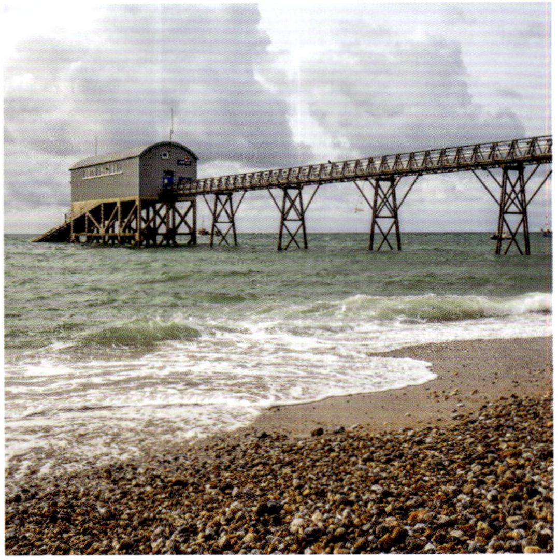

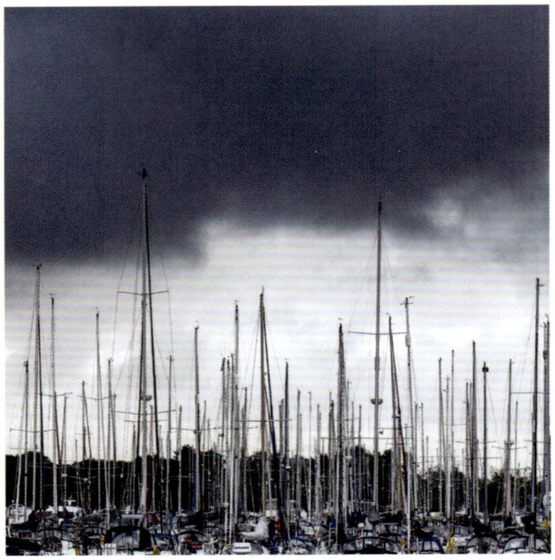

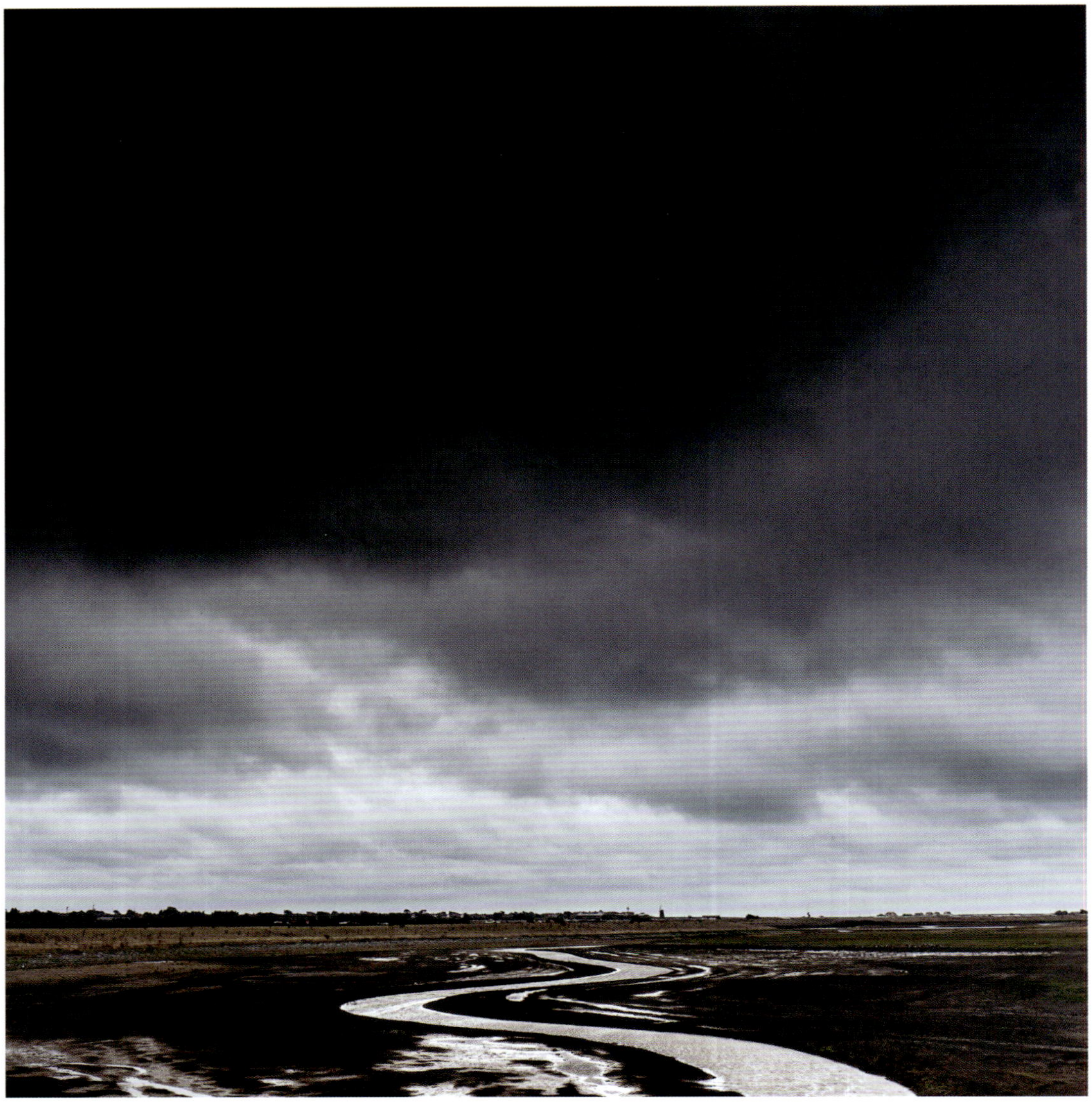

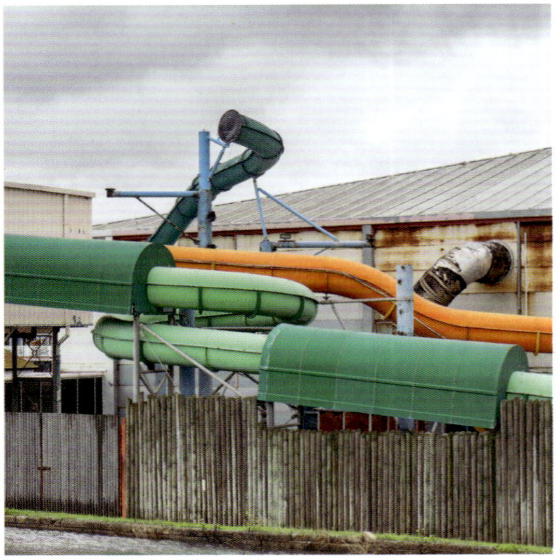

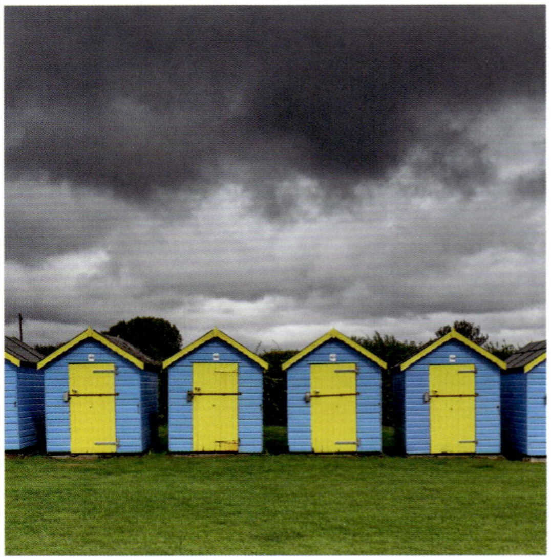

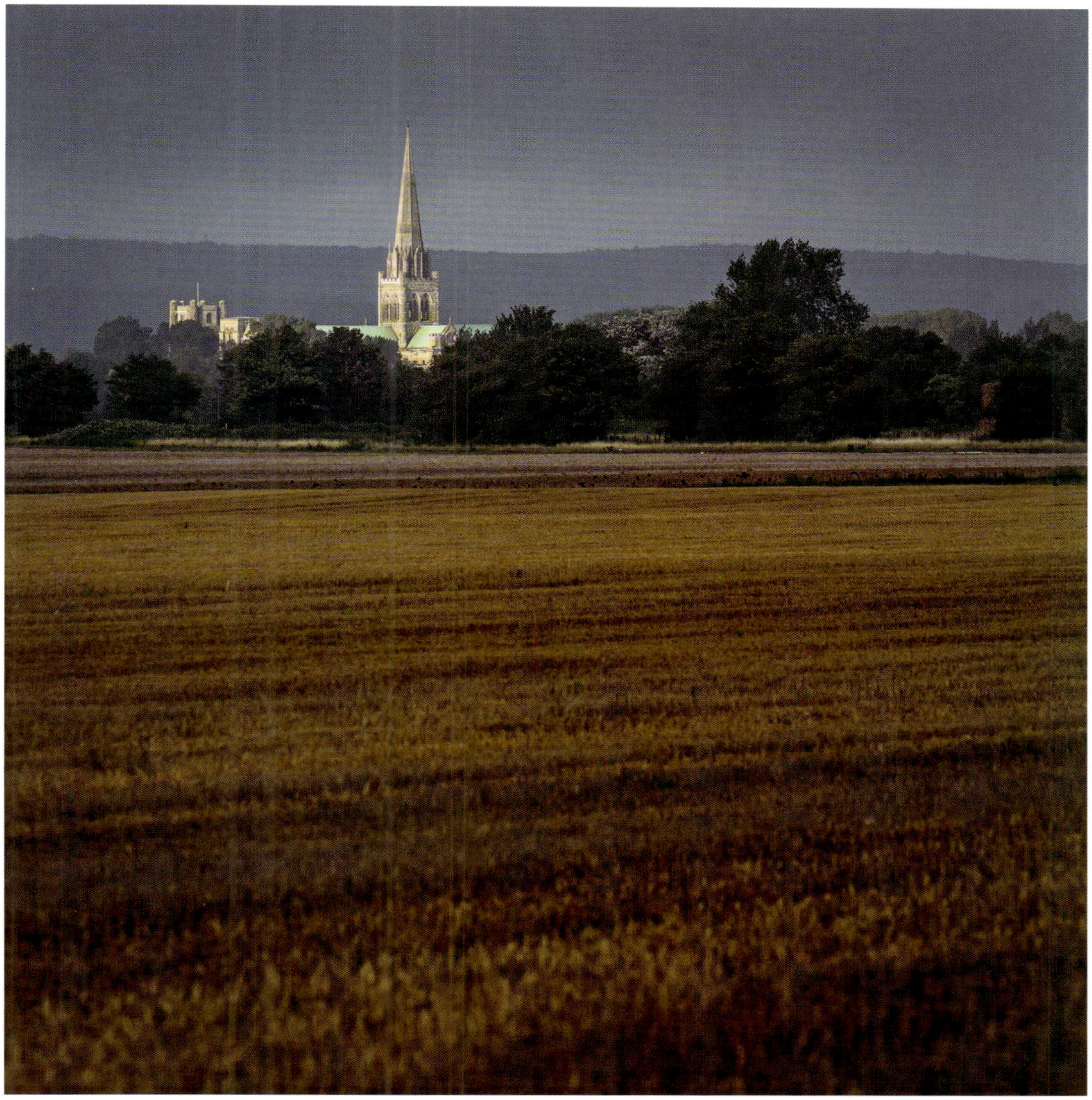

Opposite, clockwise from top left:

East Beach Cafe, Littlehampton, designed by Thomas Heatherwick in 2007

RNLI Selsey Lifeboat Station Boat House (demolished 2017)

Birdham Pool Marina, Chichester

Splash Waterworld, Butlins, Bognor Regis Holiday Park

Beach huts, Middleton-on-Sea

Medmerry Nature Reserve, Ham

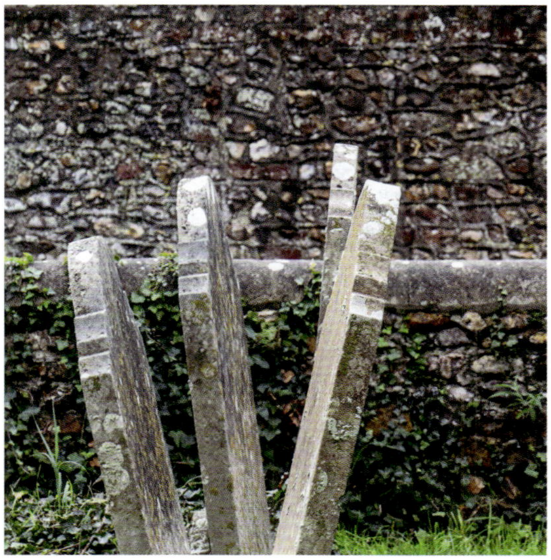

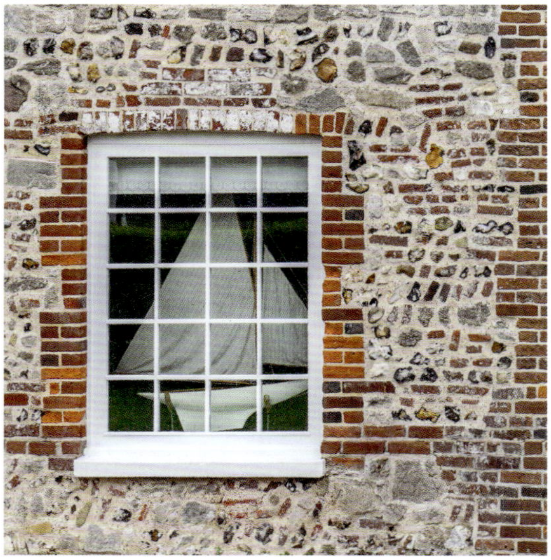

From top left:

Chichester Cathedral catches the light

Gravestones, Bosham

Nautical window, Bosham

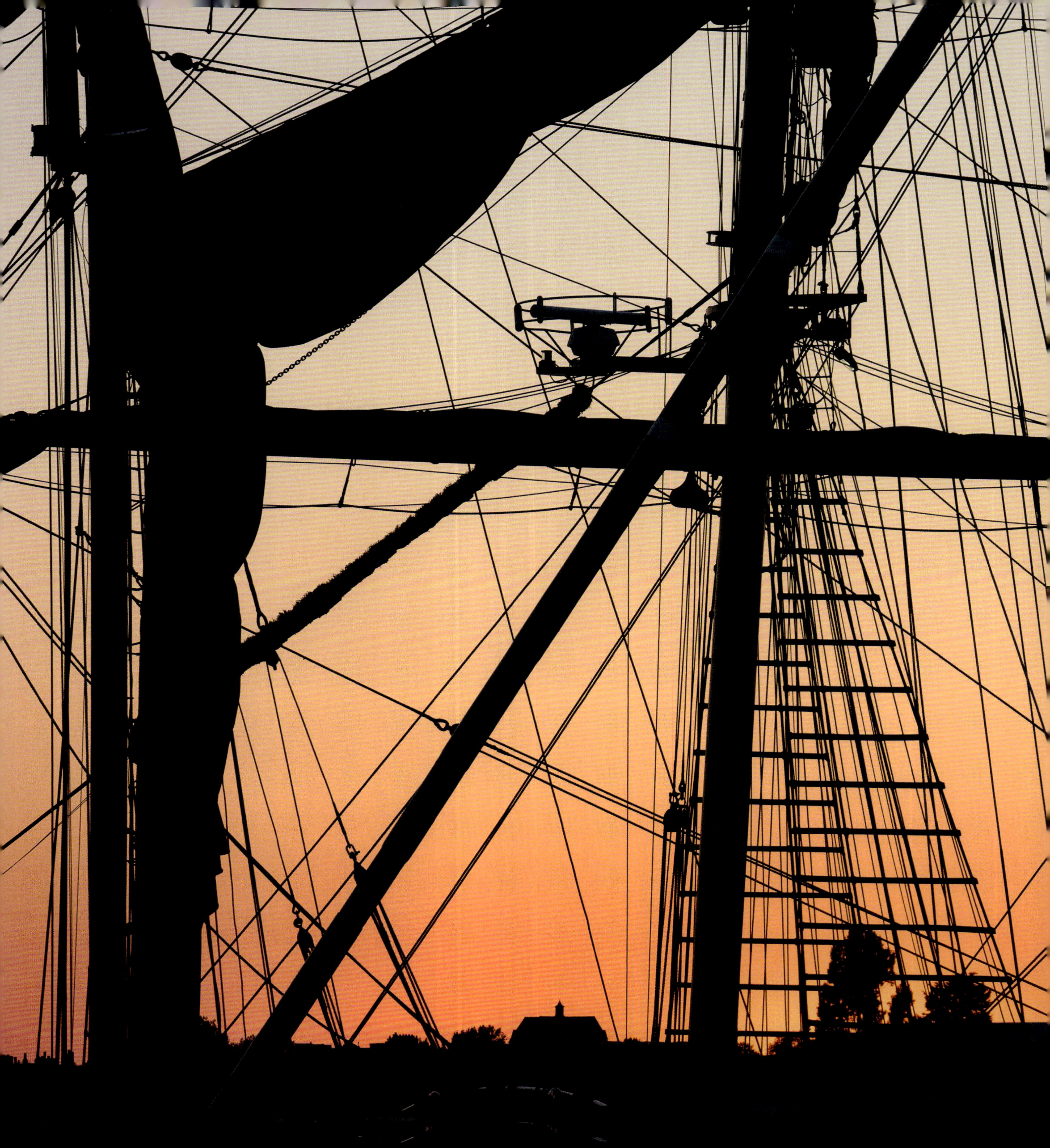

04 HAMPSHIRE

SEPTEMBER–OCTOBER 2015
DAY 023–029 | 00580–00779KM | 199KM

Opposite:

Rigging, Gunwharf Quays, Portsmouth

'Tiller away from you', 'No, tiller away from you', '. . . and go about', 'Yes, that's it, well done, Henry.' On a radiant September morning, a gentle breeze blows as children learn to dinghy sail at Emsworth. I catch snippets of conversation as I walk towards the Solent along the edge of the sheltered natural estuary that makes up Langstone Harbour. 'You been to this messy play thing at Horndean?' 'No, but I've been to Custard Club, and she loves it.' It's the perfect day to be outside and ideal conditions to cover the miles.

Near Fort Cumberland, a group of women wearing hijabs invert gender norms by fishing off the pier while black-leather-jacketed young men lean on their cars with the doors open. They listen to Arabic pop music as families picnic on the shingle opposite Hayling Island. I round the headland towards Portsmouth to be faced with the Isle of Wight very close and a busy seaway of ferries, massive container ships and a warship, all in motion. Tiny yachts dance around among the Goliaths. From here, it's easy to see how Hampshire, midway along the south coast, is blessed with protected and defendable waters that attracted trade and wealth in the age of sail.

On awakening in a B&B in Portsmouth, I hear trains rumbling into the harbour station, ships' horns sounding, and the *pssst* of coach doors opening. They're all noises of a dynamic coastal city coming to life. Once I've shouldered my bag, I gravitate to Spinnaker Tower, the city's landmark observation centre, whose sail shape evokes the place's nautical DNA. I arrive to see it undergoing a transformation, with abseilers hard at work skilfully painting the exterior gold and blue as part of an Emirates sponsorship deal. From the viewing platform, I can see the impressive scale of the historic dockyard and the vast natural harbour opening out from a narrow entrance. I realise how unassailable this harbour must have been before air power – protected both by the Isle of Wight and water on all sides. Back at ground level, I trace the public edge of the vast naval base, past numerous checkpoints of armed men clad in fluorescent jackets and peaked caps.

Over the next two days, I follow Southampton Water in a giant hairpin route, passing through Gosport, Southampton and Hythe before entering the New Forest beyond Fawley. By the second afternoon I'm well within the forest where the wild ponies of Beaulieu Heath seem to have the happiest expressions. I can't help but smile back in return. With the combination of roaming ponies and open heathland, this could be Exmoor if not for the nearby refinery chimney flaring.

As I'm approaching Beaulieu village, I try to glimpse the large manor house but can only make out a forest of elegant chimneys over the top of the encircling wall. At the shop, I enquire if the big house I've just seen is where the estate is run from. 'Oh, you can't go there; that's where Lord Montagu lives . . . though he died two months ago, now it's his son.' Soon, I pass the Montagu Arms, where a truck is emblazoned with the Montagu crest, before I open a gate into woodland carved with the same three red diamonds. It all feels a little feudal; the ultra-managed environment has the air of an elite public school. I'm reminded of Paul Theroux's observation in *The Kingdom by the Sea* that 'quaint places in England looked both pretty and inhospitable'.

On my last evening in Hampshire, I lie under a browning chestnut tree on a dry bed of fallen leaves, which feel good against my bare feet – I could easily fall asleep, but the sun has already set, and I have many miles to go. Back on the trail under the darkening sky, I lose sight first of the silhouette of the Needles on the Isle of Wight, then the horizon itself.

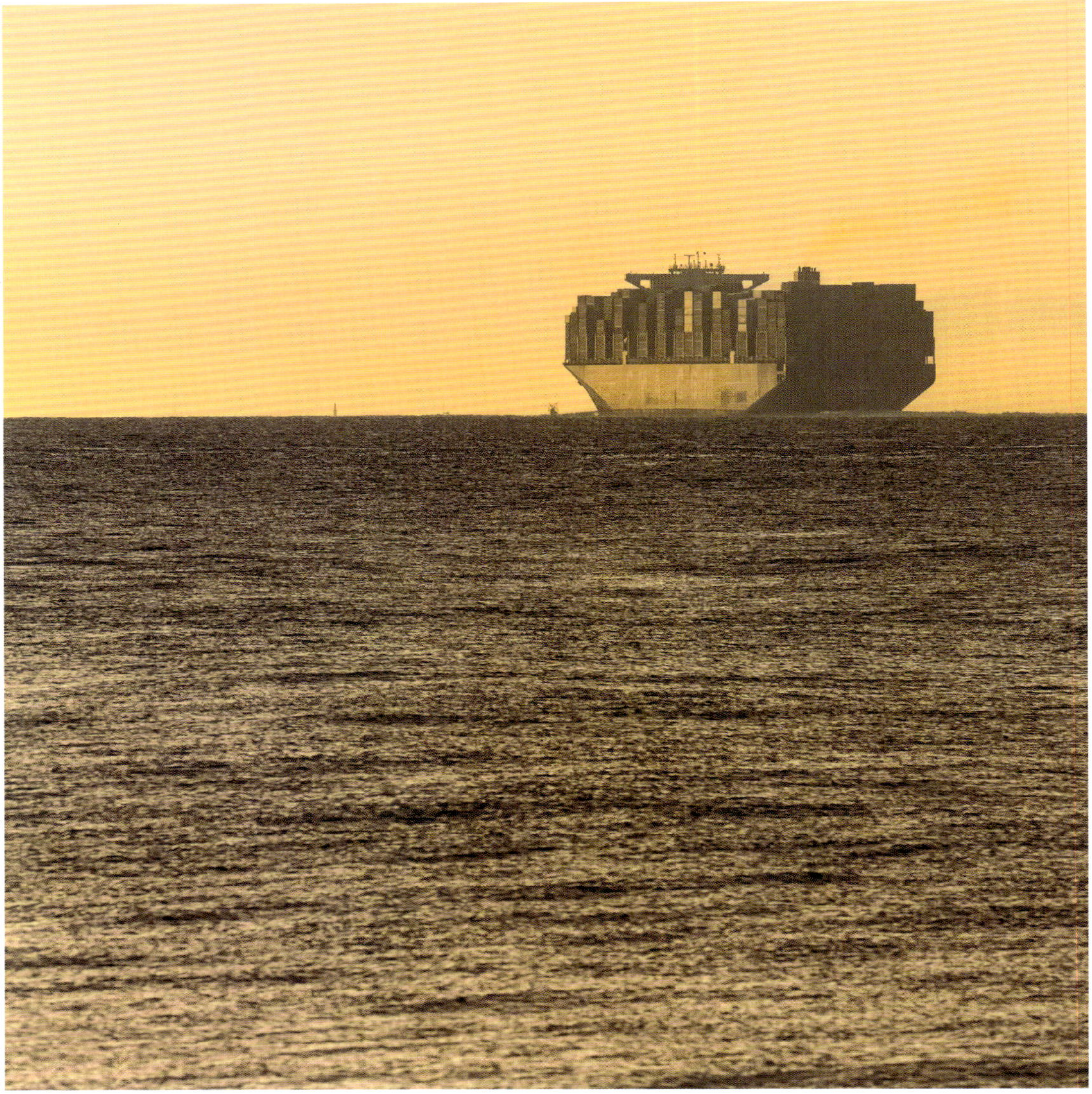

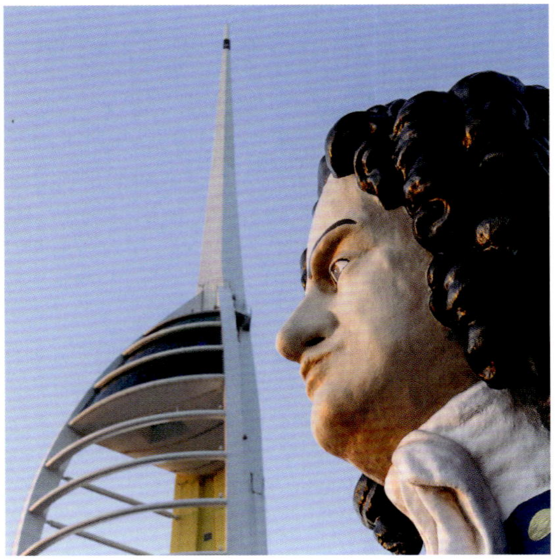

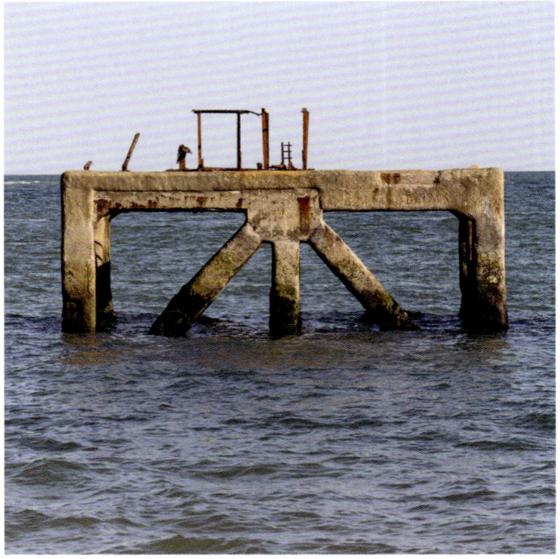

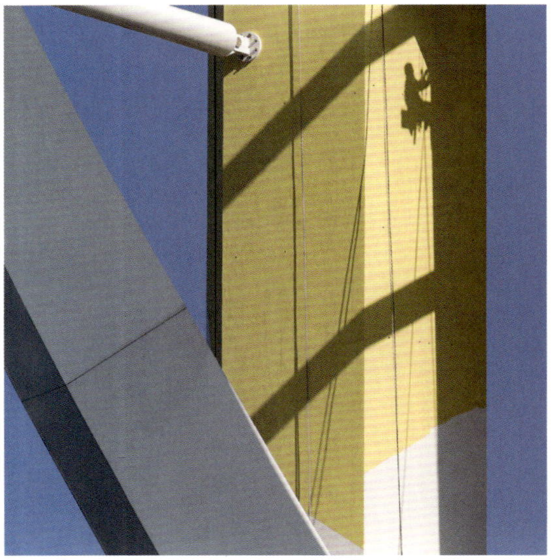

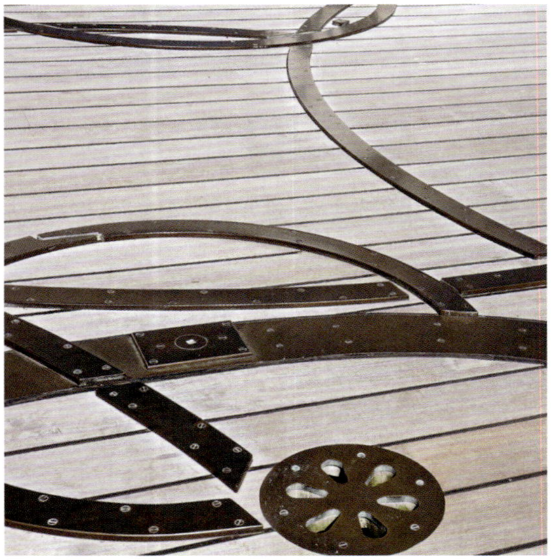

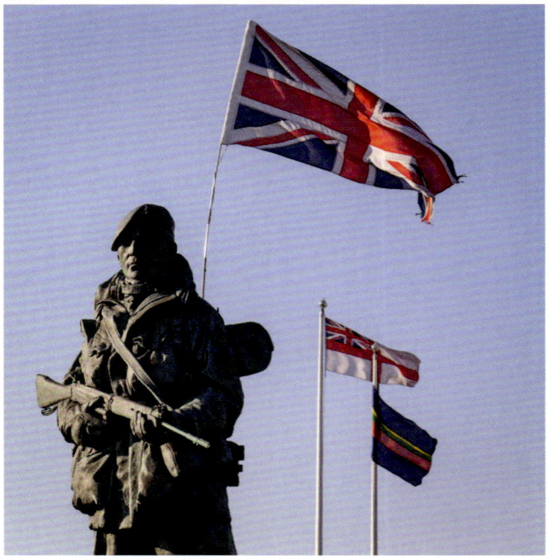

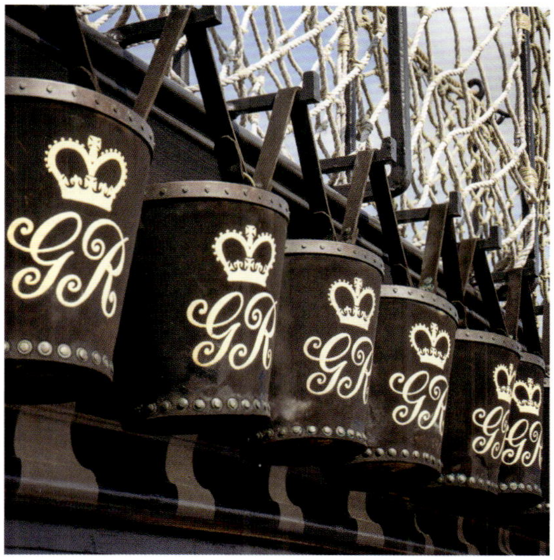

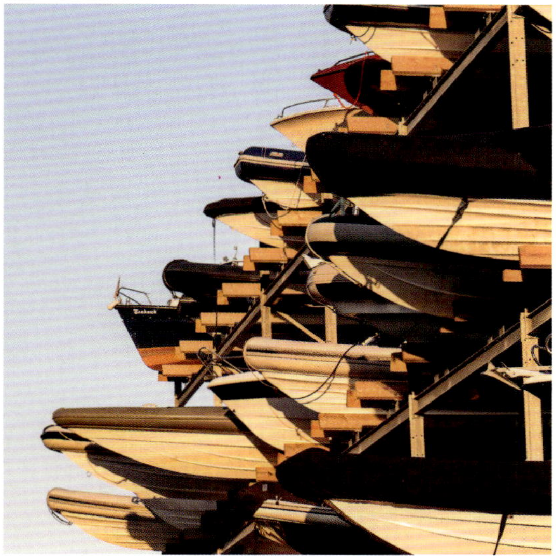

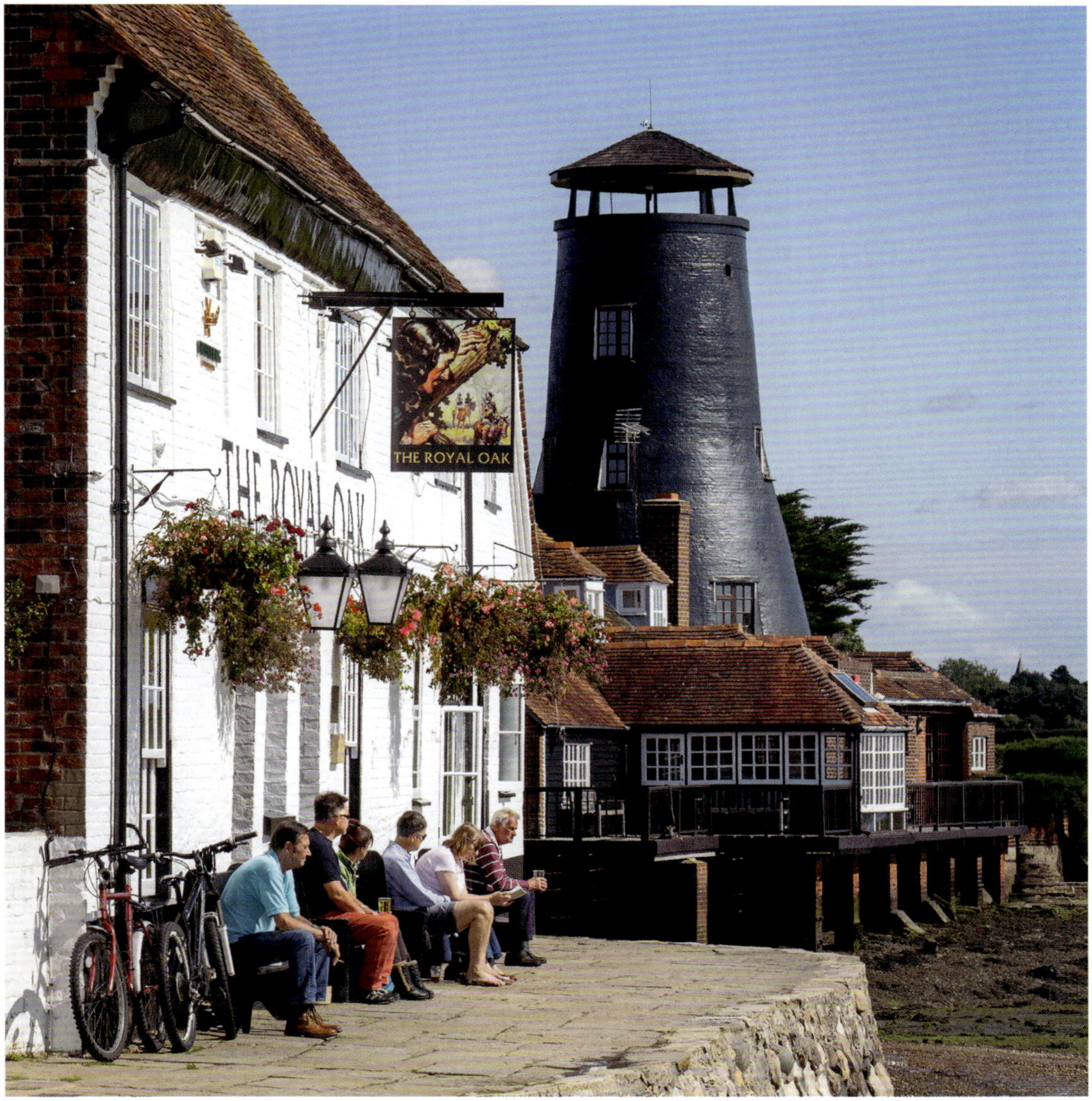

Opposite, clockwise from top left:

Container ship in the Solent from Gilkicker Point

Spinnaker Tower with a ship's figurehead of John Churchill, the 1st Duke of Marlborough, one of England's greatest generals, who led British armies to important victories over Louis XIV of France, notably at Blenheim in 1704

By Fort Cumberland, Portsmouth

The Yomper, by sculptor Philip Jackson, Royal Marines Museum, Portsmouth. It is modelled on a photograph of Corporal Peter Robinson yomping to Sapper Hill during the Falklands War of 1982

HMS *Warrior*, upper deck, Portsmouth Naval Base

Emirates Spinnaker Tower painting, Portsmouth

From top left:

Fire buckets on HMS *Victory*'s quarterdeck on which Lord Nelson was shot by musket fire in 1805, Portsmouth Naval Base

Drystack boat storage, Portsmouth

Royal Oak and Mill, Langstone

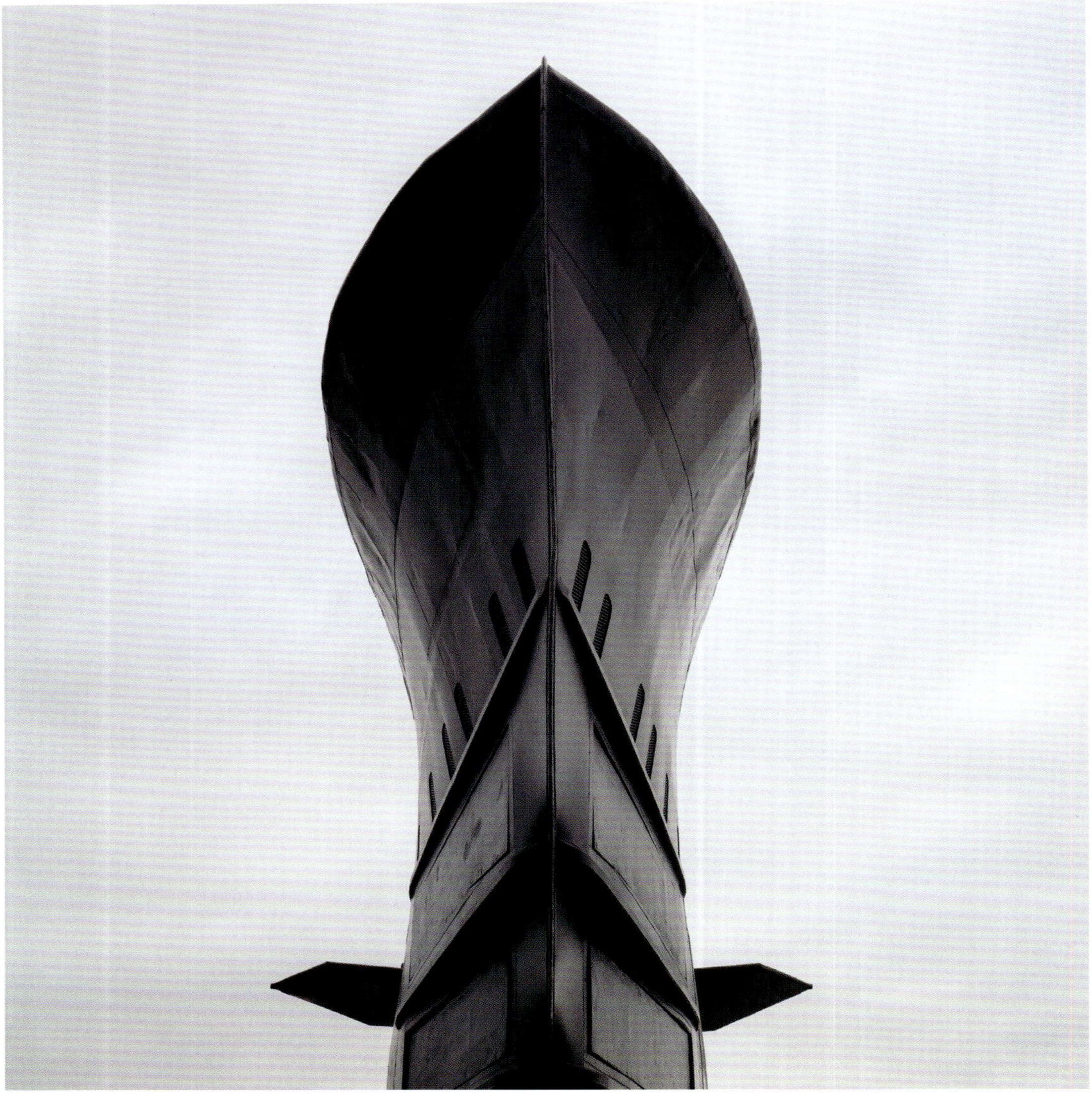

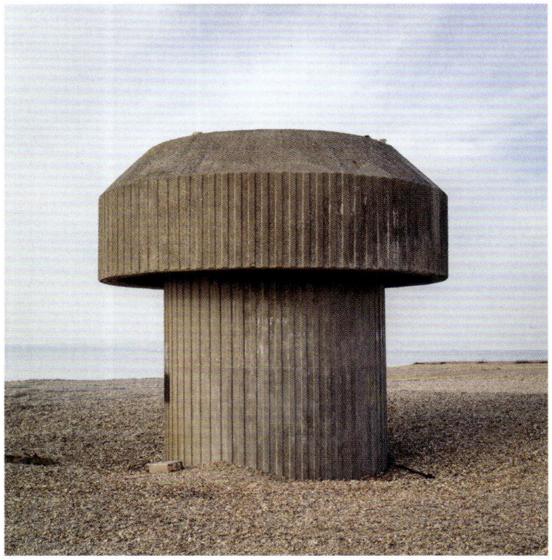

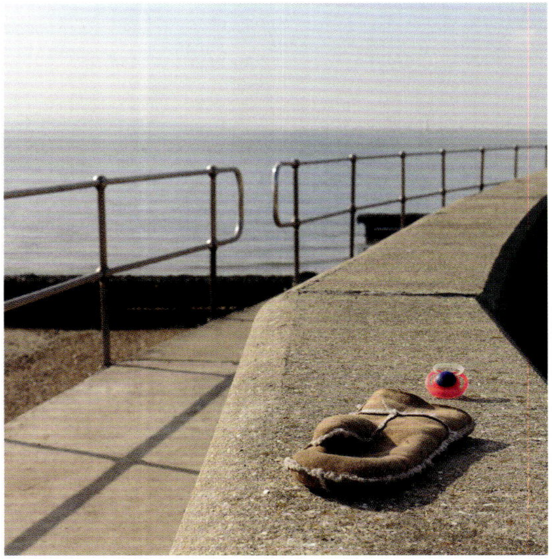

From top left:

Bow of HMS *Alliance*, Britain's last surviving Second World War-era submarine, Royal Navy Submarine Museum, Gosport

Browndown Range, outfall

Lost and found: Hill Head

Opposite, clockwise from top left:

Ashlett Mill, a water-powered corn mill, Fawley

Calshot Castle, an artillery fort constructed by Henry VIII between 1539 and 1540 to defend the sea passage to Southampton

Fawley Power Station, featured in *Star Wars* and *Mission Impossible* films (demolished 2019–23)

Turbine Hall, Fawley Power Station

Tanker, Fawley oil refinery

Fawley oil refinery from Hook Park

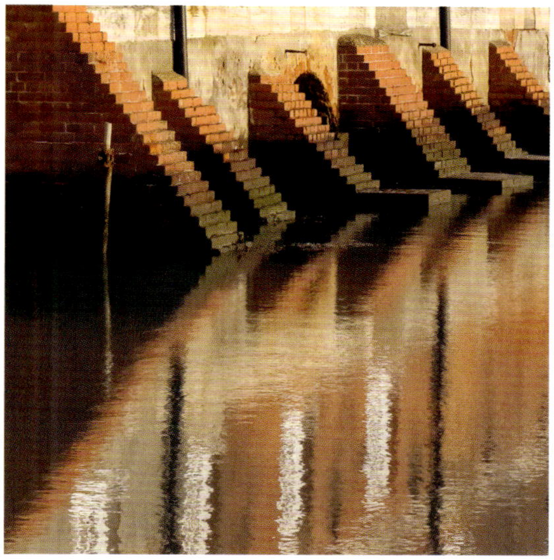
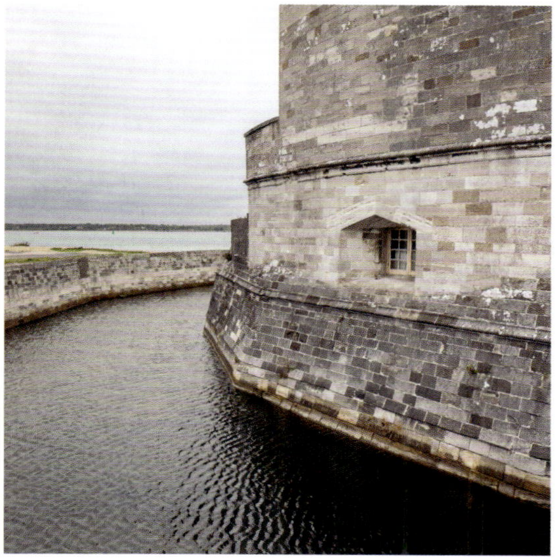
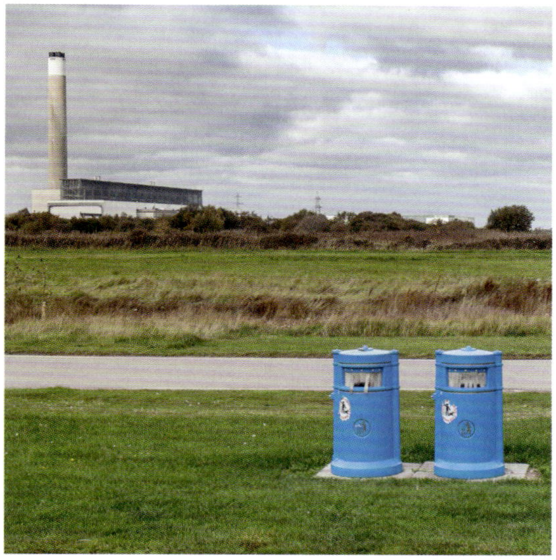
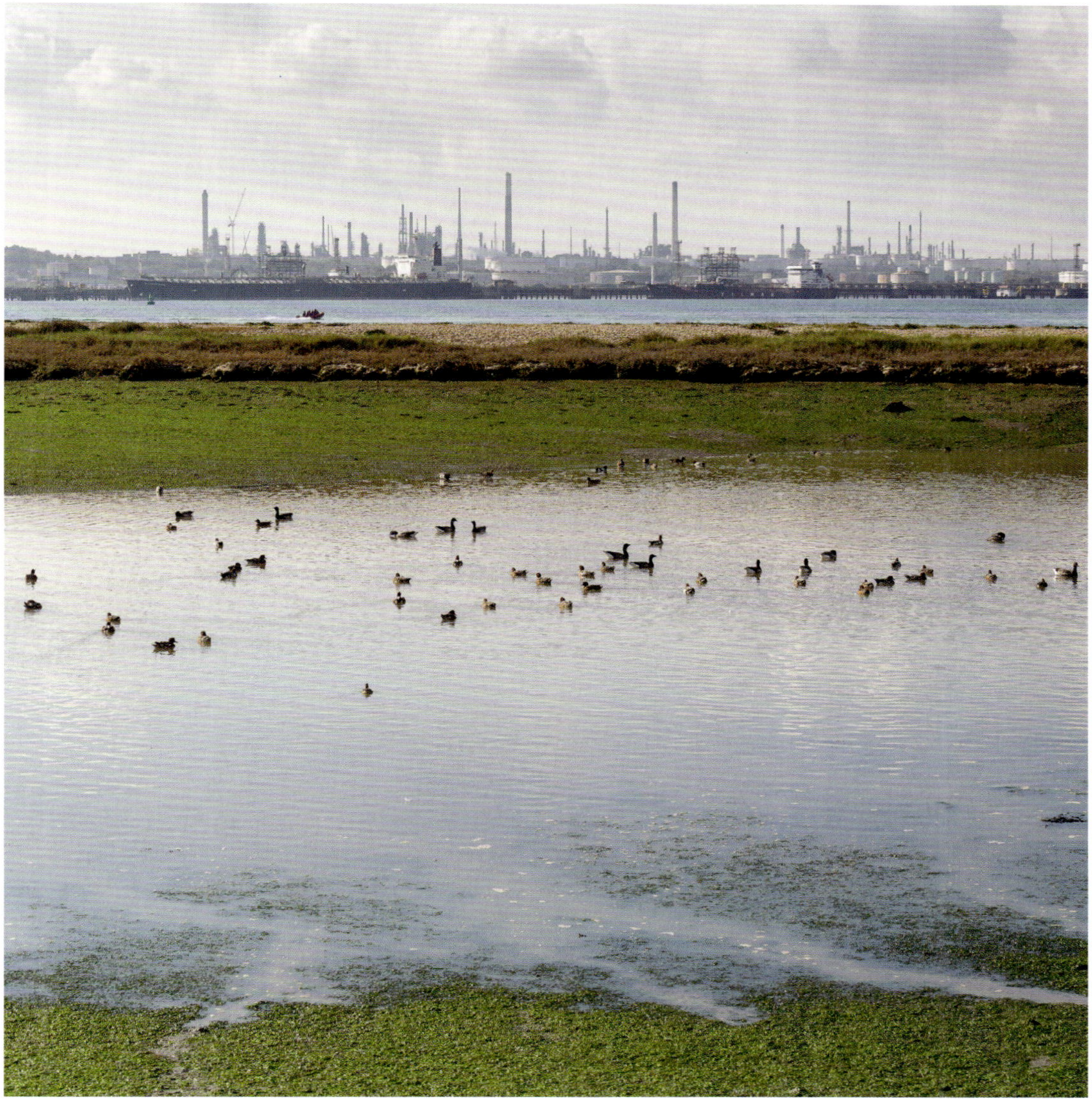
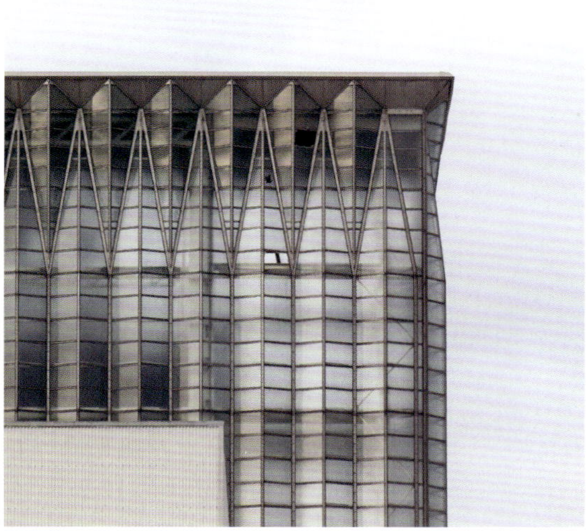
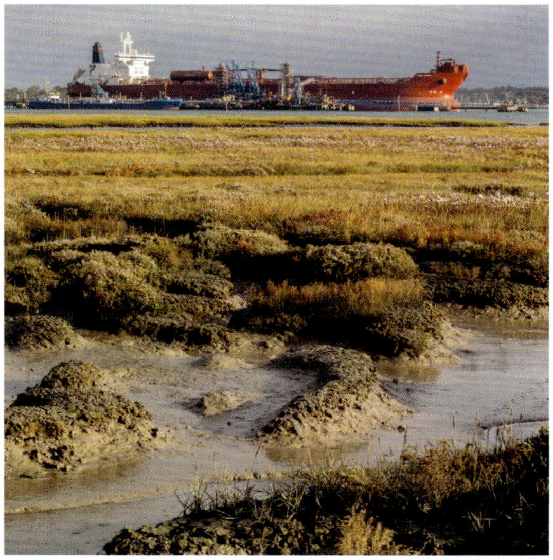

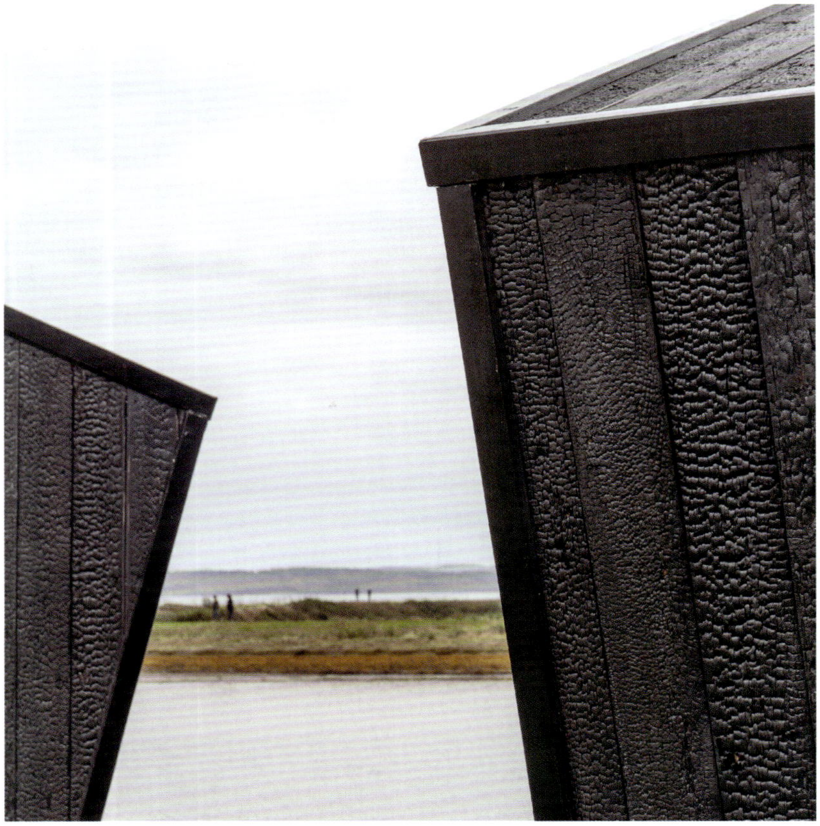
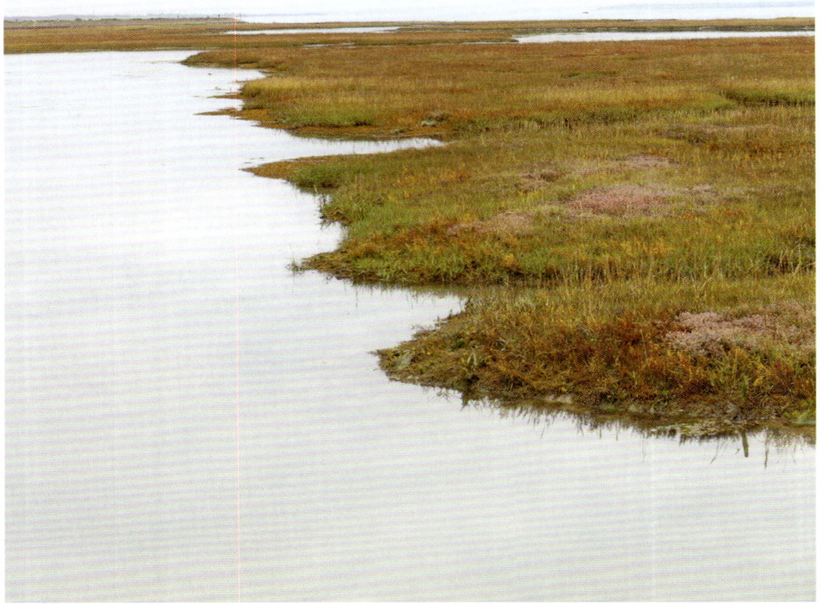
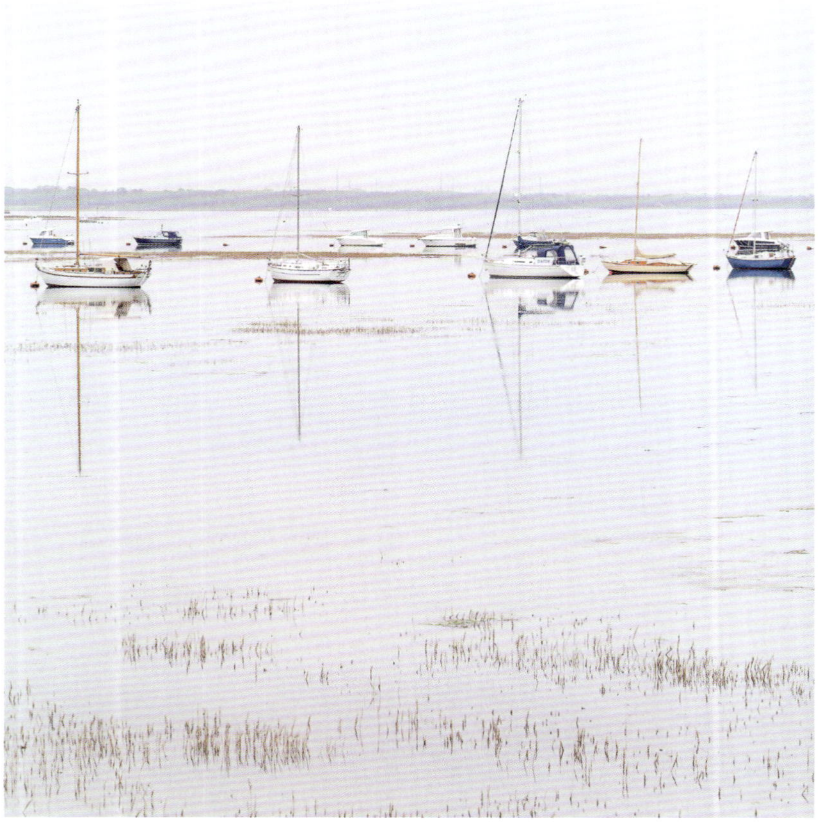
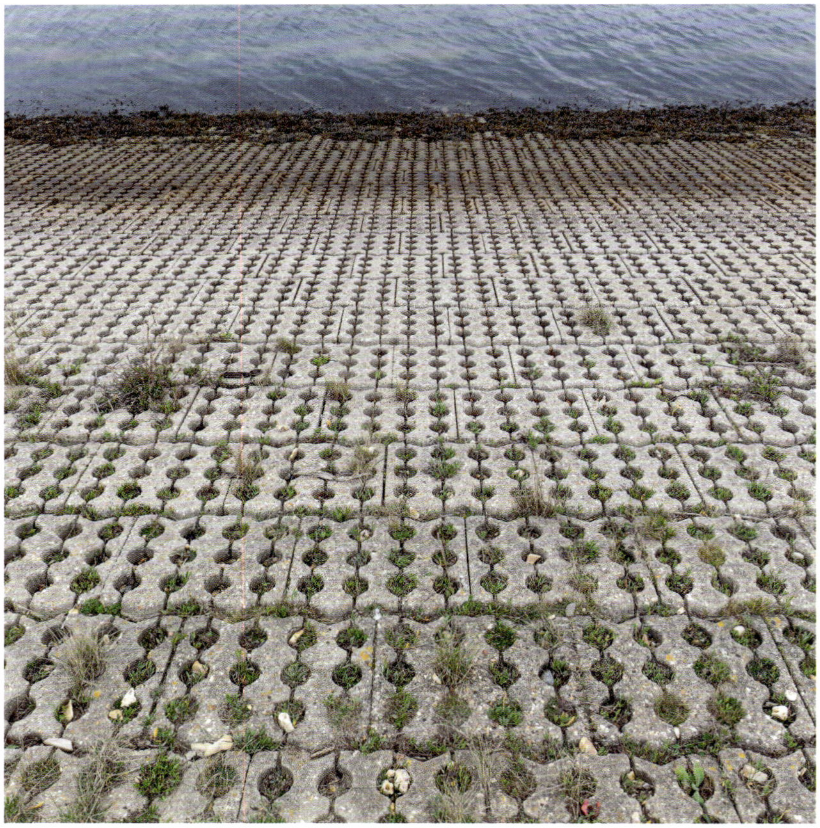

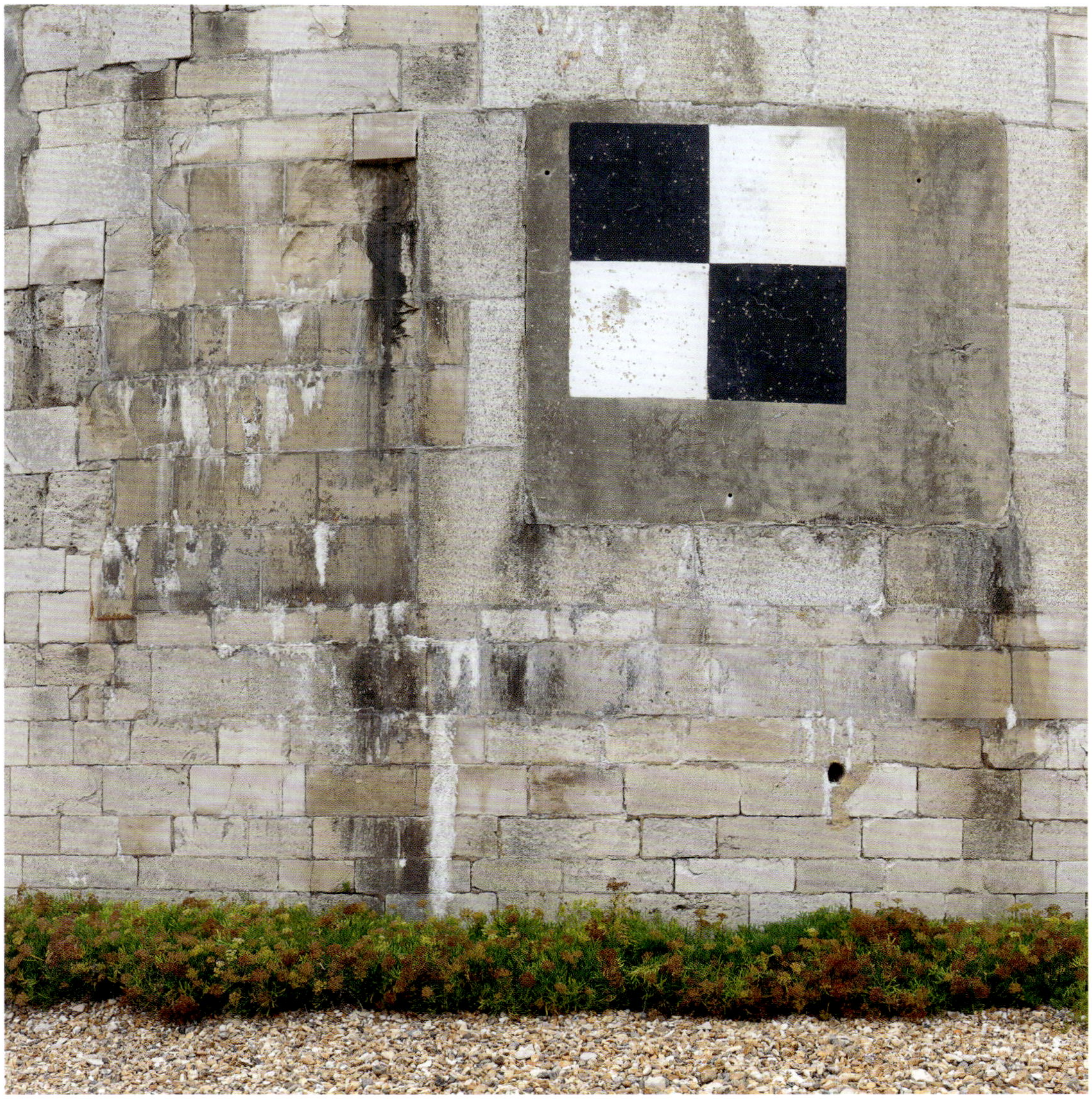

Opposite, from top left:

The Observatory, a mobile artist studio in Lymington saltmarshes designed by Feilden Clegg Bradley Studios in 2015 – detail of wood-charred cladding that uses the Japanese method of wood preservation and strengthening (shou sugi ban)

Soft edgeland, Keyhaven Marshes

From bottom left:

Moorings, Keyhaven Lake

Hard edgeland, Keyhaven Marshes

From top left:

Marker: Hurst Castle, an artillery fort established by Henry VIII by the western mouth of the Solent

Bag of blanks, Hurst Castle

Embrasure, Hurst Castle

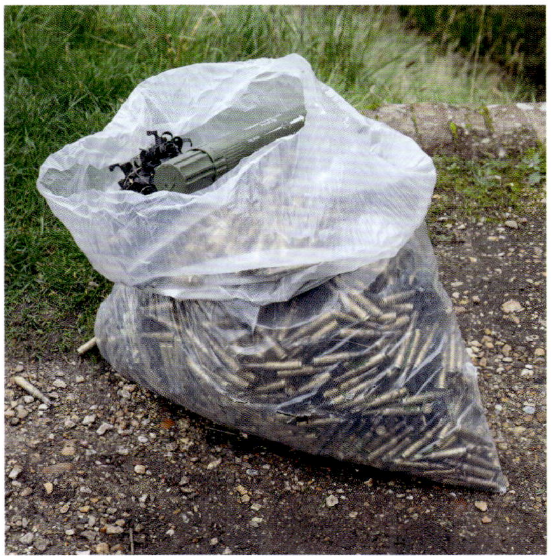

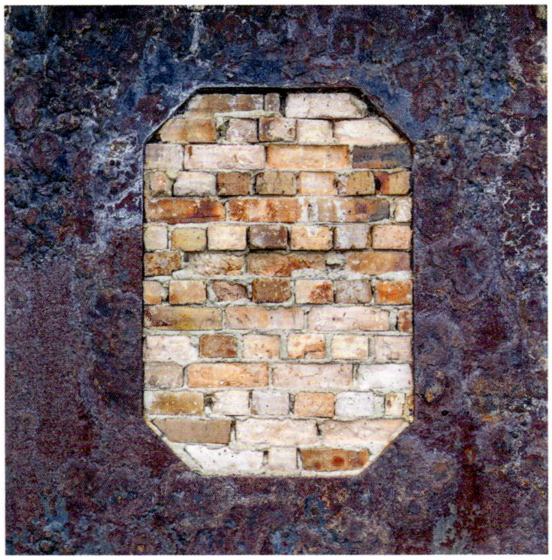

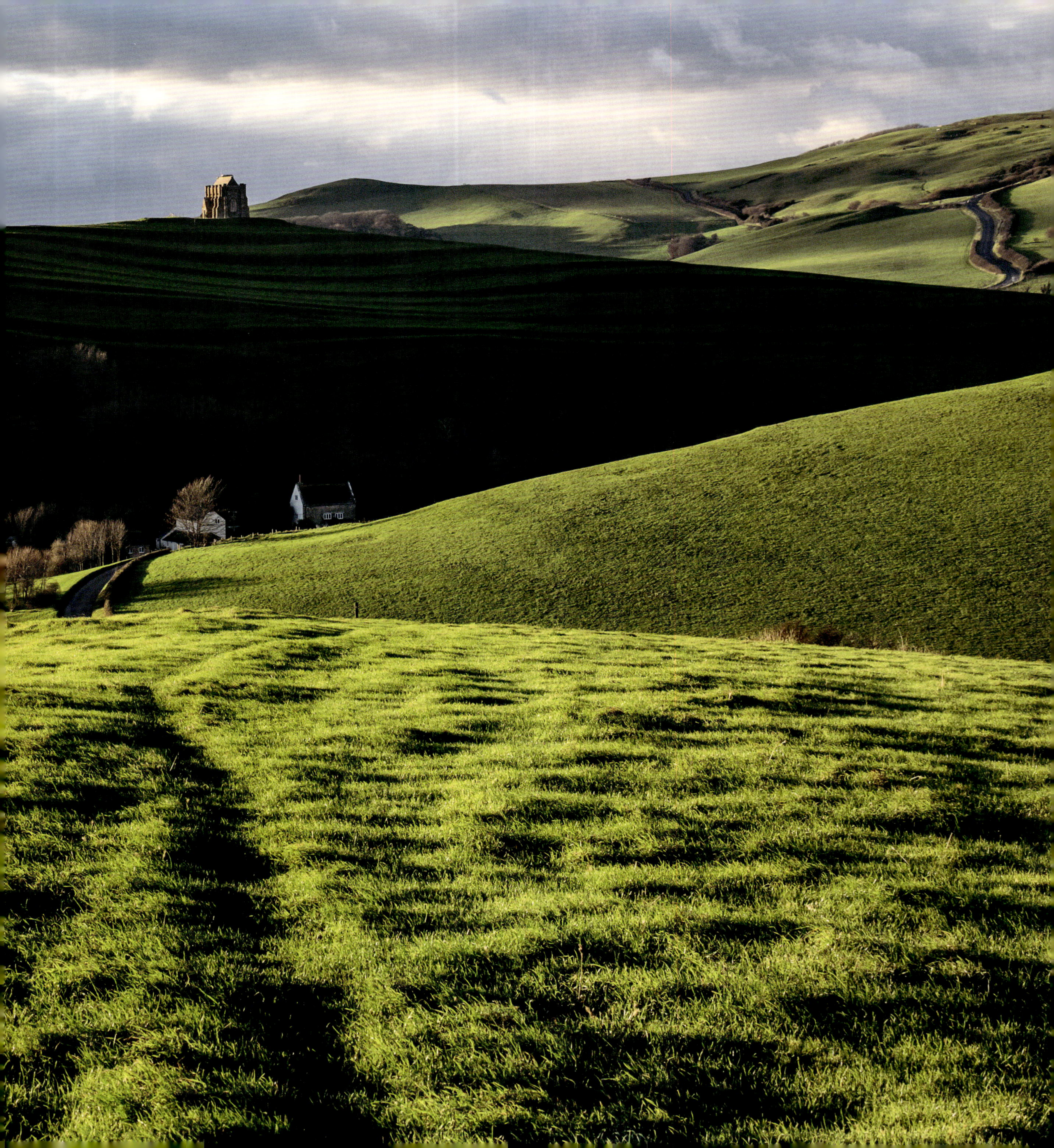

05 DORSET

NOVEMBER 2015

DAY 030–037 | 00779–01,001KM | 222KM

Thick sea mist envelops the trees in the wonderfully named Chewton Bunny, a chine that marks the border of Dorset and Hampshire and an old smuggling route. I clamber down the narrow ravine to arrive at the seafront at Mudeford, which is mirrored by a neat row of pastel beach huts where a silent couple read the *Telegraph* with mugs of tea, a golden Labrador at their side.

On the way to Poole, I peer in through the window of a Sandbanks estate agent. I'm shocked to discover that properties here are in the £1–7 million price range. Walking through the area is an underwhelming experience as the main virtue of each property seems to be its size. With their high gates adorned with CCTV and numerous *Beware of the Dog* and security company notices peppered about, I'm reminded of a damp version of Los Angeles.

Soon after leaving Poole Harbour for the Isle of Purbeck, I reach Fort Henry, a Second World War bunker overlooking Studland Bay. Here, the Allied commanders watched a full-scale rehearsal for the invasion of occupied Europe in 1944. Today, surrounded by woodland, the bunker aesthetic seems more Inca or James Turrell than military.

Near Fort Henry, the clifftops rise above the dramatic chalk sea stacks of Old Harry Rocks, marking the start of the Jurassic Coast and the much more rugged landscape of the South West Coast Path. A man dressed in a ranger uniform further along the path calls out, 'Excuse me! There must be about thirty guillemots on that ledge down there; thought you might be interested, certainly made my day!'

That evening, as the sun dips below the horizon, I enter Lulworth Ranges. The notice states they're open to the public until 8 a.m. tomorrow before closing for another week. I have to trust they will keep to schedule. The moonlight is strong enough to cast a shadow, and I use a torch primarily to be seen. To my right, signs warn of *Danger Unexploded Shells*. To my left, it's *Danger Unstable Cliffs*. The Plough, bright in the sky, marks my direction while the black water below the cliffs undulates like mercury in total silence. Distant automatic gunfire breaks the stillness. The sea glistens from the moonlight as I go up and down the black humpbacked hills before finally leaving the firing ranges and descending into Lulworth with a sigh of relief and aching knees three hours after sunset.

The following night I enter Weymouth past a floodlit skatepark where sliding figures move back and forth in the half-pipe like a pendulum. Green lasers fan out from lamps along the whole Georgian frontage. They come from an installation called *Light Veils* by artists Vong Phaophanit and Claire Oboussier. The arrangement changes every few minutes, and the overall effect is elevating and beautiful.

On my last day in Dorset, I loop around Portland and follow Chesil Beach until the cliffs rise assertively ahead. Climbing these coastal hills in the mizzle, I'm transported to the rugged landscapes of Wales or the Lake District, where sheep sit in the mist Sphinx-like while cows munch the lush grass audibly. The mud is particularly sticky here, clinging to my boots like a stubborn adversary, and I must stop regularly to peel an inch of clay off my soles. Below my feet, velvet orange mushrooms poke out of the grass, a vibrant contrast to the recently fallen cliff edge where the coast path has fallen down into the sea. A few hours later, I'm standing panting on top of Golden Cap: at 191 metres, the highest point on the south coast. Despite the mist, I can see right into Devon, a breathtaking view that makes the challenging climb all the more rewarding.

Opposite:

St Catherine's Chapel from Linton Hill, Abbotsbury

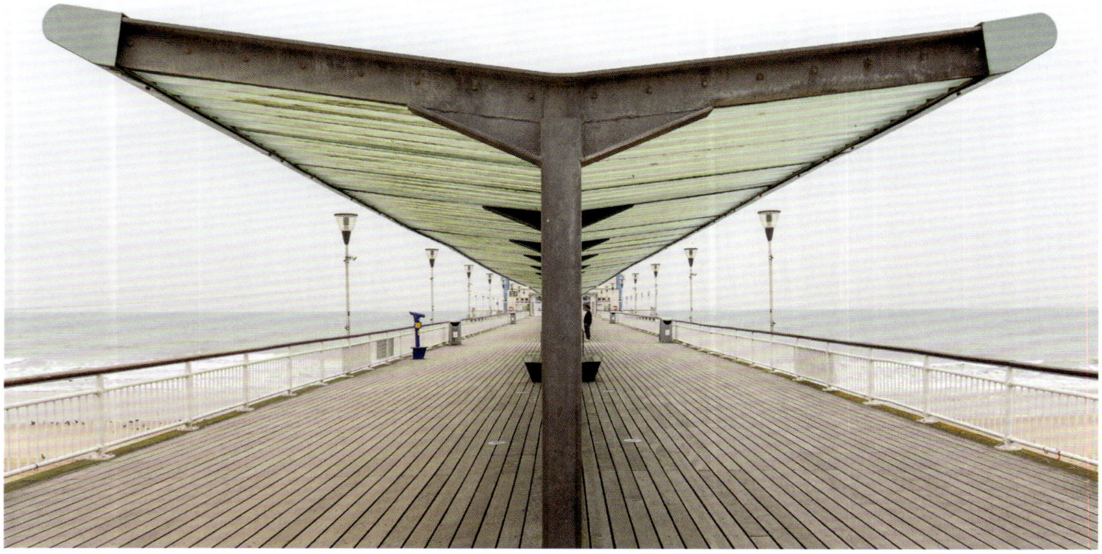

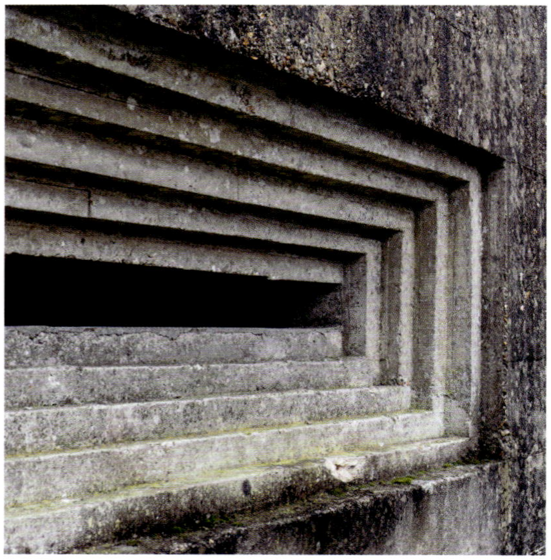

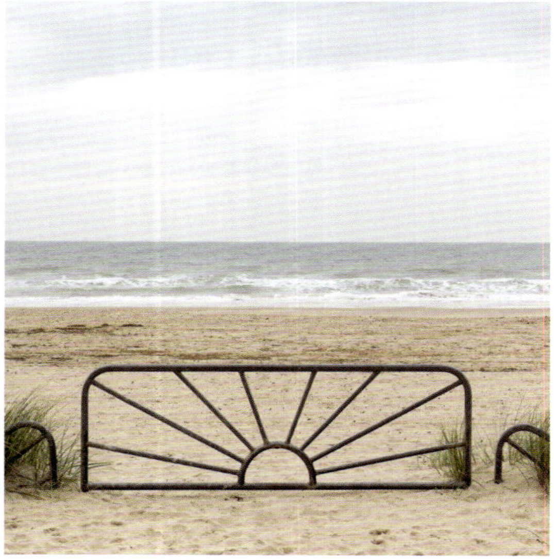

From top left:

Bournemouth Pier

Fort Henry, a Second World War observation bunker, Studland

Canford Cliffs Beach, Poole

Opposite, clockwise from top left:

Hartland Moor, Purbeck

Wytch Farm, the largest onshore oil field in Western Europe, Purbeck

Rempstone Heath, Purbeck

Chalk stack at Old Harry Rocks, Studland

Bournemouth from Warren Hill

Labrador and beach huts, Mudeford

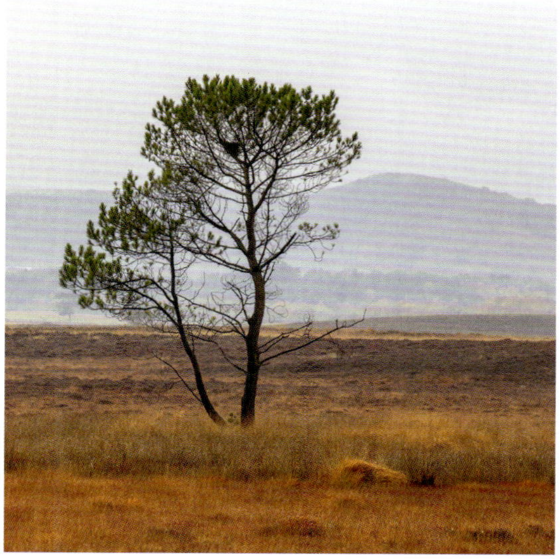
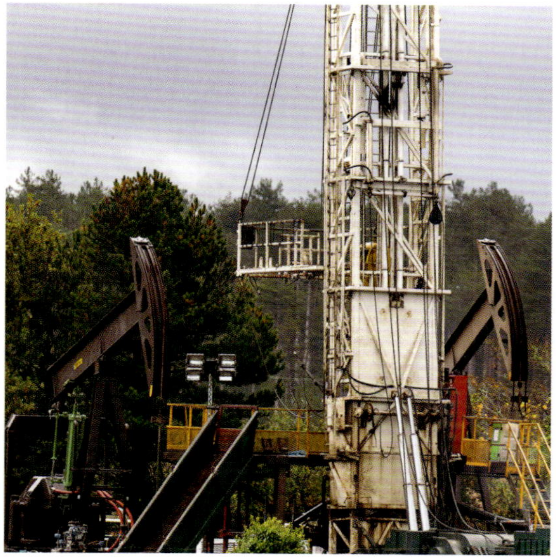
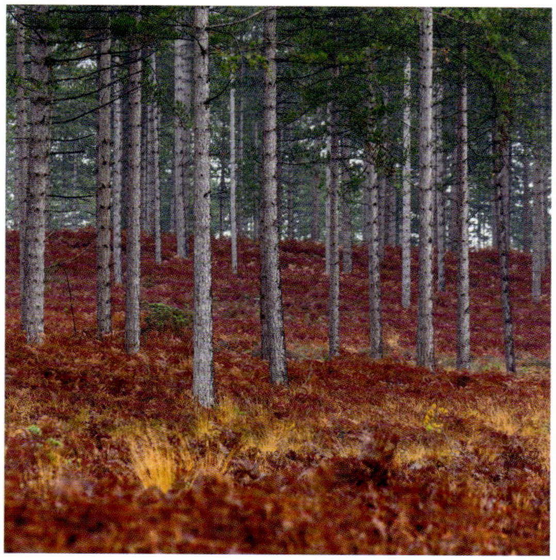
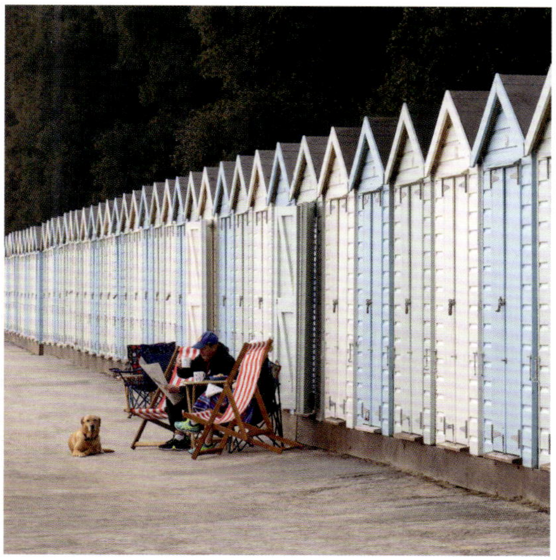
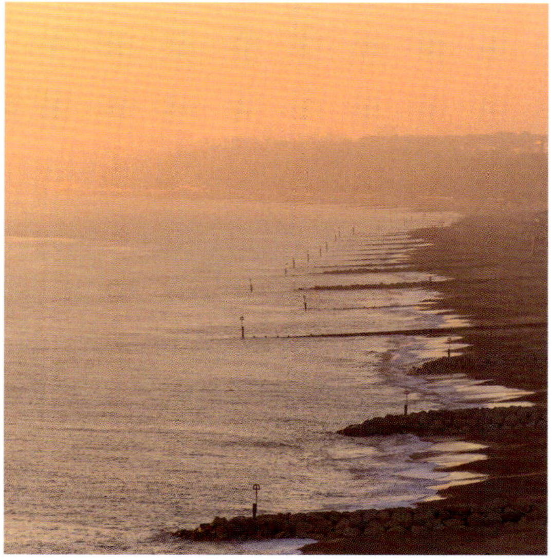
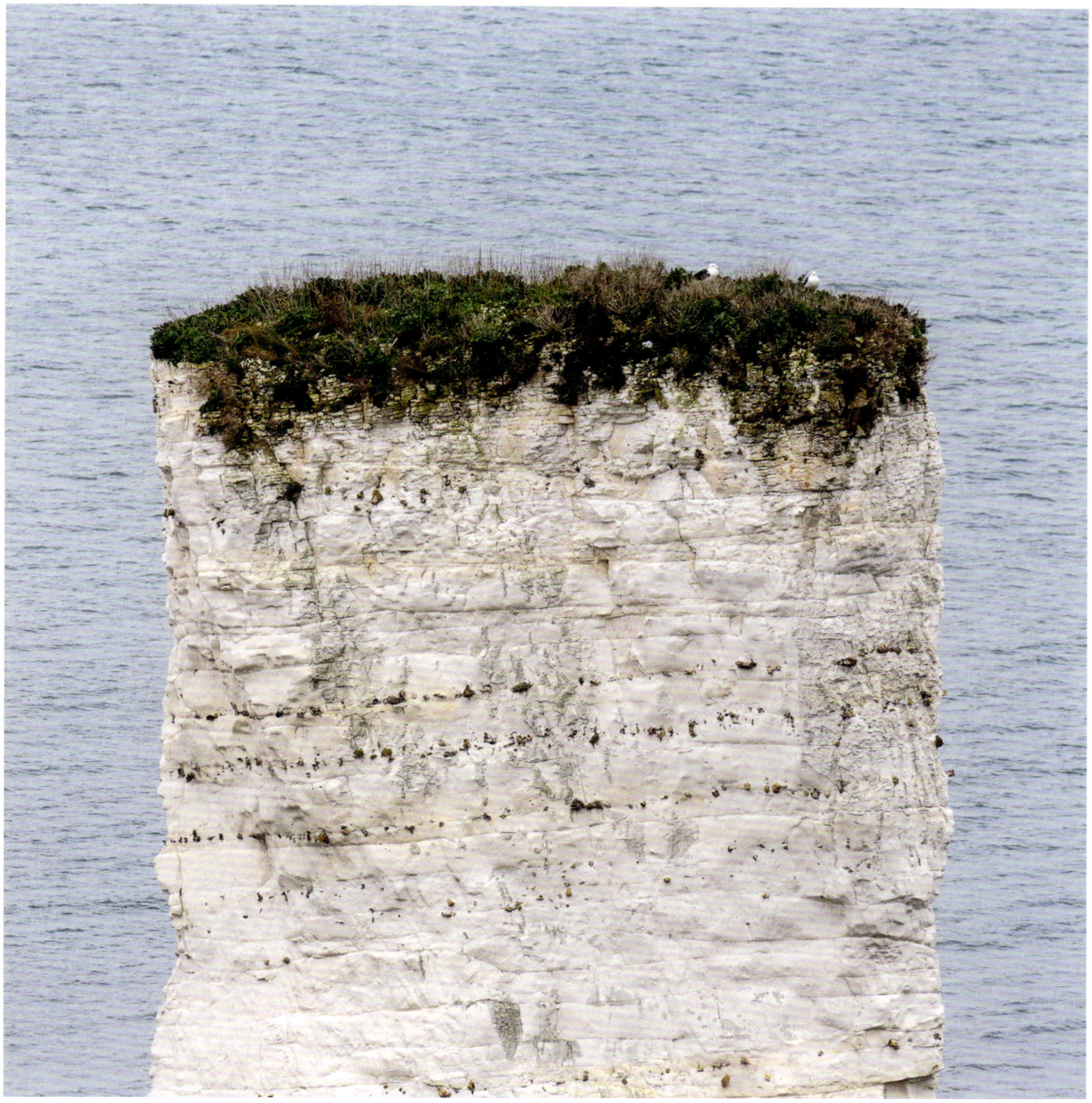

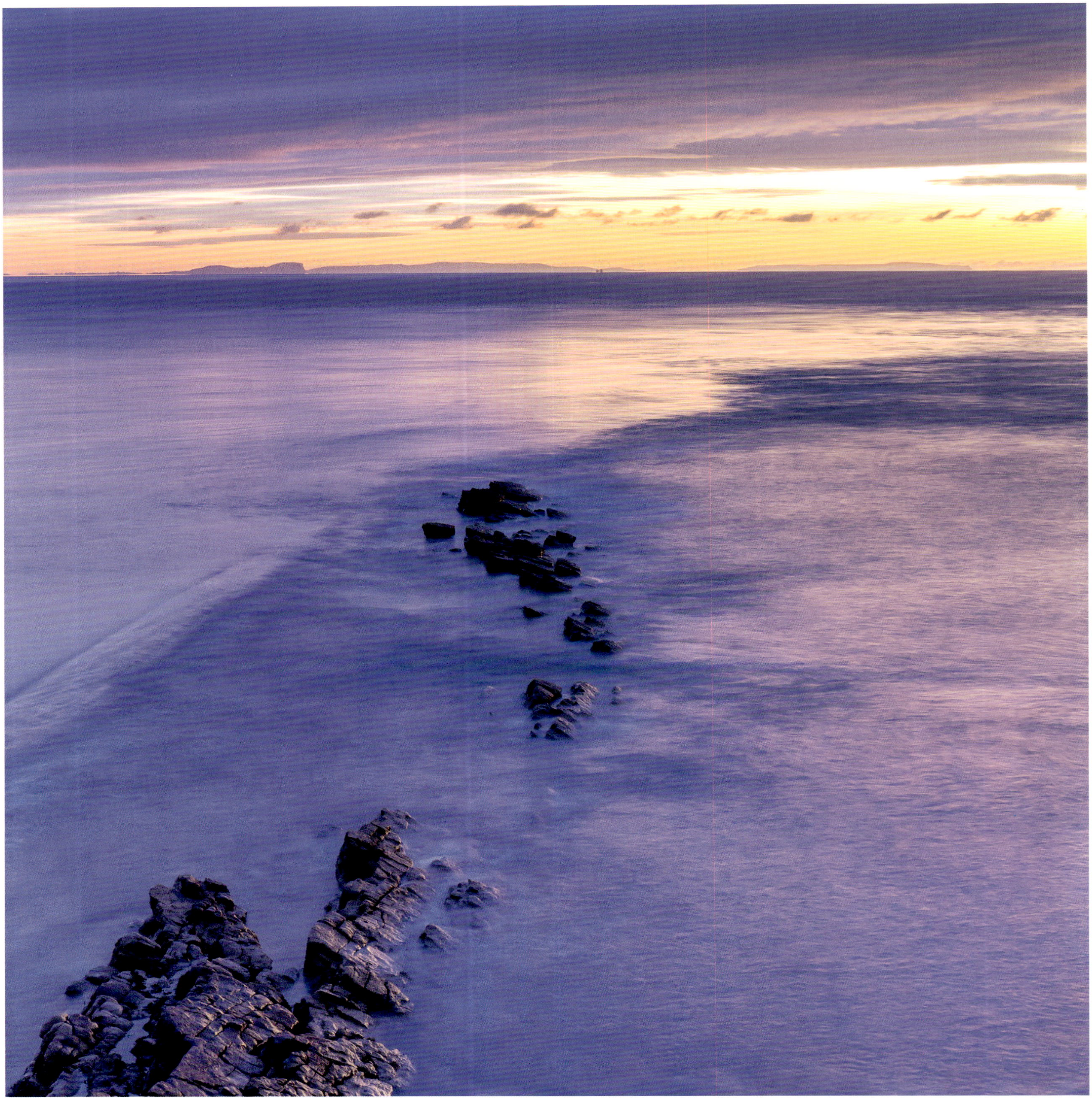

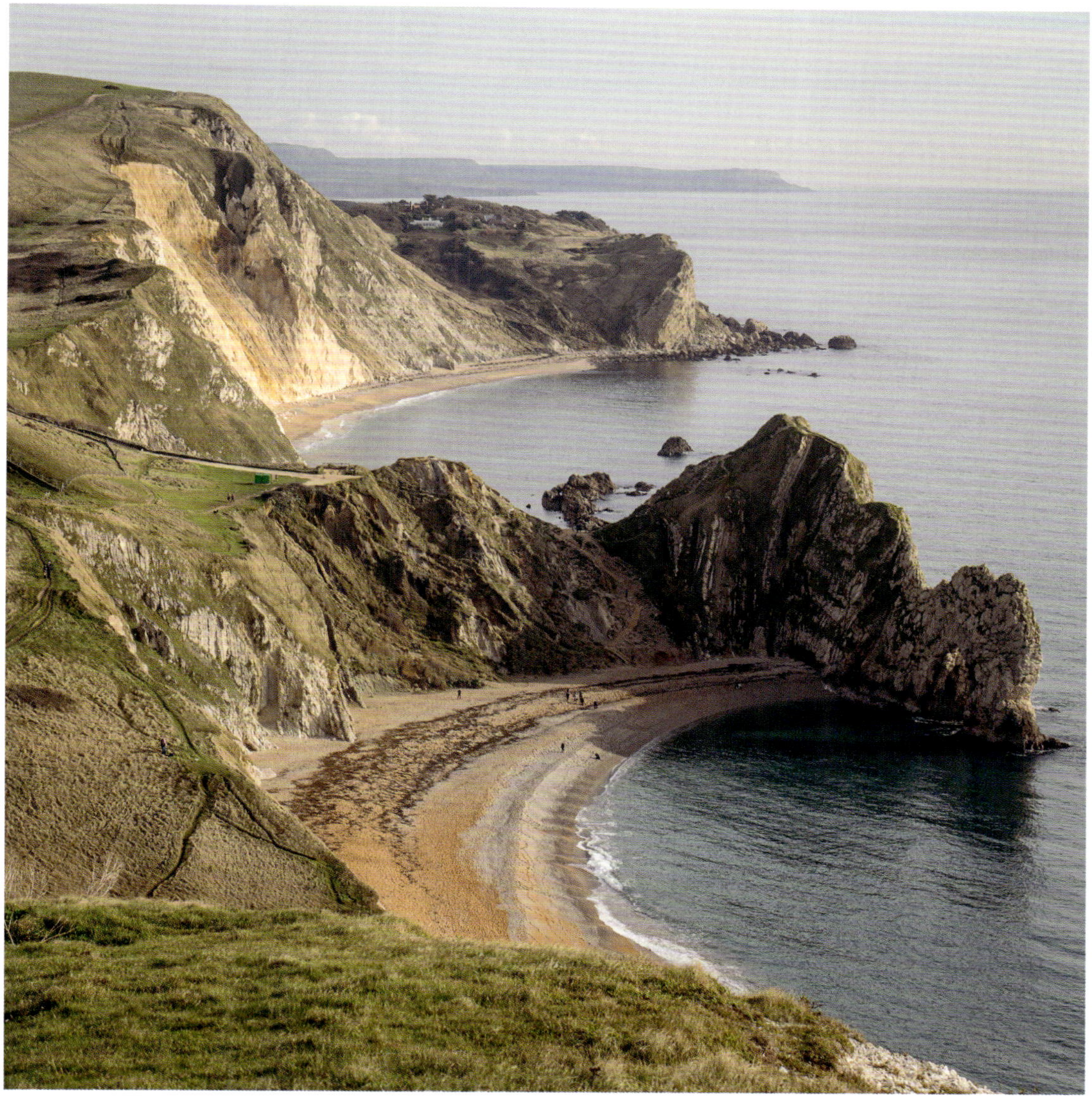

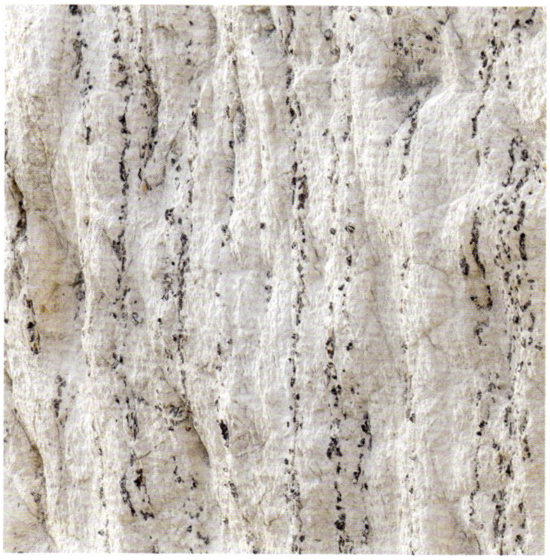

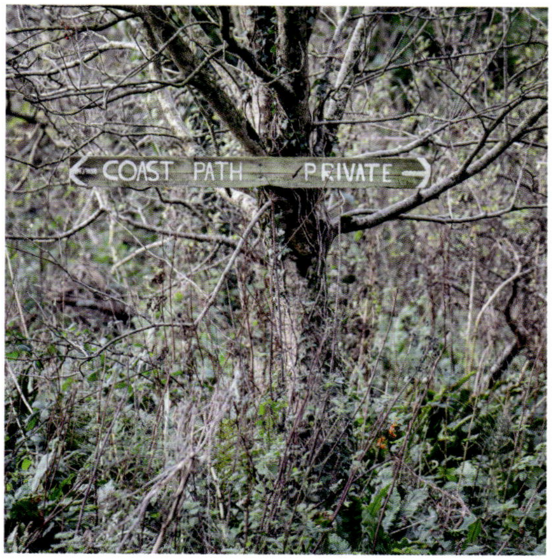

From top left:

Durdle Door, Dungy Head and beyond to St Aldhelm's Head

Vertical chalk and flint strata, Bat's Head

Duality: Ringstead

Opposite:

Peveril Point at dawn with the Isle of Wight on the horizon, Swanage

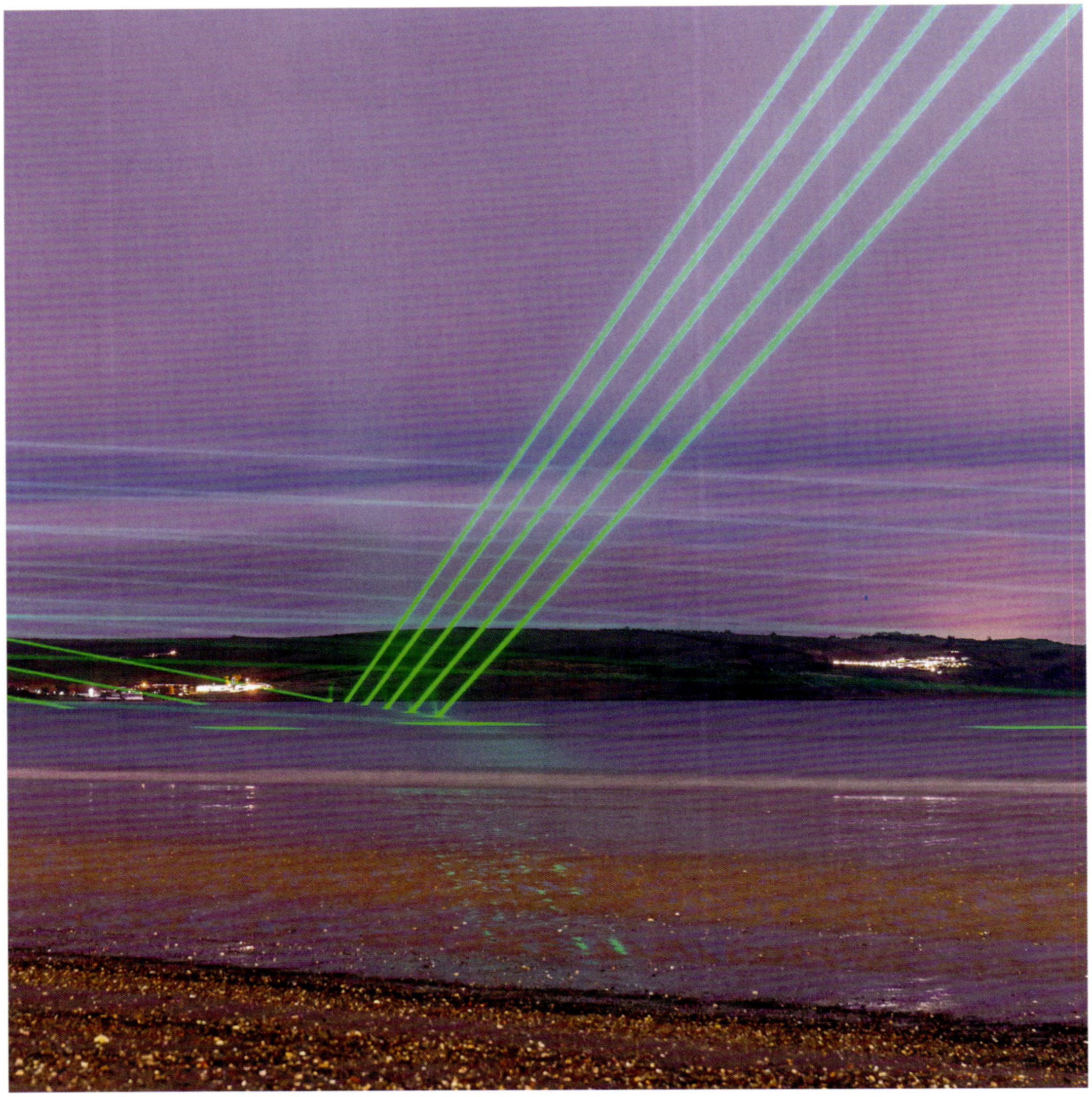

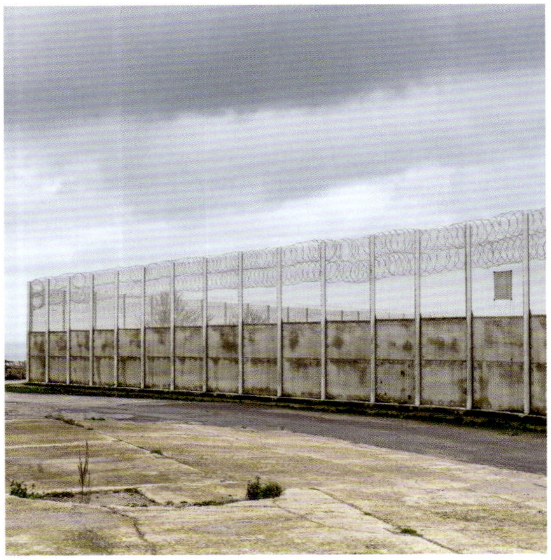

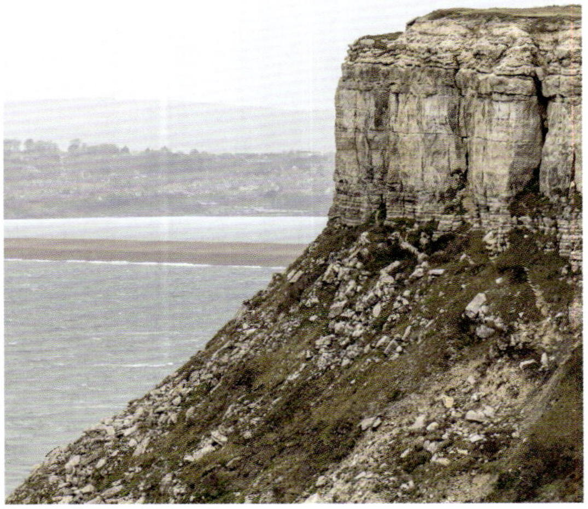

From top left:

Light Veils, permanent laser installation, Weymouth

Portland Young Offenders Institution

Blacknor Cliffs, Portland

Opposite, clockwise from top left:

Trig point pillar, Golden Cap, at 191 metres the highest point on the south coast

Lovestruck: Eype Mouth

Worbarrow Tout from Bindon Hill

East Cliff, West Bay

Thorncombe Beacon

Clavell Tower, a Tuscan-style folly built in 1830

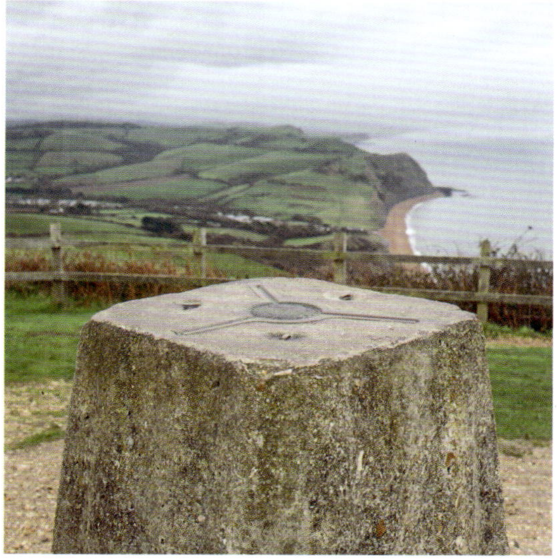
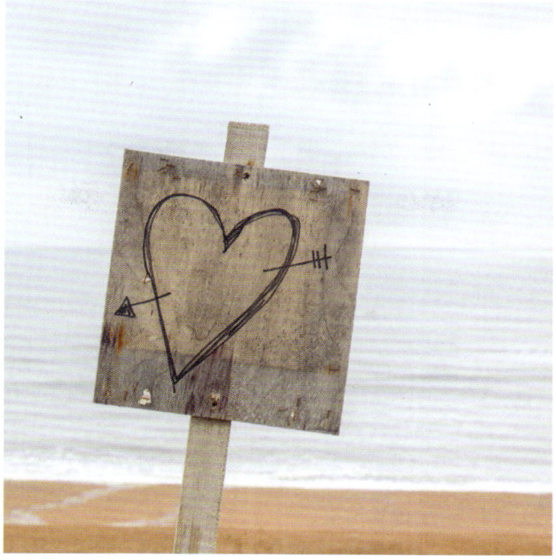
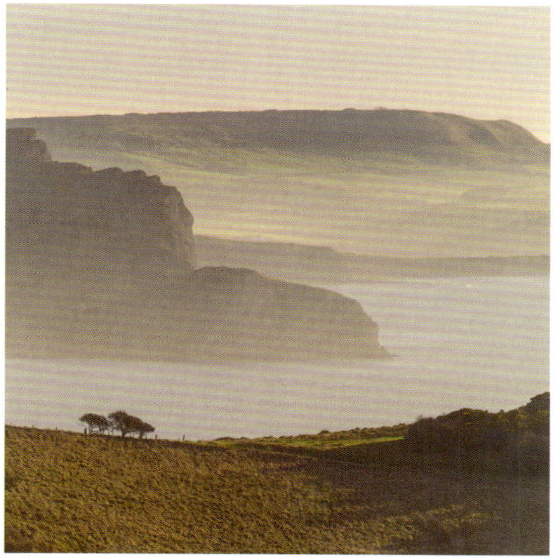
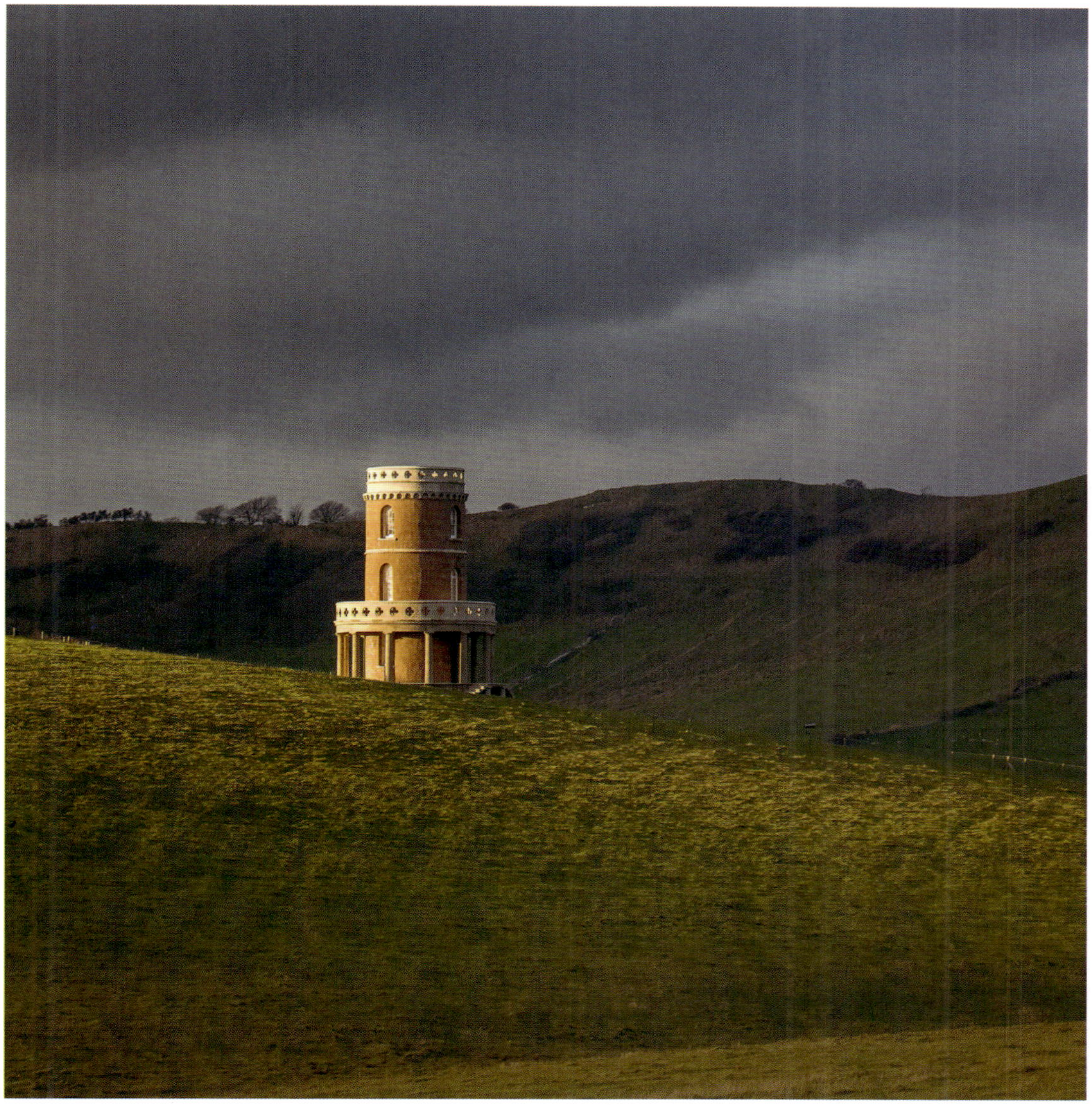
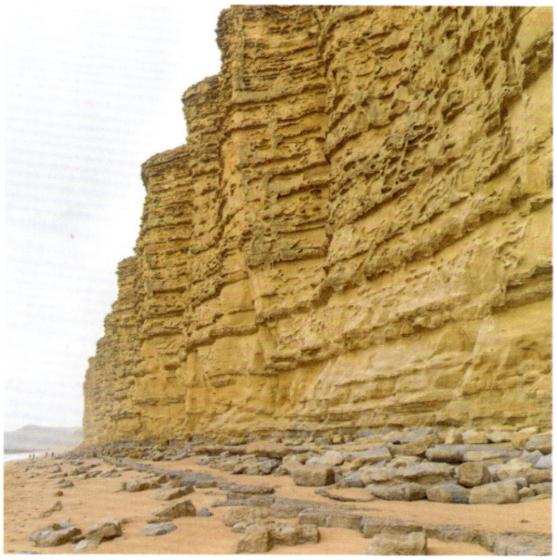
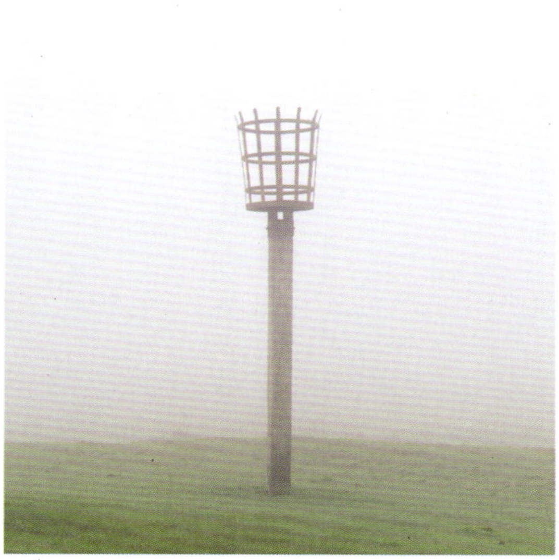

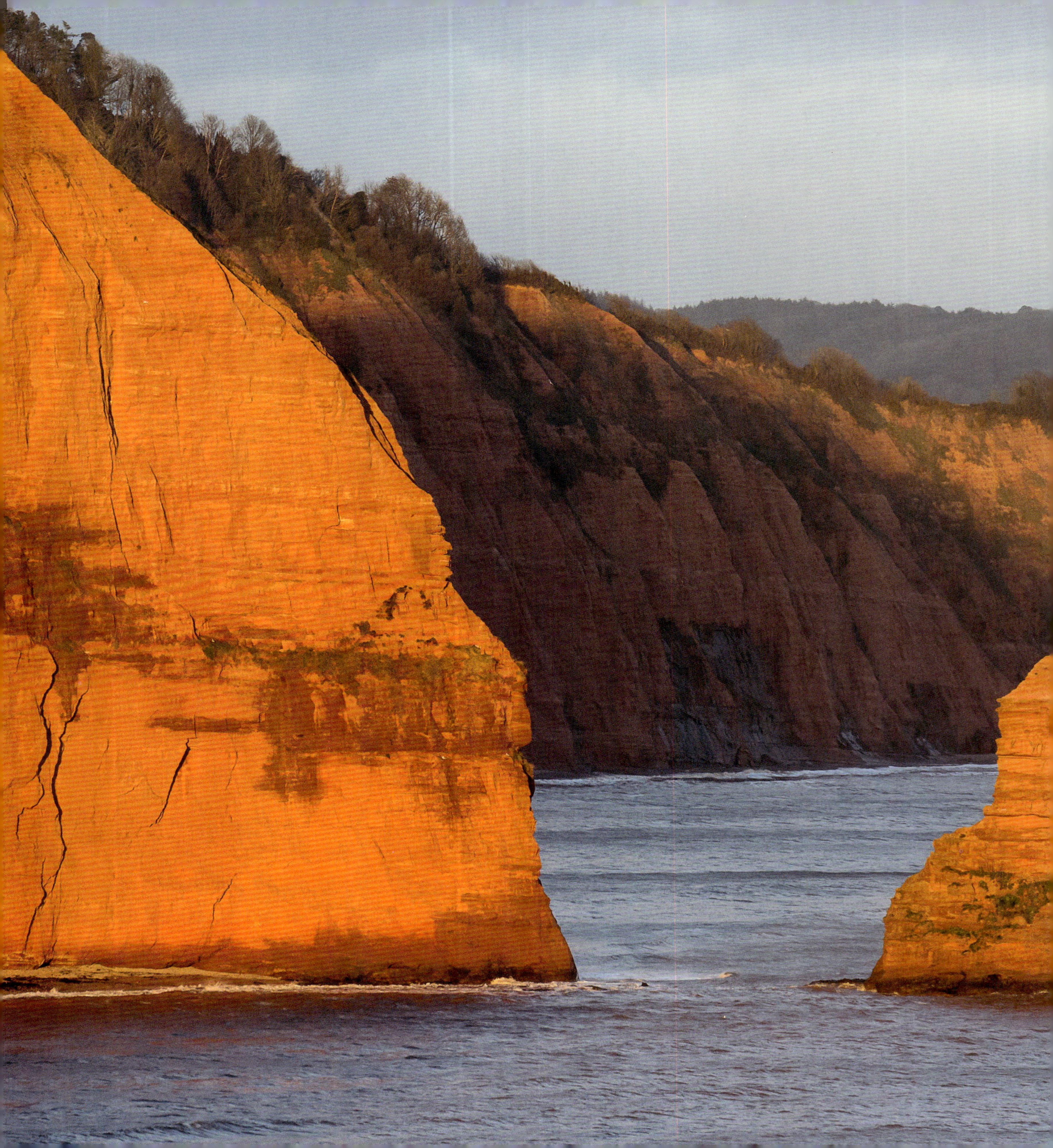

06 SOUTH DEVON

DECEMBER 2015–FEBRUARY 2016
DAY 038–052 | 01,001–01,352 KM | 351 KM

My trek into Devon starts at a deserted Charmouth Beach in Dorset, where waves break in quick succession, threatening and insistent. A red smear above the horizon hints at the verge of dawn. From afar, the cliffs of Black Ven, famous for the marine fossils discovered by the nineteenth-century palaeontologist Mary Anning, appear like a stack of coal – on closer inspection, it's a very dark, glistening clay, and the whole thing looks like it may slide into the sea at any moment. In parts, the mud oozes down the cliffs like black custard.

Devon, the first rural county on the journey with two non-contiguous coastlines, is made up of hilly landscapes, coastal cliffs and the high moorlands of Dartmoor – the largest open space in southern England and the source of many rivers I will ford or walk around. Here in the south, it faces the English Channel, where I'll walk along 724 kilometres of the Cornish coast before becoming reacquainted with Devon in the north, when it faces the Bristol Channel.

My pace quickens as I walk along the shore at Charmouth, energised by the realisation that I've covered 1,000 kilometres since London. It may be just a number, but it makes me feel the huge distance ahead isn't unfathomable – I just have to do what I've already done a few more times! I write '1,000' in the sand to celebrate as the sun rises, bathing the beach in a peachy glowing light, but the cold December wind soon prompts me to press on.

I'm keen to reach the Lyme Regis Undercliffs, an environment celebrated in John Fowles's novel *The French Lieutenant's Woman* for its other-worldly wildness in such proximity to the polite society of the town. By the afternoon, the dense foliage closes around me, moist and silent. My joyful mood on reaching 1,000 kilometres is short-lived when I find the only navigable path in the jungle at the base of the cliffs to Seaton has been severed by a large landslip, making the way impassable. *If you wish to travel along the coast, you are advised to catch the bus*, a sign advises unhelpfully; the collapsed area is two hours ahead with no side paths, so I skirt around the barrier, hoping for the best. On reaching the landslip, it looks like the ground suddenly dropped 3 metres, leaving a jagged edge of raw earth across the landscape. I negotiate this slump by lowering my pack before me, hooked on the end of my trekking pole, before ungainly sliding down. A few hundred metres on, a short scramble up the razed ground past the reverse of the *No Entry* notice gets me back to the path.

In the pre-dawn landscape of Hooken Undercliff, the wind whistles over the top, forcing me to stagger like a drunk – appropriate for a place called Beer Head. Birds glide effortlessly up above, unaffected by the gusts. This is the westernmost chalk on the English coast that I'd first encountered far to the east in Kent. I relish the last view of this iconic milky rock that has been my companion for the previous few months.

After Branscombe Beach, the colour underfoot changes from white to red. Here, the cliffs glow with iron oxide. These rocks used to be a desert-like modern-day Namibia, which resonates with me as I'd spent six weeks camping there a couple of years ago. Those distinctive golden-red hues of the rock as it catches the sun feel familiar. I almost check my footing for snakes and scorpions but a rain shower quickly brings me back to geographical reality. The sea is dyed ochre where the waves meet the shore.

The steep grassy hill leaving Sidmouth has an extraordinary number of park benches. I imagine a 'Resplendent and Copious Public Seating' trophy in the council offices. *Snow on Dartmoor, Sledges in Shop*, a chalk sign proclaims in Budleigh Salterton. There's no snow here but plenty of mud on the winding path up and down the red cliffs. 'It's like skiing, isn't it!' I tell a fellow slip-and-slider. 'It's like glissading,' he corrects me.

Opposite:

Ladram Rocks (Triassic sandstone sea stacks), Ladram Bay

There's no road crossing at the mouth of the River Exe, so I head inland to the first footbridge. The detour takes me past the Commando Training Centre at Lympstone and an extensive assault course that involves a 9-metre rope climb, a 200-metre person-carry and a rope regain. It looks like a monument to pain in brick and scaffolding. Due to their camouflage, I only notice a group of Marines sketching range cards like an incognito art class when I'm very close by. They studiously draw while looking over the Exe with binoculars as an instructor talks in a low voice.

At Exmouth, I encounter the first seaside resort to be developed in the county, which leads a day later to the English Riviera, an area that includes the coastal towns of Brixham, Paignton and Torquay, so named because in Victorian times visitors used to compare it with its subtropical climate to the French Riviera. The illusion is somewhat marred for me as I pass through in pouring rain, but when the sun comes out, and I walk past a row of palm trees, I can appreciate the exotic allure.

Beyond the Exe towards Dawlish, dog walkers scurry along the breakwater, occasionally getting splashed by mighty waves – this must be a local amusement. Inspired by their bravery, I try my luck following along. First, a wave breaks to my front, then to the back, and finally I get a wave full in the face as I shield my camera with my body like a baby. Continuing into Dawlish, the waves shift from being entertaining to alarming, and I end up being forced to backtrack and take a higher inland route.

Midway between Salcombe and Plymouth, I ford the River Erme. Though it's a dauntingly wide estuary on first sight, it's low tide, and I make my way across the sand and rocks steadily to clamber up the wooded banks on the other side. The water is piercingly cold and the strong wind leaves me feeling punch-drunk until I collapse in the lee of Beacon Hill without a thought in my head as I unpeel muddy wet socks, pus oozing from under my big toenail. I've also developed a humiliating new pain: my butt crack stings with chafing at every step.

I attend to my foot injury quickly, washing it with clean water from my bottle and putting a fresh bandage on. When I'd first started walking, the blisters, aches and pains that came with carrying heavy camping and camera gear over long distances had been a huge source of distress. But somewhere along the way, I came to accept them as the norm – a necessary evil to carrying out the task at hand.

For the next eight days, I'm put up by my friends John and Emily in Dartmouth. 'You look fucked, mate,' John, a Scottish former paratrooper, cheerily greets me as I hobble to his van. I'm happy to assure him that looks are not deceiving. On sharing my butt-related malaise, he brightens up. 'That's TRS! In Northern Ireland, we all had it: Toxic Ring Sting.' Later that evening, I humbly avail myself of their daughter's nappy rash cream.

Time and sleep do wonders to heal my battered body, and I'm soon back to the sea. Most South West Coast Path walkers (sensibly) take ferries across the mouths of the many Devonshire and Cornish rivers, but as I've set myself the challenge not to take any mechanised assistance while walking the perimeter, I'm forced to look for an alternative route. Following the spiderweb of public footpaths along the rivers adds hundreds of kilometres to the journey and I find myself meandering upstream tracing waterways like the Avon and the Yealm, which in turn bifurcate into Newton and Cofflete creeks. Away from the ravages of the coastal weather, I delight in the calm of these tranquil inland diversions through woods and undulating fields. It's not until I'm back to the cliff-lined coast on the approach to Plymouth that I come across people again – two retired lawyers, both over seventy with artificial hips, doggedly persisting in the pouring rain, determined to walk the South West Coast Path. Their grit seriously impresses me and when we stop to chat, they tell me, 'It's a bit stiff, but the trick is not to stop. Once you take to the chair, that's it; you're never getting out again.'

When I get to Plymouth, I have to remind myself not to greet every person I pass, as I've become accustomed to. As in most cities, people here walk as a means to an end and seem less receptive to new encounters. I'd anticipated that I'd enjoy being returned to civilisation, but the wind, space and freedom of living outdoors and being constantly on the move make the abundant comforts of Plymouth feel at once both miraculous and unfamiliar. After a good night's dinner and sleep in a hotel, I yearn to get back out to the trail. I leave early on Sunday morning, when all is quiet except the buzzing of a tattooist needle. A Royal Navy frigate is heading out to sea while a fast RIB of heavily armed black-clad soldiers scours the hidden corners of the harbourside.

Opposite, clockwise from top left:

Fossils on the beach near Lyme Regis, Dorset

Dawn at Charmouth with Golden Cap, the location of the first 1,000 kilometres of the walk, Dorset

Black Ven clay, Dorset

Winter pool, Lyme Regis Undercliffs

Rainbow bracket fungi, Lyme Regis Undercliffs

Hart's-tongue fern, Lyme Regis Undercliffs

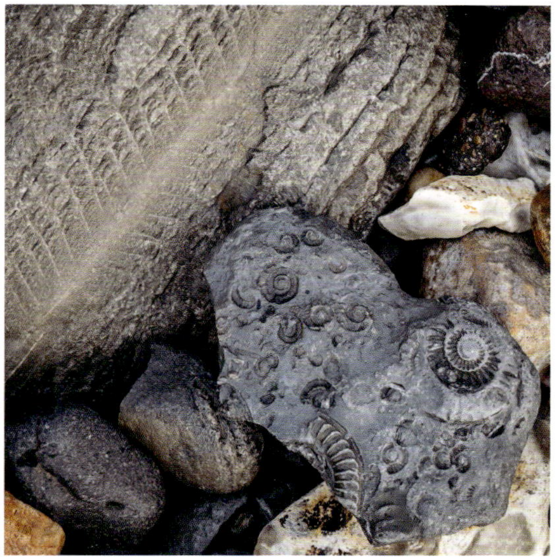
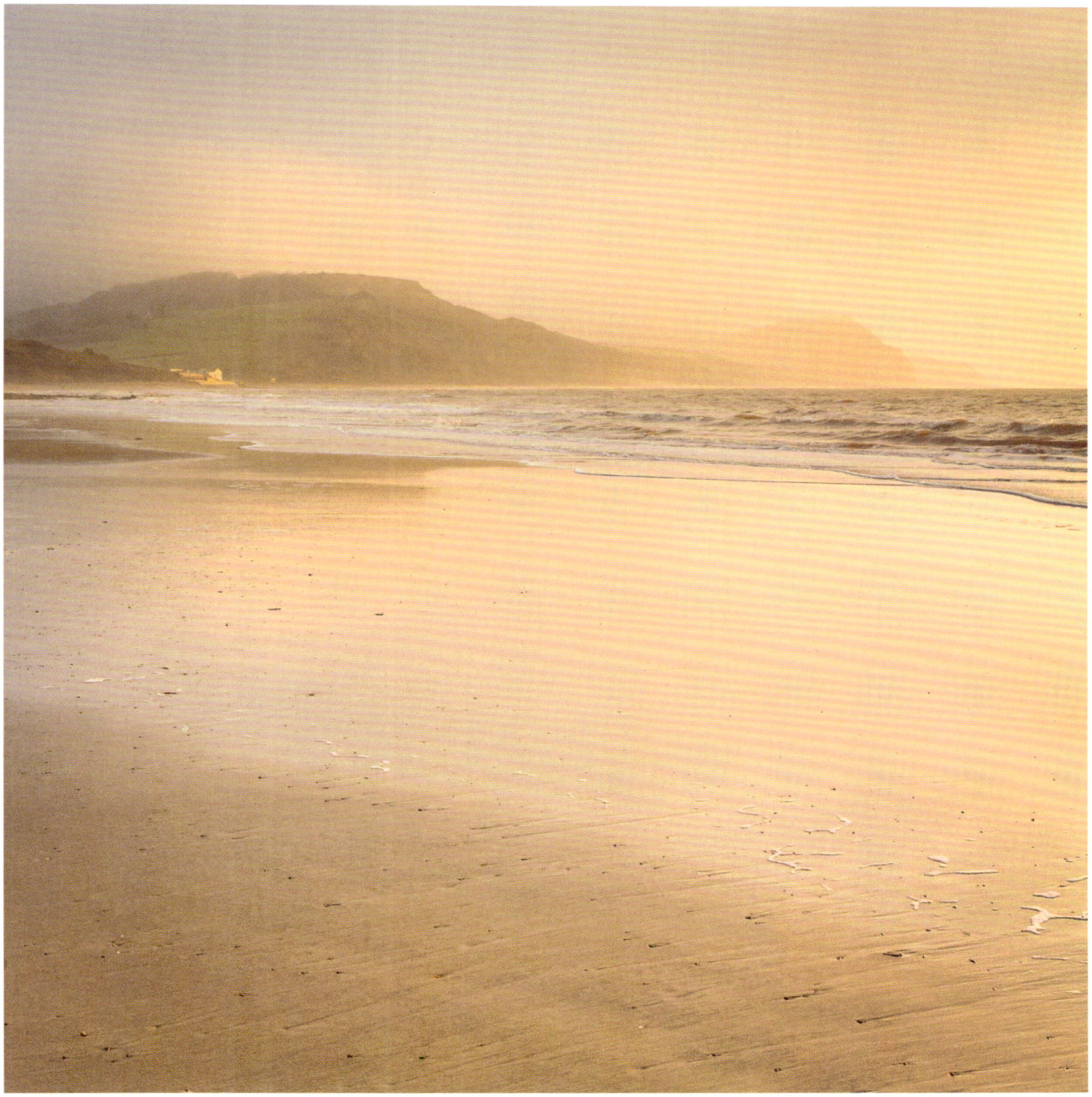
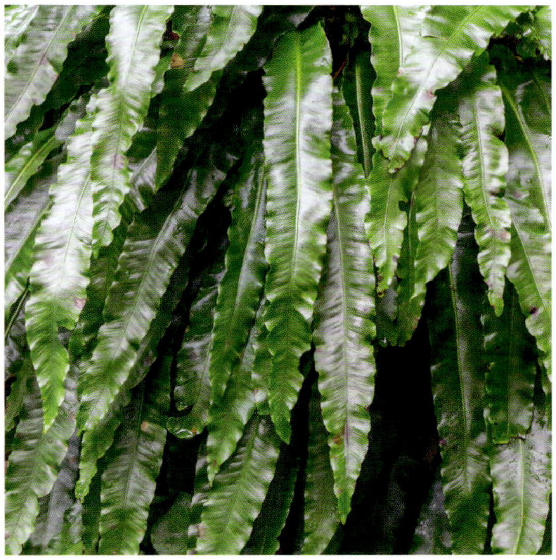
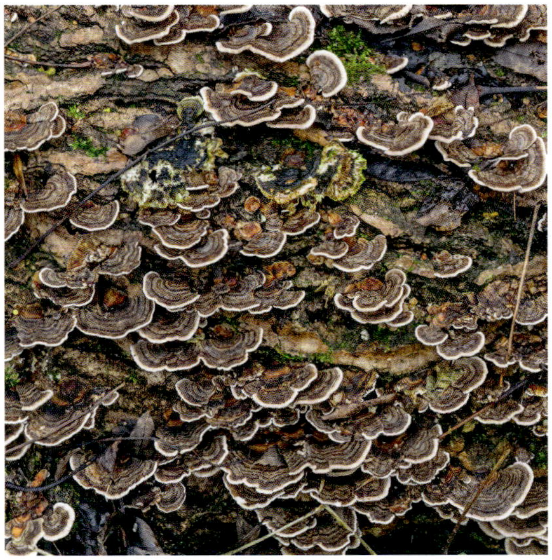
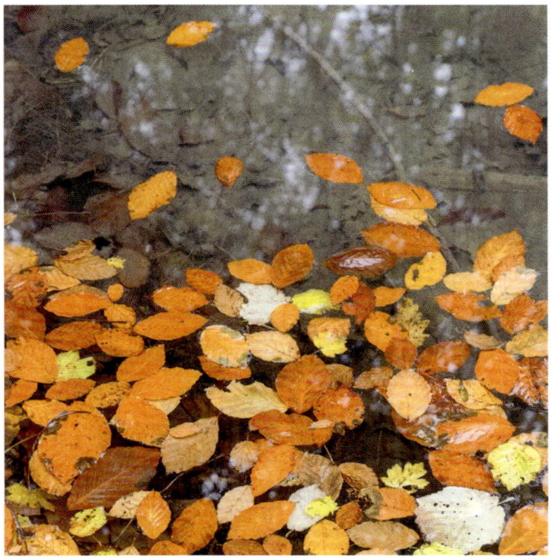
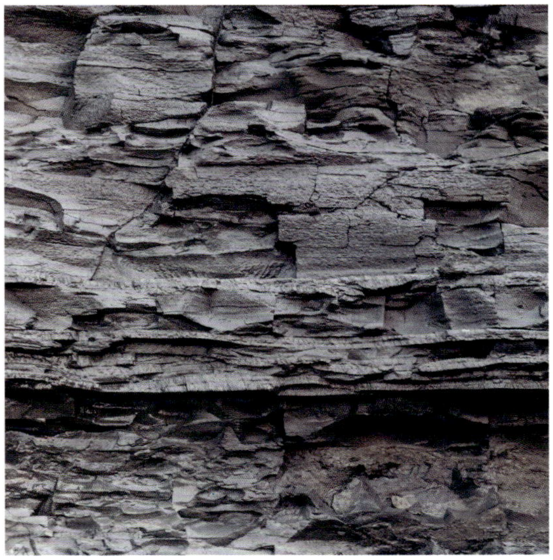

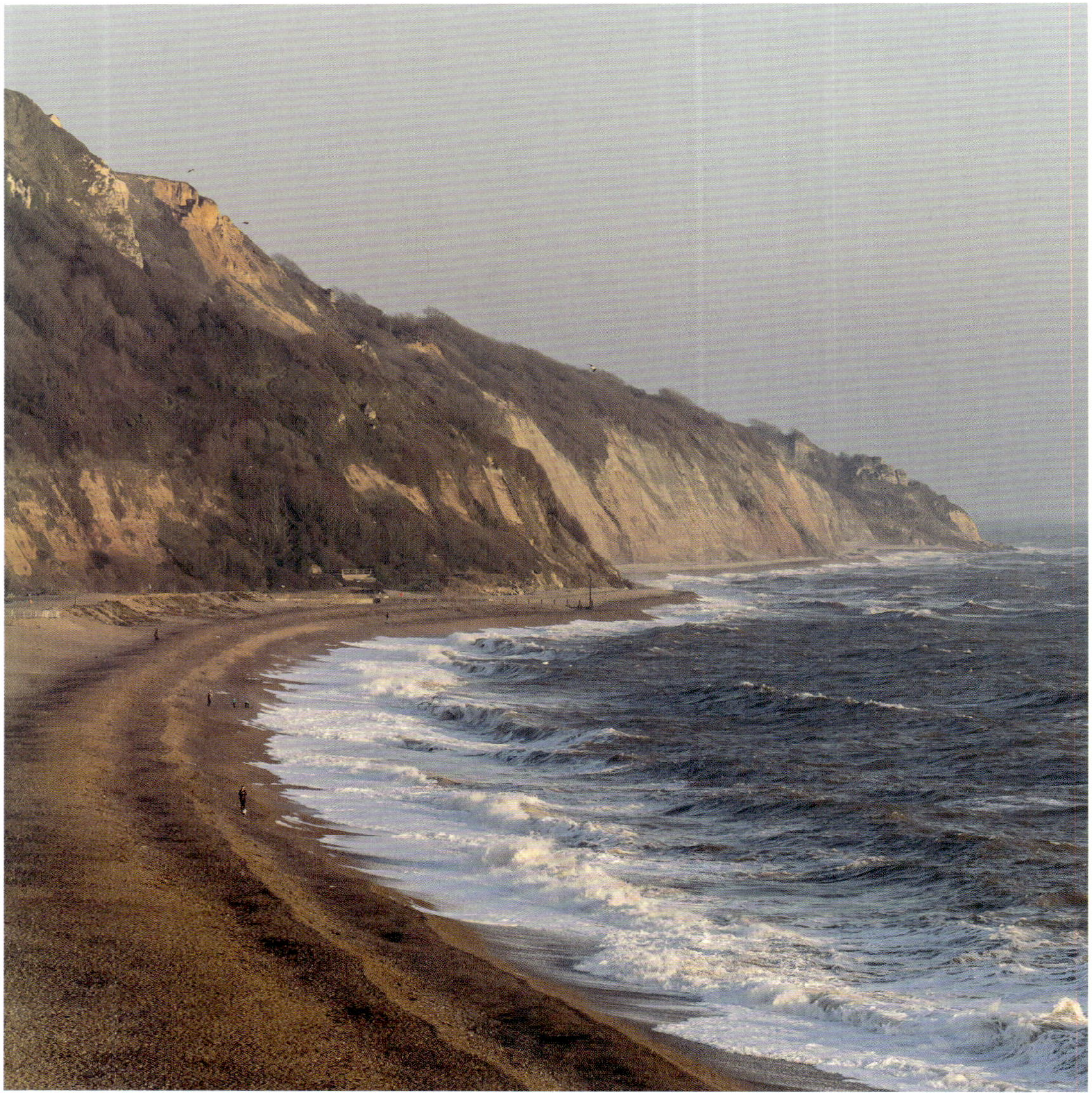

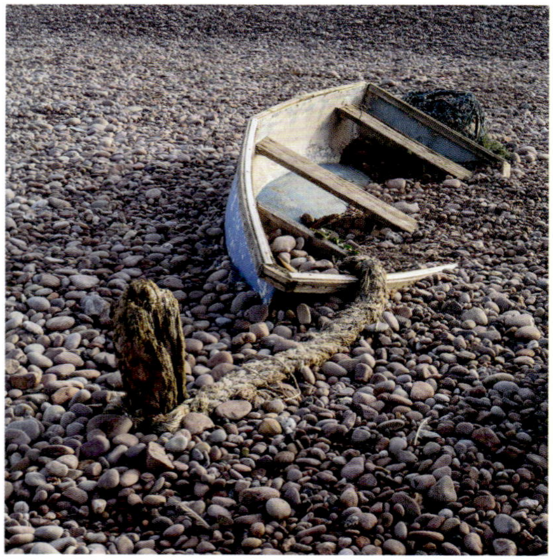

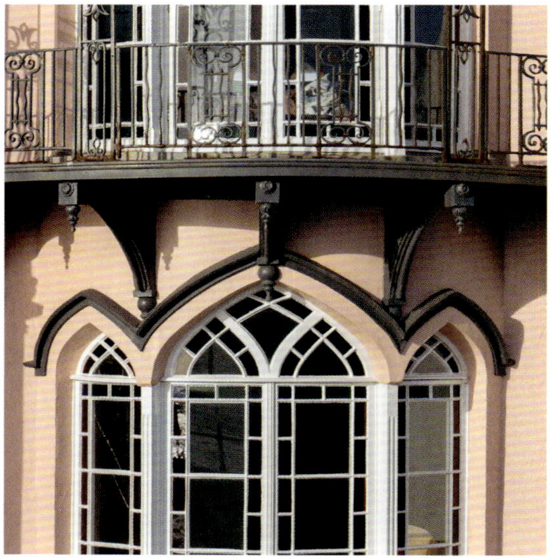

From top left:

Seaton Bay

Buried boat, Sidmouth

Beach House, a Regency villa with Gothicised details, Sidmouth

Opposite, from top left:

Dawlish breakwater

Atomised: Dawlish breakwater

From bottom left:

Exminster Marshes from Exeter Canal

Exminster Marshes Nature Reserve

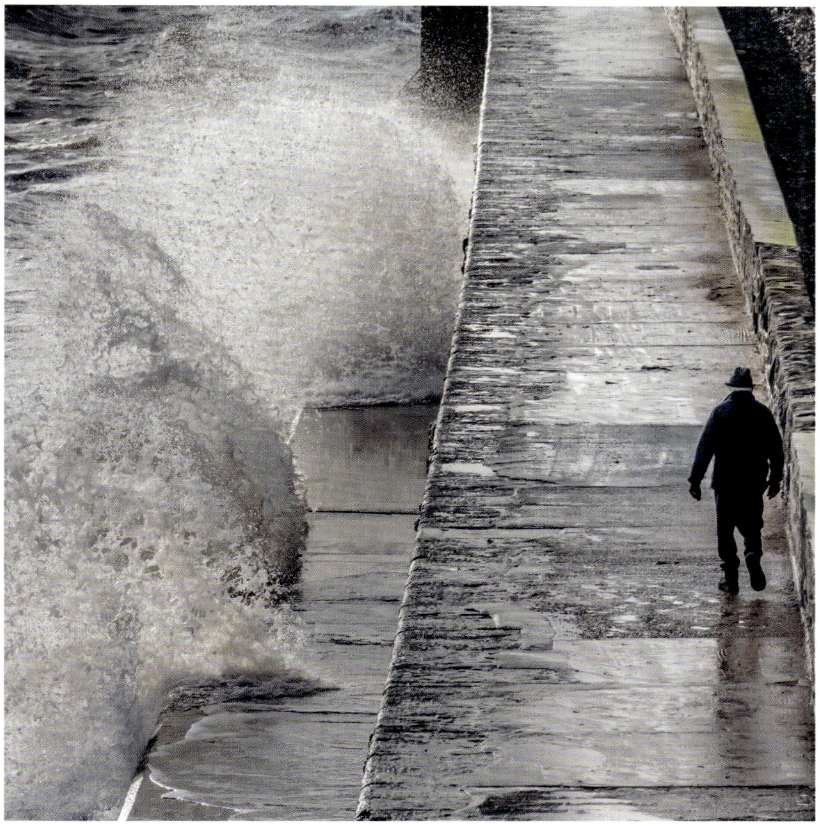

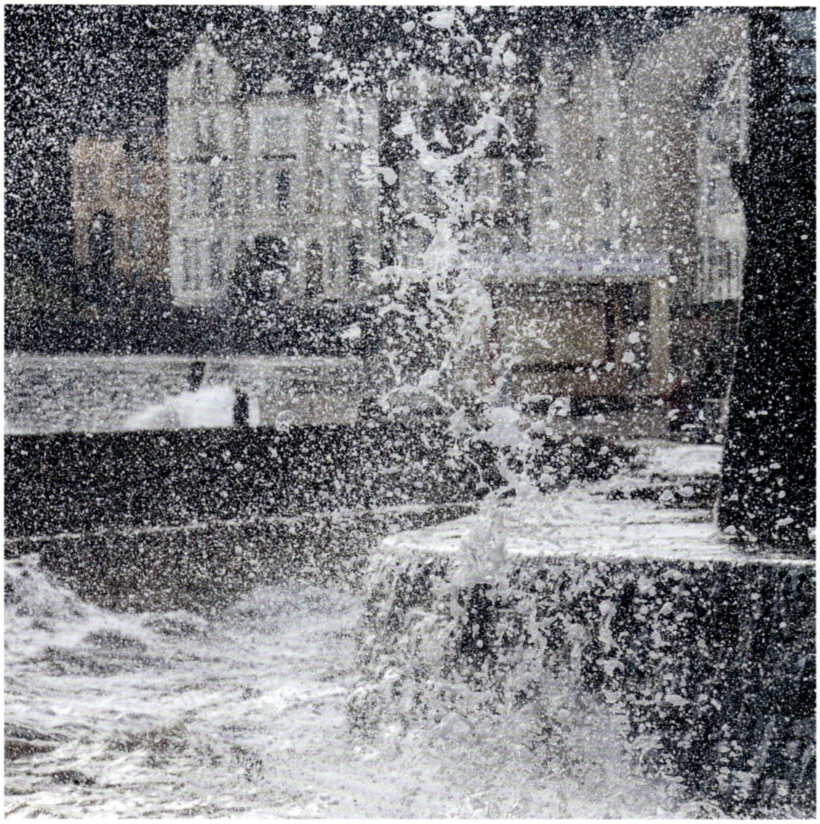

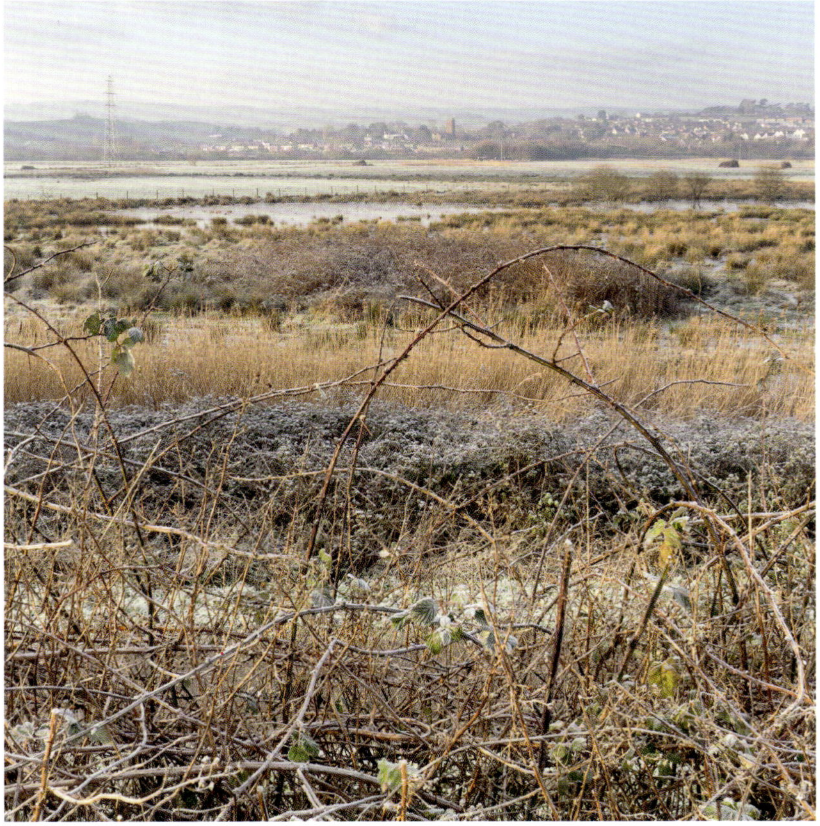

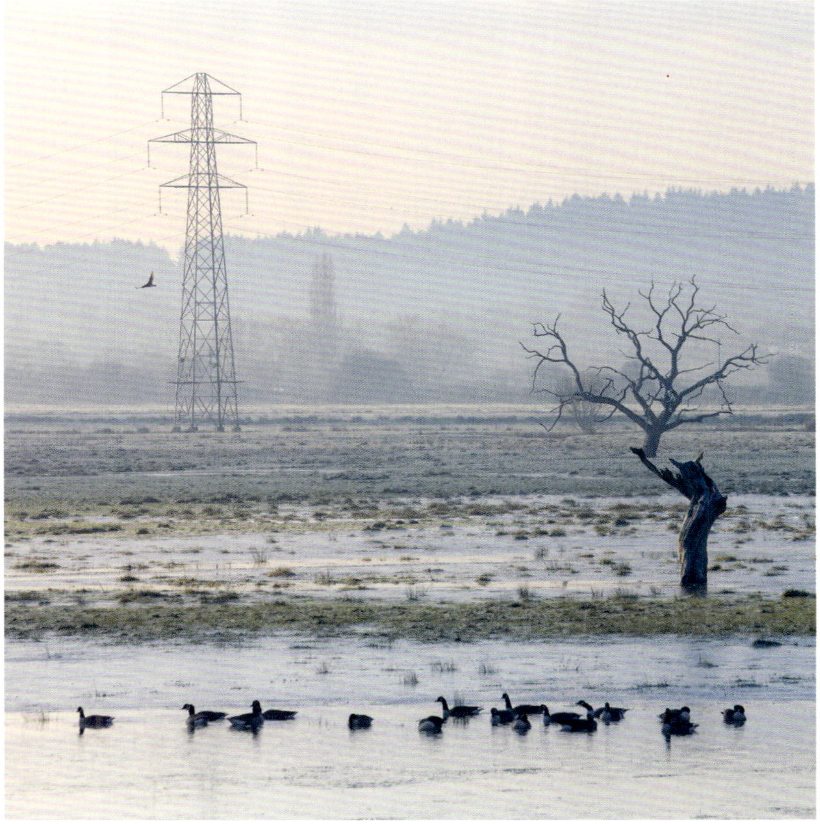

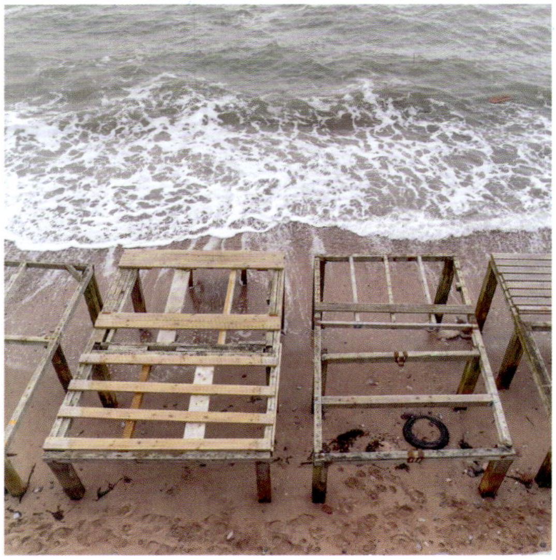

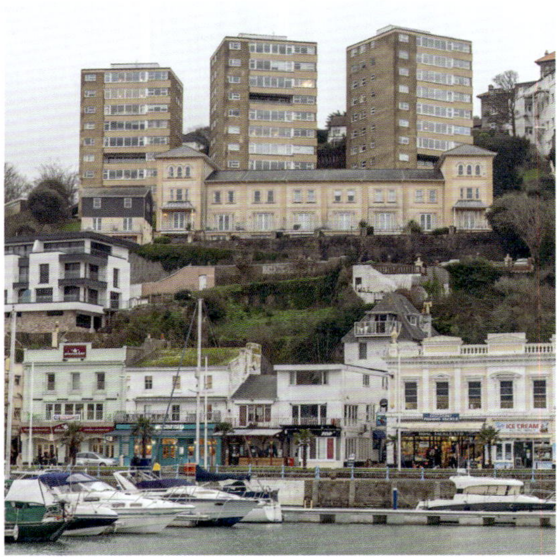

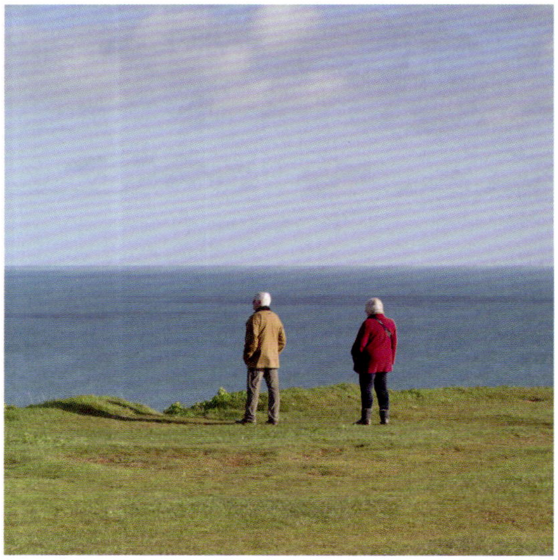

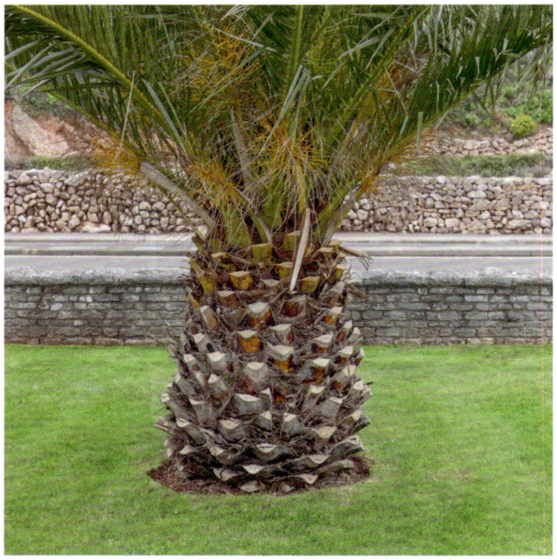

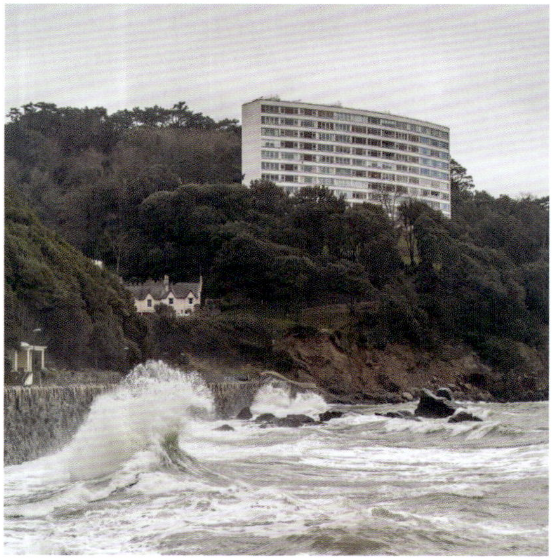

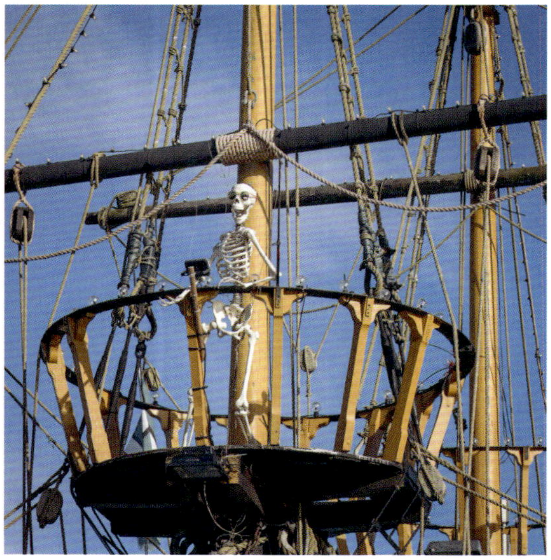

From top left:

Beach hut footings, Corbyn Head, Torquay

New Harbour, Torquay

From centre left:

Berry Head, Brixham

Date palm, Torquay

From bottom left:

Kilmorie, Torquay

'Sid the Skeleton', *Golden Hind* replica, Brixham

Opposite, clockwise from top left:

Woodhuish Farm near Scabbacombe Head

Man Sands

Seascape, Scabbacombe Head

Ashprington

River Dart boughs

Engulfed fence, Bow Creek

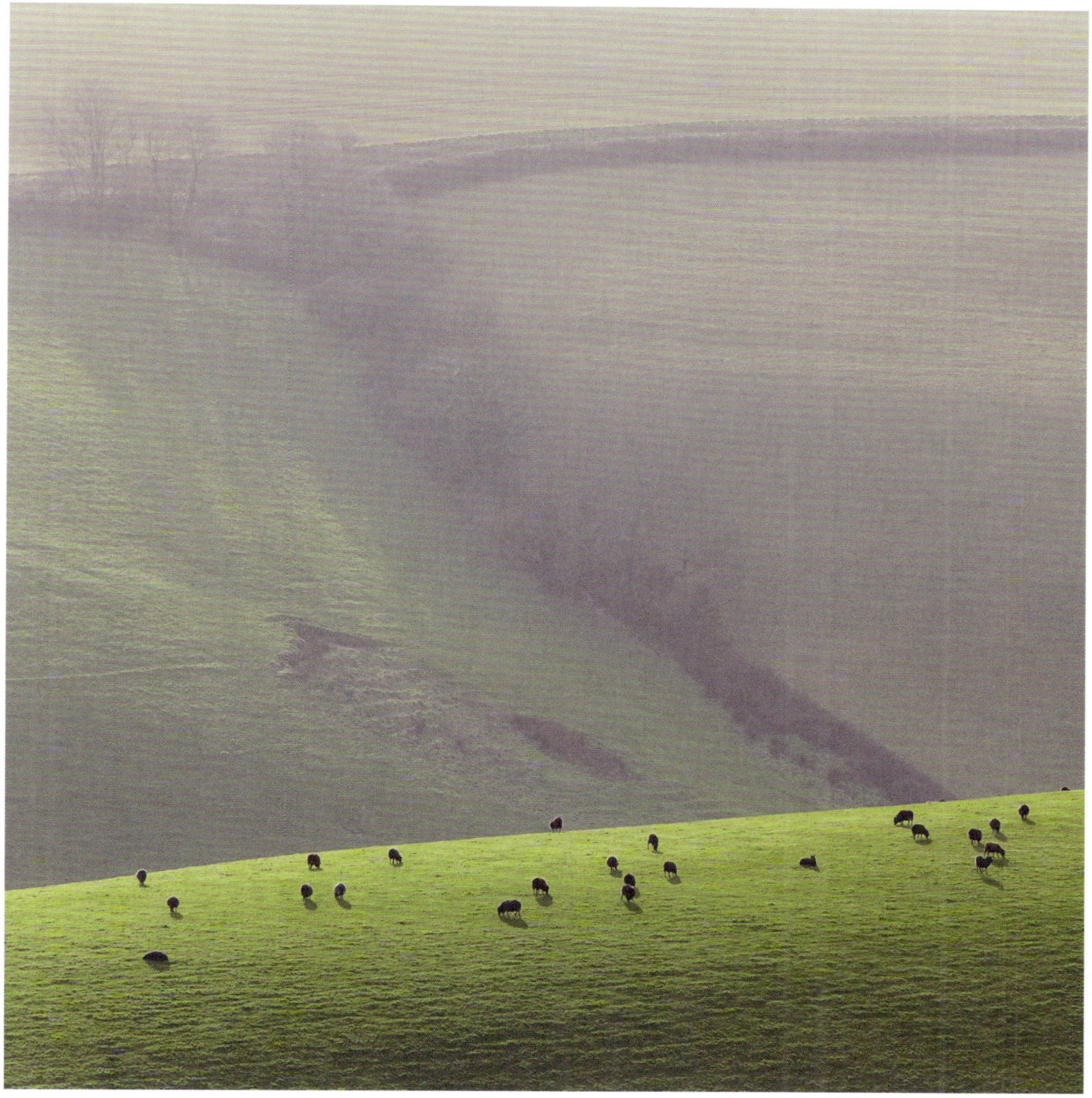
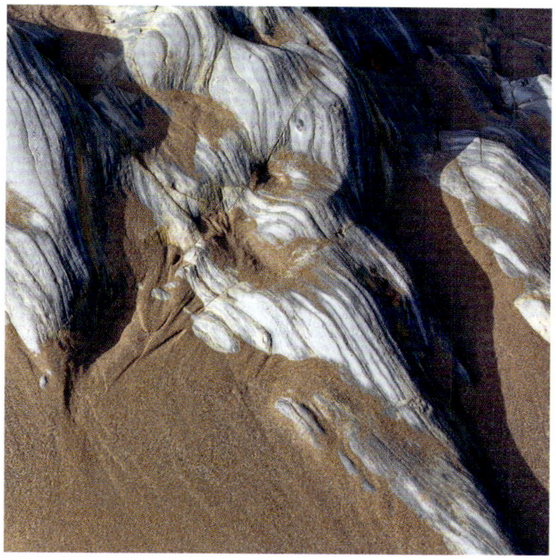
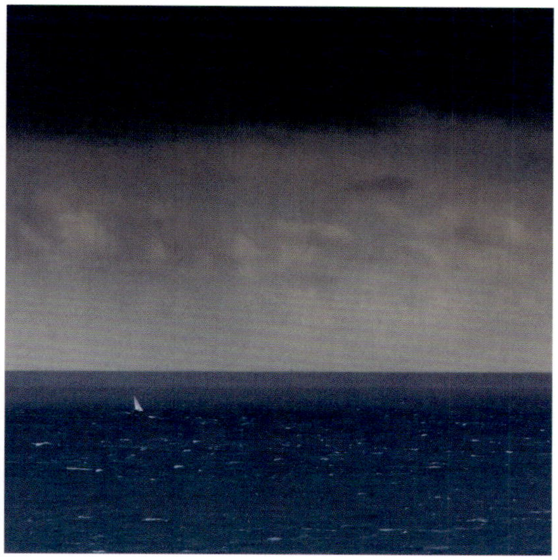
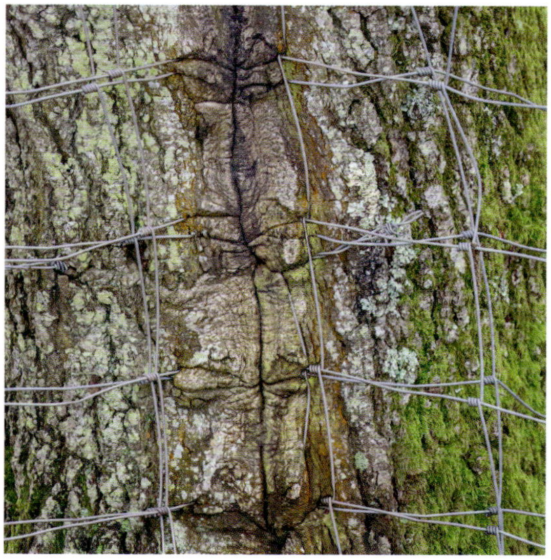
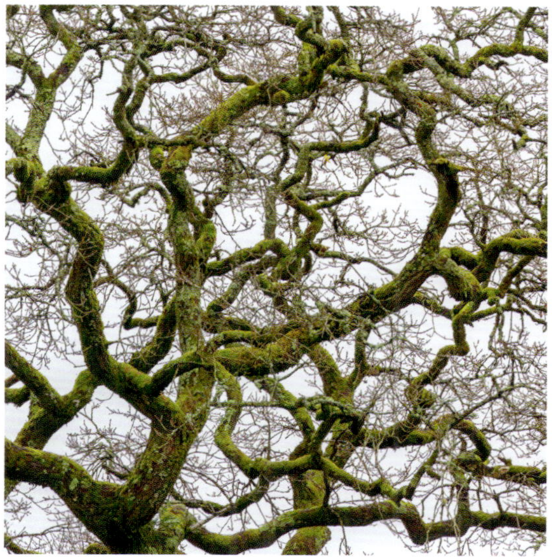
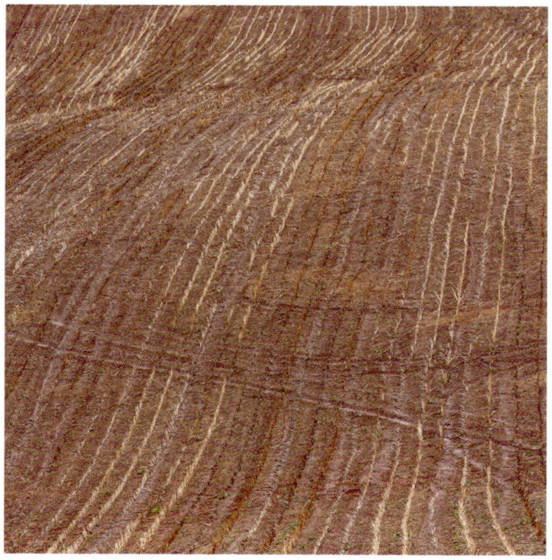

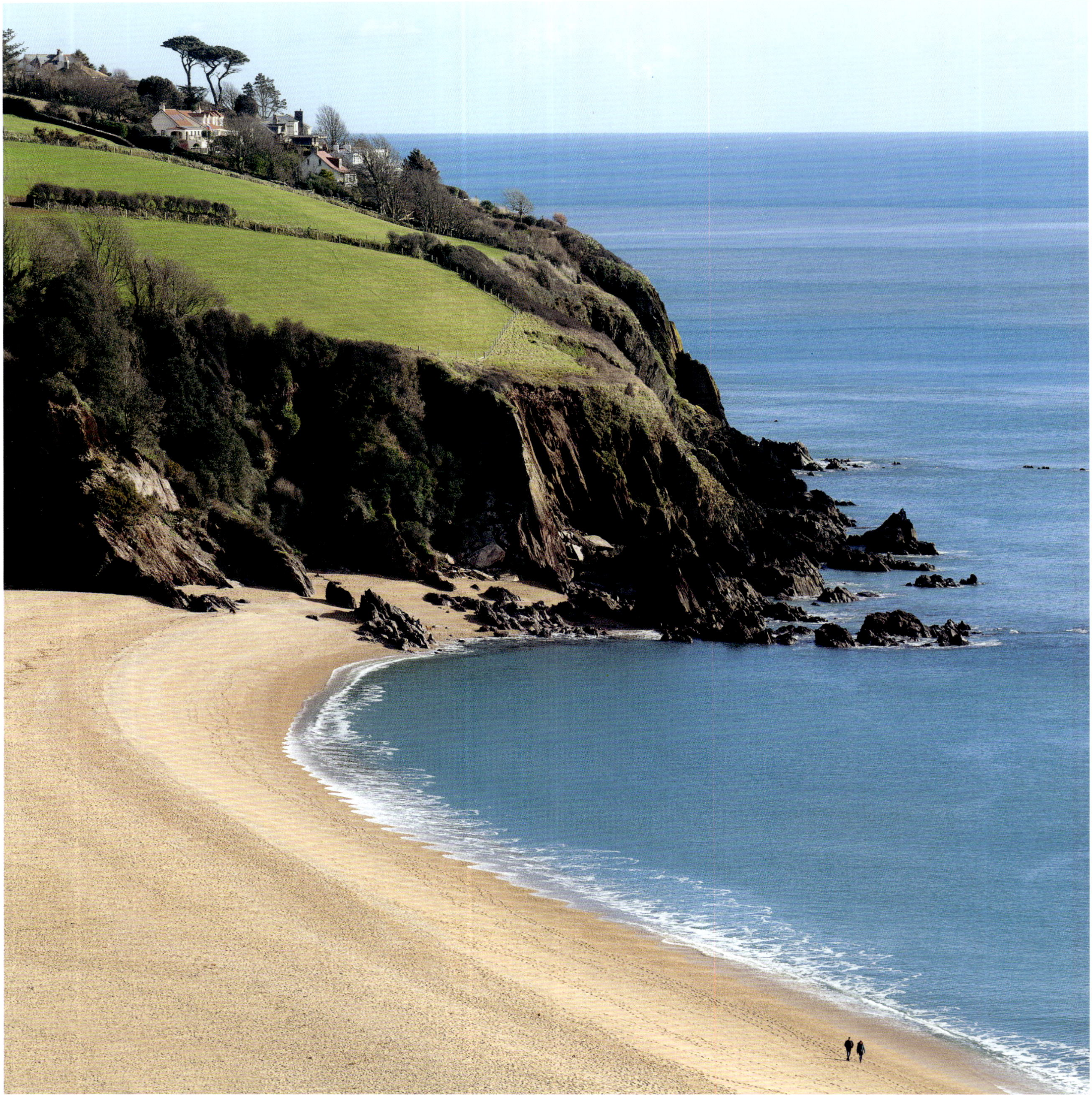

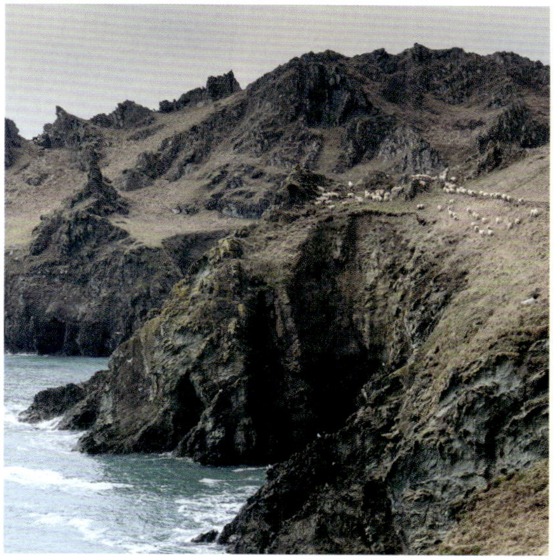

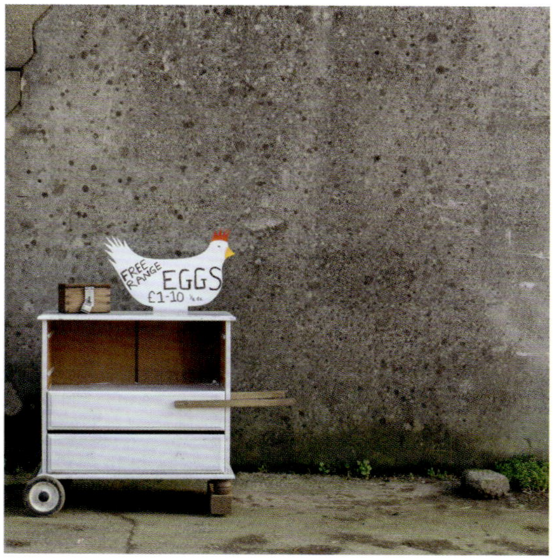

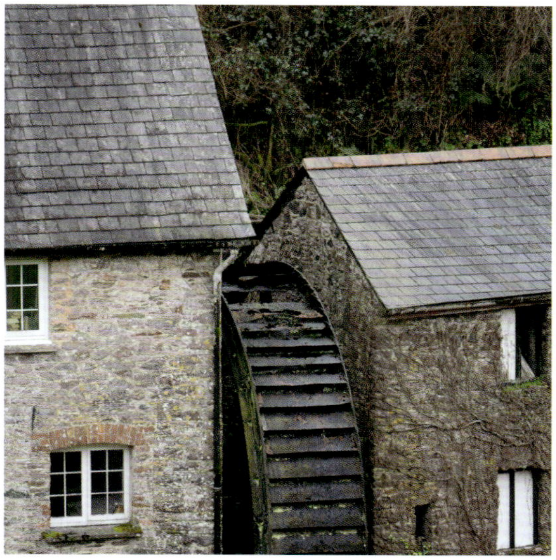

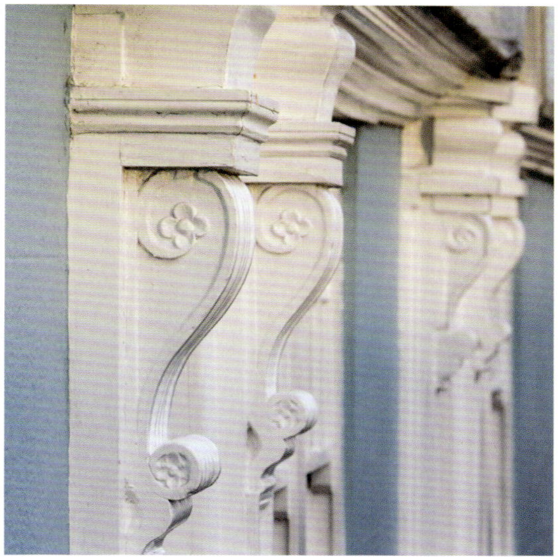

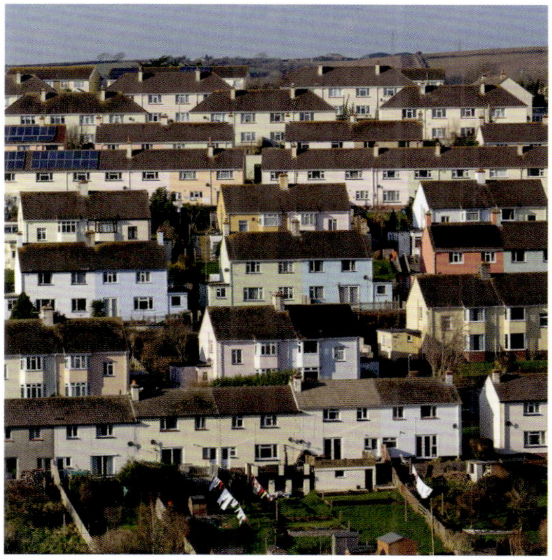

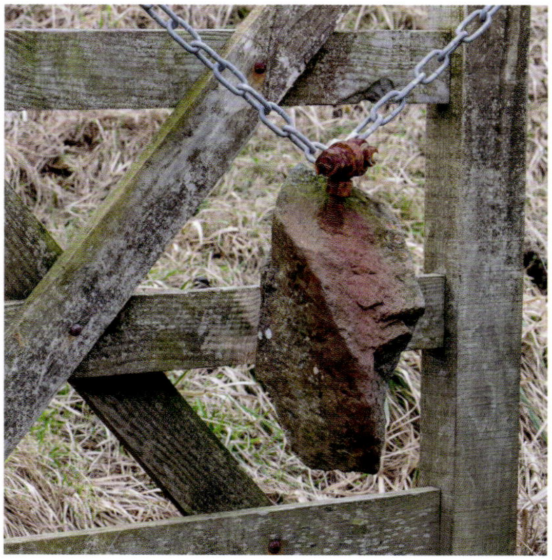

From top left:

Flock of sheep, Gammon Head

Free range: South Pool

From centre left:

Brambletorre Mill

Timber corbels, Southtown, Dartmouth

From bottom left:

Kingsbridge

Gate closer, Gammon Head

Opposite:

Blackpool Sands. In the Second World War, this was the northernmost point of the UK Battle Training Area for the D-Day landings and was used as a landing beach for fuel and stores

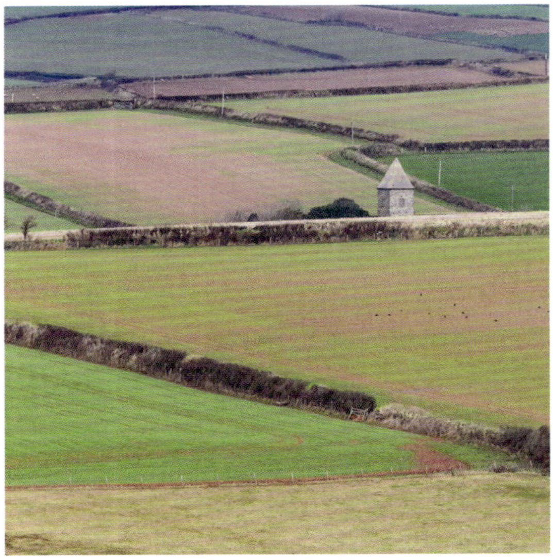
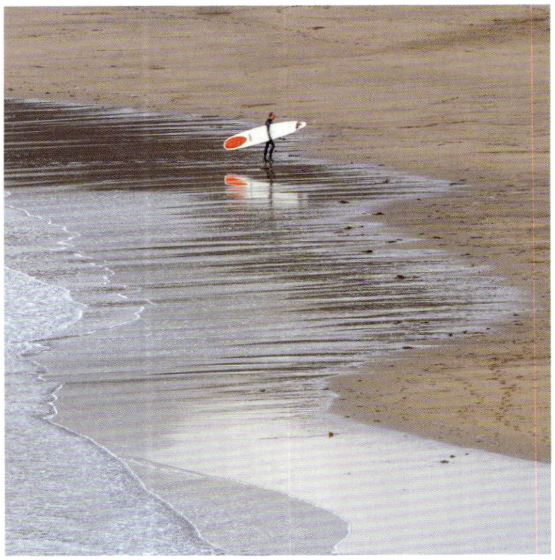
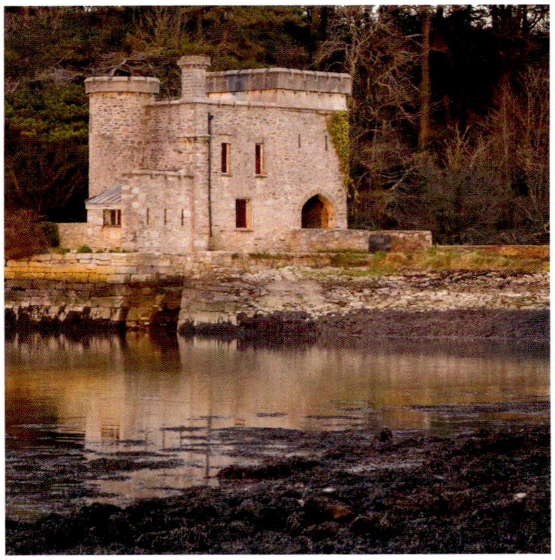
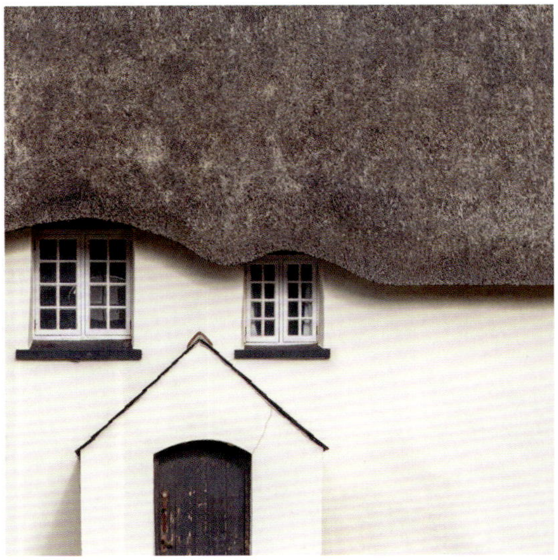
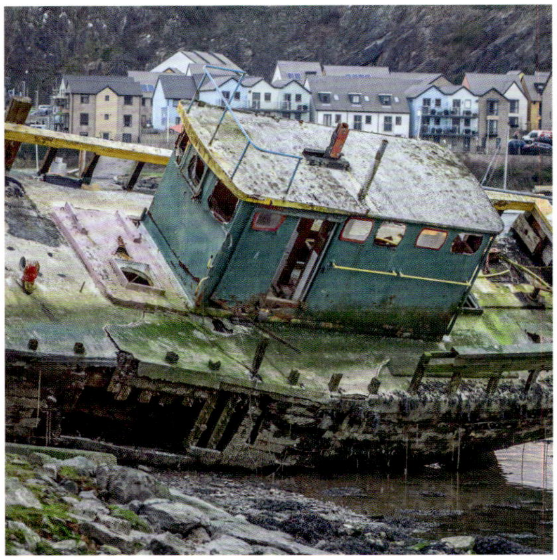
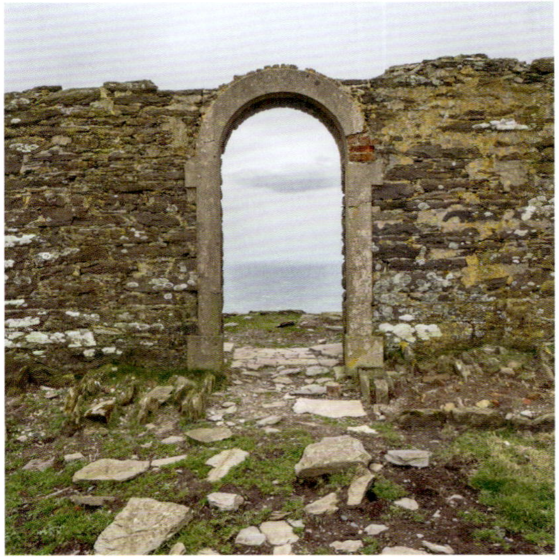
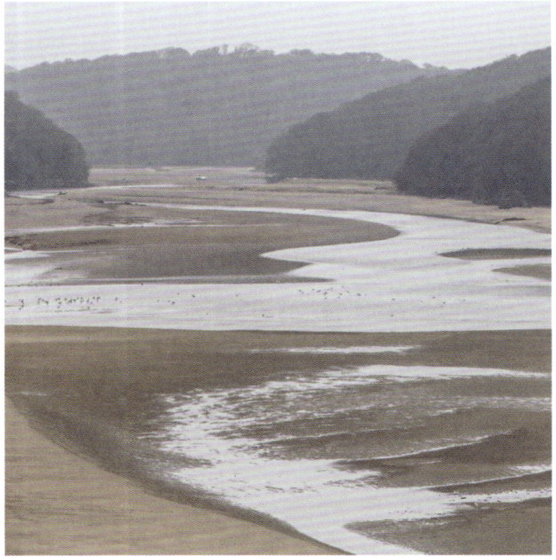
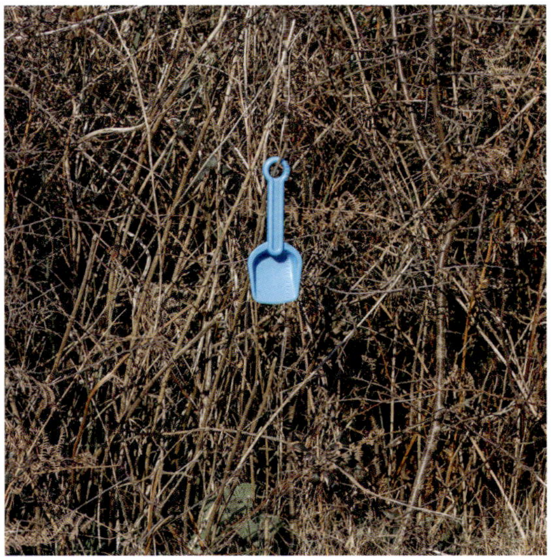
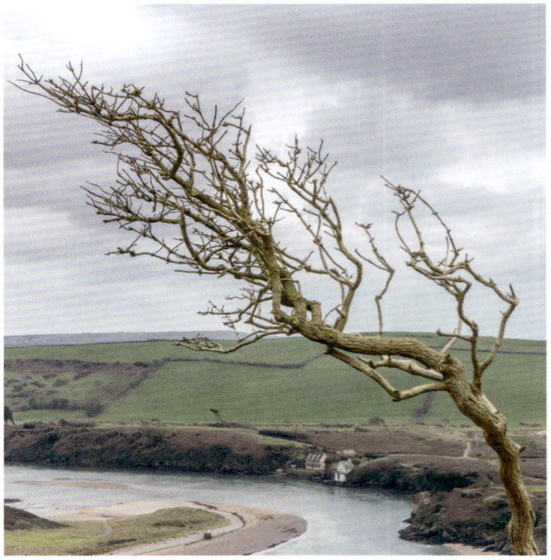

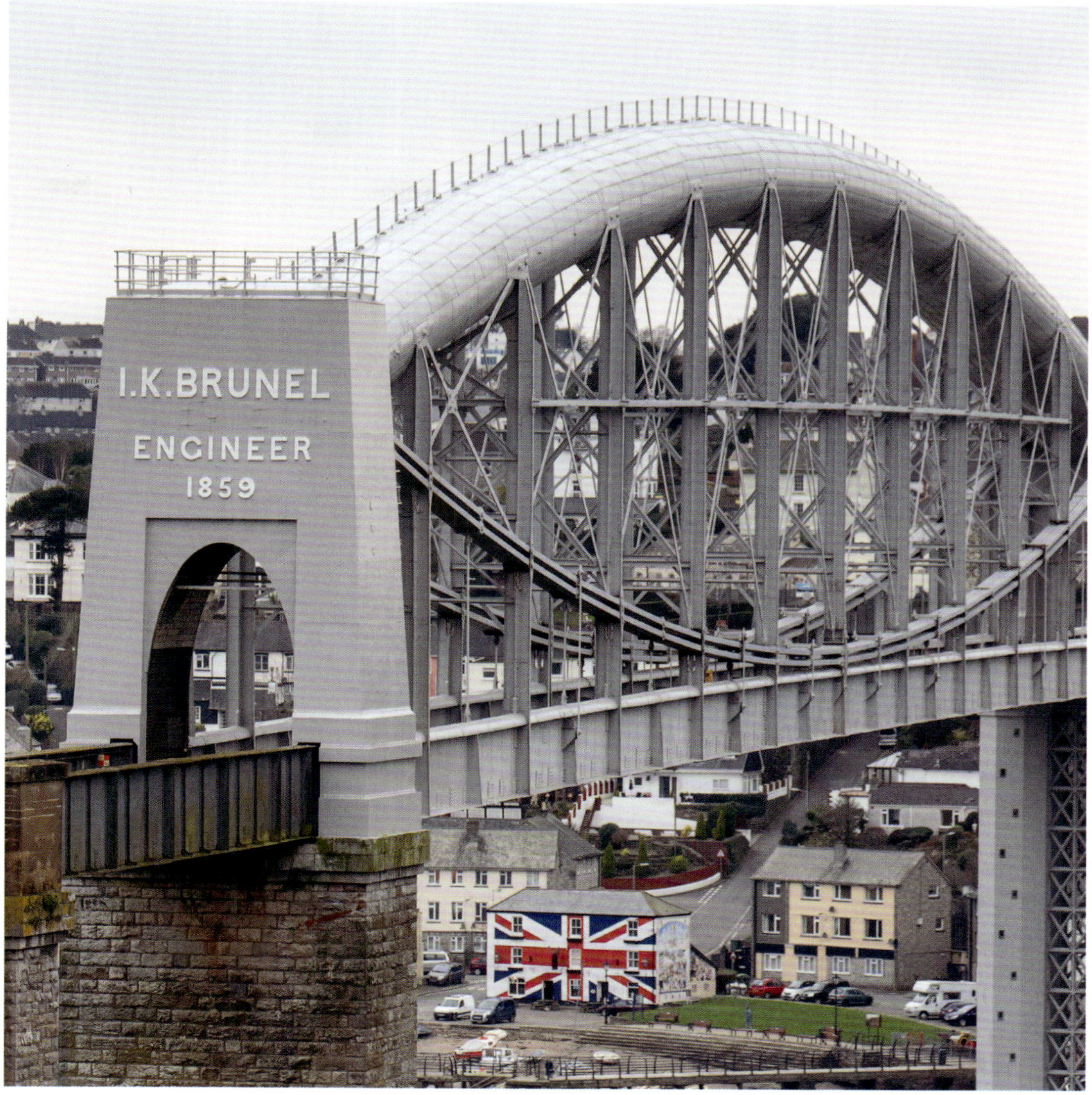

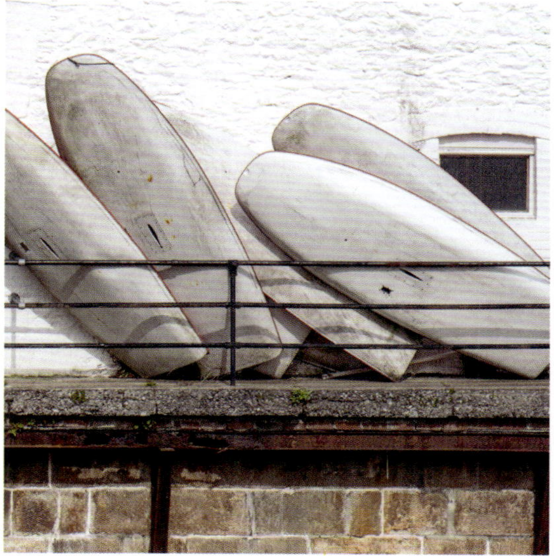

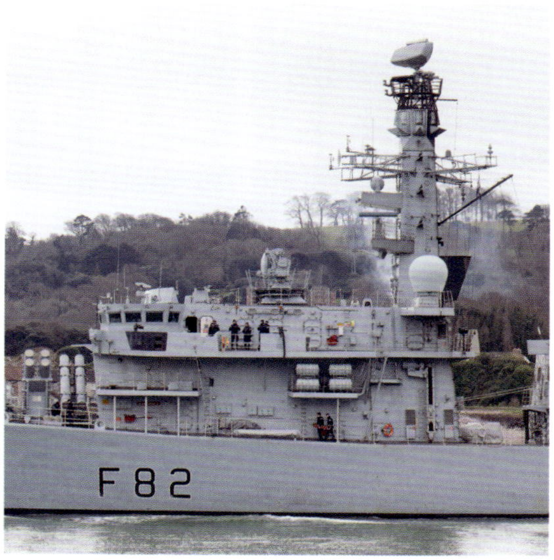

Opposite, from top left:

Holy Trinity Church, South Huish

Surfer, Bantham Beach

Radford Castle, a nineteenth-century folly, Plymouth

From centre left:

Thatched cottage, Inner Hope

The wreck of fishing boat *Dignity*, Hooe Lake, Plymouth

Beacon Hill Tea House, a folly built in 1766

From bottom left:

Low-tide fording place of the River Erme

Spade, Heybrook Bay

River Avon

From top left:

Royal Albert Bridge and Saltash, Cornwall

Dinghies, Plymouth

HMS *Somerset*, a frigate of the Royal Navy leaving Devonport, Plymouth

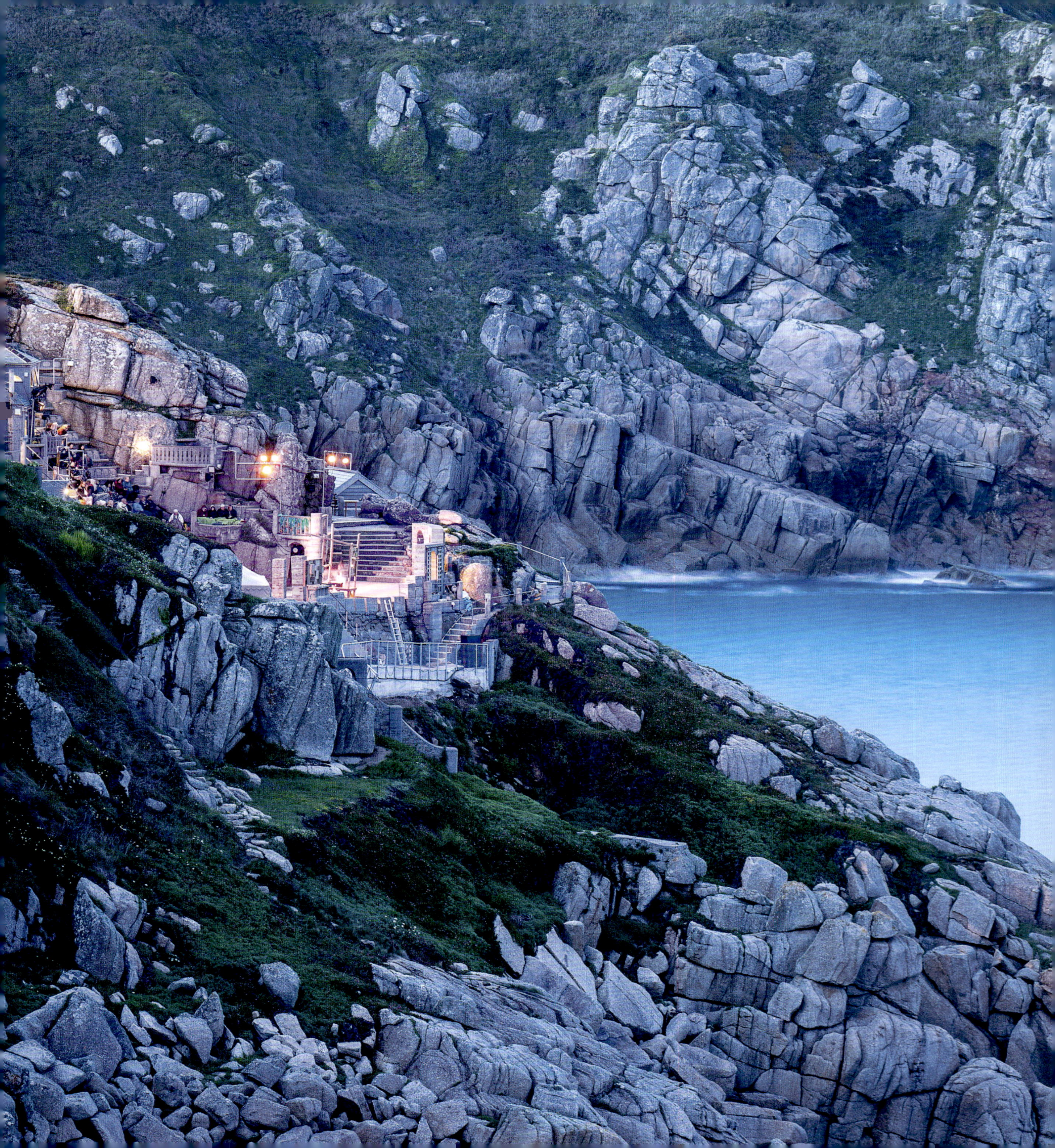

07 CORNWALL

MARCH–JULY 2016
DAY 053–081 | 01,352–02,076 KM | 724 KM

It's a grand entrance from Devon to Cornwall as I cross a road bridge high above the Tamar Valley. As I walk, I can't help but marvel at the twin curved-tube truss of the Brunel-designed Royal Albert Bridge that runs parallel next to me. Over it, a train ambles past, its speed barely surpassing my own – though beautiful, the bridge has a speed limit that forces trains to decelerate as they cross to reduce vibrations. Far below, the Tamar River slices its way across the foot of Cornwall, creating a stark divide that separates the region from the rest of the mainland.

I love Cornwall as if it were a close family member. My parents took me on holiday there as a child, and I've often brought my own family here, so it's exciting to be venturing into uncharted territory in a familiar place. Cornwall's rugged coastline is the longest of any county in England at 724 walkable kilometres, and with up to 900 metres of daily ascent and descent, it provides a great backpacking challenge.

From the Tamar, I make a 30-kilometre loop around the lush fields surrounding the Lynher River, stopping here and there to appreciate the stillness in the parish churches that pepper the landscape. The Travelodge-like campus of HMS Raleigh at Torpoint, the Royal Navy training establishment, is eerily quiet before a lone female sailor in a blue beret marches briskly between two buildings. Past an assault course, the reconstructed bow of a warship sits incongruously on-land. A dozen uniformed sailors stand in line on the deck holding a thick rope while orders are issued. As the ship looks like a theatre set, I almost expect them to break into song while wiggling their rope in a synchronised dance.

Past St Austell, where the clay spoil heaps rise like volcanoes, I reach Gorran Haven, where I've come for holidays with my children for many years. Here, I witnessed their first yelps and giggles as they came in contact with the sea, the satisfaction of creating their first sandcastles, and their fascination with the myriad creatures in the rock pools. Returning now for the first time without them, I'm conscious of how the same timeless rituals are being enacted all around me: a family unit on the pier could be a carbon copy of us.

At St Just Creek, I wake up in the condensation-filled tent to the sound of a woodpecker drumming. I'm way inland now, heading to the first bridge at Truro as silver slivers of the sea are revealed and hidden within the undulating landscape. The creeks are like fingers, and my route like the web of a duck's foot. Four days of winding hedge-lined lanes, poverty-stricken farms and stone gateposts on a heroic scale like standing stones.

It's a day's walk from Truro back to the sea, where I need to follow terrifyingly narrow roads, barely avoiding vehicles as they whizz past me. I must stay somewhere tonight to charge my batteries, but everywhere is full. 'Doubles only,' a B&B owner says before closing the door in my face. Desperate, I ask at the inn where I'm eating if I can pitch in their garden. Their expression of professional hospitality immediately hardens even as they take my money for the expensive meal, so I walk for another hour to camp under the stars on a quay. There's seaweed scattered as I put my tent up, so I triple-check tide times before falling asleep.

At Mylor Bridge, a charming village north of Falmouth, I get a cup of tea at the butcher's, where each customer is greeted by name as they come in. It must be a slow news day on the village grapevine as they all gossip about the backpacker sitting out of sight beyond the fly screen: 'He just came in for a cup of tea.' 'Nice day for it, mind.' When I return to the anonymity of the trail, white horses gallop across a field towards me, their manes dancing like fire. When they get close they vanish behind a high hedge, though I hear their heavy breath near me. I cross ancient

Opposite:

Performance at the Minack Theatre, Porthcurno Bay

slab bridges like in Dartmoor, through woodlands dripping with rain and carpeted in moss and ivy. Clusters of purple orchids by the path are so pretty that it's hard to believe somebody did not arrange them.

Near Bridge Farm by the Helford River, I meet a powerfully built man with an open, contented face going out for a walk in his shirtsleeves. In a rich Cornish accent, he tells me, 'When we first married, what with the rabbits and oysters, we pretty much lived off the land. Been here forty-nine years. No need to leave. Taught my children to swim in the river and about all the trees. They are grown up now, own family in Regis. I have been to London, but I feel like Crocodile Dundee when I go into a bar.' I tell him what I'm doing. 'Proper job,' he says, shaking my hand firmly, which is engulfed in his massive paw.

On my eighteenth day in Cornwall, the May heat is sweltering, and I can't find clear water to filter. When I come across a stream, the water is sticky to the touch, so I abandon the idea. An adder passes before me on the path, and I have to lean back to avoid stepping on him. The heat also brings on a crop of blisters, cracked lips, and sunburn that I don't notice due to the sea breeze. When I finally find a clean water source, I greedily drink a litre as an aperitif for a pint of tea.

Rounding a headland reveals the rocky island of St Michael's Mount, a famous medieval pilgrimage location topped with a castle and a chapel. The late-evening summer light bathes the mount in a yellow glow and I set up camp for a peaceful night.

I'm flattered when the BBC get in touch. They want to make a short piece for the national news, 'One man, one camera', so they send a video journalist from London to cover my story for a couple of days. He stays in a nearby hotel and within a few sweaty minutes discovers that a heavy gear trolley is incompatible with the coast path, catching on every step. I enjoy sharing the journey with someone else, trying to capture the essence of the place on film. I quickly have to overcome my fear of talking to the camera when, at busy Land's End, he wants me to do just that surrounded by a crowd. I plaintively ask if we could go somewhere nobody would hear, but he needs the background to tell the story, so I'm given my media induction with the words, 'No, get on with it!' When we're done, we say our goodbyes at the famous fingerpost, where I started a 1,677-kilometre walk to John o'Groats twenty years ago.

The path to St Ives is like a wobble board mounted on a step machine, the toughest terrain so far. It's hard to keep myself going, so when I'm exhausted, I force myself to walk fifty minutes with the promise of a ten-minute rest. The South West Coast Path has 35 kilometres of ascent and descent, and on one short break, I peel off my sweat-soaked shirt to savour the blissful warm wind on my back.

Approaching St Ives, I pass an artist sketching and, later, a man layering oil paint thickly on to canvas with a palette knife in a meadow. St Ives is where I'd spent so many happy summers as a child, and the memory leaves me nostalgic and oddly melancholy in spite of the sun. I remember only the tiniest details of the landscape – a rock I swam to, the slope up from the beach – but the feel of Barbara Hepworth's sculpture garden is firmly anchored in my mind. Where I'd reached up as a child to run my hand over her bronze sculpture *Sphere with Inner Form*, I now reach down.

I wake on the first day post-Brexit to find the tent covered in dozens of tiny snails and black slugs as fat as my thumb. It's another hot day, and most people seem to be shouting at a misbehaving child or dog. An Aussie couple ask me, 'Do you wanna buy a couple of moaning kids – really cheap?' By the time I reach Padstow, it is unpleasantly busy – slow crowds of visitors shuffle along the streets. I wonder if they're thinking, 'Is this it?' like me. It's all too clear how the influx of middle-class holidaymakers has changed Cornwall, and the sight of key safes next to almost every waterside cottage door is a stark reminder of how locals are being replaced. A street cleaner greets some friends warmly in a Cornish accent. 'You don't bloody want to go down there, I tell you – I don't have much choice, mind!'

As I leave Padstow and follow the banks of the River Camel, I enter a field where I'm charged at by a herd of heifers utterly unresponsive to the arm-waving, clapping and shouting that worked for me before in such situations. Fearing being trampled, I throw a rock at the head of the closest, giving me just enough time to clamber over the nearest wall. The next day, I eat strawberries in the churchyard around St Enodoc's charmingly wonky spire, once engulfed by sand, and the burial place of John Betjeman.

Miraculously, the summer-holiday crowds don't extend to Boscastle YHA, where I feel like a king to have a whole dorm to myself. It's been days since I've slept anywhere besides my tent – or had a shower.

Opposite, from top left:

Fifteenth-century wagon roof with carved bosses, Church of St Mary, Sheviock

Dartmoor ponies and Second World War gun emplacement, Rame Head

From bottom left:

Pane sailing: Downderry

Rainforest Biome of the Eden Project, designed by Grimshaw Architects in 2000

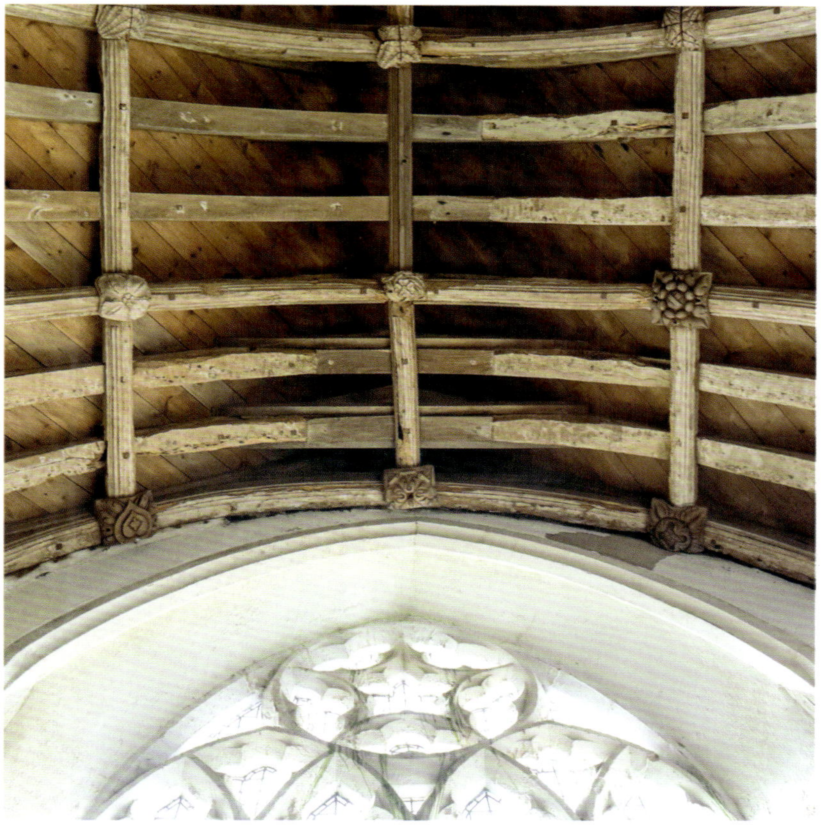

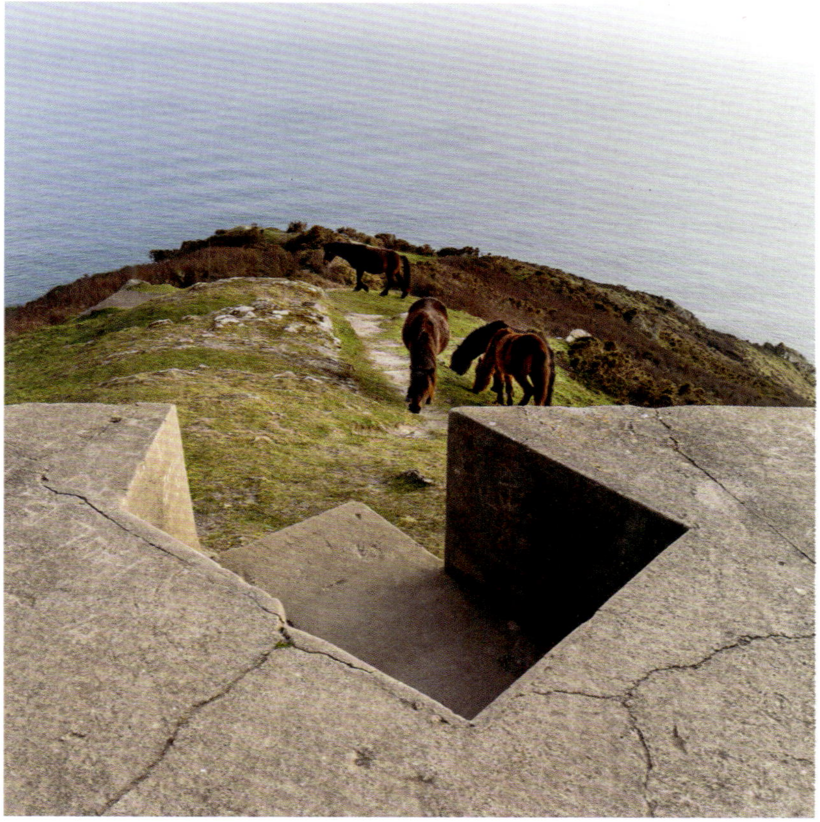

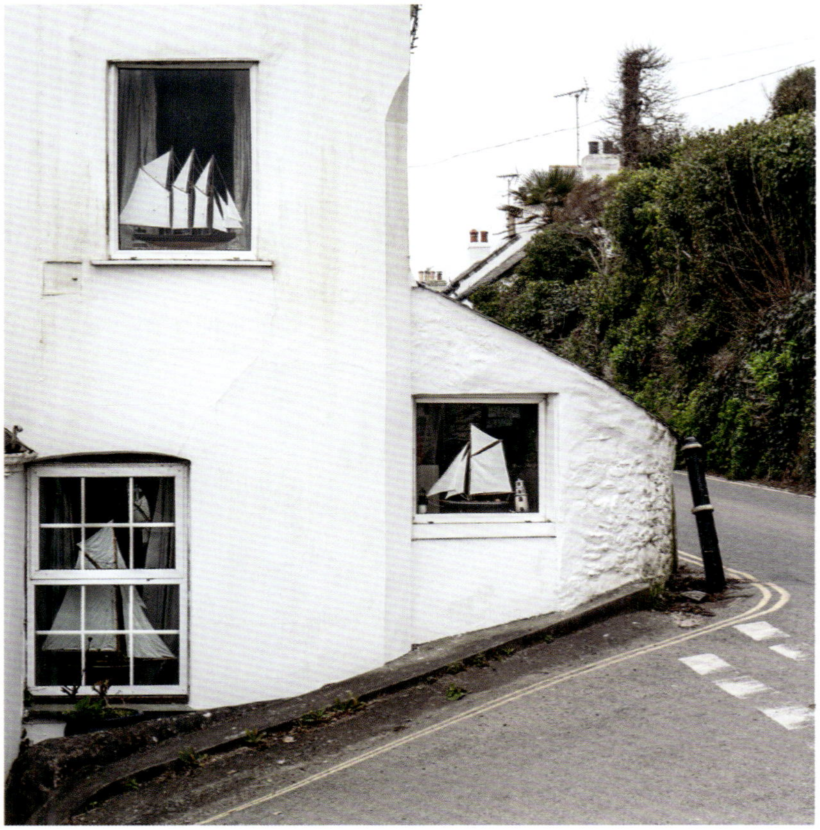

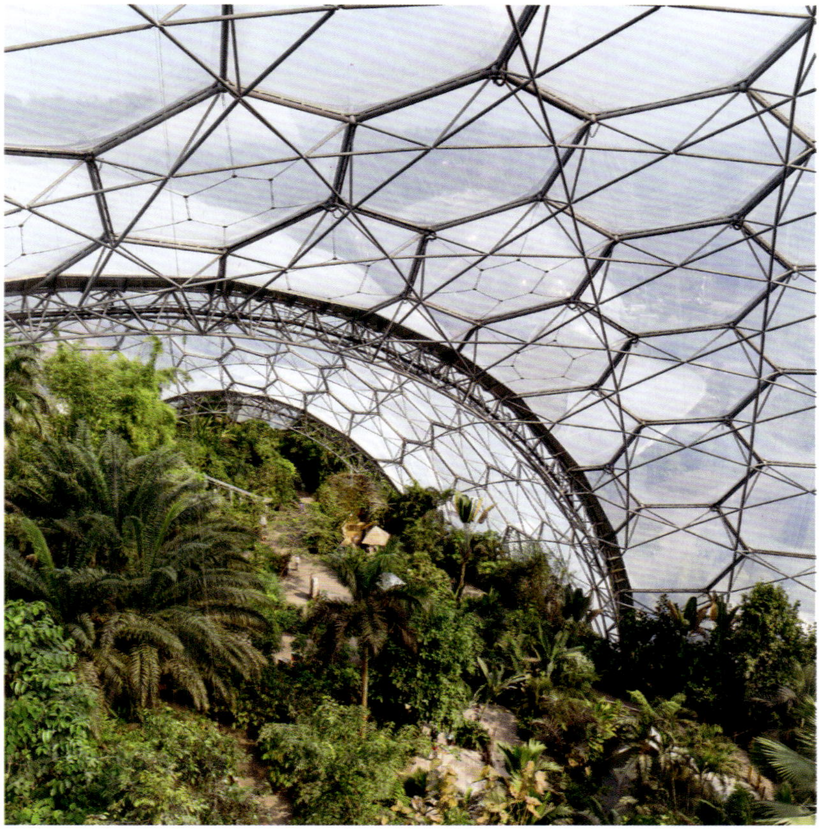

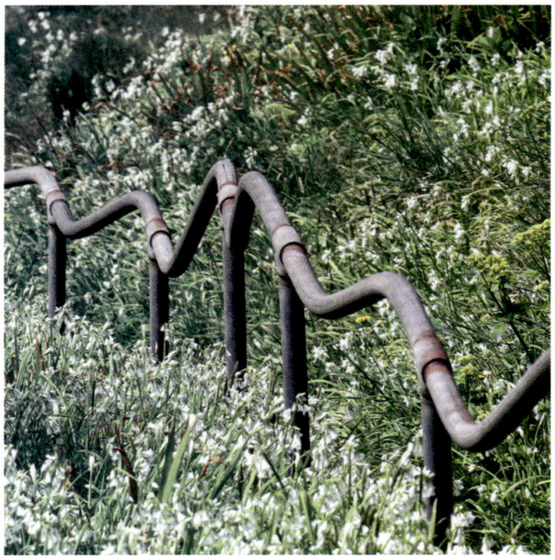

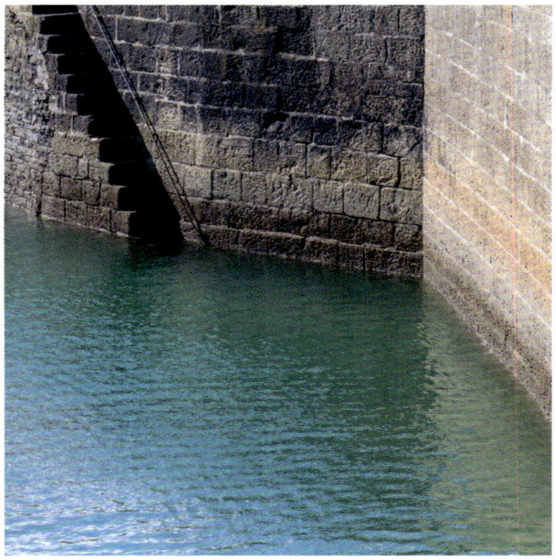

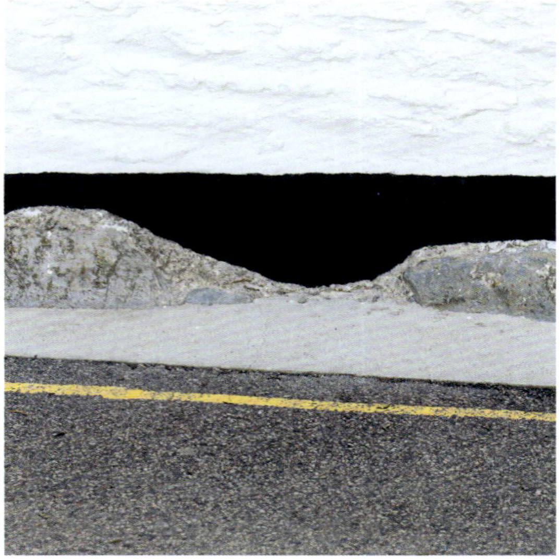

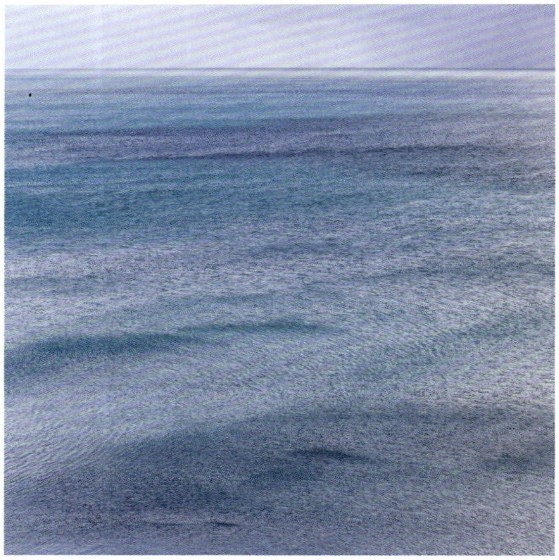

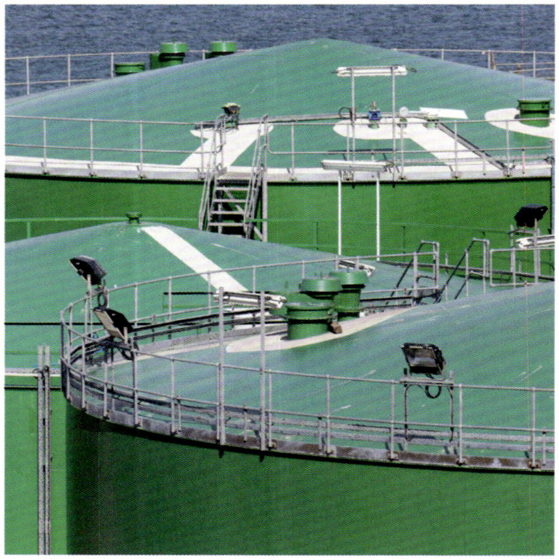

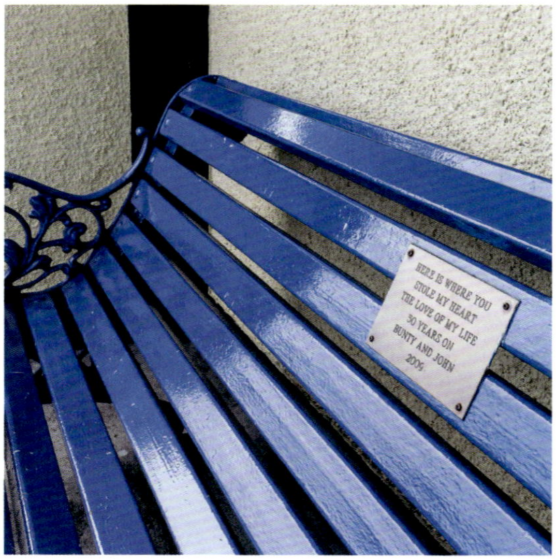
HERE IS WHERE YOU
STOLE MY HEART
THE LOVE OF MY LIFE
30 YEARS ON
BUNTY AND JOHN
2009

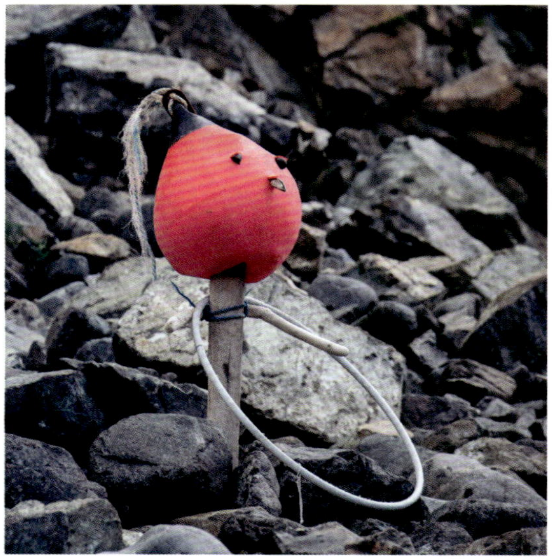

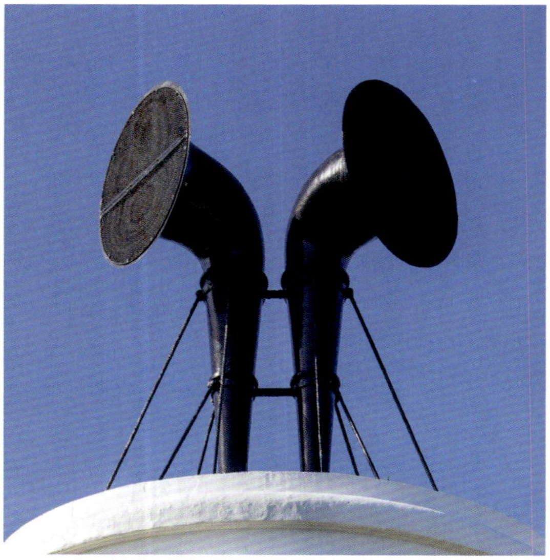

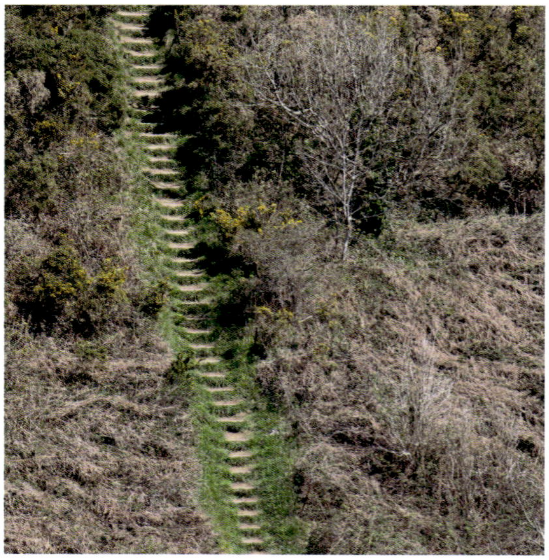

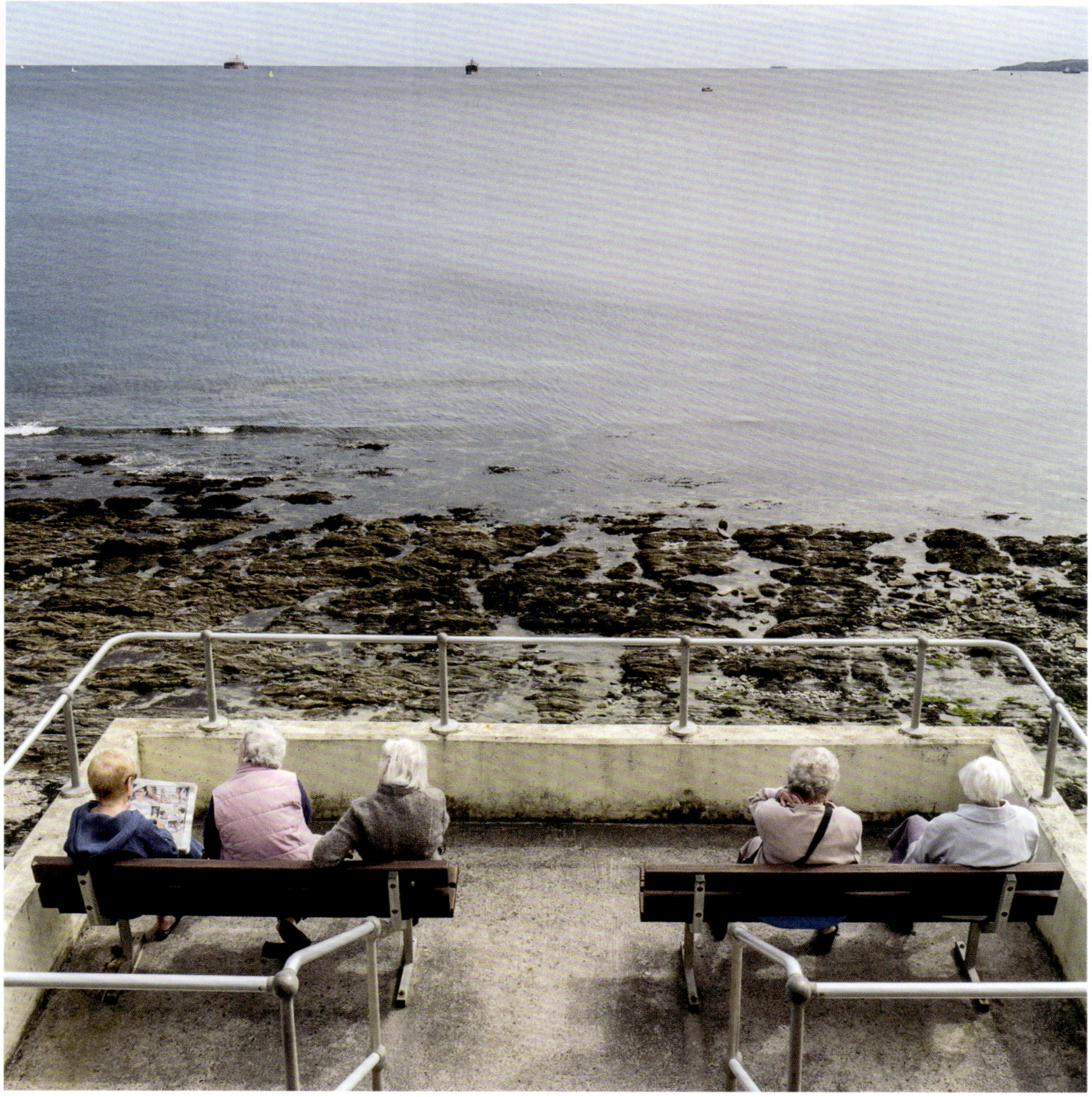

Opposite, from top left:

Path to Portloe

Docks, Charlestown

Kerb, Gorran Haven

From centre left:

Seascape after the rain, Portloe

Oil storage tanks at Falmouth Docks

'Here is where you stole my heart', Falmouth

From bottom left:

Downas Cove

Lizard Lighthouse foghorns

South West Coast Path at Silvermine Point

From top left:

Falmouth Bay

Flushing

Church Street, Falmouth

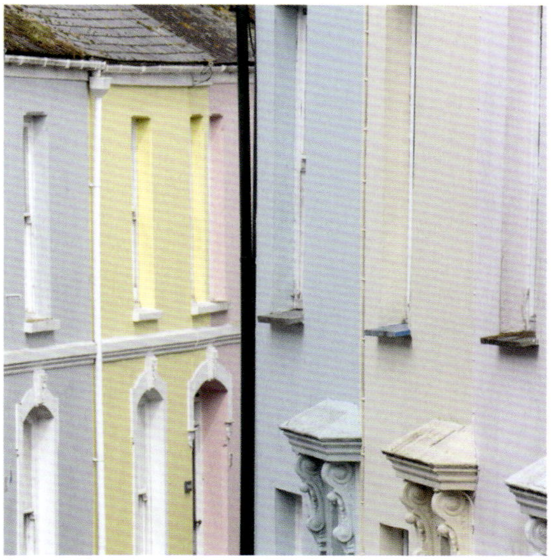

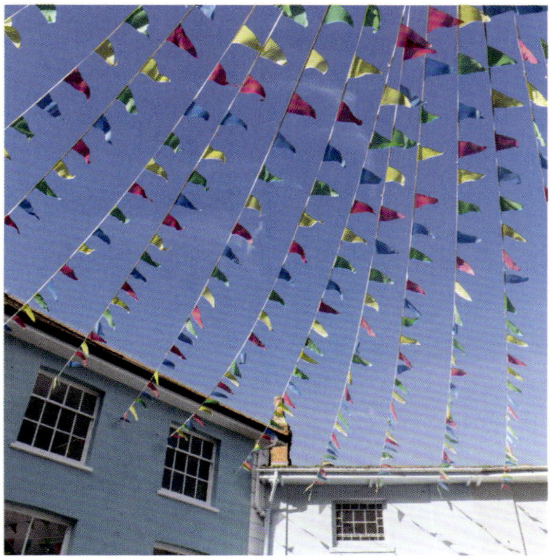

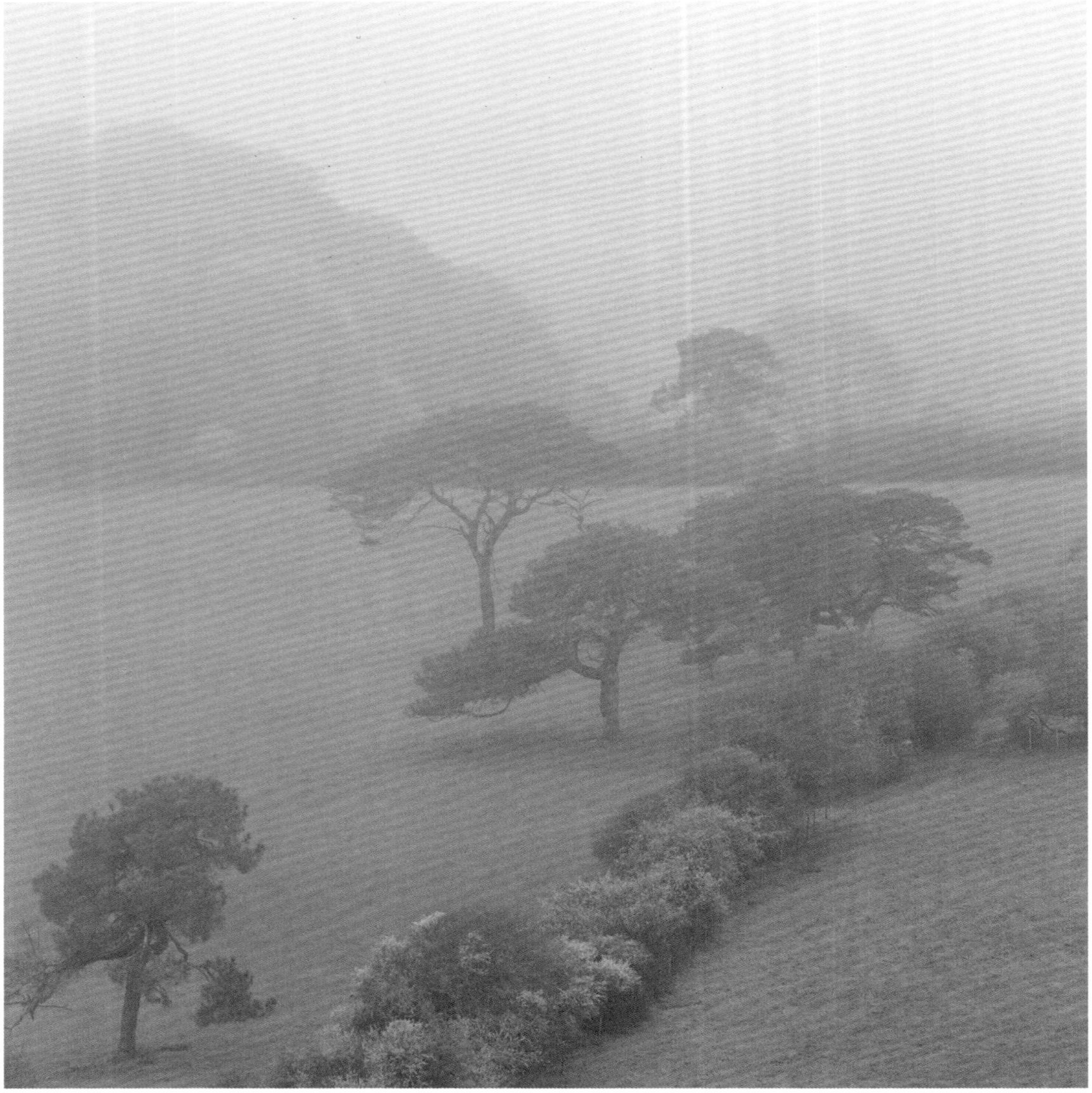

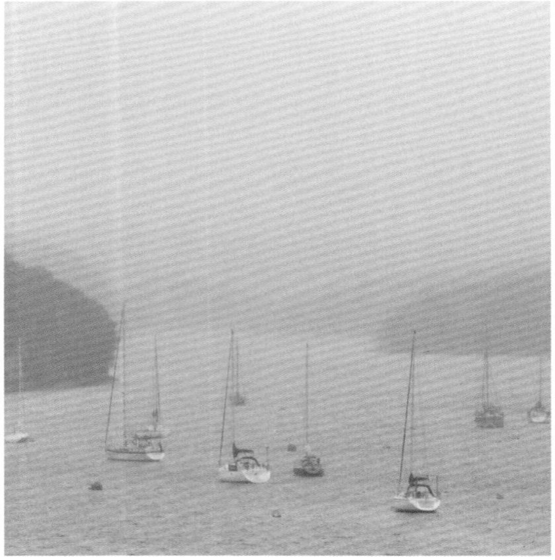

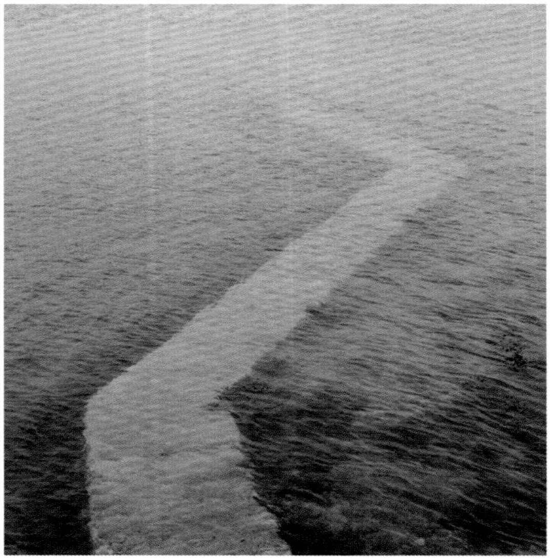

From top left:

Porth Navas

Helford River

Helford Point

Opposite:

Kynance Cove

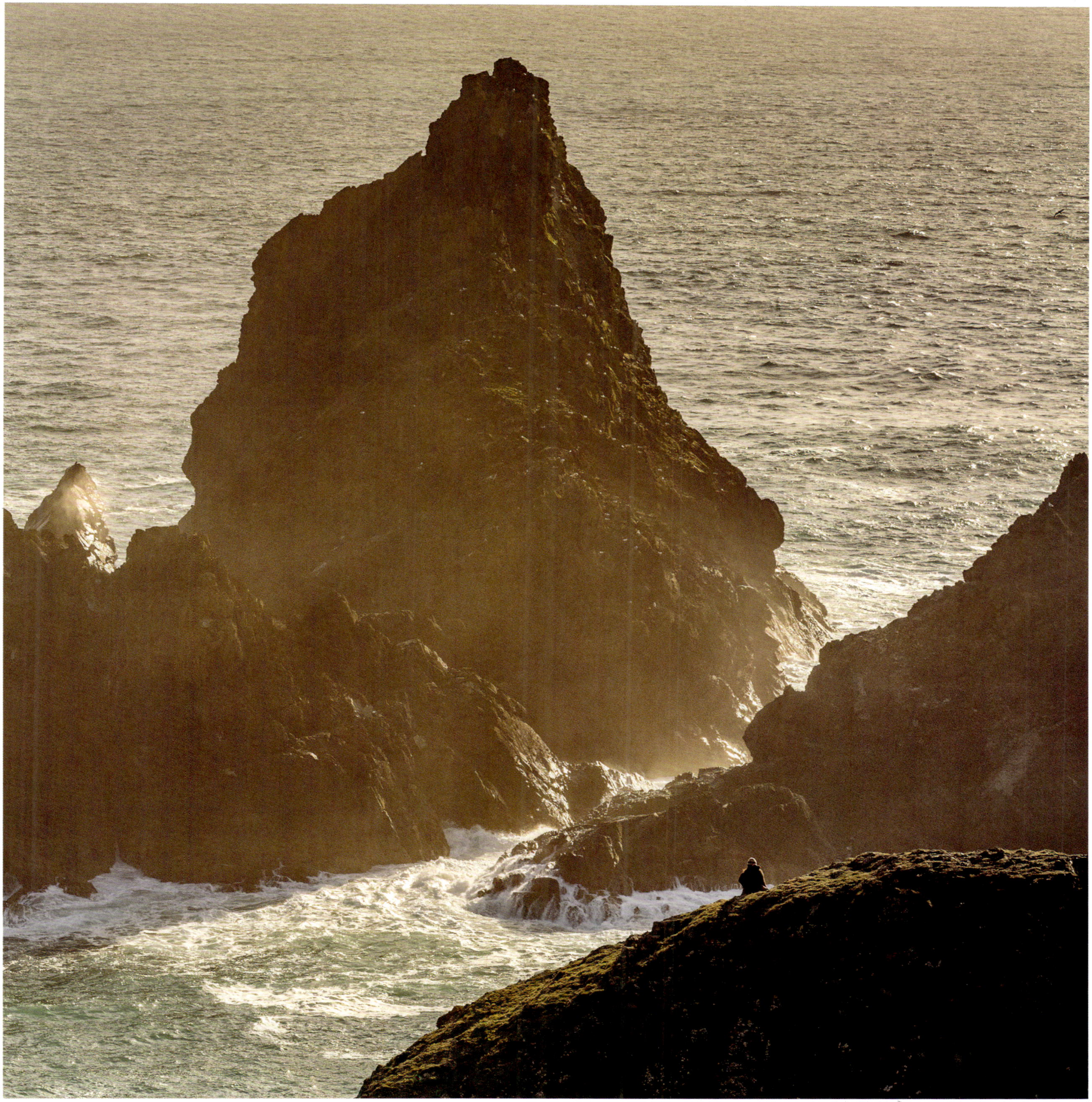

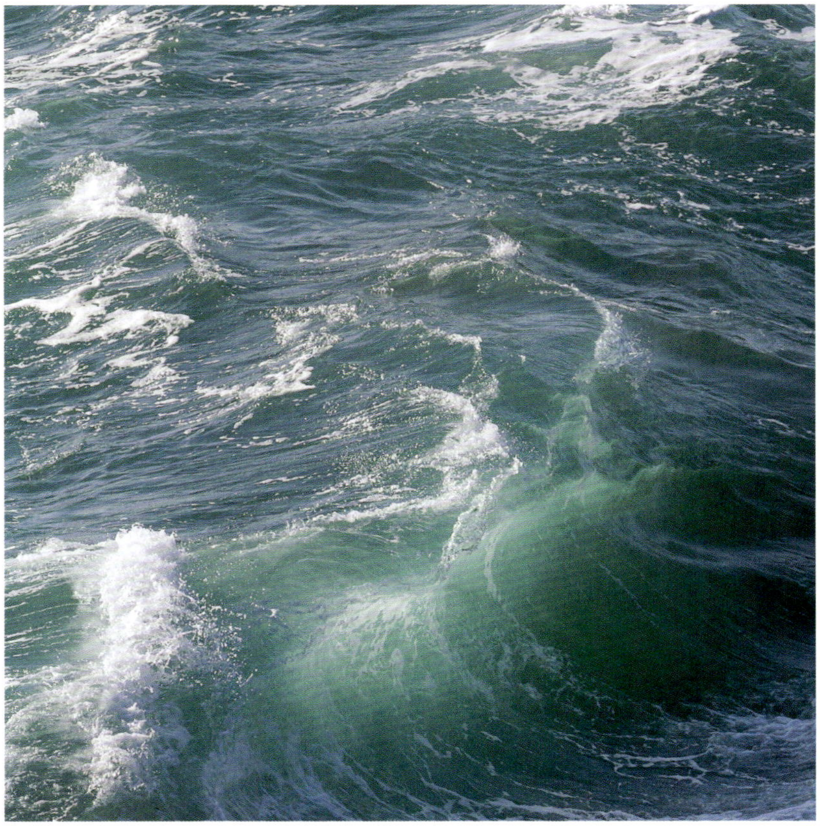

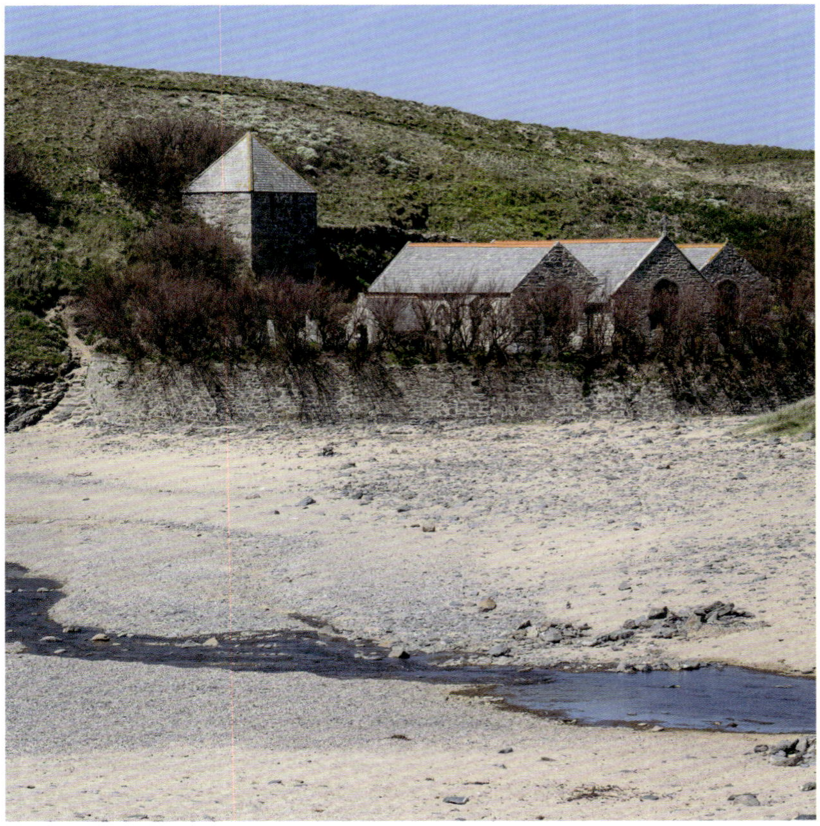

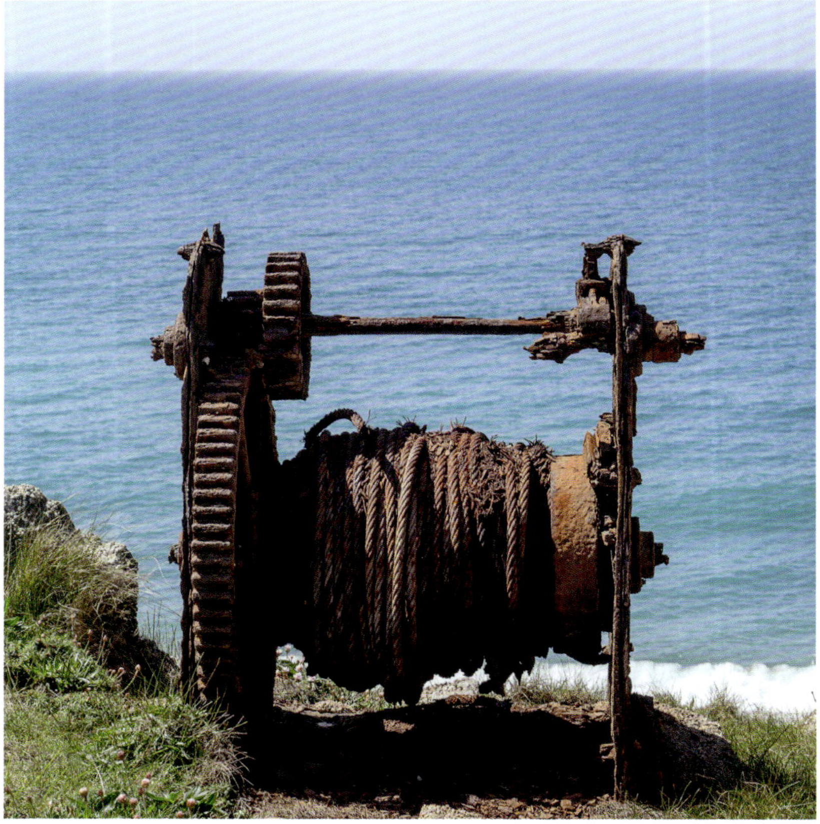

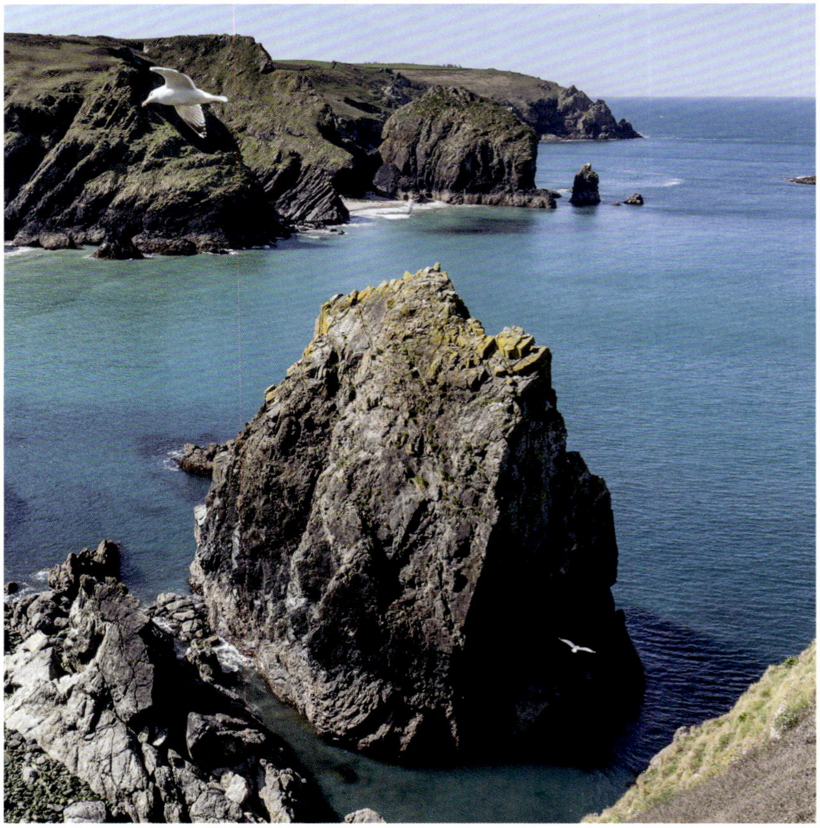

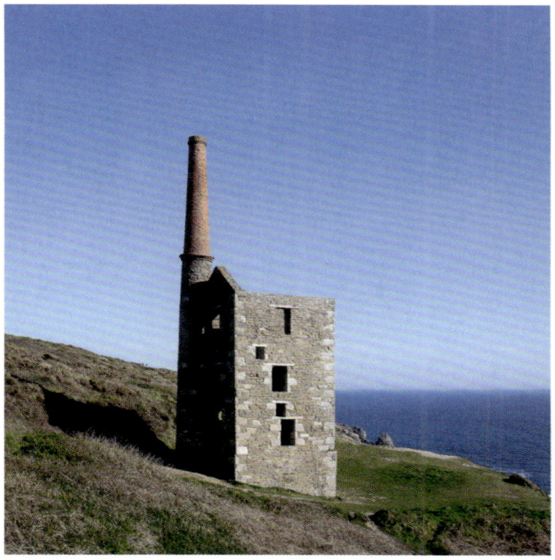

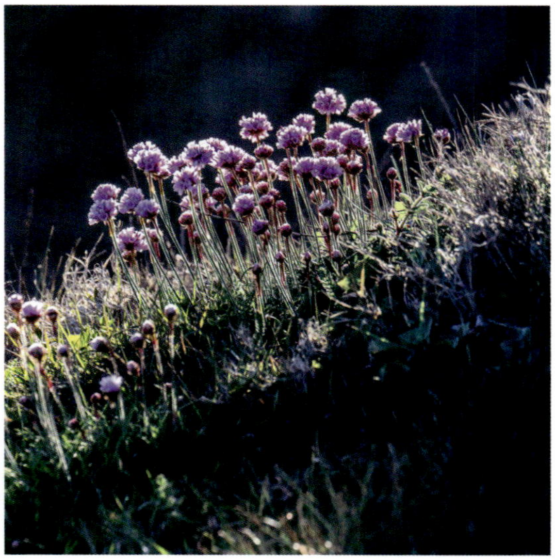

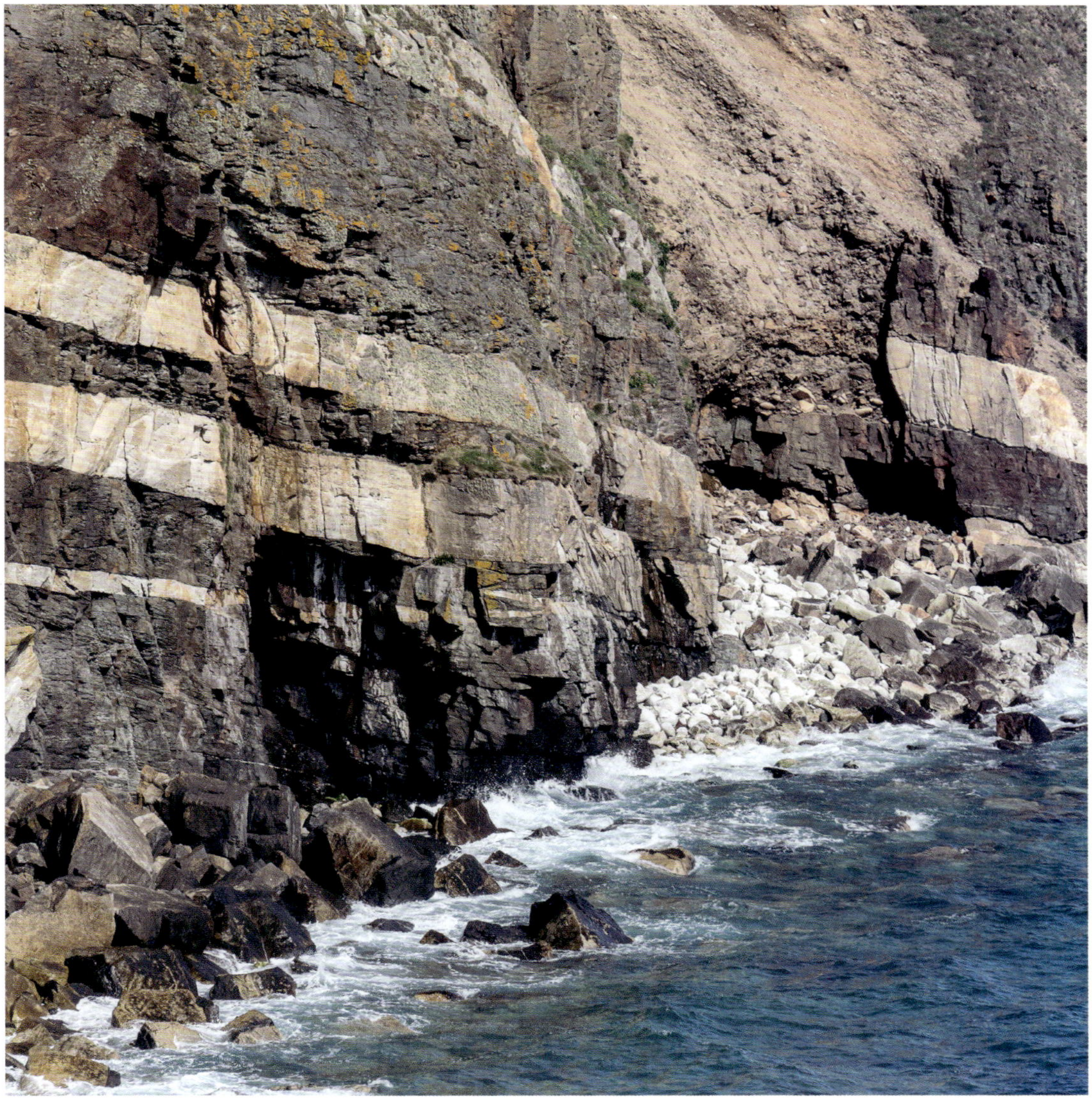

Opposite, from top left:

Waveform, Caerthillian Cove

Gunwalloe Church, Church Cove

From bottom left:

Winch, Gunwalloe Fishing Cove. The winch was used to draw the boats up the almost vertical cliff when the area was a thriving pilchard fishery

Scovarn, Mullion Cove

From top left:

Wheal Prosper Engine House, copper and tin mine from 1860 to 1866

Sea pinks, Kenneggy Sands

Strata of pale granitic pegmatites and black metasediment, Tremearne Cliff

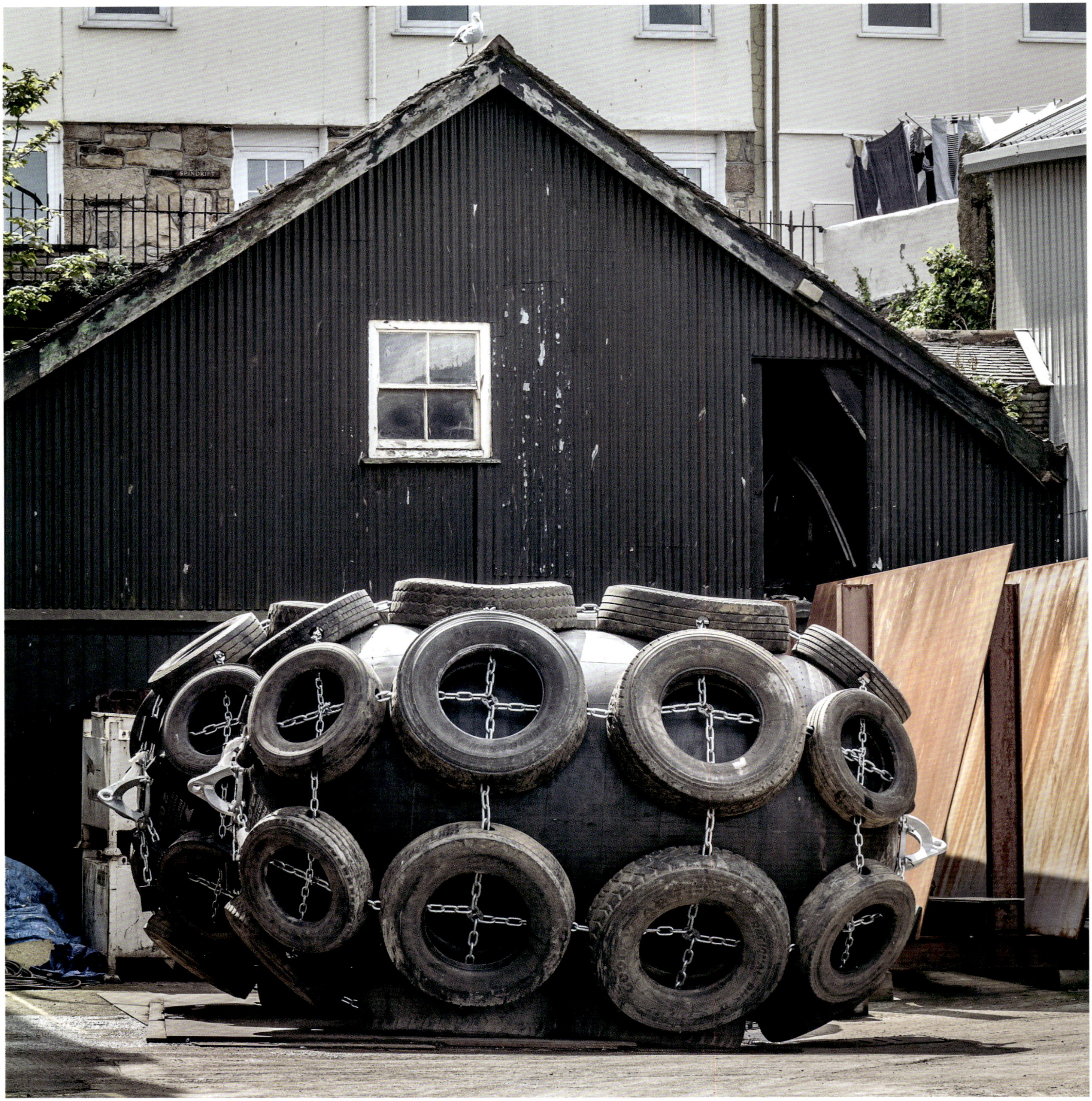

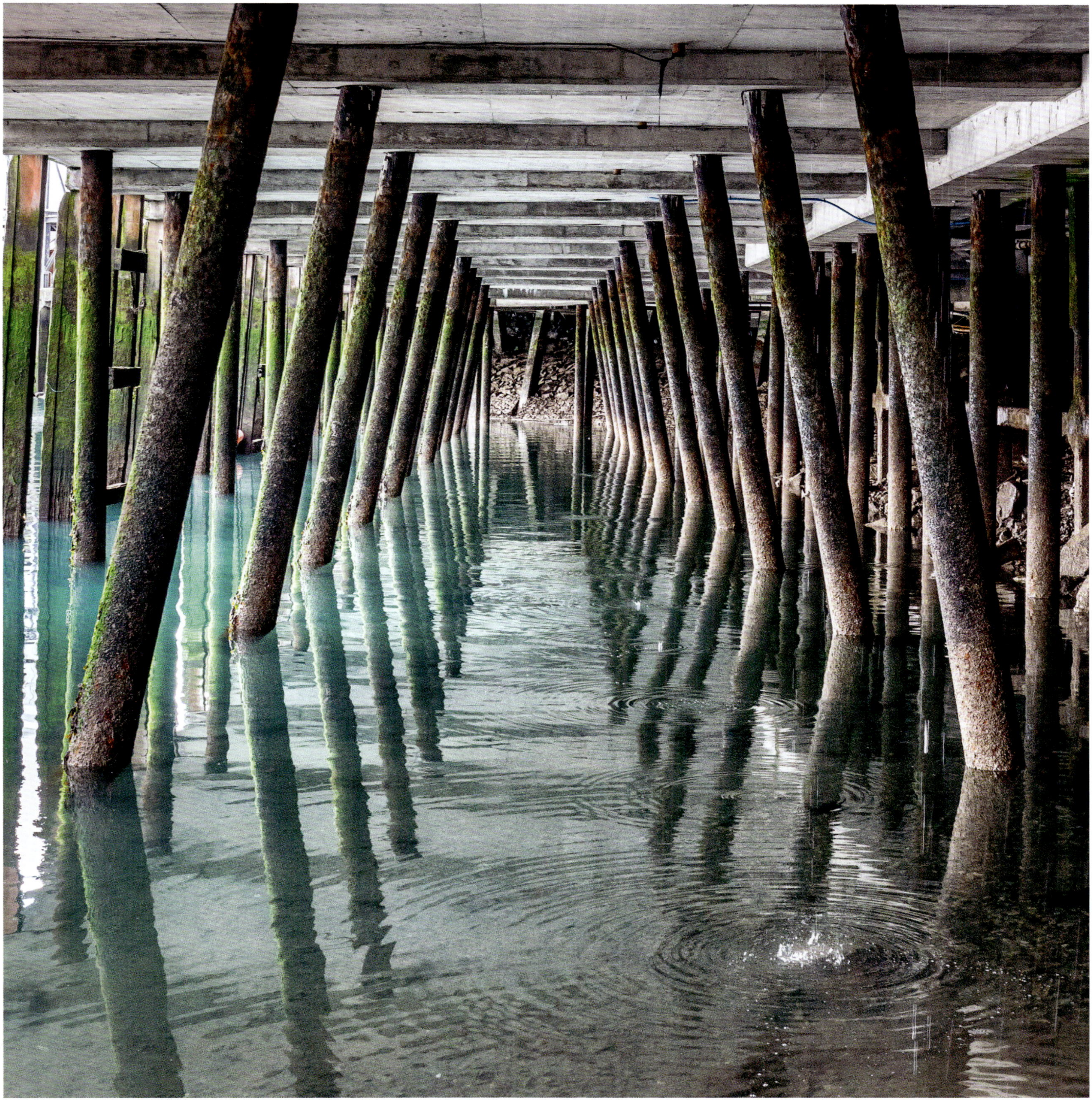

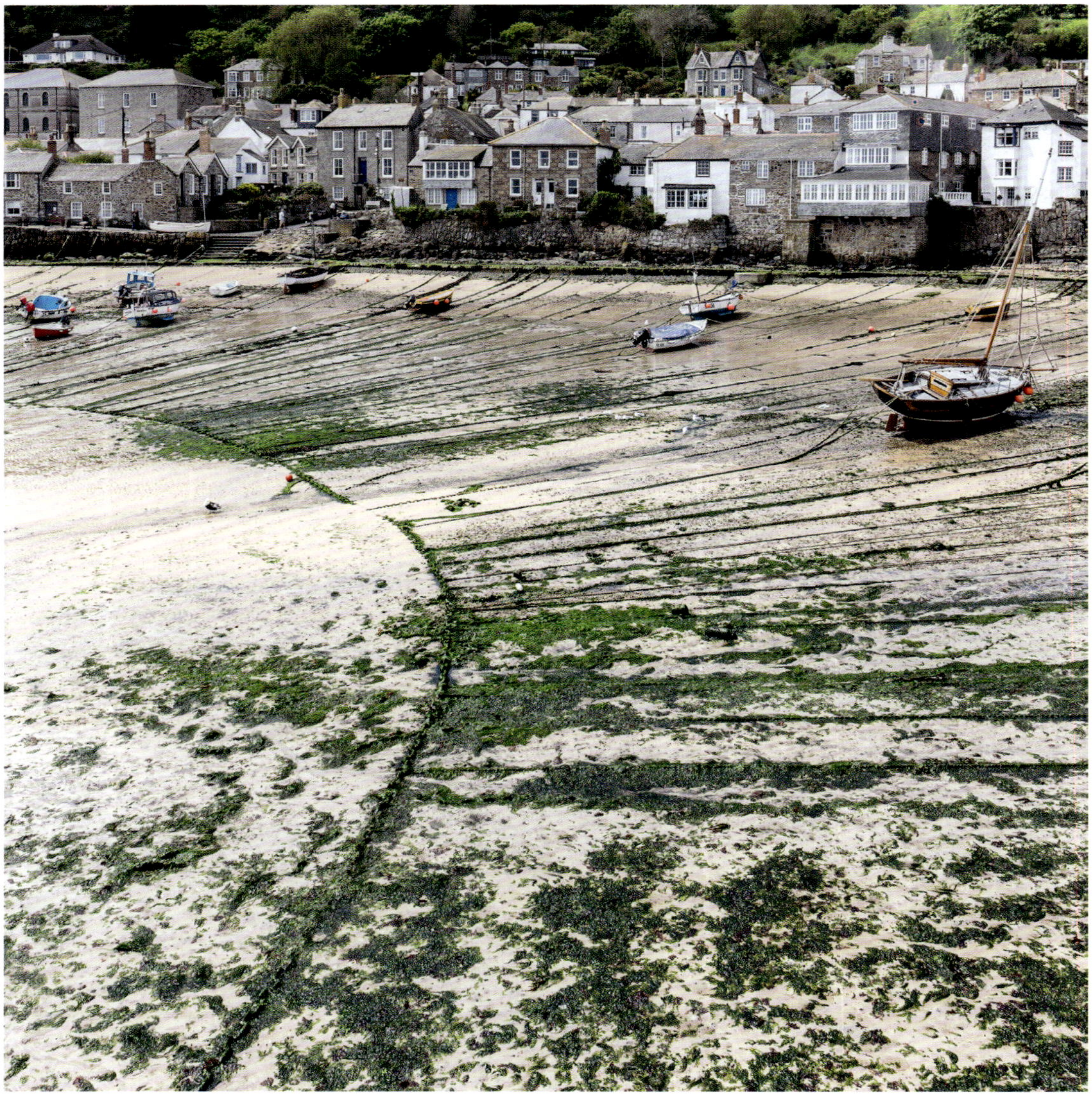

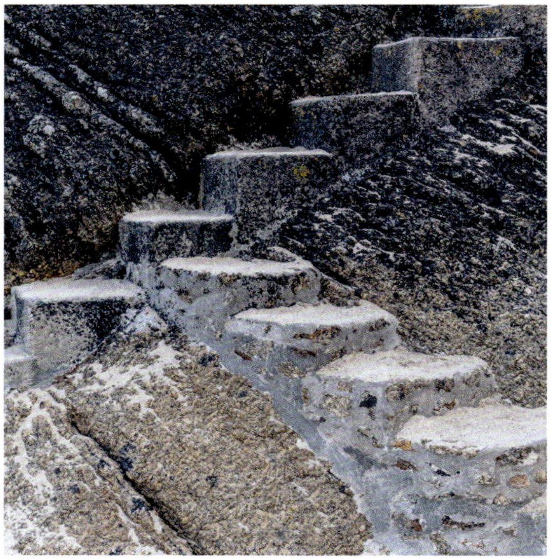

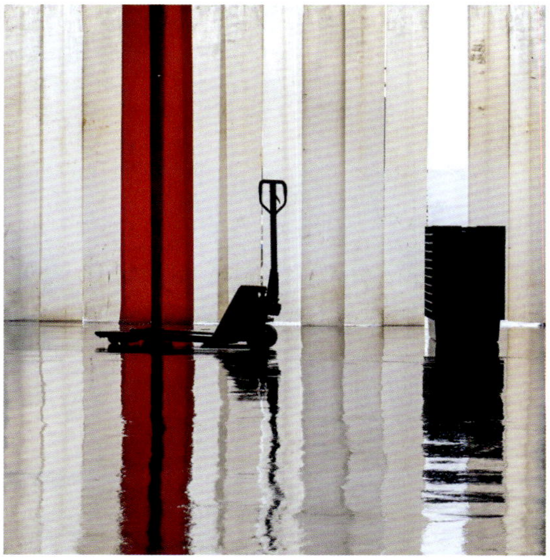

Previous, from left to right:

Yokohama fender, Penzance

Below Stevenson fish-packing plant, Newlyn Harbour

From top left:

Mousehole, Cornwall

Steps to the Minack Theatre, Porthcurno Bay

Stevenson fish-packing plant, Newlyn Harbour

Opposite, clockwise from top left:

Hella Point

Land's End signpost

Porthgwarra, artificial tunnel leading to the historic site of tidal 'hulleys', wooden containers used for storing shellfish

Porth Chapel

Whitesand Bay

Austin Sevens, Lamorna Cove

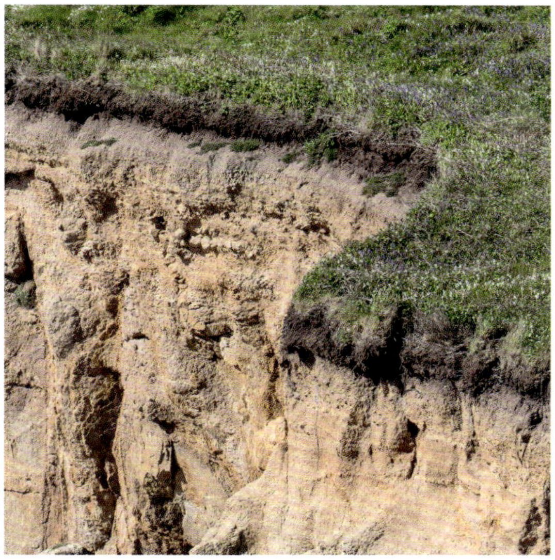

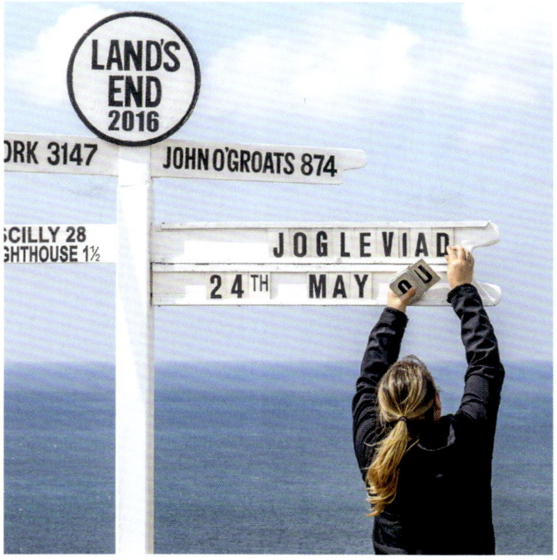
LAND'S
END
2016
JOHN O'GROATS 874
JOGLEVIAD
24TH MAY

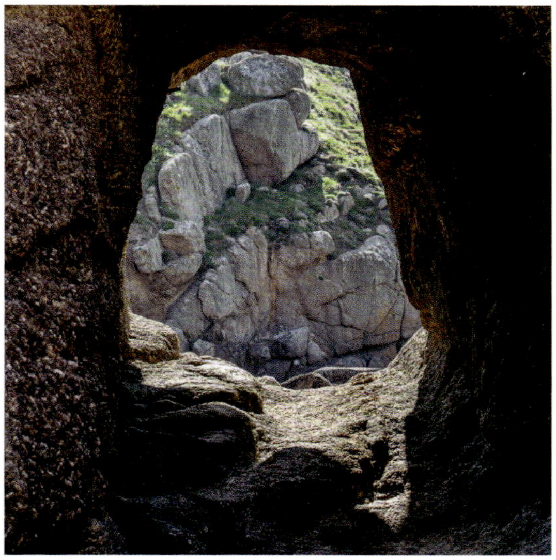

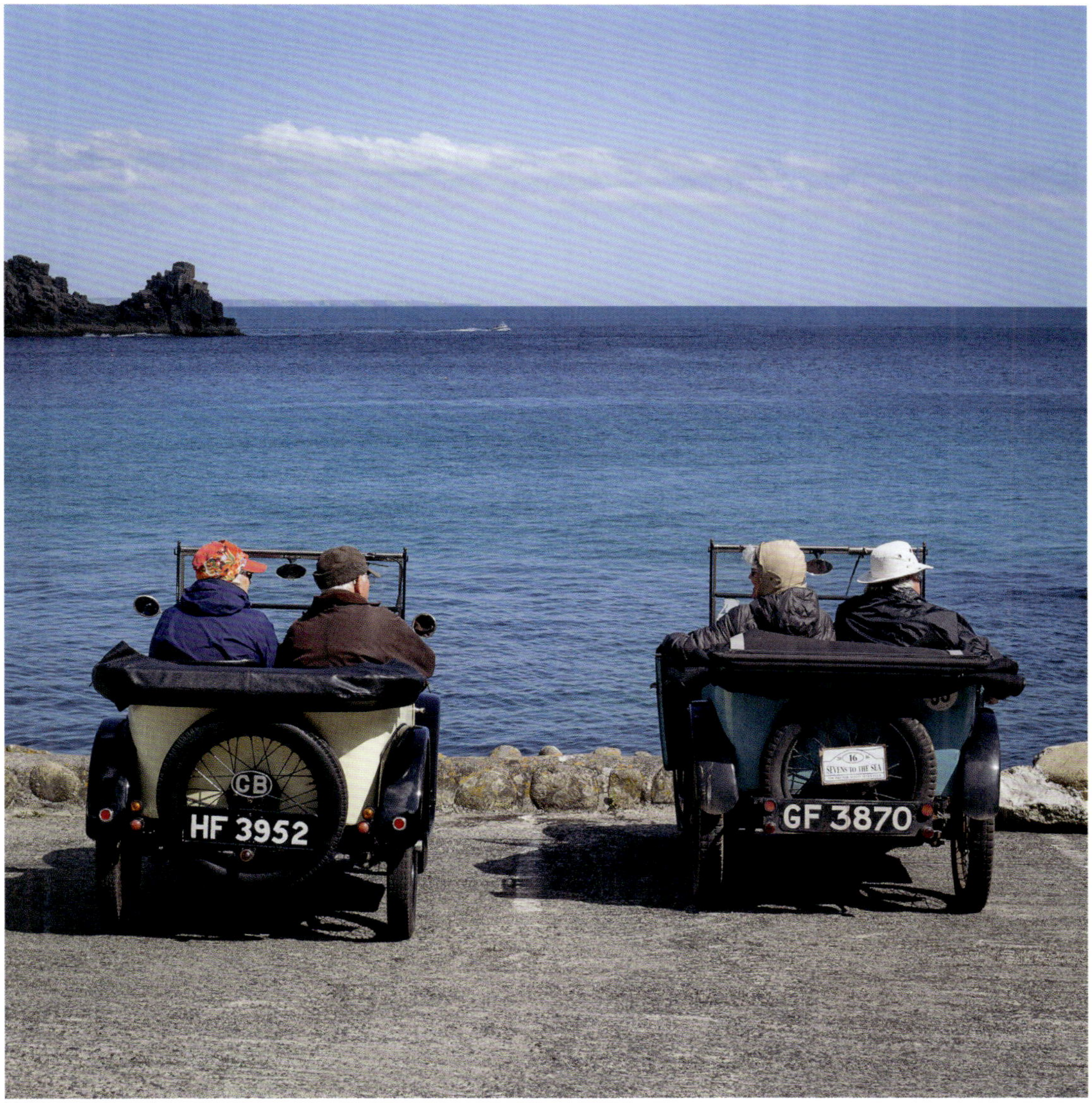
GB
HF 3952
GF 3870

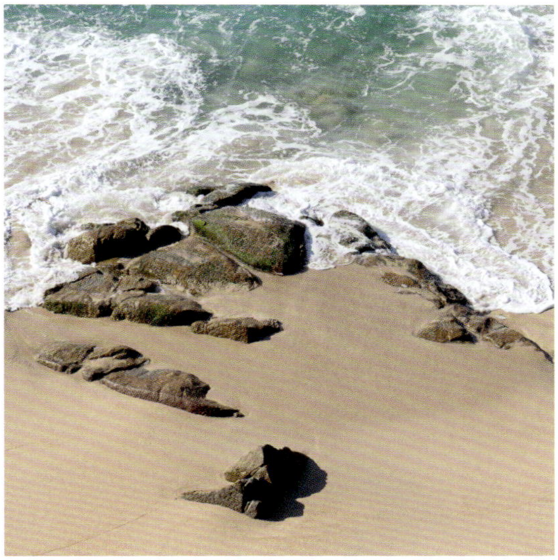

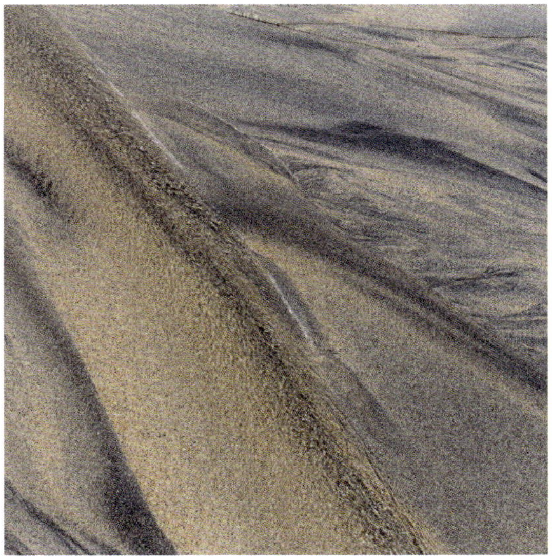

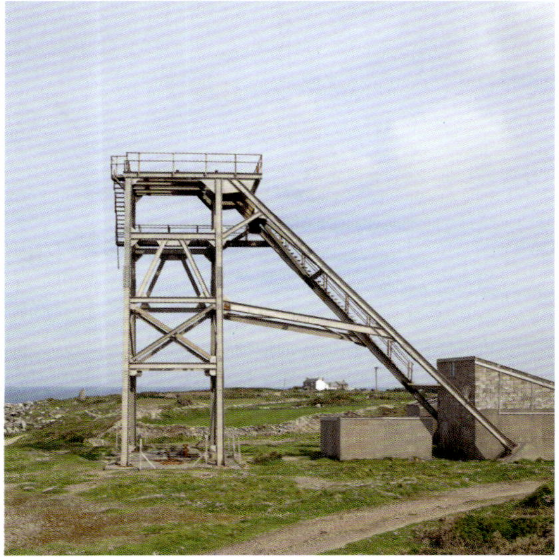

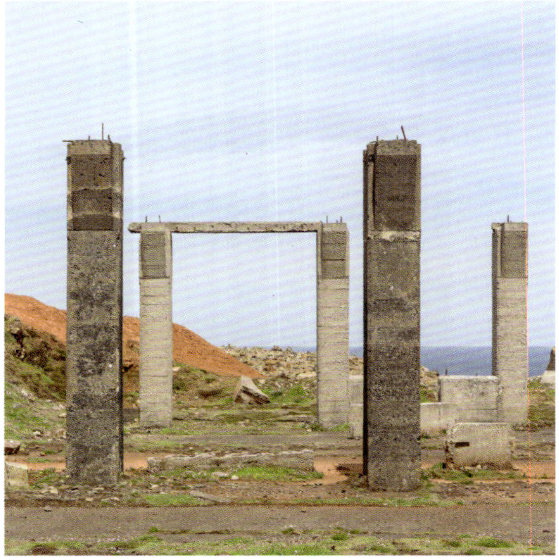

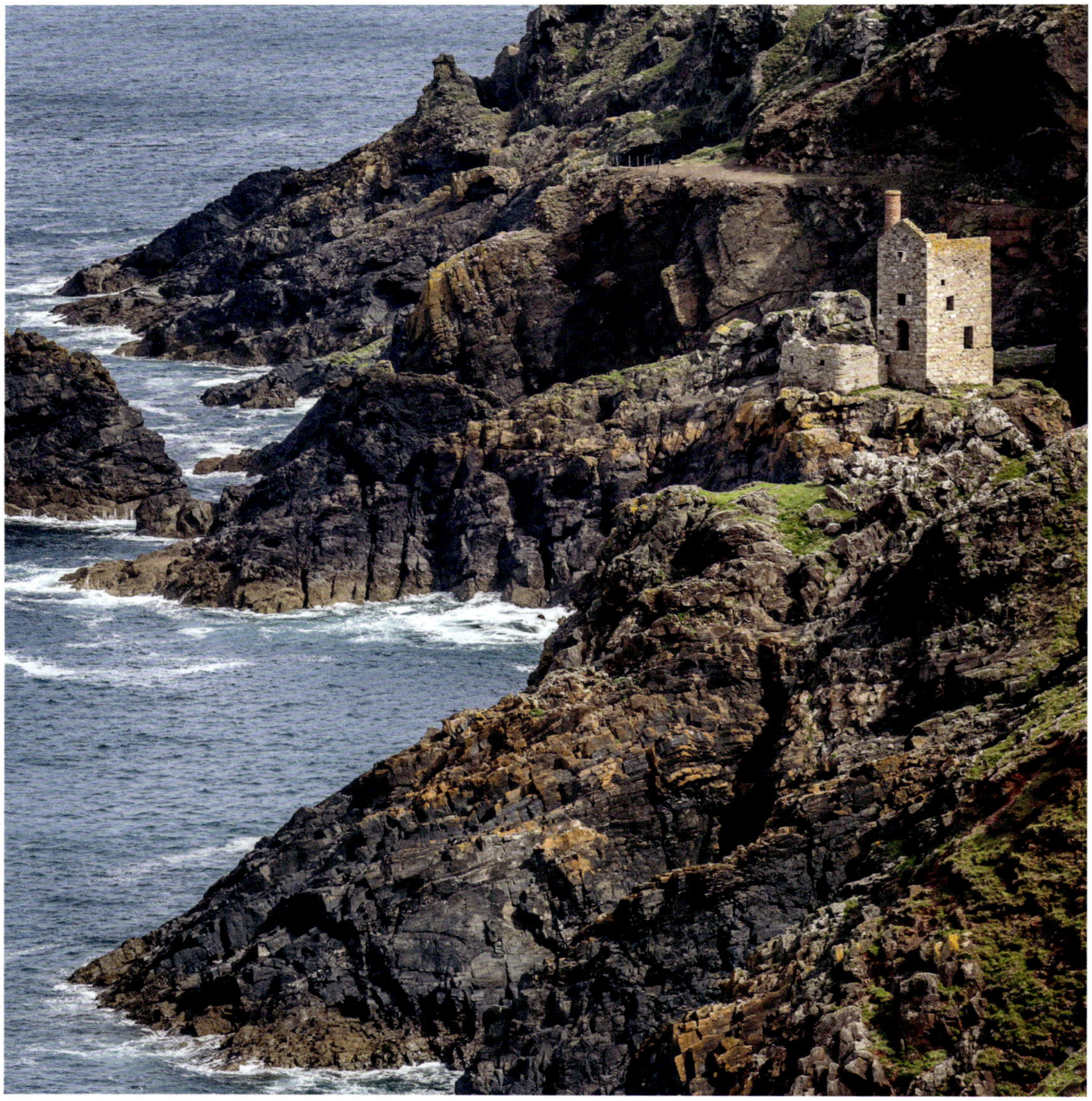

From top left:

Allen's Shaft headgear, Botallack

Geevor Tin Mine

Engine house at Crown Mines, Botallack

Opposite, clockwise from top left:

Layers, St Ives Bay

Gull Rock from Hell's Mouth

Lifeguard, St Ives Bay

Porthmeor Bowling Club, St Ives

Mineshaft cover, Cligga Head

Four-Square (Walk Through), 1966, Barbara Hepworth. Artist's studio, St Ives

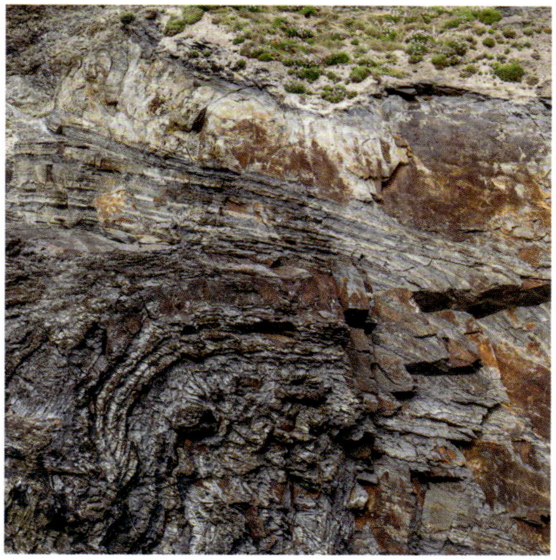
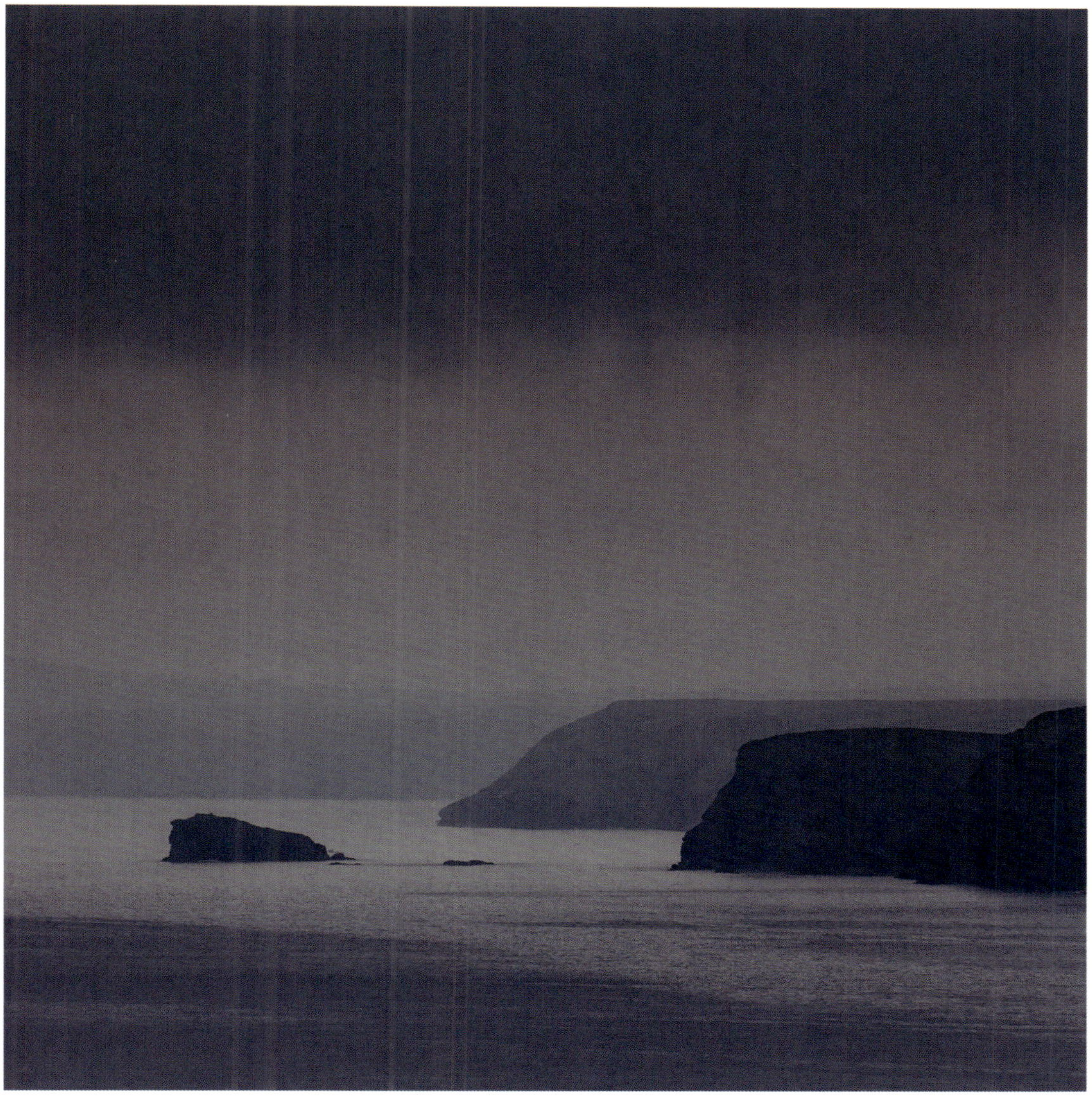
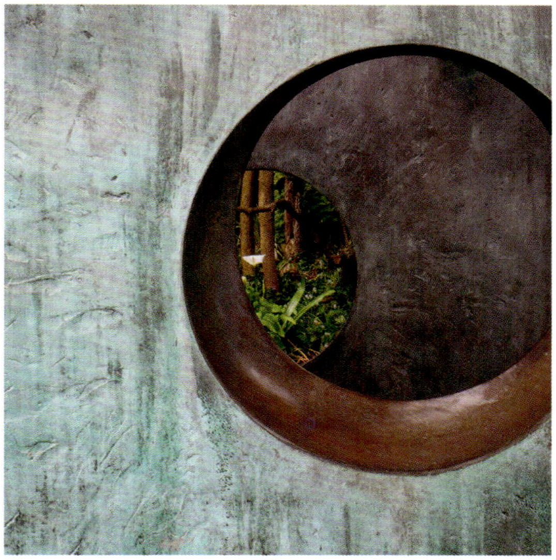
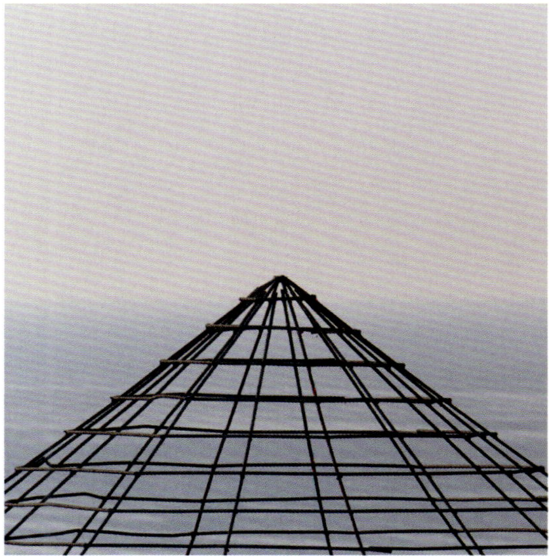
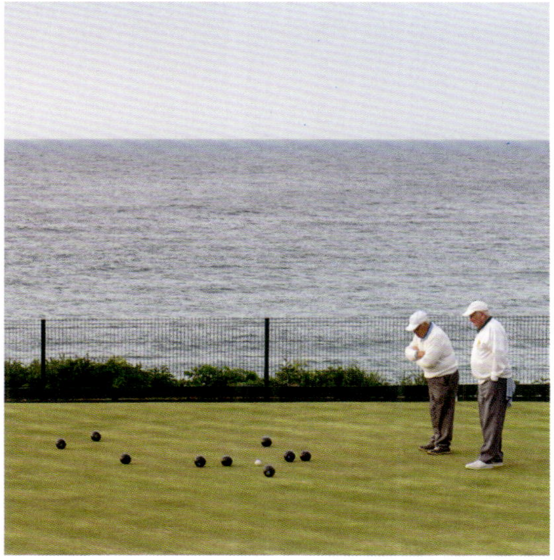
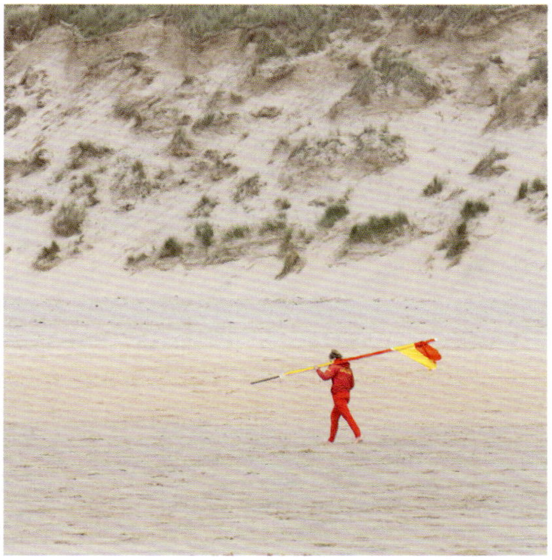

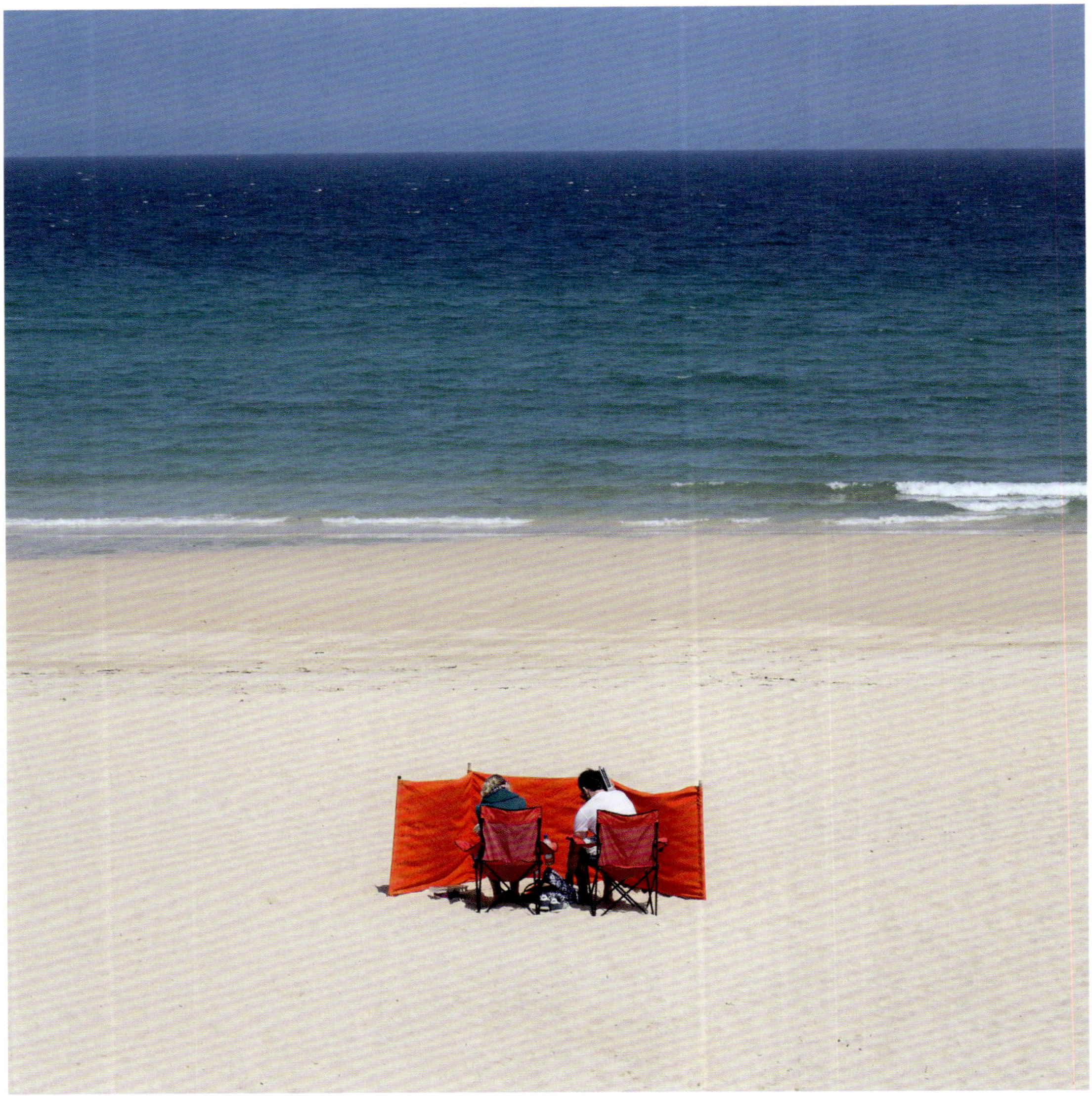

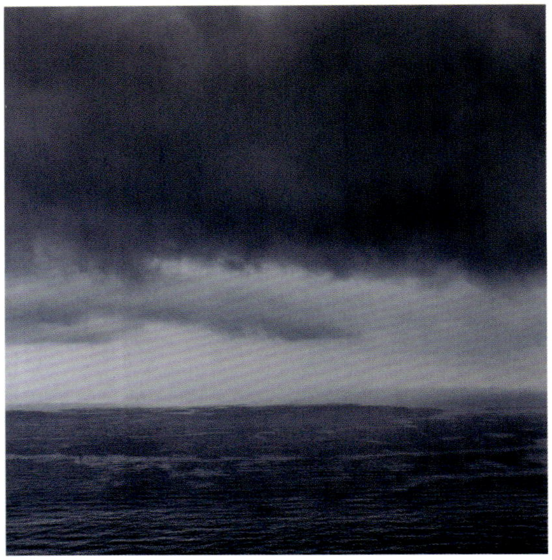

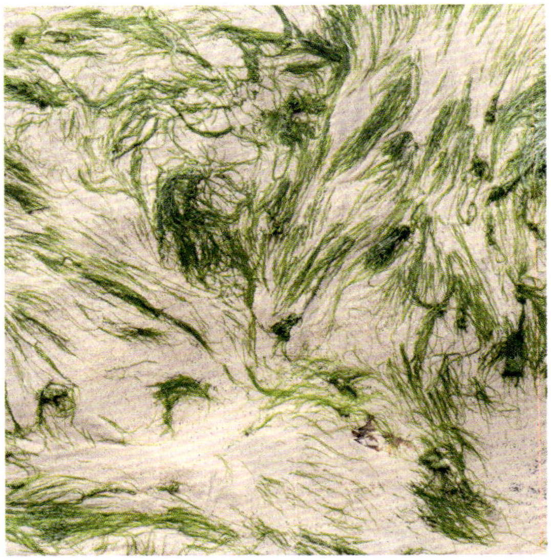

From top left:

Red and blue:
Porthminster Beach

Seascape, Derrick Cove

Frozen flow: St Ives Bay

Opposite:

Barbecue, Perran Beach

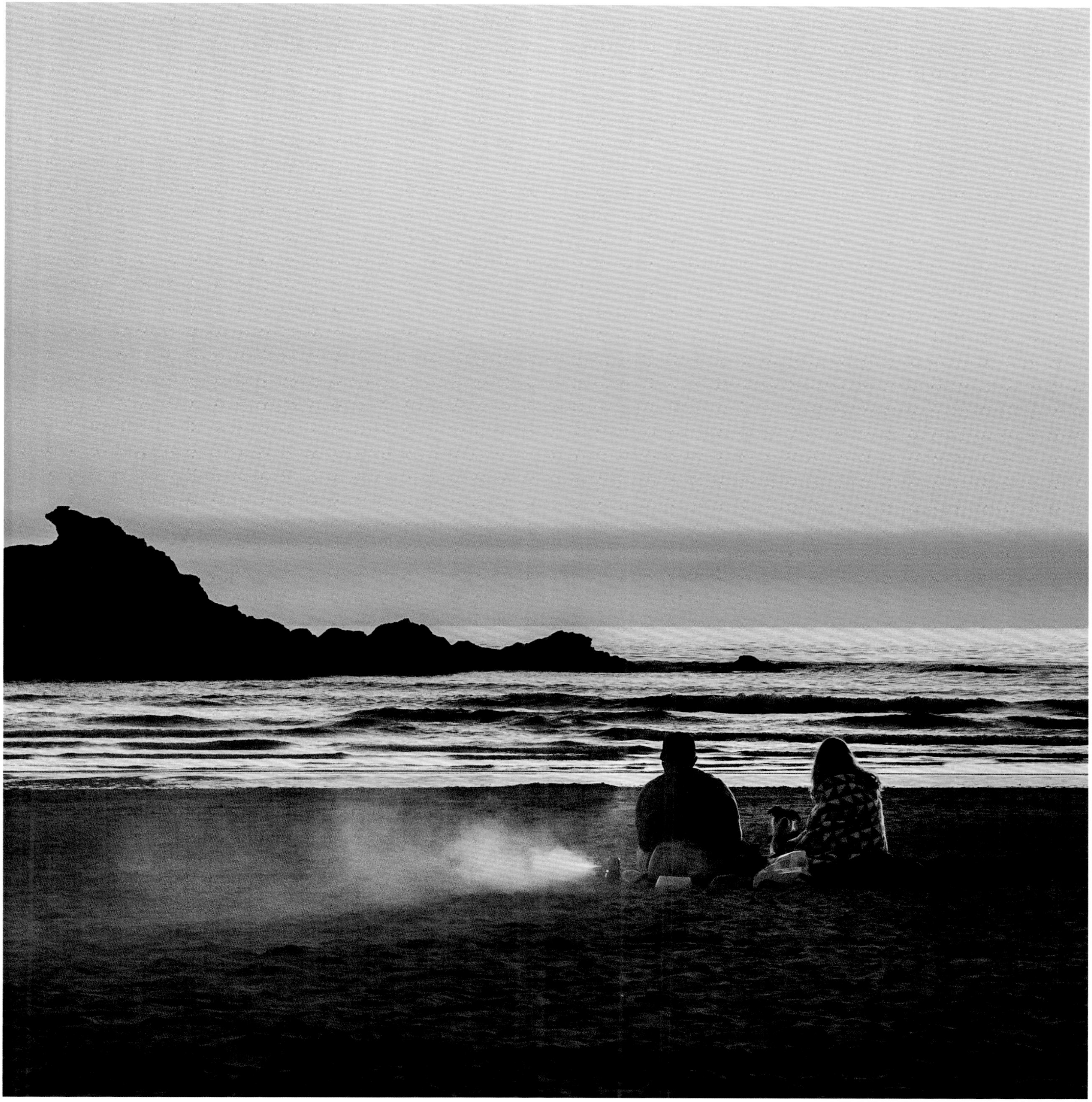

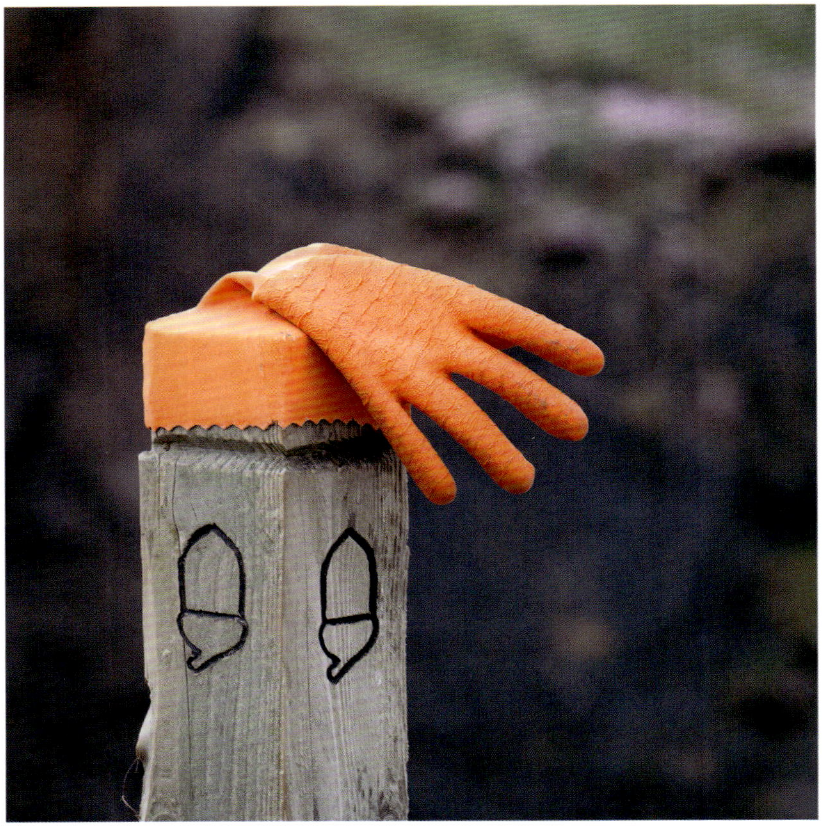

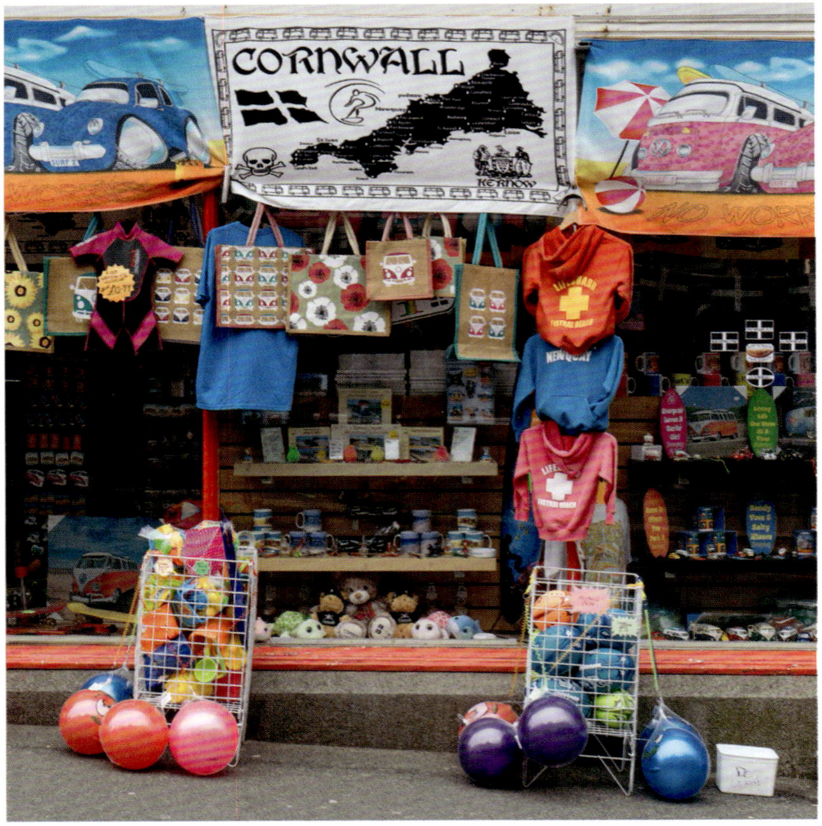

CORNWALL

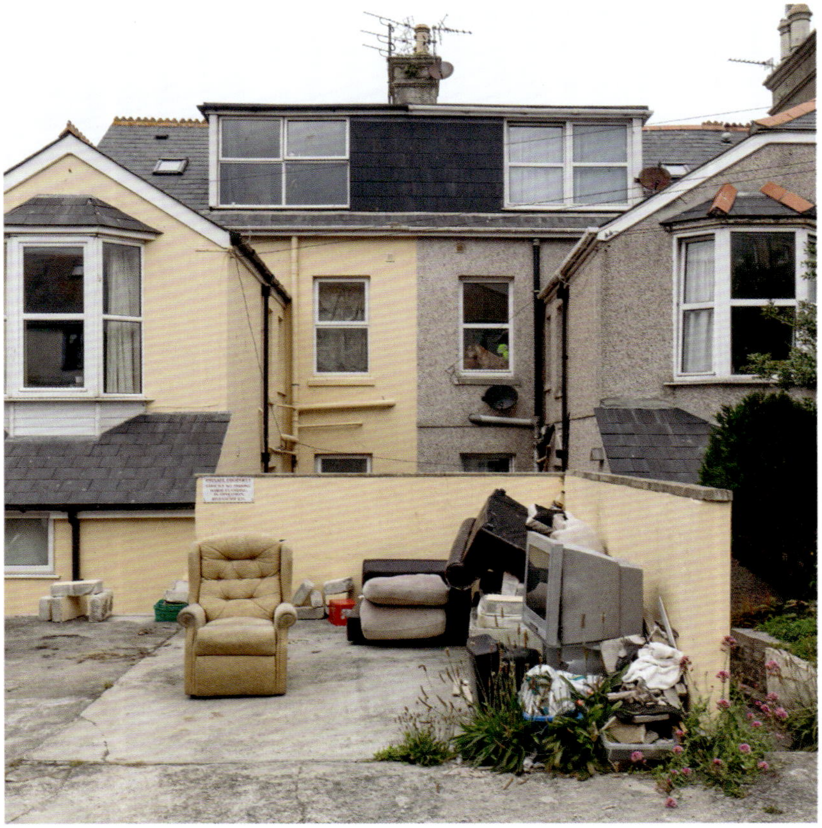

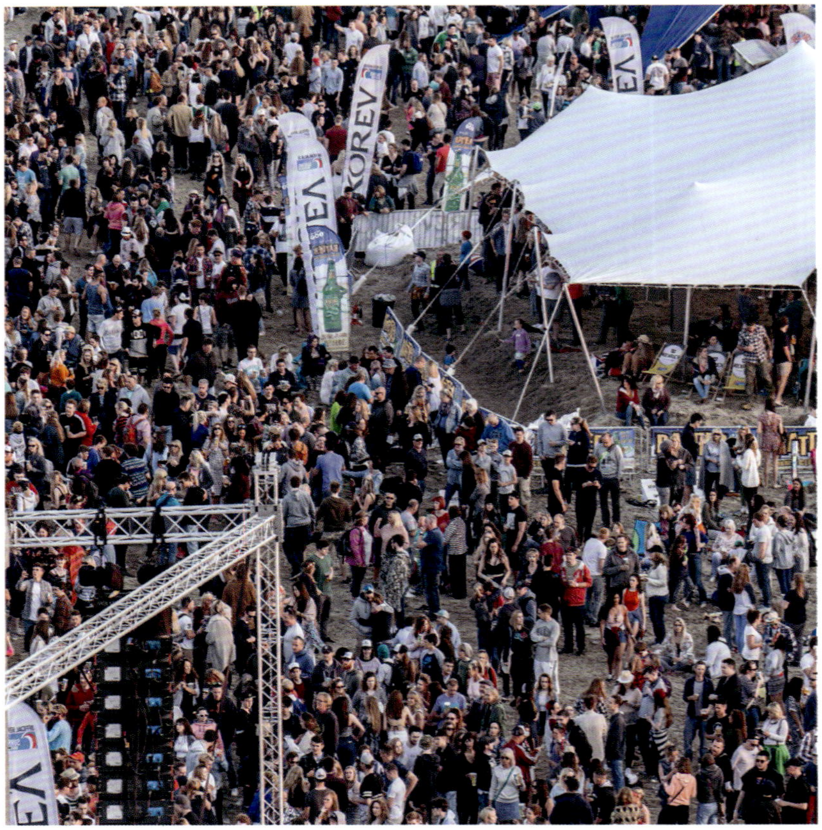

KOREV

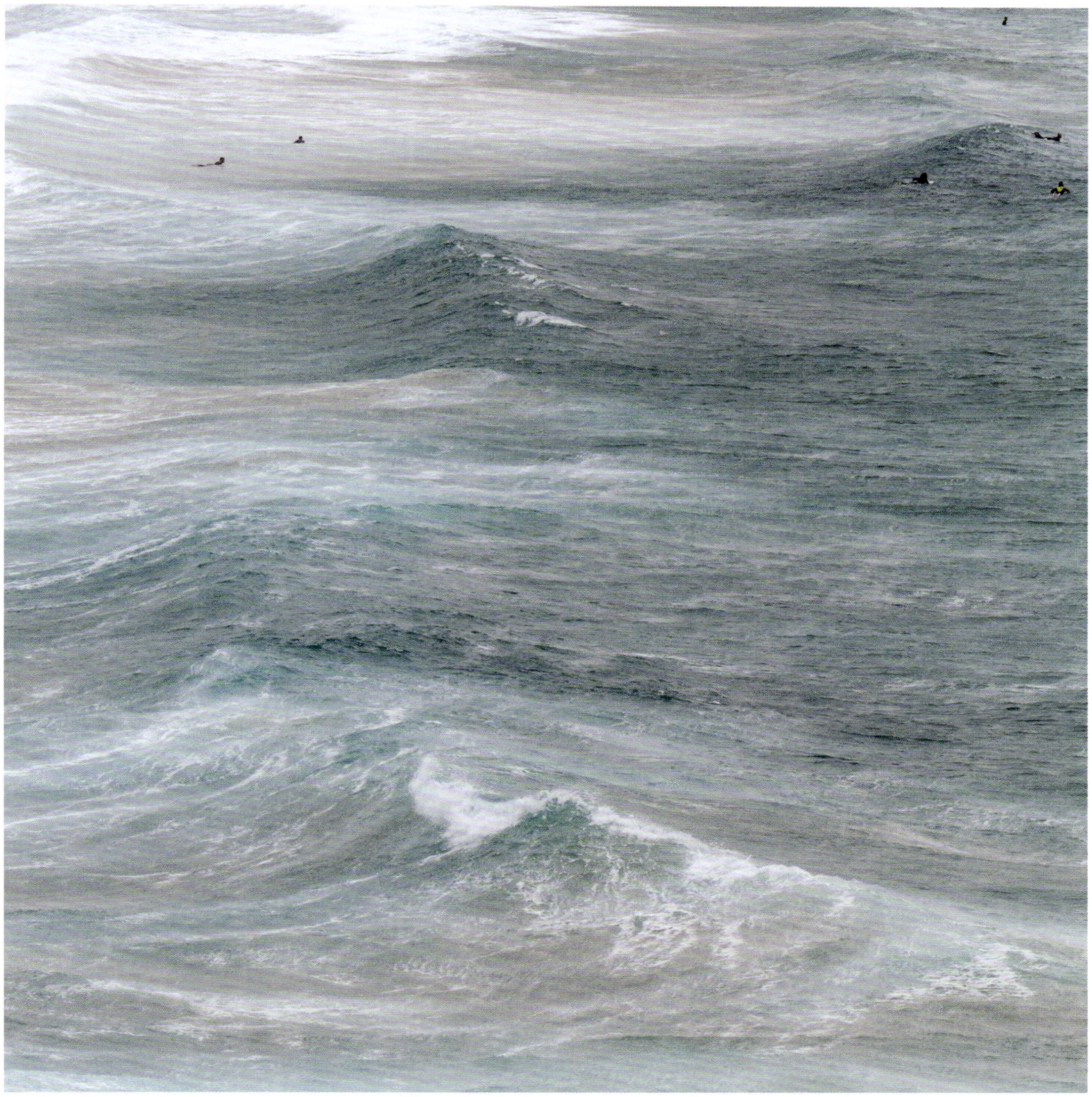

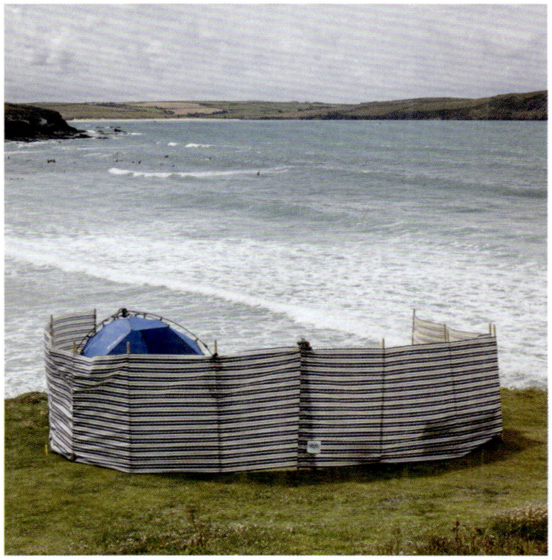

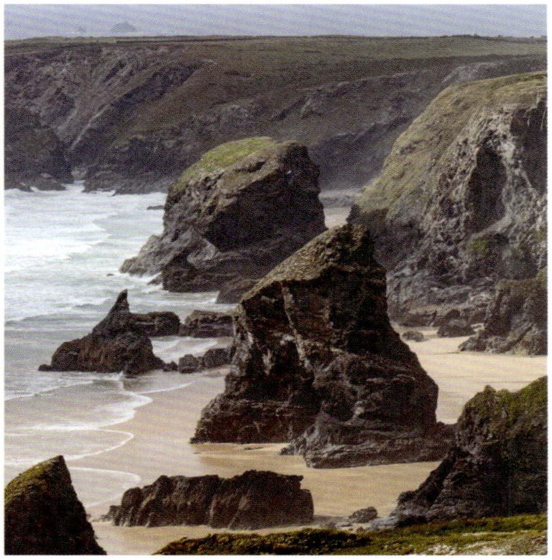

Opposite, from top left:

A tight fit: Penhale Point

Souvenir shop, Newquay

From bottom left:

Private property, Newquay

Tunes in the Dunes Festival, Perranporth

From top left:

Surfers, Fistral Beach, Newquay

Fortress: Polzeath

Samaritan Island, Bedruthan Step

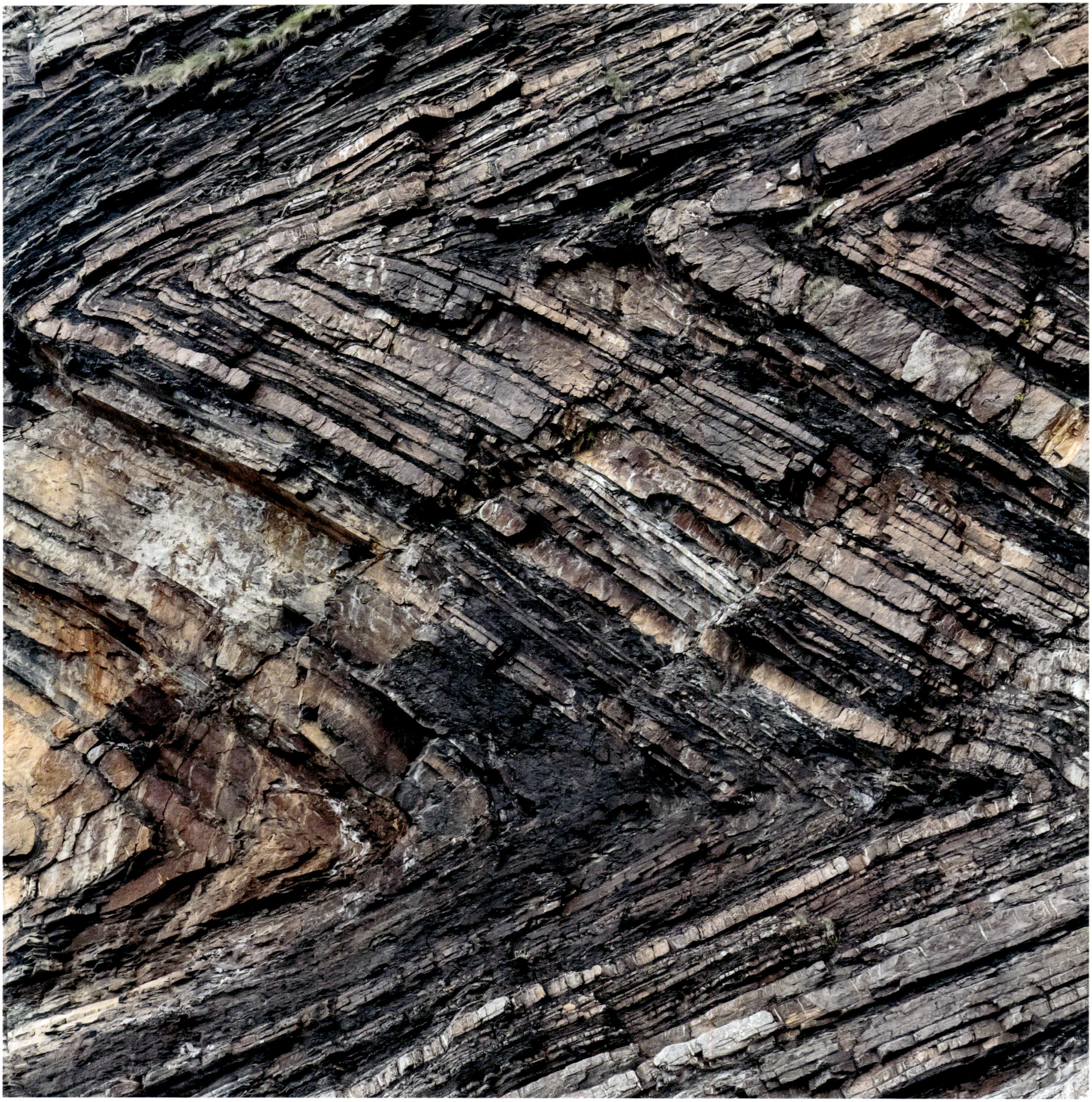

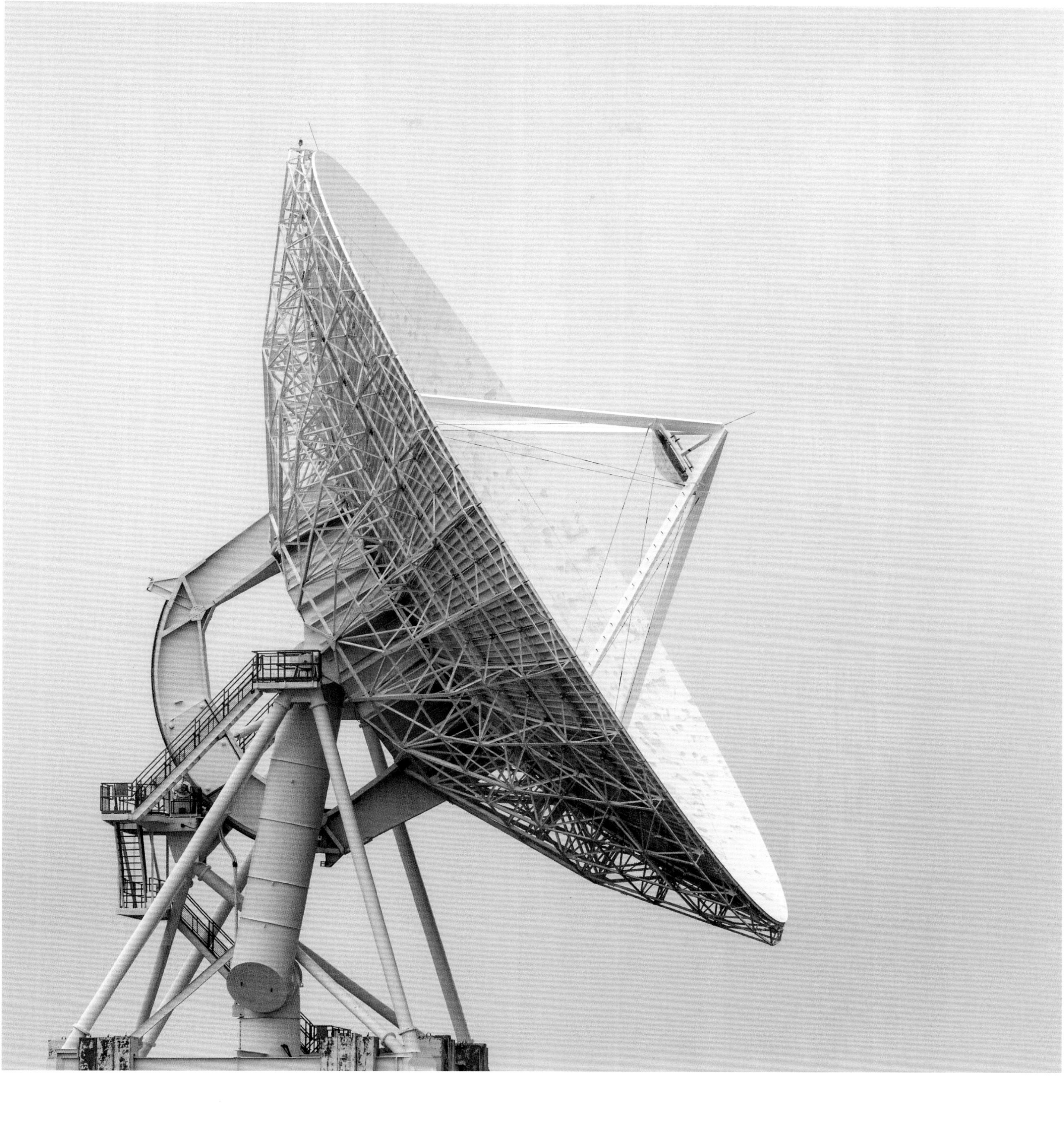

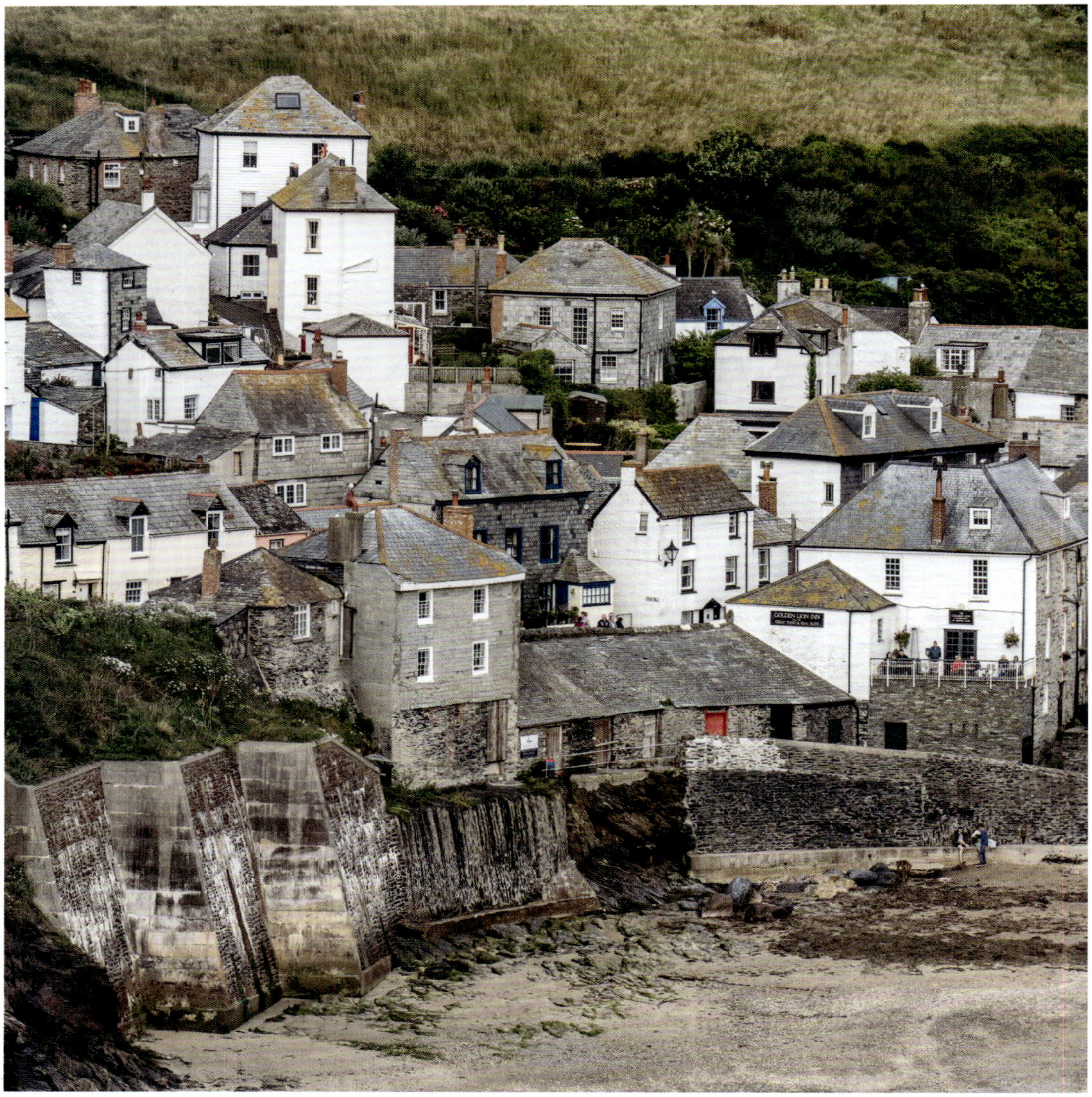

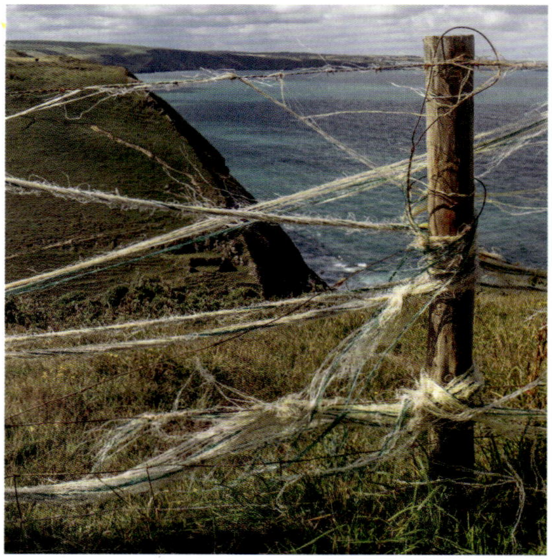

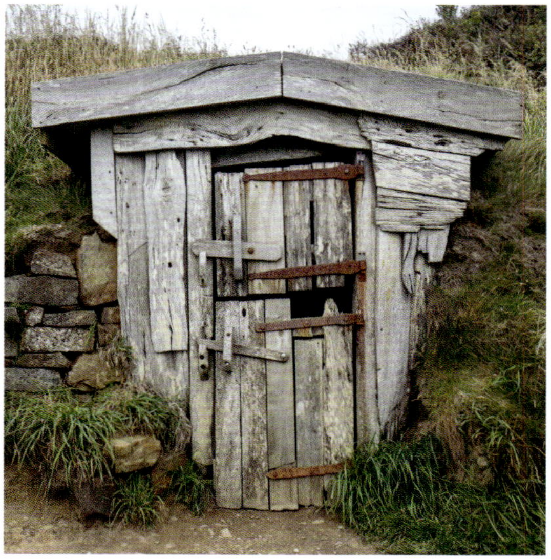

Previous, from left to right:

A dramatic example of chevron folding at Millook Haven. The inter-bedded sandstones and shales were originally deposited deep underwater. The folds were formed in the Late Devonian during the latter stages of a mountain-building event as the colliding continents compressed the basin

GCHQ Bude, a UK government satellite ground station and eavesdropping centre

From top left:

Port Isaac

Dennis Point

Hawker's Hut, where clergyman Robert Stephen Hawker (1803–75) spent many hours writing poems and smoking opium

Opposite:

Marsland Beach, near the county boundary between Cornwall and Devon

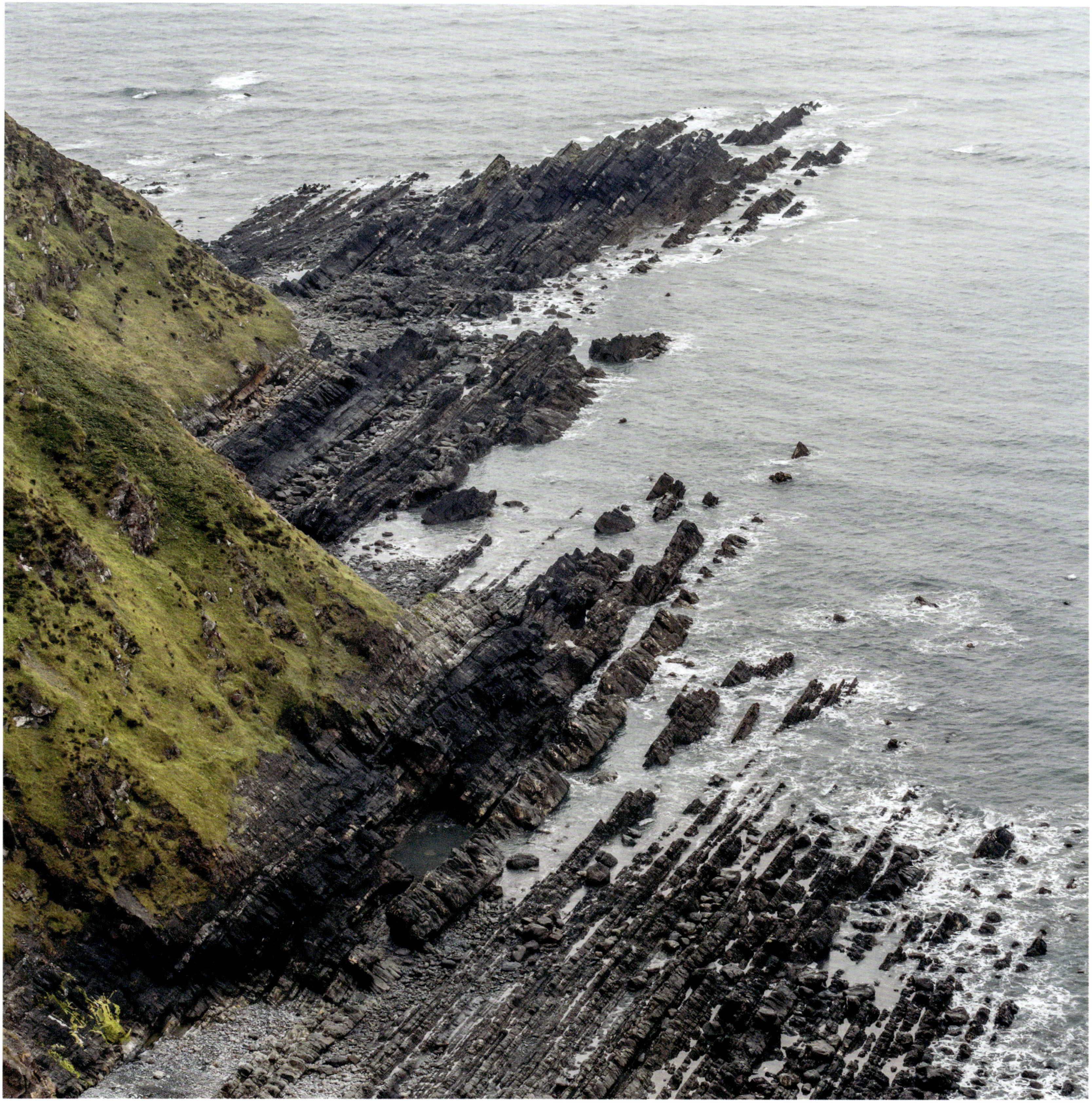

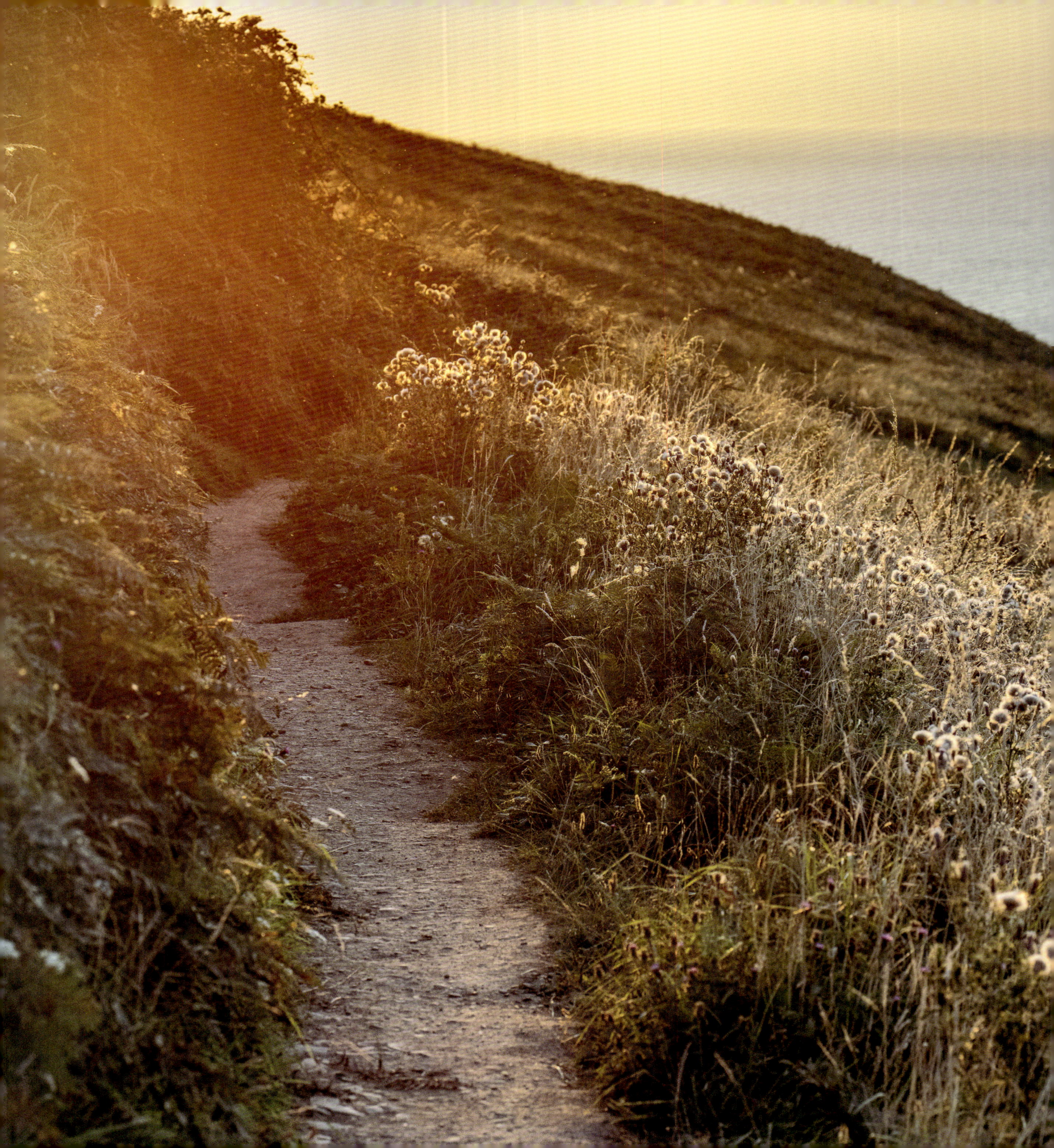

08 NORTH DEVON

JULY–AUGUST 2016
DAY 082–087 | 02,076–02,224KM | 148KM

A step across a stream reunites me with Devon, where my journey takes me into high cliffs that dissolve into still, white nothingness. On reaching the busy car park and cafe at Hartland Quay, a rugged outcrop on the north-western tip of the county, I stop to refill my water bottle and make tea on the rocks. The mist is so thick I can't see the lighthouse, and with a seaboard jagged like a saw, it's no wonder this area is often called the 'Wreckers' Coast'.

Where the last few months were defined by rain, this August has been unusually hot, humid and windless. Now the challenge of staying warm and dry is replaced by finding enough clean water to drink in the heat. I meet a German couple on the coast path who mention one of their party fainted, 'and he was the fittest'. On arduous climbing days, unable to cool down, I find myself downing two litres where a half would usually suffice.

On my second morning in North Devon, I follow the wooded coast path high above the sea towards Clovelly village. Two Americans had warned me the day before that it was like a twee Disneyland, but I am instantly charmed. Emerging from the dense, sloping woodland, I'm amazed to see a single cobbled high street flanked by sixteenth-century whitewashed cottages running steeply 100 metres downhill to the harbour. Human-powered wooden sledges deliver goods up and down; all slightly different and home-made, they lean by the door of every cottage.

At Barnstaple, I smile at the sight of a stoat, white-bellied and sinuous, rippling across the path of a disused railway line. Compared to Cornwall, which took an entire month to walk, there's a much shorter distance to cover in North Devon, and I make good progress. I beeline through Woolacombe – the busiest beach I've seen to date, crammed with hundreds of colourful windbreaks, barbecues and families – and Baggy Point, where a handful of coasteering groups return grinning with wetsuits still dripping.

The next day, I descend from the solitude of the clifftop coast path to the picturesque town of Ilfracombe; like Padstow in Cornwall, it's jam-packed with visitors, but with a reinvented cultural heart that feels more authentic. As I walk towards the harbour, I pass a theatre and art galleries, as well as the expected ice cream and fish and chips. At the pier I take off my pack and rest for a while beneath Damien Hirst's towering sculpture *Verity*.

The next day I'm thrilled to witness the grandeur of Exmoor, one of England's great wild places, and the highest coastline in England and Wales. Schlepping a heavy backpack up and down the undulating cliffs in the humid heat is near impossible and the silence as I walk is broken only by the sound of my panting breath and the occasional pheasant. A fighter jet roars unseen overhead while seven jet skis stream past in formation far below on the sea. The path soon reaches the Lynton and Lynmouth Cliff Railway where I hear two inebriated Yorkshiremen ahead teasing each other, 'You haven't got sunstroke! More like scrumpy stroke!' Turning to me with a disarming grin, one says, 'You've got to enjoy it before you die, right?'

At the wooded edge of Exmoor, I leave Devon the way I arrived, with a step across a small stream, this time at Coscombe into Somerset. As evening falls and the heat haze recedes, clarity returns both to my photos and my ability to think. Energised by the drop in temperature, I notice the landscape is in transition too: the cliffs are flattening off, the Atlantic Ocean becomes the Bristol Channel, and I can make out Wales on the horizon.

Opposite:

Last light on the coast path, Baggy Point

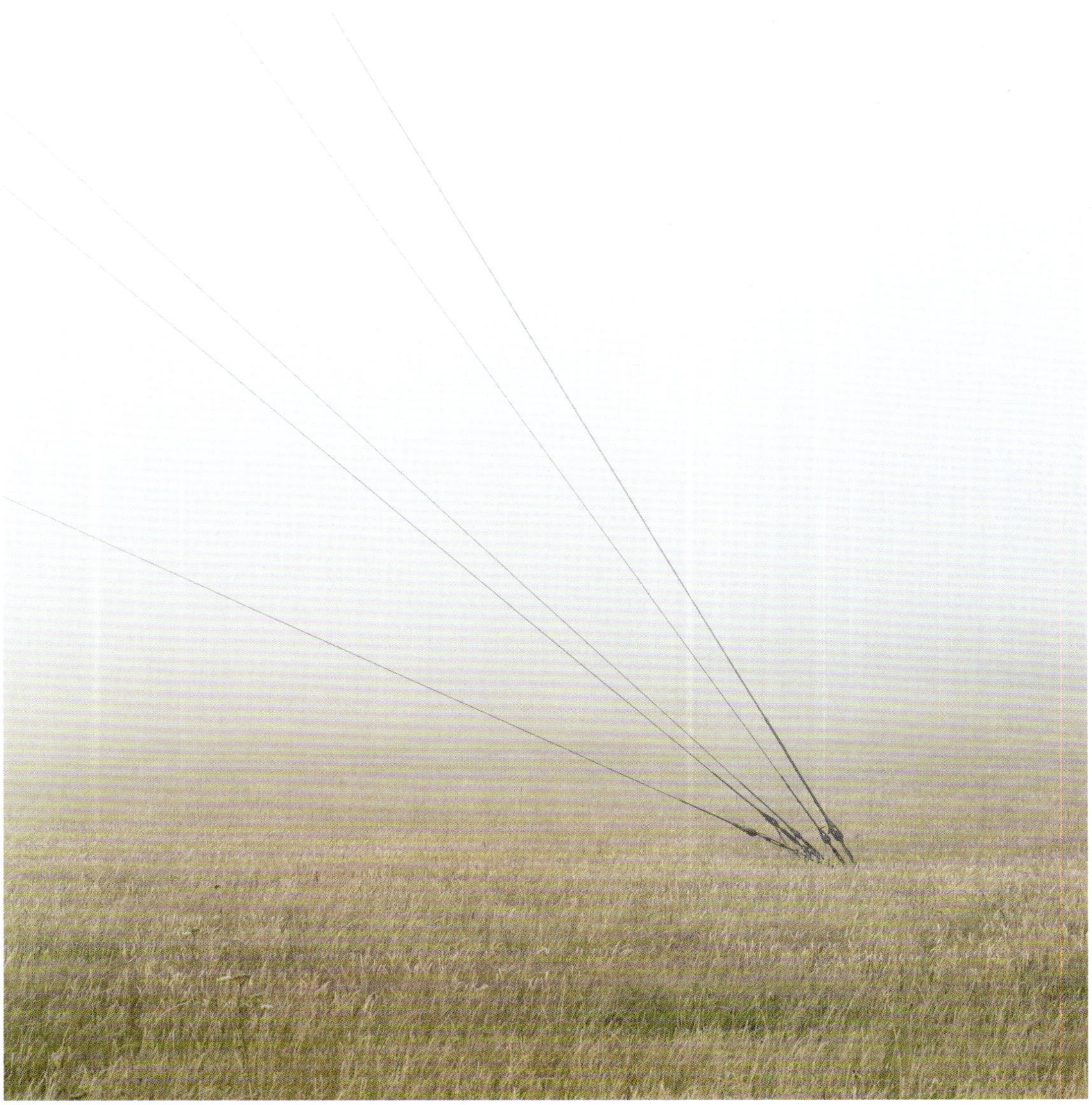

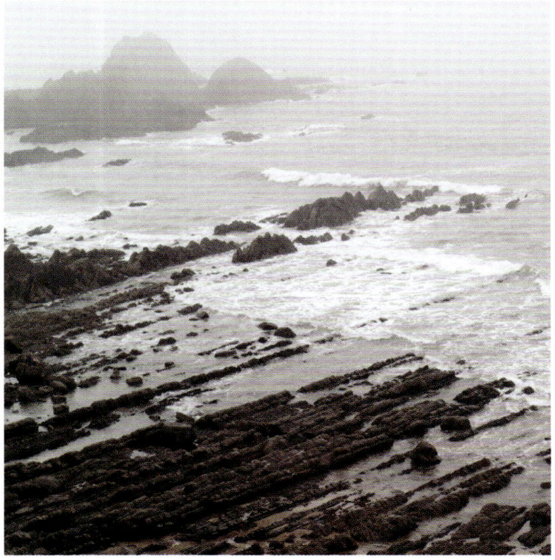

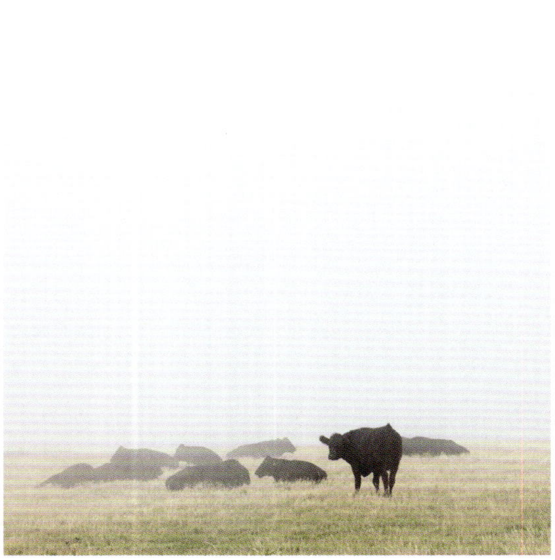

From top left:

Radio mast, Sandhole

Blegberry Beach, Iron Coast

Above Blagdon Cliff

Opposite, clockwise from top left:

Main street, Clovelly

Lundy and cloud

Cliffs towards Westward Ho!

Beech wood near Clovelly

Barley field above Babbacombe Cliff

Sledge, Clovelly

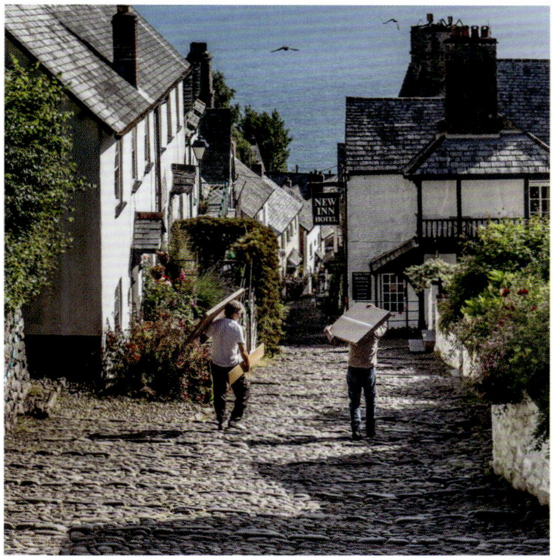

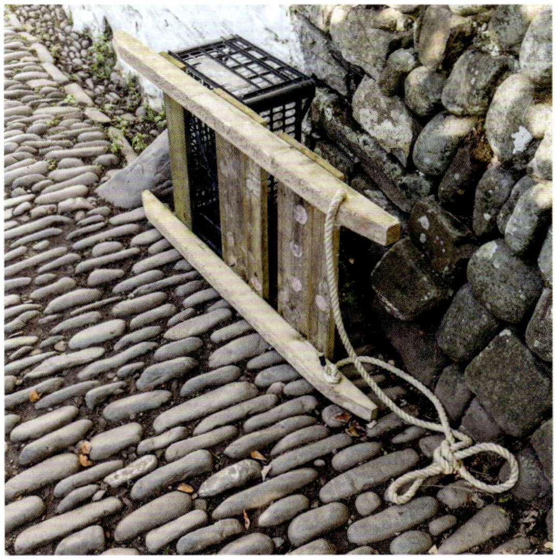

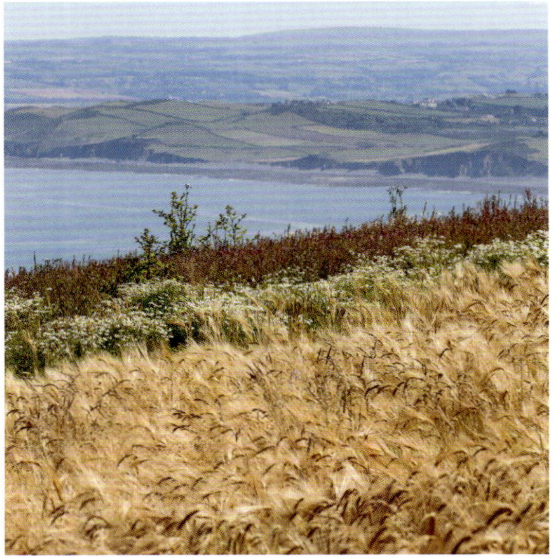

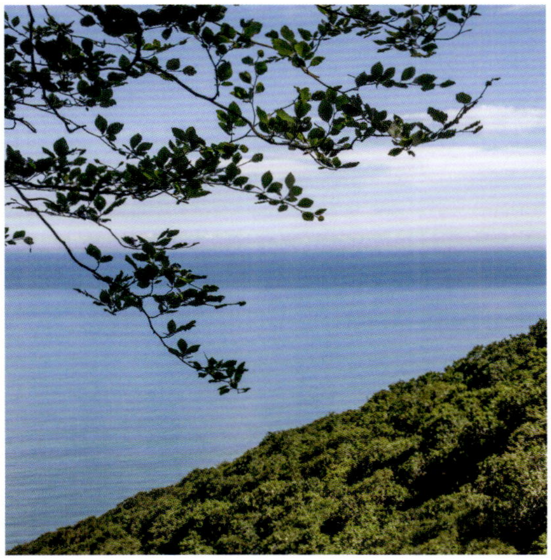

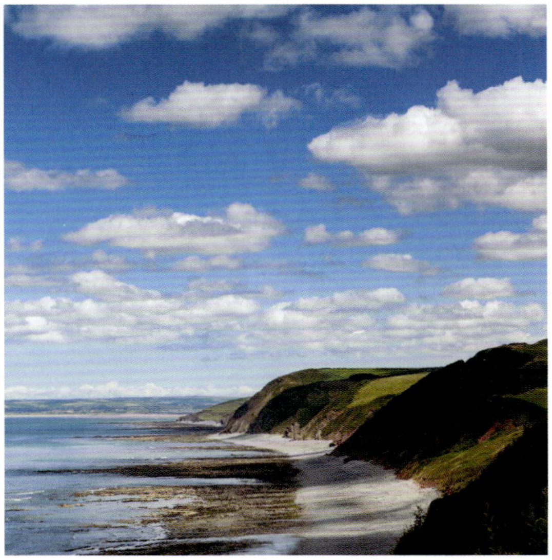

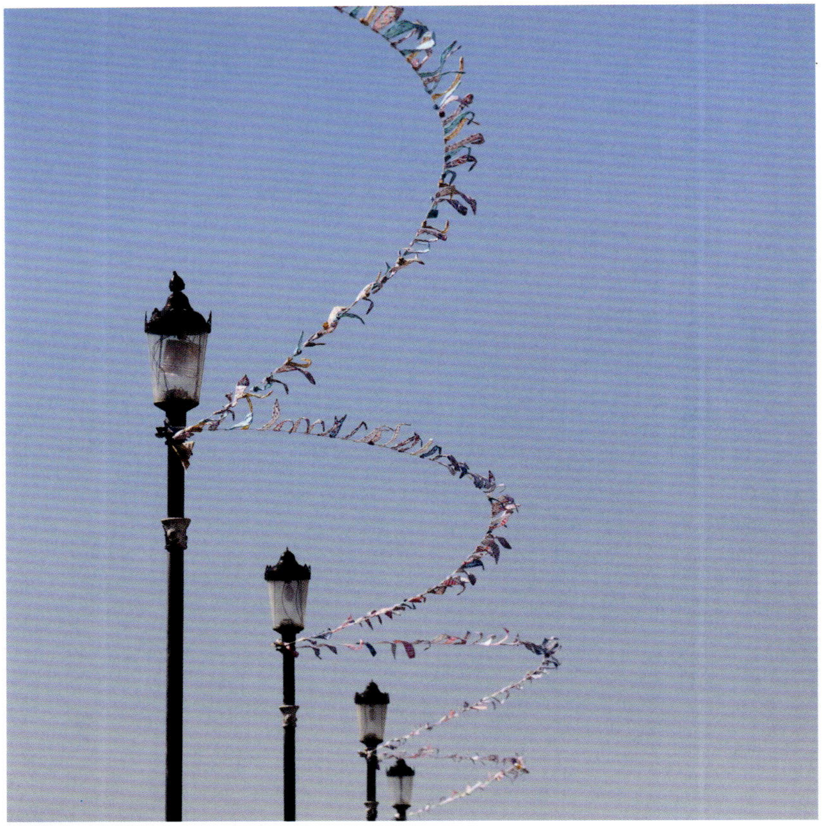

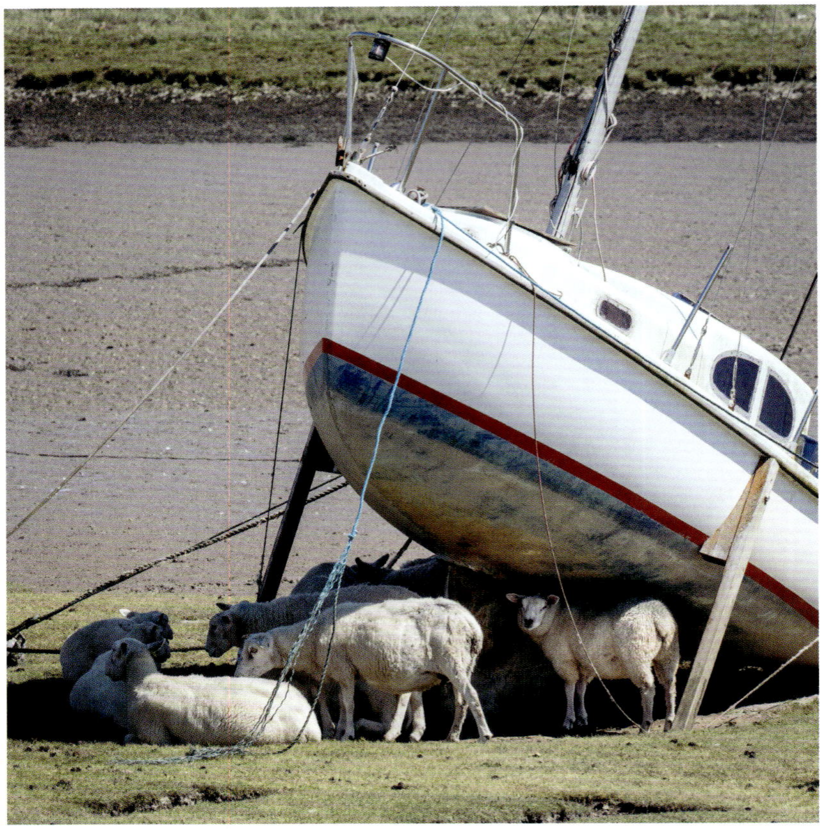

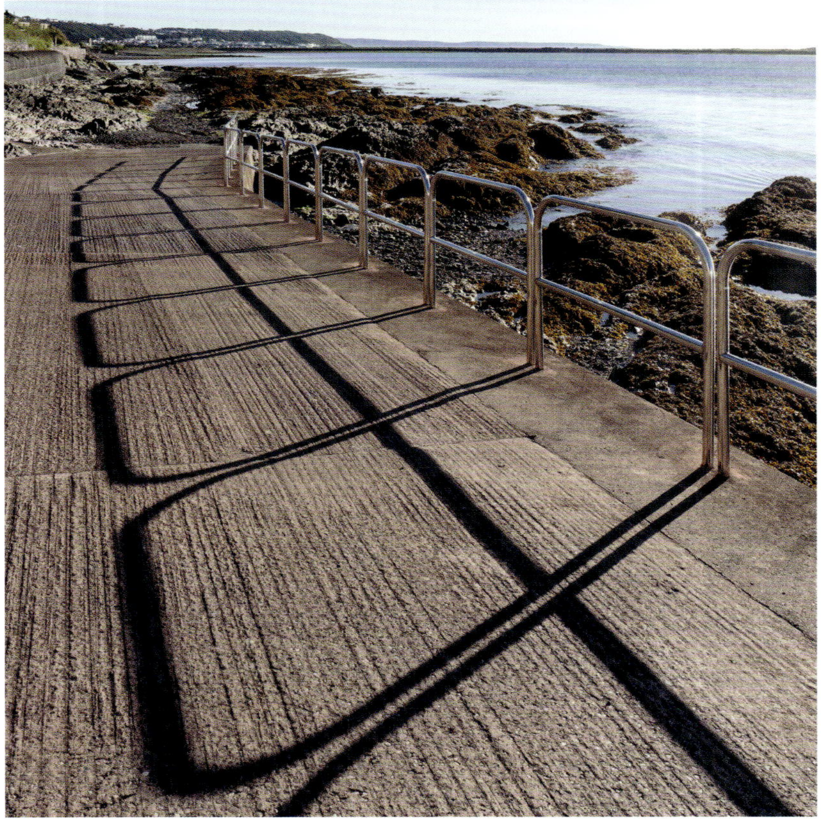

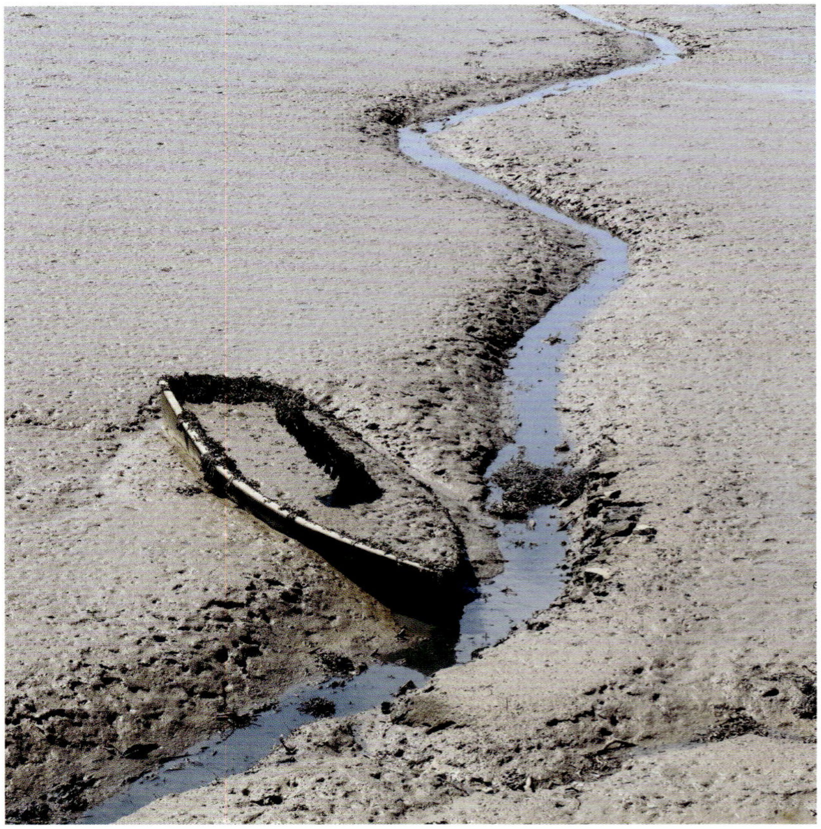

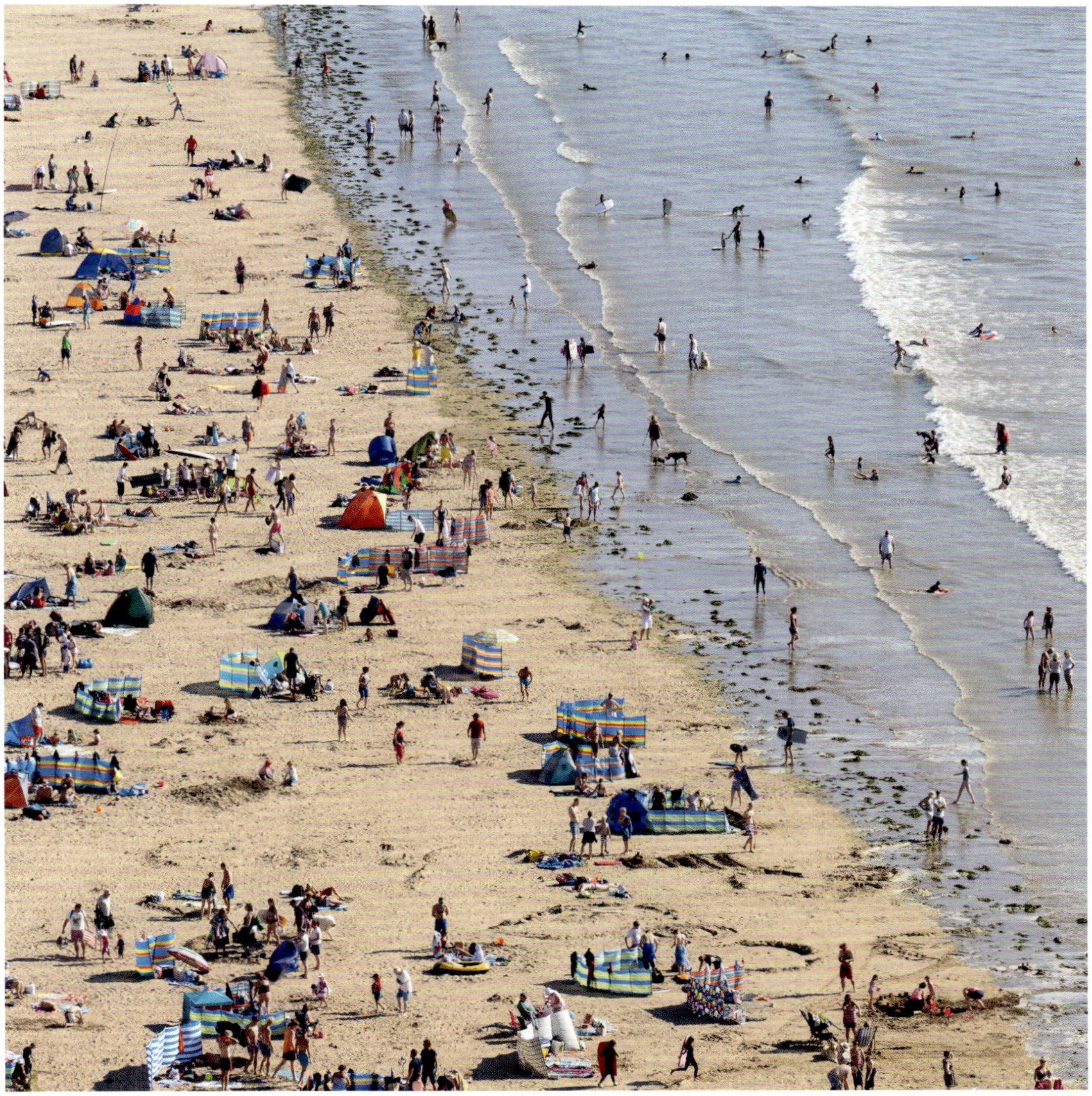

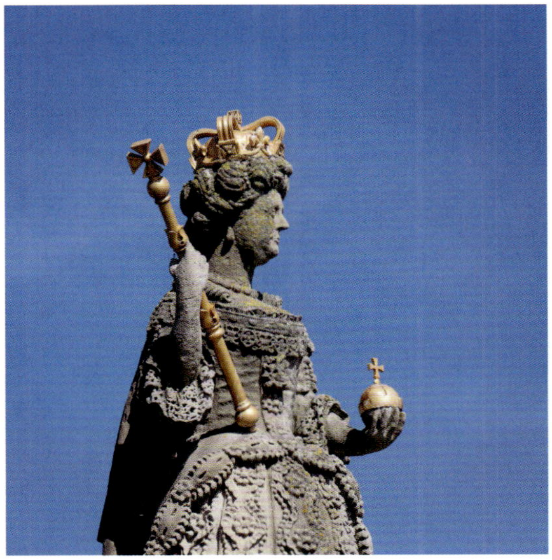

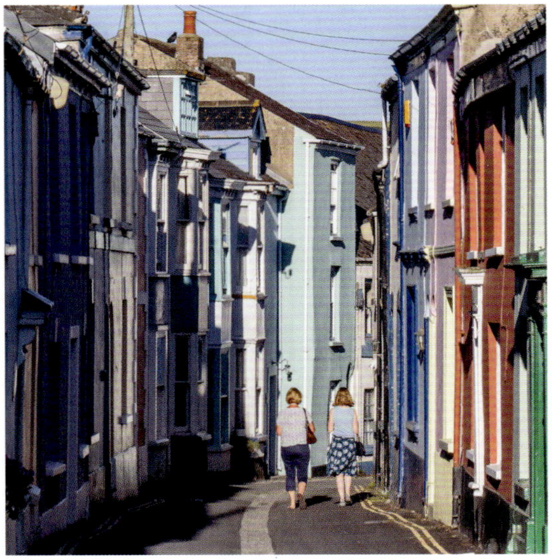

Opposite, from top left:

Appledore

Seeking shade, River Caen

From bottom left:

Slipway, Appledore

Sinking in: River Taw

From top left:

Saunton Sands in August

Statue atop Queen Anne's Walk, built in 1713 as a meeting place for the town's merchants, Barnstaple

Irsha Street, Appledore

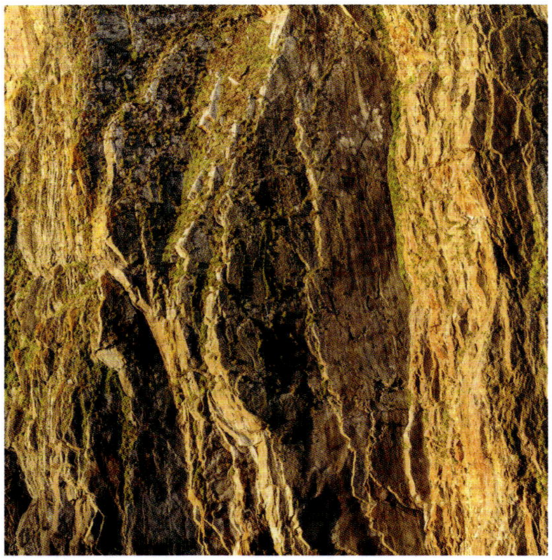

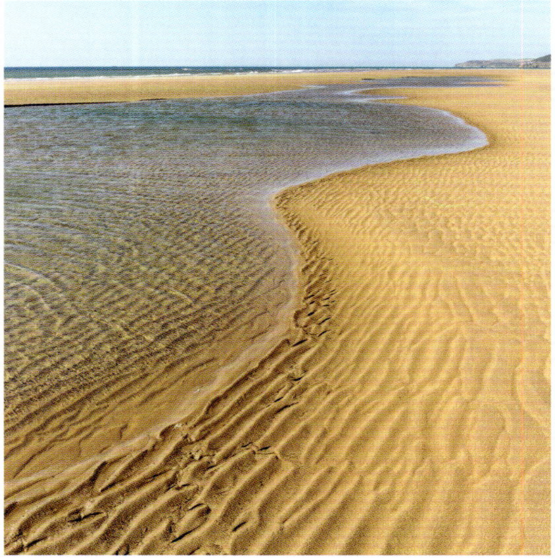

From top left:

Evening glow, Baggy Point

Baggy Point

Saunton Sands towards Baggy Point

Opposite, *clockwise from top left*

Rosebay willowherb and Little Hangman, Exmoor

Verity, a 20-metre-high stainless-steel and bronze statue by Damien Hirst, 2012, Ilfracombe

Jet skiers from Highveer Point, Exmoor

First light, Woolacombe Sands

St Nicholas Chapel, Ilfracombe

Capstone Point, Ilfracombe

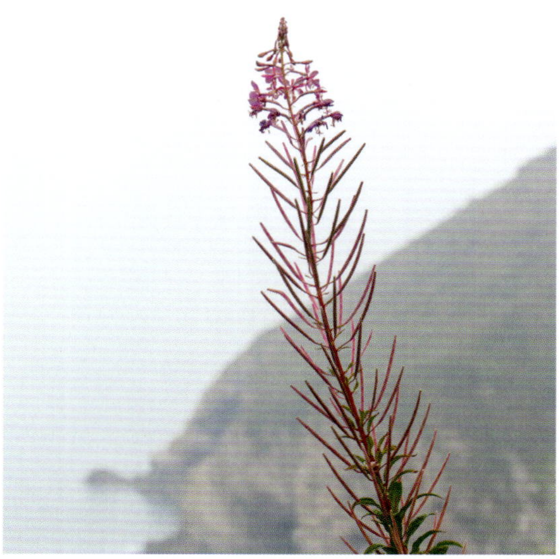
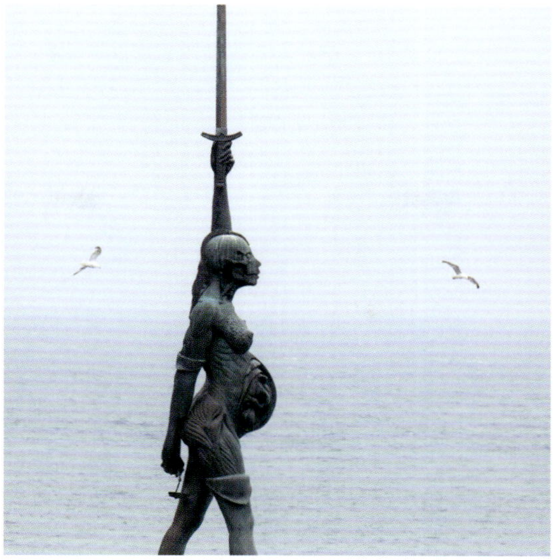
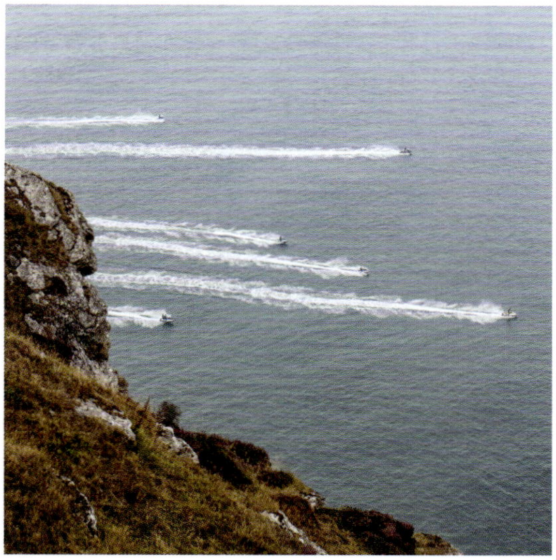
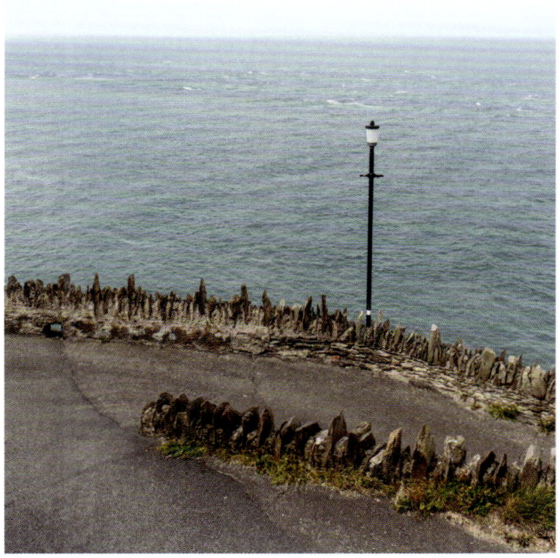
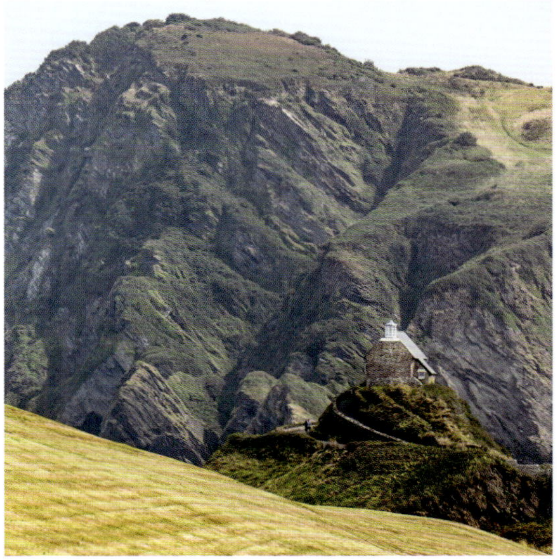
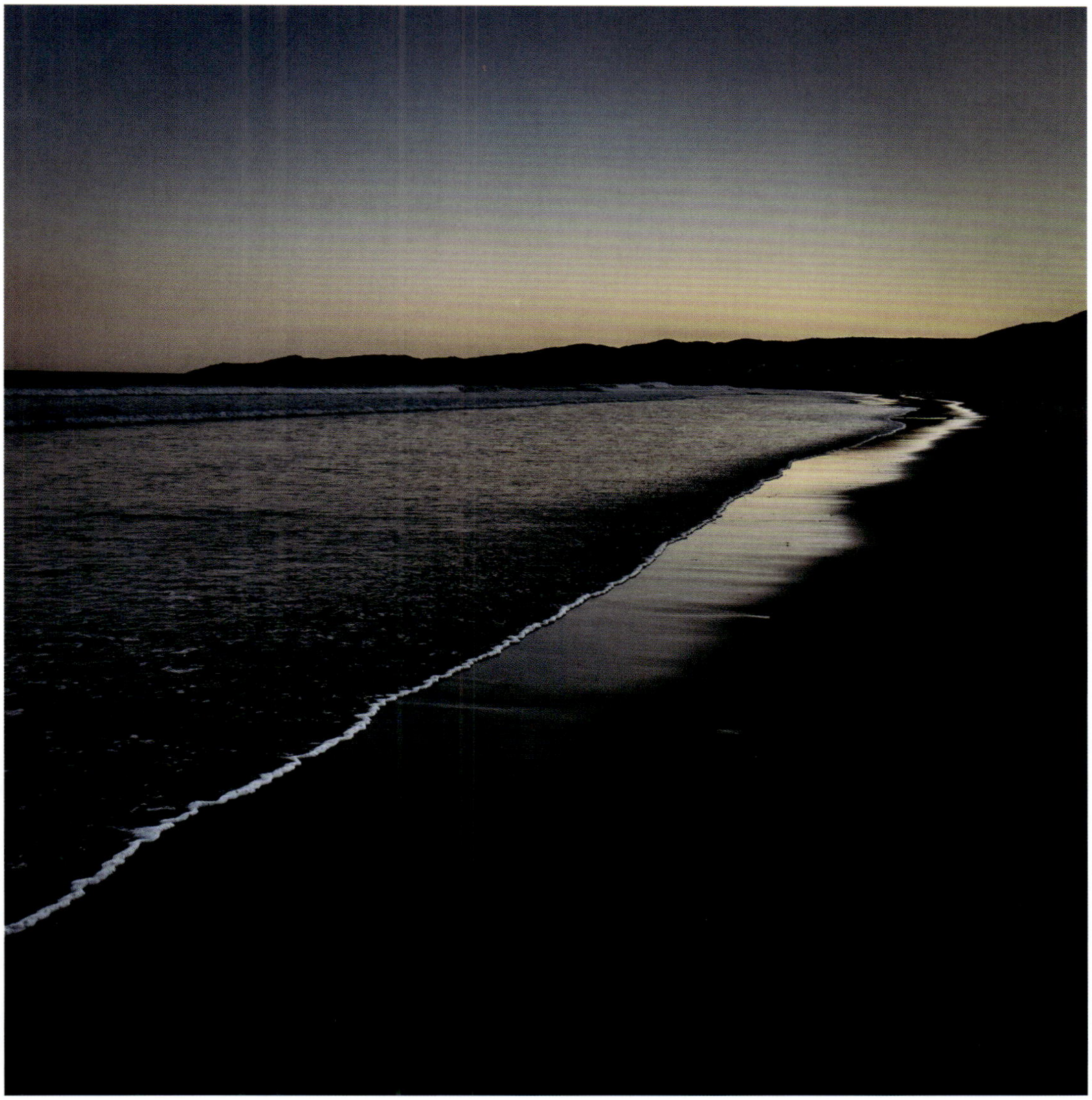

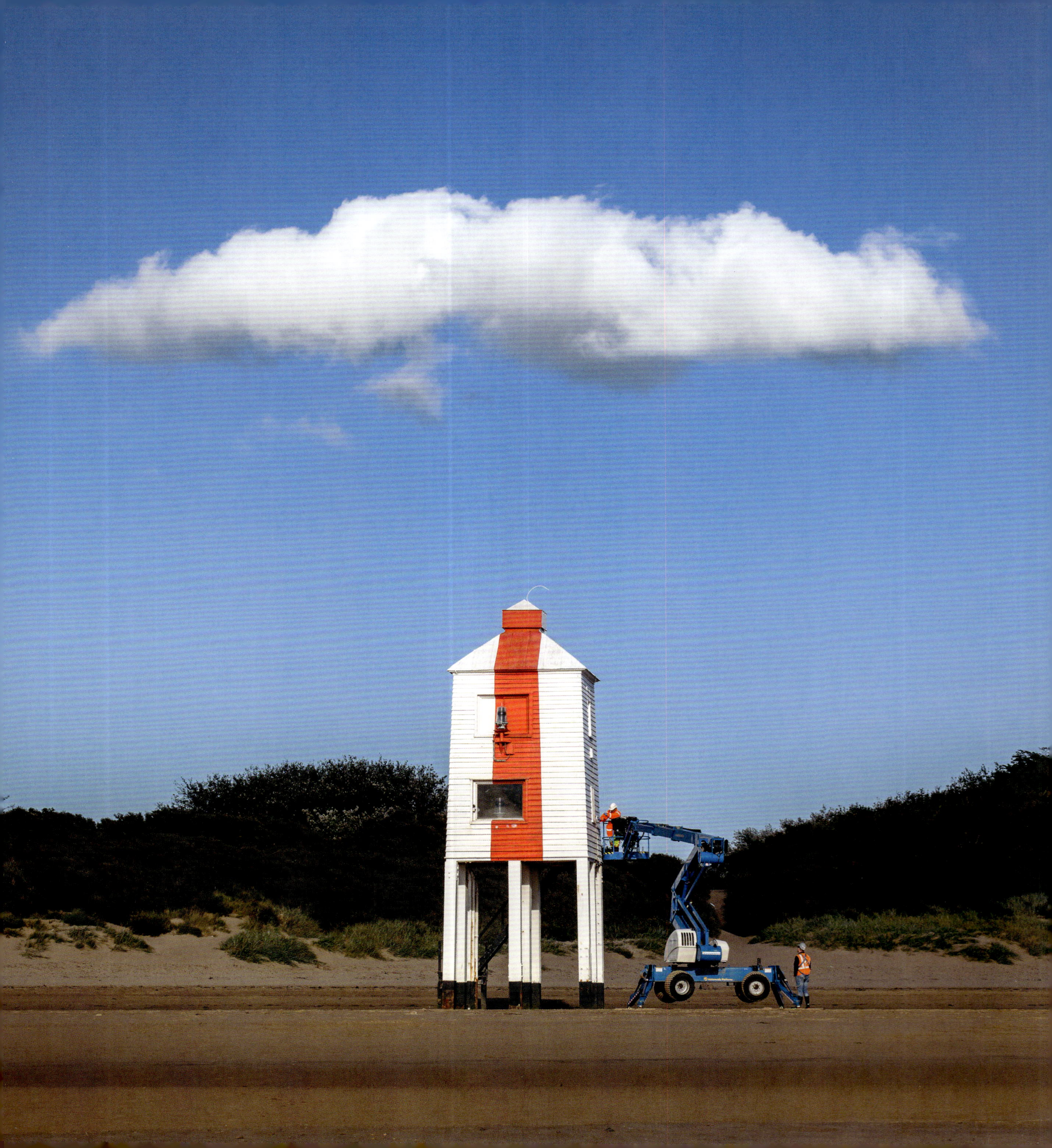

09 SOMERSET

AUGUST–SEPTEMBER 2016

DAY 088–091 | 02,224–02,361KM | 137KM

My first day in Somerset calls for a celebration when I reach the seafront at Minehead, where a statue of hands holding open a map of the South West of England indicates I've finally completed the 1,014-kilometre South West Coast Path National Trail that contains a thigh-busting 35,000 metres of ascent and descent. To mark the occasion, I leave the sea and head into town to treat myself to the king prawn special at the Taj Mahal, with fluffy naan bread and a pint of lager. It's the best Indian meal I've ever tasted, not to mention the first time I've sat down inside to eat for a number of days.

With my mind and body nourished, it's back to the trail, and the next afternoon I enter a geologist's paradise near Watchet, where coastal cliffs reveal the secrets of deep time through their fault lines and multicoloured layers of sedimentary rock. A couple of hours later, at Helwell Bay, I pick my way between bright green seaweed over expansive tidal rock beds, transfixed by the exposed ammonite spirals, some half a metre across. My sense of wonder is marred when I see where greedy fossil hunters have crudely chipped out their quarry.

At Hinkley Point, close to the power station, I pitch out of sight with a low mound acting as a windbreak. The following day, by Bridgwater Bay, I'm forced to make a significant detour around the construction site for the Hinkley Point C nuclear reactor development. The building site is a hive of activity on what looks like the groundworks as machinery and workers pass to and fro in front of giant concrete silos, but I can't make out anything that looks like a power station yet. A passing local sees me looking and tells me he thinks 'the scheme is crazy, what with the price of power and an untested design'. 'They should have started it ten years ago if we're to have any choice to stop using fossil fuels,' I reply.

September brings a bumper crop of blackberries, and they are ripe and juicy on the quiet track to Stert Point, where I can't resist climbing up a charming bird hide to enjoy the view. Three storeys up, timber-clad and with a pitched roof and overhanging eaves, the hide seems more like a child's fantasy house, and I feel deliciously separated from the cares of the world as I sit on the wooden bench looking out over the grey, flat Somerset Levels. I can see back to Hinkley Point, over the Bristol Channel to Cardiff and the immediate way ahead to Bridgwater through a landscape of seemingly endless man-made dykes and ditches.

As I approach Bridgwater, the flow of the River Parrett changes before my eyes from downstream to upstream. It's remarkable to behold as the full force of the 15-metre tidal range of the Bristol Channel comes in and overwhelms the river's comparatively gentle force of gravity. In a meander, the conflicted river flows upstream on the inside bend and downstream on the outside.

On my last evening, I reach Brean Down Fort, an impressive Victorian and later Second World War stronghold to defend the Bristol Channel. I find a flat patch for the tent on the foundations of a long-gone barracks in the lee of the headland. I am probably alone up here, but preferring not to attract any unwanted attention in the darkness, I put the tent up entirely by feel, sweeping the ground with my hand for anything sharp, unrolling the thin nylon flysheet, locating the entrance to the pole sleeve and sliding in the aluminium pole to create an arch, before kneeling beside and pegging each of the eight tie-outs as the familiar black silhouette of my tiny shelter takes shape above the mouth of the Severn.

Opposite:

Burnham-on-Sea Low Lighthouse repainting

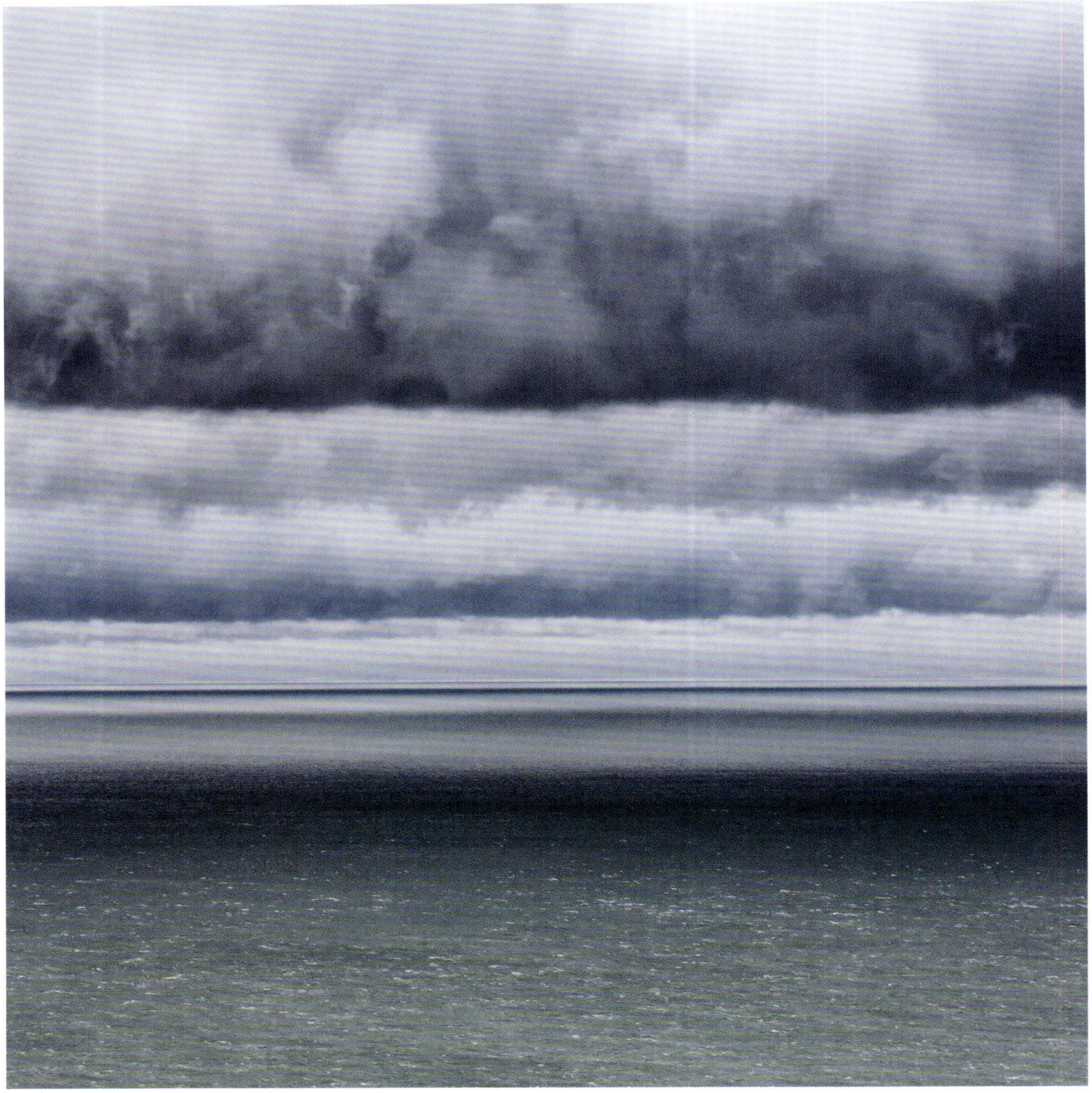

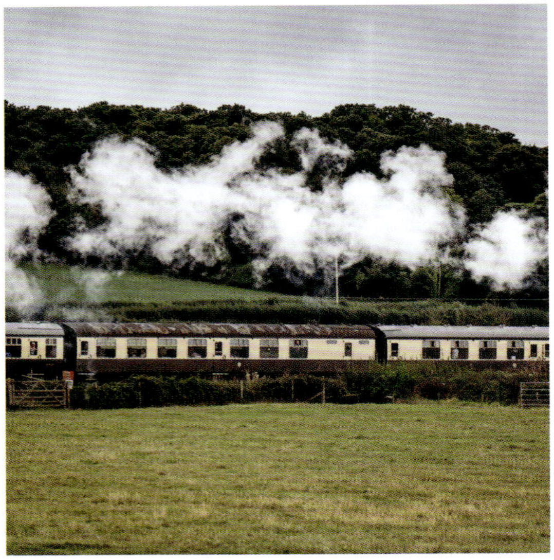

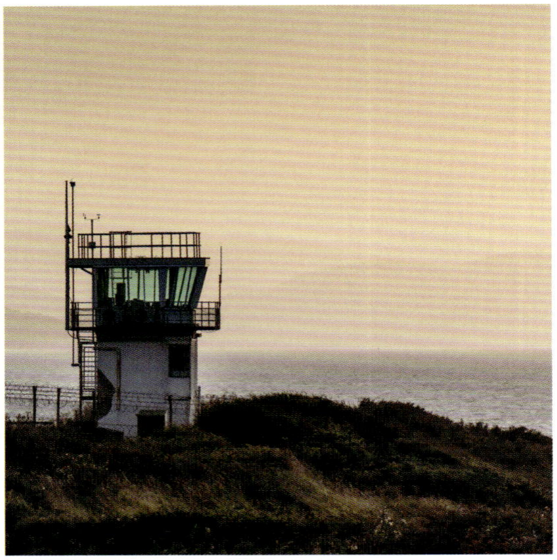

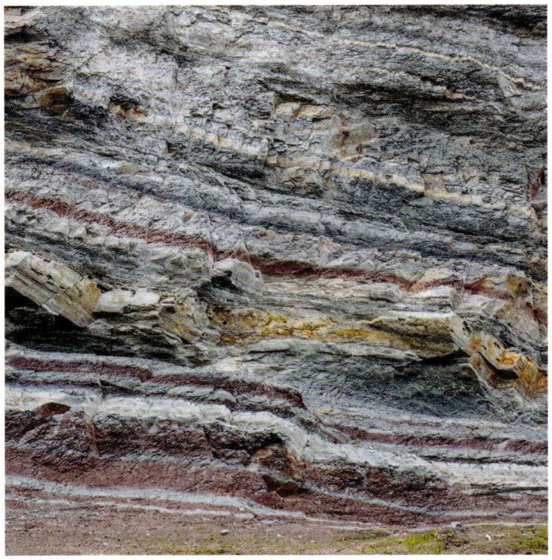

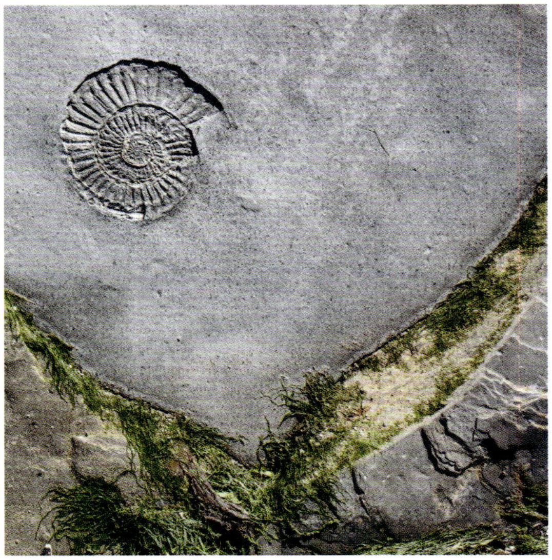

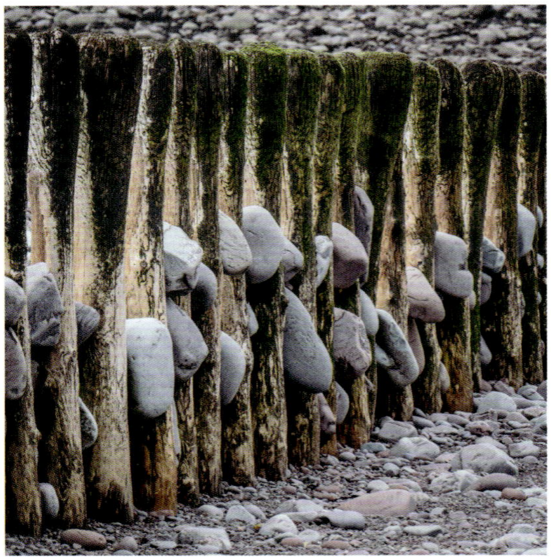

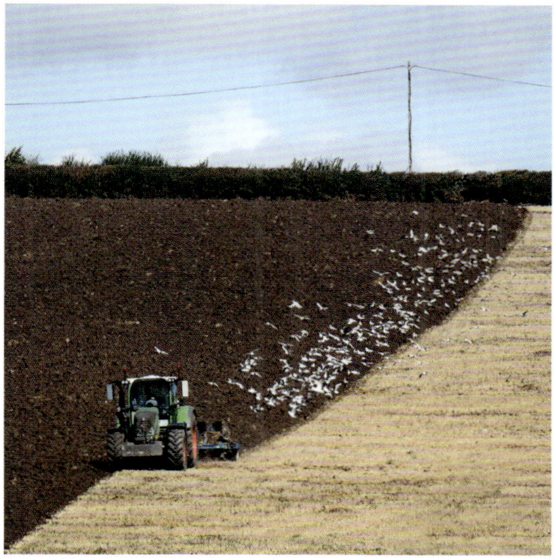

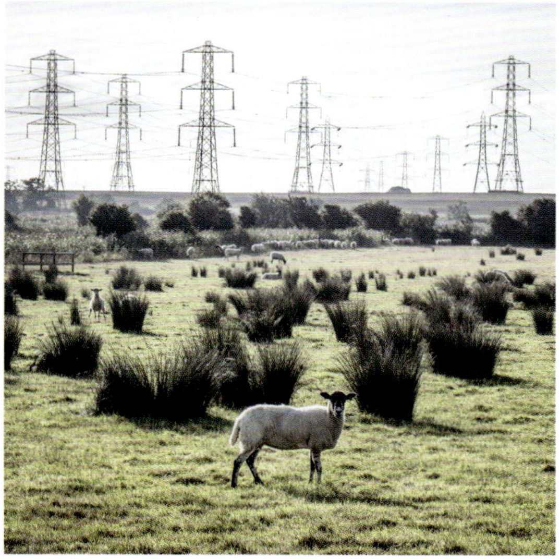

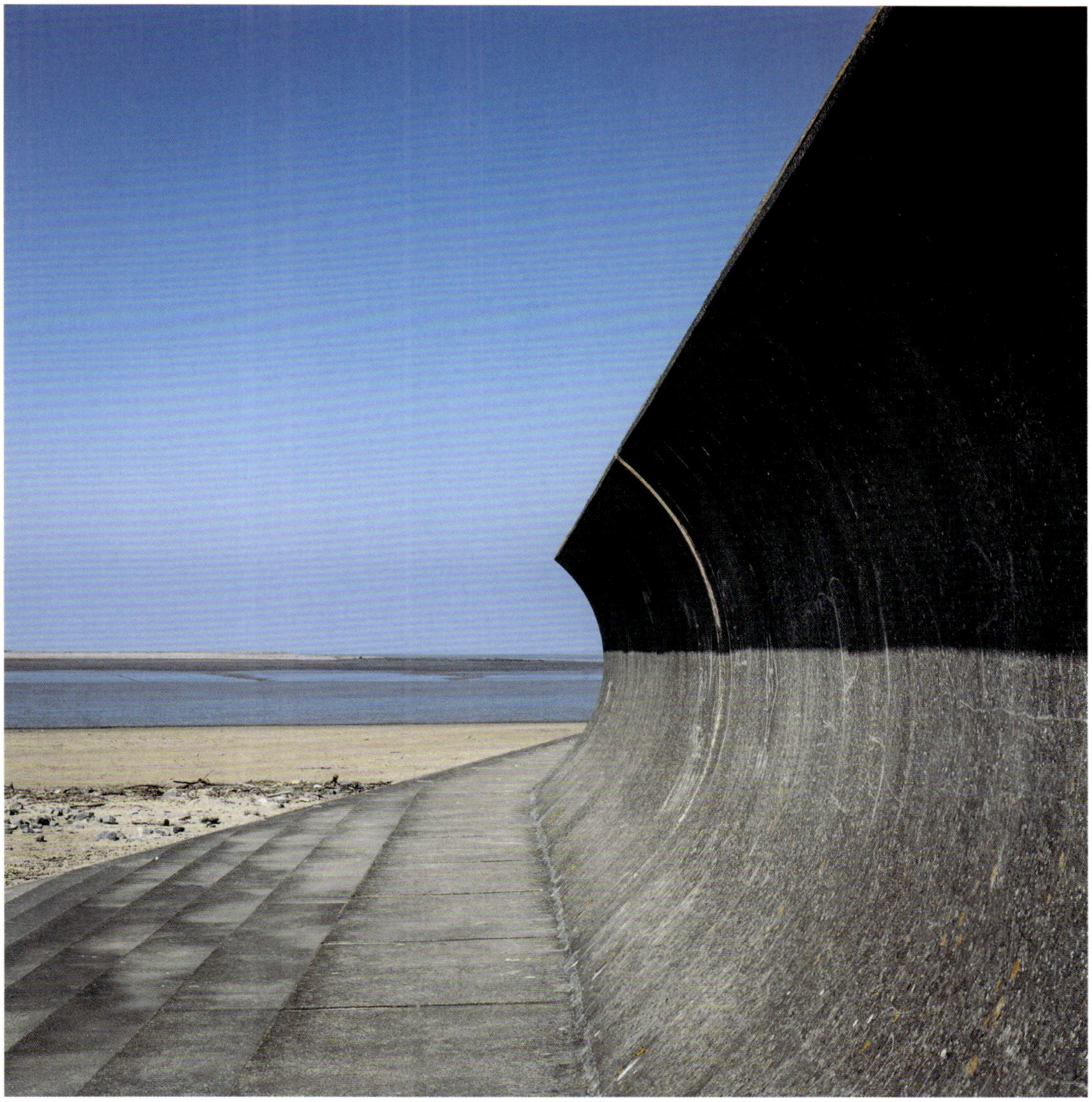

Opposite, clockwise from top left:

Banded clouds: a glimpse of Wales from Somerset

Steam train on the West Somerset Railway, near Minehead

Range Quadrant Hut, Lilstock

Groynes, Porlock Beach

Ammonite, Helwell Bay

Lower lias sedimentary rocks, Watchet

From top left:

Ploughing, Walpole

Pylons leaving Hinkley Point B nuclear power station

Frozen wave, calm sea: sea wall, Burnham-on-Sea

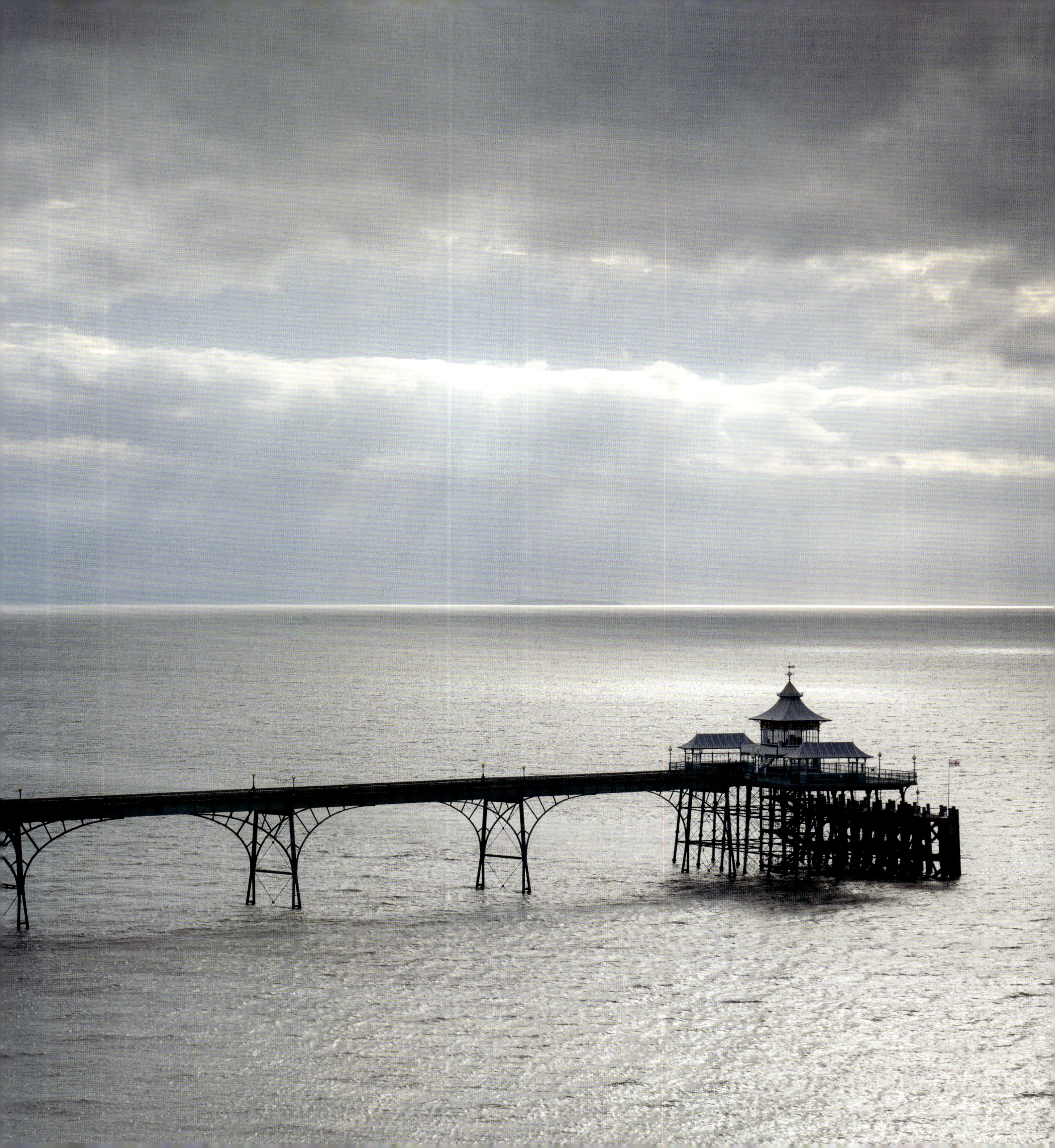

10 AVON

SEPTEMBER 2016

DAY 092–094 | 02,361–02,448KM | 87KM

My journey through Avon begins in frustration as my plan to walk along the coast from Brean Down is quickly thwarted by an impassable flood barrier across the River Axe. Forced back inland, I follow a road that's nightmarish for pedestrians, filled as it is with blind corners, and busy with buses and caravans. When I do get off the road, I soon learn why the few public footpaths here are deserted: they're either blocked off or so overgrown with brambles that I find myself criss-crossed with scratches. In contrast to the previous months in Cornwall and Devon, with their rugged terrain but easy wayfinding, here in horizontal Avon, I'm discovering the price to pay when there is no waymarked coast path.

With the labyrinth of ditches and blocked paths behind me, I'm pleased when I finally reach the streets of Weston-super-Mare early on a Monday morning. Arrows with *Banksy* are sprayed on the pavement, a vestige of his temporary art installation Dismaland, 'a theme park unsuitable for children'. In the vicinity of the Grand Pier, it's eerily quiet, with all the seaside attractions shuttered. A short distance around the headland stands Birnbeck Pier, where paddle steamers used to bring excited day-trippers from Wales. It is in a heart-wrenching state of dereliction; the timber decking of the once-handsome pier is rotten, while a rusty security camera hangs forlornly from a single cable.

It takes half a day for me to walk through the flat farmland drained by dykes that stretches from Weston to Clevedon, accompanied by the regular roar of planes from Bristol Airport. The patchwork of fields is maze-like and requires a compass bearing to find hidden stiles or gates. Then there are the green algae-filled ditches, frustratingly just too wide to jump across to make shortcuts. A stampeding herd of heifers harass me when I make the wrong turn.

More anxiety-inducing trespassing is needed to cross the River Yeo as the M5 motorway creates an impenetrable barrier inland. I scuttle through the 2 kilometres of private farmland, very visible in the uniform landscape, before crossing the private bridge. In a neighbouring field, two tractors toil away. They either don't see me, don't care or are too busy to confront me.

By the afternoon, the going is much easier from the elegantly restored Clevedon Pier, which is lapped by the gentlest of waves. An easy path guides me past a row of circular underground aviation fuel silos by the Severn that look like Neolithic burial chambers. When I reach Portishead a few hours later, I'm thrilled to make out the Severn crossing glowing in the late-evening light.

The next day, I traverse a road bridge high above the Avon, the only pedestrian beside a rush of speeding trucks. To one side are the docks at Avonmouth and on the other the edge of the city of Bristol, while below me are acres of newly imported parked cars not yet with their number plates attached, arranged in ranks, first by brand, then by colour.

I get back to ground level at Bristol Bulk Handling Terminal, where cylindrical storage tanks tower above me, and I catch a glimpse between the warehouses of a carrier being unloaded by clamshell grabbers. The sky is divided first with conveyor belts rising to a rusty red coal silo, then the giant white blades of wind turbines, before I walk below swags of power cables leading from Seabank Power Station.

A few hours later, on my last night in England, I stay at the Travelodge at Aust to be as close as possible to the Severn crossing. As expected, a sea of parked cars is surrounded by petrol stations and fast-food chains, but just a short walk away, there's a high viewpoint over the suspension bridge which reaches out to a new land on the distant shore: Wales.

Opposite:

Clevedon Pier from the coast path

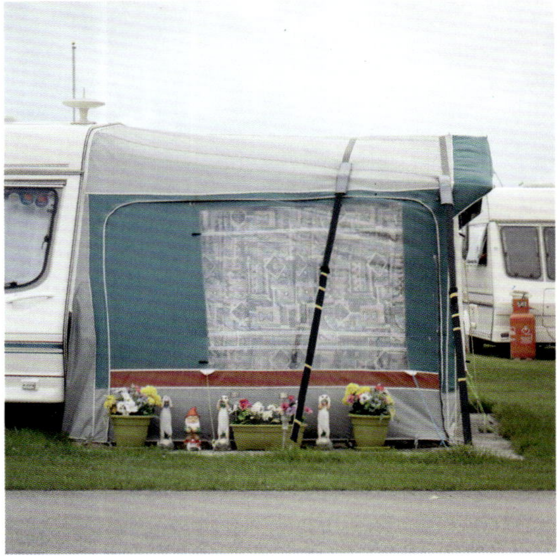

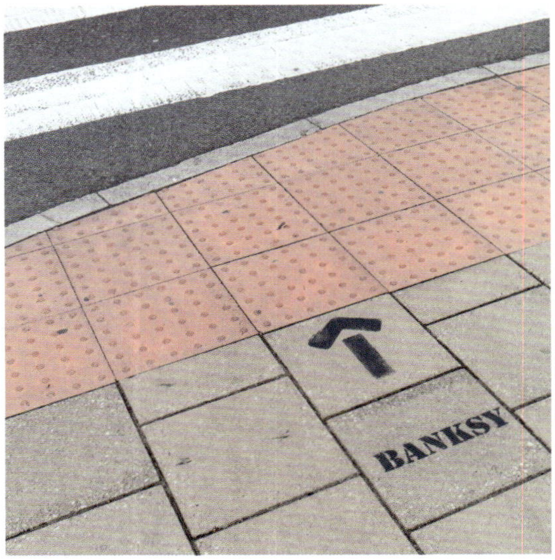
BANKSY

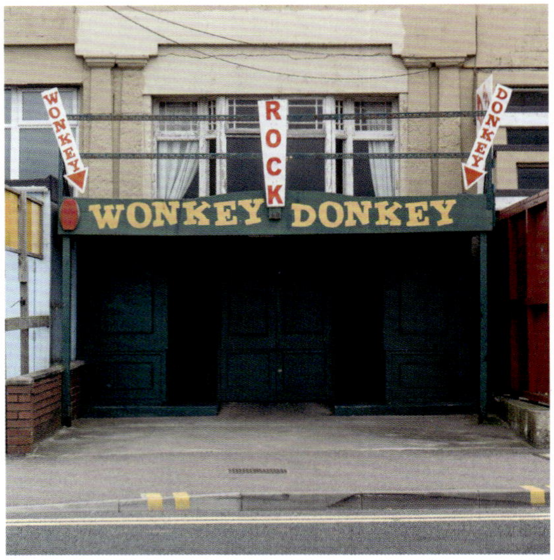
WONKEY
ROCK
DONKEY
WONKEY DONKEY

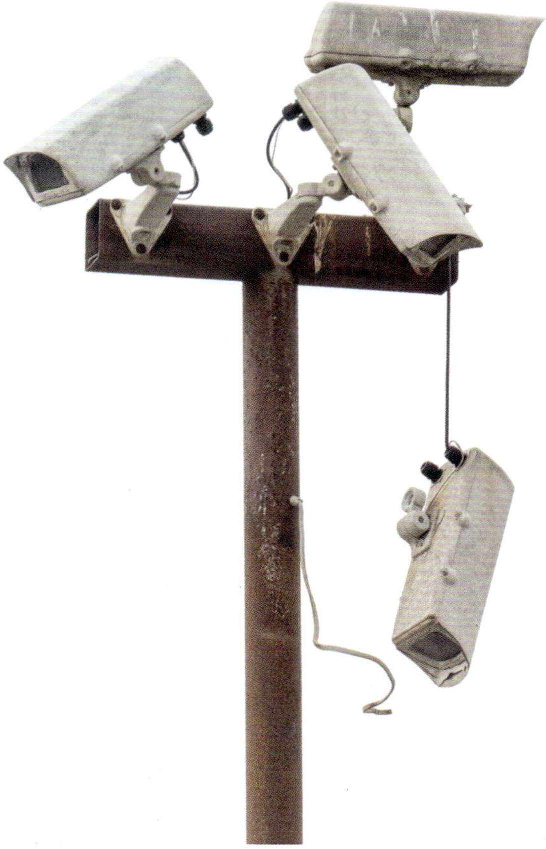

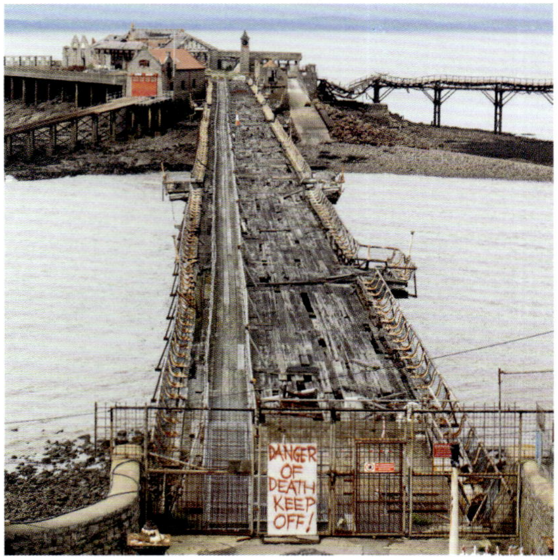
DANGER OF DEATH KEEP OFF!

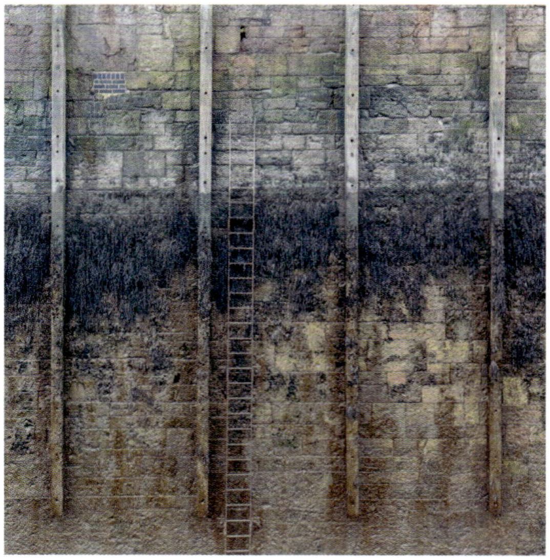

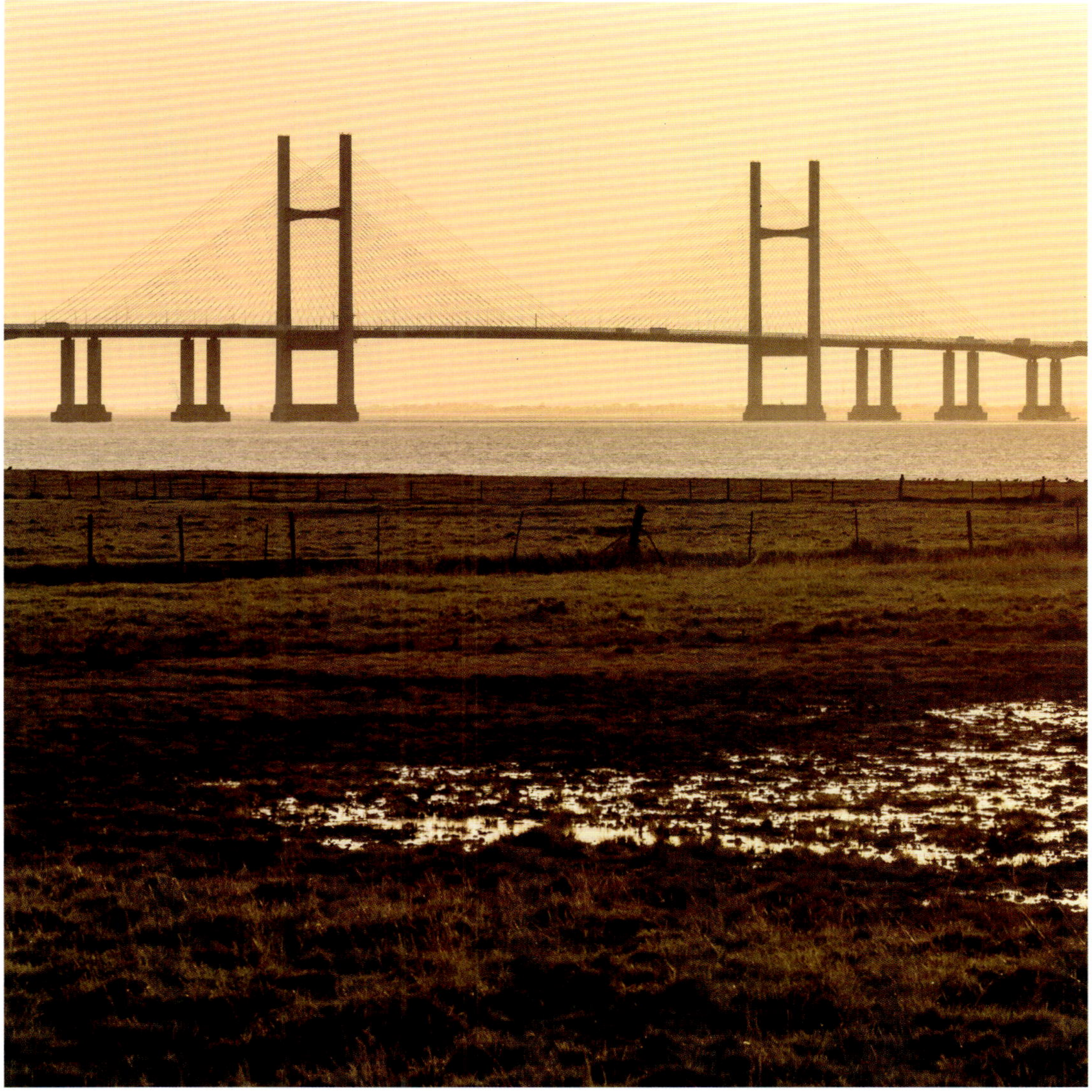

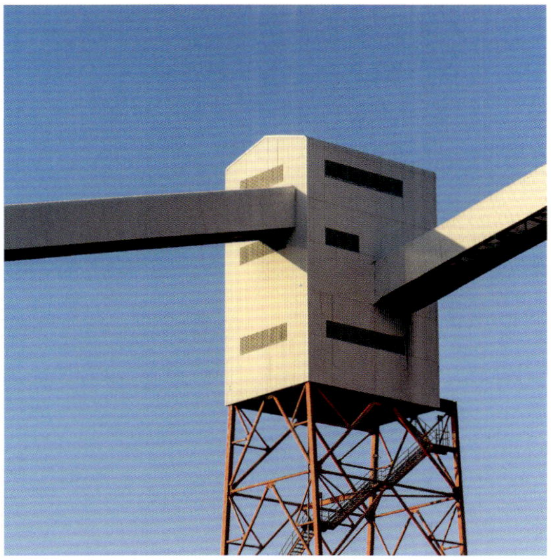

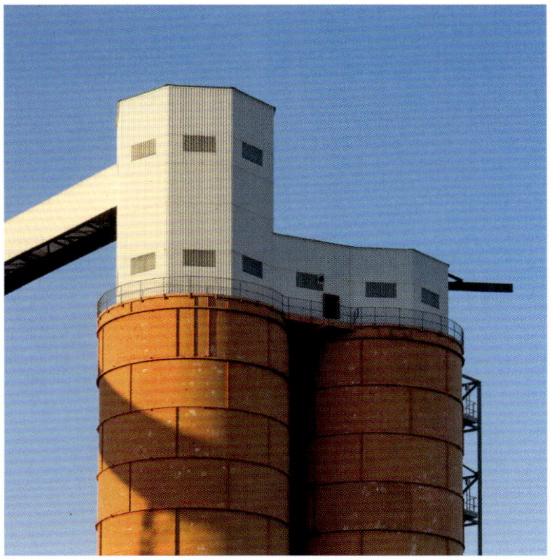

Opposite, clockwise from top left:

Home from home: Diamond Farm Caravan Park, Somerset

Remnants of Dismaland, a temporary art project organised by Banksy in August 2015, Weston-super-Mare

Wonkey Donkey gift shop, Weston-super-Mare

Danger of death: Birnbeck Pier closed in 1994 after storm damage, Weston-super-Mare

Portishead Marina Lock revealing the vast tidal range of the Severn, which can be over 15 metres

Fallen off the perch: near Birnbeck Pier, Weston-super-Mare

From top left:

Last light, Second Severn Crossing, Avon

A house in the sky: coal conveyor building, Bristol Bulk Handling Terminal, Avonmouth

Coal silo, Bristol Bulk Handling Terminal, Avonmouth

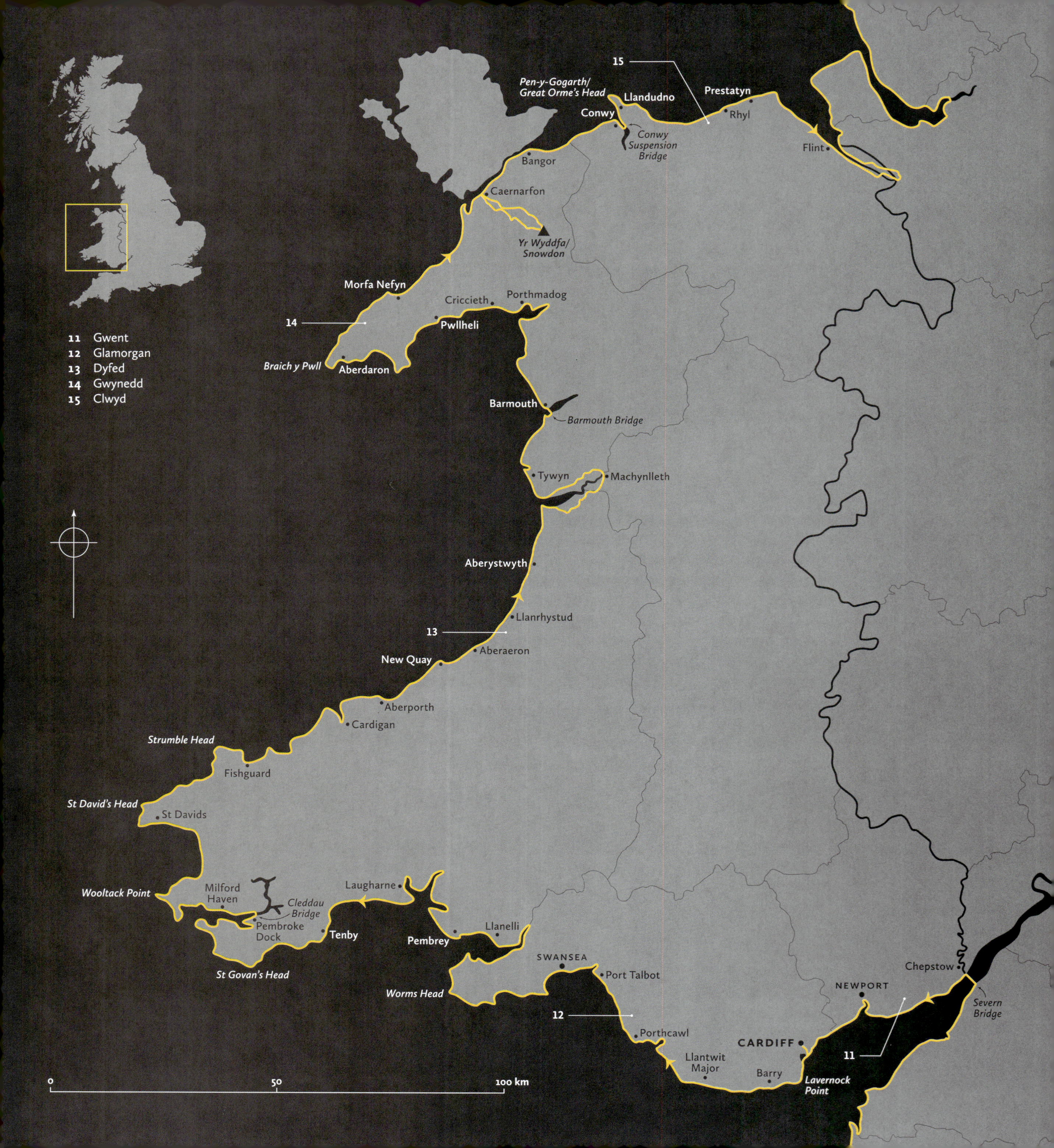
11 Gwent
12 Glamorgan
13 Dyfed
14 Gwynedd
15 Clwyd
15
Pen-y-Gogarth/ Great Orme's Head
Llandudno
Prestatyn
Rhyl
Conwy
Conwy Suspension Bridge
Flint
Bangor
Caernarfon
Yr Wyddfa/ Snowdon
Morfa Nefyn
Criccieth
Porthmadog
14
Pwllheli
Braich y Pwll
Aberdaron
Barmouth
Barmouth Bridge
Tywyn
Machynlleth
Aberystwyth
Llanrhystud
13
Aberaeron
New Quay
Aberporth
Cardigan
Strumble Head
Fishguard
St David's Head
St Davids
Wooltack Point
Milford Haven
Cleddau Bridge
Pembroke Dock
Laugharne
Tenby
Llanelli
Pembrey
St Govan's Head
Worms Head
SWANSEA
Port Talbot
12
Porthcawl
Llantwit Major
Barry
CARDIFF
Lavernock Point
NEWPORT
11
Chepstow
Severn Bridge
0
50
100 km

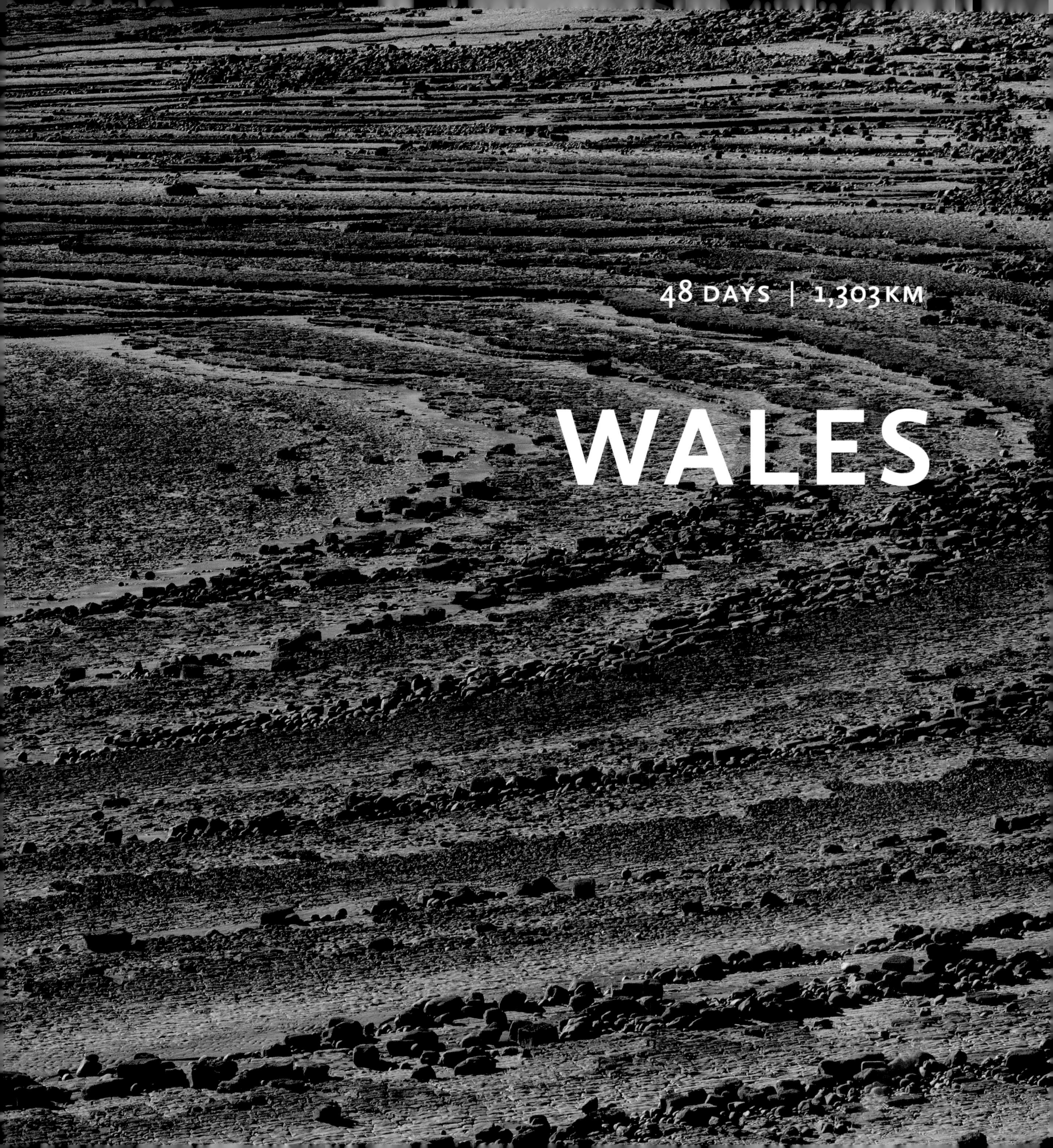

48 DAYS | 1,303KM

WALES

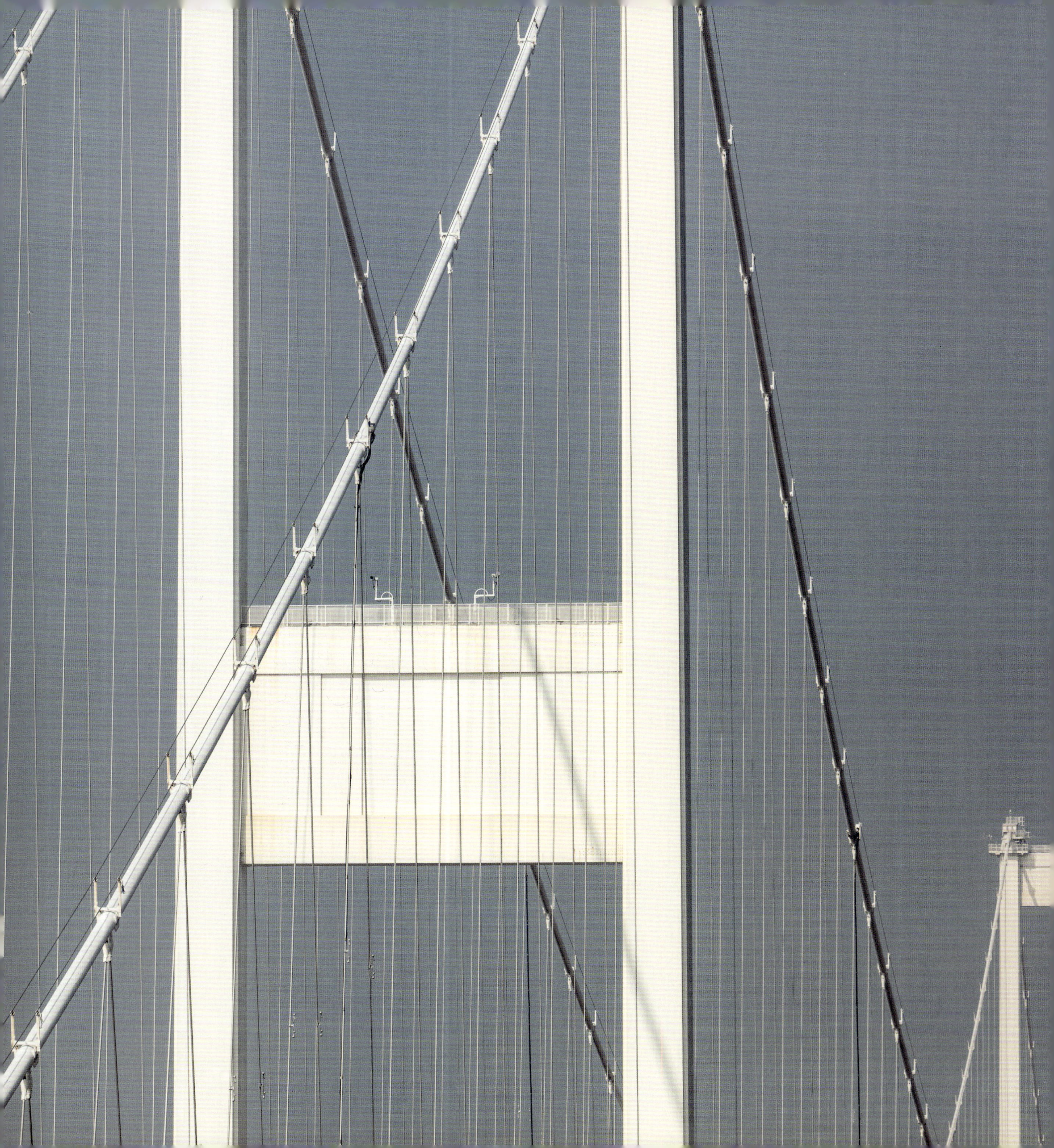

11 GWENT

SEPTEMBER 2016

DAY 095–097 | 02,448–02,526 KM | 78 KM

Previous:

Stout Bay, Glamorgan

Opposite:

The Severn Bridge, which spans the River Severn between England and Wales, was built in 1966

I'm entering a new country today, so I linger on the English bank of the Severn Bridge to reflect on the past ninety-odd days. Exposed to the wind and the rush of nearby traffic, and with unencumbered views downriver, I feel like I am standing before a portal between two worlds. In getting to this point, I've endured countless storms and blisters, and some nights I've gone to bed too weary to take another step. But each morning, the excitement of not knowing what new wonders lie ahead has kept me going.

I cross the Severn, and another bridge over the Wye, to stand on Welsh land proper. The Severn Bridge spans 1.6 kilometres, so in walking across, I have plenty of time to marvel at the engineering and construction teamwork required to build this gravity-defying finger of steel in 1966. On the other side, there's no *Welcome to Wales*, just a vast blue motorway sign with a split personality marked with Cardiff / Caerdydd, Newport / Casnewydd, and Chepstow / Cas-gwent. Beneath it, three sturdy women lean against the crash barrier puffing cigarettes, faces alarmingly scarlet from crossing the bridge.

On my last three days in England, I'd followed the banks of the Severn east towards Bristol, so it feels both familiar and alien to follow the Severn again but in a different direction and country. An intoxicating sense of peace and calm washes over me as I leave the clatter and rumble of the motorway crossings behind, and I smile with the satisfaction of reaching a milestone. Power cables grid the sky while neon-blue channel markers glow in the fields nearby.

The next day I buy my first (of many) bags of Welsh cakes in Newport to fuel myself along the sea wall towards Cardiff. There, I meet a fisherman with a lilting Welsh accent who's just landed a sizeable conger eel. 'Bit early for the cod, nice morning though, nice breeze,' he says.

I head inland up the Usk to the Newport Transporter Bridge. It's another remarkable feat of engineering that consists of two 74-metre vertical steel towers supporting a truss from which a motorised gondola is suspended. I marvel as the gondola moves vehicles back and forth slowly across the river. Using mechanised assistance is against the rules of my walk, so I happily pay £1.50 to climb up the ever-steepening zigzag stairs and cross the river. I'm less happy when I realise that it involves walking over a deck with an airy open grille. I tentatively pick my way across, gripping the handrail tightly. Where I can, I avoid standing on rusted cross-beams, eyeing the swift-moving tidal range beneath me with apprehension.

It takes an entire day of walking to reach the outskirts of Cardiff, where I get my first taste of unapologetically contemporary heavy industry. I stop to take photos at the melt shop at Celsa Steel, where mounds of coal and pyramids of scrap metal sit piled up high. There's a screeching sound as a handful of giant mechanical grabbers move scrap steel dwarfed by the looming melt shop, a grimy white rectangle from which outsize steaming pipes emerge, like a post-apocalyptic steampunk fantasy.

All along the coast, there is the rumble of trucks and a stench of waste. This is an in-between land pockmarked with piles of rubbish and scorched patches. As the wind changes and I approach the local authority Rover Way Traveller Site, the acrid smell from Celsa steelworks stings my nostrils. More stench, a sewage treatment works this time; then the heavy infrastructure gradually gives way to the Toolstations, business parks and urban bustle at the heart of Cardiff.

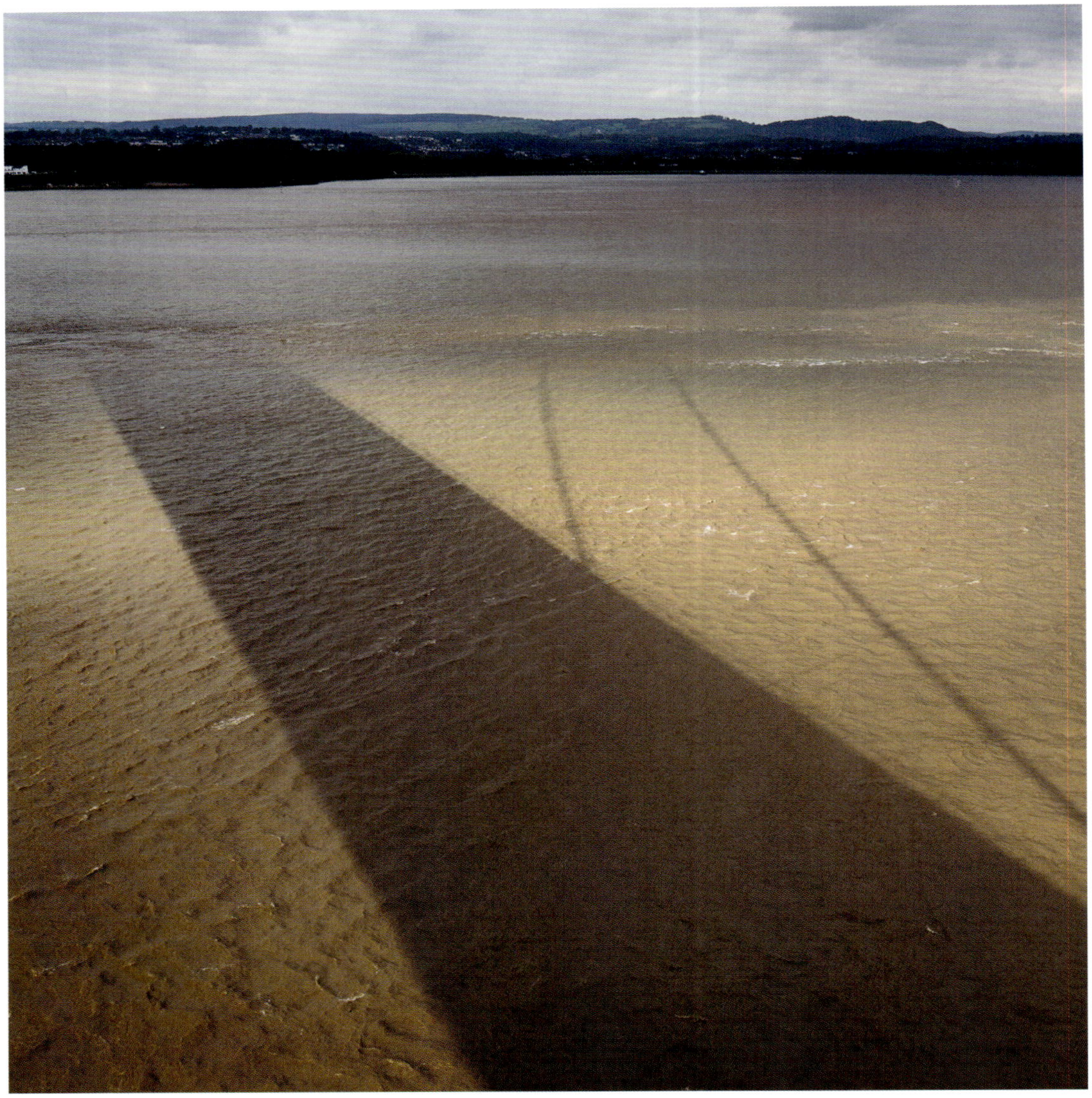

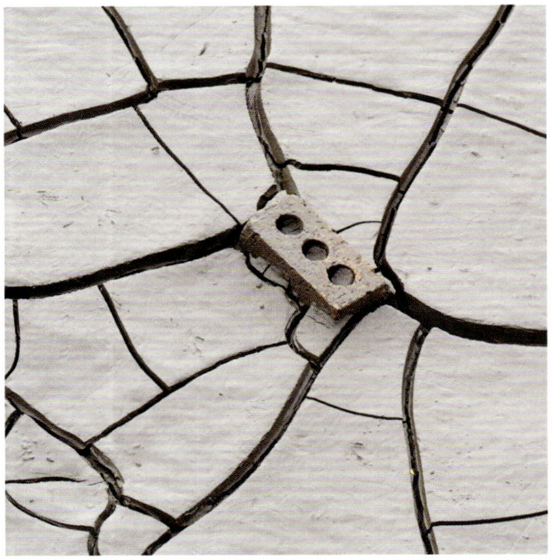

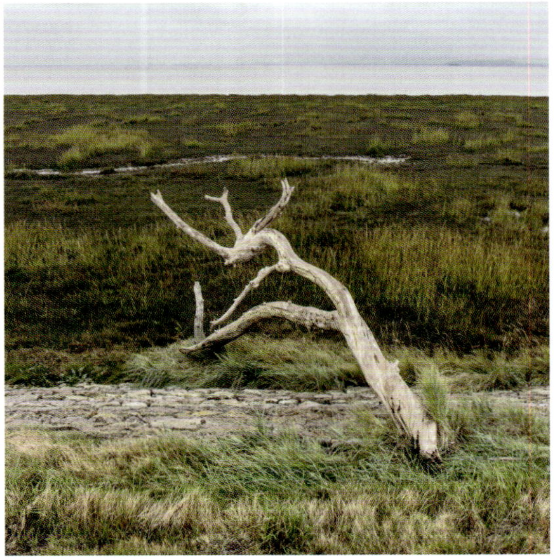

From top left:

Severn Bridge shadow

At Black Rock, Portskewett

Roggiett Moor

Opposite, clockwise from top left:

Newport Transporter Bridge, built in 1906

Yard, AIC (Arabian International Company) Steel, Newport

Melt-shop, Celsa Steel, Tremorfa, Cardiff

Wiggly sea wall, Peterstone Gout

Heavy sky over Cardiff flats

Gondola, Newport Transporter Bridge, River Usk

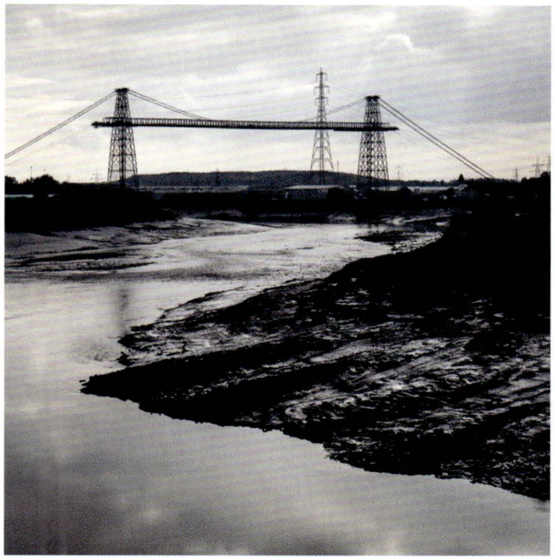

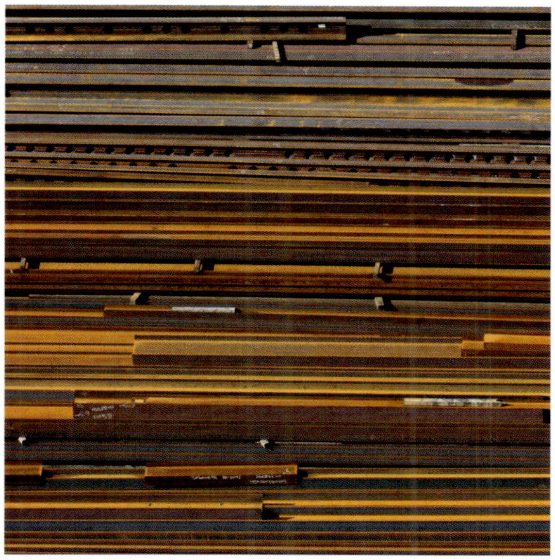

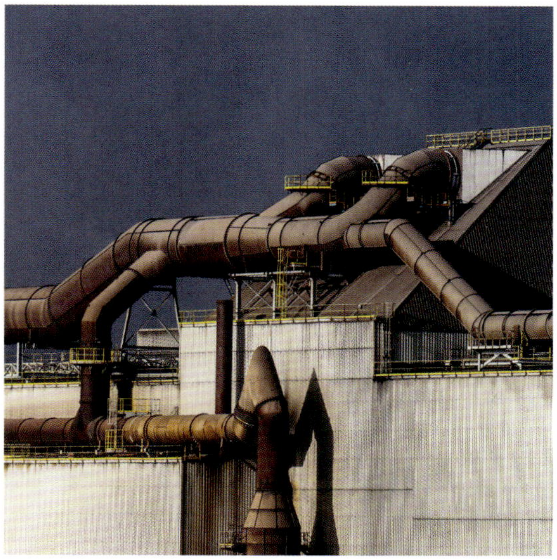

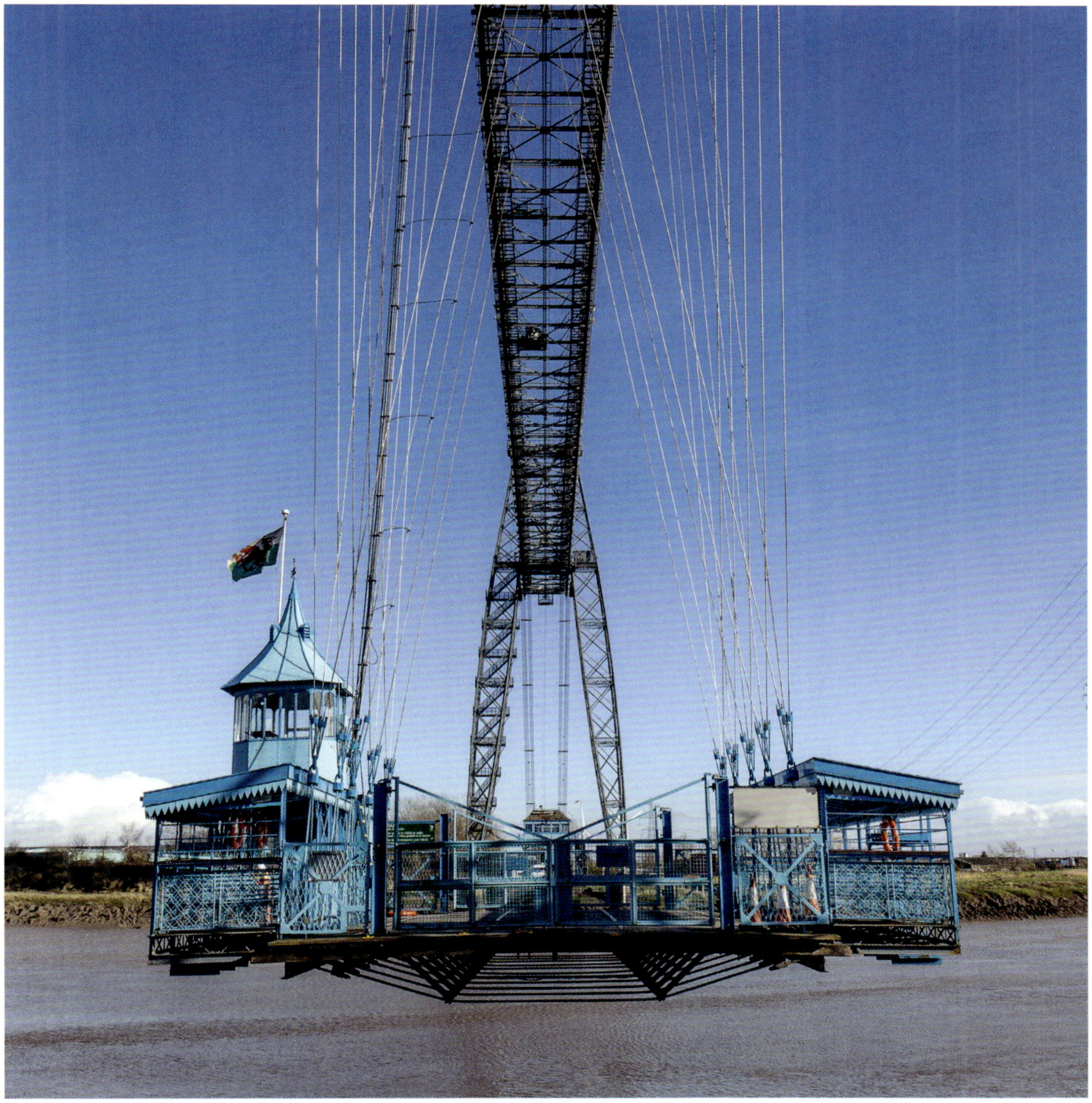

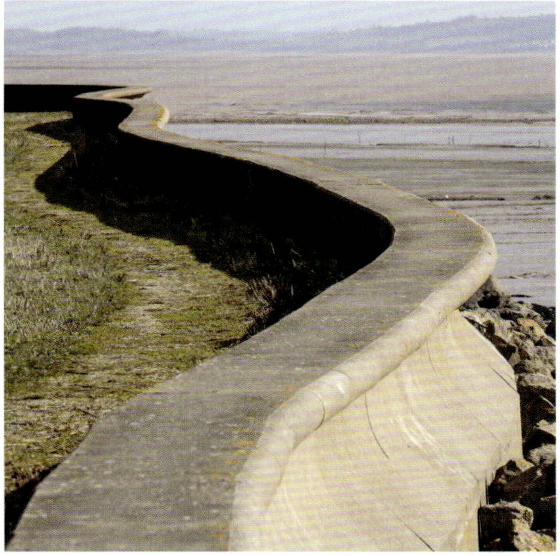

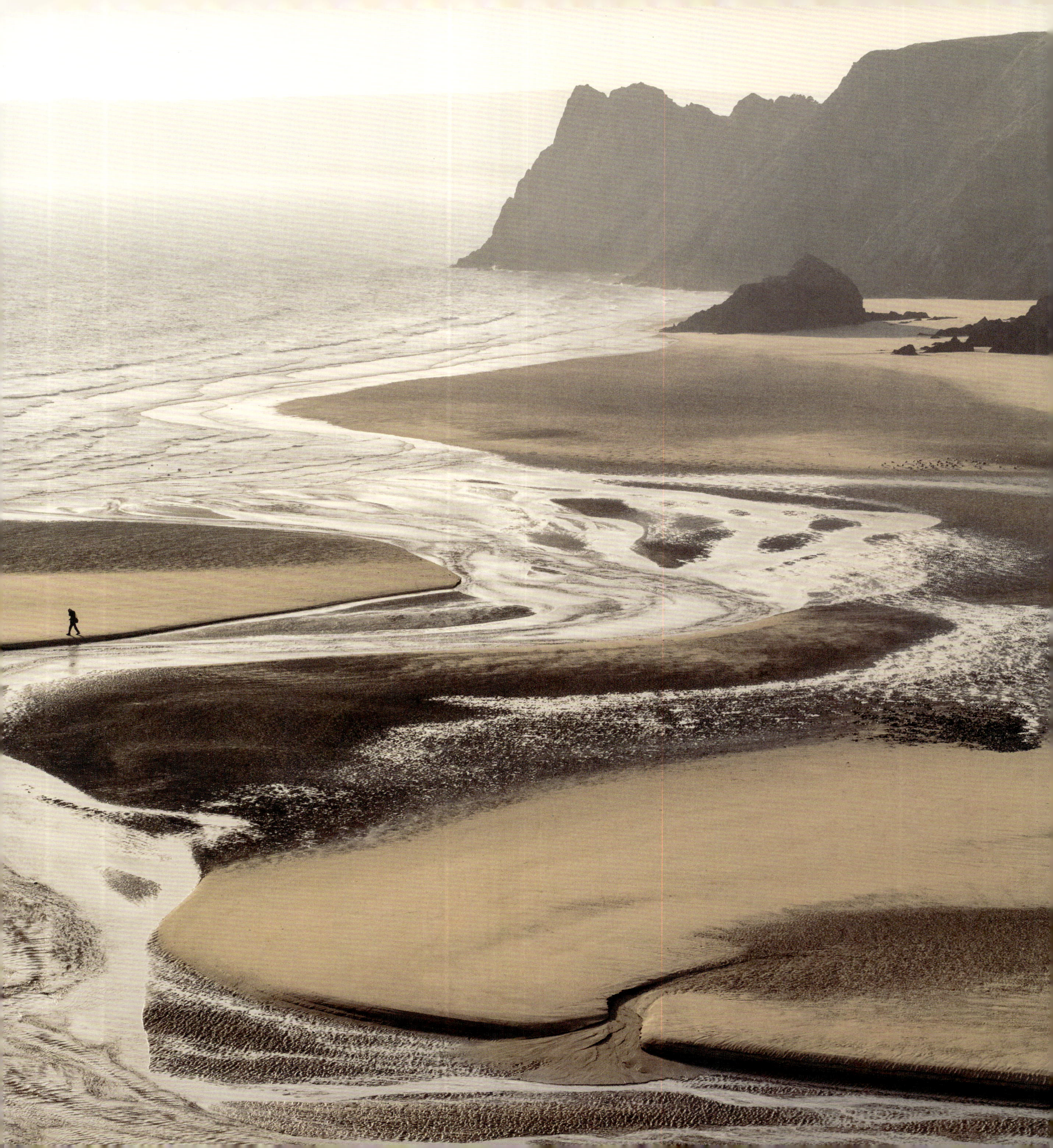

12 GLAMORGAN

SEPTEMBER–NOVEMBER 2016
DAY 098–105 | 02,526–02,753KM | 227KM

Opposite:

Three Cliffs Bay, Gower

From the bustling centre of Cardiff, I head towards the sea, pausing only at Atlantic Wharf to look out over the still water's edge. Once known as Bute East Dock, the wharf was built in the 1850s by Irish labourers for the thriving coal and iron industries. The empty vastness that stretches out ahead of me makes the lack of ships tangible, and vessels of the past spring to my imagination. But the only life here is two cormorants that stand with wings spread and drying out after the rain.

Route-finding is tricky at Bendricks Rocks, where I find myself squeezing through the bent corner of a chicken-wire fence on a derelict industrial site to emerge in Barry Docks before returning to the Wales Coast Path that leads to Rhoose Point, the most southerly bit of mainland Wales. Here, the geology of the shoreline comprises hundreds of rusted steel bolts mixed with cement nodules between the ammonites, giving it a strange mix-up of deep time and the Anthropocene. At this juncture, the Bristol Channel seems to be a funnel to the Atlantic and distant lands.

At Aberthaw Power Station, the coast path skirts past vast stockpiles of coal; three men stand on the black mounds beside heavy machinery, the colour of their hi-vis orange overalls and faces barely showing through the coating of coal dust.

On my fourth day in Glamorgan, I approach the steelworks at Port Talbot on foot via the shoreline. It's astonishing – even from miles away, I can see plumes of steam erupting into the sky like an artificial cloud machine. It looks more like an offering to the gods than the engine of the machine age. Reminded of the steel industry's perilous future and inspired by the heroic scale of the dangerous work here, I photograph a blast furnace as thoroughly as possible from public land. Afterwards, in McDonald's Port Talbot, it's crowded for lunch hour and I'm the only one not wearing Tata Steel overalls.

The following day, I arrive in the Gower Peninsula, an Area of Outstanding Natural Beauty that lives up to its designation with its intoxicating abundance of sandy beaches and rugged gorse-covered cliff edges. At the tip of the peninsula, I'm elated to get to the tidal island at Worms Head with just enough time to cross the Devil's Bridge, a dramatic sea arch at the far end. The interval timer on my camera is playing up, so it takes me longer than usual to prepare my tripod for photos. After a few shots, I look up, only to see waves rushing in angrily. Dread fills me as I realise there's a high likelihood of being marooned. I pack up quickly and jog back along the causeway as fast as I can, defying the 20 kilograms on my back with every step. To my surprise, a Coastwatch officer comes to greet me when I'm back on the mainland. 'You the last one?' he says, concerned. 'We get about one a month stranded,' he sighs. 'We have to scramble the Milford Haven lifeboat to get them off. Worst are the folks from Mediterranean countries, who don't have tides and are completely unaware.' By the time our brief chat is over, the causeway is submerged below a tumultuous sea.

Moments later, I'm luxuriating in the graceful curving expanse of Rhossili Beach that is scattered with whelks and shepherd's purses. I meet a surfer who tells me the break is good at high and low tide. 'In the summer, it's bright at 3.30 a.m., so I can get a surf in, have breakfast and watch a bit of TV before work!' As I stroll along the beach, I envision myself living an idyllic coastal life in harmony with the ebb and flow.

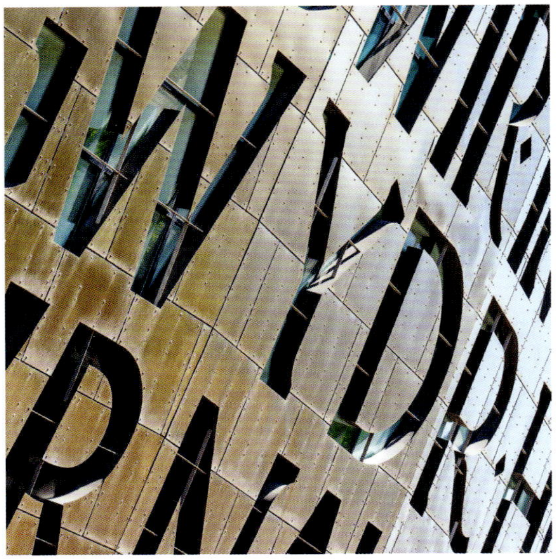

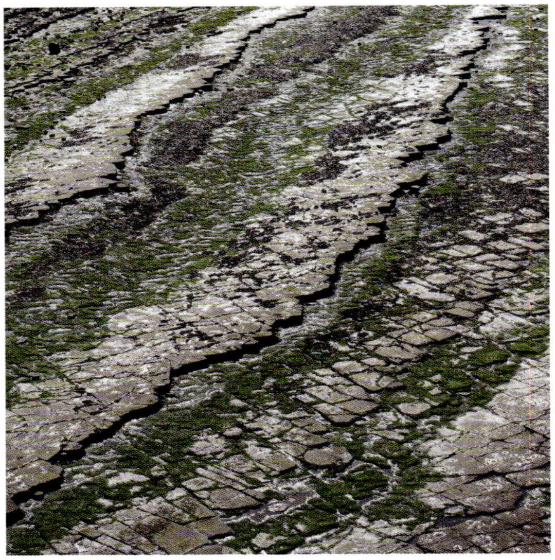

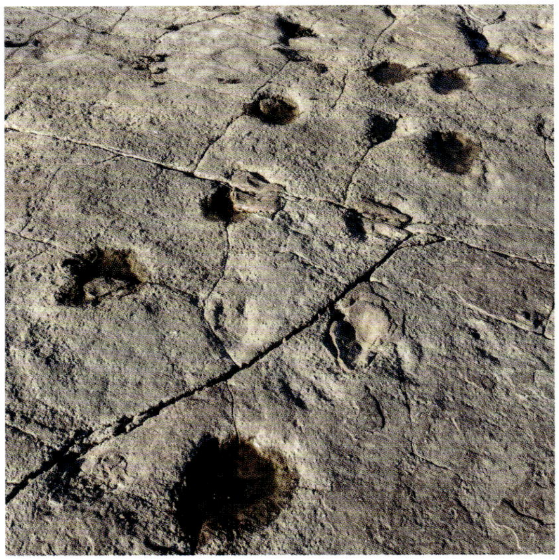

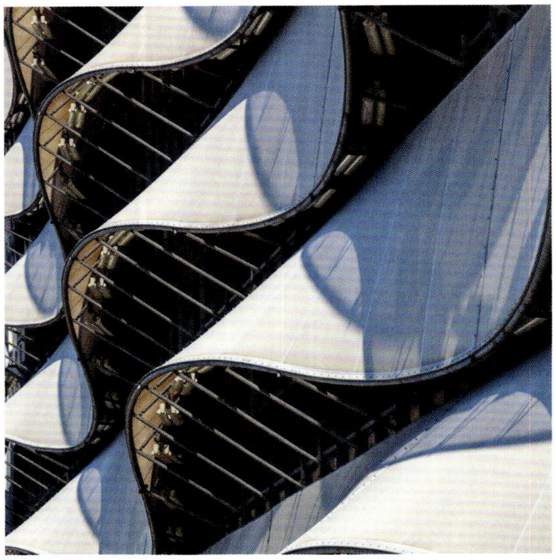

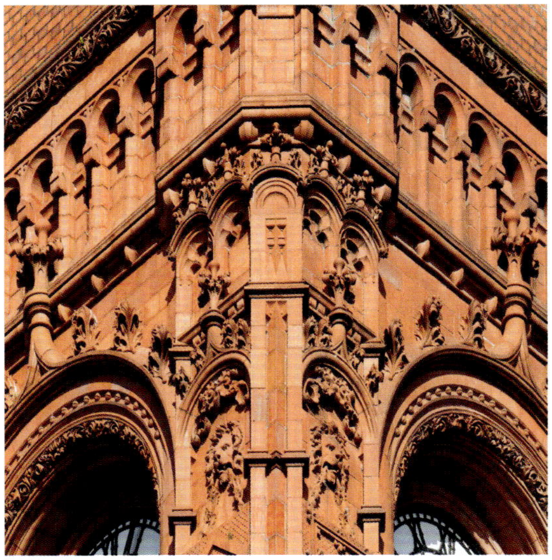

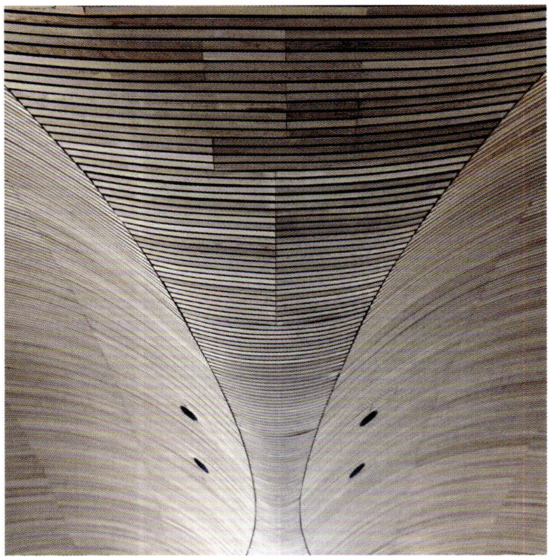

From top left:

Wales Millennium Centre, Cardiff Bay, inscribed with two lines written by Gwyneth Lewis in the Welsh and English languages

Shore platform, St Mary's Well Bay

From centre left:

200-million-year-old dinosaur footprints, the Bendricks

The Wave car park, Cardiff Bay

From bottom left:

Terracotta facade of the Pierhead Building, Cardiff Bay

Cedarwood ceiling inside the Senedd building, Cardiff Bay, designed by Richard Rogers Partnership in 2006

Opposite, clockwise from top left:

Traeth Bach

Coal bowl scraper on coal stockpile, Aberthaw Power Station (closed 2020)

Rhoose Point, the most southerly point of mainland Wales

Stout Bay at low tide

Rhoose Point, shore platform

Aberthaw B coal-fired power station (closed 2020)

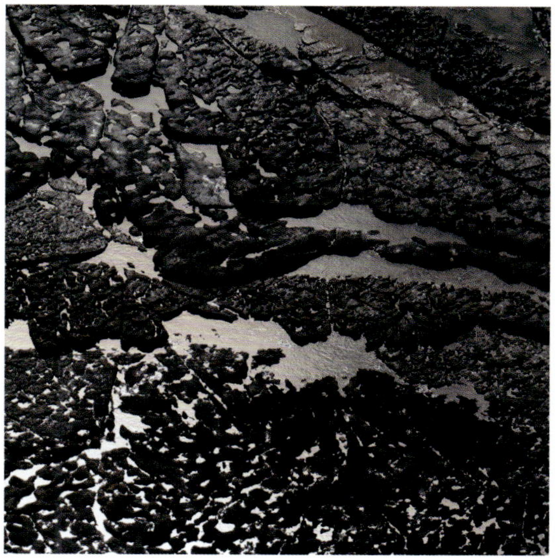
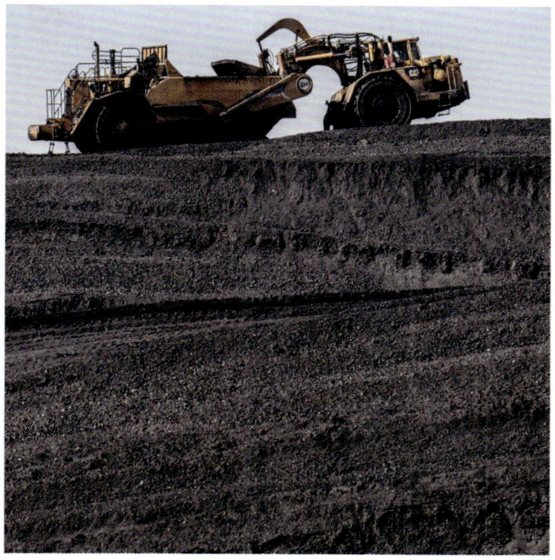
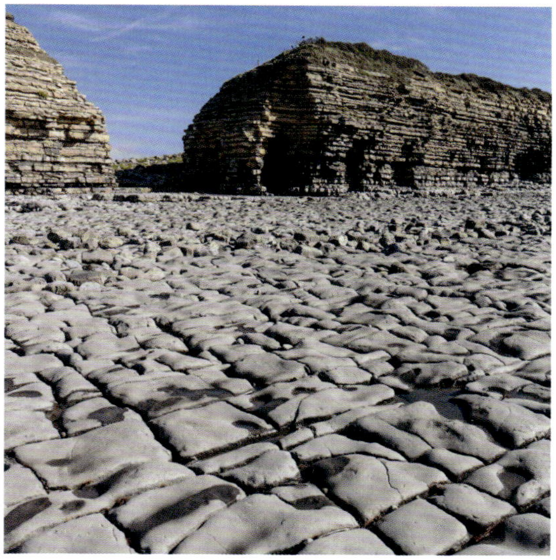
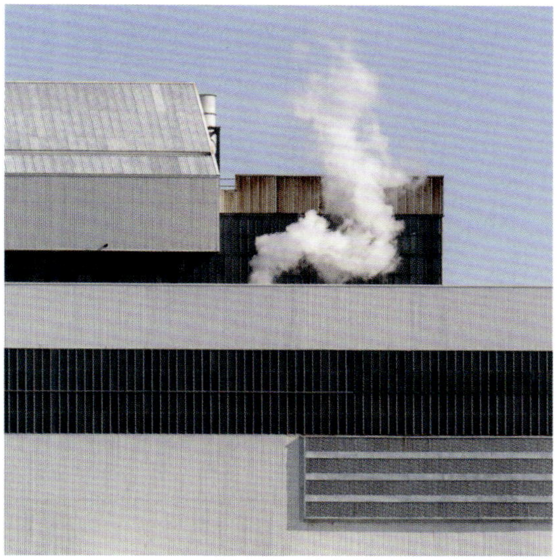
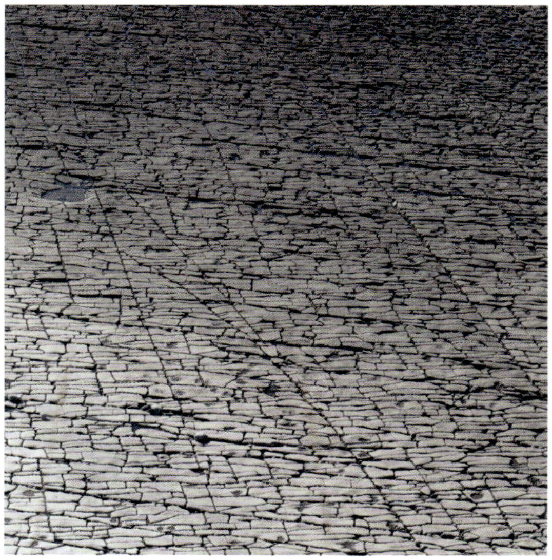
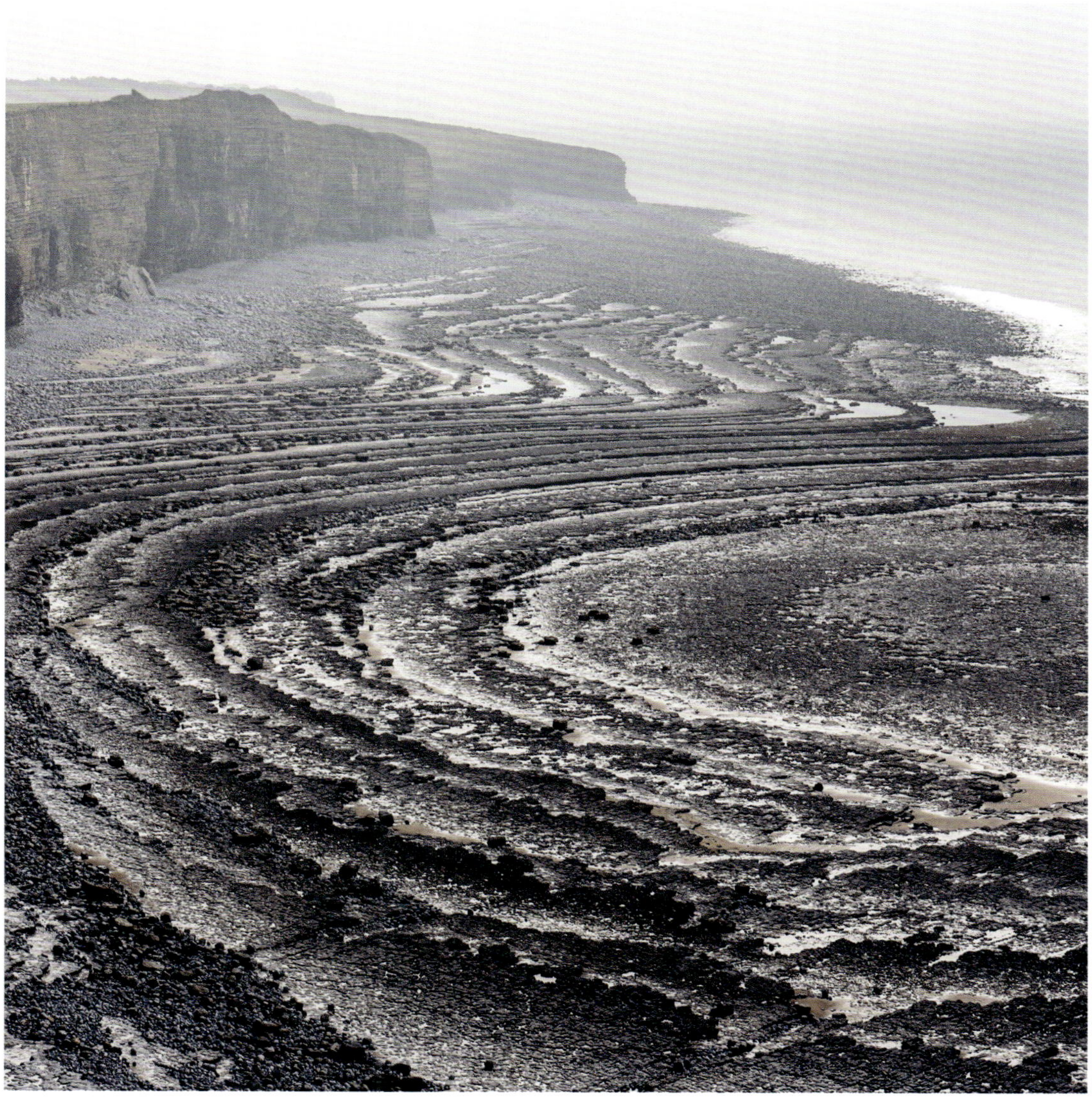

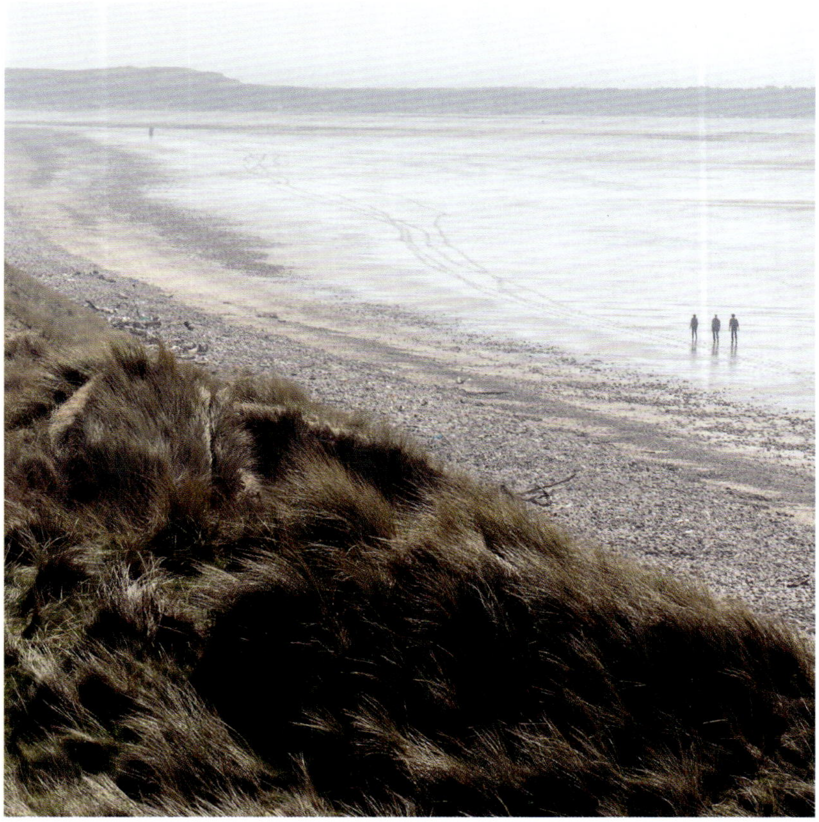

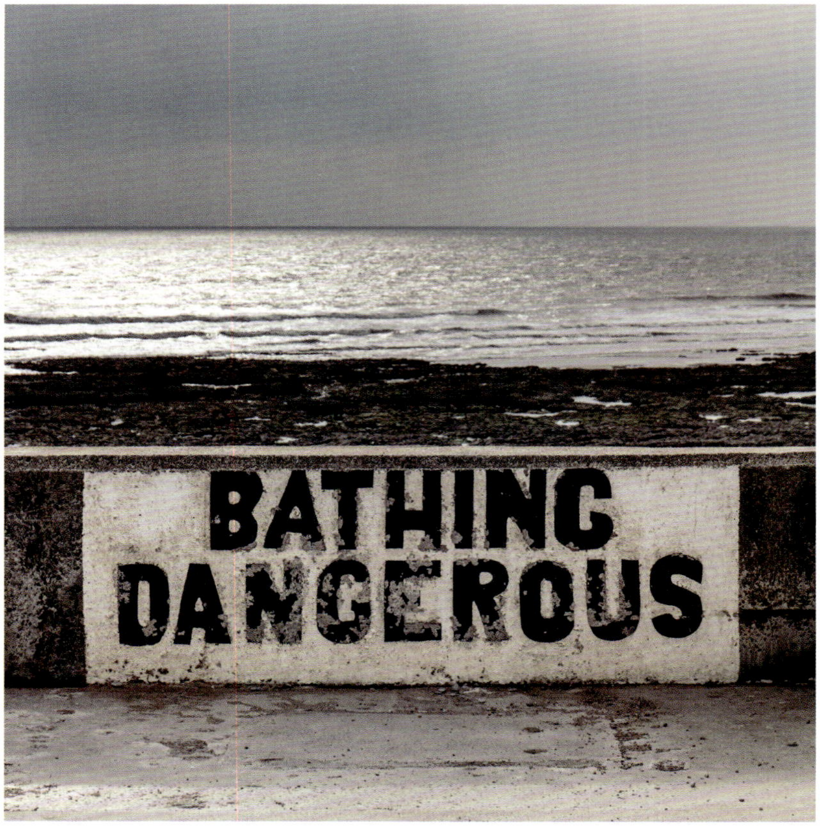
BATHING
DANGEROUS

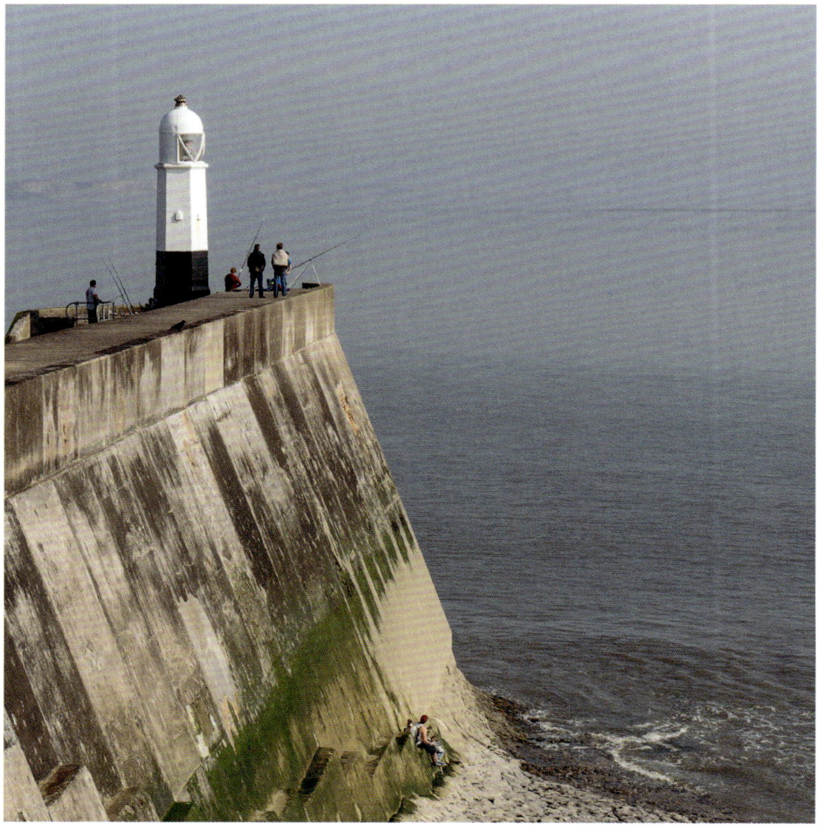

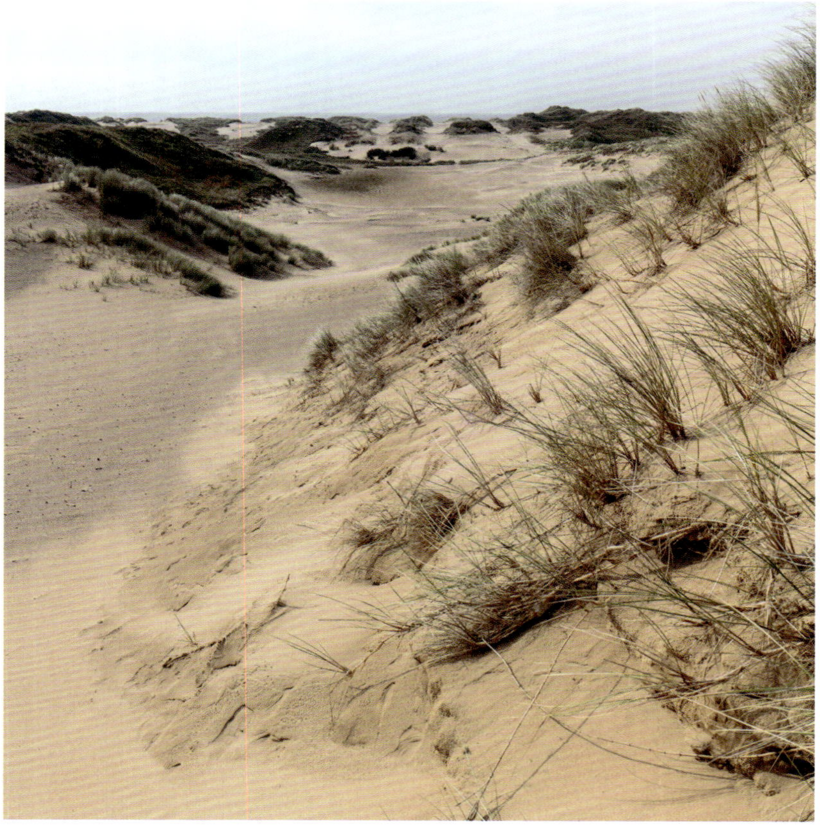

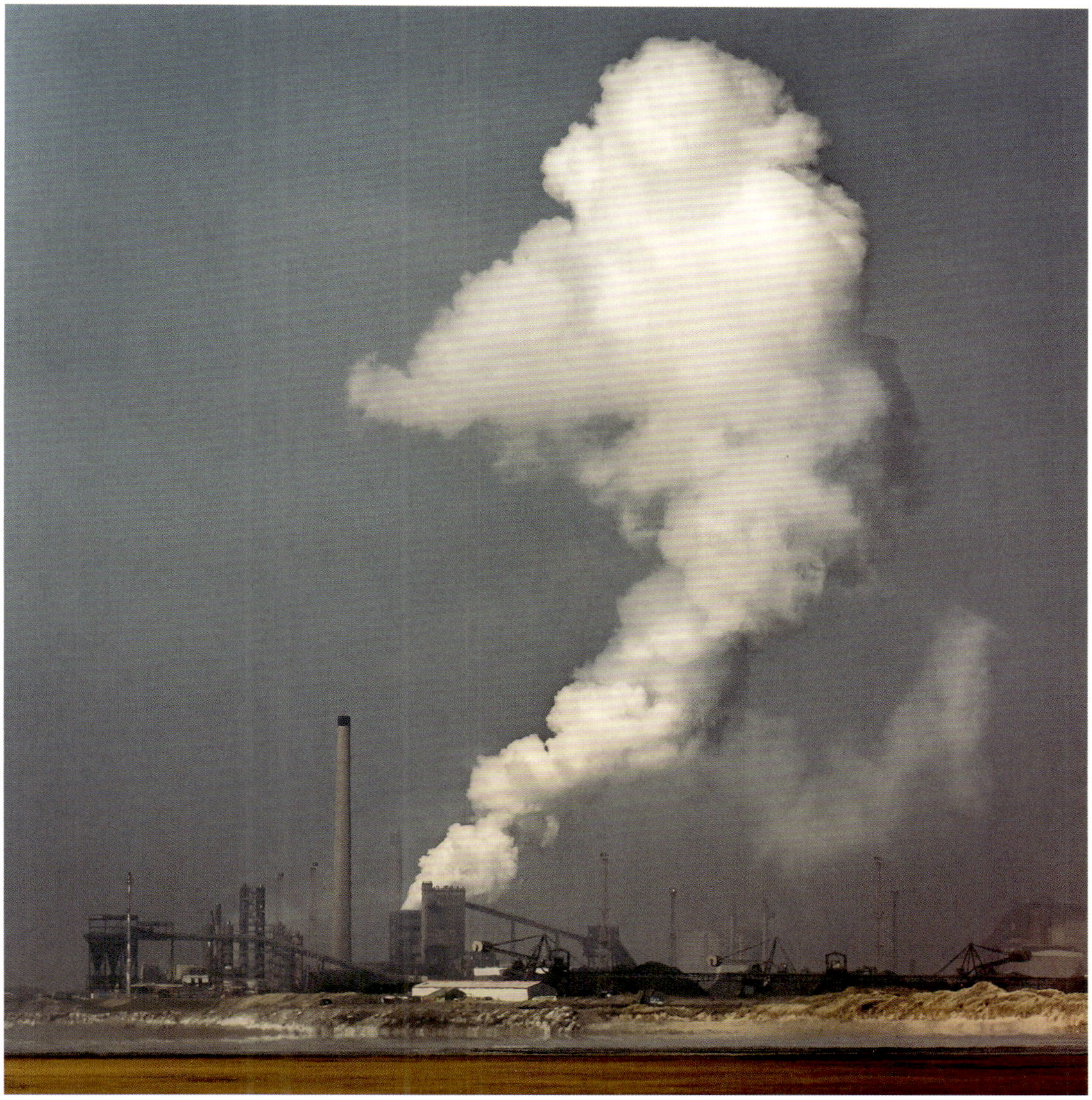

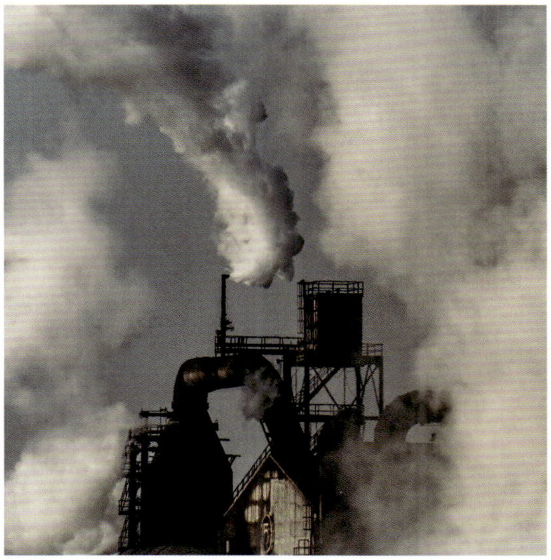

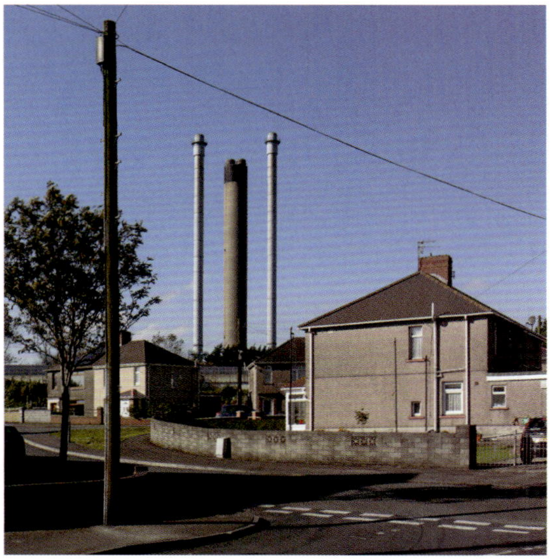

Opposite, from top left:

Kenfig Sands

Bathing dangerous: Porthcawl

From bottom left:

Porthcawl Lighthouse

Merthyr Mawr Dunes, used as a location for the 1962 film *Lawrence of Arabia*

From top left:

Steam plume, Tata Steelworks, from Kenfig Sands (the two blast furnaces closed in 2024 to be replaced by an electric arc furnace that melts scrap steel)

No. 5 blast furnace, operational from 1959 (closed 2024), Tata Steelworks, Port Talbot

Neighbours: Margam with chimneys from Tata Steelworks, Port Talbot

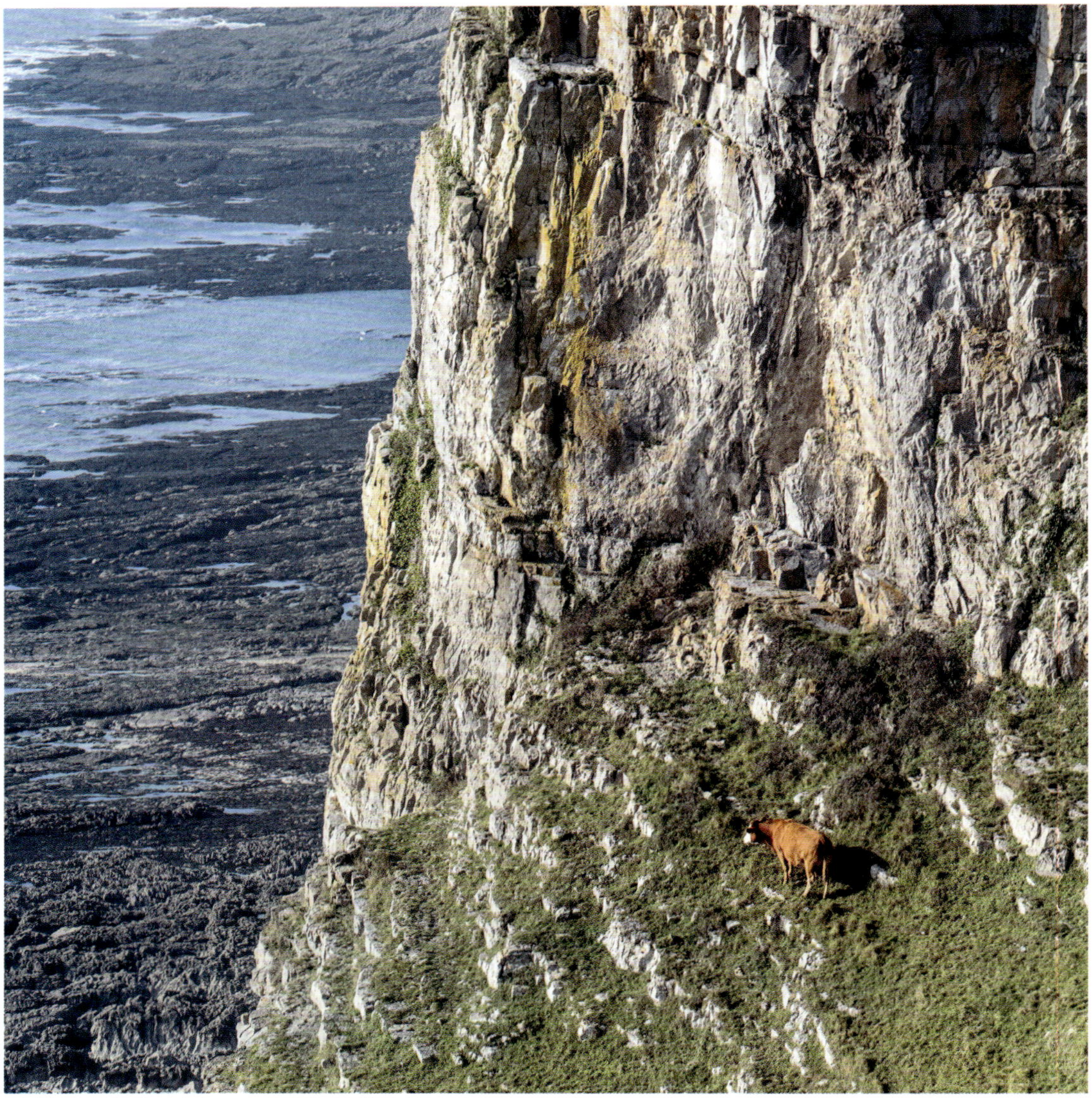

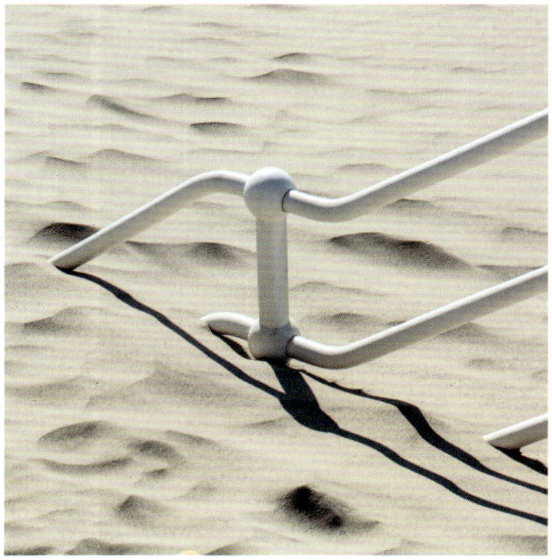

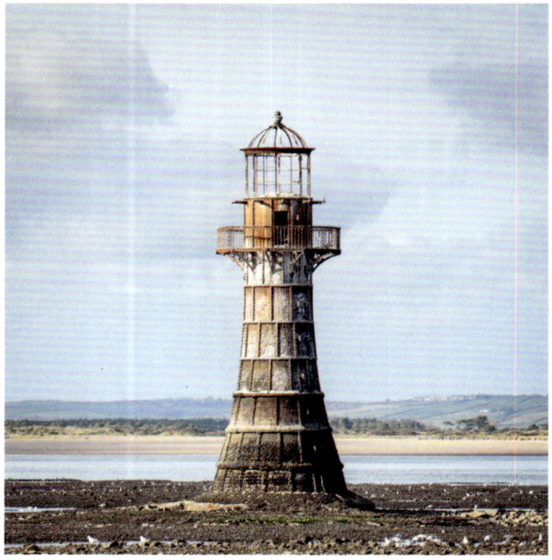

From top left:

Climbing cow, Pwlldu Head, Gower

Aberavon Sands, Port Talbot

Whiteford Point Lighthouse, Gower, a cast-iron lighthouse built in 1865 to a design by John Bowen

Opposite:

Selfie approaching Devil's Bridge, Worms Head, Gower

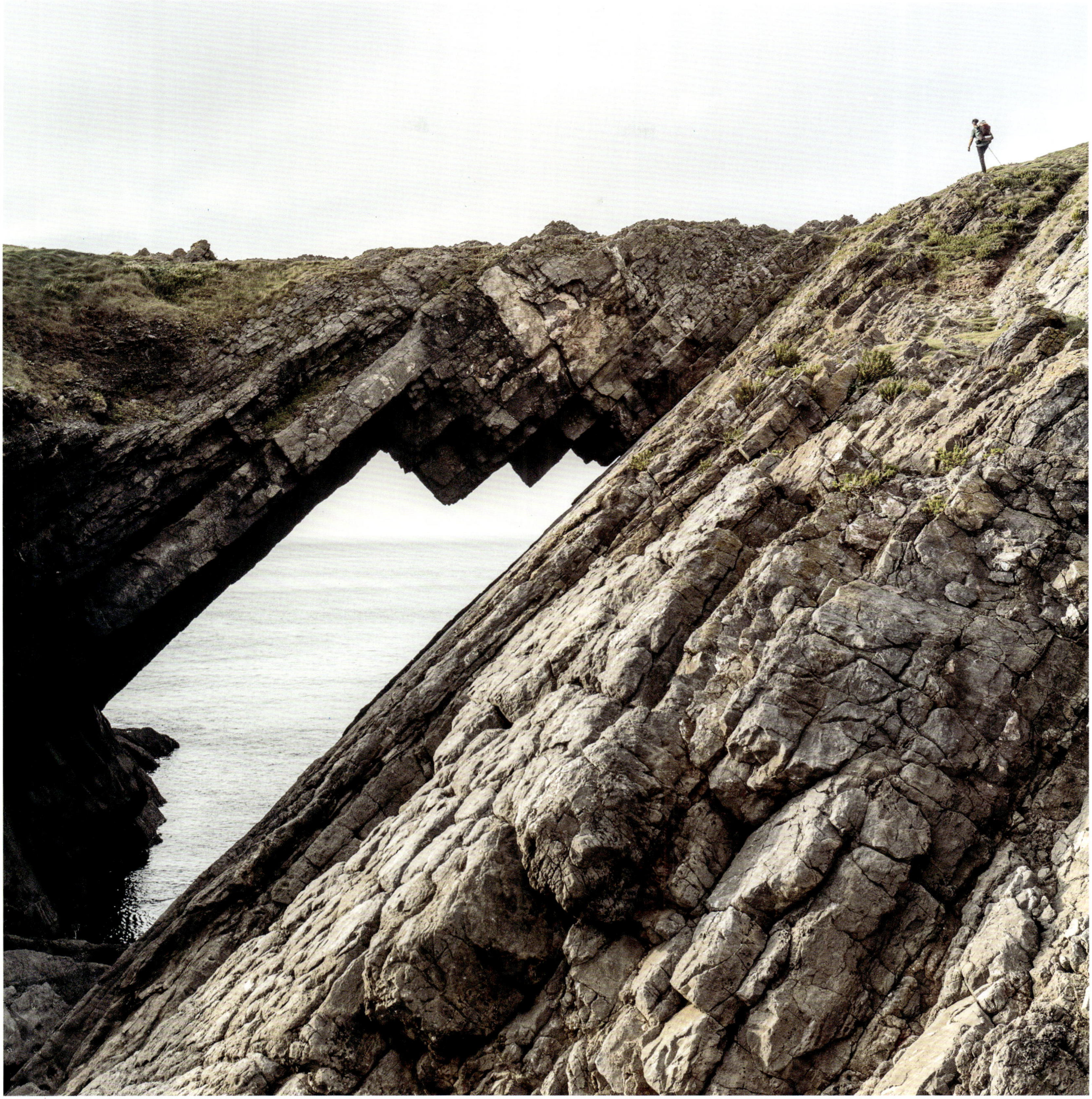

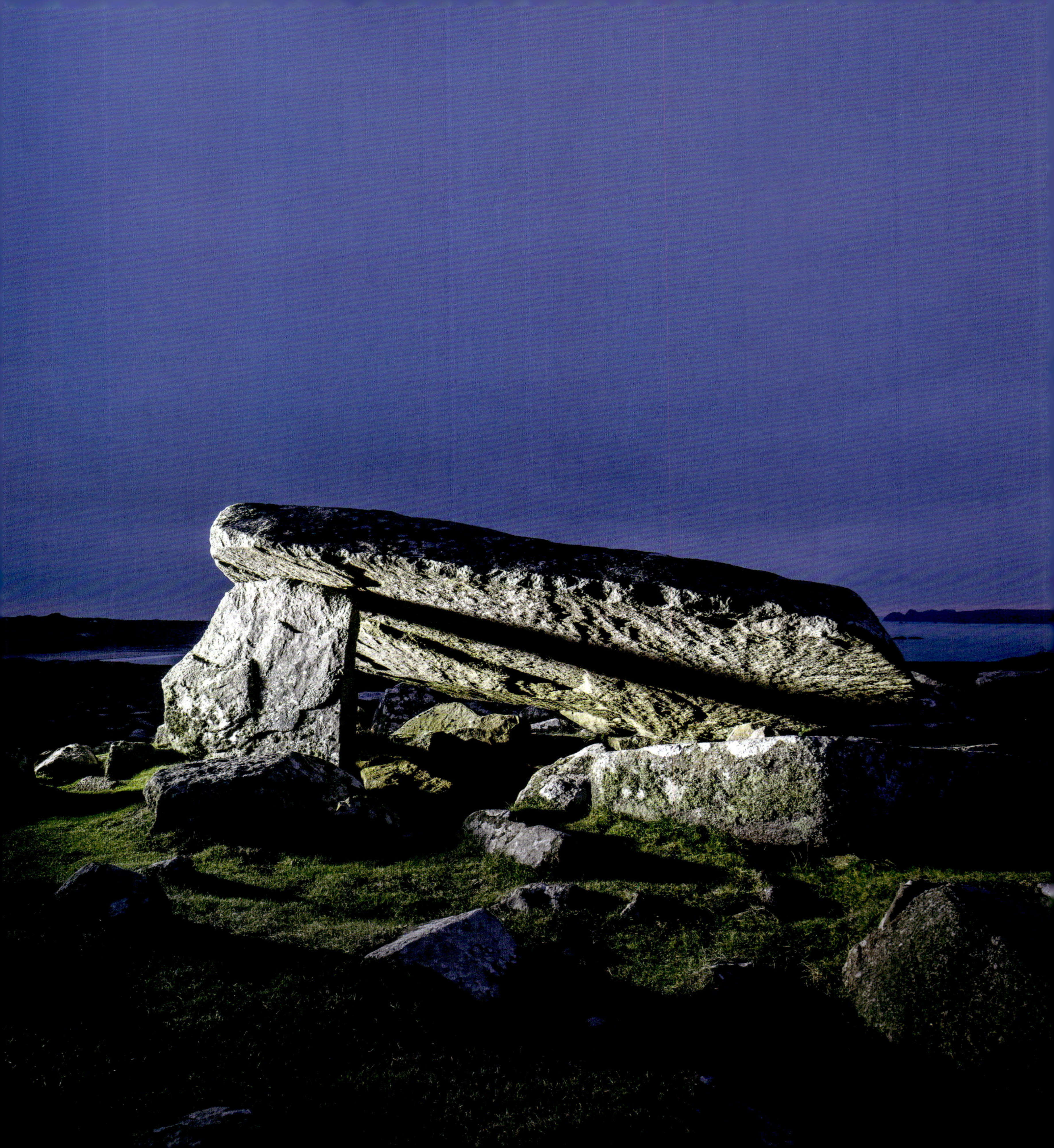

13 DYFED

NOVEMBER 2016–FEBRUARY 2017
DAY 106–126 | 02,753–03,292 KM | 539 KM

The November moon is bright, casting a shadow of my body on the silvery dune grass at the eastern edge of Carmarthen Bay. I'm grateful for the illumination, as I need to cover the miles tonight to make a good start for the next three weeks, tracing the rugged edge of Dyfed, which at 539 walkable kilometres is the longest preserved county in Wales and includes the inlets of Carmarthenshire, the cliff-lined coast of Pembrokeshire and the long seaboard of Ceredigion. I am navigating towards my first objective – a sheltered spot for my tent in the heart of a forest on the way to Carmarthen. My guide is the star at the tip of the Plough constellation, piercing through the eerie monochrome landscape.

A couple of days later my water bottle has a skin of ice when I wake to heatless sunlight under an oak tree at the side of a field near Laugharne. I pack hurriedly, keen to warm up and to see poet Dylan Thomas's boathouse and writing shed. In the first line of the poem 'The White Giant's Thigh', Thomas describes the sound of the curlews accompanying the Laugharne landscape he sees from his window. Today, the estuary is accompanied not by the sound of the curlew but by the zip of helicopter cannon fire. It's one of the dichotomies of the coast that the sound of conflict resides in a landscape of peace. The explosions make flocks of geese screech and rise.

From the Taf Estuary, I follow Carmarthen Bay past Pendine Sands, an expansive flat stretch of beach where Malcolm Campbell set a world land speed record in 1924 in his Sunbeam car Blue Bird. Pendine is also a firing range designated a 'Proof and Experimental Establishment'. From the clifftops, I hear a loud report and turn to watch the smoke from an artillery shell drift cloud-like across the beach's full width. By the afternoon, I reach Monkstone Point where I find the perfect shelter from the cold wind in which to eat my bread and ham. The simple food tastes delicious and a rare moment of warm sun bathes my face.

Approaching Tenby, a contender for the most iconic seaside town in South Wales, I become more self-conscious of my appearance and attempt to discipline my wild hair, remove my mud-covered overtrousers and generally try to look normal. It evidently doesn't work as I'm asked, 'Have you been camping?' as soon as I sit down in a cafe. Tenby is so picturesque that I find it problematic to take a photo that doesn't look like a postcard, especially in today's hard winter light, beautiful though it is.

On the seventh day in Dyfed, as the mists blow, Caldey Island vanishes and re-emerges dreamily. Sourcing food and water is more challenging because most tourist facilities are shut in the off-season. I'm relieved that Freshwater East public toilet has a tap so I can fill up with water for the next day and a closed holiday village unlocks their shop for me to get some noodles, oatcakes and frozen cheese.

Late December means that the days are short and the nights long. To keep up the pace, I begin to walk regularly in the dark with a head torch. Milford Haven oil refinery towers glitter in the distance like a magical city, and flashing bells and Santas dance in the pitch-dark in bungalow windows as I approach Pembroke. I'm knackered, and most days I only take fifteen minutes for lunch as it's too cold to stop; otherwise, I move all day. As I pass the oil refinery in the rain, I find it hard to think of photography as I only want to sleep. I've nearly walked 3,000 kilometres now. Exhausted, freezing and soaked to the skin, I reach Milford Haven train station, grateful to be heading home to my family for Christmas.

I return to the trail at the start of January, refreshed and excited to explore the cathedral city of St Davids. It's located in a hollow, tower and all, so as I approach from the cliff path, it's wholly obscured until the last minute – a ruse to deter Viking raids. Despite being remote geographically, St Davids was central to ecclesiastical history and one of

Opposite:

Coetan Arthur, a Neolithic burial chamber believed to date from around 4000 BC, Porth Mawr the most important sites of pilgrimage in the Middle Ages. As I walk around, I discover that the current cathedral was built from 1180 to 1220, and the floor of the nave slopes nearly 4 metres between the east and west ends due to subsidence. Looking up, I'm transfixed by the intricately carved Irish oak ceiling, unlike anything I've seen before. The tangible sense of ancient pilgrimage is there in the quality of devotional ornament from which the building is made. As I leave the cathedral, there's not a soul within the lovingly tended grounds; the only motion is the flight of a line of geese above a distant horizon.

Soon I reach Pen Dal-aderyn, the westernmost point of mainland Wales. There's almost nobody living on the edge here and the built-up parts are a tiny fraction, so I often walk in solitude. I enjoy the random conversation that good weather brings when the paths get busier, but the silence brings a deeper connection to the landscape, and I become attuned to spotting opportunities for photography. Without people, the nature surrounding me becomes the sole subject and focus of my lens, and I'm fascinated by the endless possibilities at hand.

Two days later, as I'm night-hiking again, Strumble Head Lighthouse pulses in the darkness in front, guiding me along the complex coastal paths like the North Star. The steeply concave ground makes it feel disconcertingly as if I'm on the brink of a vertical cliff under the torchlight. It's hard to judge distance while wearing a head torch, so I take it very slowly, testing the ground in front of me with trekking poles. Despite the caution, I slip on a patch of gravel on a smooth cliff step in the darkness; my falling body weight buckles my right trekking pole, which splinters, snapping in two. My body, with its heavy pack, pivots, but the left pole holds firmly to prevent me from falling down the cliff.

Shaken from the fall, I put the tent up as soon as I find a patch of flat ground. I'm behind schedule due to the difficult terrain so I need to start at 5 a.m. I jog on the spot to keep warm while brushing my teeth. The pre-dawn sky is swept with rays from the lighthouse even though it's not visible behind the black headland. As I walk closer, the beam dips in and out of view until it's near enough to illuminate the rocks around me with each flash. As dawn breaks I can see how the rocky tors and heather give this area of Pembrokeshire a Scottish mountain character. I hear moaning far below the sea cliff I'm walking along. To my astonishment, the sound source is a couple of dozen grey seals engaged in comical-looking grunting matches over which rock makes the ideal pillow.

The next day at Dinas Head the gale-force wind throws me about with rain stinging my face. I regularly have to stop and lean on my one remaining pole not to be blown over. At one point I'm so worried about being driven over the cliff edge that I walk on the inland side of a farmer's wire fence, grabbing on to it with every step. The steep clifftop paths are reduced to slippy mud troughs which, combined with the weather, makes this week the toughest section so far. I console myself with the thought that the drama I'm capturing with my camera is only possible in stormy weather, and that in the summer these paths would be as carefree as my time on the Cornish coast. But the strong wind and rain make it almost impossible to take photographs of the tumultuous sea, and I resort to a shutter speed of 1/2500 seconds and ISO 4000 to freeze the action in the gloom.

On my last day in Pembrokeshire, the sixteenth day in Dyfed, I photograph the inky-black weather front approaching while being pummelled with hail at Newport Sands and sense the rumble of waves far below from the clifftops past Moylgrove. I cross the bridge over the Teifi to bid Pembrokeshire farewell and head into Ceredigion, where the coastline by Cardigan Bay heads north-east with satisfying directness towards Snowdonia / Eryri.

Near New Quay, I stop by a stream to make a brew from the water source. It's sunny but only just above freezing, so as soon as I take off my backpack, I reach for my warm jacket – but it's missing! I frantically unpack everything – still nothing – and reluctantly retrace my steps along the trail, hoping to find it. After a couple of hours back along the path the way I've come, I see the jacket waving at me mockingly from a bramble that had hooked it out of my backpack like a skilled pickpocket. All in all, four hours more walking than I'd planned in the morning!

At the end of my third week in Dyfed, I pass through hilly, misty woods and mossy valley streams to arrive at the first bridge at Machynlleth. I stop to rest under an oak tree, peeling off my muddy, wet socks; not having passed anyone for miles, I absent-mindedly give them a sniff. At that very moment a woman passes and wishes me a good afternoon. As night falls, my breath looks like cigarette smoke under the head torch; I'm so busy amusing myself by pretending to be a steam train that I nearly don't see a cattle grid. I'm in grave danger of becoming far too comfortable with my own company!

Opposite, from top left:

Robin, Kidwelly Quay

River Towy, near Carmarthen

From bottom left:

Machynys, Llanelli

Bridge in a field: section of the original wooden Loughor railway viaduct designed by Brunel in 1852

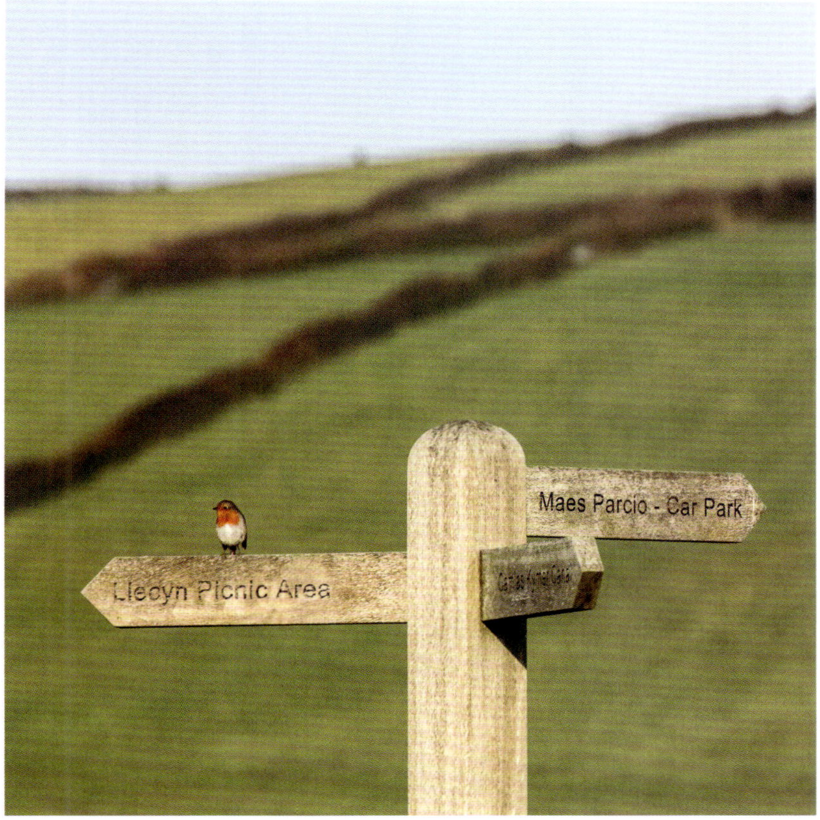
Maes Parcio - Car Park
Llecyn Picnic Area

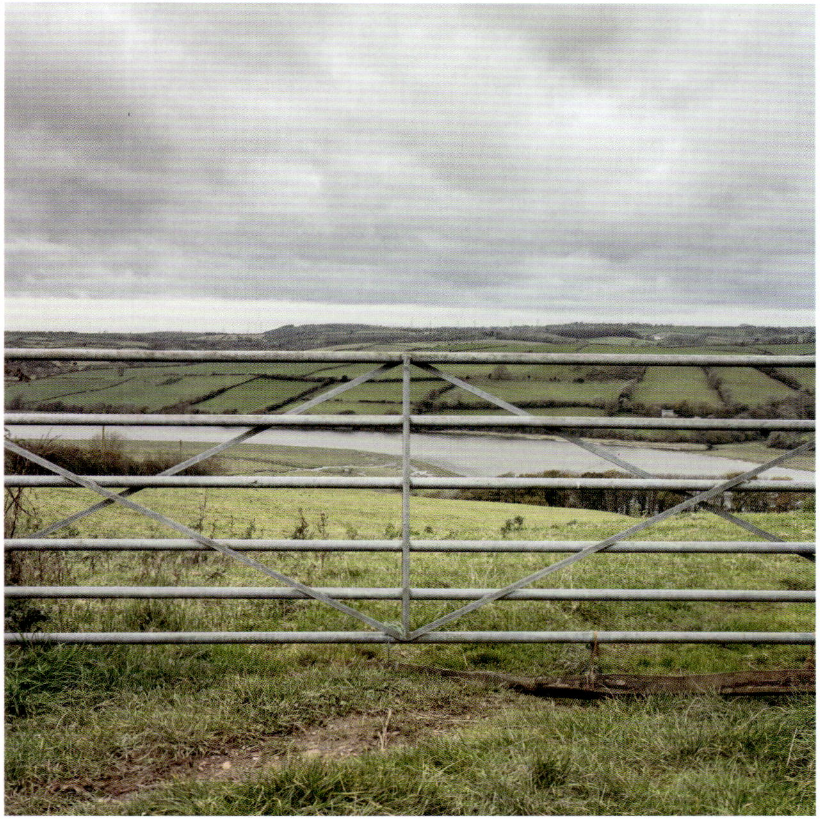

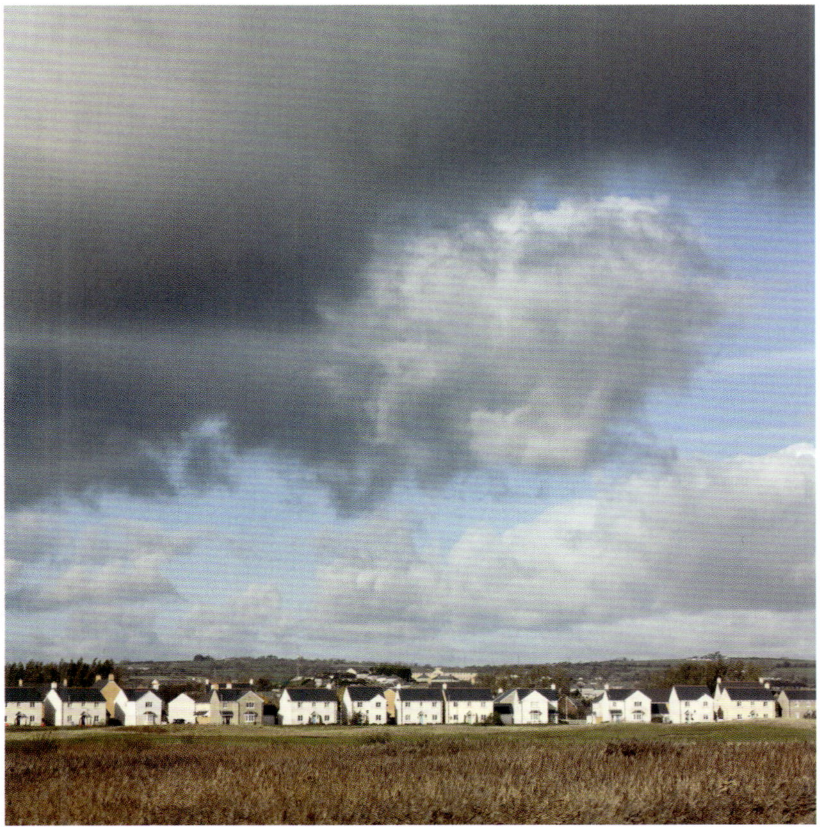

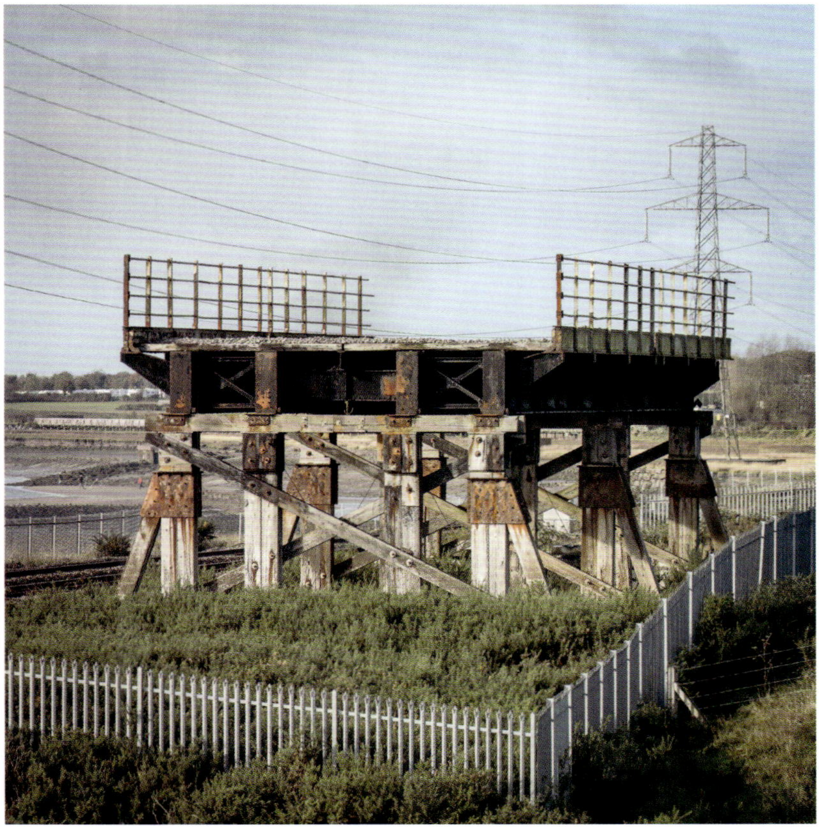

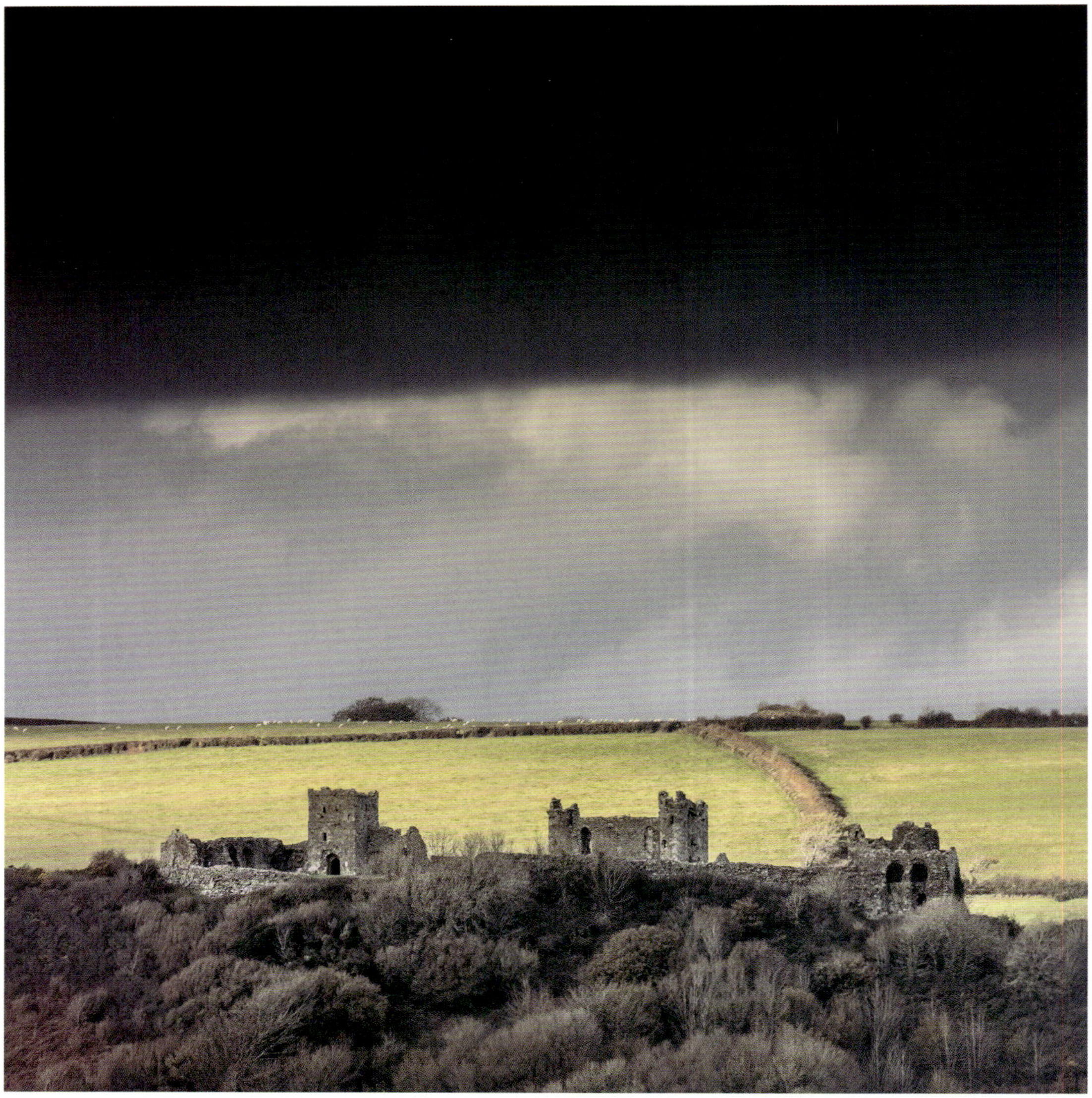

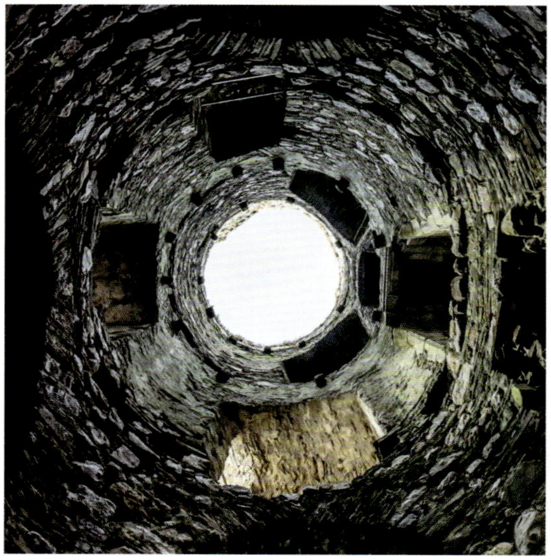

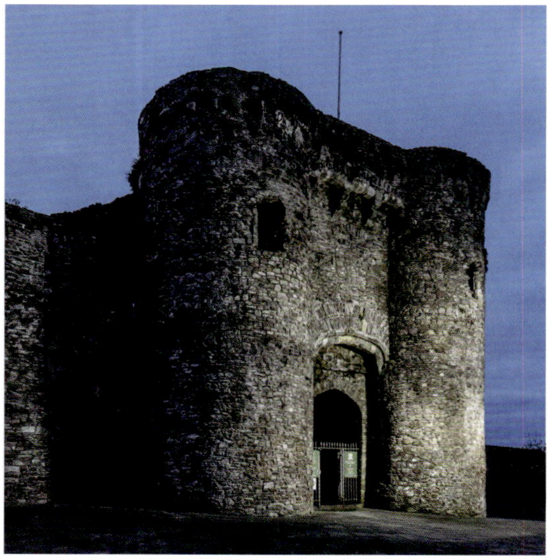

From top left:

Llansteffan Castle, built by the Normans after 1100 as part of their invasion of Wales. Llywelyn the Great recaptured the castle for the Welsh in 1215 and the castle was captured twice by the forces of Owain Glyndŵr in the 1400s

South-east tower, Kidwelly Castle, built by the Normans. The present remains of the castle date from the early twelfth century. Created as a defence against the Welsh, the castle fell to them several times in the twelfth century

Carmarthen Castle, built by the Normans, was captured and destroyed on several occasions before being rebuilt in stone during the 1190s. The castle was captured by Owain Glyndŵr in 1405. During the Civil War it was captured by Parliamentary forces and dismantled by order of Oliver Cromwell in the mid-1600s

Opposite:

Dylan Thomas Boathouse, Laugharne, in which the poet lived with his family between 1949 and 1953

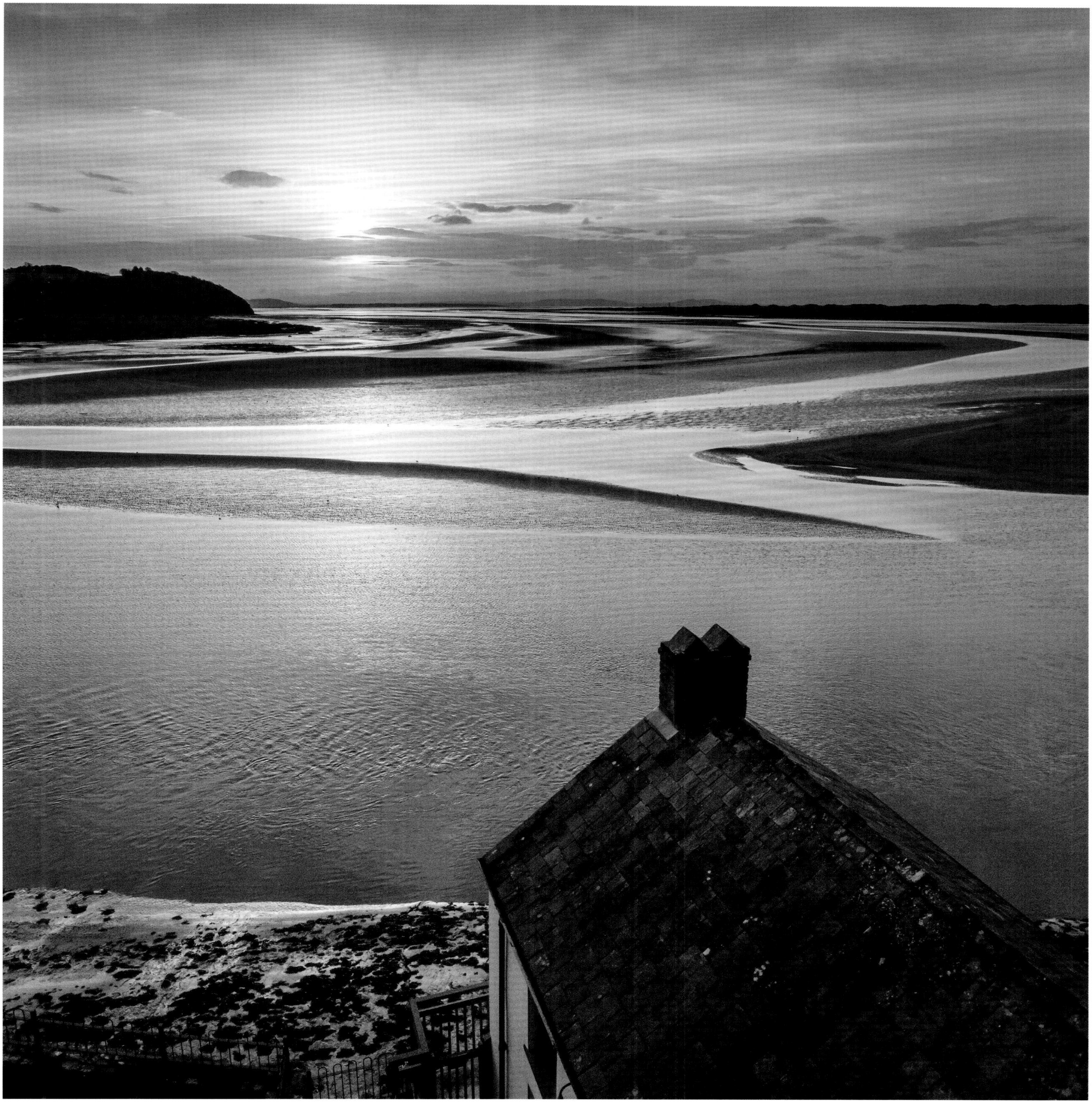

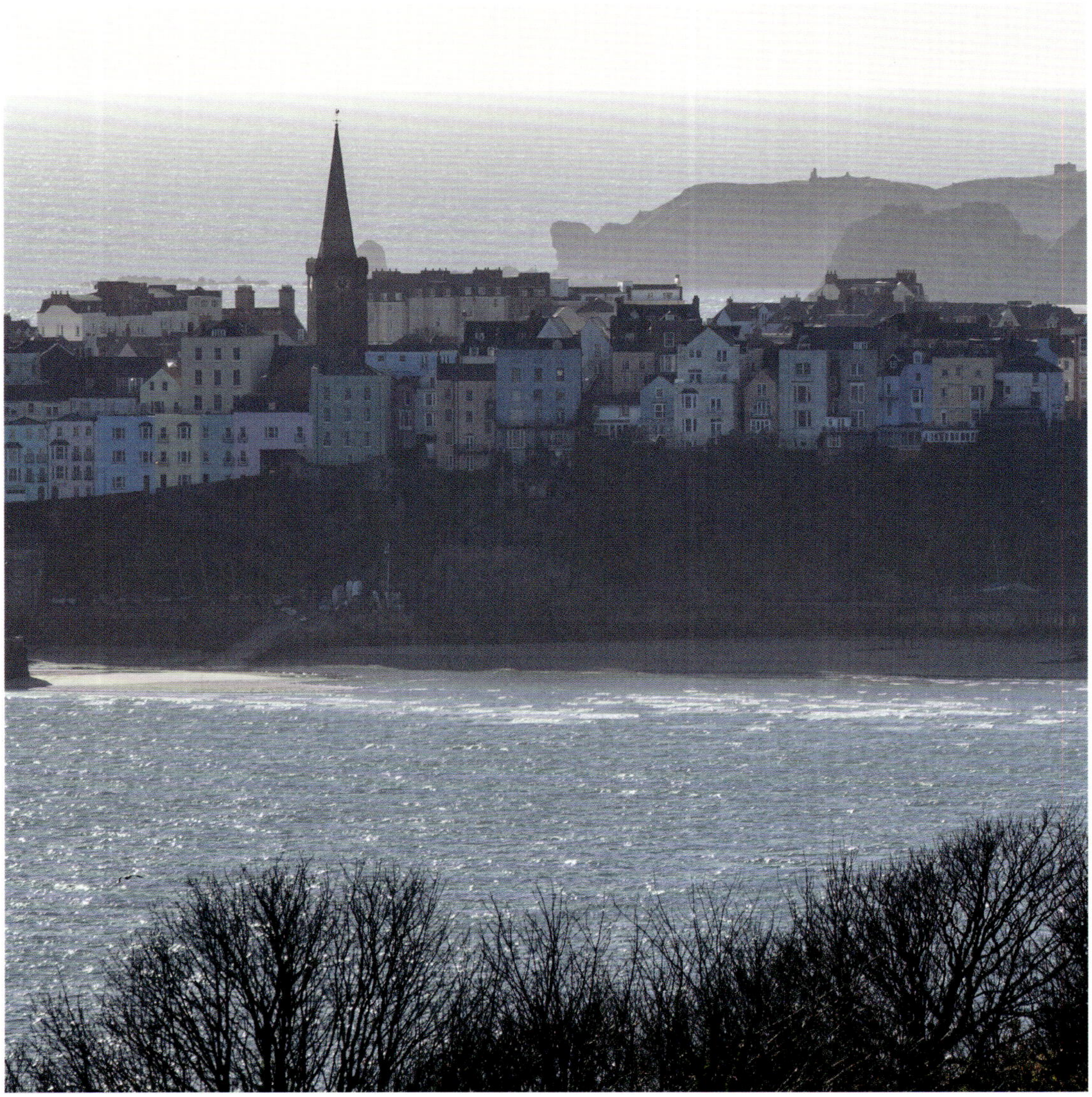

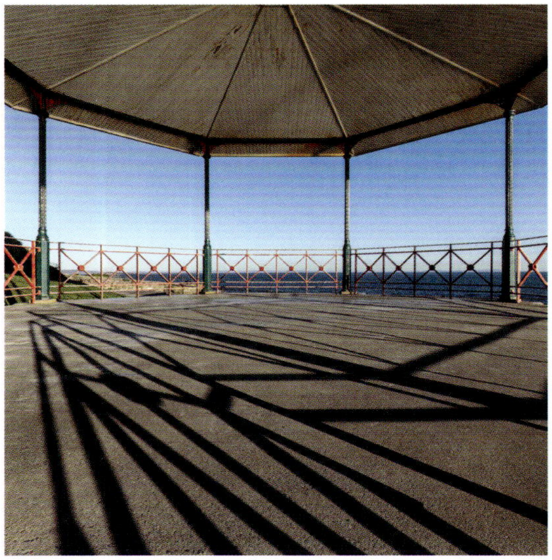

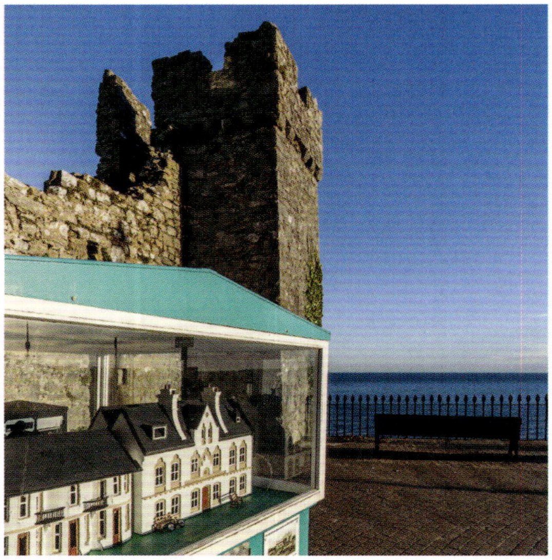

From top left:

St Mary's Church, Tenby

Winter light, Tenby bandstand

Southerndown Home for Blind Babies collection box by the medieval town walls, Tenby

Opposite, clockwise from top left:

Sentry box, Castlemartin Range East

Seascape, St Govan's Head

Air Defence Range, Manorbier

St Govan's Chapel, built into the side of a limestone cliff in the thirteenth century. Under the chapel is a huge cave system, Ogof Gofan, accessible by abseiling down the cliff

Church Rock and Broad Haven Beach

Sunrise over Caldey Island Lighthouse

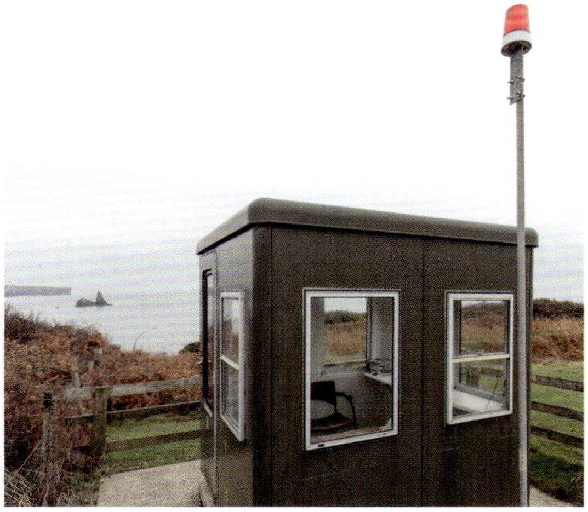

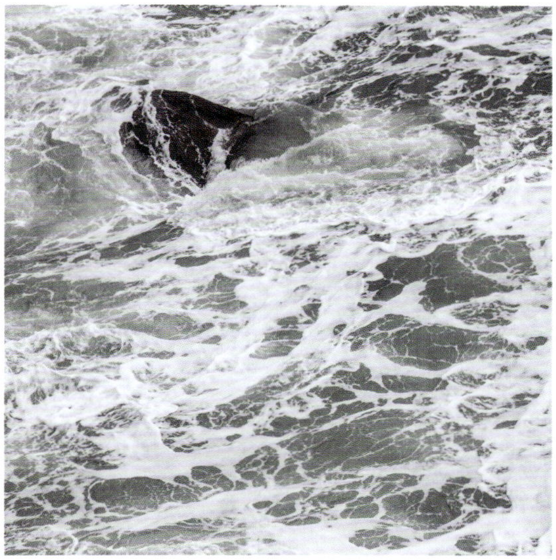

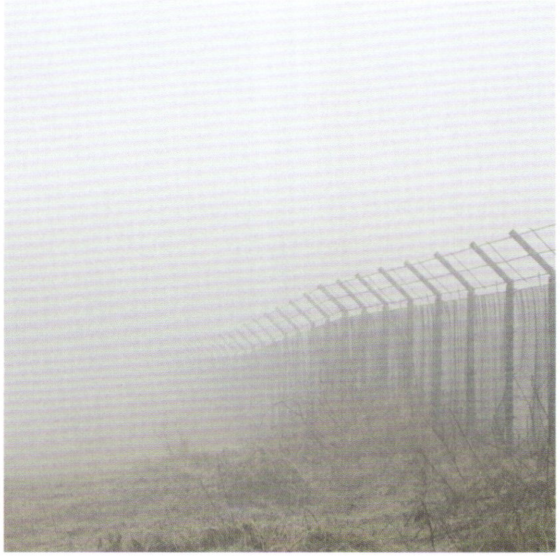

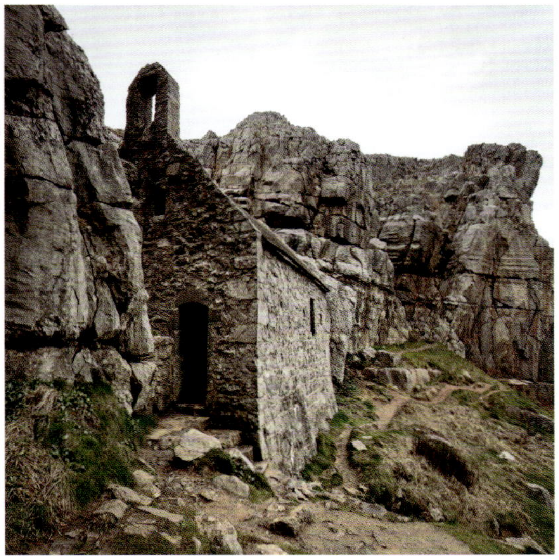

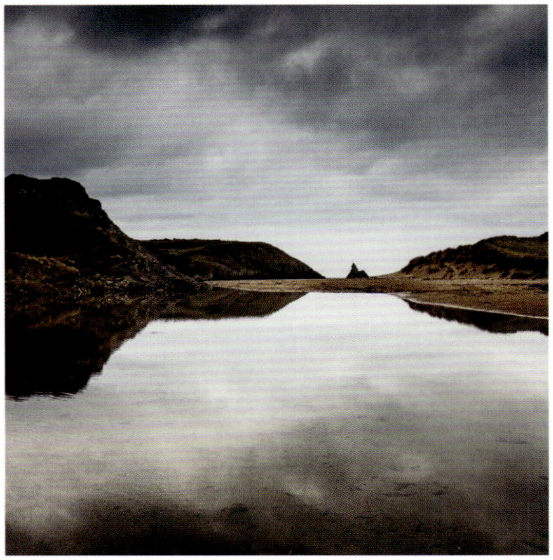

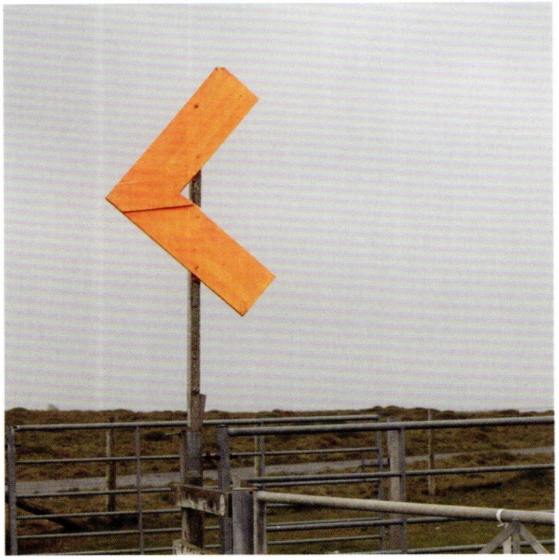

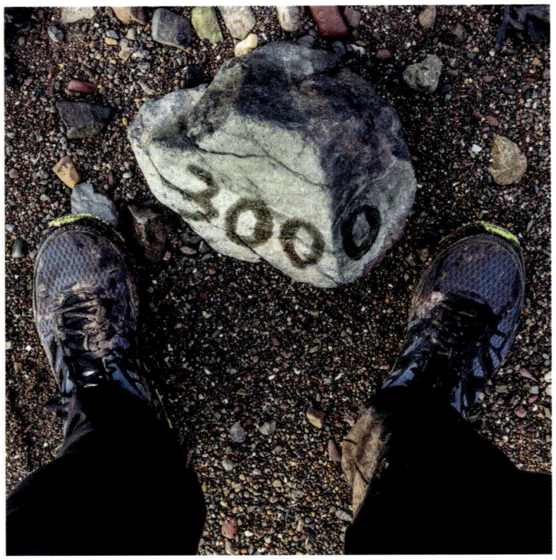

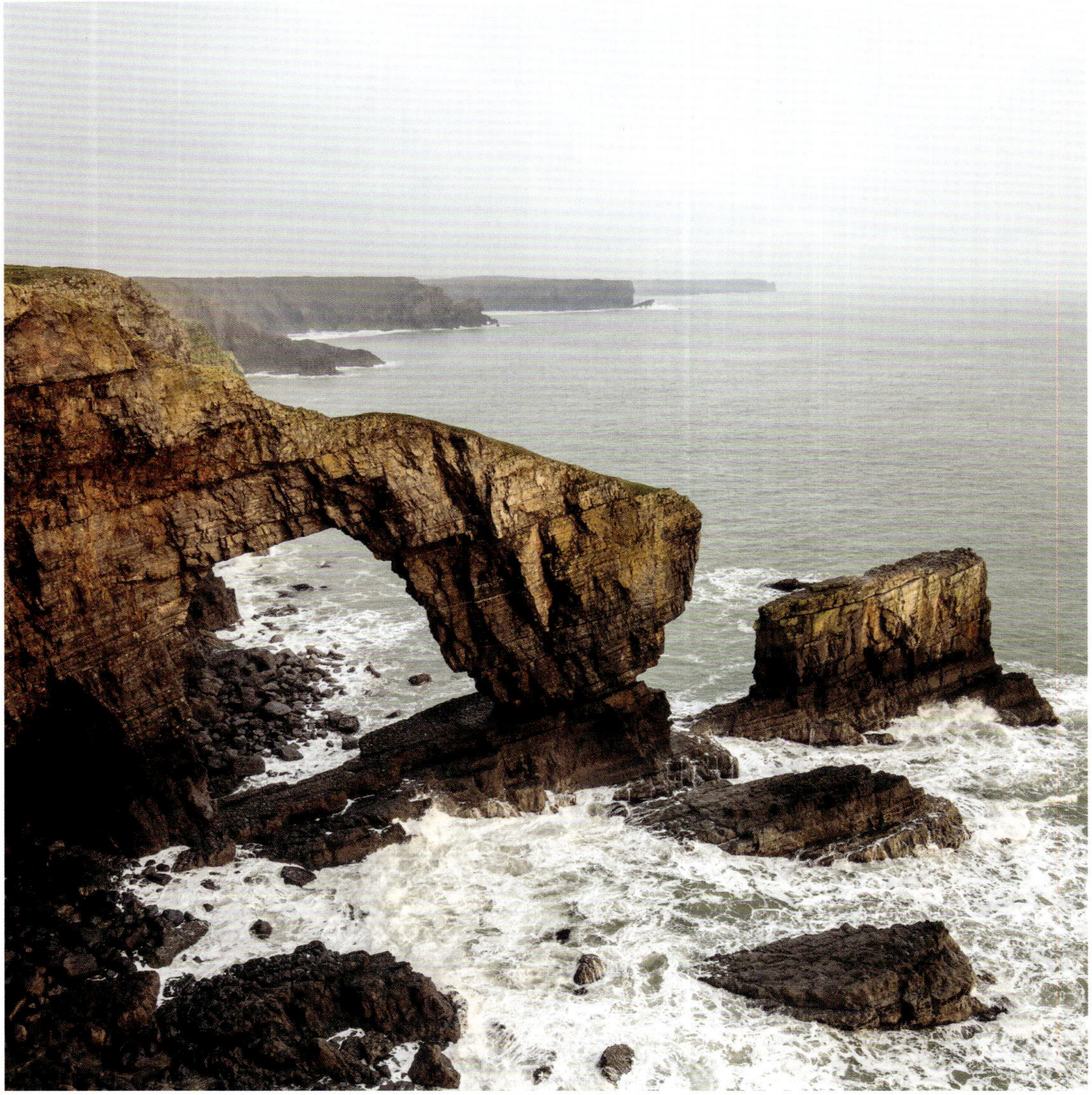

From top left:

Marker, Castlemartin Range East

Gann Beach, Pembrokeshire: 3,000 kilometres walked since St Paul's, London

The Green Bridge of Wales, a natural arch formed from limestone

Opposite, from top left:

The Old Lighthouse, St Ann's Head, Pembrokeshire

High contrast: Martello Tower, Pembroke Dock

From bottom left:

Dragon LNG Terminal, Milford Haven

Yellow and blue: Pembroke Dock

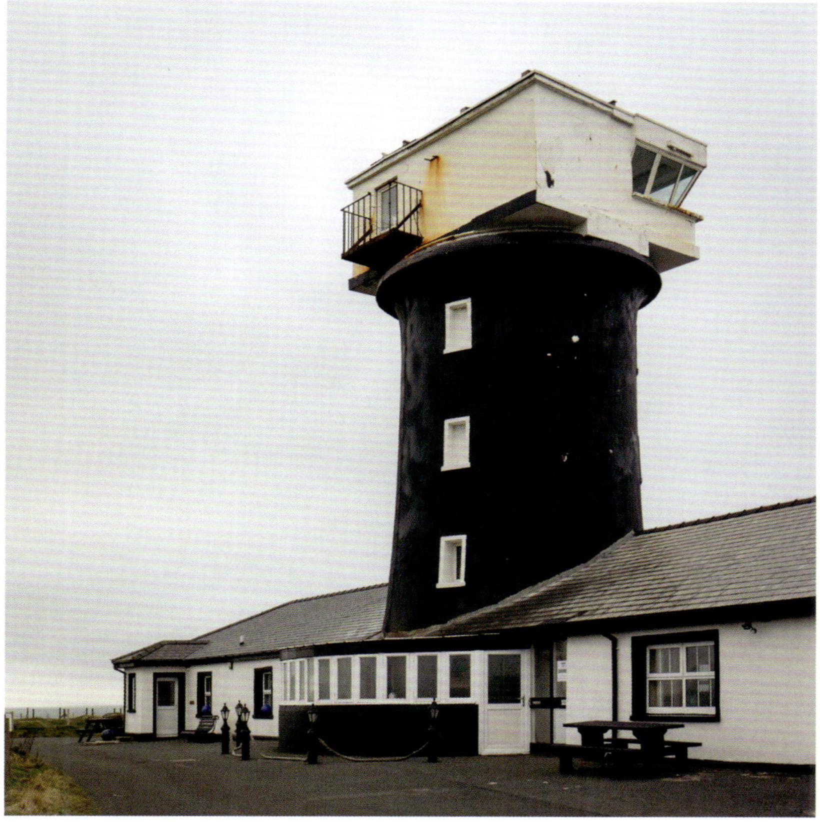

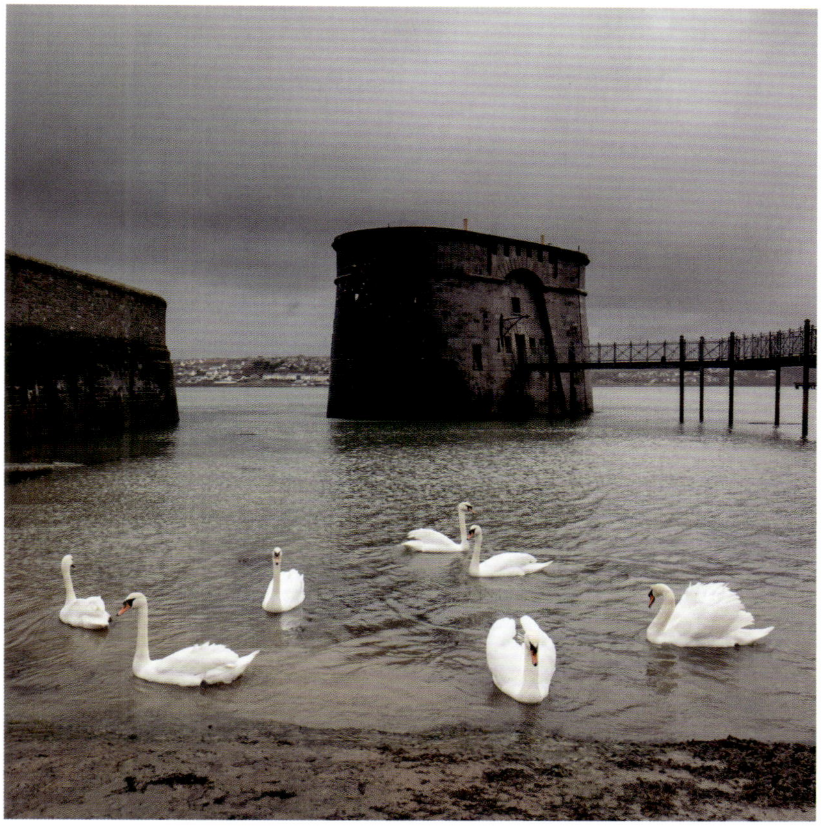

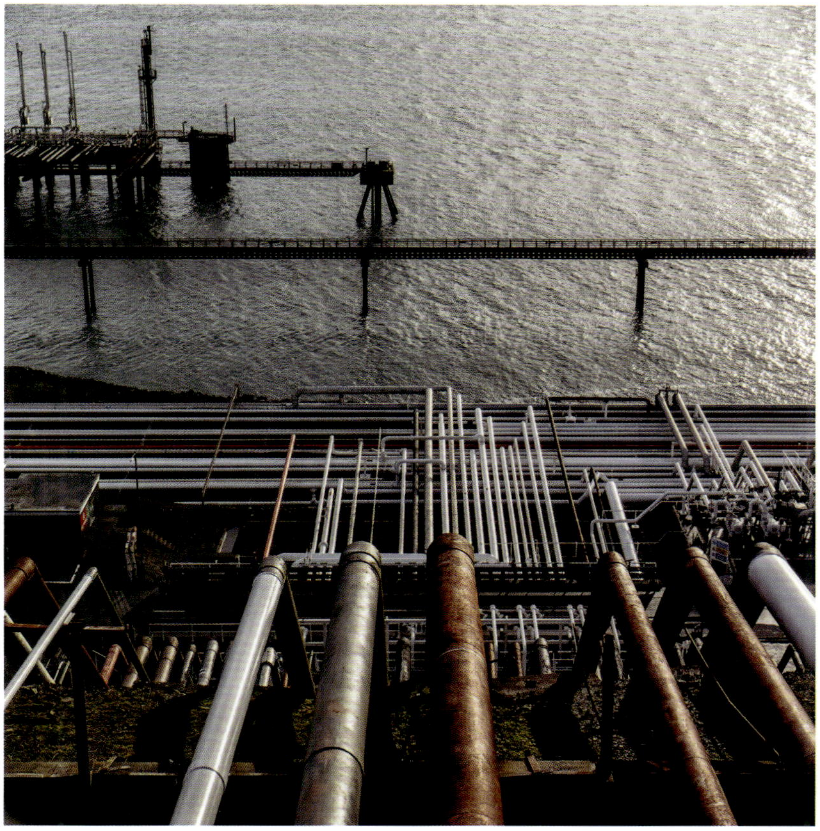

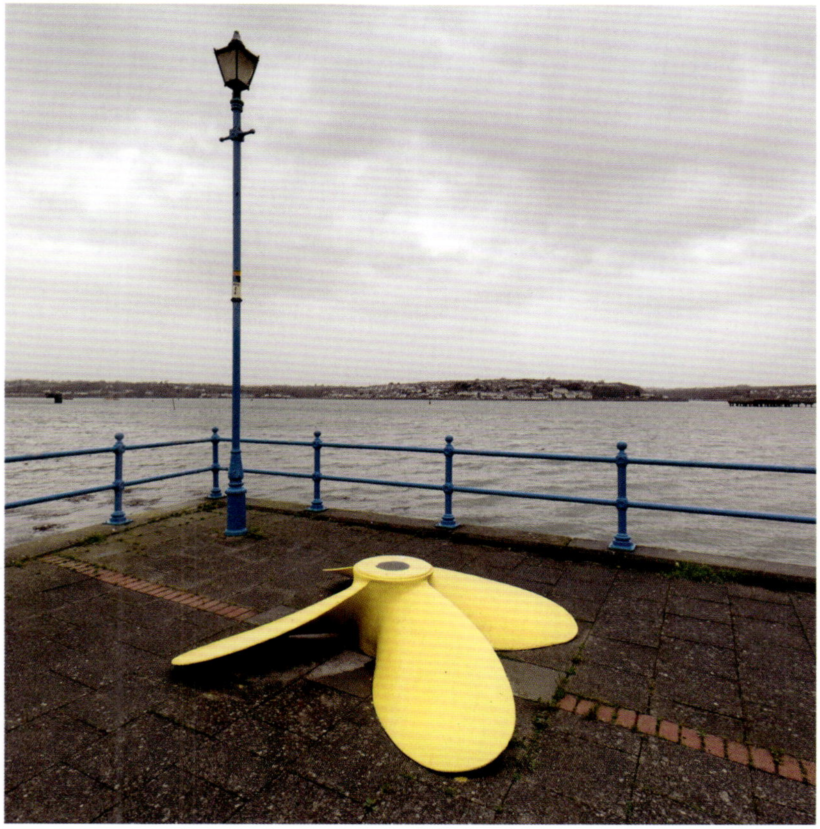

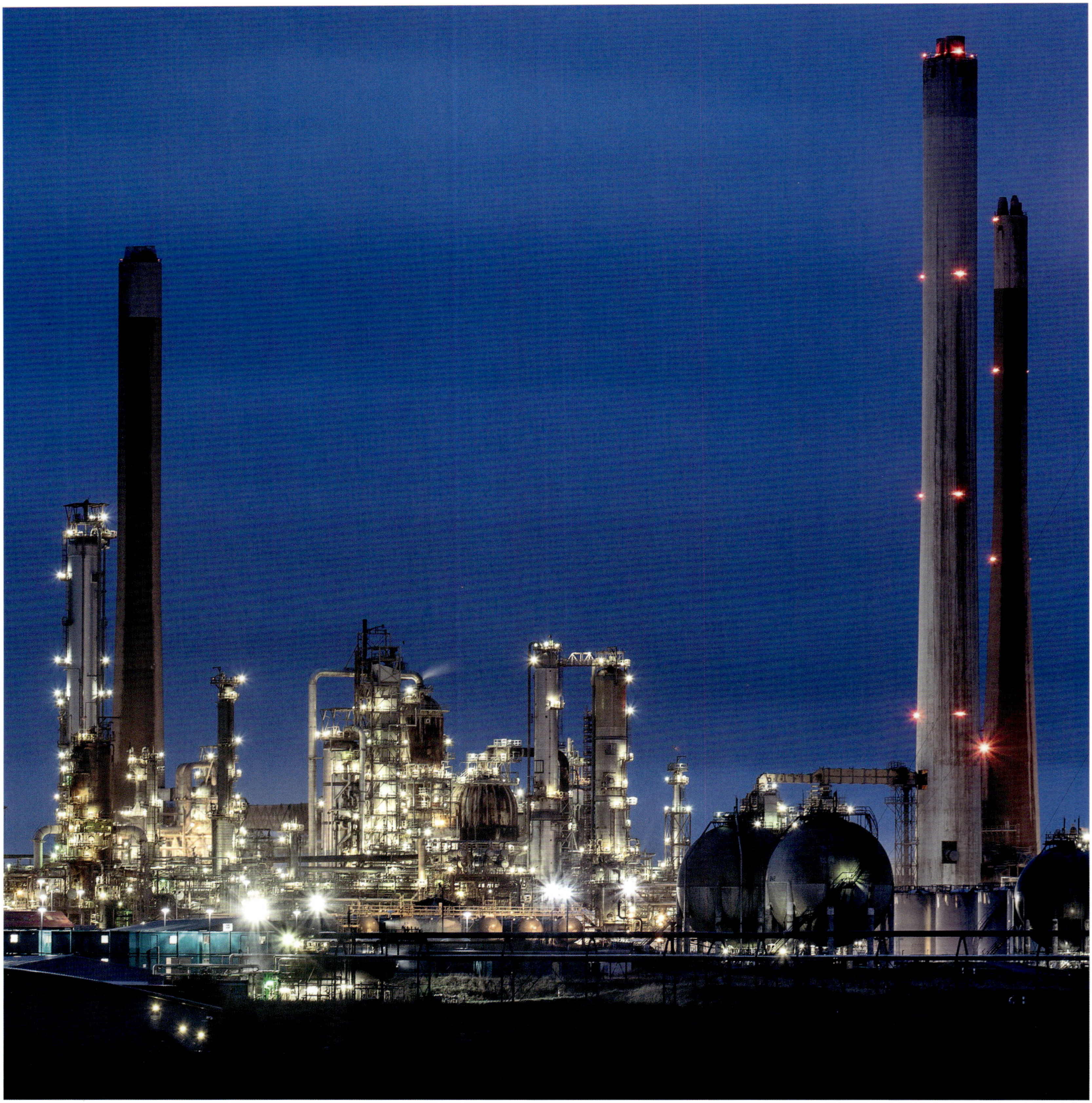

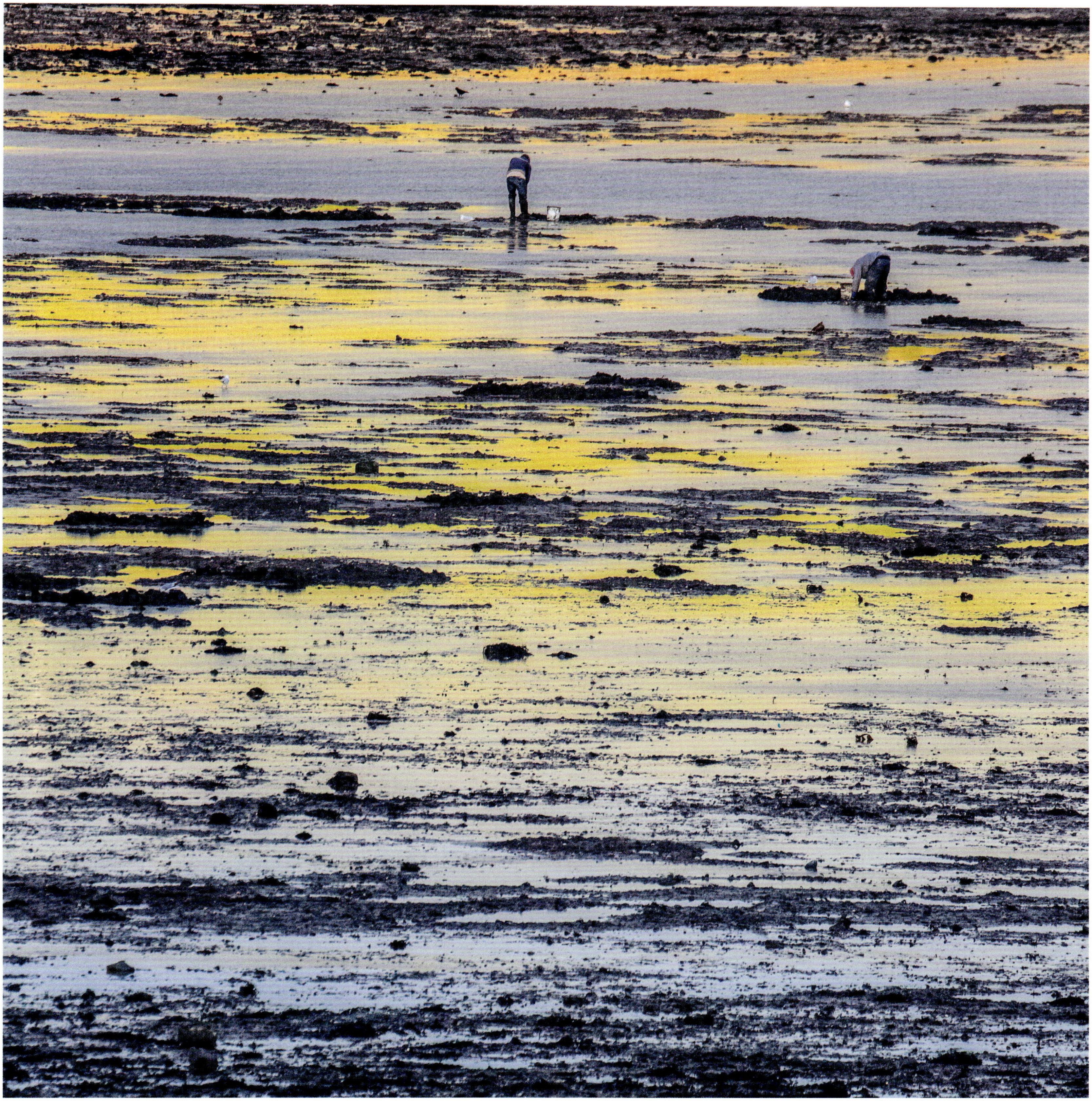

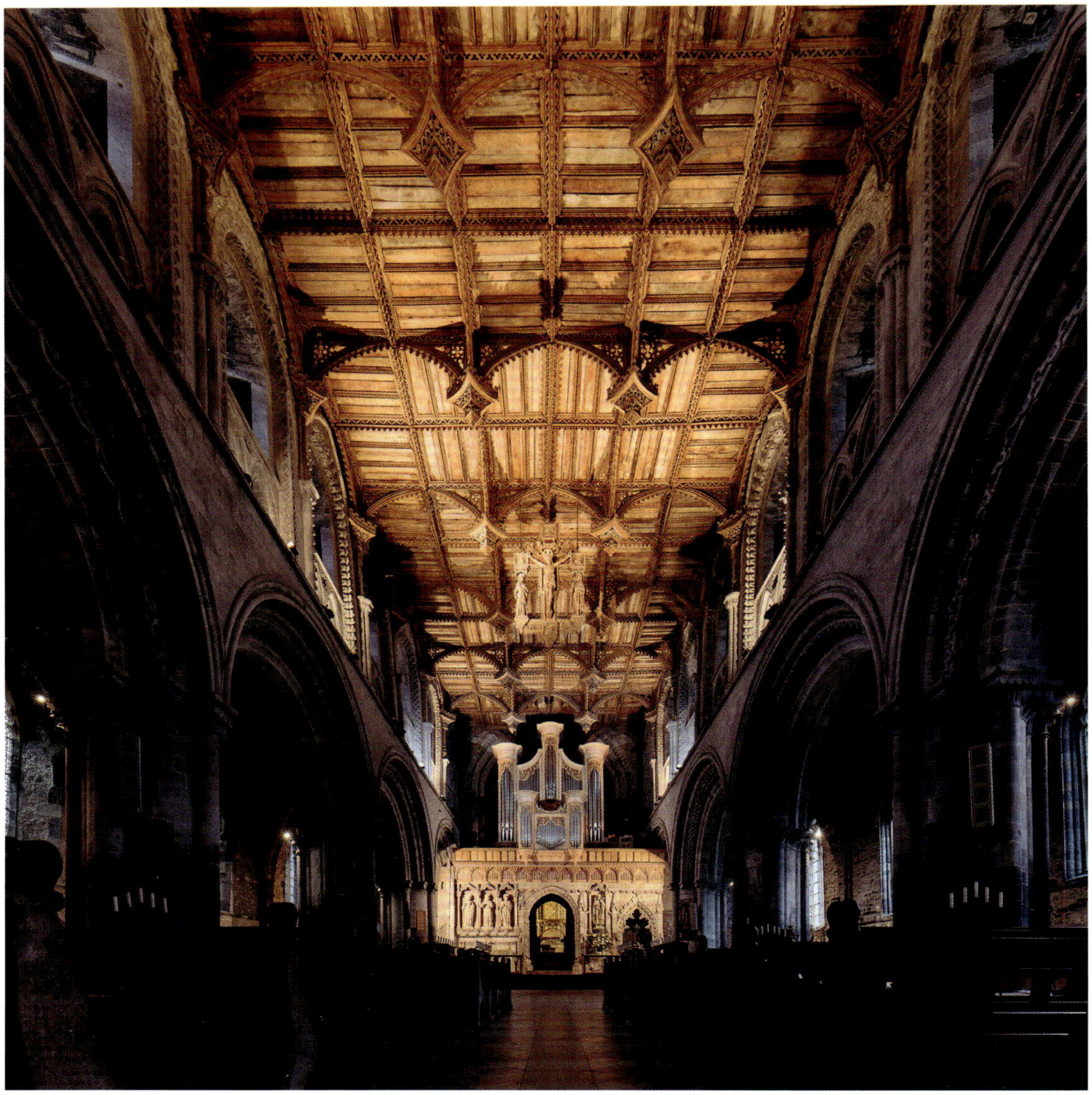
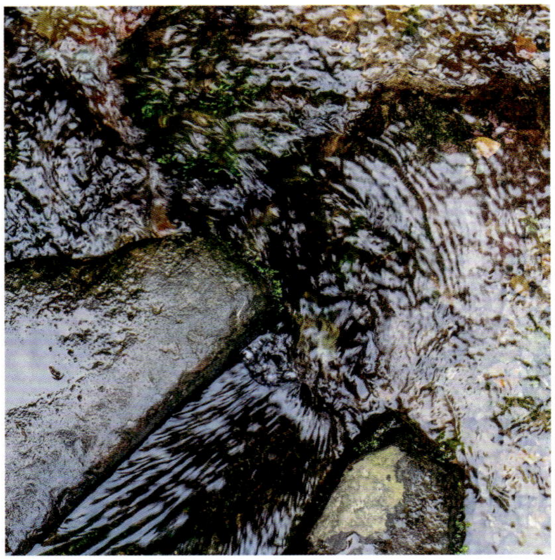
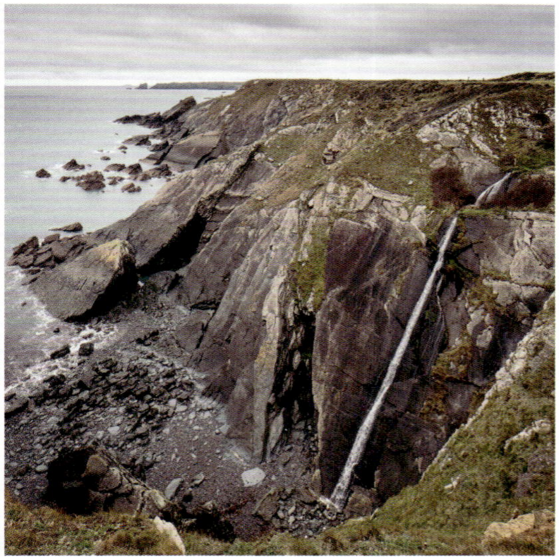
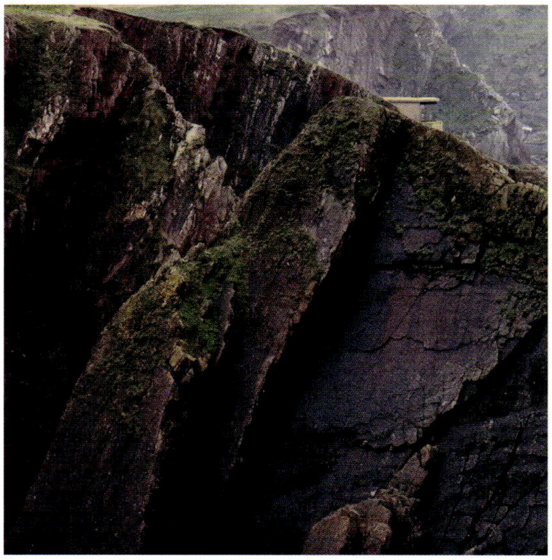
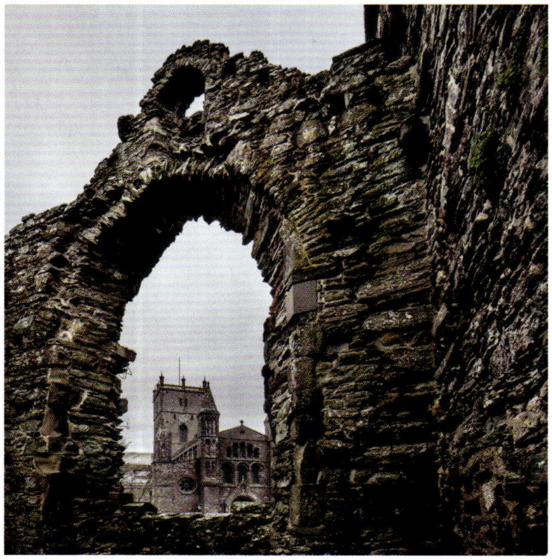
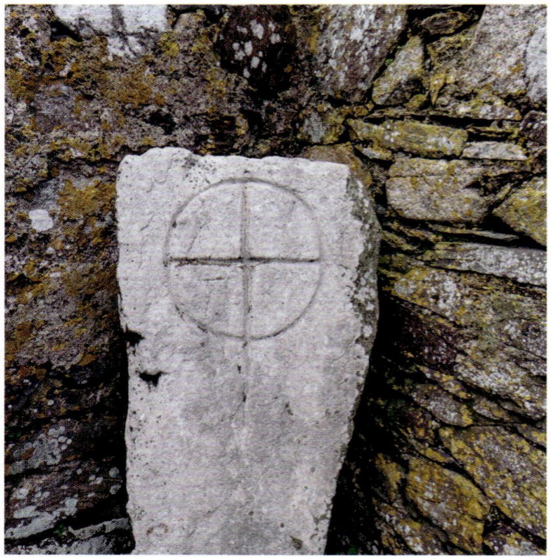

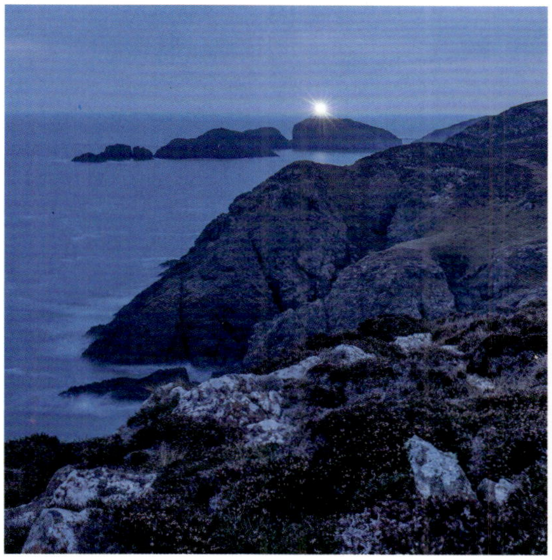

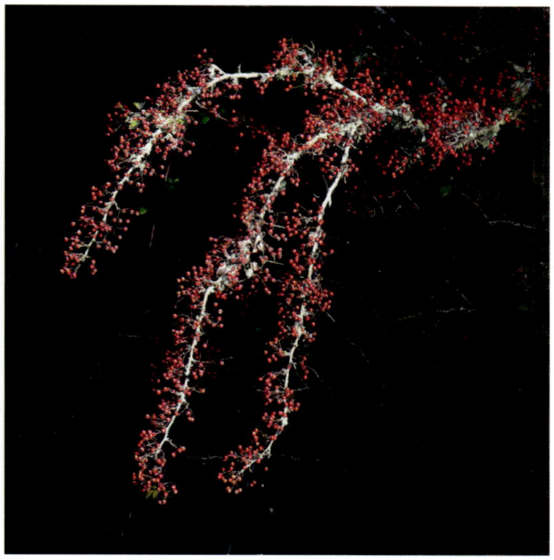

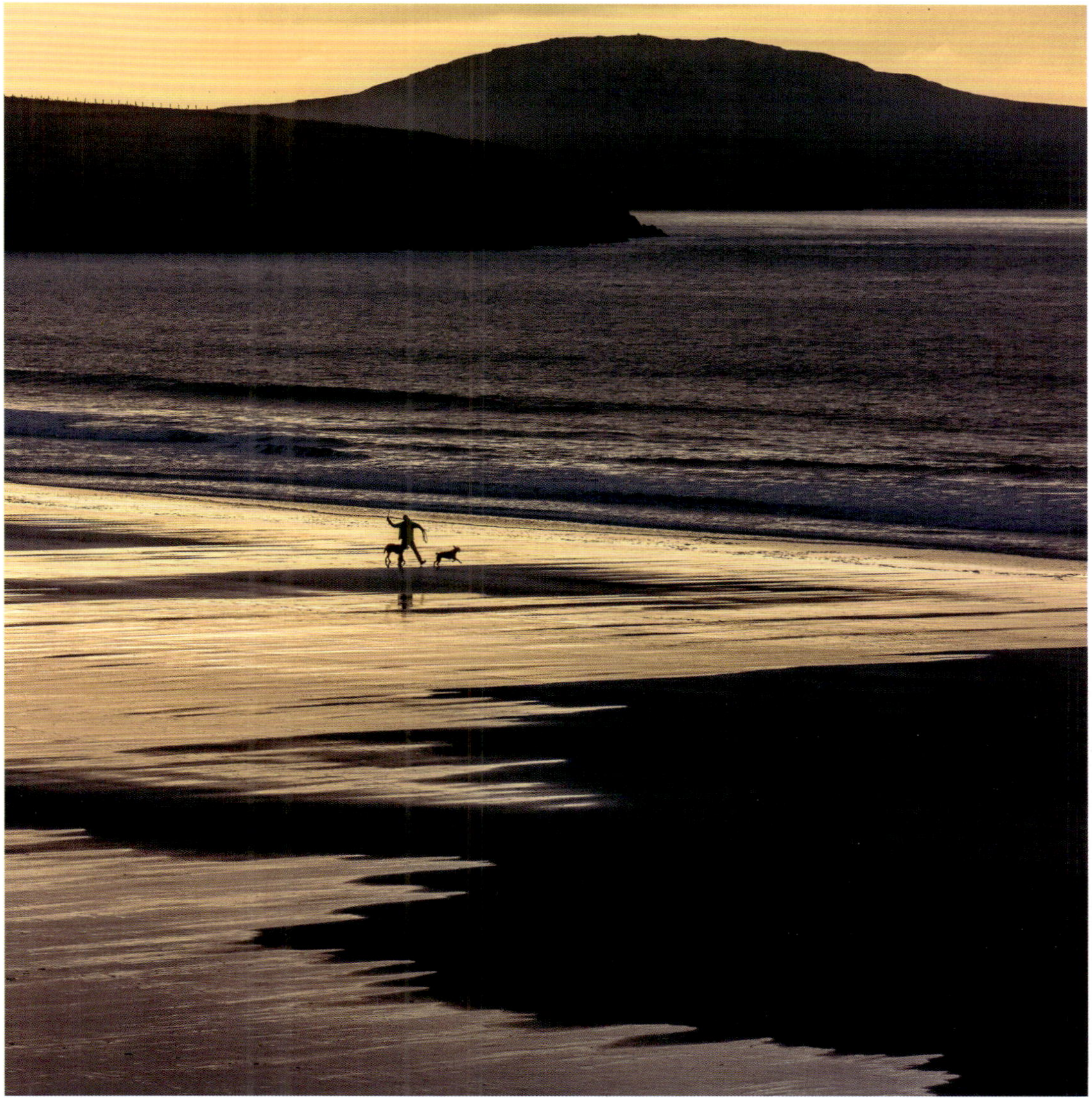

Previous, from left to right:

Pembroke oil refinery at dusk

Digging for bait, Gann Beach, Pembrokeshire

Opposite, clockwise from top left:

Irish oak ceiling constructed from 1530 to 1540 above the nave of St David's Cathedral

St Non's Well, said to have sprung up during a storm when St David was born, about AD 500. Its waters are reputed to have healing properties

Waterfall, Watery Bay, Marloes

St Non's Cross, seventh to ninth century, St Non's Chapel

St David's Cathedral from the Bishop's Palace

Second World War searchlight bunker, Angle Peninsula

From top left:

Strumble Head Lighthouse at dawn

Hawthorn berries, Kidwelly Quay

Last light, Whitesands Bay

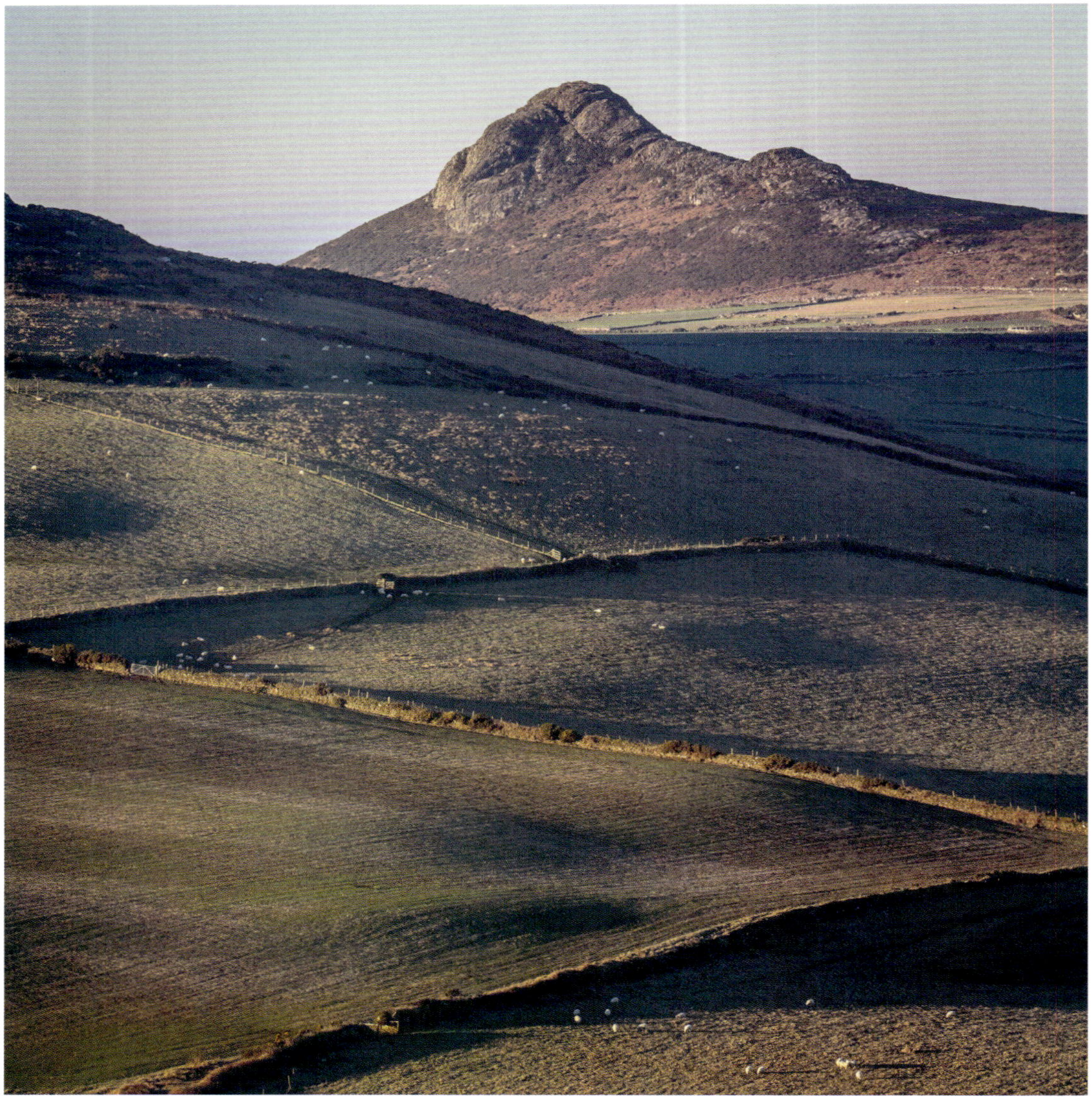

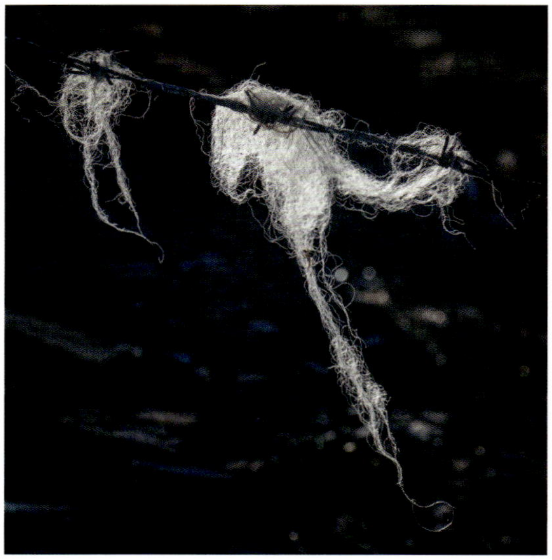

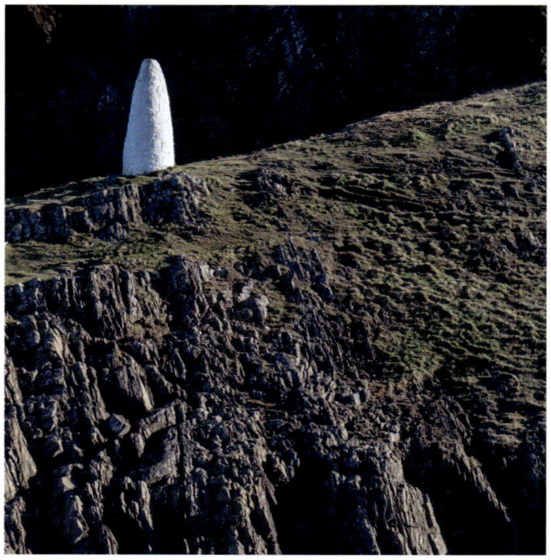

From top left:

Carn Perfedd

Snagged: Carn Penberry

Northern navigation beacon, Porthgain

Opposite:

Venus above camp at Penbwchdy, Pembrokeshire. Glow from Ireland across the sea

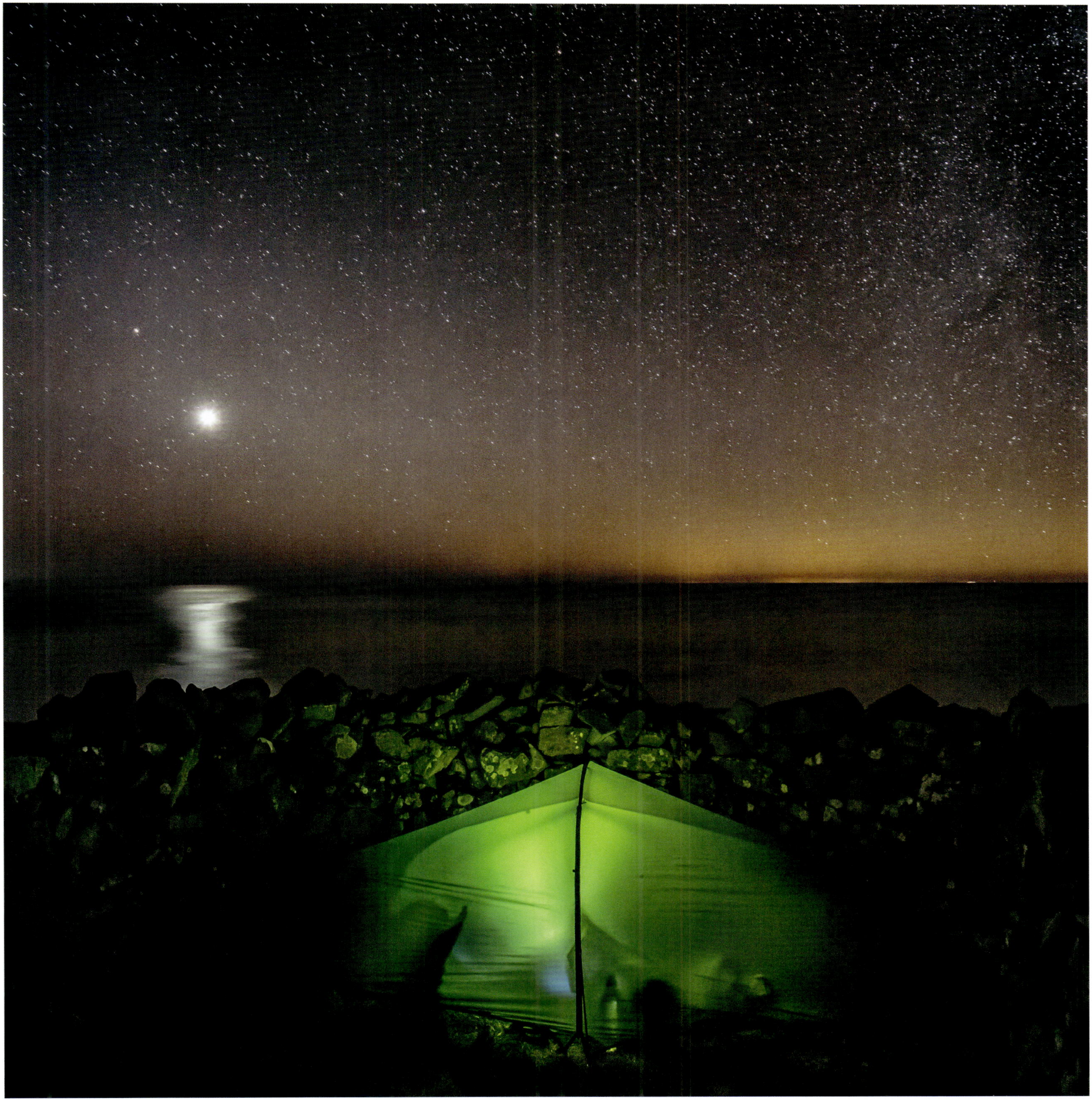

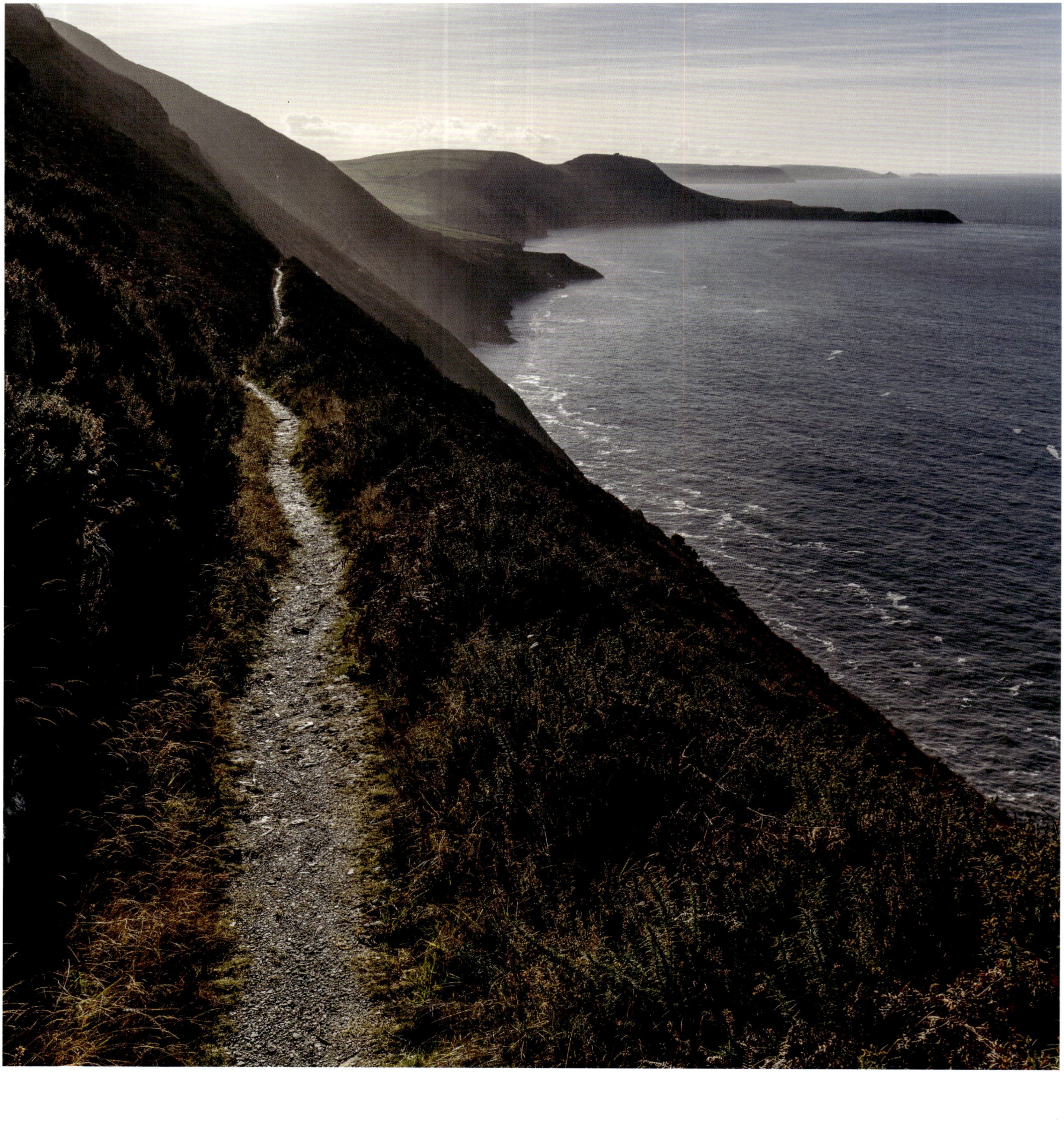

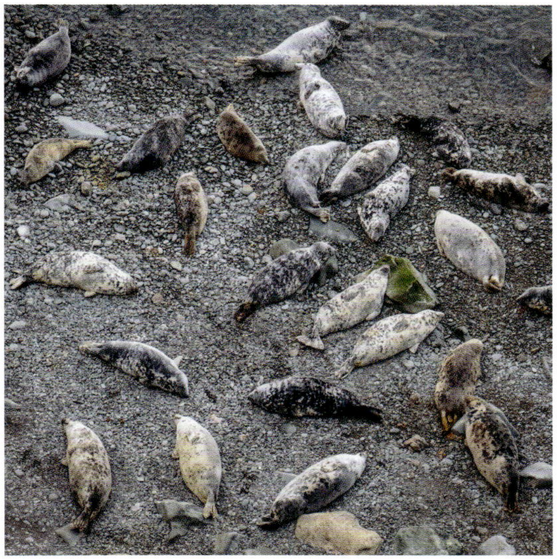

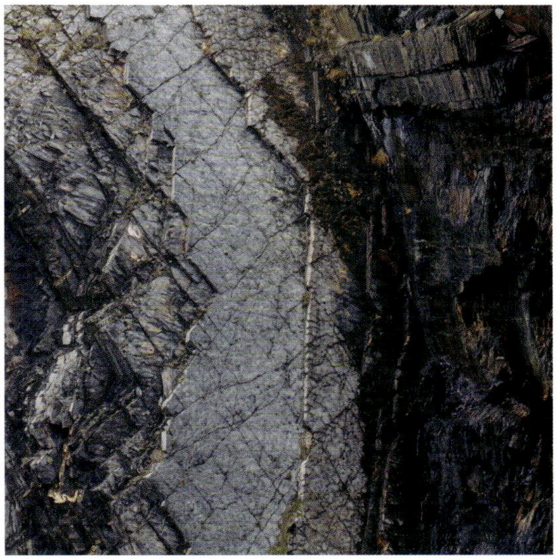

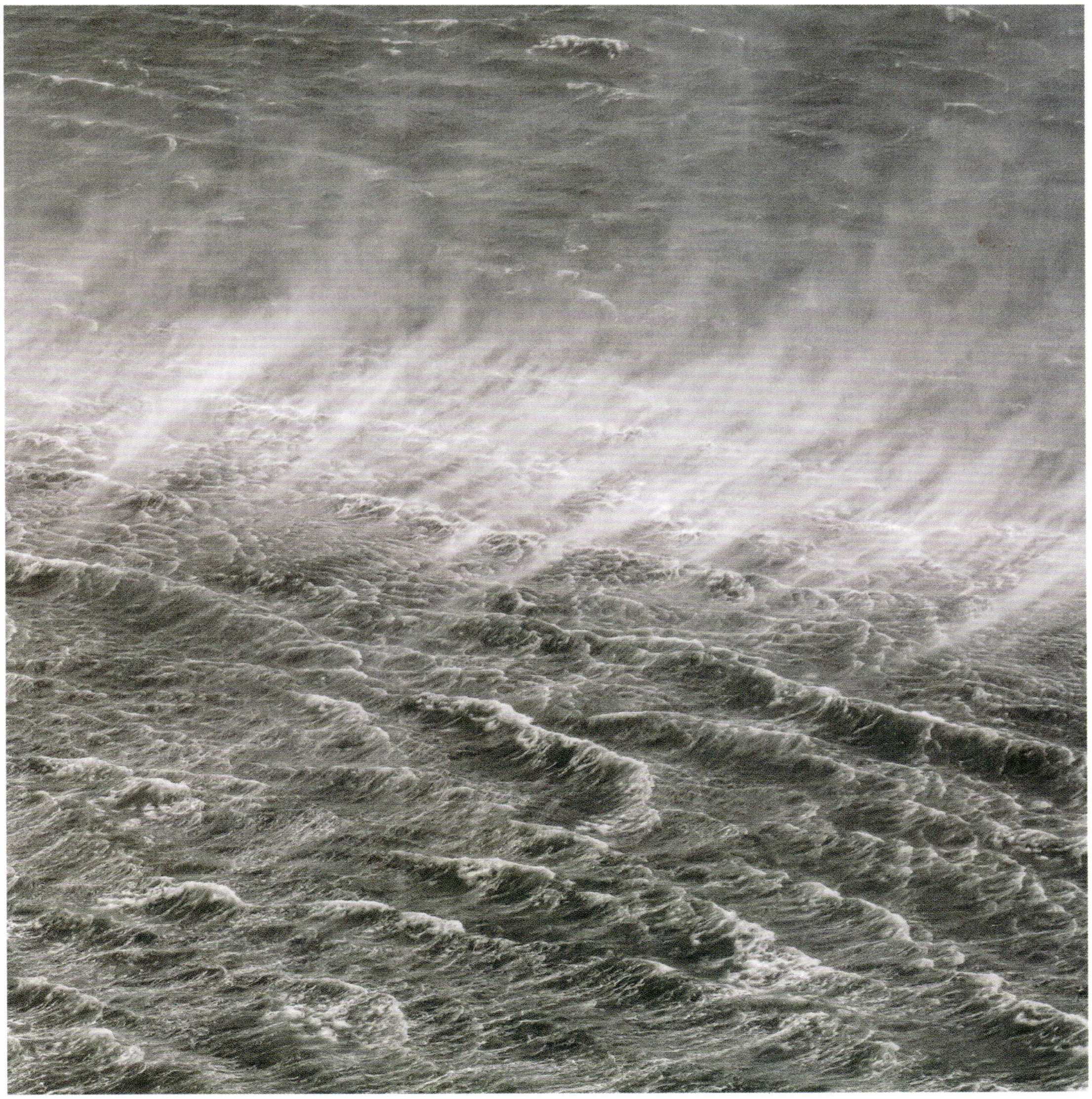

Opposite:

Ynys Lochtyn from the coast path

From top left:

Grey seals, Aber Felin

Cliff near Pen-y-Graig

Seascape in gale, Trwyn y Bwa

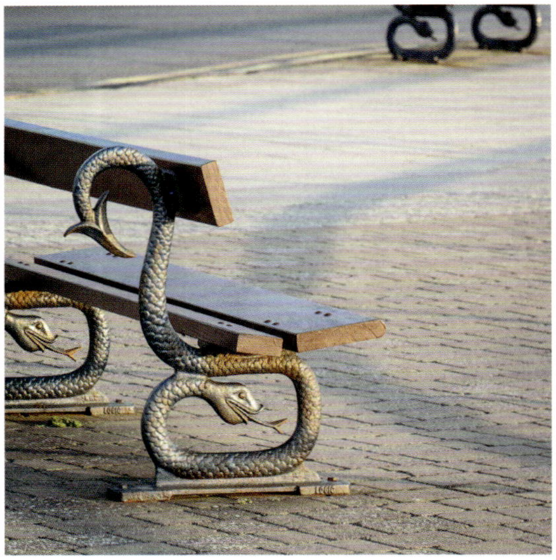

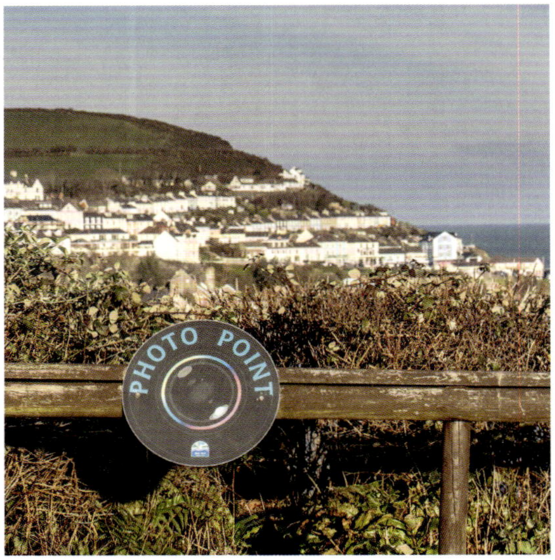

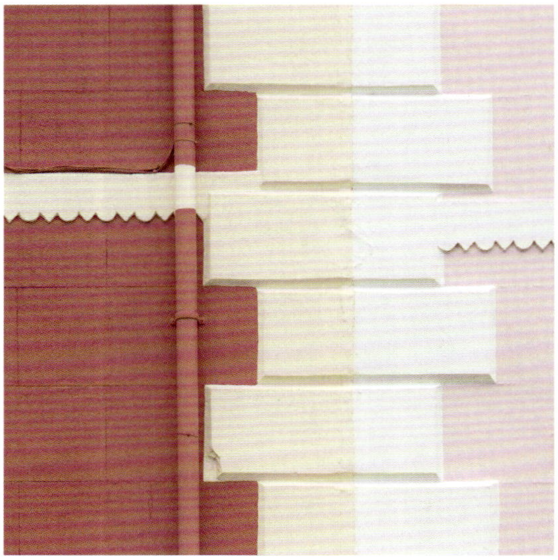

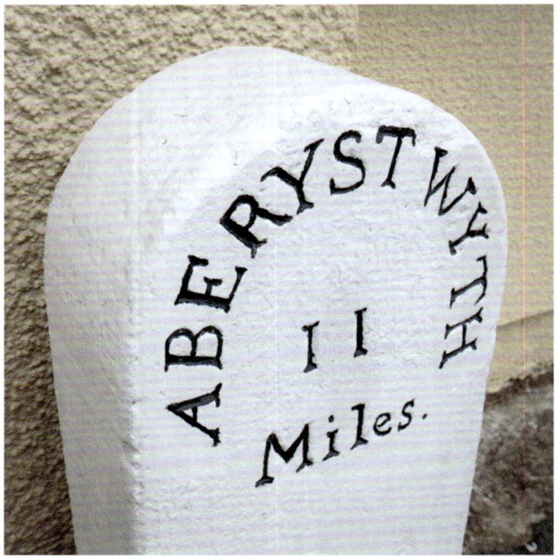

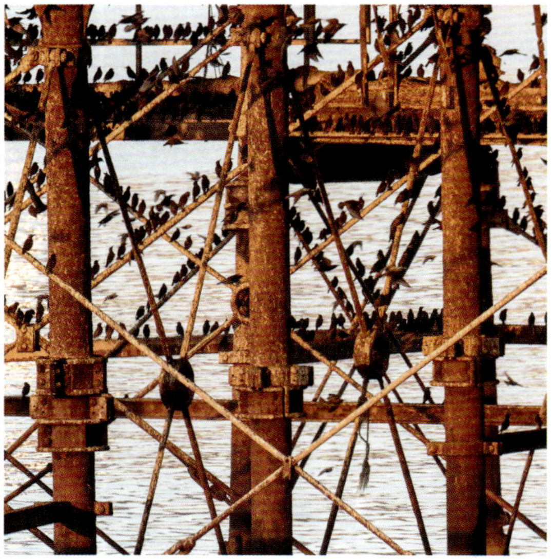

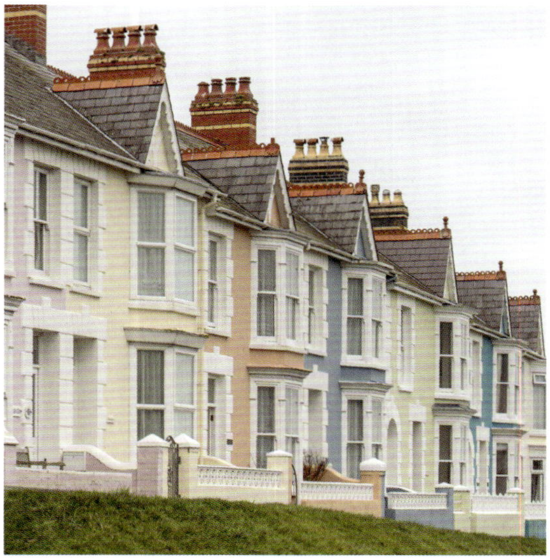

From top left:

Serpent bench-ends at Aberystwyth seafront

Photo point, New Quay

From centre left:

Next door: unusually for this part of rural Wales, the terraced houses in Aberaeron were designed in a Regency style around a principal square

Early-nineteenth-century milestone at Llanon on the Cardigan-to-Aberystwyth road. Milestones were common on former turnpikes (high-quality toll roads that have been called 'one of the central pillars on which the industrial revolution was based')

From bottom left:

Murmuration roost at sunset, Aberystwyth Pier

Harbour Lane, Aberaeron

Opposite, clockwise from top left:

Furnace from Foel Fawr

Sedimentary rock layers near Aberystwyth

Red kite near Aberystwyth

Lichen landscape, Carreg Ti-pw

Soft forest, Pantglas Mawr

Dynyn Hill from Mynydd Du

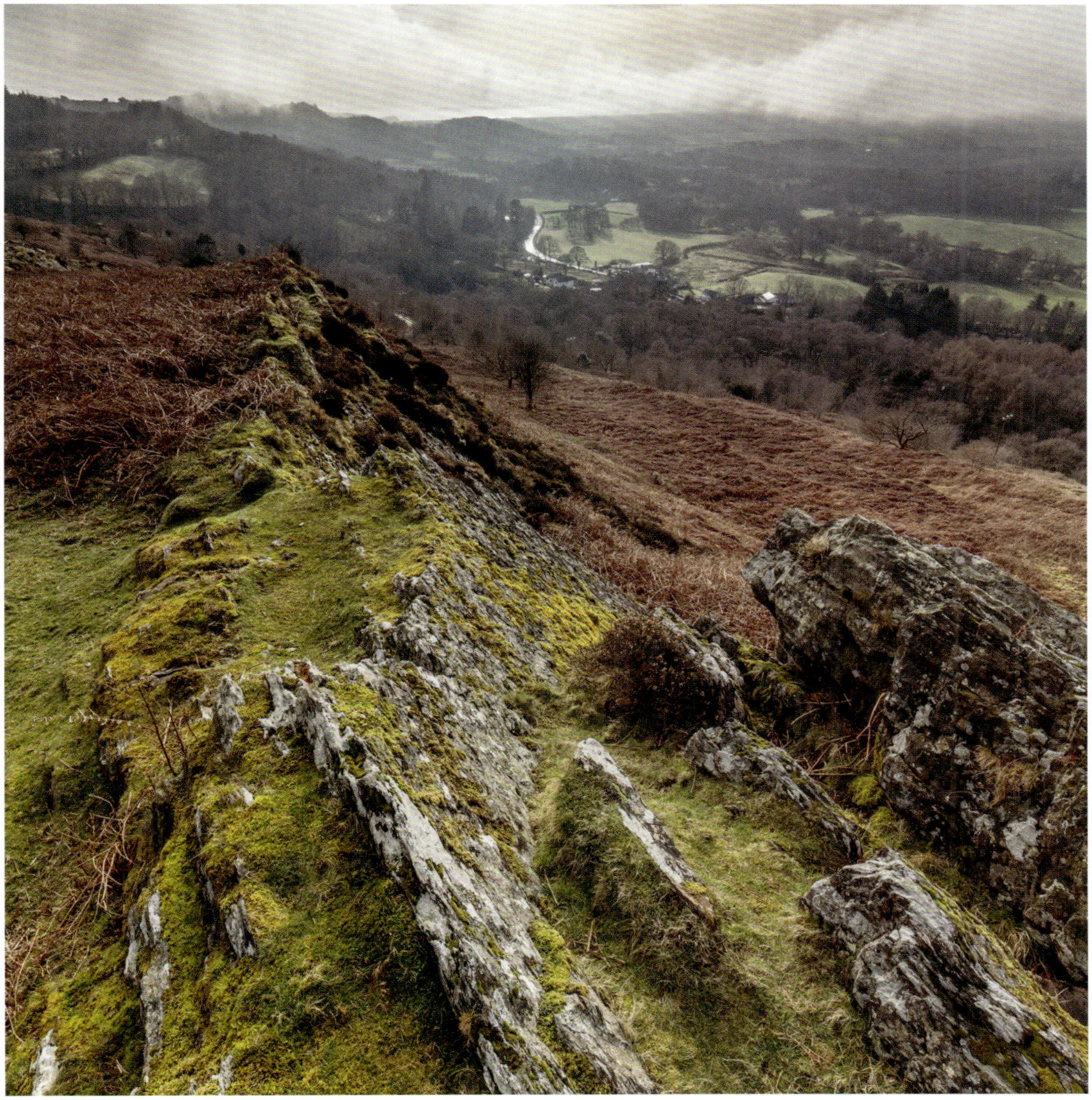
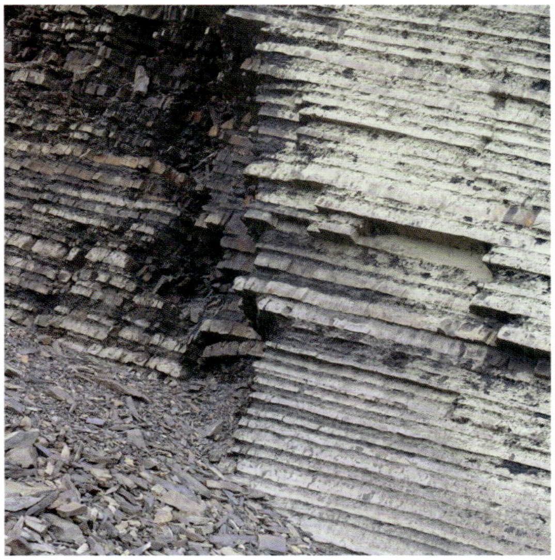
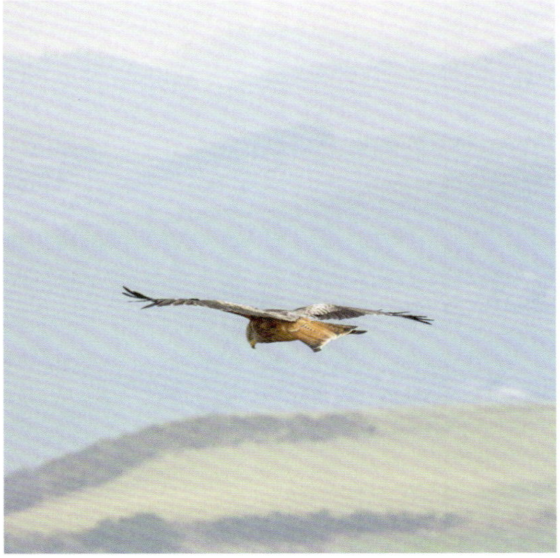

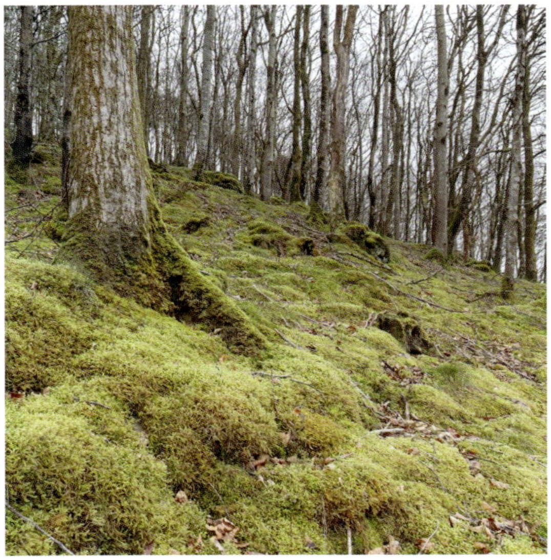
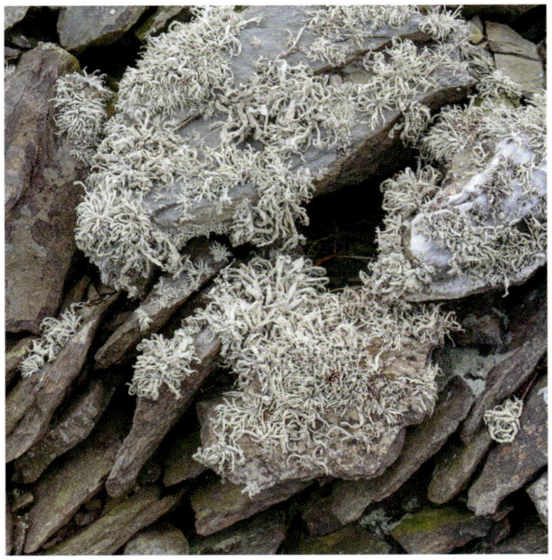

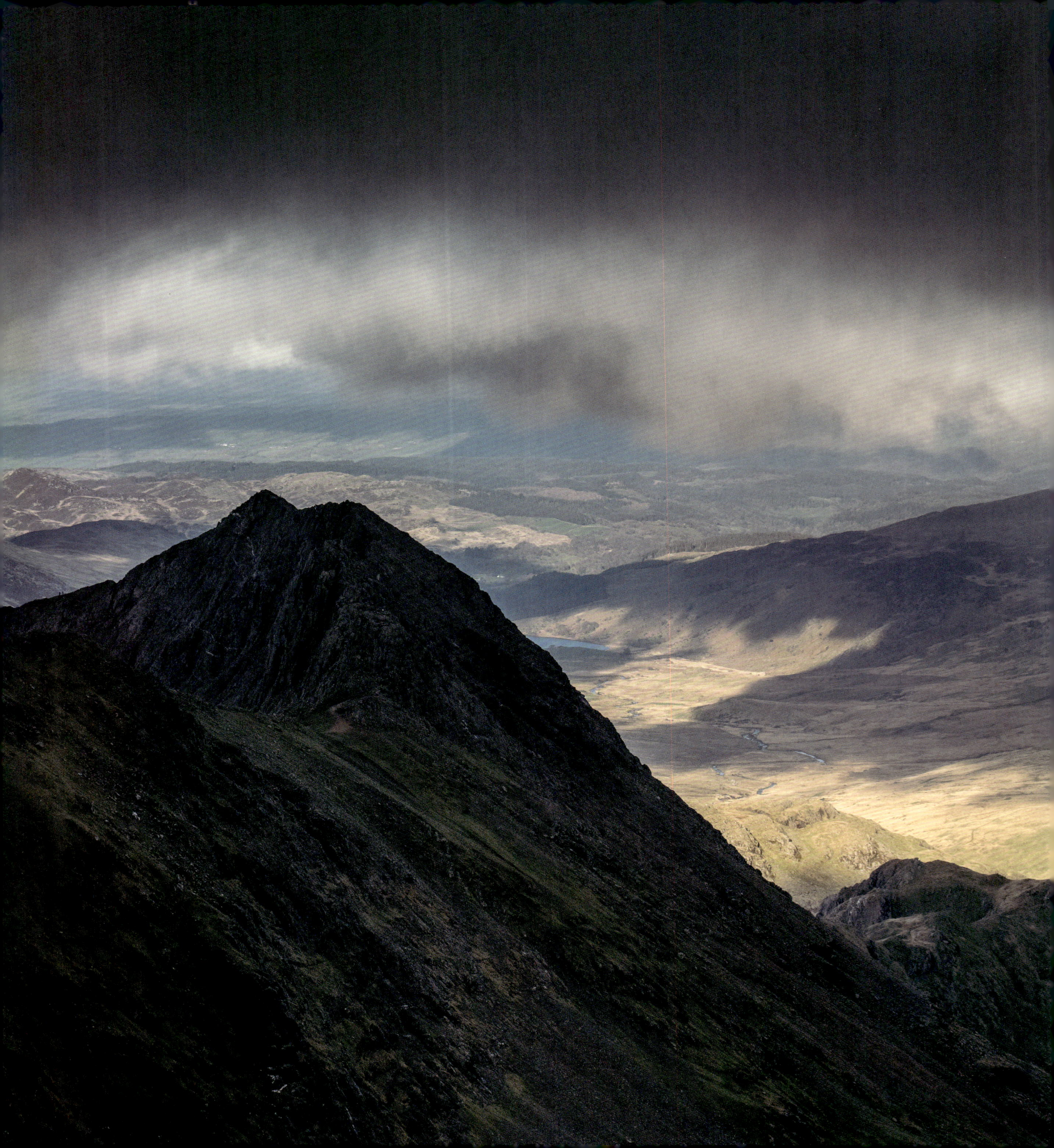

14 GWYNEDD

MARCH–APRIL 2017

DAY 127–137 | 03,292–03,621KM | 329KM

As I leave Machynlleth, the fog is so thick that it dampens sight and sound – a milky white landscape of coniferous trees, bird calls and dissolving paths. For a whole day I can't see more than a few metres ahead, and all my photos come out the palest shades of grey. But by the next day, as I'm crossing a watershed that will reveal Barmouth, the mist evaporates. As the sun emerges and the sweeping mountain vista of the Rhinogs comes into view, I forget my aching feet. It feels like spring has arrived and I sit in my T-shirt to admire this unexpected glimpse of Snowdonia / Eryri. The vivid yellow gorse, rusty bracken, verdant grass and ultramarine sky surrounding me are all the more startling after the previous colourless days in fog.

The Easter holiday is in full swing when I reach Harlech Castle, a day's walk from Barmouth. 'Ice cream, ice cream, ice cream!' a little girl wails. 'OK, let's find ice cream,' concedes her weary mother. As I approach the massive round towers of the castle on its hilltop location, I am awed by its size and dominant position. I can only imagine how it felt 700 years ago when Edward I built it as part of his Iron Ring of Castles to subjugate the Welsh. I hear the martial shouts of a rugby match from the parapets, evoking past battles between the Welsh and English that these walls have witnessed.

I arrive at Portmeirion just in time to catch the last golden light of the day. It glances off the Italianate dome and towers nestled between the woodland above the estuary, against the immense backdrop of the jagged peaks of Snowdonia / Eryri. I decide this is a vista to linger over so I pitch here and shoot the scene at dusk and dawn the next day. When I walk into the cobbled village square, I can see an ornate bell tower and what looks like a Tudor limestone doorway beside a kaleidoscope of Spanish and Greek architectural influences. Blank surfaces are adorned with frescoes and fragments of sculpture: a religious icon here, a Cupid there. A precursor to postmodernism, this is a matchless flight of fancy among coastal villages in Britain built by Welsh architect Sir Clough Williams-Ellis in 1925 to 1973, who wanted to show that natural beauty could be enhanced by sympathetic development. The village is also famous as the surreal location of 1960s cult classic TV series *The Prisoner*.

At Black Rock Sands, I'm surprised to see cars driving on the beach, leaving ammonite-like spirals in their wake where the vehicles have done handbrake turns. One car is stuck, with the driver and passengers frantically trying to dig it out as the tide approaches. At dusk, the sea is flat other than the gentlest of lapping, the full moon reflects on the high tide at blue hour, and it feels like the ocean is holding its breath. The next day, car parks reverberate to infants wailing, the beach to children screaming and the sea to motorboats roaring. For many, the pleasure of the coast seems proportional to the decibels generated. A pair of fighter jets scream past overhead as if they don't want to be left out of the ruckus.

After four days following the Llŷn Peninsula, I leave the sea at Caernarfon at 5 a.m. for a loop to the summit of Snowdon / Yr Wyddfa and back. John Merrill, the first known person to walk the entire UK coast, did the same in 1978, and it seems a fitting homage to him, not to mention an opportunity to get a different perspective. By the time I reach the summit, it's already late afternoon, but I am rewarded for my efforts as the fog clears to reveal rapidly changing views of Snowdonia / Eryri as the clouds scoot past, casting shadows on the mountains. There are glimpses of the sea back to Harlech, the Llŷn Peninsula and Conwy. I stay near the summit until my hands are too cold to take pictures before descending the mountain. It takes me five hours following ancient, silent tracks to return to Caernarfon at midnight.

Opposite:

Crib Goch, on the way down from the summit of Snowdon / Yr Wyddfa

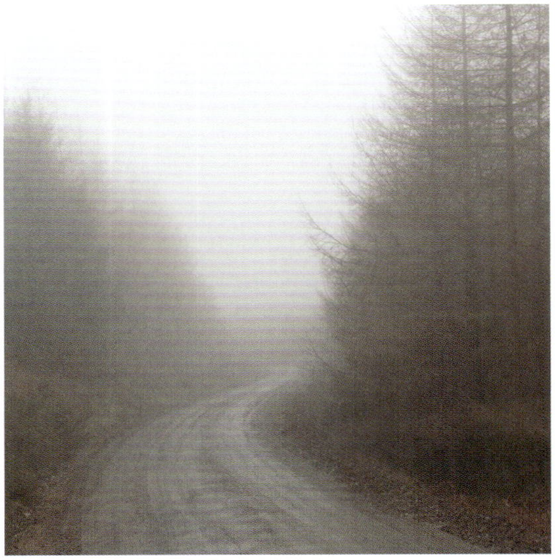

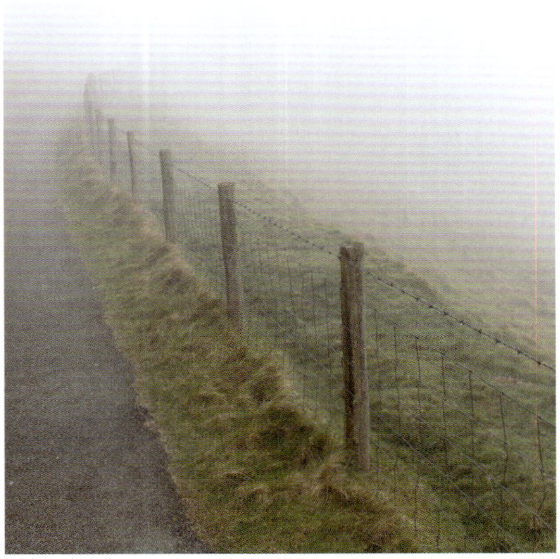

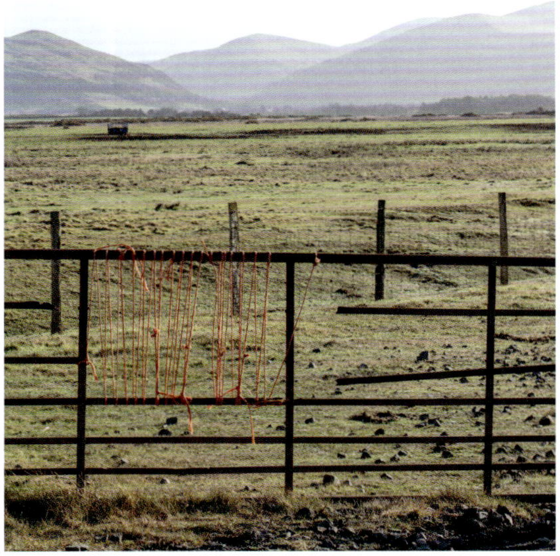

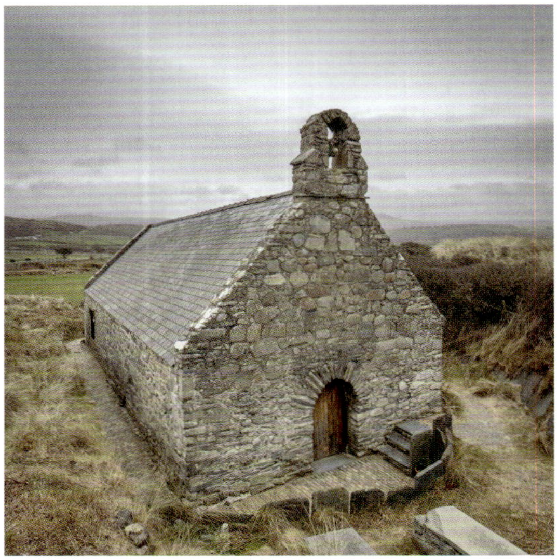

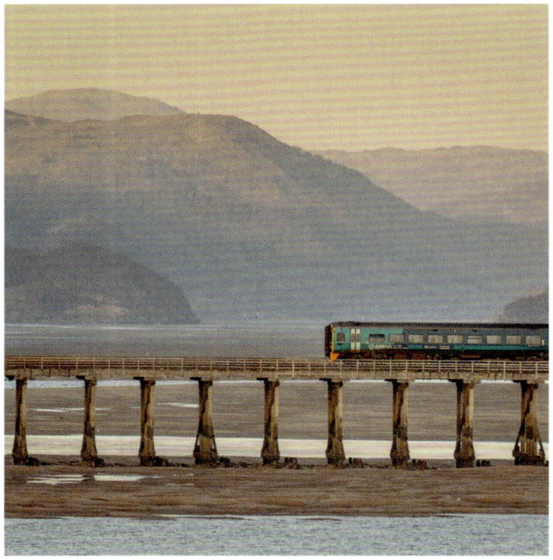

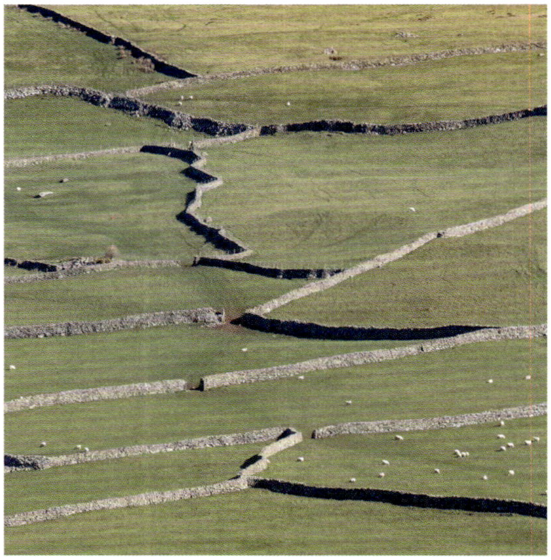

From top left:

Forestry track, Foel Goch

Road to Llyn Barfog (the Bearded Lake)

From centre left:

Baling twine, Tonfanau

St Tanwg's Church, Llandanwg, reputedly founded in the fifth century; the current structure dates from the twelfth century

From bottom left:

My dad loves trains, so I had to photograph the train he arrived on when he visited me in Barmouth

Drystone walls constructed from boulders, above Llwyngwril

Opposite, clockwise from top left:

Dragon's teeth (Second World War anti-tank cubes), Fairbourne

Barmouth Bridge at dusk, Mawddach Estuary

Flock of sanderlings, Dyffryn Beach

Boulder, Plas Bennar

Barmouth Bridge swing bridge section (no longer operates)

Dyffryn Beach

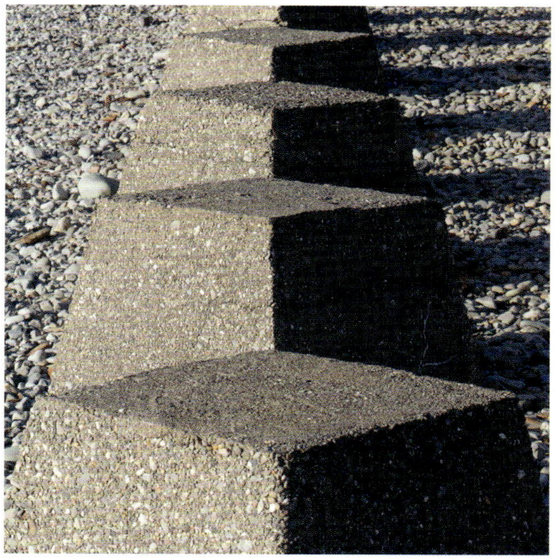
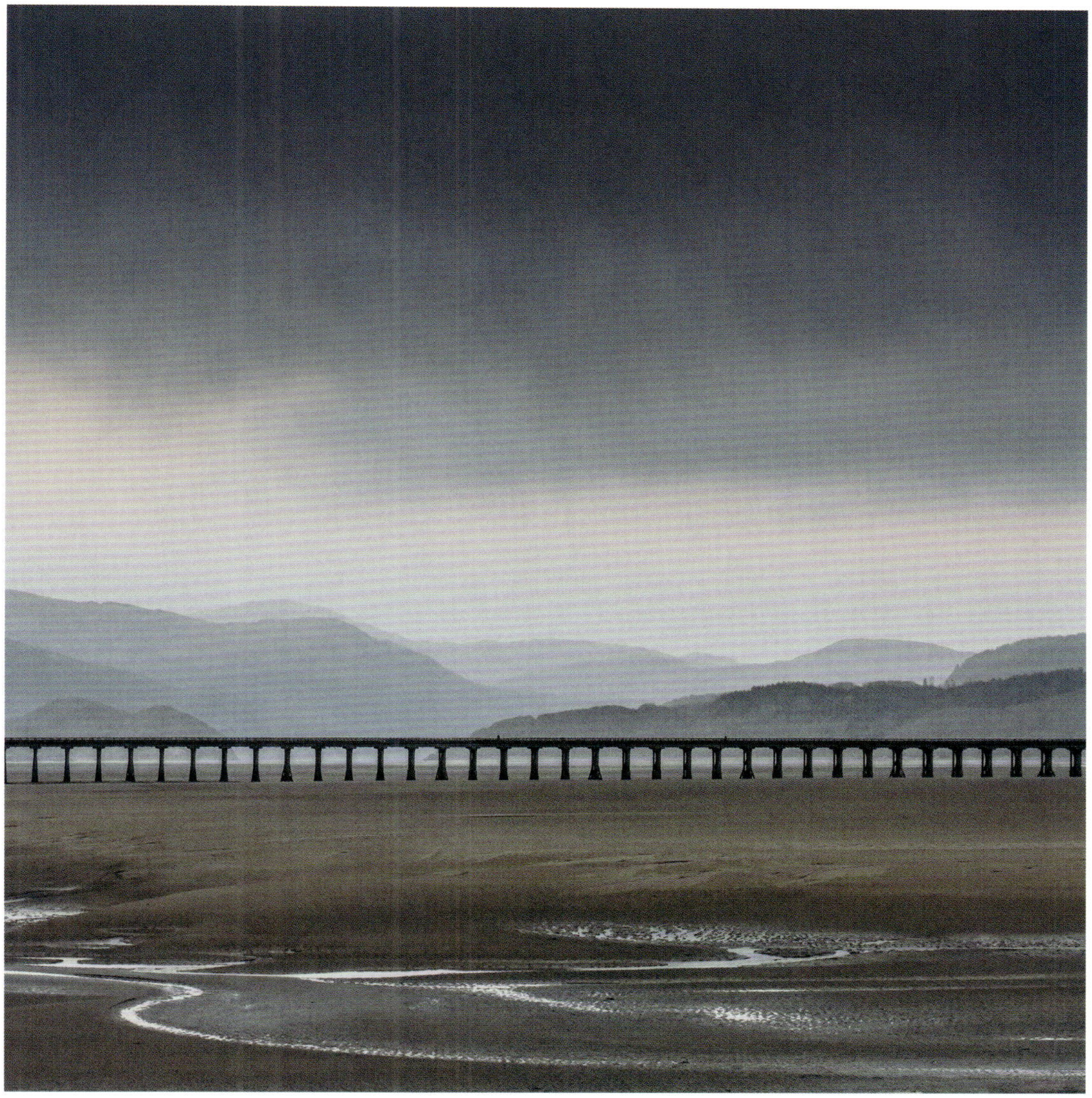
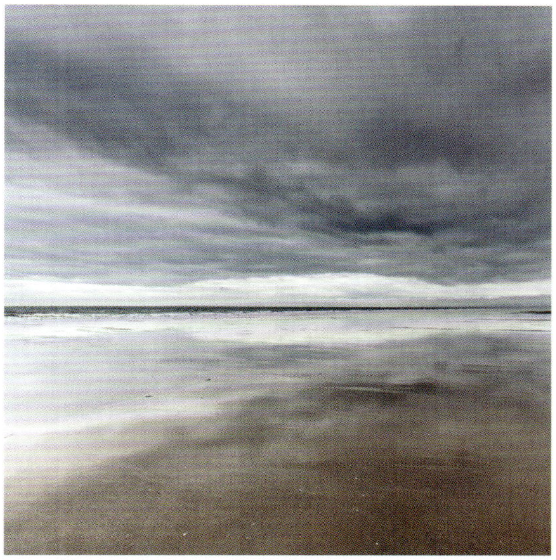
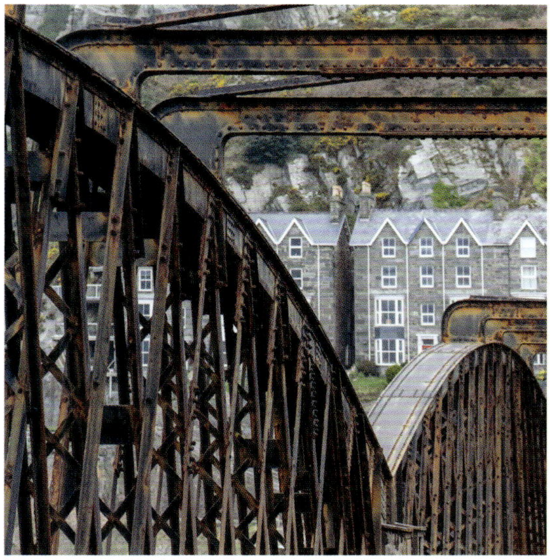
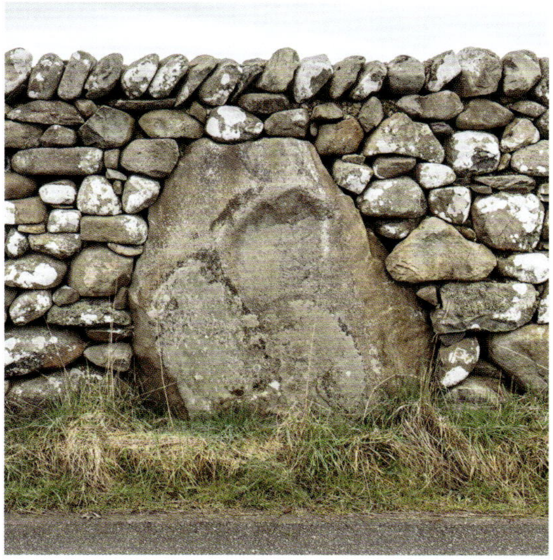
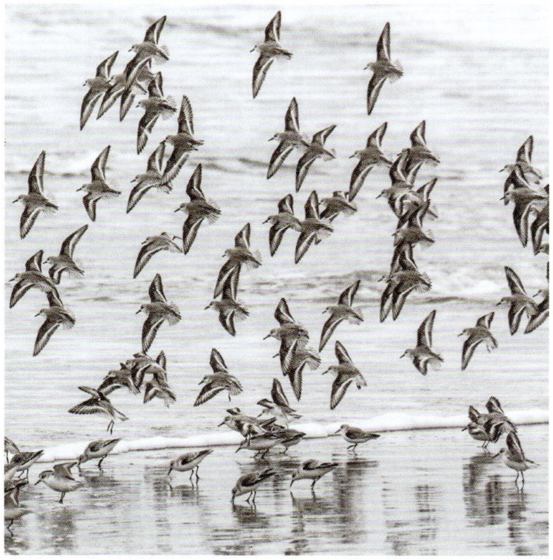

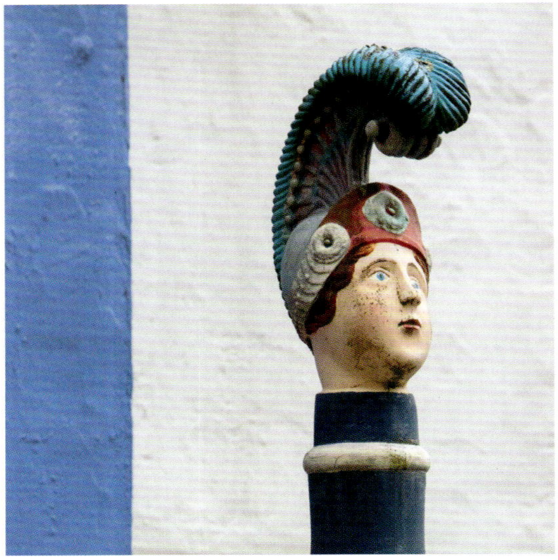

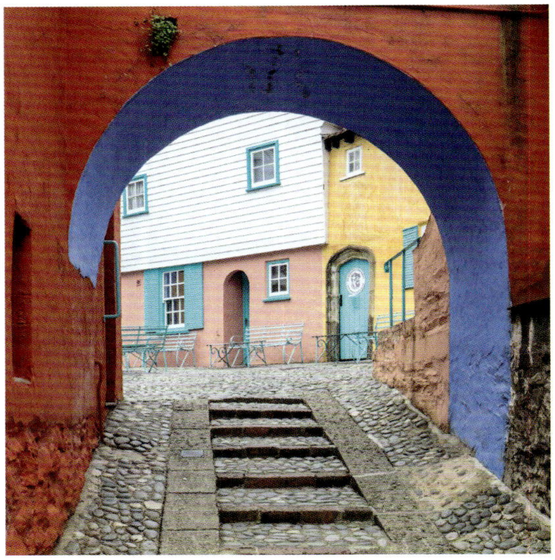

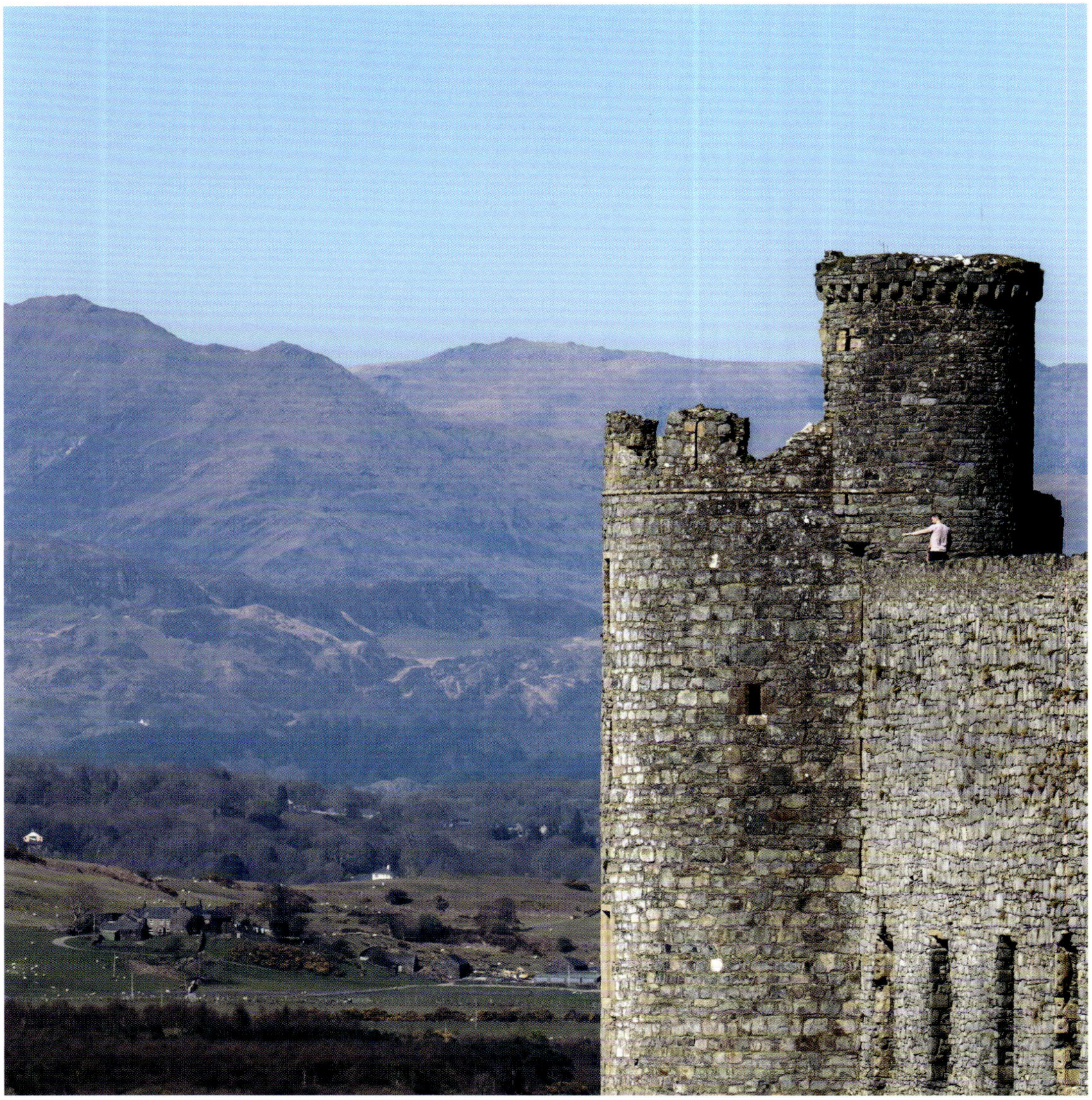

From top left:

Petrol pump figurehead, Portmeirion

Arch, Portmeirion

Harlech Castle, Snowdonia / Eryri

Opposite, clockwise from top left:

Duet: Ogof Lwyd, Llŷn Peninsula

Porth Llanllawen and Mynydd Mawr, Llŷn Peninsula

Fisherman's hut at Porth Ysgaden, Llŷn Peninsula

Yr Eifl from Porth Nefyn, Llŷn Peninsula

Nant Gwrtheyrn granite quarry, Llŷn Peninsula

Track across Yr Eifl, Llŷn Peninsula

Overleaf, from left to right:

Wild-camping group by Llyn Du'r Arddu and the Clogwyn cliffs seen from the Llanberis Path while descending Snowdon / Yr Wyddfa

Dinorwic slate quarry that operated between 1787 and 1969, Snowdonia / Eryri. At its height at the start of the twentieth century, it was the second-largest slate quarry in Wales. In 2021, the Slate Landscape of Northwest Wales, said to have 'roofed the nineteenth-century world', gained UNESCO status

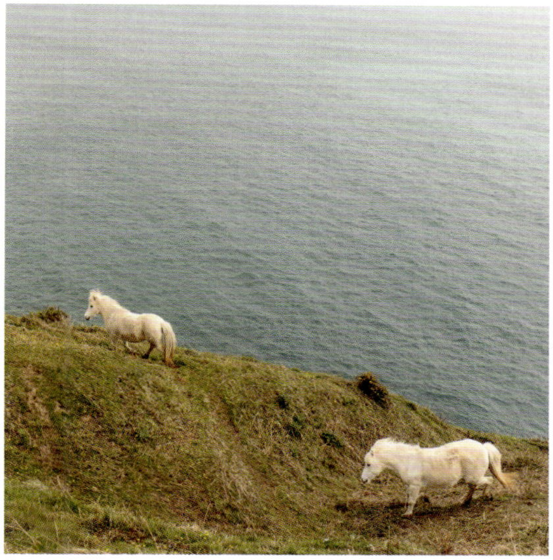
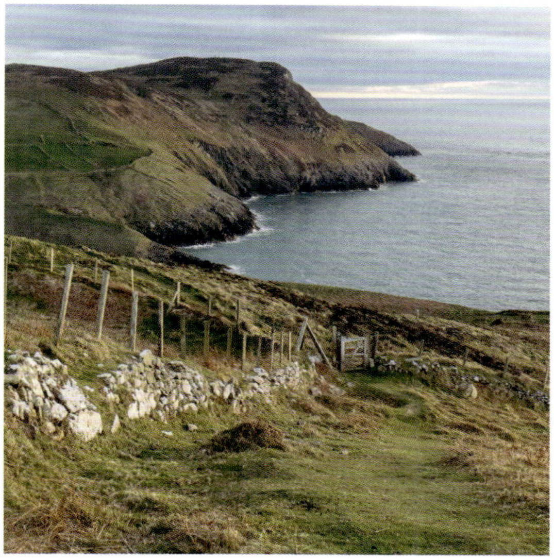
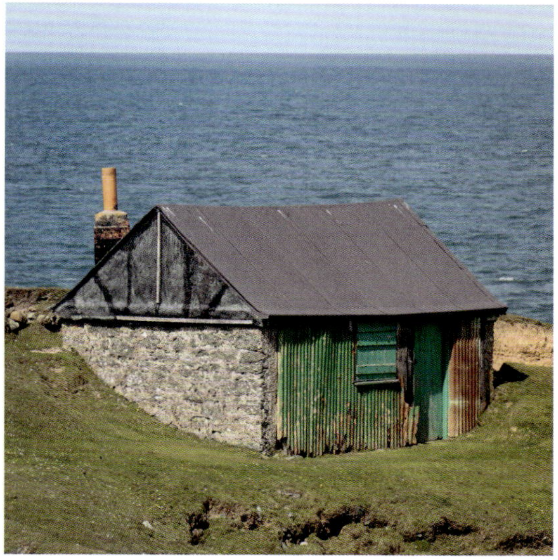
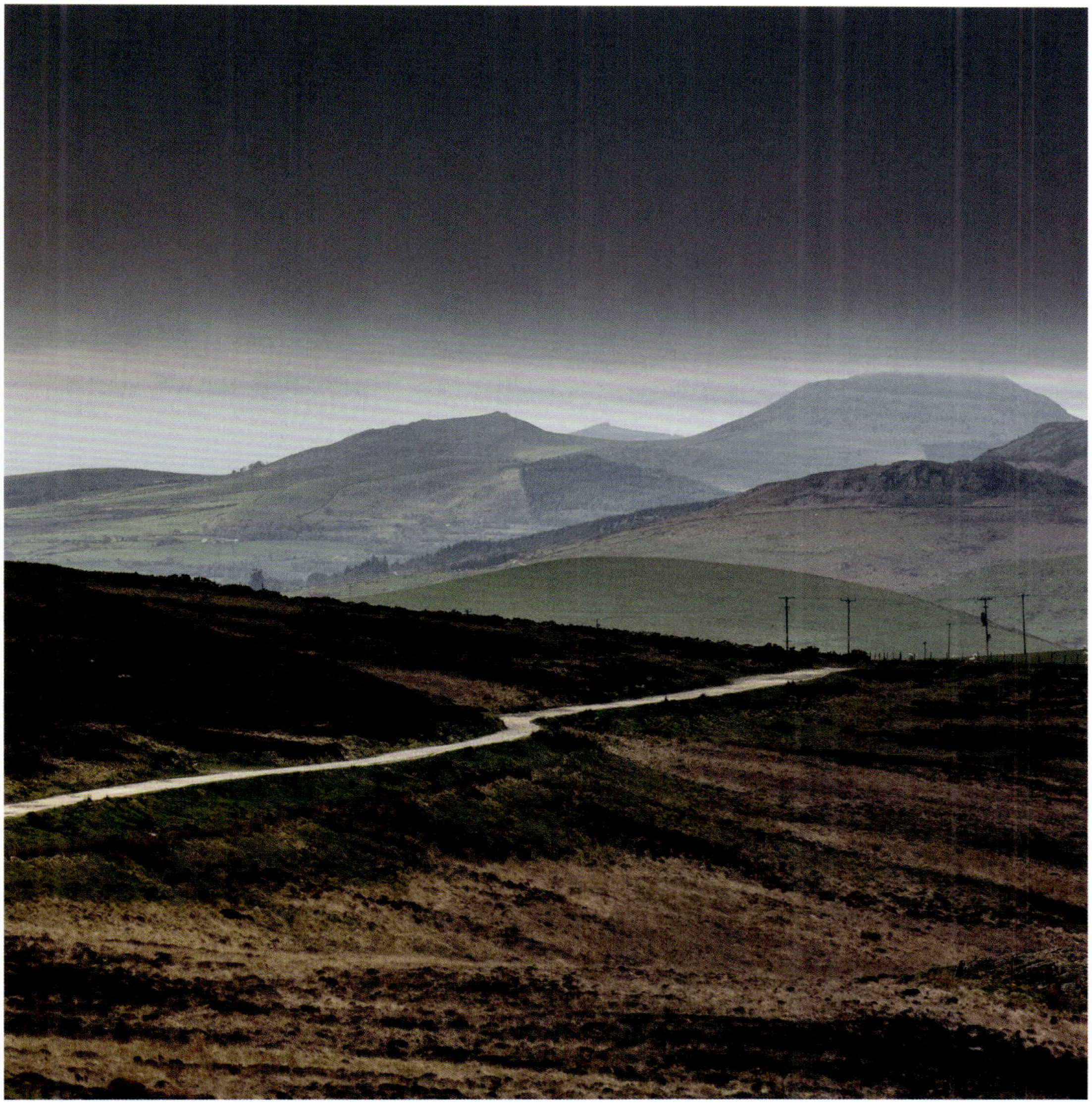
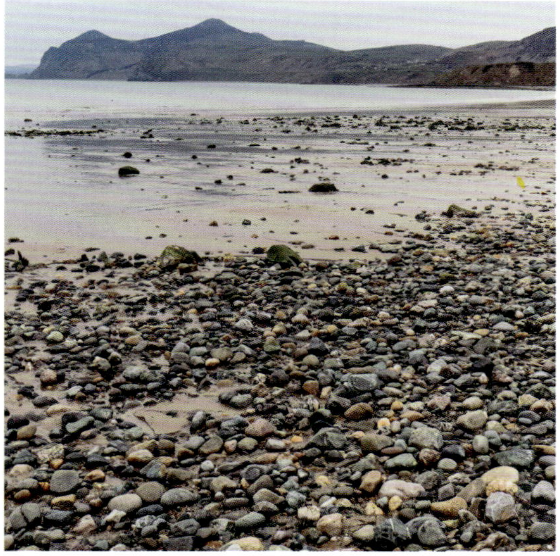
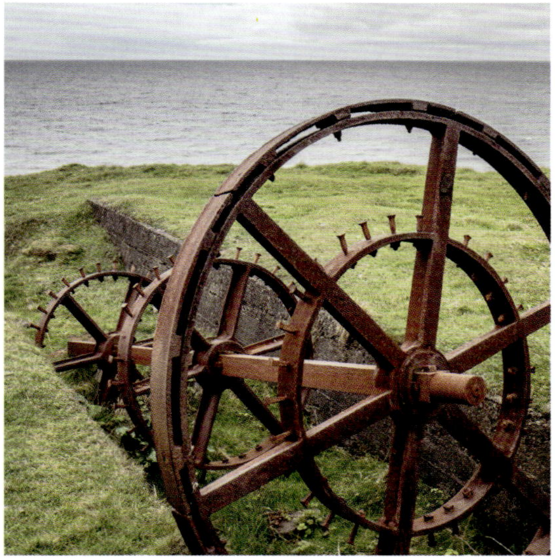

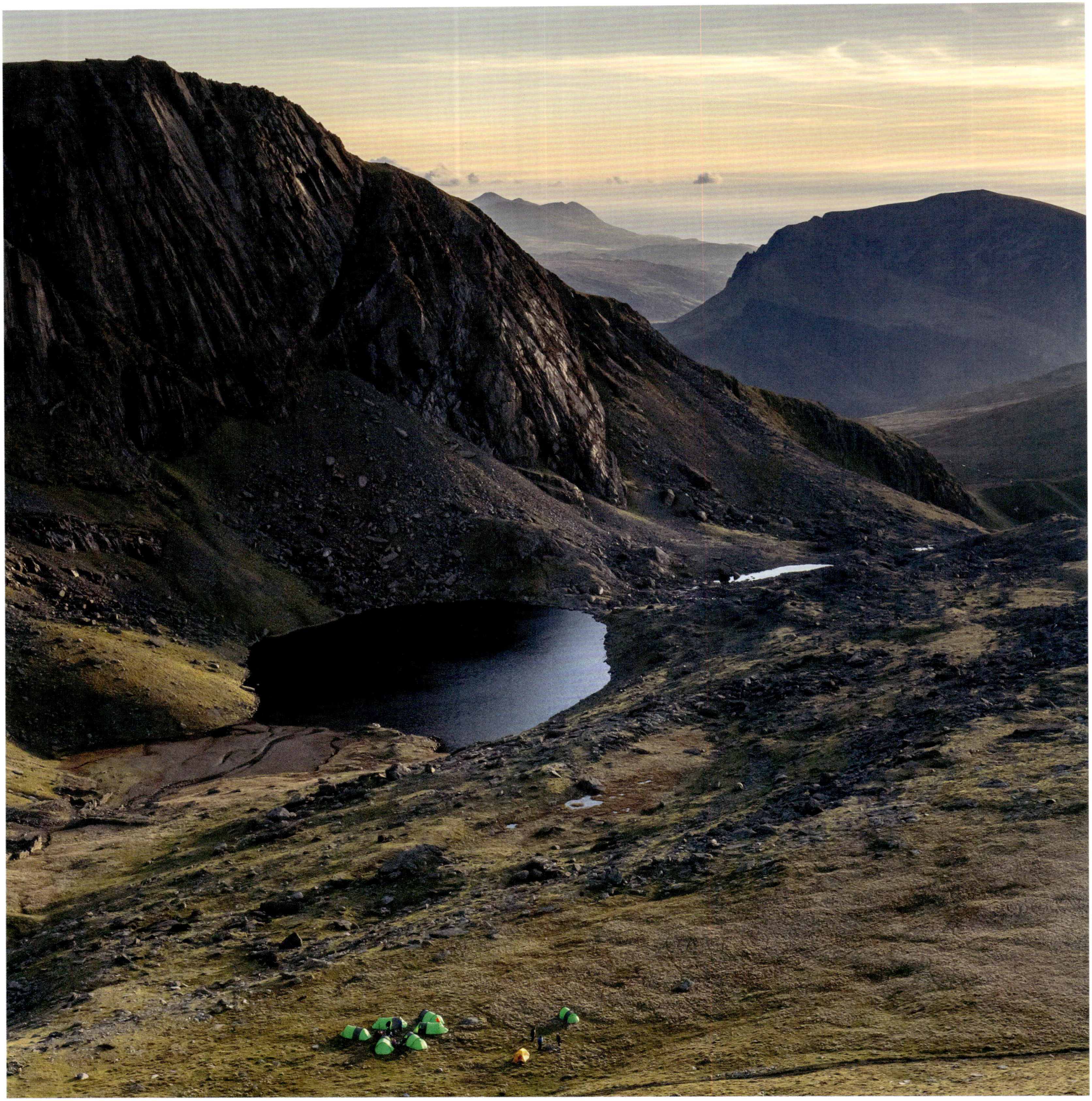

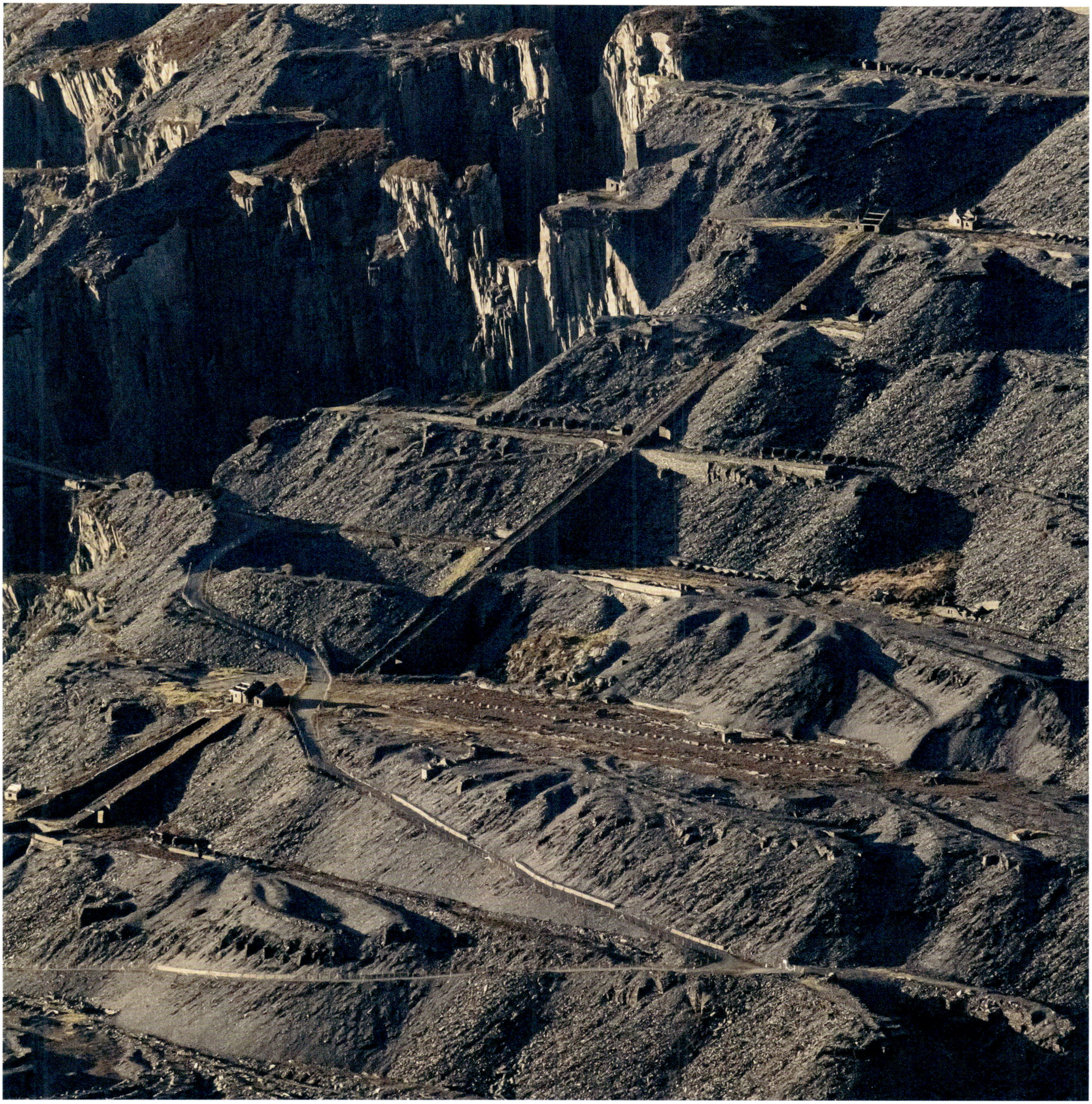

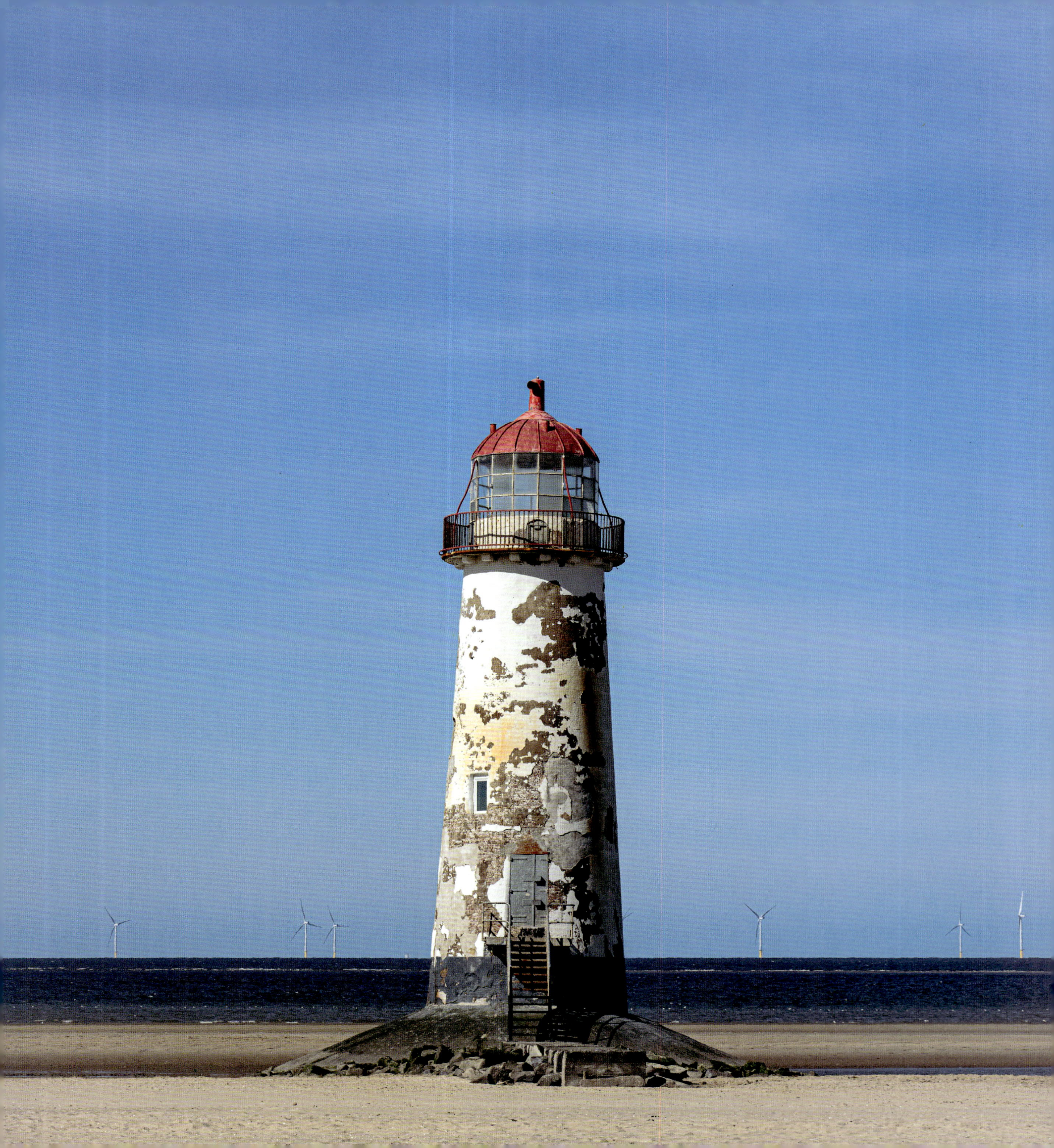

15 CLWYD

APRIL 2017

DAY 138–142 | 03,621–03,751 KM | 130 KM

As spring emerges, I leave behind the rugged coastline of the west for Clwyd, the last chapter in Wales, where a series of Victorian seaside towns punctuate the flatter north coast. Trekking up and down the craggy paths of the Llŷn Peninsula and Snowdon / Yr Wyddfa has me feeling supremely fit, and I rake up 30-kilometre days with ease as I head east along the seaboard towards England. On my first morning, opposite Puffin Island near Penmaenmawr, I walk past fields fenced with slabs of slate, the top edges of which are tied together with wire.

By evening, I've reached Conwy Castle, standing guard over the bridge spanning the River Conwy. Once painted white to accentuate its other-worldly impregnability, it's a hulking grey mass that stands today as a visible symbol of the history of English domination. The eight round towers and curtain wall are all topped with impressively intact crenellations and perforated with dozens of arrow slits, so narrow they are barely visible from a distance. When I later arrive at Plas Mawr, I see the other side of the Anglo-Welsh rivalry formed in plaster on the walls: a Tudor townhouse where three severed heads of Englishmen in Dorothy Wynn's coat of arms sit above the fireplace in the bedroom and in the dining room.

Next morning, I arrive in Llandudno, the largest seaside resort in Wales. As early as 1861, it was called 'the Queen of the Welsh Watering Places' because of its popularity as a holiday destination for rail visitors from Liverpool, Manchester, Crewe and the West Midlands. It's a different story today as cheap flights lure holidaymakers abroad, and I watch as an industrial carton of bright pink goo is poured into a candyfloss machine at Llandudno Pier, where desultory clusters of visitors wander along the deck far out into the Irish Sea below a cold grey sky. On the promenade by an unused climbing frame, I chat with an elderly lady on a mobility scooter. 'That's as far as I can go,' she tells me after we've travelled 500 metres. The lido is desolate: it's not yet warm enough for it to be filled with water – instead, it's scattered with pebbles hurled up from the beach by the storms. On leaving the promenade, my spirits rise, despite the drizzle, when I see the 200-metre-high limestone peninsula of Great Orme emerge ahead like a colossal beached whale.

On my fifth day in Clwyd, I turn inland along the River Dee, where the once-mighty *Duke of Lancaster* liner, subsequently the Fun Ship leisure and retail complex, sits rusting, graffitied and evocative. A motorcyclist, also taking pictures, tells me he worked on it in the merchant navy. 'Wanna see it before it's too late, like,' he says.

I continue along the banks of the river, past a friendly Polish group enjoying the sun with a sound system and beers, until I reach Connah's Quay. It's the last settlement in Wales, where buzzing pylons tower directly over some houses, while others, still lived in, have boarded-up windows and mounds of rubbish sitting in terraced front gardens. People I meet on the path through the industrial scrubland return earnest smiles. Soon, the Scouse accent becomes more frequent than Welsh, and I'm greeted with 'all right, fella' or 'all right, luv'.

After a total of forty-eight days in Wales, I cross anti-climactically into England at Hawarden Bridge, the first place one can travel by foot into the country. At the city of Chester, I'm welcomed by a sign advertising *A two-hour pampering session for £50* and a billboard of a woman holding a glass of champagne advertising Chester Races. I've only walked a few miles from Wales, but it feels like a different planet.

Opposite:

The Point of Ayr Lighthouse was constructed in 1776 to guide ships entering the Dee estuary, as Chester was once an important port before the development of Liverpool. It was decommissioned in 1844

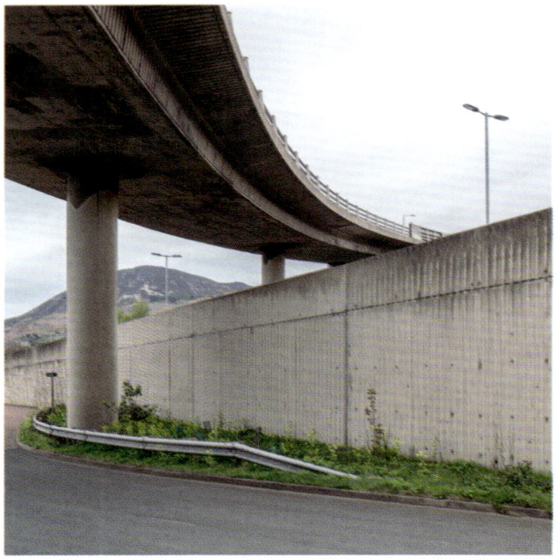

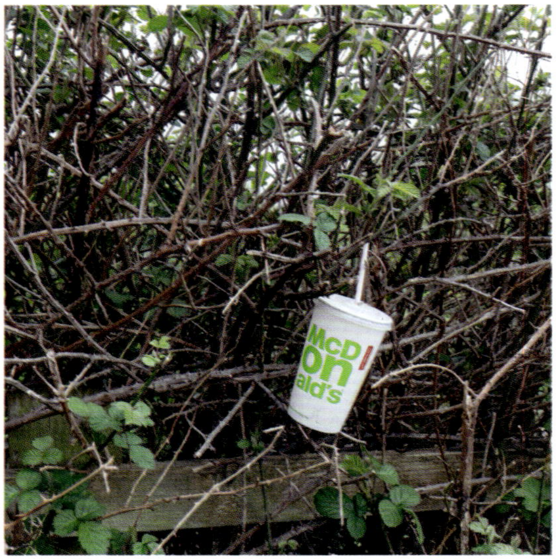

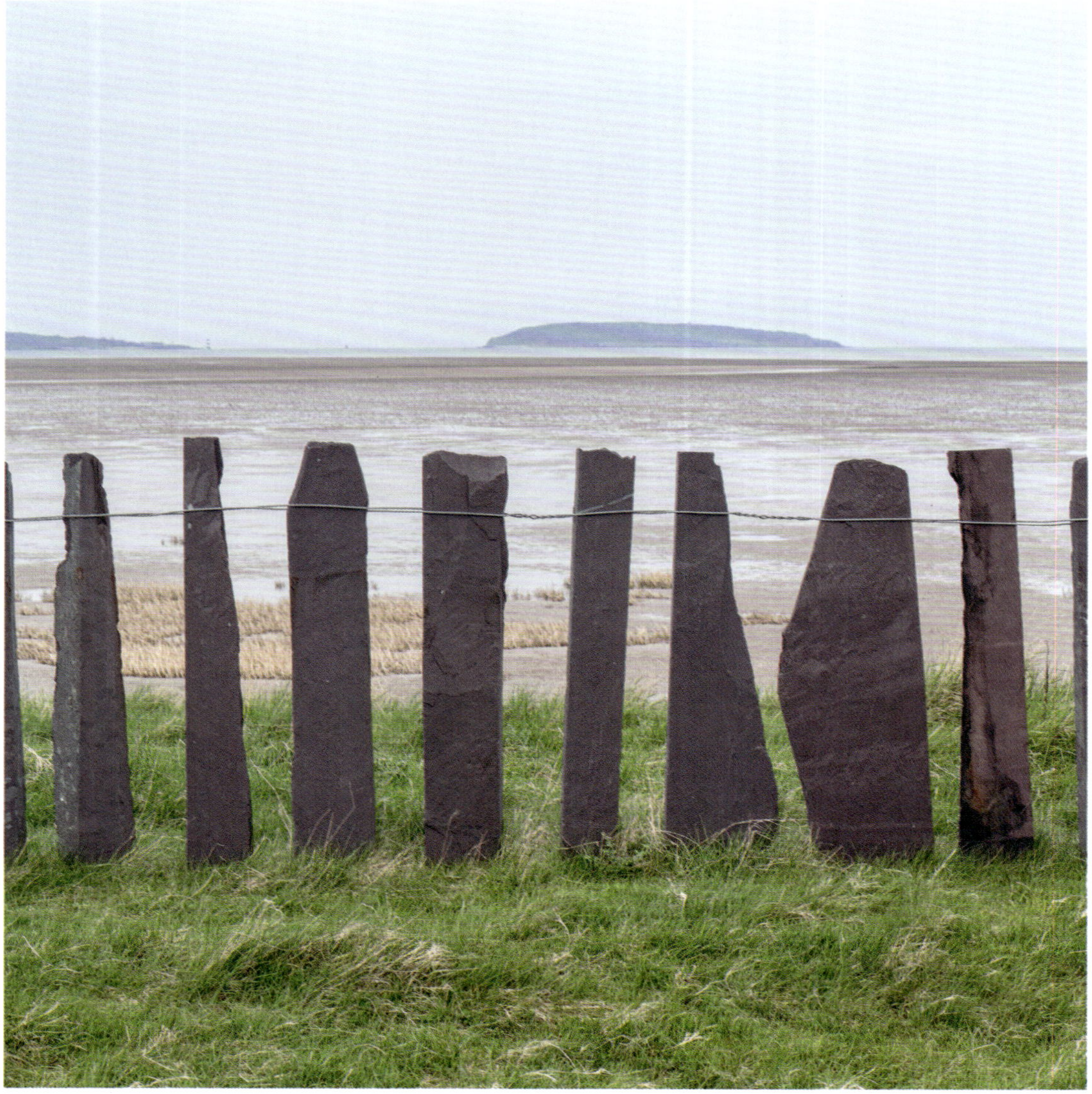

From top left:

Flyover, Penmaenmawr

Layby, Bryn, Gwynedd

Slate fence and Puffin Island, Lavan Sands, Gwynedd

Opposite, clockwise from top left:

Door detail, Plas Mawr, a Tudor townhouse, Conwy

Conwy Castle at dusk

Pantry, Plas Mawr

Plasterwork ceiling with Tudor rose, Plas Mawr

Kitchen, Plas Mawr

Severed heads of Englishmen with caryatid decoration in the Great Chamber, Plas Mawr

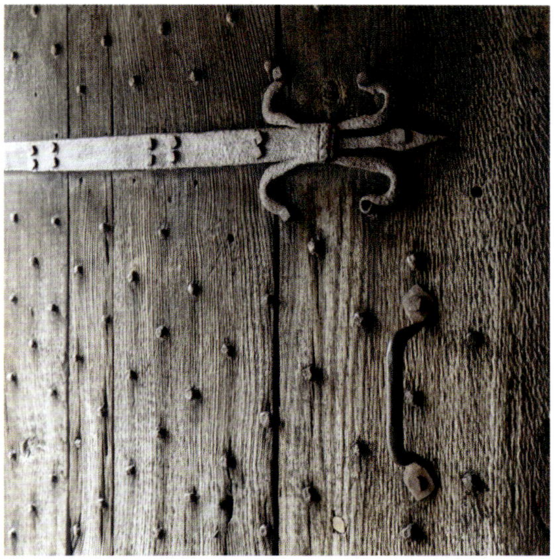
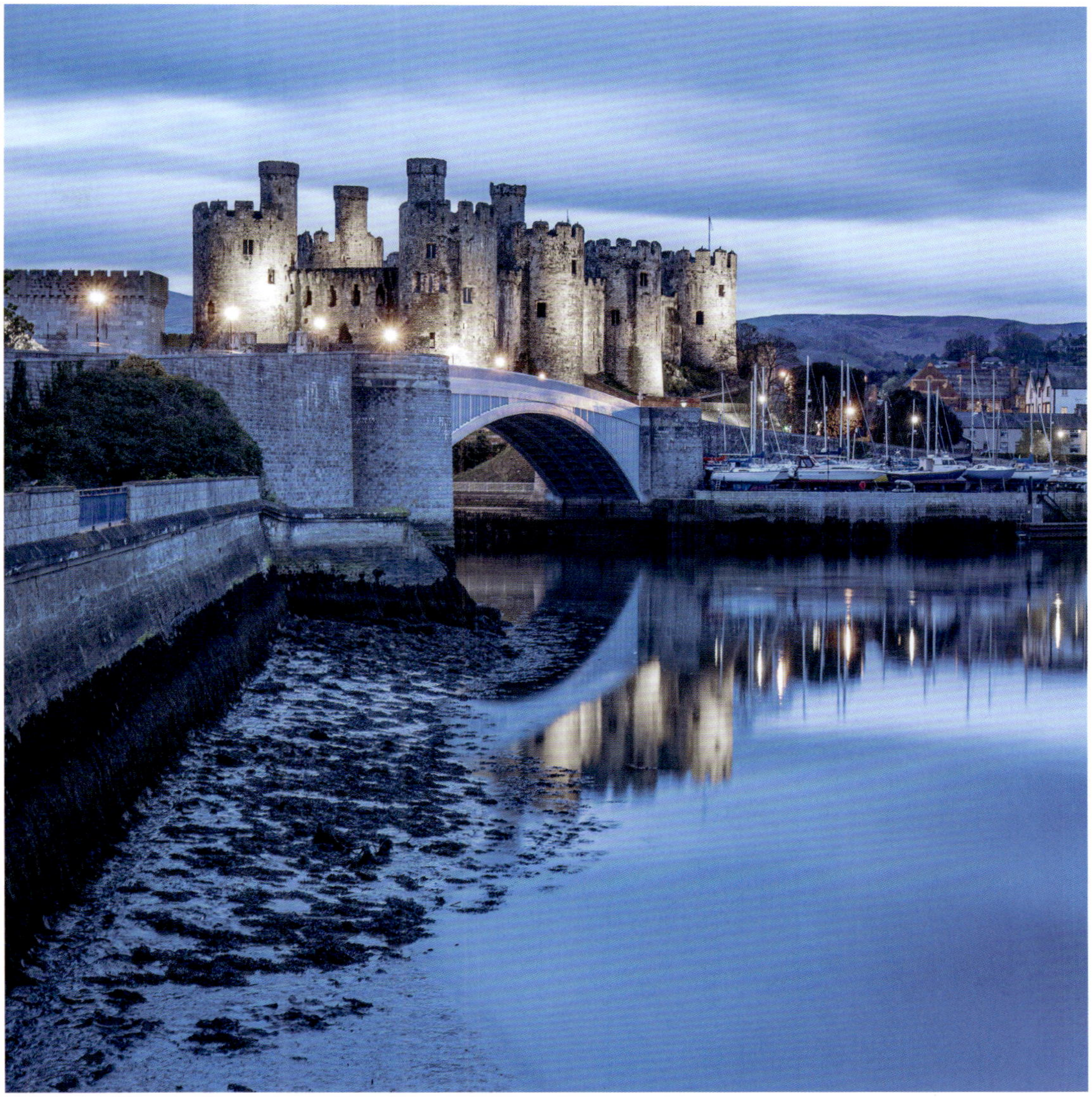
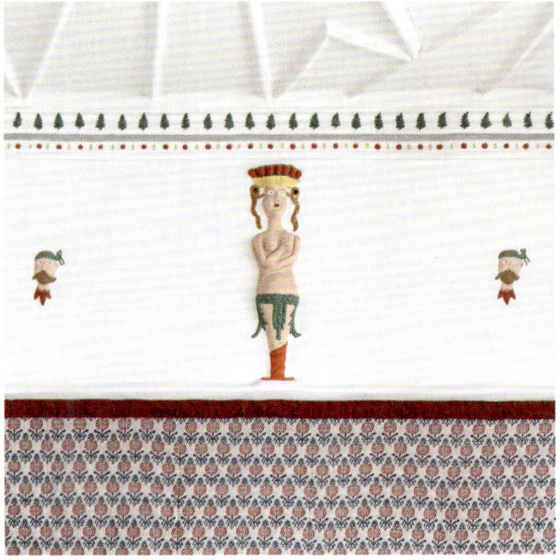
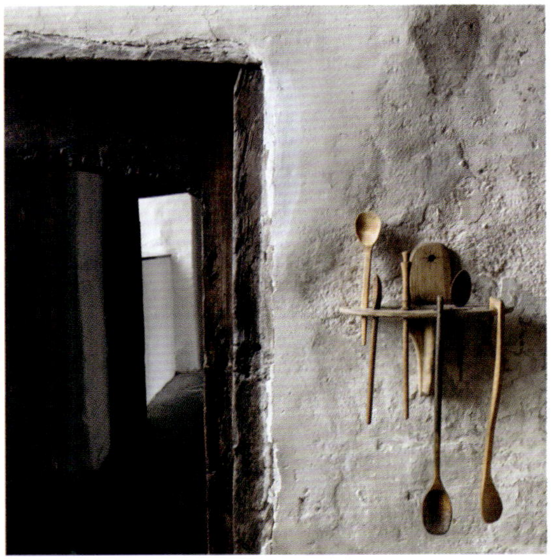
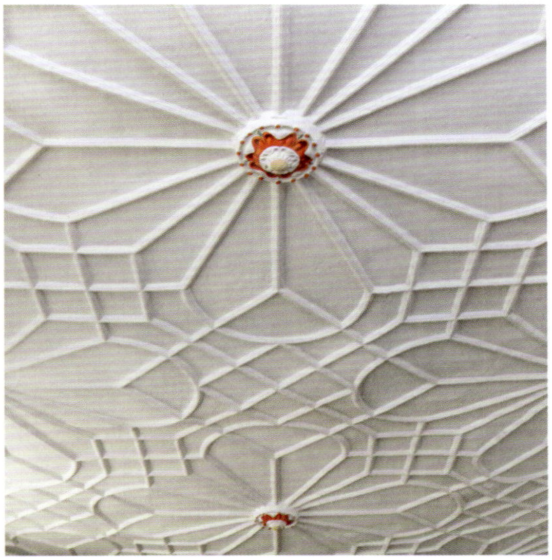
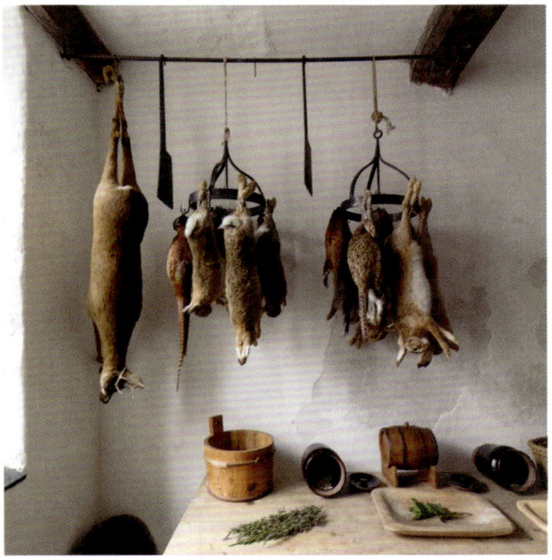

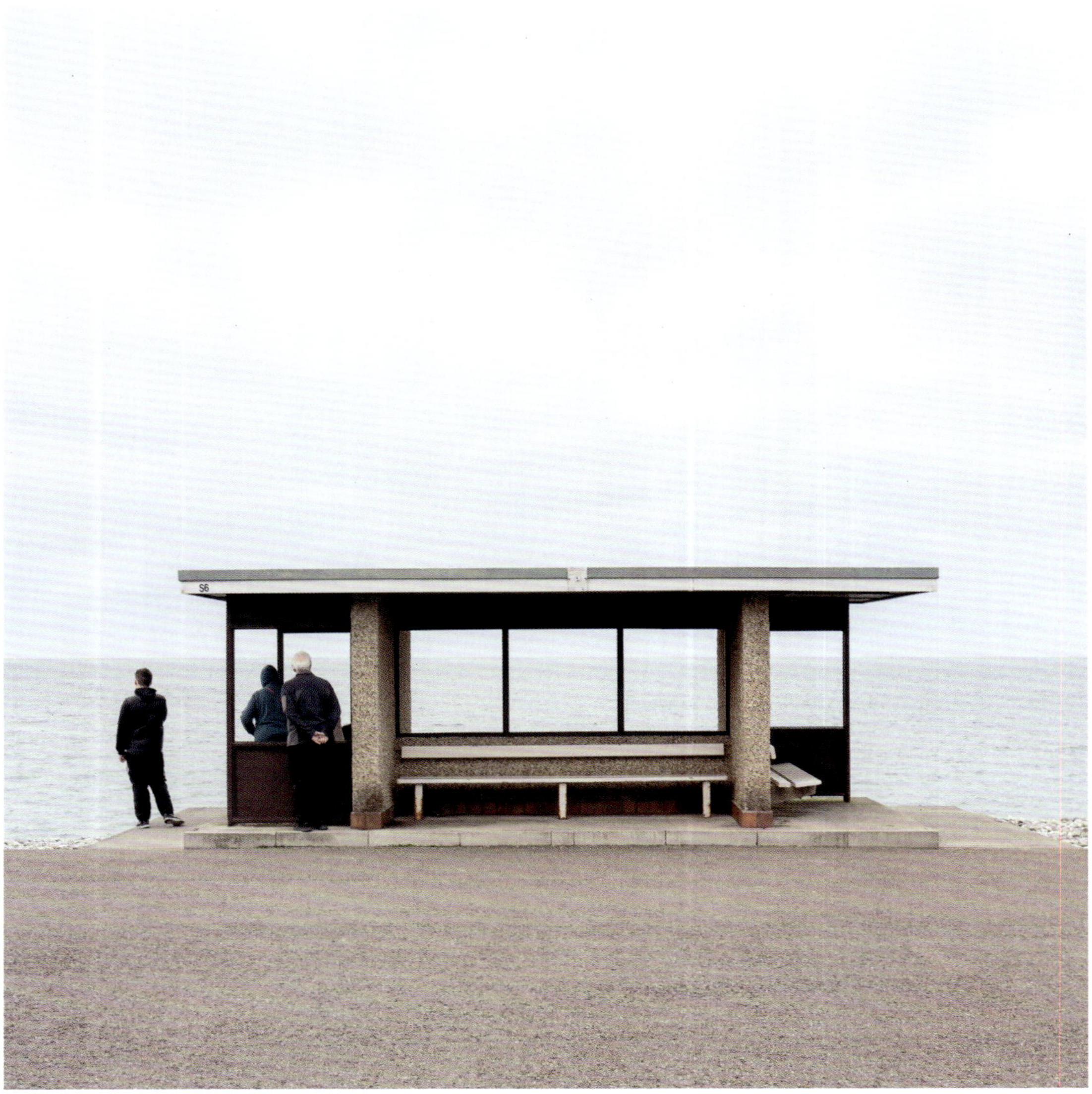
S6

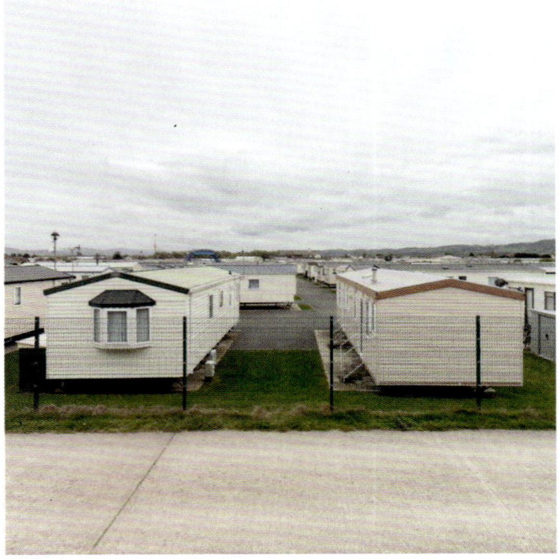

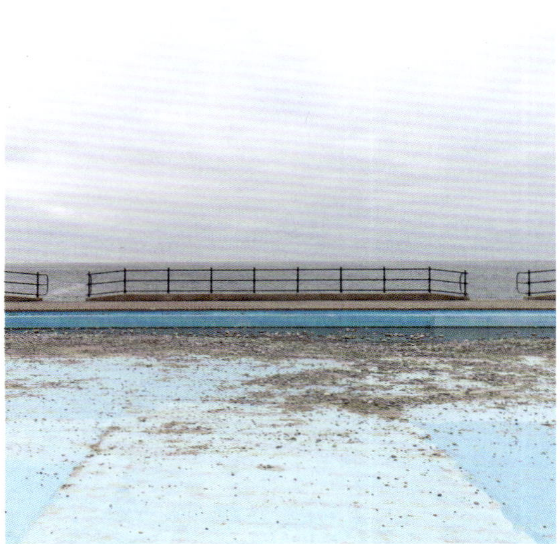

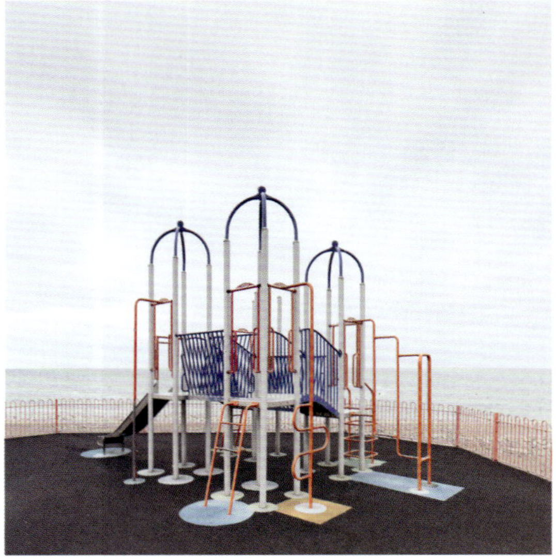

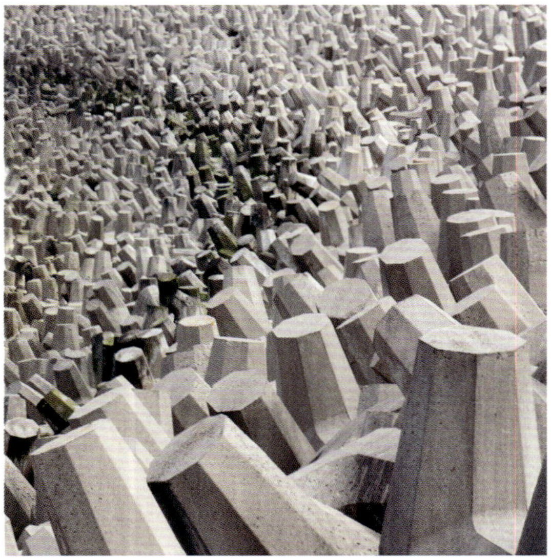

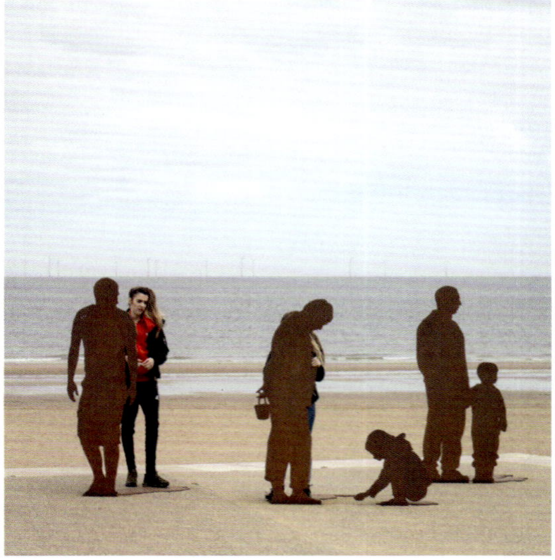

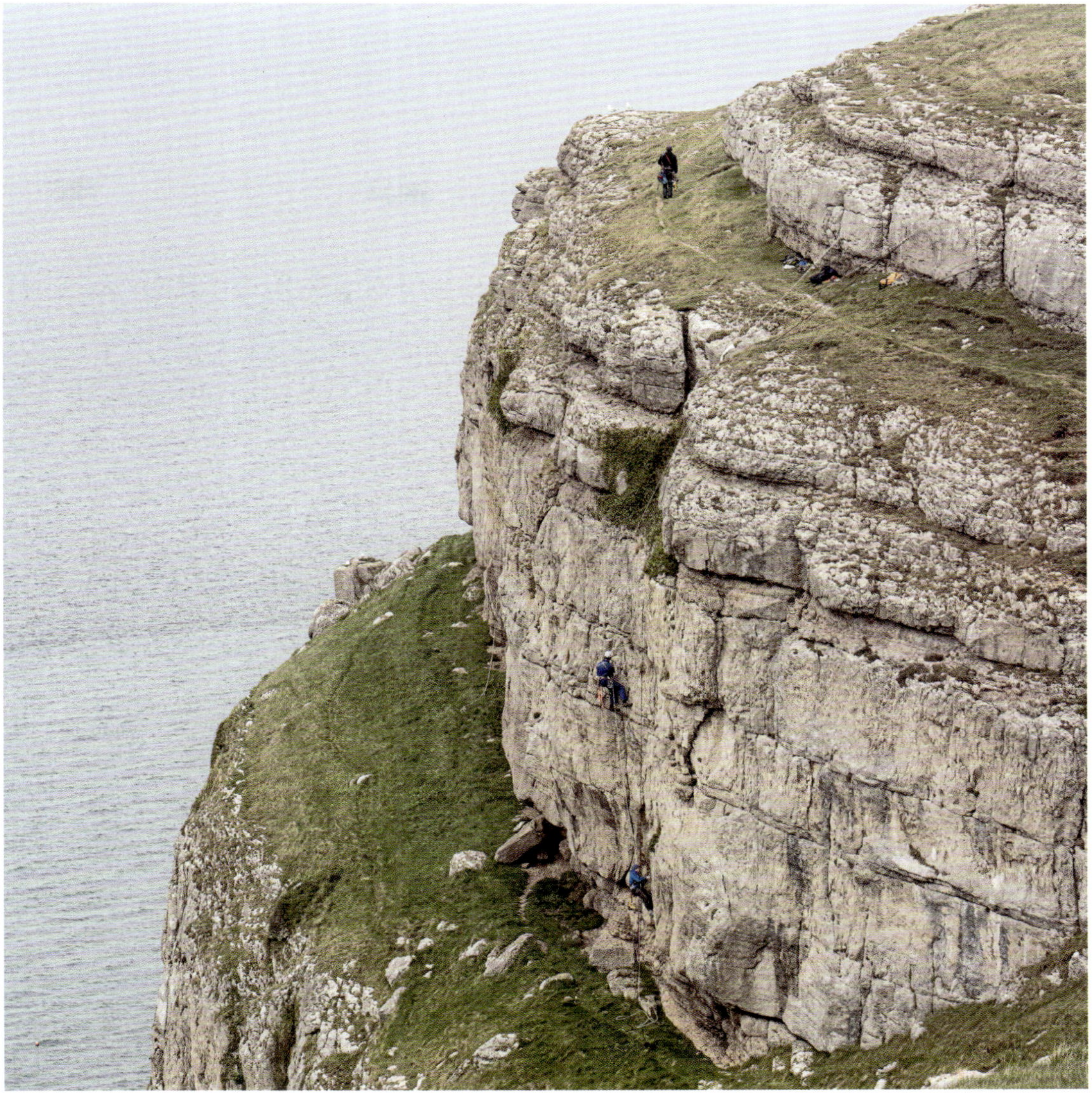

Opposite, clockwise from top left:

Promenade, Llandudno

Holiday park, Kinmel Bay

Lido in April, Llandudno

On the Beach, sculpture by Freshwest, Colwyn Bay

Dolosse landscape with tide line, near Colwyn Bay

Playground, Llandudno

From top left:

Climbers bolting limestone on Great Orme's Head

Road around Great Orme's Head

Facade, Penrhyn

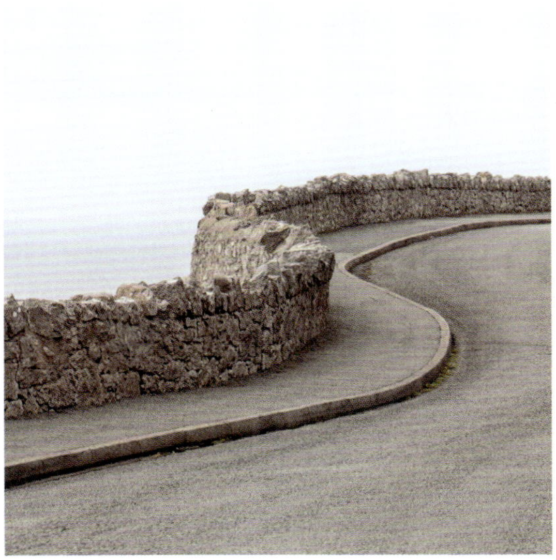

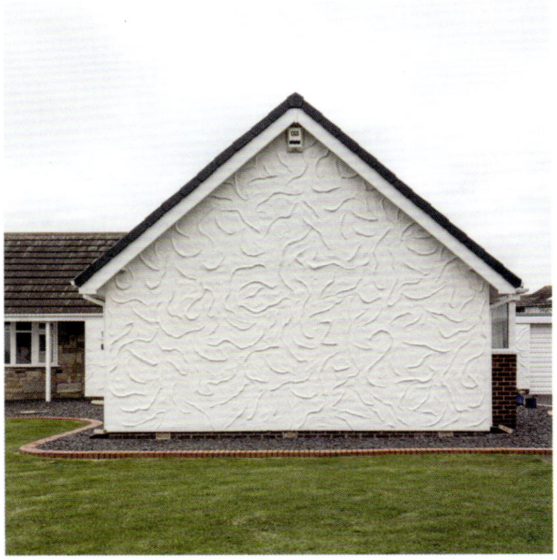

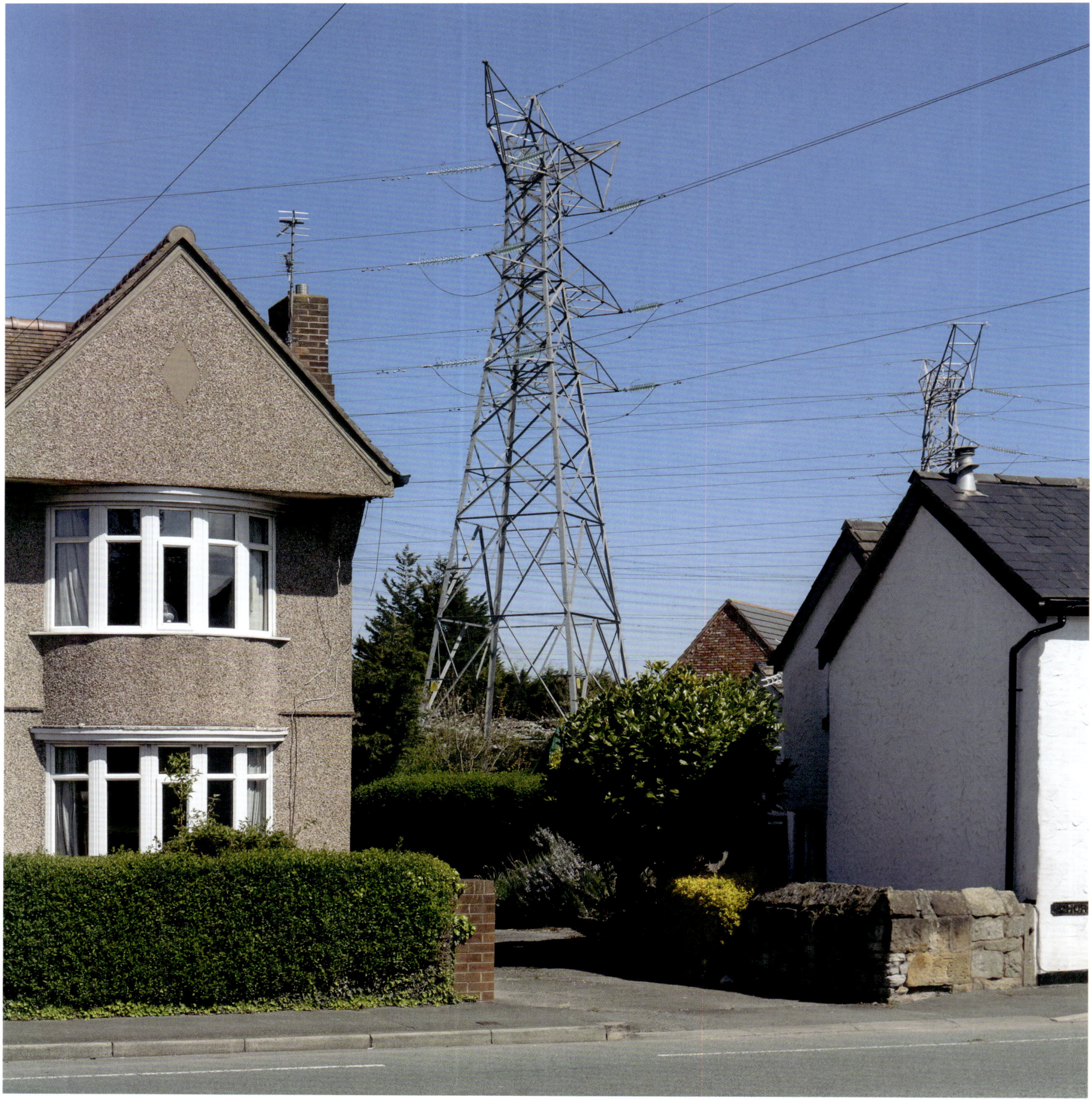

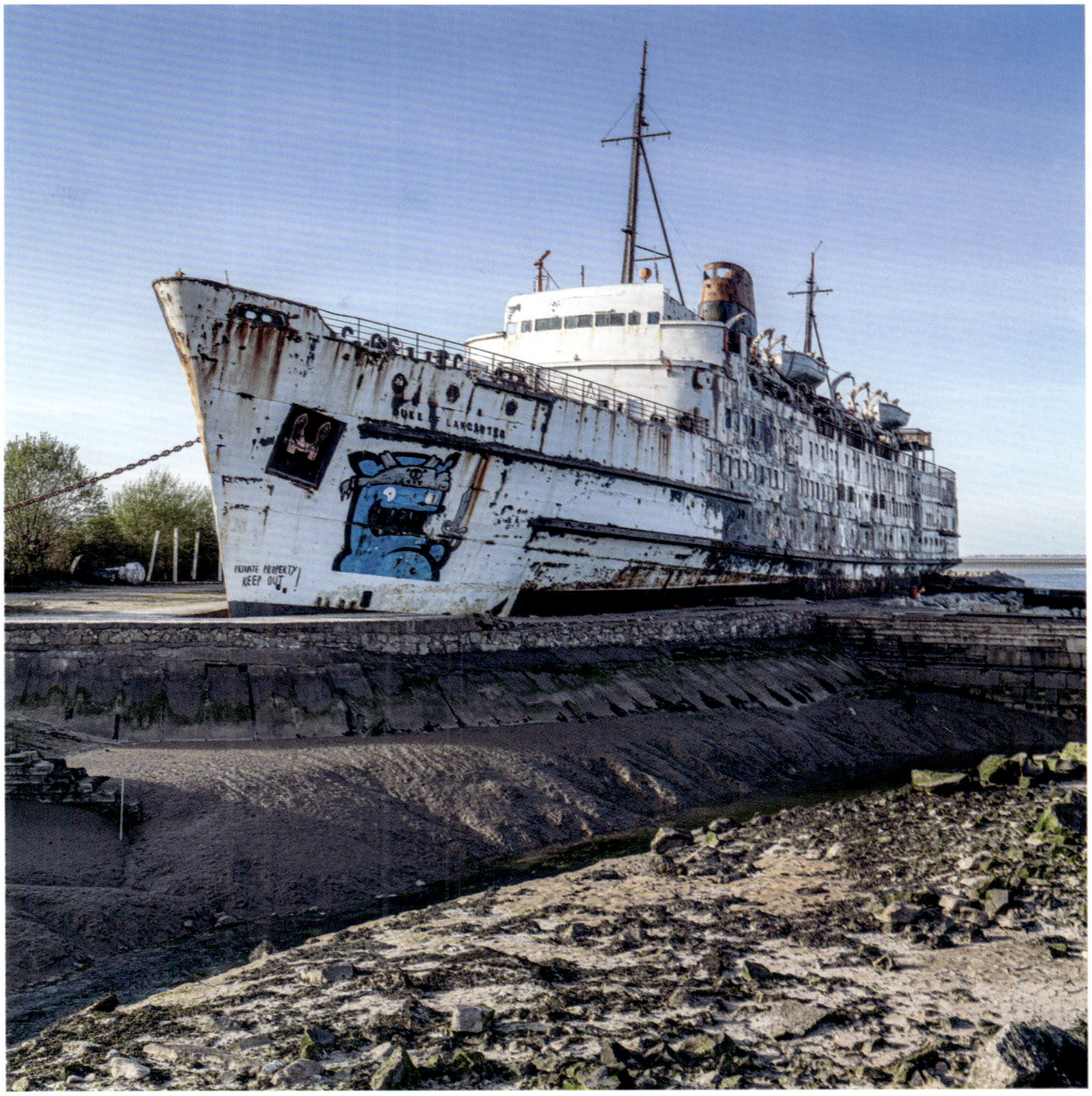

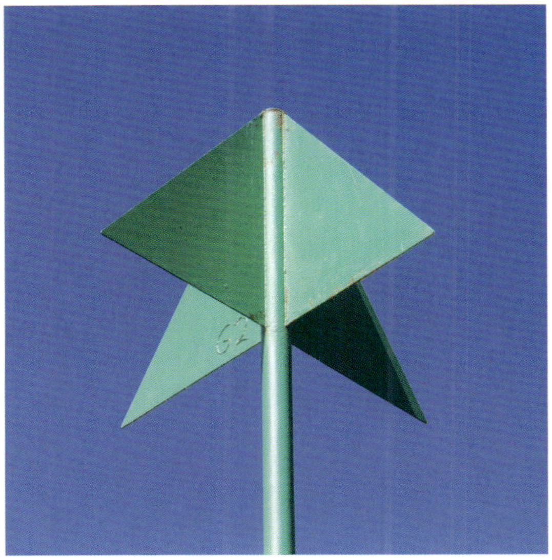

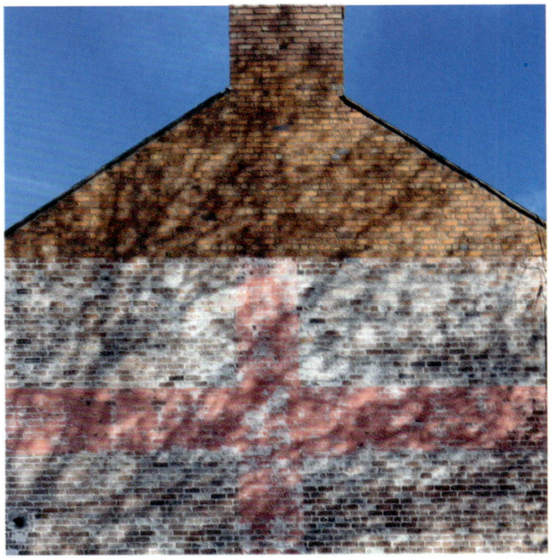

From top left:

TSS *Duke of Lancaster*, Mostyn, was a former railway steamer passenger ship that operated in Europe from 1956 to 1979. From 1979 to 2004, she started a new life as the Fun Ship leisure and retail complex to circumvent the then Sunday trading laws

Groyne marker, Barkby Beach

Across the border into England, Chester, Cheshire

Opposite:

Pylon garden, Connah's Quay

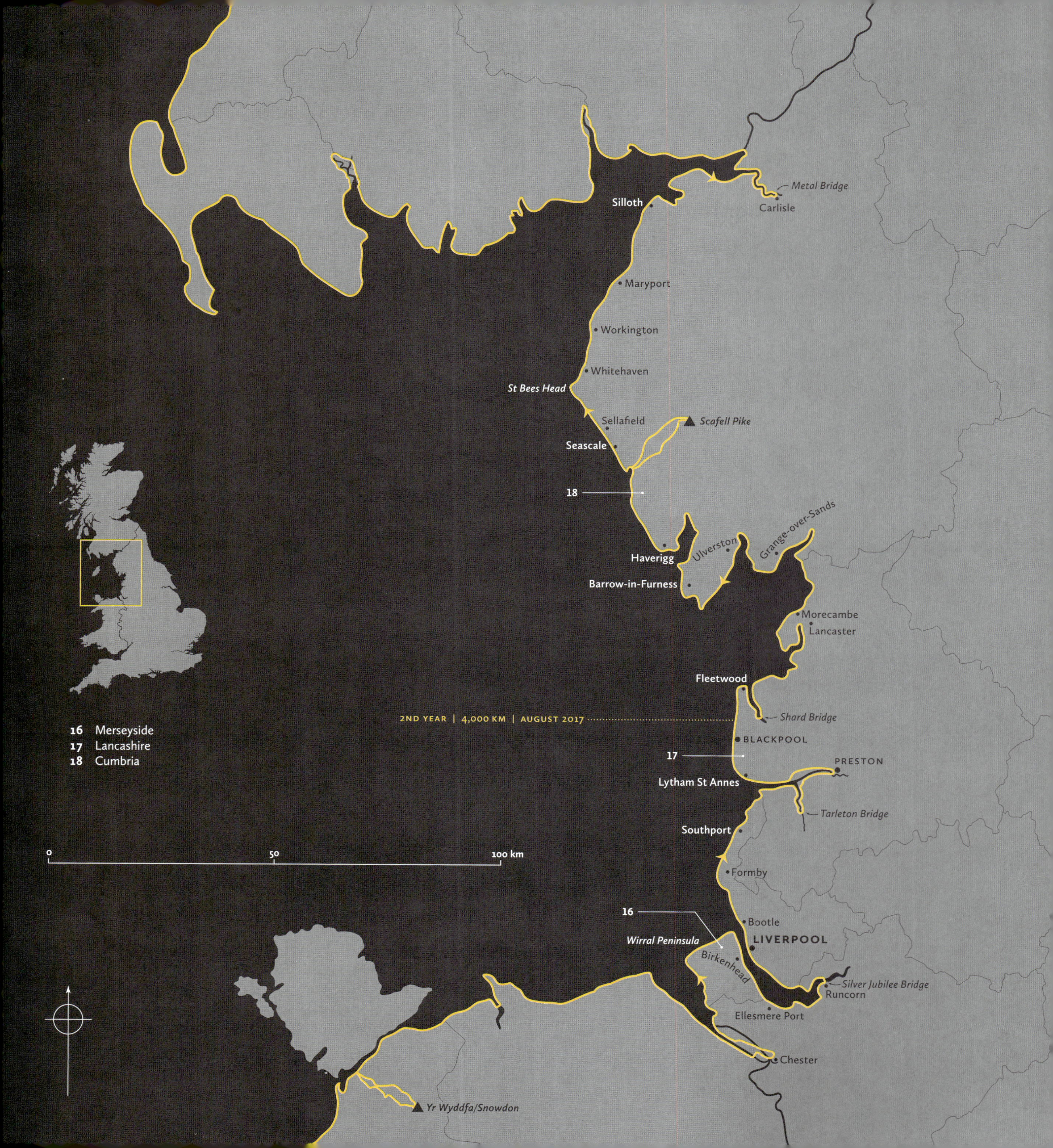

Metal Bridge
Carlisle
Silloth
Maryport
Workington
Whitehaven
St Bees Head
Sellafield
Scafell Pike
Seascale
18
Haverigg
Ulverston
Grange-over-Sands
Barrow-in-Furness
Morecambe
Lancaster
Fleetwood
Shard Bridge
2ND YEAR | 4,000 KM | AUGUST 2017
BLACKPOOL
17
PRESTON
Lytham St Annes
Tarleton Bridge
Southport
Formby
16
Bootle
Wirral Peninsula
LIVERPOOL
Birkenhead
Silver Jubilee Bridge
Runcorn
Ellesmere Port
Chester
Yr Wyddfa/Snowdon
16 Merseyside
17 Lancashire
18 Cumbria
0
50
100 km

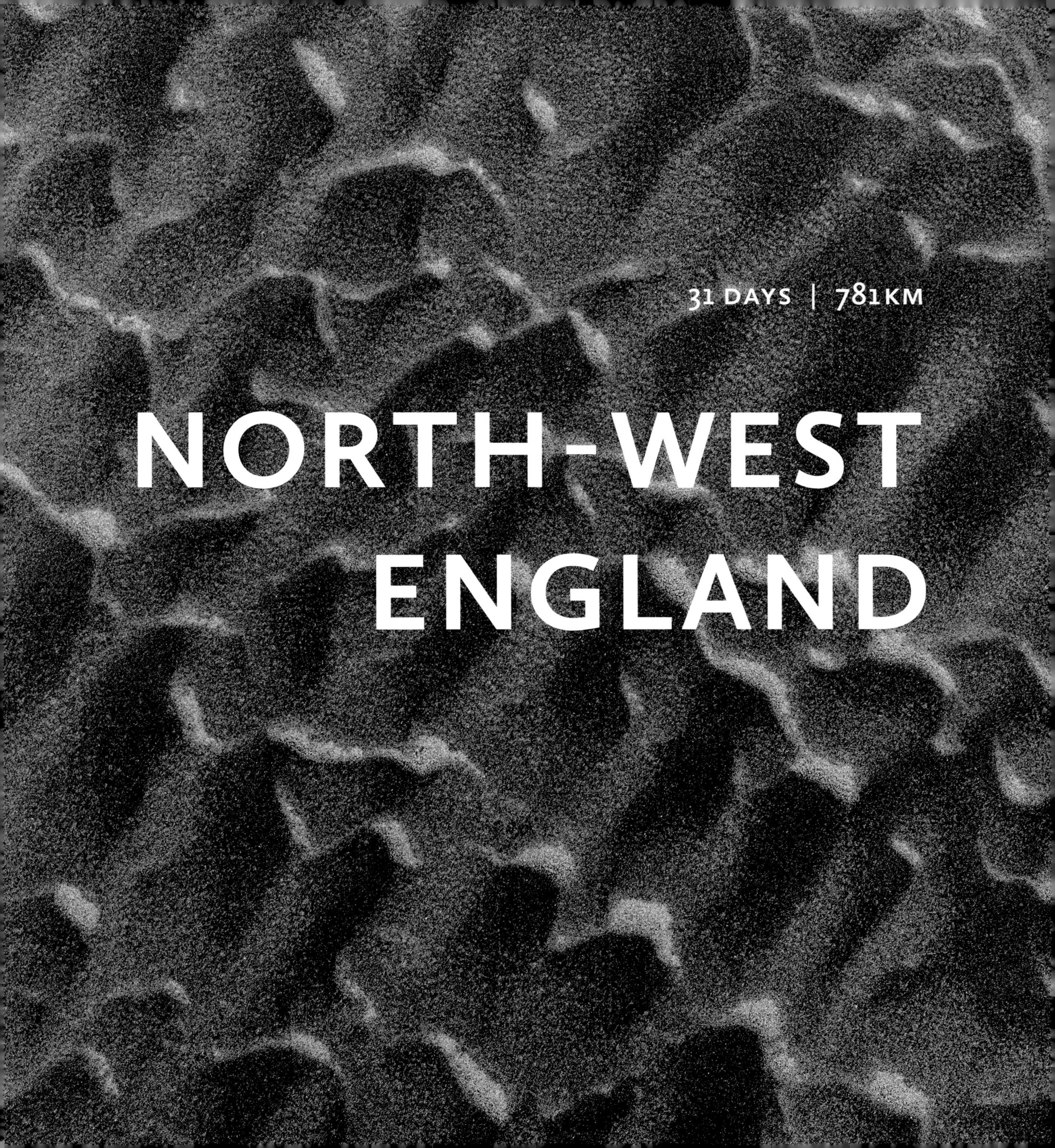

31 DAYS | 781KM

NORTH-WEST ENGLAND

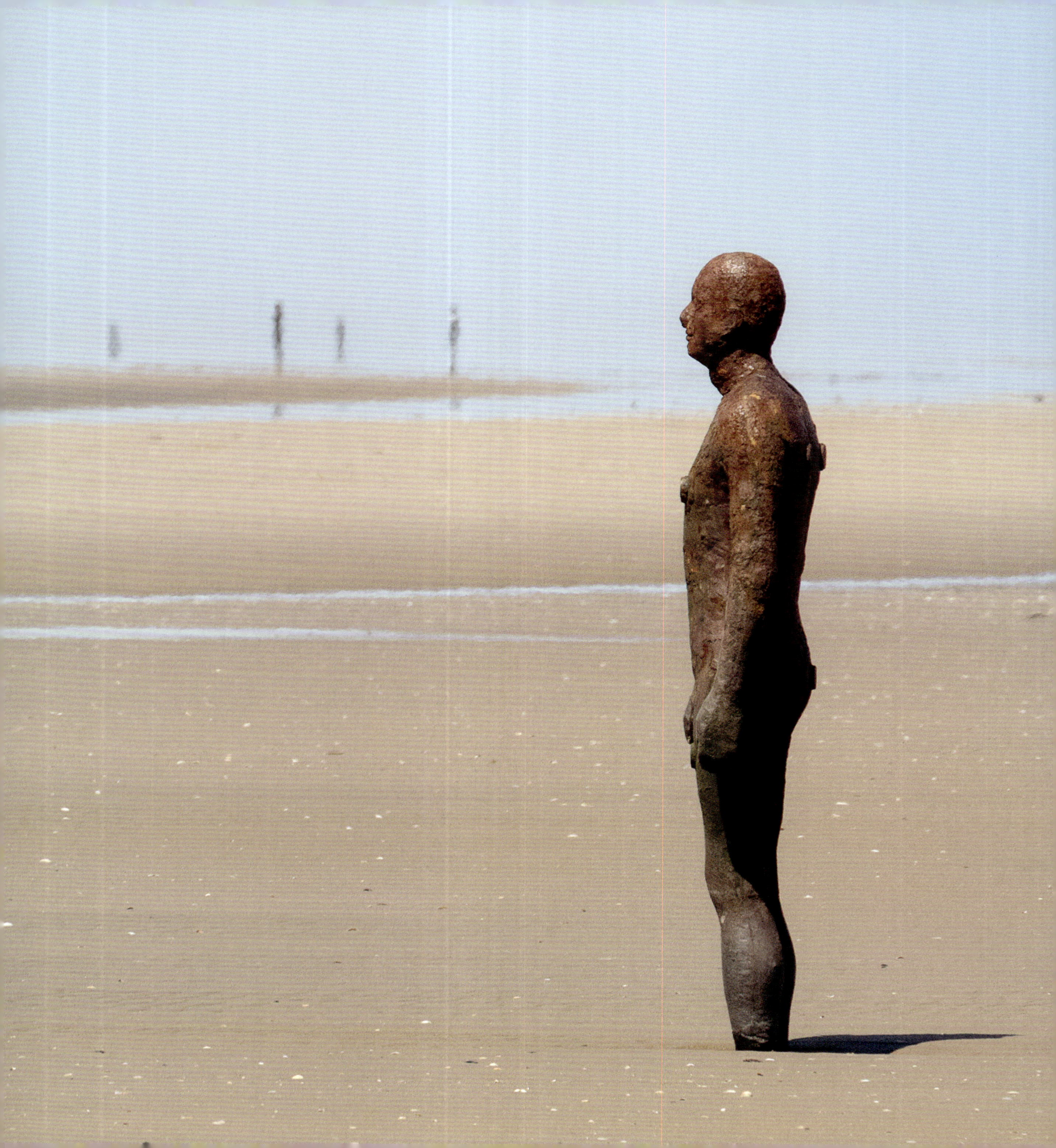

16 MERSEYSIDE

MAY–JUNE 2017

DAY 143–147 | 03,751–03,927 KM | 176 KM

Properly in the north now, my 'Hello' is greeted by folks I pass on the path with a 'How do'. I leave Chester by following the canal past a cascade of locks and red stone Roman walls leading to the Wirral Peninsula. Soon I'm at Neston, a market town that feels bereft with a quayside but no sea; the water there is silted and replaced by a saltmarsh.

The raw humanity of New Brighton immortalised in Martin Parr's book *The Last Resort* is nowhere to be seen. On the beach sits a cluster of obedient, red-uniformed schoolkids with lanyard-wearing teachers hovering over their brood. The concrete is smooth and extensive, while a large Morrisons dominates the promenade.

From Birkenhead, I can see the Liver Birds across the Mersey; what a thrill to see Liverpool so close! Pedestrians can't take the tunnels (although drunk revellers try getting home by that hazardous route regularly), so it's two more days inland through heavy industry to get to Liverpool via the bridge at Runcorn. Further south along the Mersey, a city of chimneys appear as oil refineries merge with chemical works, which become power stations. Pedestrians are not welcome here, and a map doesn't help much as I reach countless dead ends manned by security guards. I am forced to walk on the verge of main roads to make any progress.

Early the next morning, in an Ellesmere Port corner shop, a girl dressed in a Superman dressing gown and fluffy slippers tells me she's 'Never been so tired in my life, mate. Turned nineteen last night.' Somewhat wearily, I move into the landscape of chain-link fences and chimneys where the air has an acrid smell and sinister milky blue water fills the ditches. Approaching Stanlow oil refinery, signs inform me: *No photography. No stopping. No satnav*. After a roadblock, I expect to be stopped; CCTV cameras twitch regularly, but I walk on. My eyes water as I pass downwind of the nitric acid and ammonia plant at Ince fertiliser works – the steam and emissions swirl around, hiding and revealing the chimneys and structures. Over the next few kilometres, the chemical smell blends into the stench of a vast landfill. In this dystopian world, I'm grateful for a lapwing's bobbing, squeaking flight that seems miraculous among the pylons in Frodsham Marshes.

On my fourth day of walking, I say farewell to Runcorn in a downpour. 'We've had better days,' says a passing man as rain cascades off his umbrella. 'Nice summer's morning,' says a woman, sopping and laden with shopping bags. 'Lovely day for a walk,' says a cheerful dog walker. As the locals well understand, humour is essential on days like this. I do my best to see the funny side crossing the Runcorn to Widnes bridge as each passing truck covers me in a head-to-toe wave of muddy water. The stench from the chemical works blends into the more pleasant aroma of detergent from the factories on the approach to Liverpool. My excitement at arriving in the city is tempered as I start limping from a shooting pain in my right foot. I try to put the pain to the back of my mind with caffeine and ibuprofen, but by the time I reach Southport, I'm hobbling badly. Something must be seriously wrong, but I'm hopeful a good night's sleep will help. Unfortunately, this proves optimistic, and fearing a stress fracture, I make the difficult decision to head home and get medical assistance. An MRI scan shows a longitudinal tear of the tibialis anterior tendon on the top of the foot. The specialist tells me surgery won't be necessary, but I need to immobilise the foot in a 'walker boot' for six weeks before starting rehab. 'How did this happen?' I ask the doctor. He looks at me like I'm out of my mind. 'You've just walked four thousand kilometres.'

Previous:

Ainsdale Sands, Merseyside

Opposite:

Another Place, cast-iron figure based on sculptor Antony Gormley's own body, 2005, Crosby Beach, Merseyside

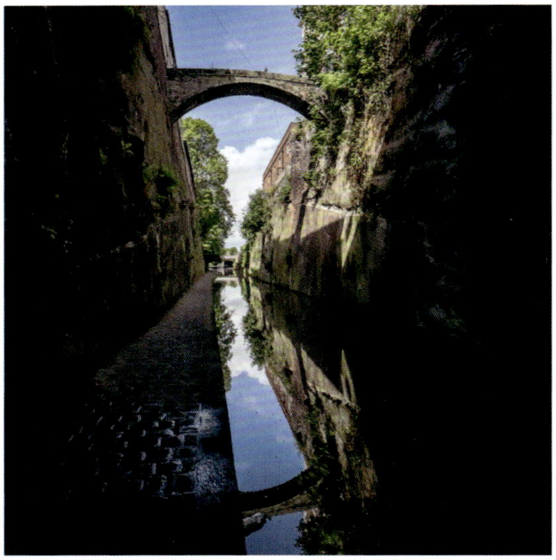

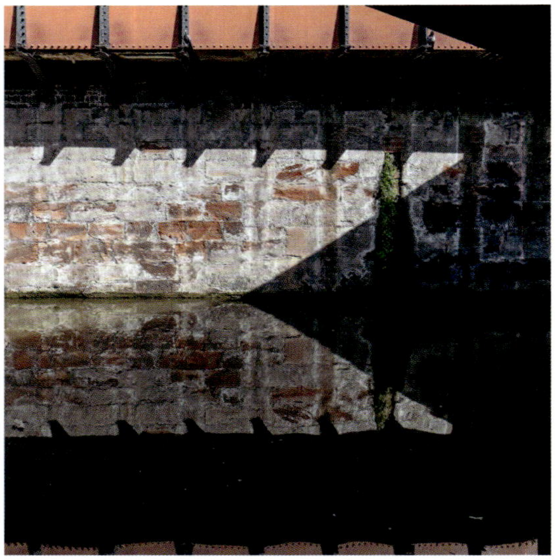

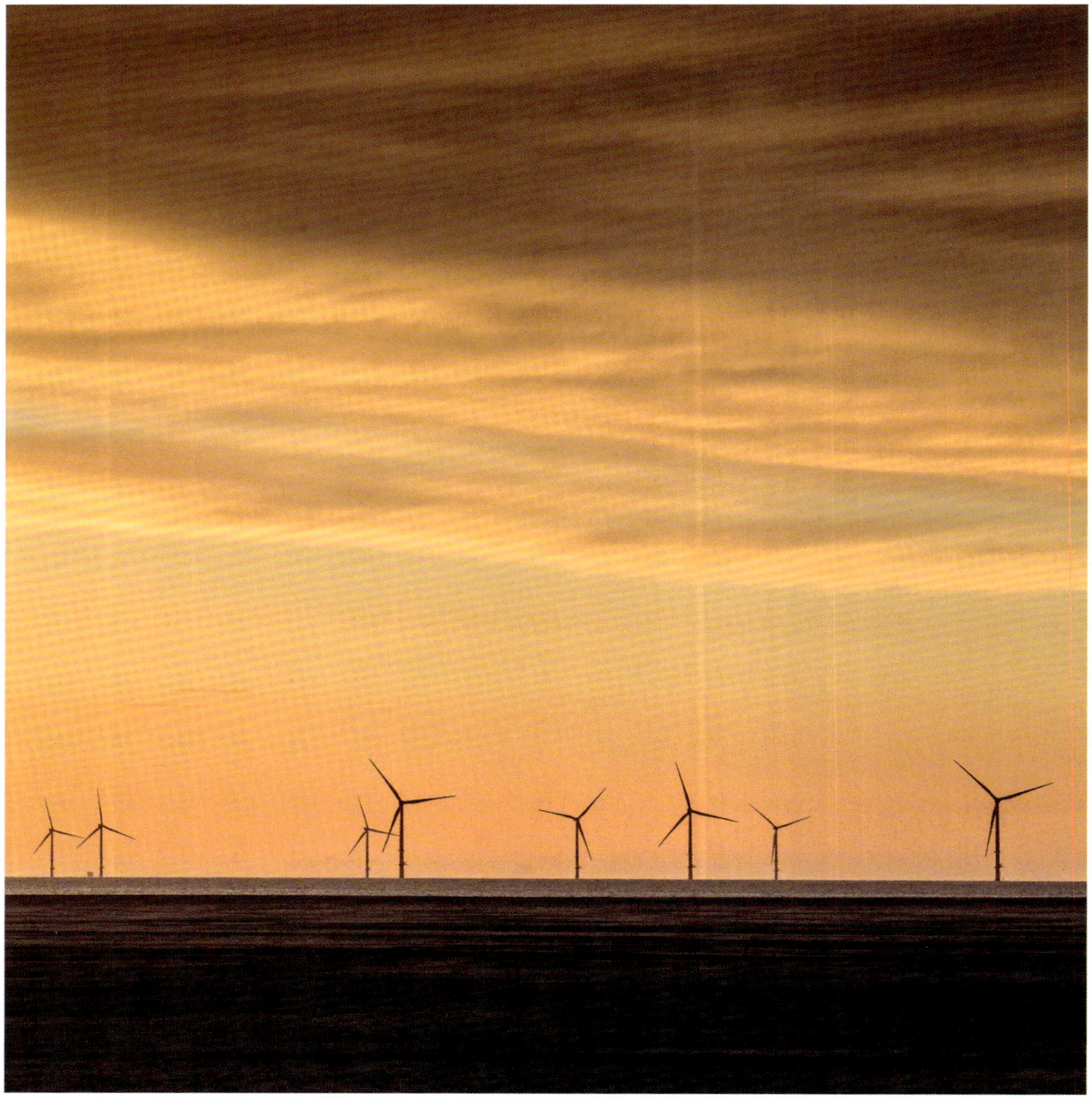

From top left:

Towards the sea along the Shropshire Union Canal, Chester, Cheshire

Shropshire Union Canal reflections

Burbo Bank Offshore Wind Farm, Hoylake

Opposite, clockwise from top left:

Marine Lake, West Kirby

Seascape, Wallasey Embankment

Mooring bollard, Birkenhead Docks

Concrete runner: Wallasey Embankment

Central hydraulic tower and engine house, Birkenhead Docks

Liverpool2, a deep-water container terminal at the Port of Liverpool

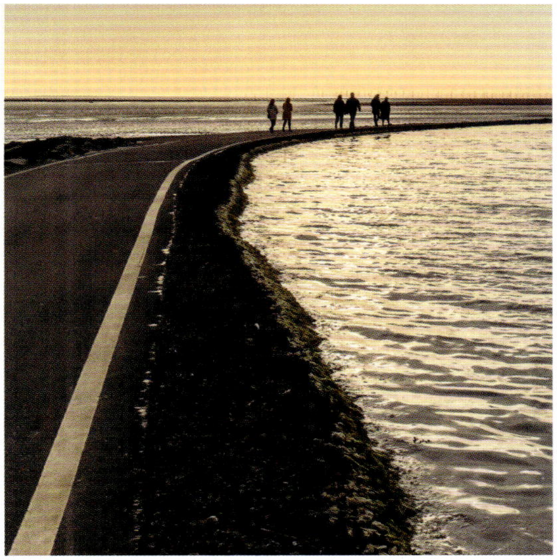
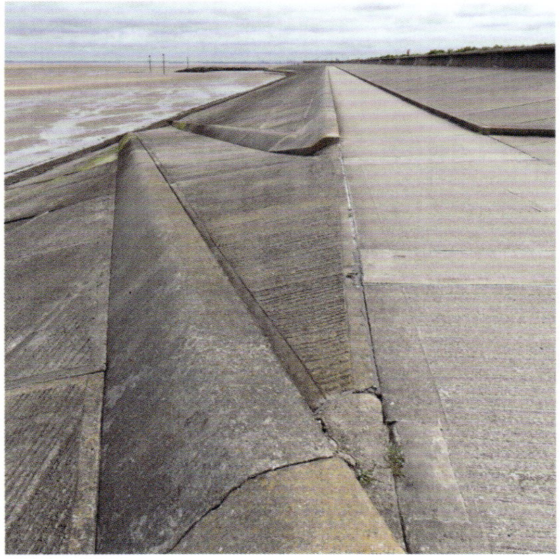
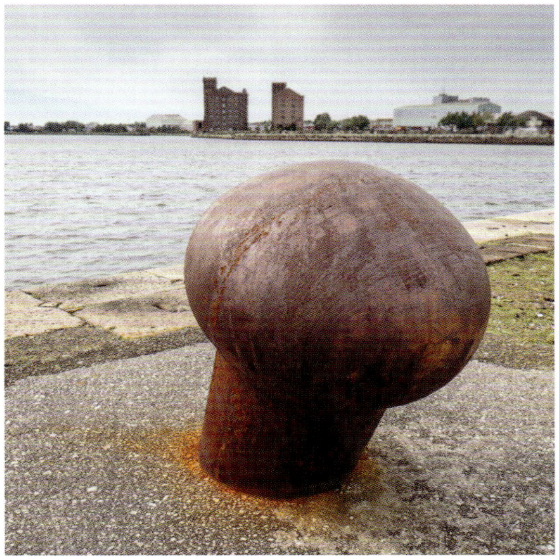
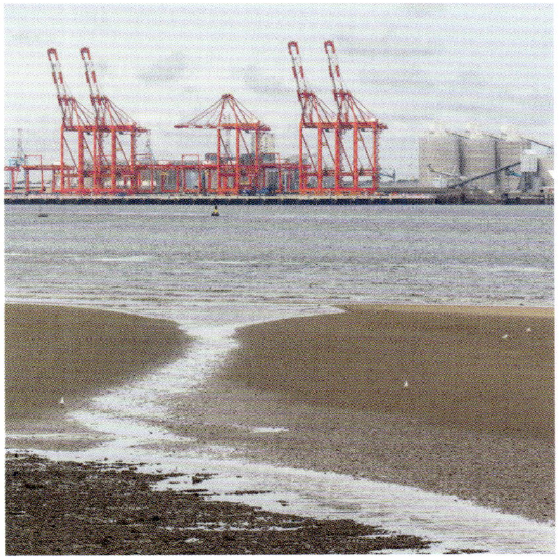
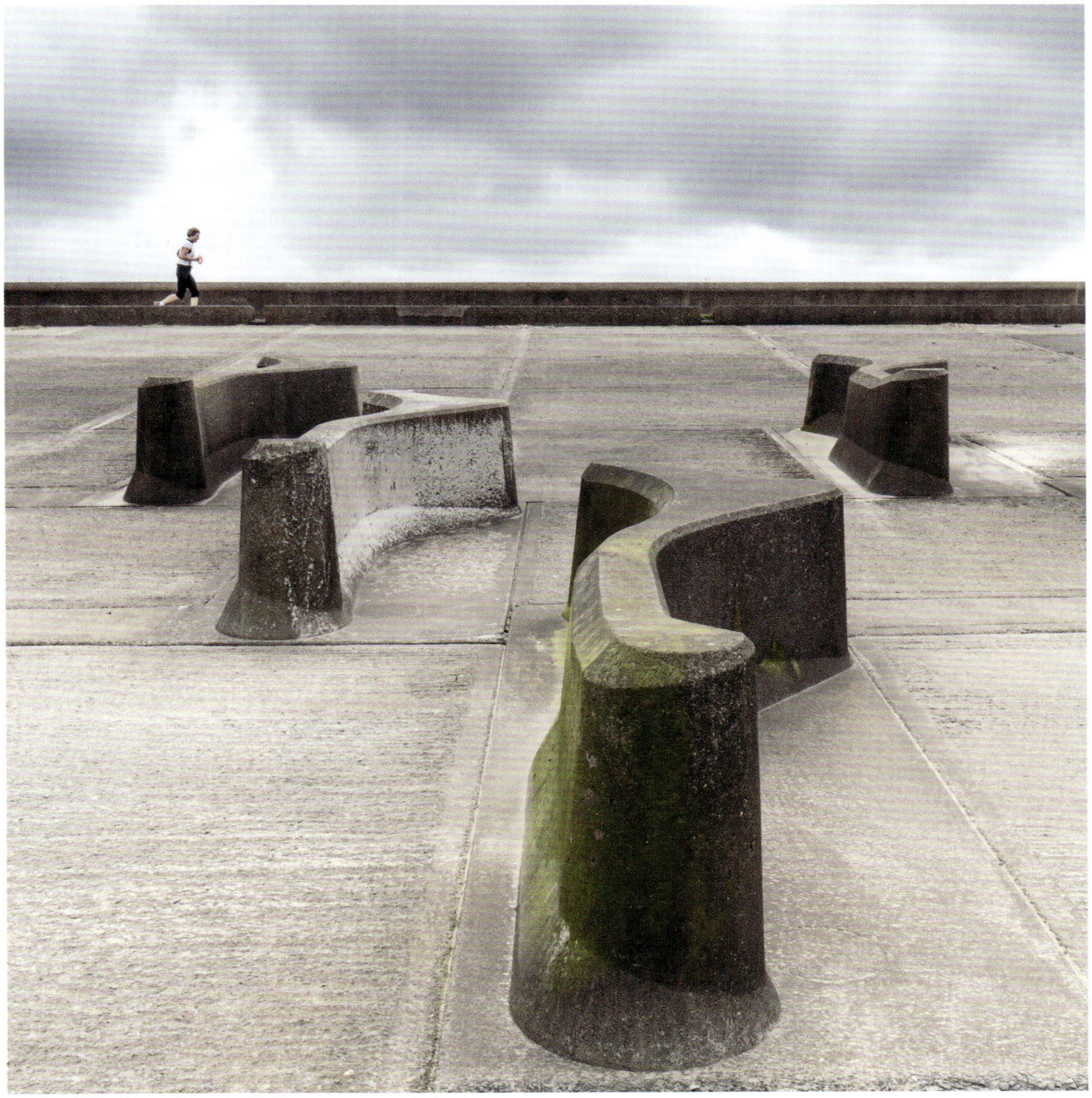
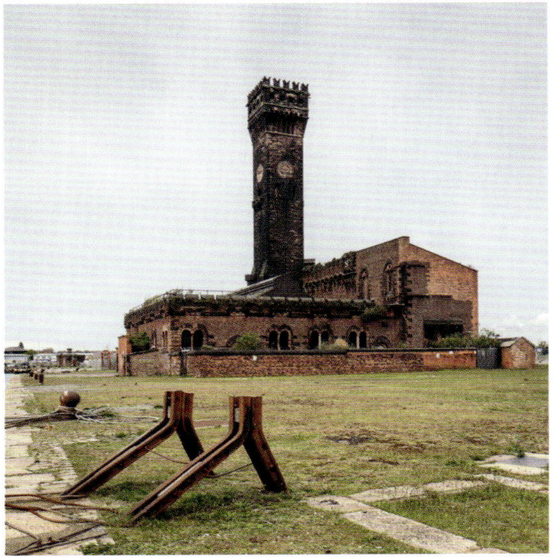

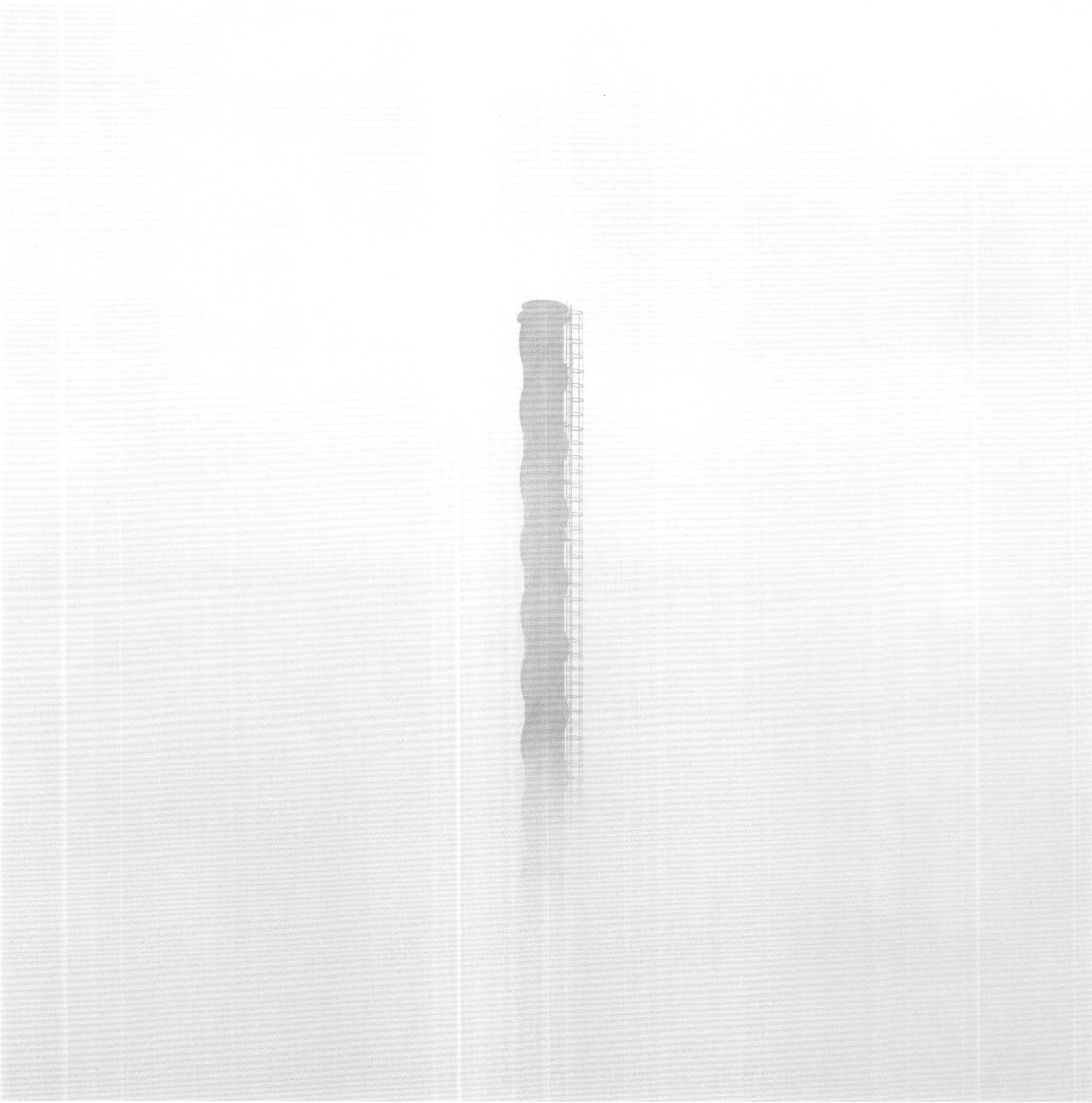

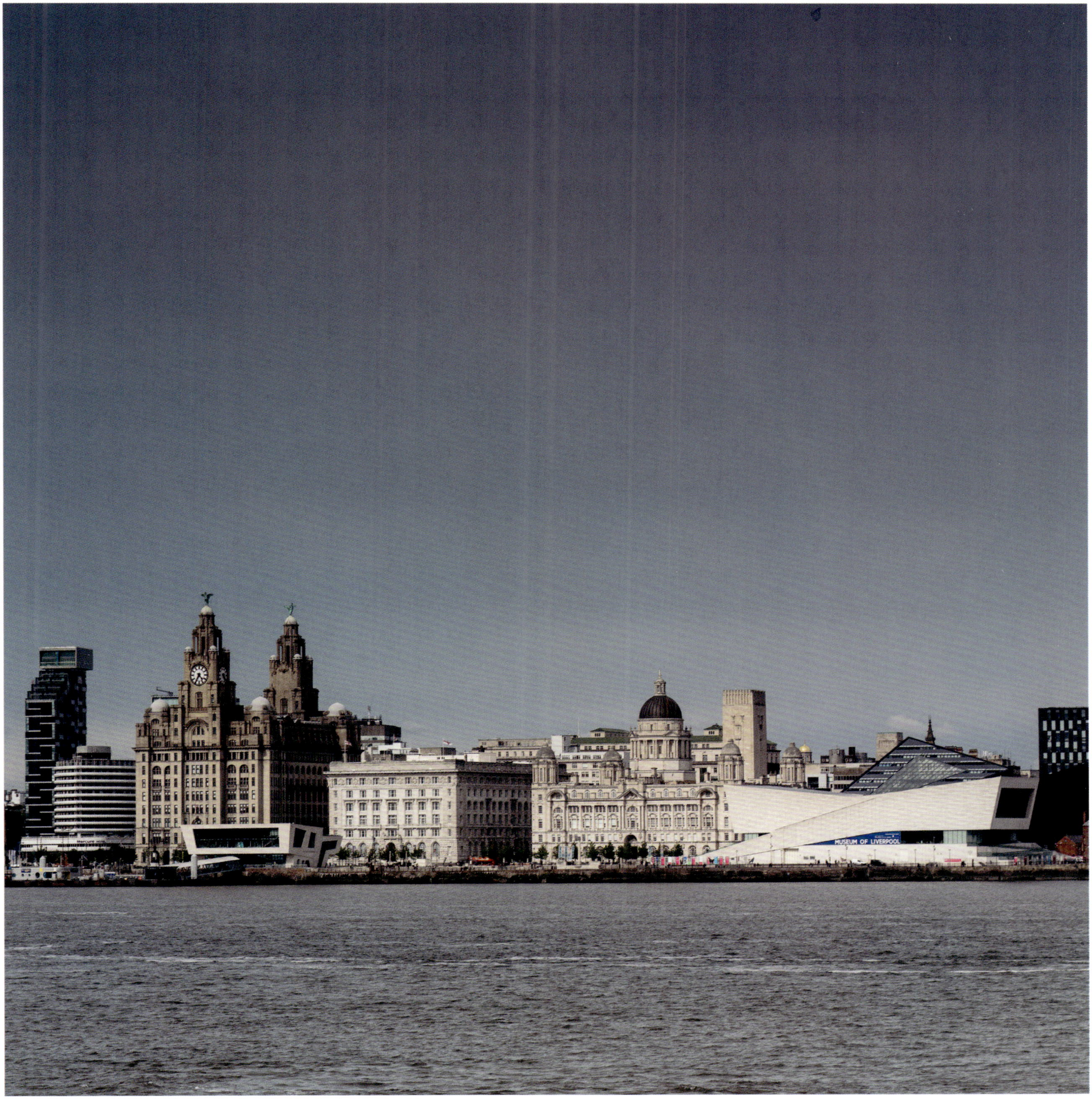
MUSEUM OF LIVERPOOL

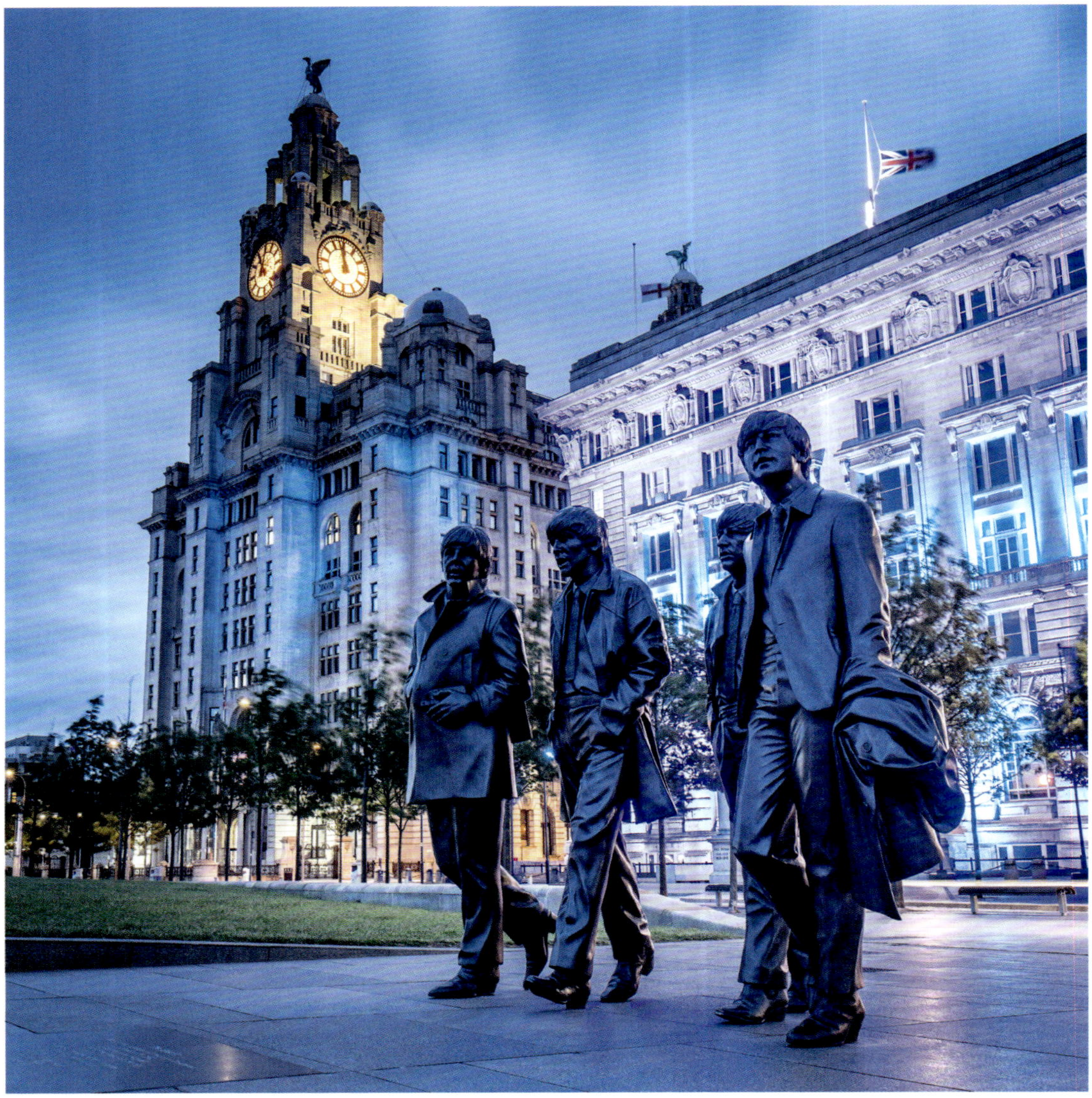

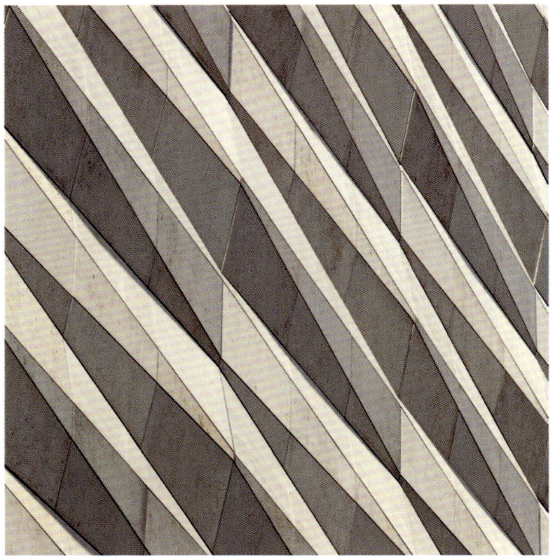

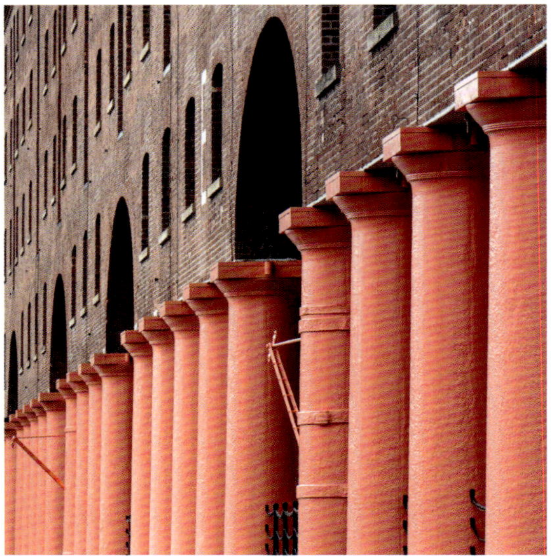

Previous, from left to right:

Fertiliser manufacturing plant, Ince Marshes, Cheshire

Pier Head from Birkenhead, Merseyside. Landmarks from left to right: the Royal Liver Building, the Cunard Building, the Port of Liverpool Building and the Museum of Liverpool

From top left:

The Beatles statue at the Pier Head, Liverpool. Created by sculptor Andy Edwards in 2015 to commemorate the fiftieth anniversary of their last concert in their home city. Union Jack at half-mast for the May 2017 Manchester Arena bombing

Museum of Liverpool facade, designed by architects 3XN, Liverpool

Albert Dock, Liverpool

Opposite:

Abandoned Stanley Dock Tobacco Warehouse, at the time of its construction in 1901 reported to be the world's largest brick building. With the decline of trade going through Liverpool, the warehouse fell into disuse in the 1980s. From 2015 to 2021, it was redeveloped into several hundred apartments

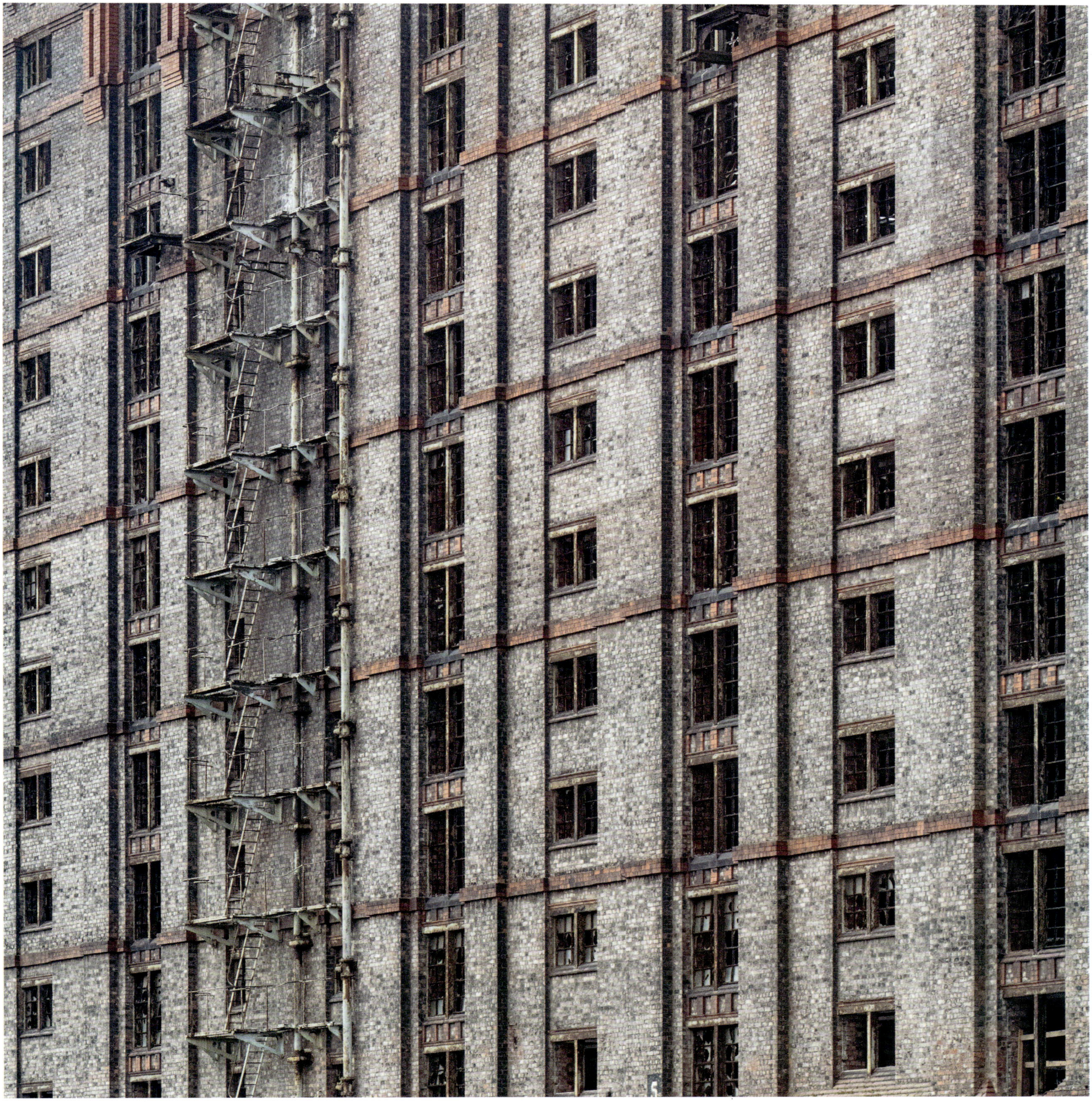

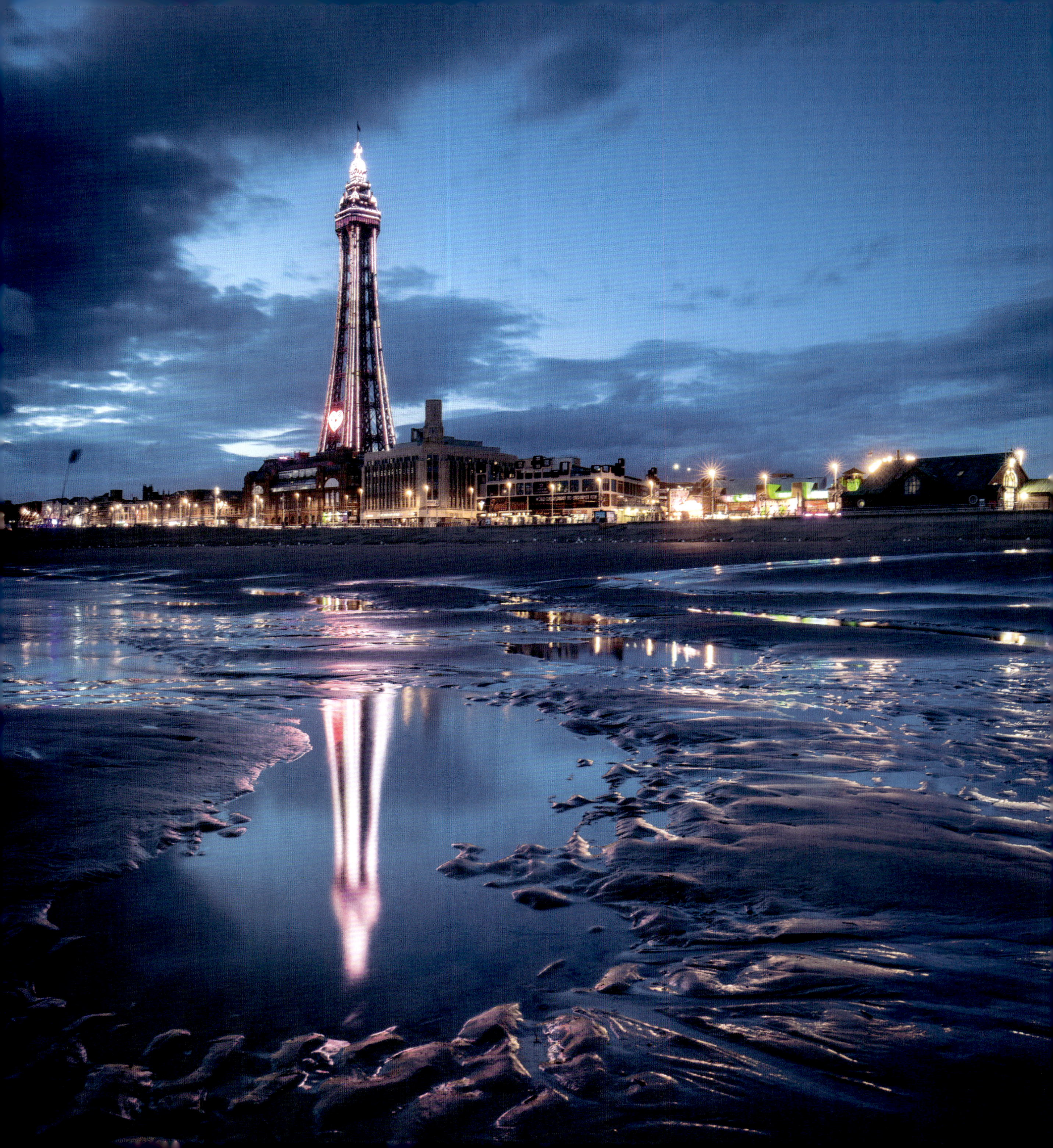

17 LANCASHIRE

AUGUST 2017

DAY 148–157 | 03,927–04,130 KM | 203 KM

After seven weeks of rest, the tendon injury in my foot starts to heal, and I return tentatively to the trail. Progress is slow, rests are frequent, but I can move forward, and the sea breeze on my face again makes me feel at home. The ground is flat, fortunately, as my ankle has lost strength, and I shuffle along like a geriatric insect with two trekking poles, mourning that my daily mileage has dropped to a quarter of what it used to be.

On my second day in Lancashire, I reach the River Ribble, where yellow and pink ribbons flutter outside every house and shop, and on every lamp post in the villages of Tarleton and Hesketh Bank. The area feels so safe, manicured and tucked away that it's a shock to discover they're in honour of two local girls who were killed in the Manchester Arena bombing.

The next day, I return to the sea from Preston and follow the Ribble to the Fylde Peninsula, a 20-kilometre coastal conurbation that runs from the affluence of Lytham in the south to Fleetwood in the north. The clatter and intermittent scream of a roller coaster marks the gateway to the centre of Blackpool, with its 400-plus hotels, three piers and famous tower. As I wander along the prom, surrounded by palm readers and shops selling lurid candy cocks, a wide-eyed man grabs my arm. 'Local idiot,' his beer-holding friend tells me with an apologetic grin; it's 9 a.m.

Most hotels near where I'm staying in the heart of Blackpool cater to the elderly. In one, live music plays, and, in another I see a white-haired older man seemingly dancing alone by the bar. Next door, a dining room full of hunched figures studiously write down their bingo scores. At the edge of it all, Blackpool Tower, illuminated by ribbons of pink lights, rises above the inky sea.

Outside Blackpool, the coastline at Fleetwood is harsh and concreted but softened as the tide reveals vast expanses of sand towards Morecambe Bay. As I walk through the town towards the River Wyre, a gaggle of dressed-up girls pass me on the way to the tram for a night out; they are all sculpted eyebrows, midriffs and tottering heels. They seem miraculously vivacious in contrast to the grey pebbledash houses and grey sky surrounding them.

Lancashire is a land rich in puns, and I pass 'Dave's tree-mendous seat', the Posh Spice Indian takeaway and a dilapidated yacht named *Who Stole My Rudder?*. The intermittent humour enlivens my route beside the river, before I skirt around yet another caravan park pressed up against stinking chemical works and concrete boarded-up houses. Then, slowly, gently, delight returns to the landscape. The tarmac gives way to a squidgy green path below the high-tide line; there's sea lavender and little egrets. The plants of the Wyre Estuary are adapted to saltwater immersion and have a waxy surface like cacti. They undulate gracefully in the water as the tide rises.

At the edge of Overton, I'm forced to practise patience as the high tide makes it impossible to continue along the tidal road through Lades Marsh to Sunderland Point. I'm not the only one, and to pass the time I strike up a conversation with a local fisherwoman who, it transpires, is the only woman in the UK licensed to use the ancient 'haaf net' for catching salmon.

By the evening, I am confident that my foot injury has healed enough for me to walk as fast as I can to the rock-cut tombs at St Patrick's Chapel, Heysham, for the last light. I arrive with barely five minutes of sunlight left, but it's enough to capture the golden glow kissing the three human forms carved into the slab of rock overlooking the bay.

Opposite:

Blackpool Tower at dusk. Inspired by the Eiffel Tower and opened in 1894, it was at the time the tallest artificial structure in the British Empire. Blackpool Tower's 'beating heart' light installation was opened in 2011

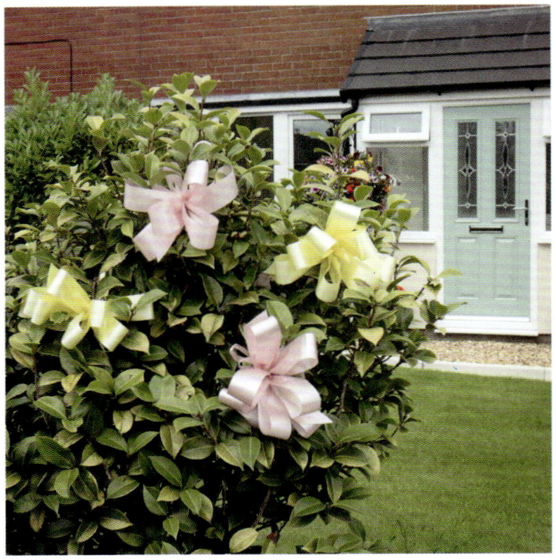

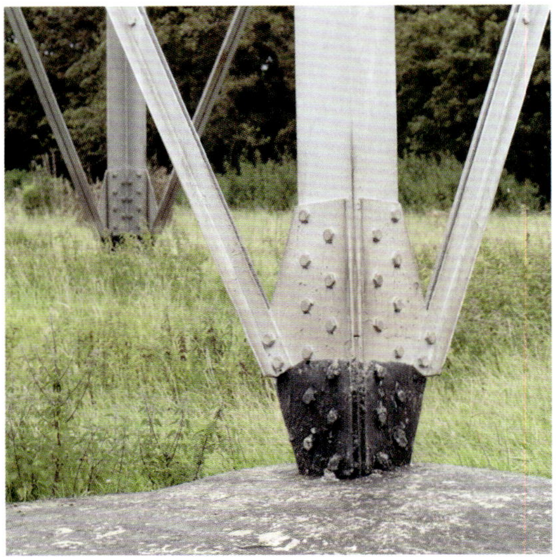

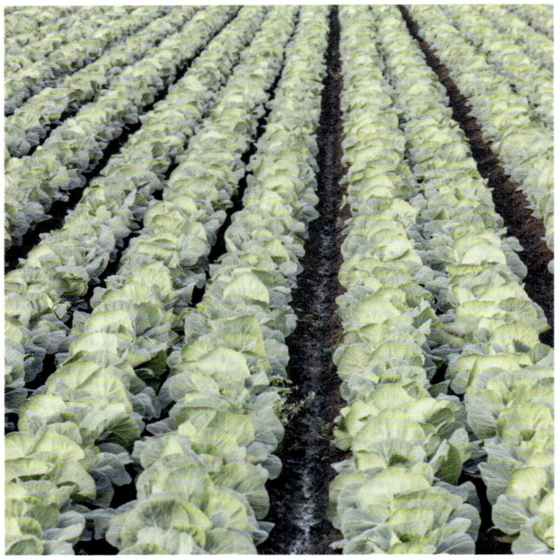

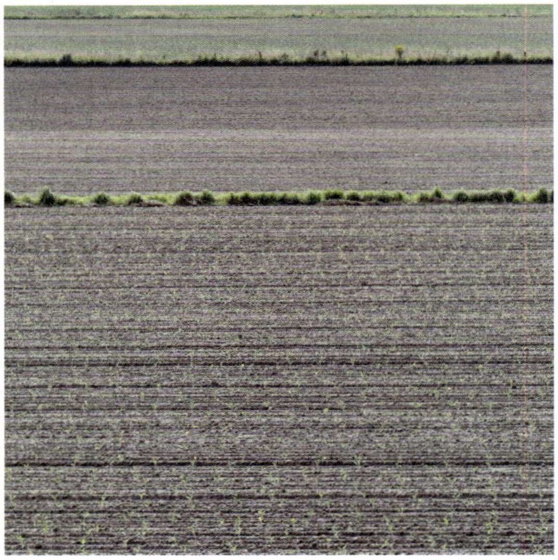

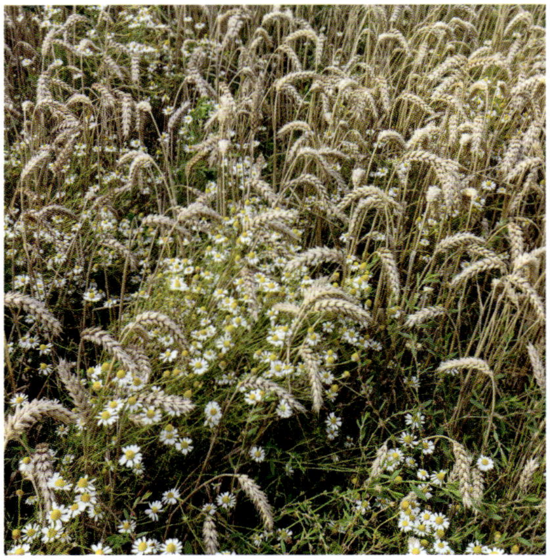

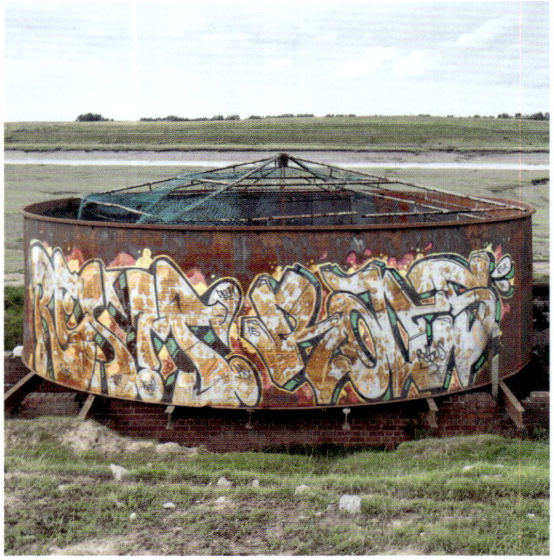

From top left:

Tribute in memory of Saffie Rose Roussos, aged eight, and Georgina Callander, eighteen, who died when a bomb exploded in the foyer of Manchester Arena after an Ariana Grande concert on 22 May 2017, Tarleton and Hesketh Bank

Pylon foot, Preston

From centre left:

Salad crops, Marsh Farm, Hundred End

Furrows, Hesketh New Marsh

From bottom left:

Corn, chamomile and wheat, Hutton Marsh

Resm and rats (I think!), River Ribble

Opposite, clockwise from top left:

Heavy sky, St Annes

Lytham Windmill

Mirror ball, Blackpool

Pirates, Blackpool Illuminations, Bispham

Breakwater, South Shore, Blackpool

Approaching Blackpool from the dunes

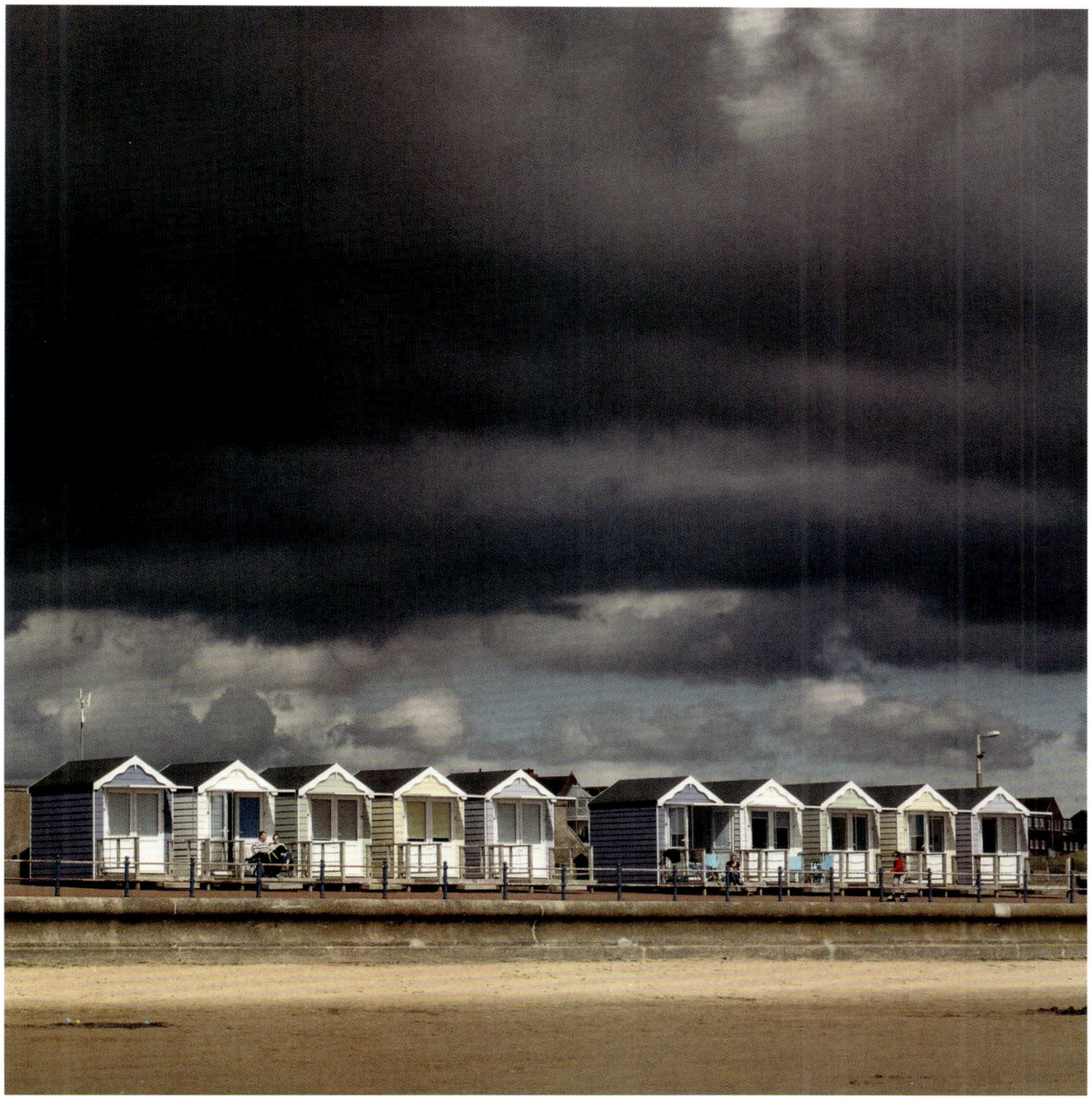
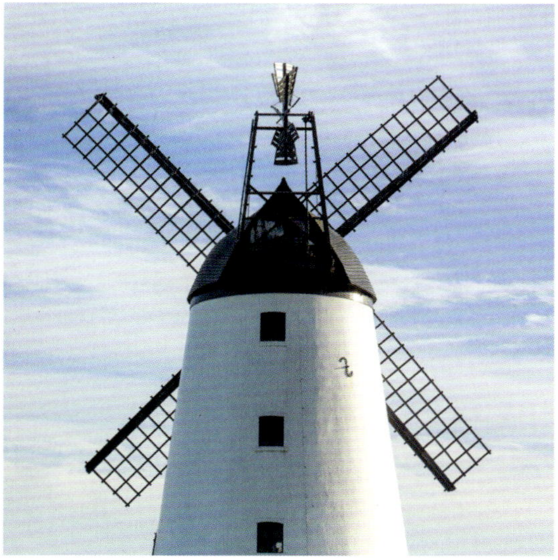
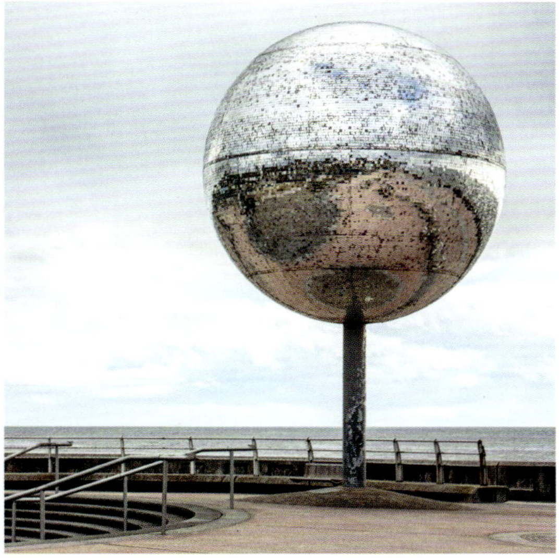
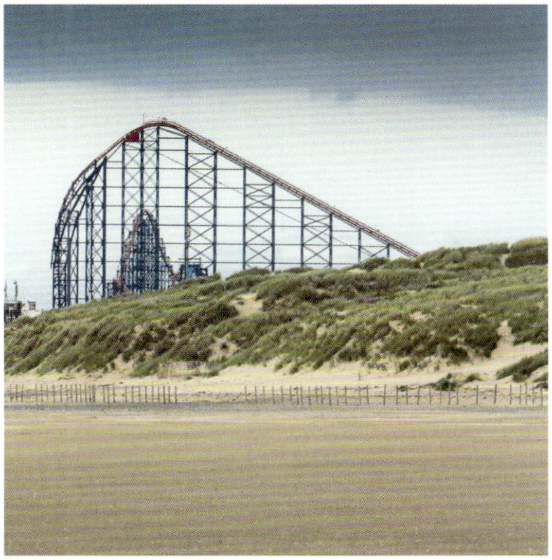
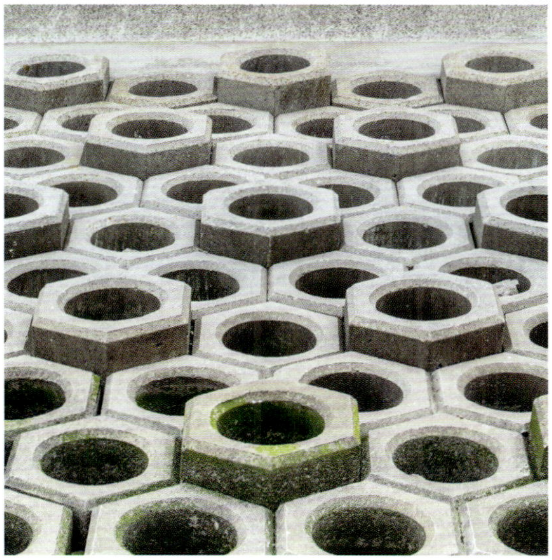
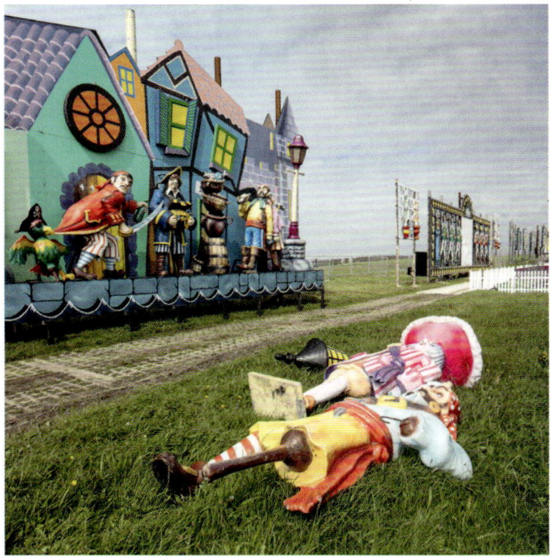

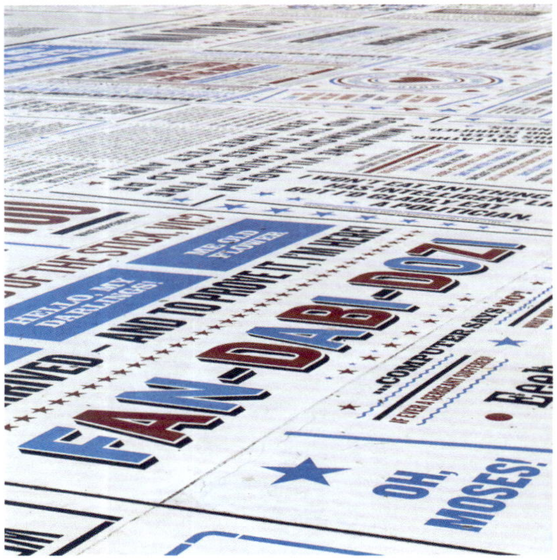

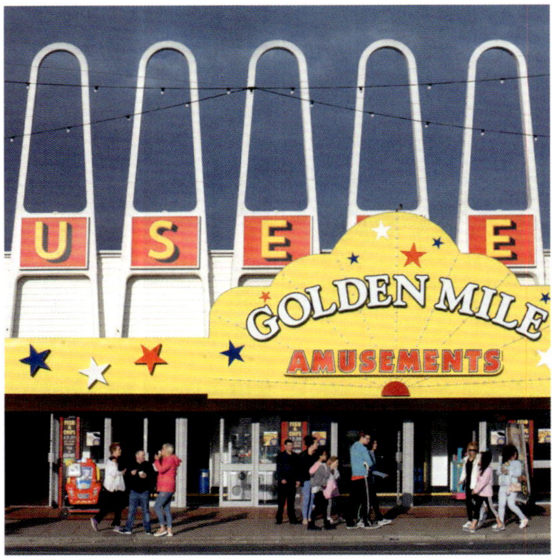

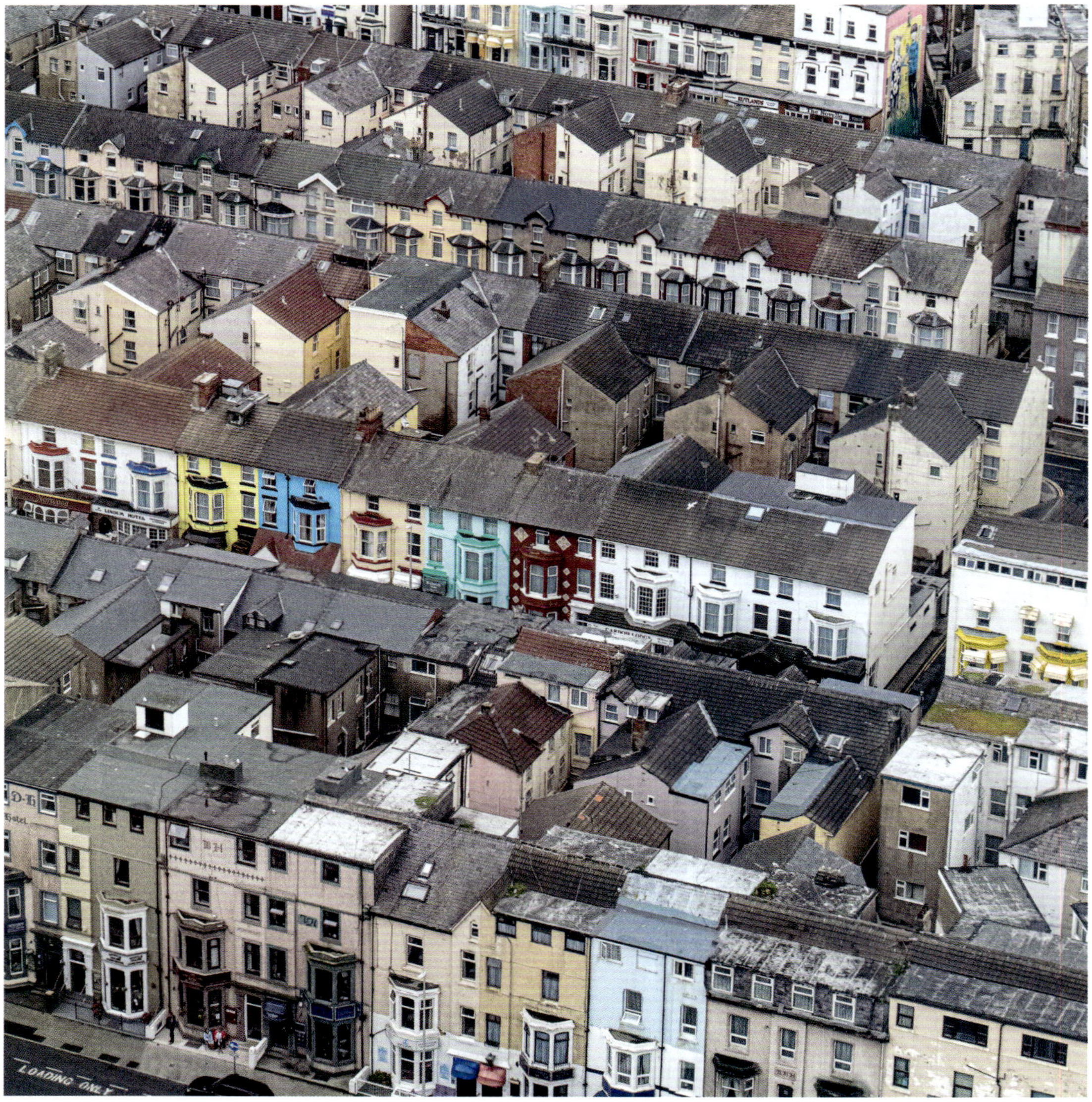

From top left:

Comedy Carpet, a work of art by Gordon Young designed in collaboration with Why Not Associates, Blackpool

Golden Mile, Blackpool

Some of the hundreds of B&Bs in Blackpool, seen from the Tower

Opposite:

Big One roller coaster, Blackpool

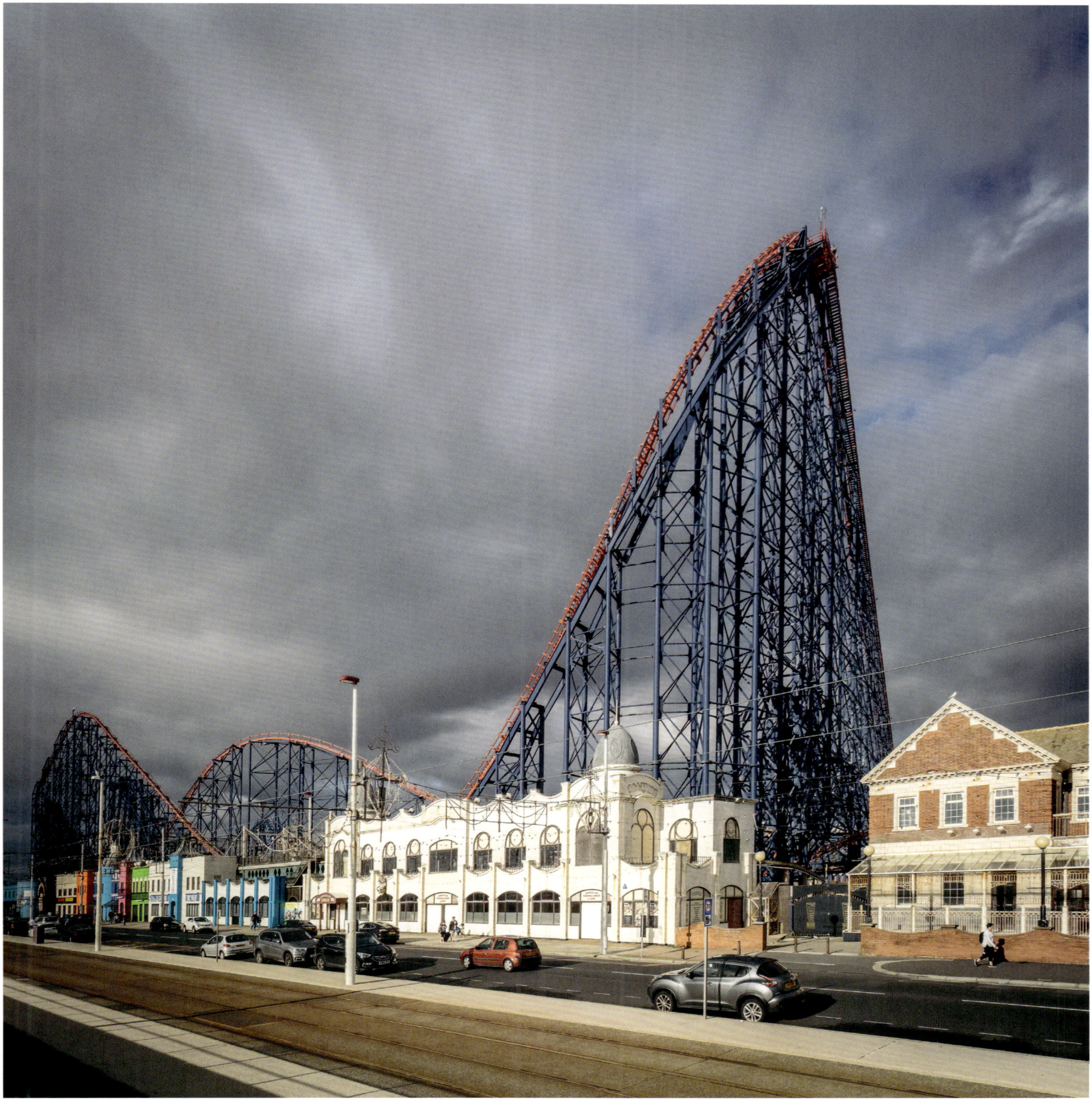

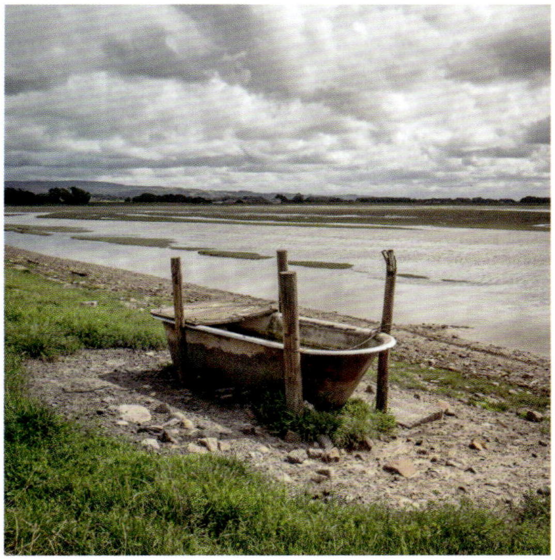
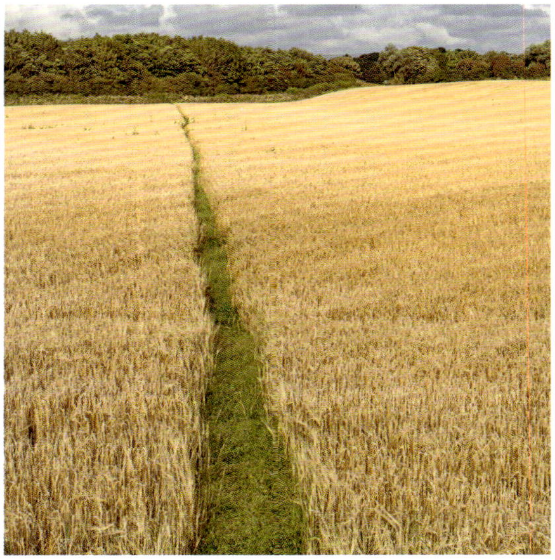
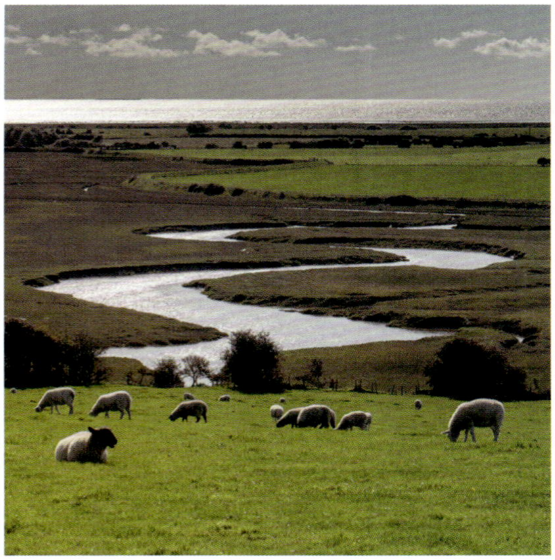
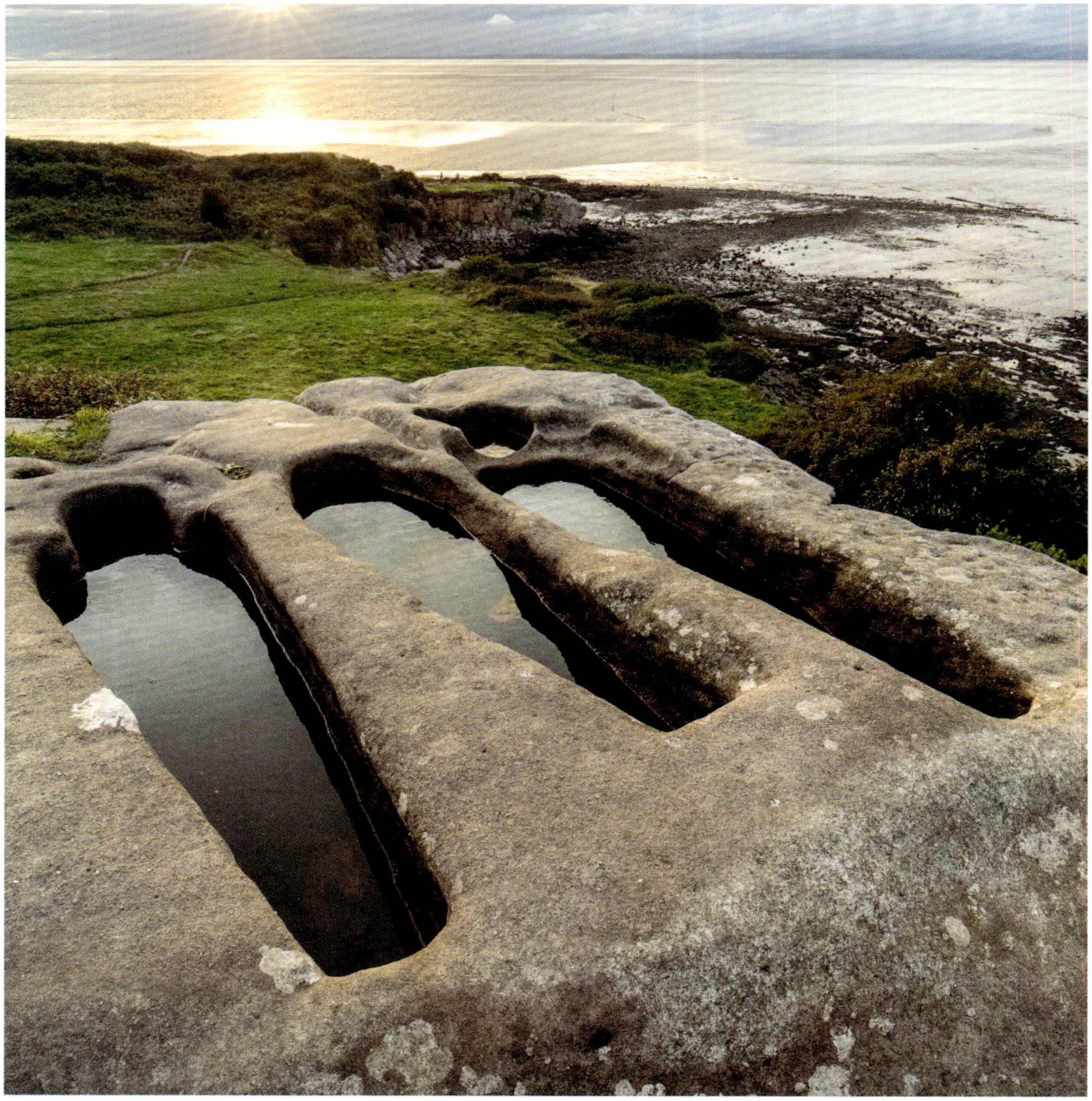
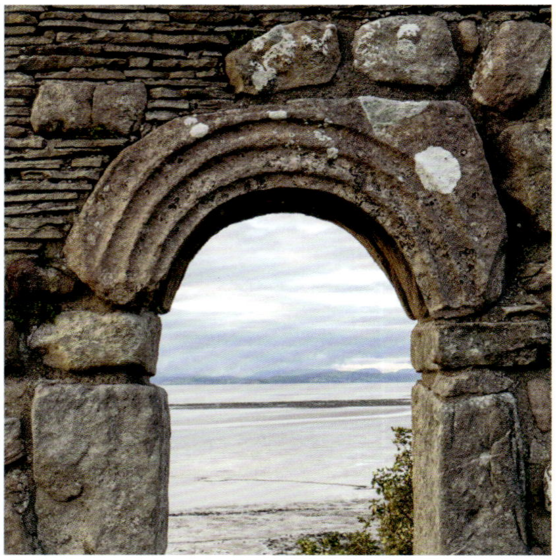
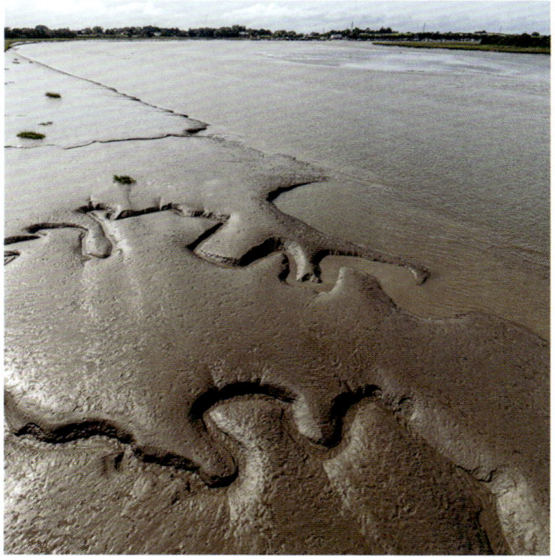

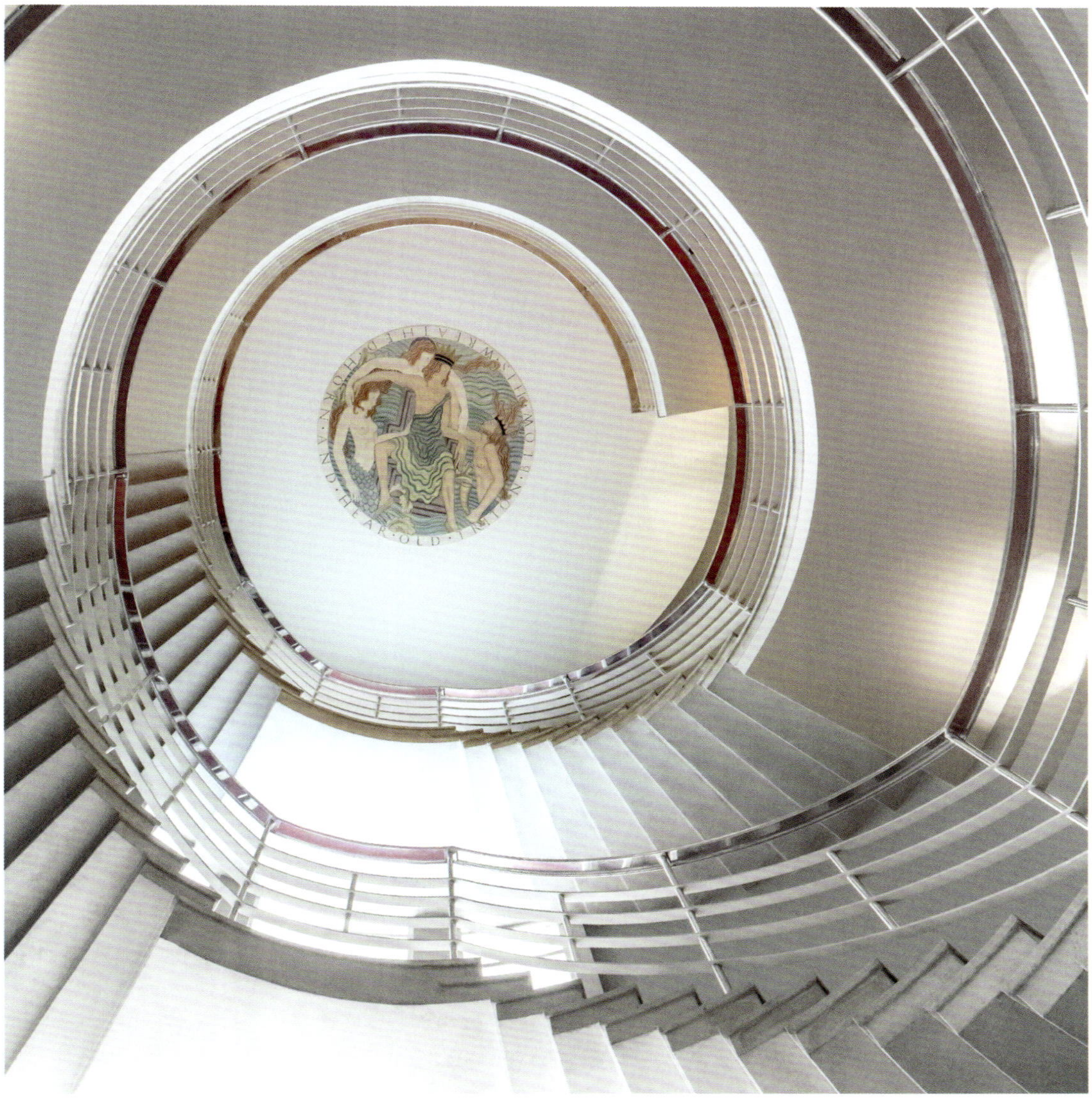

Opposite, clockwise from top left:

Four-poster bath, with snack tray and estuary views, Cockerham Marsh

A perfect path: Burrows Marsh. Reminds me of the 1967 artwork *A Line Made by Walking* by Richard Long

Lades Marsh, Sunderland

Eighth-century St Patrick's Chapel, Heysham

The River Wyre from Shard Bridge

Sunset at the rock-cut tombs, St Patrick's Chapel, Heysham

From top left:

The Neptune and Triton medallion made by Eric Gill in 1933 in the main stairwell of the Midland Hotel, Morecambe

Comedian Eric Morecambe statue by Graham Ibbeson, 1999, Morecambe promenade. He stands in one of his characteristic poses, complete with a pair of binoculars around his neck, a nod to his love of birdwatching

Beach Garage, Silverdale

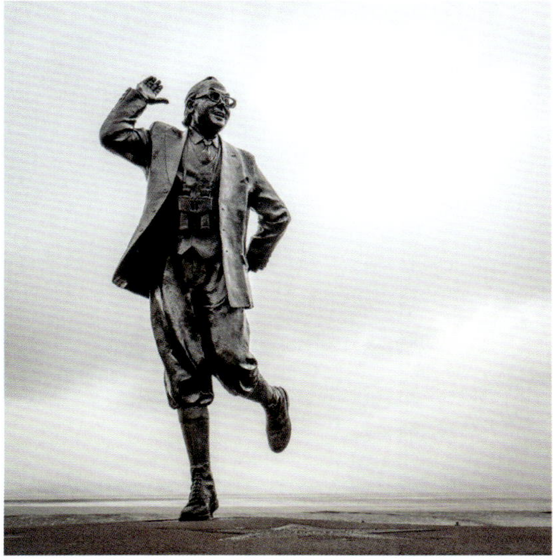

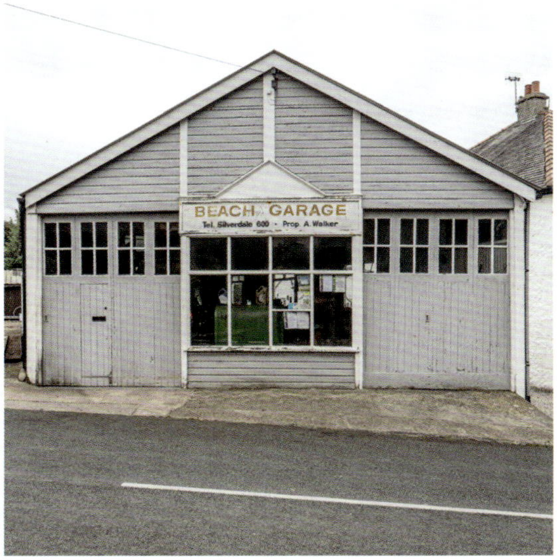

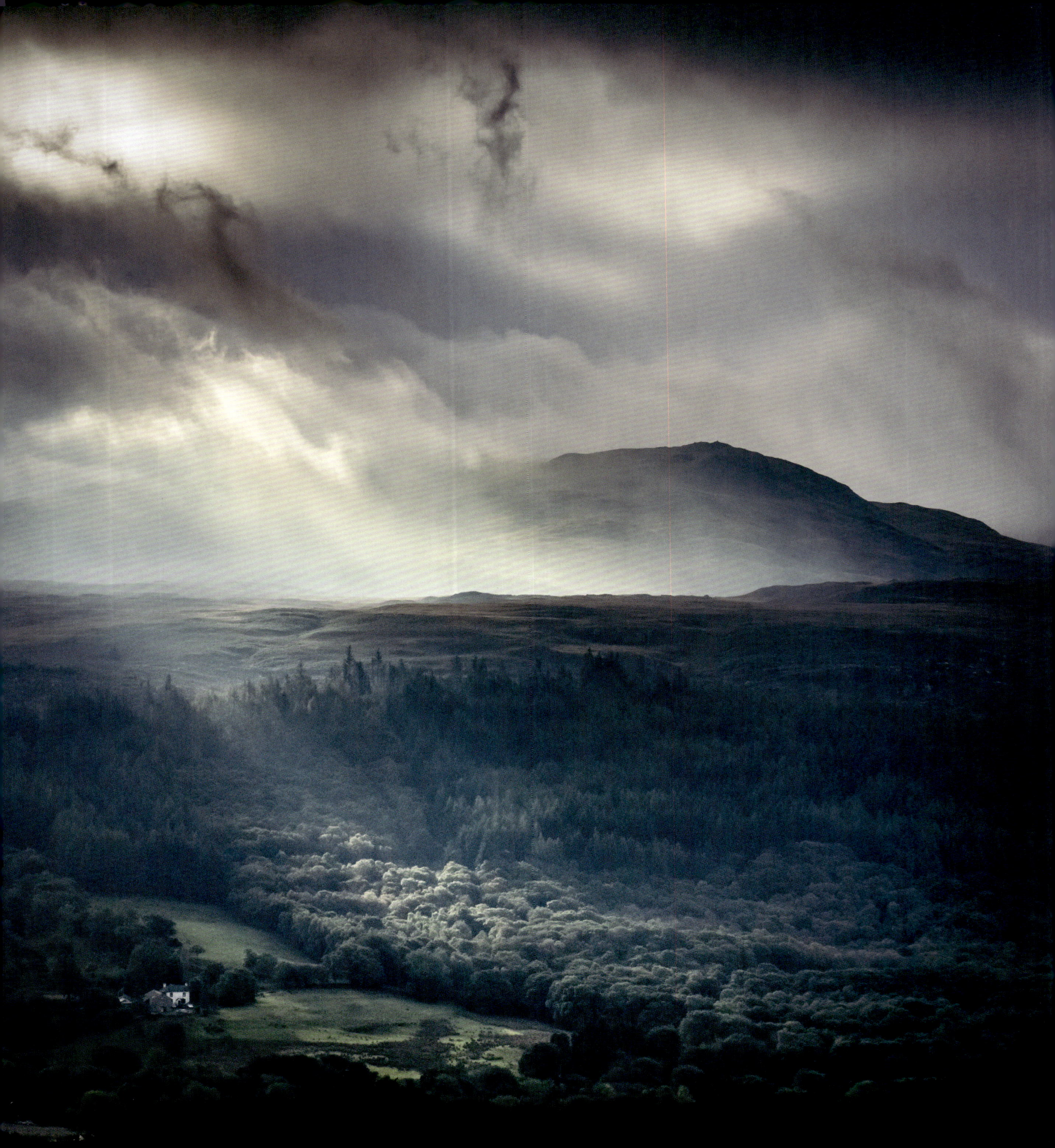

18 CUMBRIA

SEPTEMBER–OCTOBER 2017
DAY 158–173 | 04,130–04,532 KM | 402 KM

It's the fickle end of September, a time when the sensation of summer or autumn flip-flops on a whim. Clouds scud across a blue sky, their reflection mirrored in the still water of Cartmel Sands. I round a headland and am confronted with the jagged outline of the Lake District fells on the horizon. It's a startling sight, these familiar hills seen from an entirely new perspective. The beauty of the Lake District, a place I've returned to time and time again, never fails to awe me. It's where I celebrated my thirtieth birthday and spent my honeymoon, and also where I embarked on a coast-to-coast walk and countless mountain adventures. I check the map to confirm which peaks I'm looking at and relish the poetry of their names: Old Man of Coniston, Wetherlam and Black Sails, each a reminder of past journeys to their summits.

Further along Cartmel Sands, after crossing a drystone wall on a footpath, a farmer as slender and upright as the staff he holds surveys me without expression before, during and after I walk past him while doing my best to deliver a friendly hello. The coast path running by the estuary at Humphrey Head buckles and wobbles underfoot like a massive blister, giving the disturbing impression that it will burst, sending me down into a bottomless peaty mire at any moment.

Approaching Ulverston, I try my luck following a disused railway line as it represents a significant shortcut, but unfortunately it ends up in a slate depot next to a large farm, which is securely razor-wired. Feeling like a trespasser, I'm about to accept defeat and backtrack when I notice a rung of the gate has rusted away, meaning I can slip through if I take my pack and camera off and post them via the gap before me.

The next day at Barrow-in-Furness I'm expecting to encounter security guards while taking photos at Devonshire Dock, where the nuclear submarines are built, but I don't expect to be presented with such a legally balanced, if nonsensical, response: 'We can't stop you from taking photographs, but this is a sensitive area, and you've been reported for doing so.' Leaving Barrow, more strangeness ensues: a Second World War pillbox upended, the ground it once stood on having eroded away. Further along, at Lowsy Point, a collection of esoteric wooden huts includes one built around an old ship, prow and stern sticking out irreverently on either side.

As Barrow-in-Furness fades into the horizon and the expanse of Duddon Sands opens up beyond the dunes ahead, tremendous walking and landscapes unfold. The undulating panorama of the Lakeland fells spreads out before me closer than ever, and I can make out the twin peaks of Scafell and Scafell Pike in the distance. There is no path on this stretch, it's just a case of following the best route in the intertidal zone, which, combined with the dramatic scenery and absence of people, gives a deliciously adventurous feel. As darkness falls, adventure becomes frustration, and I'm caught in a labyrinth of marshy, wet channels and tall reeds. A fingerpost points tauntingly to a pitch-black body of water glimmering in my torch beam. I'm soaked to the waist, exhausted and swearing profusely. I eventually accept that the path I'm trying to follow must have been set out decades ago when the marsh was in a completely different state. I retreat wearily and find an easier route further inland.

On the other side of Duddon Sands, the 12 kilometres of shingle-walking past Millom at Haverigg Beach is slow-going, with an alarming frequency of plastic pollution along the entire length. Sports drink bottles are the most prevalent form of detritus. Finally, in the afternoon, the shingle gives way to sand, firm and fast to walk on; like riding a conveyor belt after the previous hours sliding backwards on the pebbles.

Opposite:

Illumination, Eskdale.
On the way to Scafell Pike from the sea

After a week in Cumbria I'm learning the hard way that when the map shows 'ford', they are not ankle-deep *Hay Wain*-like pastoral watercourses that I'm used to wading across down south. Eskmeals River ford is the widest and most daunting I've yet seen – 200 metres from shore to shore of fast-flowing water, too deep to see the river bed – so I'm heartened to discover that there are a dozen contractors working on the rail viaduct also waiting for the tide to drop who have their own coastguard to ensure their safety. They are a friendly lot and are happy for me to latch on to their expertise for the purpose of the crossing. After a couple of hours, the water is at an acceptable level, so they put on their waders and I strip down to my boxers and we all slosh across the broad river at knee height.

From the sea at Ravenglass, it's a 5 a.m. start to reach the summit of Scafell Pike, the second of the nation's three highest peaks that I'll be ascending on this journey. Misty bands of cloud and light play over the tops as I wrap up warmly and wait on the summit of Muncaster Fell while photographic feasts of changing vistas unfold. 'Welcome to the Isle of Man,' my mobile informs me erroneously. The ground here is a peaty, boggy slime, and I regularly sink halfway up the calf. It's ponderous work and I'm weary before I'm a quarter of the way to the summit.

On crossing over the watershed, heavy cloud hangs slicing the mountains in half and capping an exhilarating view down into Wasdale. I haven't seen many people for a few days, so it's a surprise how busy England's highest mountain can be on the weekend. My introduction to the circus atmosphere is passing a woman with a sensible daypack paired with suspenders, bunny ears, corset and hiking boots. On the mountain path, I hear mums tell their raucous teenage boys to 'be careful, or you'll break your neck'.

It's white-out conditions when I reach the rough stone pillar on the top. A couple of ghostly figures stumble awkwardly towards me as they brace themselves against the wind, their clothing flapping violently around. When they reach me, the wind tears greetings from our mouths, making conversation impossible. We give each other a thumbs-up and a grin, and I start the descent.

On the way down, I pass armies of minibused Three-Peakers, unsmiling, clad in fashionable gym attire, who march past smelling of deodorant with their earbuds in. The best light of the day occurs as I break through the clouds, the slope of Scafell velvet black in the foreground as the gusts of wind and the last rays bring the surface of Wast Water alive. I make it down to the valley floor by 7.30 p.m. while above me a procession of head torches traces the zigzag path into the darkness.

Two days' walk from Scafell Pike, I reach St Bees and the first cliffs since the Llŷn Peninsula in north-west Wales, where I get my first glimpse of Scotland across the Solway Firth. The unexpected view triggers a powerful sense of yearning to reach the grand vistas of Alba. The next day, I arrive at Whitehaven, where I stroll along the old quay, passing by rusty capstans. It's hard to believe that this place was once the third-largest trading port in the UK, exporting coal worldwide. The harbour's impressive scale and handsome engineering only accentuate the melancholy feeling now its whole purpose is redundant.

At Grune's Head, where the Solway Firth starts to turn east towards Carlisle, small pebbles mounded by the waves are delineated neatly against the sand. The pattern is so playful and systematic that it takes a moment to realise that the arrangement has been made by the tide and not humans. Near Calvo Marsh, paths are overgrown, and I get stuck in brambles trying to find my way behind an abandoned house. I'm forced to trespass to make any progress, and I greet a warm-hearted farmer mucking out his cows who tells me I can go wherever I like on his land when I fully expect him to ask me to clear off.

After days of rain, the flooding by the Solway makes national news. Tractors are pulling out school buses, and people are abandoning their cars on the higher ground. Despite all the vehicular chaos, I still do OK wading on foot. Another friendly farmer offers me a ride across a flooded track in his tractor. 'That's very kind, my feet are already wet,' I reply. 'Nae bother,' he says. Water droplets bead on the camera: it's a trust-the-weather-sealing-or-get-no-pictures kind of day.

On my sixteenth day in Cumbria and my last in England, fatigue instils a sort of rage that drives me to march 24 kilometres in eight hours through thick mud, flooded fields and roads, and barbed-wire fences. Ironically, the last stretch of road across the border has no pedestrian access, so I approach Scotland awkwardly, squeezed behind the crash barrier on the hard shoulder as trucks hurtle past. But there it is! Looking like the most beautiful thing in the world, the *Scotland Welcomes You* sign at Gretna Green. I sit on the embankment, happy and weary, airing my muddy feet and not caring how I look to the hundreds of cars racing by. It's taken 173 days and walking through two nations to get here. Tomorrow, I'll get my first taste of the third: Scotland.

Opposite, from top left:

Sheep loading, Lyth Valley

Grange-over-Sands train station

From bottom left:

Levens Hall Garden

College Green Farm, Heversham

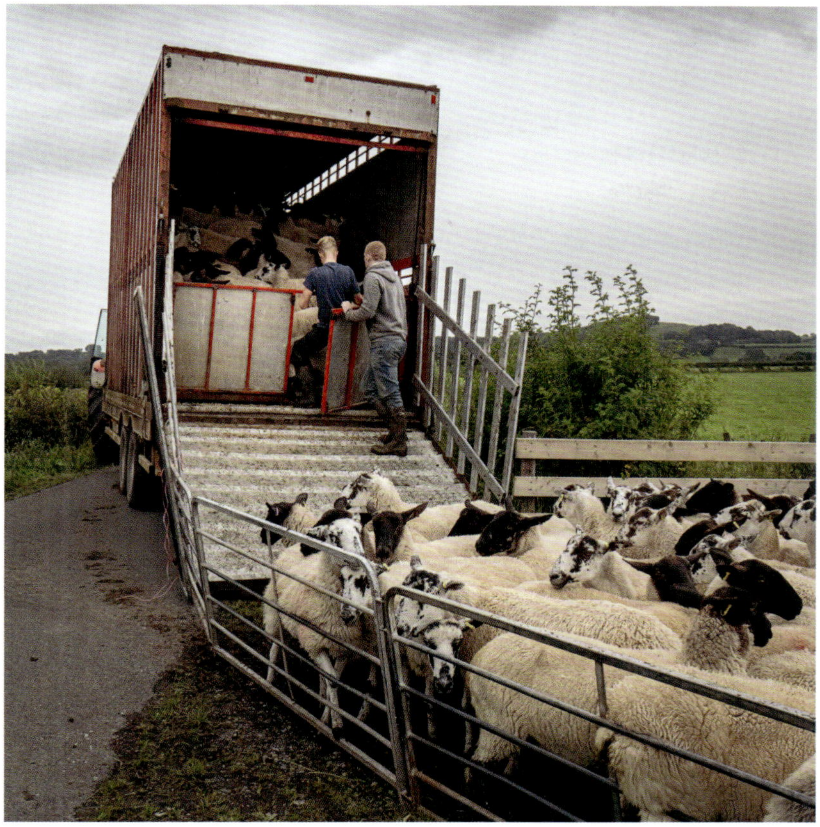

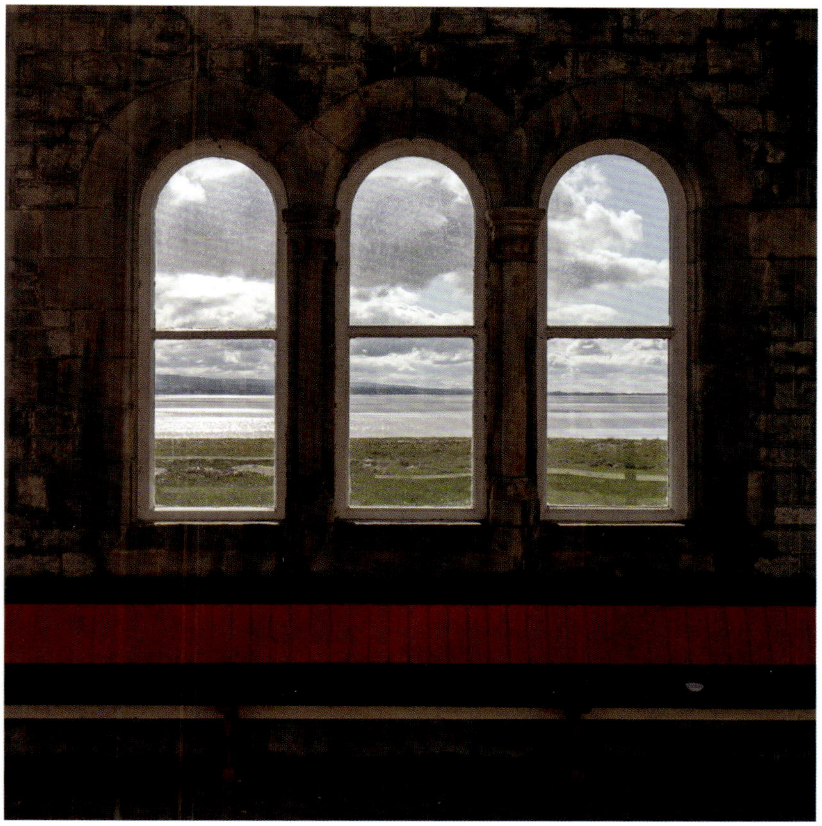

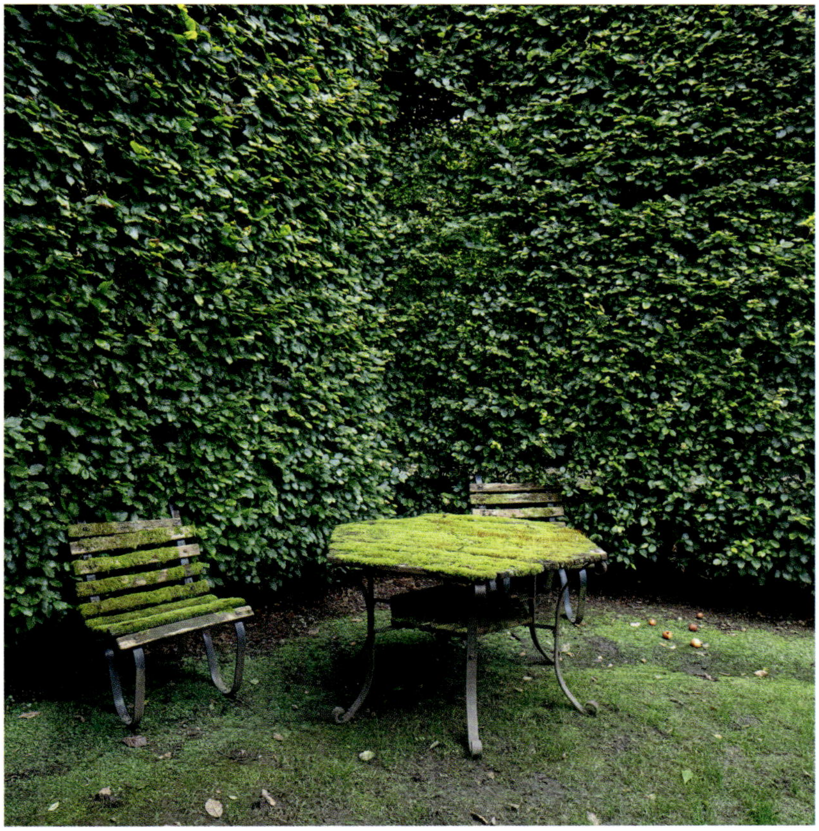

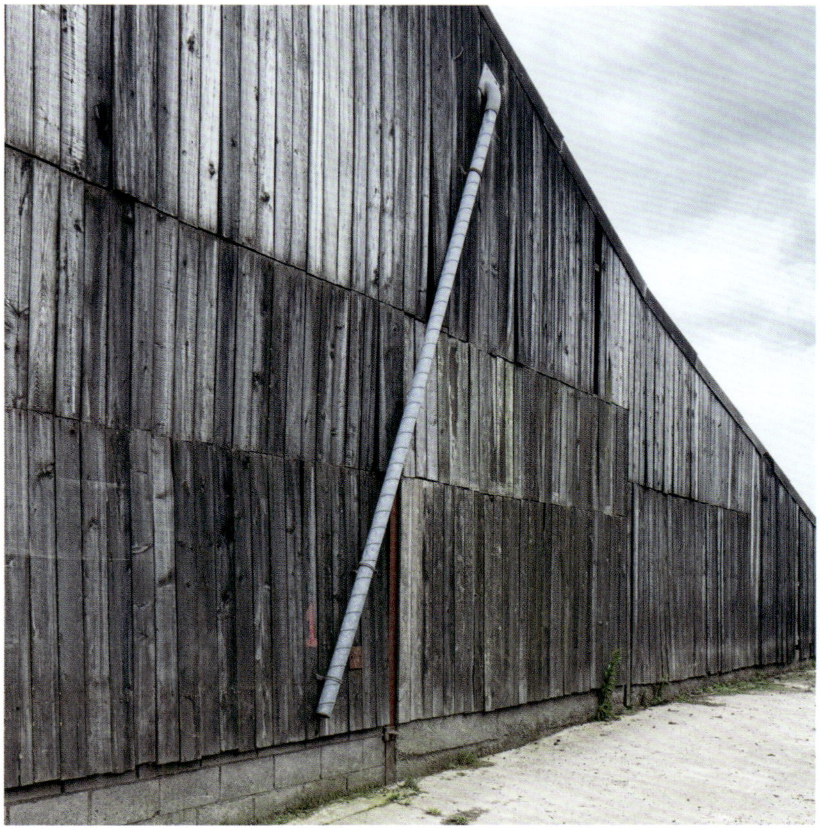

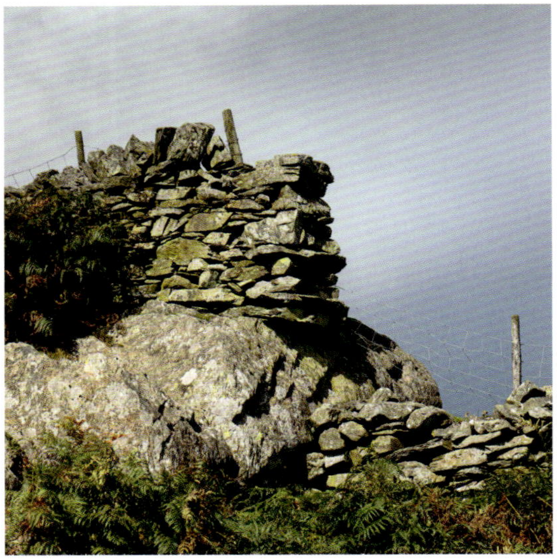
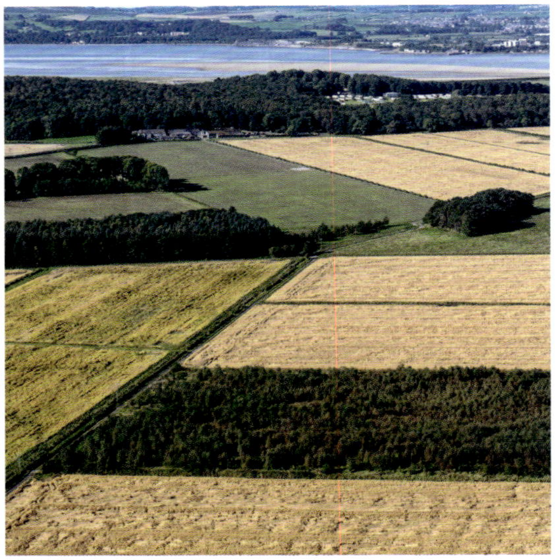
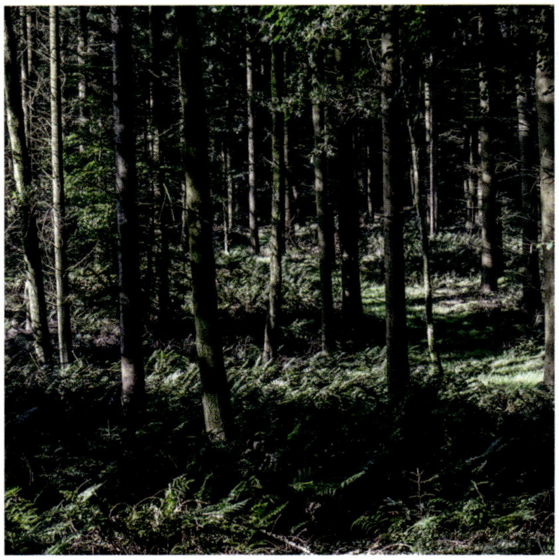
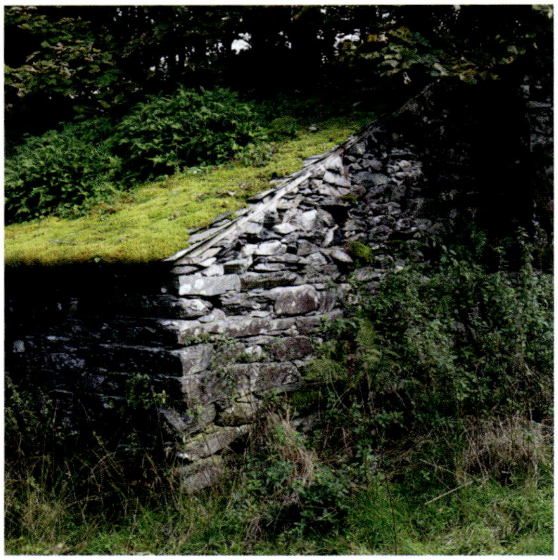
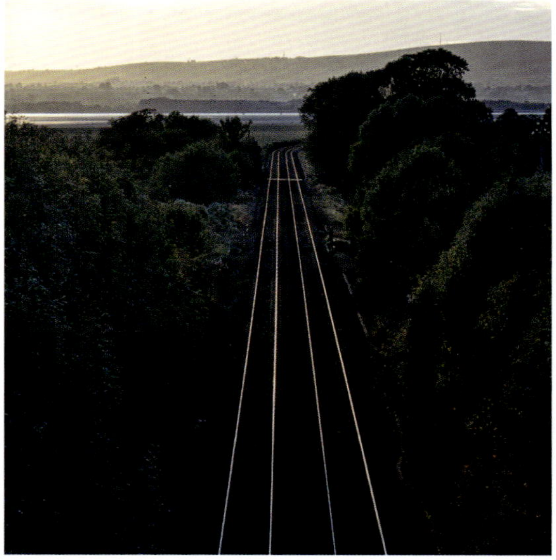
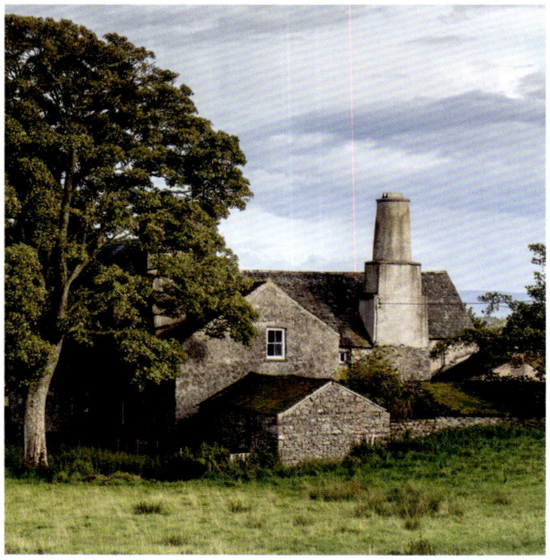

From top left:

Stepped wall, Ellerside

River Leven from How Barrow

From centre left:

Forest, Middle Scar

Reveal, Bigland Woods

From bottom left:

Tracks, Cark

Plumpton Hall with Westmorland (pepperpot-style) chimney stack, Plumpton

Opposite:

Lake District fells from Cartmel Sands

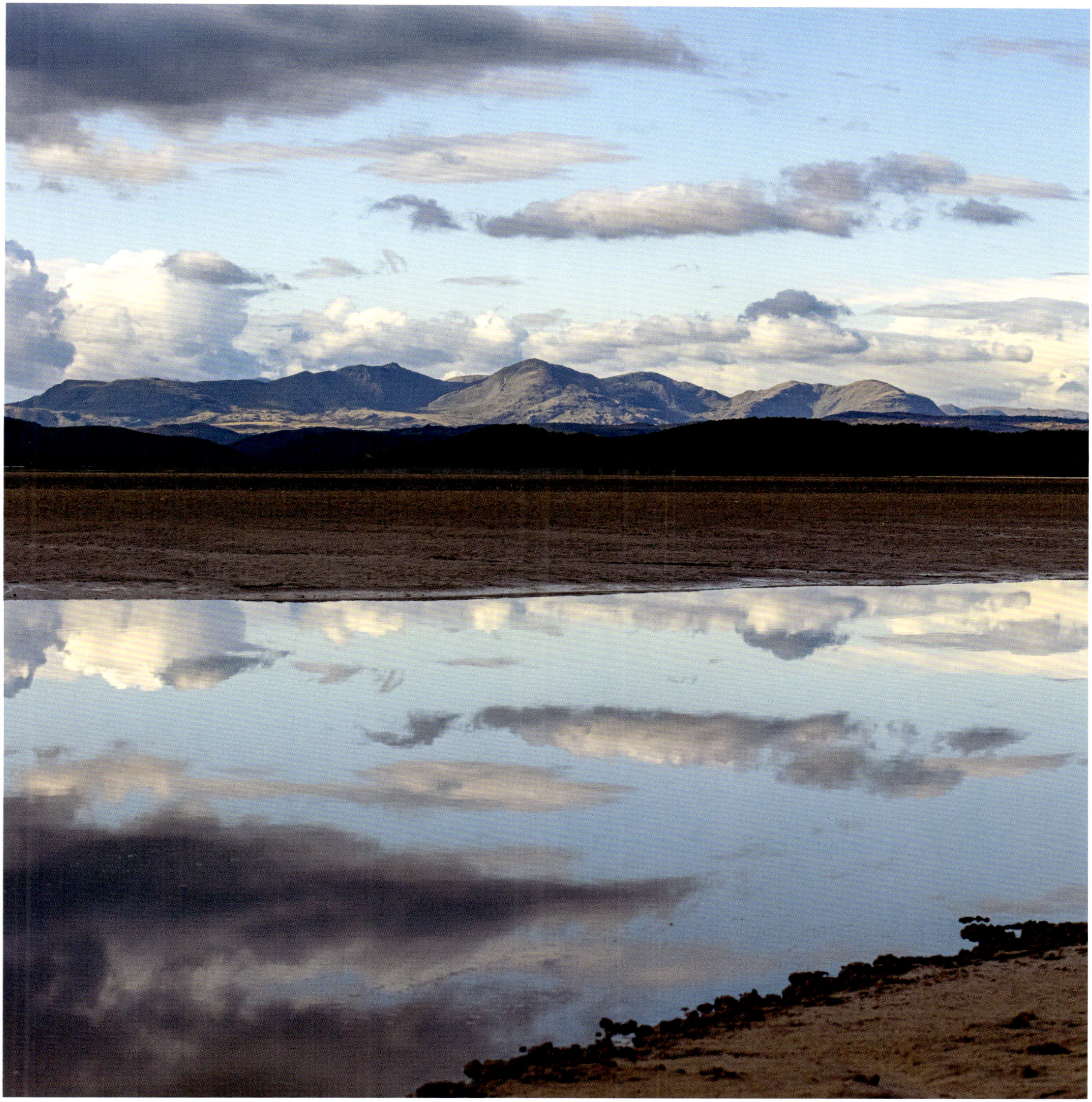

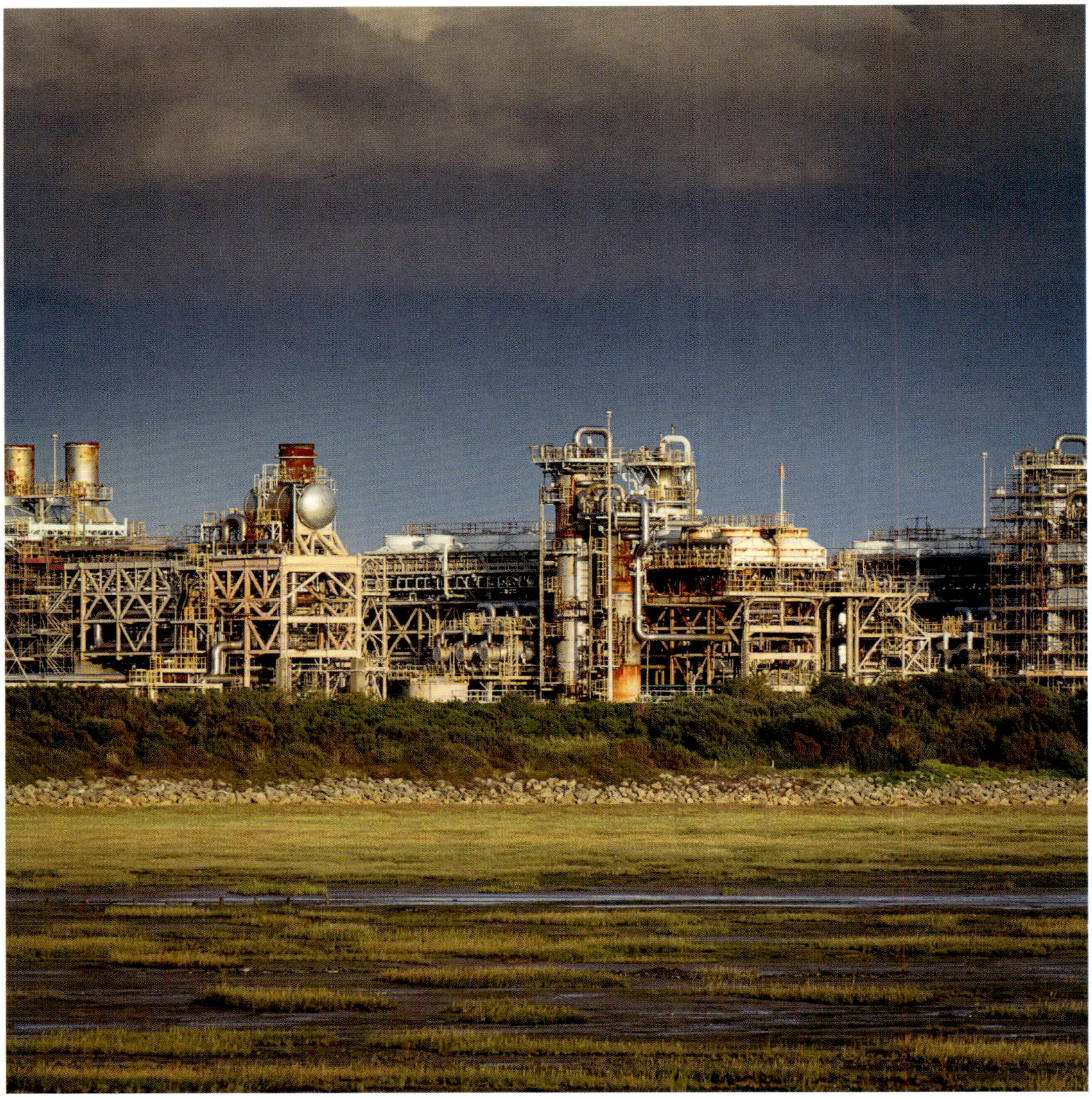

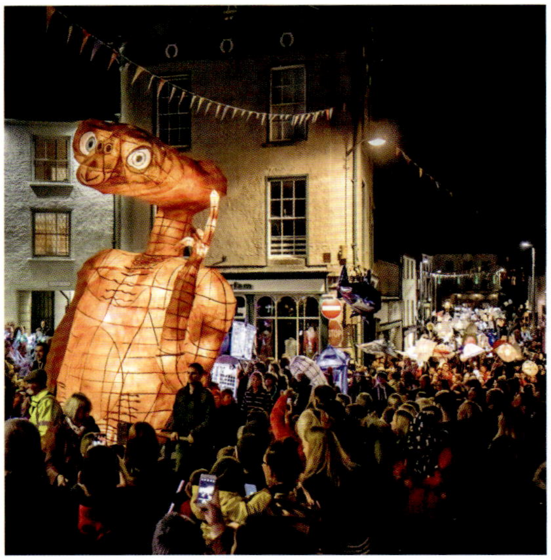

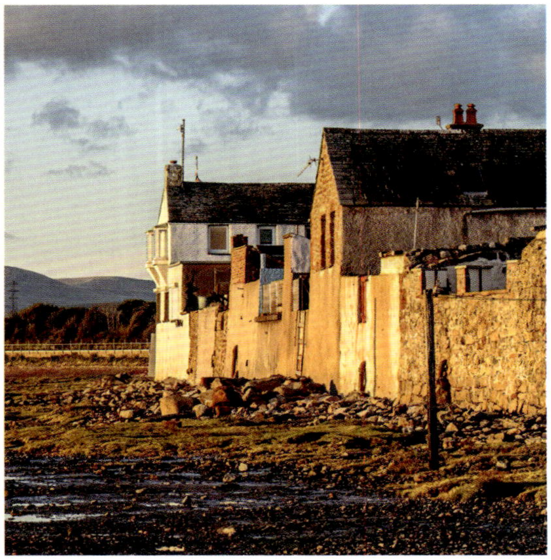

From top left:

Rampside Gas Terminal, Barrow-in-Furness

Ulverston Lantern Festival

Evening light at Ravenglass

Opposite, from top left:

Flipped pillbox, Walney Channel

Plastic pollution, Silecroft Beach

From bottom left:

Houseboat, Lowsy Point

They grow the marshmallows big up here! (The pink bale wrap is used to raise money for breast cancer)

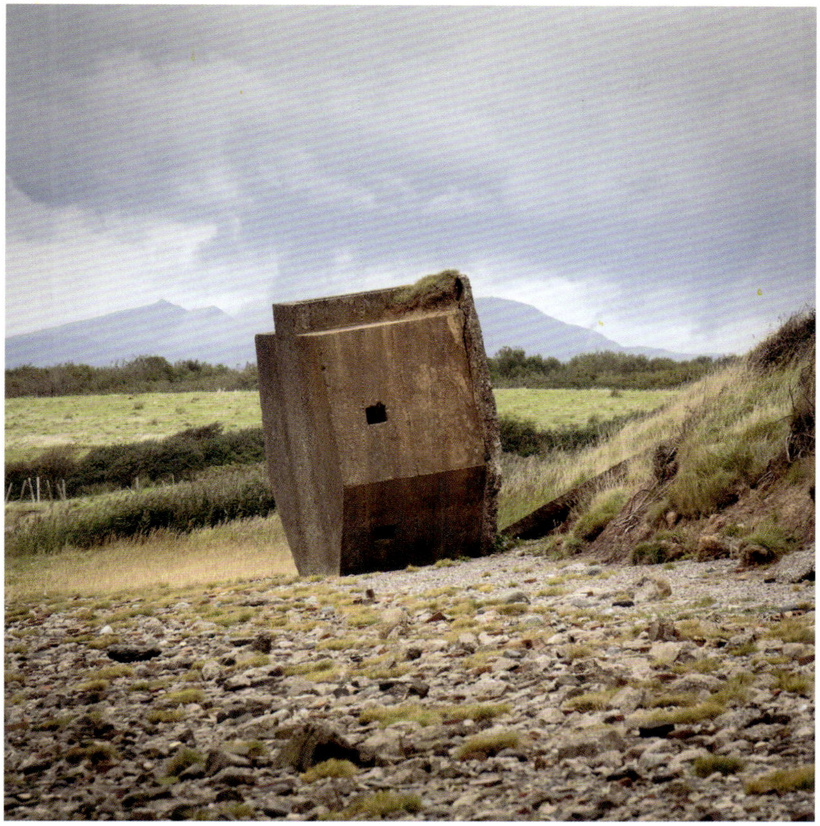

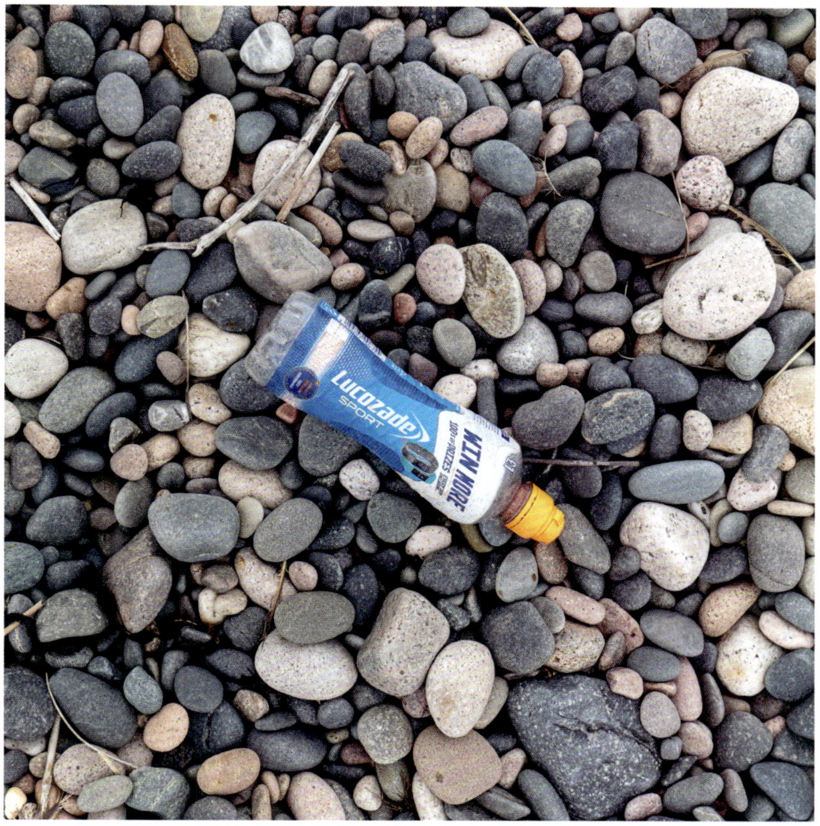
Lucozade
SPORT
WIN MORE

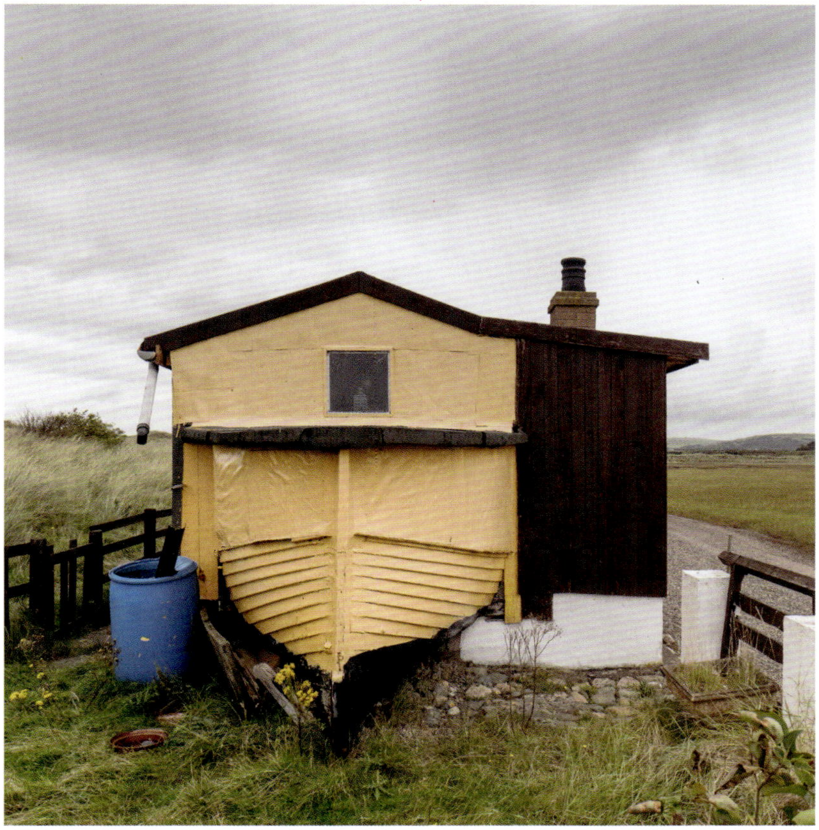

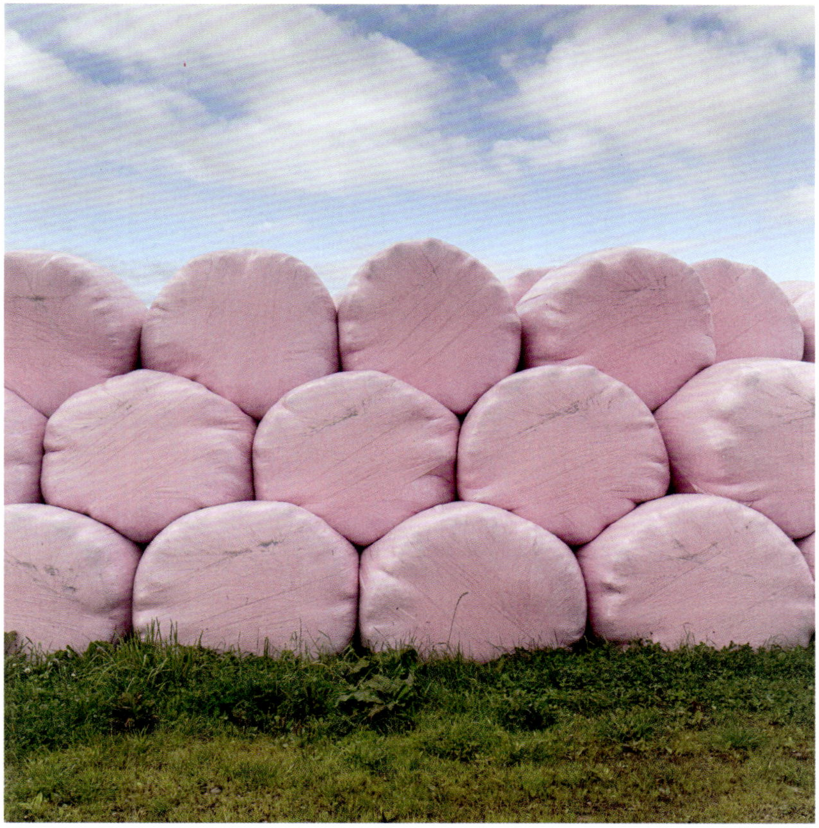

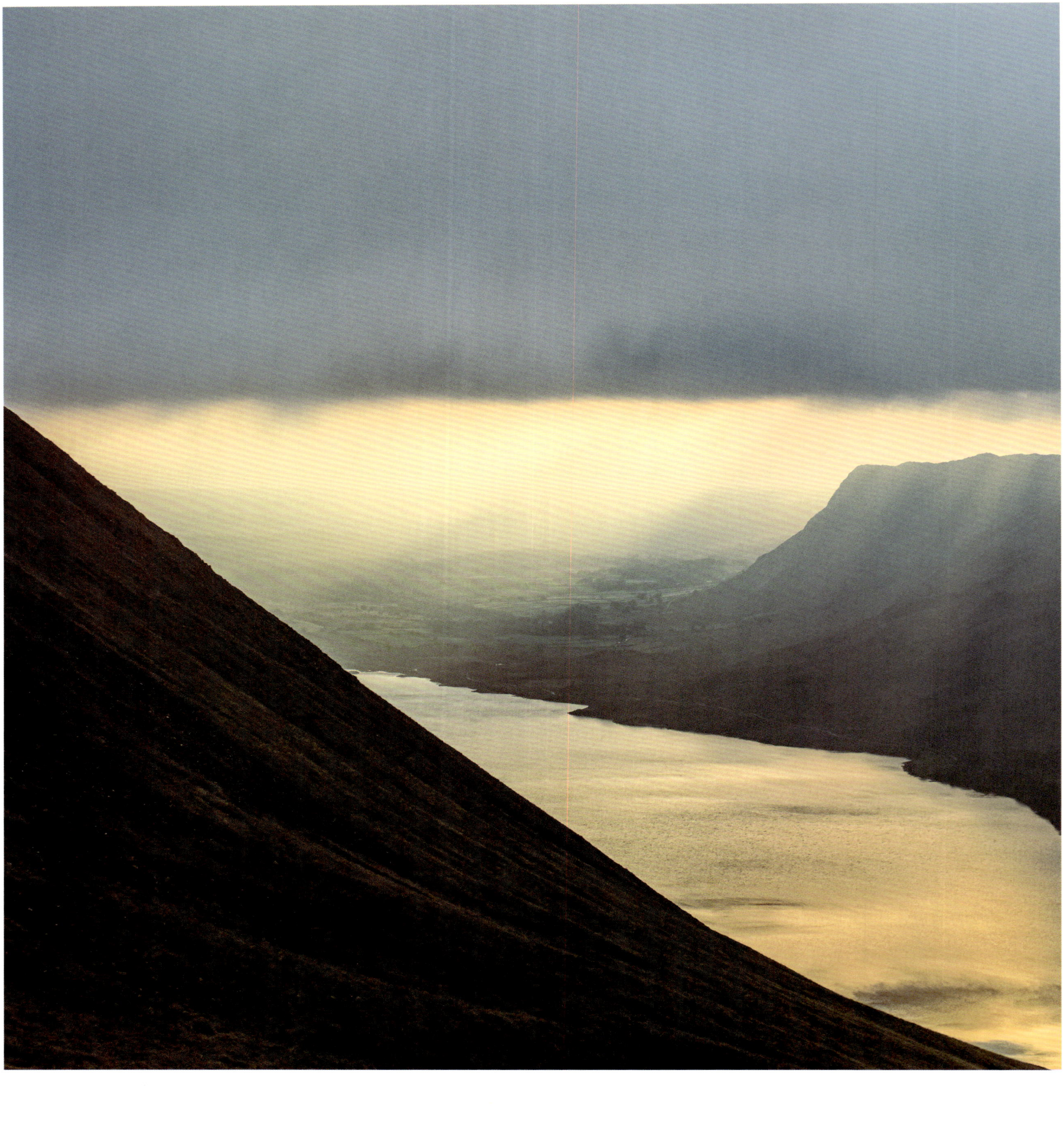

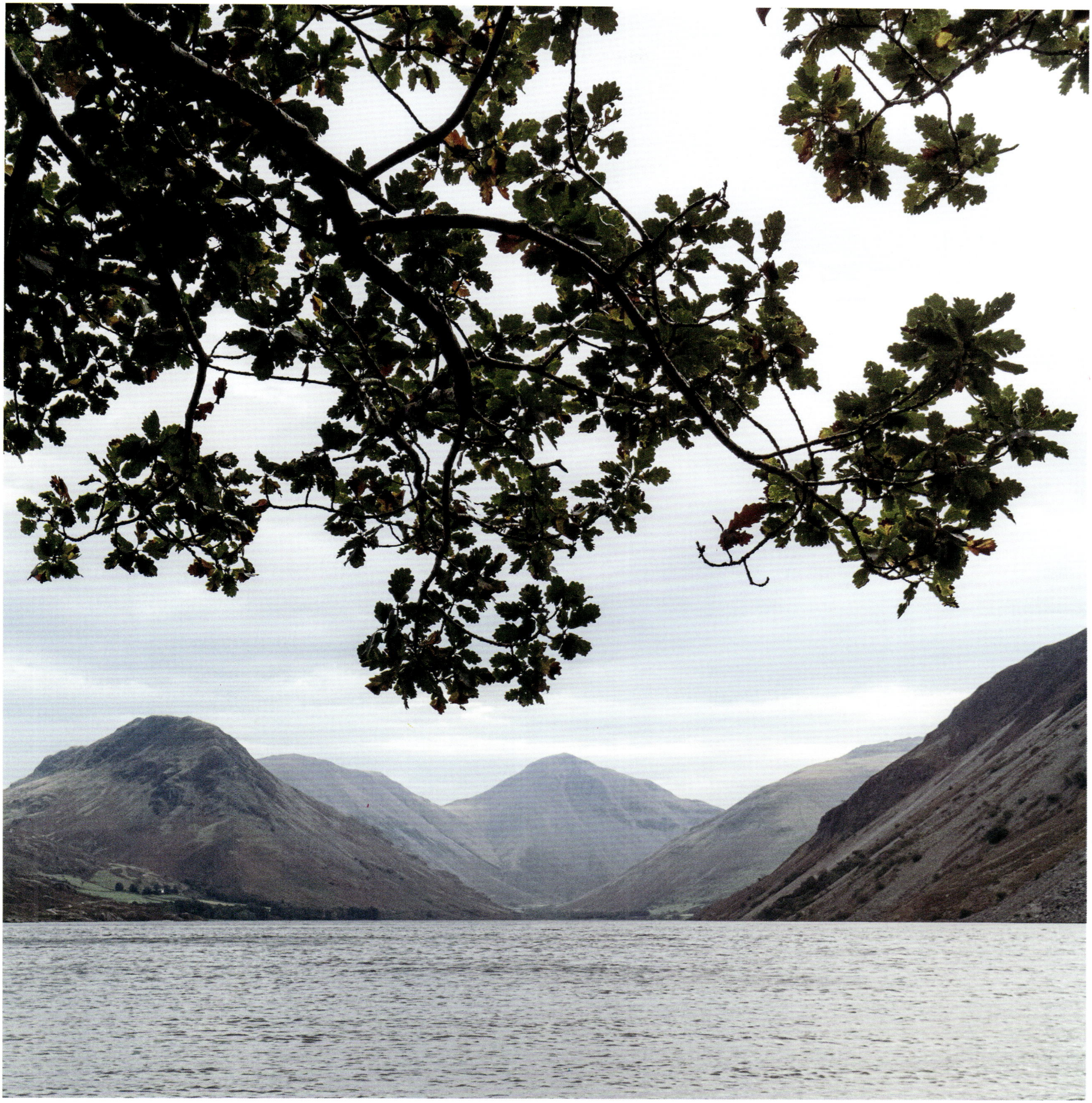

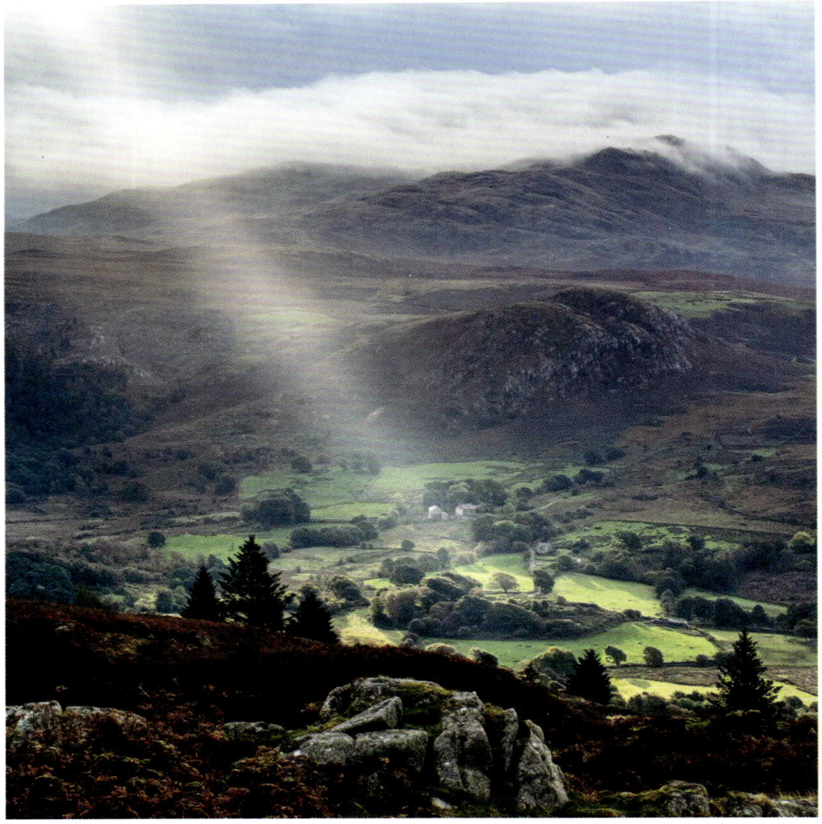

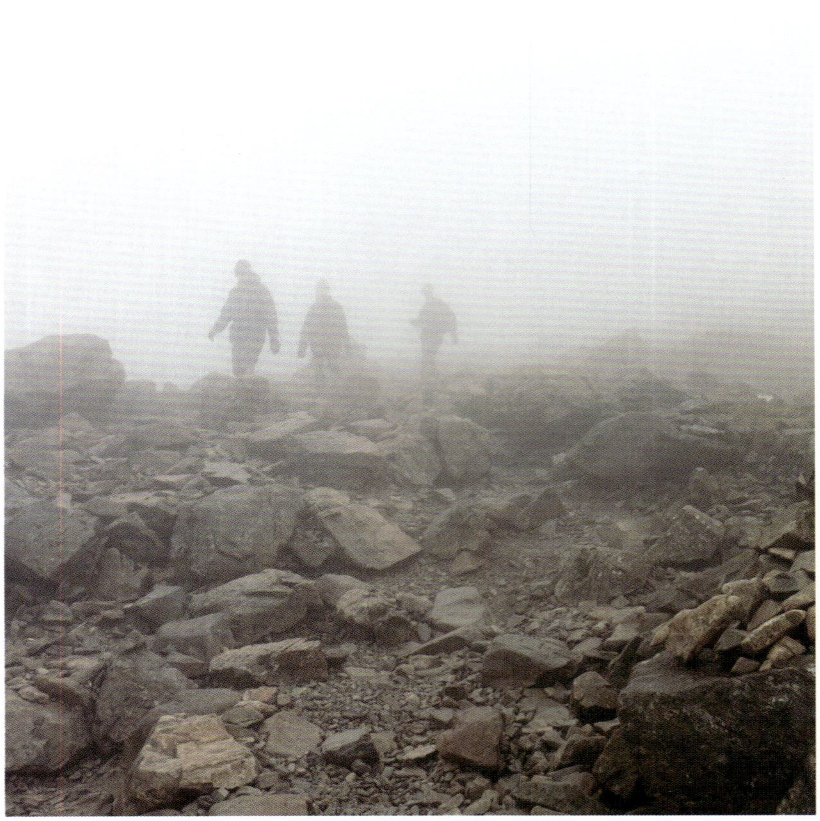

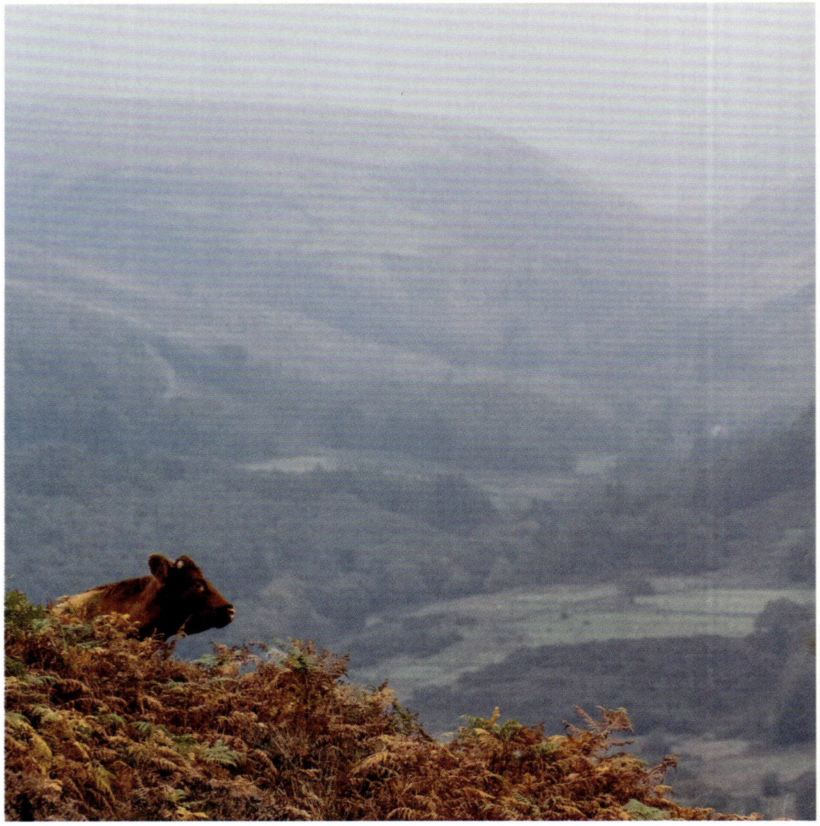

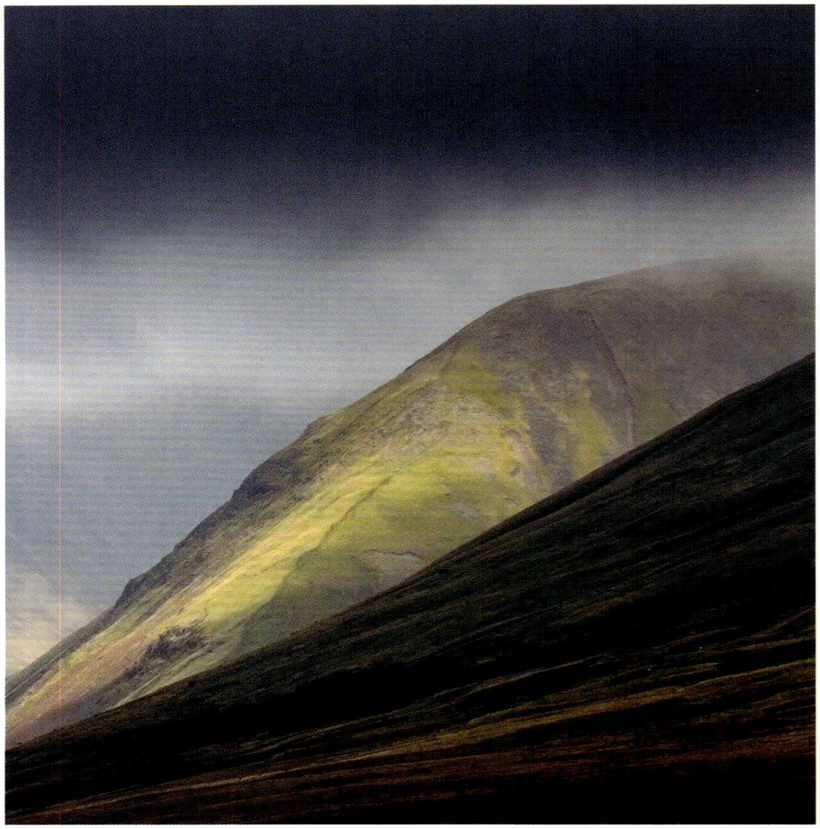

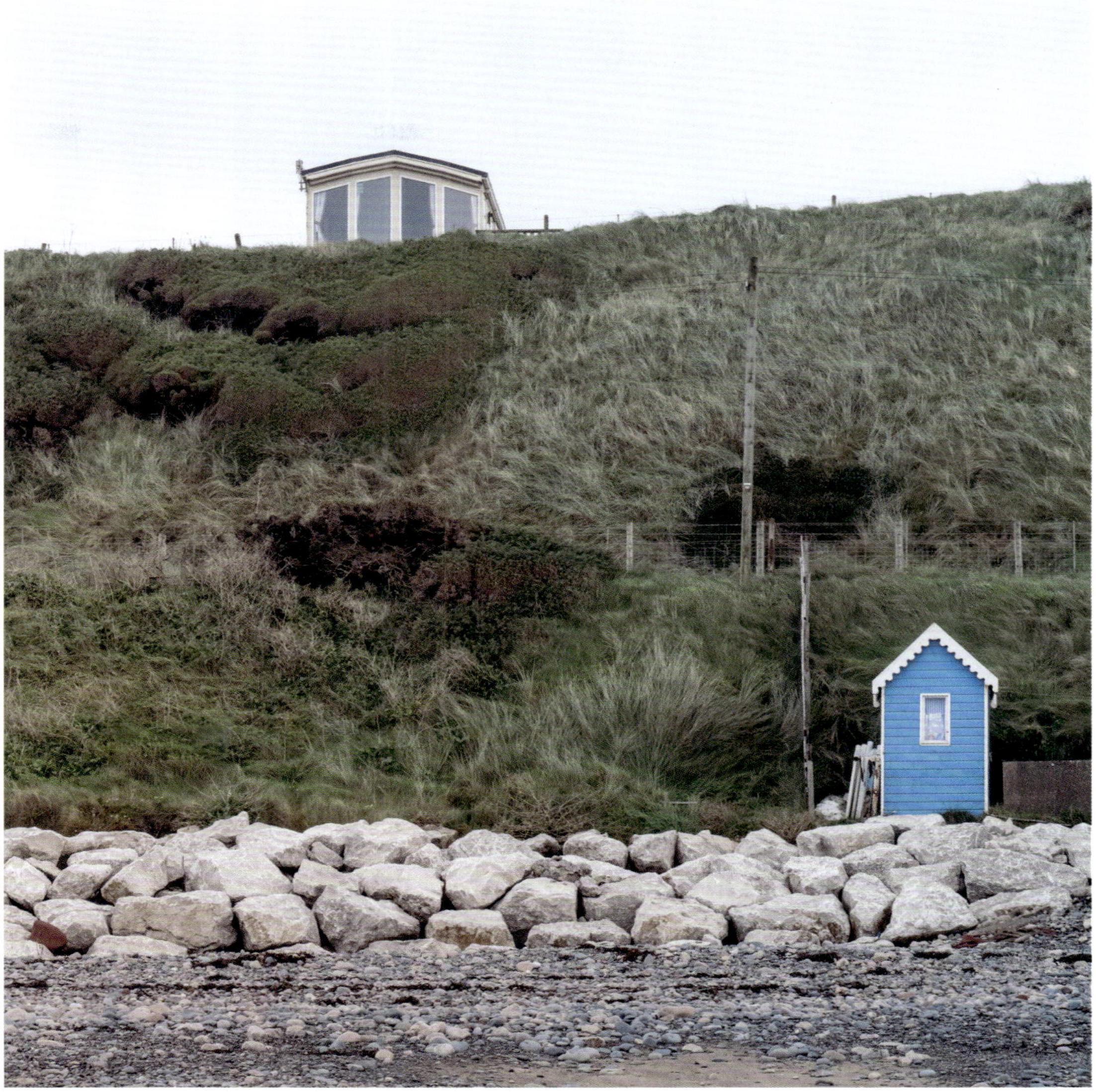

Previous, from left to right:

Last light, Buckbarrow and Wast Water from Scafell Pike

Yewbarrow, Kirk Fell and the slopes of Scafell Pike, Wasdale

Opposite, from top left:

A shaft of light, Eskdale. On the way to Scafell Pike from the sea

Ghosts: Scafell Pike

Watching over Miterdale

Lingmell, Wasdale

From top left:

English leisure: Braystones

Beach house, Braystones

Repurposed crop sprayer, Saltcoats

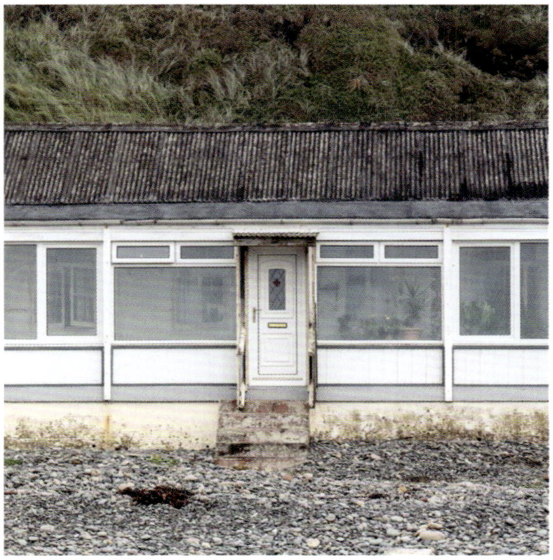

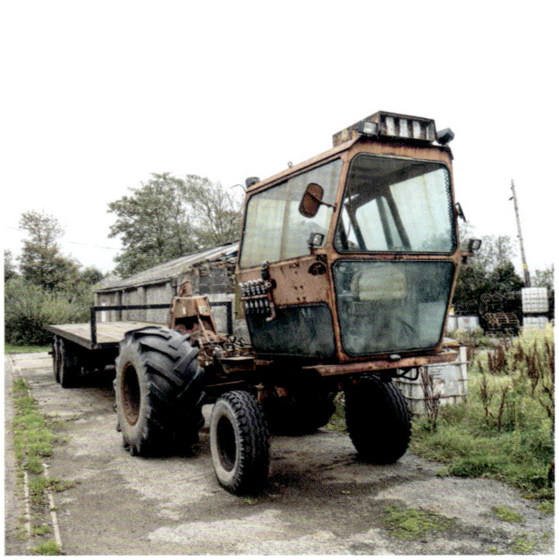

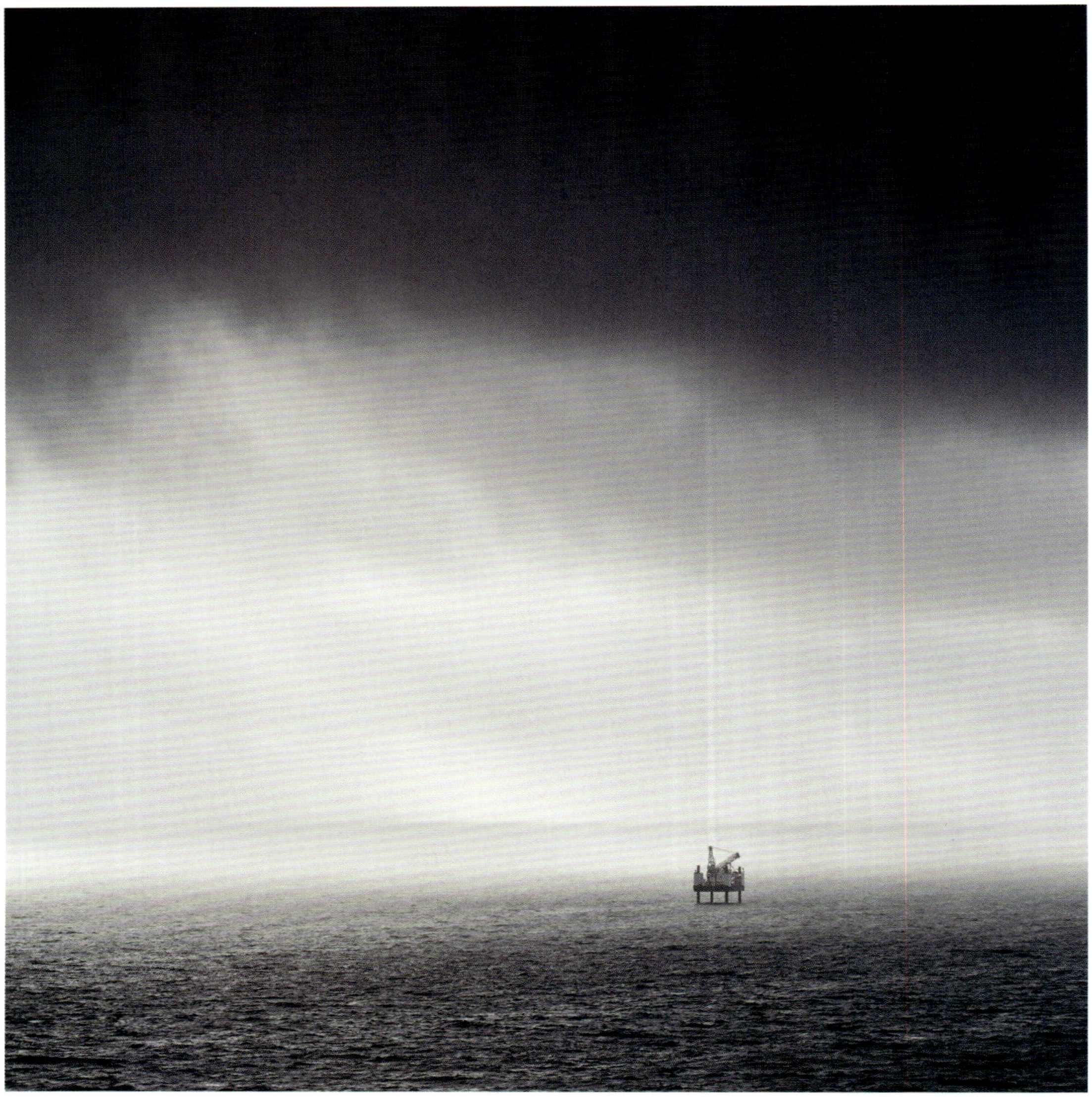

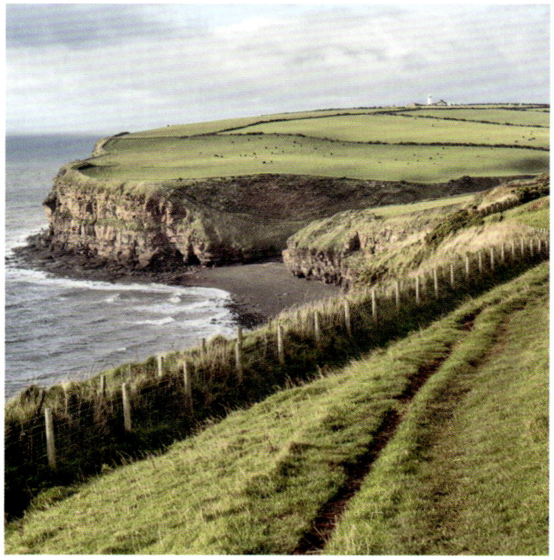

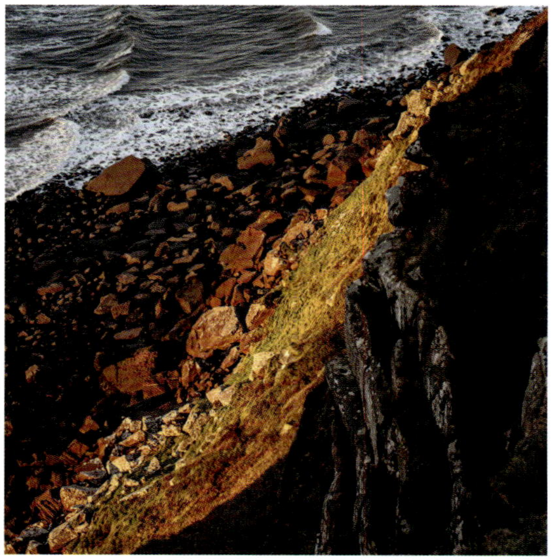

From top left:

Coal-mining borehole drill rig off St Bees Head. In July 2024 the government said that there was an 'error of law' in granting planning permission for the West Cumbria coal mine and pulled its defence of the decision in forthcoming legal challenges by Friends of the Earth and South Lakes Action on Climate Change

Path to St Bees Head

Last light by Saltom Bay, Whitehaven

Opposite, clockwise from top left:

Seaweed, Allonby Bay

Seemed like a bargain until I saw the word 'manure' hidden in the grass

Cattle sorter, Calvo Marsh

Capstan, Whitehaven North Pier

Breakwater, Skinburnessbank

Elizabethan saltpan of Crosscanonby. The large, circular, elevated structure is the sleech pit or kinch. The wall is cobble-built with a clay infill. In use, it was clay-lined and the floor was covered with reeds, acting as a filter. Salt-laden sand was gathered from the shore in a horse-drawn rake called a hap

Overleaf, from left to right:

Anthorn Radio Station by the Solway, a very low frequency (VLF) transmitter station, which is used for sending orders to submarines. The site is also used to transmit the UK's time signal

Cast-iron road sign by the Solway, Easton. The faint shore of Scotland is visible across the water

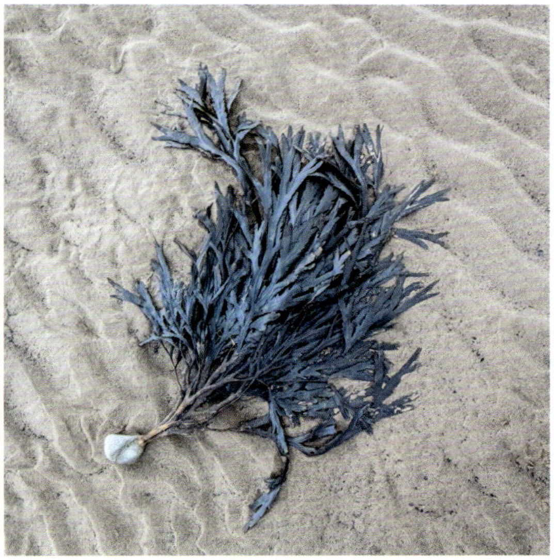

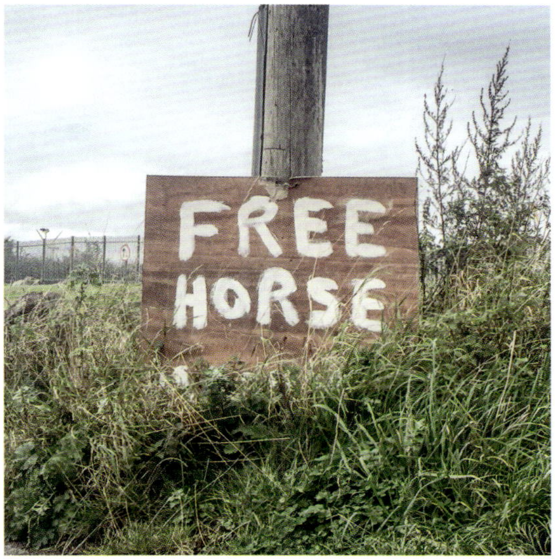
FREE
HORSE

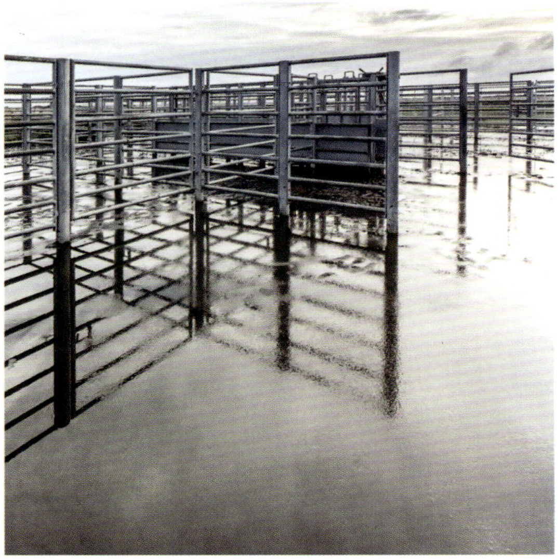

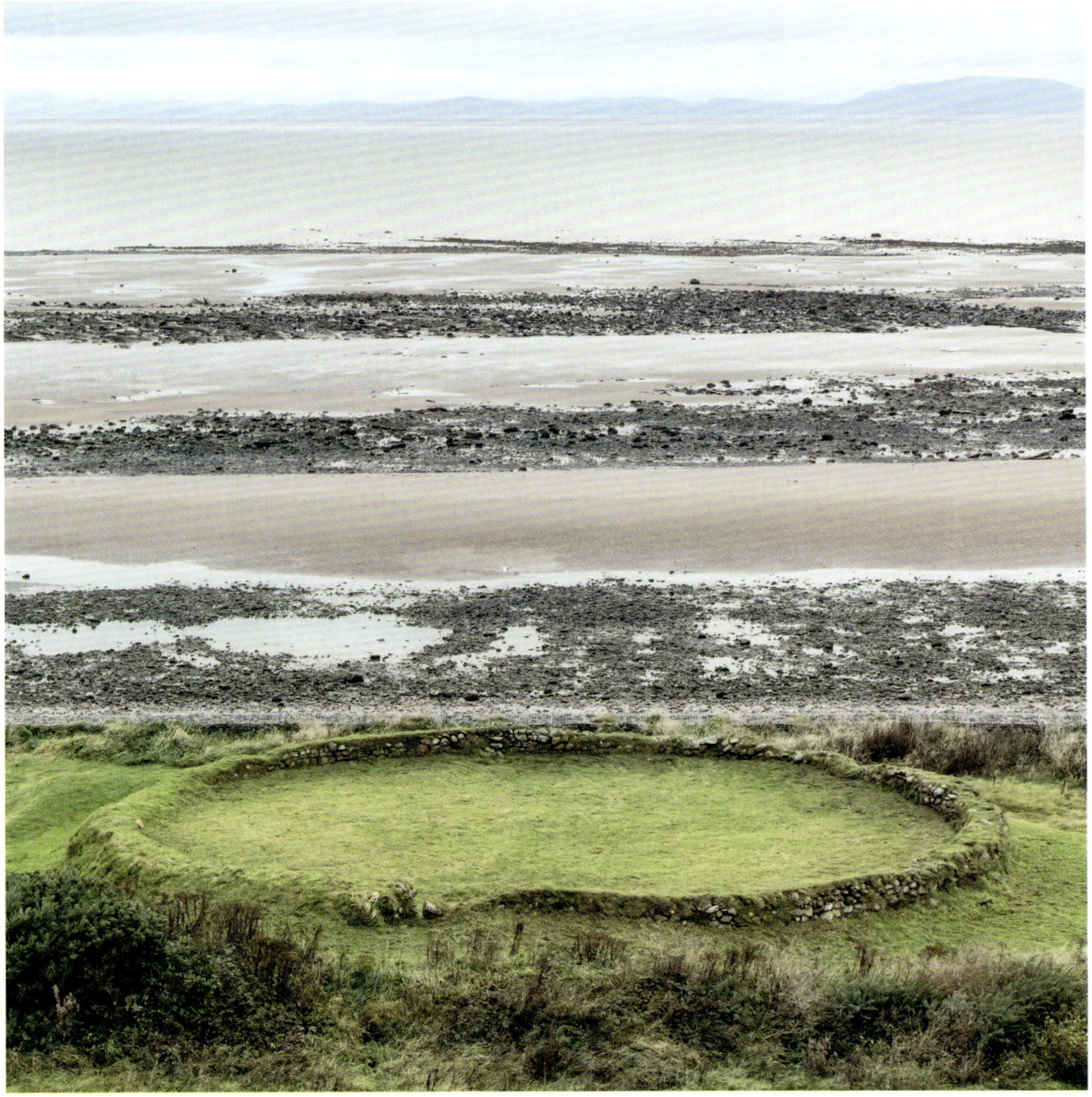

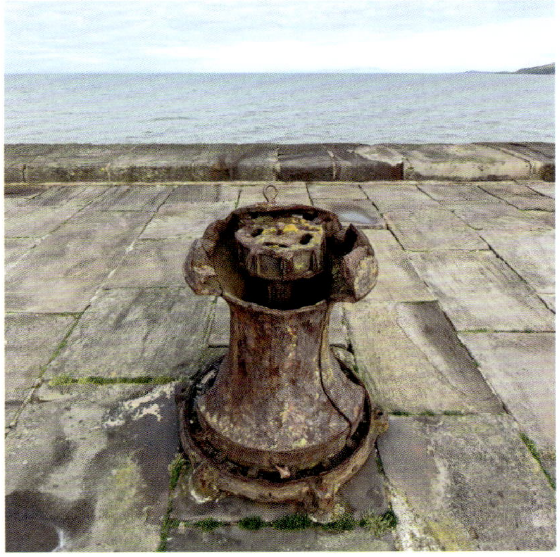

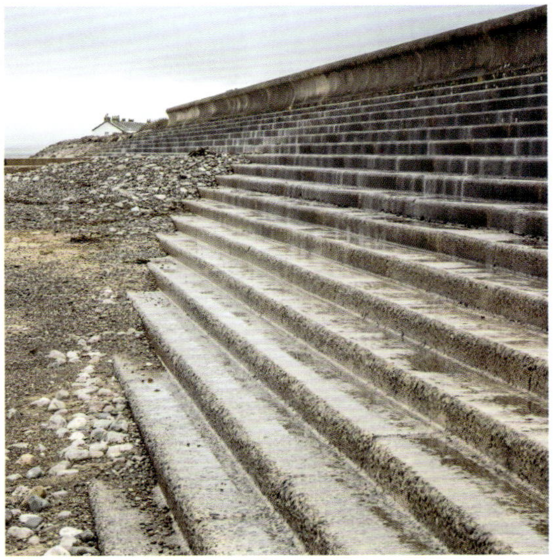

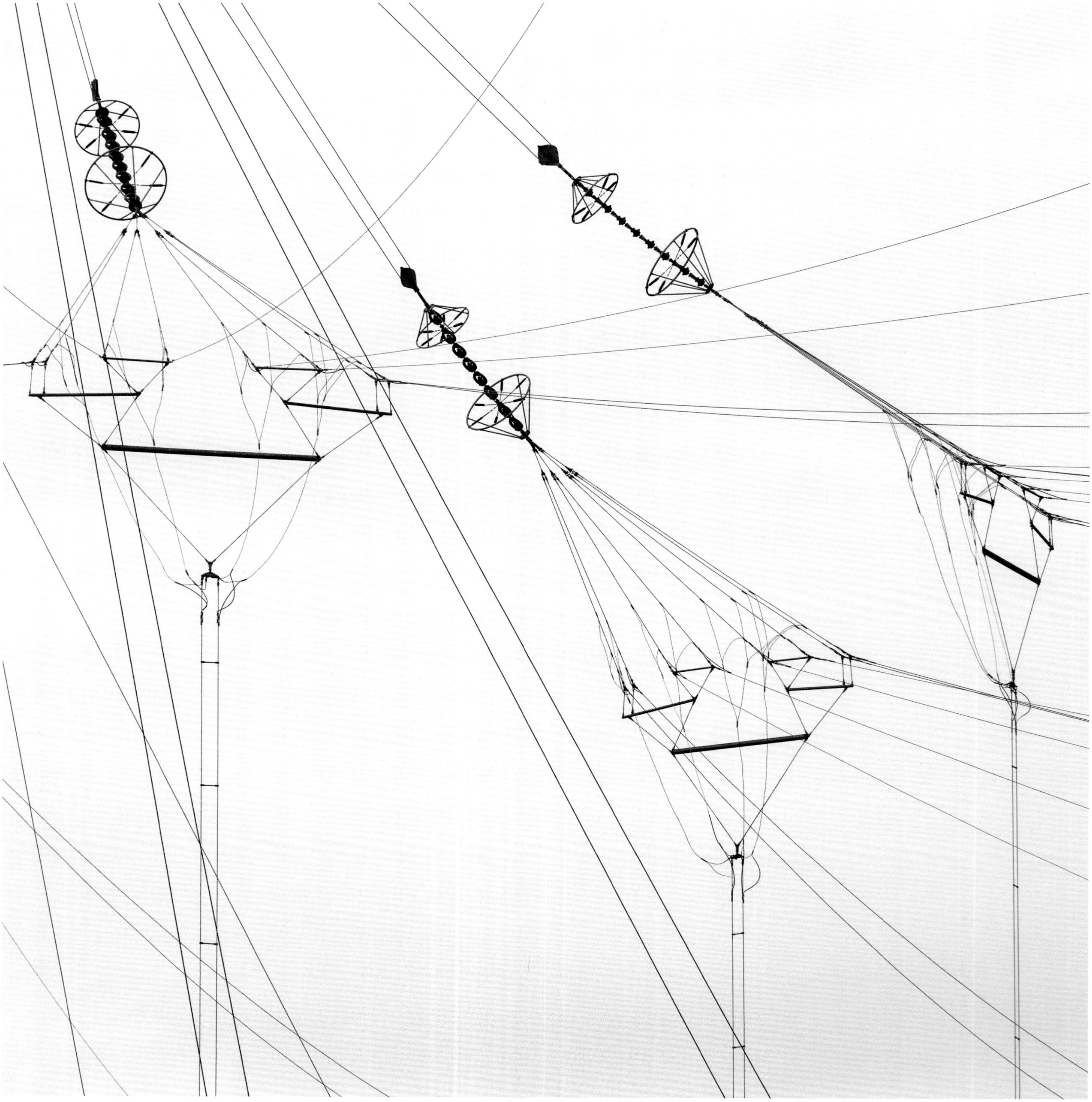

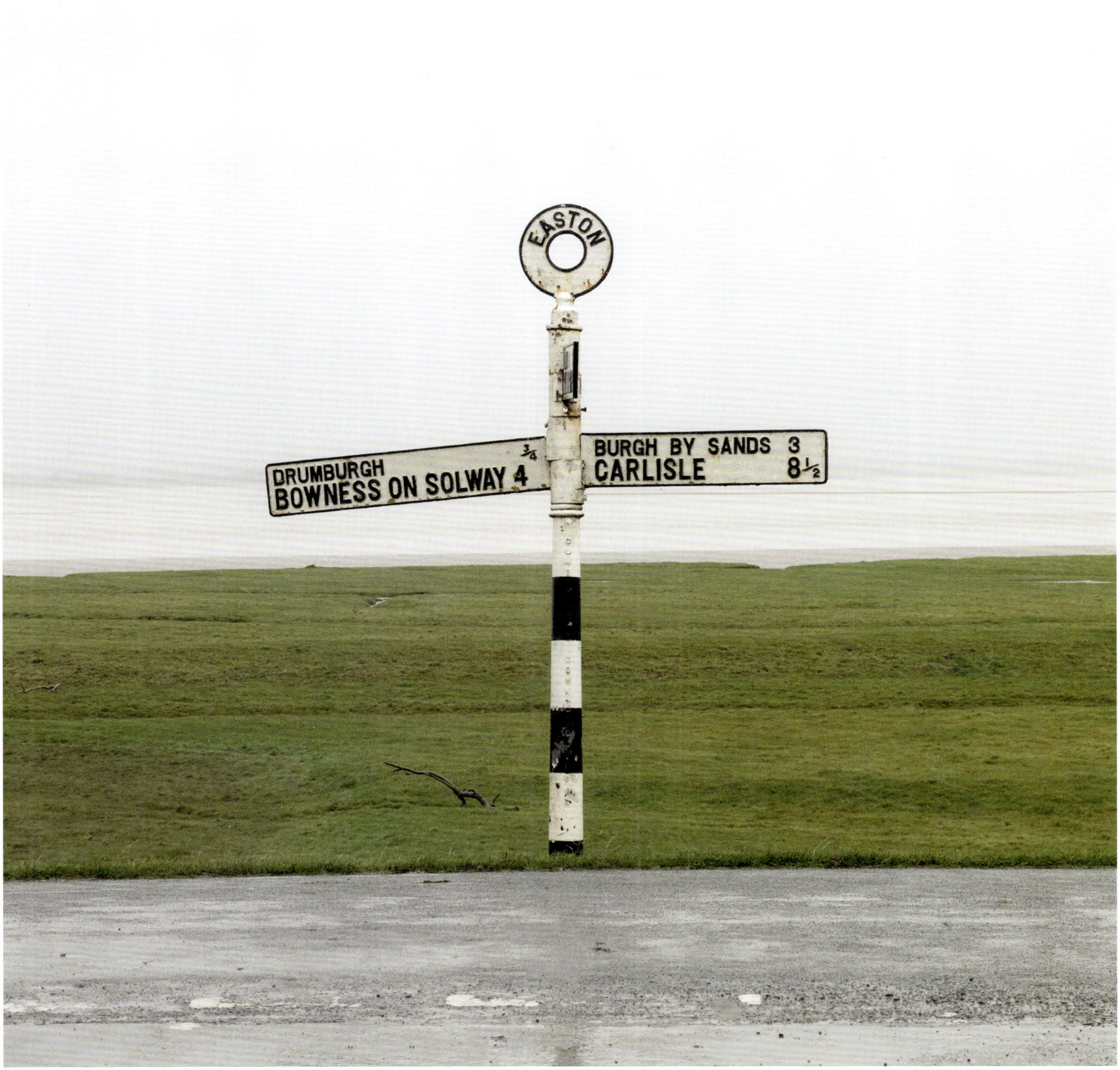
EASTON
DRUMBURGH 3/4
BOWNESS ON SOLWAY 4
BURGH BY SANDS 3
CARLISLE 8 1/2

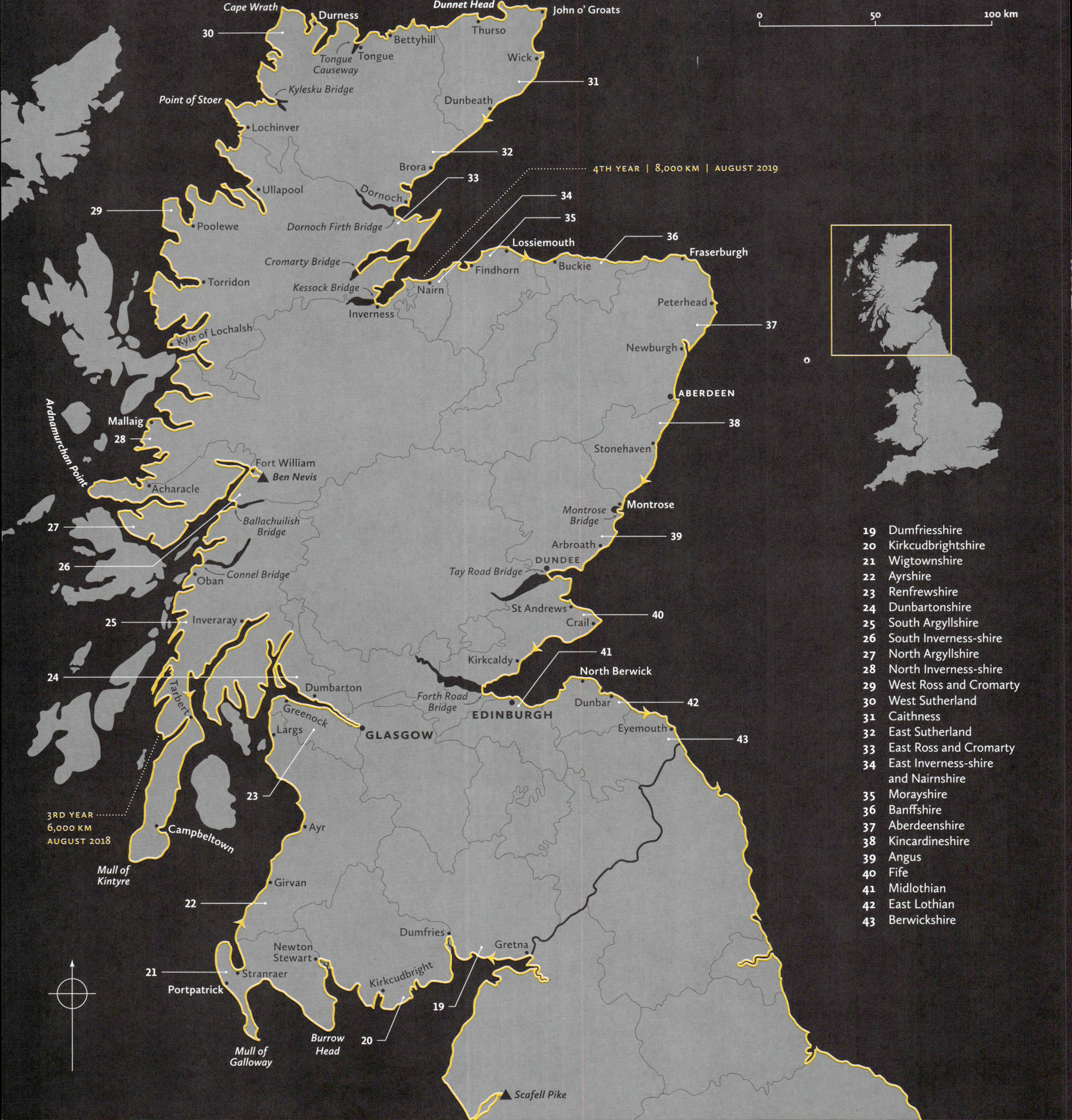

Cape Wrath
Durness
Dunnet Head
John o' Groats
0
50
100 km
30
Bettyhill
Thurso
Tongue
Tongue Causeway
Wick
31
Kylesku Bridge
Point of Stoer
Dunbeath
Lochinver
32
Brora
33
4TH YEAR | 8,000 KM | AUGUST 2019
Ullapool
Dornoch
34
29
Poolewe
Dornoch Firth Bridge
35
Lossiemouth
36
Fraserburgh
Cromarty Bridge
Torridon
Findhorn
Buckie
Kessock Bridge
Nairn
Peterhead
Inverness
37
Kyle of Lochalsh
Newburgh
ABERDEEN
Ardnamurchan Point
Mallaig
38
28
Stonehaven
Fort William
Ben Nevis
Acharacle
Montrose
Montrose Bridge
27
Ballachulish Bridge
Arbroath
39
26
DUNDEE
Tay Road Bridge
Oban
Connel Bridge
St Andrews
40
Crail
25
Inveraray
41
Kirkcaldy
North Berwick
24
Dumbarton
Forth Road Bridge
Dunbar
42
Tarbert
EDINBURGH
Greenock
GLASGOW
Eyemouth
43
Largs
23
3RD YEAR
6,000 KM
AUGUST 2018
Ayr
Campbeltown
Mull of Kintyre
Girvan
22
Dumfries
Gretna
Newton Stewart
21
Stranraer
Kirkcudbright
Portpatrick
19
20
Mull of Galloway
Burrow Head
Scafell Pike
19 Dumfriesshire
20 Kirkcudbrightshire
21 Wigtownshire
22 Ayrshire
23 Renfrewshire
24 Dunbartonshire
25 South Argyllshire
26 South Inverness-shire
27 North Argyllshire
28 North Inverness-shire
29 West Ross and Cromarty
30 West Sutherland
31 Caithness
32 East Sutherland
33 East Ross and Cromarty
34 East Inverness-shire and Nairnshire
35 Morayshire
36 Banffshire
37 Aberdeenshire
38 Kincardineshire
39 Angus
40 Fife
41 Midlothian
42 East Lothian
43 Berwickshire

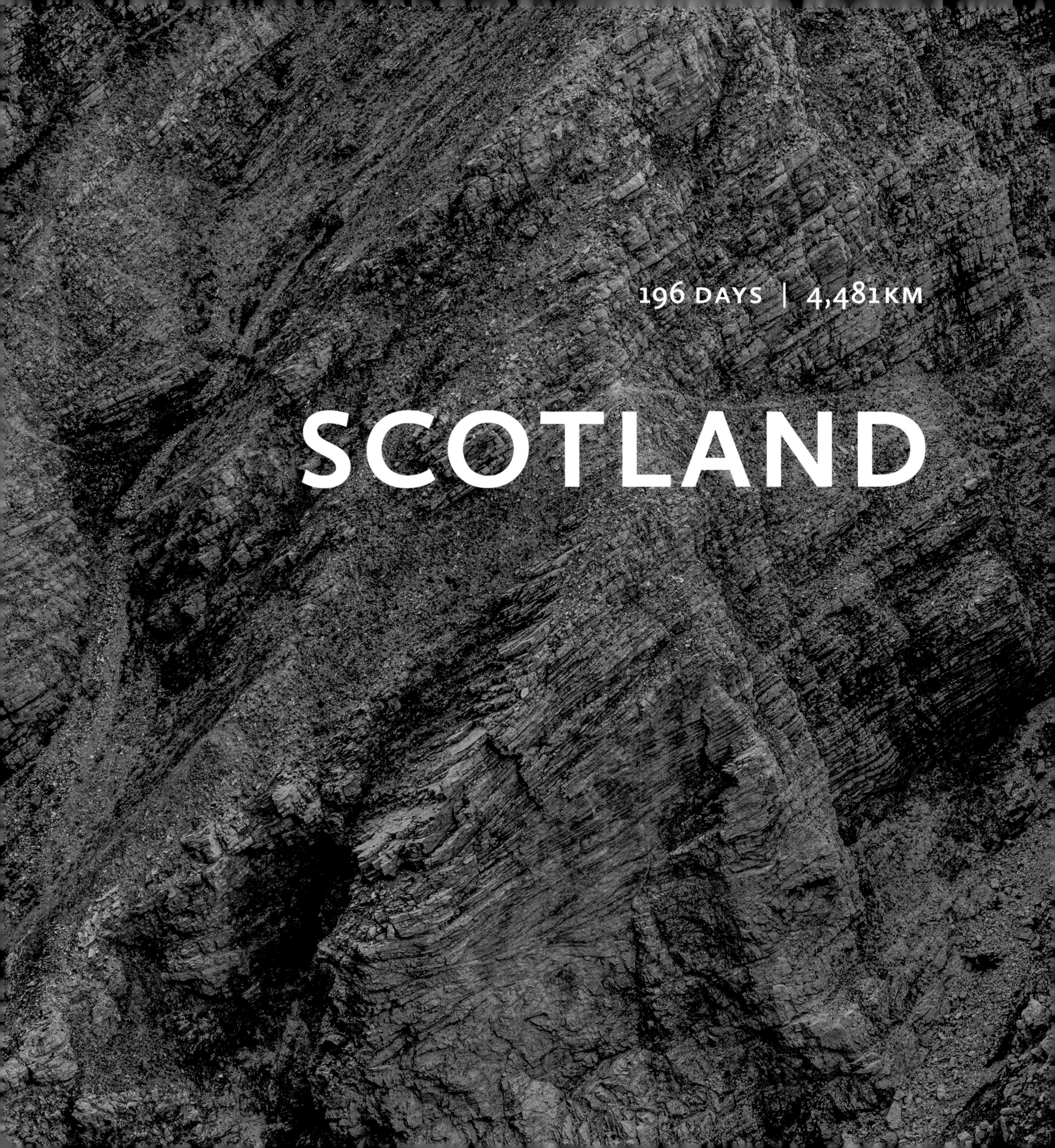

196 DAYS | 4,481KM

SCOTLAND

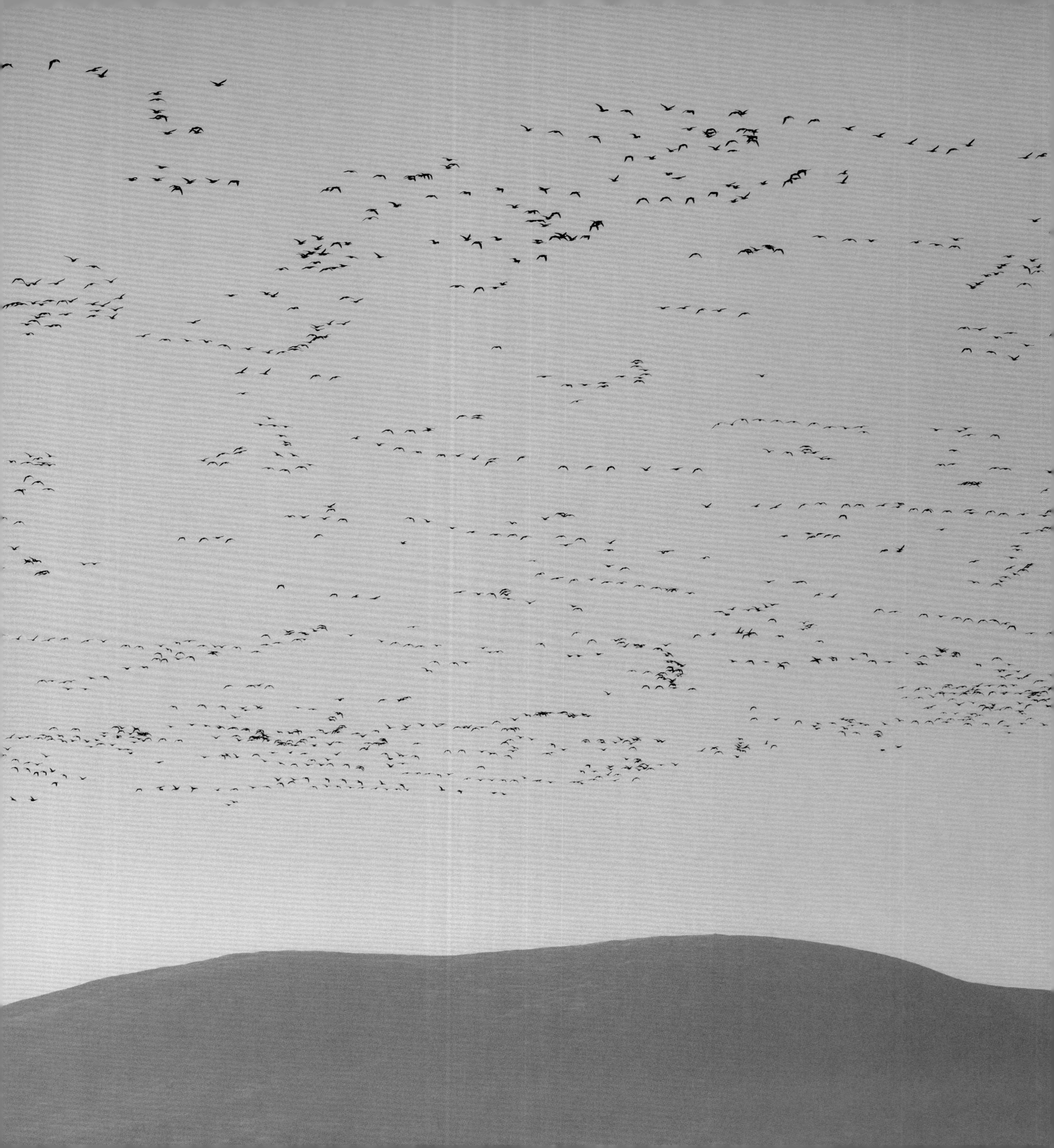

19 DUMFRIESSHIRE

JANUARY 2018
DAY 174–176 | 04,532–04,606KM | 74KM

Previous:

Whiten Head, A' Mhòine, Sutherland

Opposite:

A skein of geese above Criffel

The journey into Scotland begins with the inauspicious start of dropping my toothbrush into the toilet at Gretna Green before I head into the icy winter's dawn. Overhead, the sky is alive with flocks of migrating geese, and each wave is heralded first by honking and then a flapping of wings. I'm heading west into Dumfriesshire along the north shore of the mercurial Solway Firth. Across the water, I can see the distant Cumbrian shore where I've walked in the preceding days on the other side of the Solway.

As soon as I leave the pavement at Gretna, I'm presented with a new reality: the freedom of the Scottish right to roam. I use it immediately to detour into a field to see the Lochmaben Stone, a large and mysterious circular glacial erratic that marks the Battle of Sark in 1448 and is a landmark that has sat on the Anglo-Scottish border for centuries. When I return to trace the Solway shore, ruts of frozen mud and marshy ground have me sliding around, but despite the cold, the sky is blue and the light is golden. Long, almost horizontal shadows give the landscape a powerful tonal contrast. When I reach Annan in the afternoon and see a camper van decorated entirely in tartan, it hammers home the feeling I've well and truly arrived in Scotland.

But within hours, my exhilaration over the theoretical right to walk wherever I want is quickly tempered by physically impassable marshes and mazes of barbed wire. As there is no official public footpath network, paths aren't shown on the Ordnance Survey maps, so the route I'm trying to follow along the edge of the Solway is based on studying other walkers' blogs, the Scottish government's core paths website, and satellite maps.

I come to dread seeing the word 'merse' marked on the map. It's the Scottish name for saltmarsh, which quickly begins to represent a kind of expletive to me as they often appear flat and navigable until one reaches an unjumpable ditch, requiring a kilometre or more backtracking to passable ground. During one such zigzag, I meet a farmer wearing a woolly hat and thick red plaid overshirt. I step awkwardly across the brown frozen bracken towards him so we can hear each other. Rather than tell me to get off his land, as might happen in England, he lets me know the easiest fences to cross and asks me if I'm all right for water and provisions. This heartwarming encounter with my first Scot on the journey confirms that the right to roam is fully embraced on the ground; that land here is for sharing. I leave him with a grateful wave and he returns to fixing his fences, which, like many I've seen, have been flattened by the previous week's heavy flooding.

Throughout the second day, the distant horizon is dominated by the Iron Age hill fort of Ward Law where I plan to sleep. As night falls, I pitch my tent near the earthwork of a Roman fort on the crest of the hill to overlook the Solway. Peeking out, I can see the stars are incredibly clear against the black sky, and after making a dehydrated meal for dinner, I head out of the tent with my tripod for astrophotography. After a few moments, I'm driven back into the tent by the ferocity and bitterness of the sub-zero wind. Evidently, I'll need to reassess my clothing for winter in Scotland!

The right to wild-camp in Scotland means that there's no need to hide, and I fall asleep with the deep calm that comes from knowing I am allowed to be here, that if a farmer, gamekeeper or landowner comes this way, they will not ask me to move on. Despite the cold, it's the best night's sleep I've had in a while, and makes me realise how much low-level anxiety stealth-camping in England has given me.

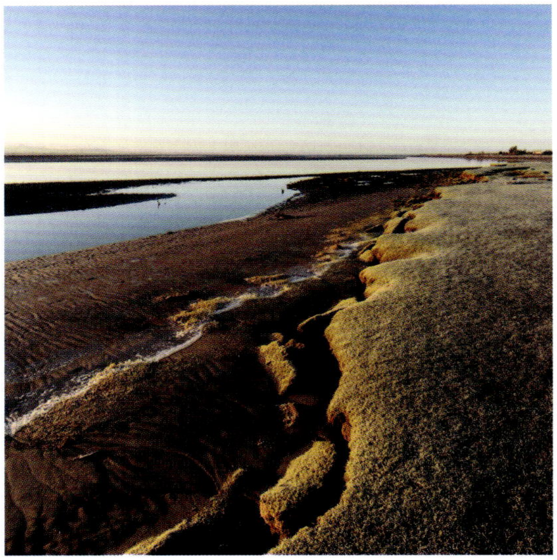
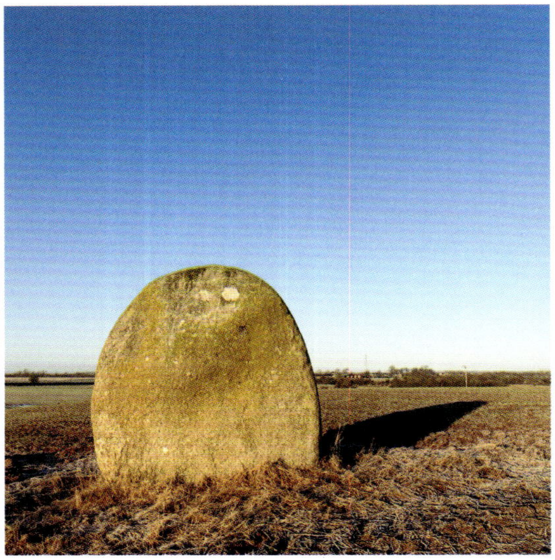
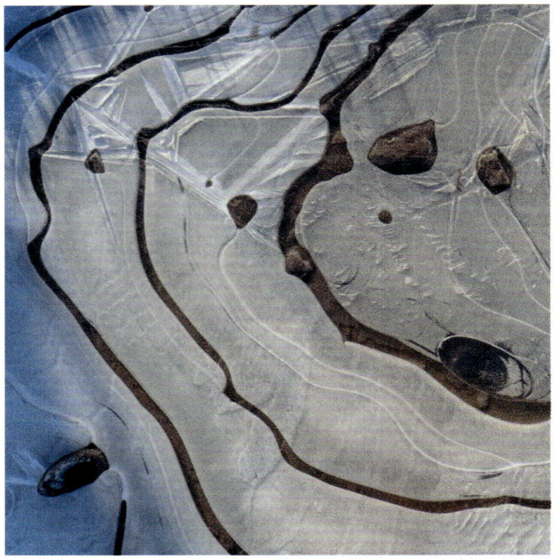
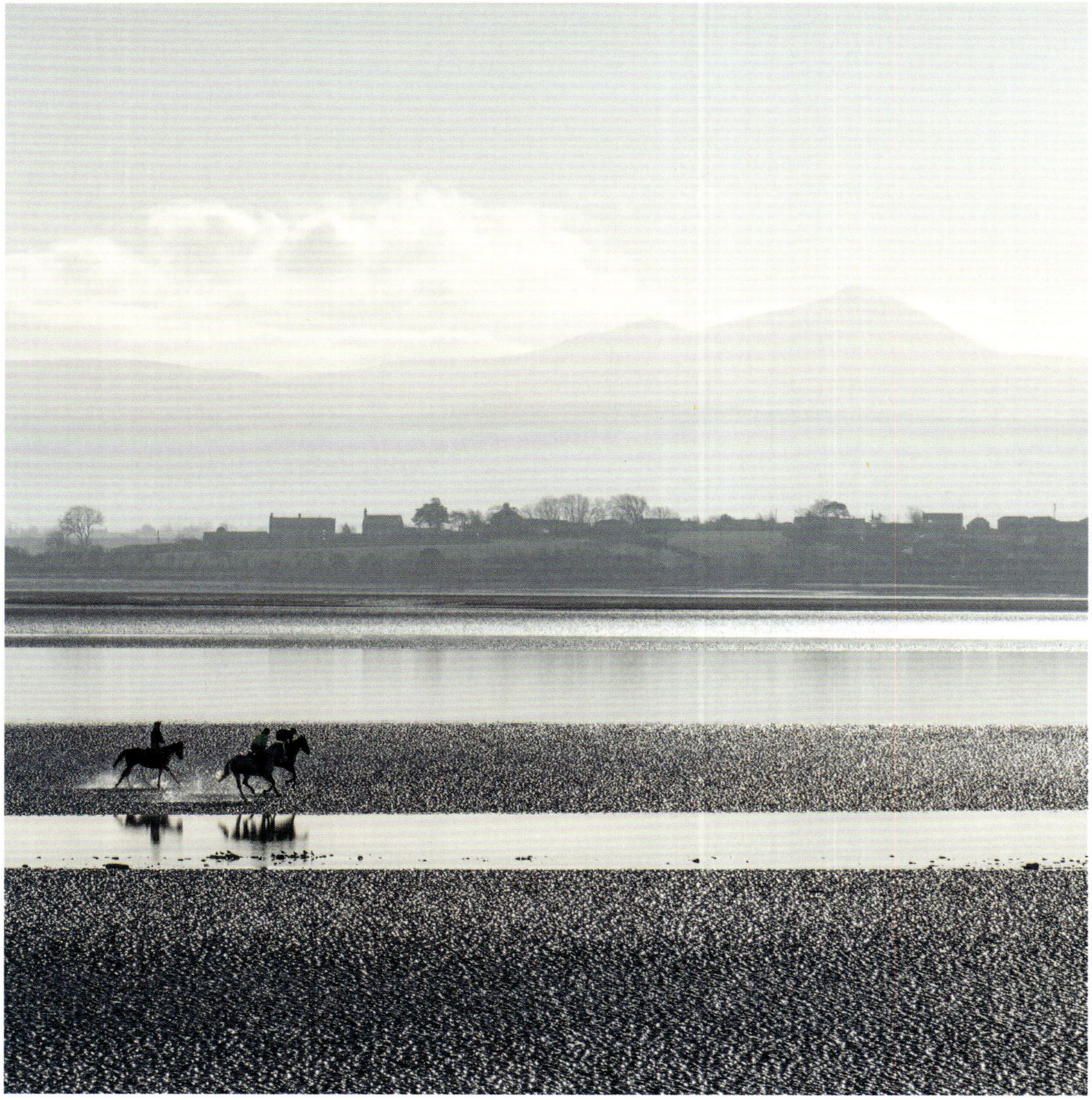
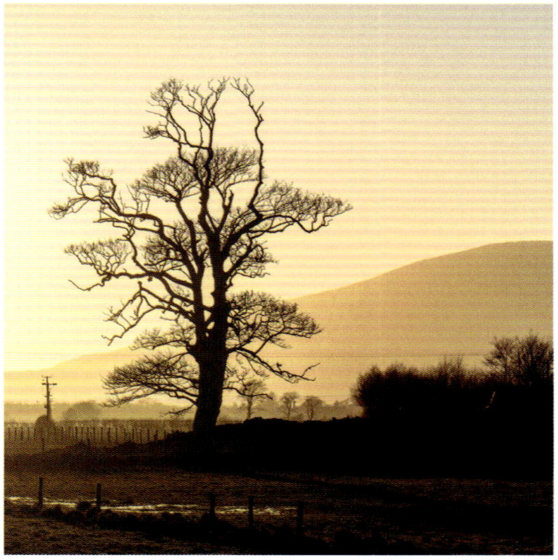
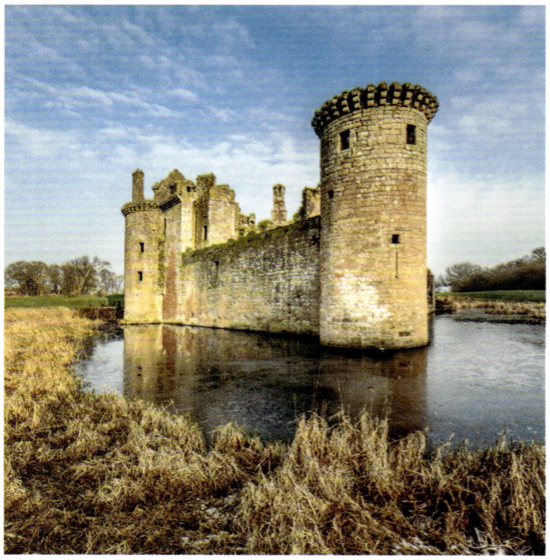

Opposite, clockwise from top left:

First light, Solway Firth, Gretna

The Lochmaben Stone, a glacial erratic and landmark for millennia. The site also marks the Battle of Sark where, in 1448, 3,000 English were killed fighting the Scots, who allegedly lost only twenty-six men!

Ice forms, Gretna

Sunset, Bankend

Caerlaverock Castle, the first of many Scottish castles I'll encounter over the two years walking in Scotland. Built in the 1270s to protect the borders region, the castle fell to Edward I of England in 1300 during the Wars of Independence. It was found that only sixty men had withstood the whole English army for a considerable period. The castle changed hands back and forth several times over the ensuing centuries

Riders on the Solway sands, Eastriggs

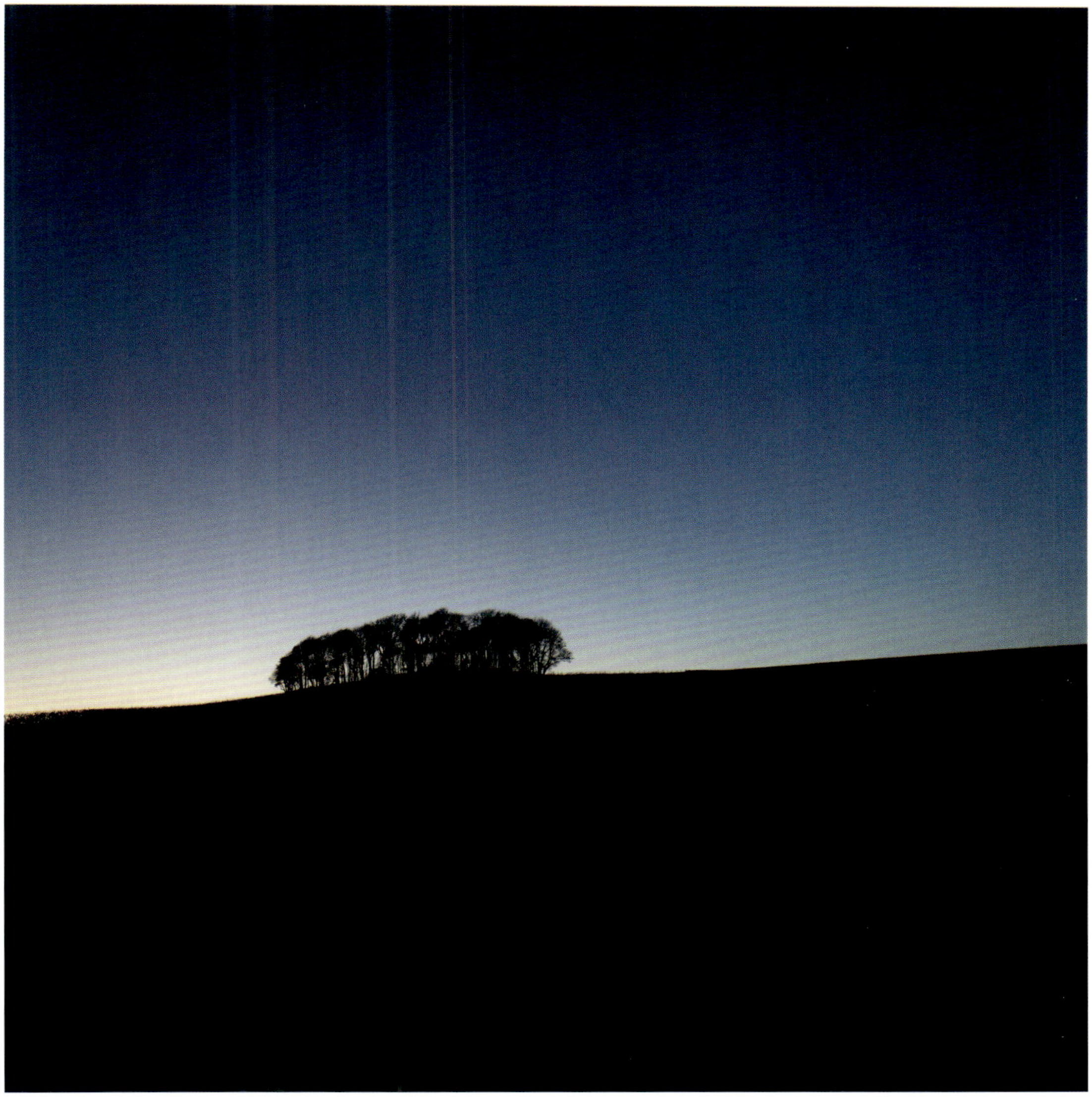

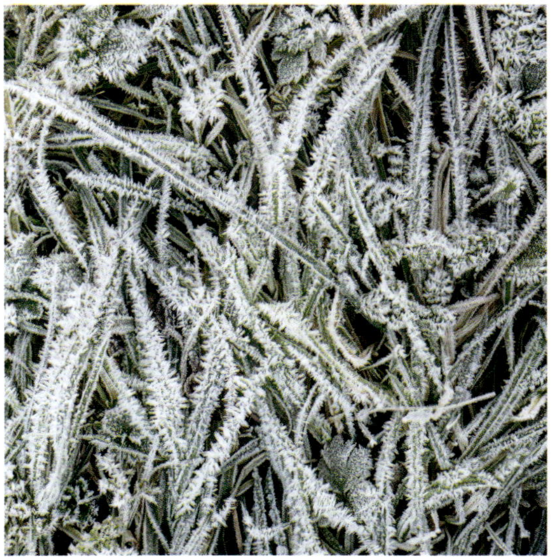

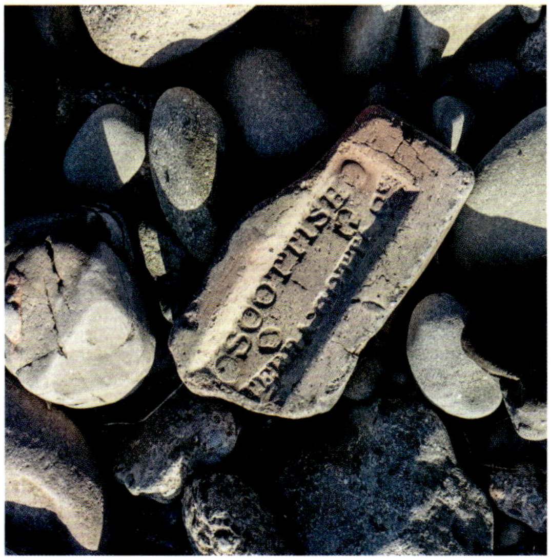

From top left:

Last light, Ward Law, where I camped one evening with a view across the Solway Firth

Frost, Barnkirk Point

Halfway to a pebble: a Scottish Terracotta Co. brick, near Powfoot

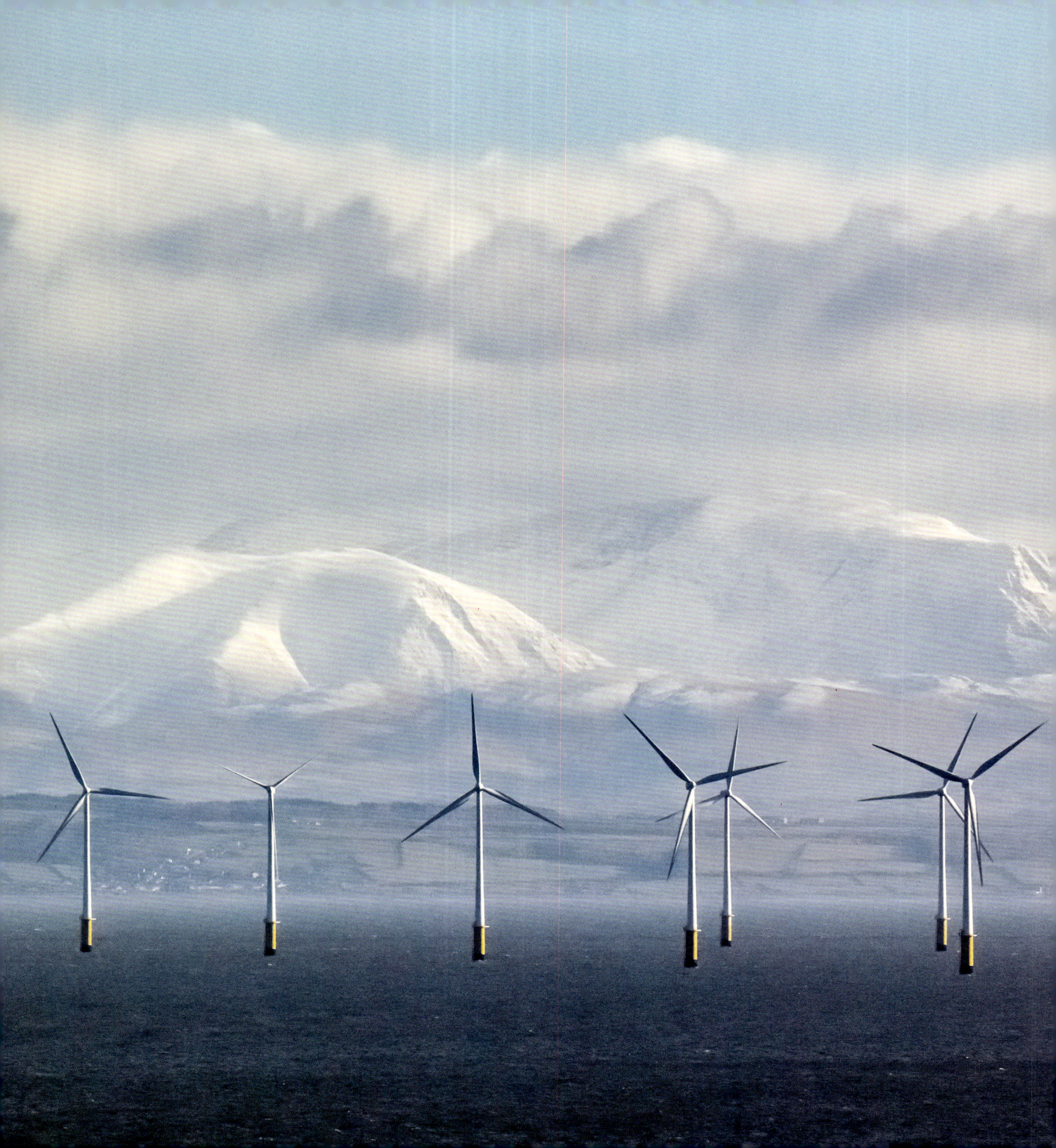

20 KIRKCUDBRIGHTSHIRE

JANUARY–FEBRUARY 2018

DAY 177–184 | 04,606–04,807KM | 201KM

It's early morning in January and a heavy mist hangs wetly in the air as I pass warmly wrapped Doonhamers – Scottish slang for the residents of Dumfries – hurrying on their way to work. I'm headed towards Devorgilla Bridge, one of the oldest bridges in Scotland, for a spot of photography. From the Robert Burns statue in the centre of town, it's a short walk, and I'm immediately transfixed as the swirling mist hides and then reveals the six handsome, slightly wonky arches that span the River Nith, made from the same red stone as much of the town. The mist is so dense it bleaches the river to a milky white, and when I leave Dumfries along the main road I can barely see beyond my feet. In an attempt to increase my visibility to the oncoming traffic, I wear a head torch, even though it's daytime.

It's not long before I encounter the wild coastline at Carse Sands, the first beach I come across in Scotland. I'd expected to have to walk further north before the landscape felt this elemental but underfoot there's an abundance of seaweed and overhead the vast flocks of geese are as much a part of the terrain here as the ever-present outline of the looming Criffel and the Solway Firth.

The next morning I arrive at Sandyhills Bay, where the air is still and sunlight vivid, with hypersaturated colours like an Instagram filter or Velvia transparency film. The Solway is very shallow here, with a texture between mercury and silk through which a complex pattern of intersecting waves gently pulsates. I marvel that, even after two and a half years of staring at the sea, it can surprise me anew.

There are other surprises, too. I soon find that sourcing drinking water is a peculiar difficulty as, although frequent, most streams are downstream of houses and farmland. I'm no stranger to filtering my own water, but the threat of agricultural chemicals here forces me to be reliant on wells, public toilets and the generosity of strangers. On my sixth day in Kirkcudbrightshire, as I'm kneeling to filter water from a well, a woman calls to me from across the road. She warns me not to drink the water, as all the sources in the area are polluted by slurry spread on the fields. I'm invited into her home for fresh water, a cup of tea and a gigantic chocolate bar, and she tells me about the legal battle she had with a local farmer, who ended up having to pay for a separate water pipe to her house after she was hospitalised from the drinking water.

Not all of nature is spoiled, though. Later that afternoon, when the rain momentarily subsides at St Mary's Isle, I spot two figures approaching along the shore. They introduce themselves as a wild-food expert and a chef, and the conversation flows as we're all pleased to be enjoying the remote and beautiful landscape together. To my delight, the wild-food expert pulls out velvet shank and jelly ear mushrooms from his bag and offers them to me. I add them eagerly into the pot of boiling water I'd been using to prepare my lunch. 'Oh, and you've got to try some of this.' He walks a few metres to gather some sea radish and scurvy grass, handing them to me like a magician. The combination of aromatic, earthy flavours with chewy and crunchy textures enlivens my bland potato powder and tinned fish. I sit back against a boulder on the shore to savour this unexpected gastronomic feast while looking out to the tiny tidal island of Inch and its crest of bare winter trees.

Opposite:

Robin Rigg Wind Farm and the Cumbrian fells from Balcary Point

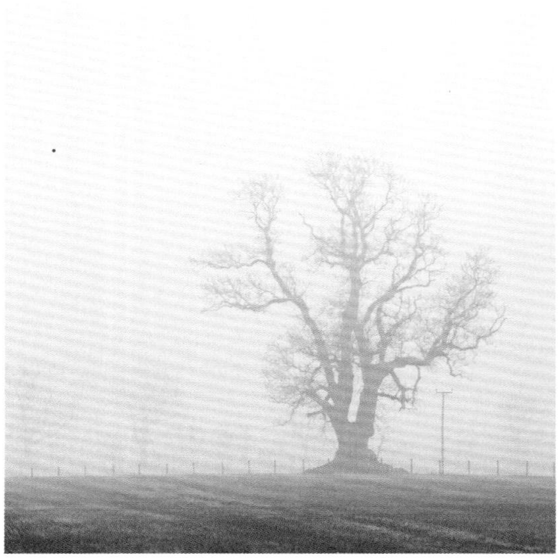

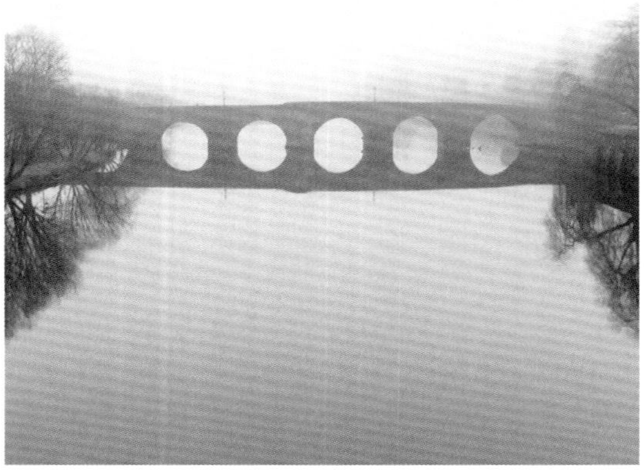

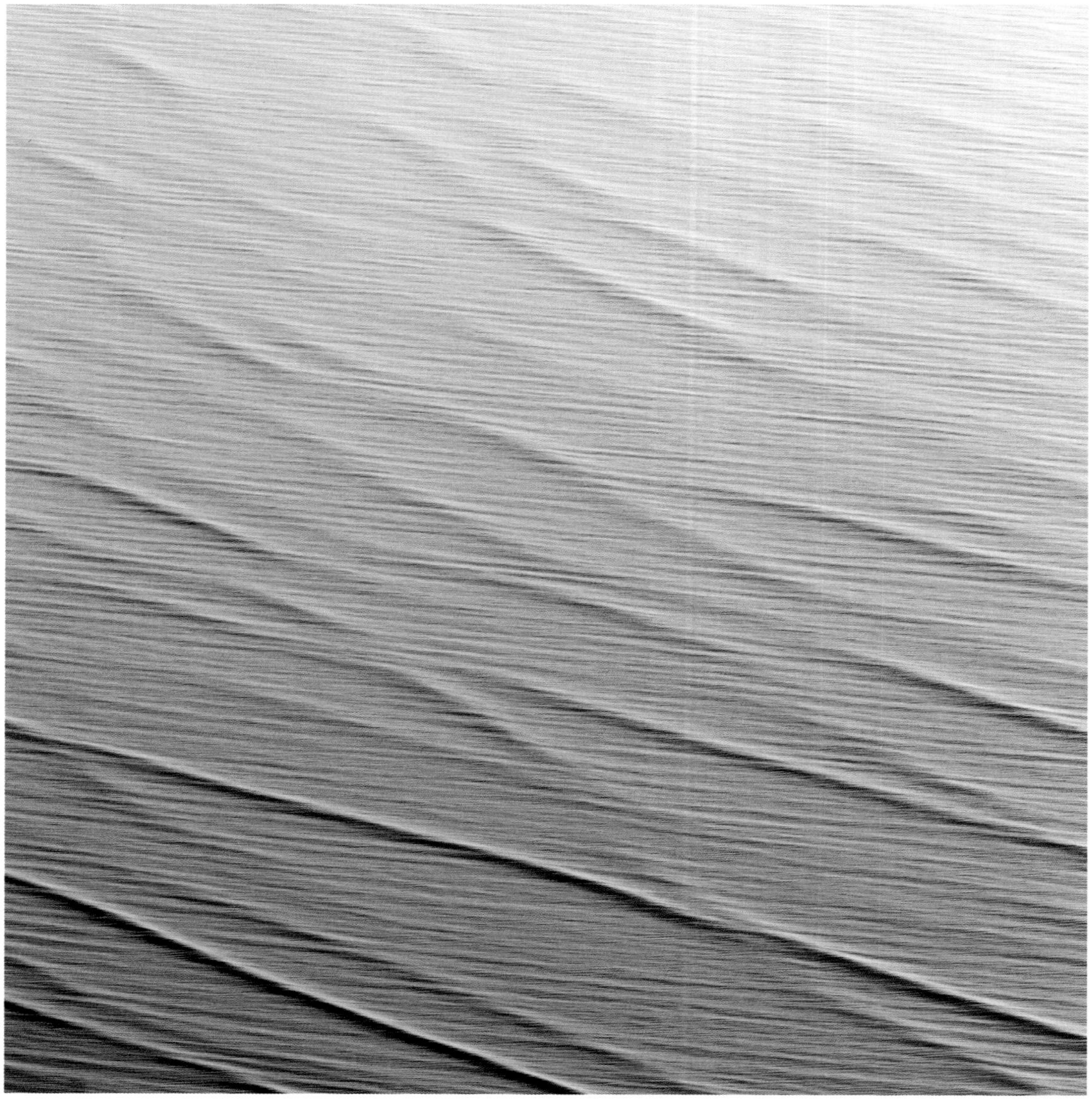

From top left:

Misty field near Kirkconnell

Devorgilla Bridge, Dumfries, the oldest surviving multiple-arched bridge in Scotland, built in the fifteenth century

Silken sea: Portling Bay

Opposite, clockwise from top left:

Salmon nets, Sandyhills Bay

Last light on Criffel from Mersehead Sands

Morning light, Sandyhills Bay

Skein of geese, Mersehead Nature Reserve

Carse Sands, the first beach in Scotland

Craigneuk Point, Sandyhills Bay

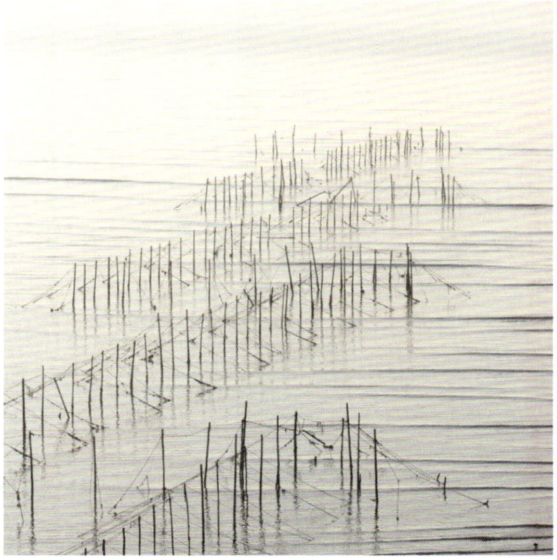
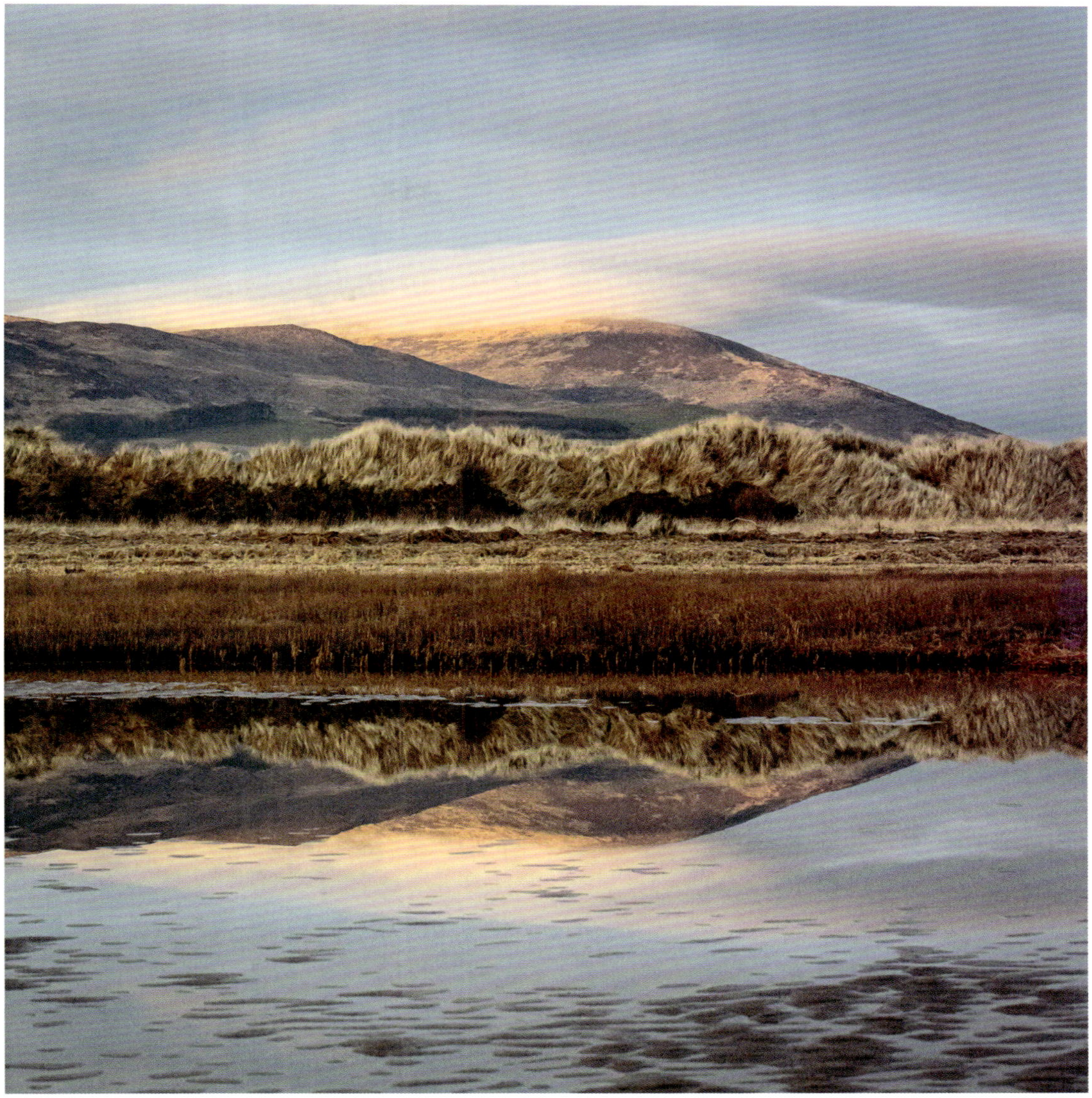
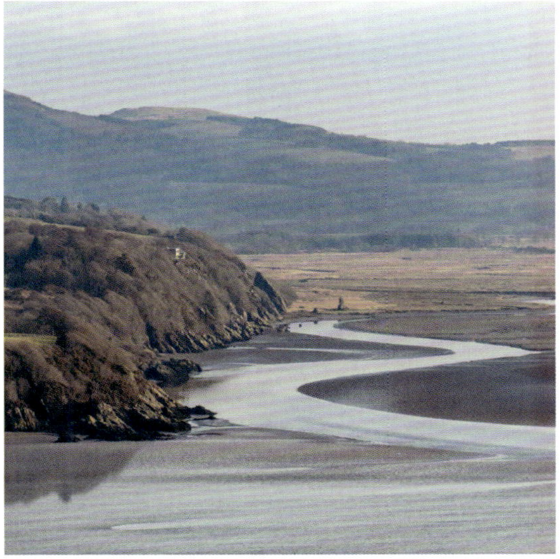
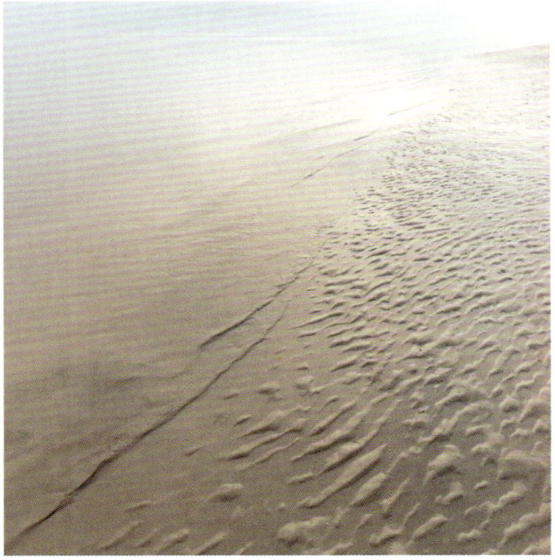
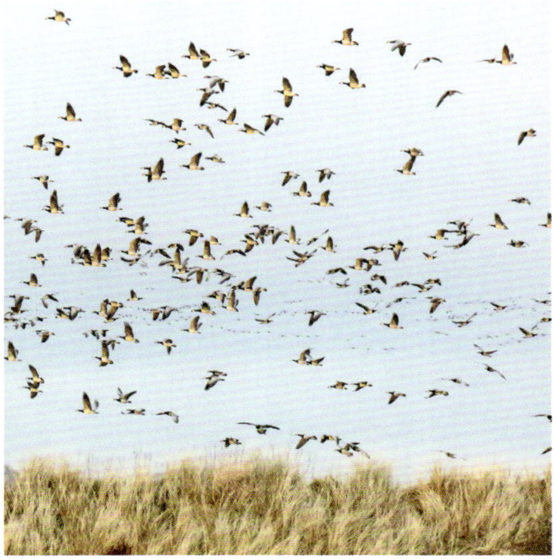
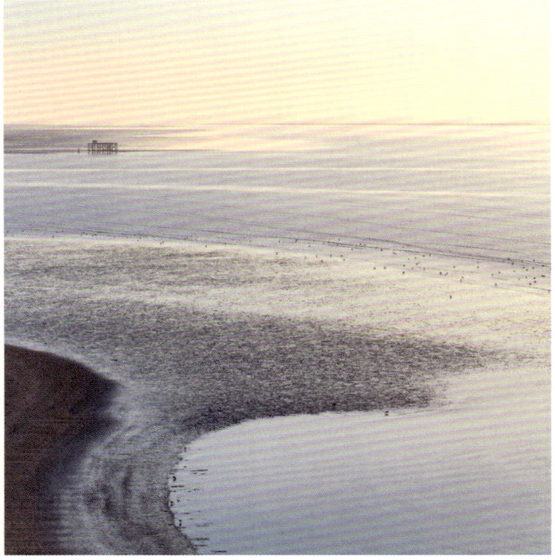

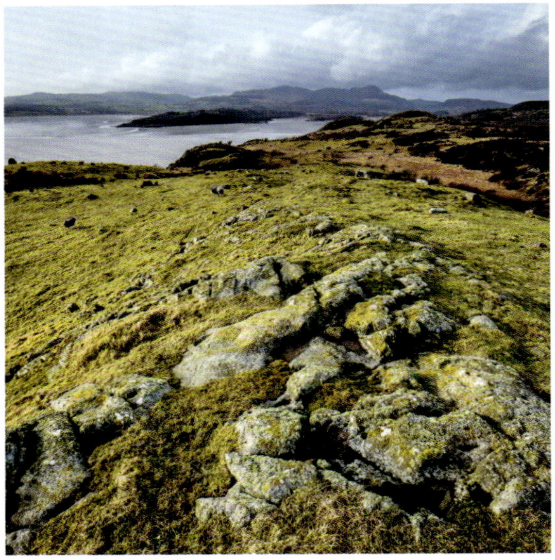

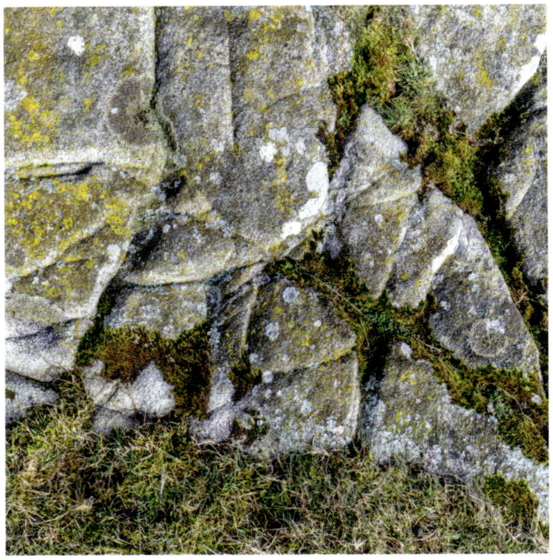

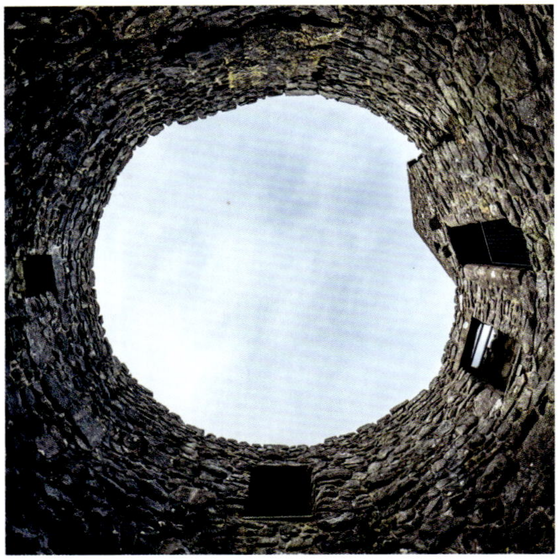

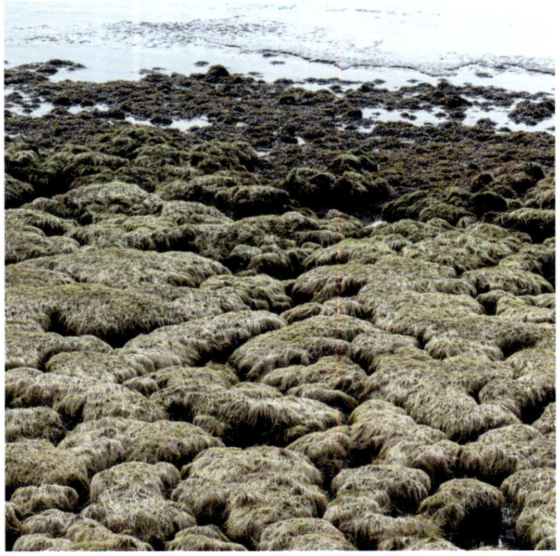

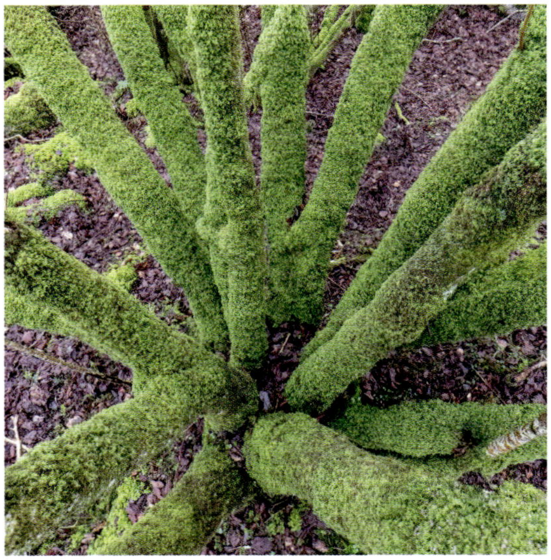

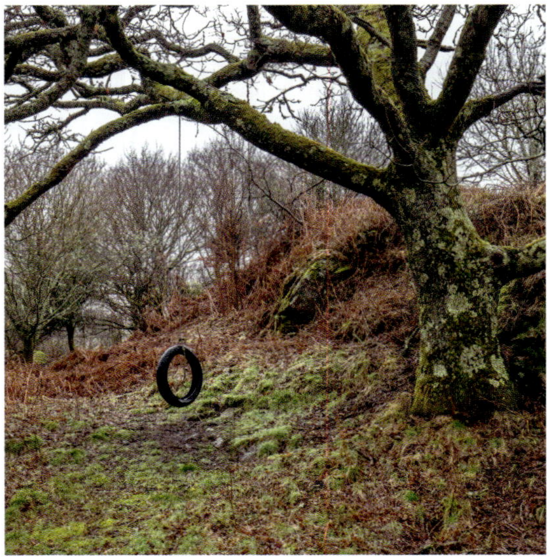

From top left:

Bengairn and Torr Point from Almorness Point

Underfoot, Almorness Point

From centre left:

The interior of Orchardton Tower, a ruined structure from the fifteenth century, that is notable for being the only round tower house in Scotland

Shore of Manxman's Lake

From bottom left:

Mossy limbs, Almorness Point

Swing, Glen Isle

Opposite:

Snow shower over the Solway Firth

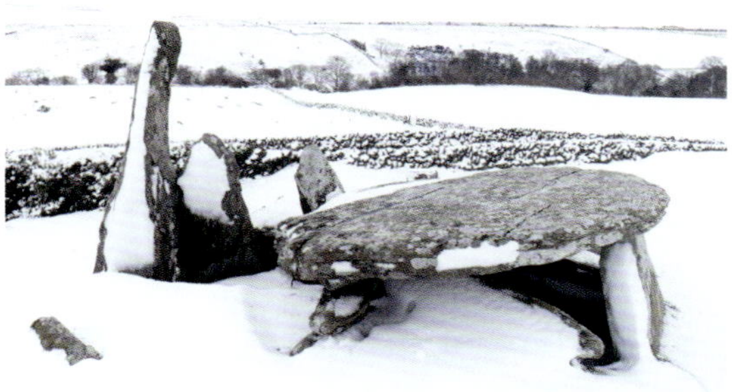
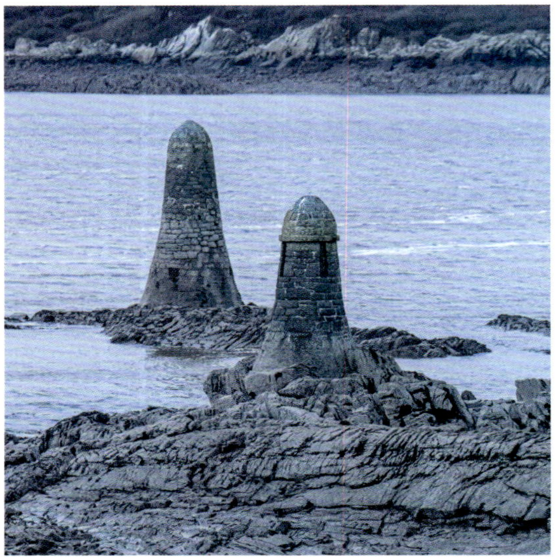
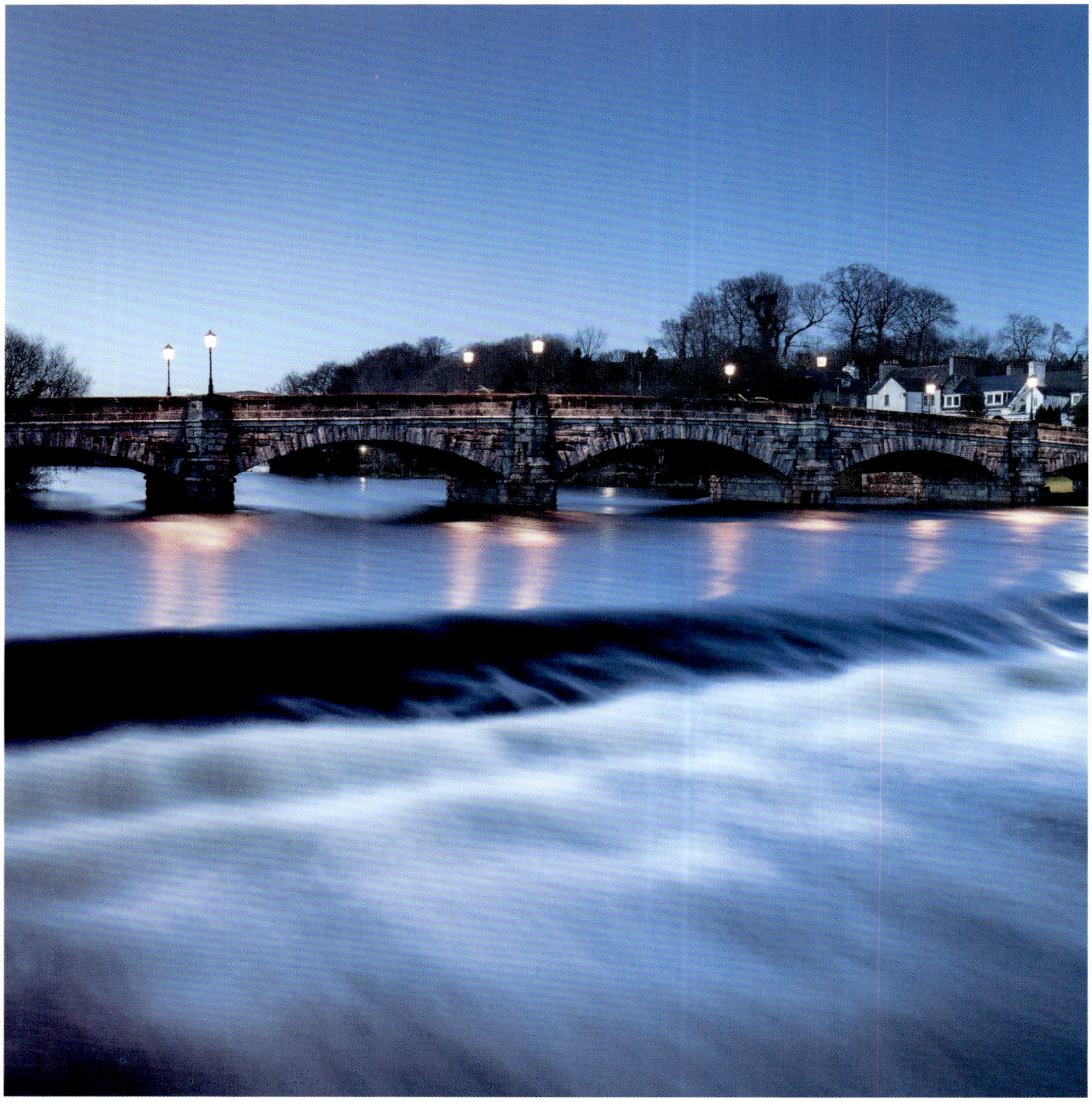

From top left:

Cairnholy, a Neolithic chambered tomb

Knockbrex Quay navigation pillars

Bridge of Cree at dusk, Newton Stewart

Opposite, from top left:

Track to Cairnholy

Ben John from Fleet Bay

From bottom left:

Wall crossing, Senwick Church

Standing stones at Cairnholy

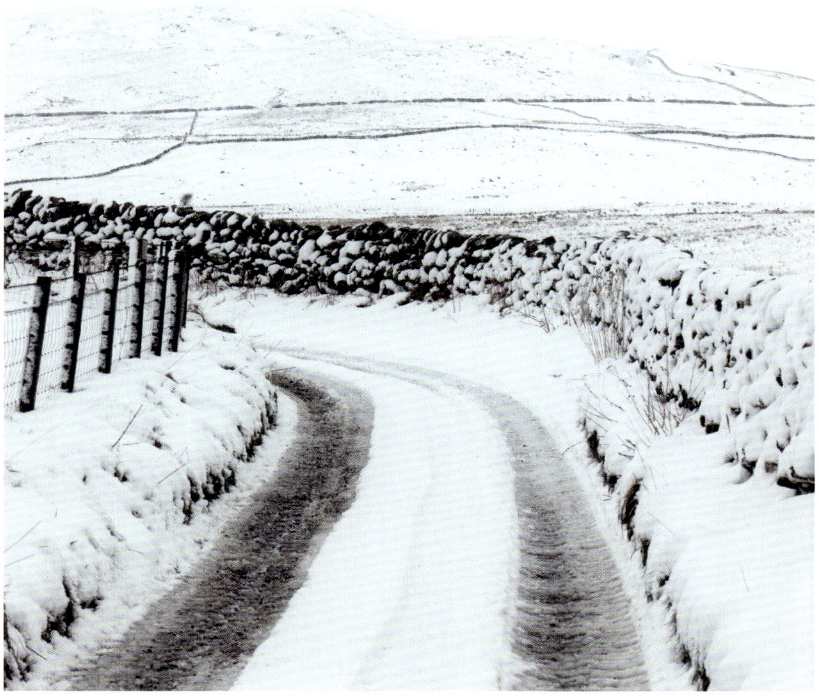

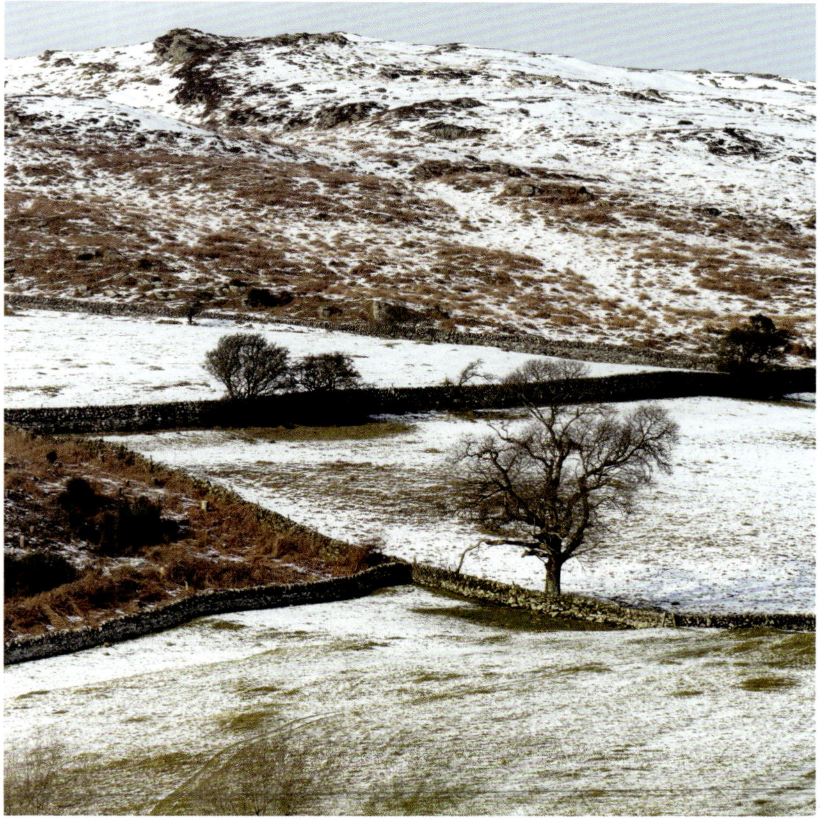

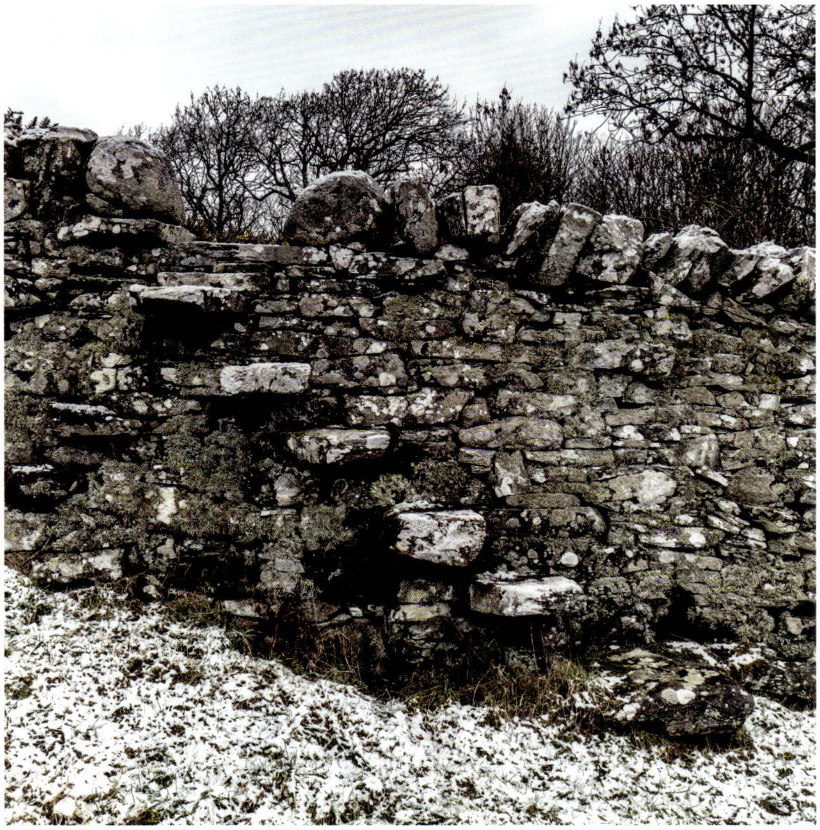

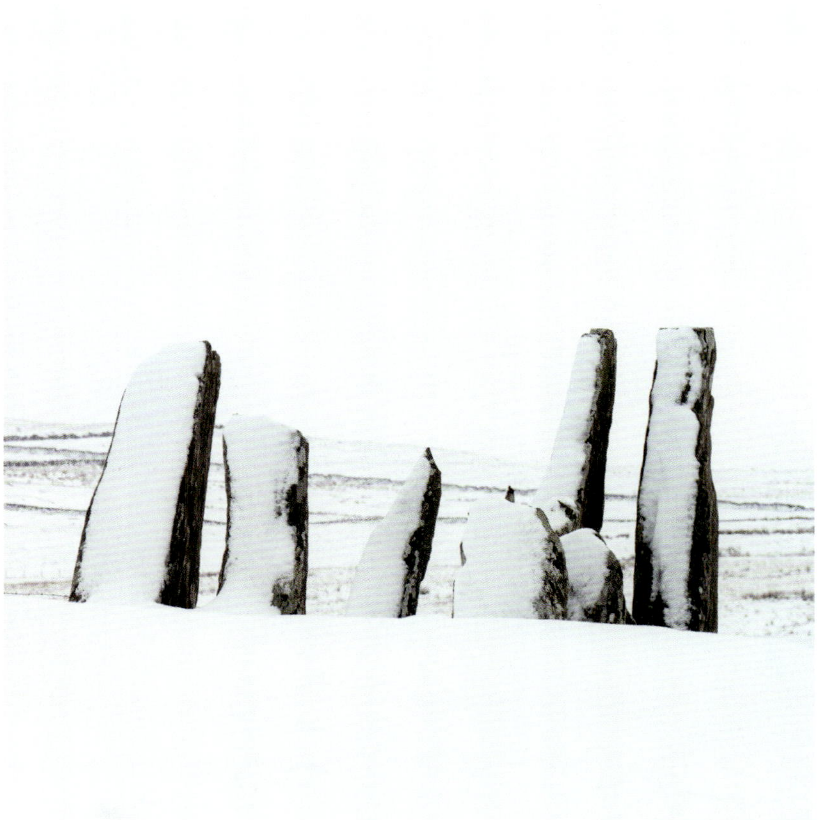

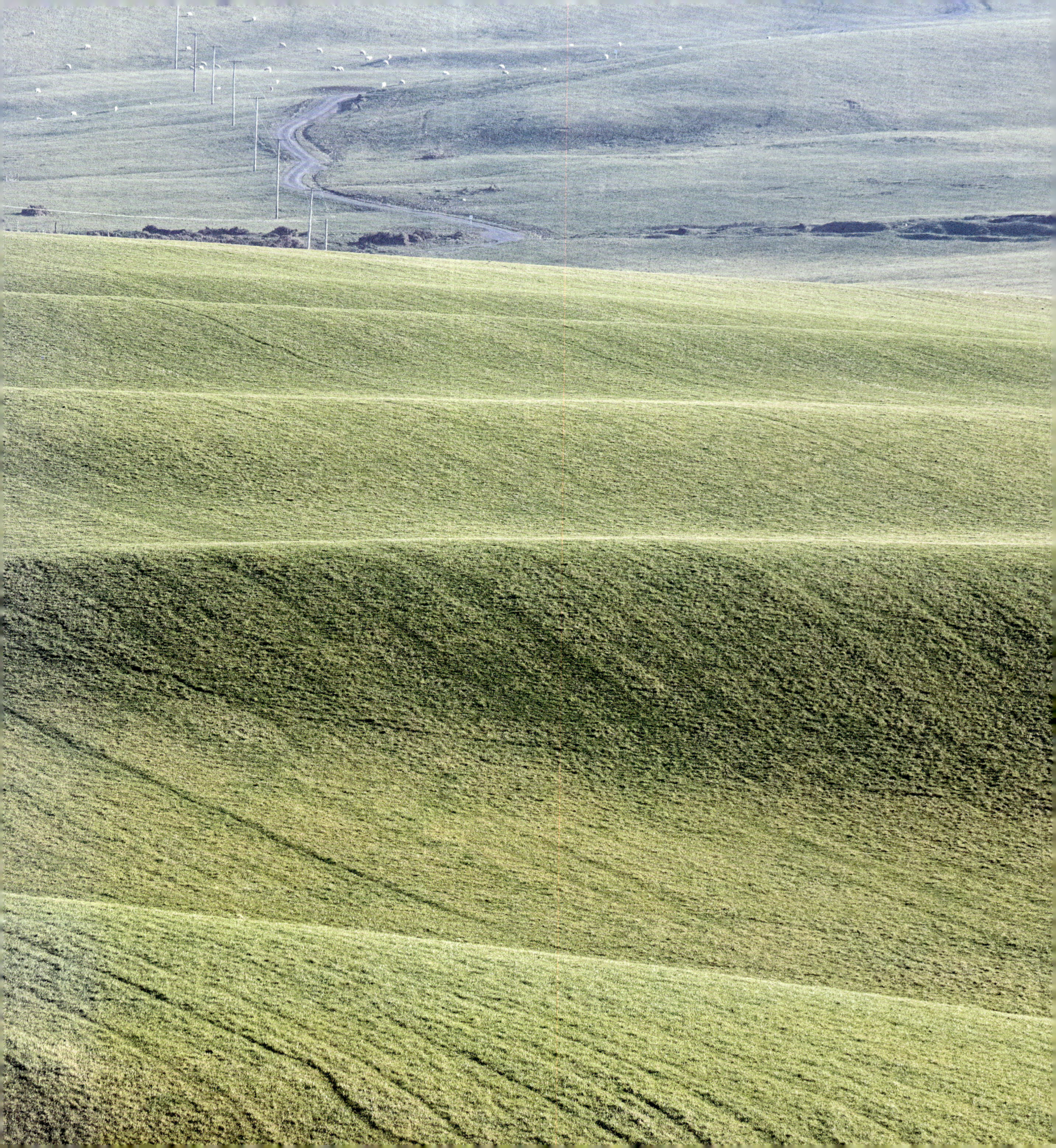

21 WIGTOWNSHIRE

FEBRUARY 2018

DAY 185–193 | 04,807–05,053 KM | 246 KM

I always love a bookshop, so arriving at Wigtown is a delight. Situated in the western region of Dumfries and Galloway, Wigtown is known as Scotland's National Book Town – and for good reason. It not only contains the largest bookshop in the country, but also has a high concentration of second-hand bookshops, all set around a charming market square. Browsing books is a welcome break from hiking in the rain, so I spend several hours ducking in and out of shops before I walk late into the night to keep on track with my daily mileage.

This part of Scotland feels deliciously untamed, and as I approach Burrow Head – the southern point of the Machars, famous for being the location of *The Wicker Man* burning scene – I spot jagged crags and unfenced coastline warmly saturated by the winter sun. It's slow-going making my way around the contorted granite cliffs, and on the third day, in need of respite from the all-too-familiar wind and rain, I take shelter in a cave at Physgill. As I lean my sopping pack against the dry rear of the cave, half a dozen driftwood crosses catch my eye. There are no obvious clues as to why they're there, and it's not until much later that I discover it to be a site of active pilgrimage – St Ninian's Cave, allegedly the place where the saint who introduced Christianity to Scotland first found sanctuary after arriving from Ireland.

It requires a couple more days of navigating rugged coastline to reach Scotland's most southerly point, the Mull of Galloway Lighthouse. I arrive at night with only a few metres of visibility, and even the beam of the lighthouse itself can only be seen close-up. It's not until the morning that I make out the mountainous horizon of Cumbria in the far distance. I savour my last glimpse of England, knowing it will be months before I see it again.

The landscape changes to a sea of green as I head north, where rolling fields of velvety grass bordered by granite cliffs that drop into the Irish Sea characterise this area known as the Rhins. Although the pastoral scene is charming to look at, the barbed wire, electric fences, fields of bulls and paths overgrown with gorse make progress slow and frustrating. Looking for an easier way to progress, I descend a hill to the nearest farm and follow the lanes. By a gate to the yard, I meet a farmer clad in an argyle sweater and tweed flat cap. He's carrying a pickaxe, broom and spade, and seems surprised to see anyone coming from my direction. With a warm, beguiling accent somewhere between Irish and Scottish, he tells me with a vitality that belies his eighty years that he manages the farm mostly alone, though once a handful of derelict crofts on his land housed seven people who worked with him. 'All the young ones leave after school these days,' he says wistfully. 'I don't have to join the army or anything now!' he jokes when I ask to take his picture.

The sky is a brilliant blue on the road to Portpatrick the next day and the good weather has people leaving their front doors open, engaged in wholesome activities and up for a chat. The scattered dwellings here are whitewashed, slate-roofed bungalows or farmhouses, each nestled within undulating fields of livestock with the greenest grass I've ever seen. I have a friendly yet shouted conversation about the best pubs in Portpatrick with three feisty women across a large meadow.

All this enjoyable banter means I have much night-hiking ahead of me to keep to my schedule. This is no hardship as it's a magical moonlit approach along the cliffs to Portpatrick, with the lights of Belfast twinkling in the distance.

Opposite:

Undulating landscape of the Rhins, Mull of Galloway

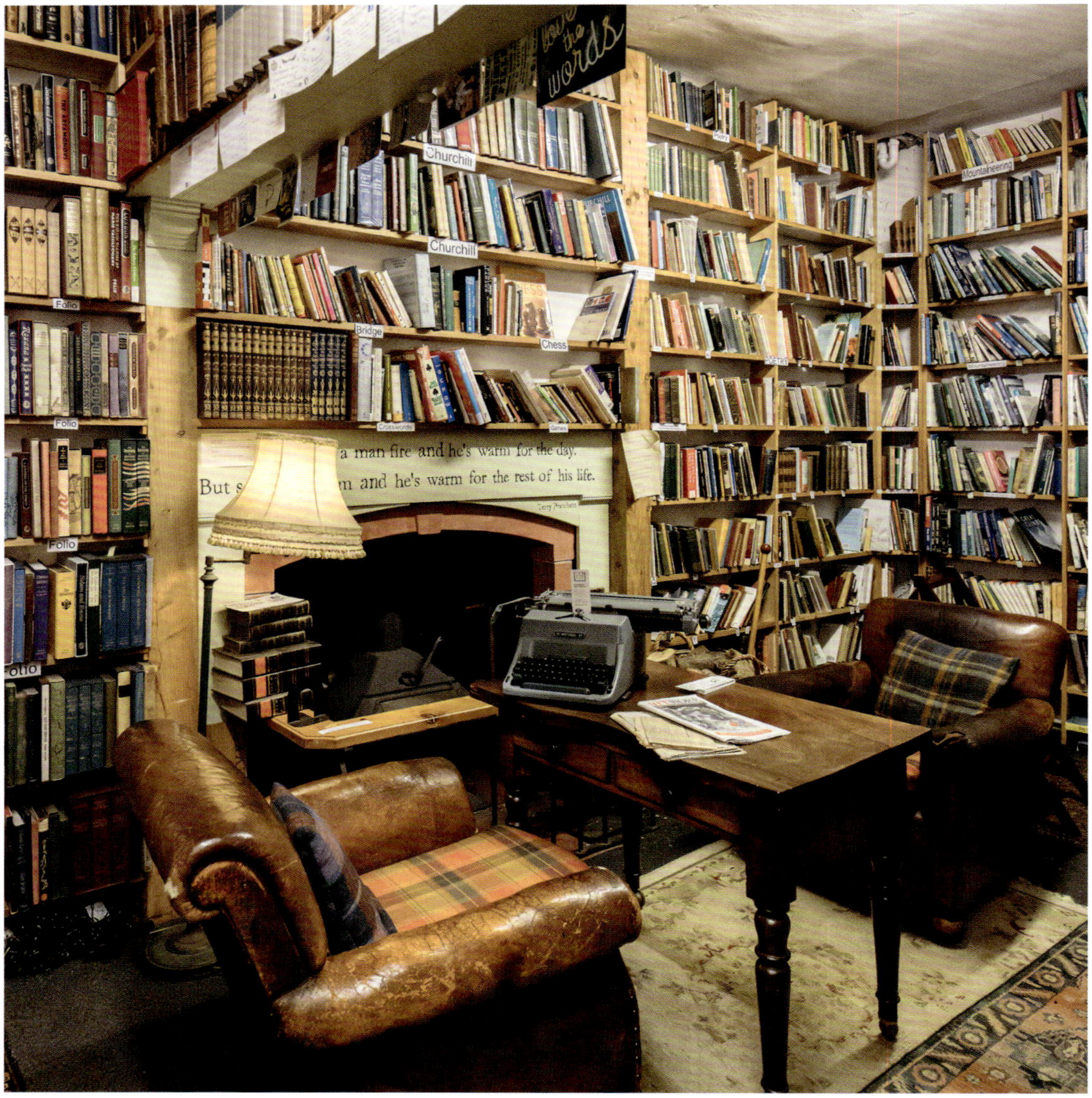

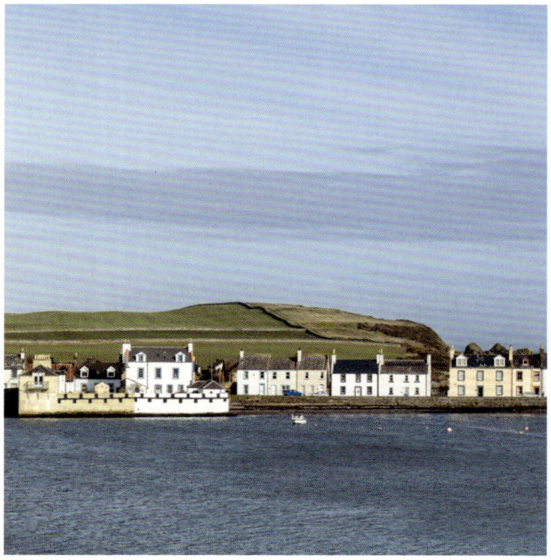

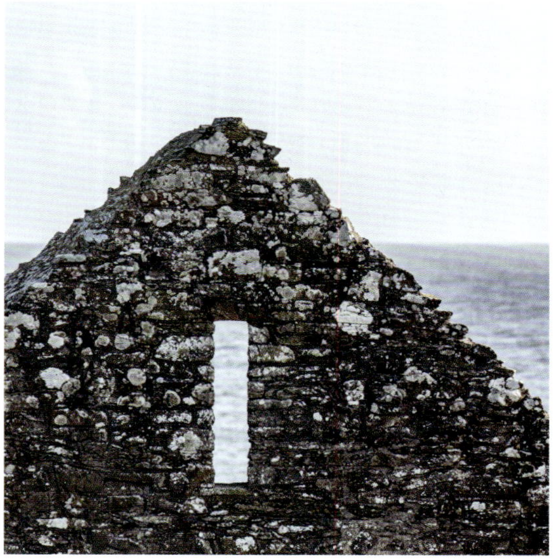

From top left:

The perfect respite on a rainy day, The Bookshop, Wigtown

Isle of Whithorn Harbour

St Ninian's Chapel, Isle of Whithorn. The original chapel on this site was built in the 1100s, when many would have walked from the shore and thanked God for their safe passage

Opposite:

St Ninian's Cave, Physgill. The Christian missionary St Ninian (360–432) was the first in Scotland, and the cave was reputedly used as a place of personal prayer. The site remains an important place of Christian pilgrimage

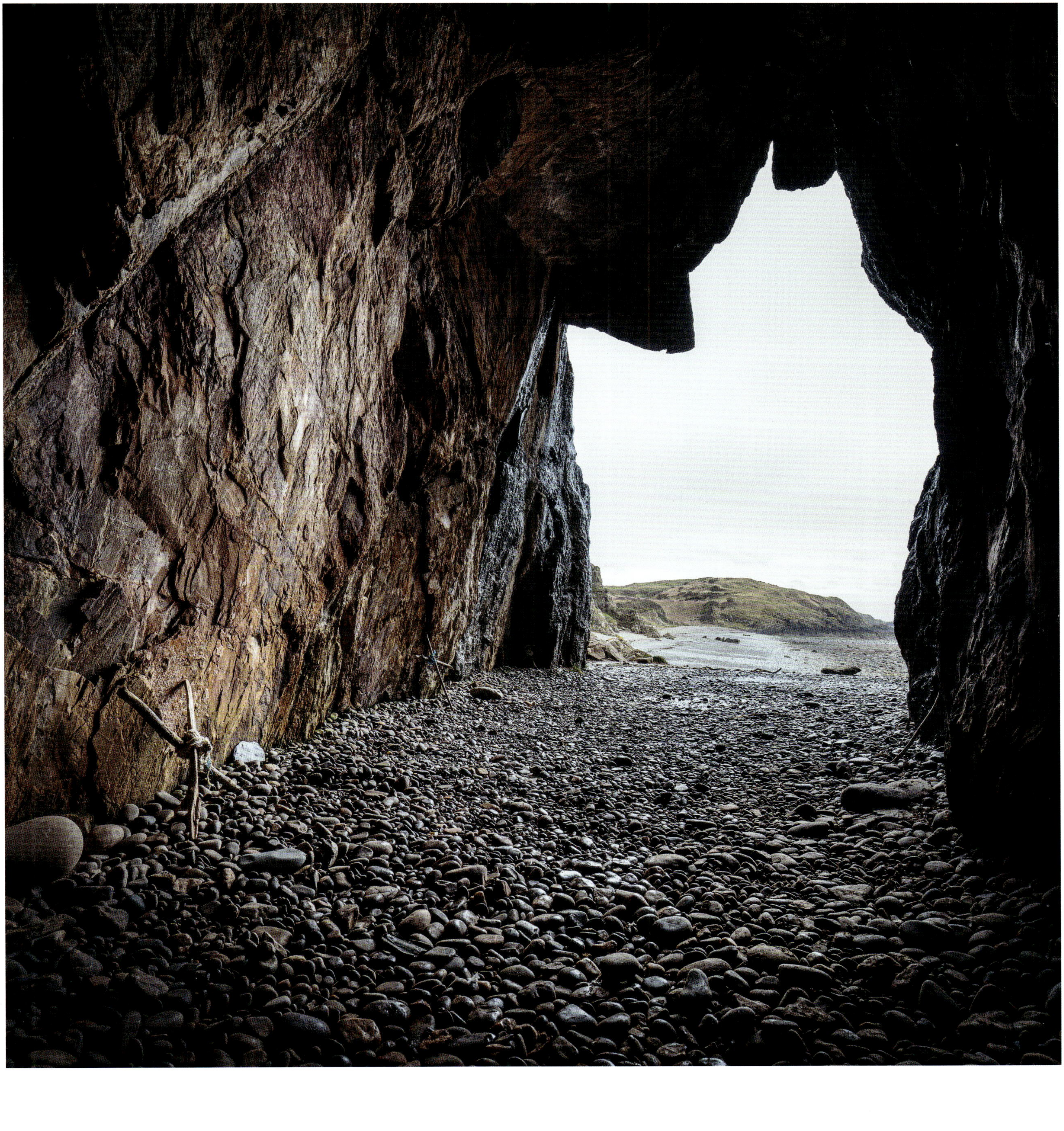

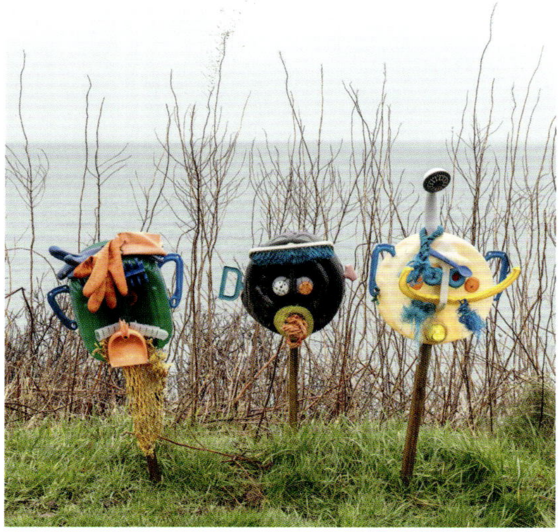

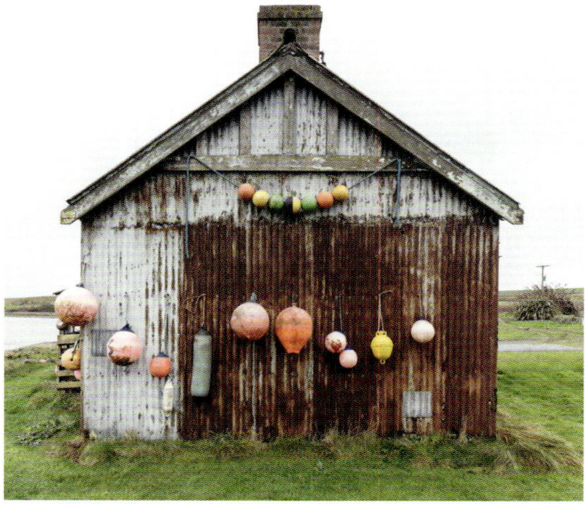

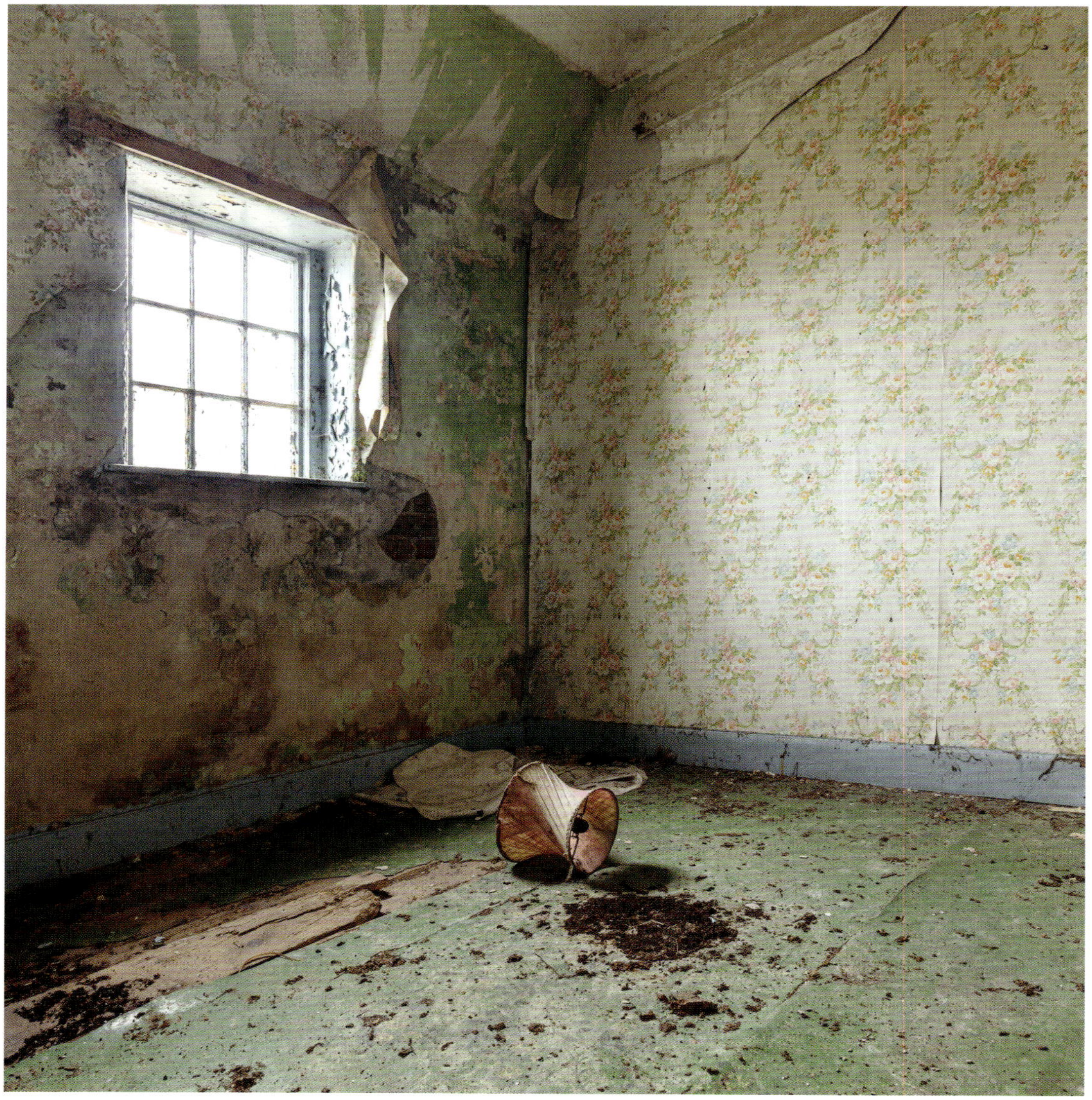

From top left:

Sea beasts: Drummore

Buoy house, Portacree

Bedroom in a house by the sea, Portacree

Opposite:

Mull of Galloway Lighthouse in a rainstorm

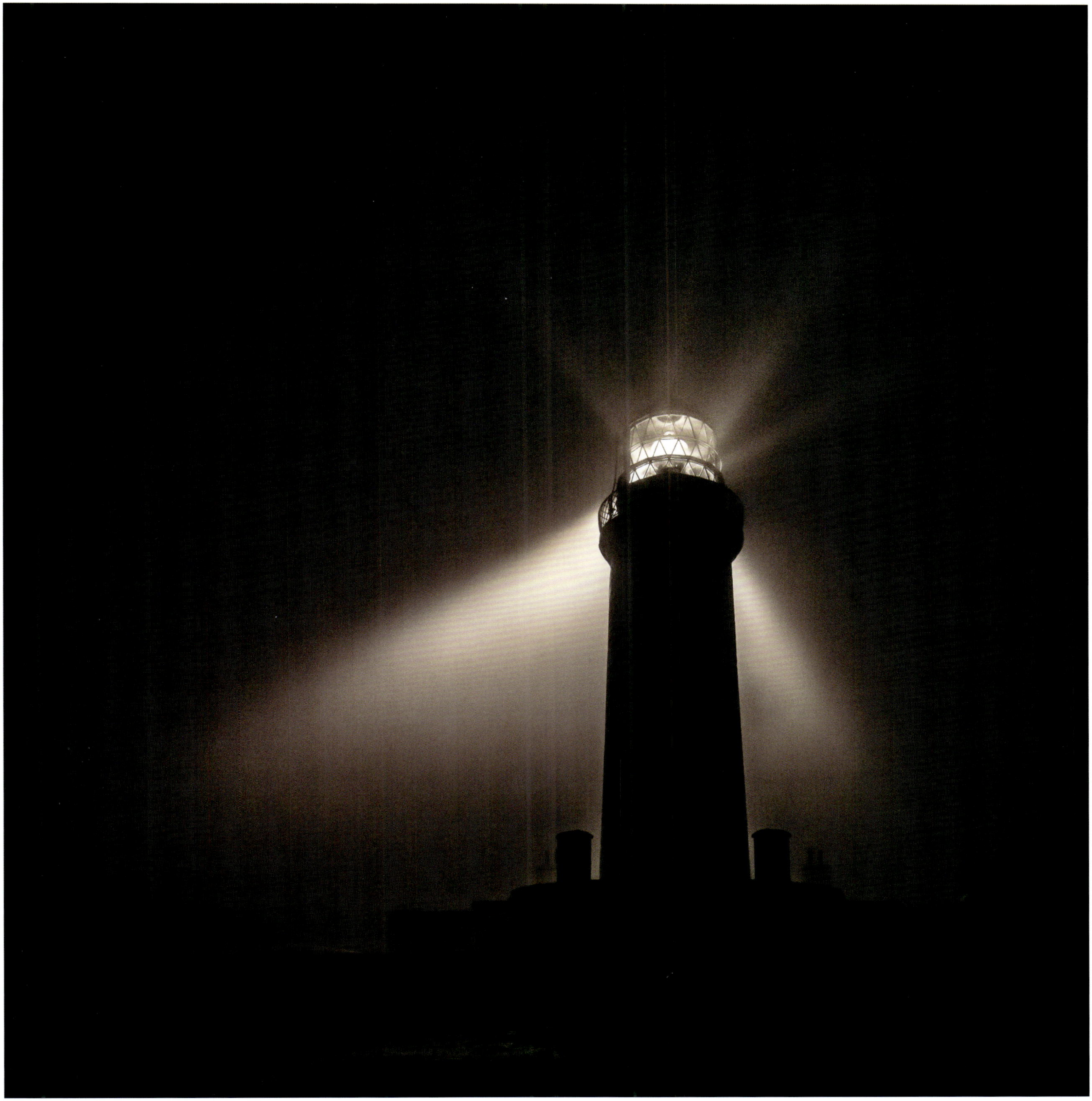

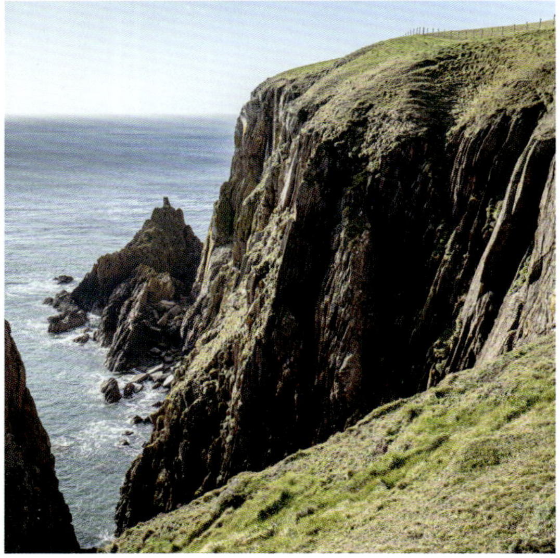
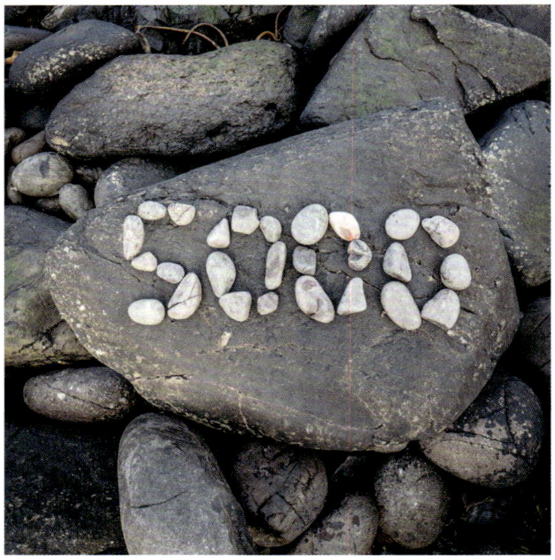
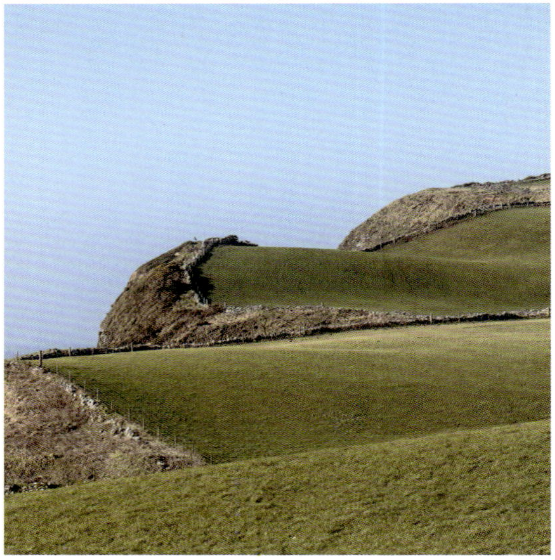
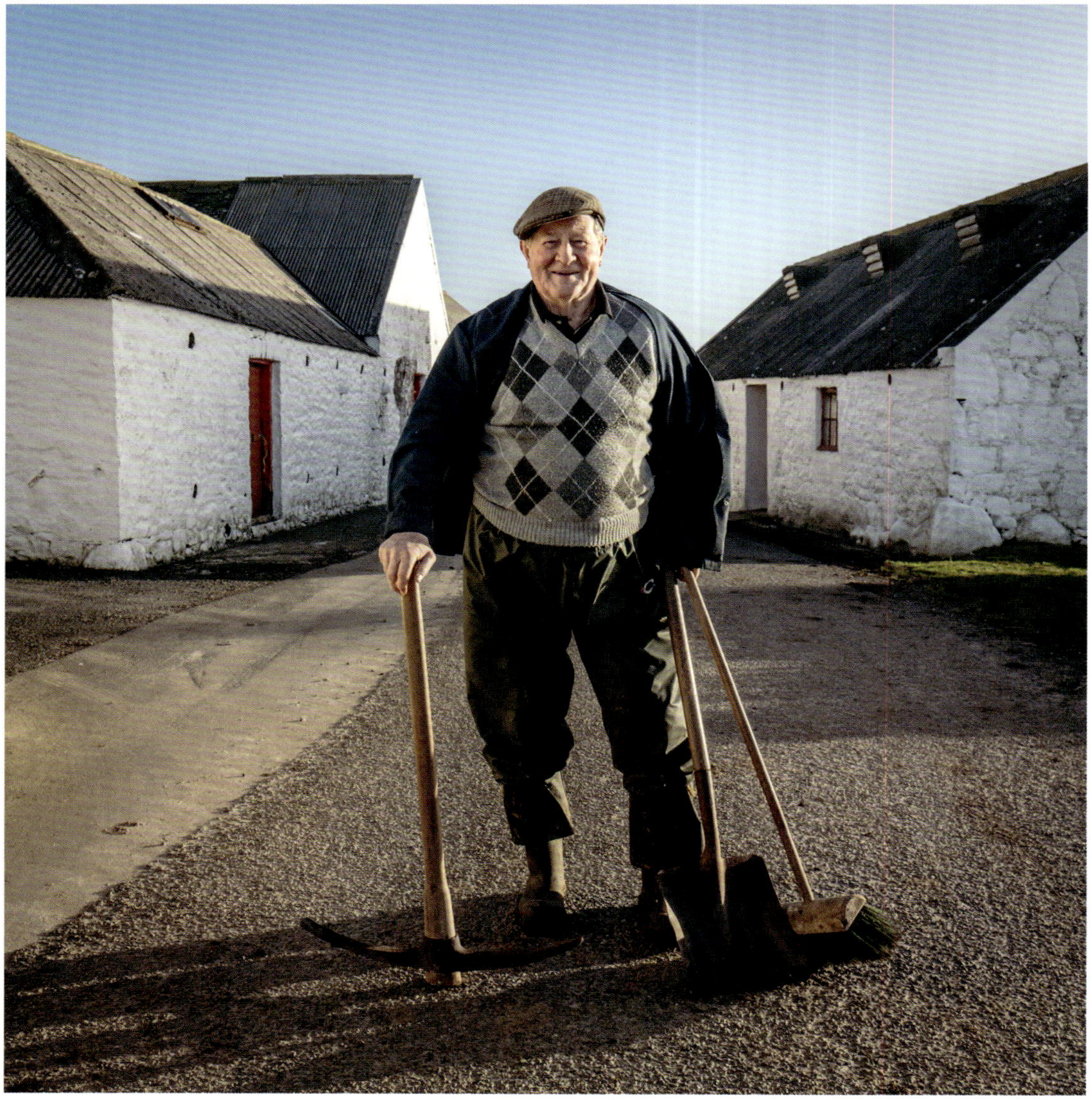
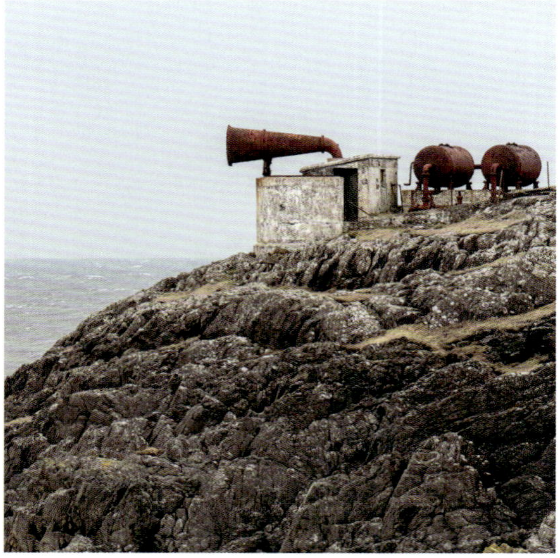
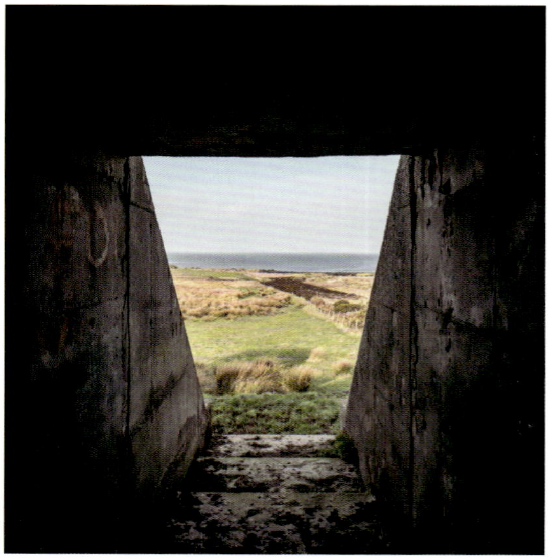

Opposite, clockwise from top left:

The Mull of Galloway cliffs

Milestone: 5,000 kilometres walked since London. At the time, I celebrated reaching the halfway point here, thinking the total distance of the walk was 10,000 kilometres. As I progressed further north, the terrain got more challenging, adding 1,000 kilometres to the total

The Rhins landscape

Foghorn at Killantringan Lighthouse

RAF North Cairn, a Second World War chain home radar station bunker

Farmer Hughes of Knockencule Farm on the way to feed his cows. There is a handful of derelict crofts on his land that once housed seven people who used to work with him. Today he manages the farm mostly alone

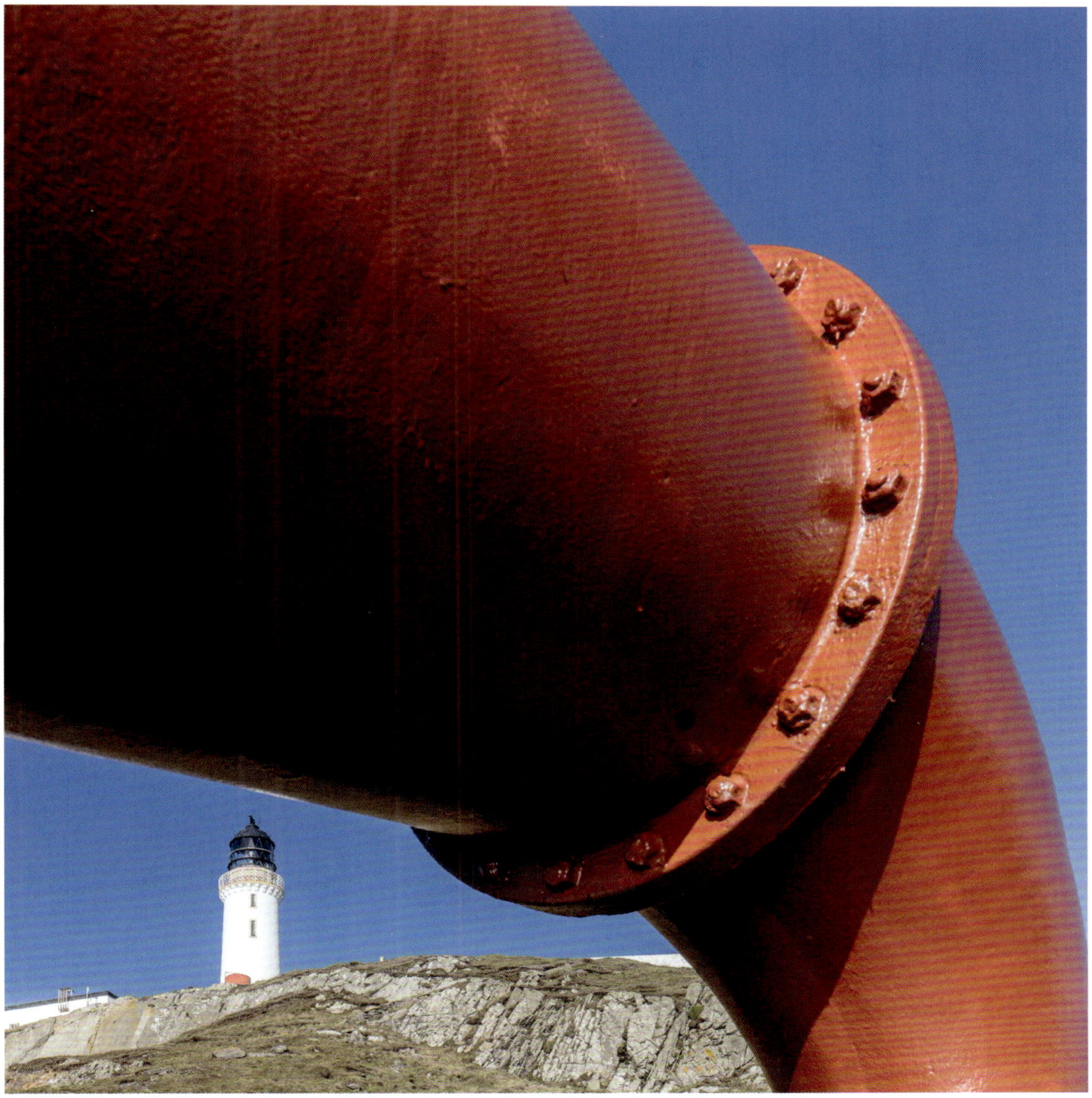

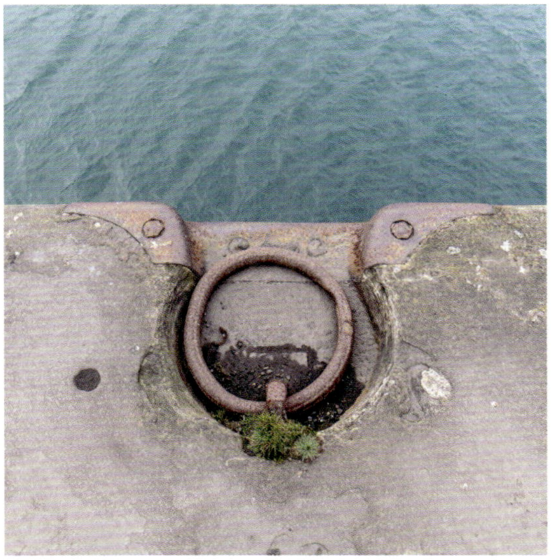

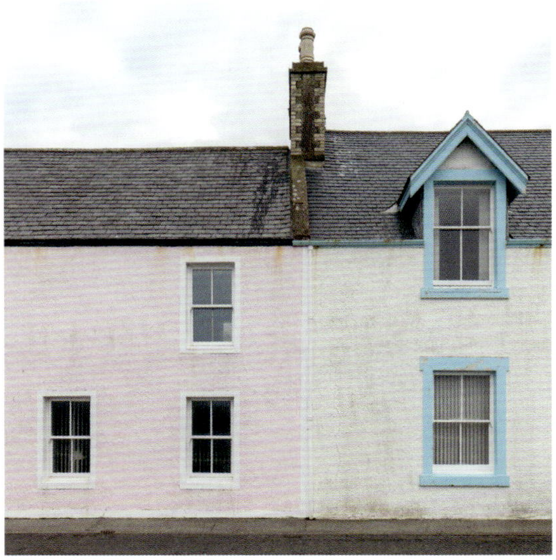

From top left:

Foghorn at the Mull of Galloway Lighthouse, Carrickcarlin Point

Portpatrick Harbour

Portpatrick harbourfront

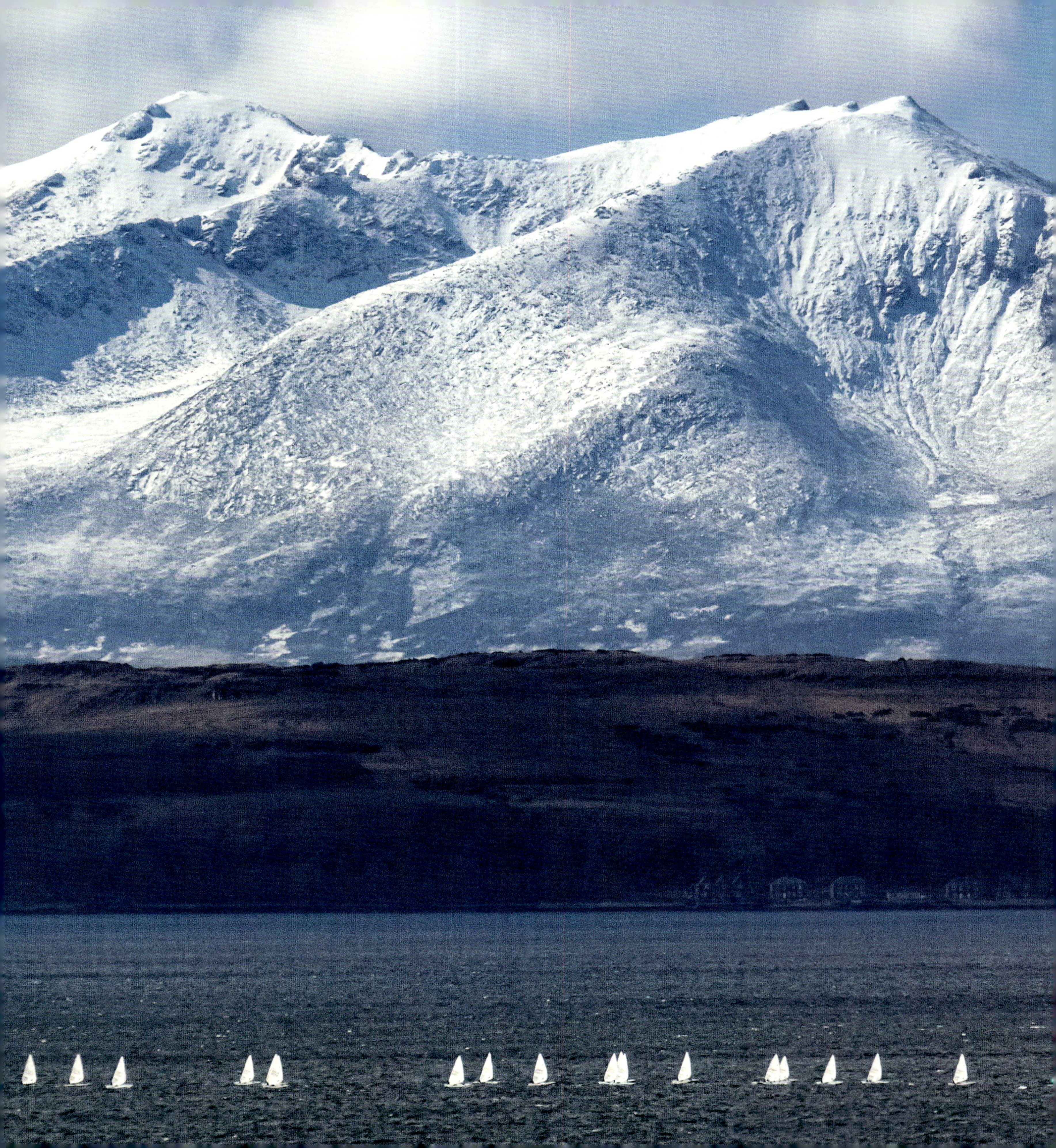

22 AYRSHIRE

MARCH–APRIL 2018

DAY 194–200 | 05,053–05,222 KM | 169 KM

A step across the diminutive Galloway Burn and I'm into Ayrshire. The coast stretching northwards towards the Clyde is gratifyingly direct, and with a marked path to follow, I feel like I'm flying along. However, the weather gods don't want me to get too smug, and it rains for five days solid. Seeing me trudging along in the rain, a highway maintenance truck driver offers me a lift. 'Aye, nae bother,' he says when I explain that I'm walking along the coast and can't accept.

The next day I'm following a disused, overgrown section of the old coast road when I duck into a cave facing the sea to escape the rain and eat my lunch. The cave entrance is walled off, with a neat void where a door once hung, and there's a second walled-off chamber deep inside. Nearby, overlooking the waves, stands a carefully made conical cairn in memory of the wayfarer who lived here. It is inlaid with a plaque that reads: *Henry Ewing Torbet (Snib) of Bennane Cave 1912–1983. Respected and Independent.*

For the rest of the day I'm staring out to sea as I walk along, transfixed by Ailsa Craig, the small steeply-sided island named from the Gaelic for 'fairy rock' and also known as 'Paddy's Milestone'. Lying 16 kilometres offshore, it's my constant companion on the walk to Girvan, and I immediately dub it a contender for the most beautiful Scottish island. By the afternoon, the vast expanse of the Irish Sea clears just enough to reveal the Mull of Kintyre. It's only about 50 kilometres away as the crow flies, yet the coast is so convoluted beyond Glasgow that it will take me many months to reach it.

In a chippy in the harbour town of Girvan, I meet the jovial inventor of the Blaggis: half haggis, half black pudding, sliced lengthwise and battered. The next morning, while staying in a B&B, I April Fool myself by accidentally googling the weather (sunny and hot!) in Italy before opening the curtains to the cold grey reality in Ayr.

At Culzean Castle, I leave my muddy backpack in the National Trust ticket office to enjoy the elegant oval staircase, painted ceilings and delicate frieze of the romantic fantasy dwelling built by Scottish architect Robert Adam in 1777–92. This intense dose of rarefied culture seems all the more remarkable in contrast to my previous days in an elemental world of rocks, waves and wind.

On my sixth day in Ayrshire, I reach Stevenston Beach Park where the focal point is a burnt-out fridge freezer whose charred husk sits proudly in a circle of singed grass. Dog owners park and release their hounds into the rain without leaving their cars. I can't see any trees, and the sea, sky and concrete sea wall are all shades of grey.

After skirting around the menacing hulk of the Hunterston nuclear power station, the atomic theme continues at Skelmorlie Secret Bunker which was operational during the Cold War. Terrifyingly, I discover that back in the day, a steel drum mounted on top of the bunker would have recorded the position of the nuclear blast on light-sensitive paper through a pinhole, allowing its position to be triangulated.

On my last day in Ayrshire, the sky clears to reveal glints of blue. At Blackhouse Moor, my mood lifts further as I see the magnificent mountainous view across the Isles of Great Cumbrae, Bute and Arran. I spot a wind turbine installation vessel gliding by the snowy peaks of Arran before heading up the River Clyde to Port Glasgow and I follow suit, turning my back on the mountains to join the ship towards the heart of the Glasgow metropolis.

Opposite:

Sailing school with Bute and Arran, from Skelmorlie

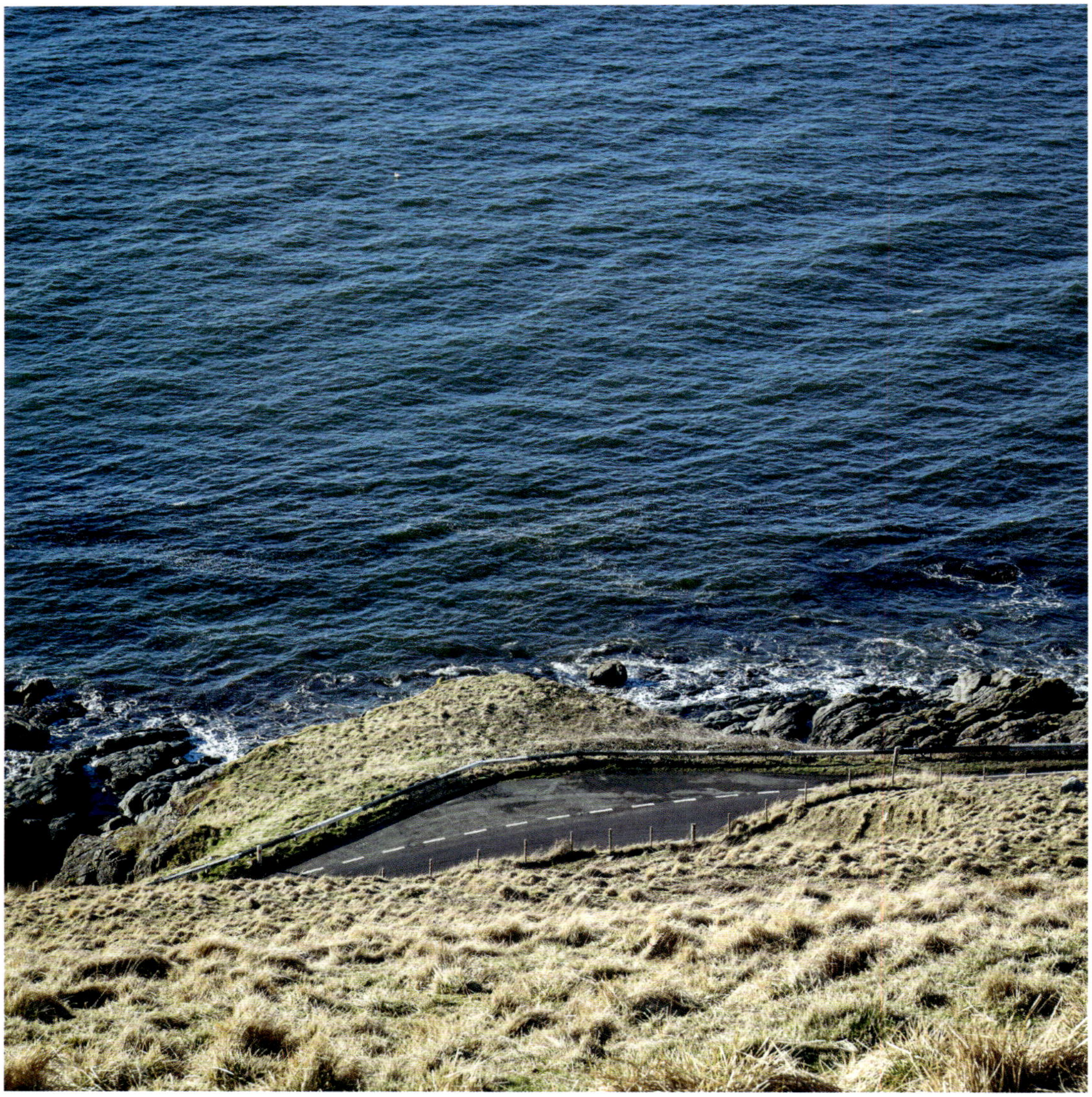

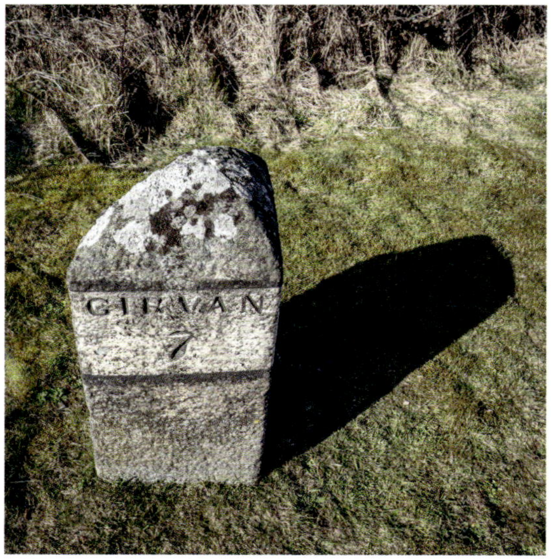

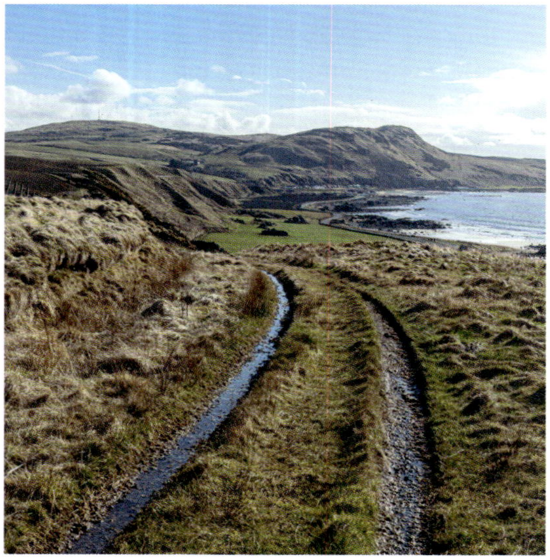

From top left:

A glimpse of the A77 from Pinbain Hill

Milestone, Lendalfoot

The Ayrshire Coastal Path on Pinbain Hill

Opposite, clockwise from top left:

Potatoes under plastic, Girvan

Potato harvest, Girvan Mains (in Scotland, mains was usually the principal farm on an estate, or at least the one with the most fertile ground)

Chocks, Girvan Harbour

Fishing hut, Carleton Bay

I can neither confirm nor deny the nature of the event: Turnberry

Tumbleweed: Blarbuie

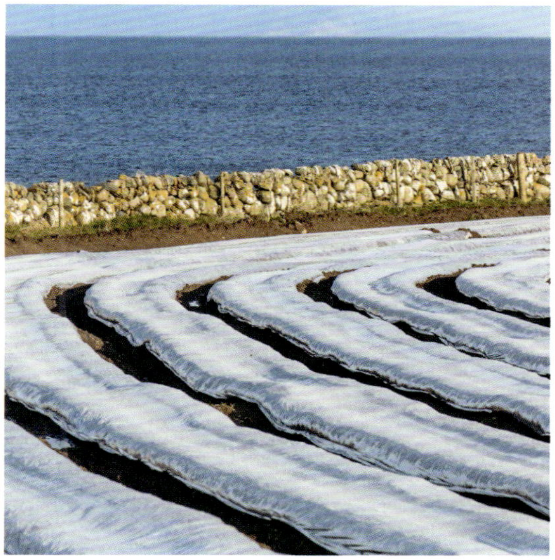
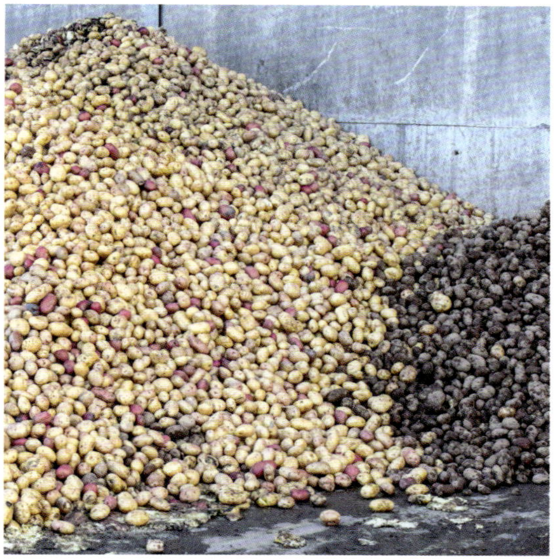
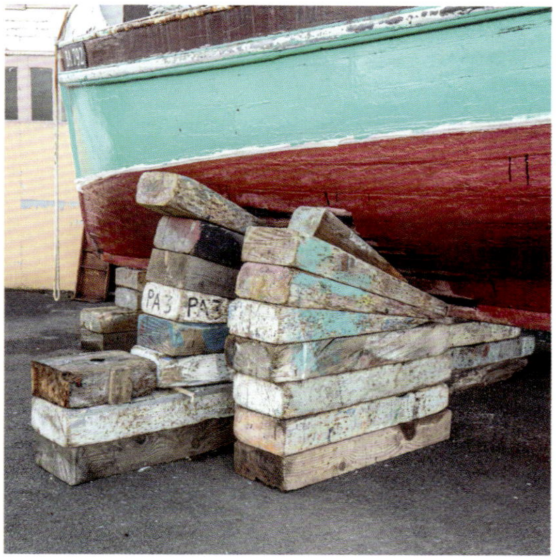
PA3 PA3
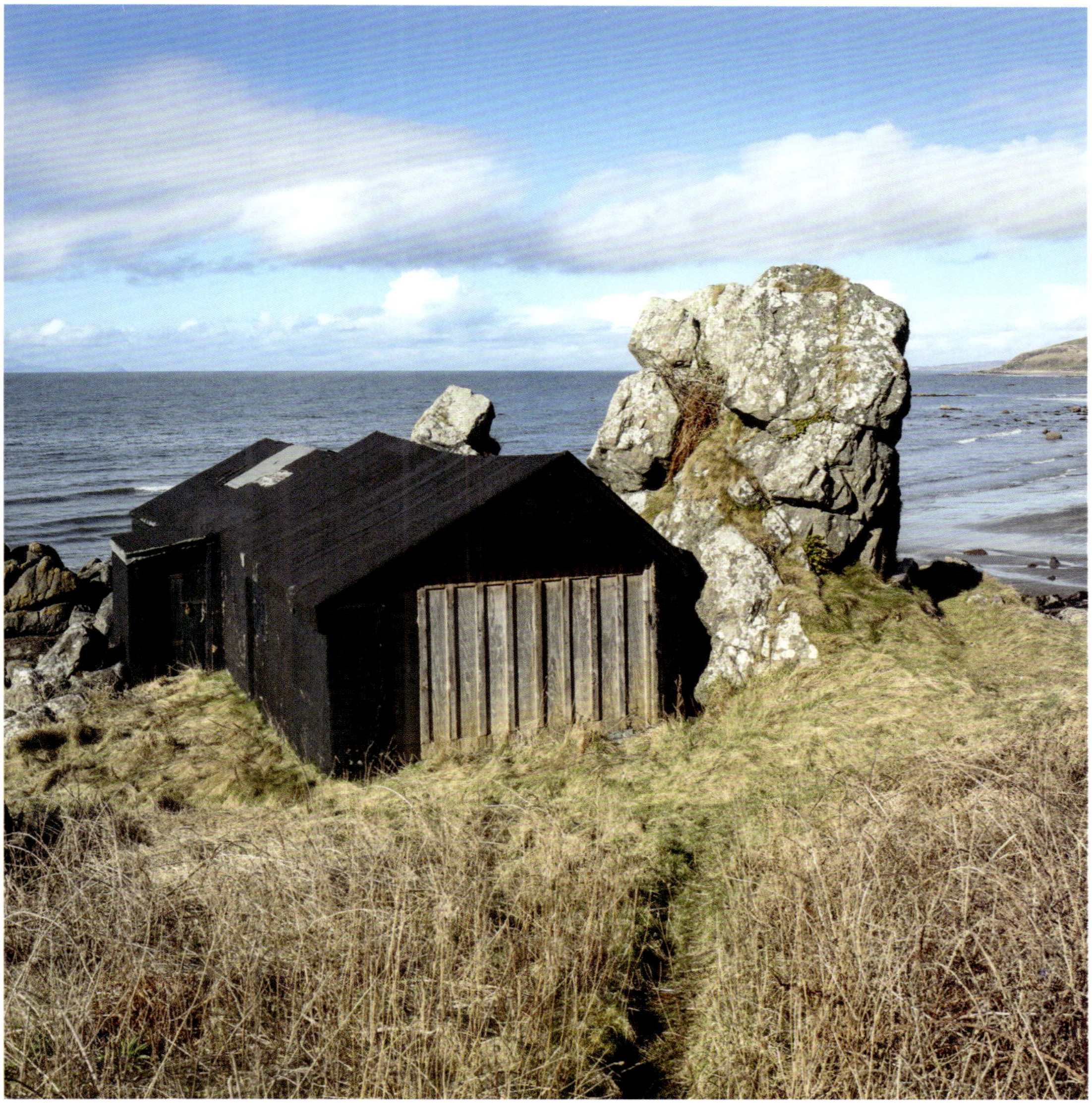
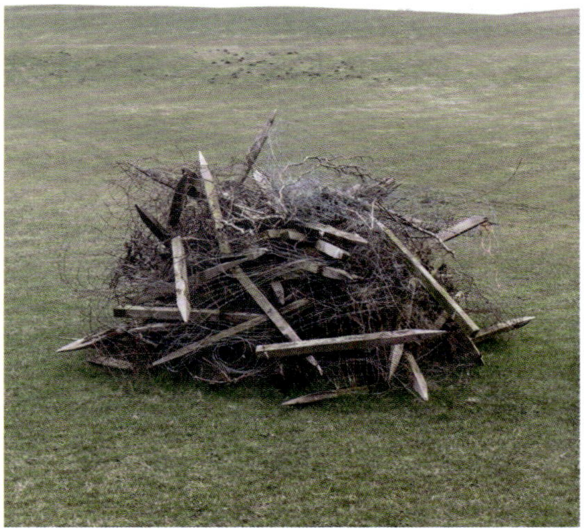
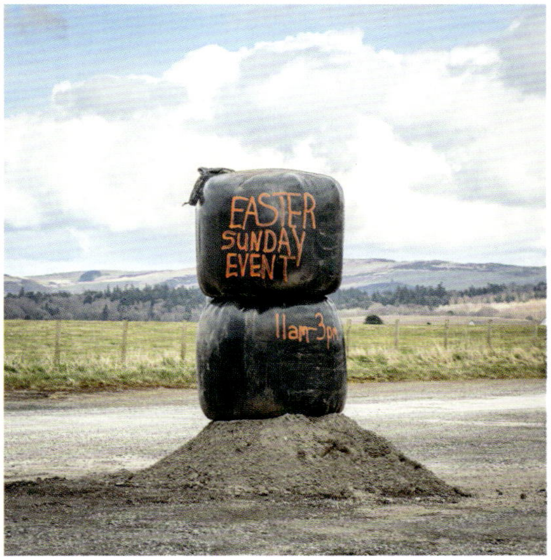
EASTER
SUNDAY
EVENT
11am-3pm

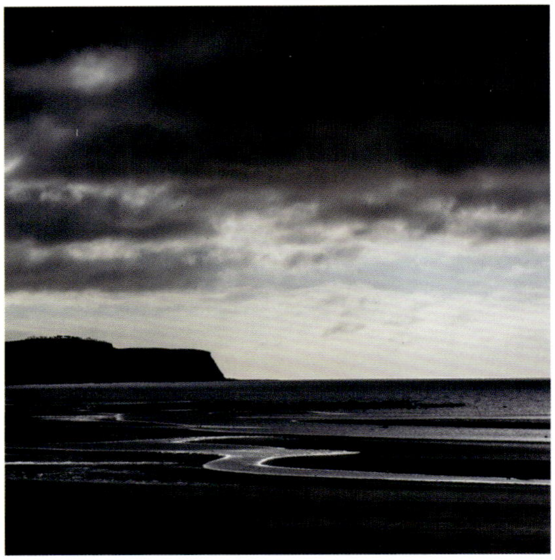
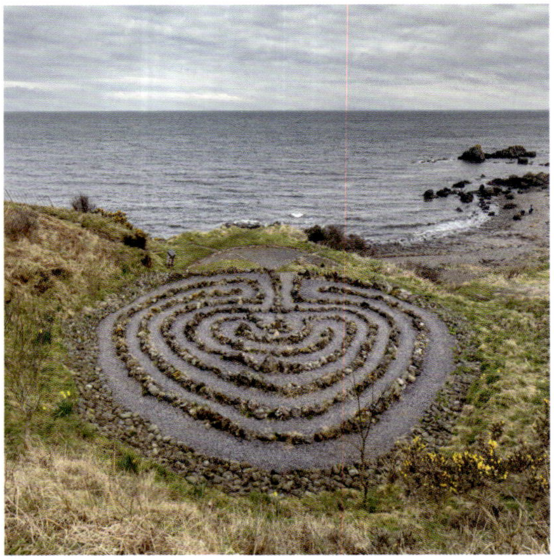
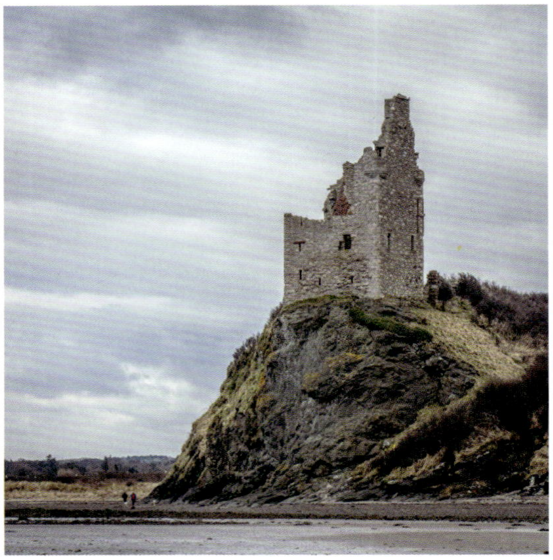
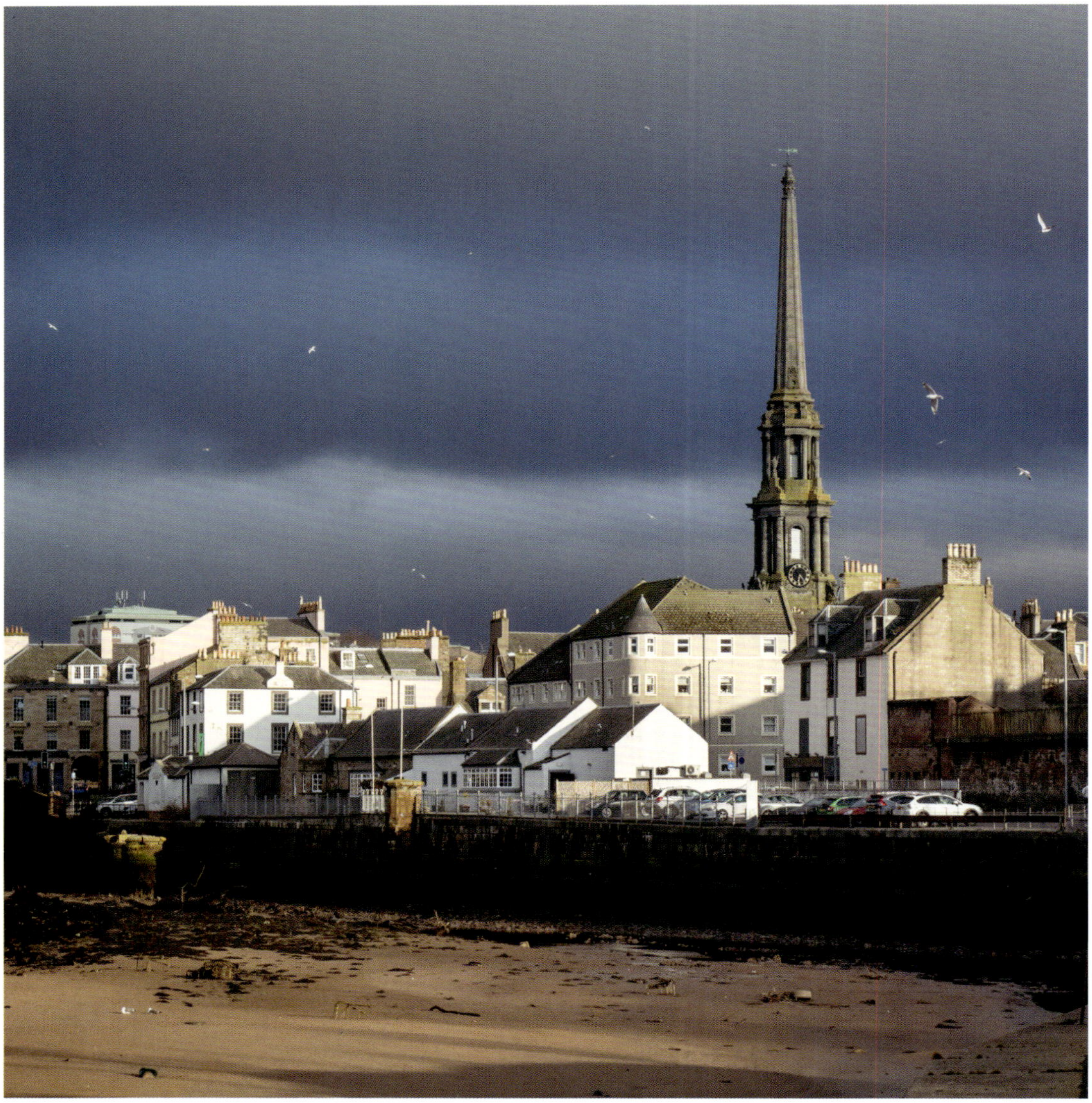
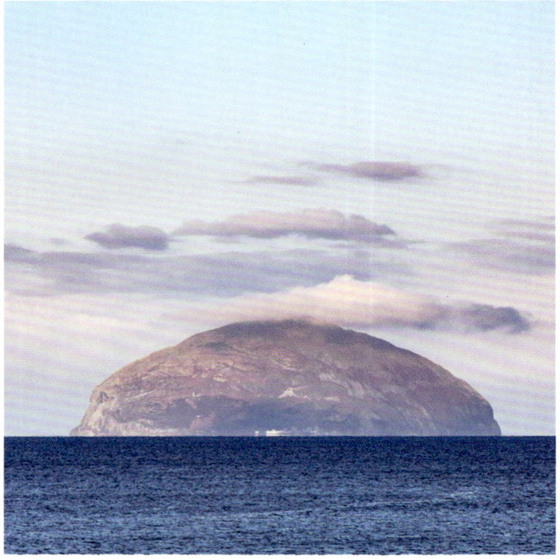
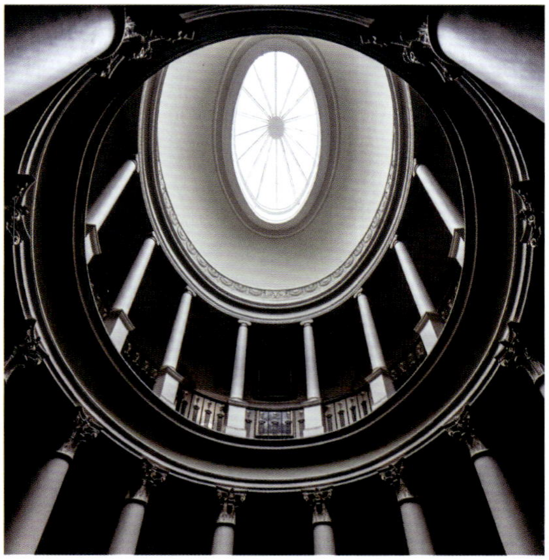

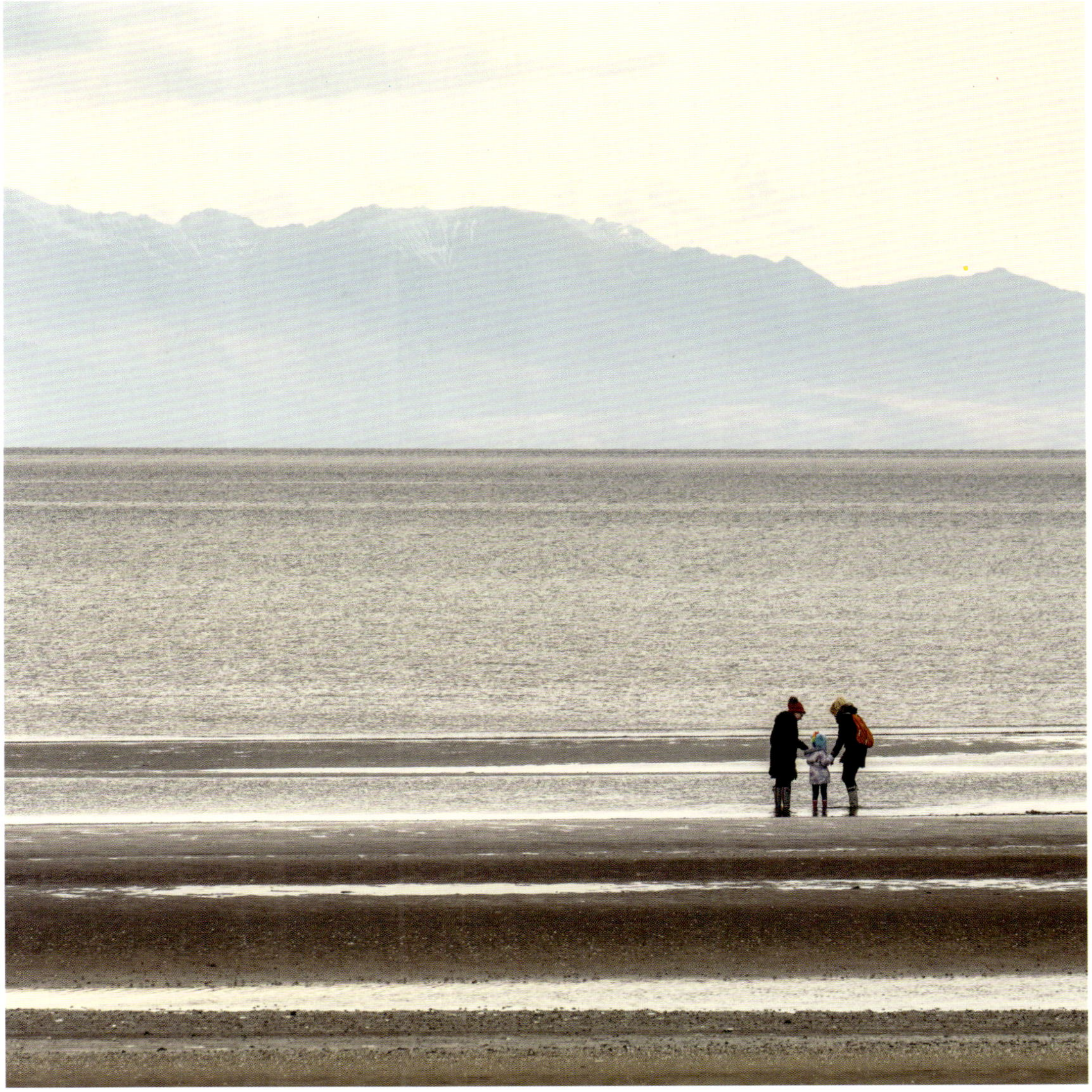

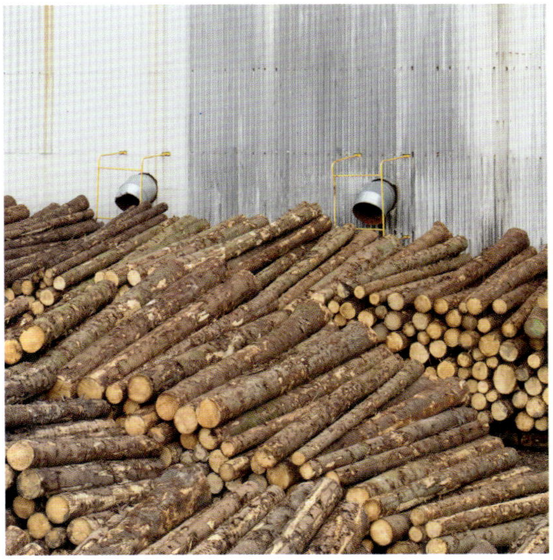

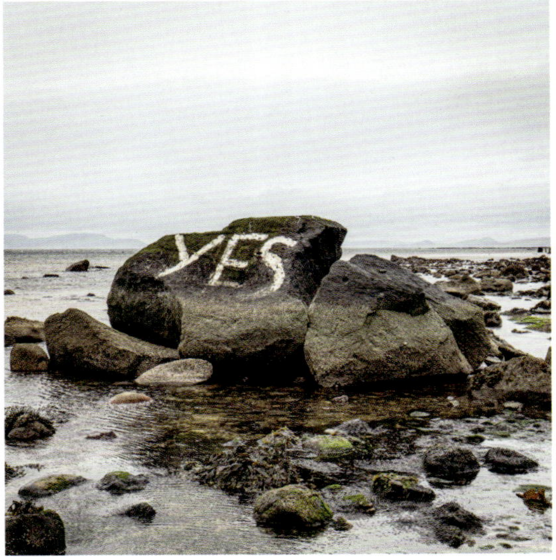

Opposite, clockwise from top left:

Heads of Ayr after the rain

The Dunure Labyrinth, built in 2008

Greenan Castle, a sixteenth-century tower house, Ayr

Ailsa Craig, a plug of dense rock left over from a long-extinct volcano. Its blue hone granite is used for the manufacture of curling stones

The oval staircase, Culzean Castle, was designed by neoclassical architect Robert Adam in 1792, who died before the final phase of the building – the staircase – was completed

Ayr, with town-hall spire

From top left:

Barassie Sands

Glennon Brothers sawmill, Troon Harbour

Yes: Boydston Shore

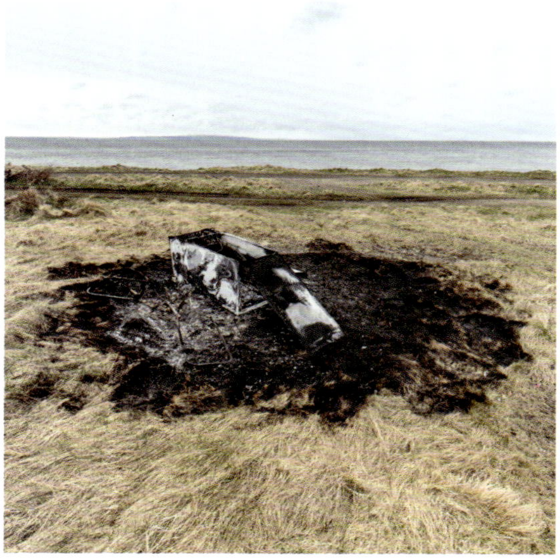

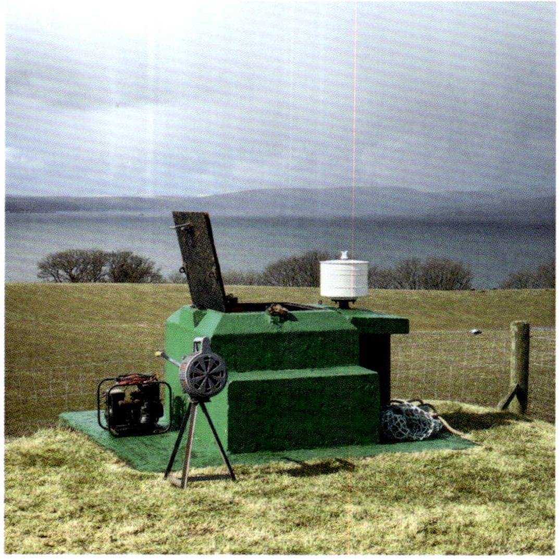

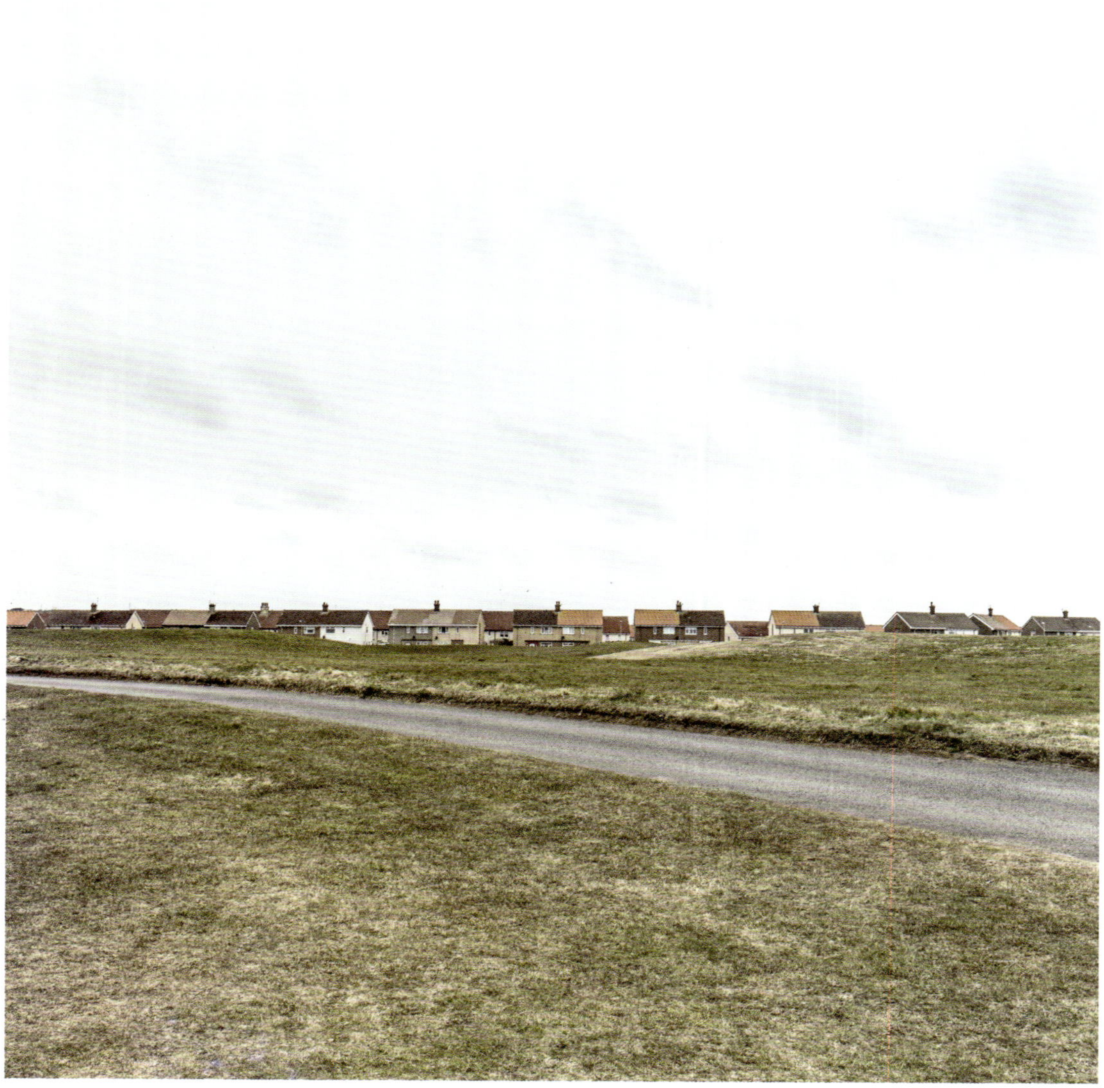

From top left:

Alfresco fridge-burning, Stevenston Beach Park

Skelmorlie nuclear bunker, operated by the Royal Observer Corps from 1965 to 1991. The white drum would record the position of a nuclear blast on light-sensitive paper through a pinhole allowing its location to be triangulated

Stevenston

Opposite:

MPI *Adventure*, a wind turbine installation vessel, passes the peaks of Arran en route to Greenock from Robin Rigg Wind Farm. Viewed from Blackhouse Moor

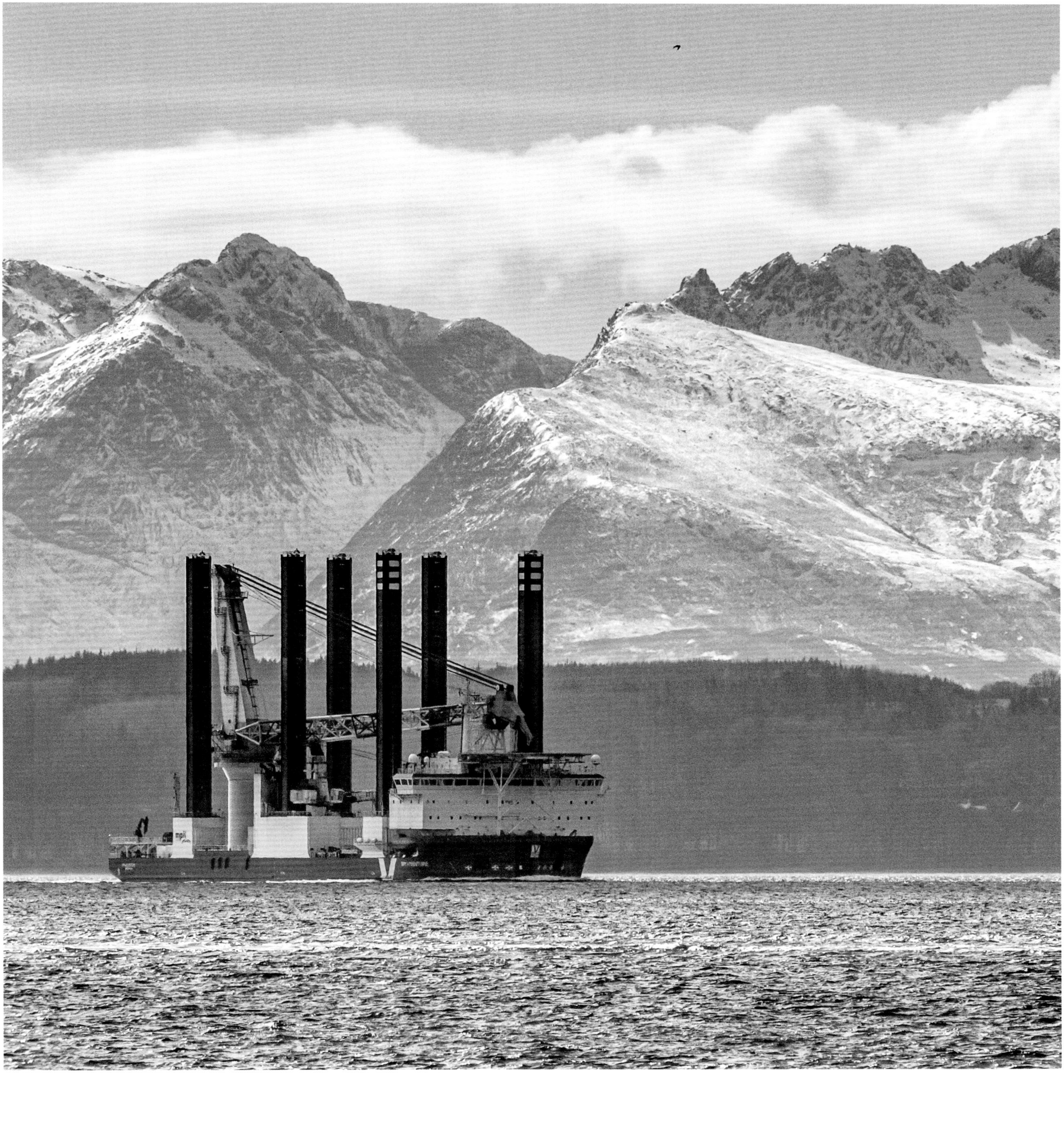

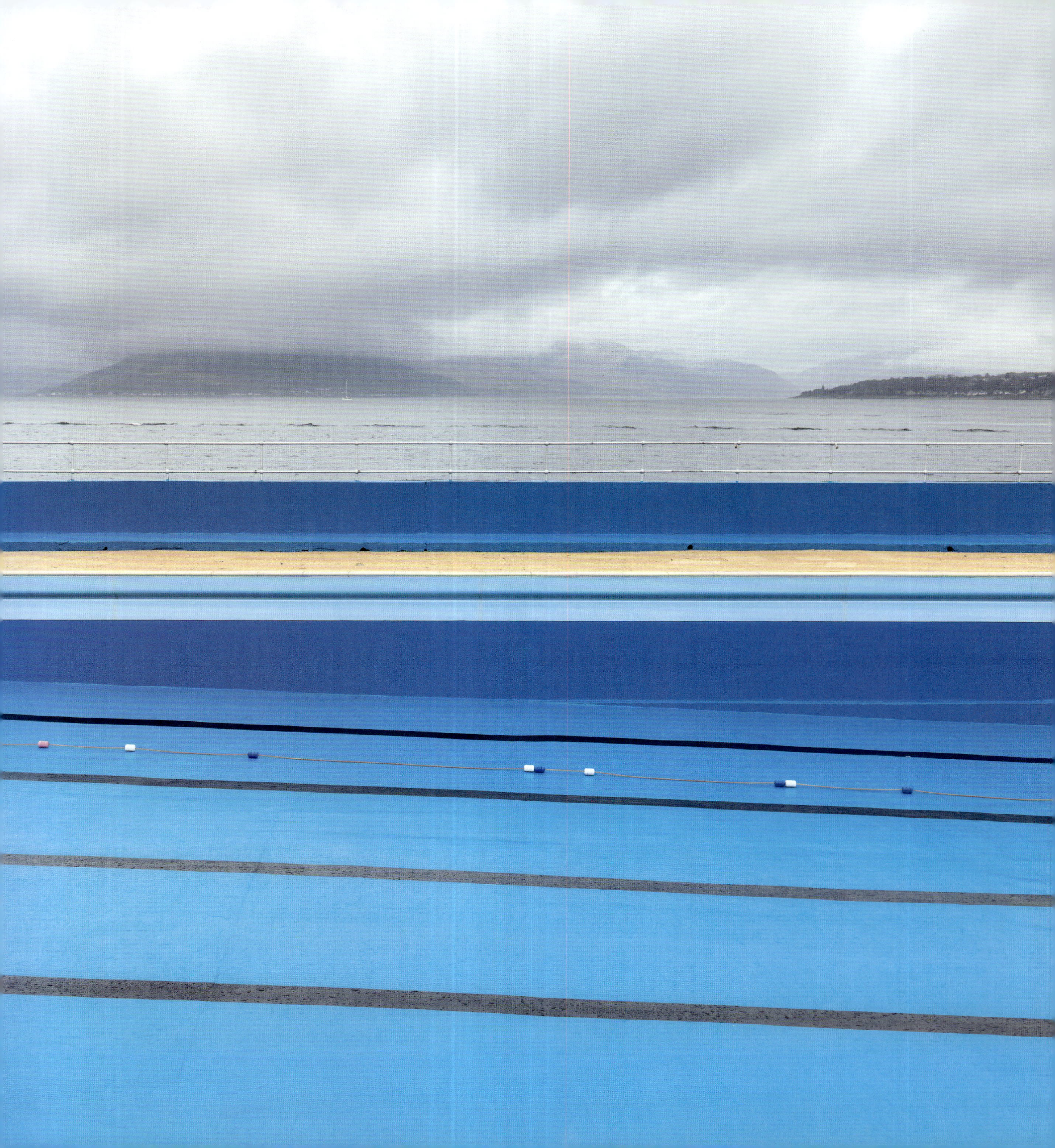

23 RENFREWSHIRE

APRIL 2018

DAY 201–204 | 05,222–05,293KM | 71KM

As I enter the sheltered embrace of the Firth of Clyde, the water is alive with myriad ferries. They pass to and fro along the intricate, rugged coastline on the north bank of the Firth, where the sea lochs Long, Gare and Holy intersect. I'm headed towards Glasgow, a three-day walk away, and it's the first day of the year that I don't need thermals. I dare to dream that warmer weather is on its way – only earlier in the week, it had been so bad that I'd picked up two Scots words in conversation: 'oorlich', meaning damp, chilly and utterly unpleasant; and 'drookit', meaning drenched or soaked through.

I'm soon wandering along the densely populated shore at Greenock, on the south bank of the Clyde. Here the river widens into the Firth of Clyde, making it an ideal location for a deep-water port. I pause to gaze up at the impressive neoclassical customs house built when the town's prosperity was fuelled by colonial trade. The Doric columns symbolise the borrowed authority of classical civilisation, which contrasts with the building's current use as indeterminate rental office space.

Past Greenock's bustling container port, I see an Aldi and a Halfords Autocentre before coming face to face with the Glebe Sugar Refinery, an artefact from a different era. This handsome, five-storey brick warehouse, once the hub of a globally dominant sugar trade, now stands silent, with half its windows broken.

A leisurely forty-minute stroll along the waterfront brings me to the James Watt Dock Crane. The imposing structure, one of the four remaining Titan cantilever shipbuilding cranes along the Clyde, stands frozen in time with nothing to lift, overlooking a riverside development of apartment buildings and a marina of leisure craft.

I soon reach the east end of Greenock, where I can see holes in the tarmac exposing the old rail lines that once serviced the port by Scott's Dry Dock, now derelict. Its ship-shaped stepped interior is encrusted with tassels of seaweed below the tide line and a thick layer of grass and weeds above.

The next day, near Port Glasgow, the timber ponds along the Clyde are as beautiful as any land art and make for a thrilling photographic subject in the motionless reflective water. In the eighteenth century, they were used to store and season imported wood by floating the logs in the Clyde; now all that remains are the posts that delineate rectangles in the shallow water. Beyond the timber ponds, the twin mounds of Dumbarton Castle are mirrored on the far shore.

Approaching Glasgow along the bank of the Clyde, I expect some banter with gangs of bored lads as I've had on the edges of other coastal cities. In fact, the whole area is eerily sanitised, filled with new housing estates and generic retail parks and few people. The recent developments, constructed over the remains of the once-unsurpassed shipbuilding industry, have left the southern side of the Clyde feeling bathetically lobotomised: all Krispy Kreme, Ikea, Sainsbury's and a couple selecting the colour of their BMW. At least fusion cuisine seems alive and well – haggis pakoras jump out at me from a takeaway menu at Bishopton Tandoori, along with Irn Bru, Scotland's ever-popular lurid orange soft drink.

I continue up the, now much narrower, Clyde below the Erskine Bridge, which towers above on slender concrete columns, before passing scrap-metal yards on the outskirts of Glasgow. 'Glasgow! The third capital city on this coastal walk,' I tweet with a jubilant selfie once I reach my destination. People respond to my tweet like I've made a joke, leaving me flummoxed. Suddenly, the realisation dawns on me that Glasgow is not the capital of Scotland. How did I not know that! I delete the tweet with a flush of embarrassment and cross to the north bank to lick my geographical wounds in a B&B.

Opposite:

Gourock Outdoor Pool

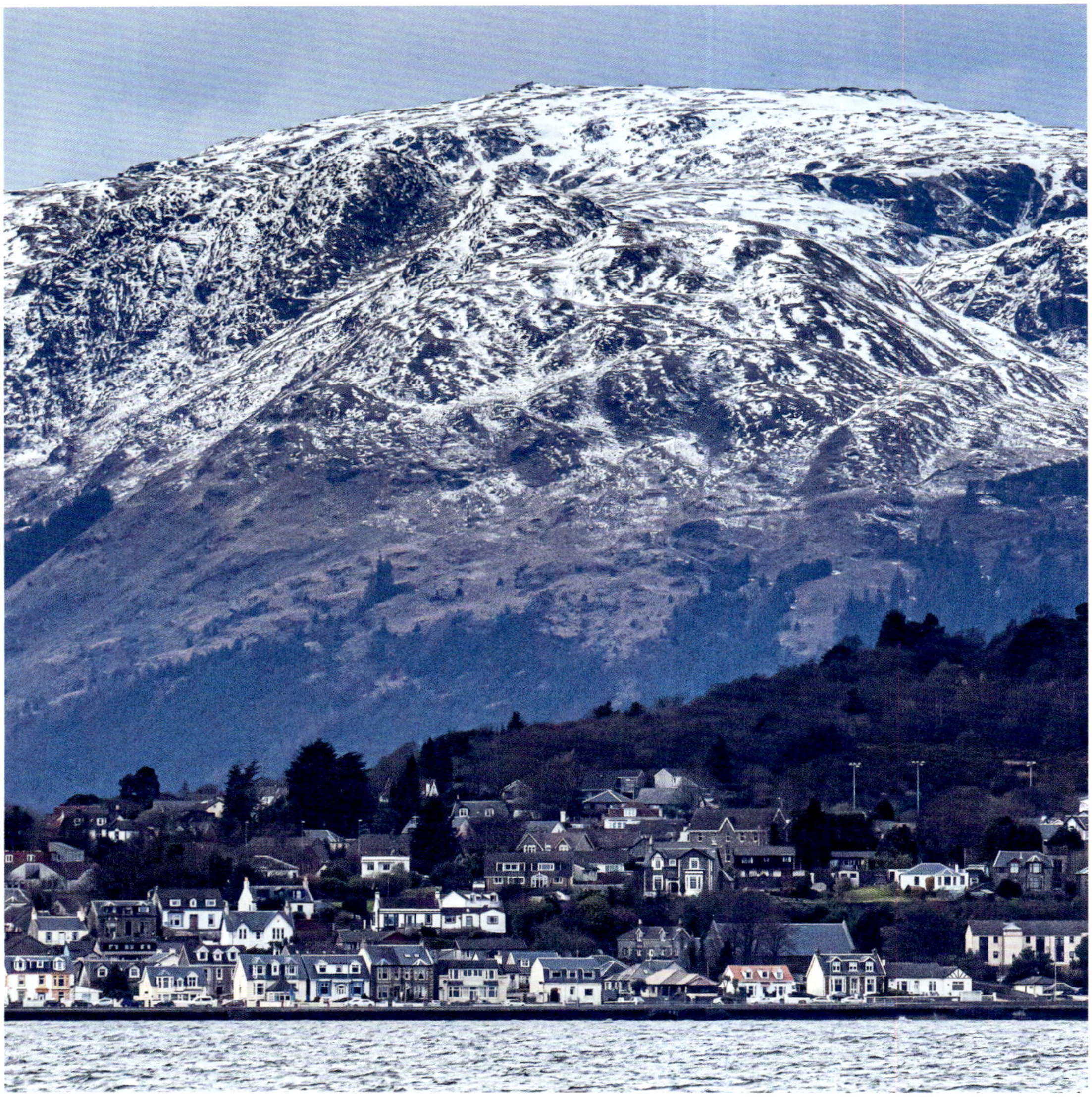

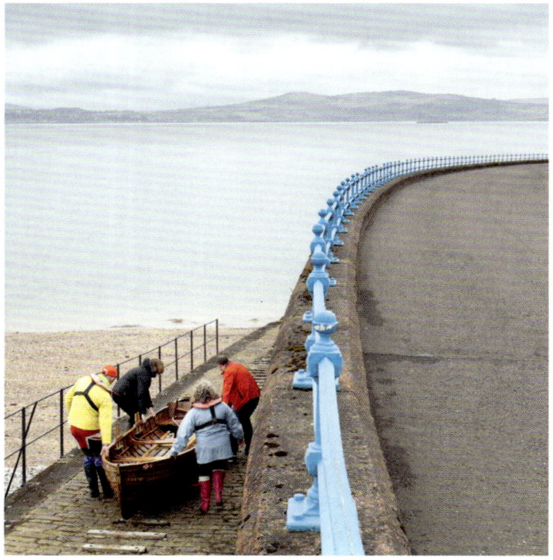

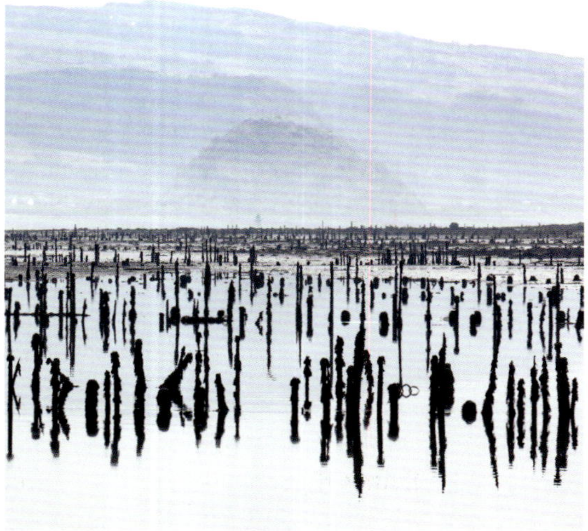

From top left:

Dunoon across the Clyde from Inverkip Bay

Launch: Royal West of Scotland Amateur Boat Club, Greenock

Timber ponds at Kelburn Park and Dumbarton Castle. Dating from the eighteenth century, the ponds functioned as storage for timber from North America prior to its sale to local shipyards

Opposite, clockwise from top left:

AAM (American Axle & Manufacturing) Works, Scotstoun, from Braehead

Buried rails, Victoria Harbour, Greenock

Clyde Auditorium, Finnieston Crane and SSE Hydro at dusk, Glasgow

Golspie Street housing designed in 2012 by Do Architecture, Govan

Erskine Bridge spanning the River Clyde

Scrap metal (with Yoker tower blocks), Christie & Son, Renfrew

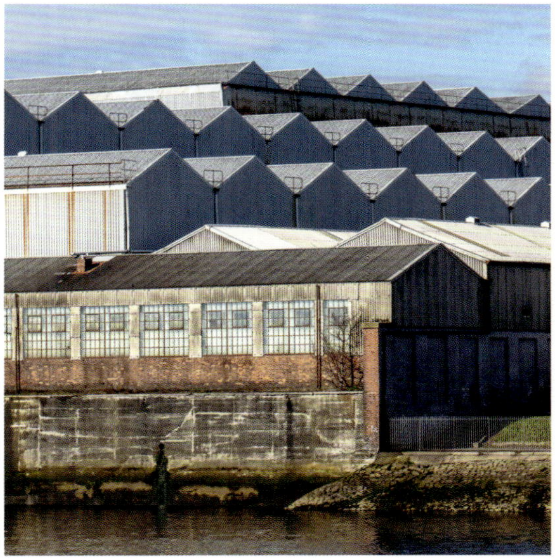
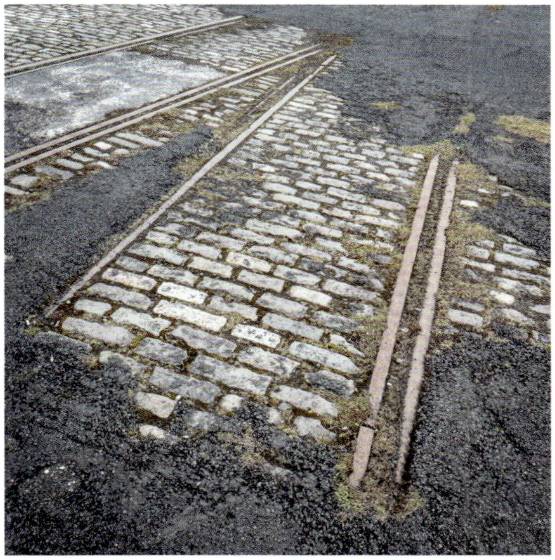
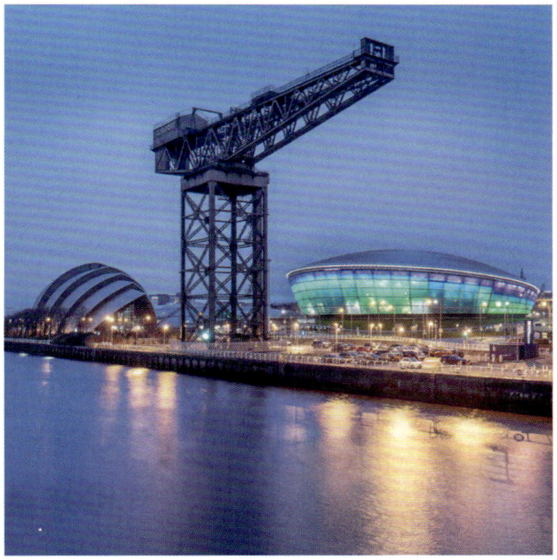
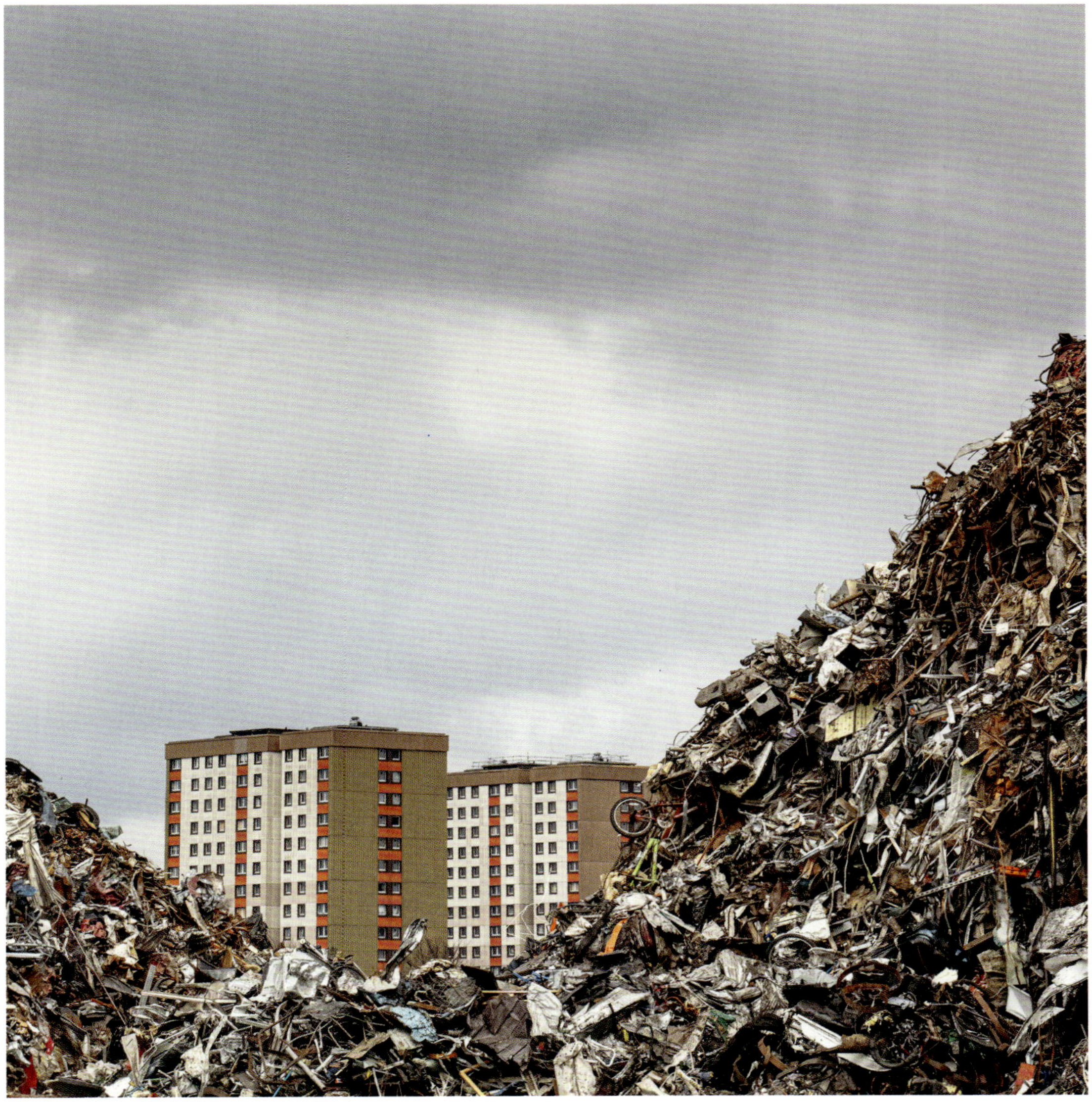
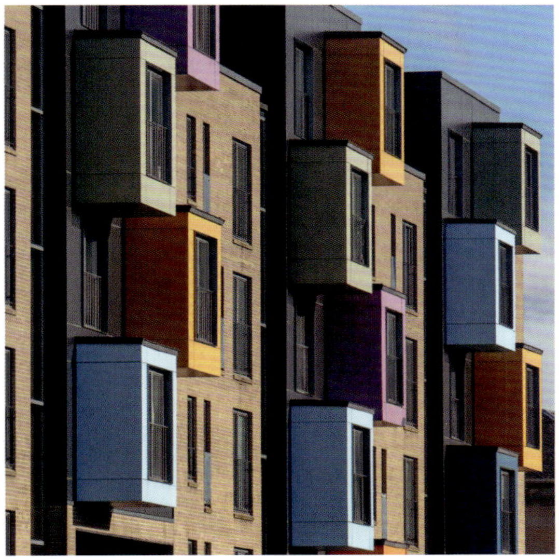
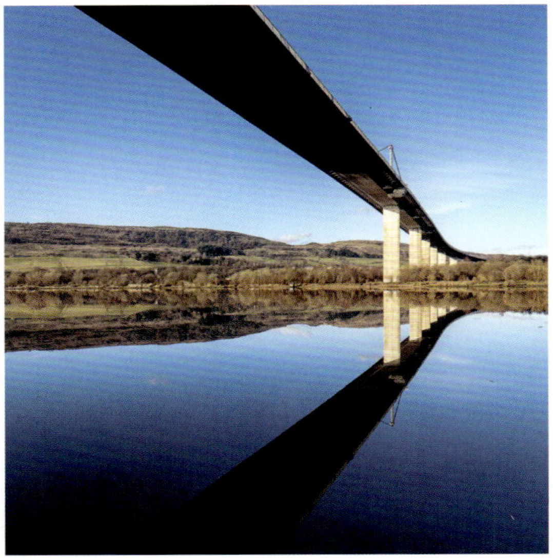

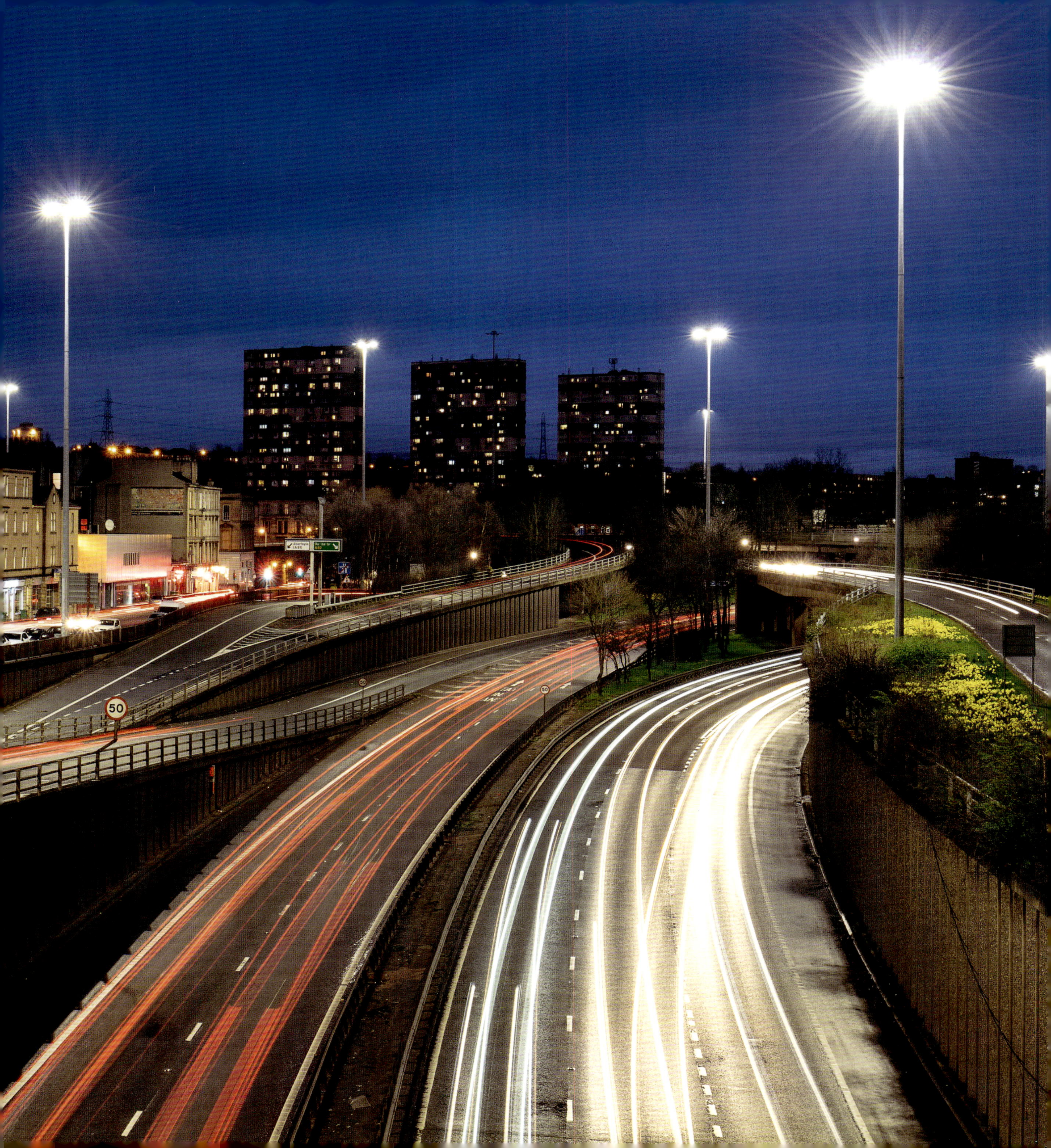
50

24 DUNBARTONSHIRE

APRIL–MAY 2018

DAY 205–209 | 05,293–05,425 KM | 132 KM

I stay a few days in Glasgow before continuing my journey. It's been a while since I've been in a city, and I'm wide-eyed and appreciative of the comforts and achievements of civilisation. To be able to buy food when I'm hungry and find shelter when it rains seems miraculous. As I head west along the north bank of the Clyde towards Dumbarton, it's impossible not to notice how alive the shipbuilding industry is here compared to the south bank, and I pass the scaffolded bow of a warship while clusters of men in oil-stained overalls lean on the counters of snack vans.

At Cardross, opposite Port Glasgow on the north bank of the River Clyde, I detour from the coast to St Peter's Seminary, a derelict modernist masterpiece. I'm unsure if there will be any security or how well protected the site will be, so I'm relieved and amused to find a narrow gap in the fence with a hand-painted *This Way* sign. There's not much space, and after posting my backpack through and squeezing after it, I'm glad I've been cutting back on the cooked breakfasts. Only the lichen-stained concrete frame remains in the main block of student accommodation, and with its dematerialised walls, roofs and floors, the structure feels like a ghost – more the idea of a building than a physical one. Despite its ruined state, I can still see the majesty of what once was. Looking up, I can't help but marvel at the scalloped roof of the refectory, and at how the beauty of modernist architecture has endured over the years. I spend five hours photographing here and leave buzzing and unconcerned that I'll need to walk into the night to make up time.

Three days later, as I cross from the Lowlands into the Scottish Highlands, I find myself at geological and ethical fault lines when I encounter the Faslane nuclear submarine base and Faslane Peace Camp, a permanent encampment of anti-nuclear weapon protestors. It is a thought-provoking couple of days walking the actively defended and razor-wired edge of the UK's nuclear weapon facilities: the submarine base at Faslane and the nuclear warhead store at Coulport. I pass groups of hyper-fit Marines on training runs, vigilant police patrols, and numerous caravans at Faslane Peace Camp emblazoned with *Killer Trident* slogans. I've always understood nuclear deterrence as a hidden-away strategic concept, but to see it in the flesh reminds me of my childhood fears of a nuclear apocalypse.

Unsurprisingly, there's no pavement alongside much of the 30 kilometres of electric fence that protects the site. Together with the constant rain, the occasional clipped and disembodied tannoy announcements and prison-camp lookout towers add to the sense of foreboding. The few people I meet ask if I'm 'working at the base'; the thought of visiting the area for any other reason seems incomprehensible to them.

With a tangible sense of relief, I leave Ministry of Defence land to follow Loch Long north towards the distinctive silhouette of the Cobbler. A porpoise bobs up and down in the loch playfully, but as I lift the camera in its direction, a blurred, dark object covers much of the scene. It takes me a while to realise it's a giant black slug slithering across the lens's front element.

I quickly acclimatise to being surrounded by nothing but nature again. As I head further north, shops become increasingly sparse, and I find myself regularly carrying three days of supplies. However, the plentiful drinking water in the tiny burns means I need to shoulder much less water and I no longer have to hunt for a suitable stream in the evenings. There's a lot of plantation-forest walking, and I let myself drift into the introspective mood that comes from the monotony of staring at miles of identical trunks and branches without any distant horizons.

Opposite:

M8, Glasgow

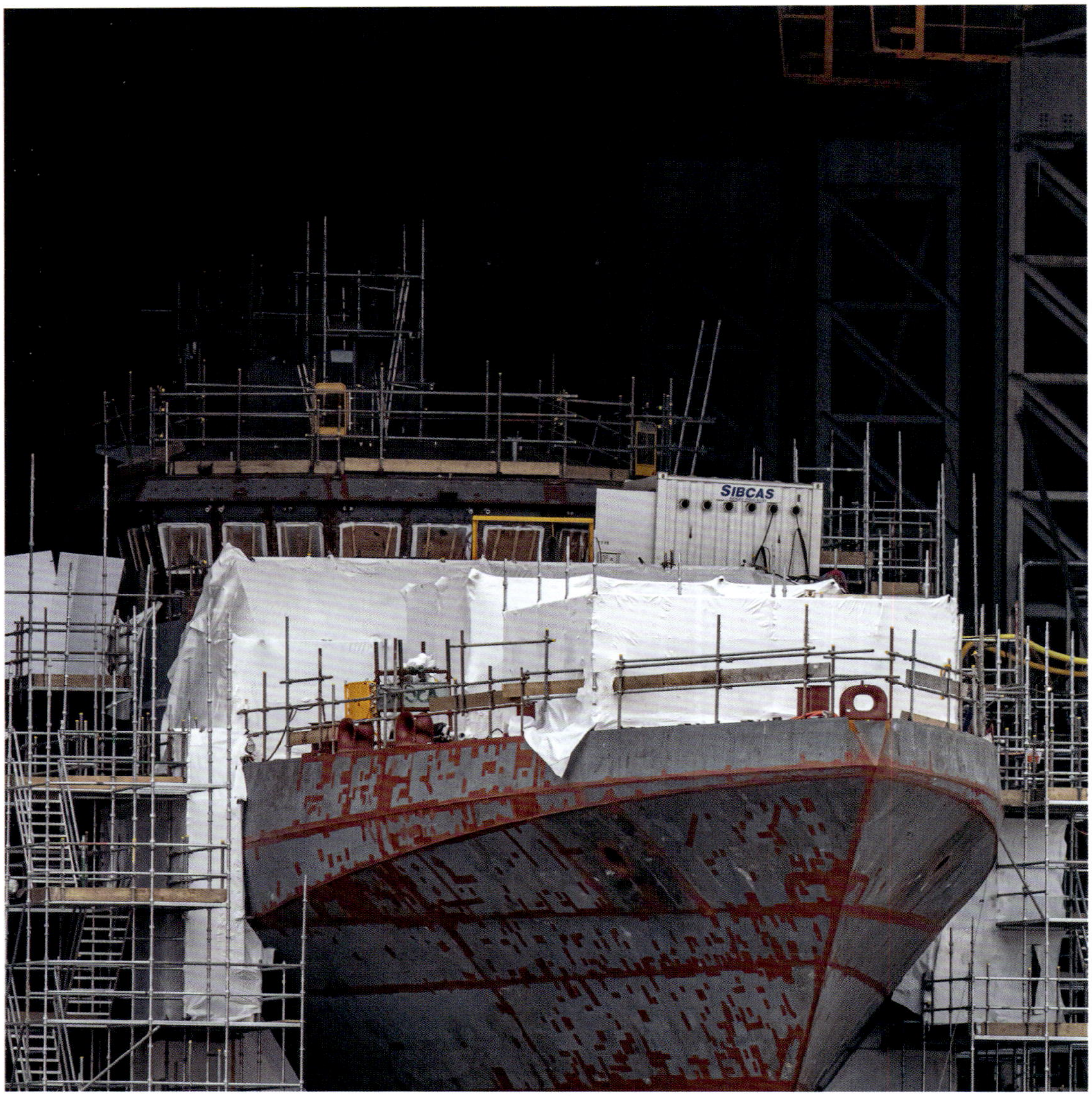

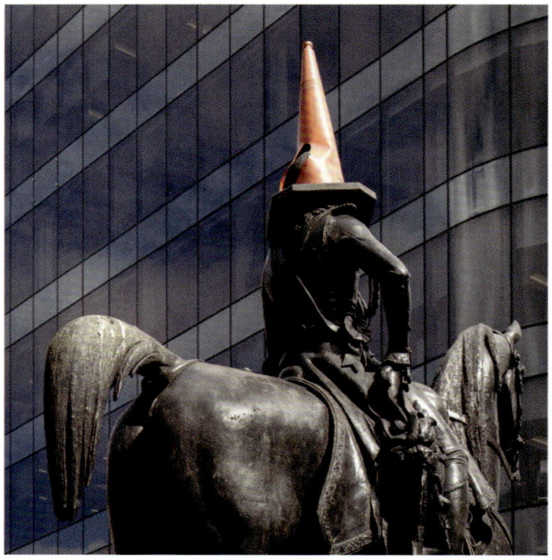

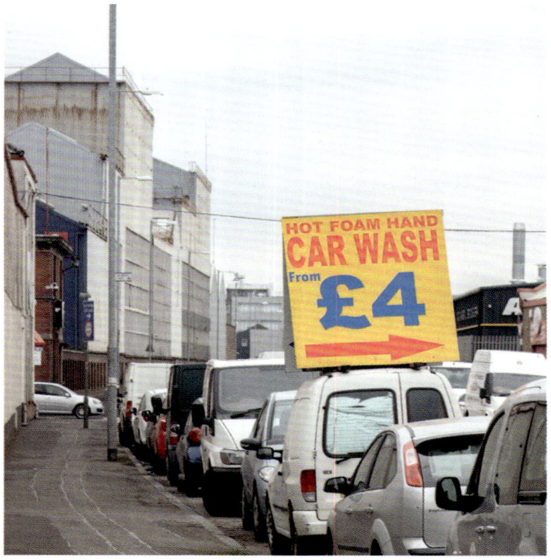

From top left:

Royal Navy offshore patrol vessel under construction at BAE Systems, Govan

Statue of the Duke of Wellington, Glasgow, which has been capped with a traffic cone for over thirty years

Car wash, Scotstoun

Opposite, clockwise from top left:

Lightwell in the Reid Building, Glasgow School of Art. Designed by architect Steven Holl, 2014

Wardrobe with chair back, Hill House, Helensburgh. Created by architects and designers Charles Rennie and Margaret Macdonald Mackintosh in a British art nouveau style in 1902–04, the furniture being an integral part of the overall architectural effect

Red sandstone tenement with satellite dishes, Yoker, Glasgow

Kibble Palace, designed by James Boucher and James Cousland in the nineteenth century, Glasgow Botanic Gardens

The late-nineteenth-century Gothic Revival cloisters inside the Gilbert Scott Building, University of Glasgow, are named after its designer

The Riverside Museum of Transport, Glasgow, designed by Zaha Hadid Architects and engineers Buro Happold in 2011

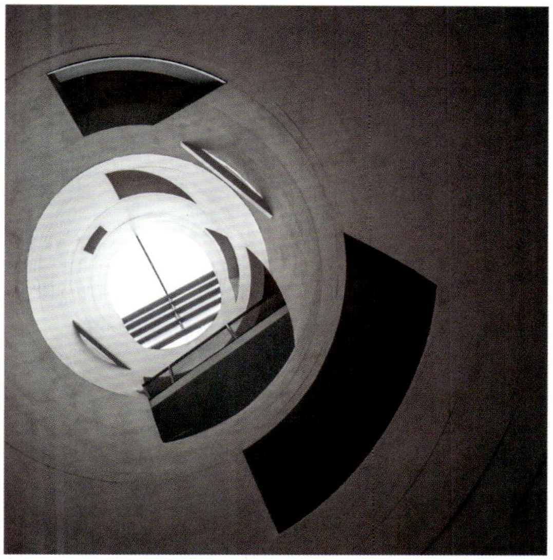
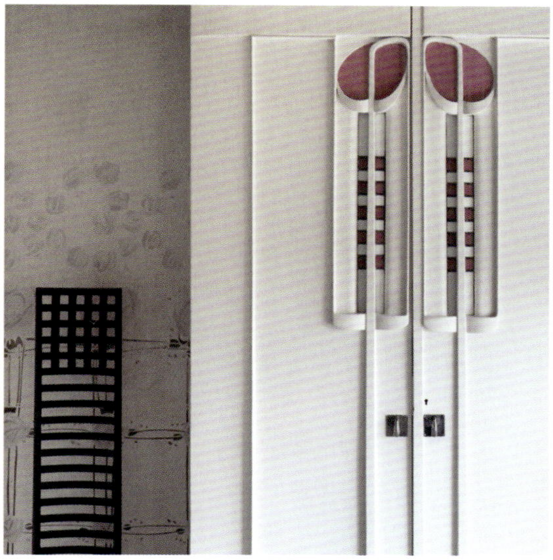
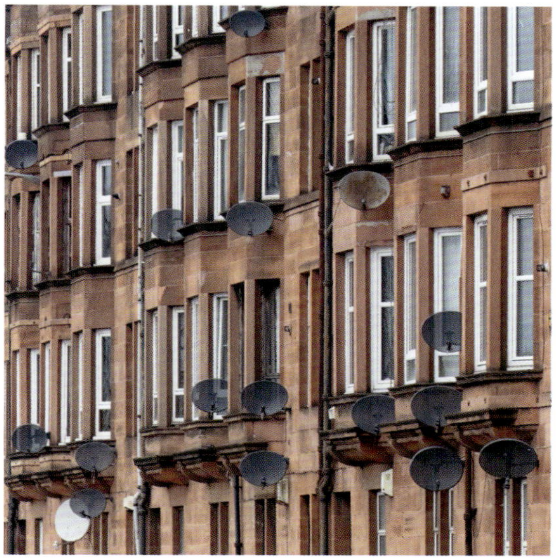
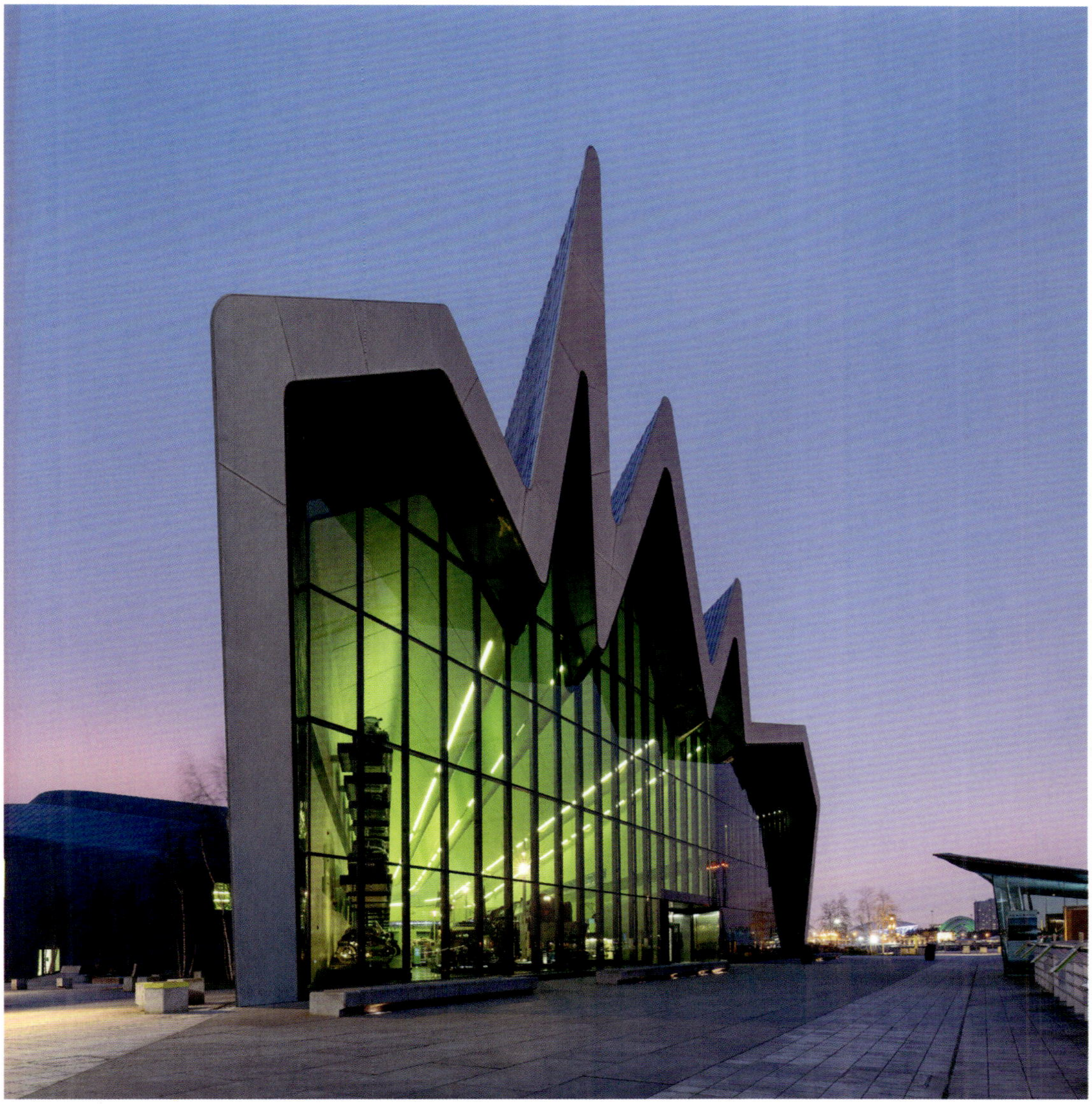
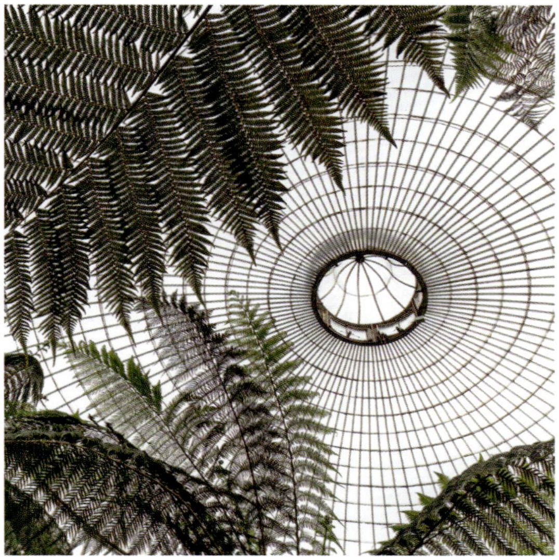
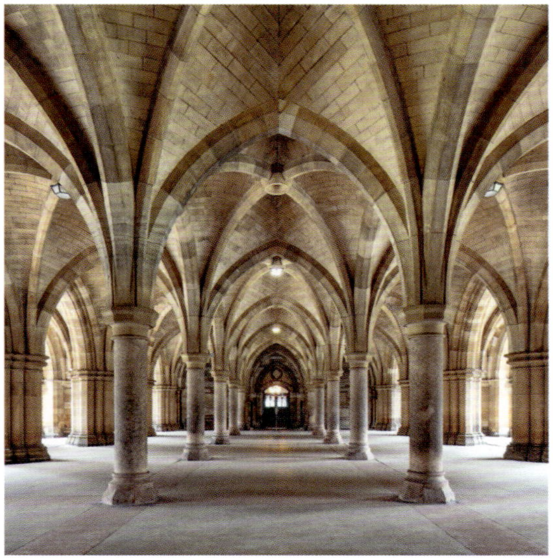

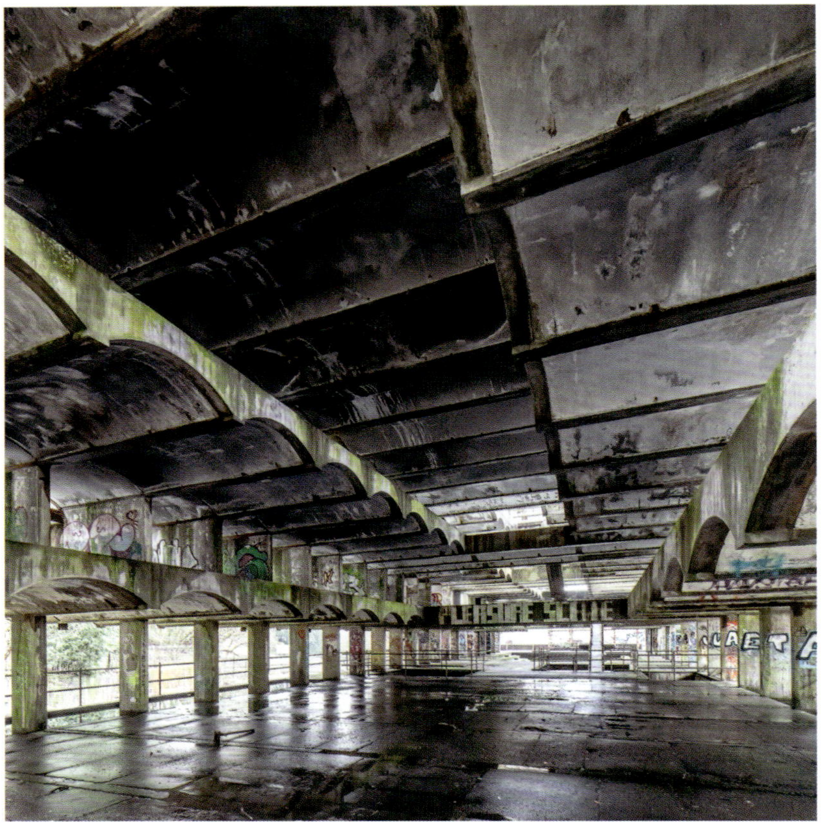

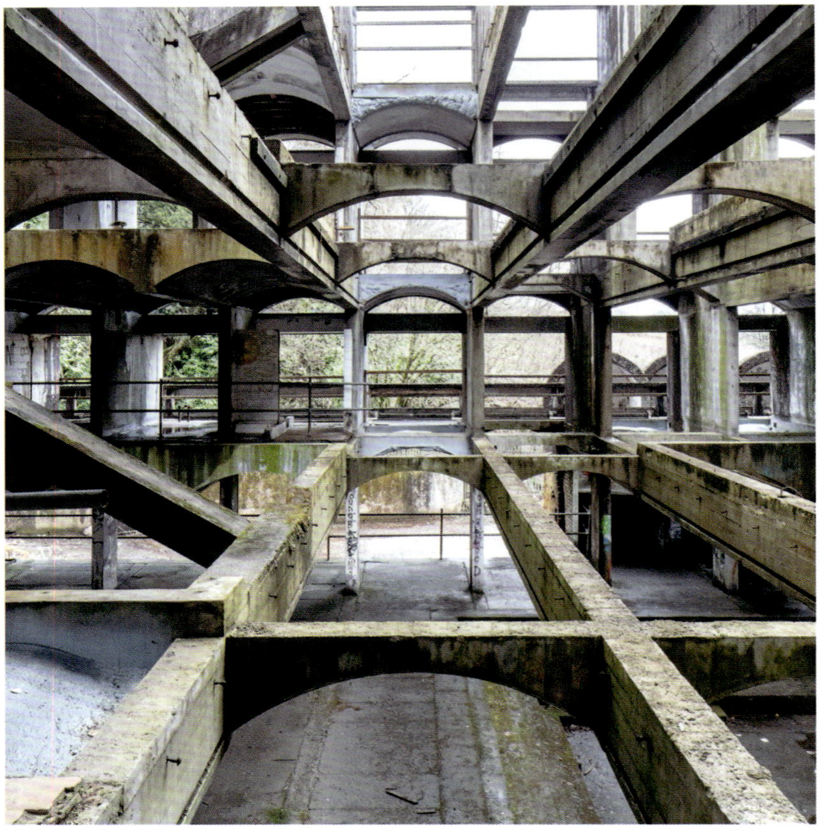

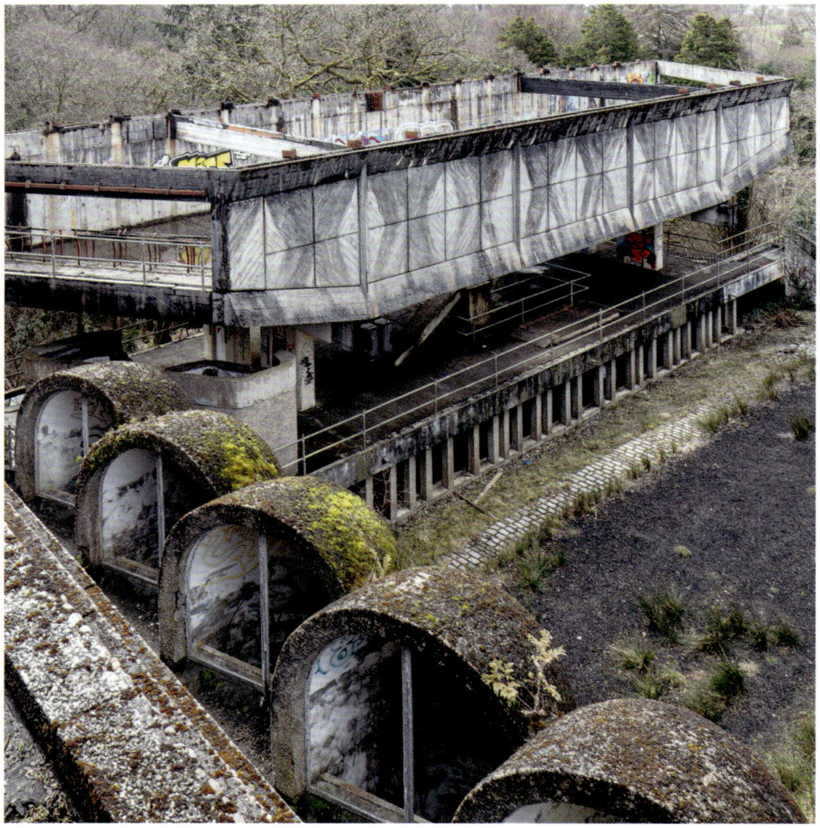

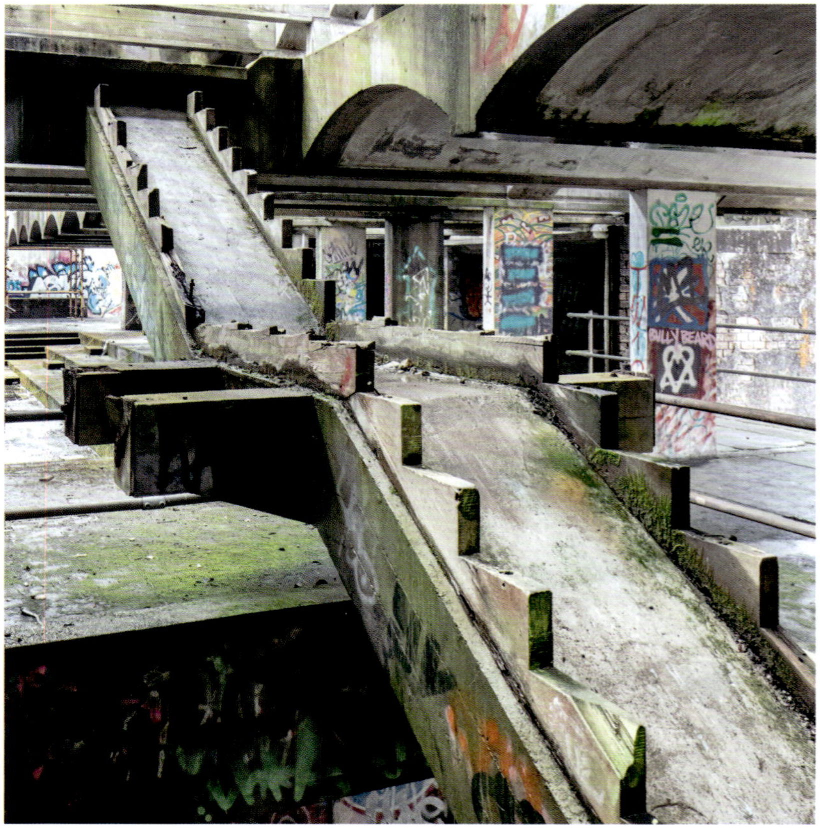

Opposite, from top left:

Refectory, St Peter's Seminary, Cardross. Designed by architects Gillespie, Kidd & Coia in 1961–66. Abandoned since 1987, it is one of only forty-two modernist buildings in Scotland to be listed as Category A

Former bridge between student rooms, St Peter's Seminary

From bottom left:

Private prayer chapels and the teaching block, St Peter's Seminary

Stairs in the hall, St Peter's Seminary

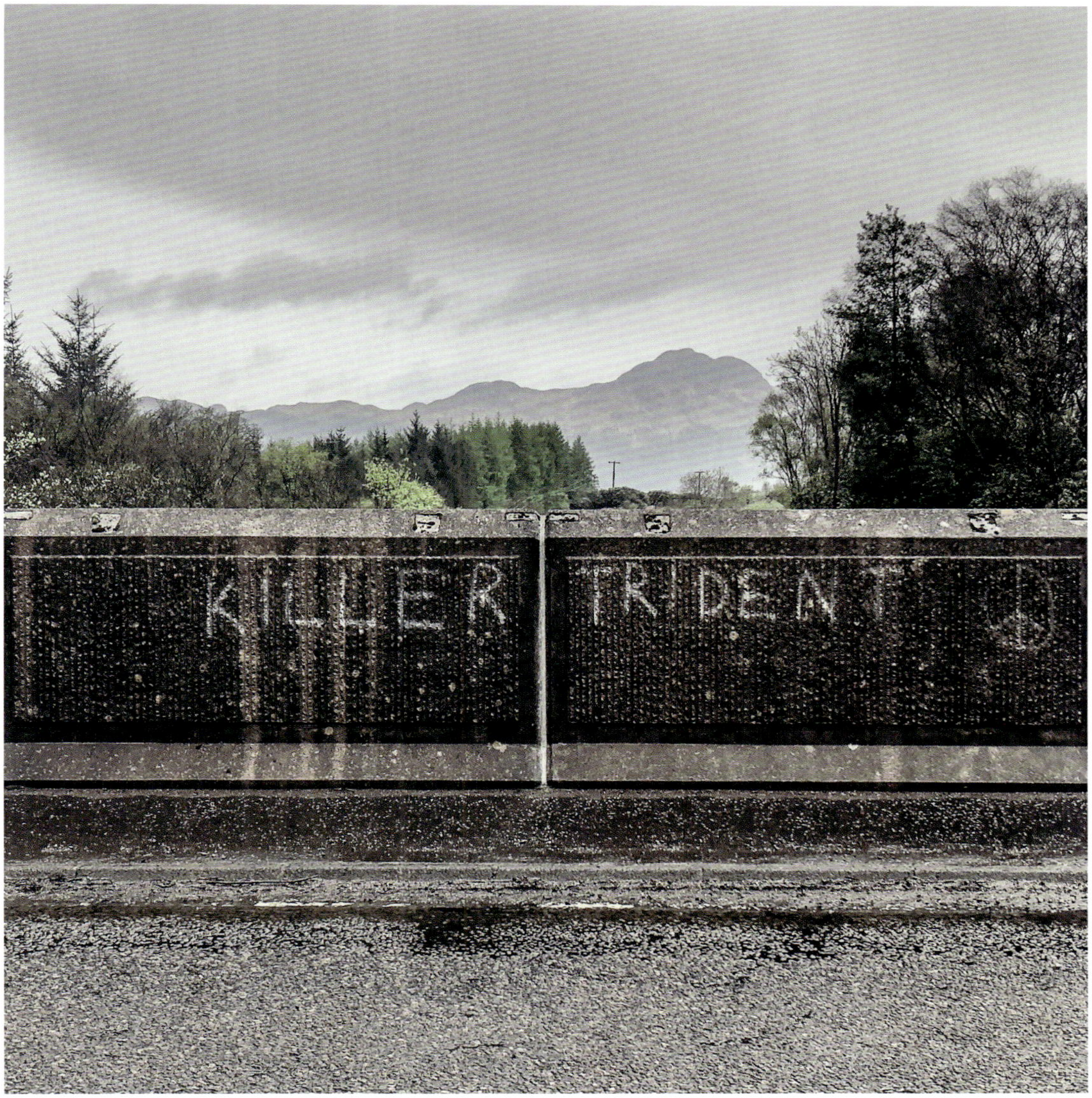

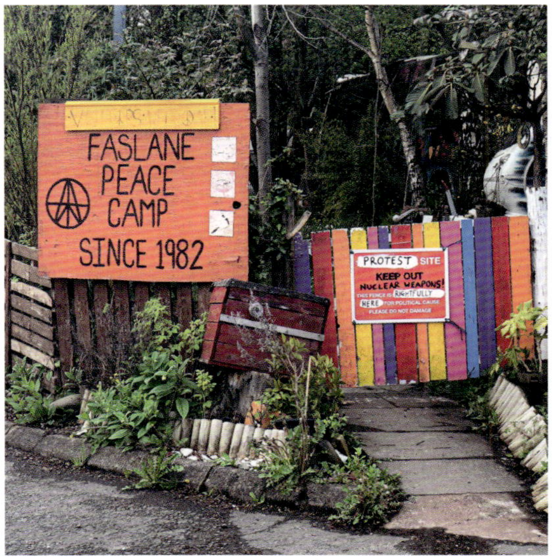

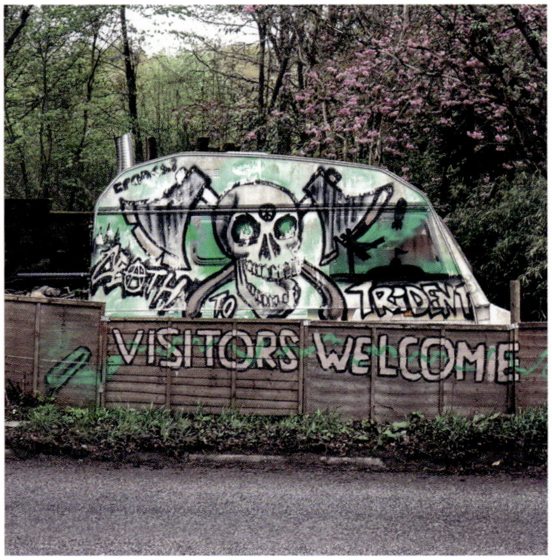

From top left:

Access road to Royal Naval Armaments Depot Coulport

Faslane Peace Camp, a permanent camp opposing the deployment of nuclear weapons at nearby His Majesty's Naval Base, Clyde

Caravan at Faslane Peace Camp

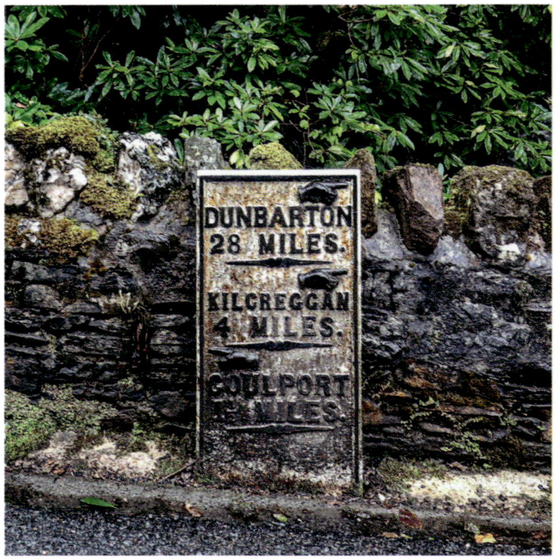

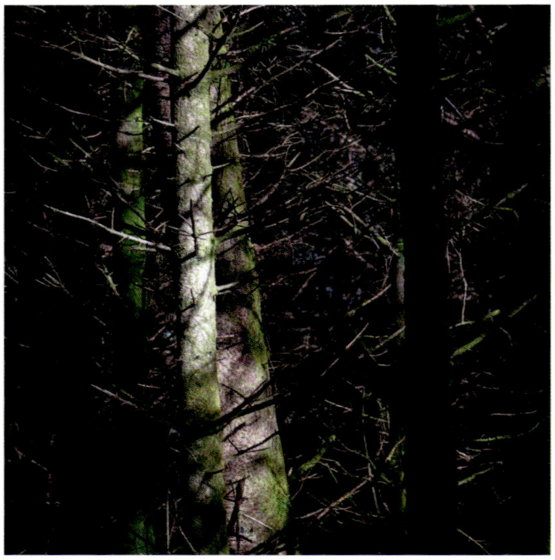

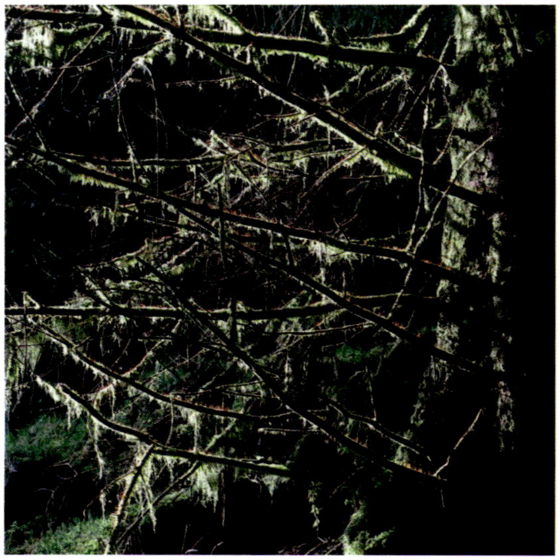

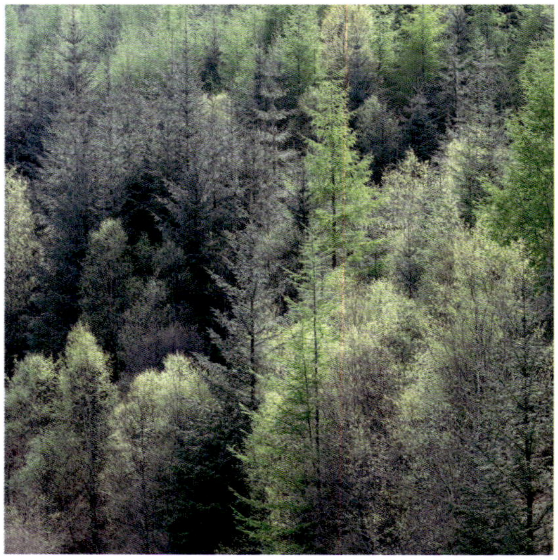

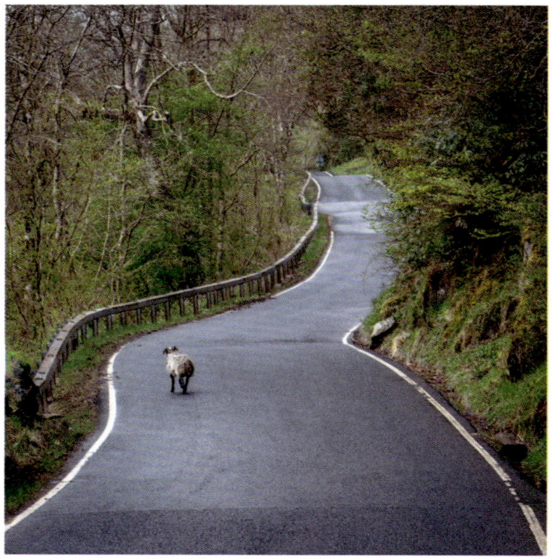

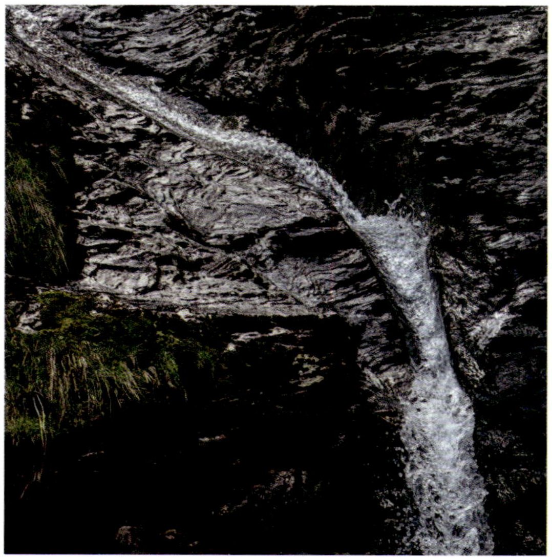

From top left:

Milepost on the Rosneath Peninsula

Illumination: Ardgartan Forest

From centre left:

Backlight, Ardgartan Forest

Ardgartan Forest textures

From bottom left:

Traffic on the road by Loch Long

Burn, Ardgartan Forest

Opposite:

Last light, Ardmay with Arrochar beyond, Loch Long

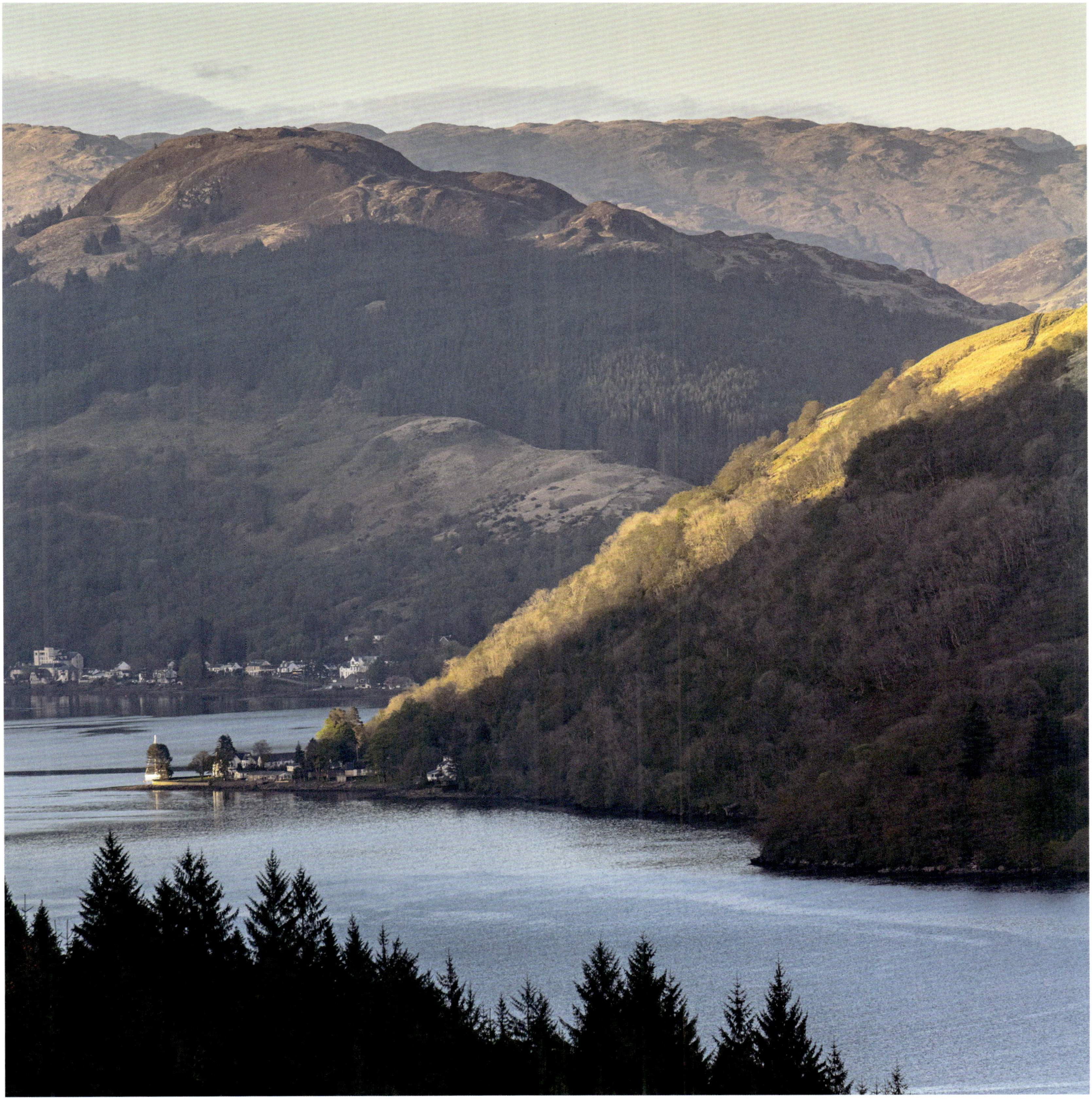

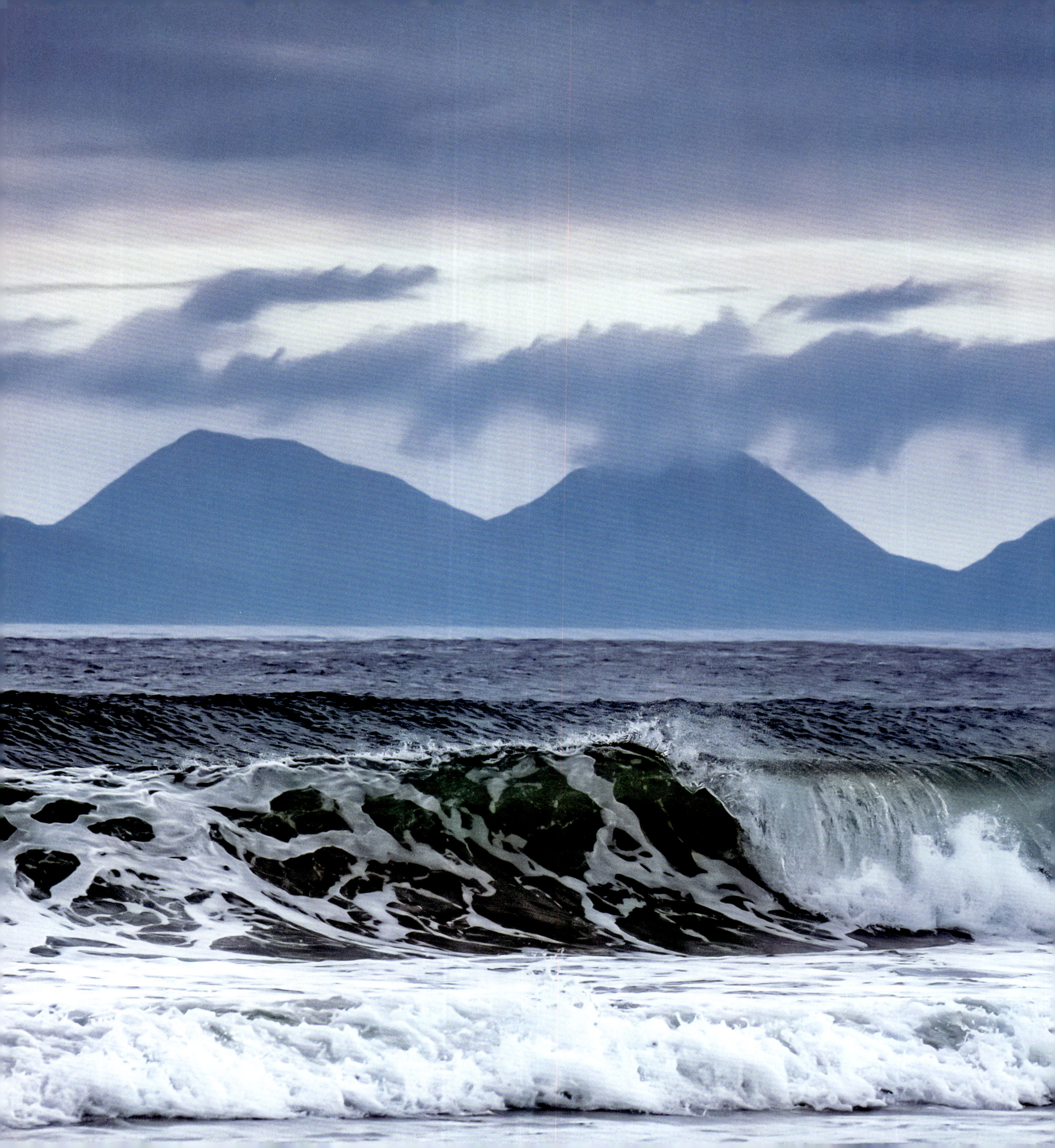

25 SOUTH ARGYLLSHIRE

MAY–NOVEMBER 2018

DAY 210–244 | 05,425–06,282KM | 857KM

At 857 walkable kilometres, South Argyllshire is the longest county I plan to cover on this journey, with a complex coastline that is sparsely populated and mountainous. I arrive during a heatwave in the Cowal Peninsula, and quickly find myself battling not just the dense vegetation along the lochside, but the humidity and relentless midges that swarm at sea level. In search of cooler climes and relief from insects, I pitch my tent at the top of a mountain only to find that it is equally windless and infested. Only a mosquito net keeps me from being attacked, and as I cower in my sweatbox of a tent, I get the feeling that conquering South Argyllshire won't be easy.

The next day, when I return to the shore of Loch Striven, I nearly step on oystercatcher eggs just above the tide line. Yellow flag irises flank the beach, and it remains humid and still. I walk through chest-high bracken when the shore gets too steep, which leaves my skin and clothes crawling with ticks. A proprietorial red deer bark emanates from deep within the forest and I follow their faint tracks through the undergrowth. In contrast to the winter, swarms of midges, mossies and horseflies make stopping even for a moment difficult. As I follow the Kyles of Bute, I tuck in my socks and spray myself with repellent, but it's so hot my sweat seems to wash it away immediately. I filter a litre of water and drink it in one sitting without removing the bottle from my lips.

For two days, I trace the east shore of Loch Fyne, where, at low tide, the barnacle-covered rocks give me a good grip, and the air is so unpolluted that the lichen grows thick like grass above the golden-yellow and black bands of lichen below. On the second night, countless thousands of midges crawl on my tent, trying to get in, creating a shimmering black surface and sounding like the patter of fine rain. Eating in these conditions involves dashing out with a zipped-up anorak and head net, lighting the stove, jogging about until the water boils, pouring it on to the dehydrated food, and diving back inside. I soon discover that lighting a fire has the dual effect of not only keeping the pests away, but generating a heat that is so relaxing I fall asleep the instant the embers are covered and I'm in my sleeping bag.

After nine days following the indentations of the Cowal Peninsula, I head south down the limply suggestive outline of the Kintyre Peninsula on the other side of Loch Fyne. I enjoy picking my own path along the west shore of the loch, where I find an intact urchin shell like a porcelain pincushion. By Point House at Lochgair, a two-storeyed pyramidal-roofed tower built in the eighteenth century, I watch the tide fall, concentrating on a single pointed boulder just below the surface. As the water recedes, concentric rings appear above the rock before it pierces the surface tension and steadily emerges, encrusted in barnacles.

At Carradale, opposite the Isle of Arran, my sixth pair of shoes starts to fall apart, which, combined with the heat, gives me foot problems. I'm sitting down to tape up both when a man comes up to me. 'You here for the otters?' he says by way of an introduction. It turns out he's an ecologist who does bird surveys for the offshore wind farm industry. He tells me how not to confuse a seal with an otter from a distance (their heads look similar in water, but an otter will always also show its tail above the surface) and advises me to keep my eyes open for golden eagles nearby.

Further south down the peninsula, I notice on the map that a hill I'm walking past is called 'The Bastard'. 'Only in Scotland,' I think to myself with a chuckle. But by the afternoon, my sense of humour dissipates when I realise I'm out of water. The mewing call of a buzzard overhead torments me as I pass dry stream after dry stream. To fill my bottle, I'm forced to detour to a larger burn marked as 'The Snout Waterfall' on my map. Still, even this is a barely perceptible trickle, and it takes me pulling foliage apart and listening with my ear to the ground to locate the source.

Opposite:

The Paps of Jura from Machrihanish Bay

At the end of a long, winding road through moorland, I reach the lighthouse at the Mull of Kintyre. The headland rises to 400 metres above the sea and feels like no place to linger with its crashing waves and raging torrents. I head inland and, after several more days of wild camping along the roadless south-west of Kintyre, make it to the Argyll Hotel in Bellochantuy just before the kitchen is due to close. My pack contains an empty food bag, 10 per cent of battery left on the phone (which also doubles as my map), a power bank with no charge and a blinking last bar on the camera. I try to sound casual when I ask if they are still serving food.

Beyond Ardpatrick Point, I encounter hostile terrain along the off-track north-western section of Kintyre. A pretty appearance disguises narrow, sharp rock bands, like upturned axe heads, that run against the grain of travel. Rain and seaweed make the lower shore too slippery to walk. Dense growth of bracken hides sudden vertiginous drops along the only passable route. Going further inland is impossible due to dense walls of scrubby thickets. I'm using my hands continuously, and in many instances, my shoes wedge between rocks and need to be wiggled backwards to extricate them.

At Crinan, the only paths are deer tracks and the wild landscape towards Ardfern, with its views over to Jura and Scarba, is more like mountaineering than coast-walking. In the middle of a forestry plantation, I'm delighted to encounter the mysterious 4,000-year-old Ormaig rock carvings overlooking Loch Craignish. The site has just been strimmed, obscuring the artworks under loose grass. As it's getting dark and I want a photo, I make a brush from bracken to hurriedly clear the cut grass from the rock, revealing the carvings like some form of ancient devotion. Dozens of outlines of cups and rings emerge, some the size of dinner plates, which adorn the rocky incline in a compelling but indecipherable code.

I leave the Ormaig rock carvings in the dark and clamber over giant mossy stumps covering the steep ground, hoping unsuccessfully for an easier route to walk along towards the road. I follow a solitary power line through a plantation, as there is less vegetation below it. To my alarm, the head torch picks out great swags of cable drooping down to the ground in front of me, intertwined with a messy nest of upended tree roots; storm-felled trees have smashed the post holding up the power line. To bypass this, I'm forced to crawl under the lower branches to reach the edge of the forest, where a tall wall stands between me and a road. At the limit of my endurance, I trace the wall, looking for a way over. I'm relieved when my torch illuminates the improbable sight of an aluminium ladder, which I climb quickly to escape.

Weeks of bogs, wobbly tufts of grass, impenetrable thickets of bracken and steeply undulating terrain take their toll, and I have a few nasty falls at the end of an especially long day. At Ardfern, I start to develop moderate pain in the front of my left shin. I hobble on for two more days, but when the pain worsens, I cut my day short and camp by the Ardmaddy Wishing Tree. The next morning, I can only manage a handful of steps at a time before the pain becomes overwhelming, so I admit defeat and call a taxi from Oban to get medical attention. I'm amazed to have had a phone signal, but now the only catch is that I'm in the middle of nowhere, a few hours away from the nearest road. The painkillers I carry have no effect, so I shoulder my pack to wince and shuffle my way down the hill like I'm walking on hot coals. I'm not surprised when the doctor confirms I have an emergent stress fracture from overuse, but when he tells me I'll need nine weeks of rest and recovery with my foot immobilised, frustration overwhelms me. It's the second time that an injury has forced me to put a pause on this journey, and it's discouraging to know that I'm in this state already when the hardest terrain is yet to come.

By the time I've recovered, it's November, so I no longer need to contend with the summer heat or midges. On my first day back, I take it gently and am pleased to discover the off-trail sections are more manageable in winter when the bracken has died away. I make good progress and by the afternoon I've reached the Clachan Bridge, a beautifully simple, single-arched, hump-backed masonry bridge spanning the Clachan Sound to the Island of Seil.

On my last days in South Argyllshire, I lap up the walk north-east along the Great Glen fault beside Loch Linnhe. The walking is mercifully easy, yet across the loch rise the remote and mountainous regions of Kingairloch and Ardgour that appear like sheer walls of fissured rock. Crossing the bridge at Ballachulish, surrounded on all sides by mountains, with a glimpse inland into Glen Coe, feels like a big moment: I'm in the heart of the Highlands now.

Opposite, from top left:

Path to Loch Goil from Corran Lochan

Finnart Oil Terminal, Loch Long

From bottom left:

Perimeter fence, Royal Naval Armaments Depot Coulport, the storage and loading facility for the nuclear warheads of the UK's Trident programme

Denuded forest, Shepherd's Point, Loch Long

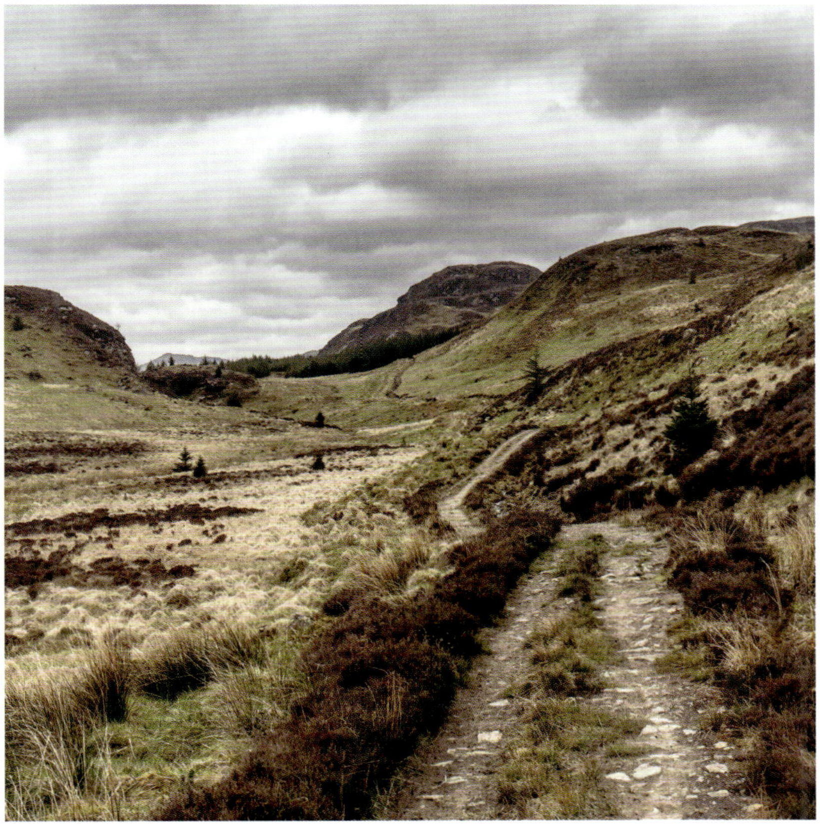
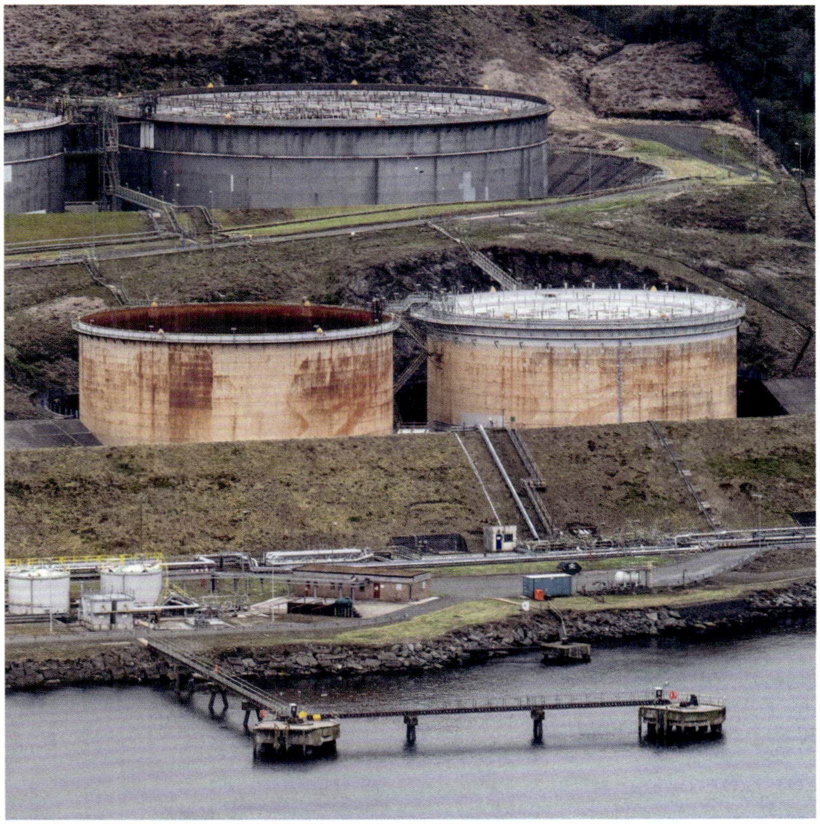
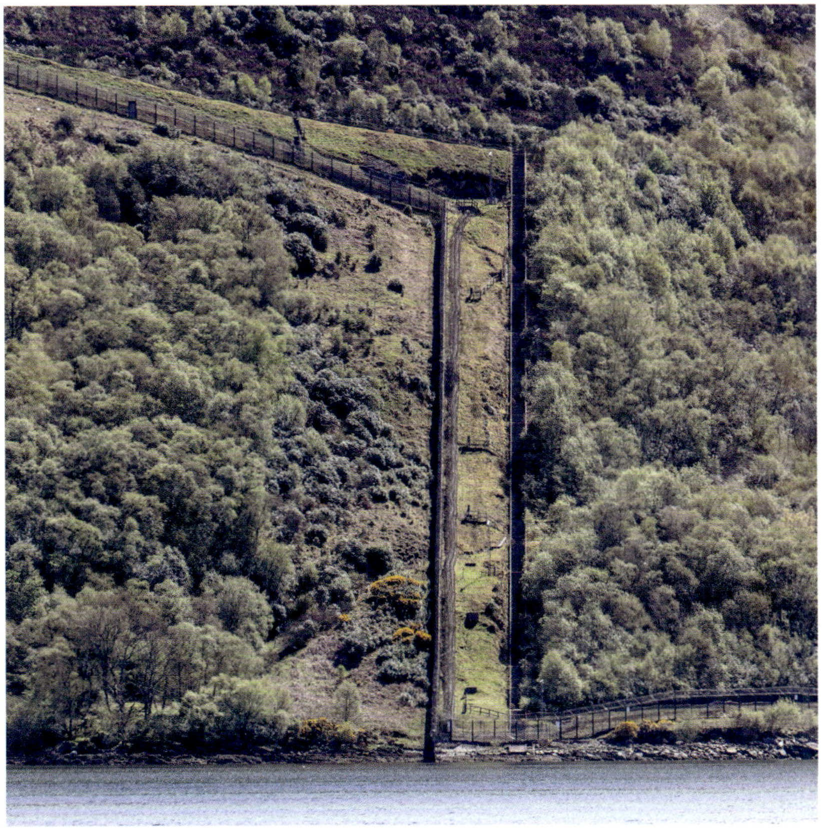
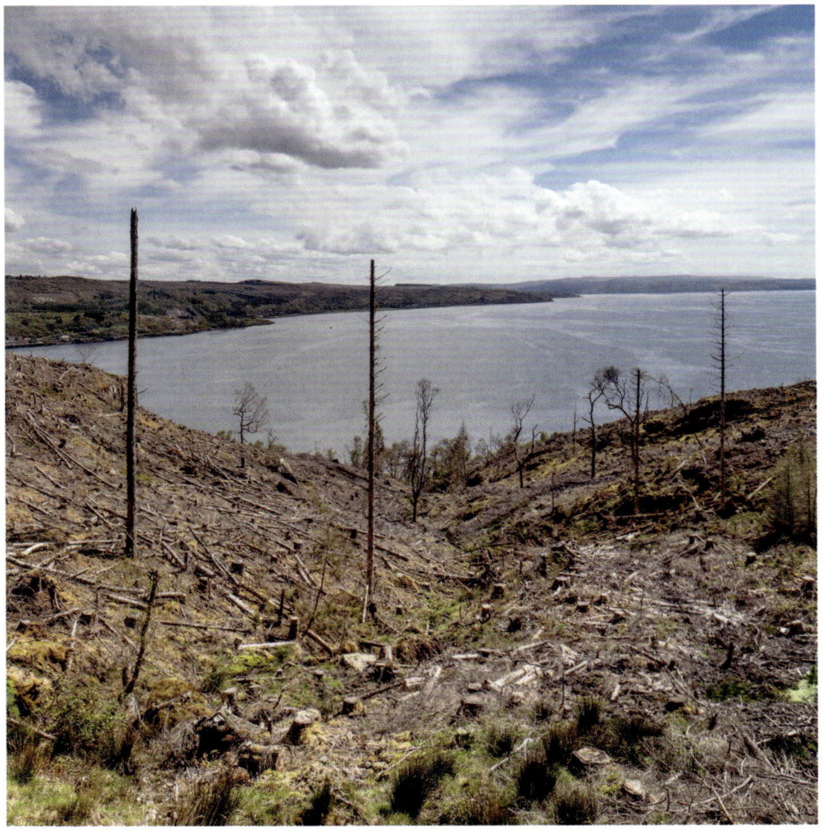

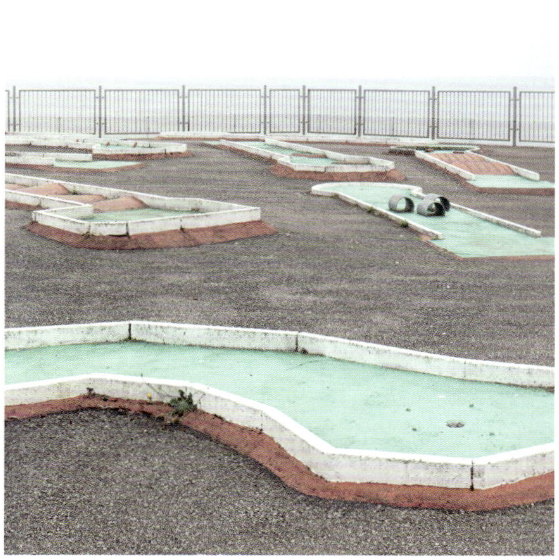

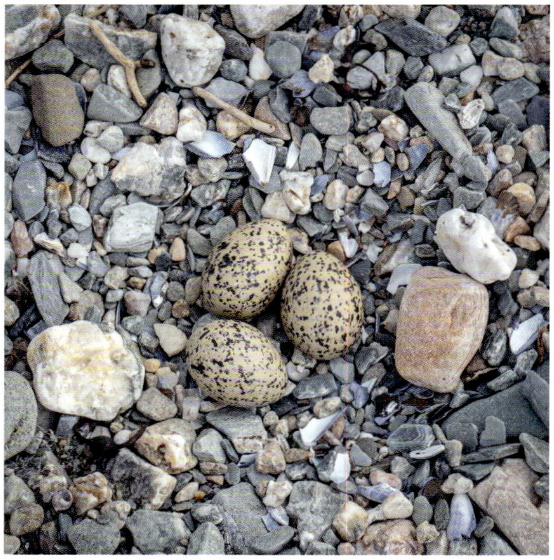

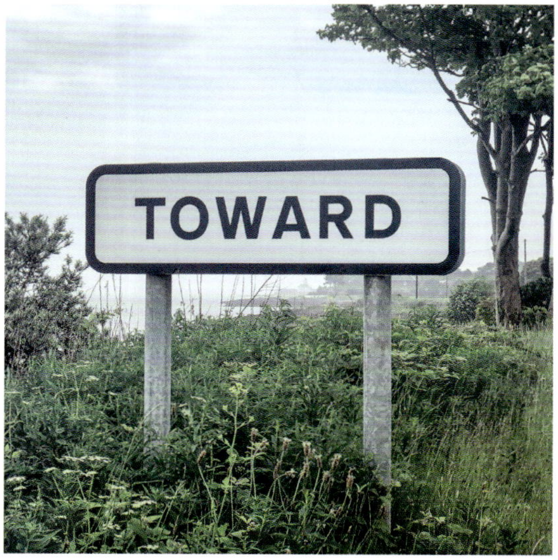

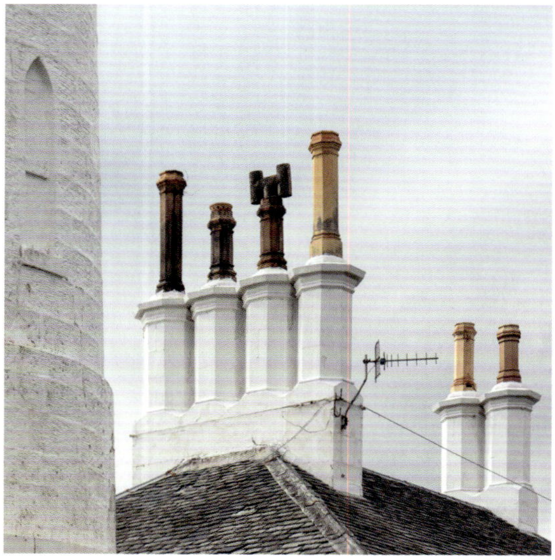

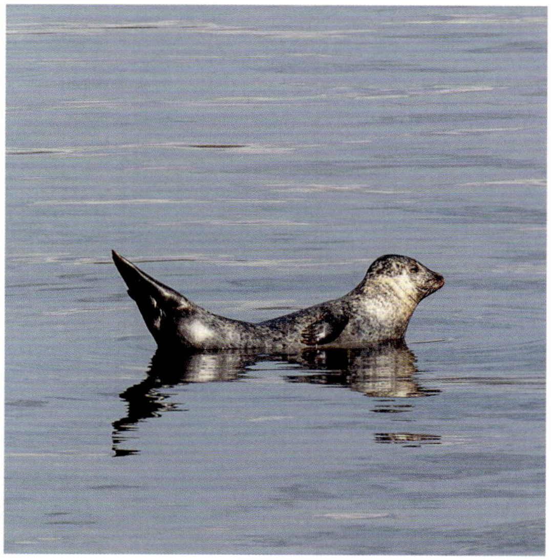

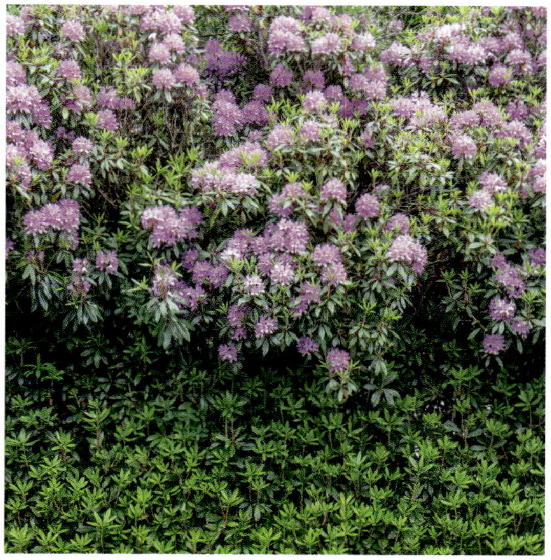

From top left:

Crazy golf, Dunoon

Oystercatcher eggs just above the tide line on the shore of Loch Striven

From centre left:

Towards Toward

Toward Point Lighthouse

From bottom left:

Common seal, Loch Long

Rhododendron hedge, Toward

Opposite:

Last light, Holy Loch, Ardnadam

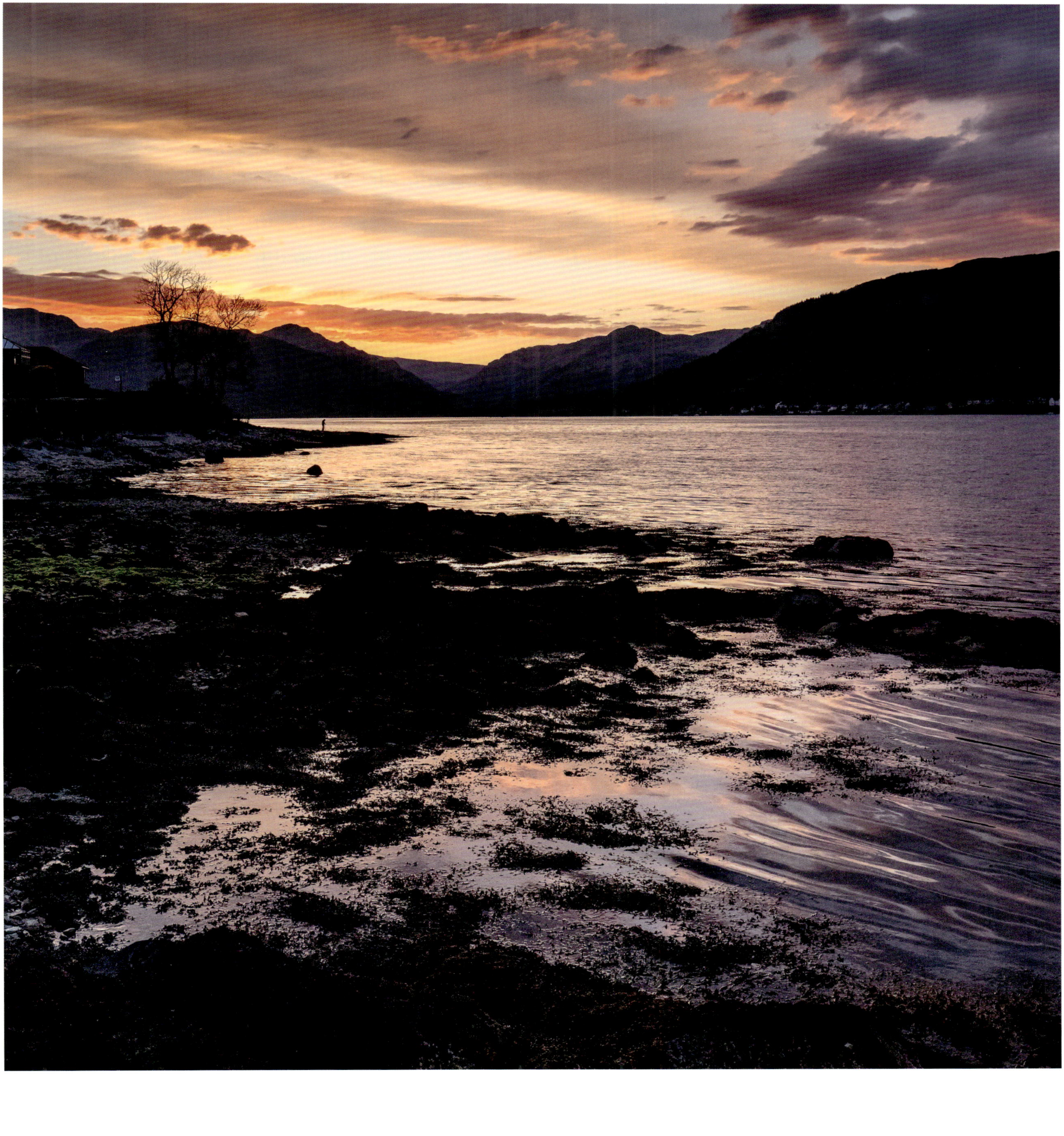

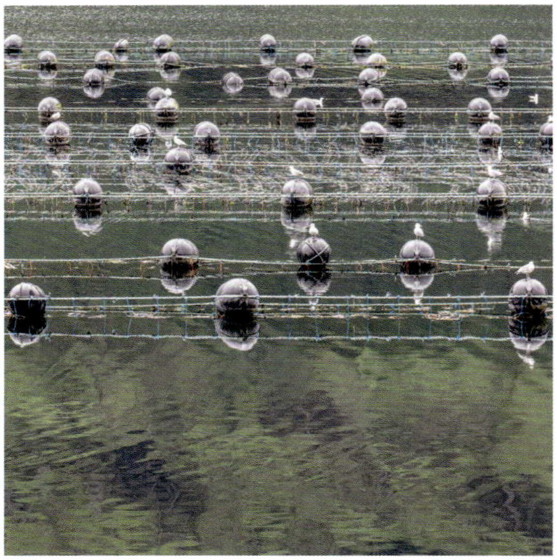

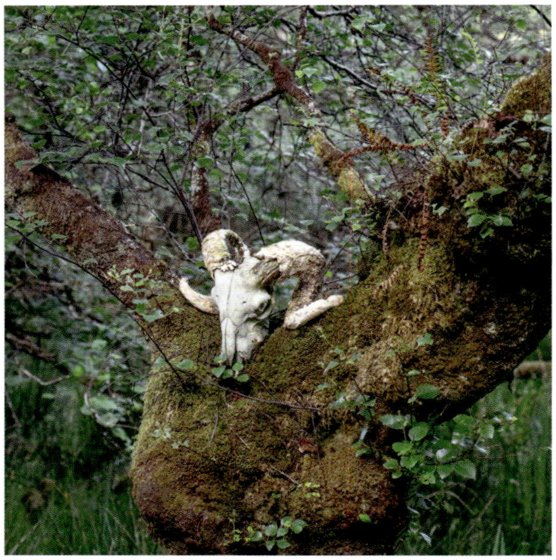

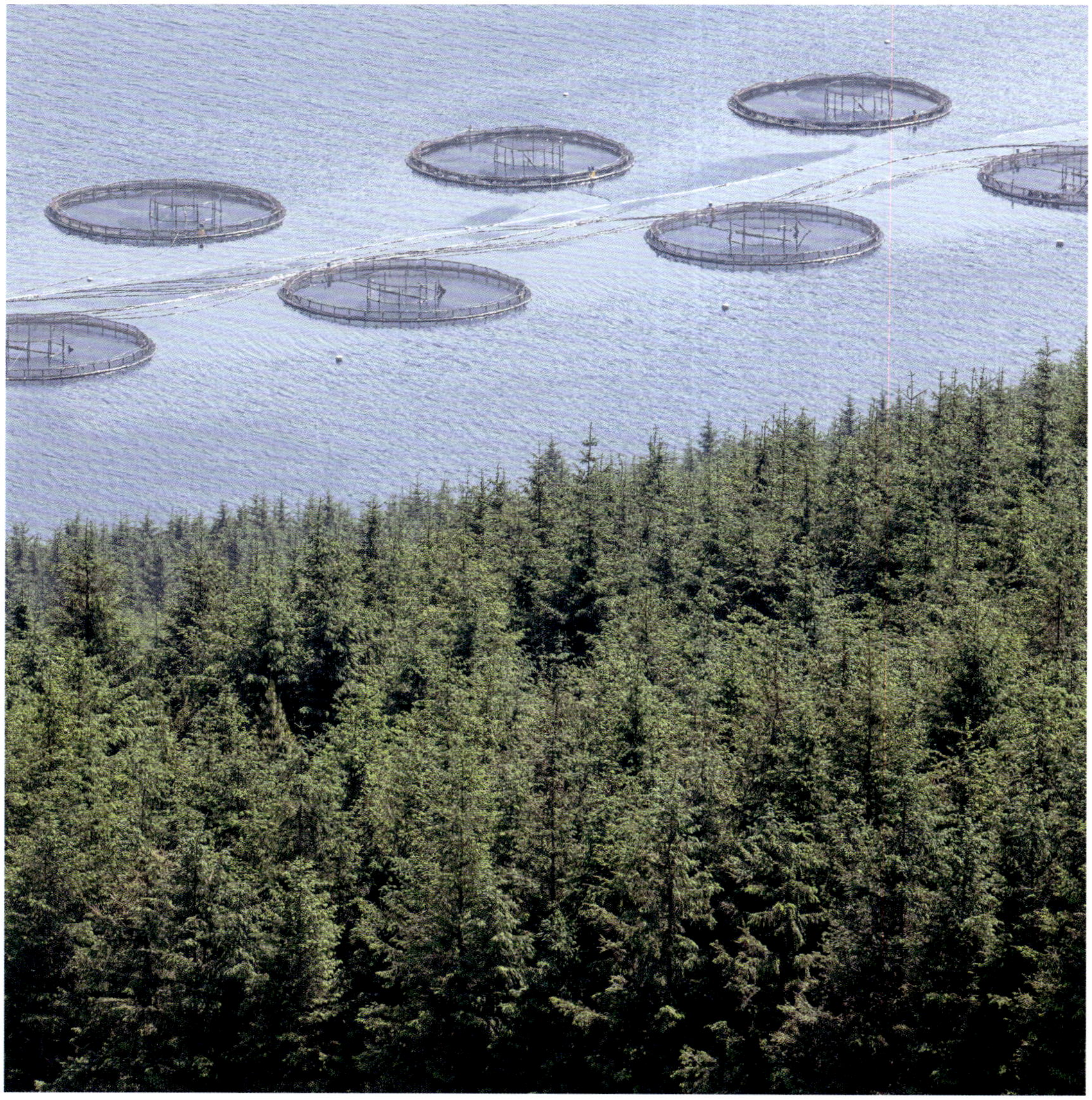

From top left:

Mussel farm, Loch Striven

Warning: Loch Riddon

Fish farm, Loch Striven

Opposite, clockwise from top left:

Rough foreshore walking near Portavadie

Arran from Kilbride Bay

Kilbride Bay textures

Glenan Bay

Arran from Salann Bay

Sea pink, Asgog Bay

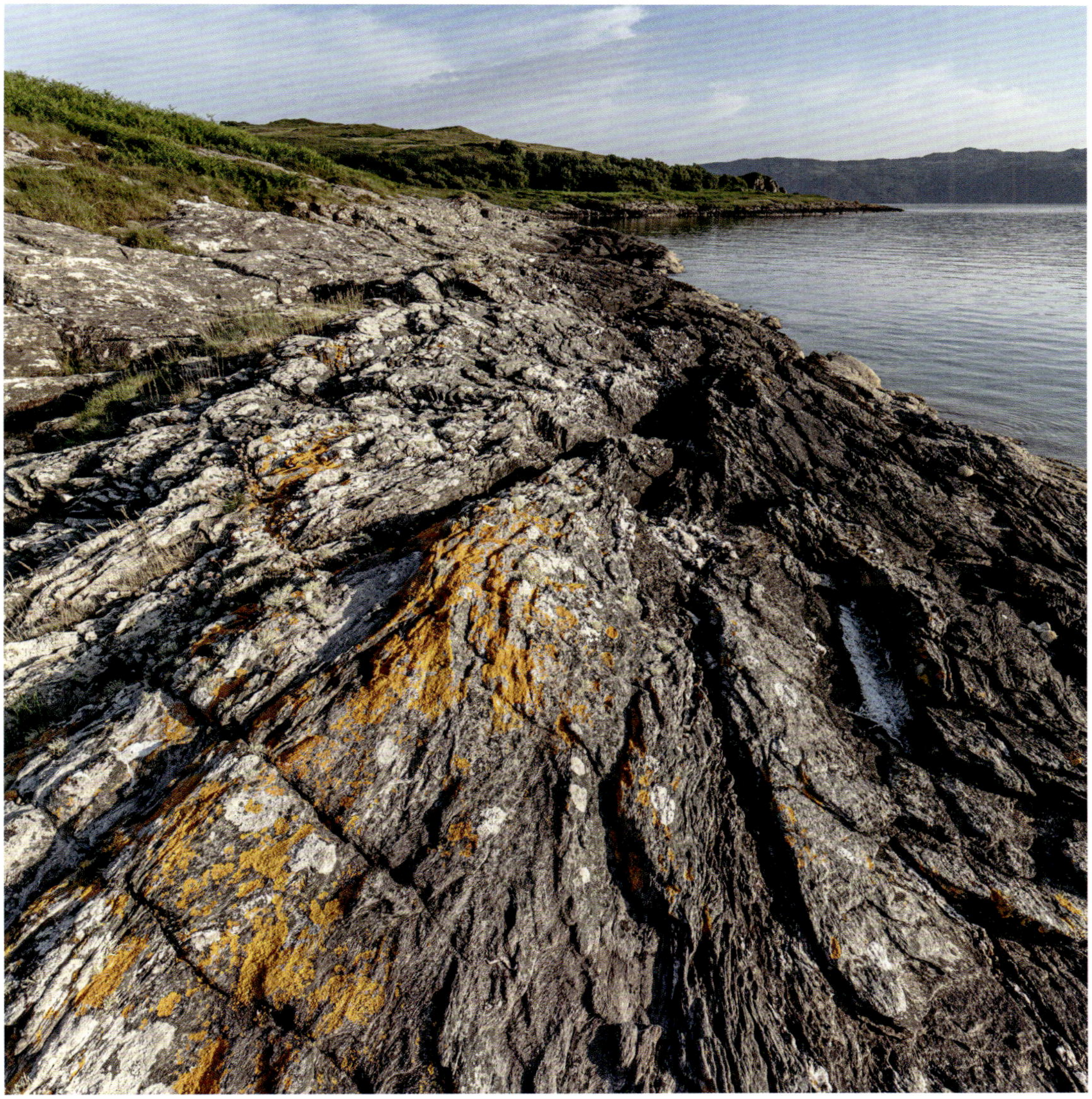
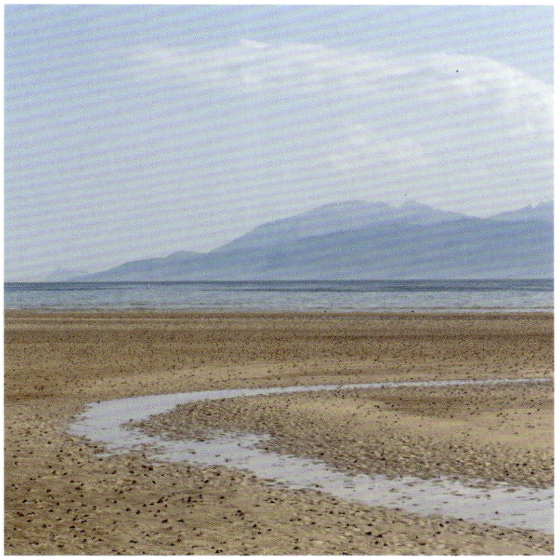
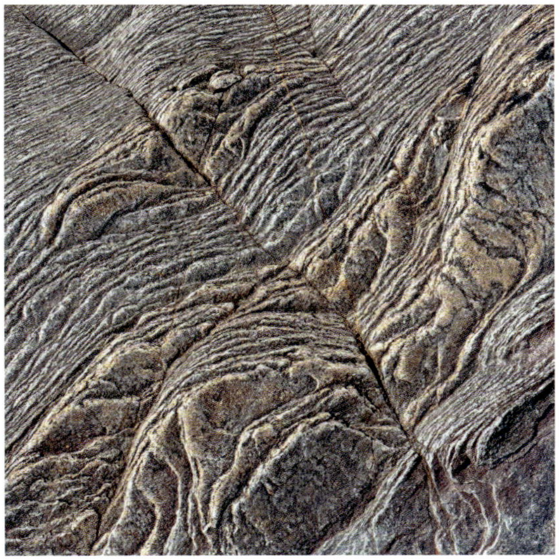
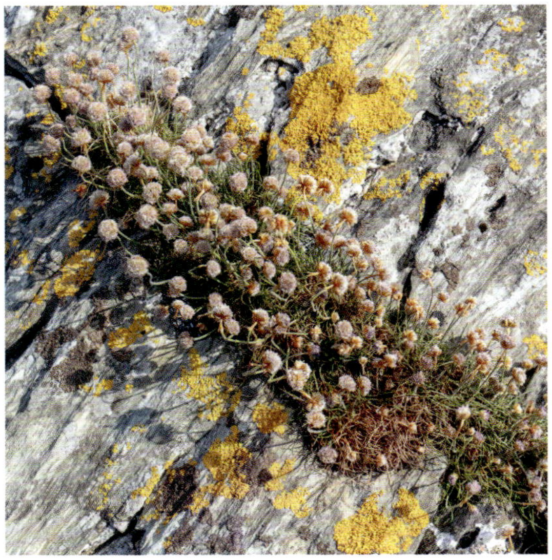
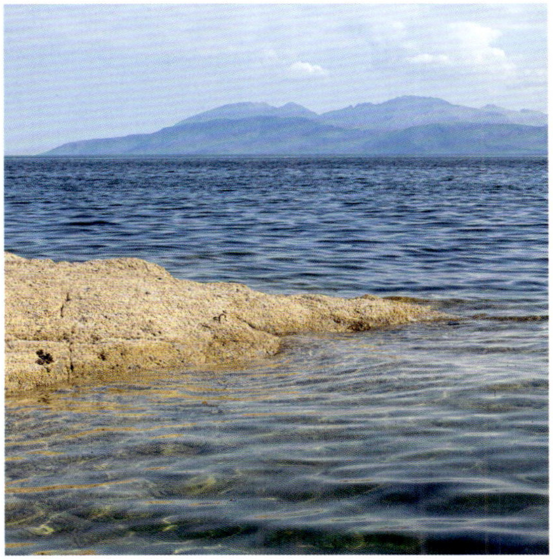
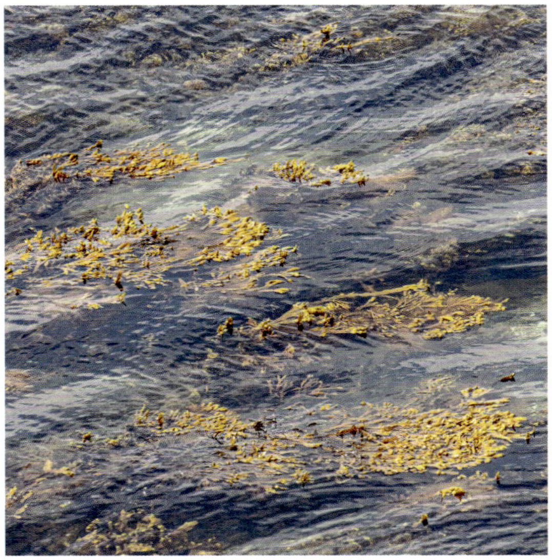

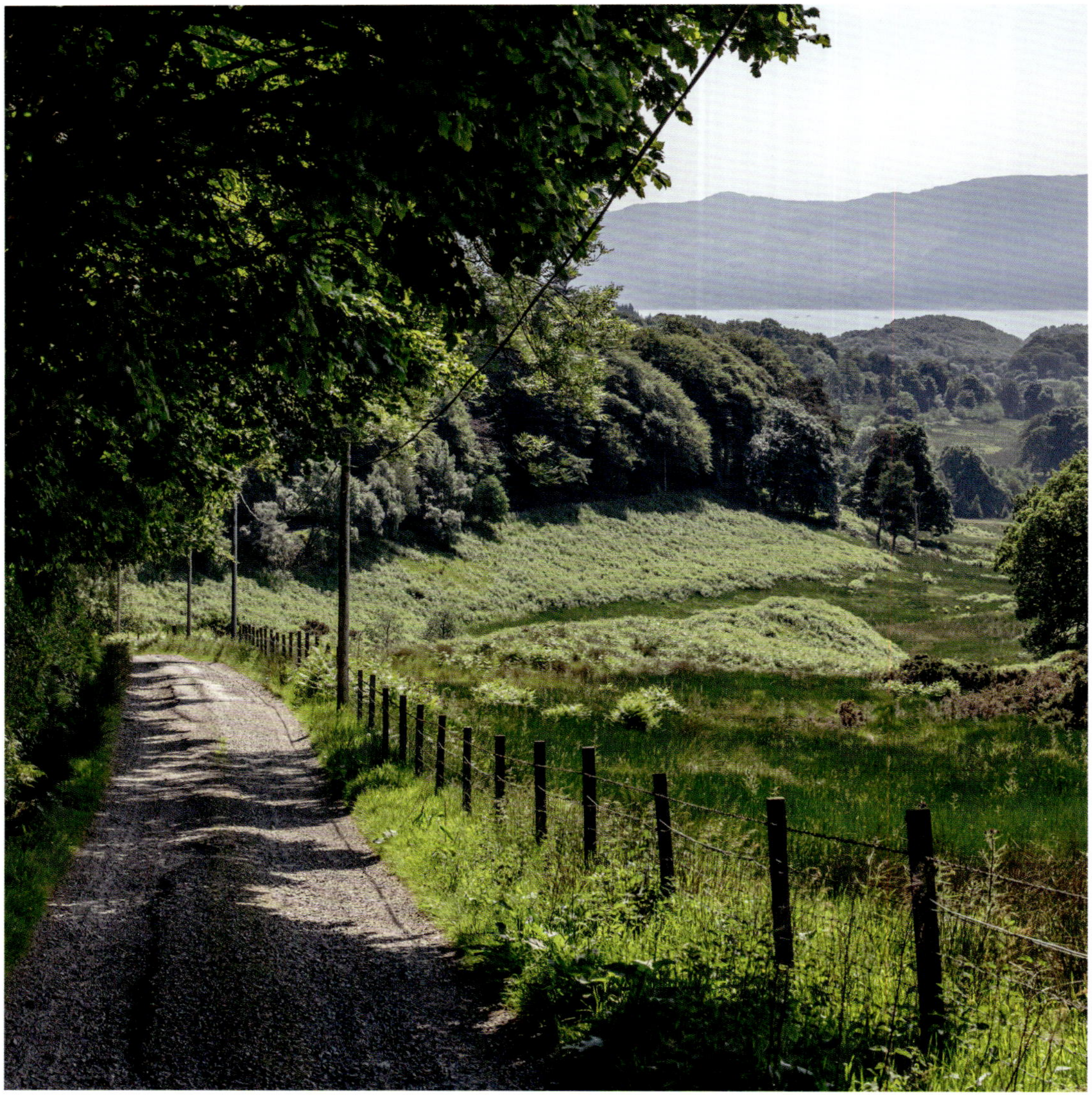
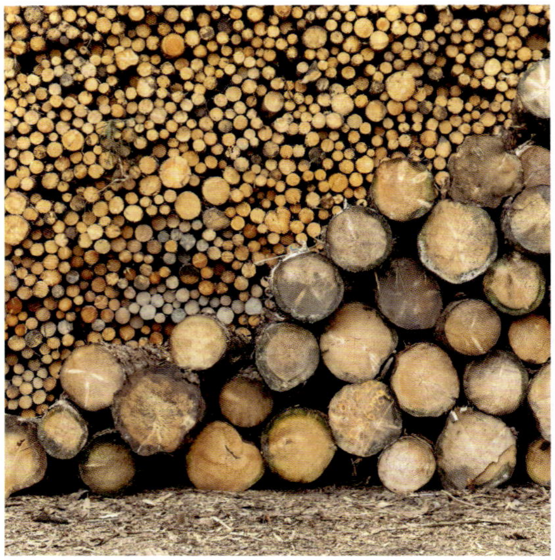
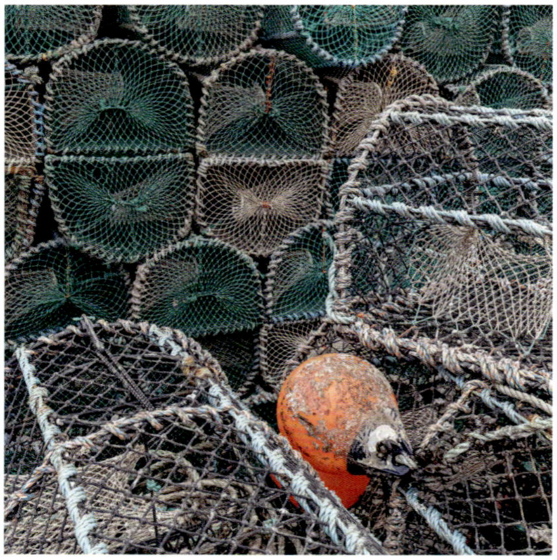
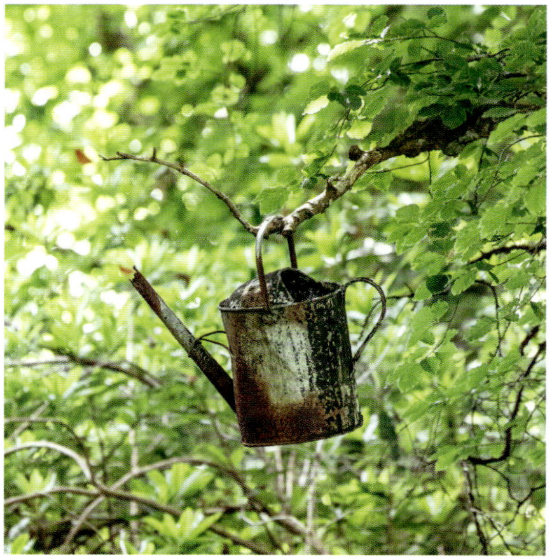
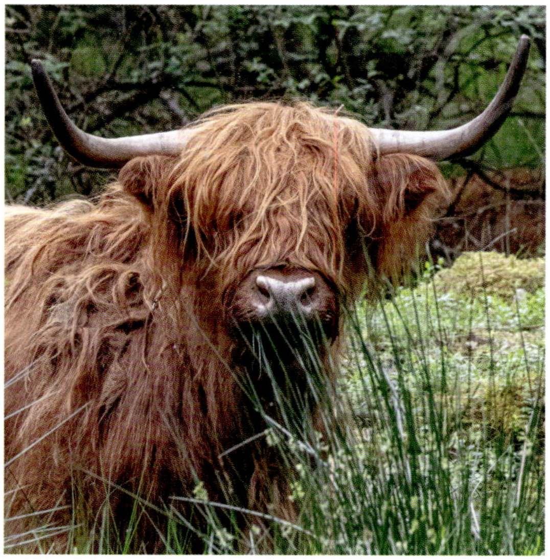
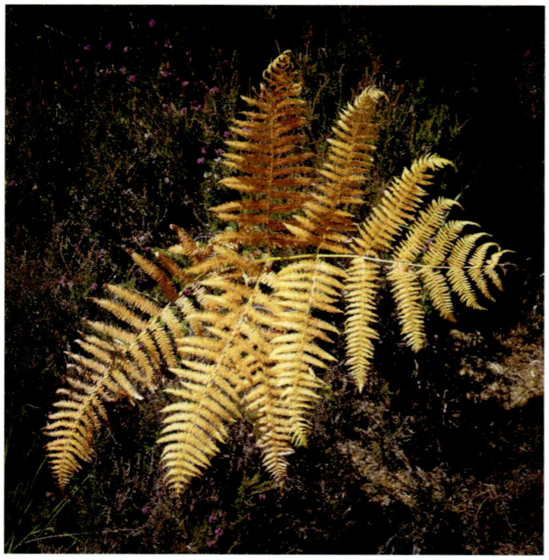

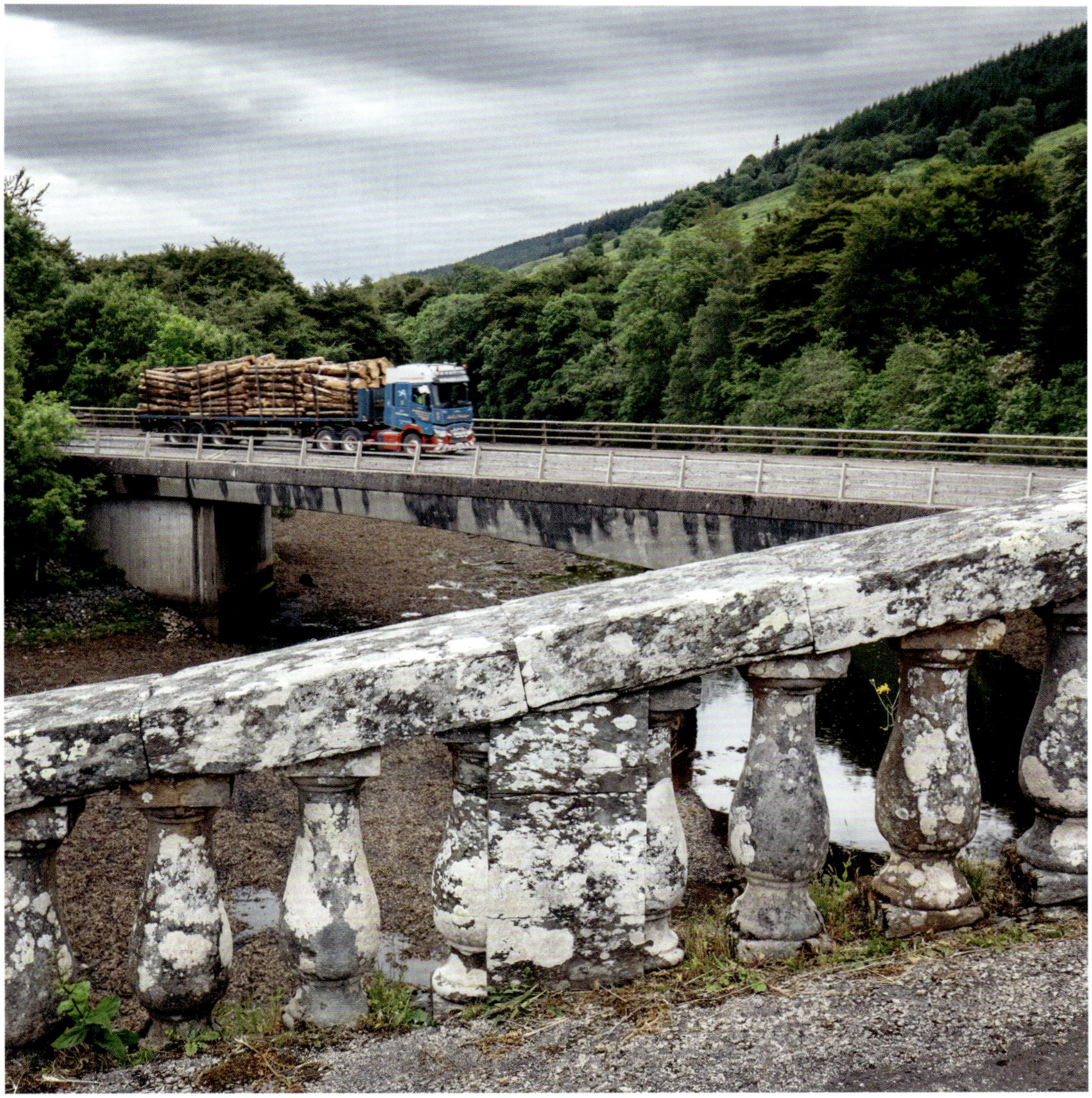

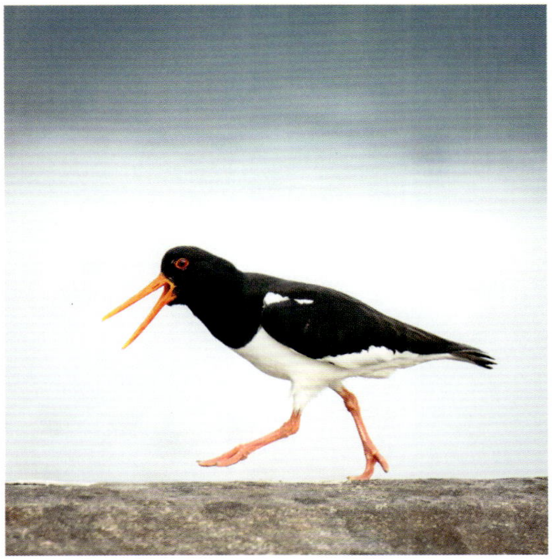

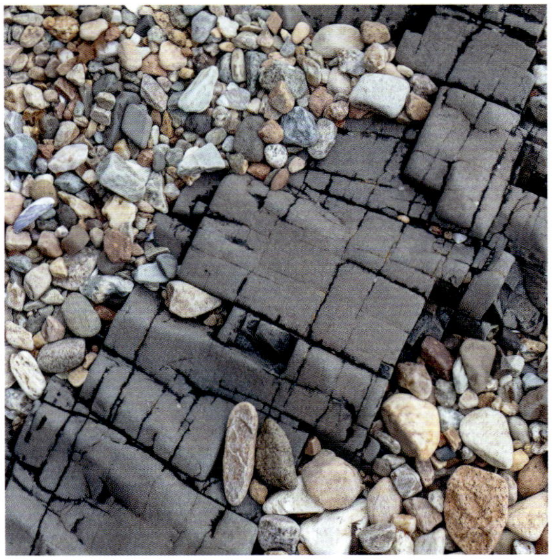

Opposite, clockwise from top left:

Track to Crispie by Loch Fyne

Logging, Ardcastle Wood

Creels, Tarbert

Bracken, Port Ann

Highland cow, Ardkinglas

Hooked: Ardmarnock

From top left:

New bridge across the River Shira from the disused Garron Bridge near Inveraray

Strutting oystercatcher, Aray Bridge, Inveraray

Loch Fyne shore near Inveraray

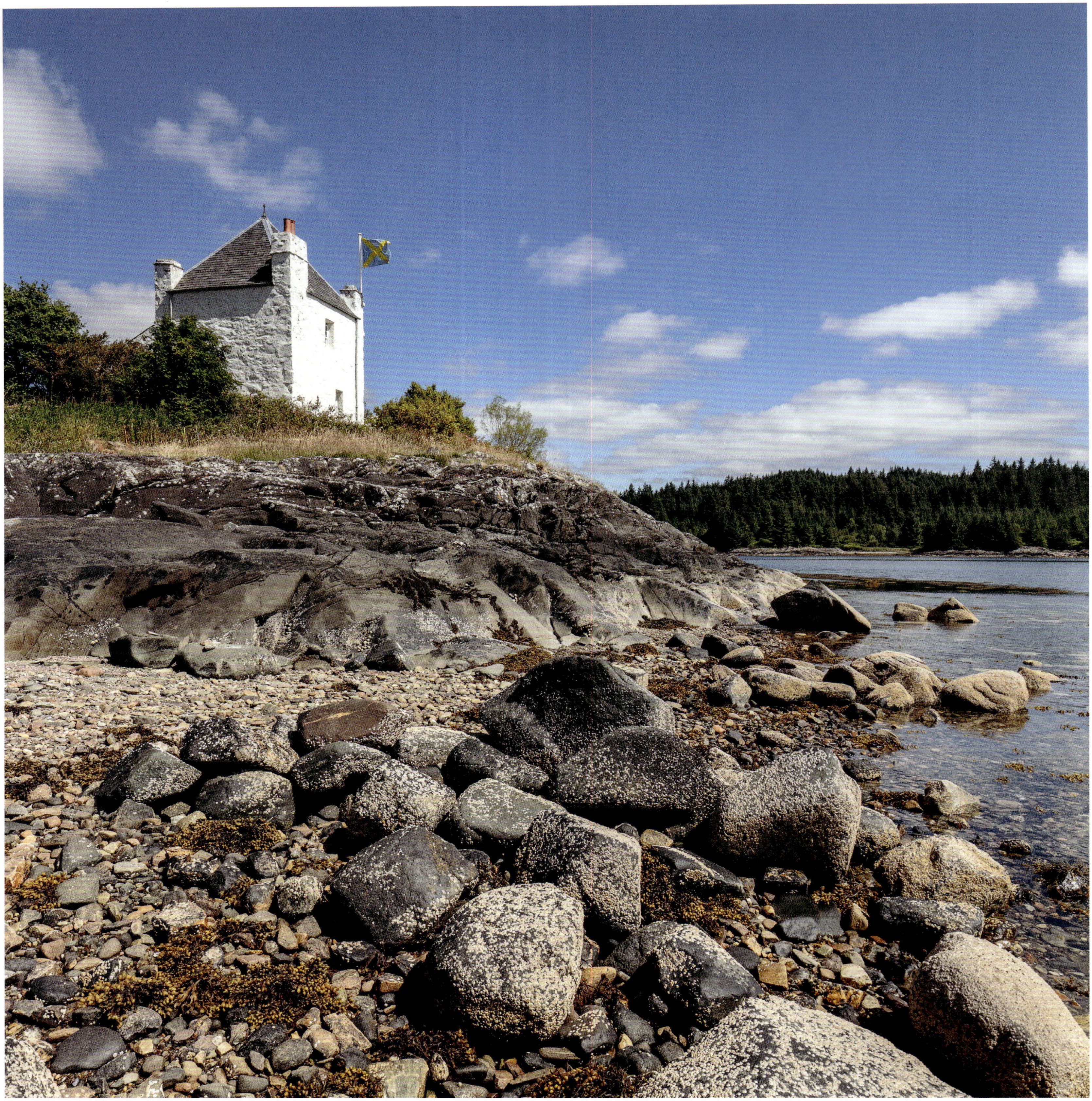

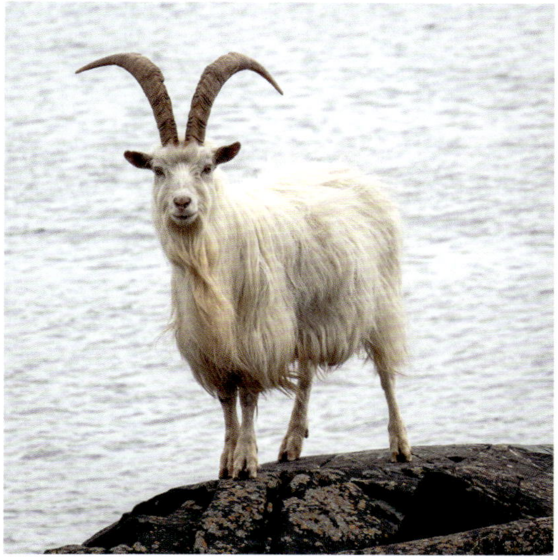

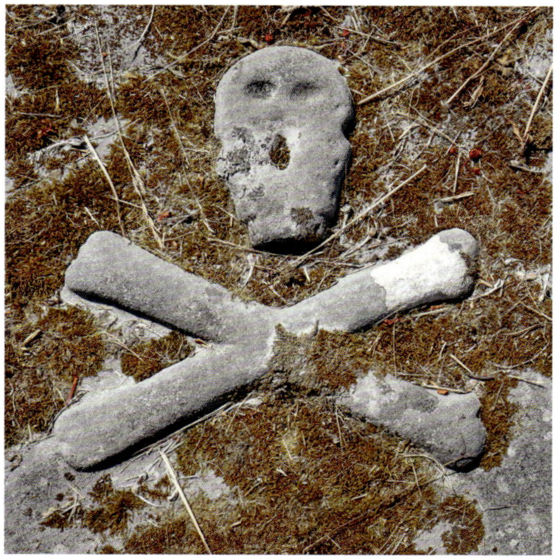

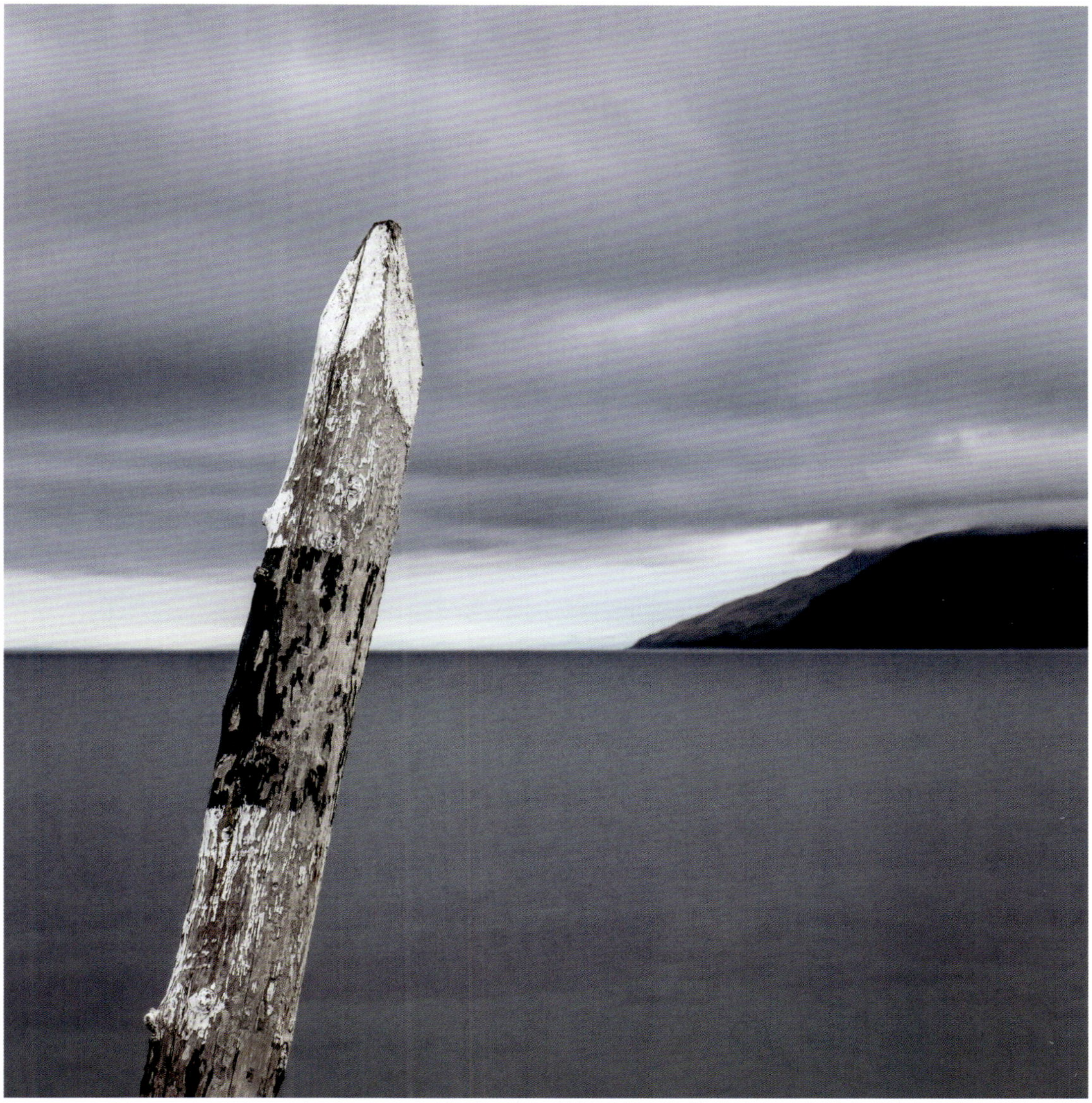

Opposite:

Point House, Loch Gair. The building, also known as Catherine Castle, is probably late eighteenth or early nineteenth century and may have served as an eyecatcher for Asknish House

From top left:

Wild goat at Carradale Point

Tombstone, Saddell Abbey

Arran from Kintyre

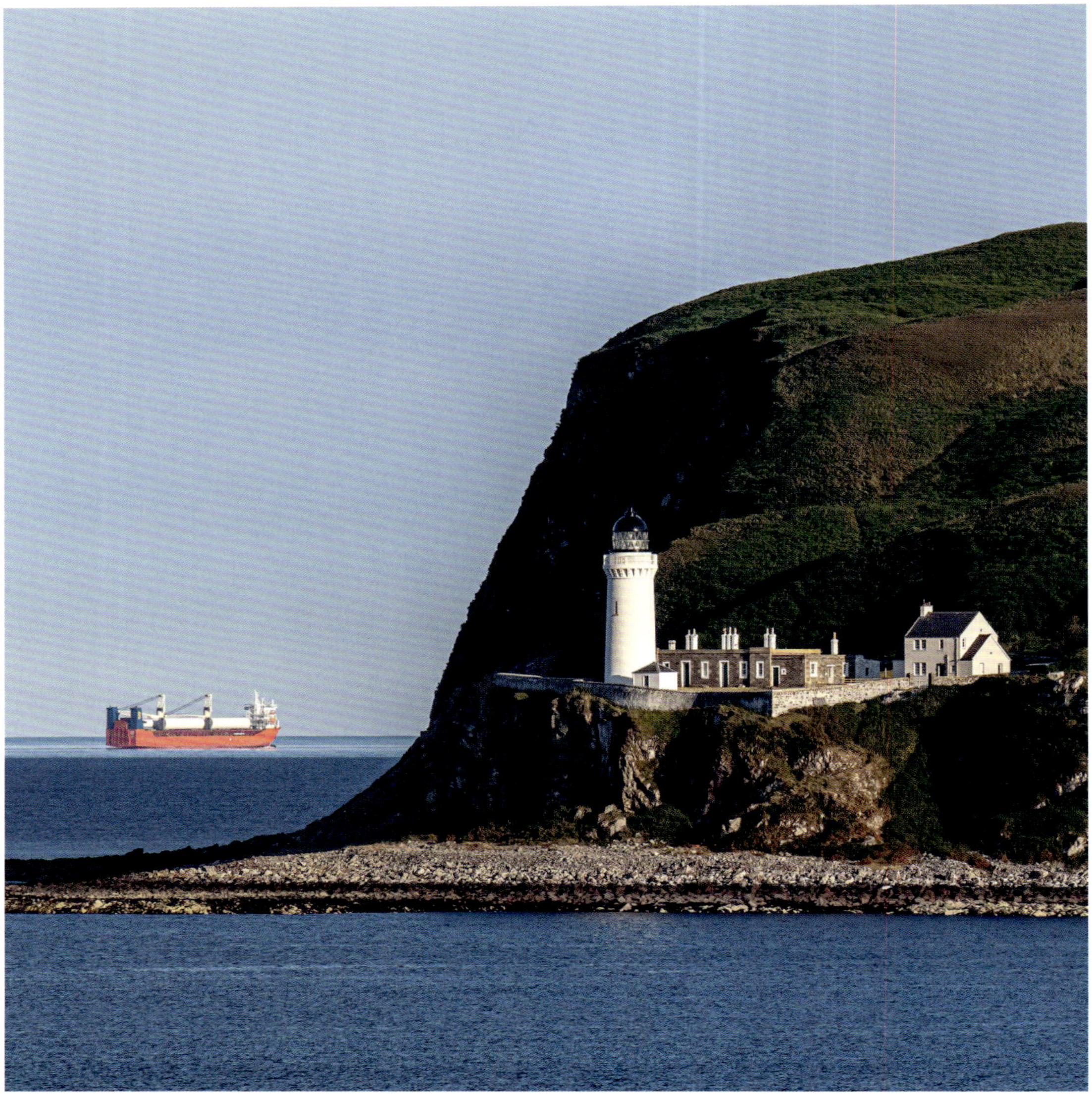
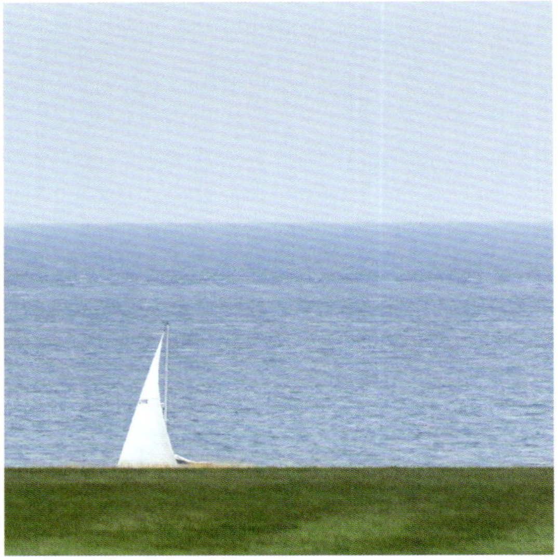
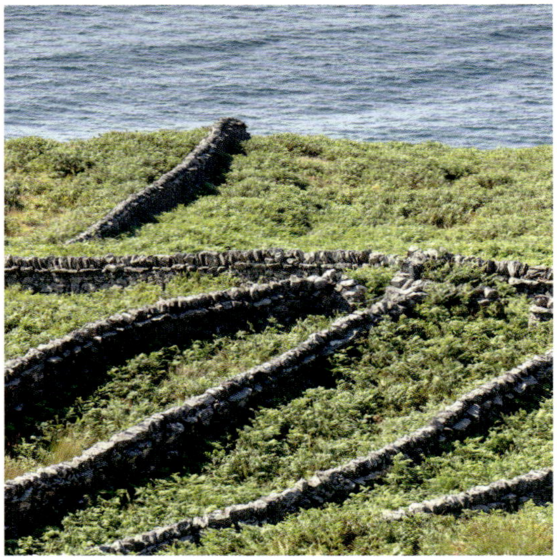
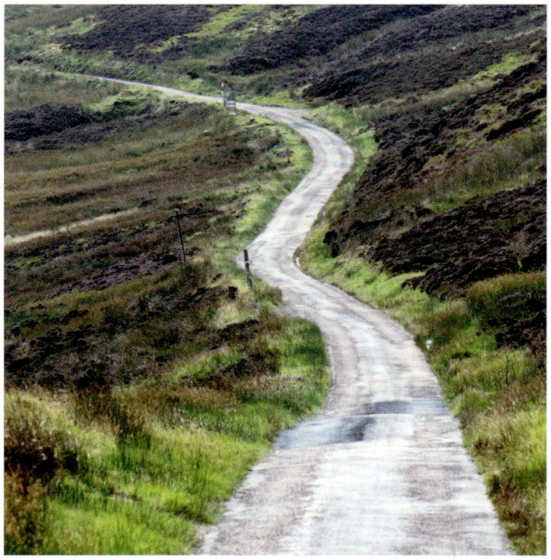
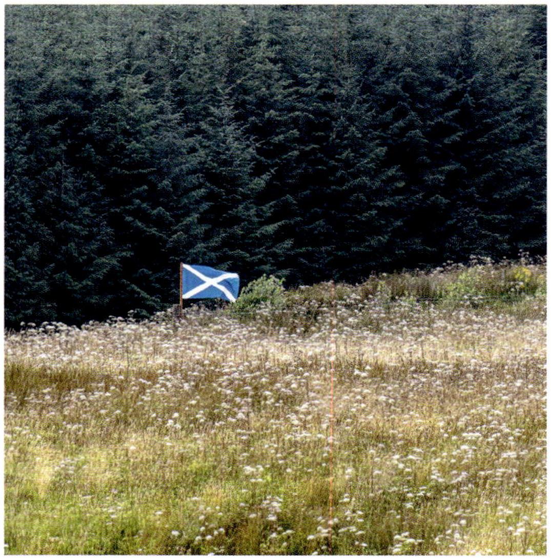
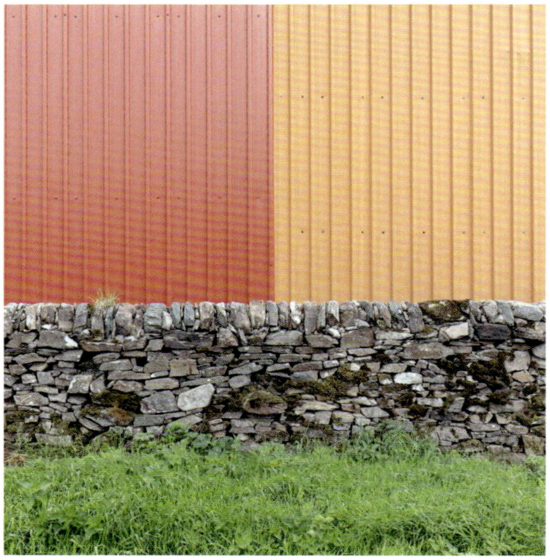

Opposite, clockwise from top left:

Davaar Lighthouse, Campbeltown

Shark's tooth: Sound of Sanda

Black Point, Mull of Kintyre

Lephenstrath Farm, Kintyre

Saltire, Shenachie

Road to the Mull of Kintyre

From top left:

Memorial to the 1994 RAF Chinook crash, Mull of Kintyre

Dragonfly and lochan, Beinn na Lice, Kintyre

From centre left:

Bus stop Mondrian: Glenbarr, Kintyre

The remains of a Lockheed Neptune MR.1 from No. 36 Squadron based at Topcliffe in Yorkshire. It crashed on Beinn na Lice on 10 October 1956

From bottom left:

Island Queen, Rhunahaorine Point, Kintyre

Rhunahaorine Point Second World War lookout post

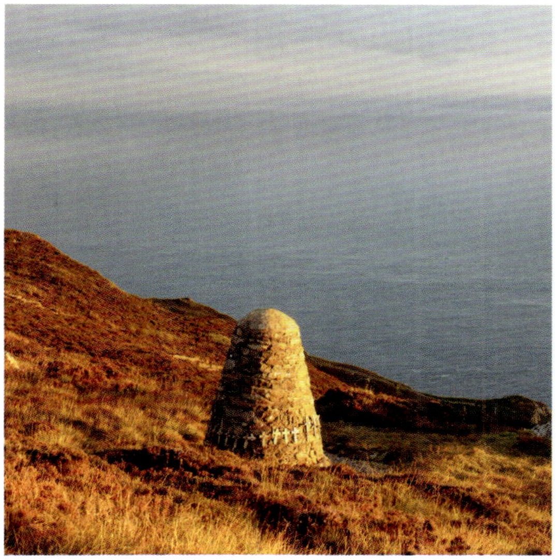

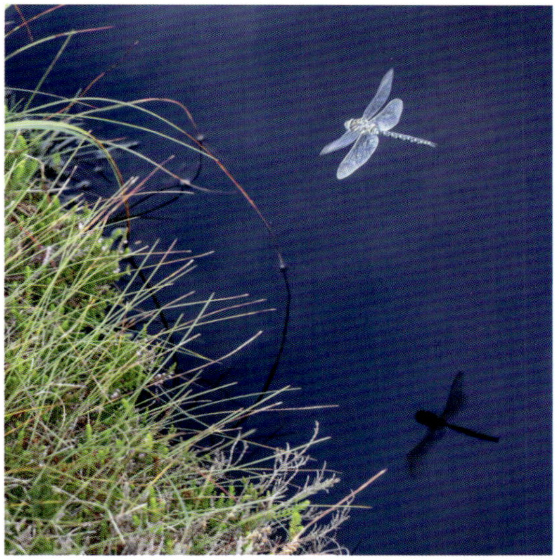

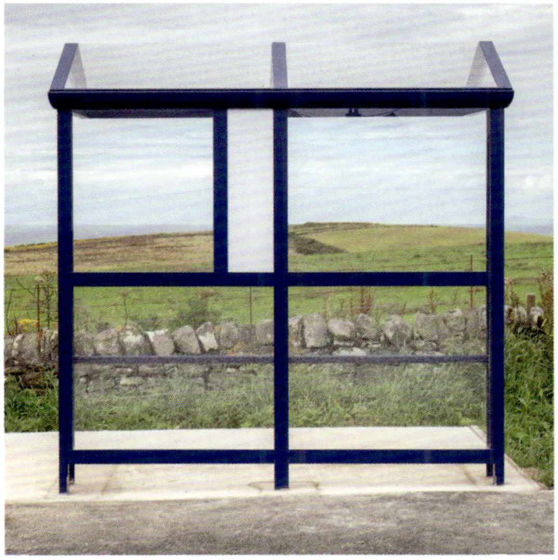

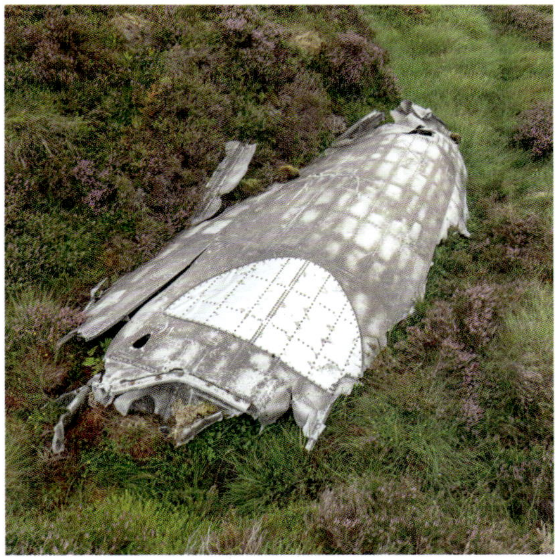

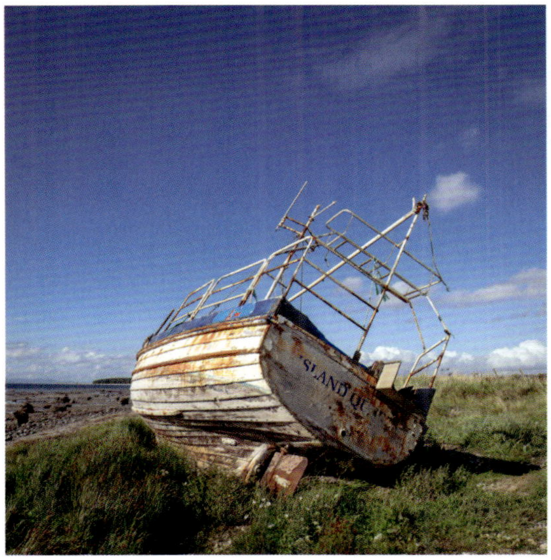

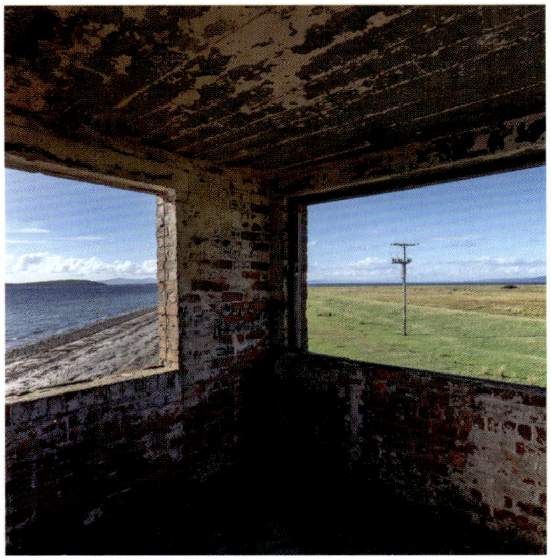

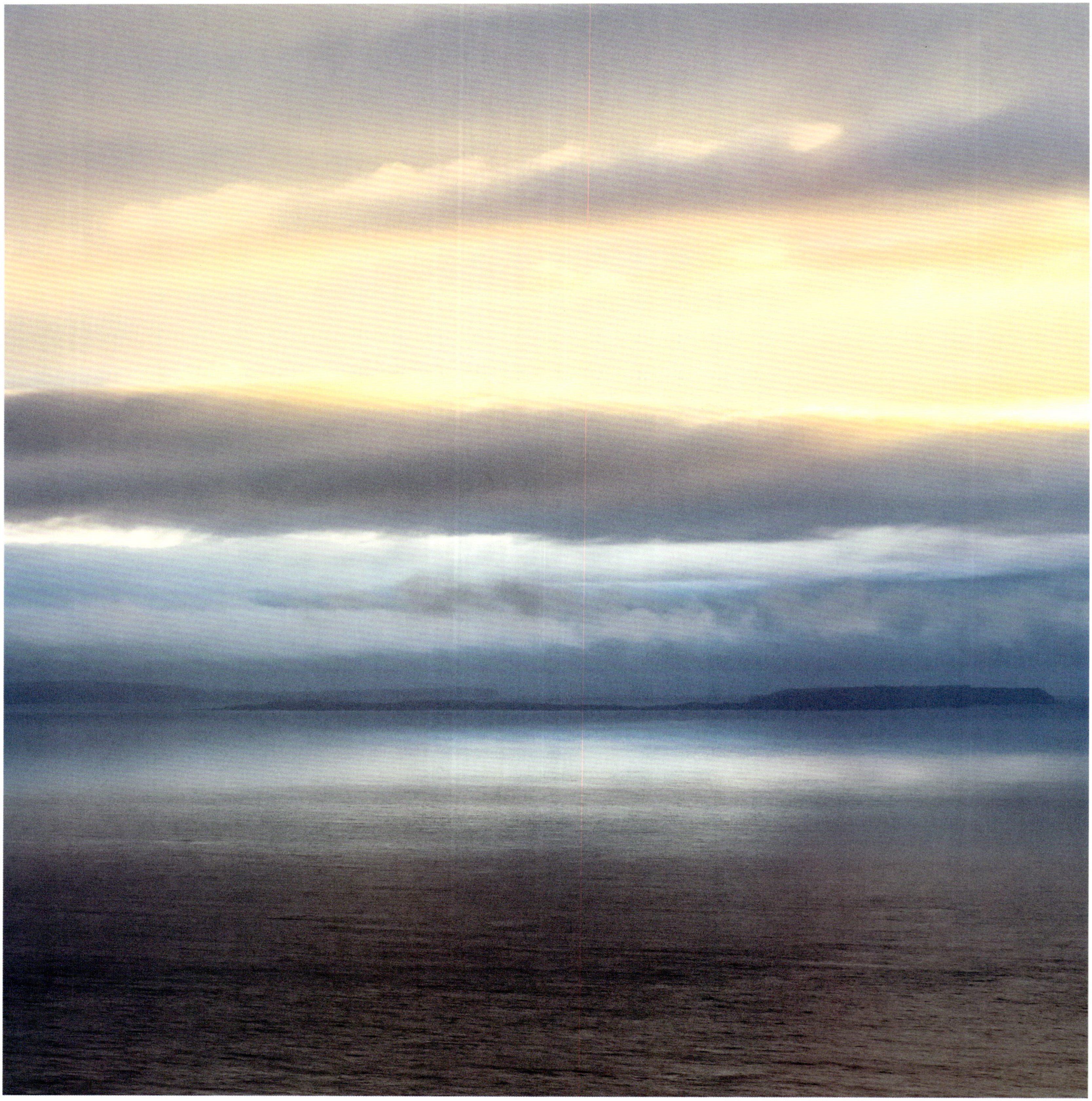

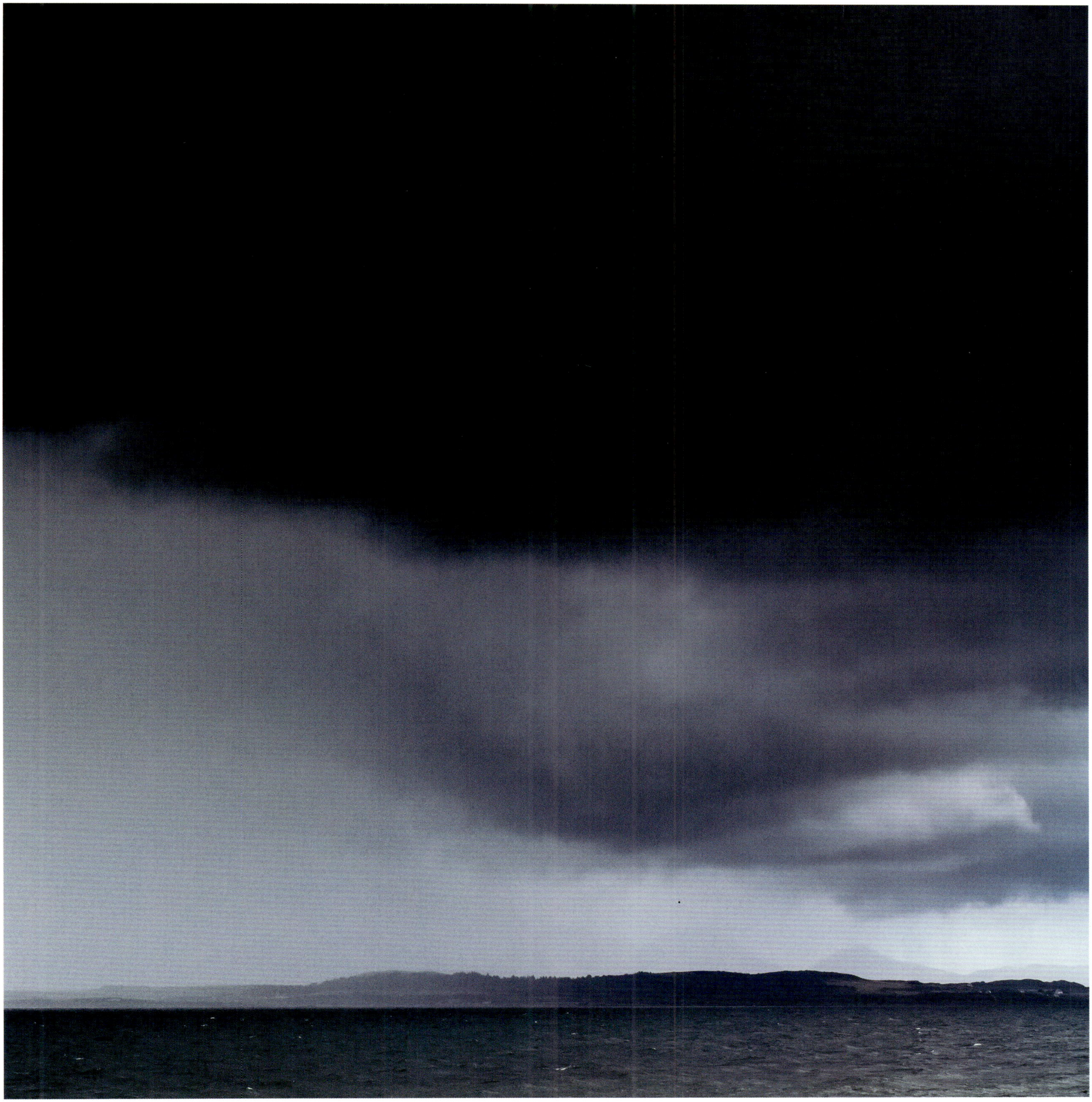

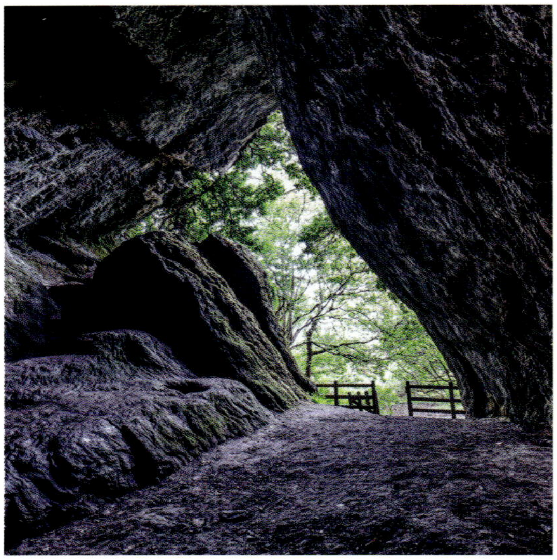

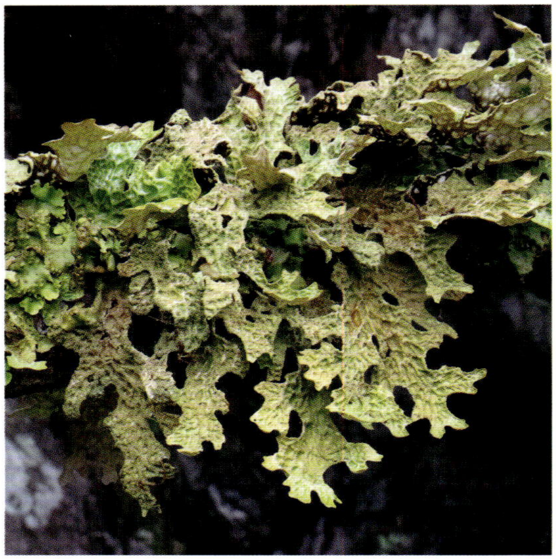

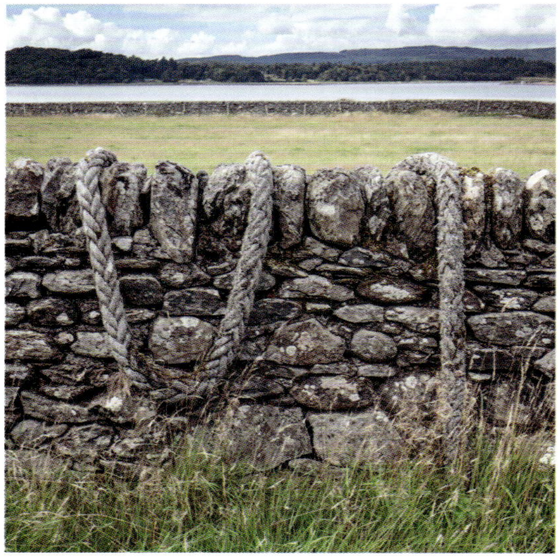

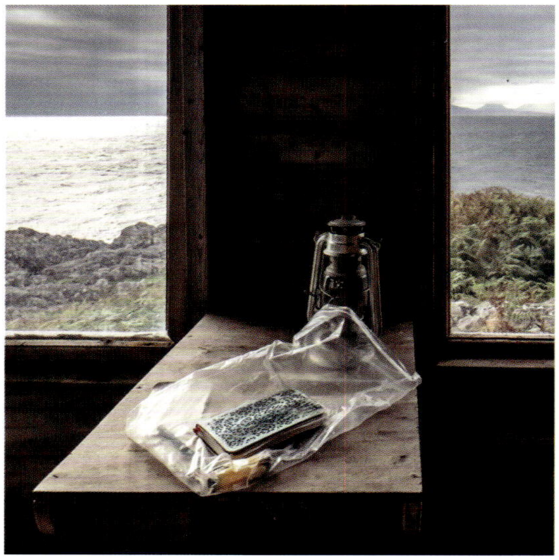

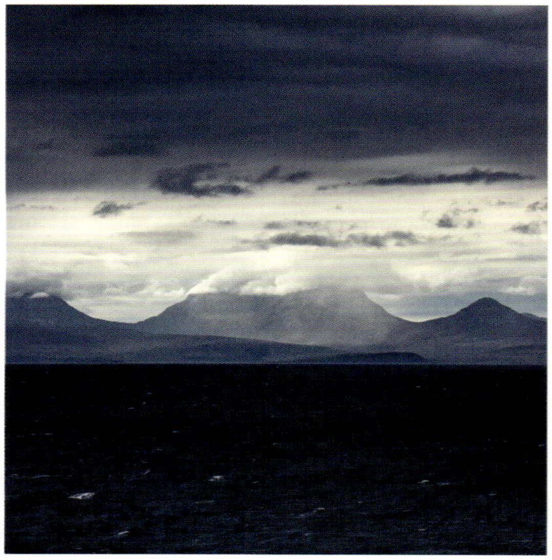

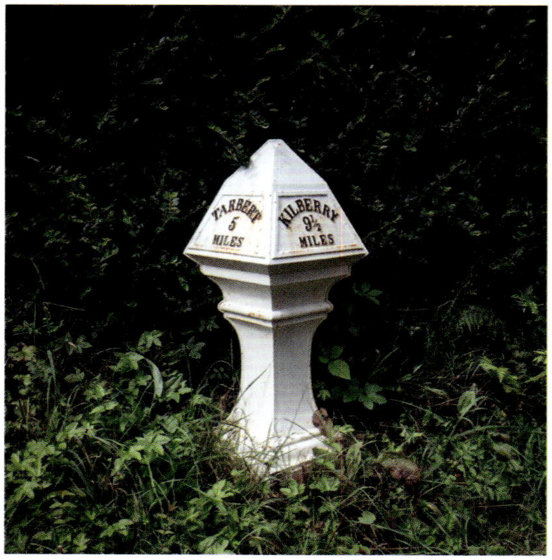

Previous, from left to right:

Rathlin Island, part of Northern Ireland, from the Mull of Kintyre

Squall over the Sound of Gigha, Kintyre

From top left:

Entrance to St Columba's Cave. The cave is thought to have been used around 563 by the saint who is credited with spreading Christianity in what is now Scotland

Lichen at Uamh Niall Cave, Ardminish

From centre left:

Draped: Corran, West Loch Tarbert, Kintyre

Bothy at Ardpatrick Point

From bottom left:

The Paps of Jura from Ardpatrick Point

Milepost, West Loch Tarbert

Opposite, from top left:

Alex, on his last day of holiday, Ormsary

Carse Neolithic Standing Stones East, Loch Stornoway

From bottom left:

Like walking in a row of upturned axe heads, an exceptionally unpleasant surface underfoot on a pathless stretch north from Ardpatrick Point

Bothy at Ardpatrick Point

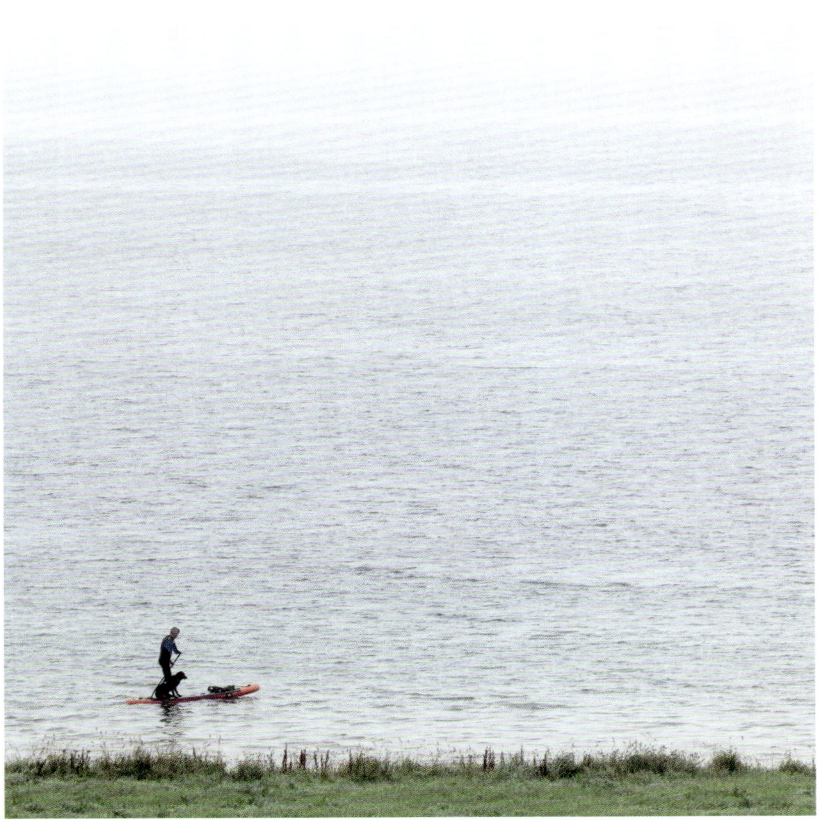

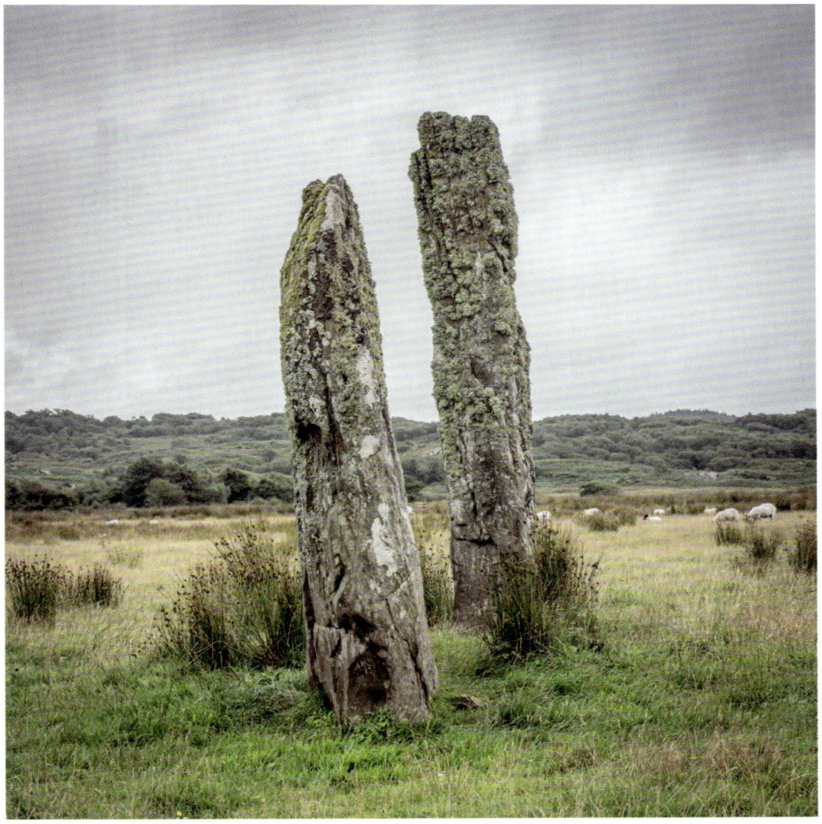

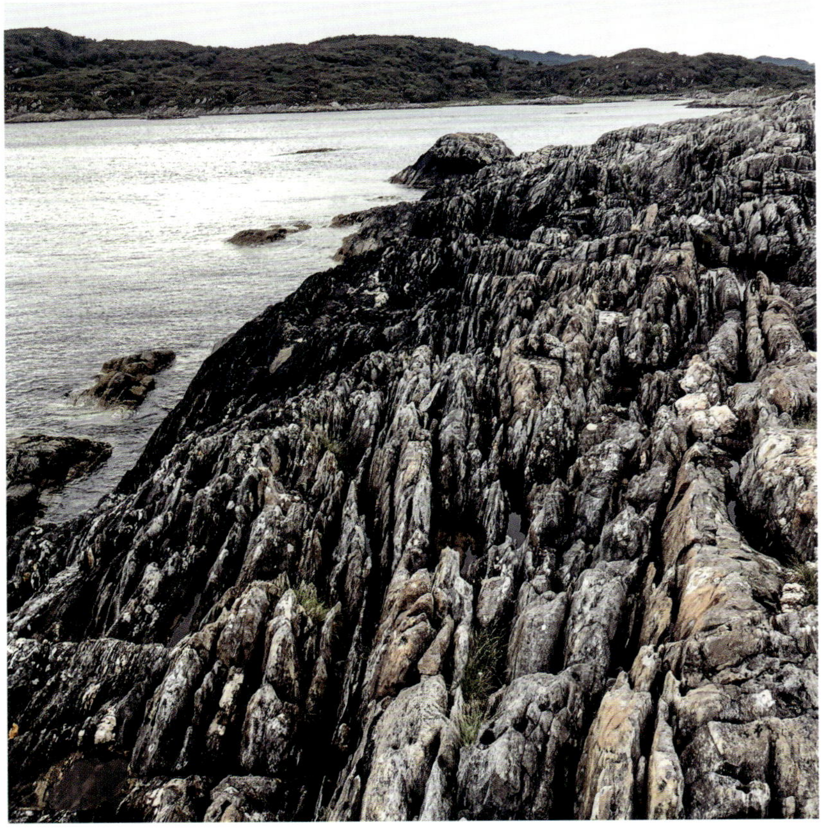

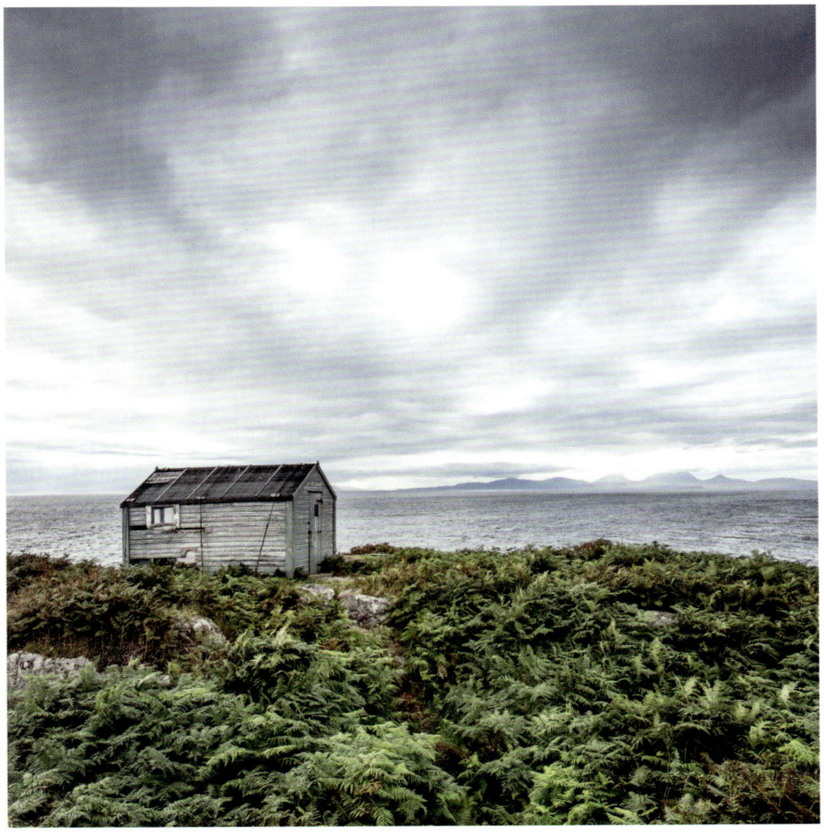

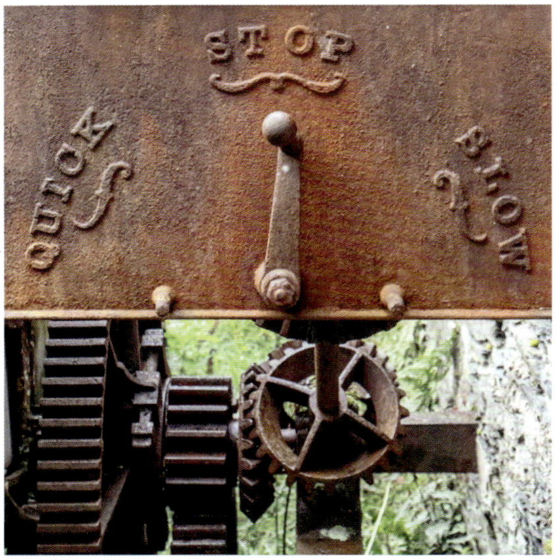

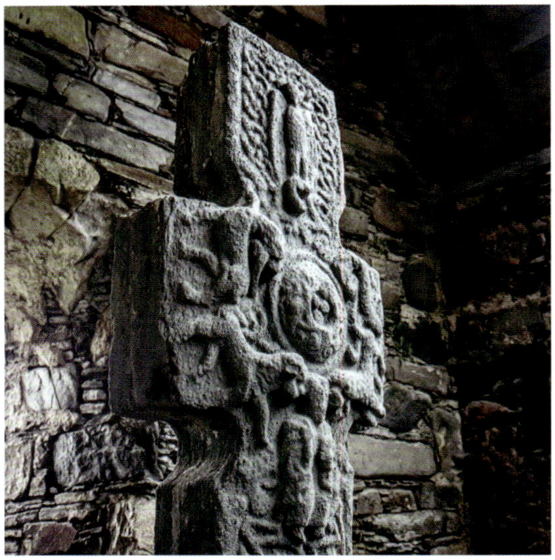

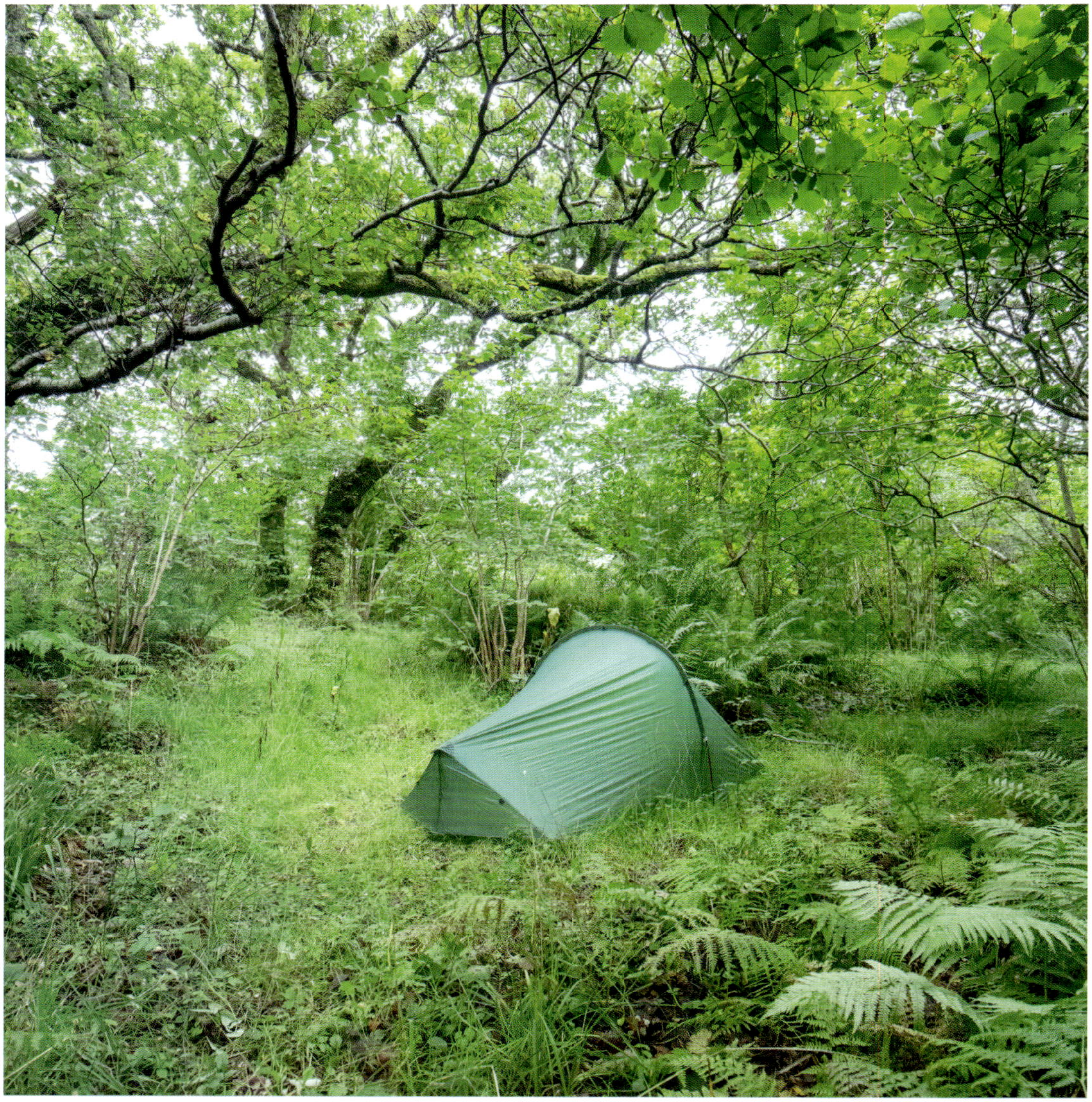

From top left:

Barnashaig farmstead, Tayvallich Peninsula

Keills Chapel Cross, dating from the late eighth century

Camp in a magical glade near Mefort

Opposite, clockwise from top left:

Loch Coille-Bharr

The largest rosette on Ormaig East Rock. Part of the 4,000-year-old Ormaig cup and ring marks on the west slope of Creag Mhor overlooking Loch Craignish. Their purpose and meaning remain unknown

Creagach Crosgach, Bagh Ban

Bridge to a small island from Craignish Castle

Medieval grave slab, Keills Chapel

Duntrune Castle in rain

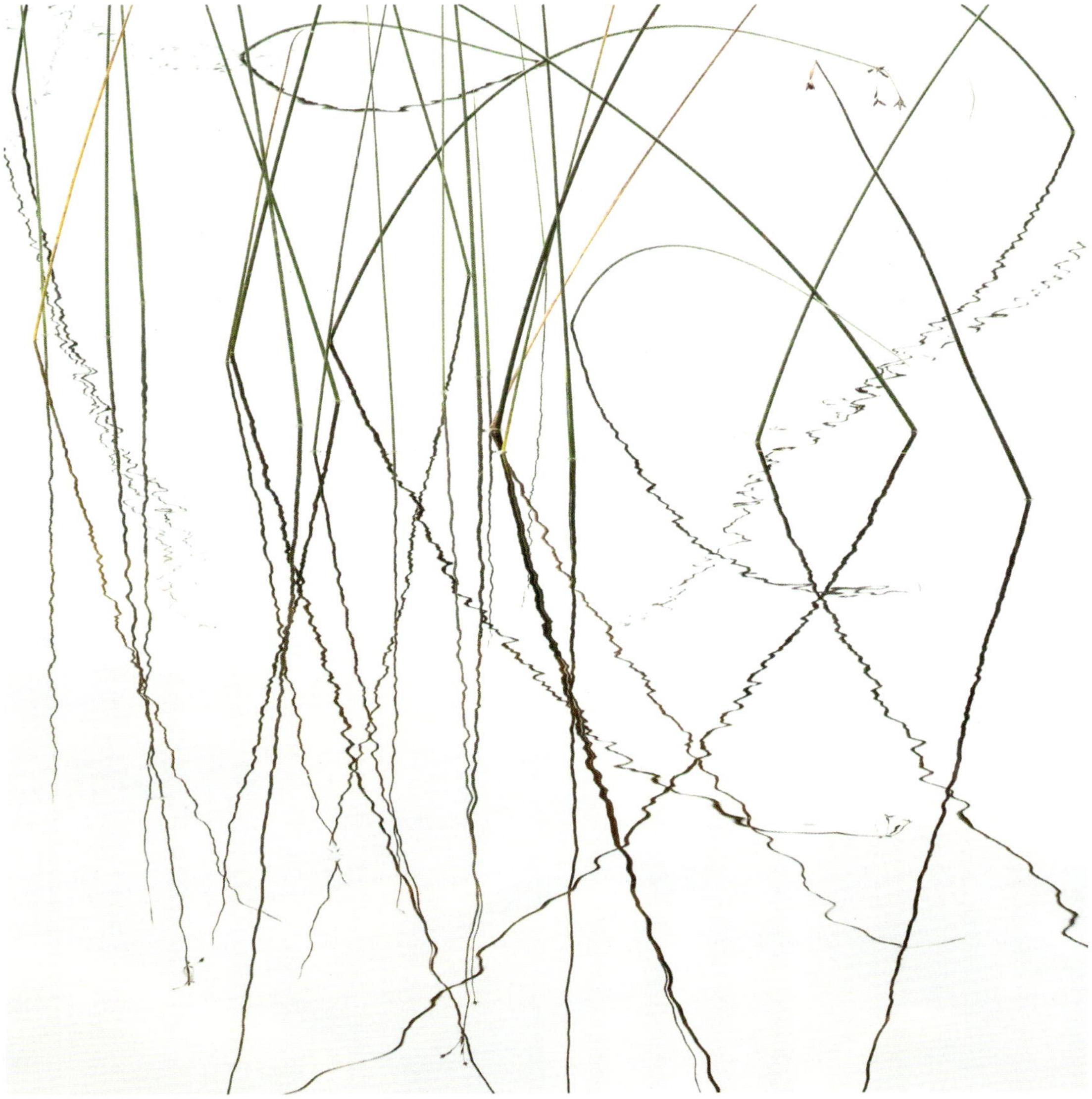
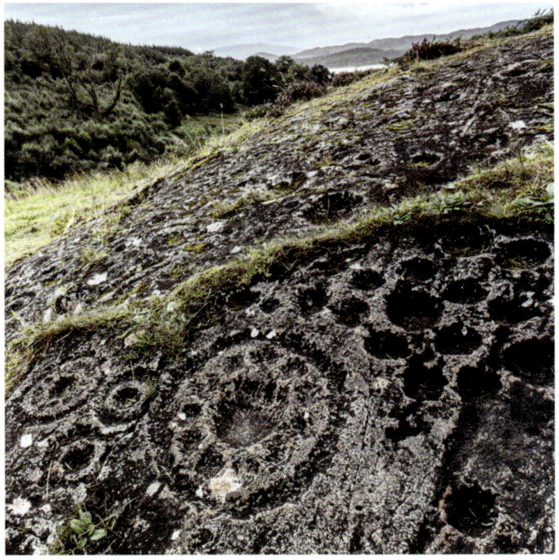

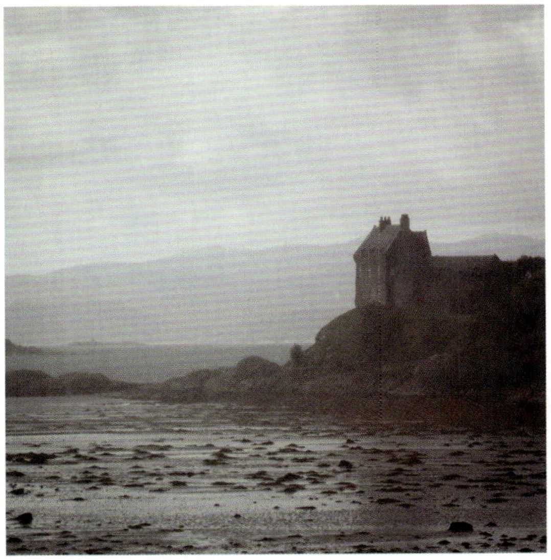
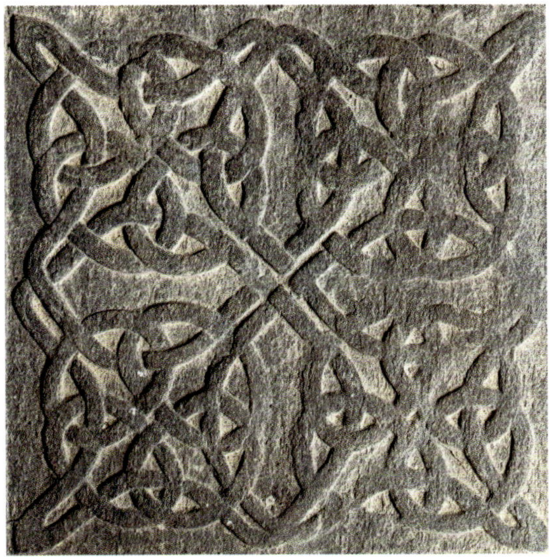
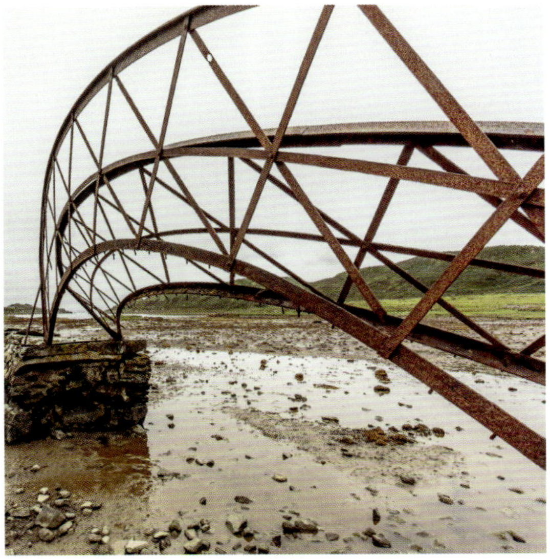

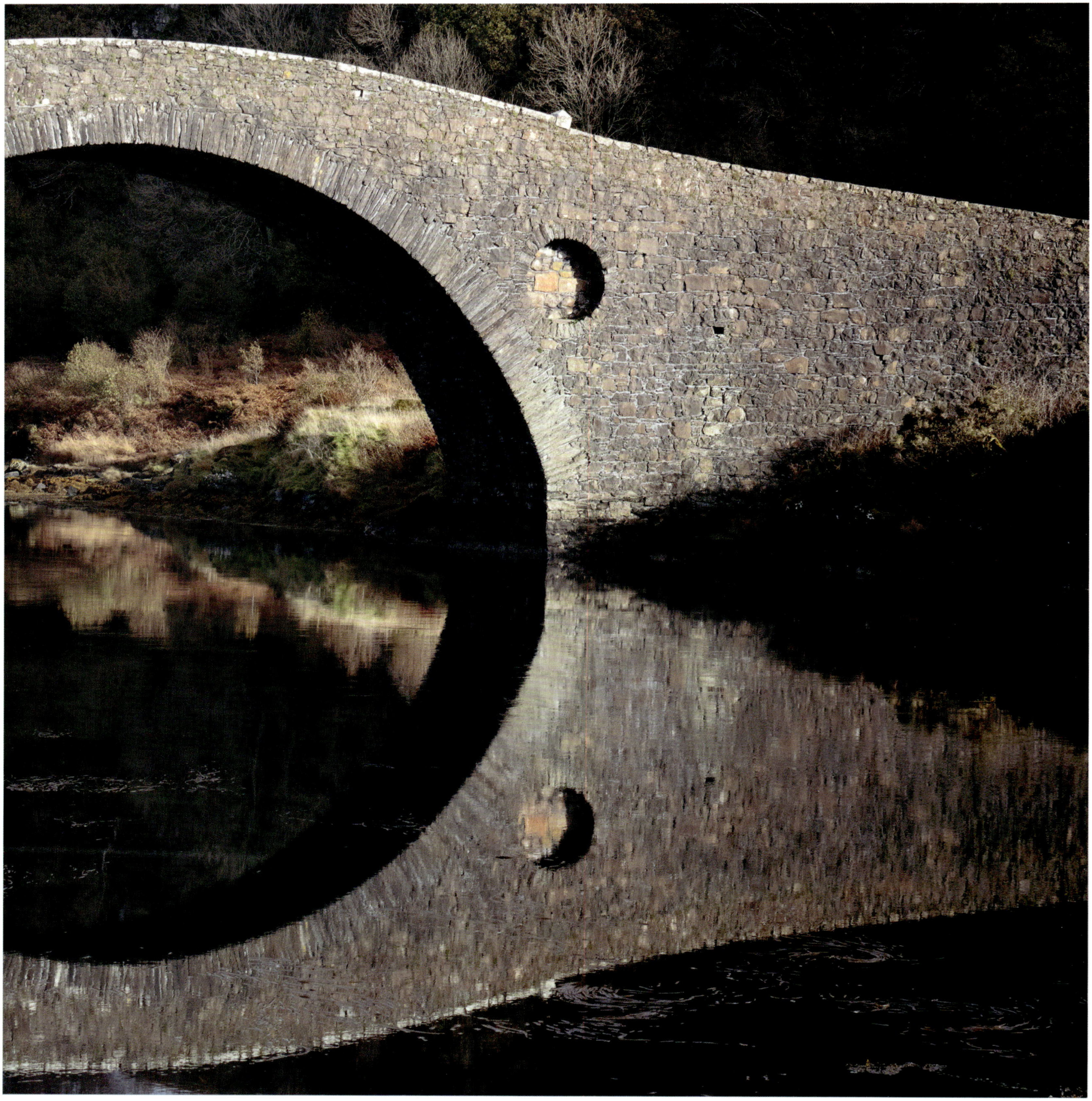

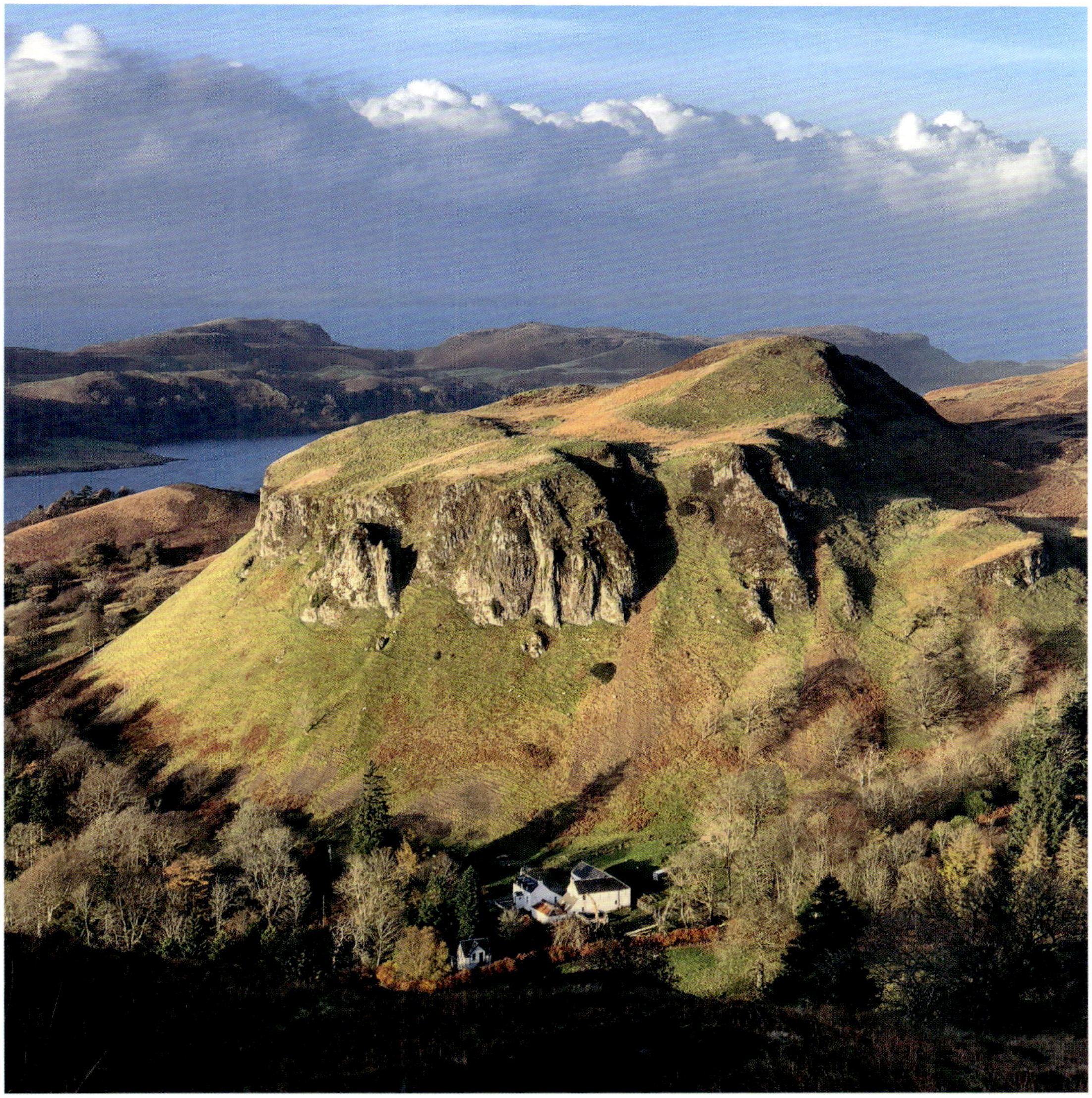

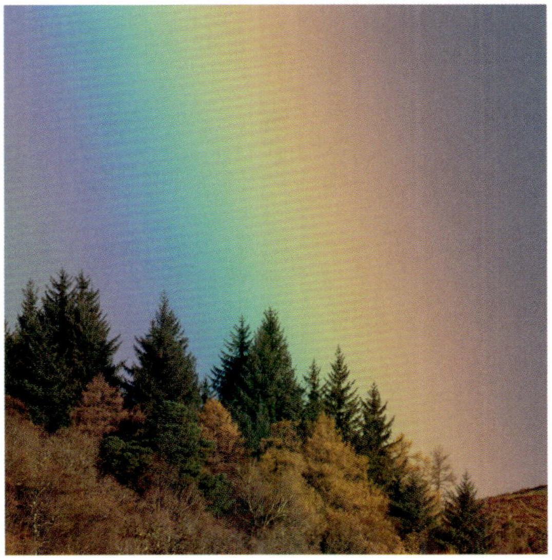

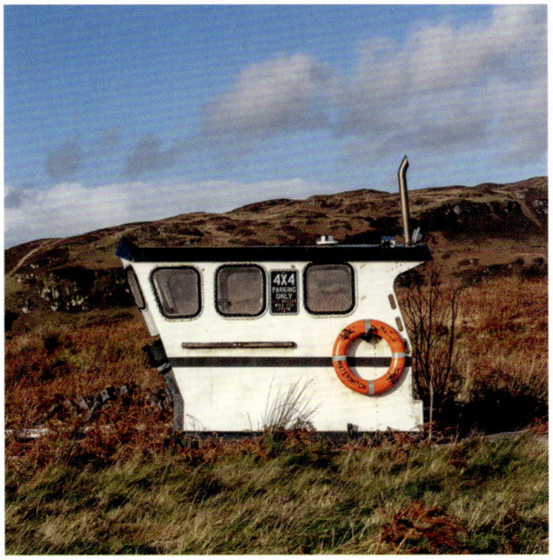

Opposite:

Clachan Bridge, which links the mainland to the island of Seil and is also known as the Bridge over the Atlantic

From top left:

Dun Ormidale, an Iron Age fort that occupies the whole of the sloping summit of the hill

Rainbow's end above Oban

The Wheelhouse at Ardentallen Point

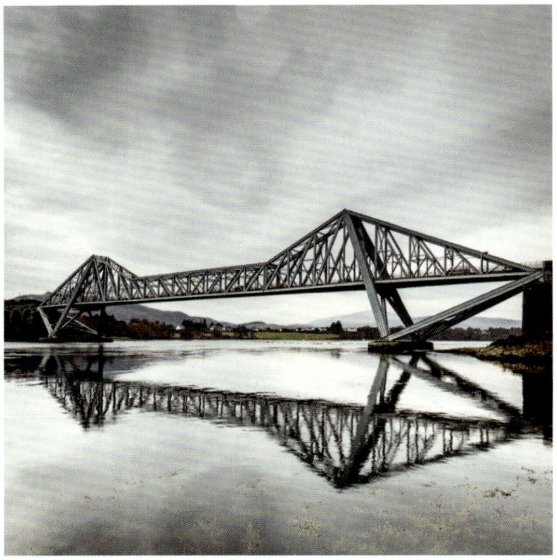
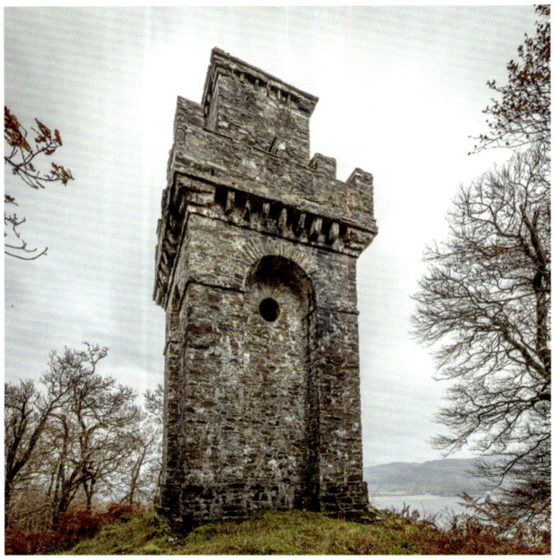
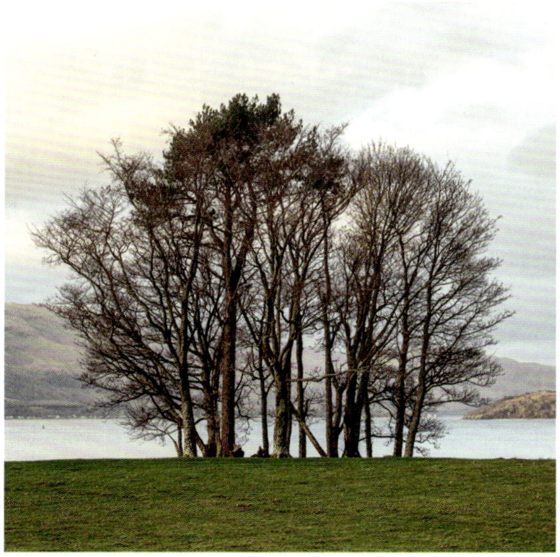
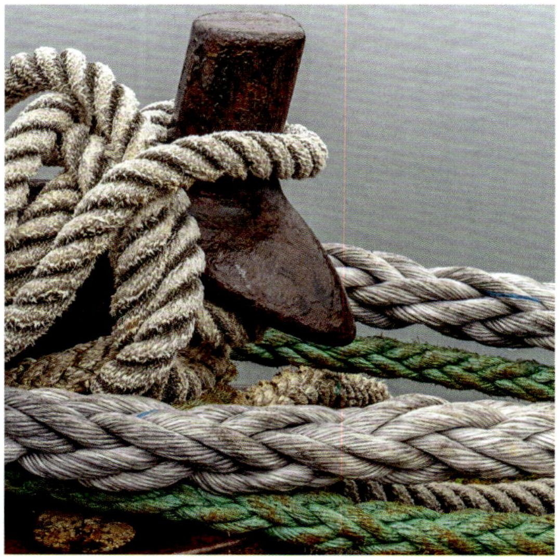
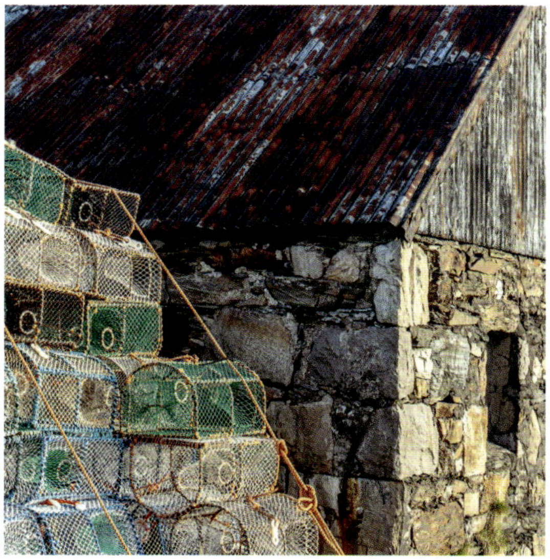
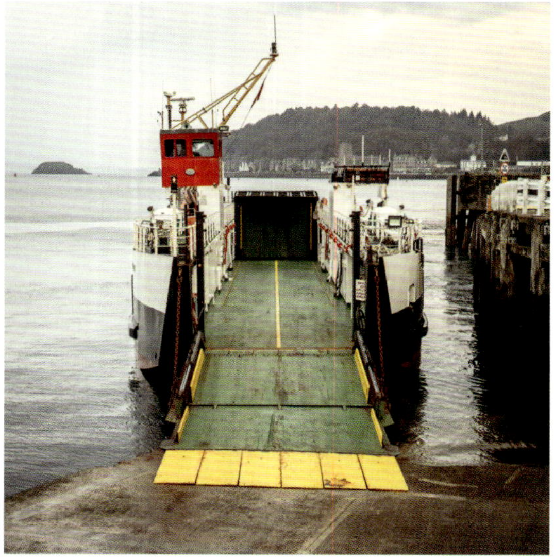

From top left:

Connel Bridge that spans Loch Etive, designed by John Wolfe Barry in 1903

Lady Margaret's Tower, an observatory built in 1754, Lochnell House

From centre left:

Copse, Crom-Roinn by Loch Linnhe

Oban Quay

From bottom left:

Fishing hut, North Cuil

Lismore ferry, Oban

Opposite:

Sgorr Dhonuill, a Munro just south of Ballachulish

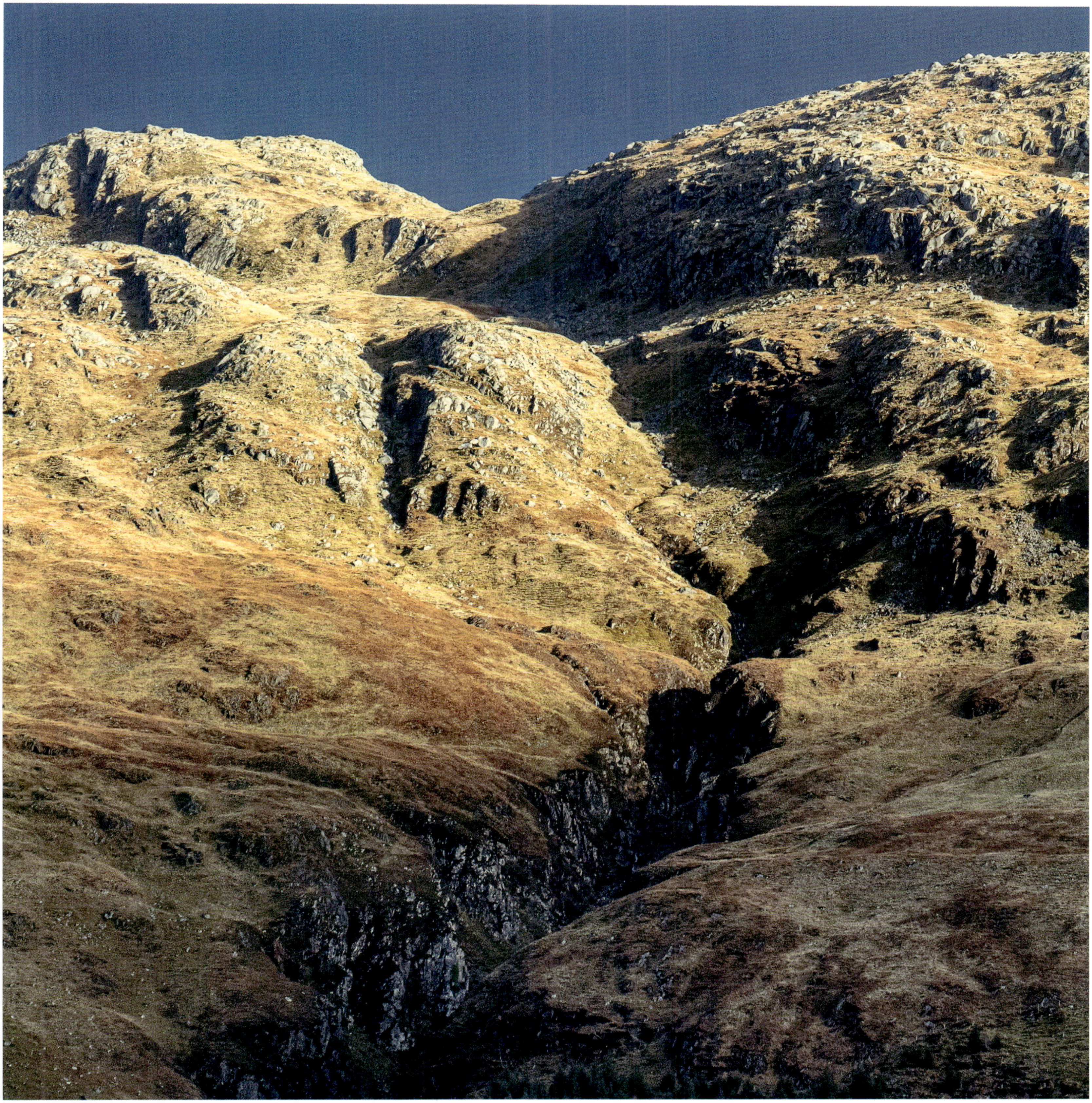

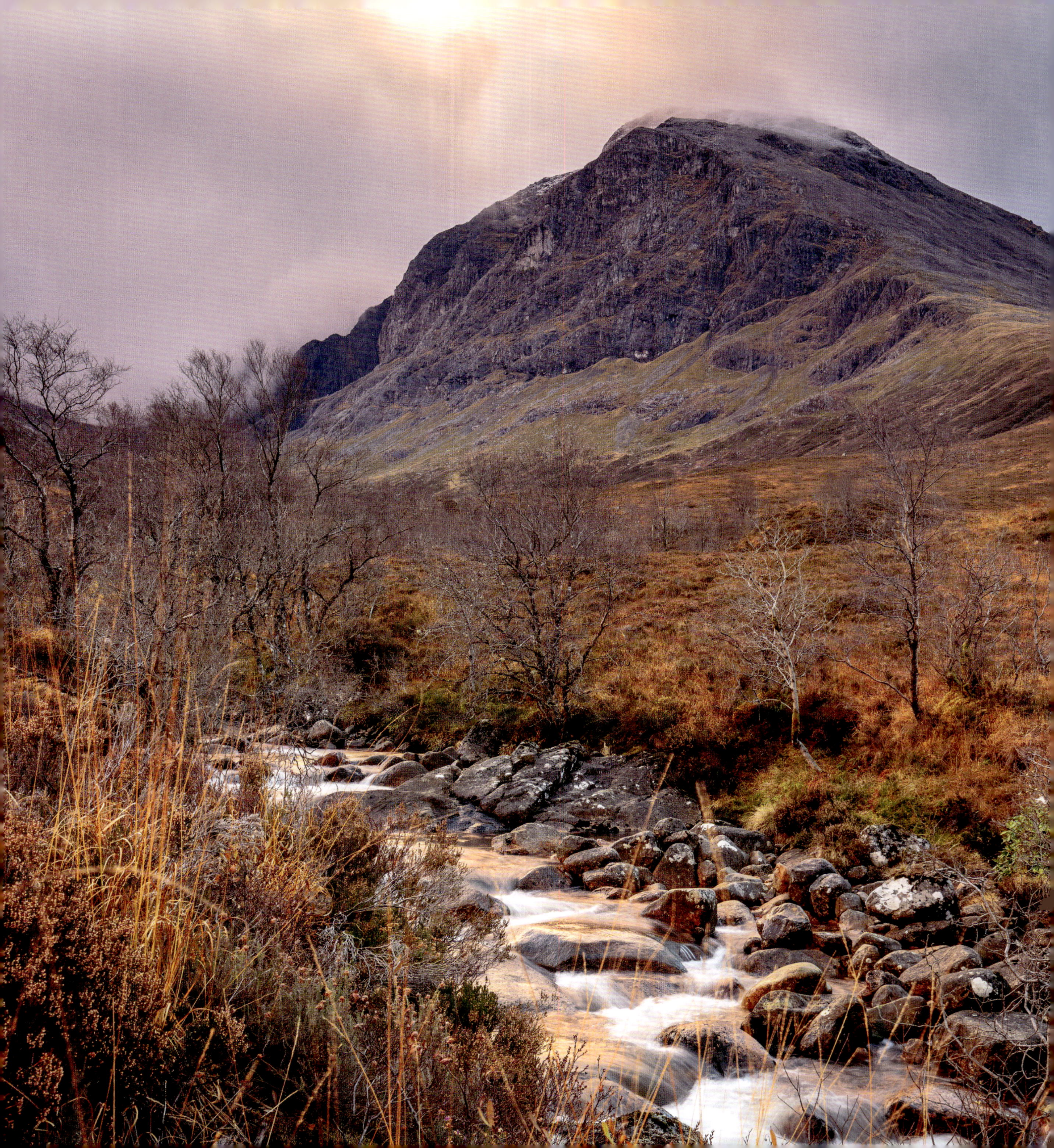

26 SOUTH INVERNESS-SHIRE

NOVEMBER 2018

DAY 245–246 | 06,282–06,324 KM | 42 KM

The A82 from Onich to Fort William is a particularly nasty bit of road for a pedestrian to follow as it is cut into the cliff without a walkway or hard shoulder, leaving few spots of refuge. I wear a hi-vis hat and panel across my pack for stretches like this, but the concentration required to dodge cars for hours makes walking extremely tiring. When I finally reach a pavement at Fort William, I head to my digs, where my room has a magnificent view of a wheelie bin. I share my good fortune by posting a photo on Twitter. 'Ah, the famed Bin Nevis' is the first comment.

The next morning, I plan to conclude the trilogy of walking to the summit of the highest mountains of England, Wales and Scotland as a loop from the sea in a single day. The stars are bright overhead as I leave the kebab-strewn streets of Fort William at 5 a.m. My head torch guides me past a steaming distillery, through a golf course into a knotted birch wood and out on to the open hill. The higher I climb, the more ferocious the wind becomes. At 500 metres up, I'm forced to take shelter behind a boulder to admire the clear views across the mountains.

As I approach Carn Mor Dearg Arête, the ground is covered in snow and mist swirls around Castle Ridge menacingly. I spot a group of ptarmigan, a plump gamebird that breeds in the highest mountains of the Highlands, well camouflaged with their winter white plumage, except for their distinctive red arc above the eye. The snow cover is extensive but grippy. Foolishly, I don't have an ice axe or crampons, so I double-check every step I take and follow a slow, careful route at the side of the arête so that a slip can be controlled. The white-out conditions help me concentrate: hand, foot, hand, foot, hand, foot.

As I clamber over the jagged boulders towards the summit, the ice-covered ruins of the meteorological observatory emerge from the whiteness. The summit of Ben Nevis is other-worldly at the best of times, but the colourless surroundings accentuate the strangeness. The absence of a view comes as no surprise as, at 1,345 metres high, the summit is allegedly clear only once every ten days.

I've been out for ten hours now and haven't seen a soul, but as I approach the raised refuge near the summit cairn, two Polish men are inside and gesture for me to enter as the wind is too strong to talk. They shuffle along to make space for me and we enthusiastically compare notes on how we came up. I discover they've just climbed the Ledge Route, a classic summer scramble and Grade II winter climb, and their rope sits between them. Although I'm warmed by the shelter and the conversation, I decline their offer of whisky, feeling I need all of my faculties for the descent.

As I make my way down, I'm grateful for the cairns along the tourist track. The summit is a featureless plateau, but the path down to Fort William dog-legs around a treacherous cliff called Gardyloo Gully which is difficult to see when cornices form in winter. Earlier that morning, I'd made a sketch map of the summit, with the bearings and distances needed to descend from the top, and I refer to it frequently, needing the extra reassurance that I'm heading the right way. Dropping out of the monochrome world of the summit, the snow line ends abruptly, the wind softens, and the temperature rises. I exhale. The rich autumnal colours of the surrounding glens and mountains return. Soon, I spot the faraway lights of Glen Nevis sparkling in the darkness.

The loop is complete after fifteen hours in motion, and I'm back to Fort William. When I review the photos from the day, it looks like I've taken a week's worth of images comprising two distinct outings – one in autumn and one in winter.

Opposite:

8.03 a.m.: Allt a'Mhuilinn and the north face of Ben Nevis

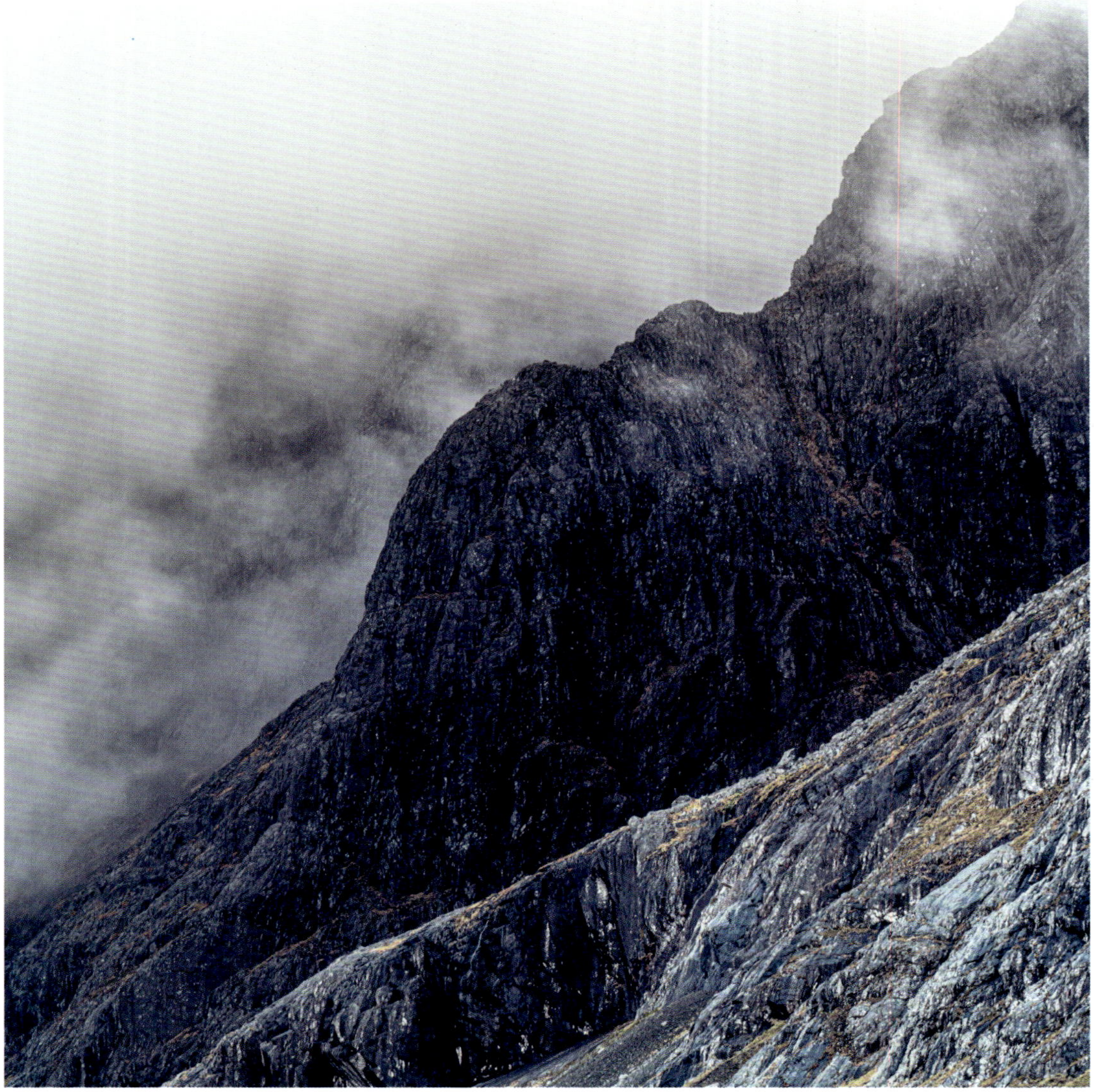

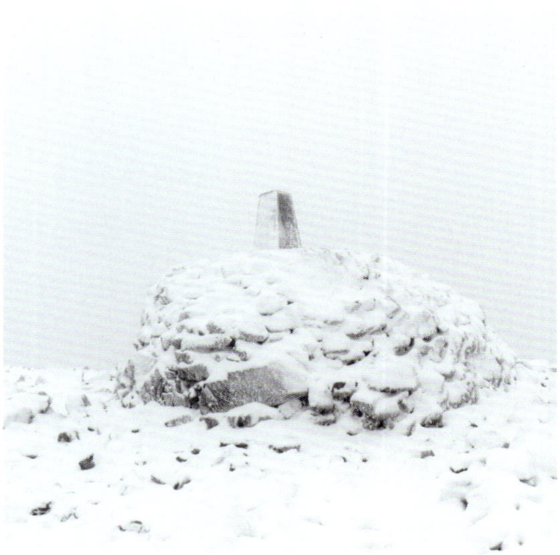

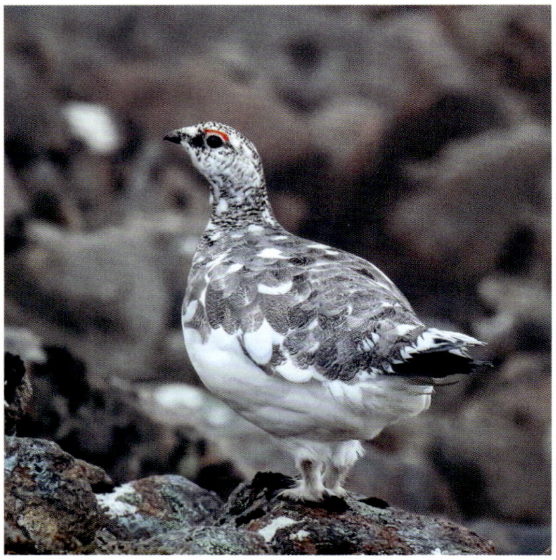

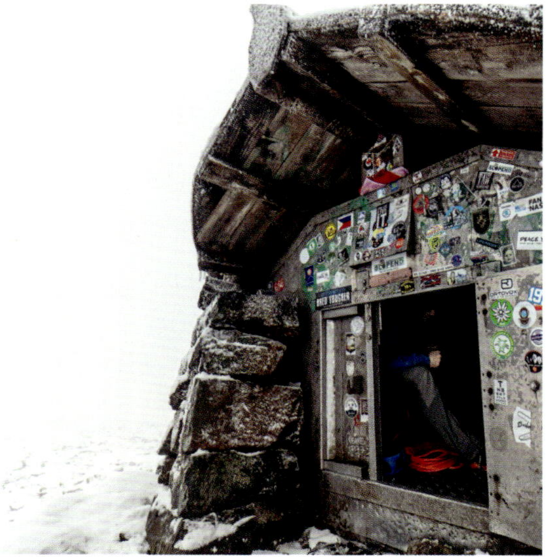

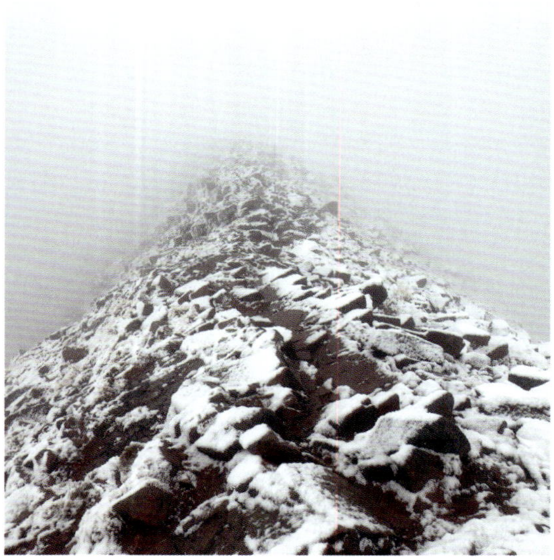

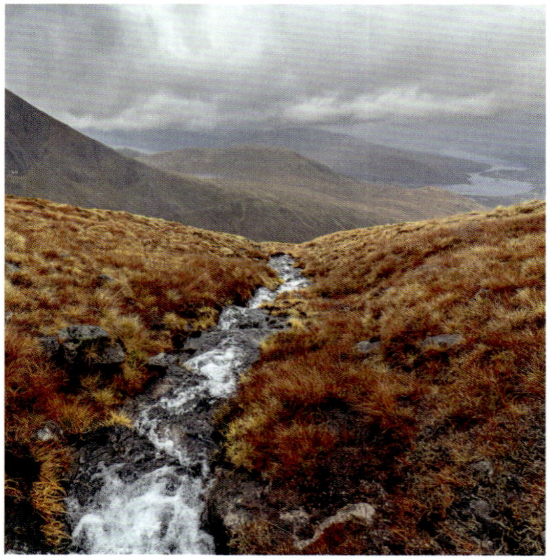

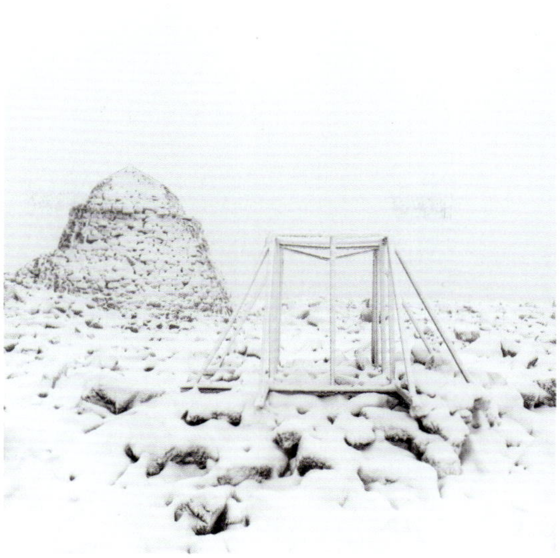

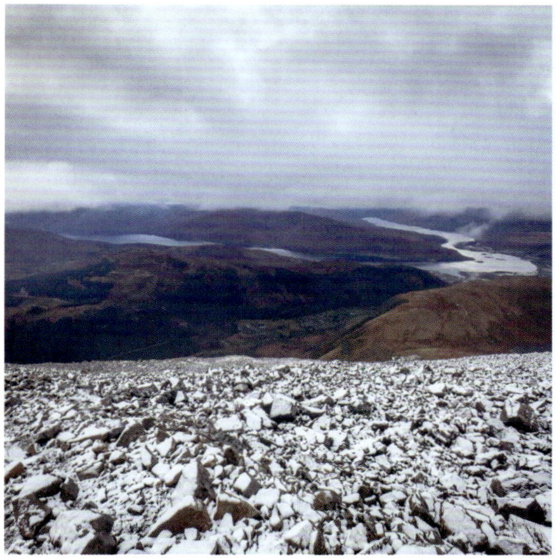

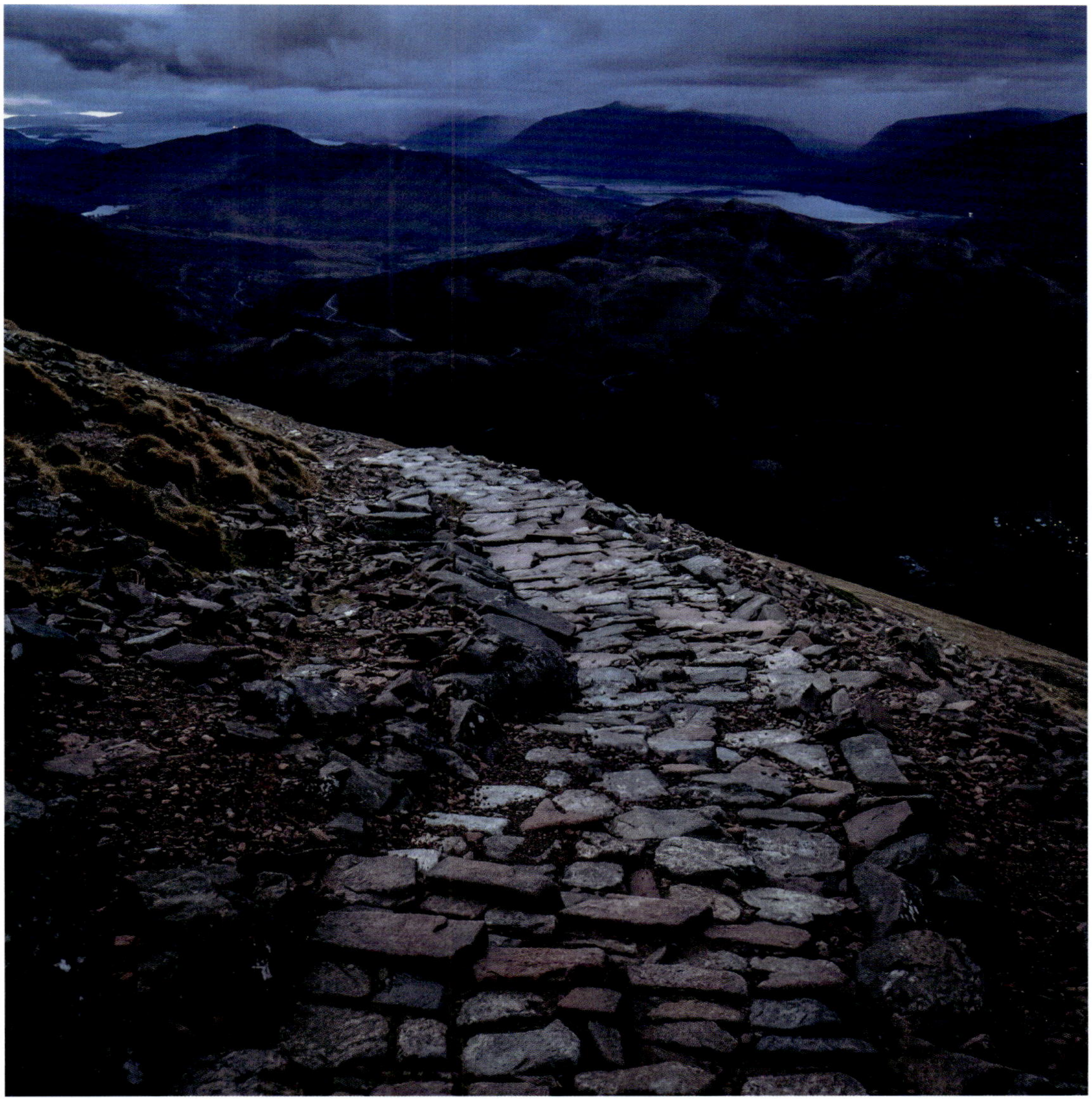

Opposite, clockwise from top left:

8.20 a.m.: Tower Ridge, Ben Nevis

2.34 p.m.: Ben Nevis summit trig point at 1,345 metres

11.06 a.m.: ptarmigan, Carn Dearg Meadhonach

10.17 a.m.: burn, Carn Beag Dearg

12.15 p.m.: Carn Mor Dearg Arête

3.27 p.m.: summit refuge, Ben Nevis

From top left:

2.33 p.m.: meteorological instrument frame with summit refuge. For twenty-one years from 1883, scientists worked and lived on the summit of Ben Nevis at a purpose-built observatory recording weather conditions

4.12 p.m.: Glen Nevis from the snow line on Ben Nevis

4.50 p.m.: last light above Glen Nevis, Ben Nevis

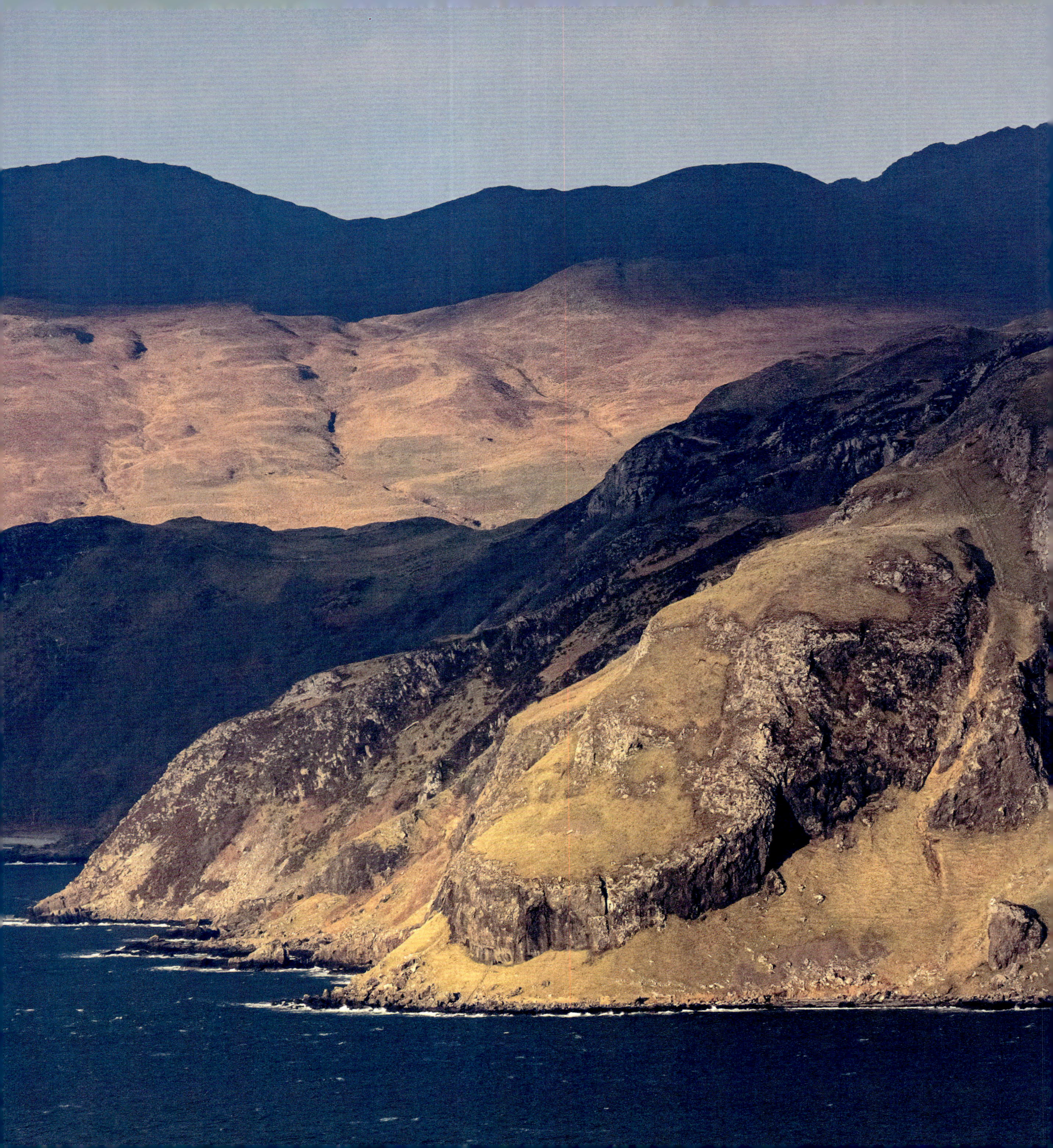

27 NORTH ARGYLLSHIRE

NOVEMBER 2018–JANUARY 2019
DAY 247–262 | 06,324–06,630KM | 306KM

Opposite:

Maclean's Nose, Ardnamurchan

I just found myself talking to a goat. The descent into madness begins. But to be fair, I am walking into Ardgour, which is from the Gaelic for 'height of the goats', so maybe it's OK. Today is the first time I'm carrying over 20 kilograms on this journey, twice what I needed for the south coast of England in summer. The extra weight comes from winter gear and food, and one of the latest additions is a morale-boosting string of Christmas lights for the tent. As I walk along the shore of Loch Linnhe, with mountains rising steeply at my side, I look up to see a pair of white-tailed eagles with wings like barn doors flapping close overhead. I've never seen this bird before, rare as they are, and I'm amazed to see these two close enough to spot that one is carrying a bloodied fish in its talons.

It takes three days of walking for the mountains to swallow me whole as I push on towards the Morvern and Ardnamurchan Peninsulas. The sparse population and difficulty of the pathless terrain in winter mean there's no easy way out once I've started, so I prepare myself to be self-sufficient for the next five days. The consequences of getting lost are severe, so in another first, I carry a paper map as a backup to my digital version.

Beyond Ardgour, the coastline gets wilder and steeper. Only the occasional ruined croft hints at human intervention and the mountains hide a secret: Glensanda super-quarry, the largest granite quarry in Europe, where I'm forced to ask for permission to walk through the complex. The site, surrounded by mountains, is only accessible by sea, so it's like a world of its own. It includes a processing plant, an aircraft landing strip, a coastal deep-water berth on Loch Linnhe, and a harbour that receives a ferry from Port Appin, bringing workers to the quarry. Coastal hikers are usually driven through the site for safety reasons, but when I explain that I'm trying to walk the entire coastline of Britain, I'm given a set of hi-vis overalls and a helmet and am escorted past towering piles of aggregate and an enormous shiploader, a building-sized conveyor structure that can be rotated into place when needed. 'We're a big employer in these parts. It's either the fish farms or here if you don't work for the council,' one of the men tells me. They give me two bags of food and take a picture of me for their newsletter. I leave with big smiles all around to head up into the open hills towards Leacraithnaich Bothy. There's nobody in when I arrive, so I light a candle to cook dinner as the wind rages outside. The wooden sleeping platform is hard and cold but drier than the tent.

The following day, I arrive at a B&B in Lochaline, where I'm happy to be reunited with my dehydrated food and fuel parcels for the next four days around the Morvern Peninsula. Walking in the winter with a heavy pack off-trail takes a lot of energy and I have to consume around 4,000 calories a day to keep myself going. The coast in Scotland is so sparsely populated that wild camping becomes my default shelter most nights, so I'm careful to buy and send ahead dehydrated backpacking food in bulk to pick up from hostels or B&Bs whenever I can. I settle in and hang up my wet camping kit to dry. In the corner of the room, my camera, torch and power bank battery lights flash reassuringly as they recharge.

A few days into Morvern, a car pulls up, revealing a friendly bearded face. 'Don't see many backpackers here; stop in at the next house over the hill, and I'll give you a cup of tea.' A few minutes later, I'm nursing a brew from a retired air-force pilot and indefatigable explorer of the local area, who unfolds a meticulously annotated map. The pilot gives me invaluable advice on the best route to take through the pathless regions. His straight-to-the-point military speech makes me feel like I'm being briefed for a mission. 'Walking around the coast here is much worse than up on the mountains, some very bad ground. You be careful.

There's no mountain rescue here,' he warns. I stand to leave, but am stopped in my tracks by his partner, who puts her fingers to her lips and beckons me to look out the window of their kitchen. Outside, a Scottish wildcat, extremely rare, stands a few metres away from us. I attach my 70-300mm as swiftly and silently as possible and capture a handful of frames before it darts away. Later, as we say our farewells, the pilot calls out, 'When you write your book, only mention Morvern in passing; we don't want too many people here!'

At Ardnamurchan, I encounter one of the remotest peninsulas in Britain with a fiendish topography. A high cliff halfway along the southern edge called Maclean's Nose makes any attempt to follow the coast here a climbing expedition. I discover the closest walkable route is skirting around the mountain of Ben Hiant by following a faint path a couple of kilometres inland. The goal is to reach the westernmost point of mainland Britain by New Year's Eve. The heavy rain cuts visibility most of the time on this peaty, mountainous terrain, but a lighthouse flashing in the distance keeps me feeling grounded. It's rocky and boggy everywhere, so I'm delighted when I find a patch of short, flat grass, like a putting green, next to a small bay with beautiful white sand on which to put up my tent.

I arrive in sun at Ardnamurchan Point on New Year's Day, where the wind blows into the foghorn with a continuous eerie low tone and I can see all the way out to the Isle of Rum. There's an uncharacteristically good path towards Sanna Bay from which I see the first people of the day, a group of friends screaming in turn while taking a rapid and cold New Year's Day swim before going back to their beach fire and bottles of beer. I walk away into the uninhabited north of the peninsula as the light starts to fade, and their bonfire turns into a flickering speck in the distance.

I stop for a break in the afternoon to photograph the sunset beyond Ardnamurchan Point Lighthouse. Winter photography has many challenges, with short daylight hours, poor weather and low light levels throughout the day. However, the landscape at this time of year has a unique look, with heavy skies, very long shadows and moody tones. Plus, it gets dark so early it's easy to stay up for astrophotography.

There's still enough light in the sky to appreciate that this leg is turning out to be the most thrilling part of the peninsula as I'm heading between the shore and the volcanic centre near Sanna Bay, where the curvature and scale of the remains of the 3-kilometre-wide caldera can be clearly seen. I share this part of the journey with a large herd of deer and a solitary golden eagle that flies right down the valley towards Fascadale.

At Port Eigin-aig, on my thirteenth day in the county, I camp by a trickling stream and wake to find my boots frozen solid. To prepare myself for the unexpected cold therapy, I make a steaming cup of coffee and try to recall the warmth from last night's beach fire. Once packed, I head east back to the mainland along tussocky headlands; the view out to sea is an ever-changing vista of rocky islets, a breathtaking sight that leads the eye towards the misty, mountainous islands of Skye and Eigg.

I celebrate surviving five days of wild camping around the Ardnamurchan Peninsula in a warm B&B in Acharacle, where everything in the room, including the bedspread, cushions, coasters and artwork, is decorated with a Highland cow.

Next morning, as I head into the Ardtoe Peninsula, a flock of black and white sheep run towards me and start trailing behind me on the road. 'I received a lot more followers today,' I tweet along with a photo of my entourage. At first, the company is amusing, then it becomes disconcerting. I'm relieved when finally, after this woolly posse has followed me for a couple of miles, they decide they've come far enough. Further down the road, I pass the Monster Midge of Ardtoe, a huge boulder with painted teeth as large as a dinosaur's and dripping with blood.

As I prepare dinner on my last evening in North Argyllshire I can't help but feel a sense of anticipation. Tomorrow, I'll embark on the next chapter of my walk, venturing into the Rough Bounds, a notoriously remote part of Scotland that culminates in the wilderness of Knoydart. This area, steeply mountainous and with some roads built as recently as 1966, was previously only accessible by foot or boat. I shake my head to free it from thoughts of the future as I boil water and set up the tripod to photograph Castle Tioram on the far side of Loch Moidart. Its mirrored reflection in the water, paired with the winter hues and textures, reminds me of a Rorschach ink-blot test, encouraging and yet defying comparison to other ideas.

Opposite, from top left:

Loch Eil watercolour

Mist above Loch Eil

From bottom left:

Golden symmetry: Loch Eil

Greylag geese with Garbh Bheinn, Loch Sunart

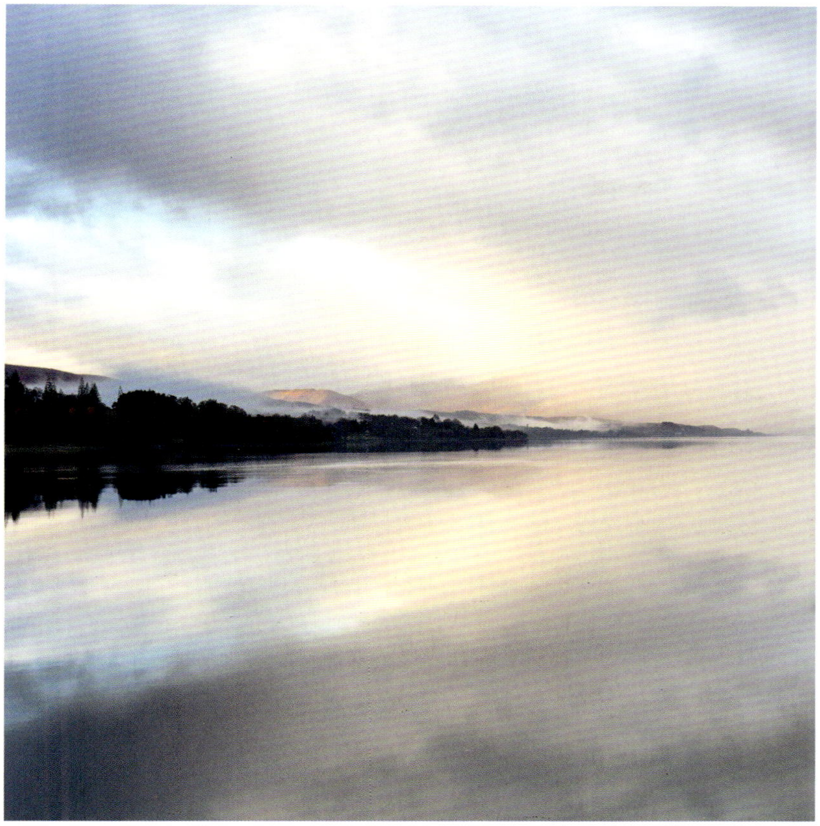

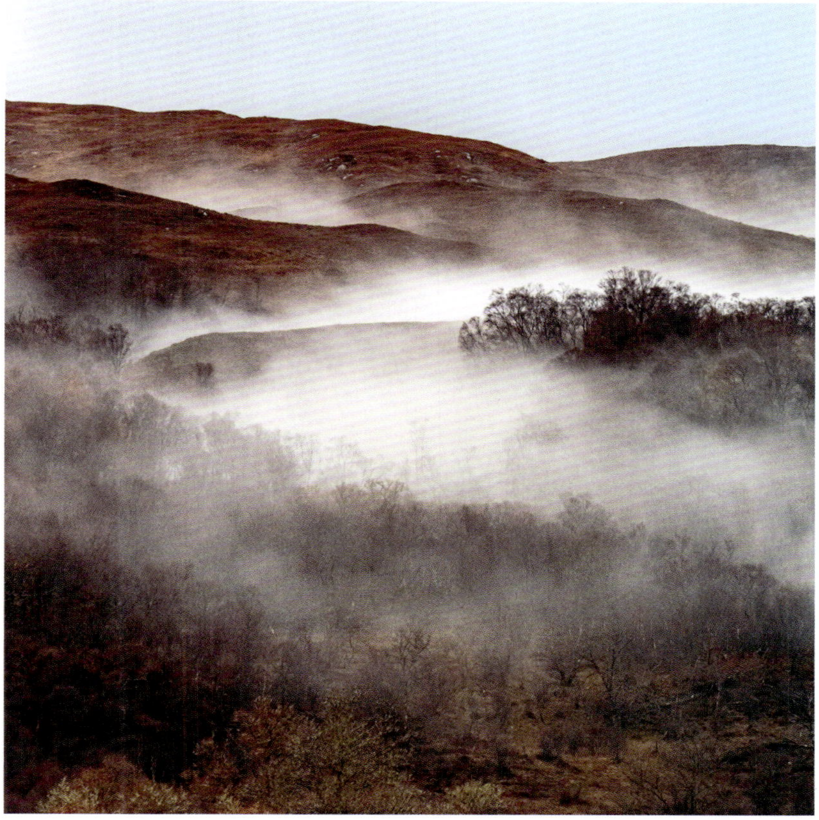

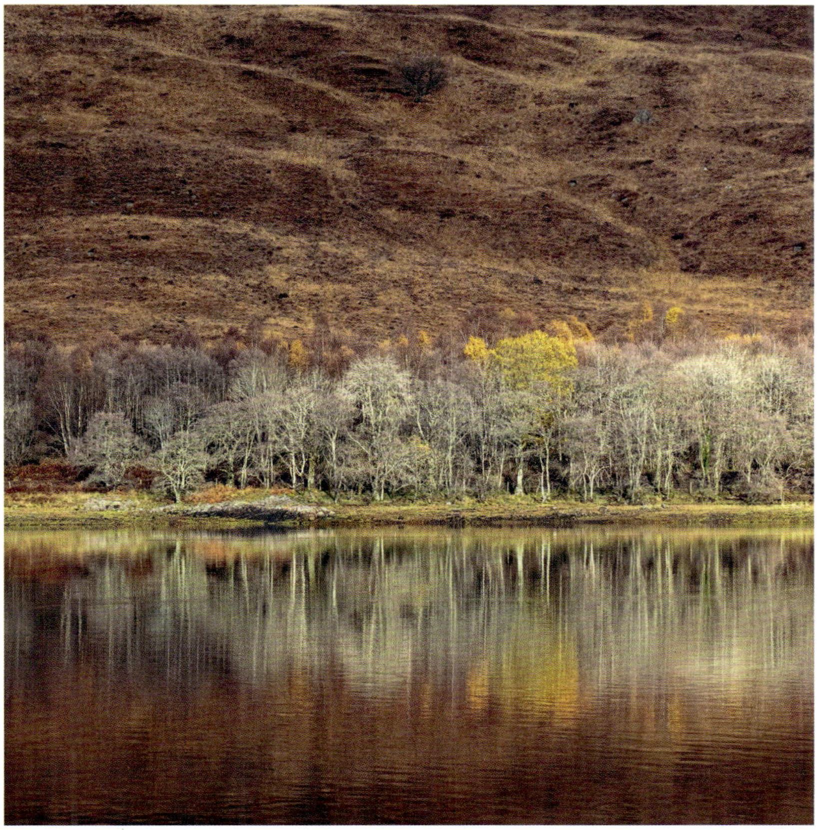

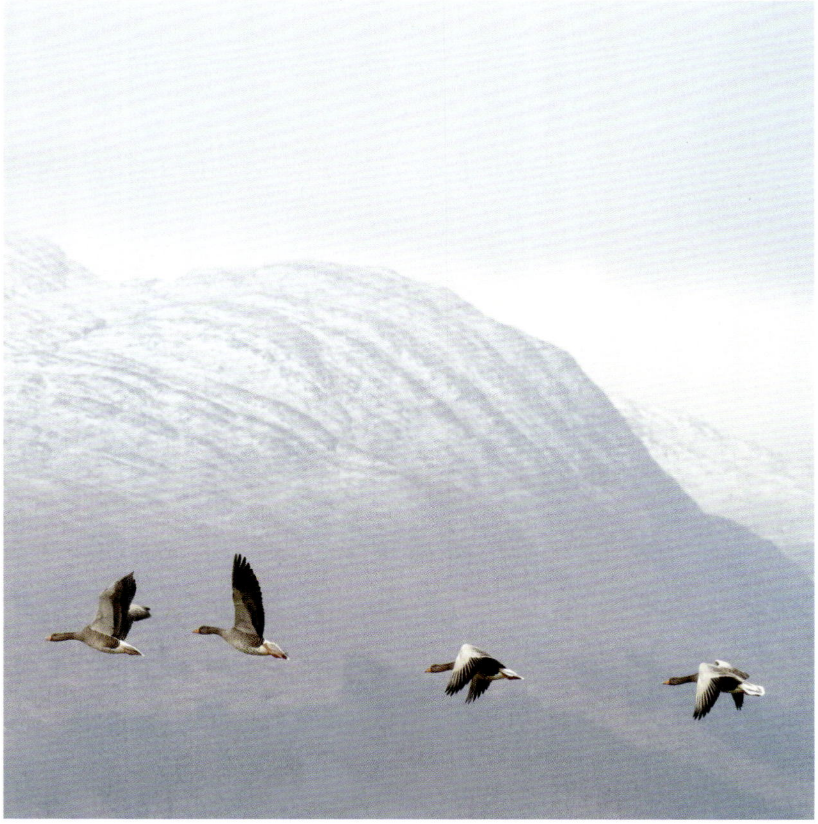

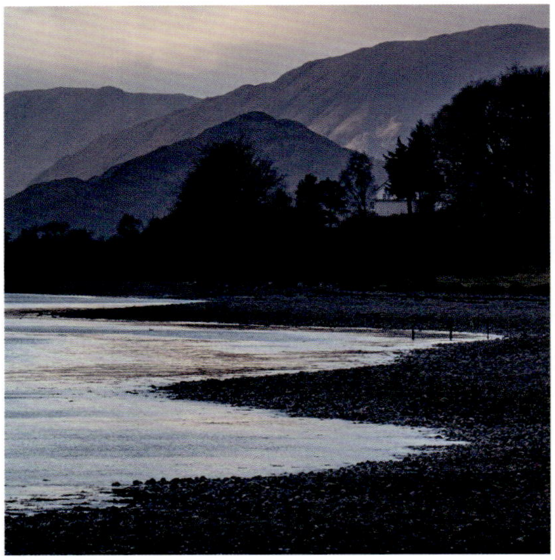

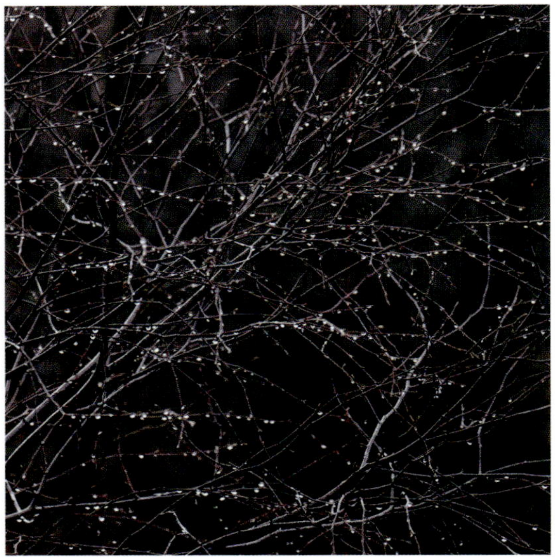

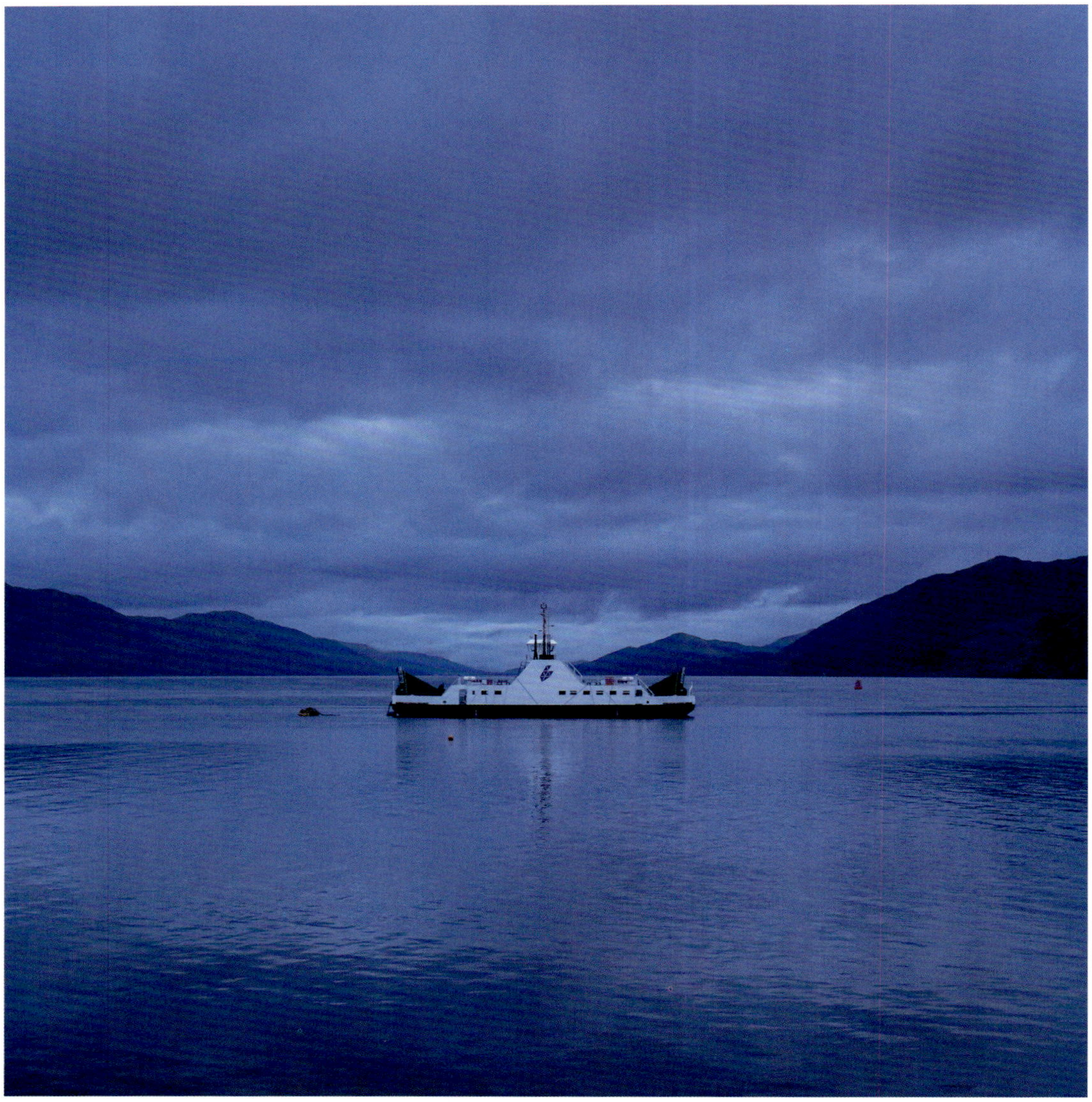

From top left:

Towards Kingairloch, Ardgour

Winter constellation by Loch Linnhe

Ferry at dusk, Corran

Opposite:

Coast road to Kingairloch

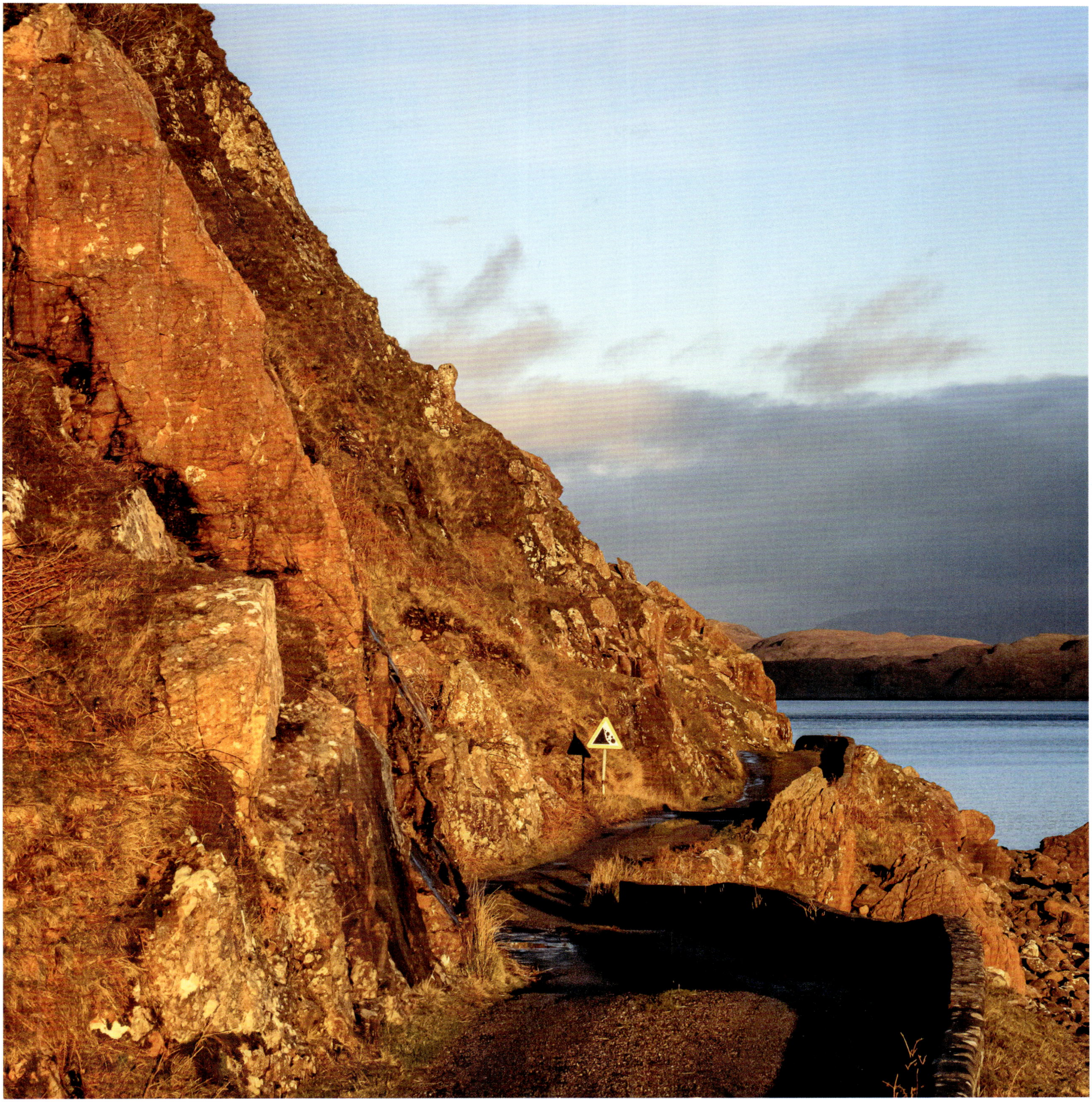

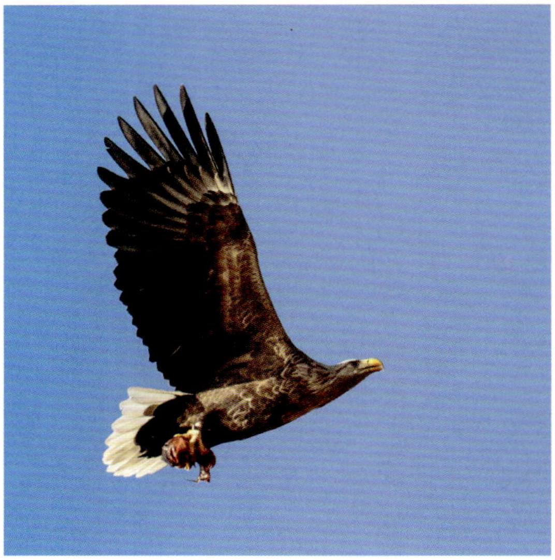

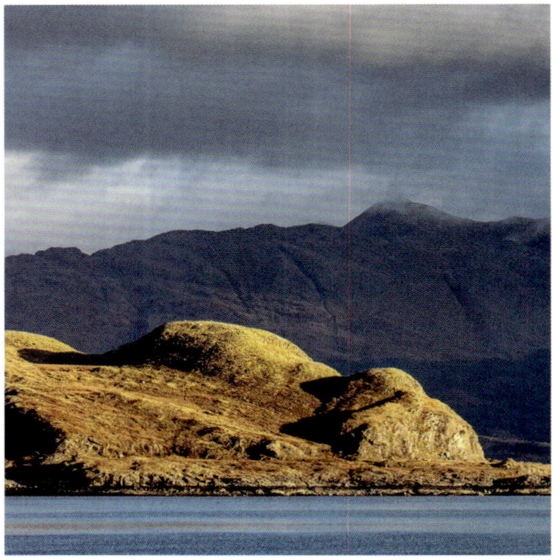

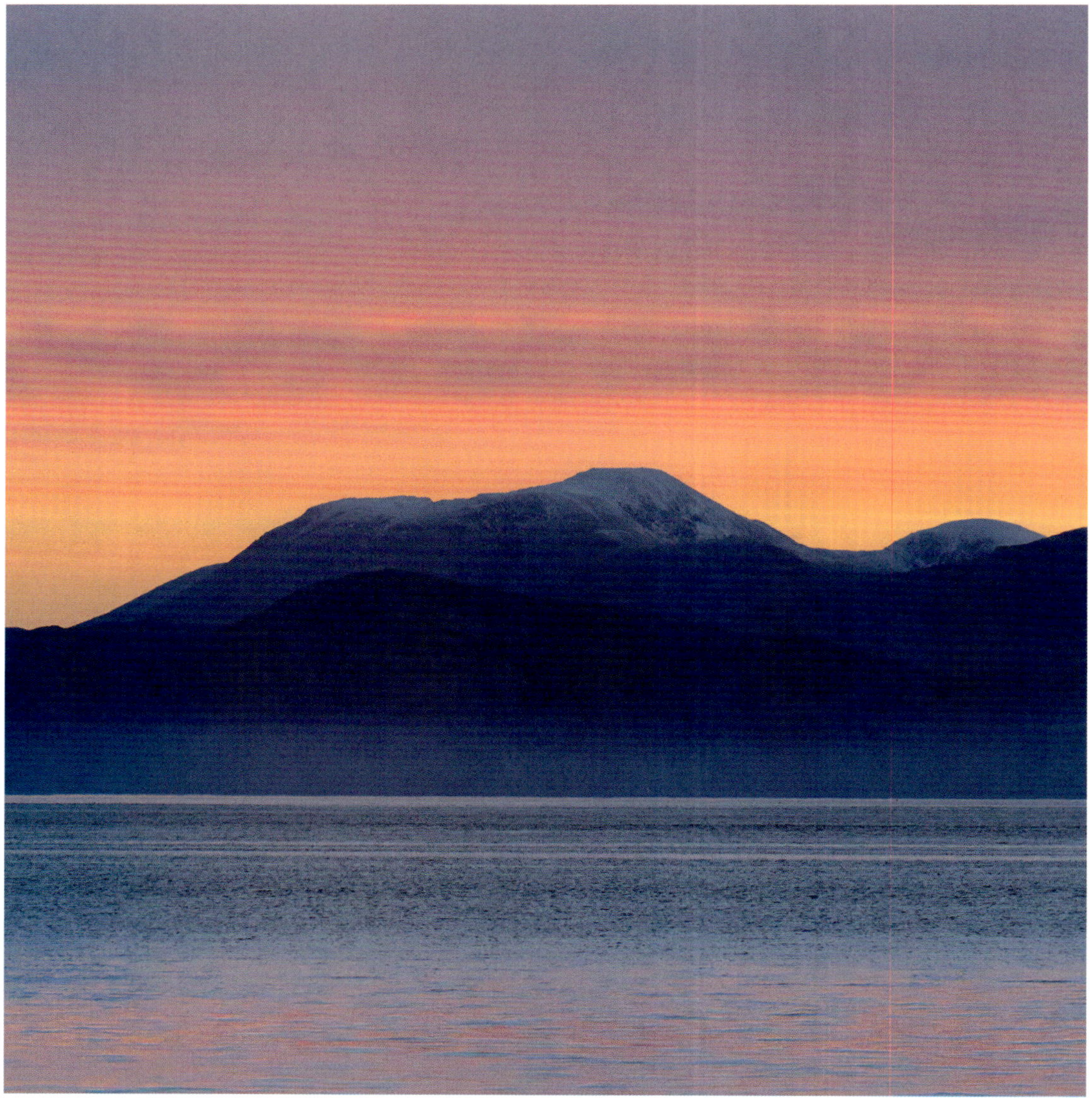

From top left:

The sea eagle (aka the white-tailed eagle) is the largest bird of prey in the UK, Kingairloch

Rubha na h-Earba and Mam na Gualainn beyond, Ardgour

Ben Nevis from Kingairloch

Opposite, clockwise from top left:

Provisions, Leacraithnaich Bothy, Ardtornish

Gather: Allt a Chaigin

Essentials, Leacraithnaich Bothy

Burn by Loch Aline

From Leacraithnaich Bothy

Morning light at Leacraithnaich Bothy

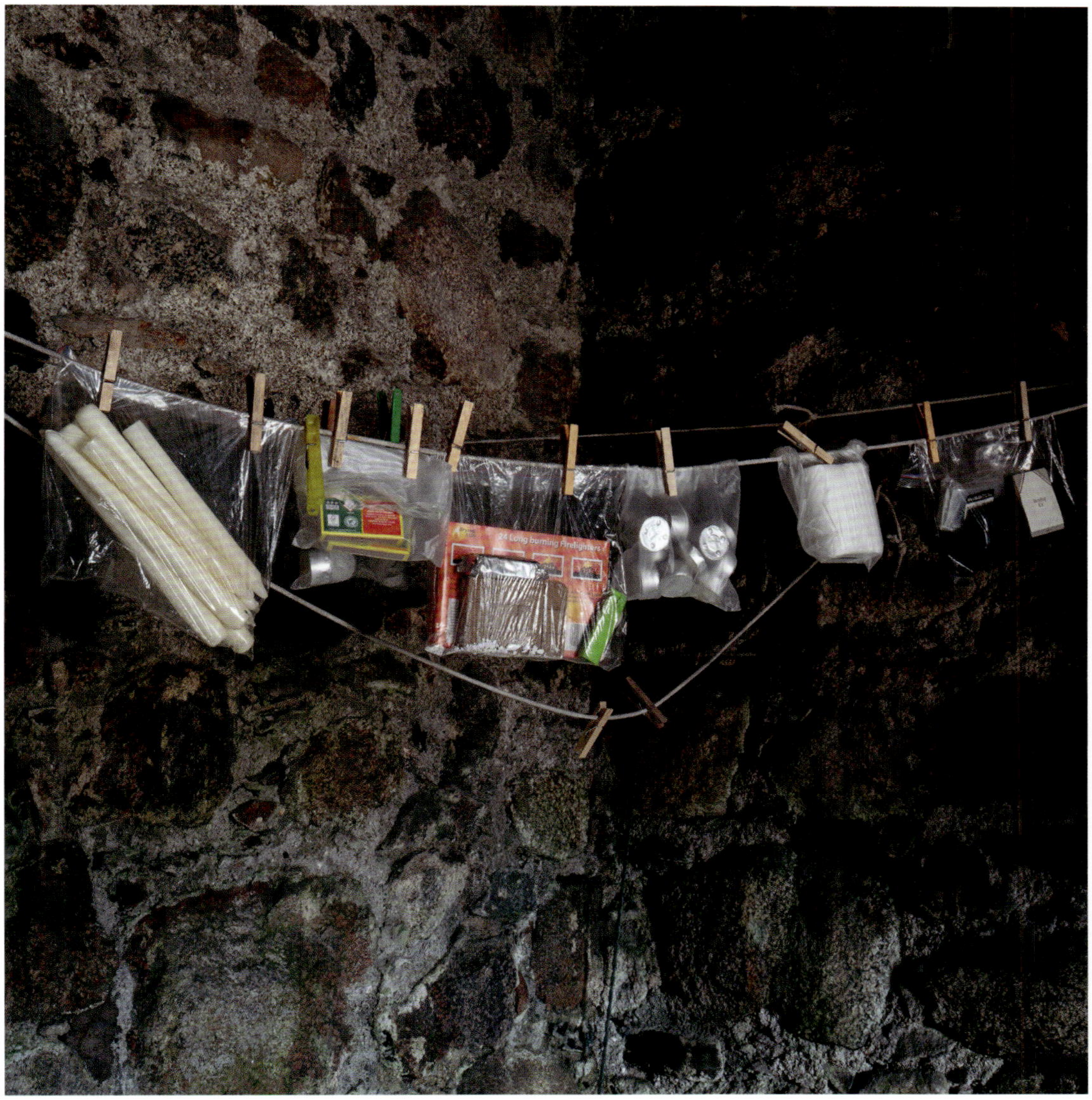

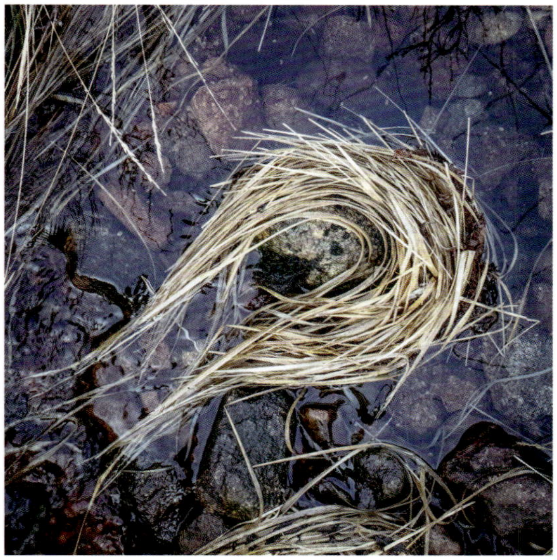

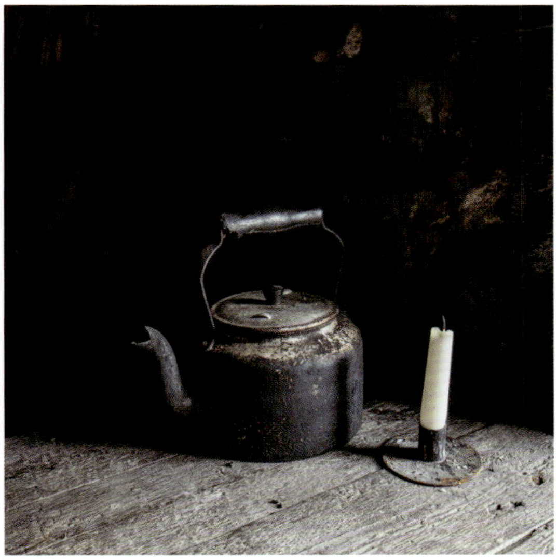

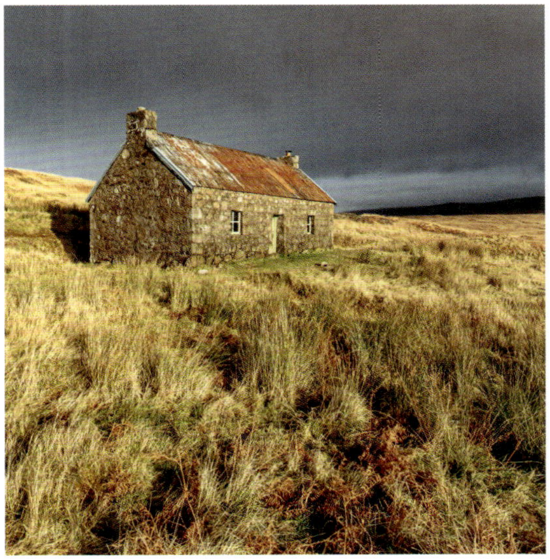

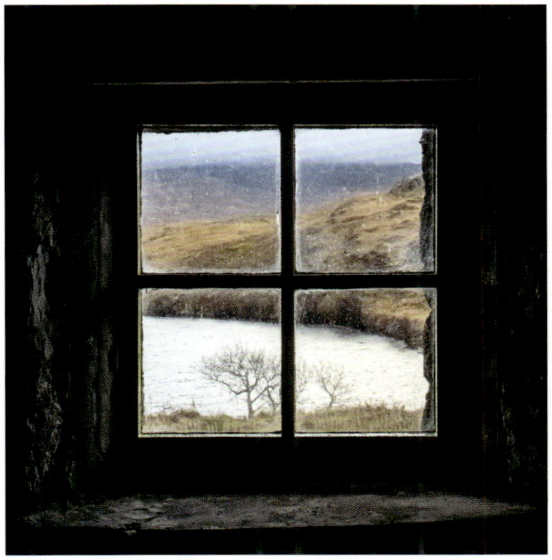

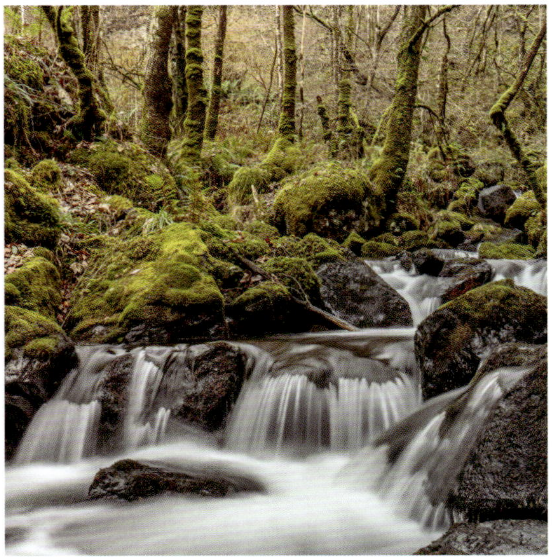

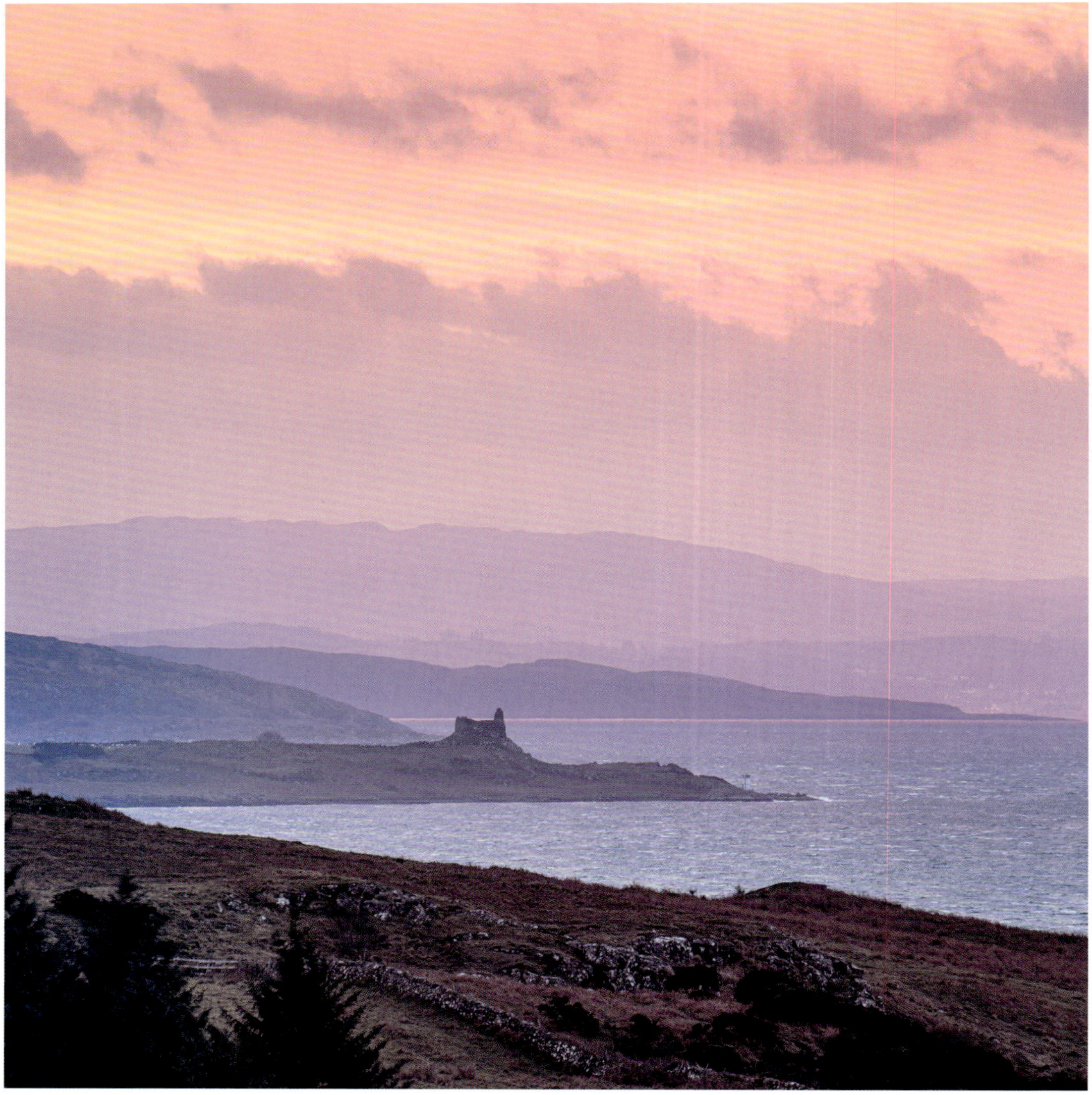

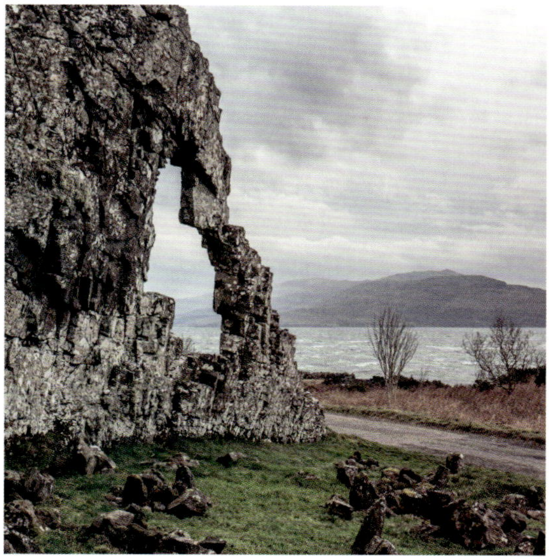

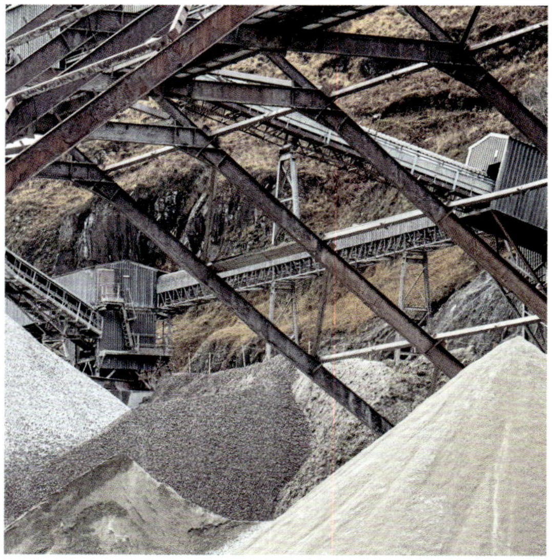

From top left:

Dawn at Ardtornish Castle and the Sound of Mull

Clach na Criche, or the Wishing Stone, in Morvern which once marked the border between Gaelic and Pictish lands. The cairns were built by mourners on funeral processions in memory of the dead

Glensanda Quarry

Opposite, from top left:

Dorlin (formerly Doirlinn), an eighteenth century former ferryhouse, Morvern

Carna Island, Loch Sunart, Morvern

From bottom left:

Track from Loch Teacuis, Morvern

Drimnin to Dorlin milepost, Auliston, Morvern

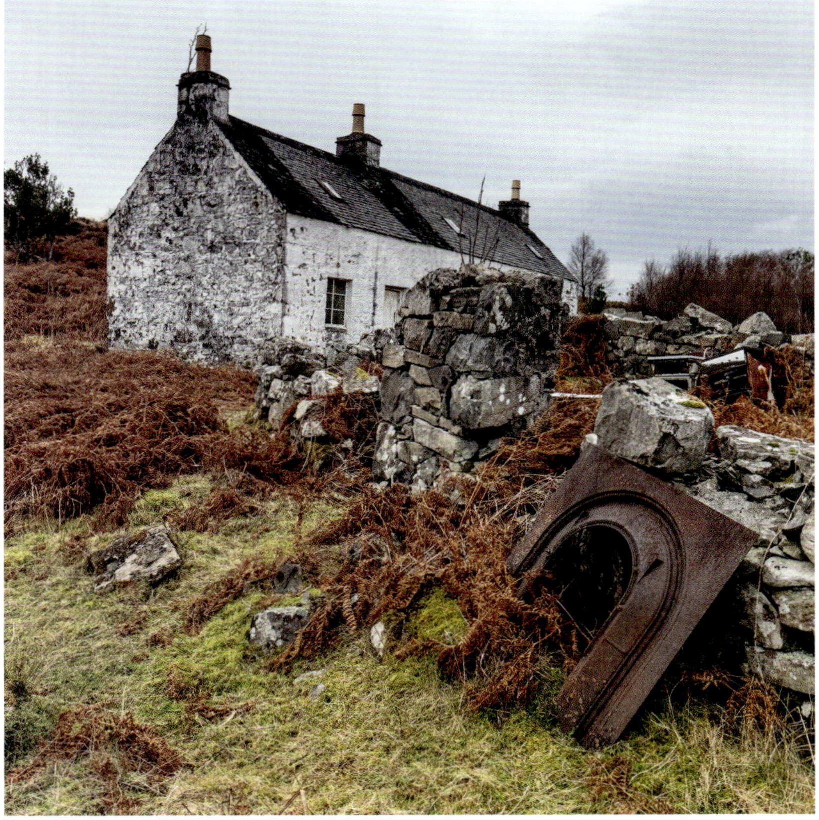

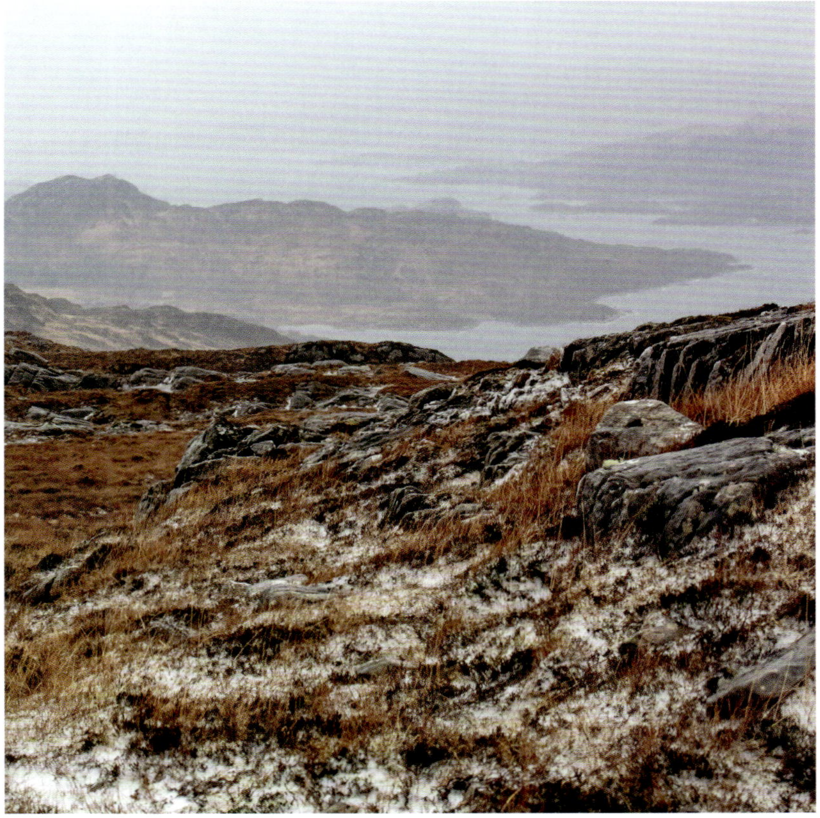

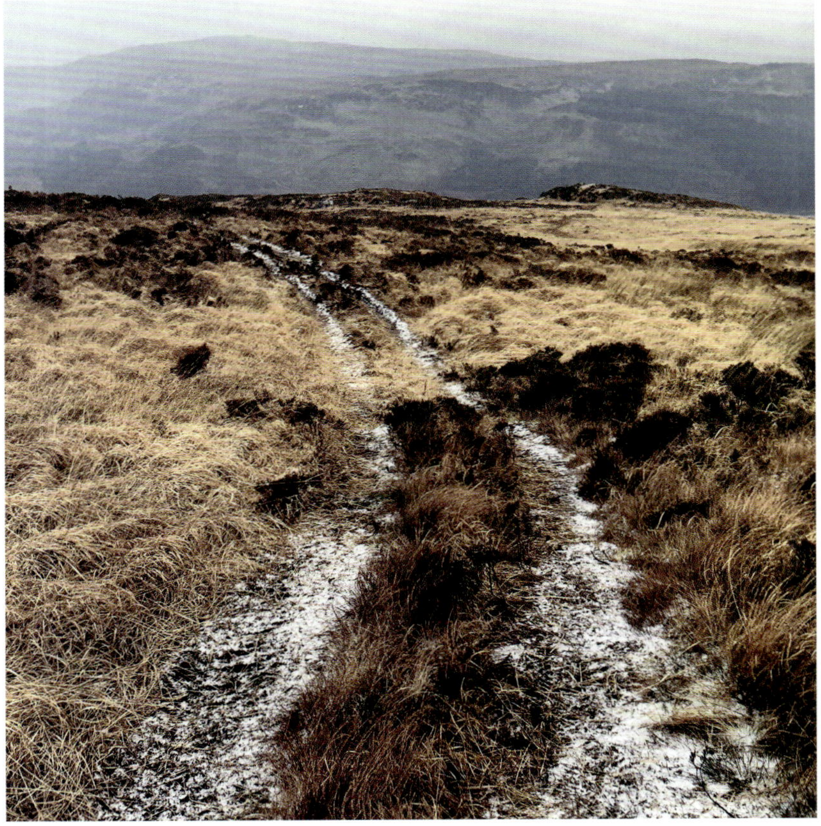

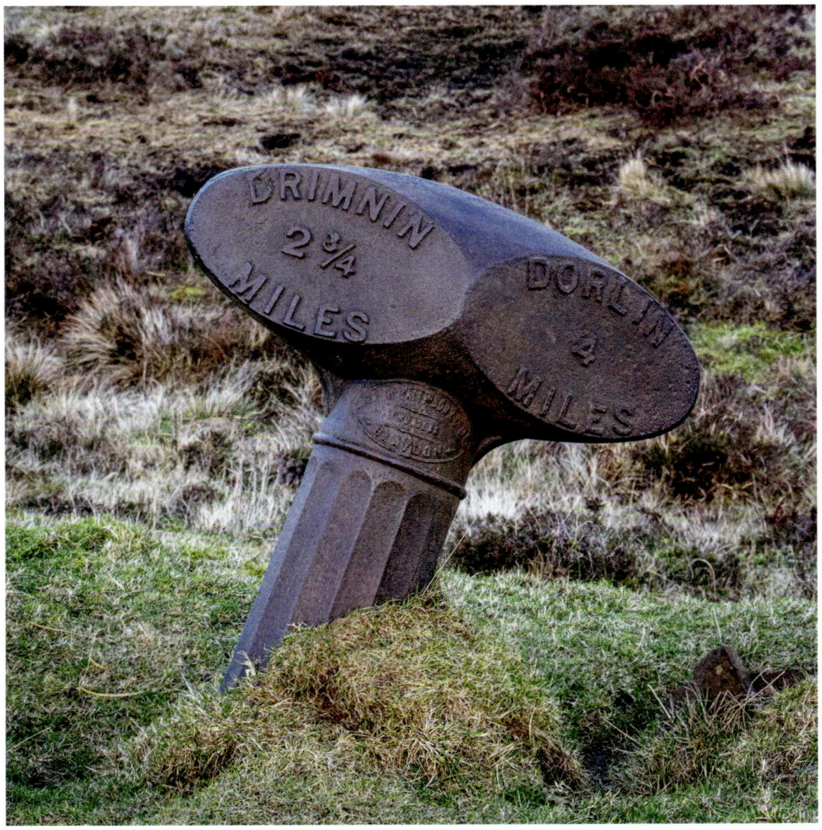
DRIMNIN
2 3/4
MILES
DORLIN
4
MILES

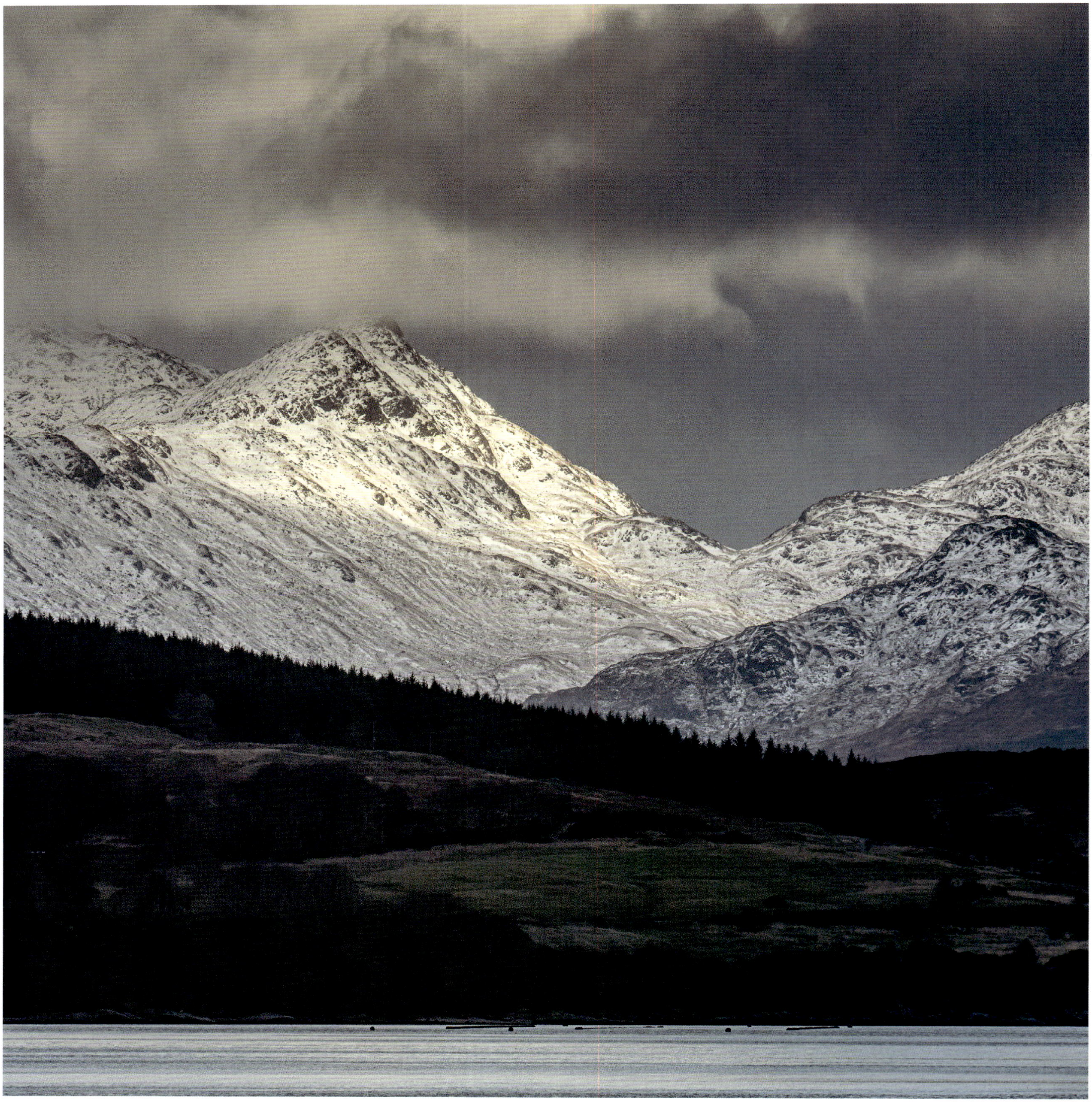

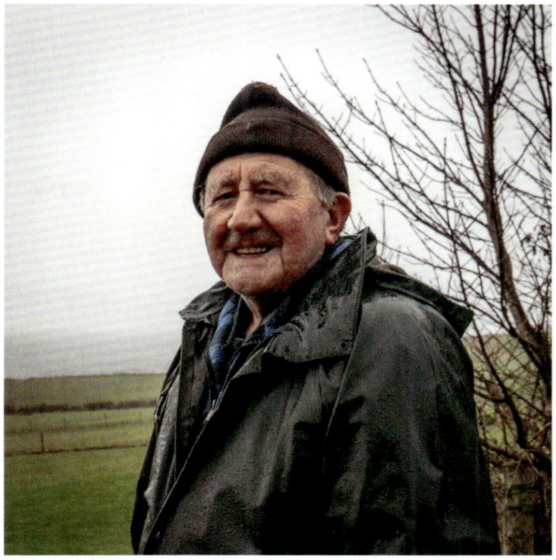

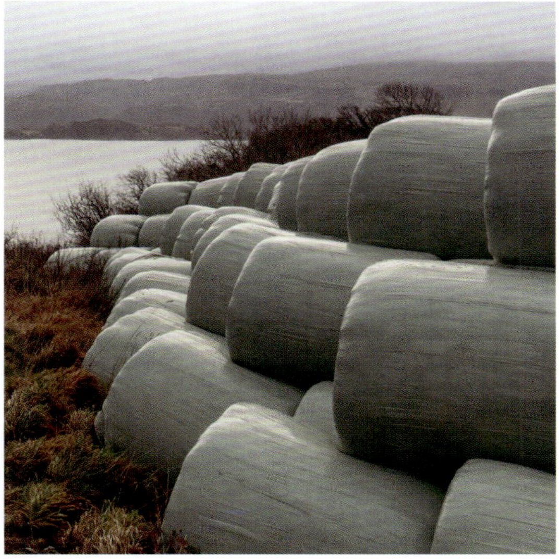

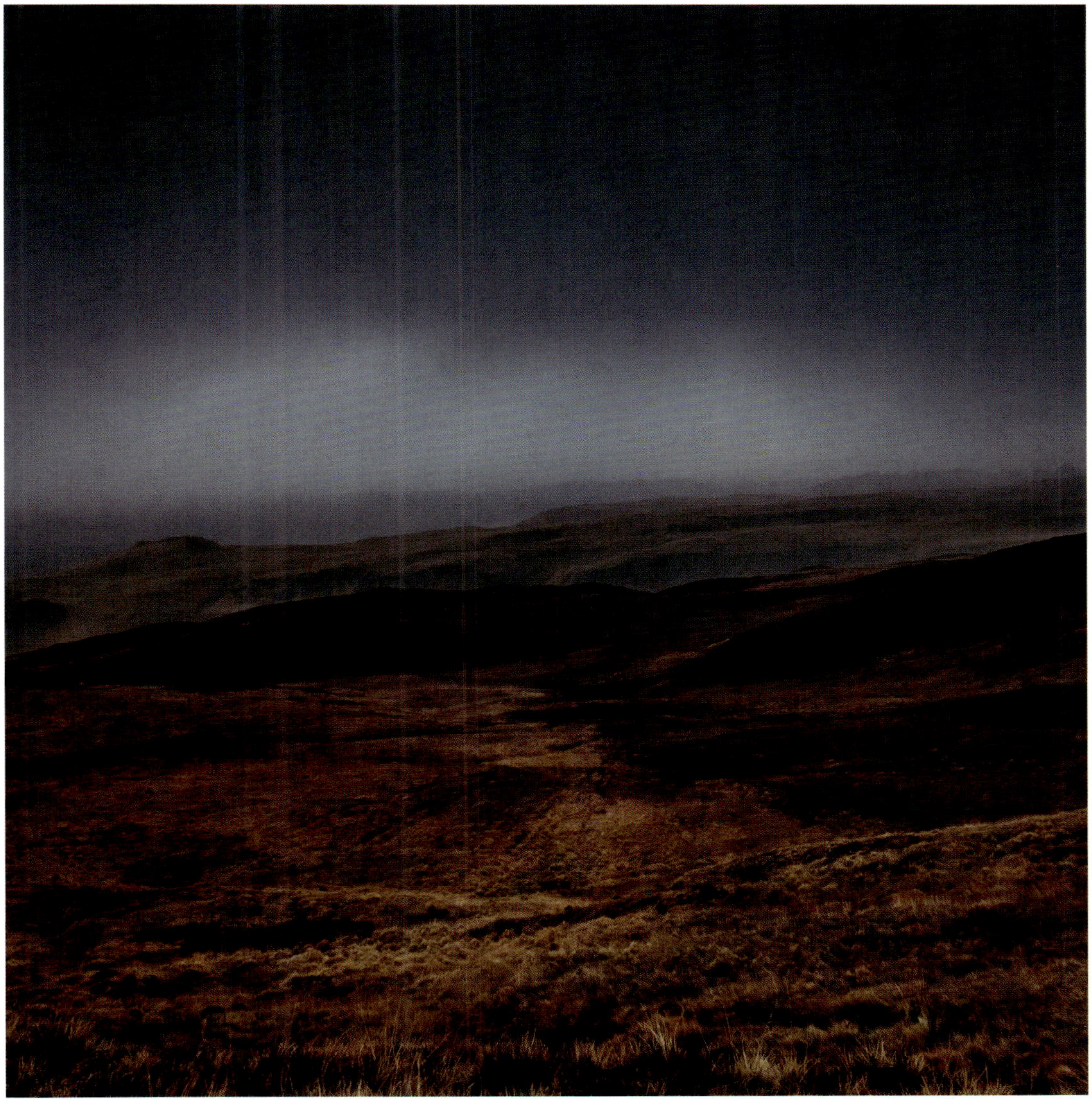

Opposite:

Sgurr na h-Ighinn and Loch Sunart

From top left:

Crofter Alistair Campbell, Kilchoan, Ardnamurchan

Loch Sunart from Port na Gall, Ardnamurchan

Below Ben Hiant, Ardnamurchan

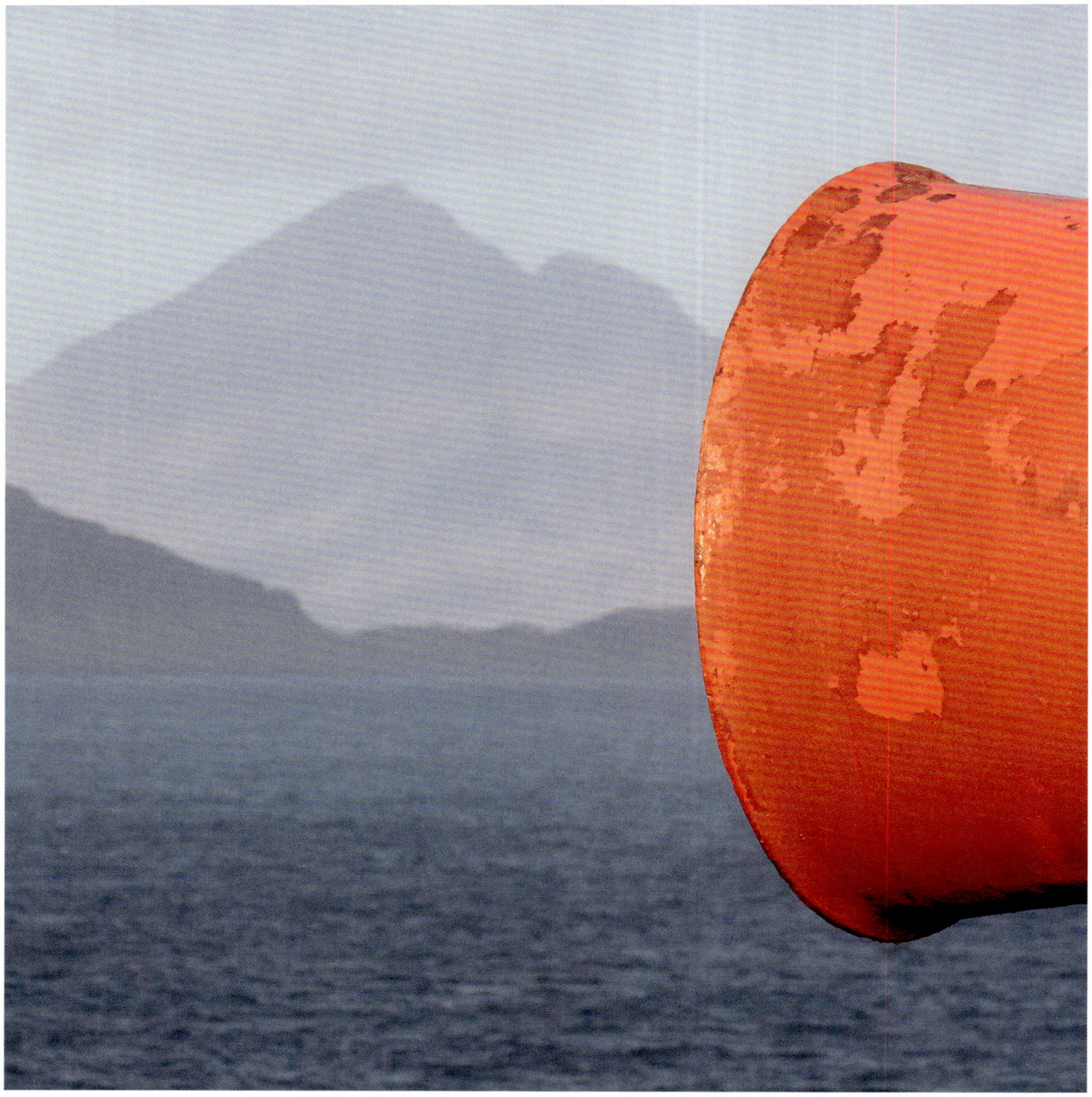

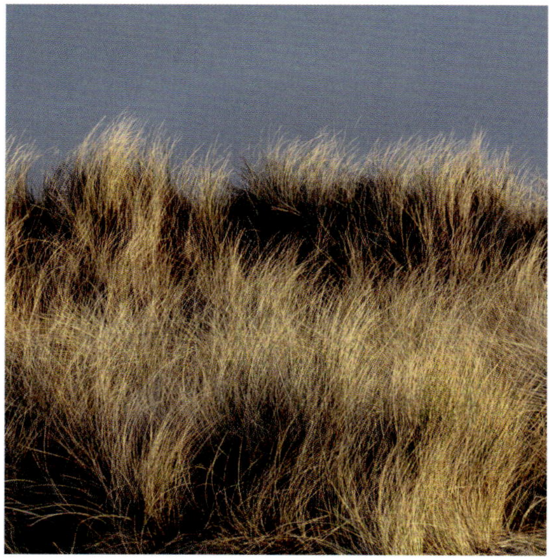

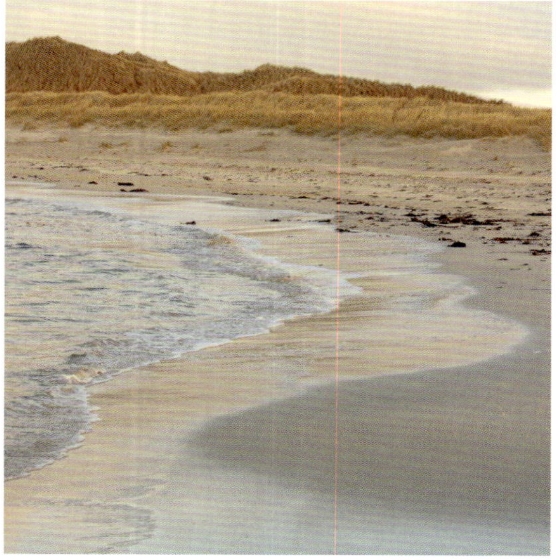

From top left:

Foghorn with Rum, Ardnamurchan Point Lighthouse

Beachgrass, Sanna Bay, Ardnamurchan

Golden shore on New Year's Day, Sanna Bay, Ardnamurchan

Opposite, clockwise from top left:

By the fishing huts, Acarsaid Bheag, Ardnamurchan

New Year's Day bonfire on Sanna Beach, Ardnamurchan

Lookout: Sanna, Ardnamurchan

Sunset on New Year's Day, Ardnamurchan Point Lighthouse

Rockform, Rubha Ruadh, Ardnamurchan

Skye from Kilmory Bay, Ardnamurchan

Overleaf, from left to right:

Singing Sands, Kentra, Ardnamurchan

Fishing huts, Acarsaid Bheag, Ardnamurchan

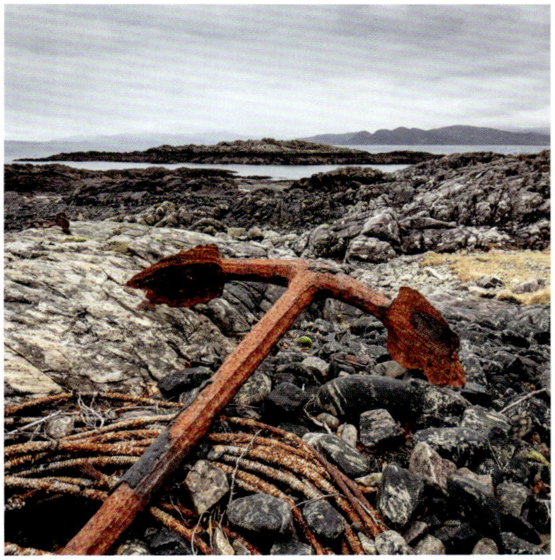

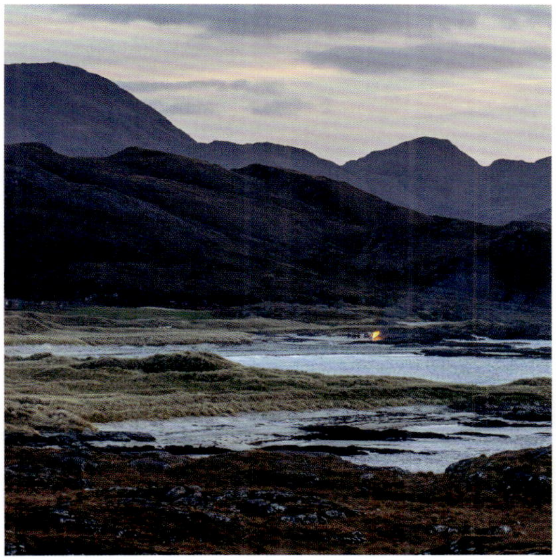

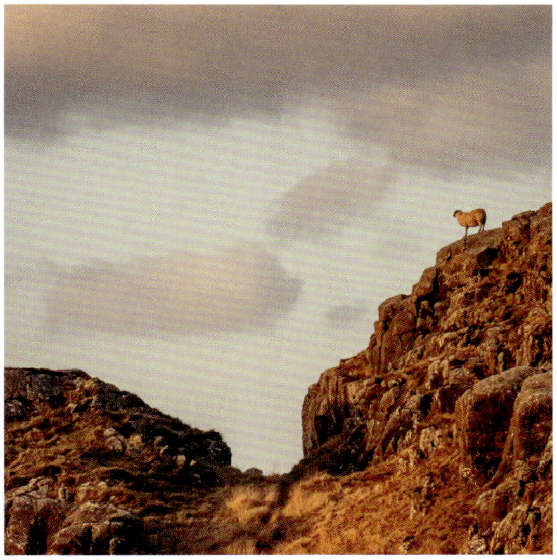

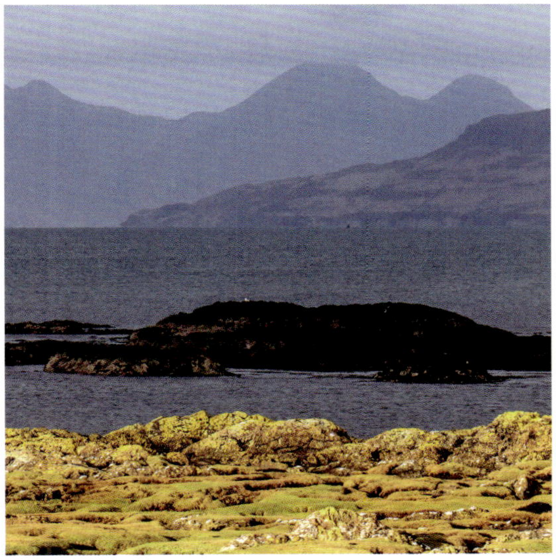

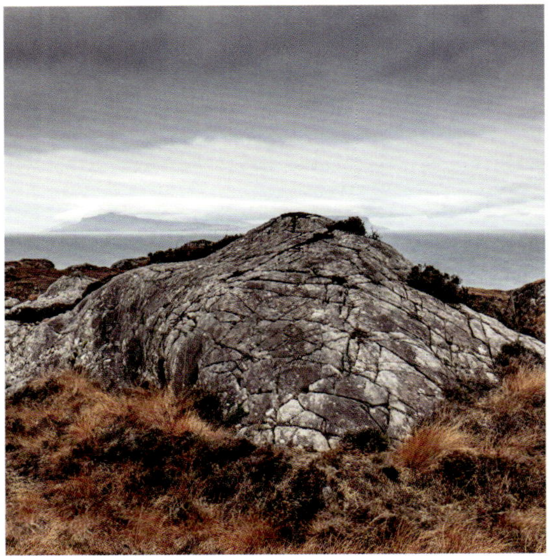

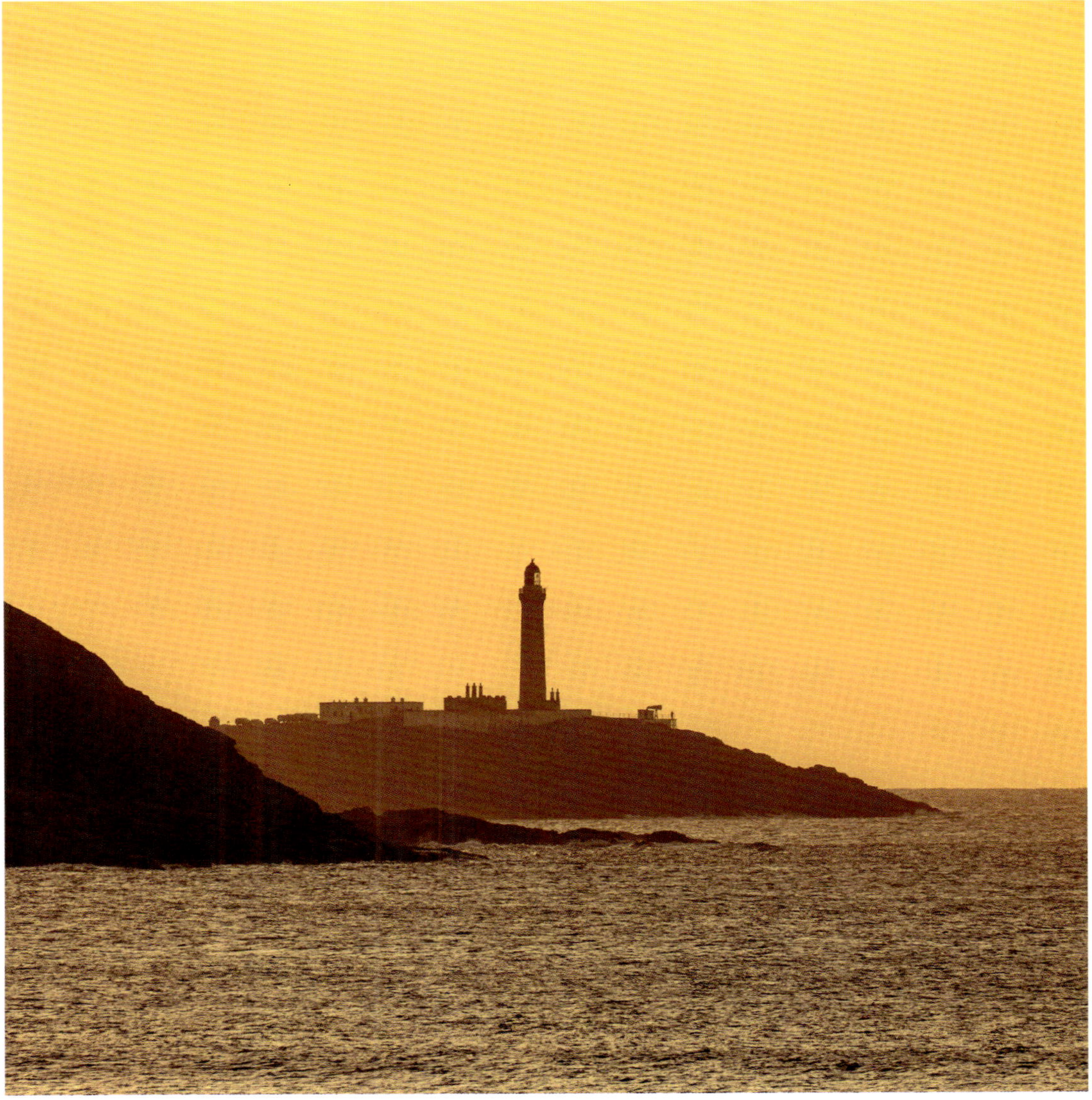

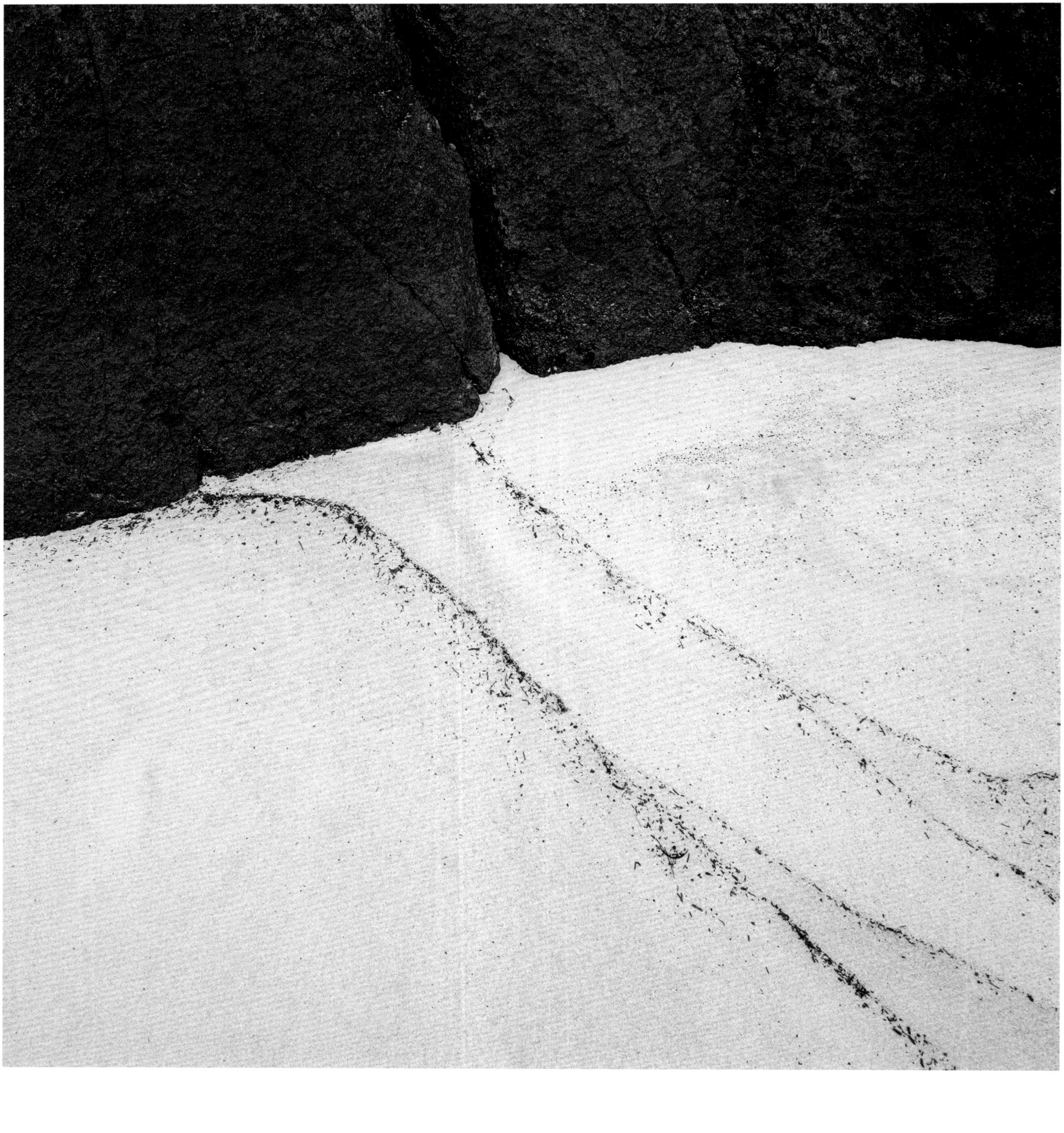

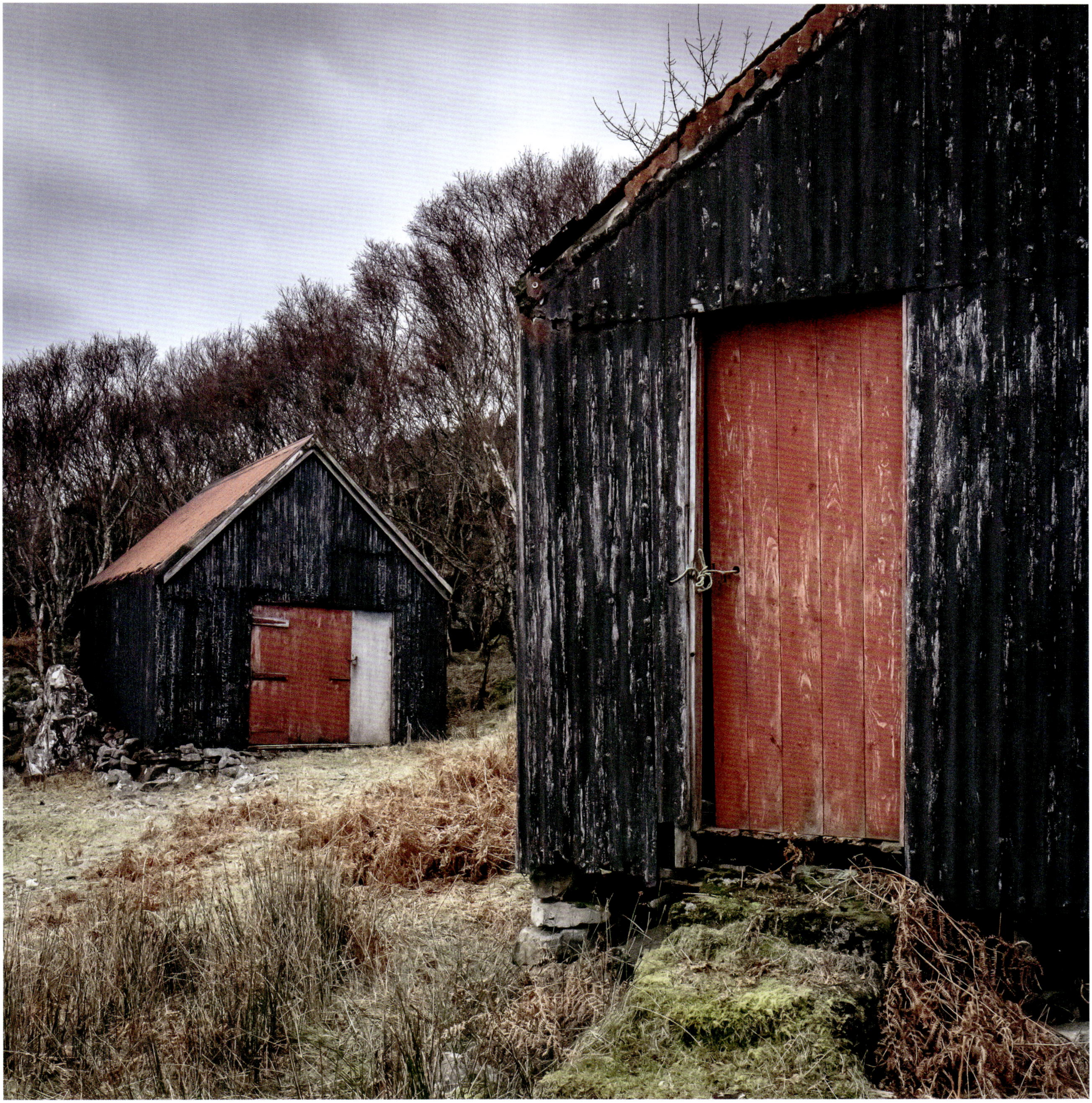

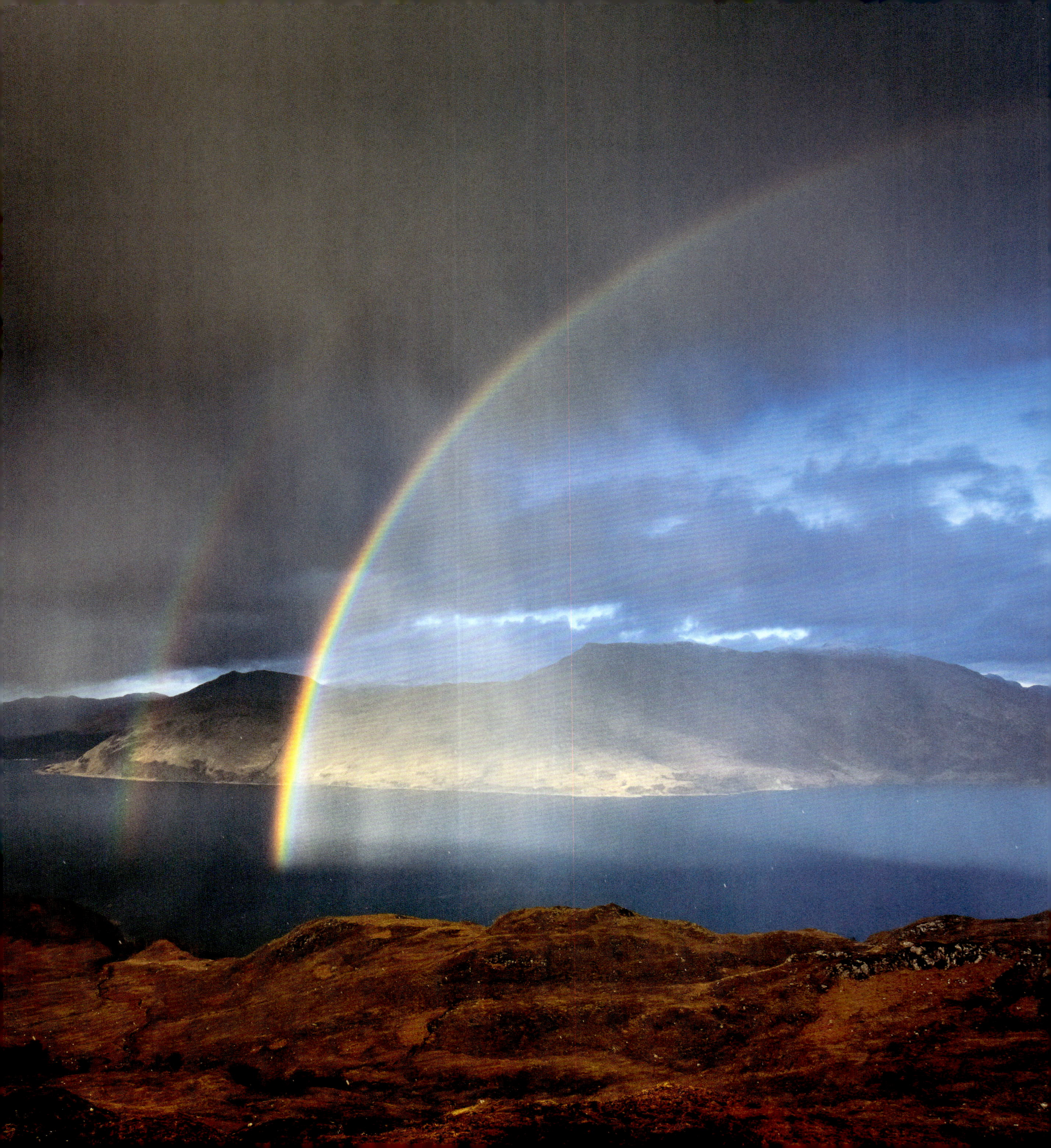

28 NORTH INVERNESS-SHIRE

JANUARY–MARCH 2019
DAY 263–277 | 06,630–06,867KM | 237KM

My thighs are burning and I'm panting for breath as I haul myself up the mountainside above Mallaig. It's been a week of hiking through the Rough Bounds, of slogging through pathless moorland and sparse settlements, wading through bogs and wobbly tussocks of grass, and climbing around the sides of jagged, granite, snow-peaked mountains as they plunge down to the sea. This part of Scotland has a reputation for being incredibly difficult to traverse on foot, and as I catch my breath and survey the scene across Loch Nevis to the hulking Knoydart massif, I can see why. On top of the regular challenges that hiking in Scotland involves, the coast here includes sheer cliffs dropping into sea lochs and small crags that I can already tell will require constant detours to make progress. And the weather is brutal and mercurial – my face is numb from wind chill.

I forget my aches and pains when a brief slice of wonder emerges: a rainbow framing Knoydart against a backdrop of mountains, menacing cloud and swirling mist. It's a sight that takes my breath away and reminds me of a Caspar David Friedrich painting. Slowly, it dawns on me that only by taking on the challenge of hiking into Knoydart could I have experienced this sublime moment. All at once I am glad that I came and a sense of accomplishment washes over me.

I fight hard to hold on to that feeling as the sleet and rain pummel me relentlessly for the next few days. On my fifth day of walking, I wake in my tent on the north shore of Knoydart, the remotest of the Rough Bounds' peninsulas, opposite the Isle of Skye. I'm sipping on my coffee when I discover a juicy, highly caffeinated slug curled around the bottom of the mug. It wakes up me like nothing else and I rush to pack my things away and get back on the road. But much like the slug, I find myself making slow progress. Where I used to average 3 kilometres per hour, the hilly, broken terrain and mounting fatigue force me to cover ground six times slower. I'm so dispirited that after the fourteenth hour on the move, I collapse in exasperation on a clump of moss while descending a steep valley.

The following day, I wake up to alternating rain and snow flurries by Loch Hourn. It's so cold that I walk quickly not only to cover miles, but to stay warm. As I make my way around one headland, a magnificent sight emerges: a tiny, solitary, resilient cottage by the shore of the loch, above which rises the mountain like a never-ending wall of rock, the top half snow-covered and the transition between the snow line accentuated by a swirling sheet of mist. Looking through the viewfinder, a tingle runs up my spine as I capture what I know will be a special photo.

That evening I'm woken after midnight by gale-force winds and torrential rain. I notice with alarm that the tent has started to leak badly, so I cover my sleeping bag with my jacket to keep it dry. When the gale pushes the tent poles forcefully against my body, I worry they'll snap. Adrenaline courses through me – my lightweight tent isn't designed to withstand even half this 60-miles-per-hour-wind force. I pack up all my gear except the sleeping bag and stay wearily awake throughout the night, fully expecting the tent to collapse.

Five days later, when I finally leave Knoydart, my face feels like it is in a permanent squint from the days of storm-force hail driven into it. Knoydart will remain in my heart as the journey's most beautiful and challenging section. It is a landscape that required the most persistence to traverse yet repaid it many times over with the most intense photographic reveries.

Opposite:

Hailbow over Loch Nevis and Knoydart, North Morar

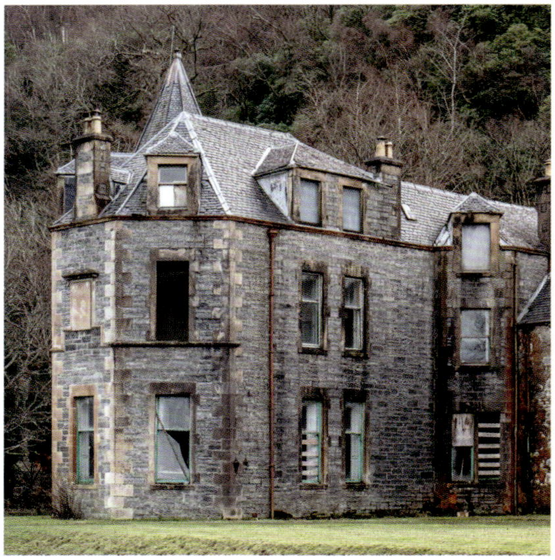
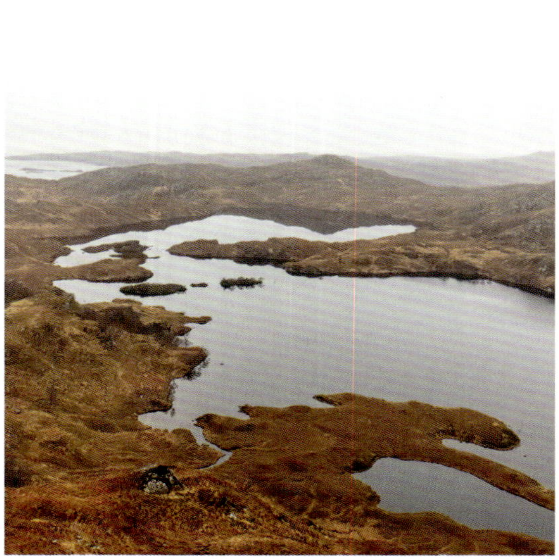
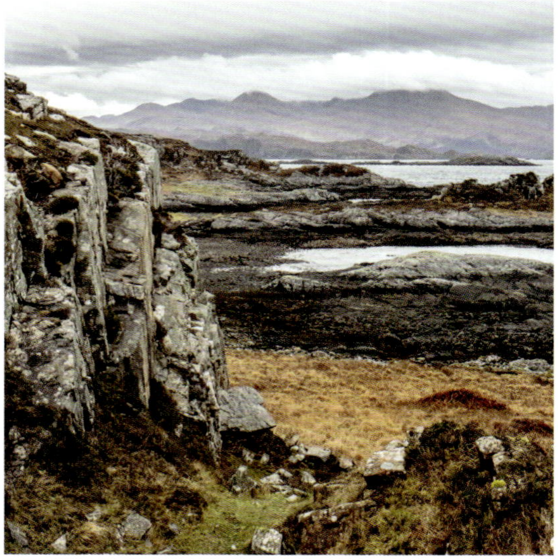
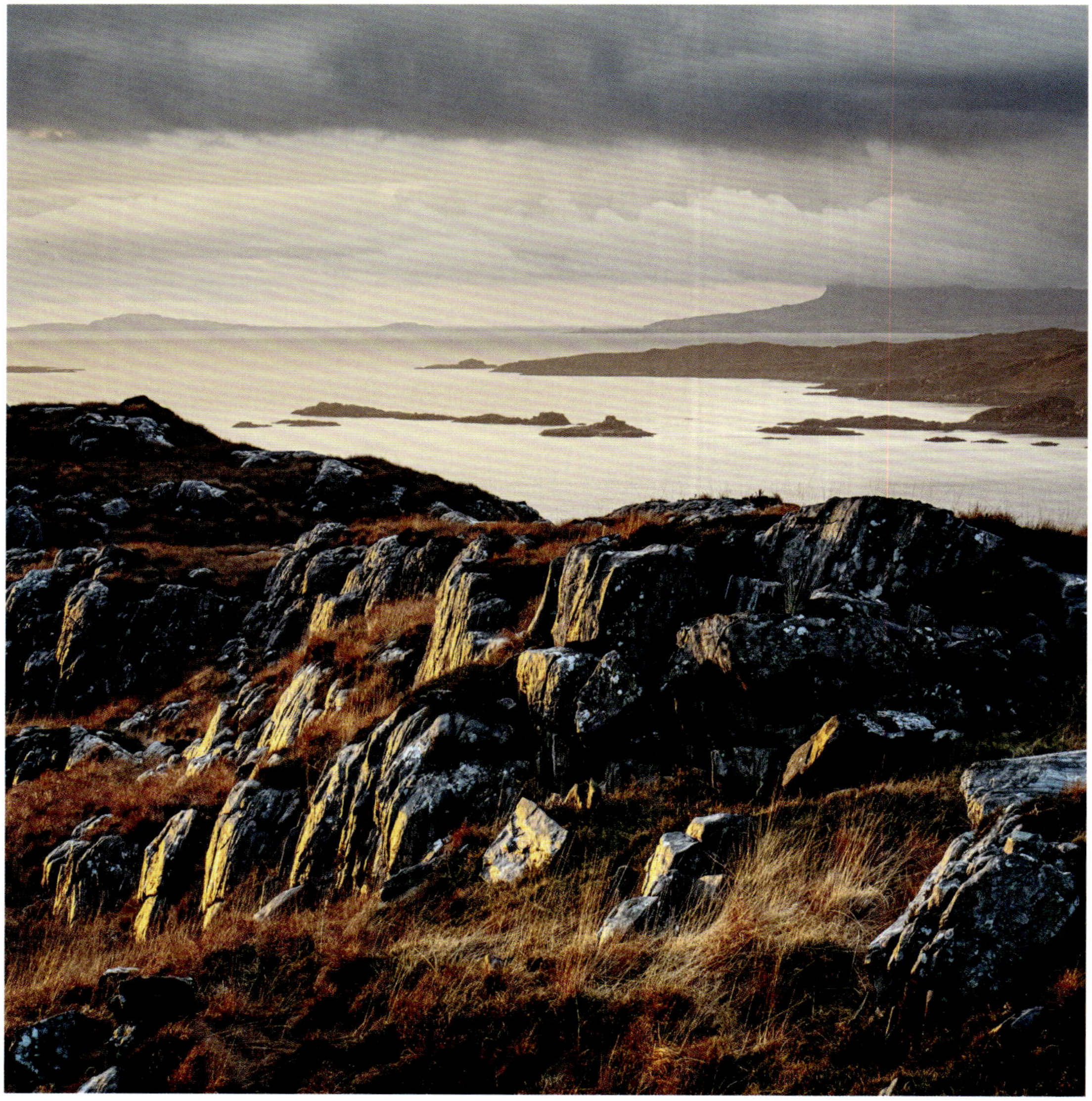
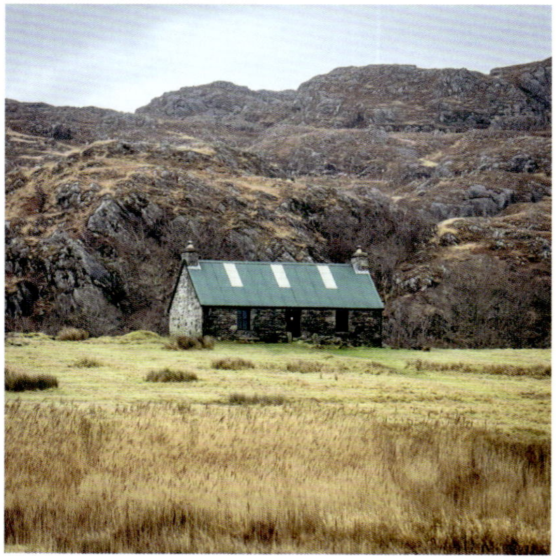
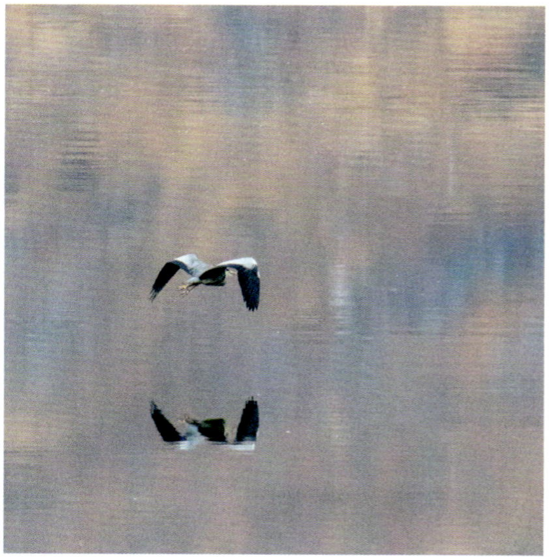

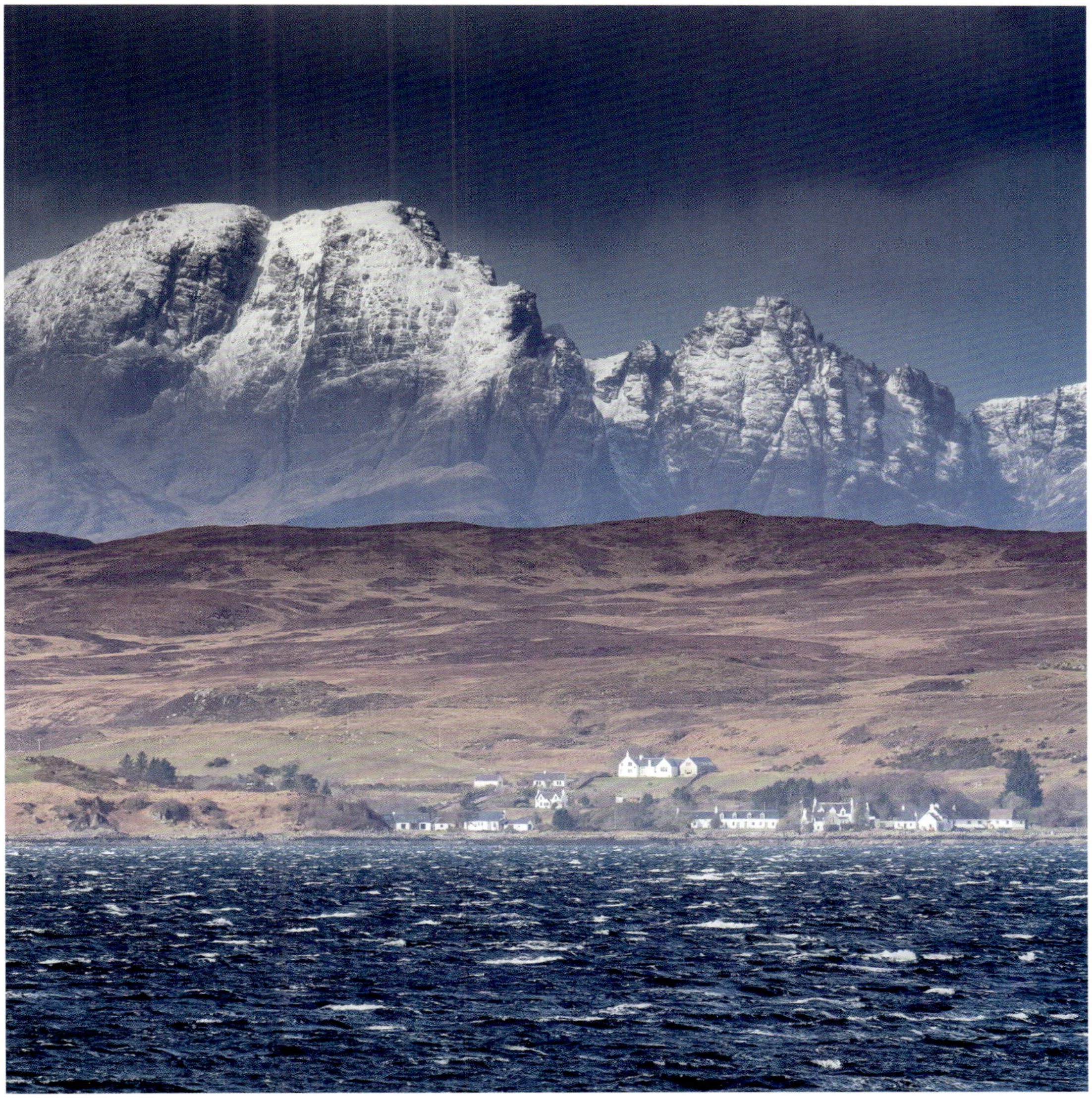

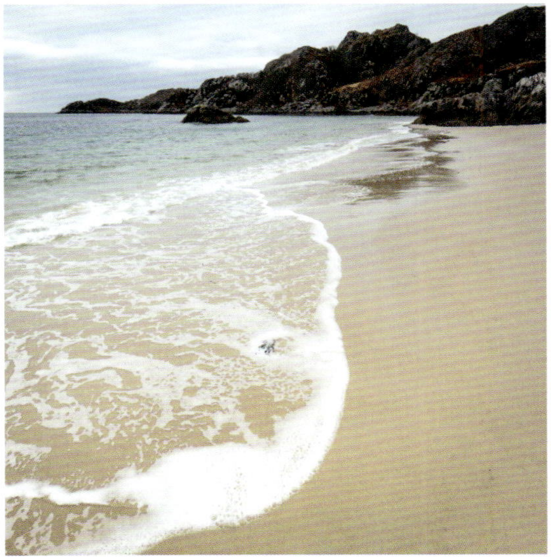

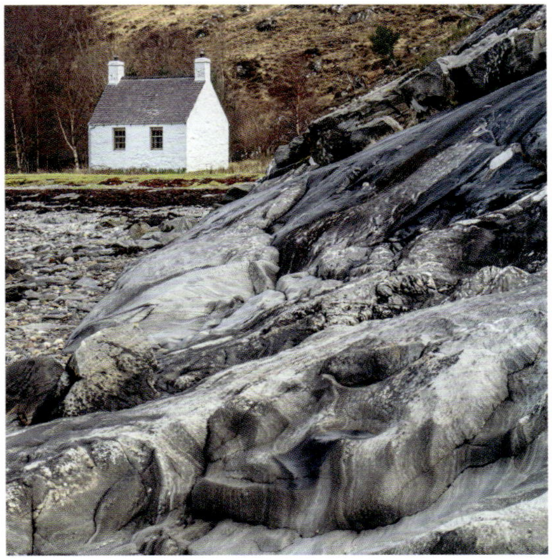

Opposite, clockwise from top left:

Inverailort House, Loch Ailort, once a base of the Second World War Special Operations Executive and commando training. British agents were trained here in ruthless techniques of intelligence gathering, sabotage and survival, which were later directly adopted by the CIA

Loch Doire a' Ghearrain, Ardnish Peninsula

The Rhu Peninsula

Peanmeanach Bothy, Ardnish. In the 1841 census, Peanmeanach's seven houses were home to forty-eight people, the Highland Clearances having pushed people on to the peninsula. The final resident, Nellie MacQueen, lived in the house that is now the bothy. She finally moved on during the Second World War, unable to survive on wartime rations; one candle a week was simply not enough to see her through the long nights of a Scottish winter

Flight: grey heron, Loch Ailort, Lochaber

One minute of sunlight before nightfall after a day of rain. The Sound of Arisaig from Ardnish

From top left:

Blà Bheinn looking fierce above Isleornsay on Skye. View from Knoydart

Exhale: Ardnish

Old Schoolhouse, Kylesmorar, Loch Nevis

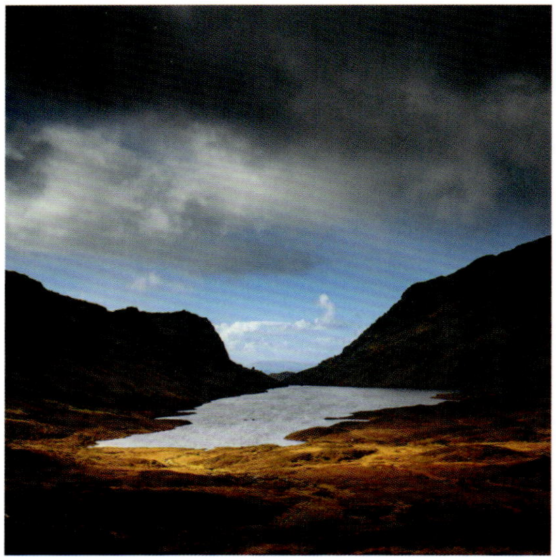

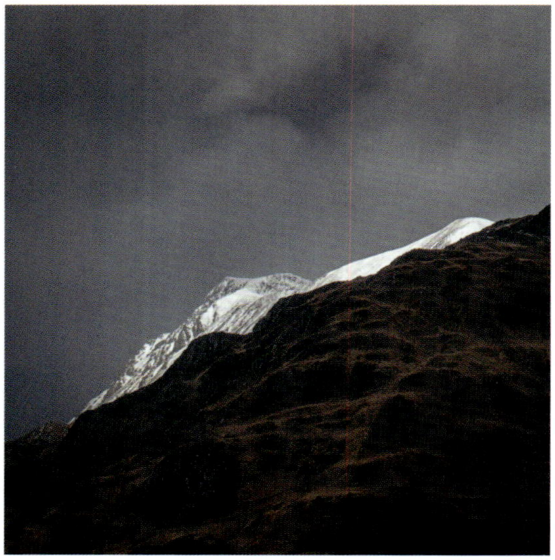

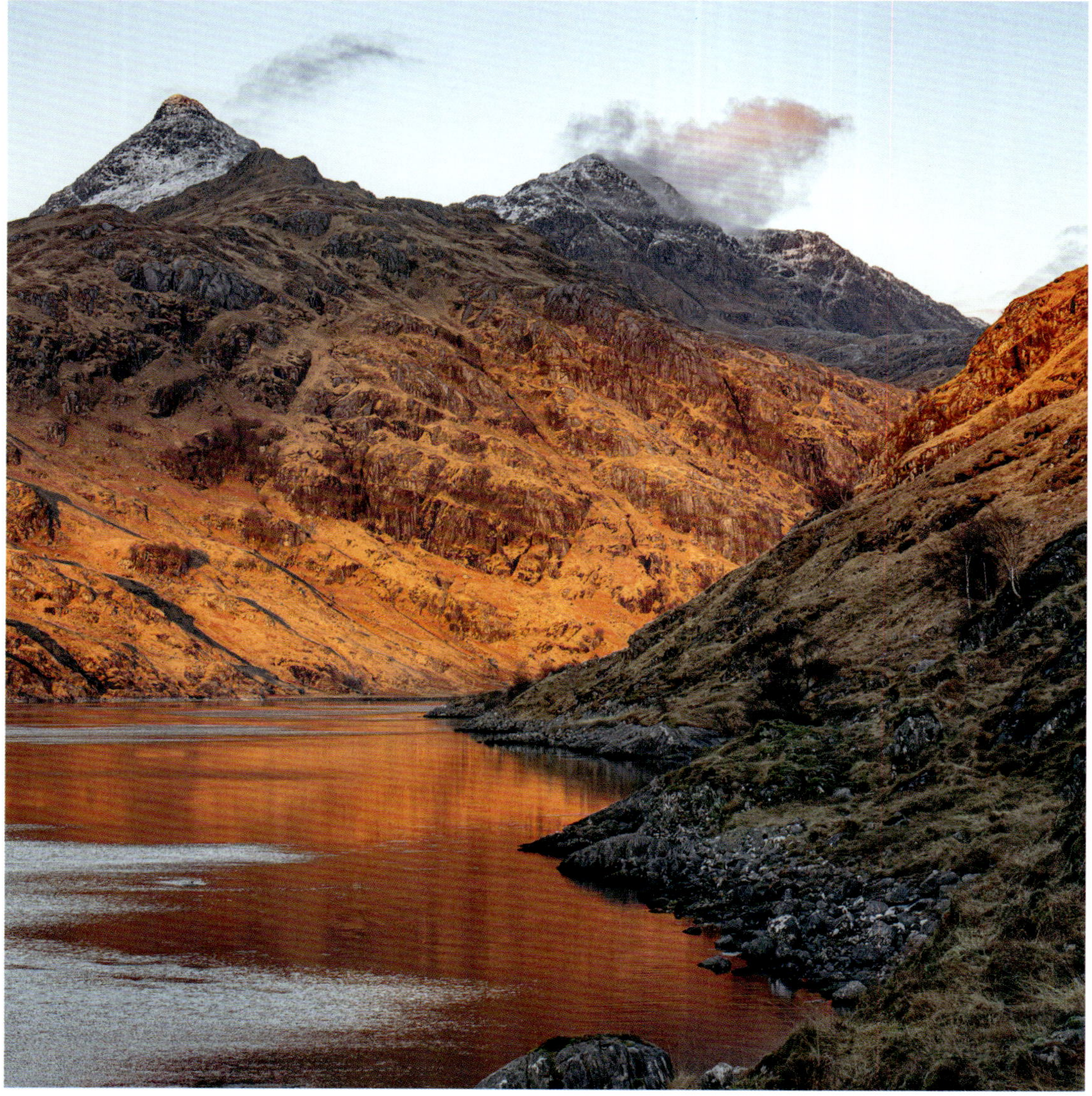

From top left:

Loch Eireagoraidh (Loch of the Shieling of the Corrie) above Mallaig with Mullach Mor on Rum in the distance

A slice of Beinn Sgritheall from Glen Arnisdale

Sgùrr na Cìche in Knoydart catches a few moments of golden light before sunset, Loch Nevis, North Morar. In the water, a small flat object can be seen, which turned out to be a pair of otters that came ashore and walked close past me as I was sitting motionless by the tripod

Opposite, from top left:

Deer pen at Ardnamurach, Loch Nevis, North Morar

'Moby' Prince of Whales, Tom McClean's boat at Ardintigh, which completed a circumnavigation of Britain in 1996; he plans to take it across the Atlantic in future

Tom McClean, seventy-eight, SAS veteran and adventurer. He holds the world record as the first man to row across the Atlantic Ocean from west to east solo, and numerous other feats of endurance

From centre left:

Steve and Alan, Cape Wrath trail hikers, Sourlies Bothy

Target, Camusrory, Knoydart

Ardintigh, Loch Nevis, North Morar

From bottom left:

Gate to nowhere, Knoydart

Honda, Airor, Knoydart

A charismatic Knoydart beastie, Croulin

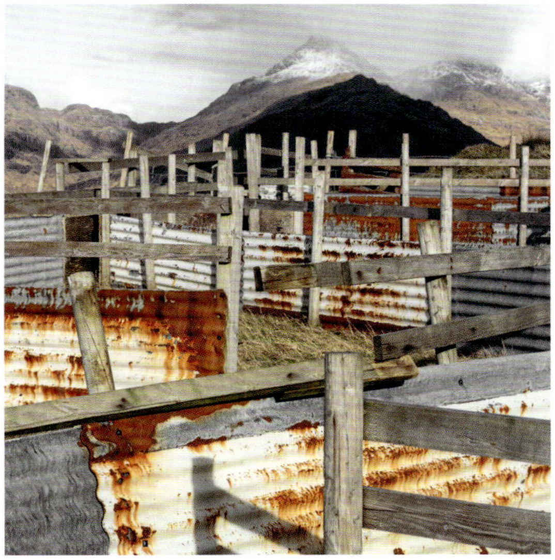

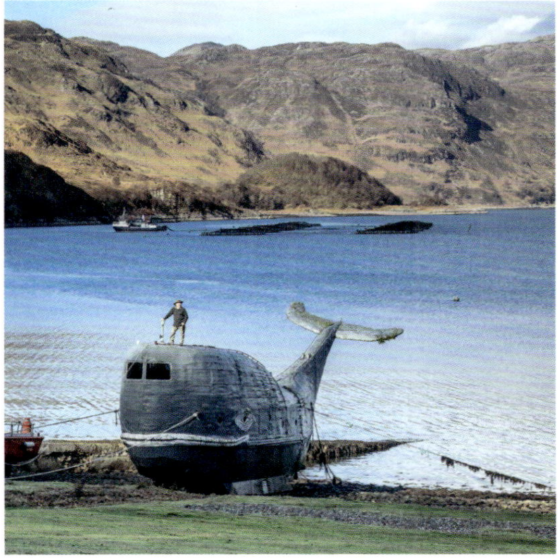

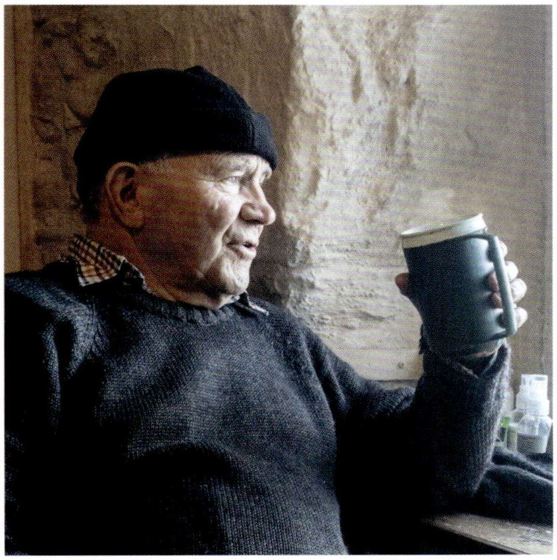

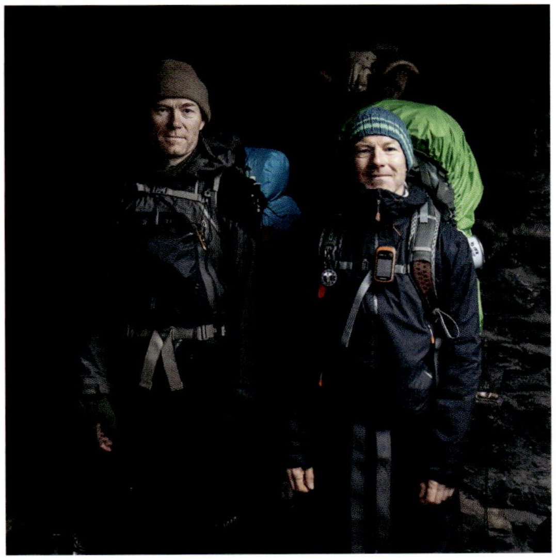

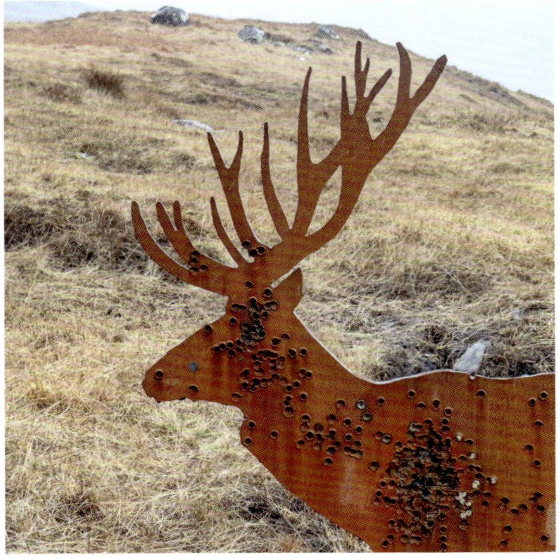

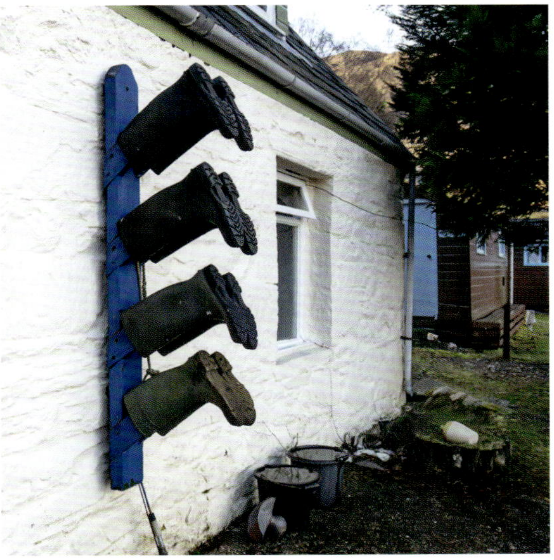

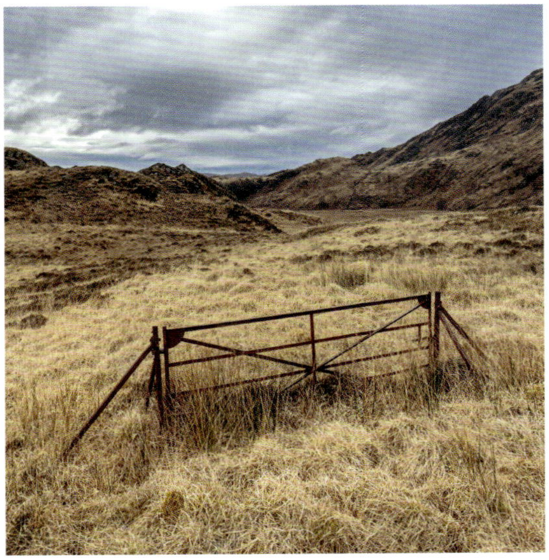

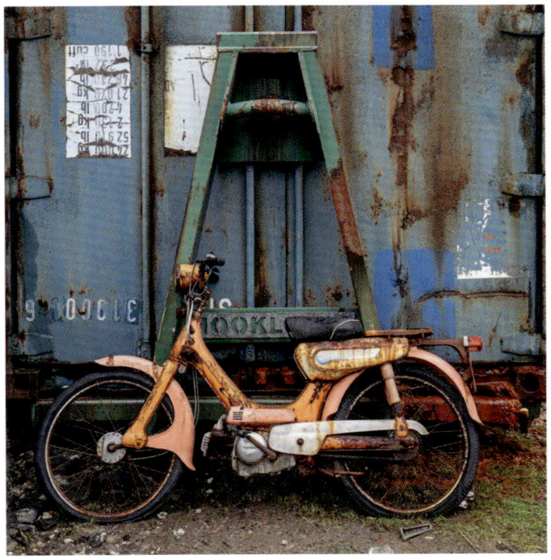

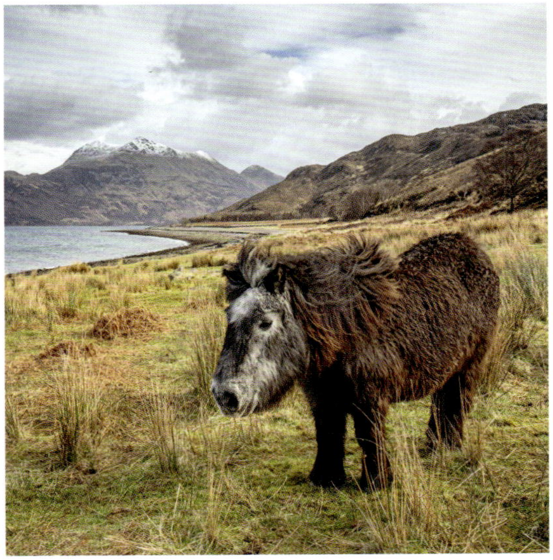

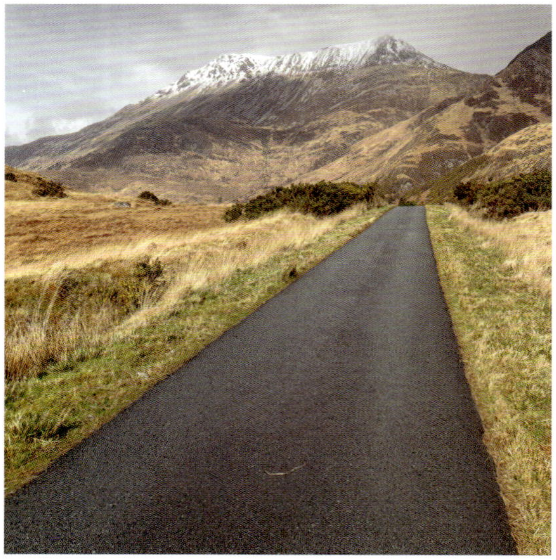

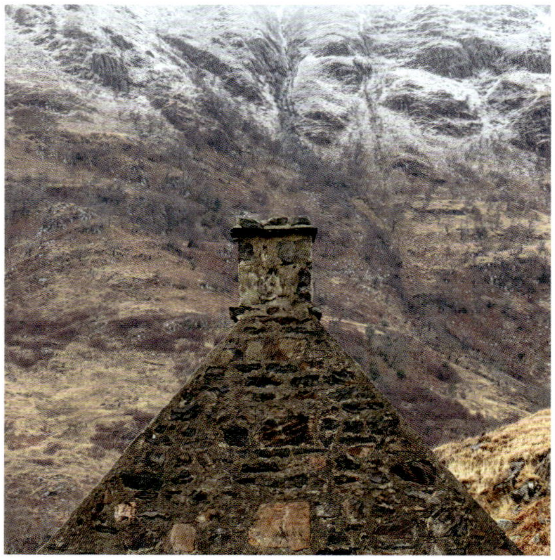

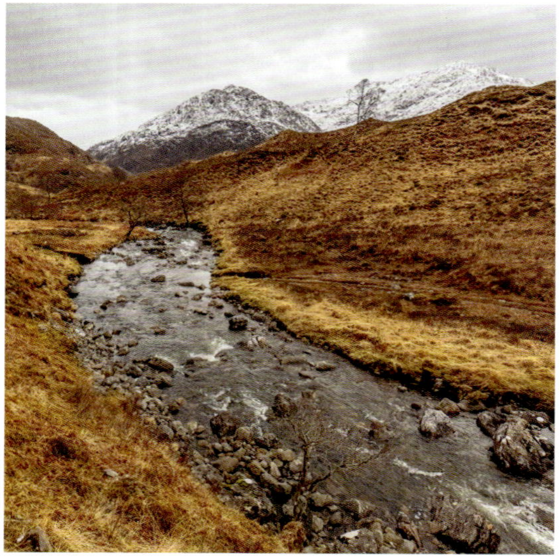

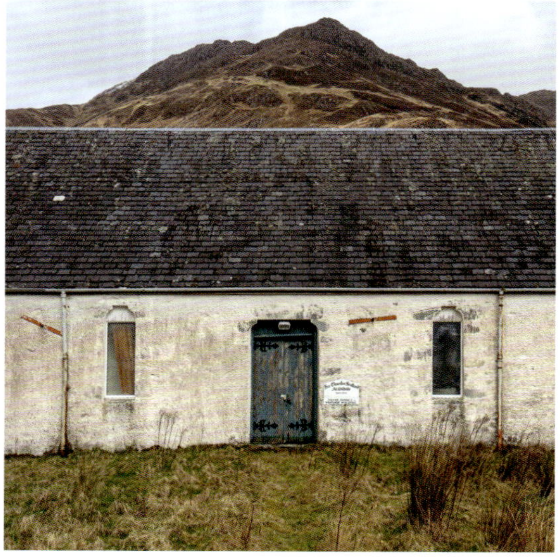

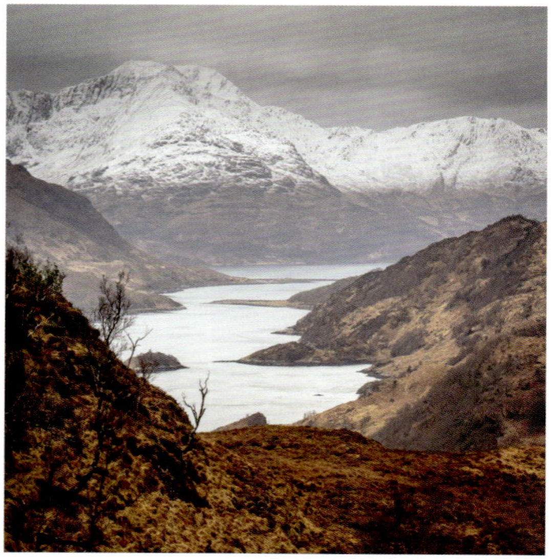

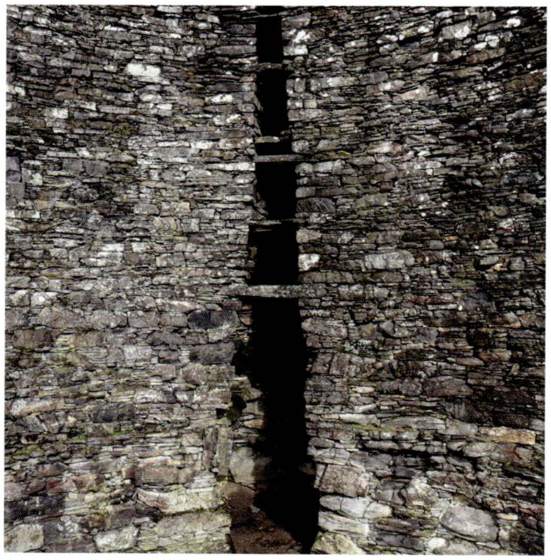

From top left:

A strand of grass at Arnisdale on the road to Glenelg. The road felt astonishingly fast to walk on after weeks of rough ground preceding this

Gable, Barissdale, Knoydart

From centre left:

Allt a' Choire Reidh

Arnisdale Free Church

From bottom left:

Ladhar Bheinn beyond Loch Hourn, Knoydart

Interior of Dun Troddan, an Iron Age broch at Glenelg, revealing the double-skinned drystone walls

Opposite:

Skiary, Loch Hourn from Knoydart

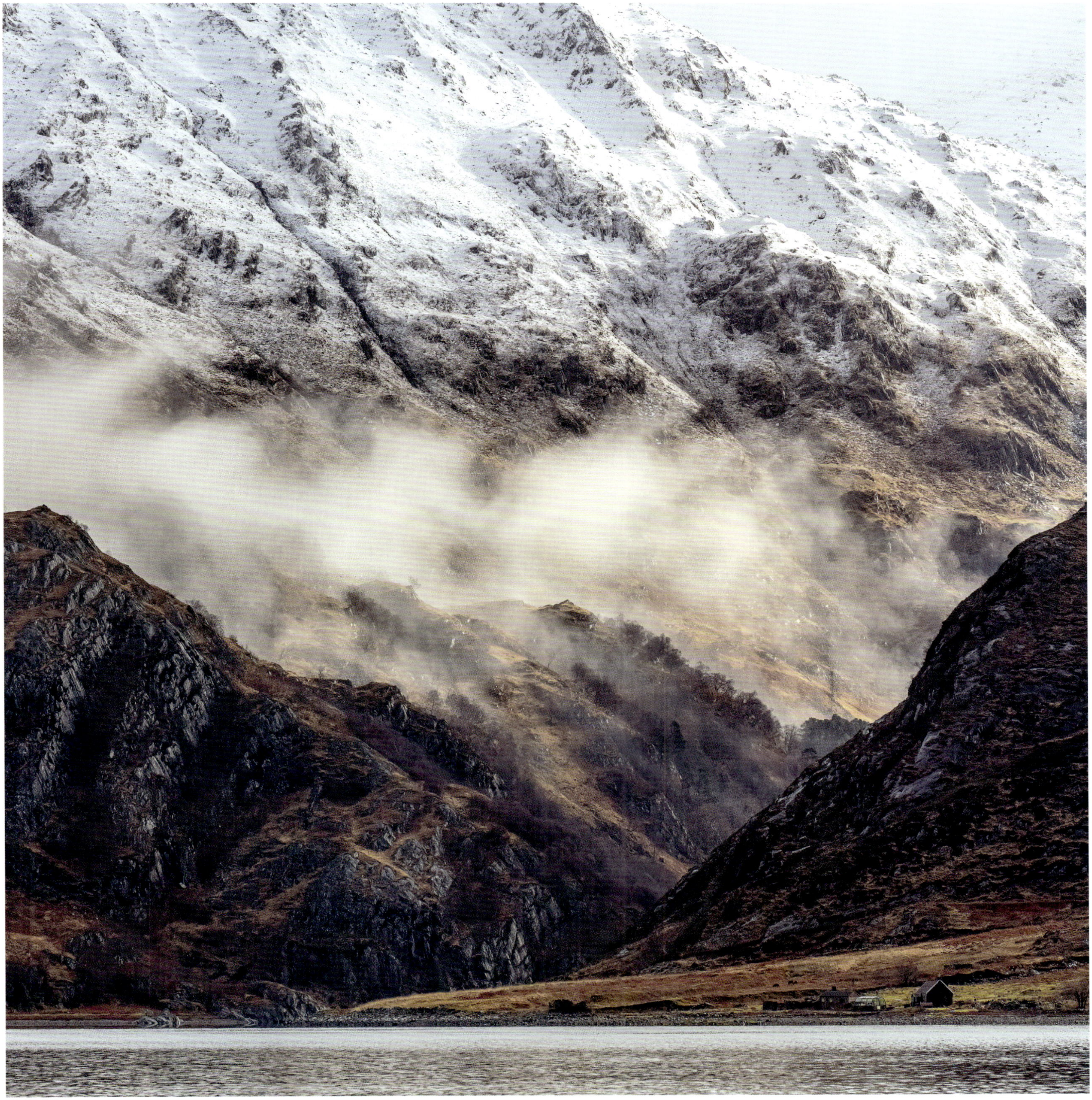

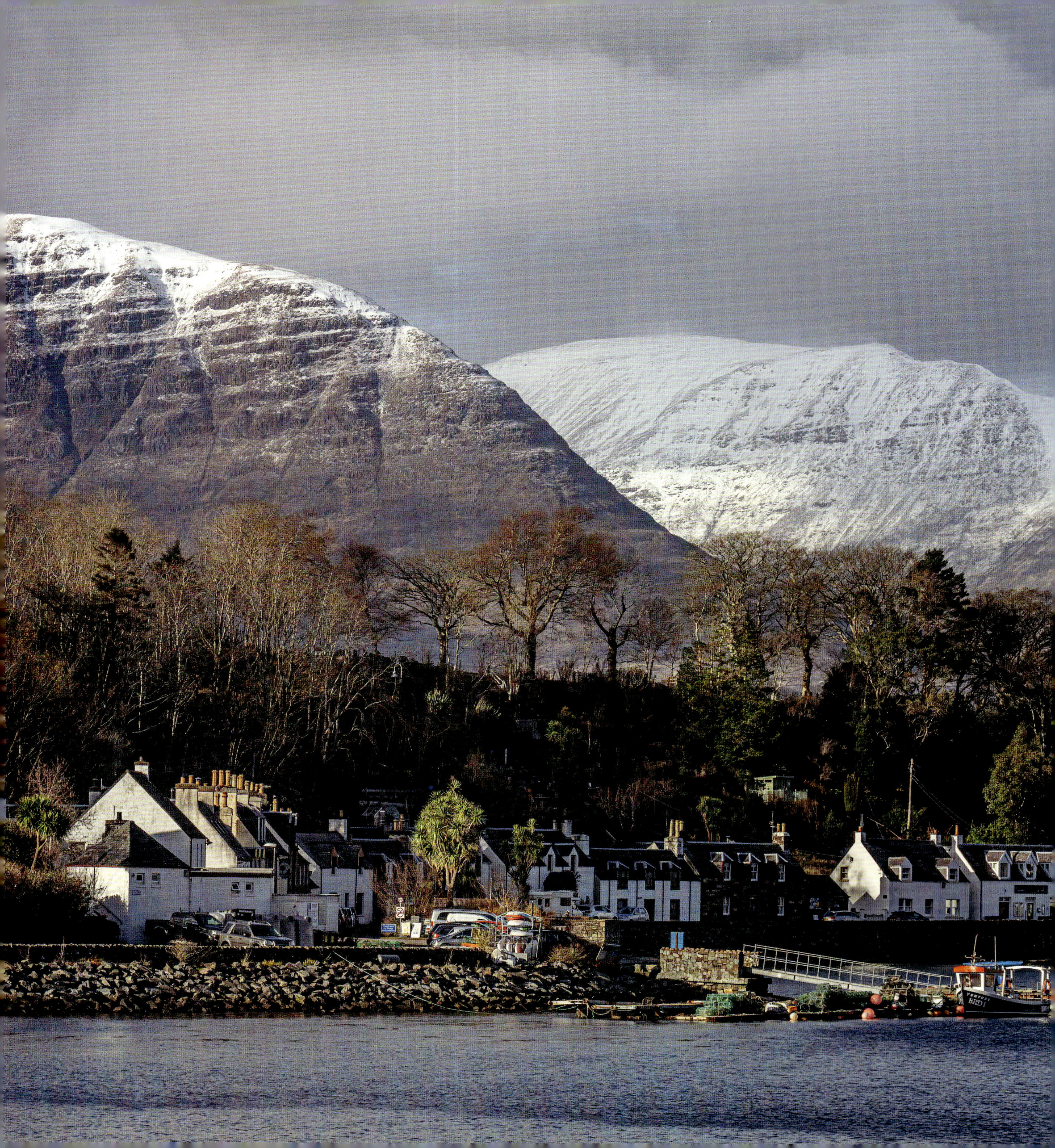

29

WEST ROSS AND CROMARTY

MARCH–APRIL 2019

DAY 278–300 | 06,867–07,373KM | 506KM

A clear spring morning from Glenelg brings me to the narrowest point of the Sound of Sleat, a body of water that separates the Isle of Skye from the mainland, where cattle used to swim tied nose to tail on their way to market in the days of the drove roads. Today, the crossings are mainly in the form of a vehicle ferry whose concrete slipway gently emerges as a mysterious object from the surprisingly azure sea.

I'm in a jubilant mood as I've got a lot to look forward to in the next three weeks exploring Wester Ross, which continues the north-west Highland trend of achingly beautiful, sparsely populated, highly fractured coastline adjacent to mountainous scenery. To the north of Wester Ross, beyond Ullapool, lies the historic county of Cromarty, which includes the Coigach Peninsula and the Summer Isles. In 1889, Ross-shire and Cromarty merged to form Ross and Cromarty.

I walk beside Loch Alsh through a forest for the rest of the day before emerging opposite Eilean Donan, the iconic island castle. Often described as one of Scotland's most photographed monuments and featured in the 1986 movie *Highlander* and countless other cinematic cameos and adverts, I wonder if it's possible to photograph it with any semblance of originality. Despite the ancient appearance of the castle's weathered stonework, most of what stands today was built in the 1920s and 30s in a mock-medieval style on foundations that date back to 1200.

I camp on the opposite shore to capture Eilean Donan at dawn and dusk. The next day, having walked for hours around Loch Duich, I find the castle's car park is full of coaches, and it is my startling first taste of mass tourism in Scotland now that the winter is over. Between hail showers, sunlight flits in and out, illuminating the bridge and castle, making for photography of rapidly changing mood separated by mere seconds.

The following evening, I approach the Kyle of Lochalsh where the road bridge springs elegantly, reuniting me with the Isle of Skye. I pause for a moment, remembering my parents driving us on to the ferry to the island before the bridge was built in 1995. It's Friday night, and the bar is heaving with a kilted and saltire-emblazoned rugby team and their entourage; I tuck myself into the corner, the only one ordering food among a sea of pint glasses.

The next morning, I pass the picturesquely sheltered village of Plockton to accompany Loch Carron as it winds its way inland. Following a sea loch deep inland on one shore before returning on the other gives the walking an unhurried rhythm: it's not about getting from A to B but about relishing the moment. After the road ends at Ardaneaskan, I carry on into the moorland and check the depth of a bog ahead of me with my trekking pole. I am alarmed when it sinks without resistance down to my hand.

The weather in springtime changes so quickly it gives me whiplash – I often find that, within minutes, I'm swapping between a sun hat and two layers of insulation. Along the rugged shore of Loch Kishorn, there are no paths and indeed no people, so I take the opportunity to bathe in a stream. Despite the golden light, I can only manage momentarily dunking in the frigid water. As daylight wanes, I take a bearing to Uags Bothy, a few kilometres away; it corresponds to the position of the crescent moon, which acts as my signpost for the rest of the night's walking. When I emerge from the stone cottage into the sun the following day, I discover it has the most spectacular location of any I've stayed in, situated on a raised grassy terrace beside a crystal-clear burn with a view across the Inner Sound to the mountainous horizons on Skye.

Two days later, I'm heading north up the Applecross Peninsula where the open rolling lands of Wester Ross

Opposite:

Plockton with Sgurr a'Chaorachain and Beinn Bhàn

now have a grandstand prospect of the neighbouring isles. I share the road with the famous North Coast 500 motoring route, which is filled with people in super-cars. A herd of shaggy, large-horned Highland cows aren't too impressed, refusing to budge off the tarmac, causing a tailback of sleek vehicles.

The next morning, near Shieldaig in the north of the peninsula, my thoughts revolve entirely around food. I may be in one of the most beautiful places in the world, yet all I can think of is the black pudding roll I'd seen on Tripadvisor is available in Torridon. I haven't done a long stretch of road walking for ages, so I've forgotten how fast progress can be when the conditions are good, especially when I'm driven by hunger. Soon, I'm well fed and rested and able to properly appreciate the distinctive pink jagged stone of the Torridon Hills paired with the soft, exotic texture of the Scots pines.

On the tenth day in the county, the path from Torridon is glacier-smoothed red limestone, which often, and pleasingly, resembles high-street pavement slabs. Leaving the mountains and wind behind, I enter the shelter of Craig Bothy, which I share with two Belgian students, a family from Inverness and a Glaswegian man with his young son. Convivial conversation flows in many accents as we all cook by candlelight on our individual camp stoves while occasionally feeding a branch into the hearth.

Beyond the dead-end track to Rua Reidh Lighthouse on the Melvaig Peninsula, I look up, not quite believing my eyes, to see plumes of smoke rise from the headlands ahead as wildfire burns along the horizon at Greenstone Point on the far side of Loch Ewe. Fortunately, Melvaig and Greenstone Peninsulas create a narrow mouth and protective embrace around the loch. At the eastern mouth, I come across a jetty that was once used for loading Arctic convoys bound for Russia during the Second World War. Nearby, the hooked concrete weights remain of a submarine net that ran from this point to the opposite mouth of the loch, as do the concrete naval gun and anti-aircraft emplacements. 'They said when the Arctic convoy was here, you could walk from one side of the loch to the other, there were so many ships,' a local fisherman tells me. 'I had three boats once, but I sold them now. The industry's changed; fish farms are all big corporations today. When I started, the fish were in wooden cages, and we fed them by hand; now, the fish barges feed the pellets in by machine, and each barge has one operator who controls everything by a computer on-shore.'

The following day, I reach the Greenstone Peninsula where the traces of war are absent but the landscape is charred from the wildfire. Fence posts have been burnt away, leaving their wires draped and exhausted across the landscape. Walking through the ravaged heather, my trousers look like a toddler has attacked them with a stick of charcoal. In places, peat still smoulders, sending up twirls of smoke. This unexpected transformation makes an interesting photographic subject as what one expects to be green is now black. At the tip of Greenstone Point, I enjoy the rare luxury of being able to delay putting up the tent as there is no wind. Sleeping on the dry peat is as comfortable here as a mattress at home. In the morning, I am excited to see my first glimpse of the isolated peaks of Assynt, the very far north.

A couple of evenings later, I have a sinister night's sleep, having pitched my tent opposite Gruinard Island, where, in 1942, biological warfare tests using anthrax took place. It was only in 1990, after forty-eight years of quarantine, that the island was deemed safe and the warning signs were removed. Needless to say, I collect my water for dinner a couple of hours away!

Scoraig Peninsula to Ullapool passes by in a blur. Hot, sunny skies make walking a brain-dead act and my world becomes timings and points to aim for – I set myself the goal of walking for fifty-five minutes at a time, with five-minute breaks in between. It's cooler as I head into the Coigach Peninsula along the postman's 'path' to Culnacraig. It's an alarmingly steep walk and I spend most of it watching my footing.

From Coigach headland, I have a panoramic view of Assynt, where the isolated mountains of Suilven and Quinag rise steeply from the flat moorland like totems in the landscape. For three nights in a row, the sunset appears with a vivid intensity. The entire sky glows red and pink, with the mountains burning fire orange. I look down at my hand to see that it shines as gold as if I'd illuminated it with a gelled theatre spotlight. When I preview the pictures on the camera, the images appear unreal, like I'd applied an extreme Instagram filter.

On my last night in Ross and Cromarty, the spot I've chosen for my tent above the dunes and tranquil sandy beach at Achnahaird feels safe and sheltered; the nearby archaeological remains of duns (ancient forts) and Viking hut circles suggest I'm not the first to think so. With only five hours of semi-darkness, I need an eye mask to fall asleep, making me aware of how far north I am now.

Opposite, clockwise from top left:

The Thomas Telford slipway to Skye covered with a modern concrete screed, Glenelg

Silence: Ardintoul Wood

Some weather over Loch Duich and the Five Sisters of Kintail

A glimpse of Eilean Donan Castle at dusk across Loch Duich. Soon, the rain started up again, and I retreated to the tent

The massive triangular lintel over the doorway of Totaig Iron Age Broch near Loch Alsh

Last light, Ardelve Point

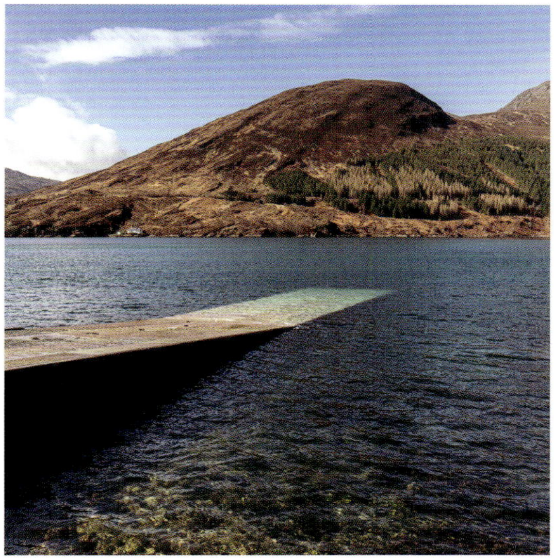
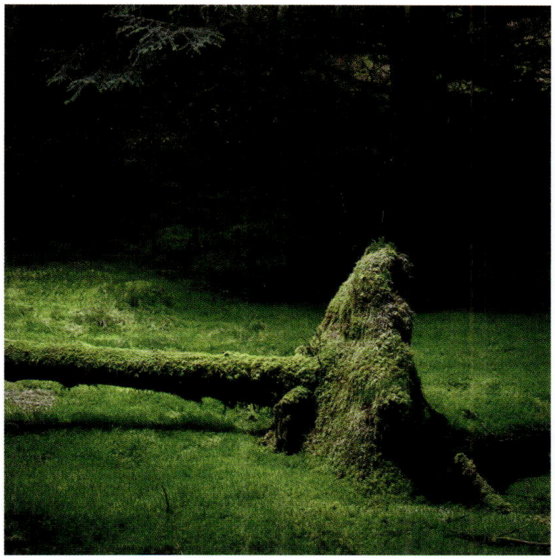
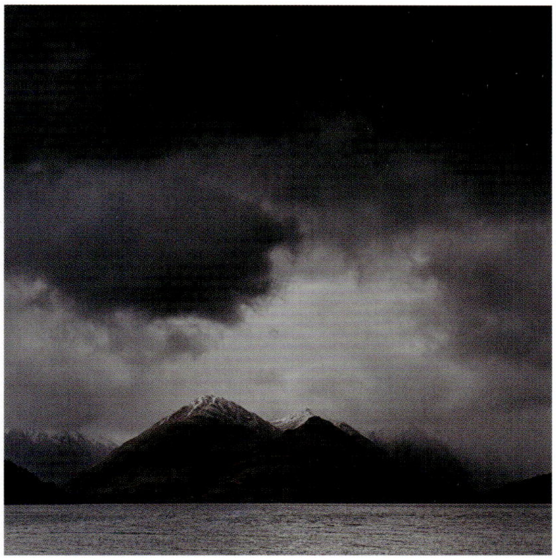
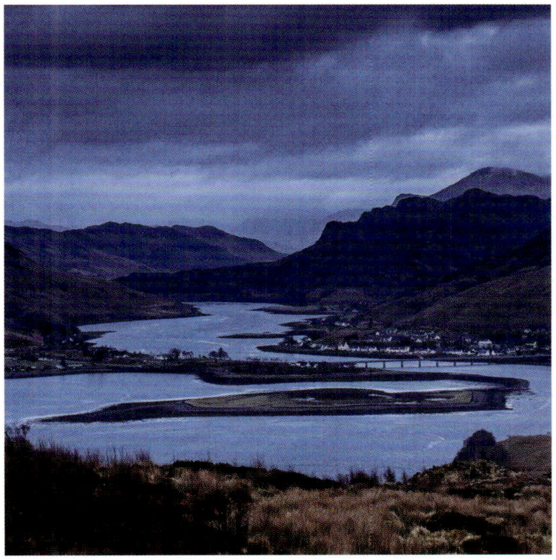
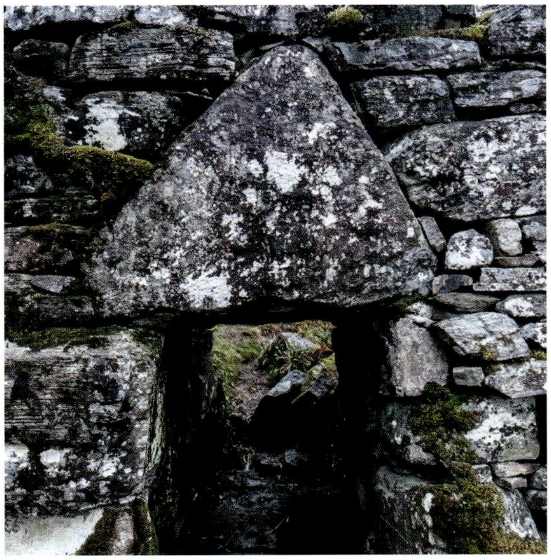
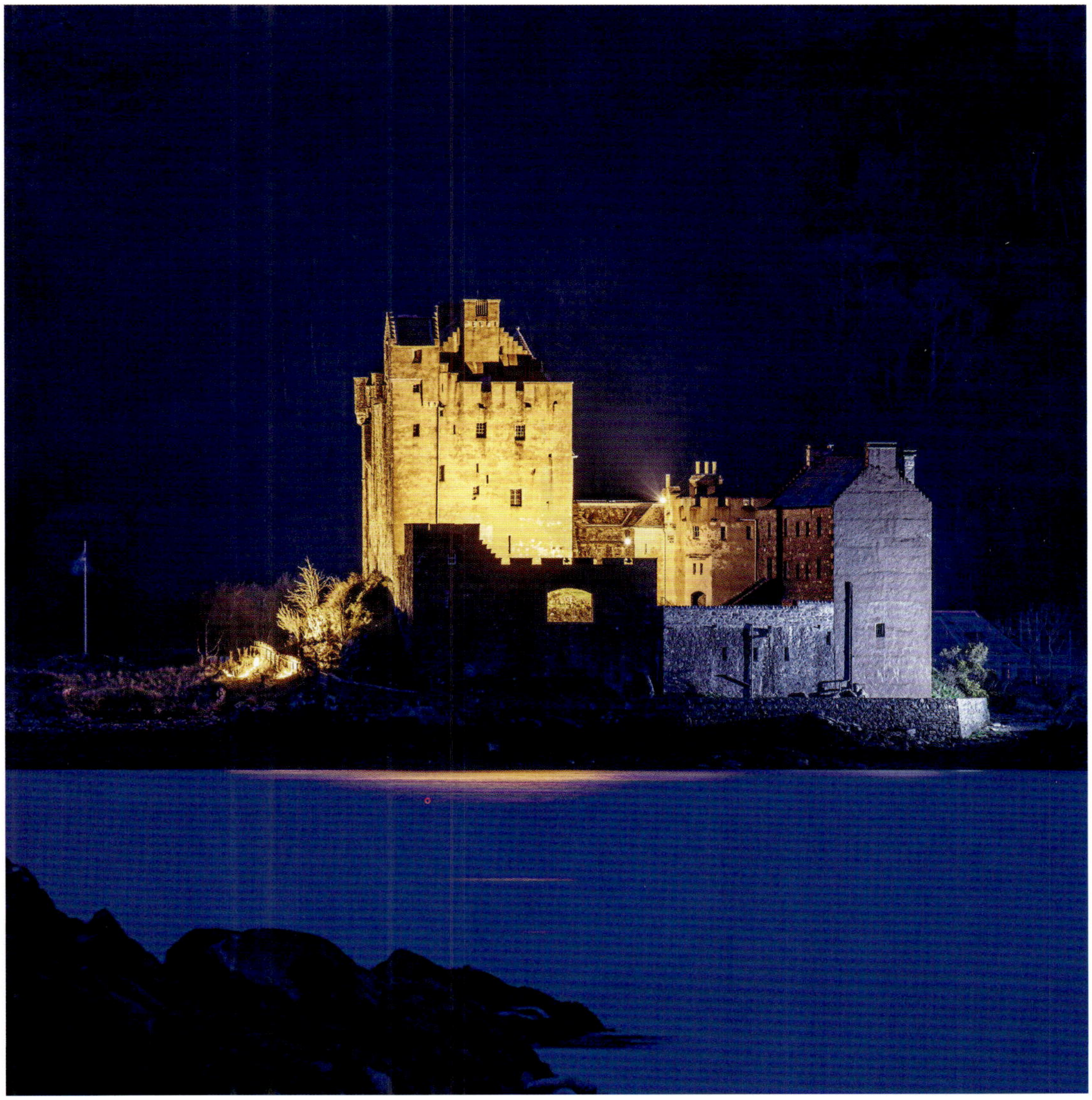

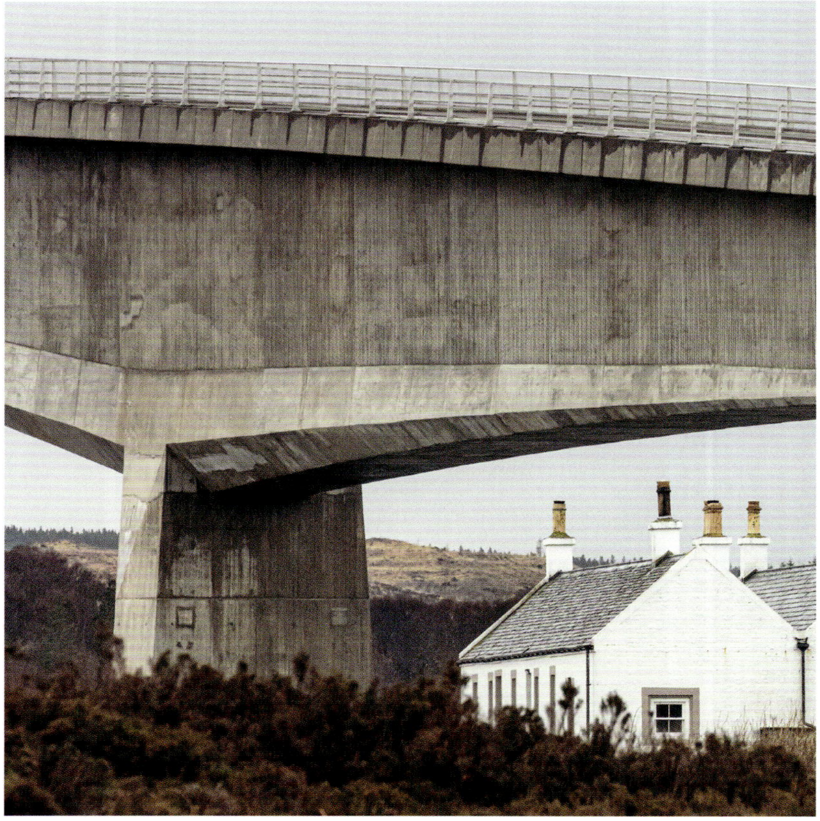

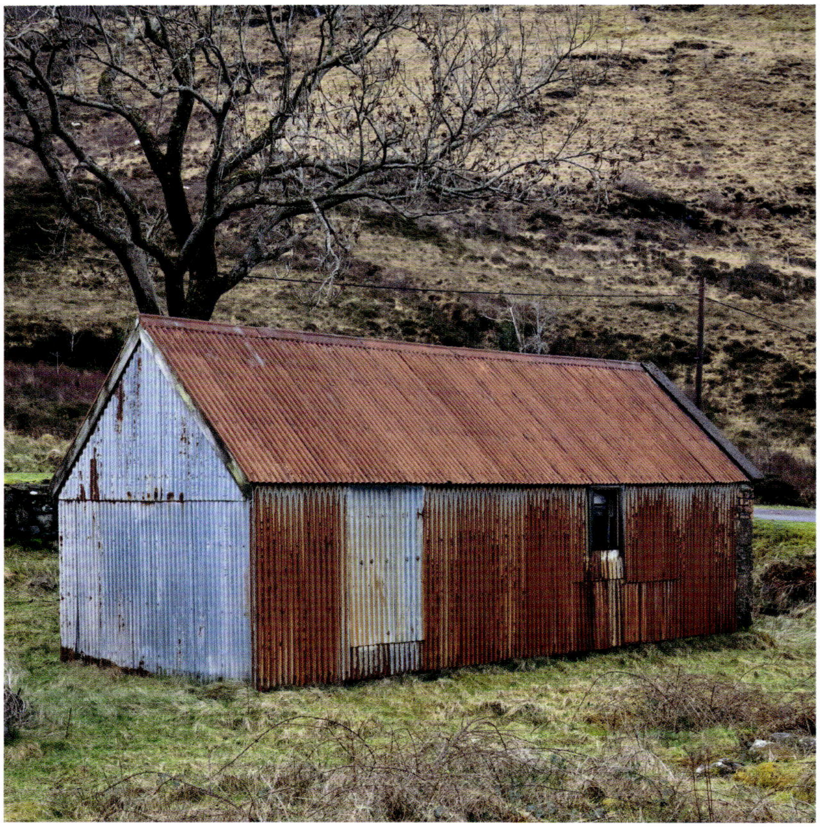

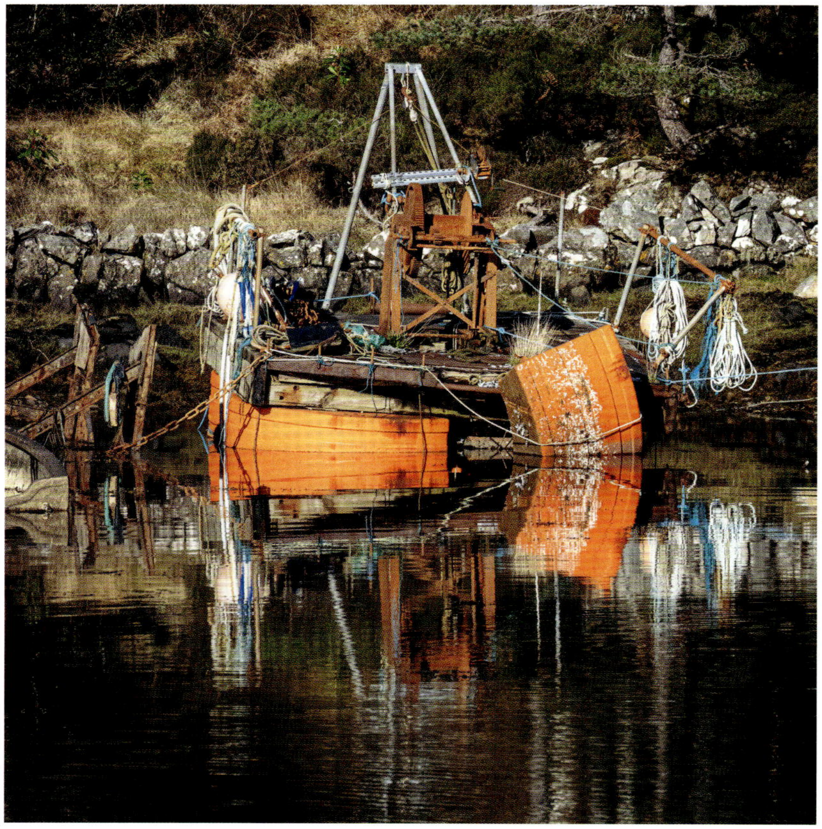

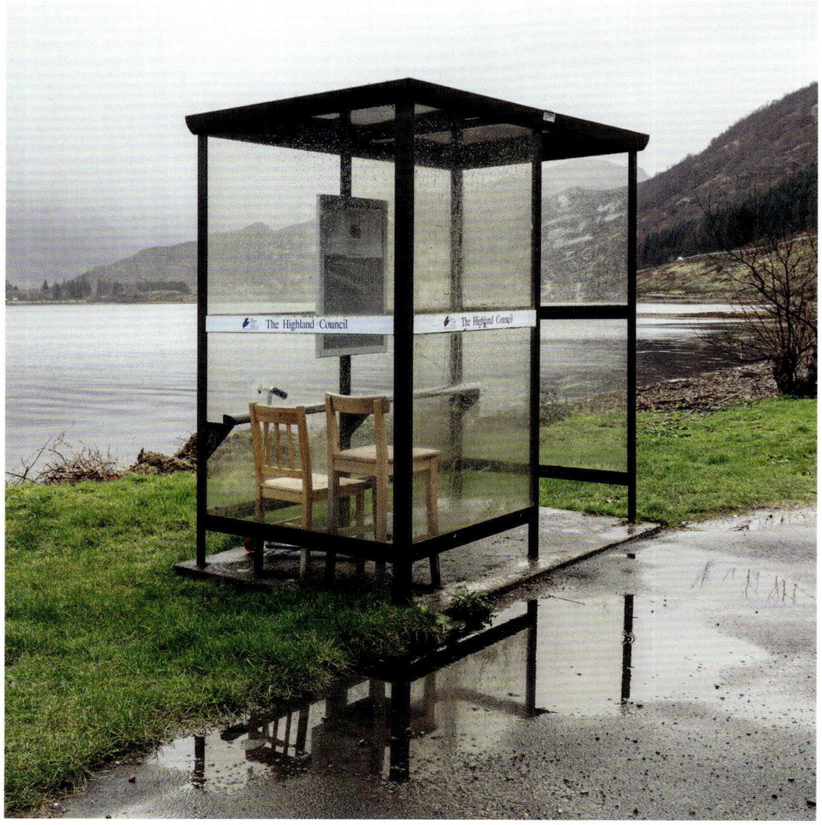
The Highland Council

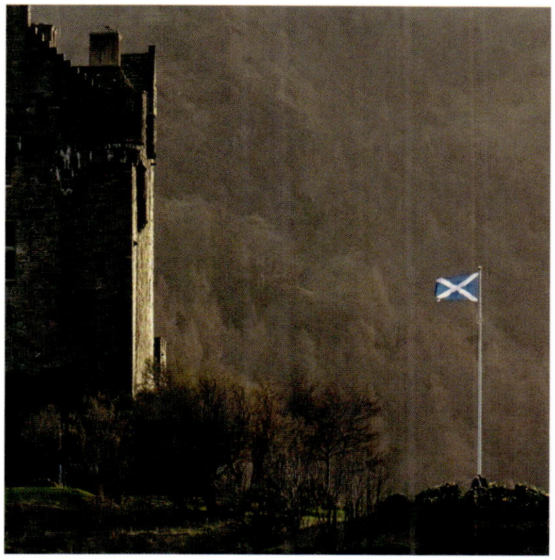

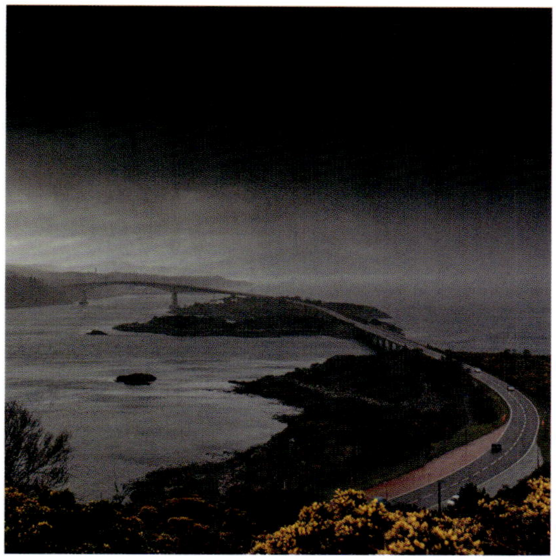

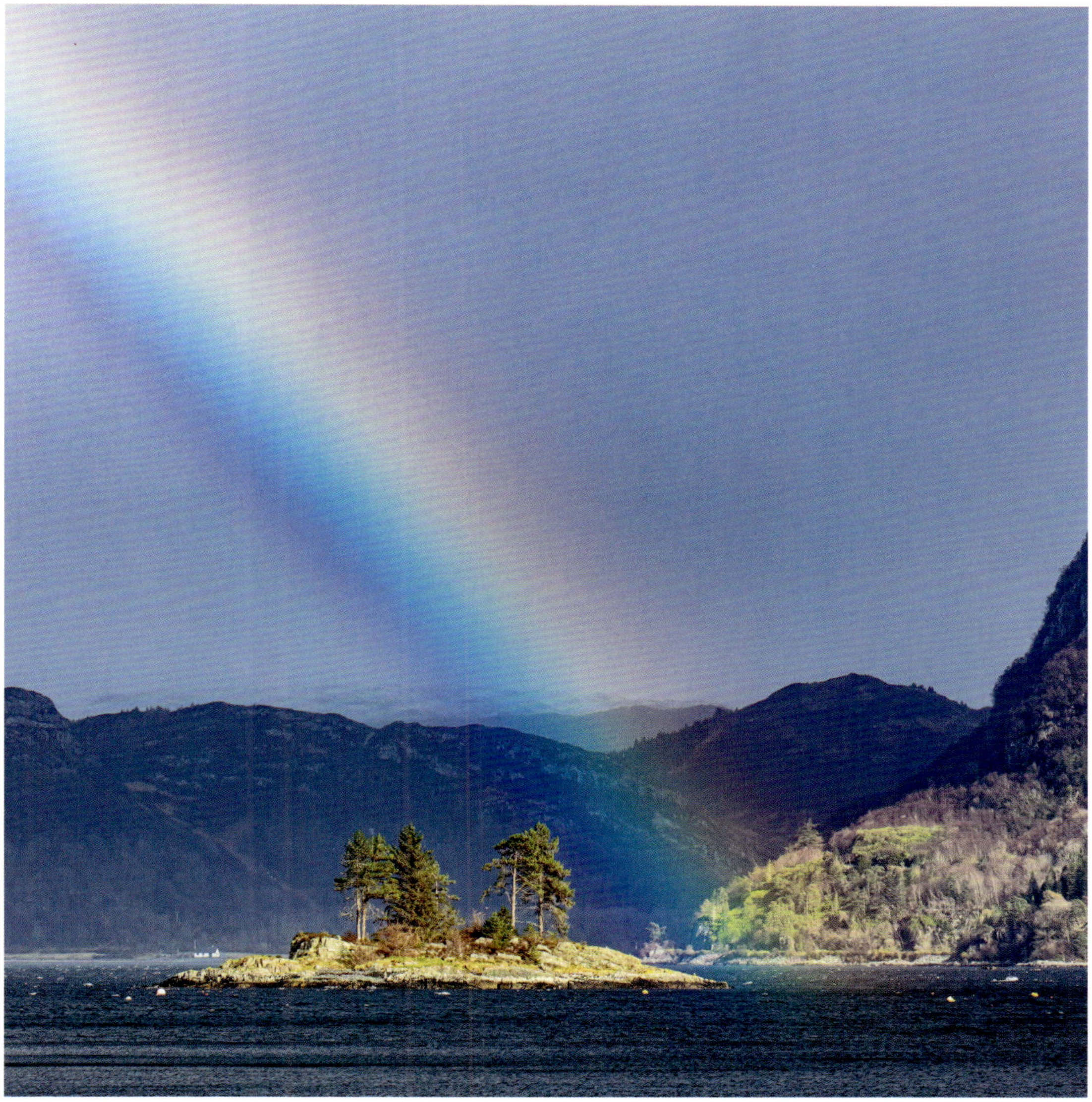

Opposite, from top left:

Gavin Maxwell Cottage on Eilean Bàn below Skye Bridge where the author of *Ring of Bright Water* lived in the last years of his life after his Sandaig home was destroyed by fire

Shed at Invershiel, Loch Duich

From bottom left:

Winch near Plockton

By Loch Duich

From top left:

Eilean Donan with Saltire

A passing rain cloud over Skye Bridge from the Plock of Kyle

Rainbow with Sgeir Bhuidhe and Loch Carron from Plockton

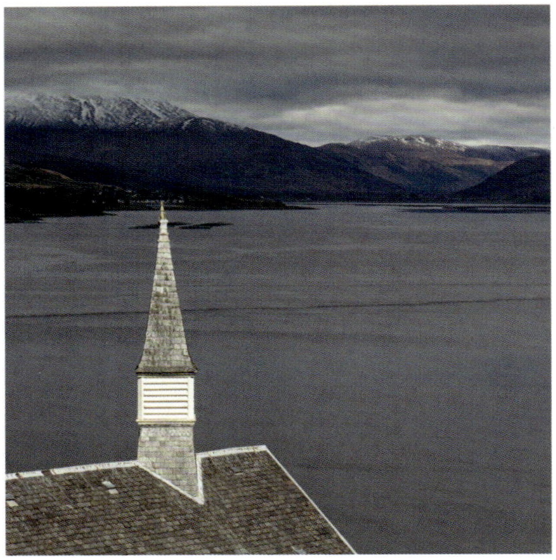

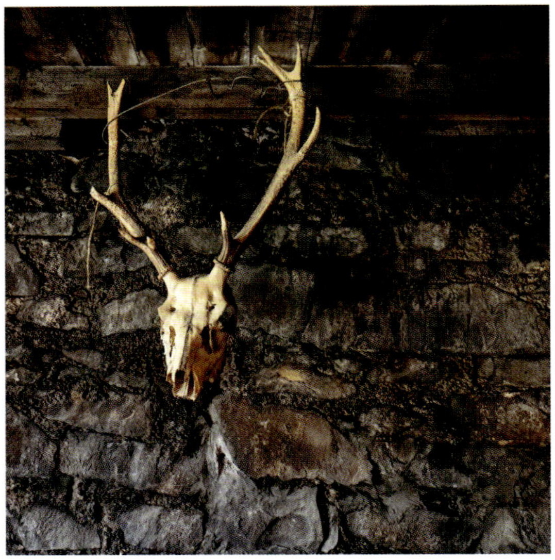

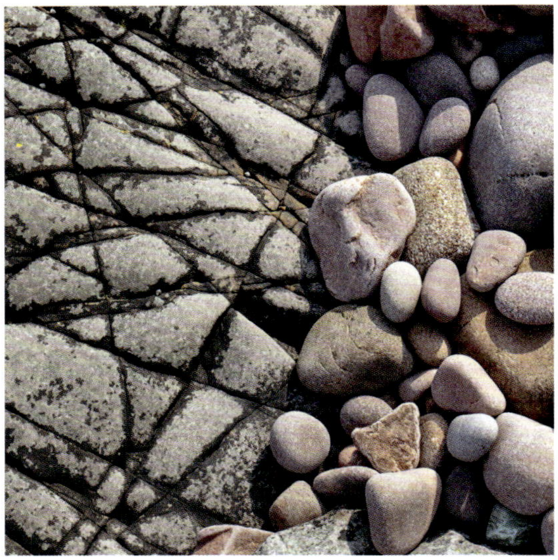

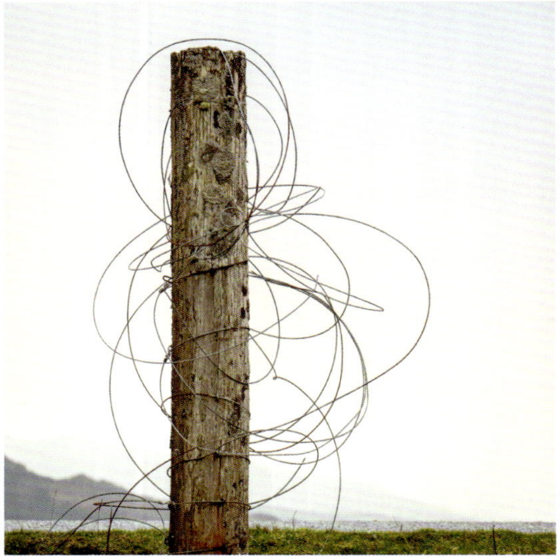

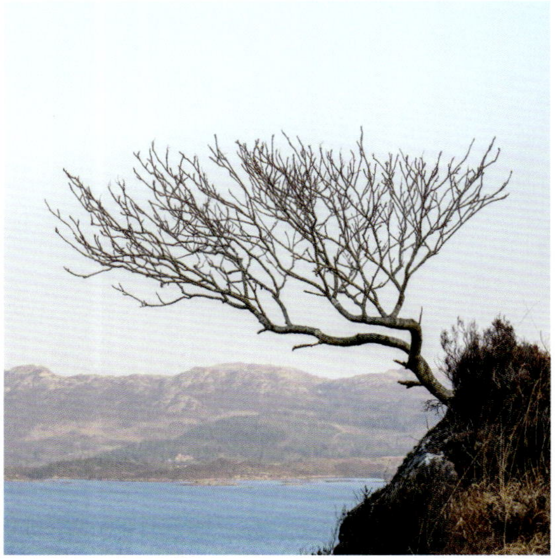

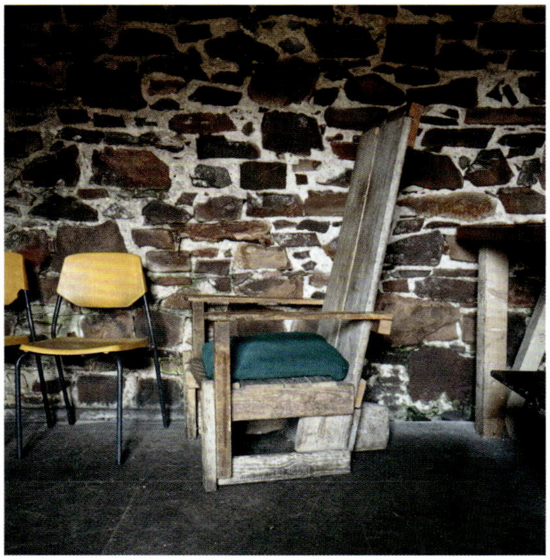

From top left:

Stromeferry (No Ferry), Free Church Mission Hall

Above the hearth, Uags Bothy

From centre left:

By Loch Carron

Fence post by Loch Carron

From bottom left:

Nature's Bonsai: Loch Carron

The throne: Uags Bothy

Opposite:

Uags Bothy and Skye the morning after sleeping inside

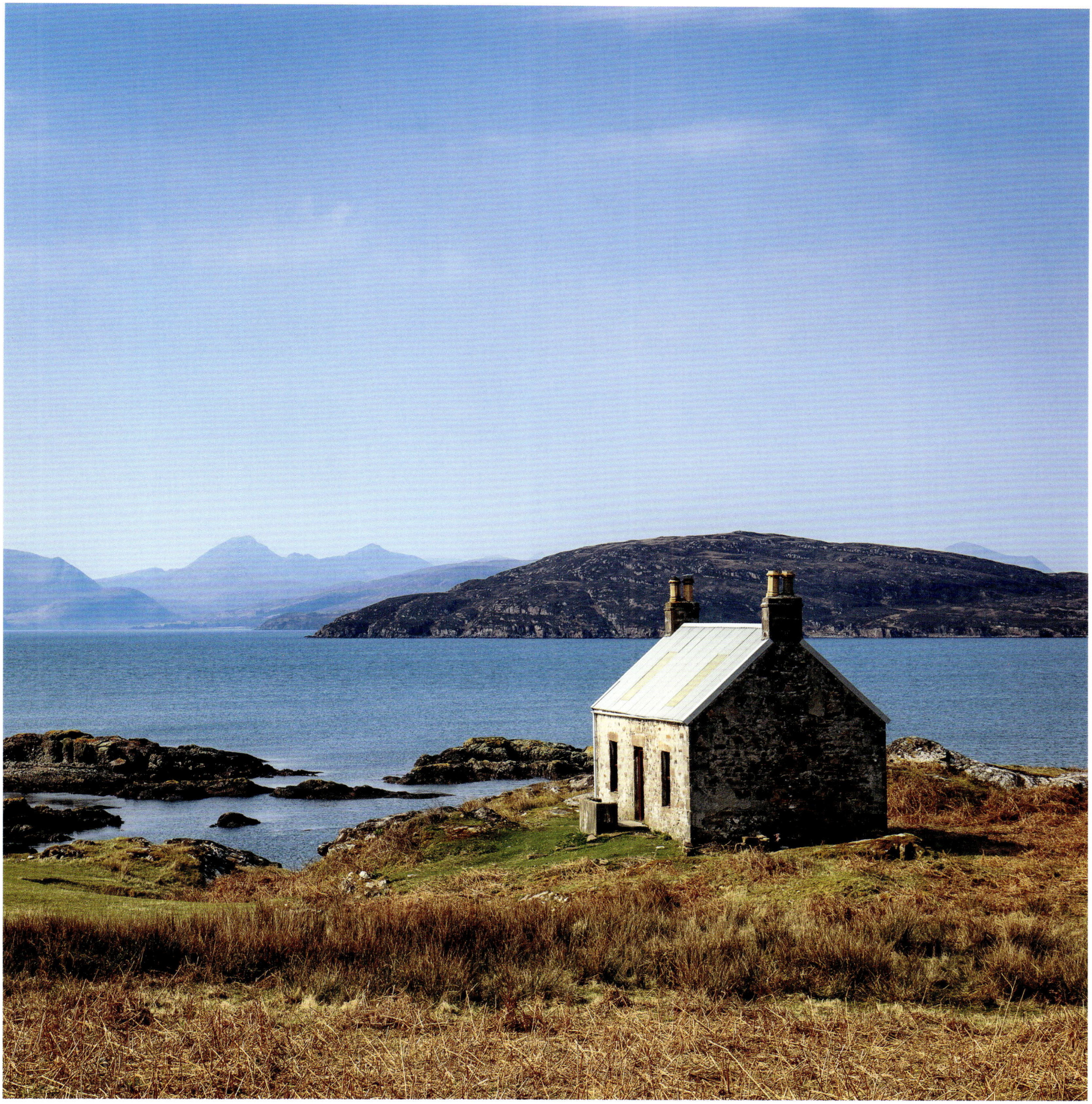

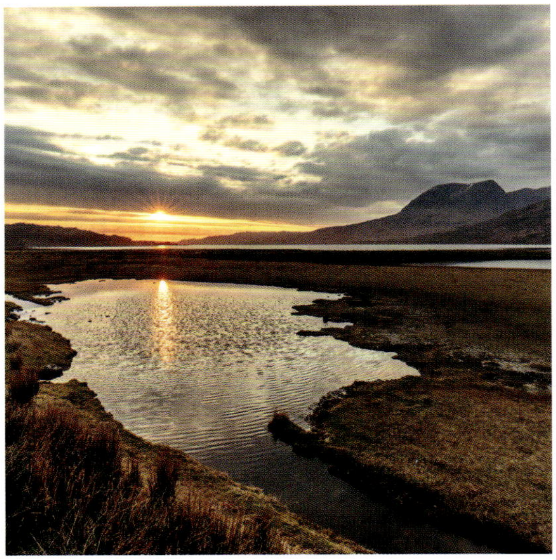
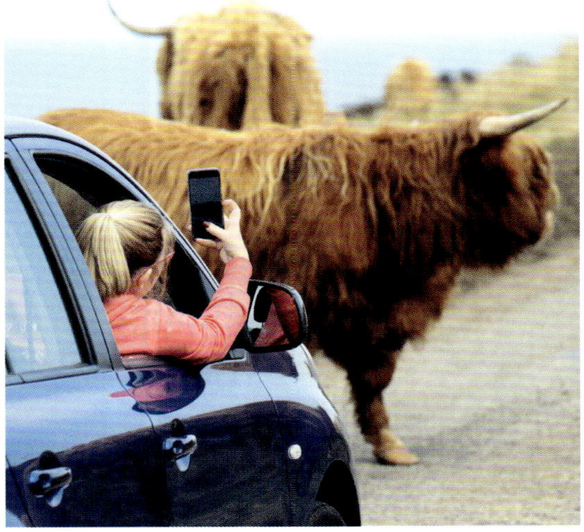
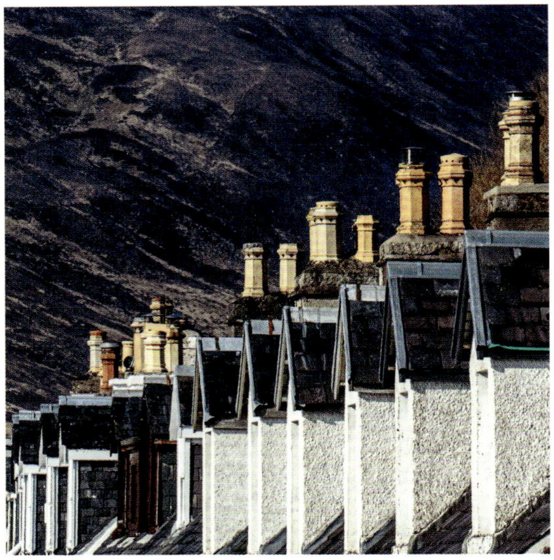
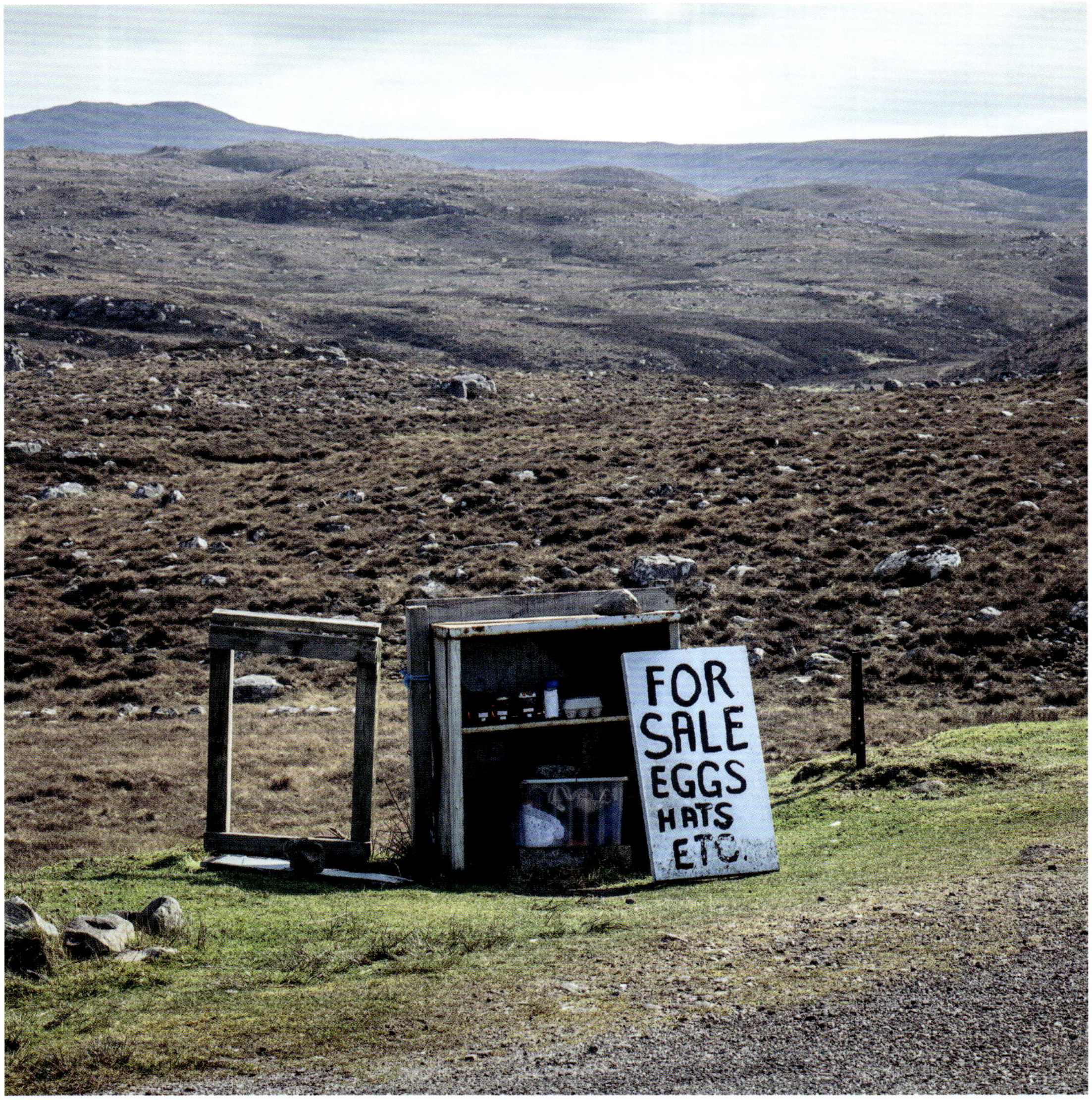
FOR
SALE
EGGS
HATS
ETC.
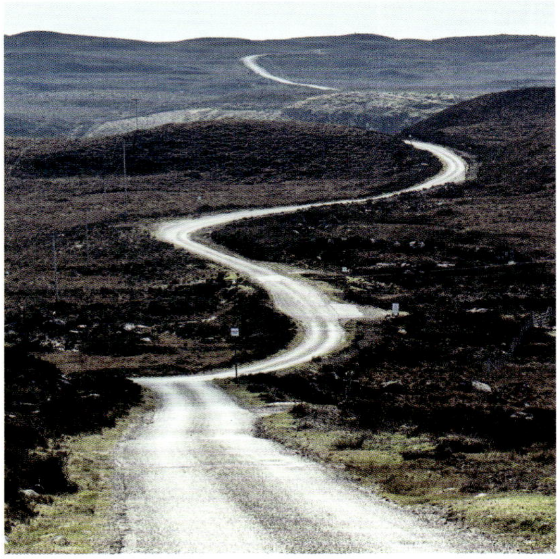
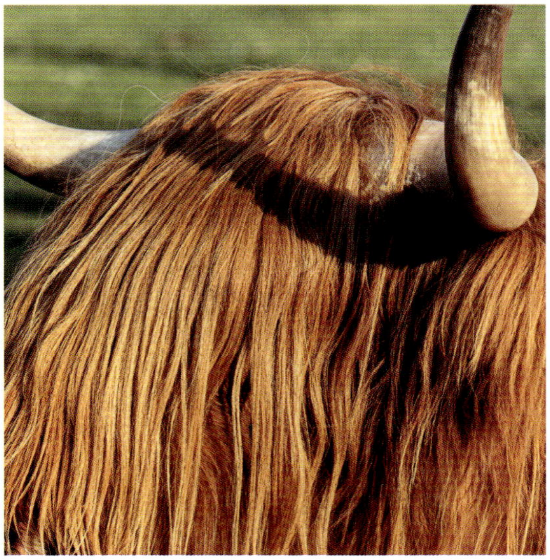

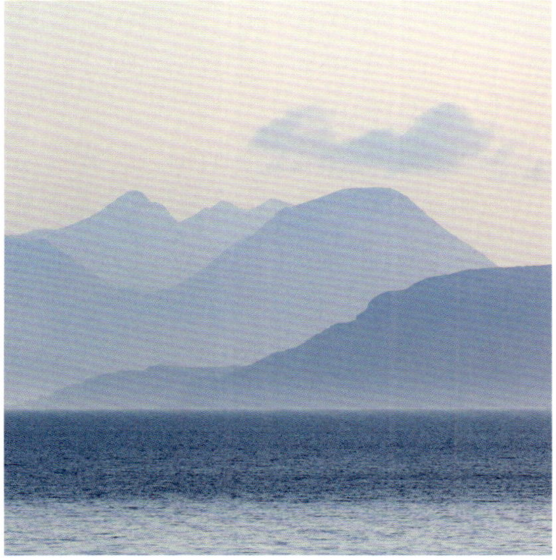

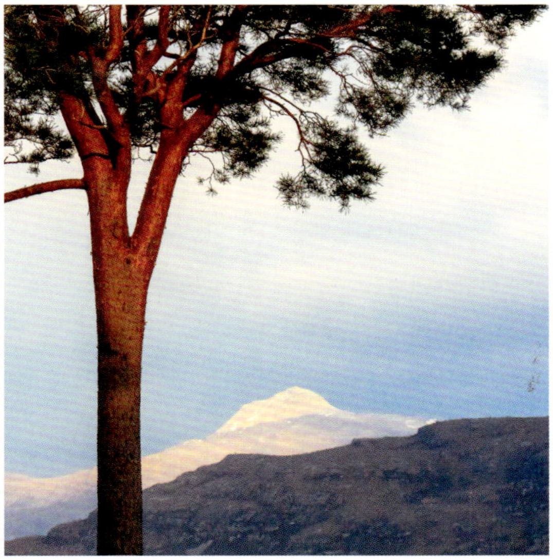

Opposite, clockwise from top left:

Last light, Upper Loch Torridon

Making the most of the traffic jam, Applecross Peninsula

Applecross

Easy to see the appeal of the North Coast 500 on the Applecross Peninsula

I don't want a haircut, OK! *slams door, stomps to bedroom*

Etcetera: Cuiag

From top left:

Shieldaig blues

Landskein, Skye and Raasay

Last light, Torridon

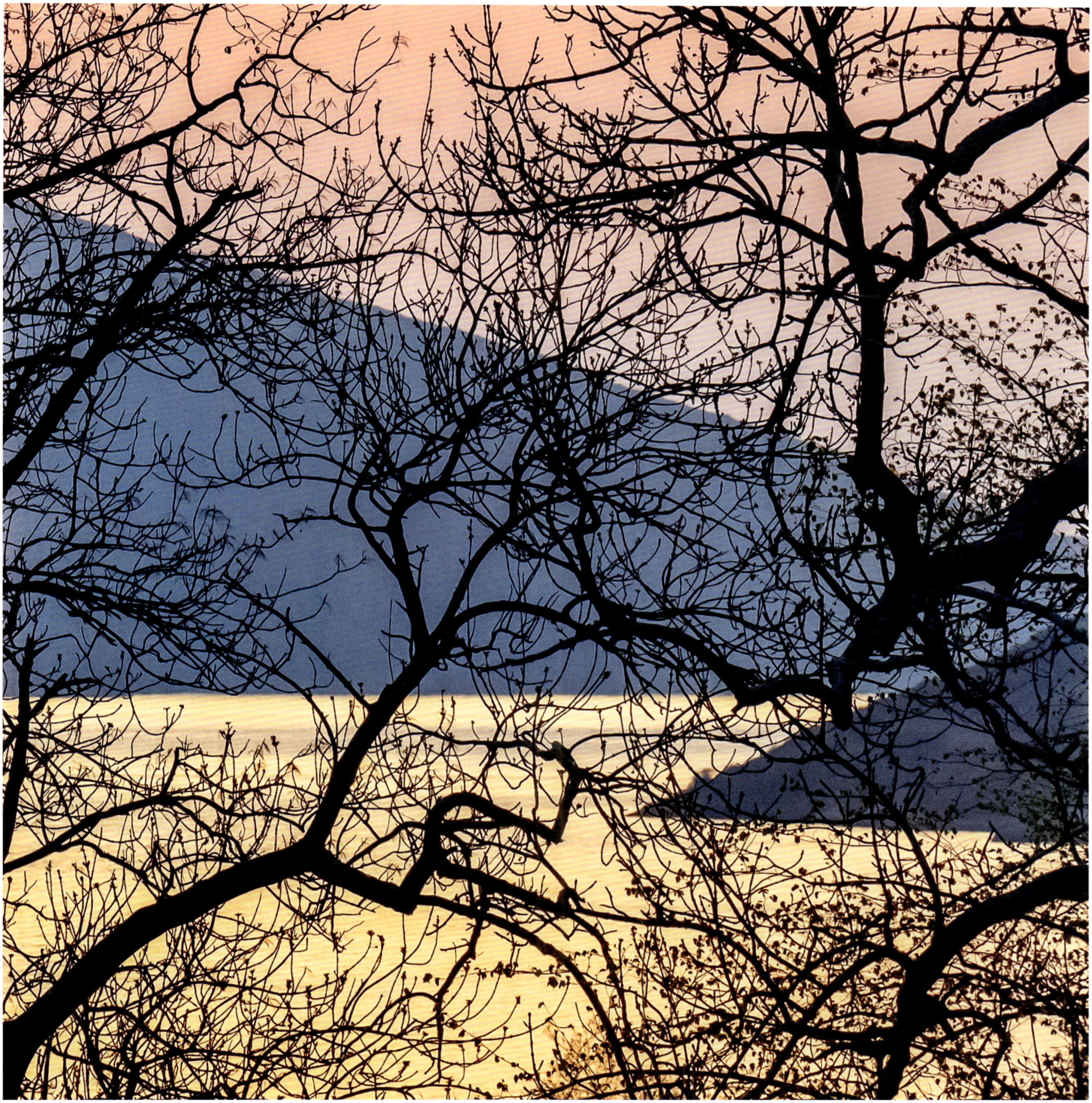

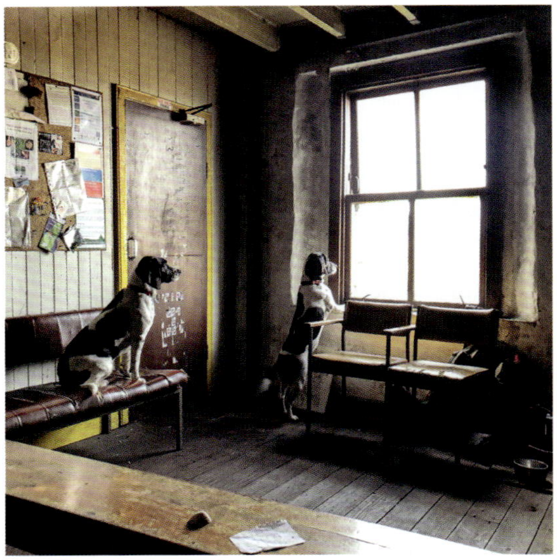
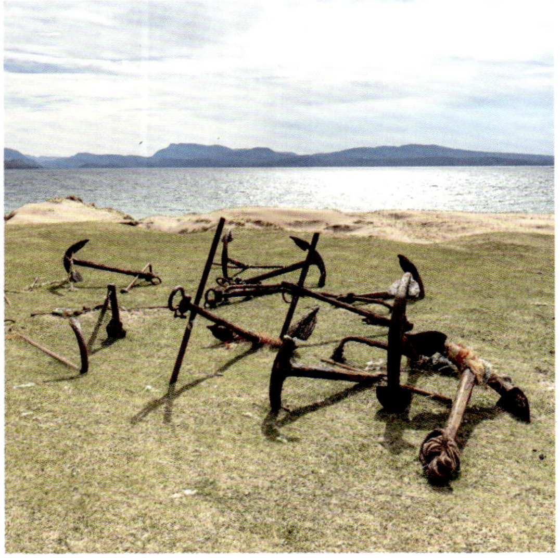
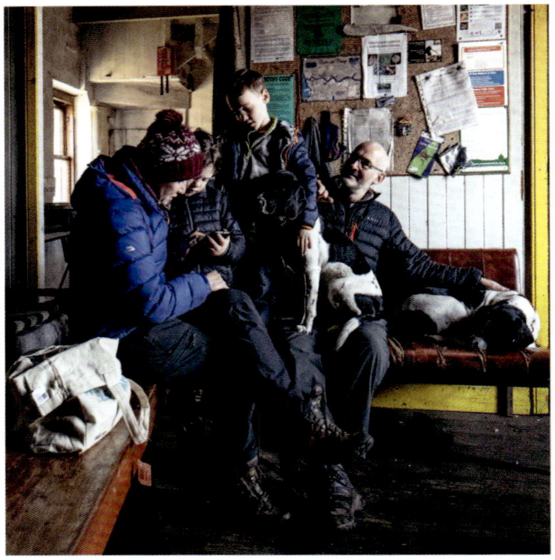
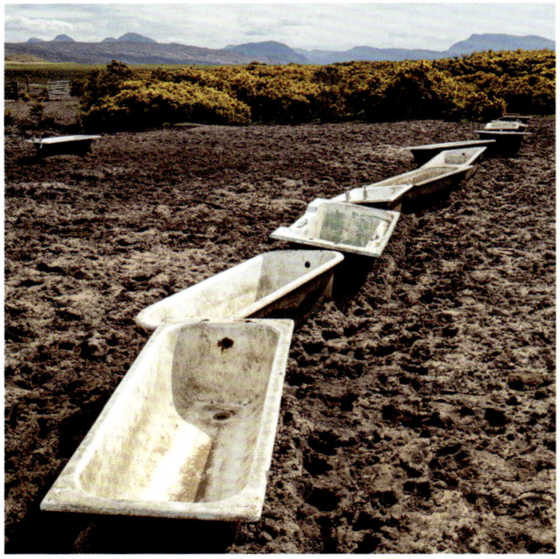
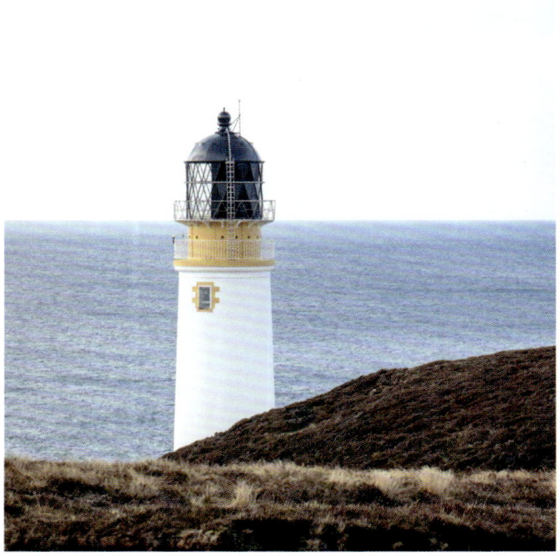
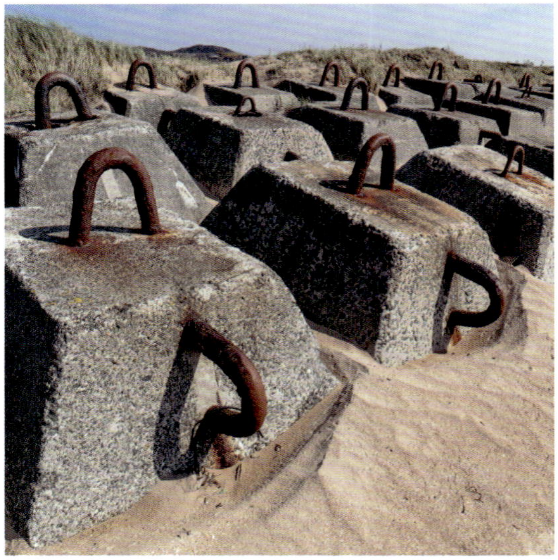
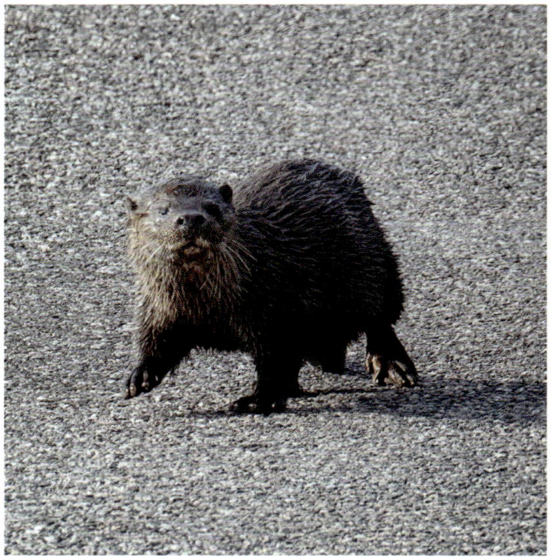
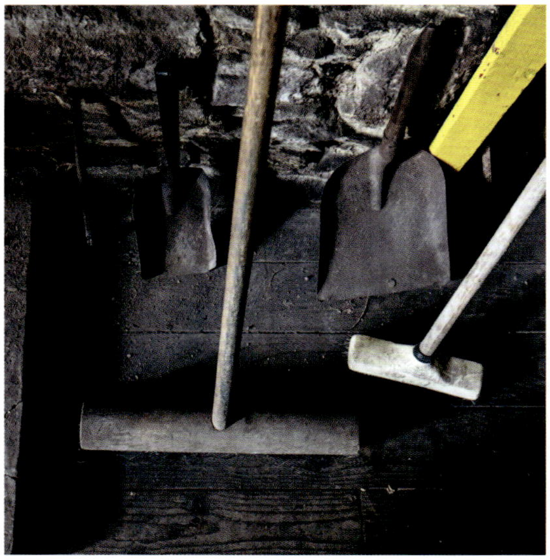
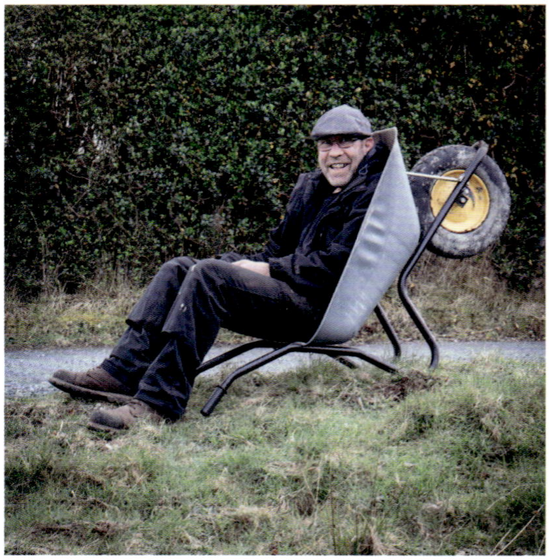

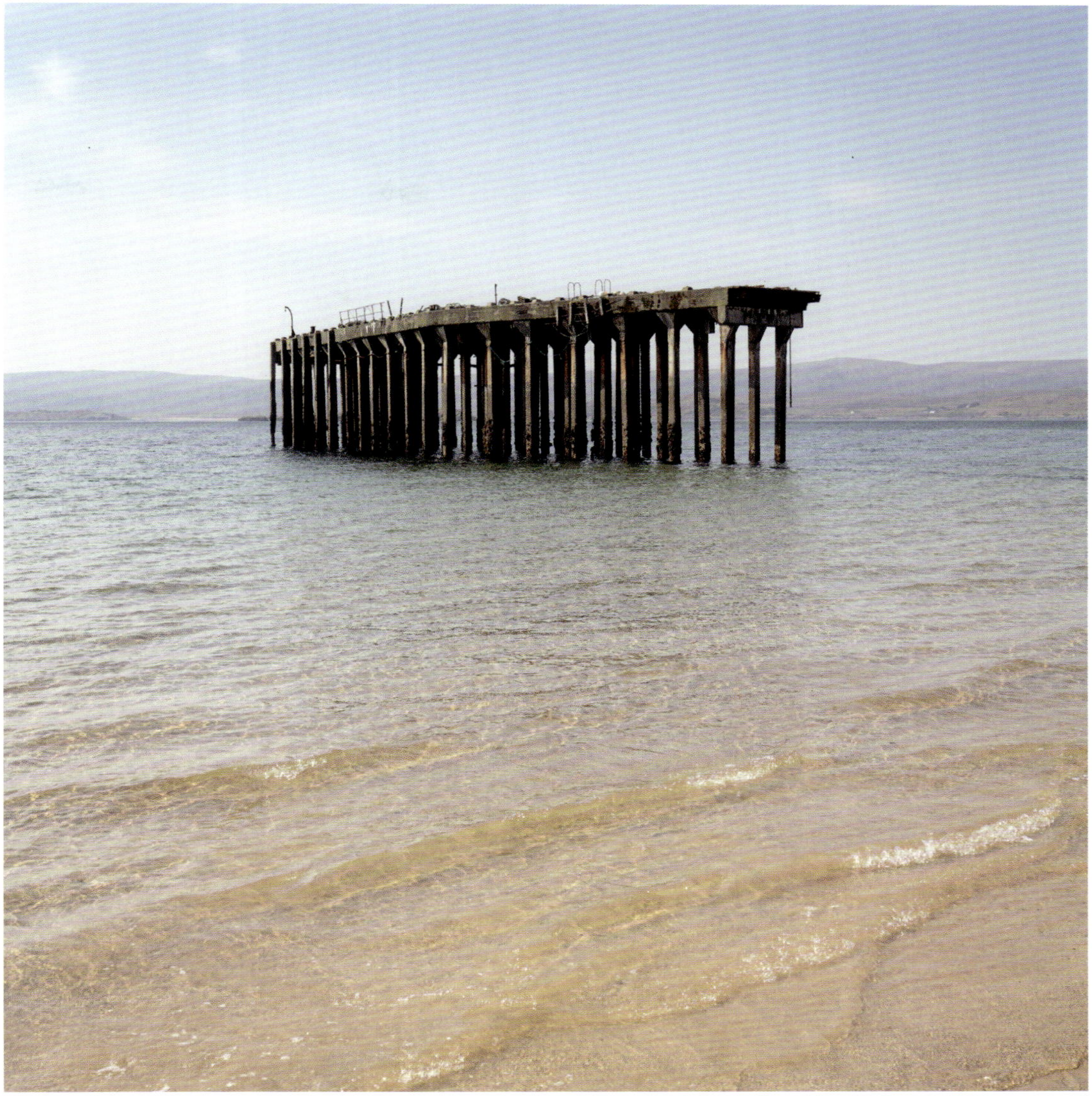

Previous, from left to right:

Upper Loch Torridon

Last light by Loch Broom

Opposite, from top left:

Millie and Patch, Craig Bothy

Anchors at Red Point salmon-fishing station

Lenka, Lilly, Ben and Simon with their dogs, Millie and Patch, Craig Bothy

From centre left:

Bathtime: Red Point

Rua Reidh Lighthouse overlooking the Minch

Blocks used to secure an anti-submarine net across the mouth of Loch Ewe in the Second World War at Mellon Charles

From bottom left:

An otter crossing the road at Rubha Reid Lighthouse

Craig Bothy

Mark, who subsequently offered me a brew and some food, at Brae by Loch Ewe

From top left:

This structure in Loch Ewe is the remains of a jetty used for loading the Arctic convoys in the Second World War, where they began their perilous journey. A submarine net ran from this point to the opposite mouth of the loch

Searchlight position, Cove Battery, Loch Ewe

Red Point salmon-fishing station

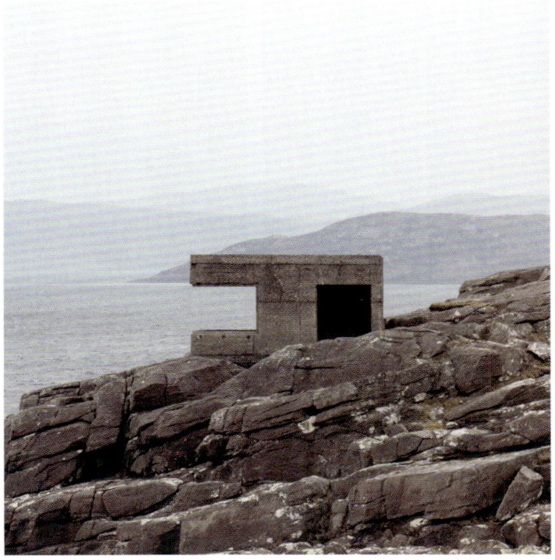

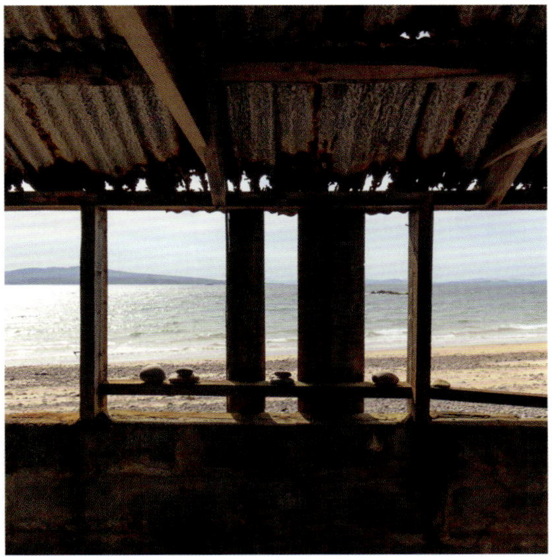

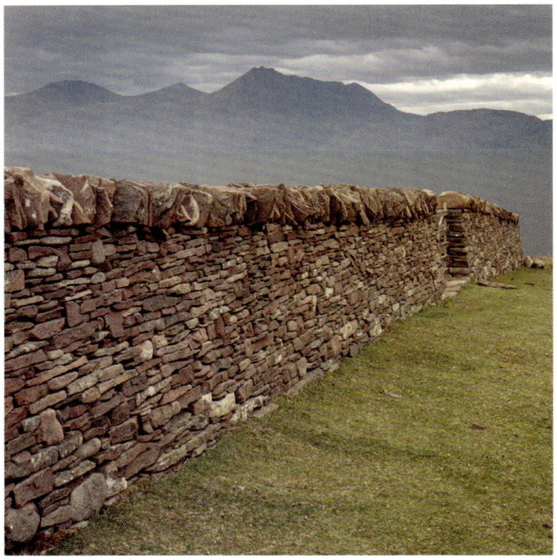

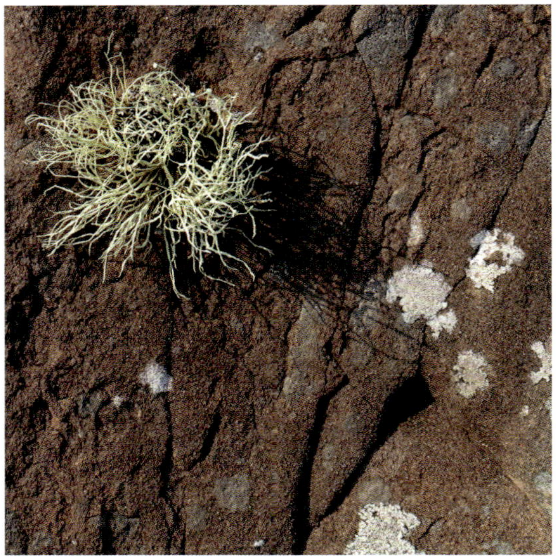

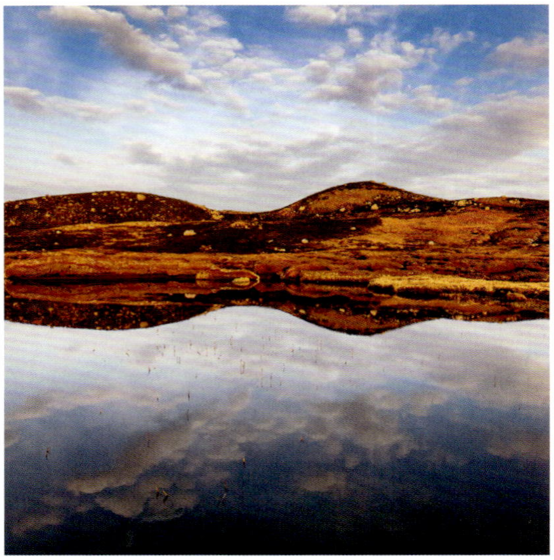

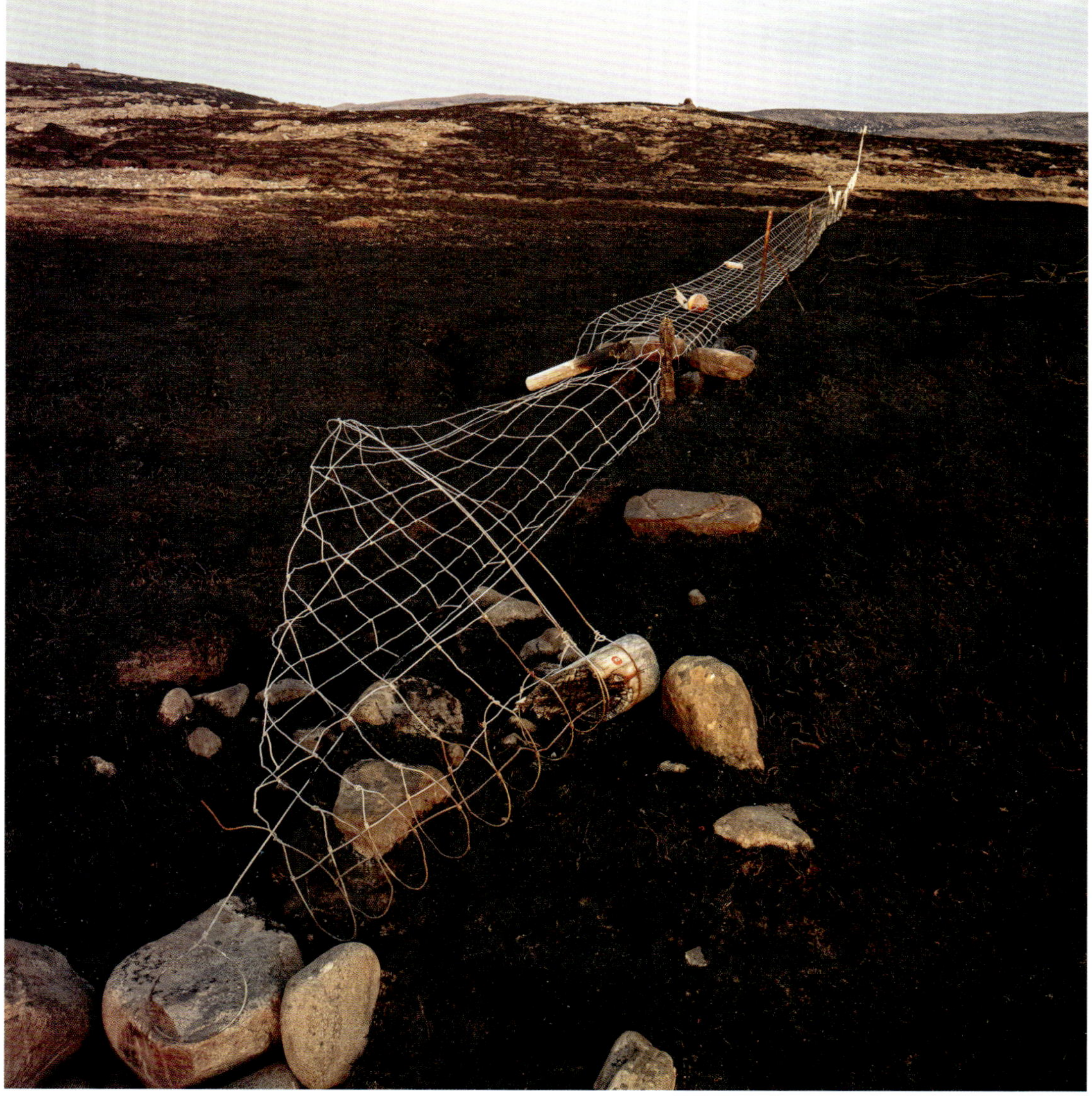

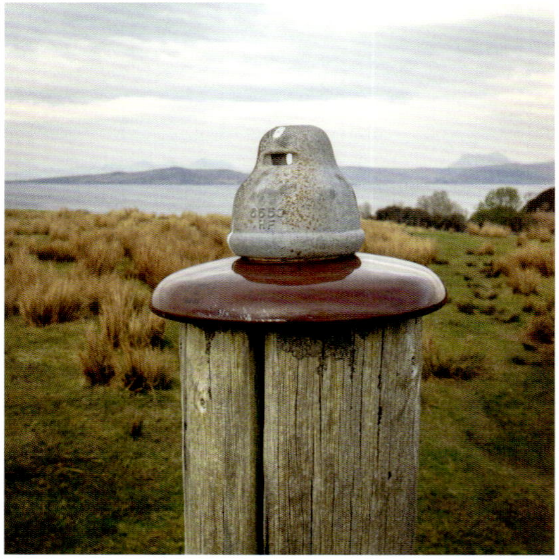

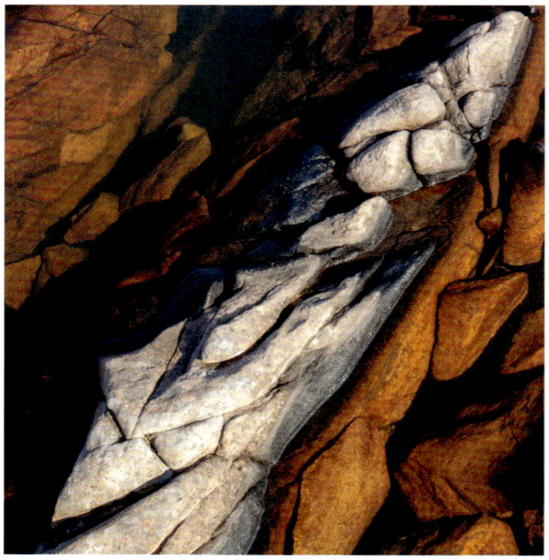

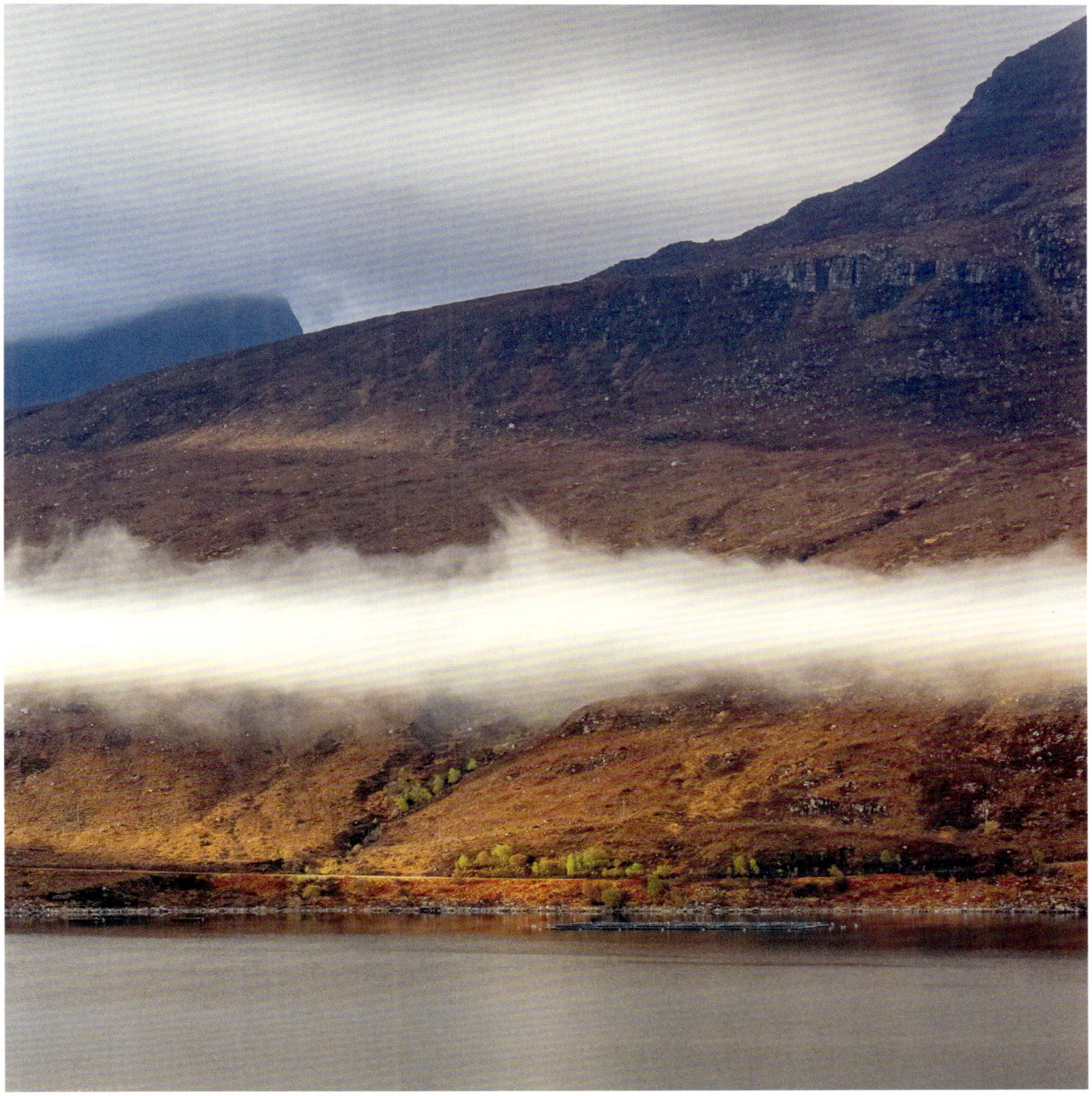

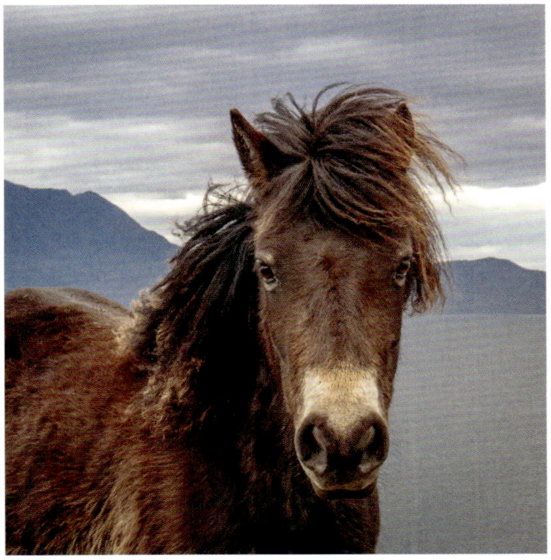

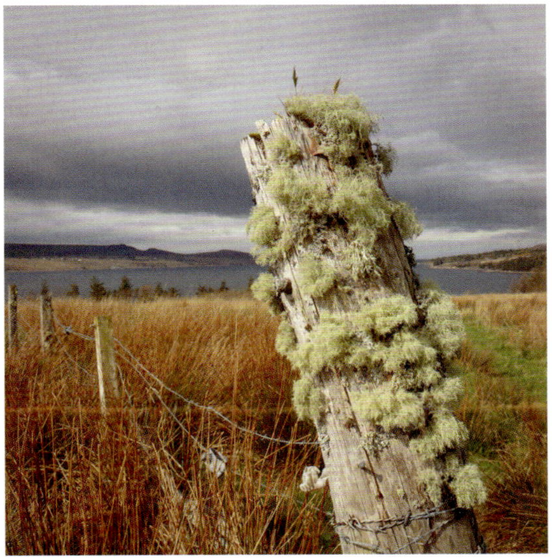

Opposite, clockwise from top left:

Annat, Scoraig Peninsula

Underfoot, Greenstone Point

Lochan near Greenstone Point

Fence cap, Gruinard Bay

Tidal pool, Greenstone Point

After the wildfire, Greenstone Point

From top left:

Morning band of sea fog, Little Loch Broom

A spirited horse at Annat, Scoraig Peninsula

Hairy fence post, Scoraig Peninsula

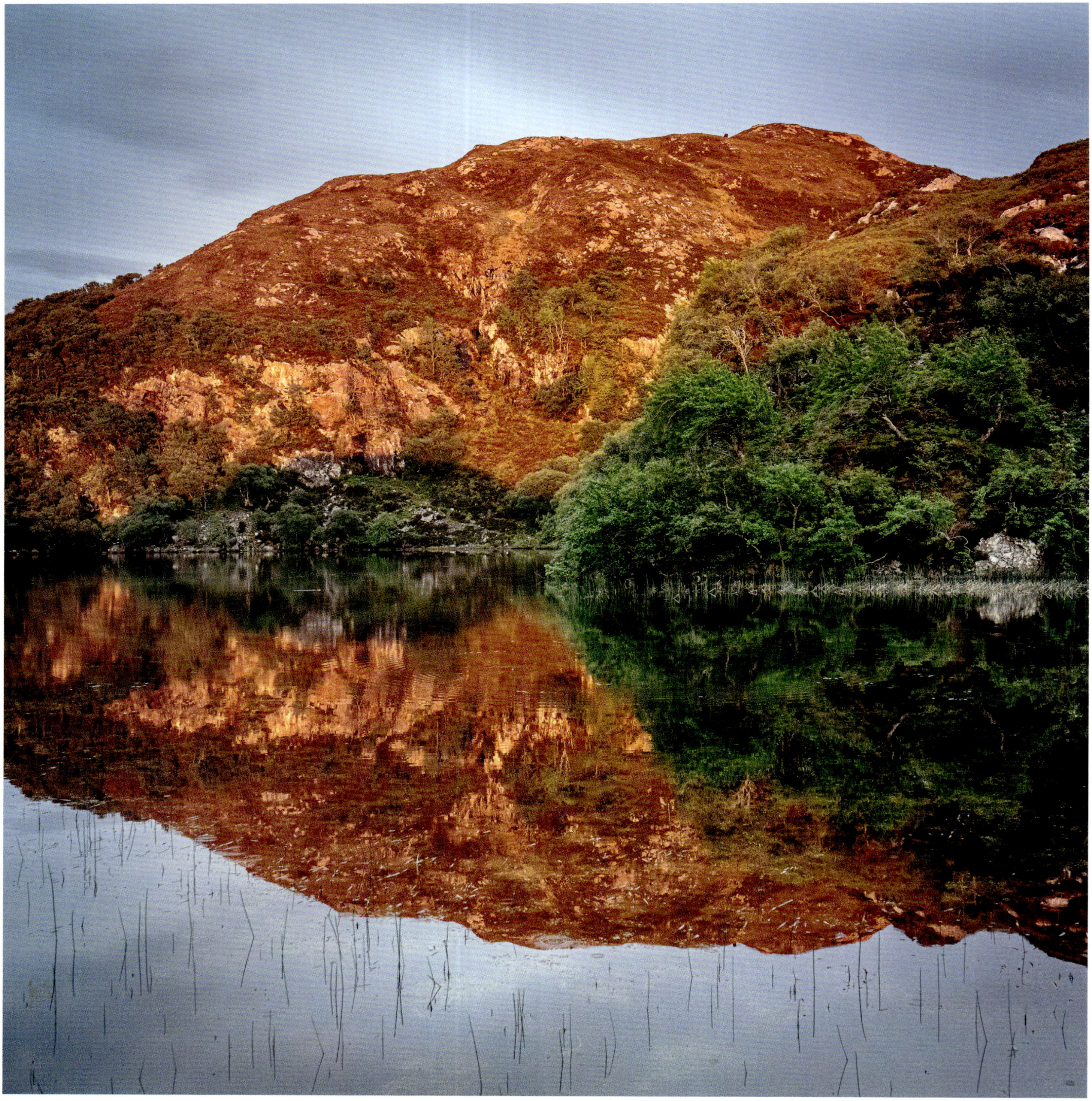

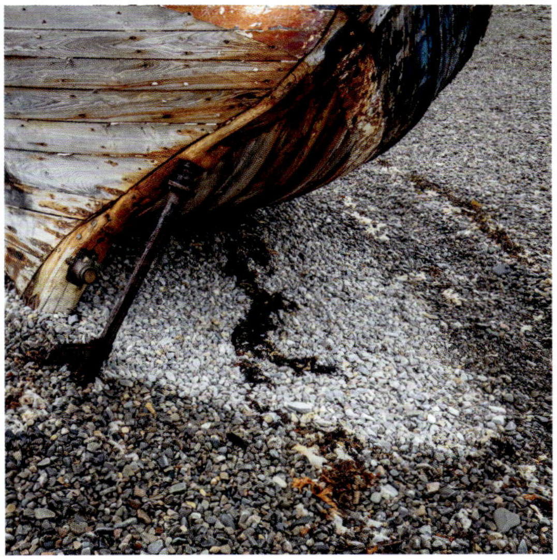
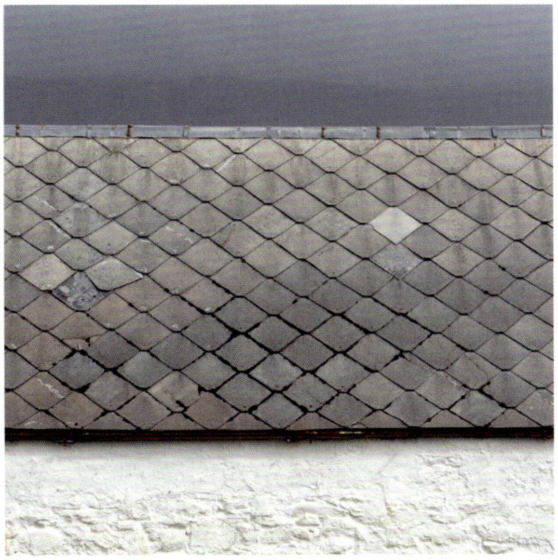
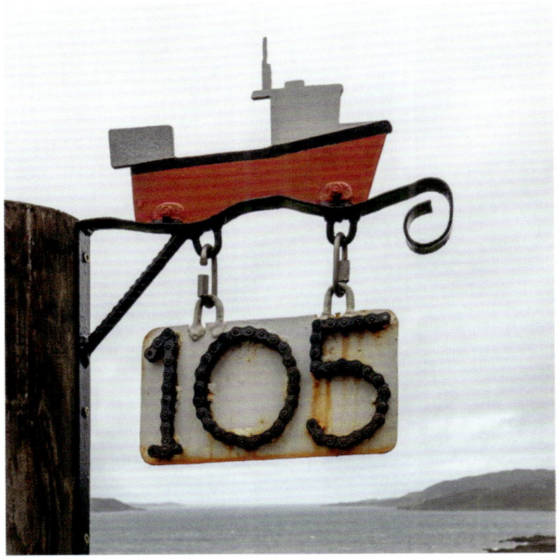

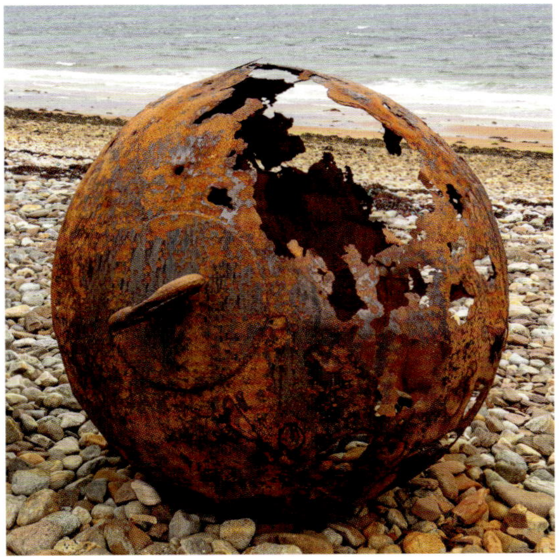
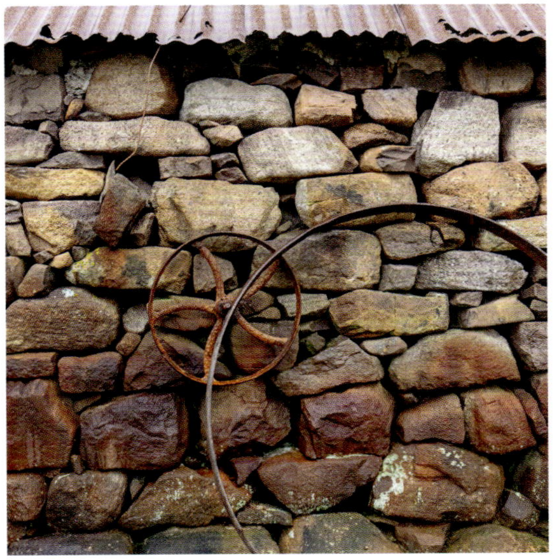
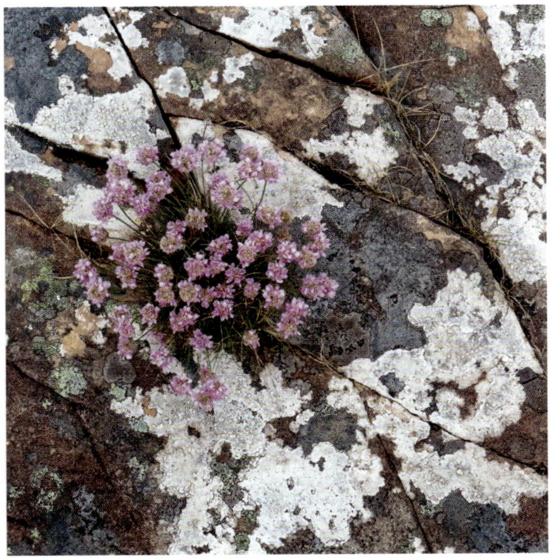

Opposite:

A luminous moment before sunset by Lochan Sal, Assynt

From top left:

Rain shadow, Luib na Mor-choille, Ullapool

Asbestos diamond cottage roof, Polbain

From centre left:

Achiltibuie

Terra incognita: Badentarbat Bay, Achiltibuie

From bottom left:

Culnacraig

Sea pink at Garvie Bay

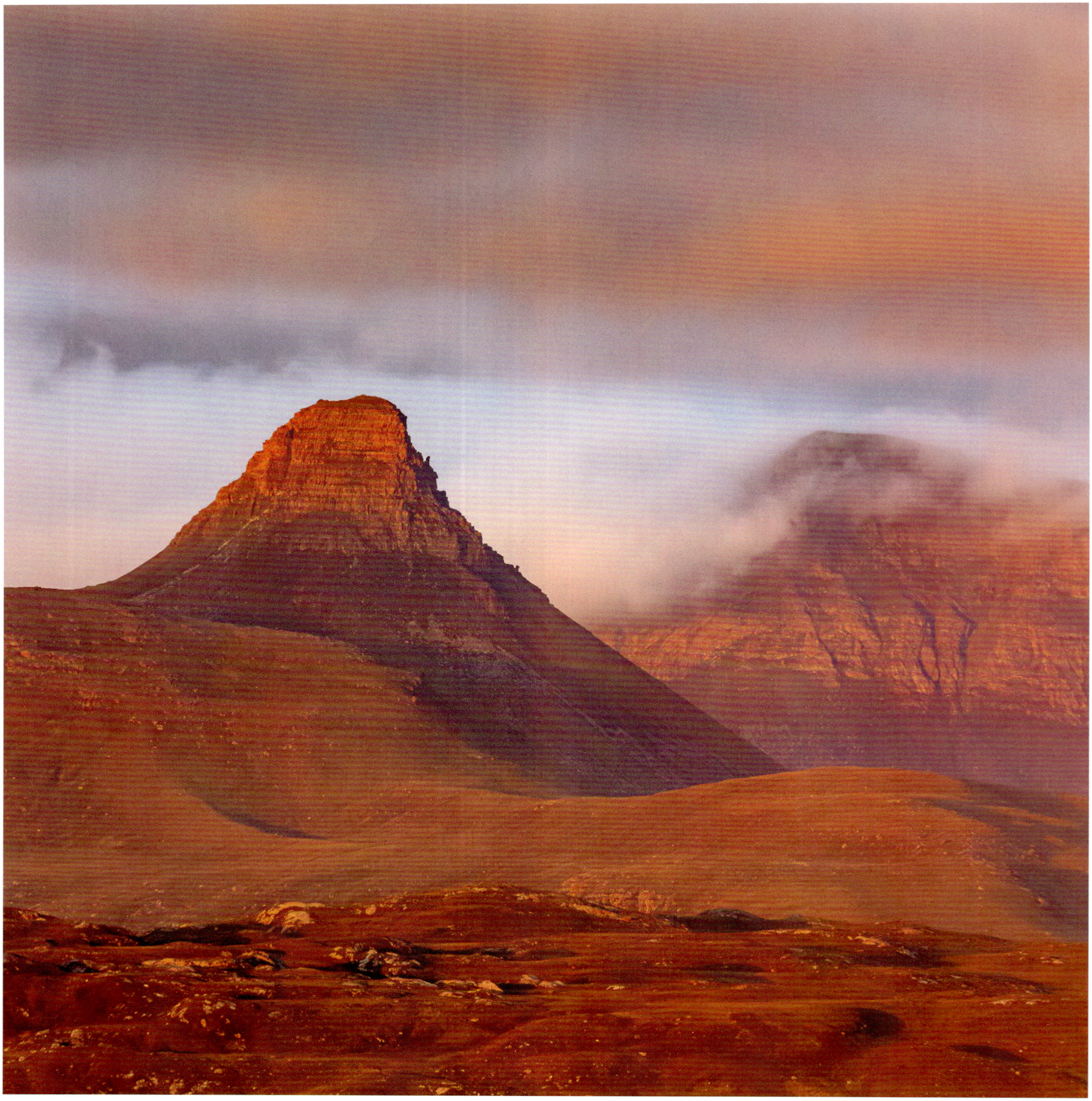

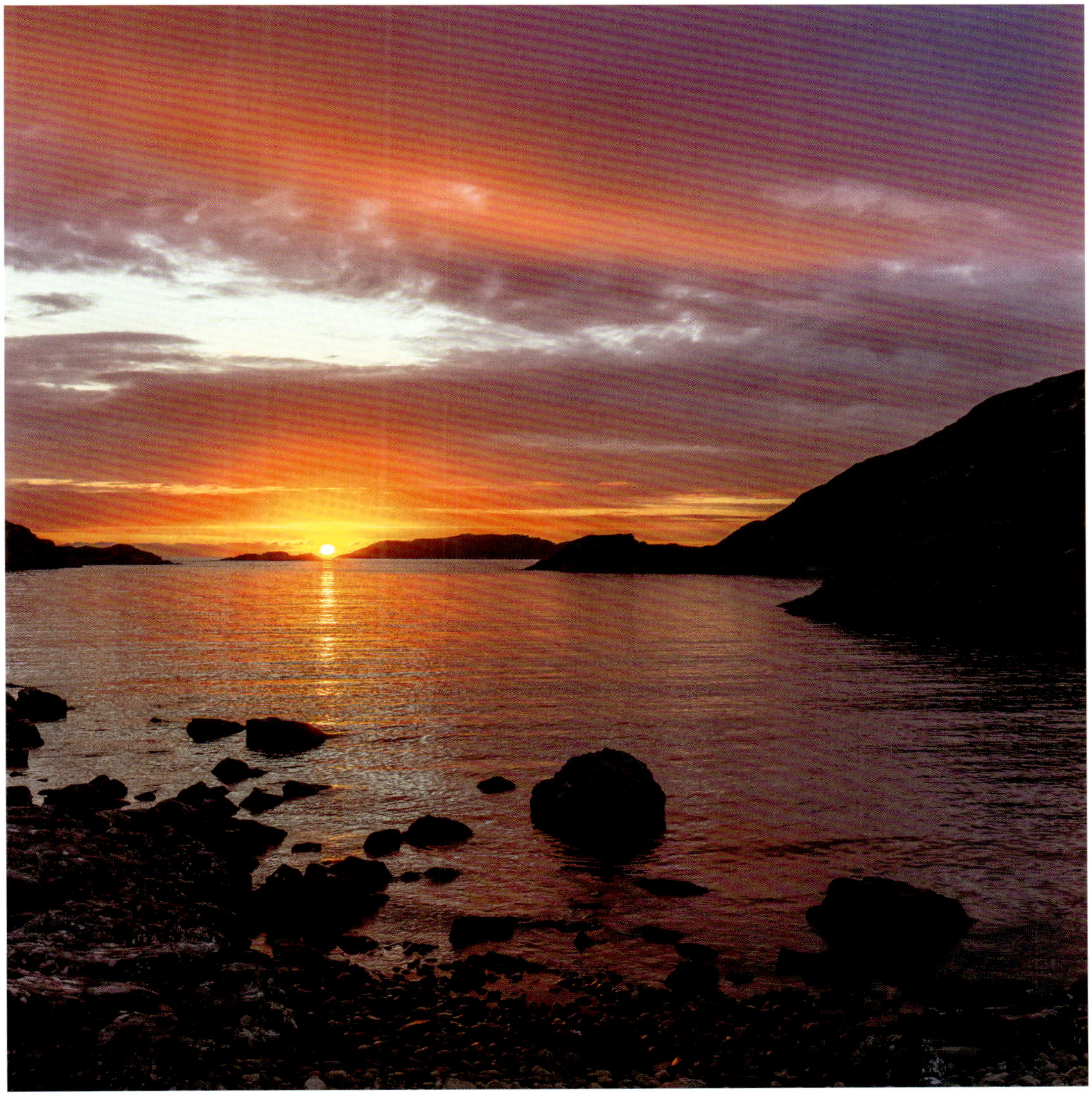

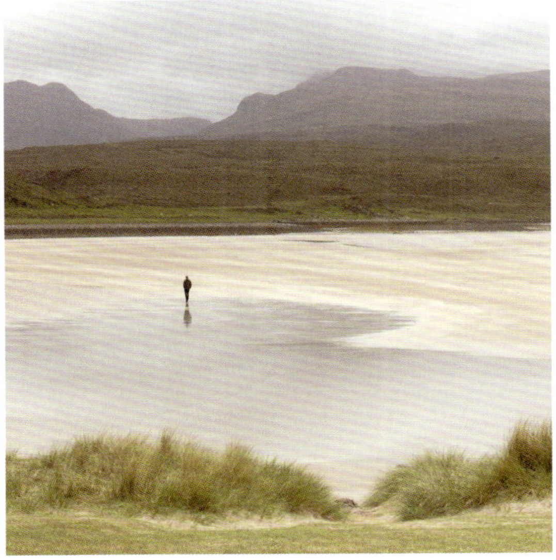

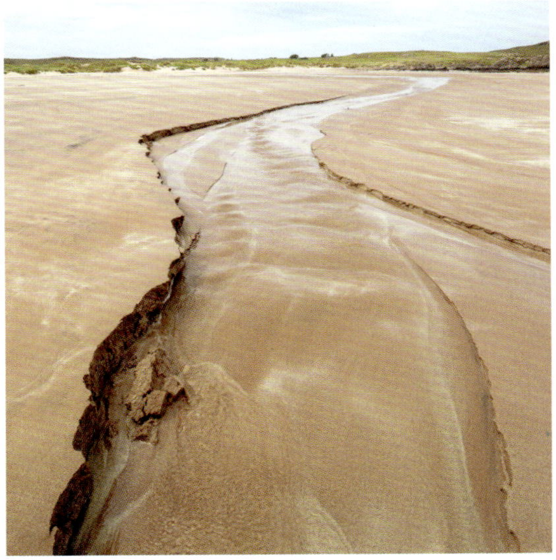

Opposite:

Last kiss of light on Stac Pollaidh and Cùl Beag, Assynt

From top left:

Sunset at Enard Bay, Assynt

Solitude: Achnahaird Bay

A tiny landslip, Achnahaird Bay

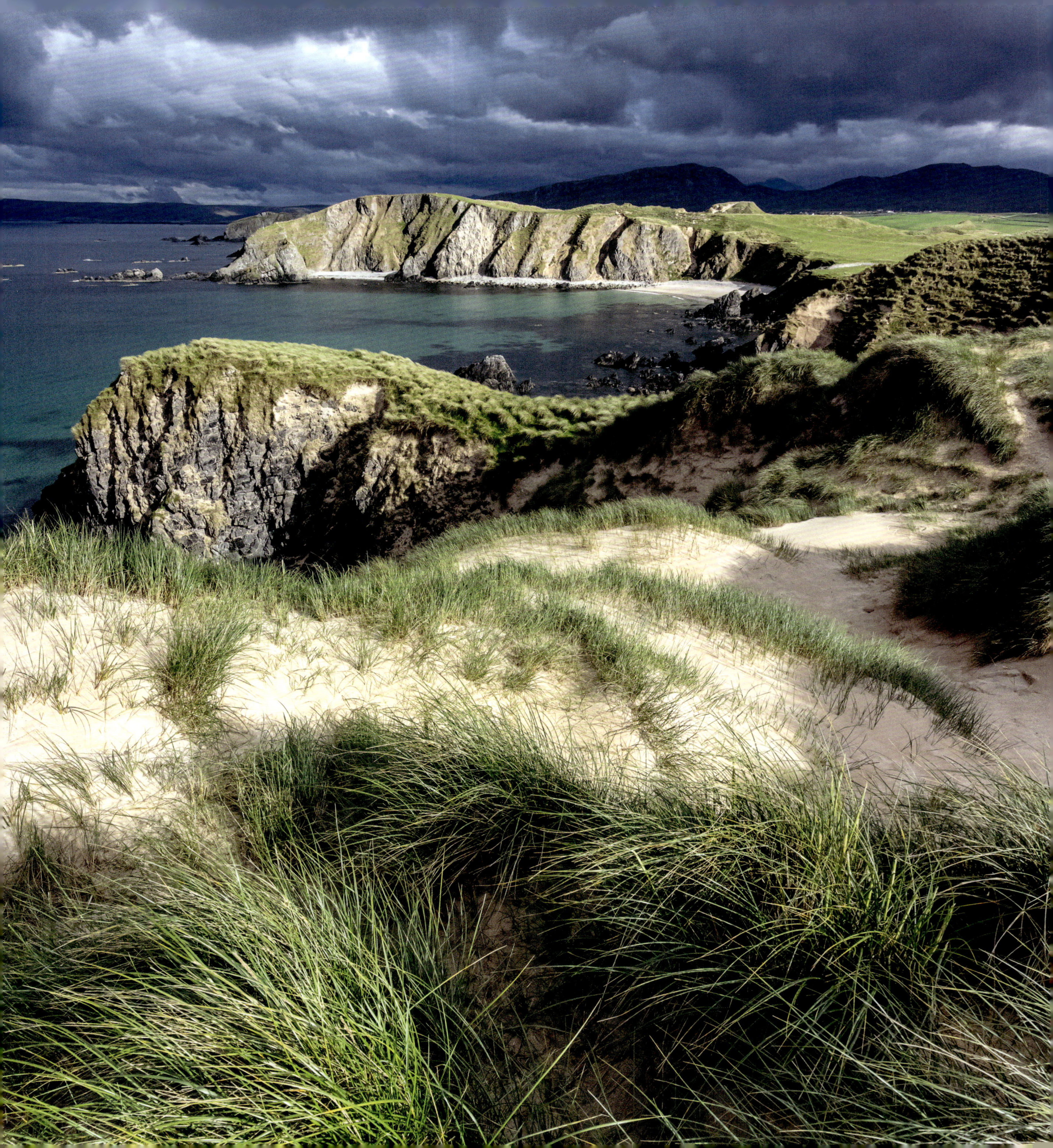

30 WEST SUTHERLAND

JUNE 2019

DAY 301–317 | 07,373–07,742 KM | 369 KM

With the long days and the especially luminous light at the top of Britain, Sutherland may represent the far north to many, but to the Norsemen, the north of Scotland was south of their colonies in the Orkney and Shetland Islands, hence why they named it Suðrland ('land to the south') in Old Norse. For the last few months, I've noticed the Norse legacy on the names on the map: names I can pronounce correctly, like Mallaig, scattered among the Gaelic names that I inevitably mangle. The Norse explored the countless sea lochs and headlands along the west coast of Scotland by longboat, but as I'm on foot I've been taking them one at a time to avoid feeling overwhelmed by their numerous indentations. Now, as I enter Sutherland, there are only three more peninsulas to the north-west corner of Britain at Cape Wrath and the thrill of reaching the top is tantalisingly within my grasp. If I can cross the wilderness separating Cape Wrath from the rest of the mainland, then the hardest terrain will be behind me.

On a fresh June morning, I stop to cook a late breakfast by the shore of Loch Inver with a view to a tiny lush and rocky island that characterises this section of coastline. Sea pinks bob next to yellow lichen-clad boulders nestled against the golden-green seaweed. The whole scene has the luminosity and invigorating harmony of a Monet. A pair of seals splash playfully, performing forward rolls in the water; their closed flippers appear above the surface as if in prayer.

The next afternoon, as I head north to the Point of Stoer from the village of Lochinver, I marvel at the turquoise sea and fine white sand at Achmelvich Bay. If I didn't know better, I'd mistake the bay for a tropical paradise. All the timeless beach rituals are in full effect; toddlers dig with spades assisted by attentive mothers, middle-aged couples sit in silence on folding chairs, while young lovers hold their shoes in one hand and their partner's hand in the other, walking slowly through the lapping tide.

The Shetlanders call the energising summer twilight 'simmer dim', and tonight it's bright enough to walk until midnight. I camp on the highest ground above the jutting headland of Stoer Point, famous for the Old Man of Stoer, a 60-metre-high sea stack of Torridonian sandstone. When it finally gets dark in the early morning, I can see lights from four lighthouses: north towards Cape Wrath, west to Lewis, south at Loch Inver and close by at Stoer Point.

Assynt, the area I'm walking through, is characterised by isolated mountains rising dramatically from the lochan-strewn moorland. On my fourth night in Sutherland, I camp with a clear view of the mountain range Quinag to maximise opportunities for photography in the last of the evening's golden light, but the midges around my tent are so dense they appear as a grey fog, bringing my photoshoot to an abrupt end. When I boil water for my morning coffee the next day, the surface immediately forms a thick skin of hundreds of the little blighters.

By the afternoon, I'm walking across the graceful lines of the Kylesku Bridge, marvelling at how Ove Arup & Partners' good engineering design has created a modern structure both true to itself and so complementary to the Highland landscape. After many days of exclusively appreciating the beauty of nature, I'm particularly receptive to enjoying the work of humankind.

It takes three more days of persistent northward travel to arrive at the desolate Ardmore Peninsula. It's a place that seems to have been forgotten by the very earth that birthed it, with raw, menacing rocks jutting out around me. I feel a sense of being trapped in the angry, muscular folds of these rocks, and I scramble to the highest point of the bleak, glacier-smoothed hills to gain some perspective and plan my next move. In the distance, I spot two golden sickles, the twin beaches at Oldshoremore, a hint of softness ahead amid the harshness.

Opposite:

Dunes, Faraid Head

On my eighth day in Sutherland, I should be tired, but my proximity to Cape Wrath pulls me onward. The path to the mile-long Sandwood Bay is busy with hikers deposited by coach, but they don't walk far and soon it's just me, the rain and boggy, featureless moorland again as I navigate the 12 kilometres to Cape Wrath. It is a challenging route to find: pathless, undulating boggy tussocks where I need to avoid the towering cliffs, deep lochs, wide gullies and unfordable rivers; I take a sequence of bearings backed up by my GPS to zigzag forwards. After 6 kilometres, a wire fence stretches across the moor emblazoned with yellow signs at regular intervals: *Do not touch any military debris. It may explode and kill you*. The north-west of Scotland is a giant firing range, but I've planned my passage when this one is inactive. I climb over the fence, squelching ever on.

It's midnight and pouring with rain when I leave the moorland to reach the track to Cape Wrath Lighthouse. With the west coast now complete, I'm overcome with a sense of relief. I collapse to my knees to kiss the road in gratitude. A few minutes later the lighthouse beam swings diffuse through the rain above as I pitch my tent, and when I finally crawl into my sleeping bag, I notice my feet are white and crinkled thanks to constantly walking through boggy ground.

The next evening, I pick my way through the craters at Cape Wrath's bombing range. The pockmarked landscape is scattered with armoured personnel carriers in varied states of destruction. Although I'd triple-checked that the range isn't firing, it's still disconcerting to walk across fresh peaty craters with their edges folded back and surrounded by scattered gobs of earth. In some areas, artillery shells poke out of the wasteland, the whole scene littered with white parachutes from illumination flares. It's like walking into a First World War painting by Paul Nash.

After thirteen days, I'm about a quarter of the way along the top edge of Scotland, excited to enter the uninhabited wilderness of the A' Mhòine Peninsula. Within a few hours following a faint trail up and down valleys, I push through a sea of waist-high bracken, where I unexpectedly find a croft with an intact roof. The building is Freisgill Bothy and it sits alone, unconnected by road and miles from anywhere. I stop inside to get out of the rain and make a brew when an alert-eyed bearded man enters wearing a wetsuit. We are both surprised to meet anyone else here. Still, we soon share our stories, as is the bothy way, and I learn he is a nuclear physicist and retired Dounreay engineer who's sea-kayaking alone along the dramatic cliff-lined coast.

Having walked past so many of Britain's nuclear power stations, all located next to the coast so they can have a ready supply of cool water, I'm curious what he thinks this country should do about power generation. 'Well, I don't believe in wind; it only works economically because of subsidies. If we want to reduce carbon, we need to stop driving; it doesn't make sense to save carbon in energy production and then drive. We need new nuclear reactors.' Are the new ones more efficient? I ask. 'No, but they are much safer.'

A couple of days later, I stop at an isolated croft for some pest control. Since the expansive sandy beach at Torrisdale Bay, a collie has been following me for over an hour, and I feel responsible for finding its owner. A man puts down an angle grinder when I ask if he might know anything. 'No, but he'll find his way back.' I take comfort from his words and fall into easy conversation with him and his partner. On hearing where I've come from, they tell me there are few people who can say they've walked all around the A' Mhòine Peninsula. I ask to take a photo of them both, and they suggest a fishing boat as a background. They tell me it was once a lifeboat on the RMS *Lusitania* that survived an attack from the German Navy during the First World War, and precipitated the US entering the fray.

On my penultimate evening in Sutherland, I venture through Kirtomy. In this small crofting community, I traverse fields of freshly cut hay, arranged in parallel mounded strips and filling the air with its aroma. As I ascend a hill away from the settlement, I realise this is the first time in a long while that the landscape looks fertile and inviting. Scanning back over the way I have come, inhospitable folds of rock retreat into the distance through which the misty outline of Ben Hope emerges far away. It's the summer solstice, and I walk late into the night, the brightness of the moon guiding my path across the moor without a torch. More frequent paths, fields, trees and houses gradually add to the increasingly benign feeling. After midnight, I reach a high point to see the flatness of Caithness ahead; it looks like the landscape is taking a deep breath after all the contorted drama of the north-west.

Opposite, from top left:

Achmelvich Bay

Shoreline, Achmelvich Bay

From bottom left:

Ripples and light, Achmelvich Bay

Path to Achmelvich Bay

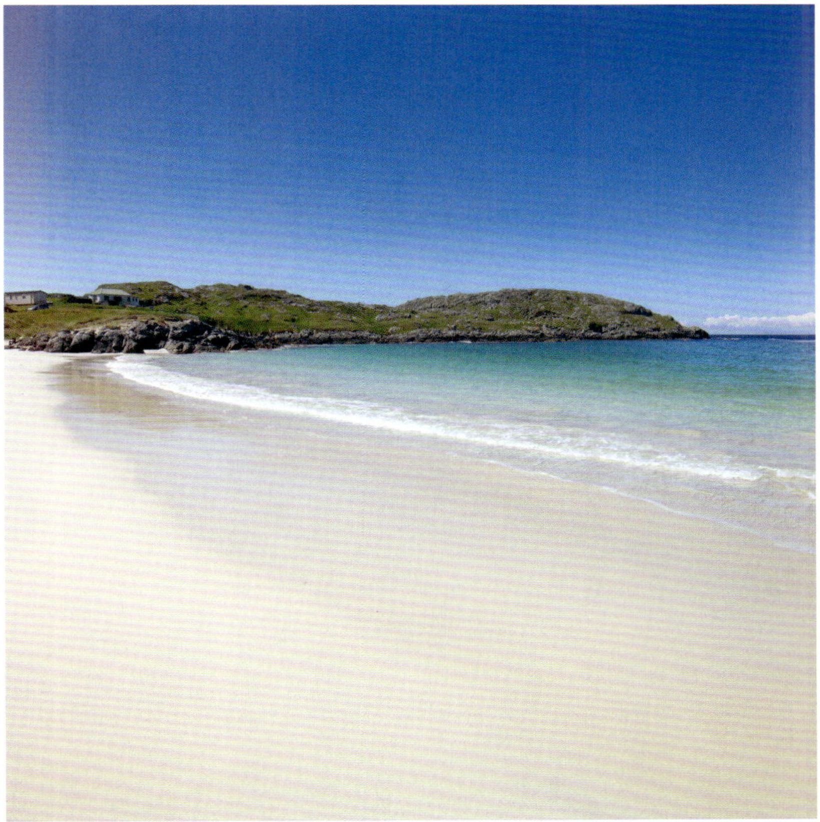

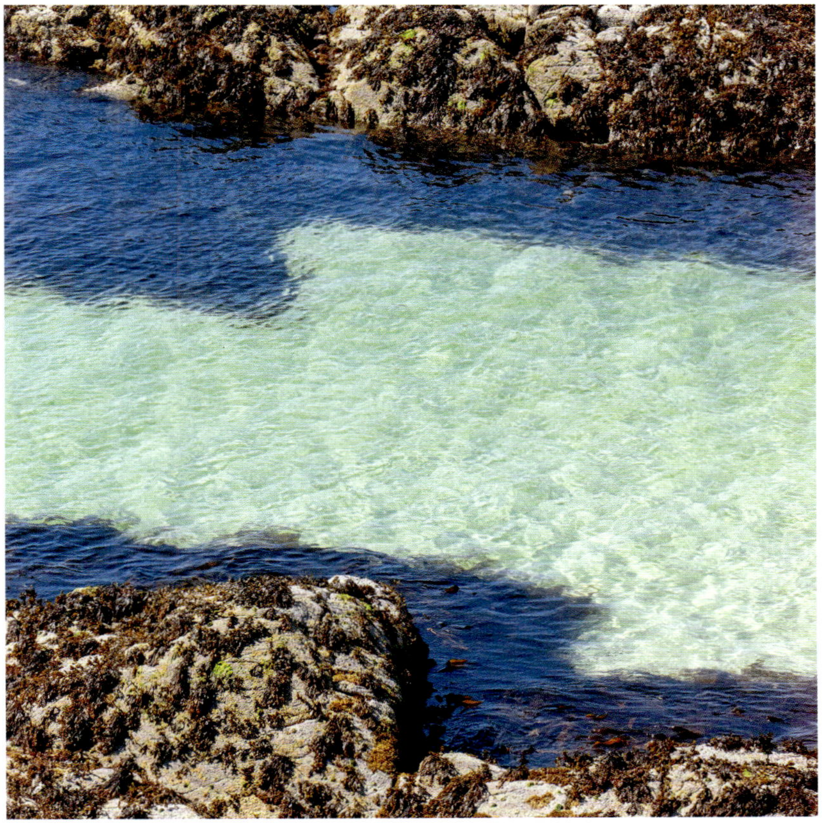

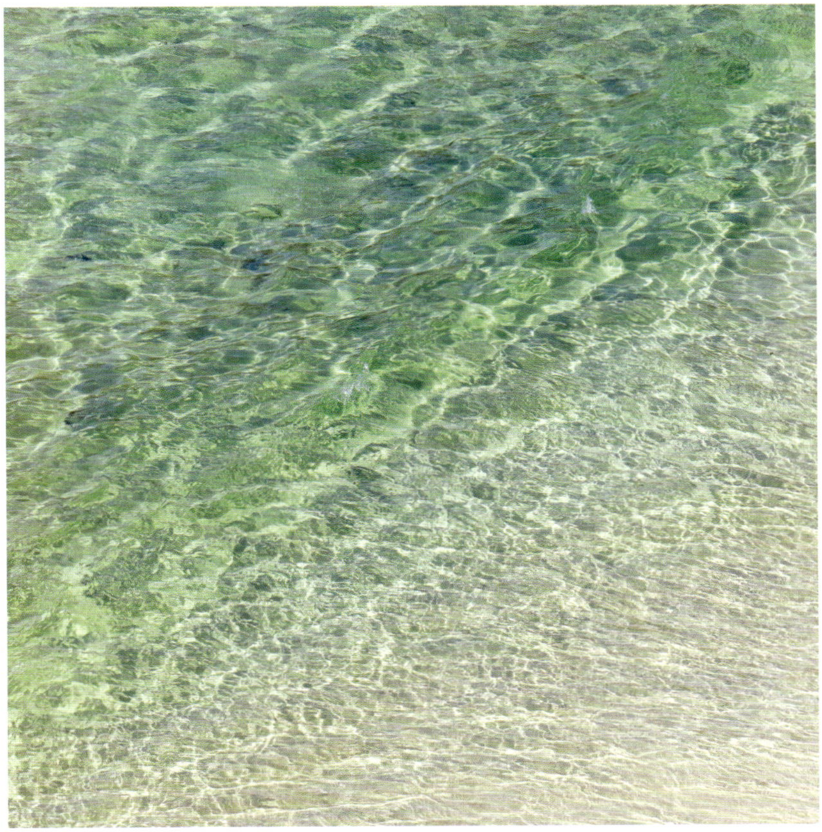

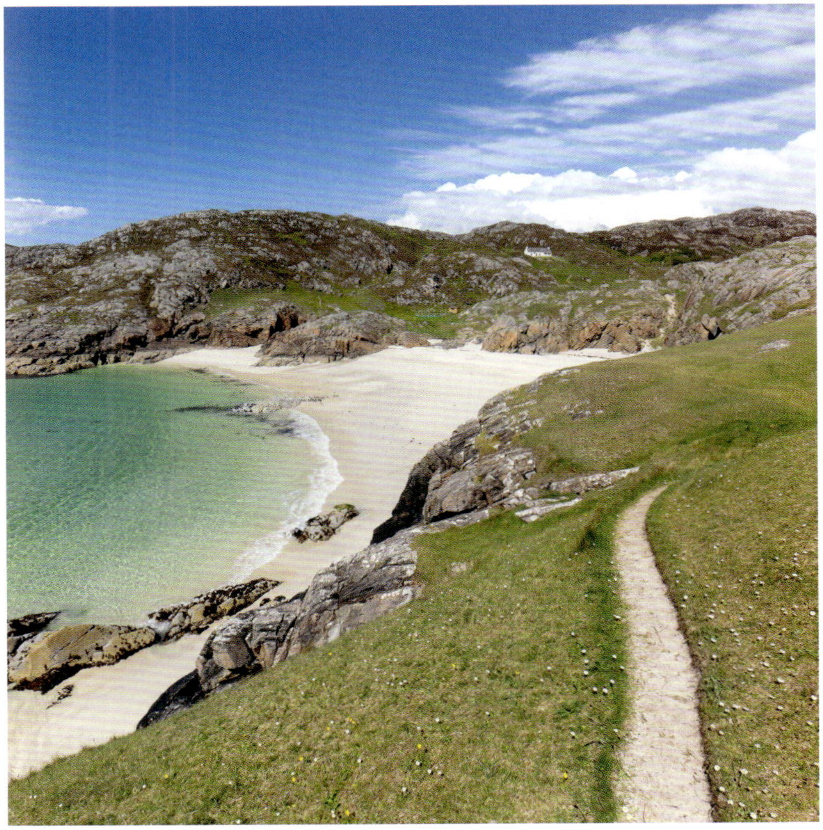

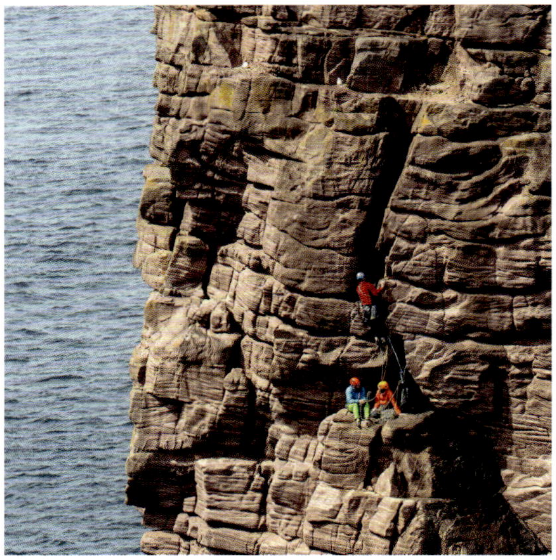

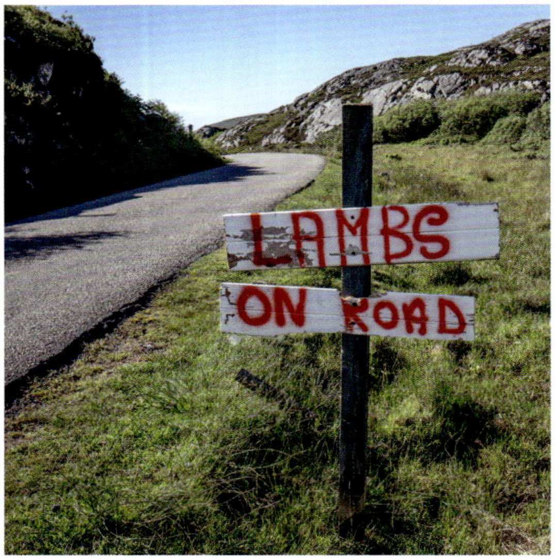
LAMBS
ON ROAD

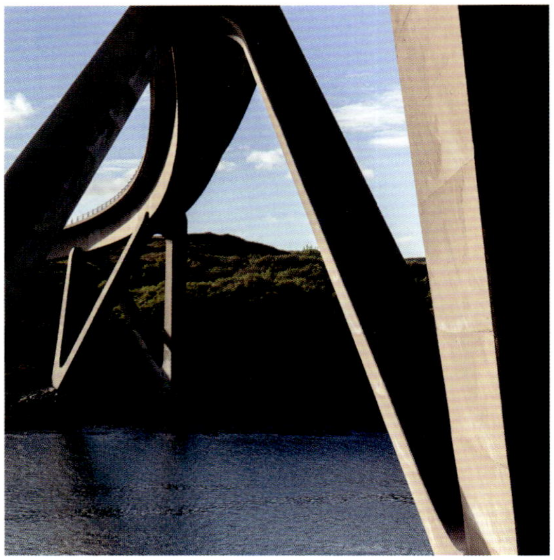

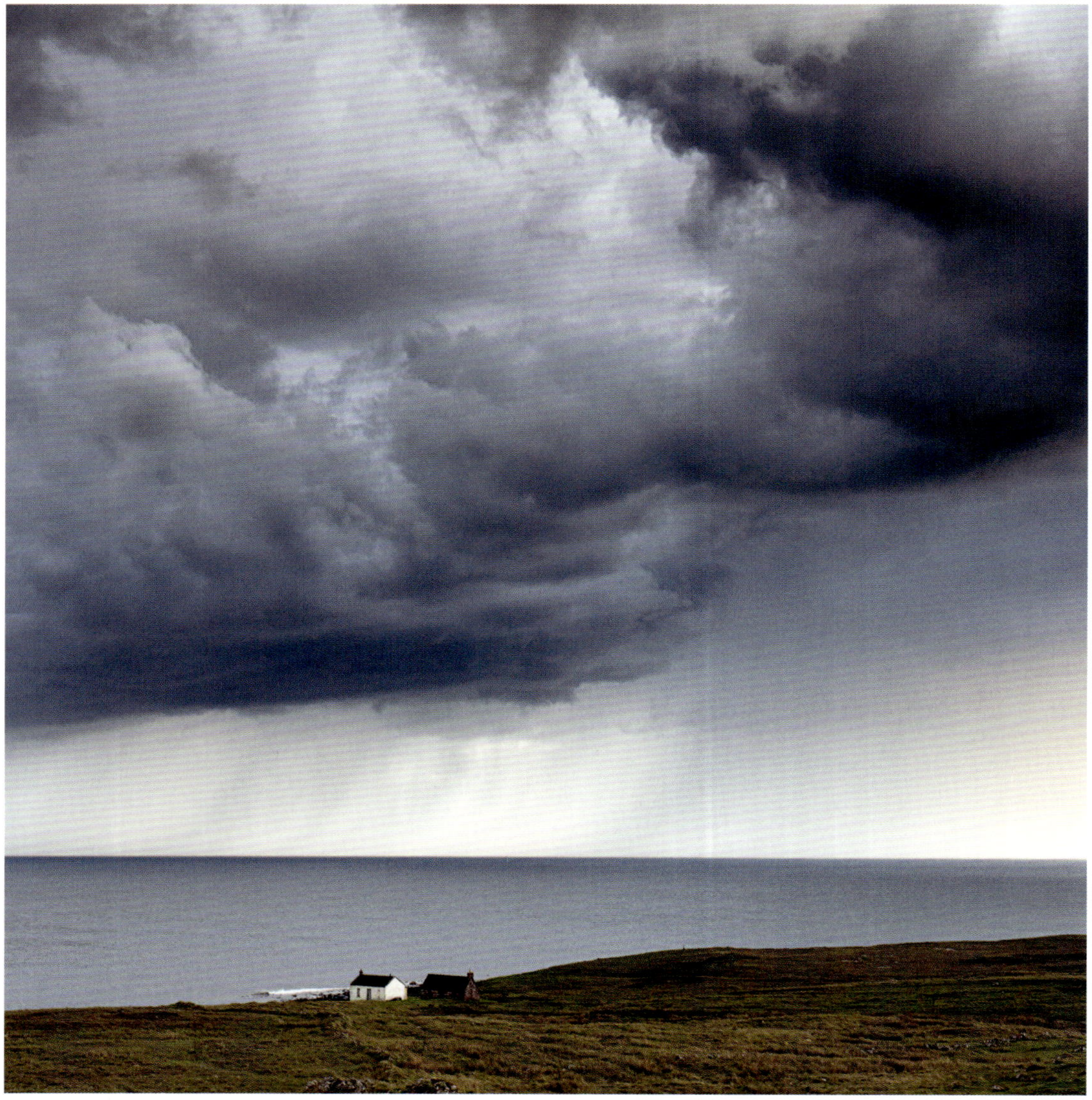

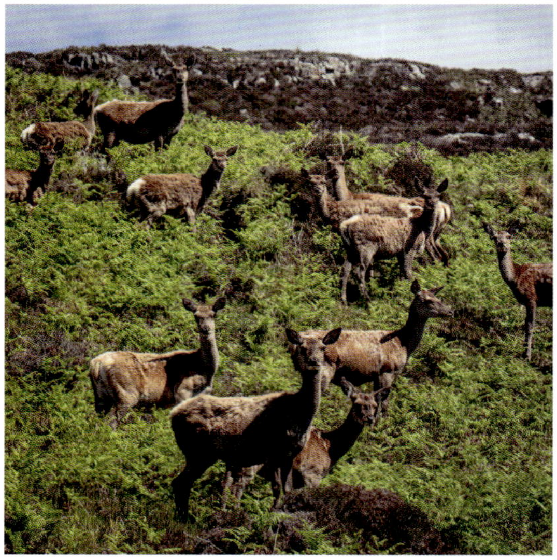

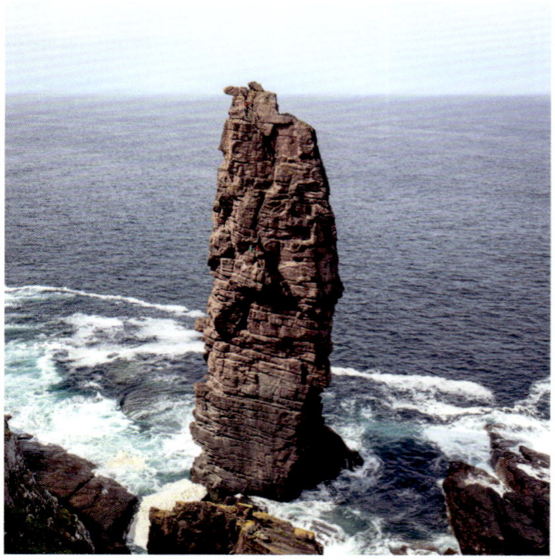

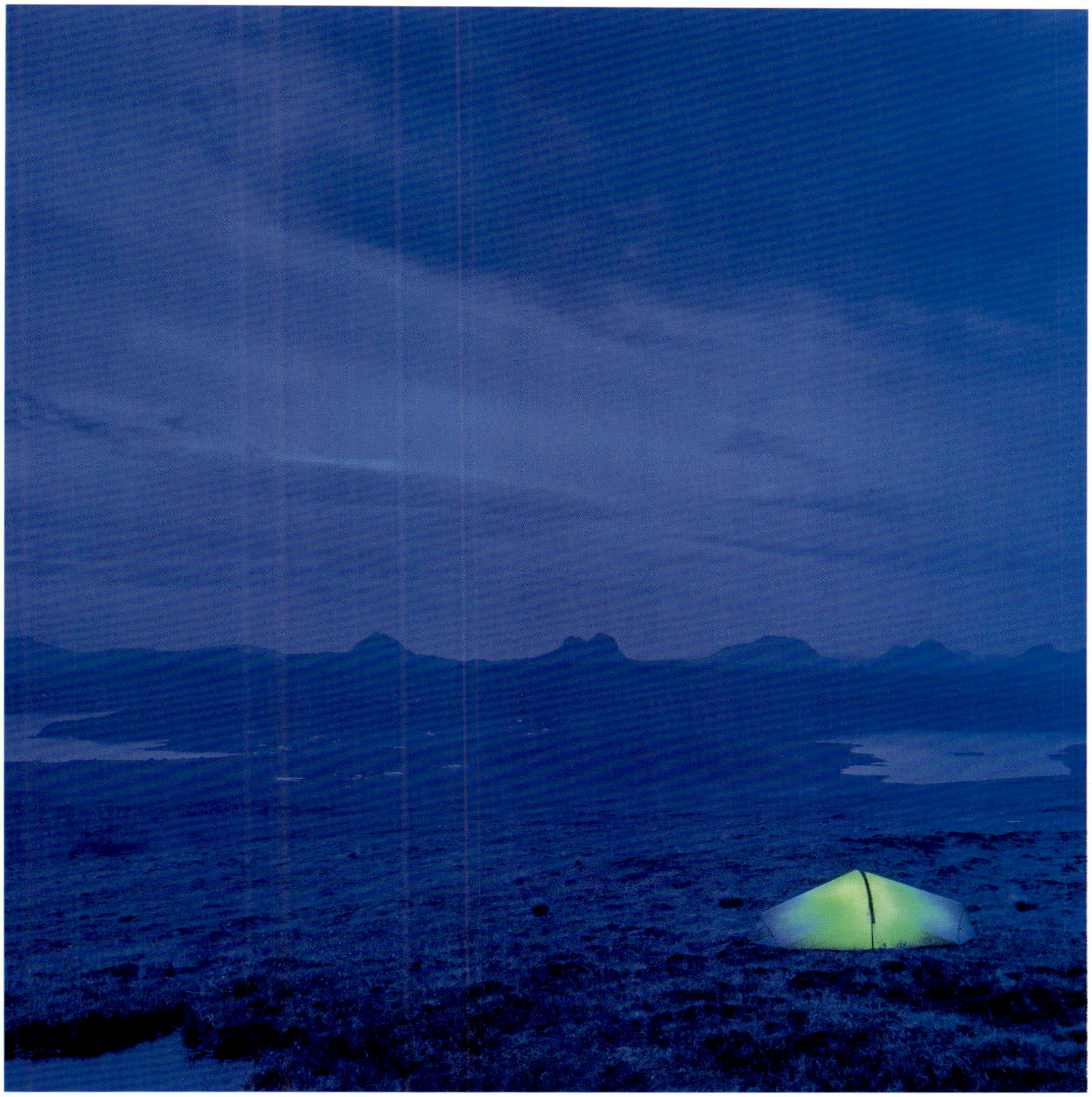

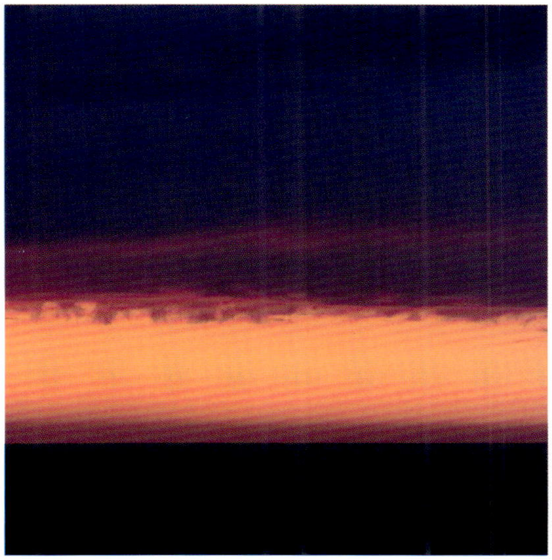

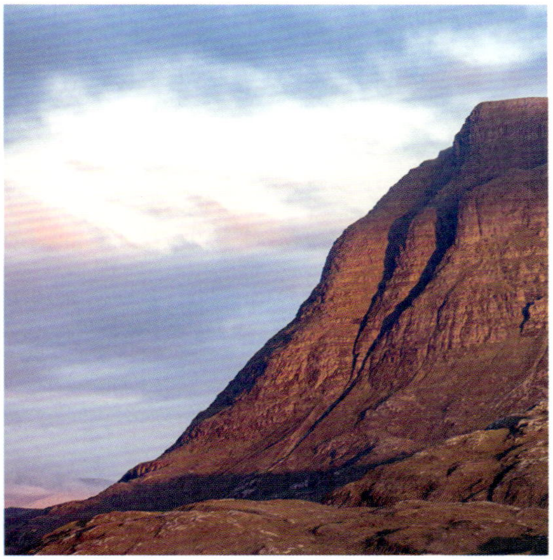

Opposite, clockwise from top left:

Climbers on the Old Man of Stoer, a 60-metre-high sea stack of Torridonian sandstone

Signage of the lambs: Achmelvich

When engineering becomes art: Kylesku Bridge, designed by Ove Arup & Partners, 1984

Ever get the feeling you're being watched? Loch Ardbhair

The Old Man of Stoer

Storm off Stoer Head

From top left:

Camp at the Point of Stoer overlooking the Assynt peaks

Colour field seascape: it never really gets dark this far north in the summer, but this Rothko moment at Stoer Head over the Minch marked the end of the day

Last light on Quinag, Sail Gharbh

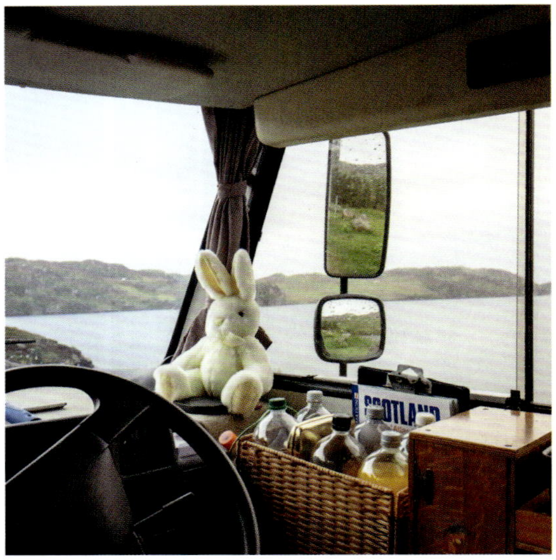
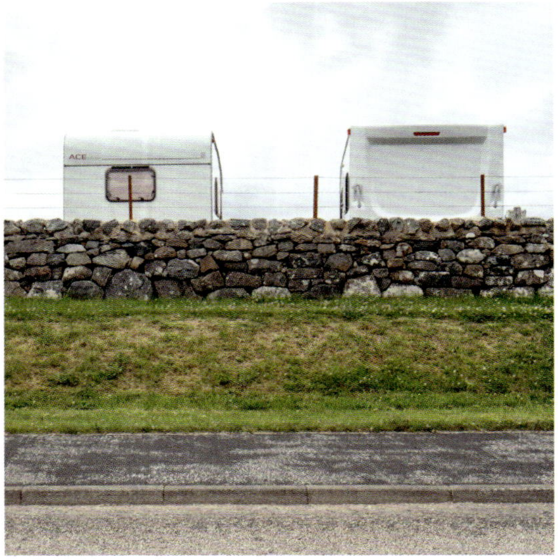
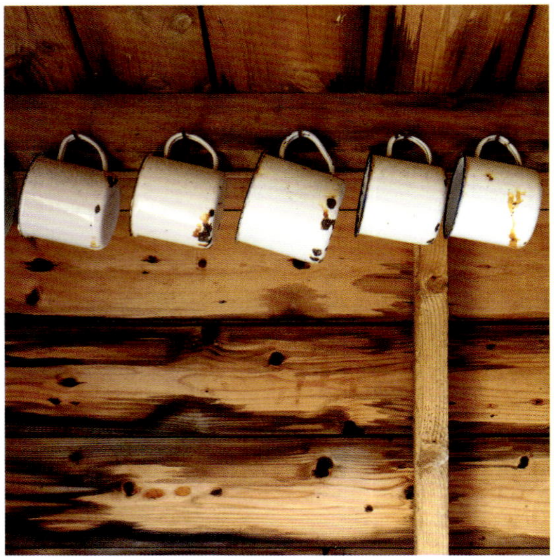
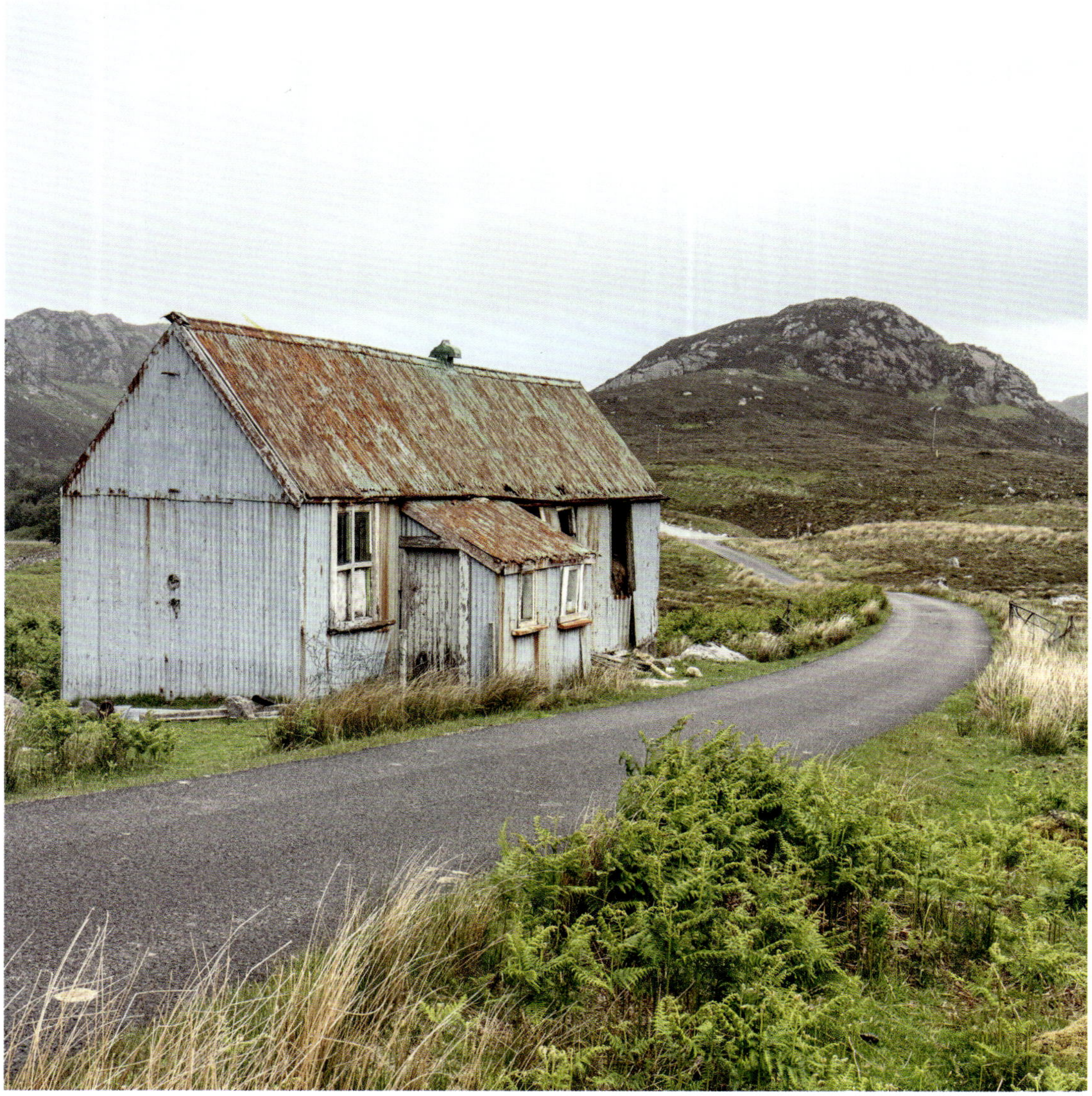
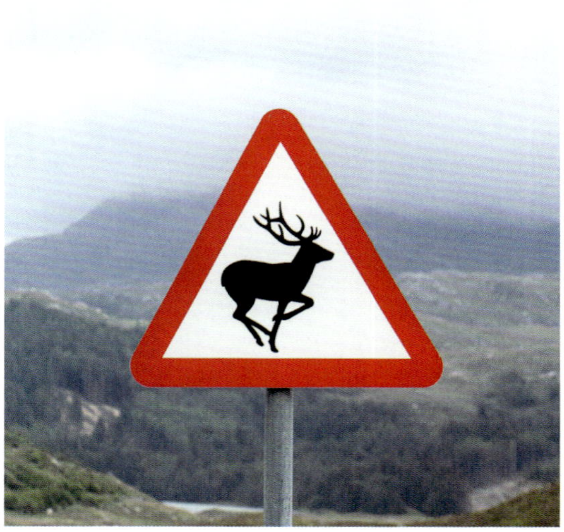
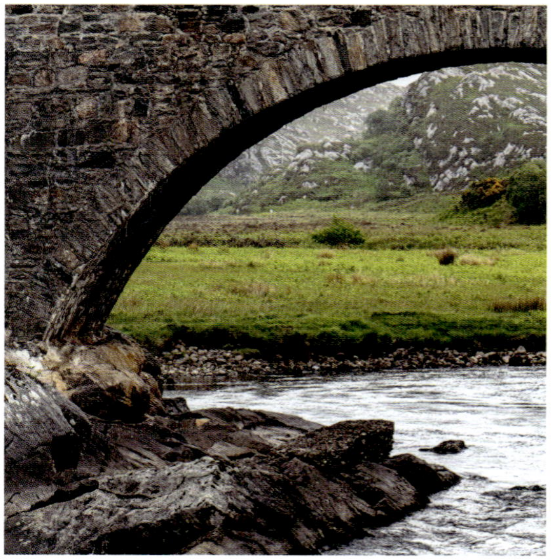

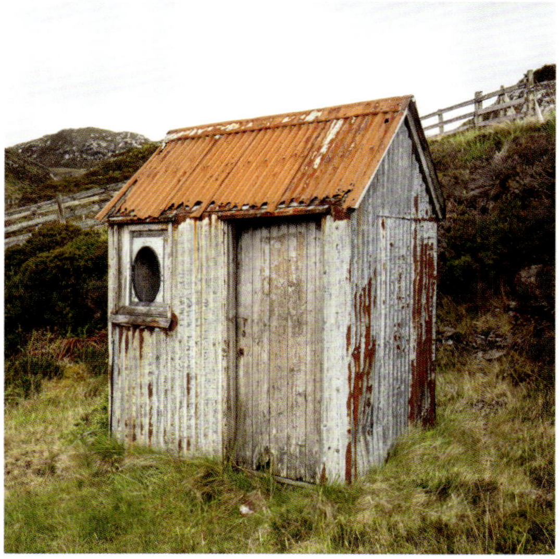

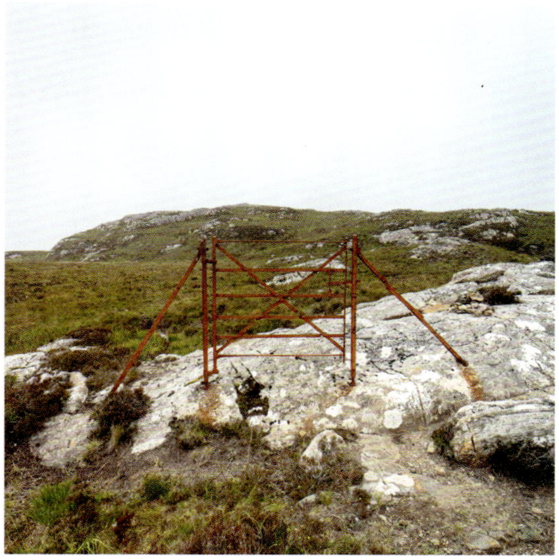

Opposite, clockwise from top left:

Peter and Friday's motor-home by Loch Inchard

Caravans, Scourie

Hut in the Ardmore Peninsula

I've always found deer warning signs evocative of the wild out there, but this one also has barely visible magical stars in the white background that I only just noticed while editing the photo taken on the road to Laxford Bay

Laxford Bridge

House used for storing hay, Achlyness

From top left:

Shed goals: Scourie

It gave me great pleasure to divert my course to this gate at Scourie, lift the latch, step through, and then close it diligently behind me

Crow-stepped gable, Scourie Lodge

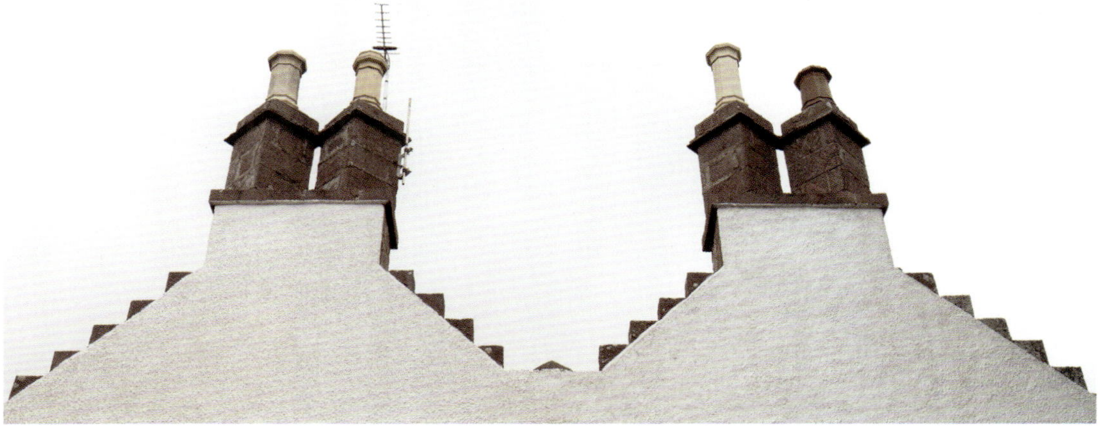

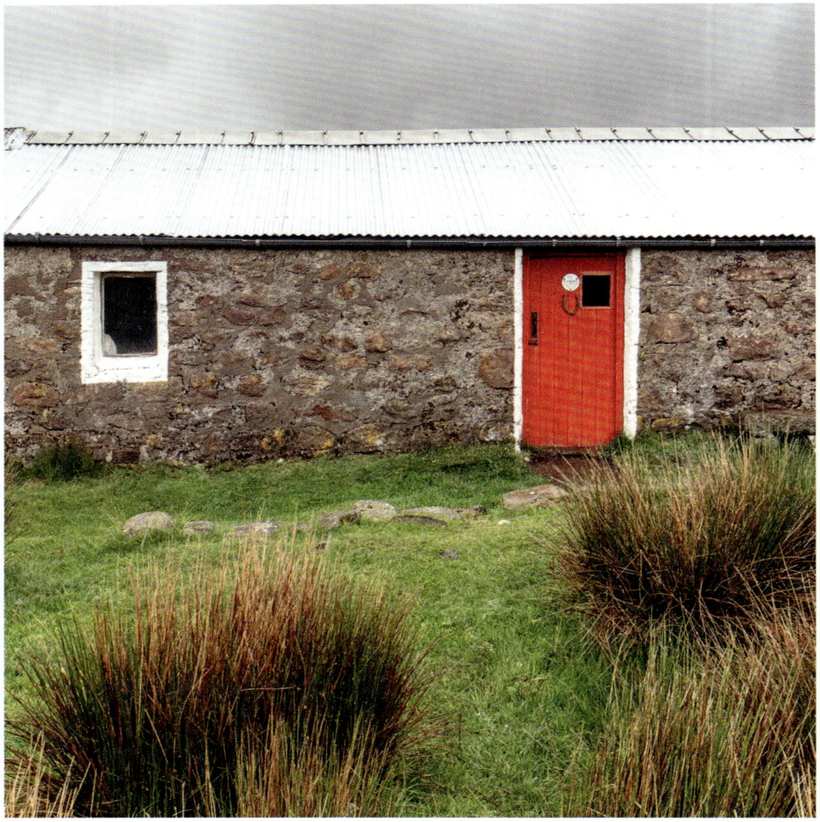

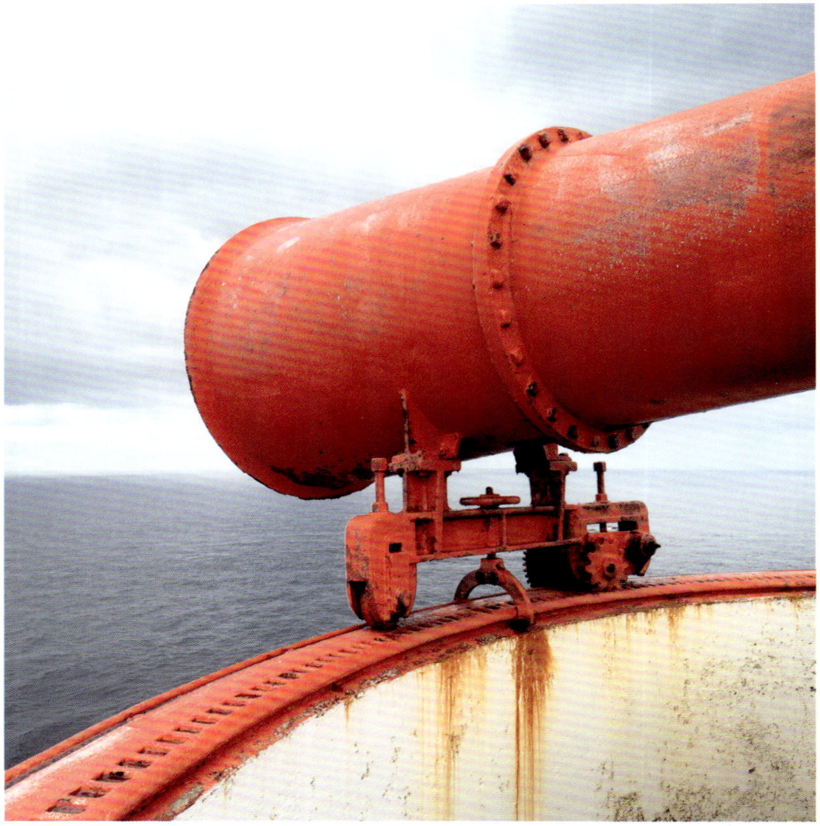

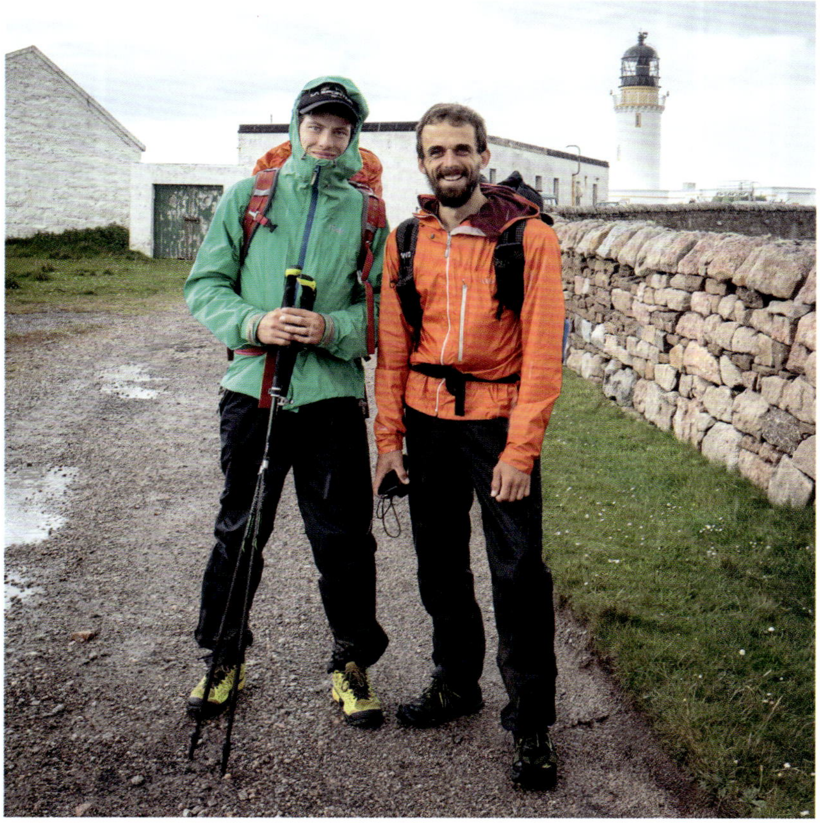

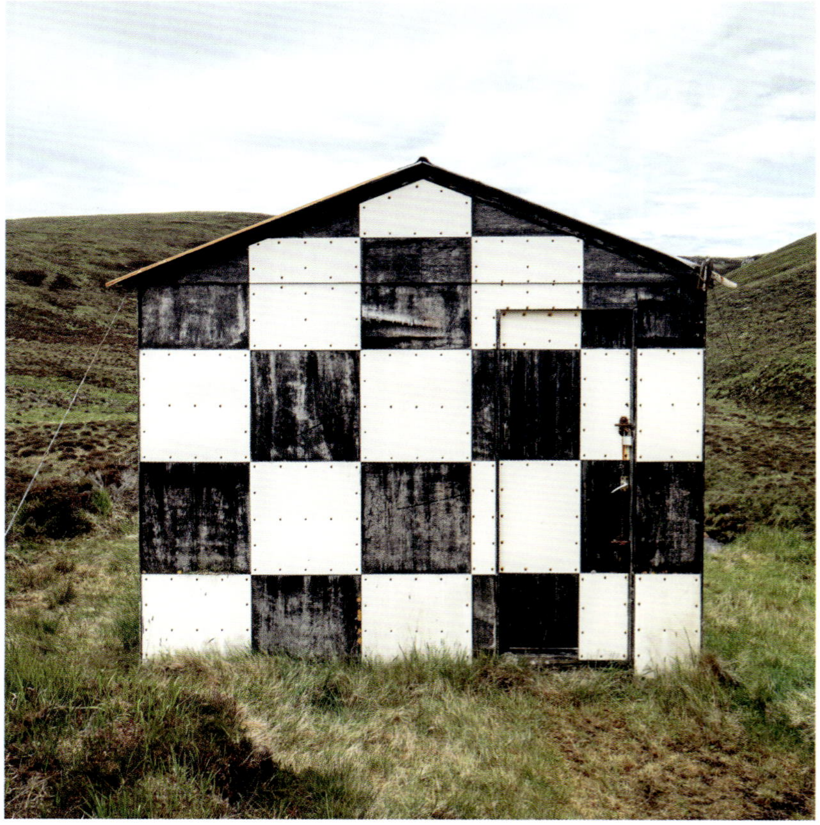

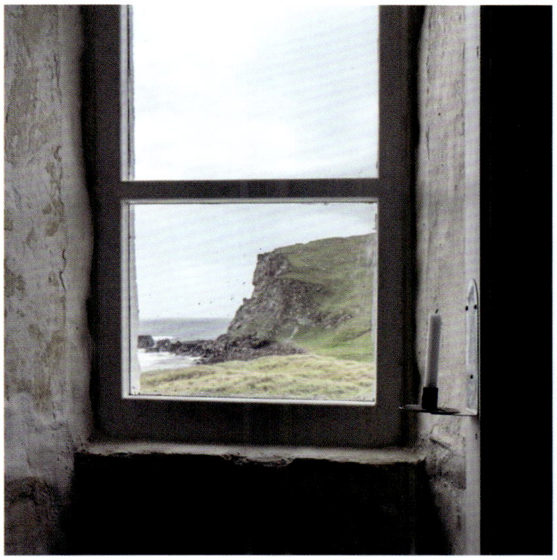

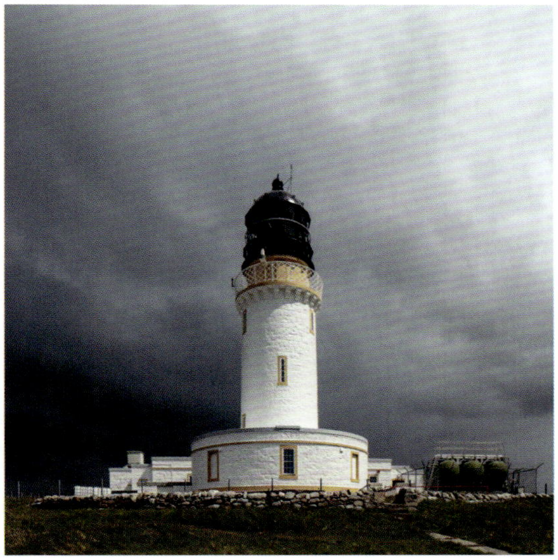

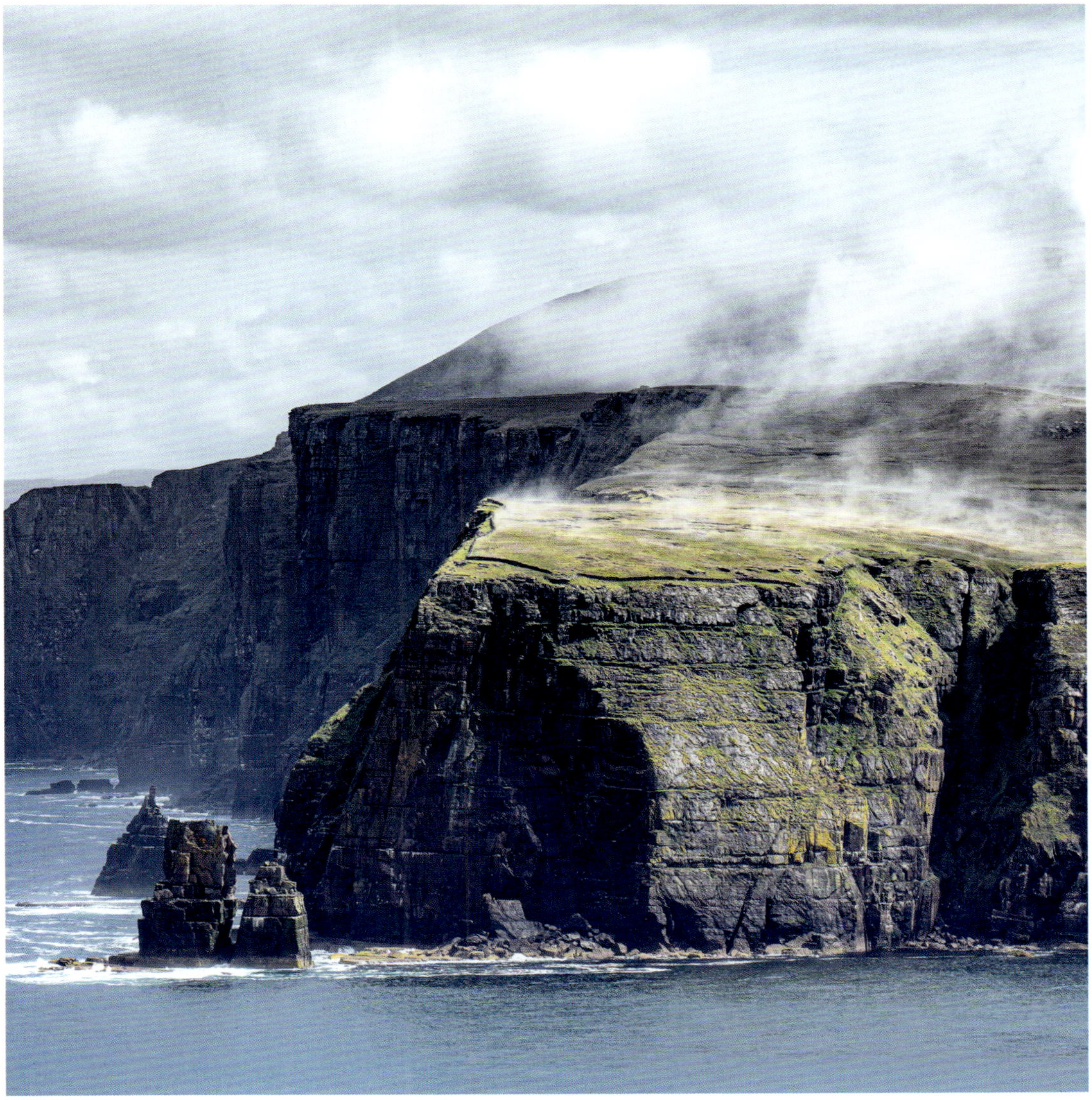

Opposite, from top left:

Entrance to Strathchailleach Bothy

Foghorn, Cape Wrath Lighthouse

From bottom left:

Ross and Tomáš, from Czechia, on their completion of the Cape Wrath Trail, which runs 370 kilometres from Fort William to Cape Wrath

Checkpoint buildings, Cape Wrath bombing range

From top left:

Kearvaig Bothy

Cape Wrath Lighthouse, the north-westernmost point of mainland Britain

At 281 metres, Clò Mór are the highest vertical sea cliffs in mainland Britain. Stack Clò Kearvaig is in the foreground

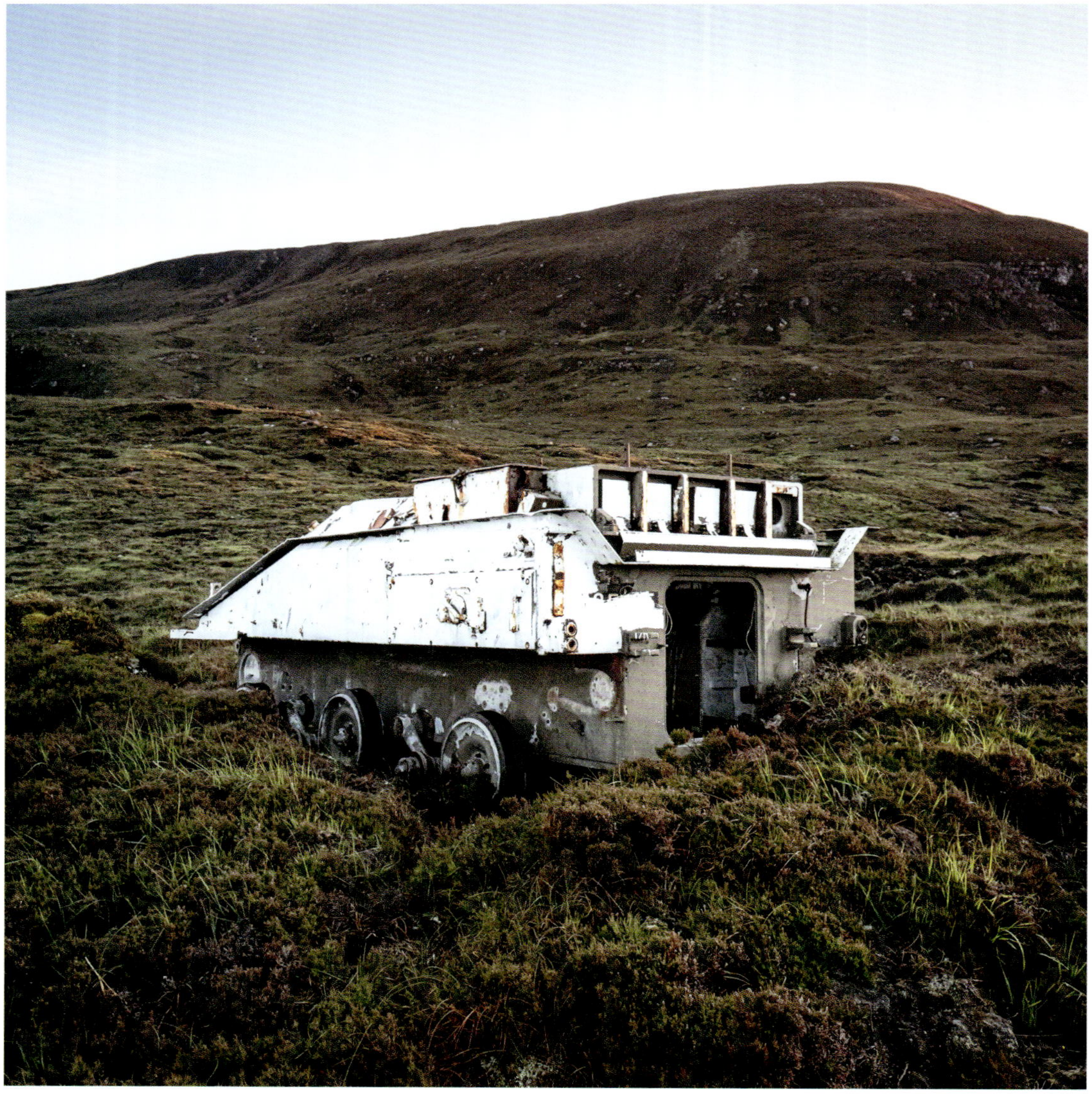
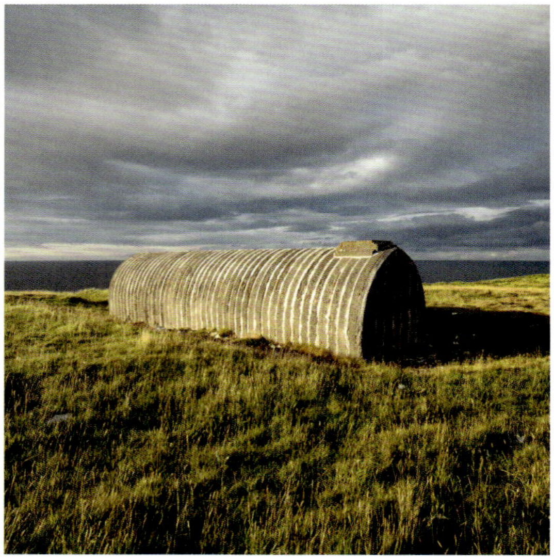
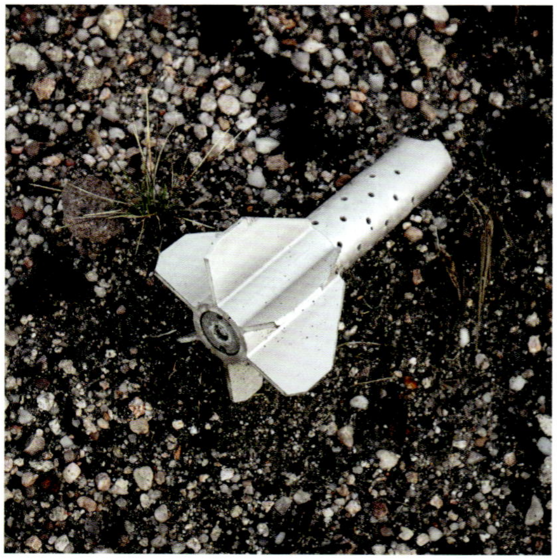
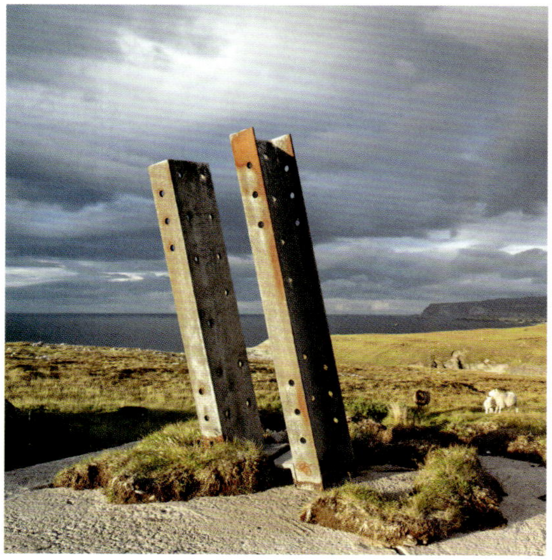
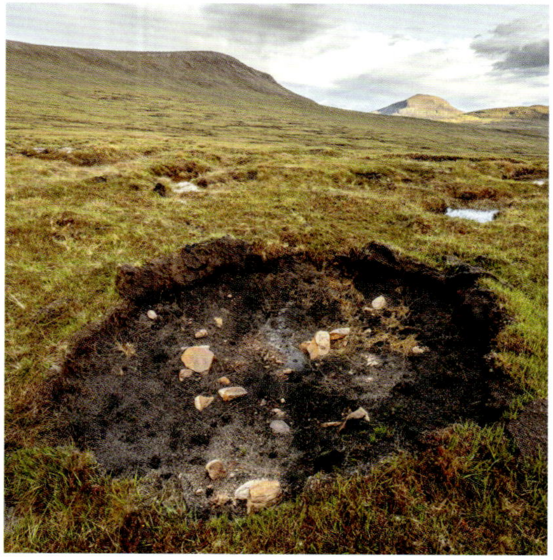
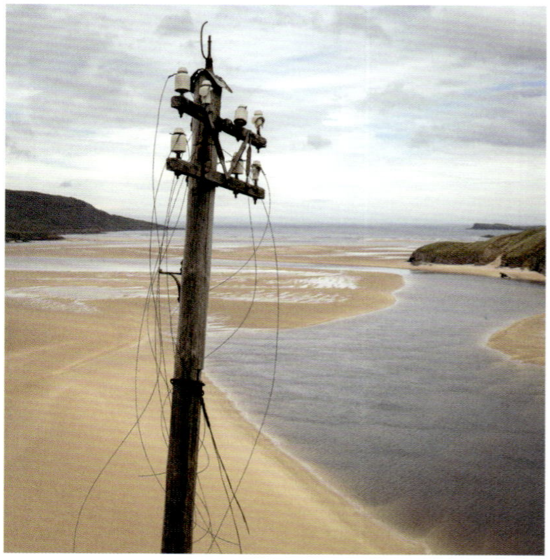

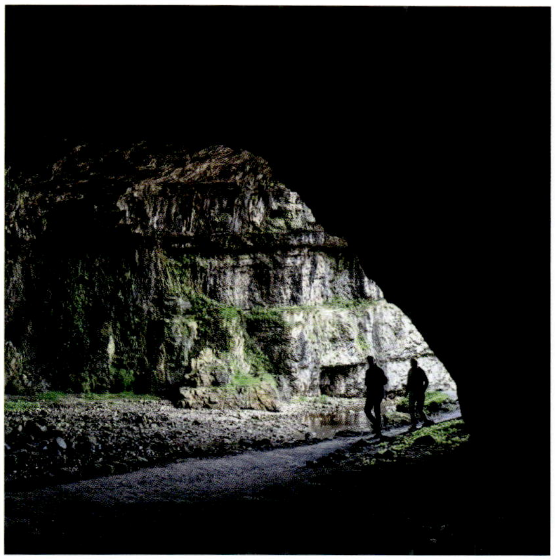

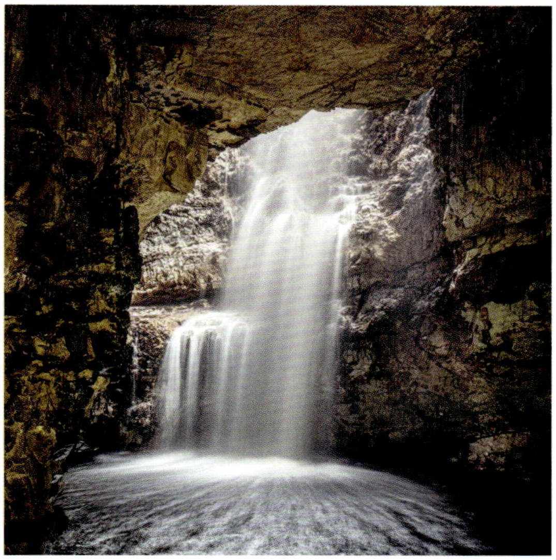

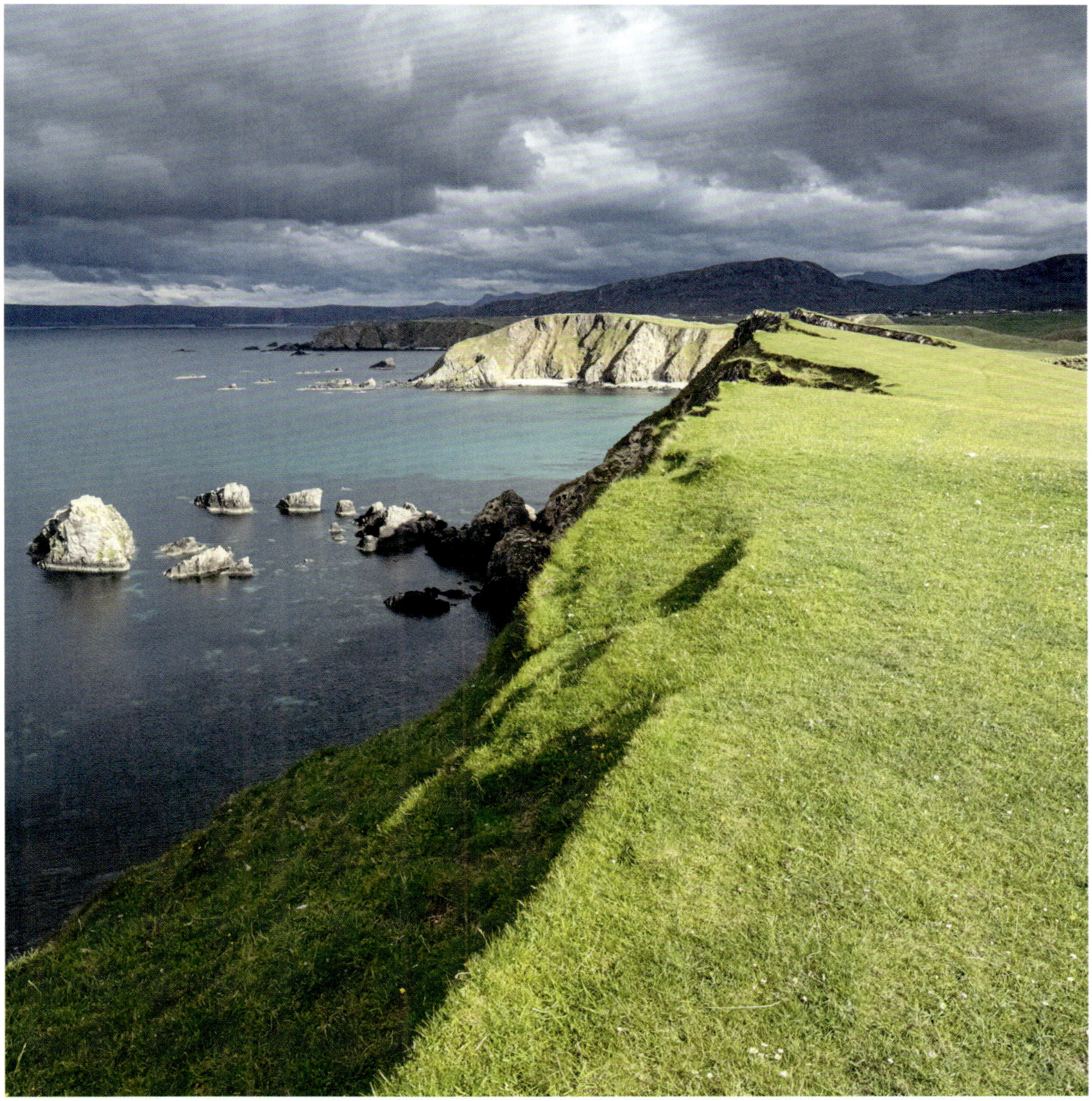

Opposite, clockwise from top left:

Spartan armoured personnel carrier, Cape Wrath bombing range

Stanton air-raid shelter, Sango Bay Chain Home Radar Station, Durness

Mortar tail fin, Cape Wrath bombing range

Cut off: the Cape Wrath side of the Kyle of Durness

Crater, Cape Wrath bombing range

VEB (variable elevation beam) mast base, Sango Bay Chain Home Radar Station, Durness

From top left:

Smoo Cave, Durness. The name is thought to originate from the Norse *smjugg* or *smuga*, meaning a hole or hiding-place. The front of the cave is formed by the sea whereas the rear is formed by freshwater

The Smoo Burn that drops into Smoo Cave through a sinkhole

Evening light at Faraid Head

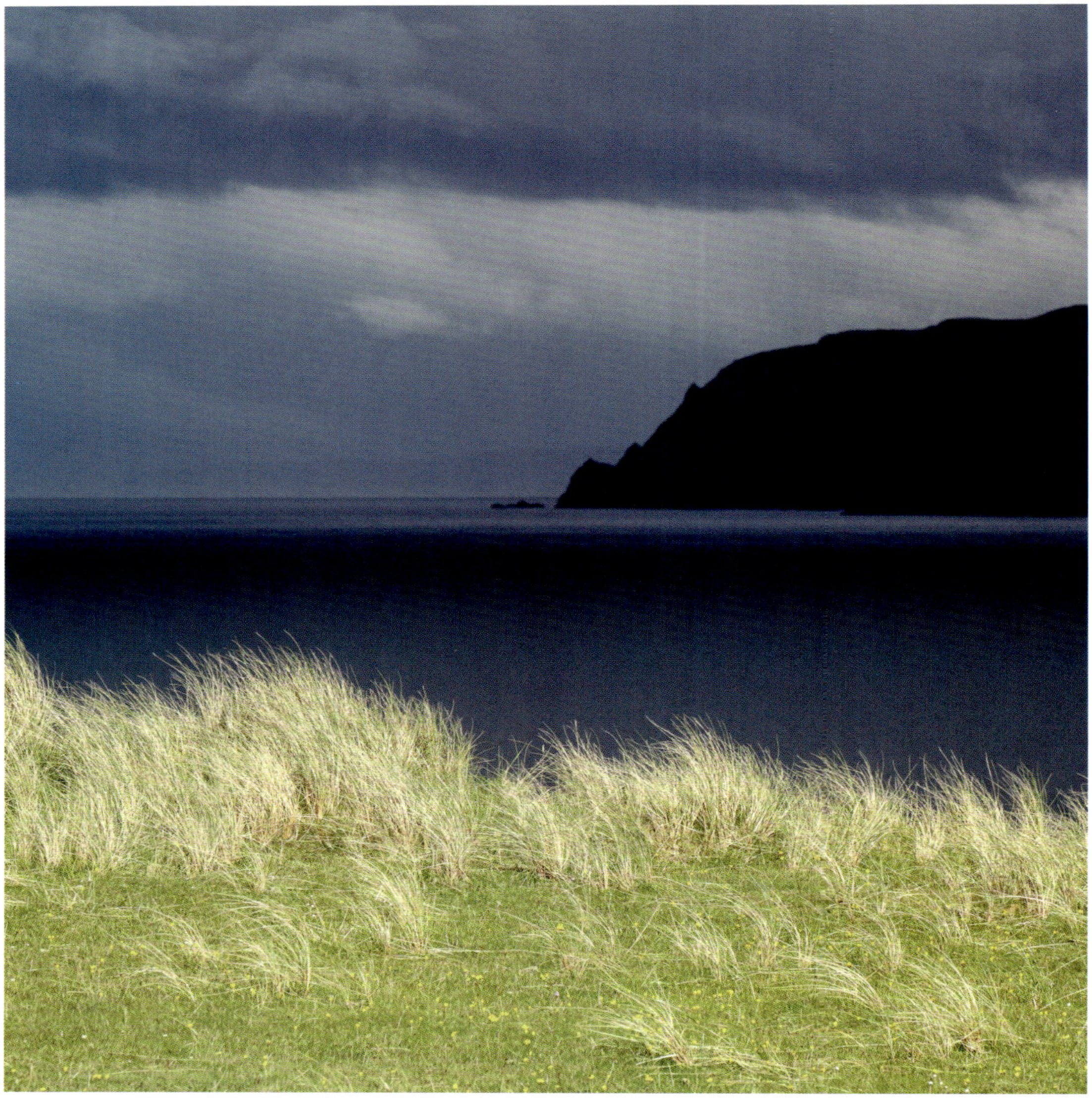

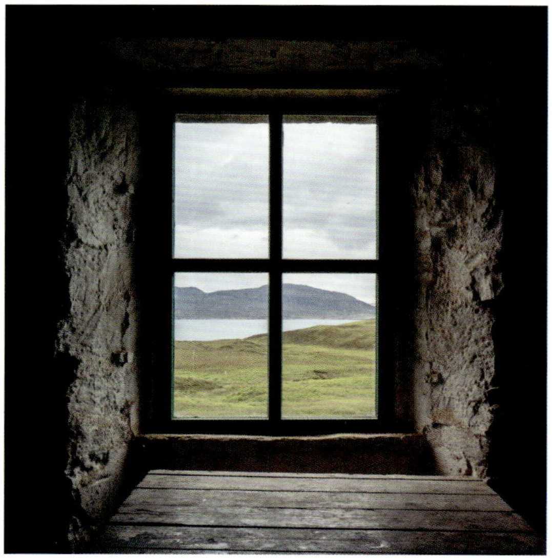

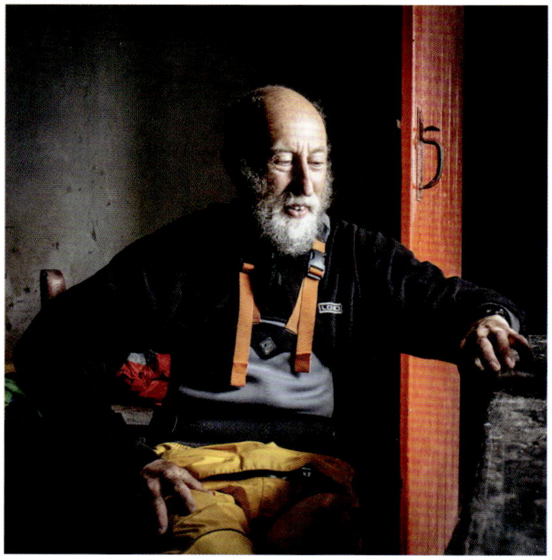

From top left:

Whiten Head from Faraid Head

From Freisgill Bothy, A' Mhòine Peninsula

Ben MacGregor, Freisgill Bothy

Opposite:

Pixel glitch: Balnakeil Bay

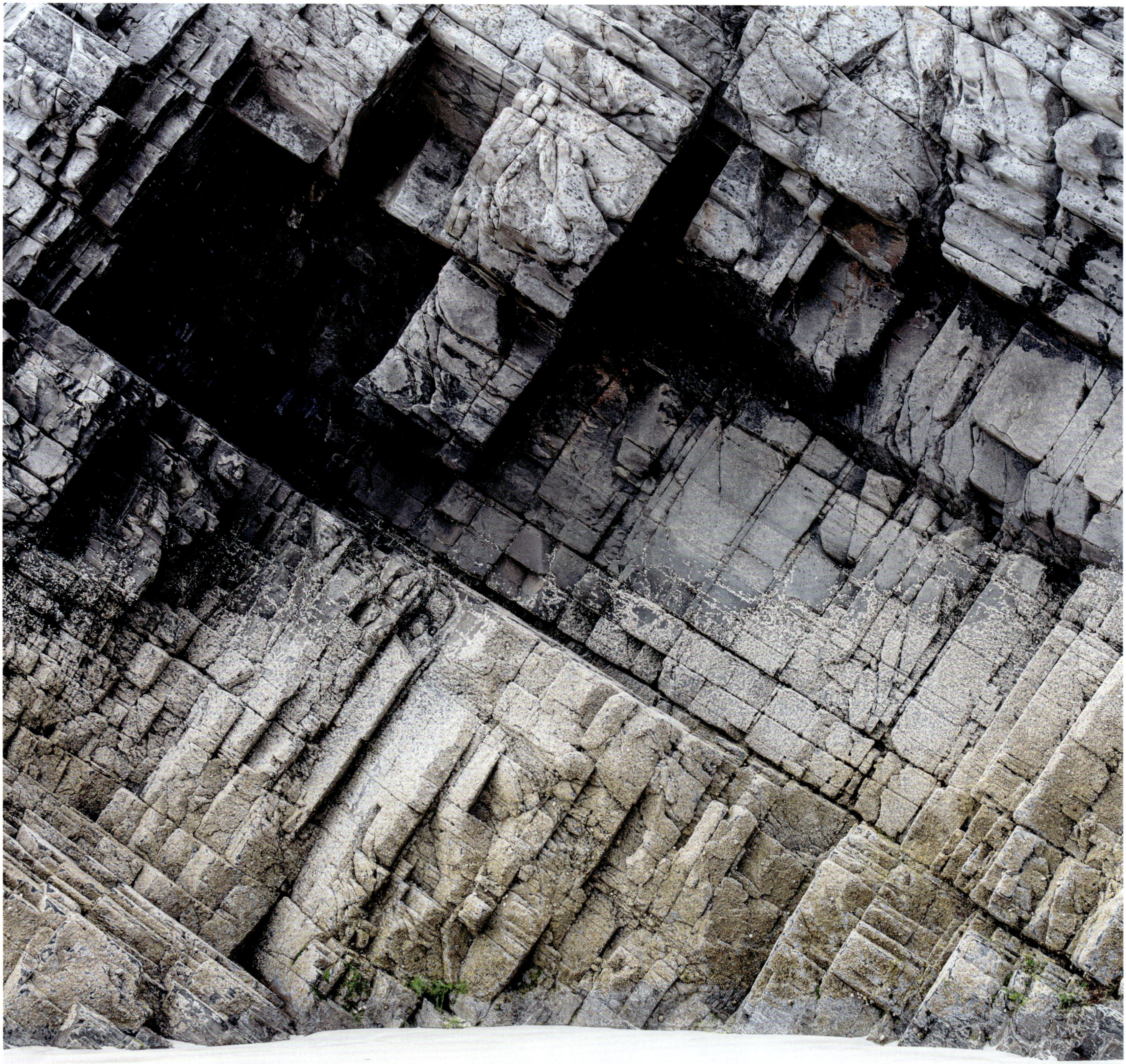

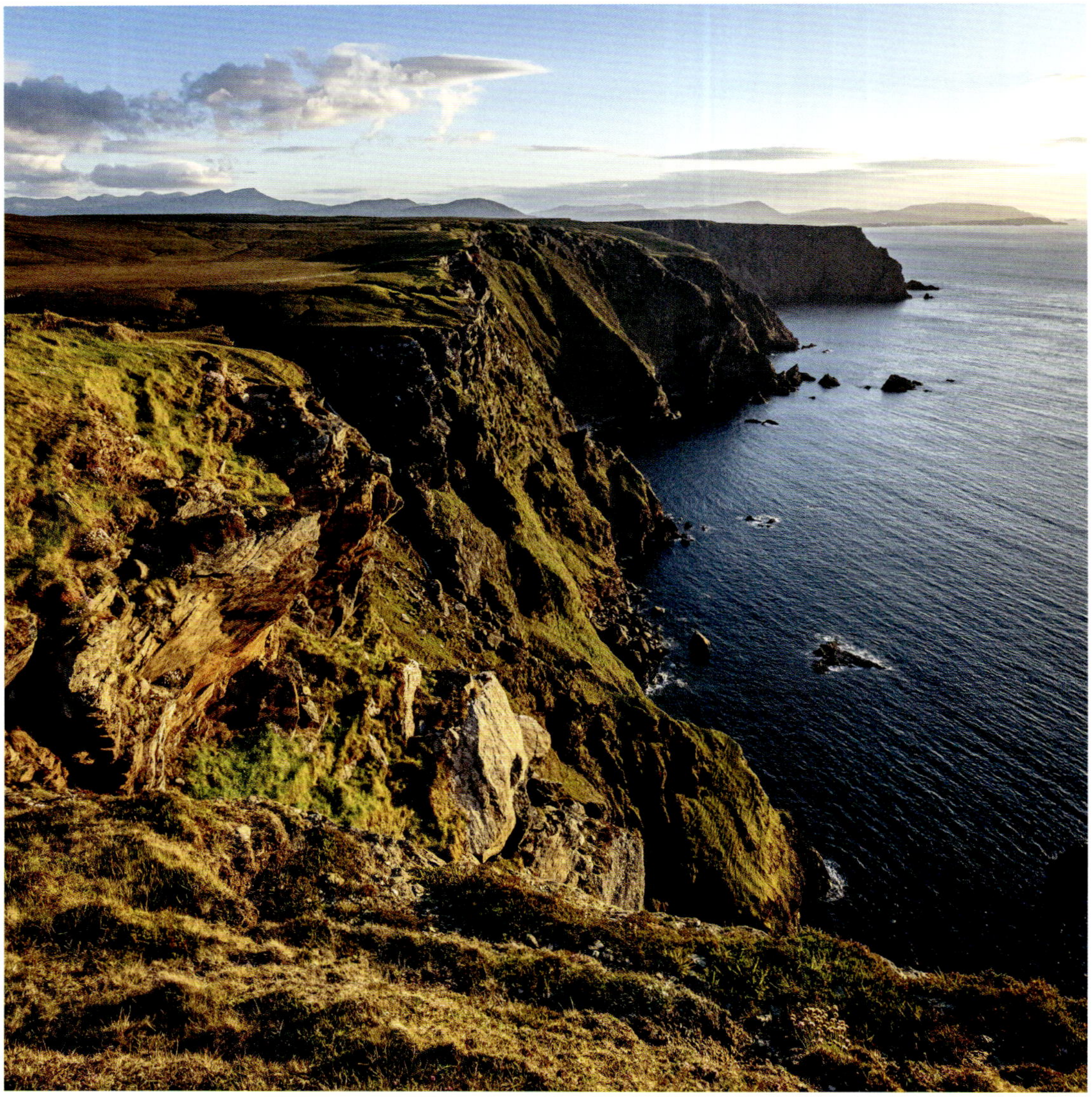

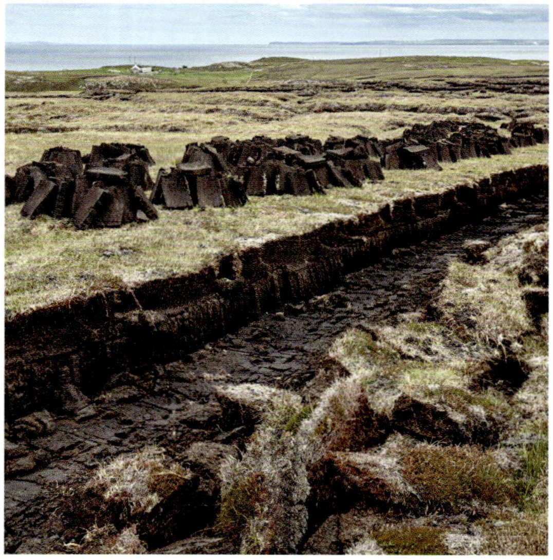

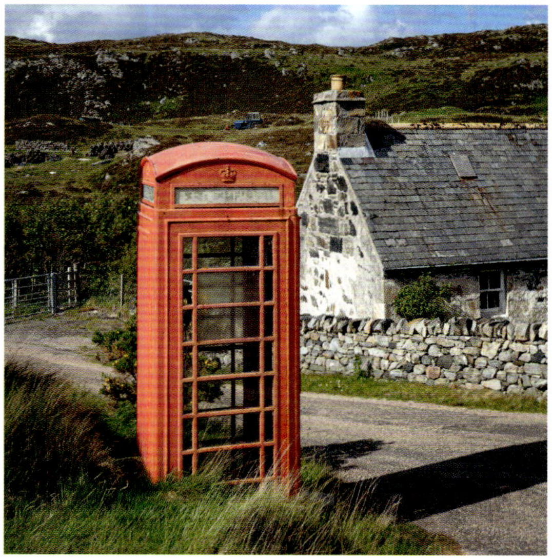

From top left:

Looking west along the A' Mhòine (meaning The Moss or The Peat in Gaelic) Peninsula towards a distant Faraid Head and Cape Wrath

Peat cutting on Strathy Point

Skerray phone box

Opposite:

Emma and Shane, in front of a surviving lifeboat from RMS *Lusitania* that was converted to a fishing boat

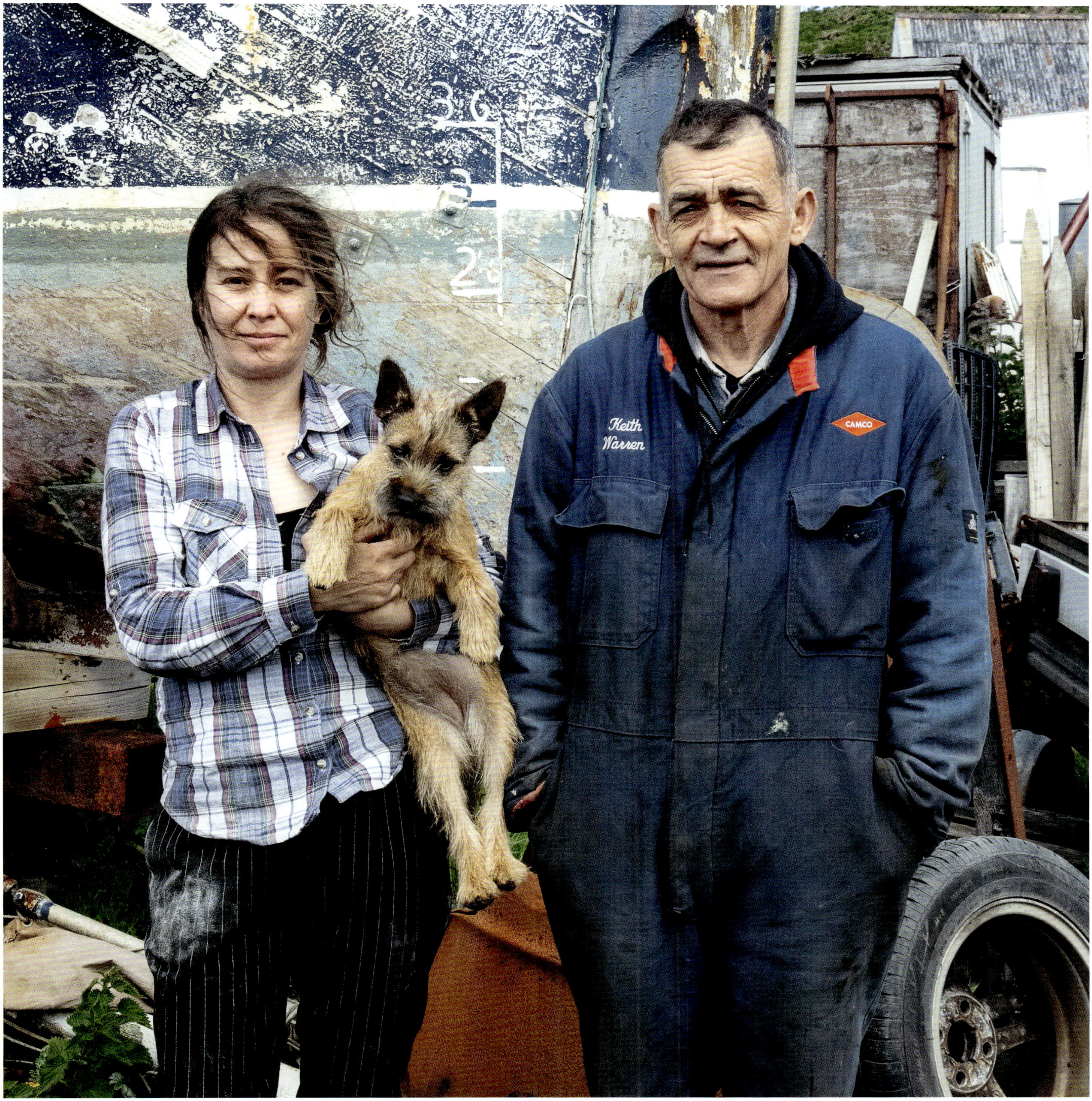
Keith
Warren
CAMCO

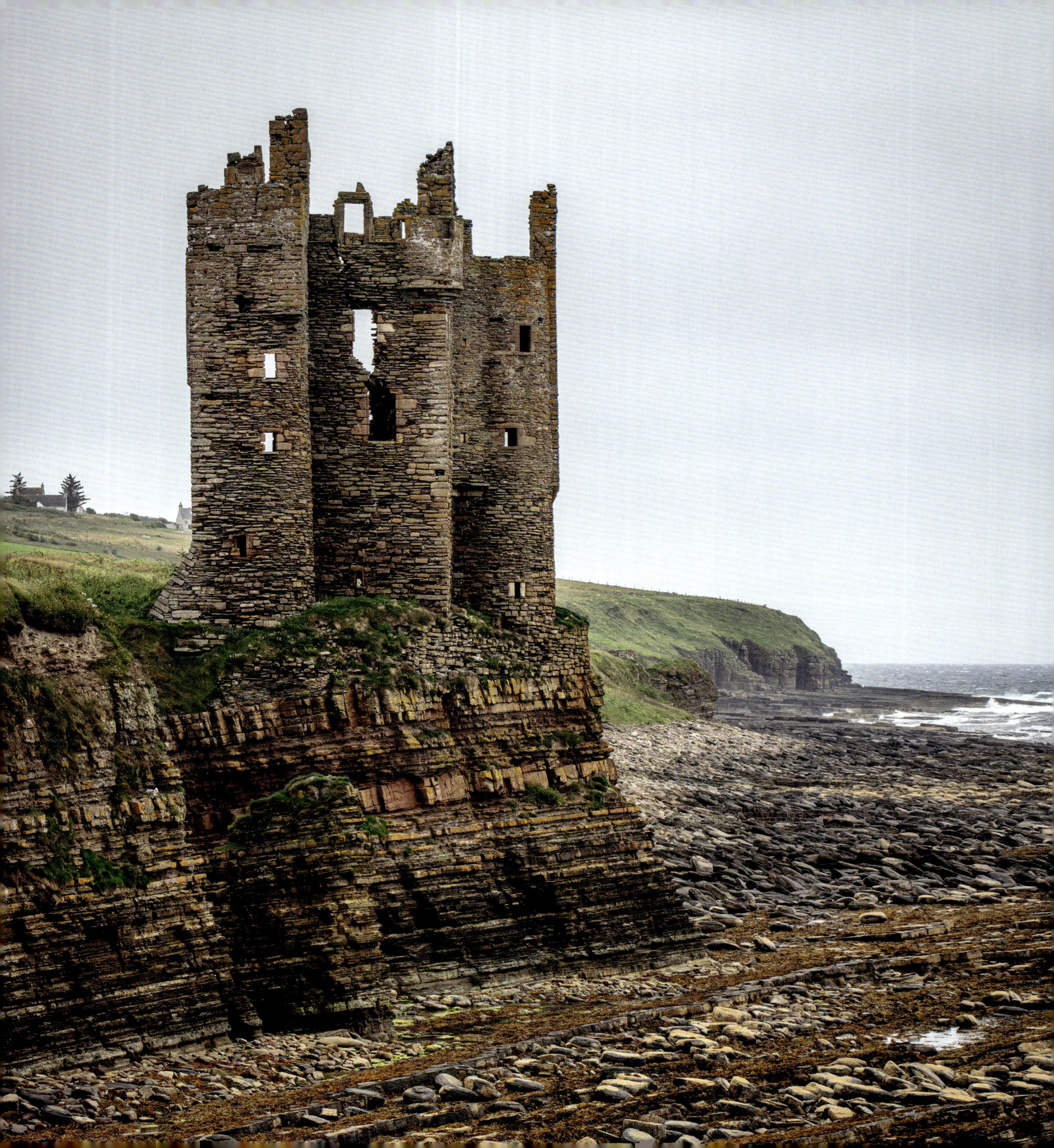

31

CAITHNESS

AUGUST 2019

DAY 318–326 | 07,742–07,933KM | 191KM

As I cross the border into Caithness, the wild flowers are in full bloom, forming a purple sea of heather and thistles offset by the fluttering of common blue butterflies. They're a beautiful diversion, but I refuse to be distracted: today is all about puffins. I'd been tipped off a few days ago that they liked to nest on the cliffs, and as I tread along the coastal path, my eyes are peeled. The first indication that I'm in luck is a photographer with a large white lens stood on the distant sea cliffs. I make my way closer to him eagerly. It's slow-going and at first I don't see anything – then all at once, there they are: thousands of birds, standing just a few metres away on the clifftops. It's my first time seeing one in the flesh and I'm instantly captivated by their black and white plumage – which appears more like fur than feathers – their joyfully vivid orange beak, and constant sense of busyness, simultaneously gossiping and bickering. Suddenly, it makes sense that they're known as 'the clown of the sea'.

'They'll be gone to the Atlantic in a couple of days; you're lucky to have caught them,' says the photographer, who tells me he knows the site like the back of his hand. There's limited space to get a good angle, so he moves over in order for us to share a narrow patch of flattish ground above the cliffs. The photography is thrilling, but as the light fades, midges begin to devour me. Even after applying repellent, I'm forced to wipe a black tide of the beasties from my face. Still, I'm too excited to stop, and we both don head nets to keep photographing as the sun sets. That evening, I pitch the tent nearby to stay as close to the puffins as possible. There's not much flat ground, and the only spot I find is a couple of steps from a sheer drop. I've never sleepwalked before, but I don't want to start tonight, so I tie my tent door closed with my bootlace just in case.

Over the next few days, I discover Caithness is a photographer's paradise in more ways than one. At the bulging peninsula of Dunnet Head, the most northerly point in mainland Britain, I approach the lighthouse from the tussocky moorland, where visibility varies from white-out conditions to complete clarity within a few minutes due to sea fog. I wait with my camera above a precipitous cliff until the swirling fog reveals a glimpse of both the lighthouse and the cliff on which it stands, capturing the treachery and mystery of the location.

As I make my way from the tourist shops at John o'Groats to the drama of the sea stacks at Duncansby Head, it's the practicalities of taking photos that prompts the startling realisation that I've begun to hike south and back towards home for the first time. Walking into the sun means that the landscape ahead is silhouetted more often than not, and the best pictures require looking behind, which means I'm often missing the best light on a subject. It's tricky adjusting to the shifting light and perspective along the clifftops, but I'm grateful it gives the sunburn on the back of my neck a chance to recover.

The thought that I've walked over three quarters of the perimeter makes me want to savour every second, even as it adds a renewed energy to my stride. With my newfound home-bound momentum and one of the straightest coastlines of any county, Caithness comes to an end all too quickly. As I zip up the tent on my final night, I can't help but feel that now I'm descending down the side of Britain towards London, the peak of the journey is behind me.

Opposite:

Keiss Castle, built in the sixteenth century

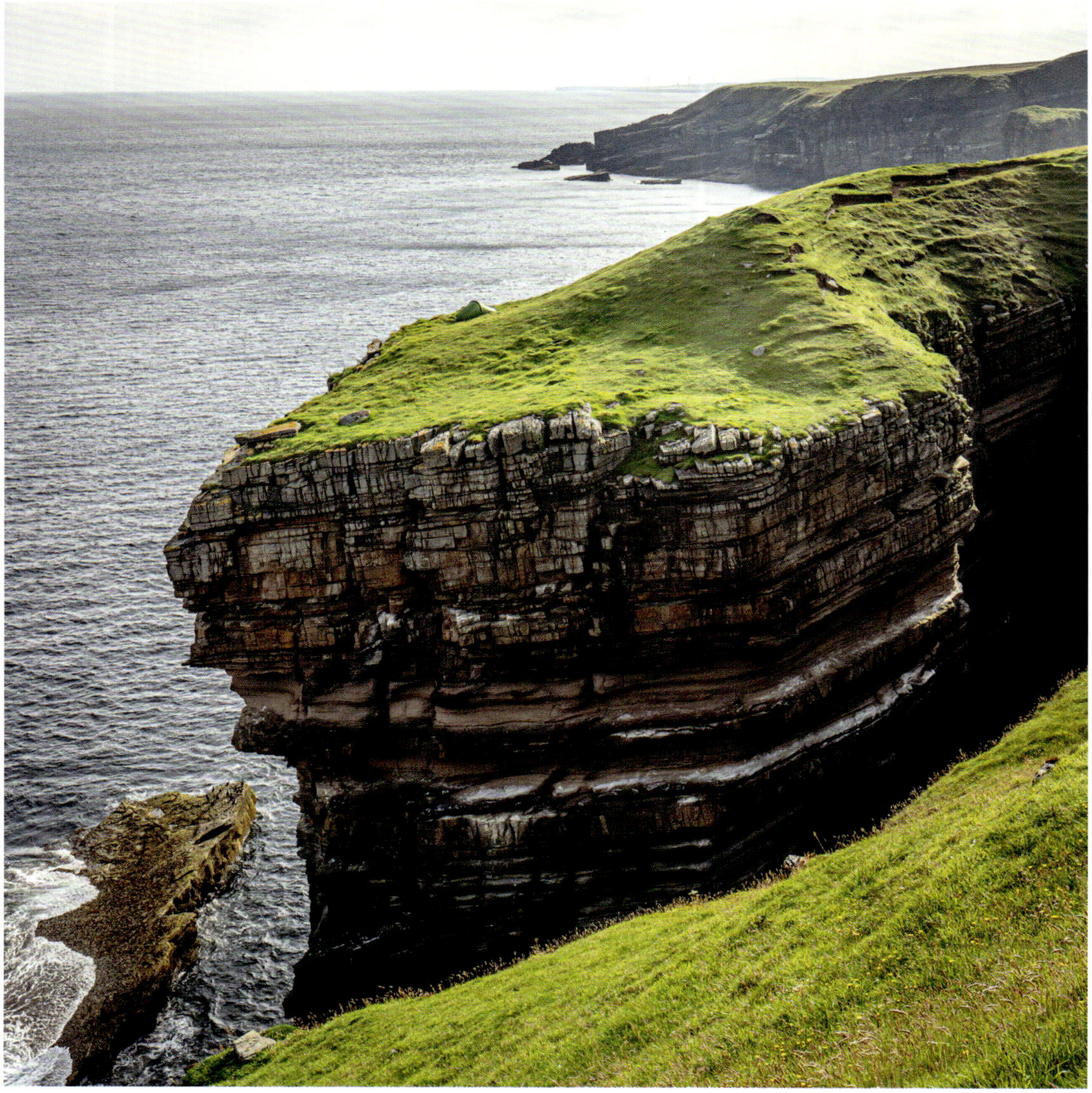

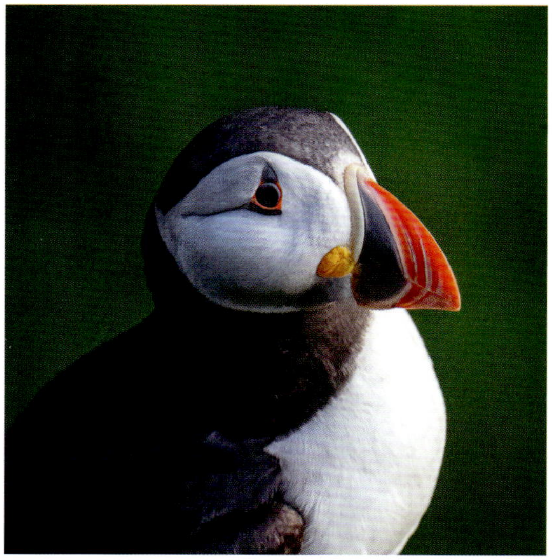

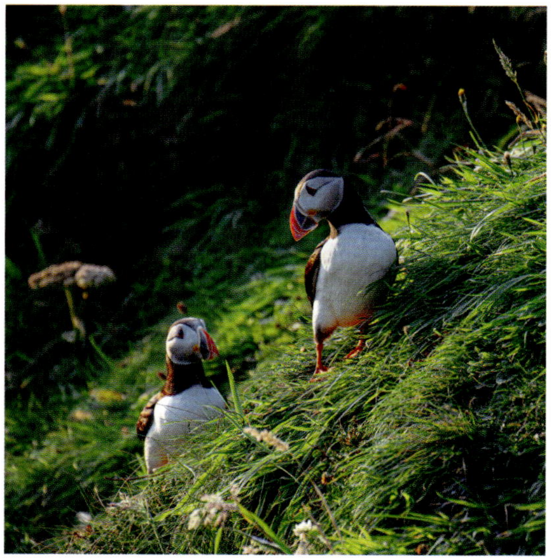

From top left:

No exit tonight: I tied the tent door shut at Middle Clett just in case I decided to make a sleepwalking debut

Puffin at Wester Clett

Puffins perched on the clifftops, Wester Clett

Opposite, clockwise from top left:

Sandside Harbour, Fresgoe, with Dounreay nuclear site

Links, Sandside Harbour, Fresgoe

Forss Wind Farm

Sea mist swirls around Dunnet Head Lighthouse, the extreme north point of mainland Britain

Line and stone, Sandside Harbour, Fresgoe

Weathervane, Crosskirk

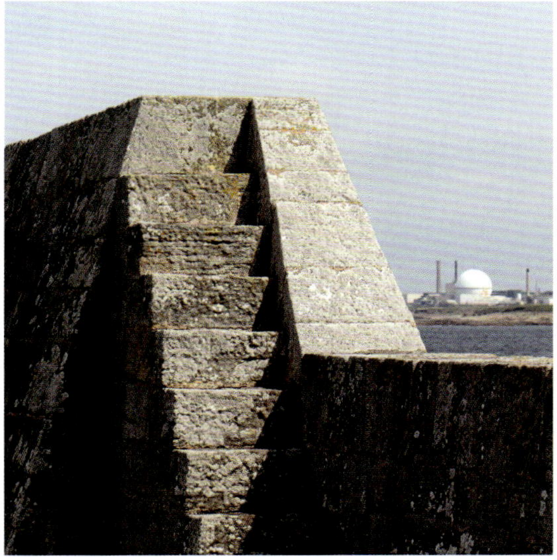

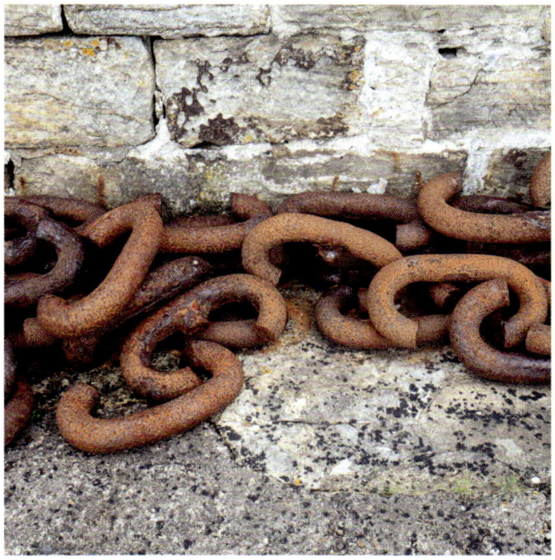

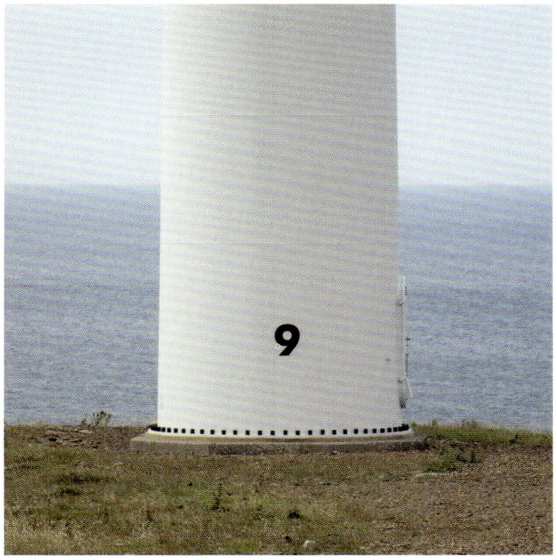
9

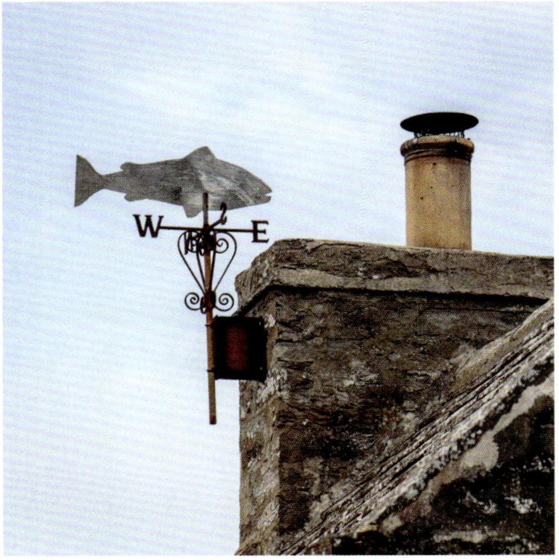
W
E

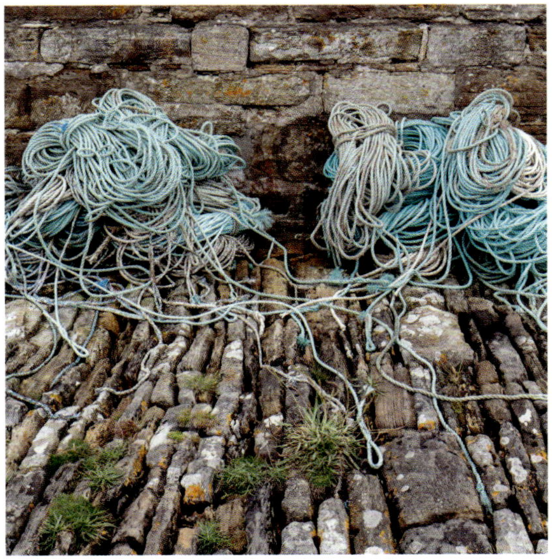

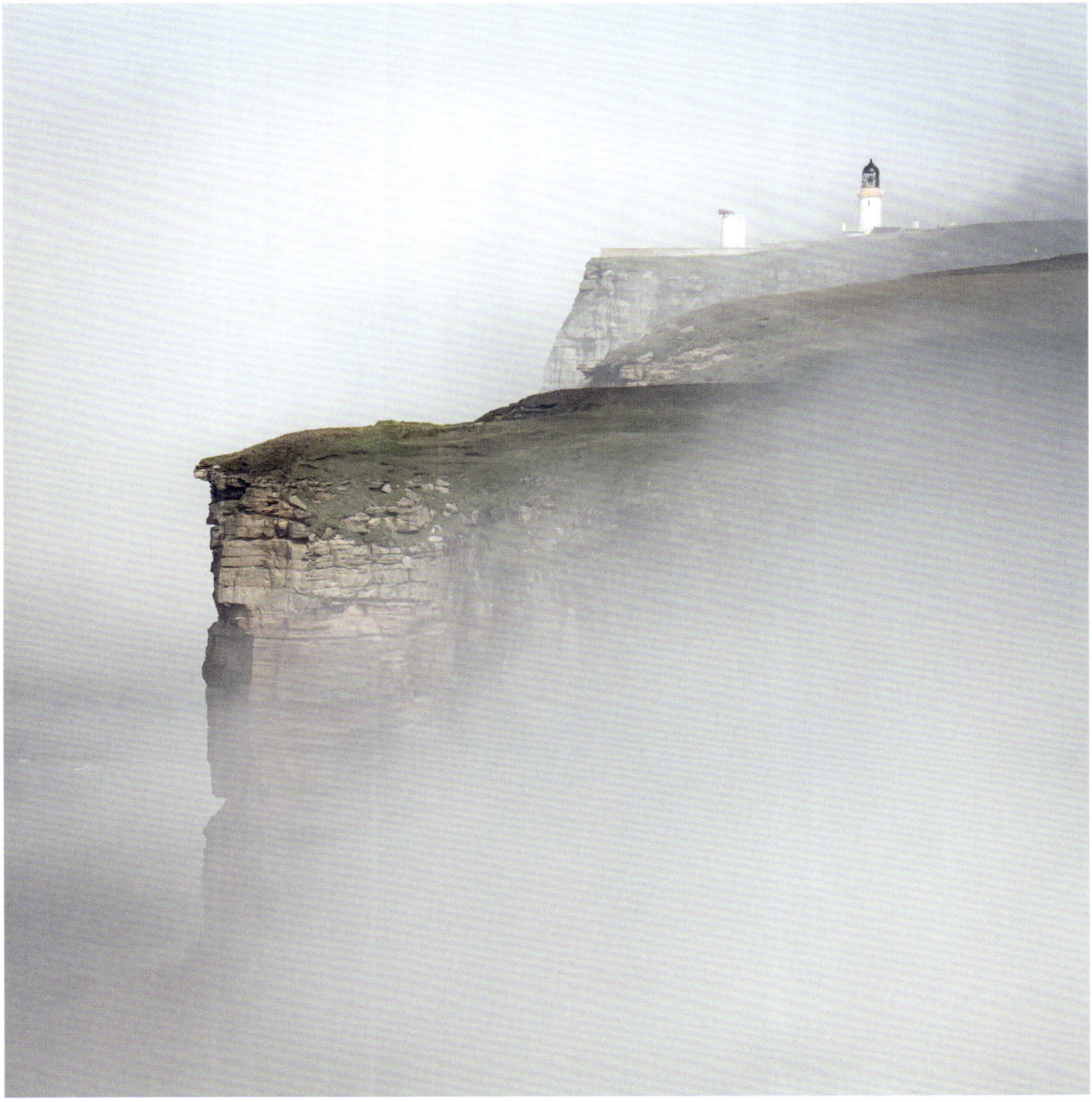

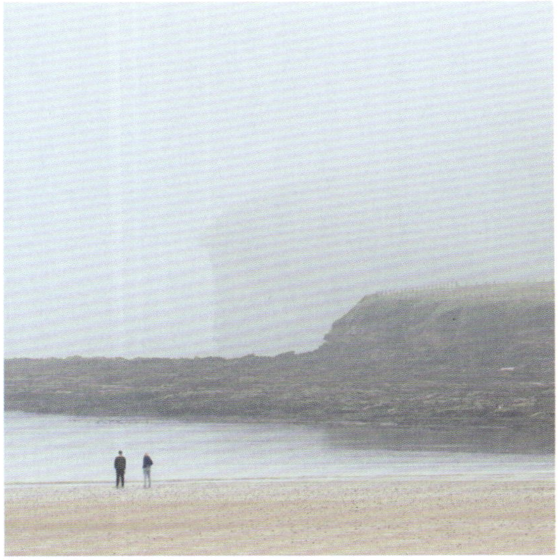

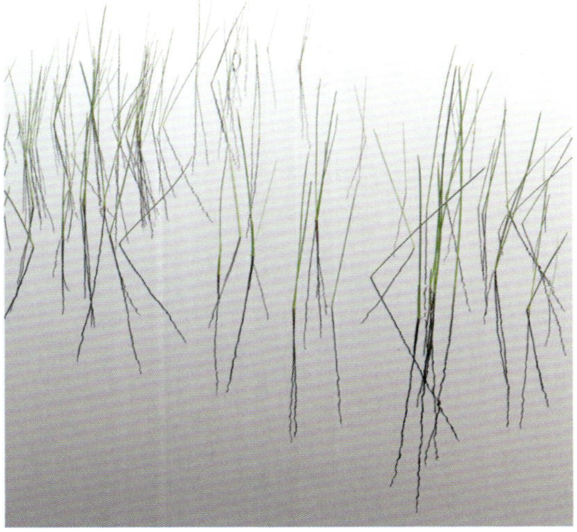

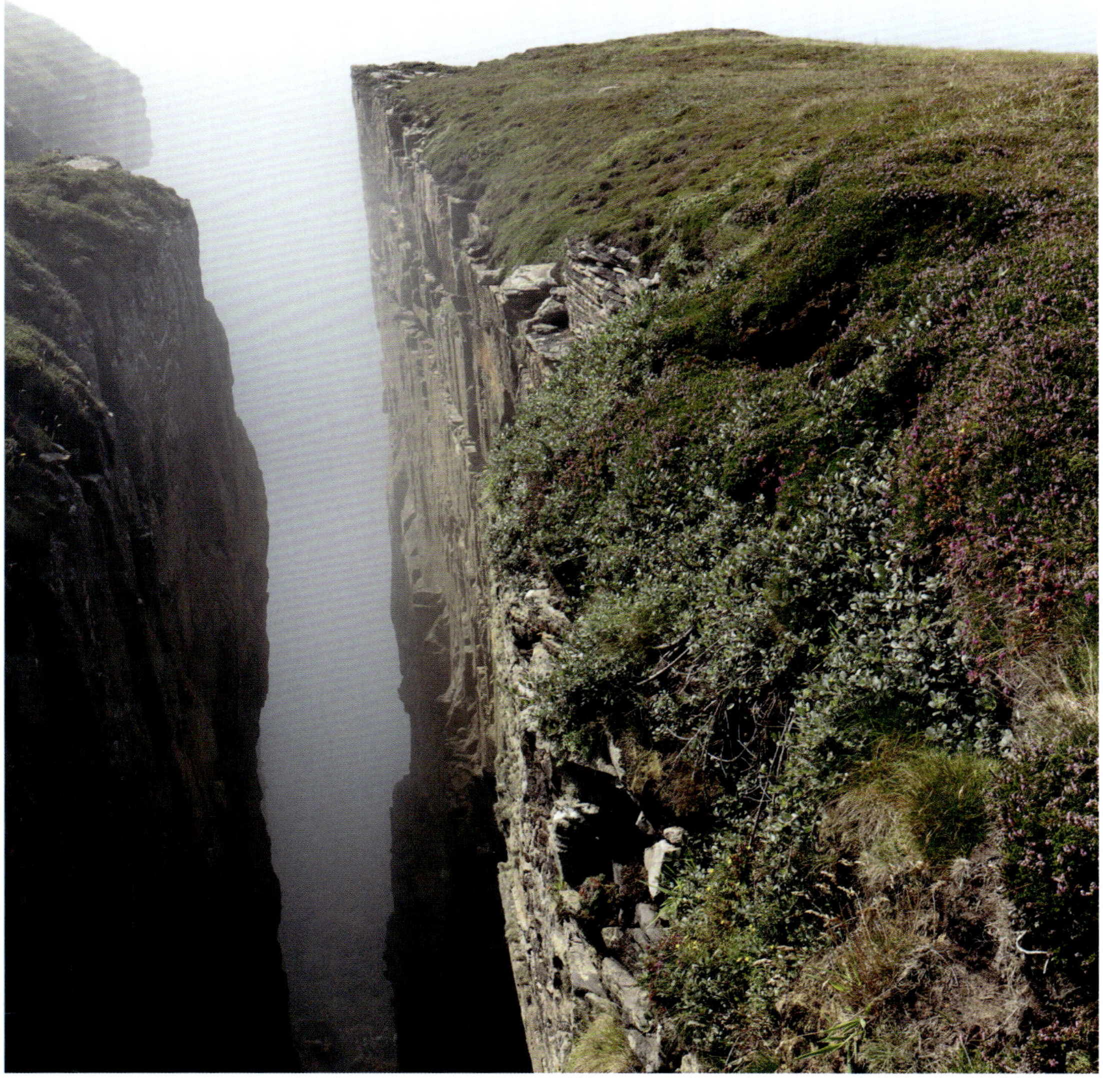

From top left:

Figures, Dunnet Bay

Loch of Easter Head, Dunnet Head

Black Geos (a geo being a narrow and deep cleft in the face of a cliff, a common feature in Caithness), Dunnet Head

Opposite, clockwise from top left:

Scarfskerry

Car park at Duncansby Head

Field boundary, Castle of Mey

Canisbay Parish Church dates to the early 1600s and is the most northerly church on mainland Britain

Fingerpost at John o'Groats, which lies on Great Britain's north-eastern tip (actually, it's Duncansby Head, a mile and a half away, but there's no village there, so it tends to get overlooked) and is popular with tourists as one end of the two extremities of the mainland with Land's End in Cornwall lying 1,410 kilometres south-west as the crow flies. This was the second time I'd walked between these two points; the last time I was here was in 1996, having walked 1,677 kilometres from Land's End over eighty-one days, when I got so drunk on drams of whisky proffered by friendly locals in the pub that the best I could do in putting up the tent was wrap it loosely around my body. This time, my coastal Land's End-to-John o'Groats walk was 6,315 kilometres and involved no whisky!

Shoreline, Ness of Huna

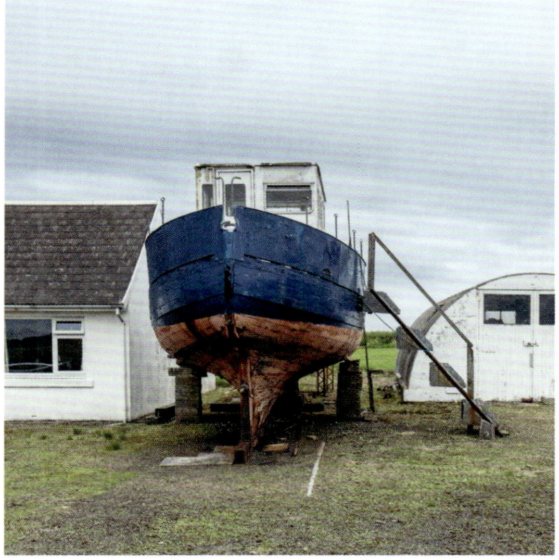

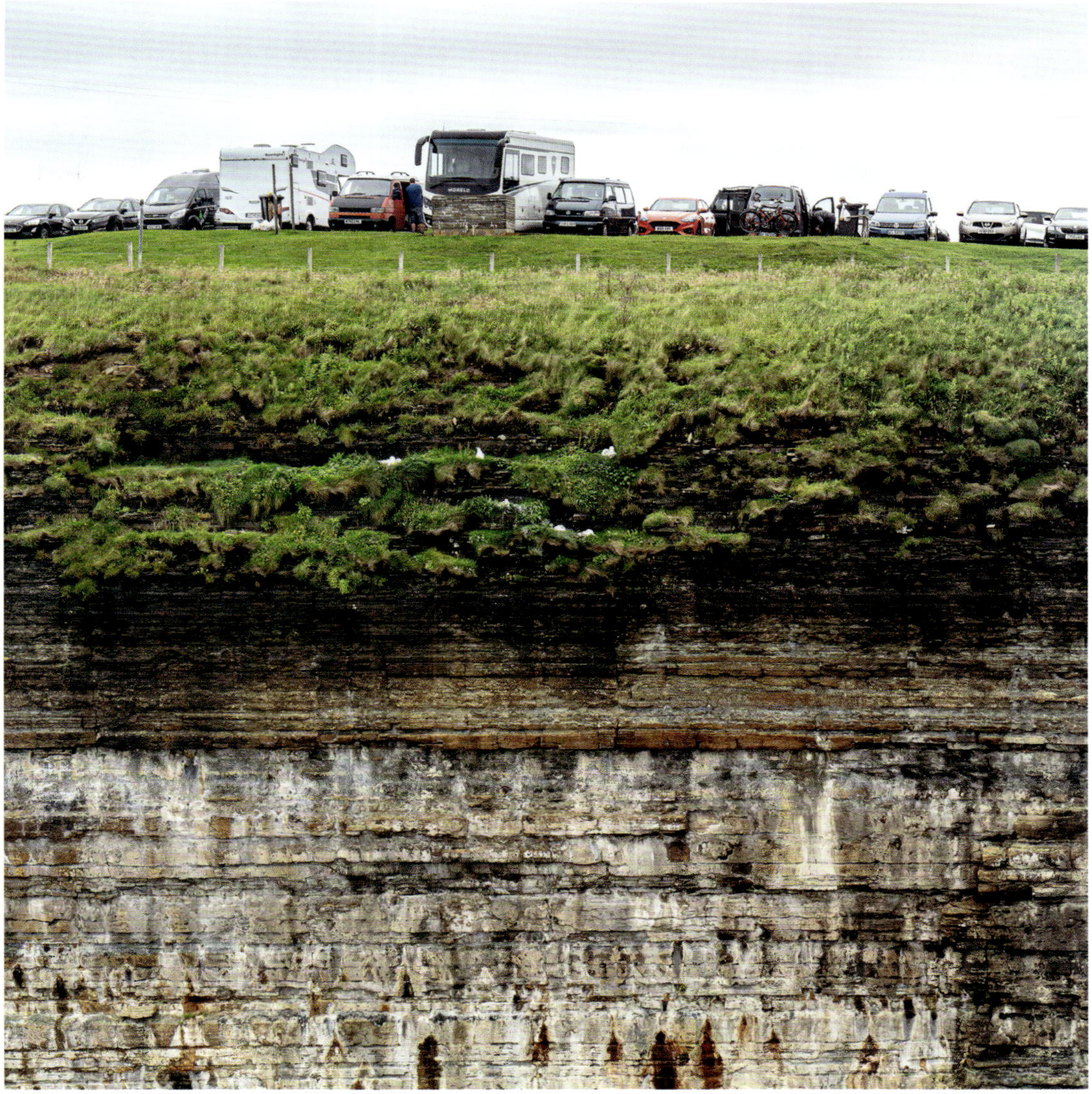

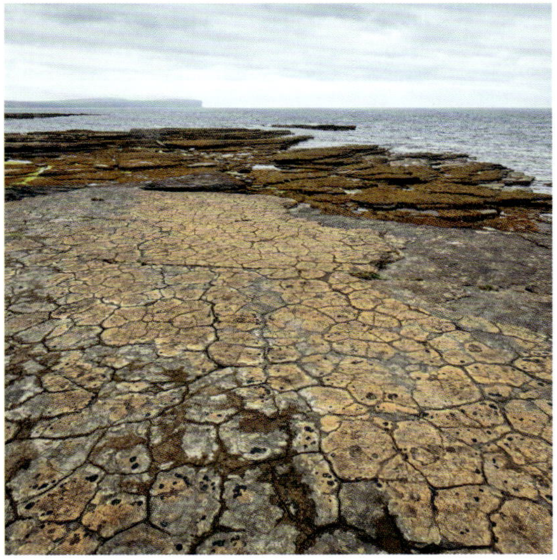

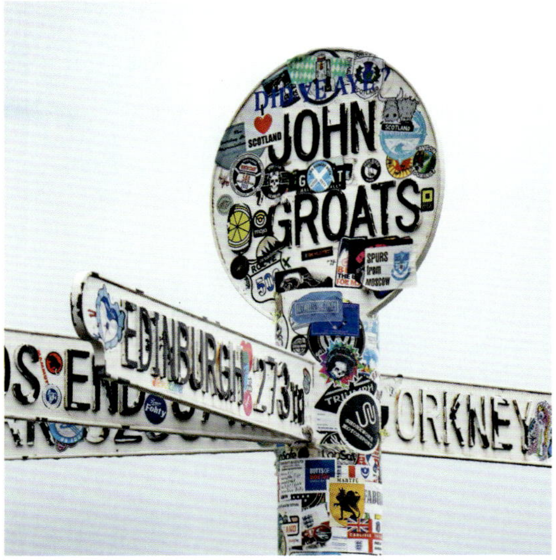
JOHN
GROATS
EDINBURGH
ORKNEY

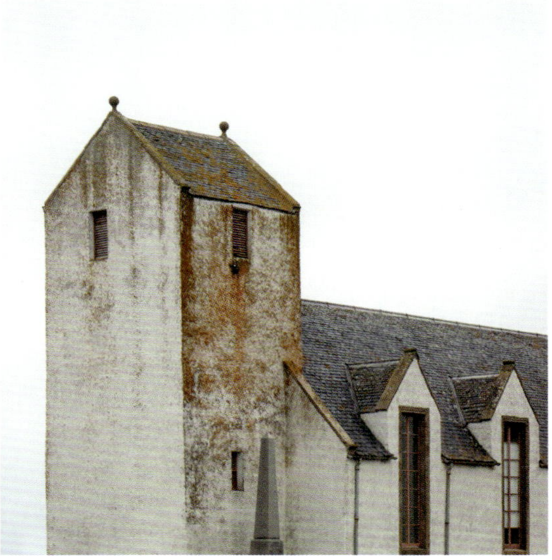

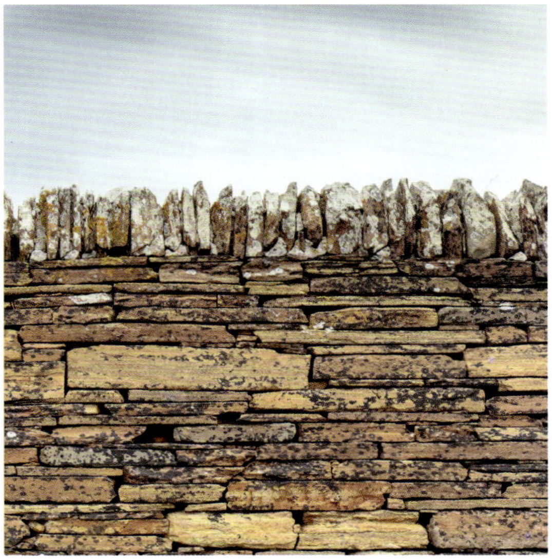

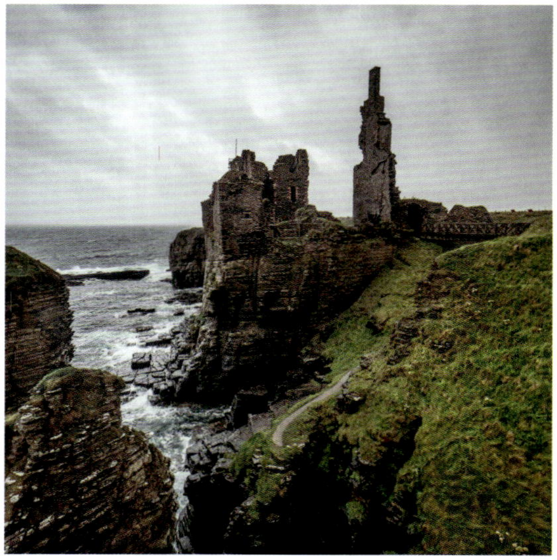

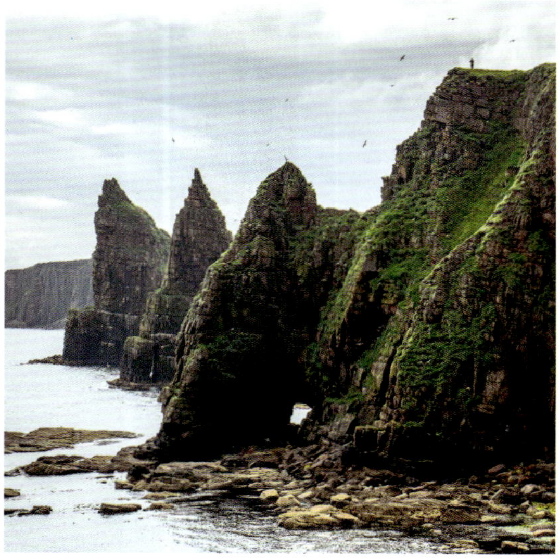

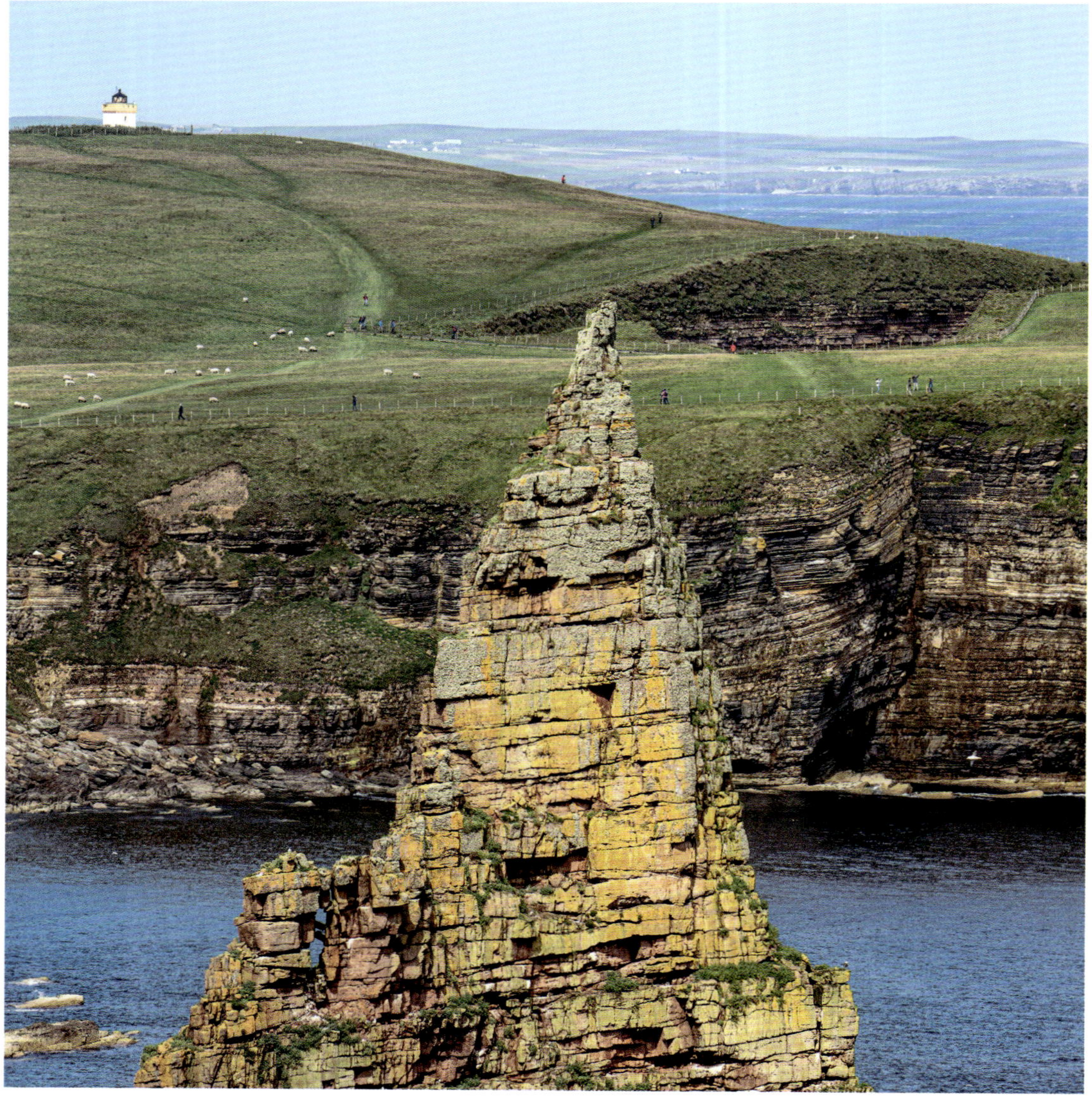

From top left:

Castle Sinclair Girnigoe in the rain, comprising the ruins of two castles: the fifteenth-century Castle Girnigoe and the early-seventeenth-century Castle Sinclair

Thirle Door and the Stacks of Duncansby

The Witches' Hat Stack and Duncansby Head Lighthouse

Opposite, clockwise from top left:

Hearth in the mausoleum at Mains of Ulbster

Kitchen with a framed lintel of seventeenth-century chimney piece with centre coat of arms of Sinclairs of Ulbster (probably from earlier house on site), Mains of Ulbster. The kitchen is floored with huge slabs of Caithness flagstone

Mausoleum at Mains of Ulbster with the North Sea

Mid Clyth graveyard

Keiss Harbour

Navigation beacon tower, Berriedale

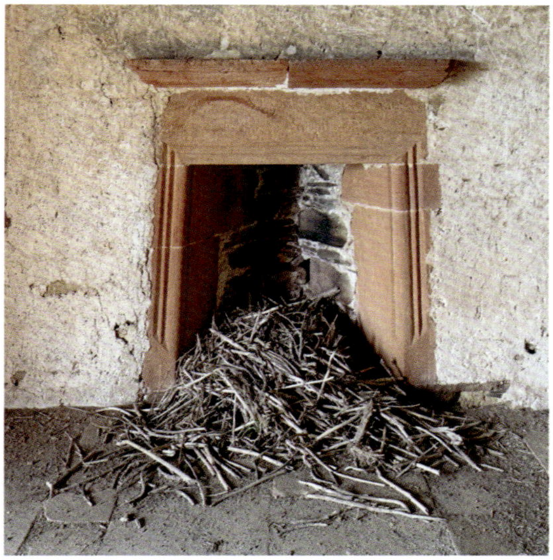

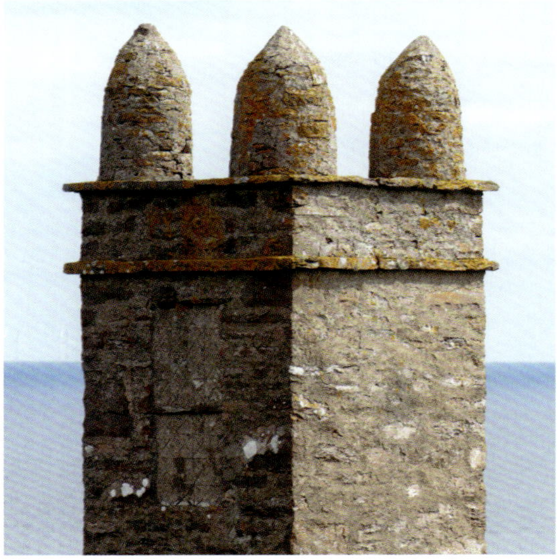

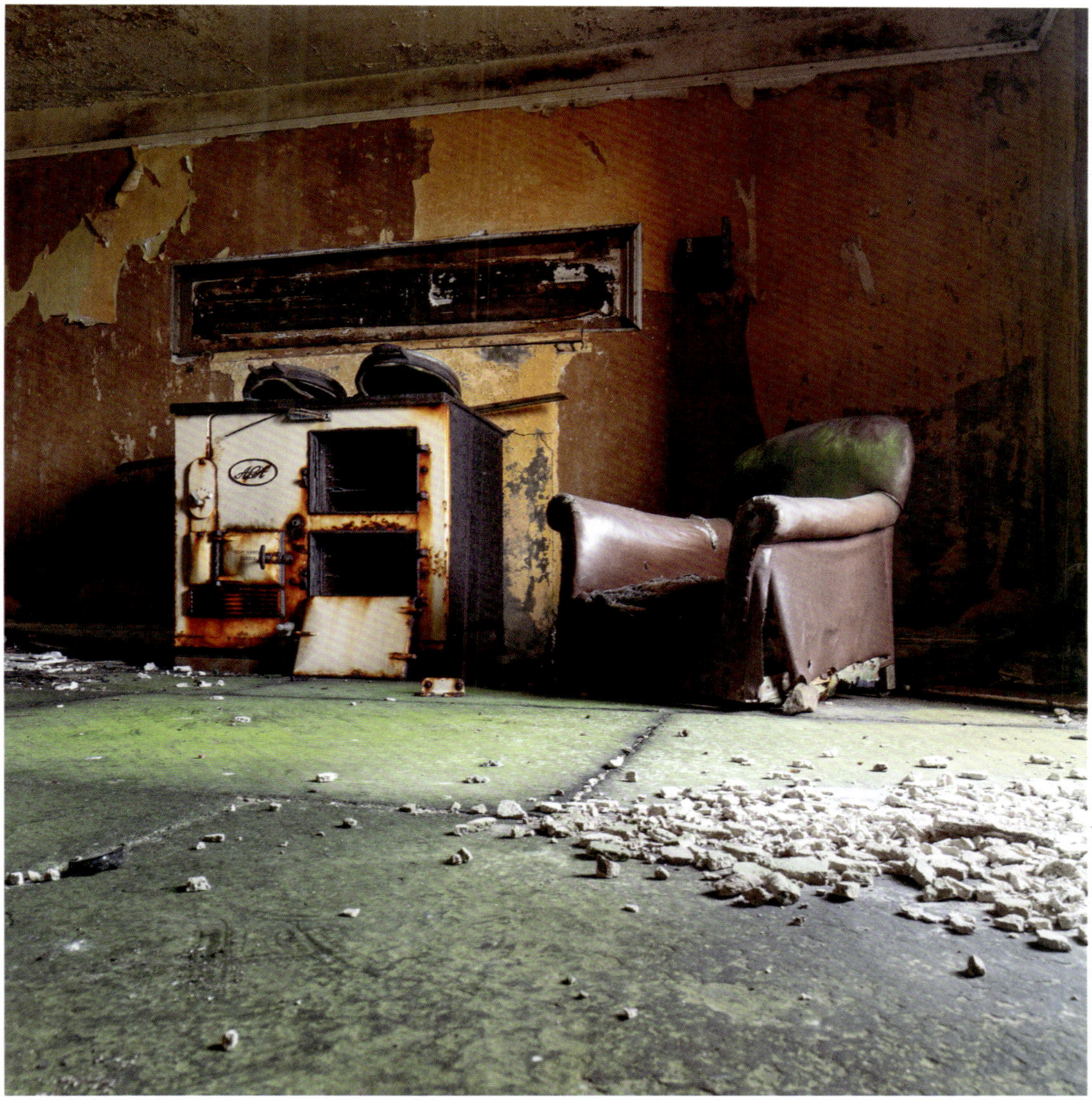

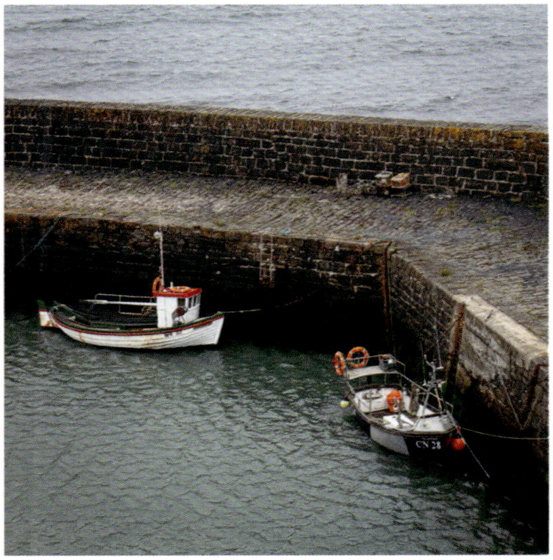

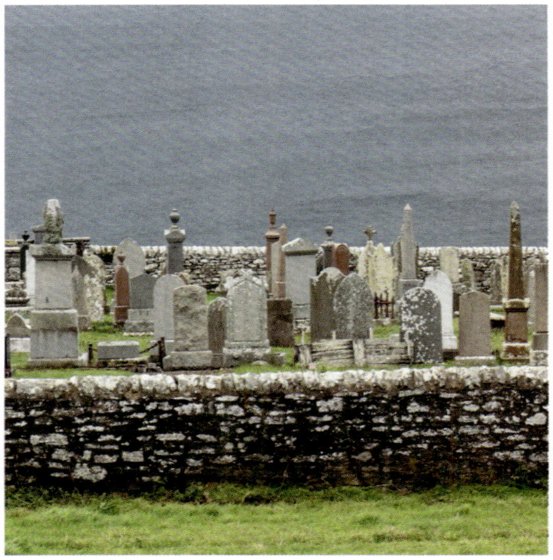

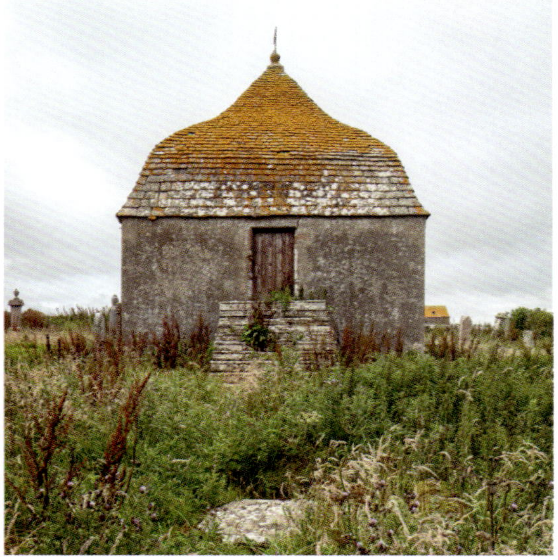

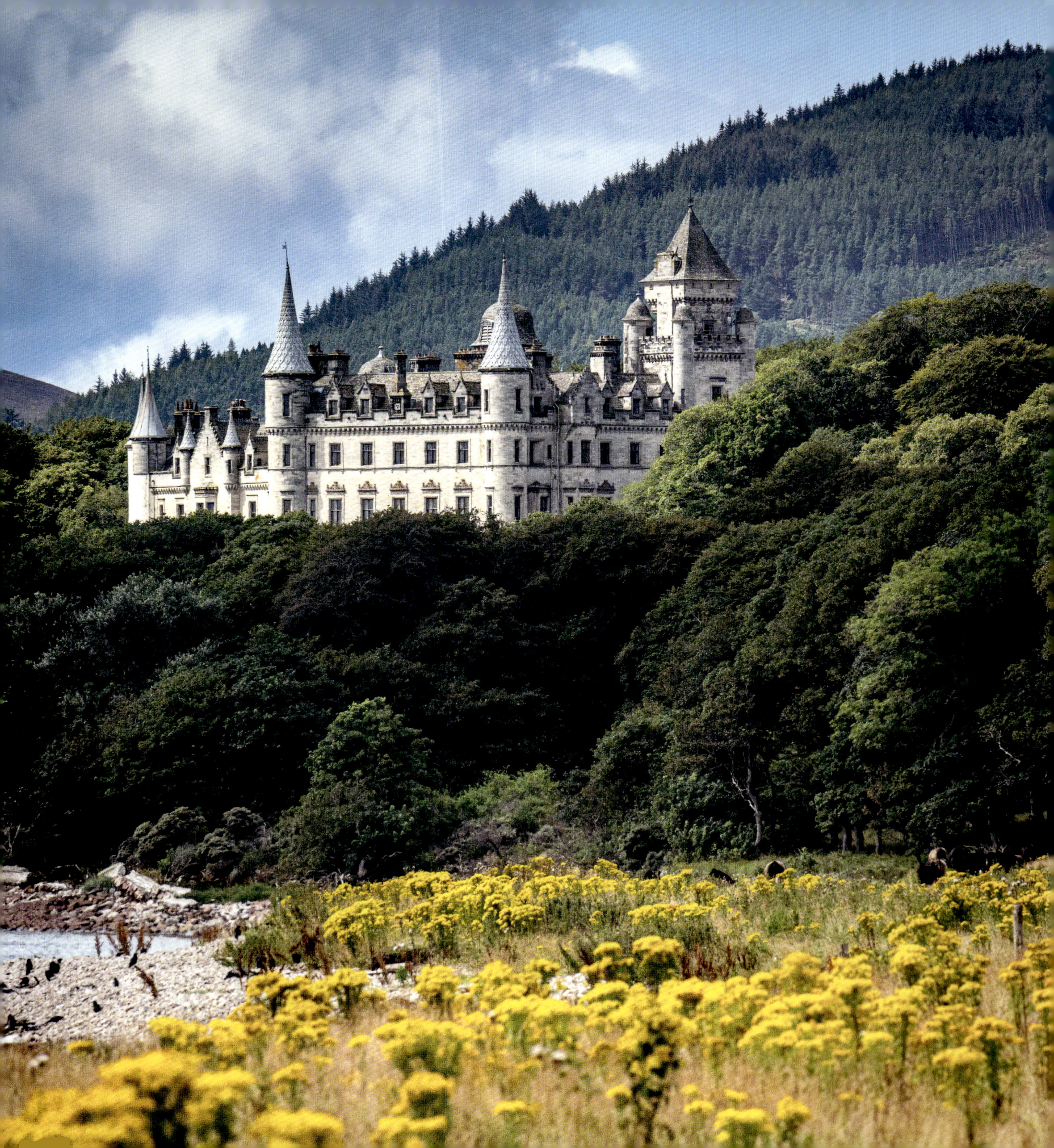

32 EAST SUTHERLAND

AUGUST 2019

DAY 327–328 | 07,933–08,003 KM | 70 KM

The enduring architectural character of the last few months walking the Highland coast has been the ruined croft and the clearance village, so the fairy-tale splendour of Dunrobin Castle seems to mark the start of different forces set among the fertile lands of the east coast. As I leave behind the carefree golden beaches of Brora, my eyes are drawn to its cluster of turrets, each topped with a curved, conical pale lead roof in a fish-scale design, which stands in contrast to the dark forest that envelops it. It's the kind of building that makes you wonder if anyone knows how many rooms it contains. Up close, the castle's ornamental details become more apparent: crests and carved crowns above the windows, as well as filigree on the ridge lines.

This sudden manifestation of wealth and power was constructed for the 1st Duke of Sutherland, a figure impossible to miss because his statue, immodestly perched on the top of Ben Bhraggie, had dominated the skyline all morning. The duke was one of the key players responsible for relocating thousands of people from the fertile valleys into clearance villages to make way for more profitable sheep farming. This must have been galling for the inhabitants of the Badbea clearance village that I'd passed just yesterday, who in the early nineteenth century had to tether livestock – and children! – to rocks or posts to prevent them from being blown over the cliffs or into the sea by fierce winds.

Far more intriguing to me than Dunrobin Castle are the unpretentious ruins of the nearby Carn Liath Broch, a gently tapered drystone roundhouse perched on raised ground a short distance from the shore. Stepping into the building, I'm taken aback by the intact guard cell at the entrance, a unique feature that evokes the defensive strategies of the Iron Age. I crouch inside the dark, small room, trying to fathom the lives of those who occupied this space 2,000 years ago. From the interior, I climb the remarkably preserved stone stairs between the inner and outer walls, which lead me to panoramic views of the Moray Firth. As with Glenelg Brochs in the west, I leave the structure with my imagination ablaze, inspired by this distinctly Scottish form of architecture.

It's a 47-kilometre slog to get from Dunrobin Castle to the historic town of Dornoch, so I march steadily for the rest of the day, following a disused rail line to arrive at my hotel just before midnight. I plan for only a short reunion with Sutherland, so the next day is spent enjoying simple pleasures: a relaxing hot bath and a satisfying meal. Feeling refreshed, I leave Dornoch and pass pastel-clad golfers wrestling with umbrellas during a shower to follow the shoreline at Dornoch Beach. Bizarrely, it's scattered with hundreds of white spherical objects which, on closer inspection, I realise are sea potato shells, a kind of urchin that lives buried in the sand. Each shell is exquisite and looks like it could have been made by a porcelain ceramicist.

The tide is low at Cuthill Sands, enabling me to take a vast, exhilarating shortcut across the estuary, with the wet sand mirroring the clouds above. As I look back to land, the squat tower of Dornoch Cathedral catches the evening sunlight. A flock of sanderlings rise with a lonely oyster-catcher in their midst. The sand below my feet is marked with myriad web-footed bird prints through which my solitary boot tracks appear like those of an alien outsider.

Opposite:

Dunrobin Castle, the family seat of the Earl of Sutherland and the Clan Sutherland. Dunrobin's origins lie in the Middle Ages, but most of the present building and the gardens were added by Sir Charles Barry, the architect famous for designing the Houses of Parliament, between 1835 and 1850

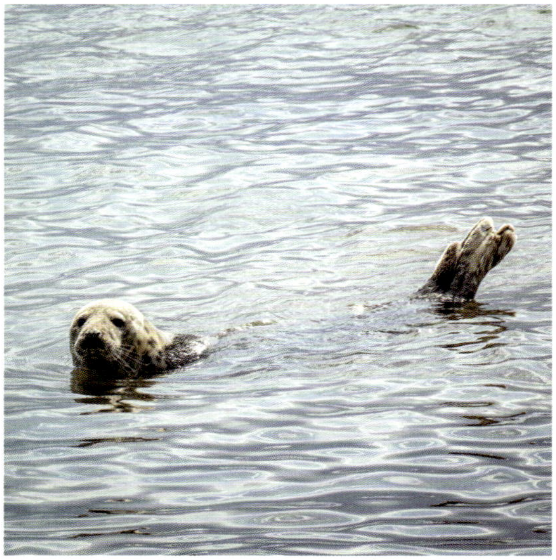
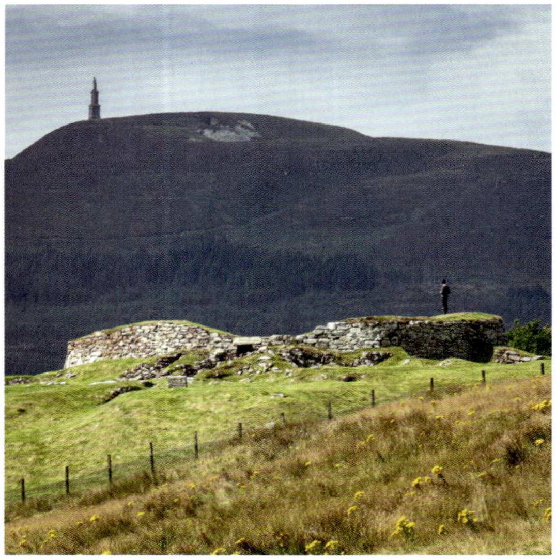
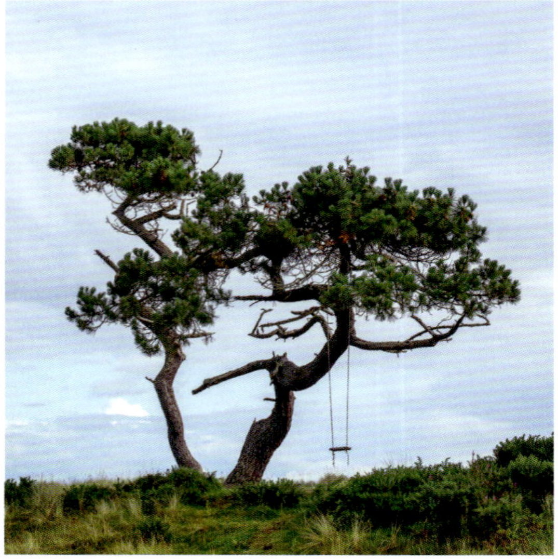
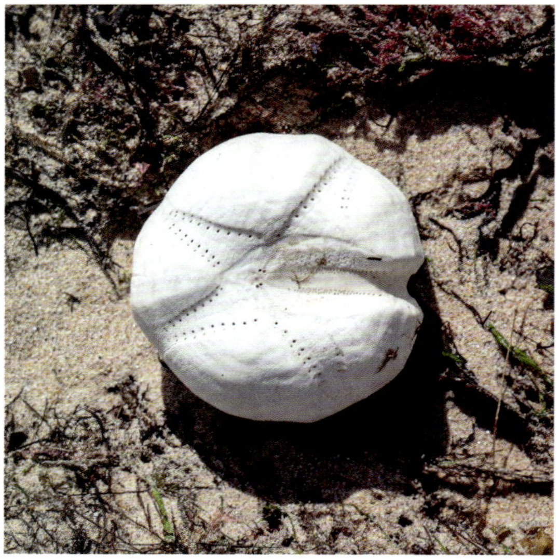
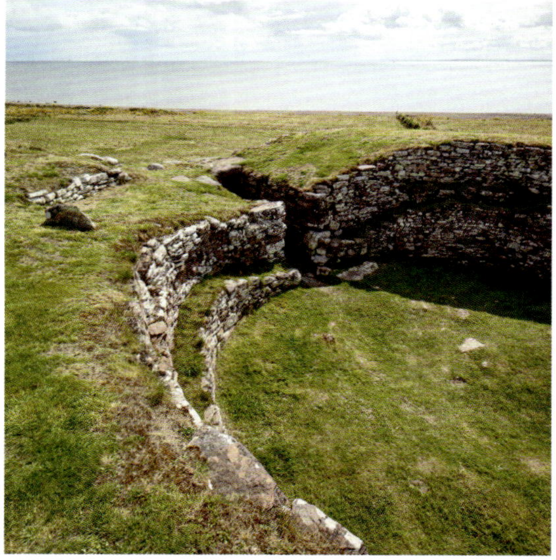
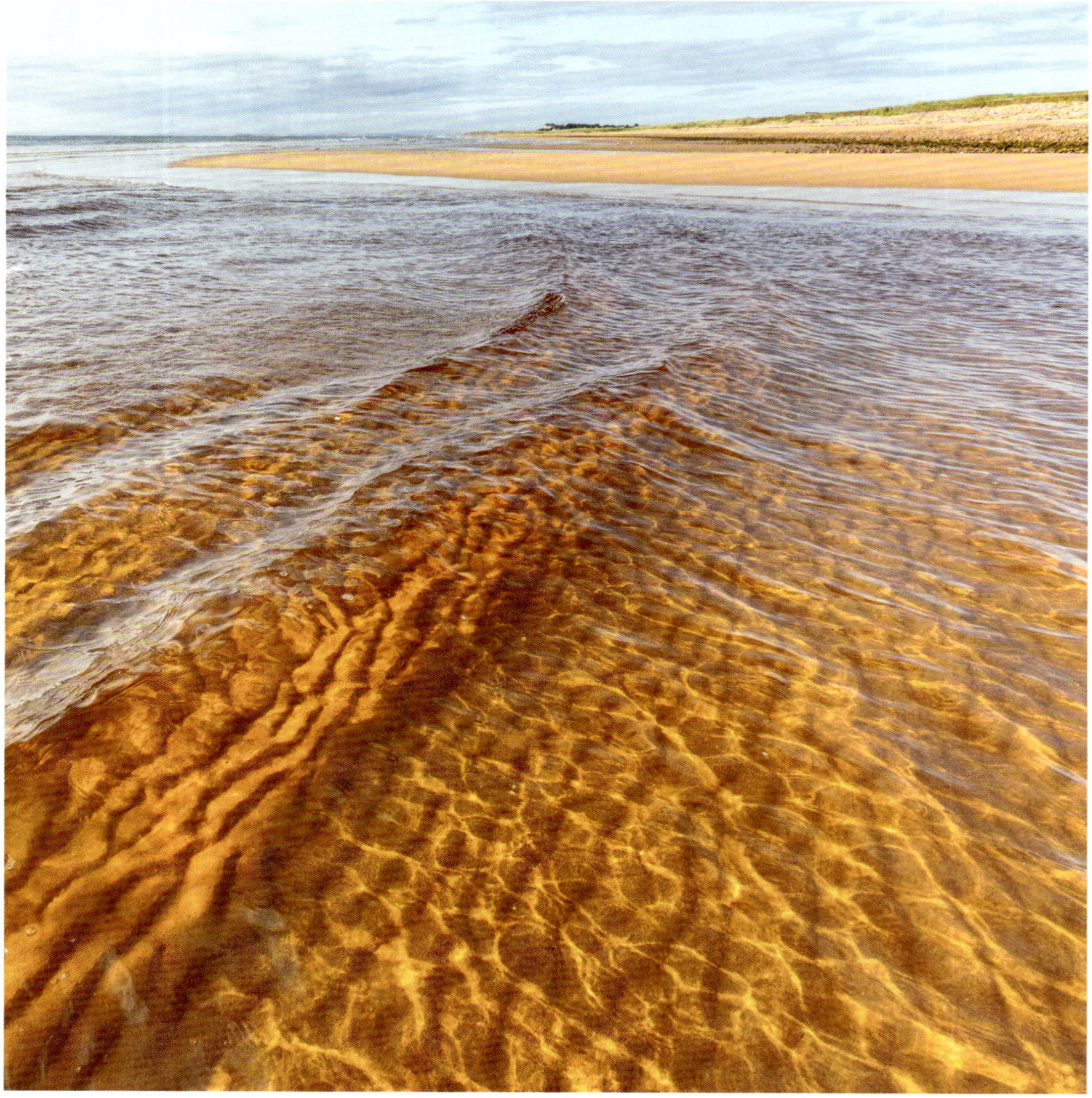

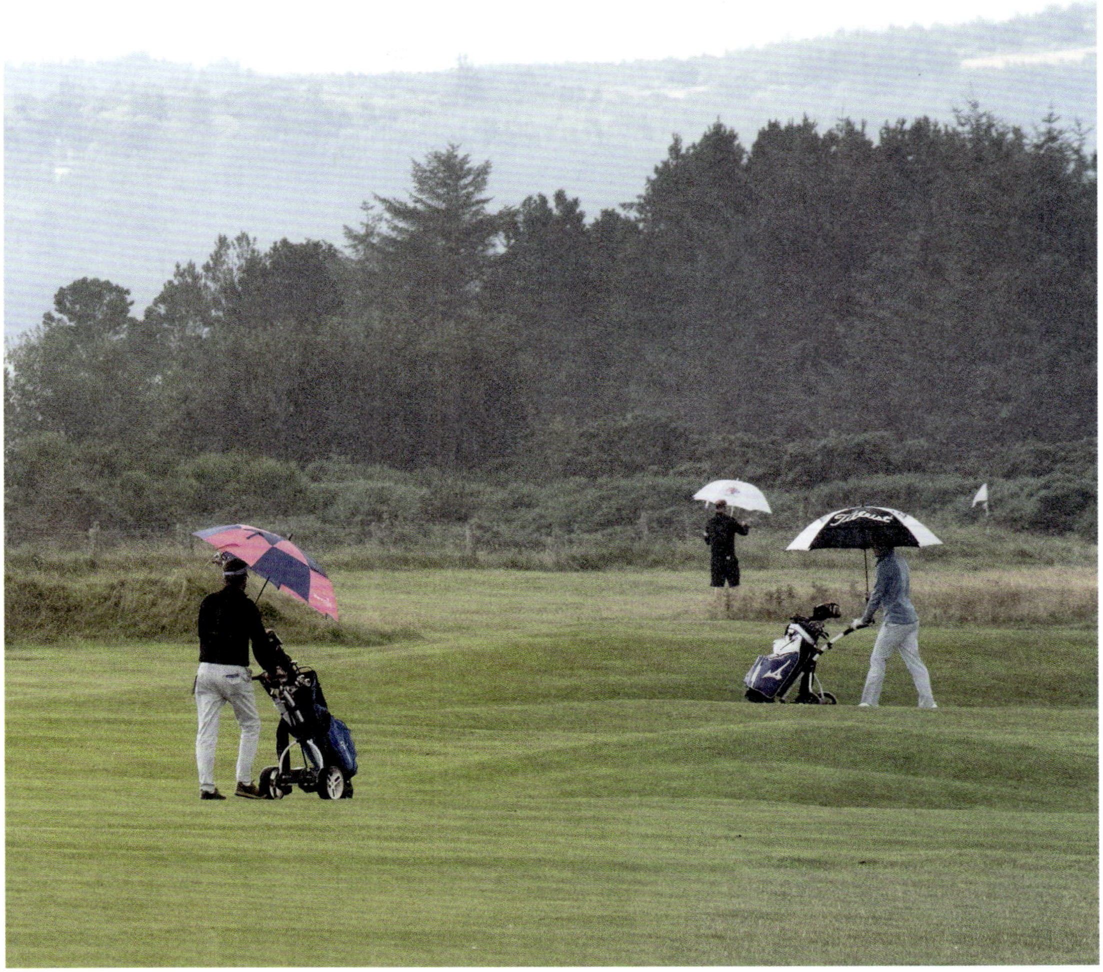

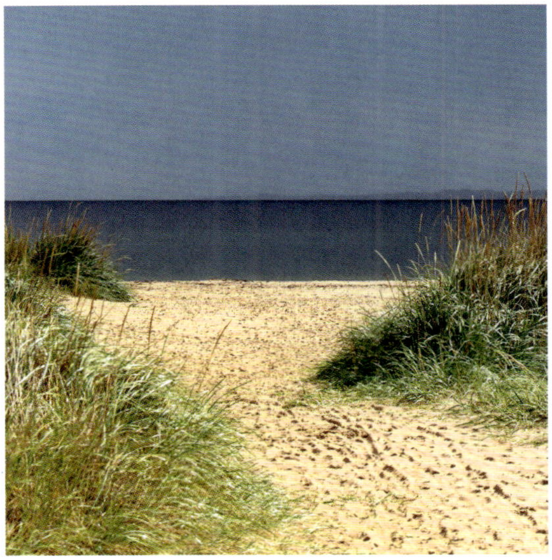

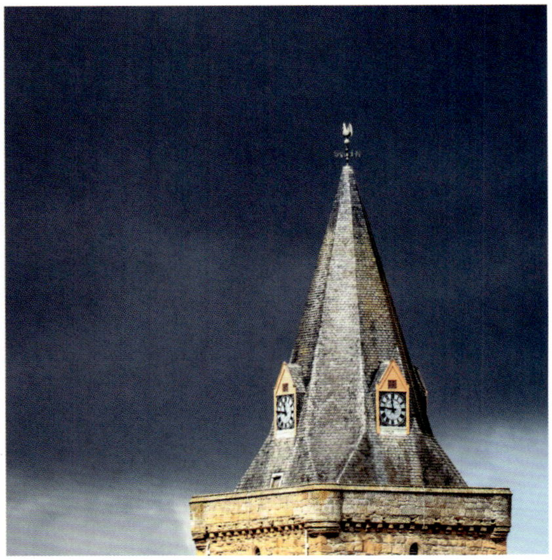

Opposite, clockwise from top left:

Grey seal near Brora

Carn Liath Broch and the Duke of Sutherland Monument, Golspie. (The statue is highly controversial and several attempts have been made to topple it due to the Duke's role in the Highland Clearances)

Swing, Littleferry

Brora Beach (the peaty colour from where the Clyne Burn meets the sea)

The entrance and interior of Iron Age Carn Liath Broch, Golspie, overlooking the Moray Firth

Sea potato (a type of sea urchin), Dornoch Point

From top left:

Royal Dornoch Golf Club

To the beach at Dornoch

Dornoch Cathedral tower

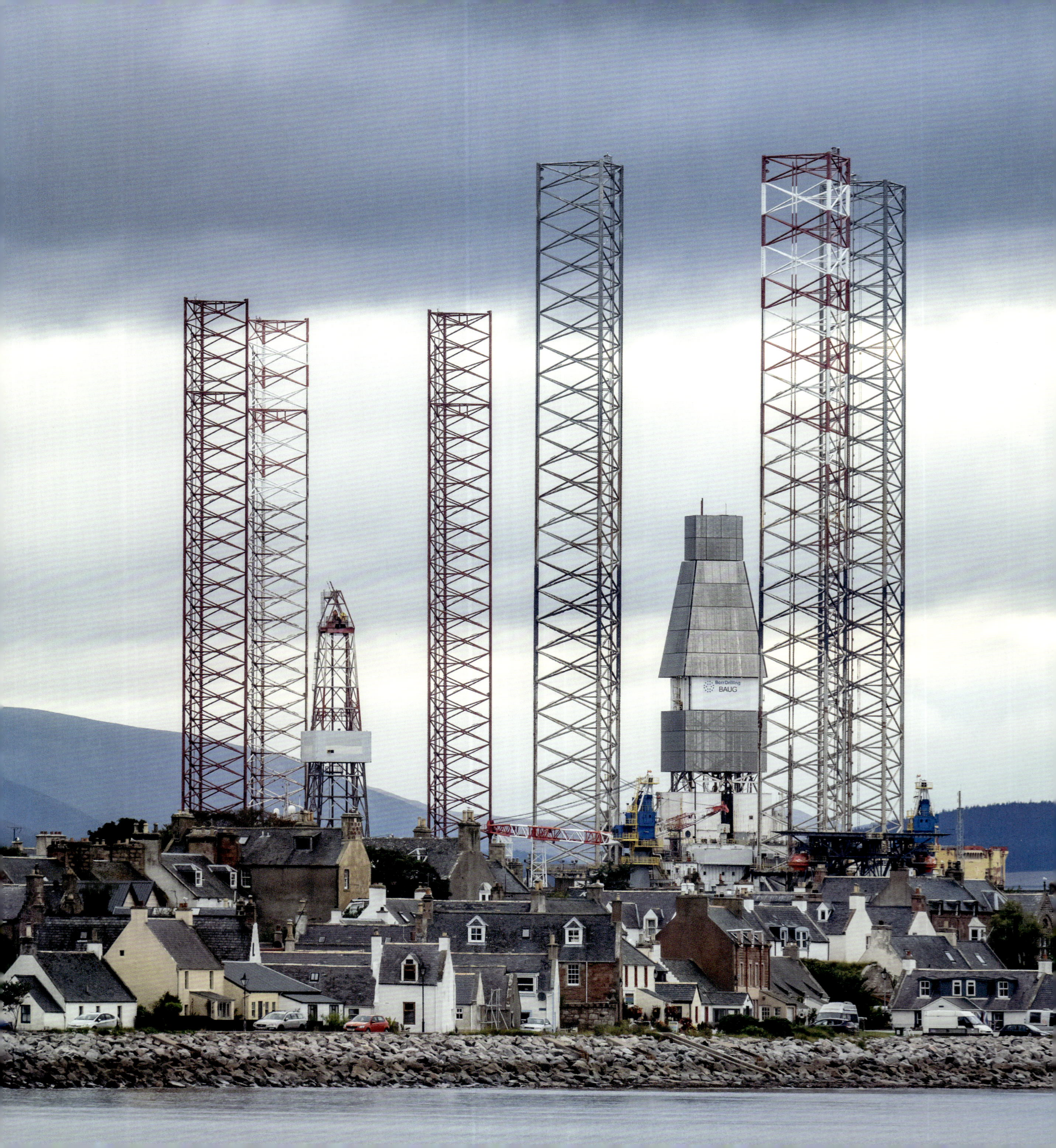
BAUG

33 EAST ROSS AND CROMARTY

AUGUST 2019

DAY 329–335 | 08,003–08,193KM | 190KM

Travelling along the edge of Easter Ross is an exhilarating journey through a faintly understood past. The Tarbat Peninsula is littered with enigmatic carvings left behind by the Picts – a group of people from the northern and eastern parts of Scotland circa AD 300–900. I first encounter one of these carvings in the gorgeous interlocking spiral designs of the Pictish Dragon Stone, at the tiny museum in Tarbat Old Parish Church at Portmahomack. Every part of their history and culture seems to be debated, which only adds to their allure, and for a few days I become obsessed with finding traces of their remains.

On the eastern shore of the peninsula, I visit the Hilton of Cadboll Stone. Standing at eight feet tall, it's easy to spot, but even with the nearby interpretation panel, the sheer riches of ornament and unfamiliar symbolism are mind-boggling. I learn this slab-stone is especially important because it shows that the Picts of Easter Ross adopted Christianity: the seaward-facing side depicts a Christian cross; and the landward-facing side, which shows a secular hunting scene, is believed to depict Christ.

The following day, I reach the most impressive of the Pictish symbol stones, the Nigg Stone, remarkably even more sculpturally dense, with layers upon layers of decoration so not a single part of the slab-stone remains flat, which gives me a tangible sense of the sculptor's joy in the creative act. The sign beside it tells me it's one of the last records of the Picts in Easter Ross, as their distinct culture was lost when their land was amalgamated with the Scots in the ninth century in response to Viking raids. My eyes wander over the bas-relief as I try to decipher their meaning, to no avail. A few hours later, my mind still full of Pictish spirals, I'm brought abruptly into the twenty-first century as the oil platforms moored in the Cromarty Firth come into view. I linger, trying to capture these enormous structures on camera, wondering if I might also be recording the last traces of engineering ingenuity from the fossil fuel age. The locals I speak to have mixed opinions: some tell me they're waiting to be scrapped, while others say they are in for repairs.

The next couple of days of walking brings me to remnants of the world wars. At North Sutor, a rocky promontory at the southern tip of the Tarbat Peninsula, I wander around a concrete bunker complex, part of a naval defence battery, still covered in its original camouflage paint. I slide down an artillery shell elevator chute and discover an extensive network of pitch-black underground rooms. I'm surprised by how dry and clean it is down here and how well the wooden racking that once held the shells has endured. It's much harder to get back out of the ramp than expected, as there's so little friction on the smooth concrete. After sliding back to the bottom three times, I feel the first twangs of panic before I spot a couple of bolts that once held the conveyor, giving my boots just enough purchase to launch myself up to ground level.

Back in fresh air, I start the two-day loop around the edge of Cromarty Firth. I pass another mysterious Pictish symbol stone, Clach a' Mheirlich, or the 'Thief's Stone'. Only the faintest outline of the carvings is visible. There's a step symbol on one side and what could be a crescent with a pair of pincers on the other.

At the edge of the fertile peninsula of the Black Isle, I rest awhile in Cairds' Cave, near Rosemarkie, where samples of charcoal and animal bone found in the bottom layers of the floor were carbon-dated in 2010 and show that the cave has been in use since 300 BC. Perfectly sheltered from the wind and rain and with direct access to the sea, it's just as useful to me today as it was to those in the late Iron Age.

Opposite:

GSF Monarch and Baug jack-up rigs tower above Cromarty

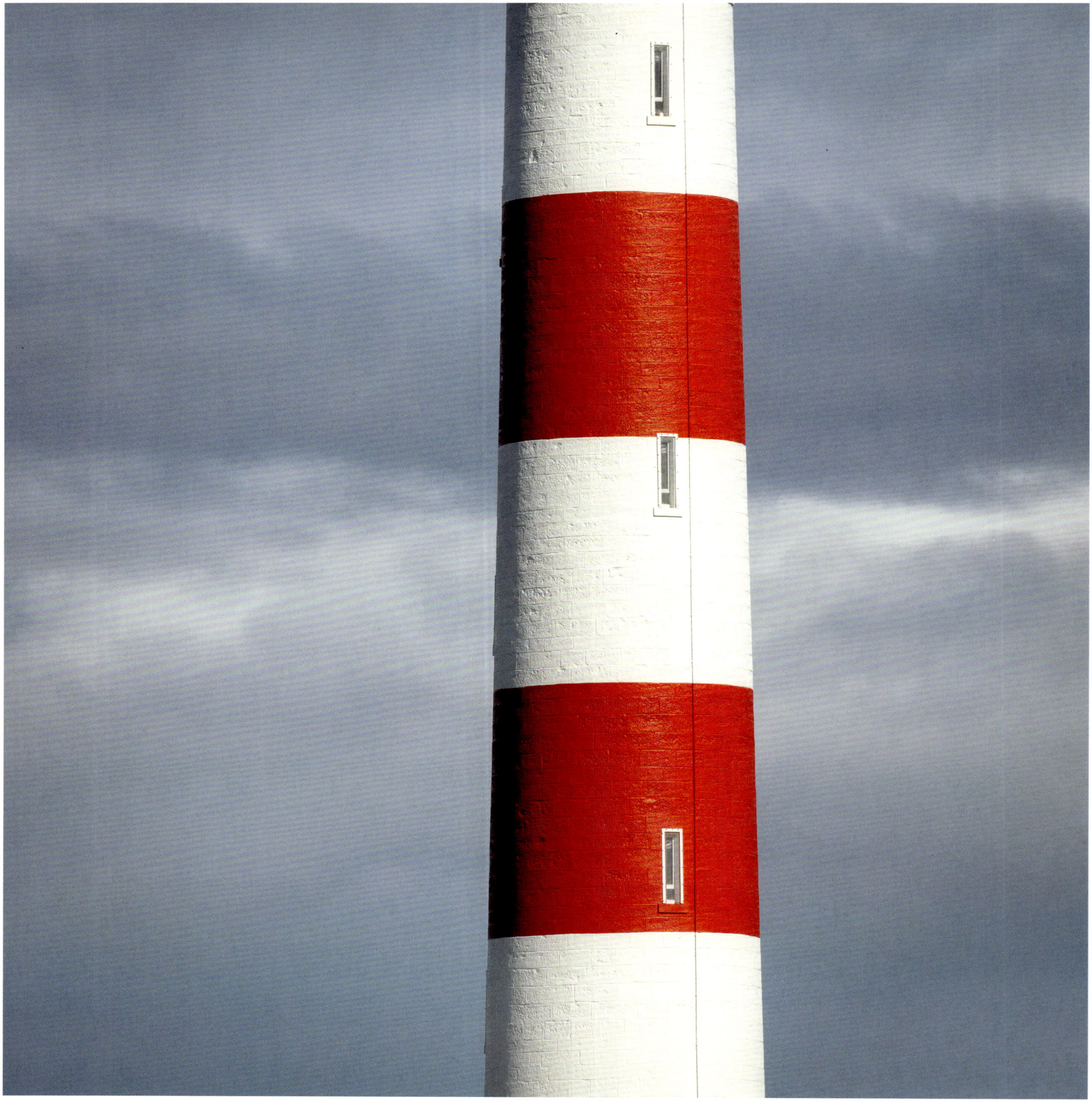

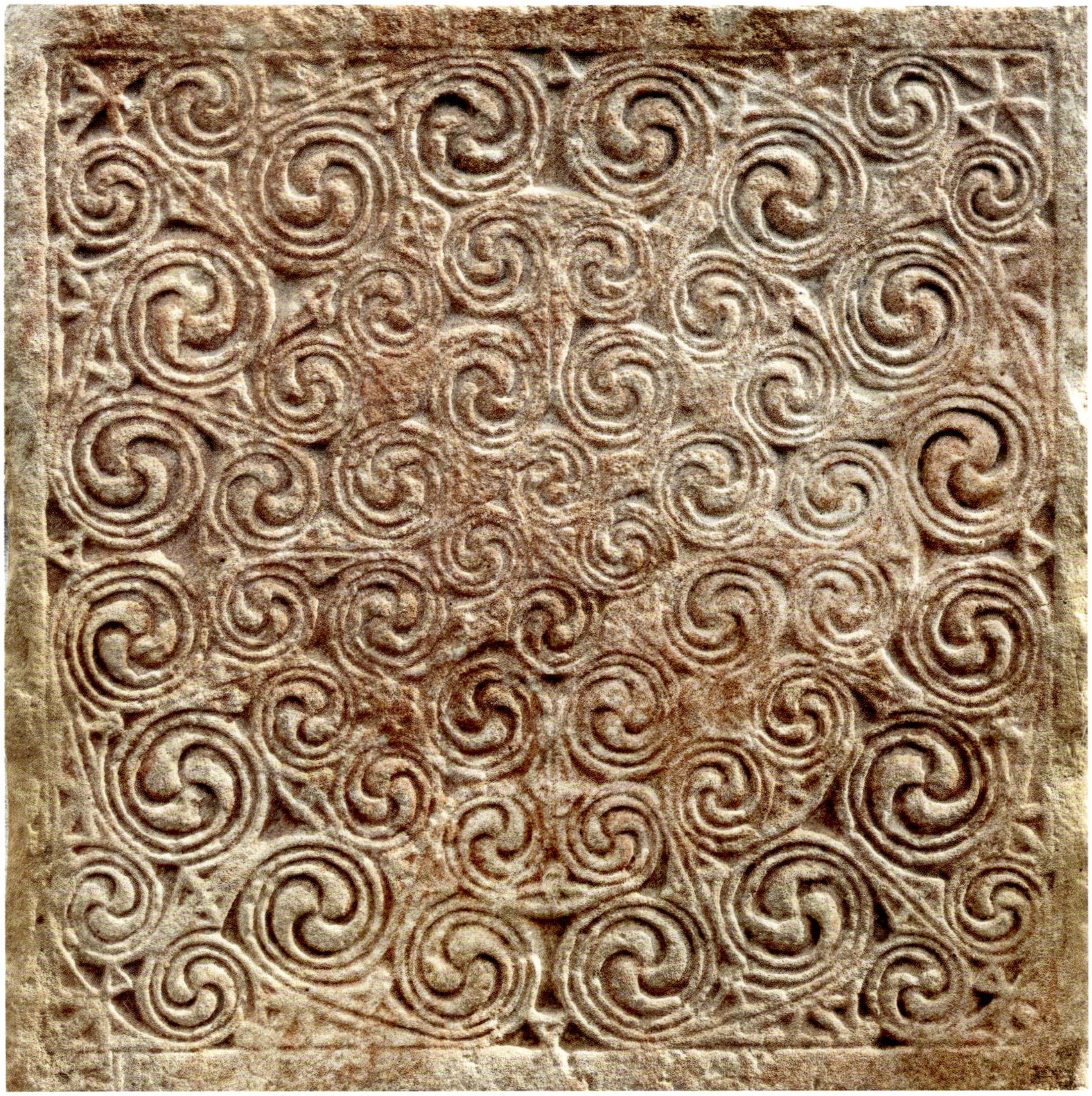

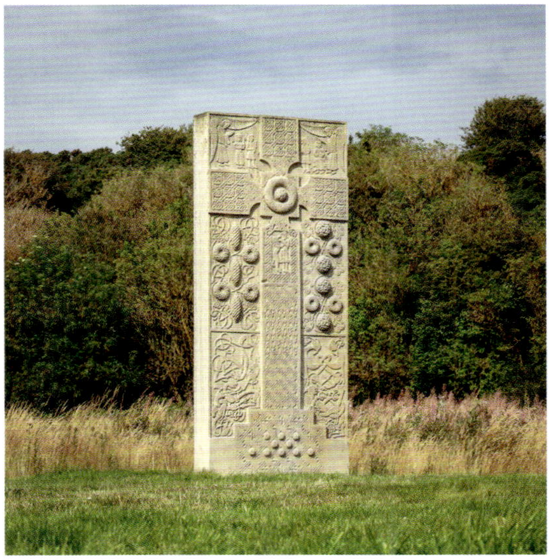

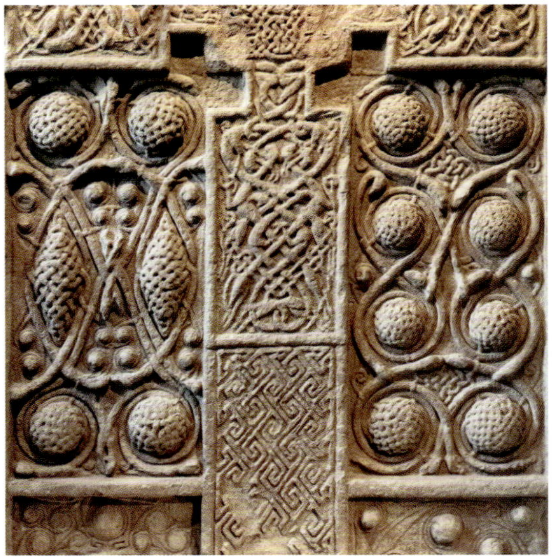

From top left:

Detail of abstract patterns based on triskeles (three-in-one spirals) on the western or landward-facing side of the Shandwick Stone, a Pictish cross-slab dating from AD 780, Tarbat Peninsula

The Christian cross on the seaward-facing side of the Cadboll Stone, a Pictish cross-slab reconstruction by Barry Grove in 1998 (the original, dating from about AD 800, is in the Museum of Scotland), Tarbat Peninsula

Detail of the Pictish Nigg Stone, dating from the end of the eighth century, Nigg Church

Opposite:

Tarbat Ness Lighthouse

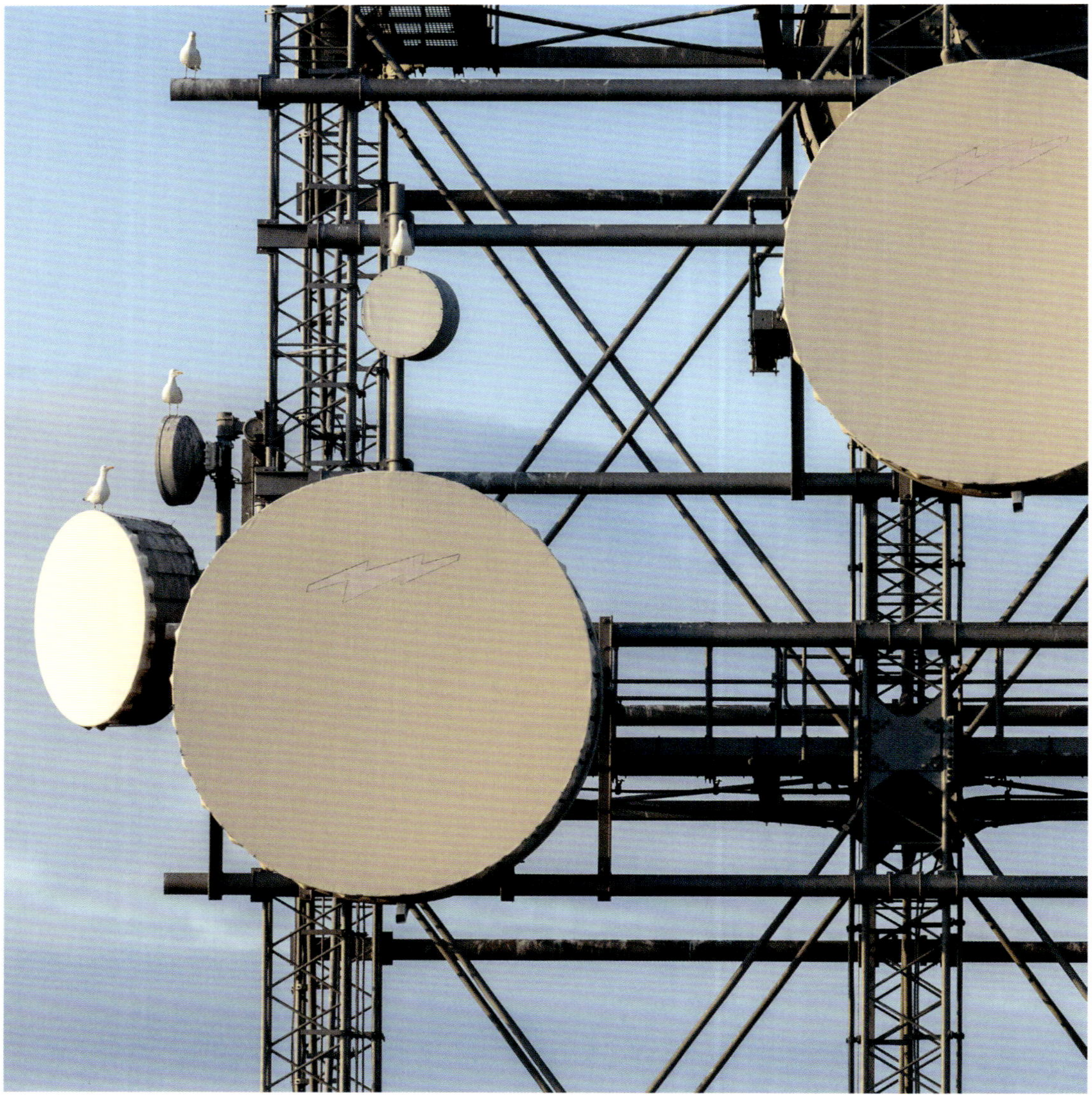

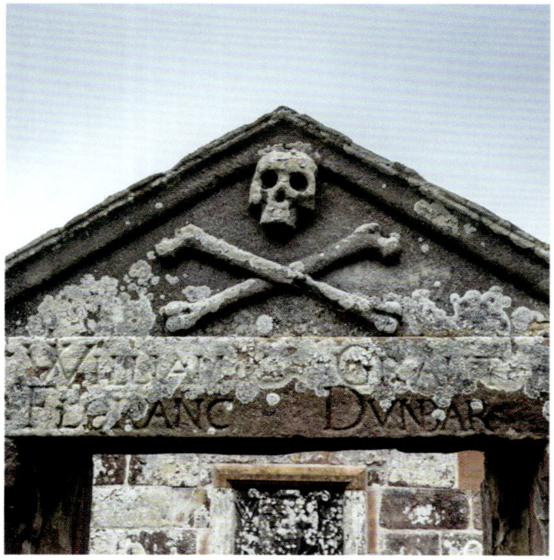

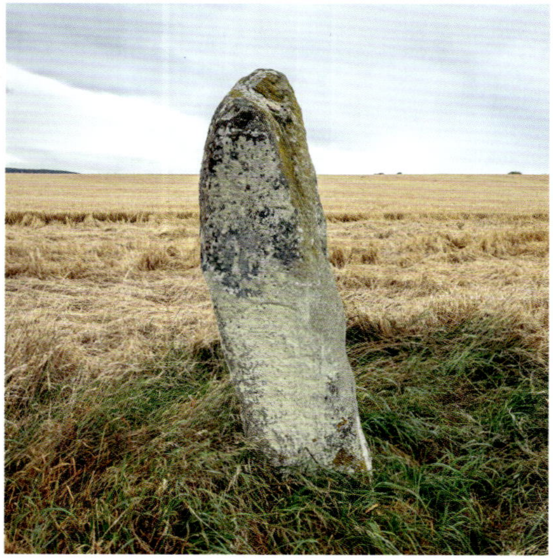

From top left:

Microwave antenna tower with gulls, Easter Bindal, Tarbat Peninsula

Symbols of mortality above a tomb in the graveyard of St Michael's Church, Black Isle

Clach a' Mheirlich, or the 'Thief's Stone', a Pictish symbol stone at Rosskeen. Only the faintest outlines of the carvings are visible. There's a step symbol on one side and what could be a crescent with a pair of pincers on the other

Opposite, from top left:

Ocean Vanguard semi-submersible drilling rig, Cromarty Firth

Topless rig, Cromarty Firth

From bottom left:

Bike and rigs, Cromarty

Baug jack-up rig, Cromarty Firth

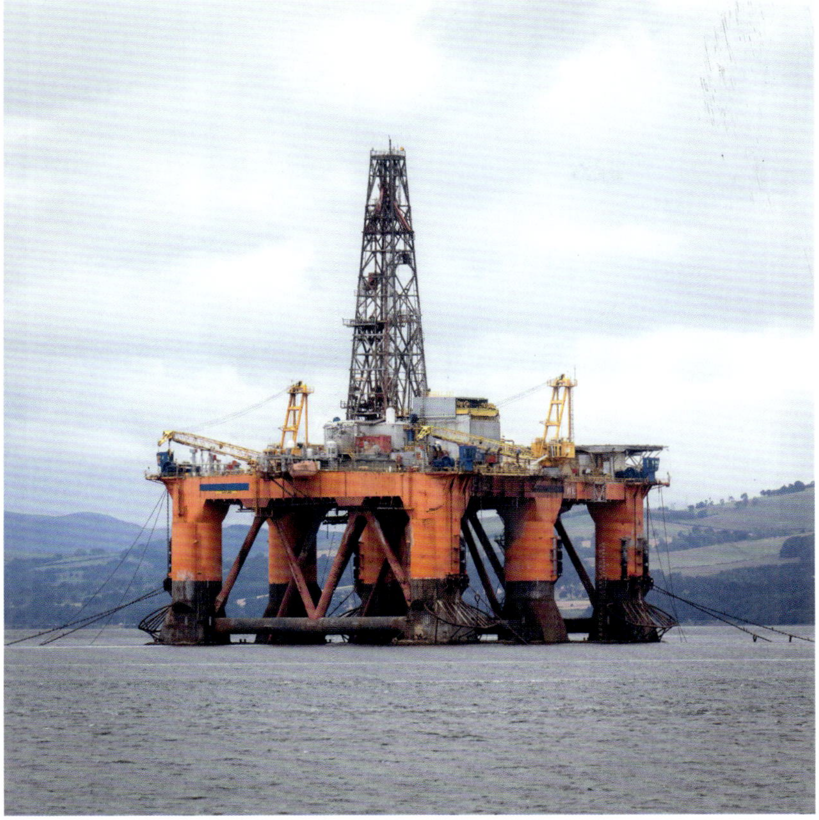

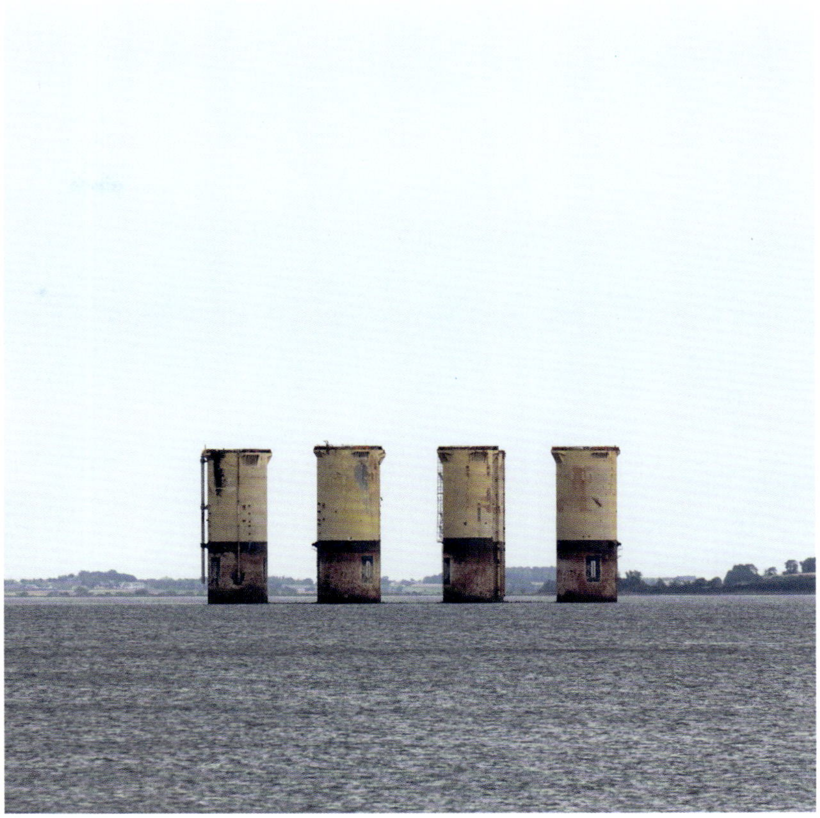

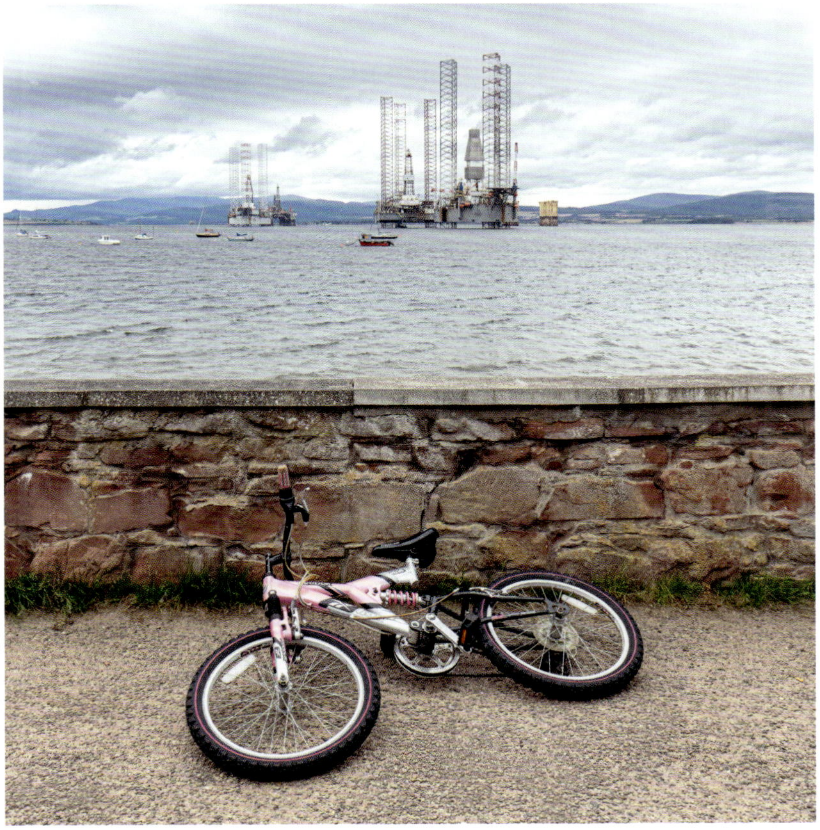

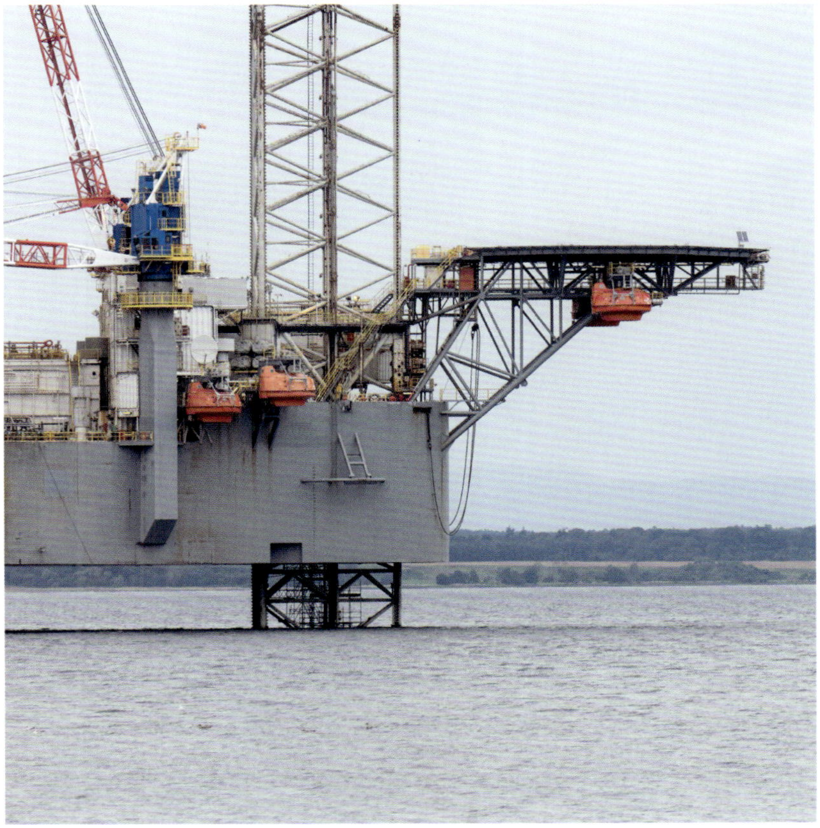

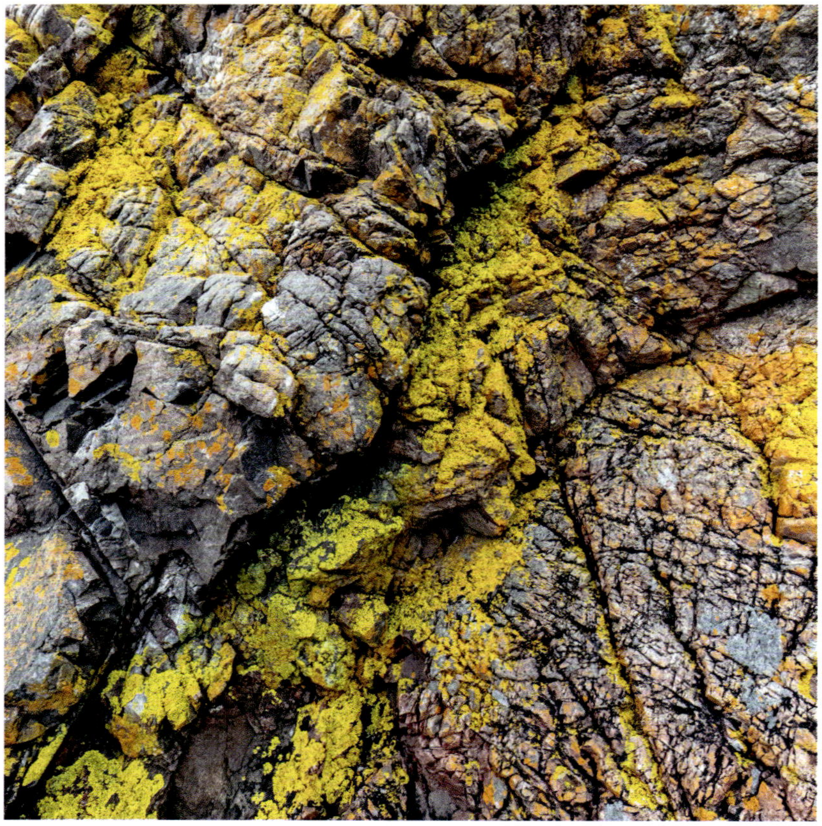

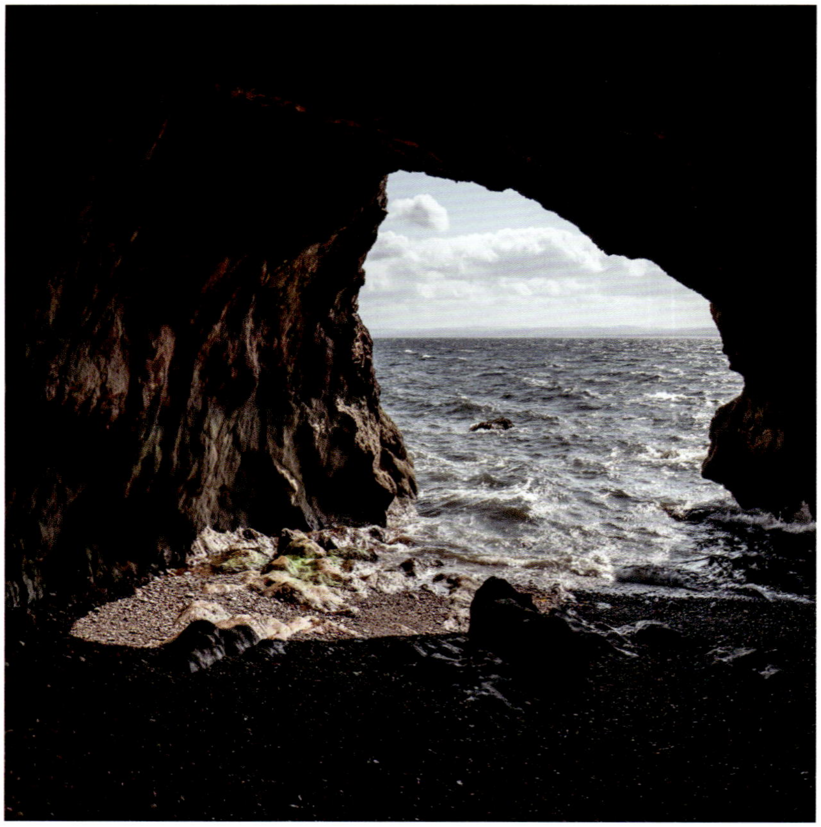

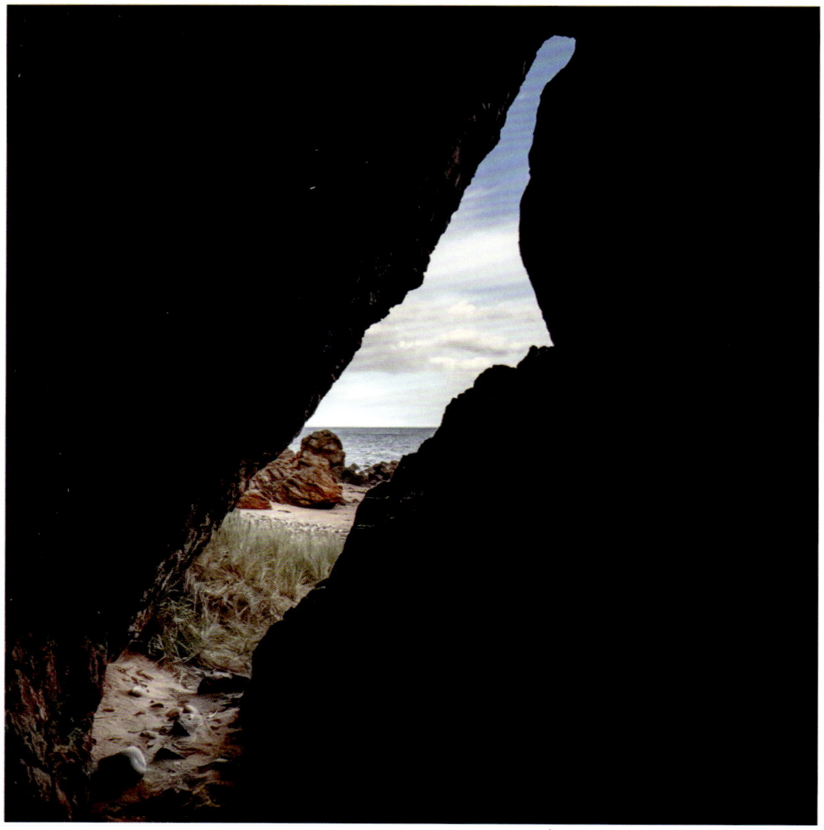

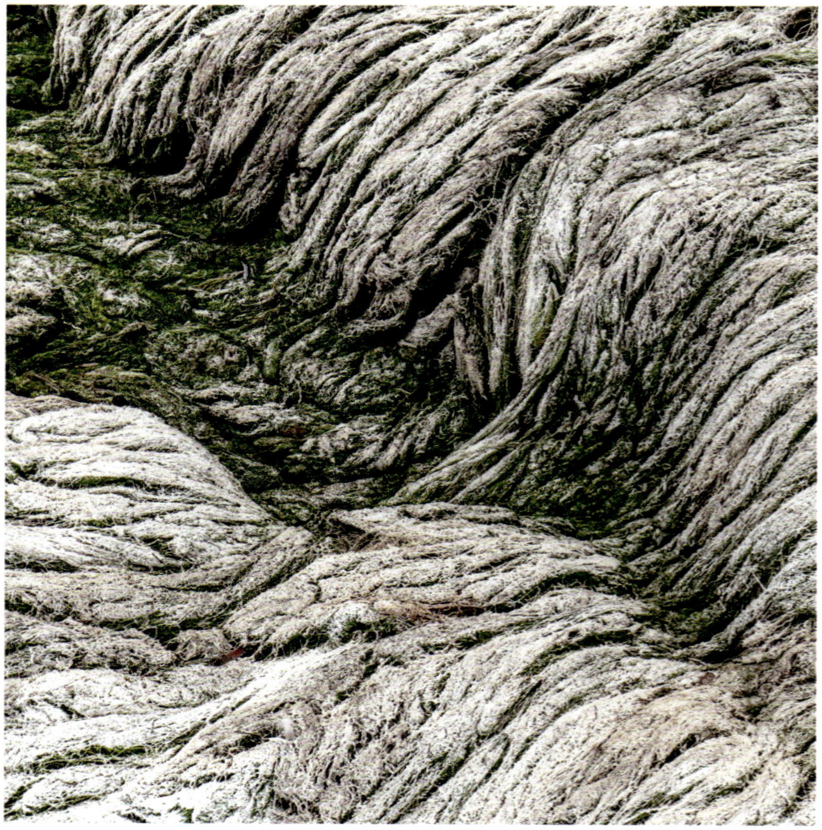

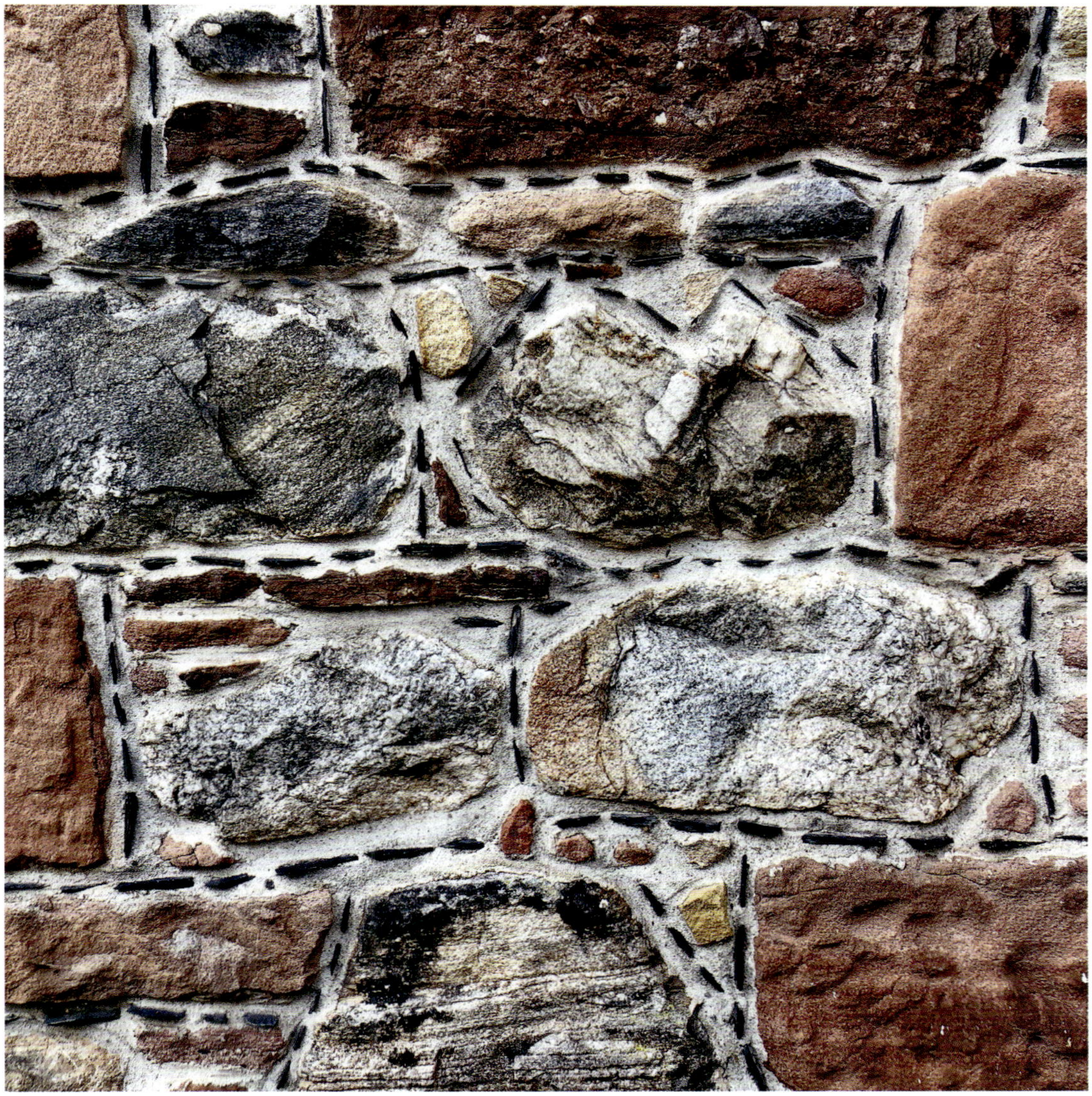

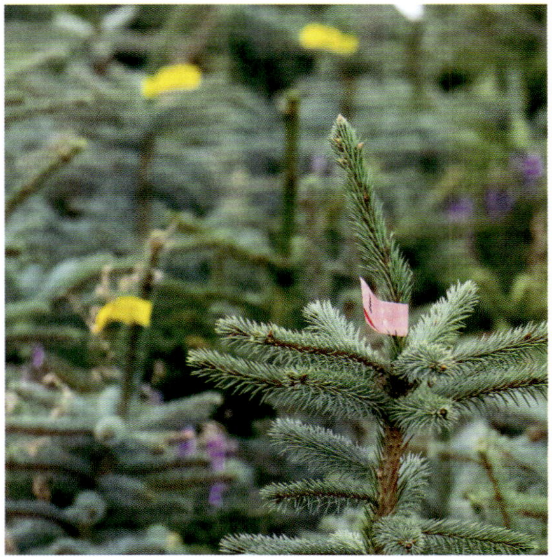

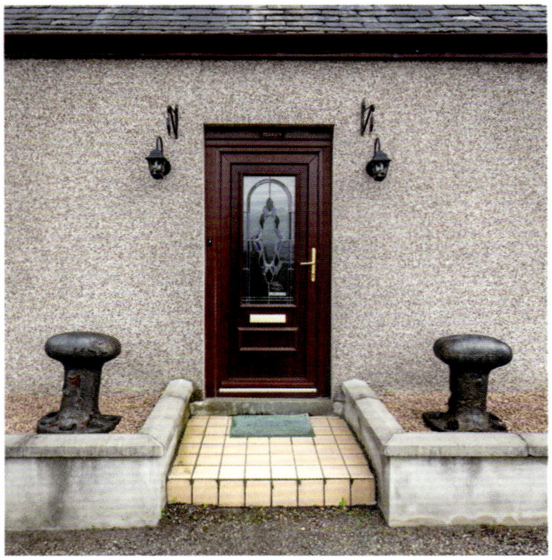

Opposite, from top left:

Rocks painted with lichen by the Moray Firth, Black Isle

Cave at McFarquhar's Bed, Black Isle

From bottom left:

One of nineteen Rosemarkie Beach Caves, Black Isle, some inhabited since 300 BC

Felted gutweed: Munlochy Bay, Black Isle

From top left:

House detail, Fortrose, Black Isle

Christmas tree farm, Craigiehowe Wood, Black Isle

Seems like the builder's merchant and marine salvage are the same place in Avoch, Black Isle

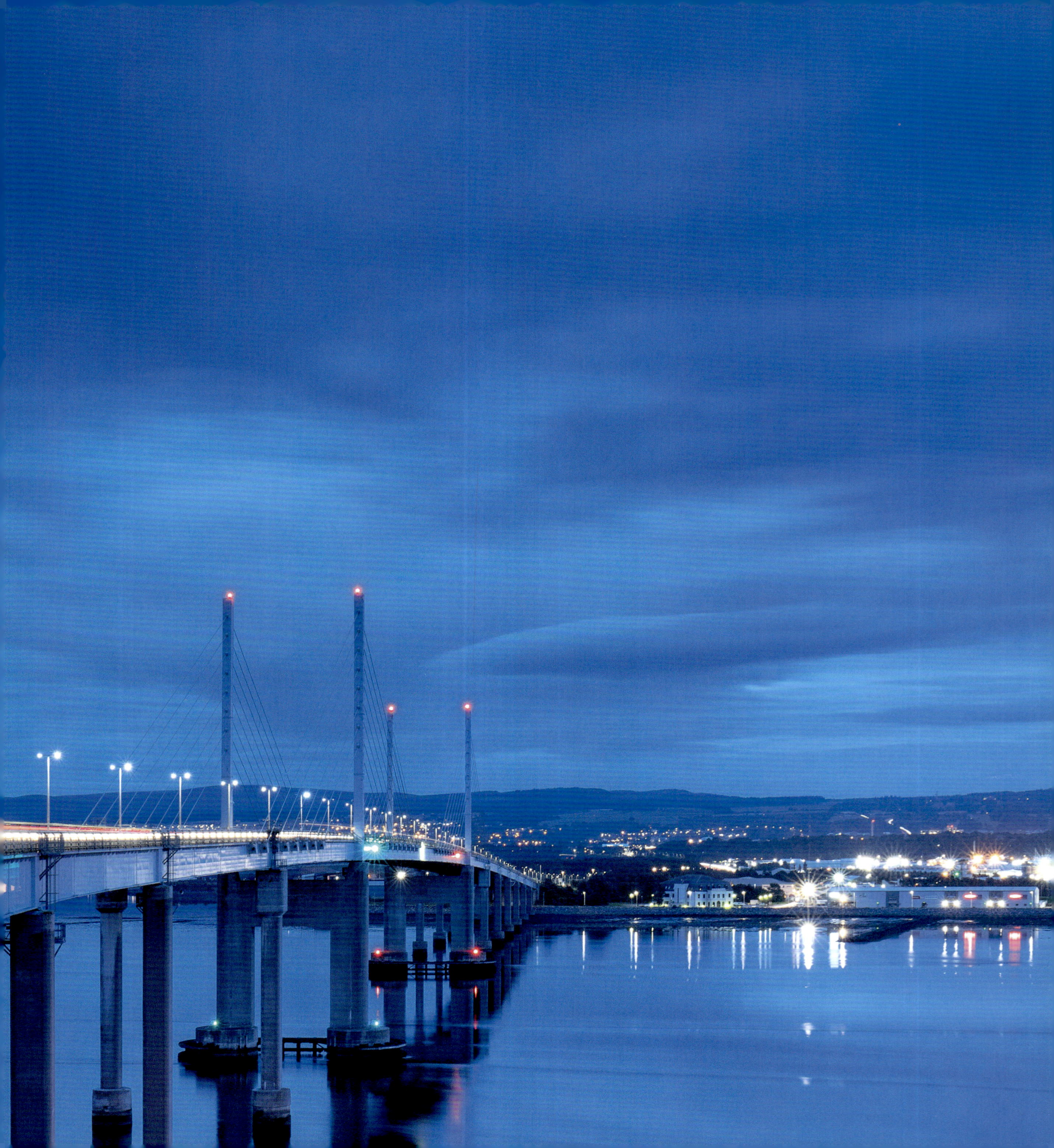

34 EAST INVERNESS-SHIRE AND NAIRNSHIRE

AUGUST 2019

DAY 336–337 | 08,193–08,250KM | 57KM

Walking across the Kessock Bridge high above the Beauly Firth leads me to Inverness, the biggest city I've seen in a long time. With its cosmopolitan offerings and handsome sandstone houses, it seems to mark the end of the wild north. I trace the River Ness before winding my way between the bridged islands, where the riverfront teems with French and Italian tourists alongside spired and gabled architecture. I peek into the river, hoping to see Nessie, when I spot a heron scritching atop a lamp post. Within a couple of hours the city is behind me and it's back to the open coast.

Like Dunrobin, Fort George feels like a historical pivot point, but it is also a reminder of the history of tension between Scotland and England. As I approach the angular defensive walls along the shingle beach, I realise it's also the first time I've thought about England since being in the Highlands. I buy a ticket to enter the fort, where I learn it is the mightiest artillery fortification in Britain, built to control the Scottish Highlands following the 1746 defeat at Culloden of Bonnie Prince Charlie. Culloden, only 12 kilometres away near Inverness, was the site of the last pitched battle fought on British soil. The historical significance and unbridled display of the Crown's power here sends a shiver down my spine.

I enter the immaculately preserved star-shaped fort via a wooden walkway and drawbridge and then through two 6-metre walls. Inside, I see soldiers walk smartly between the garrison buildings wearing berets with a distinctive red plume. It turns out the fort is home to the Black Watch, 3rd Battalion, Royal Regiment of Scotland, which was originally established to sit 'watch' over rebel activity in the Highlands. In November 2016, the Ministry of Defence announced that it would close in 2032. Defence Minister Sir Michael Fallon said it was no longer needed because 'the Highland rebellions are over'.

The next day, I follow a path through a rifle range and past rusty armoured personnel carriers of the Fort George training area. The route takes me through the apocalyptic landscape of the Ardersier Oil Rig Construction Yard. Not knowing what it is I'm looking at, I search the name on my phone and learn that the site opened in 1972 to fabricate and construct huge oil rig legs and offshore platform structures used in the newly established North Sea gas and oil industry. At its height, the yard employed around 4,500 people and was the largest private-sector employer in the Highlands until it closed in 2002, as demand in the UK oil industry declined.

It seems like they left in a hurry: I wander around a vast hangar-like structure, whose walls are lined with oil drums and piles of discarded chairs. In the rear, there's a Portakabin shower block still with shower curtains intact. Outside, cables of thick braided steel and bent girders poke out of the scrubland among the gorse and rosebay willowherb. Severed colour-coded pipes and cables emerge and re-emerge through the complex. In the development centre, there are scattered fax machines and piles of training manuals covered in pigeon droppings. I leave the site past four giant lighting towers and the decommissioned security checkpoint before following an abandoned but dead-straight, metalled road towards Nairn. With nothing to occupy my mind but the rhythm of my feet on tarmac, I contemplate how many grand dreams, now derelict, I've witnessed on this walk.

Opposite:

Inverness and the Kessock Bridge at dusk

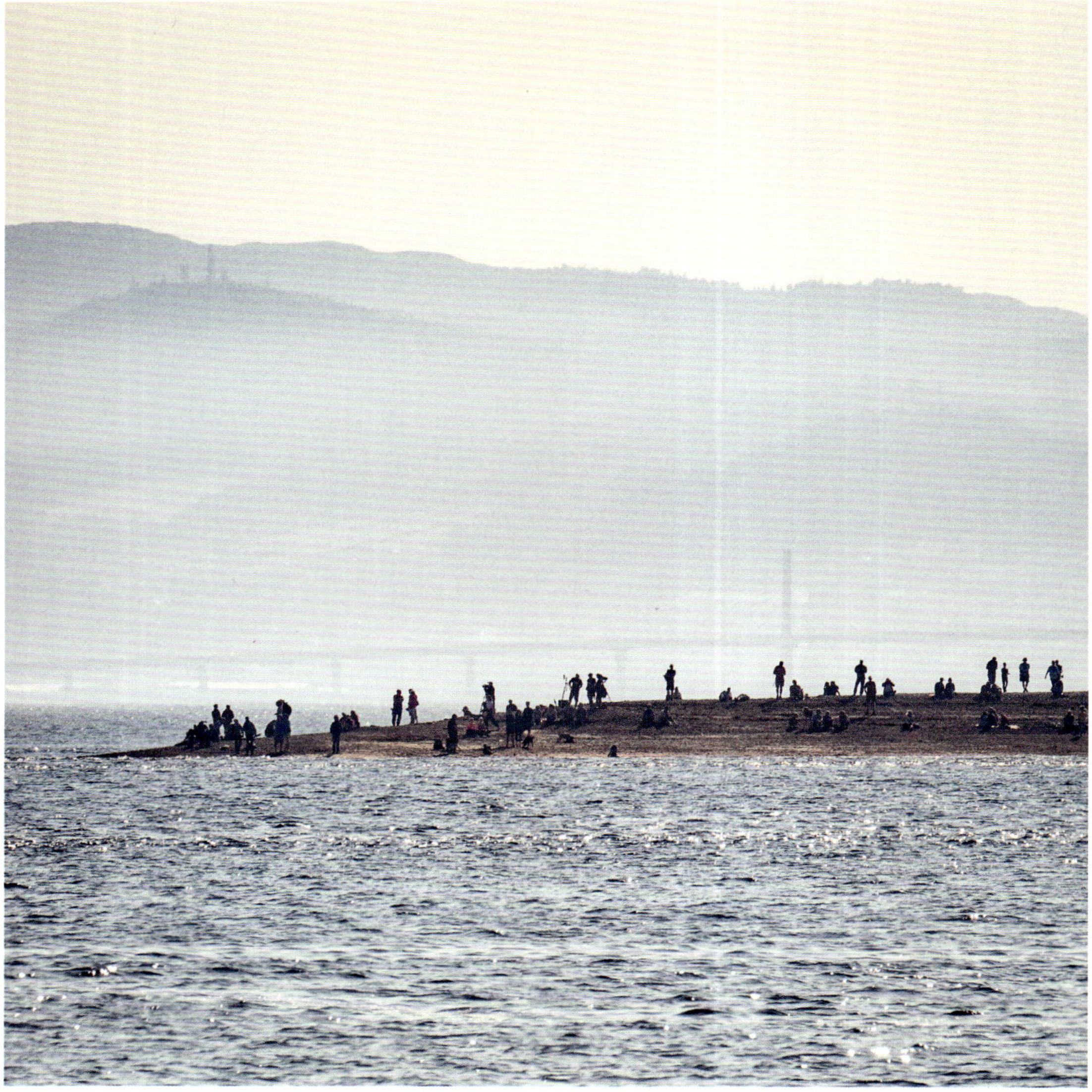

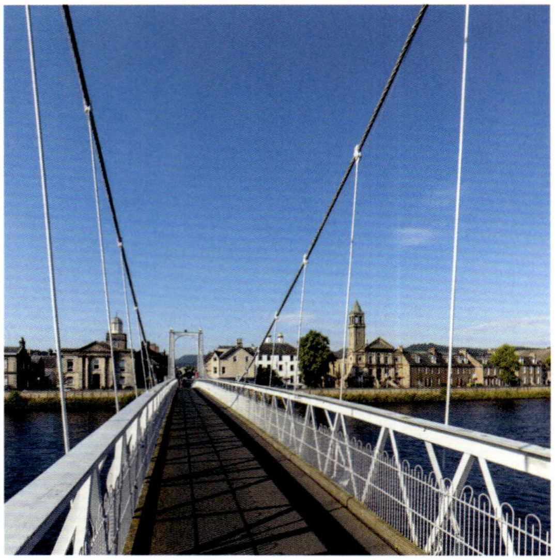

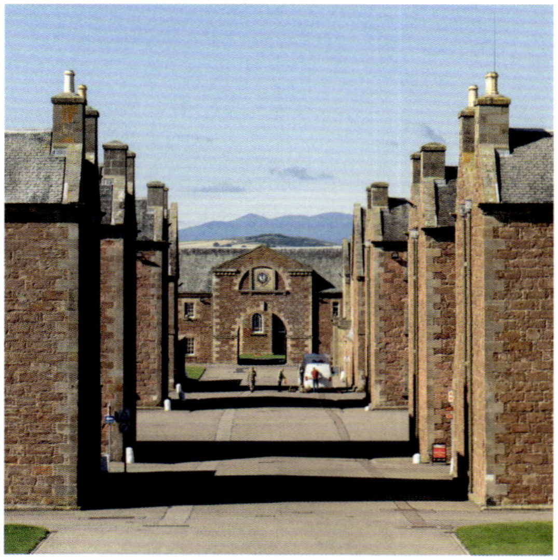

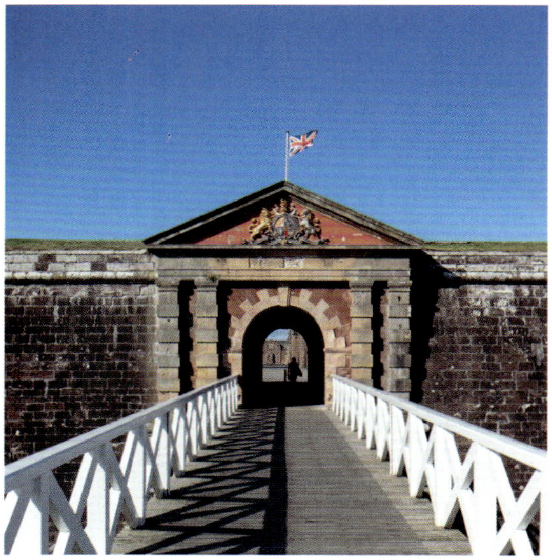

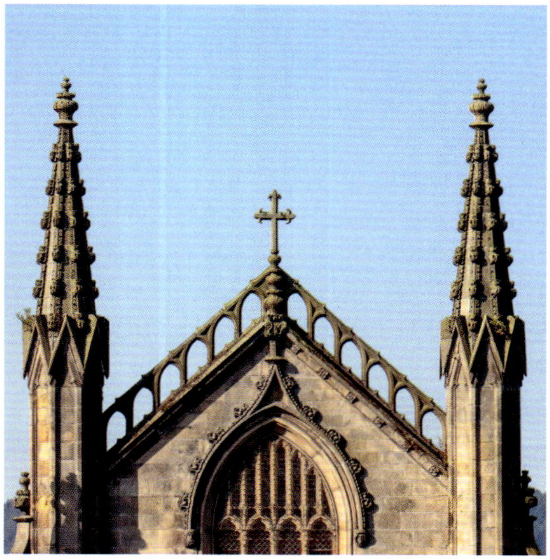

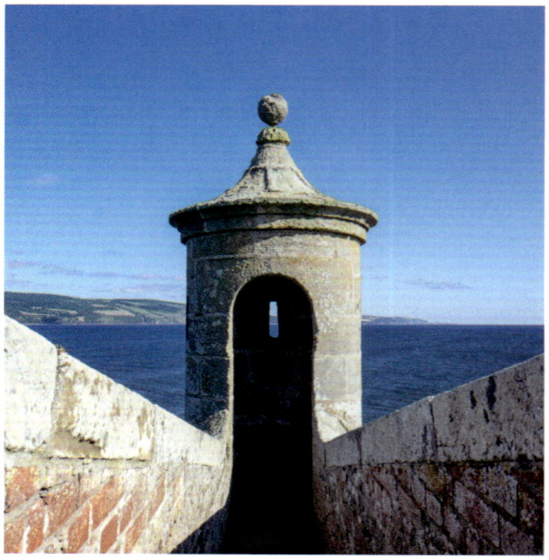

Opposite, clockwise from top left:

Dolphin spotters at Chanonry Point with Kessock Bridge, from Fort George

Greig Street Bridge, built 1881, across the River Ness, Inverness

Fort George is currently the home of the Black Watch, 3rd Battalion, the Royal Regiment of Scotland

Bartizan overlooking the Moray Firth, Fort George

St Mary's Roman Catholic Church, Inverness

Entrance to Fort George

From top left:

If Roy Lichtenstein designed a firing range: Fort George, Ardersier

Waste oil: Ardersier oil rig construction yard that was in use from 1972 to 2002

From centre left:

Severed pipes and cables, Ardersier oil rig construction yard

Inside the hangar, Ardersier oil rig construction yard

From bottom left:

Colour coding: Ardersier oil rig construction yard

Disused road to Ardersier oil rig construction yard

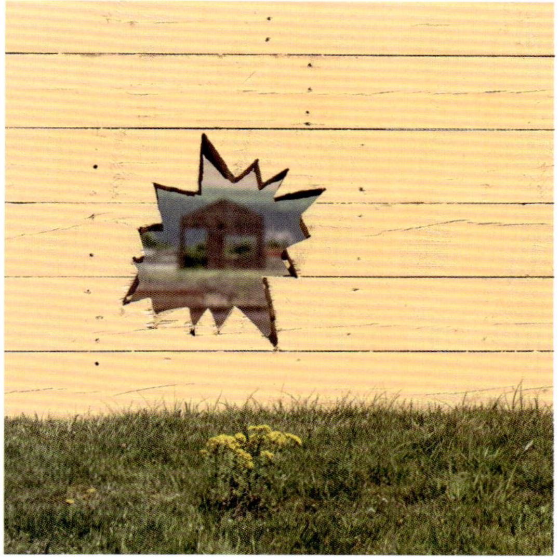

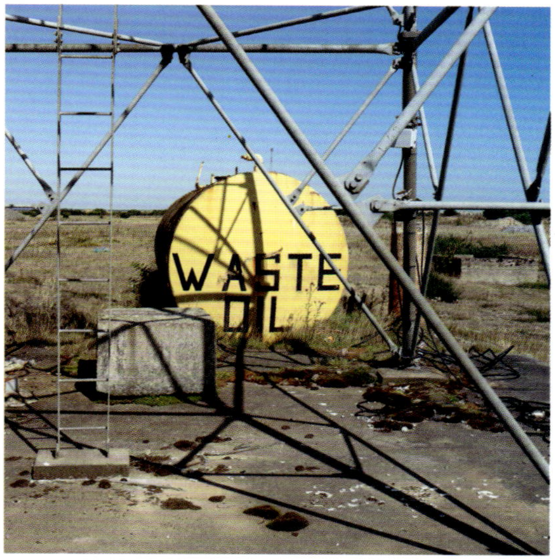

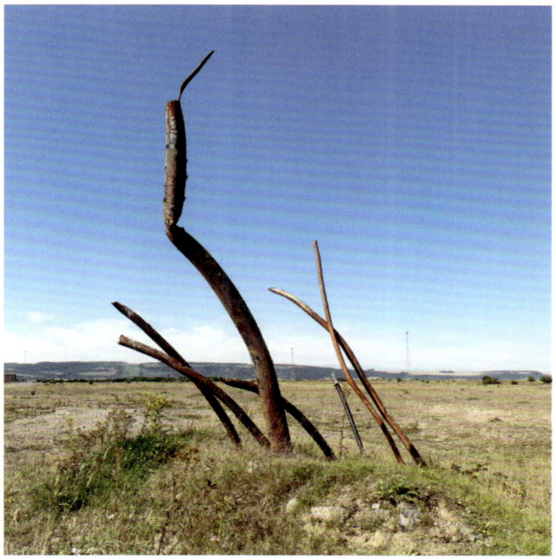

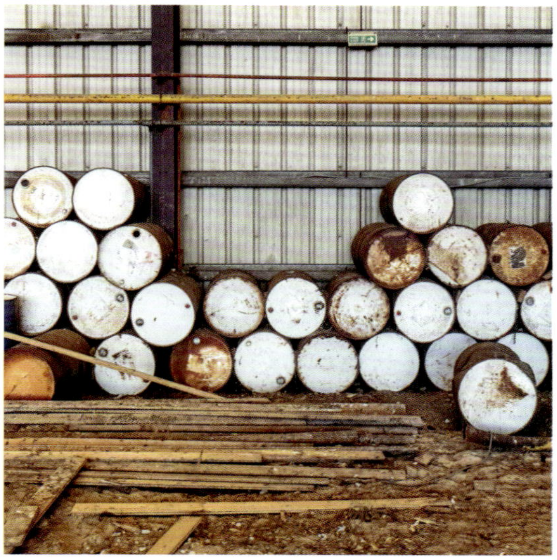

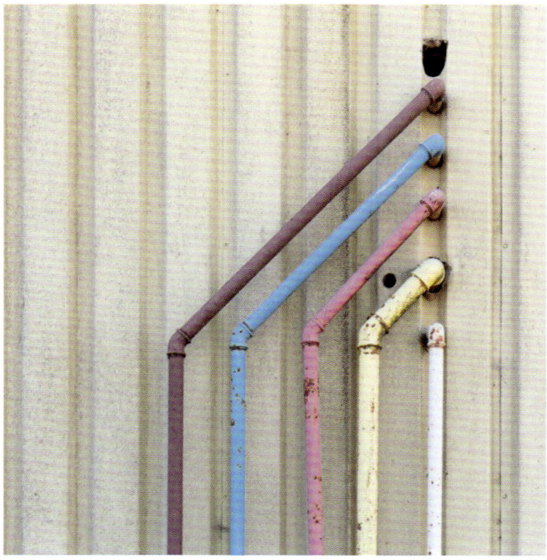

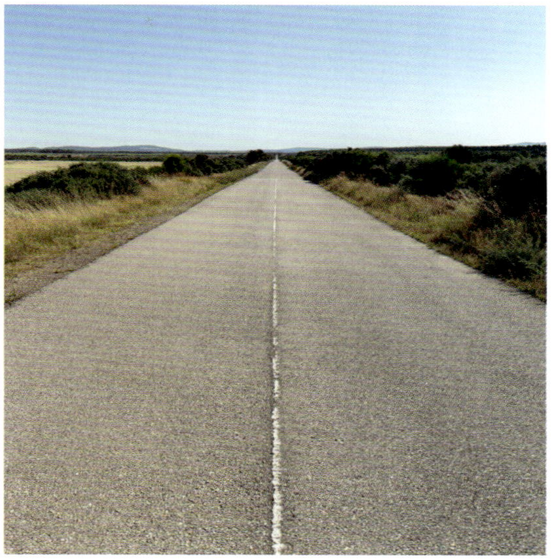

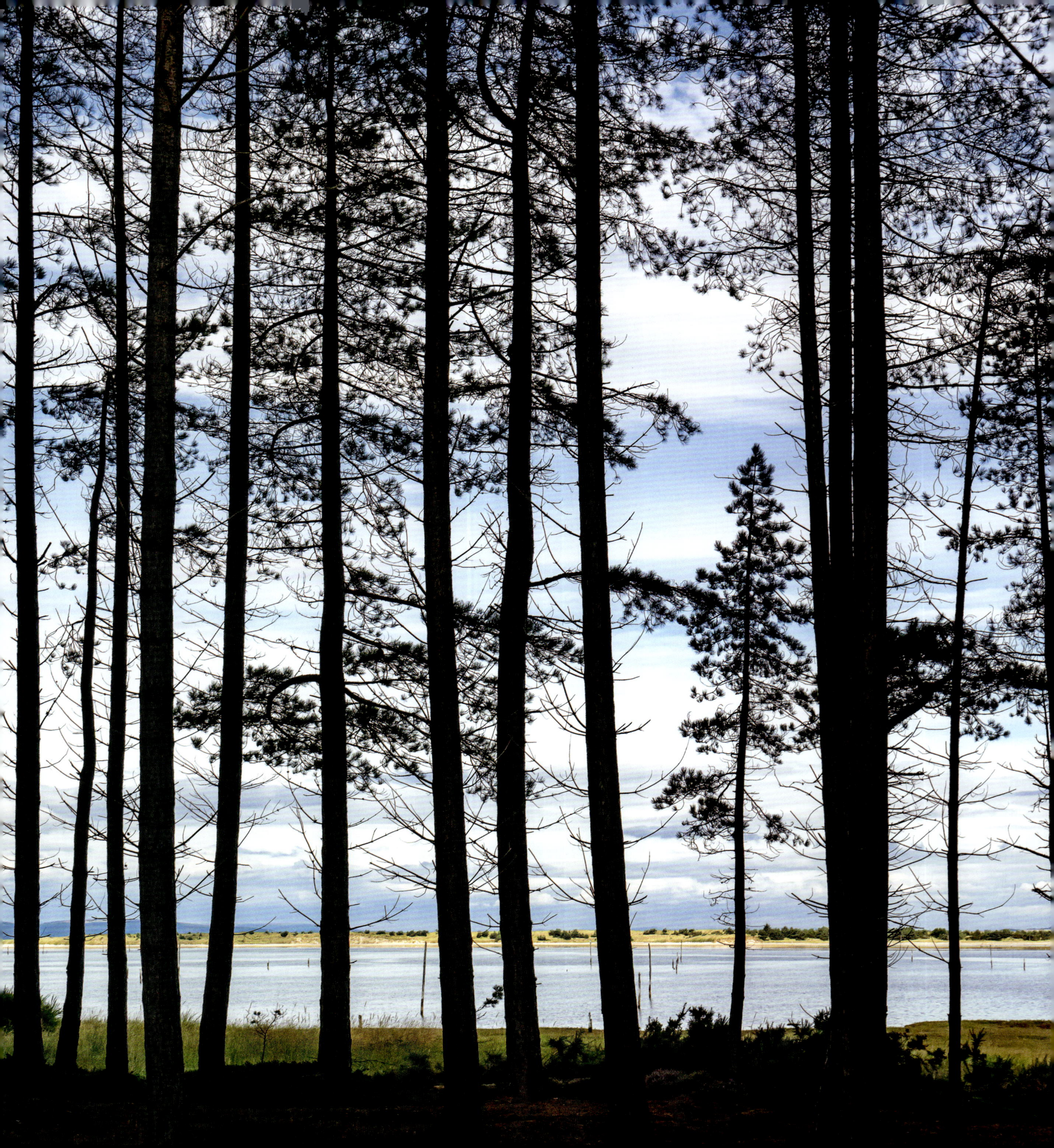

35

MORAYSHIRE

AUGUST 2019

DAY 338–340 | 08,250–08,332KM | 82KM

Opposite:

The Moray Firth and the remains of the Second World War anti-glider defences on Culbin Sands seen through Culbin Forest

I emerge from the tranquillity of the lavender and moss-carpeted Culbin Forest to a broad expanse of sand revealed by the low tide. Here, a secondary forest of Second World War anti-glider defences stands – parallel lines of thigh-thick poles emerging a few metres from the sand, many of which have now deteriorated to no more than rotten stumps. From the forest it takes a whole day to walk around the muddy shore of Findhorn Bay, and as the sky greys I find myself zoning out, eyes roving restlessly, hungry for more than the muted tones I'm surrounded by. So as the summer light fades on a dreary evening near the Findhorn community ecovillage, my eye is drawn to the only colour in the landscape: a bright TV blaring through a living-room window, momentarily reconnecting me with society.

I press on past Findhorn, navigating by torchlight past clanging boatyards and through the dunes to pitch up at the tip of Findhorn Spit. I check the map and realise that, due to the bay's bottle shape, I'm only 200 metres from where I started in the morning! The second I finish putting my tent up, I fall asleep to the sound of seals moaning. The following dawn, I sit cross-legged inside the tent where I have the joy of removing a pair of freshly laundered socks from my clothes bag that I'd been saving for weeks; the smell of home fills the tent.

That afternoon I see a monument at Burghead Harbour prophetically quoting a line from Robert Burns's 'Tam o' Shanter' – *Nae man can tether time or tide* – erected *To all that lost their lives to the sea*. I climb the worn steps from the harbour as dozens of small birds take off from a bush behind which an open window reveals a woman with curls of blonde hair contemplating the horizon, surrounded by canvases. I, too, pause to admire the panorama until I am unexpectedly engulfed by the intoxicating stink of hash.

The next day starts with the prospect of a long walk ahead to Buckie. I wake tired, with alarming stiffness in my injured tendon, despite a long sleep and plenty to eat. Getting on the road doesn't help as it usually does, so I dose up on ibuprofen and dump any weight that isn't essential, retaining the bare minimum of consumables like water, insect repellent, sun cream and food. I trudge on like a zombie, but the going gets tougher underfoot with miles of pebble beach that seem specifically devised to absorb any attempt at forward motion.

As a distraction from the aches and pains, I immerse myself in discovering the history of the militarised coastline on the edge of Lossie Forest. It's impossible to avoid the traces of war, and just above the high-tide line, I find myself walking along the best-preserved length of Second World War anti-invasion cubes and pillboxes in Scotland, which comprise strategically arranged rows of 1.5-metre blocks of concrete with small hexagonal fortified structures set at regular intervals, designed to slow down the progress of an armoured beach landing.

As I look out over the long, shallow beach, I can see how vulnerable this area would be to invasion, with its close proximity to Nazi-occupied Norway and the need to protect Bomber Command at RAF Lossiemouth on the other side of the forest. I soon discover that hours of walking on shingle beside identical concrete cubes and the bleak association with human conflict are soul-destroying, but the pillboxes mean there are regular places where I can duck inside to get out of the wind and I find that the machine-gun platform makes a handy table for my stove. As I sit drinking my tea, the ever-present roar of Eurofighter Typhoons swooping overhead makes this place still feel like the front line.

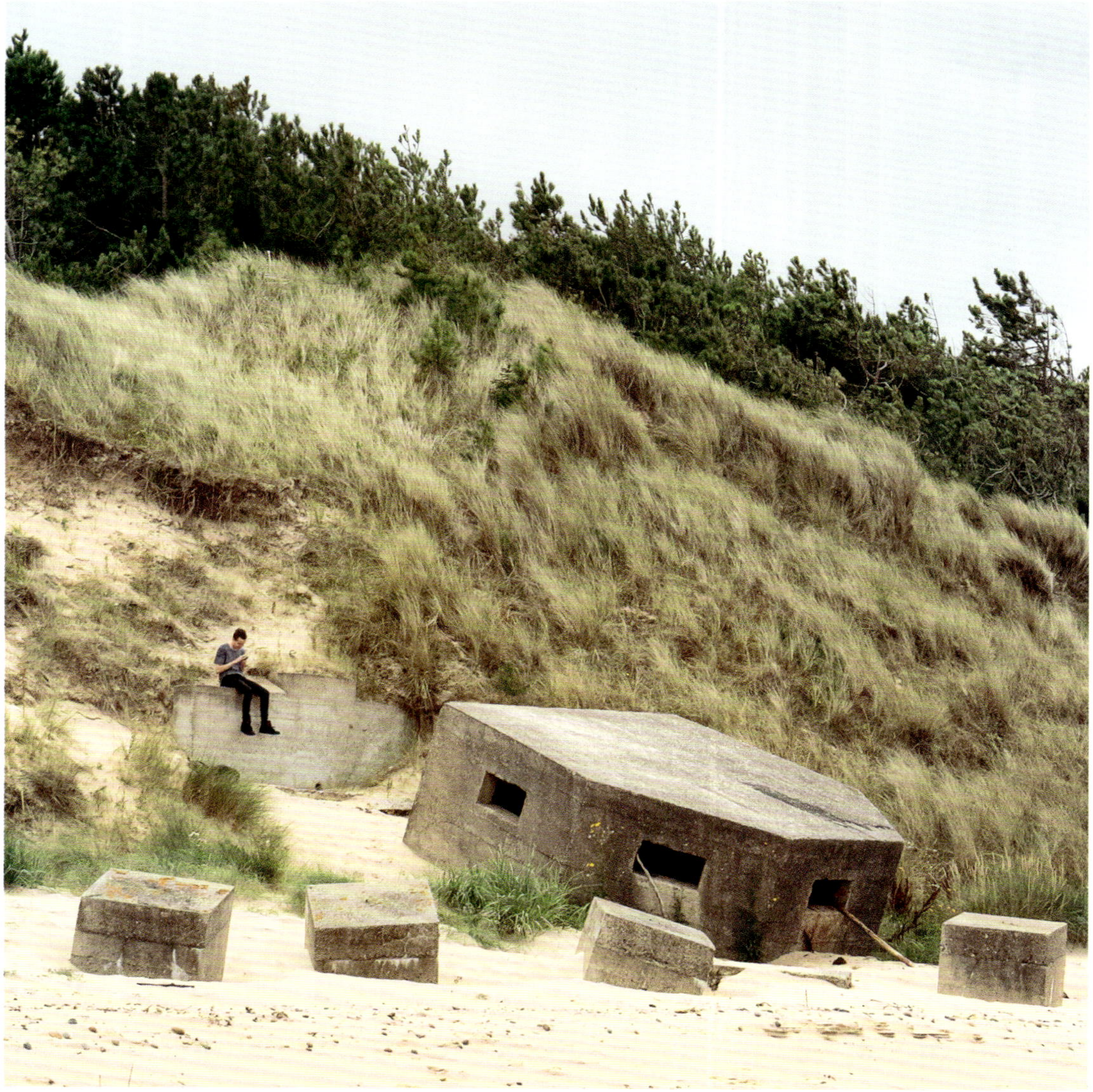

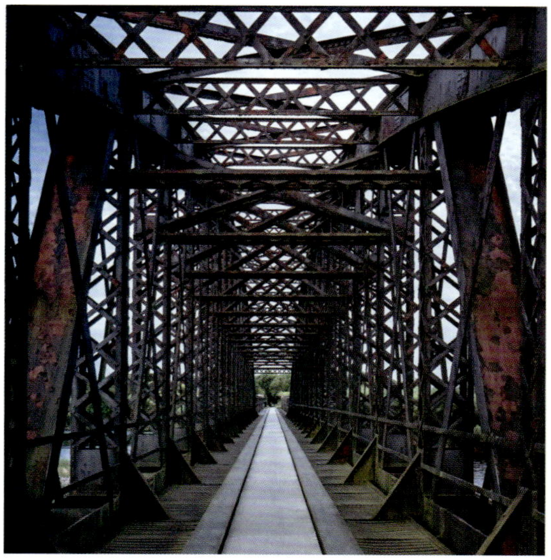

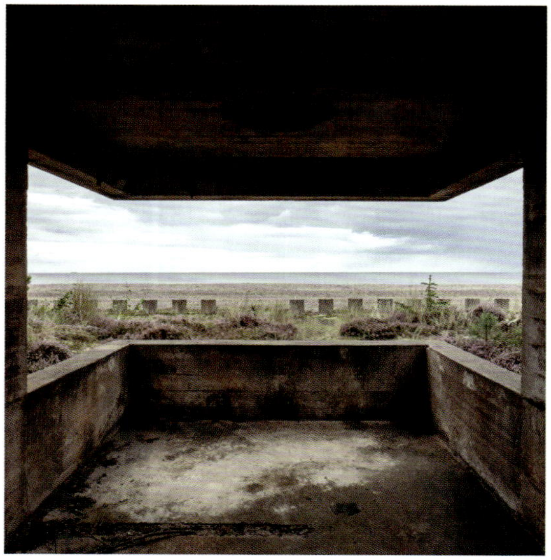

From top left:

Second World War anti-invasion defences, Burghead Bay

Spey Viaduct

Searchlight position, Second World War Innes Links Emergency Coastal Gun Battery, Lossie Forest

Opposite, clockwise from top left:

Covesea Lighthouse

Precarious Second World War anti-tank cubes, Findhorn

Shingle beach by Lossie Forest

Lossie Forest anti-invasion defences. At over 8 kilometres, the coastal defences in Lossie Forest comprise the longest and best-preserved length of anti-invasion cubes and pillboxes in Scotland

Burghead Harbour

Second World War anti-invasion defences, Burghead Bay

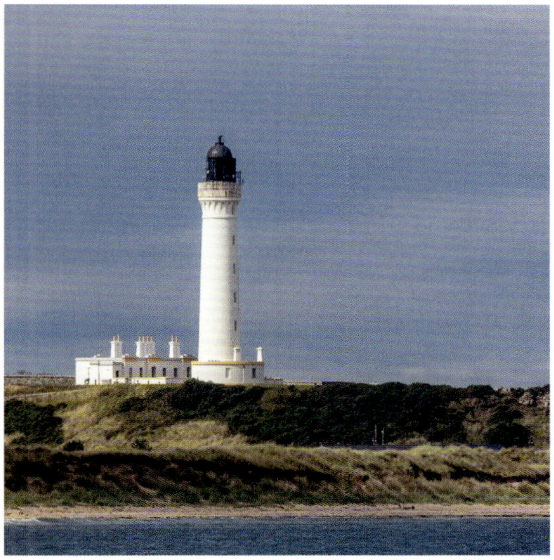

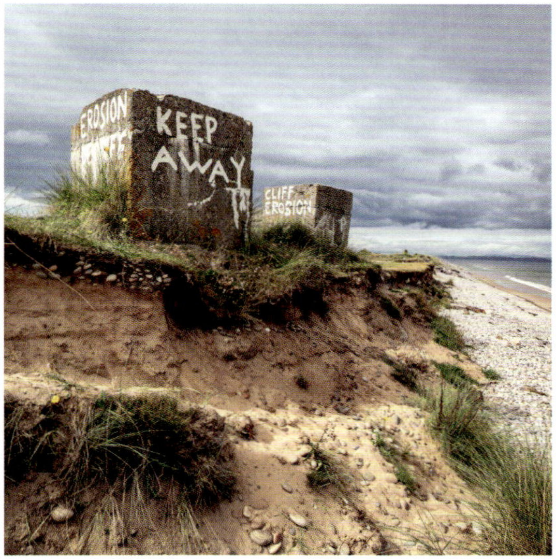
EROSION
KEEP
AWAY
CLIFF
EROSION

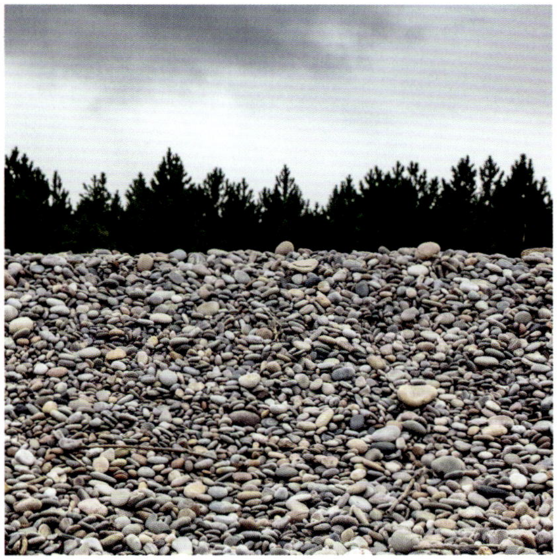

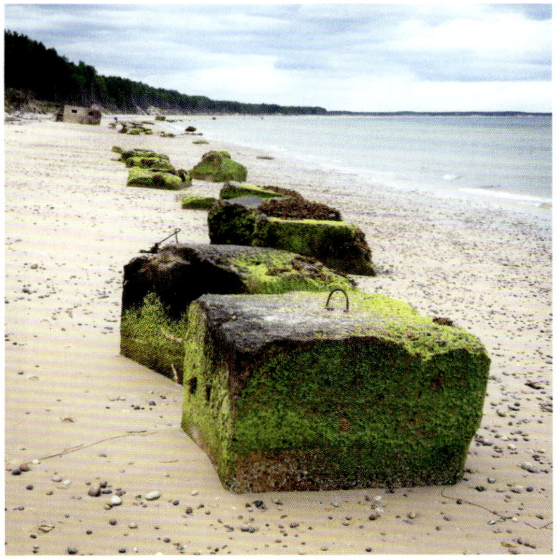

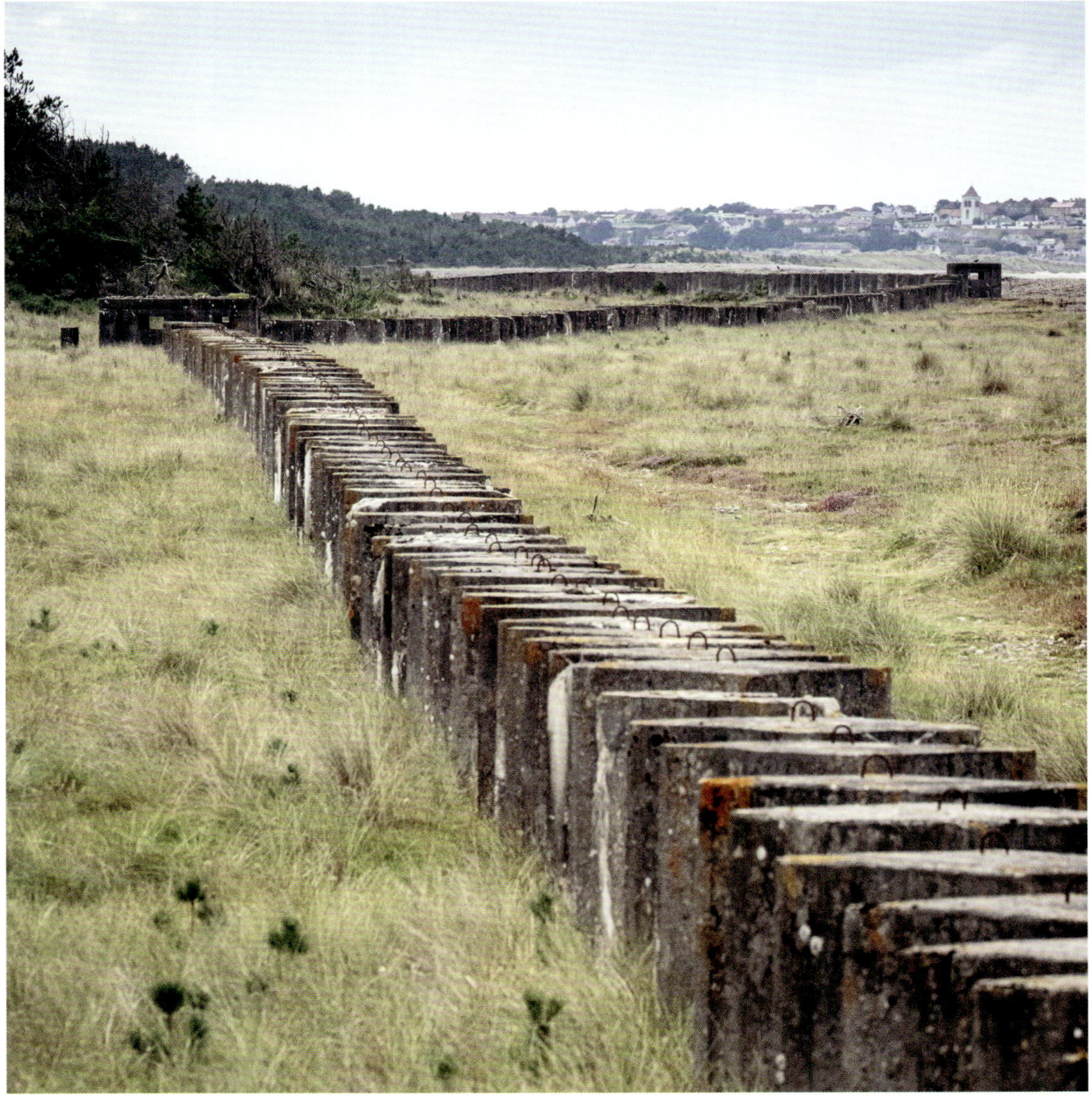

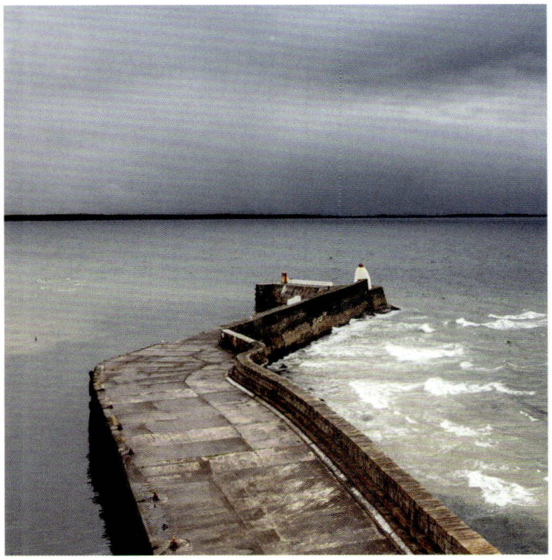

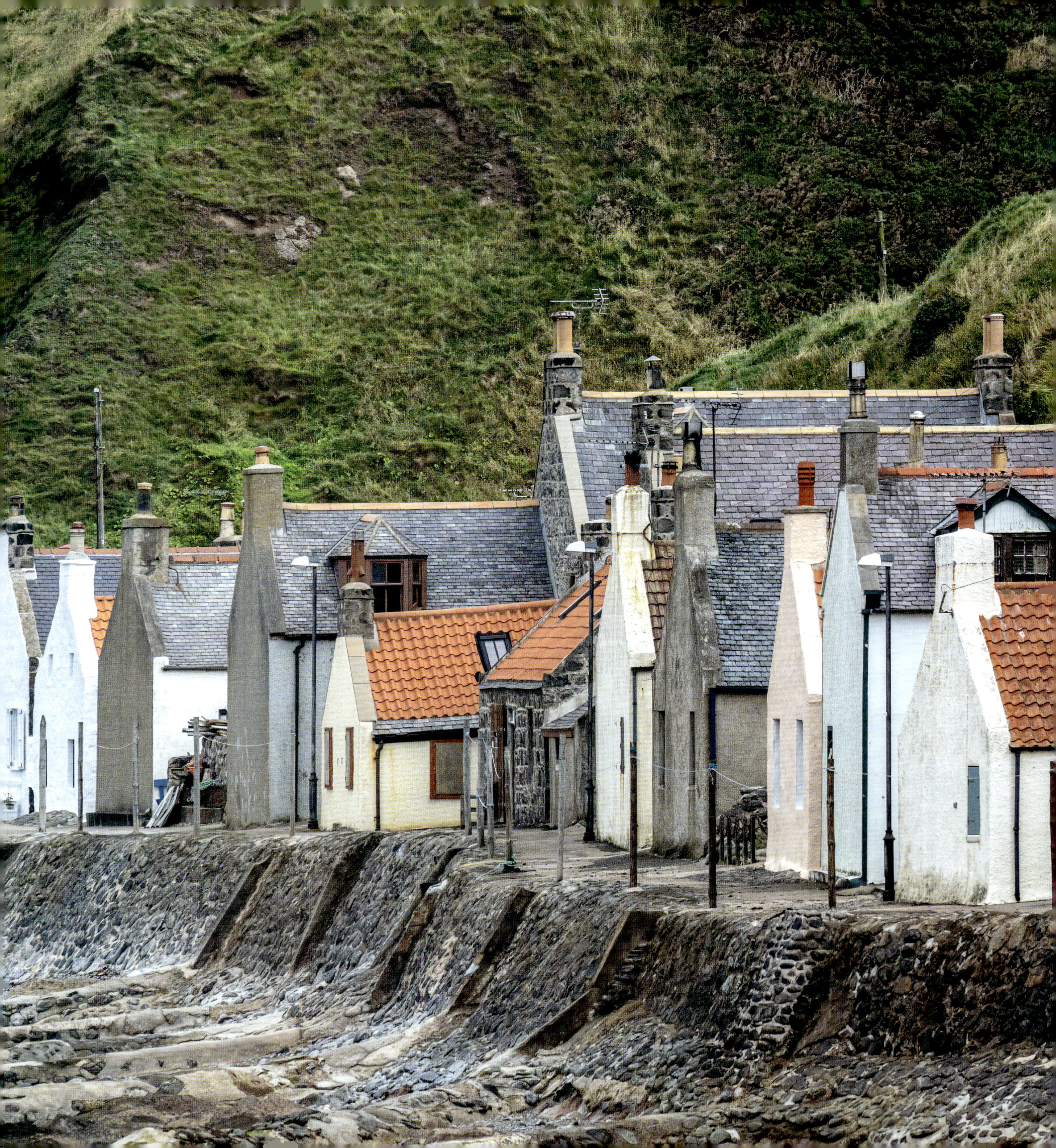

36 BANFFSHIRE

AUGUST–SEPTEMBER 2019

DAY 341–344 | 08,332–08,413KM | 81KM

I arrive at the fishing village of Findochty cheered by the colourfully painted houses and matching boats lining the harbour. The seafront at Portgordon had been covered with beige pebbledash and concrete, so it's a delightful change of pace to be confronted with an eruption of vibrant tones. The fishing industry feels like an integral part of life here and the jetty is stacked with creels. I even walk past a car with a F15SHY number plate.

The road to the harbour at Portknockie is closed, so I rely on directions from locals to get to Bow Fiddle Rock. Even in the rain, the view is impressive, and it's easy to see how the sea arch got its name – it bears a remarkable resemblance to a violin bow tip. Something bobs in the middle of the arch so I look through the telephoto lens to see a bright blue fishing boat with a man in oilskins busy on deck.

The next day I reach Macduff, an even busier working harbour. In the late afternoon, the dock is full of stout trawlers preparing to depart for the ocean. The trawlers are well maintained, but each boat's stern remains unadorned, scratched and rusted, where the nets are hauled in over steel rollers, hinting at the violent struggle needed to land every catch. The nightwatchman checks the mooring lines for all the trawlers: too long and the boats crash into each other; too short and the boats get lifted out of the water as the tide falls, he tells me. He has a fantastic Doric accent, a kind of Geordie hybrid, unlike anything I've heard before, punctuated with rich, distinctive phrases such as 'Ay ay, fit like?' (Hello, how are you?)

As evening falls, I make a long detour to Gardenstown Beach to set up my tripod for a good view of the heavens. Despite all the fantastic things I've seen, auroras have proved stubbornly elusive so far, but I'm hopeful I might see one if the clouds clear up. When the conditions are favourable, it's not unusual to see the aurora borealis from the north of Scotland right down to the Moray coast. But like every other time I've patiently waited by the tripod for that mystical green shimmer, I get rained into submission. Dejected, I return to my B&B, where the comfort of a roof over my head consoles me.

The next morning, daylight allows me to appreciate how Gardenstown, like many fishing villages in Banffshire and Aberdeenshire, sits snugly nestled beneath the cliffs. Each one is a hidden treasure that can only be accessed by a single road. As I walk along the seafront here, I admire how these villages, with their gable ends facing the weather, exude a sense of seclusion and tranquillity. A winding path below the sea cliff leads me to car-free Crovie, the most enchanting of these coastal villages. So limited is the space below the cliffs that gardens are out of the question: washing lines are strung out front, adding a touch of practicality to the charm. I'm so captivated by the peace of Crovie that I sit for a while wondering how many other places could be improved by keeping cars at bay.

On the last day I'm enthralled by Troup Head Nature Reserve, the mainland's only gannet colony, teeming with squawking life. Thousands of the majestic white birds, with their spear-like beaks, cover the dark vertical cliffs while hundreds more reel through the sky, revealing their black wing tips. I hoped I'd get to a town tonight, but it's been slow-going up and down pathless cliffs and over innumerable barbed-wire fences, so dinner is all my remaining food: a spoonful of peanut butter and a single sachet of sugar.

Opposite:

There's no vehicular access to the houses at Crovie, which are tucked in tightly below the cliffs

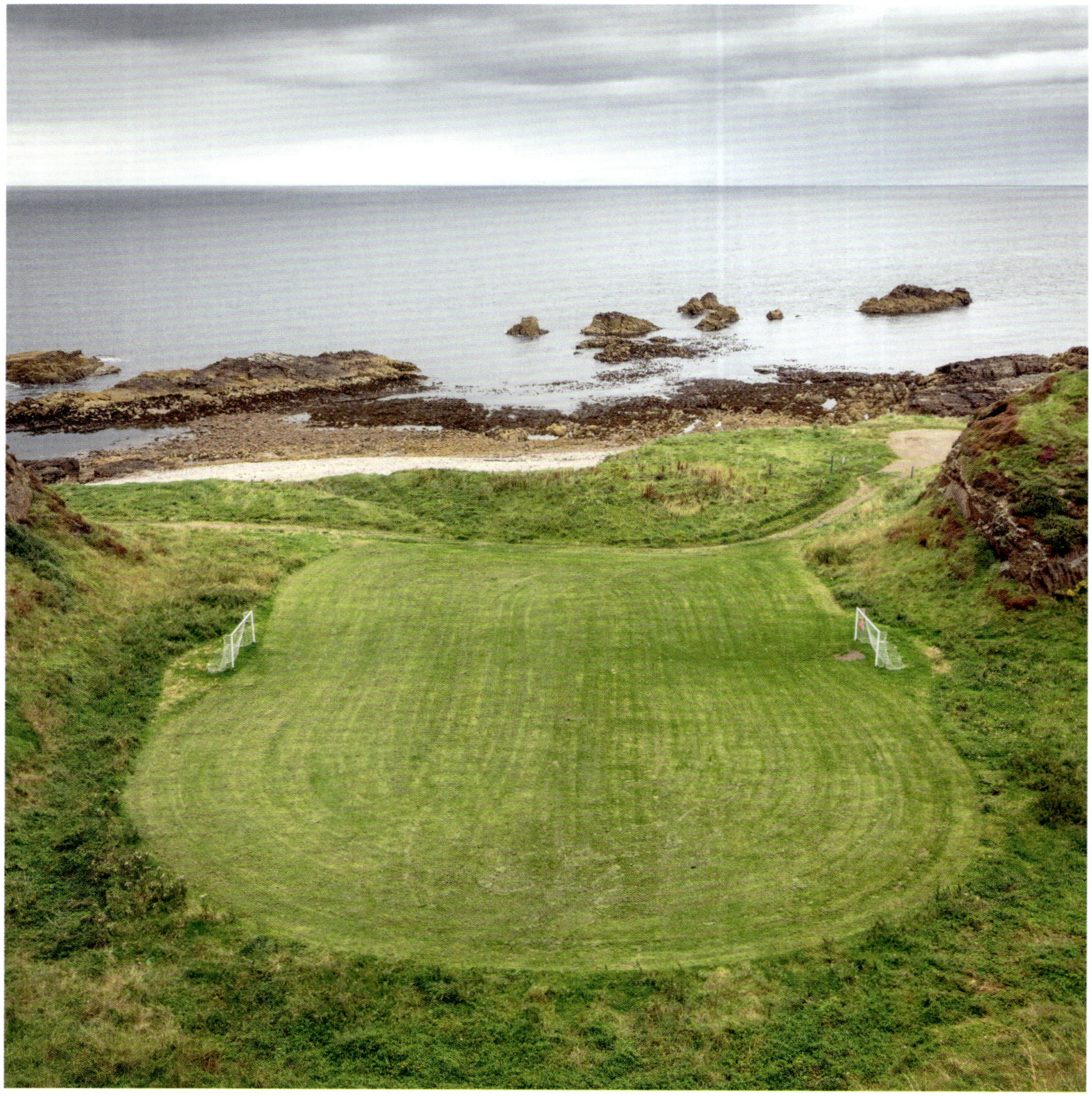
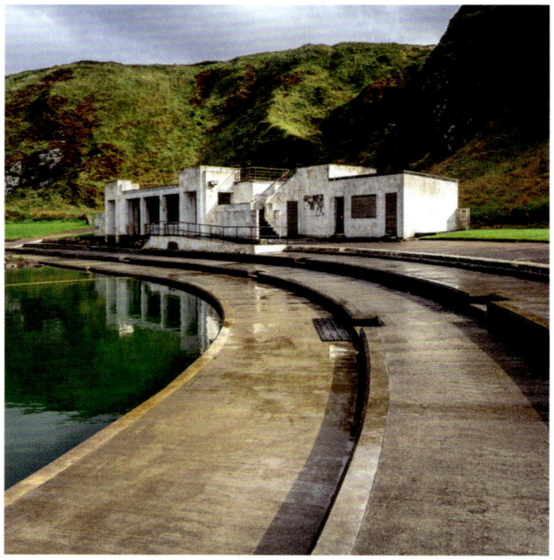
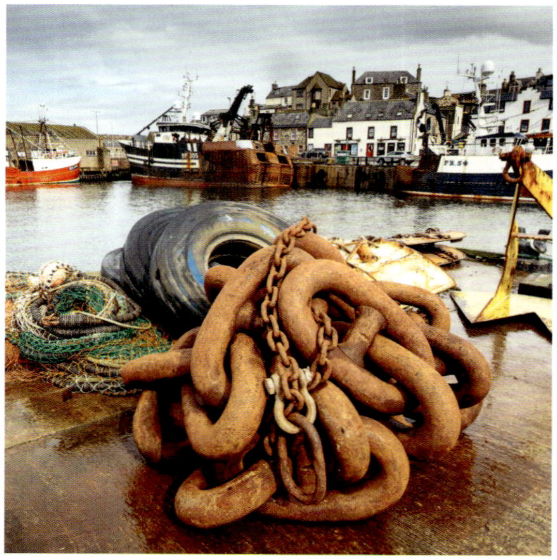
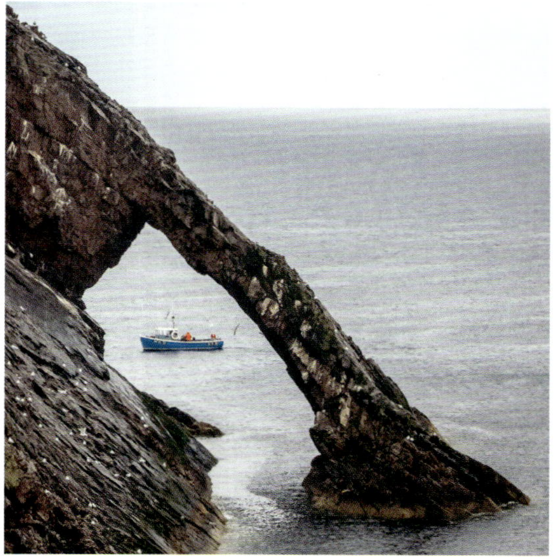
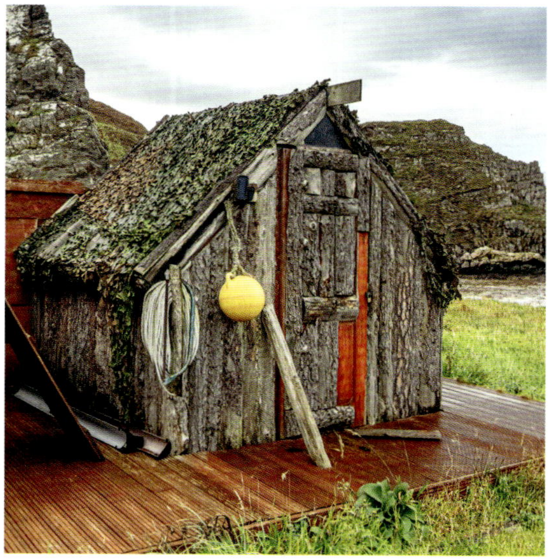
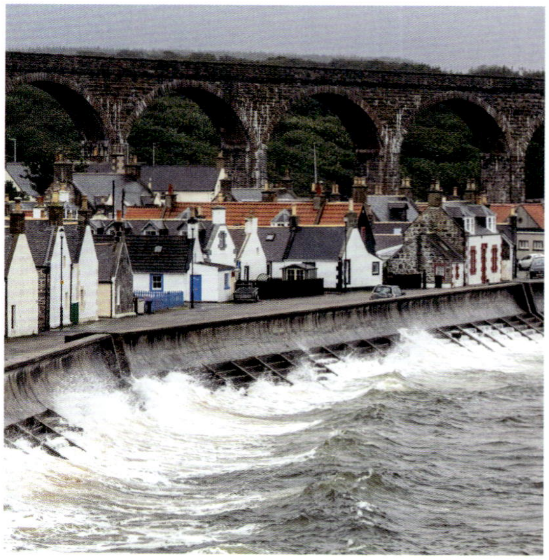

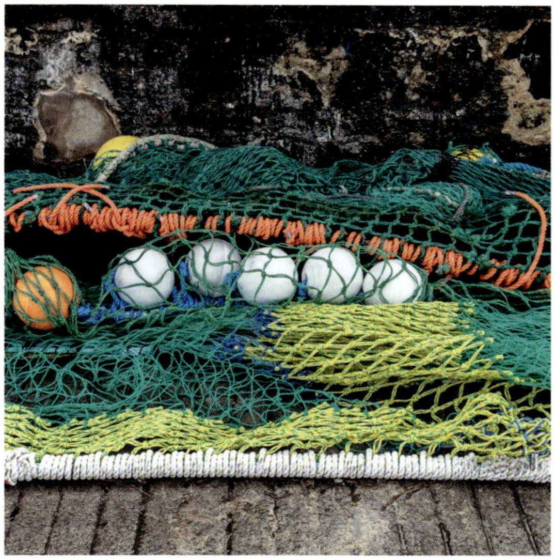

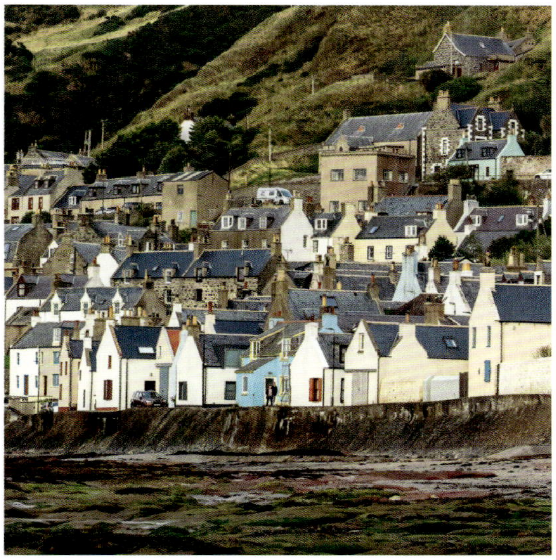

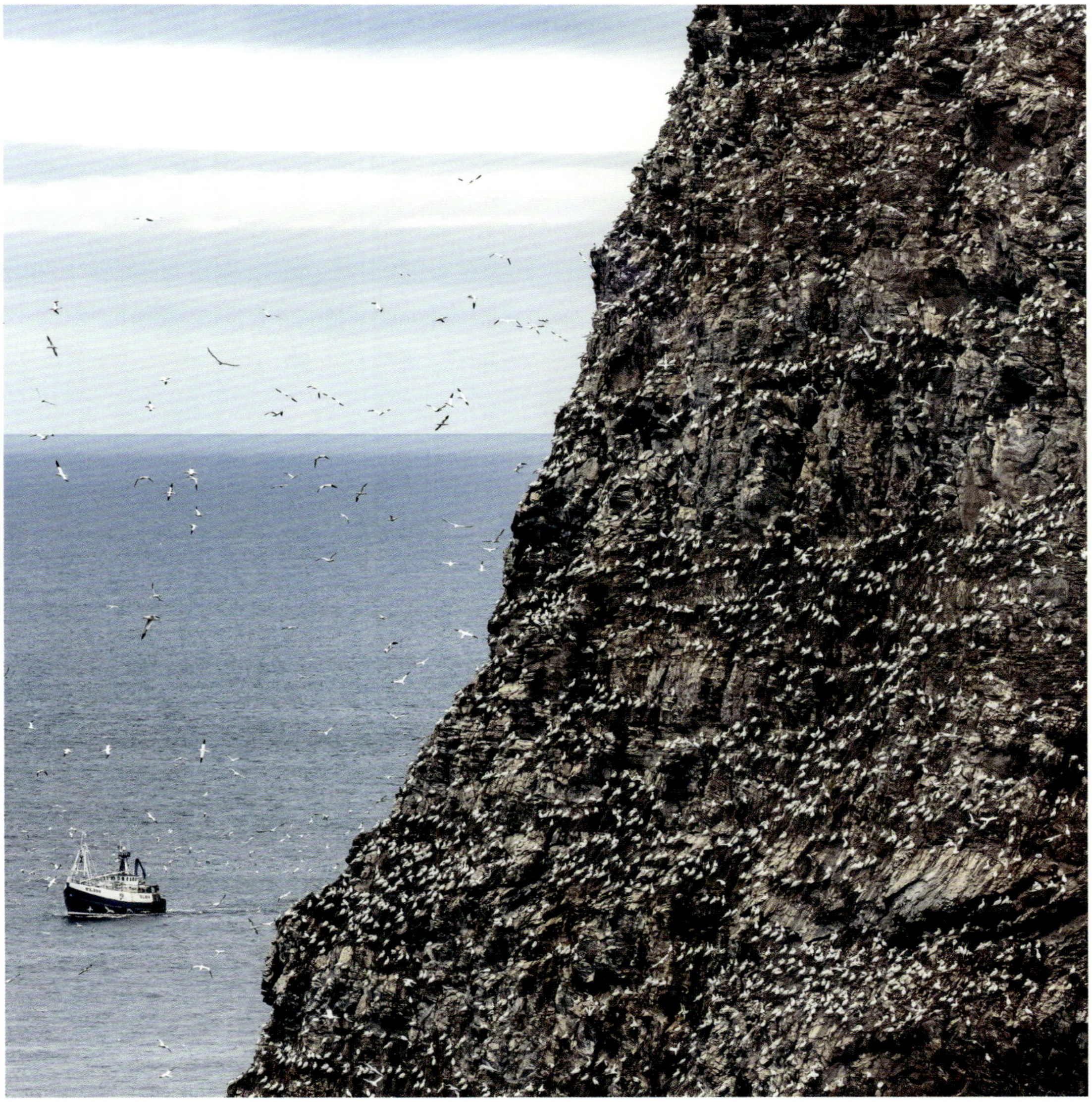

Opposite, clockwise from top left:

Coastal goals: Findochty

Tarlair Swimming Pool, a disused lido by Macduff

Heavy chain at Macduff Harbour

Cullen Viaduct

Shed, Old Haven

Bow Fiddle Rock, Portknockie

From top left:

Nets, Macduff Harbour

Gardenstown from the beach

Troup Head gannetry

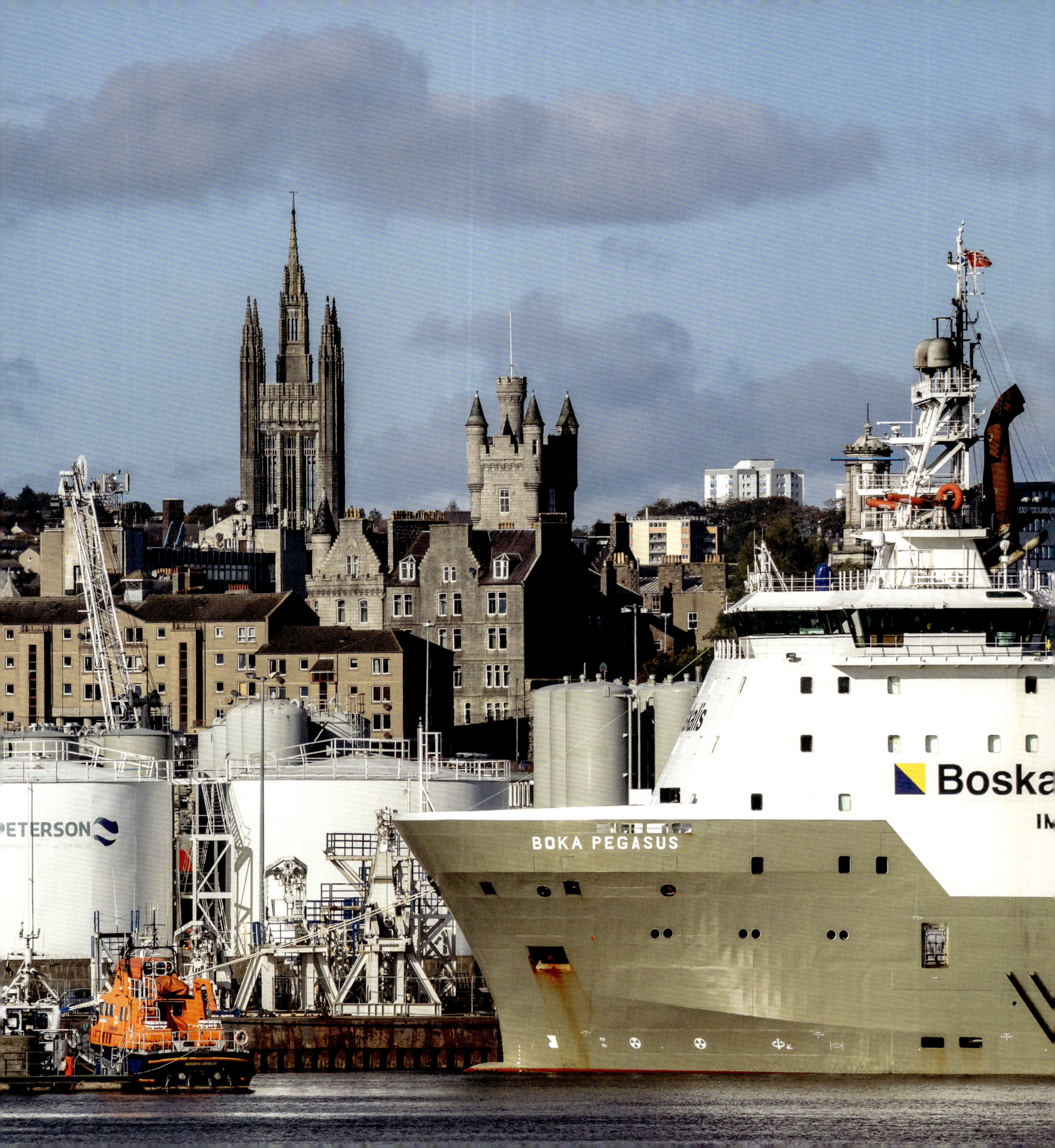
PETERSON
BOKA PEGASUS
Boska

37 ABERDEENSHIRE

SEPTEMBER 2019

DAY 345–348 | 08,413–08,549 KM | 136 KM

Long before I stepped foot in Aberdeenshire, the village of Pennan was one of the places I really wanted to visit. I'd first come across it in the film *Local Hero*, which tells the story of an oil executive tasked with buying out the village to build a refinery. In the movie, the village (fictionalised as Ferness) is filled with vivacious characters and a bustling community so full of warmth that the oil executive has a change of heart. I'd fallen in love with what I'd seen on-screen, so I can't help but be disappointed when I realise that the real-life Pennan is nothing like the Bill Forsyth version. Far from the lively village of his imagination, the only other visitors I spot as I meander about are a couple taking elaborate selfies with a harbourside phone box similar to a prop featured in the movie. I search in vain for the tight-knit community portrayed in *Local Hero* and am disheartened to discover the village only has twelve full-time residents as half the houses sit empty for much of the year due to the rise of Airbnb and second-home holiday rentals.

It's not until I arrive at Fraserburgh that my surroundings come to life again. The fishing port is busy with the cacophonous sound of metal grinding and forklift trucks scooting along, and men in fluorescent coveralls marching past piles of ice dumped unceremoniously about. It's a nice change of pace to be surrounded by so much activity, but as the wind and rain picks up, I do too, conscious of the need to find shelter for the night. By the time I leave Fraserburgh, the wind has become gale-force, buffeting me about as I attempt to walk in a straight line along the beach. I feel a spike of adrenaline when I spot a trawler floundering on the rocks near Inverallochy. In the fading light of day, I check my rain-splattered phone to see if there's enough signal to call the coastguard. Relief washes over me when I get closer and make out that it's a historic wreck.

The following day, as I walk along the expansive beaches at Rattray Head, the real-life oil industry rises unexpectedly above the dunes. The flare towers at the St Fergus Gas Terminal, with their flaming baskets held aloft, remind me of the signal towers on the south coast of England. Might it be that engineers make the most radical sculptors? Improbably, a cluster of wetsuit-clad surfers catch impressive rollers below this industrial scene.

On my way to Peterhead's lively fish market, a friendly local on the coast path engages me in conversation. Awkwardly, I find myself struggling to comprehend half of his words. After he departs, I embark on a linguistic adventure with Google, to learn more about the unique Doric accent and phrases from this part of Aberdeenshire: 'Foo're ye deein?' meaning 'How are you doing?' One phrase that quickly becomes part of my vocabulary is 'fair trauchled' (exhausted).

On my final evening, dark skies and golden light pick out the ruins of the Scots baronial mansion Slains Castle on the clifftops. Bram Stoker was a visitor in its heyday, and the sprawling building is believed to be the inspiration for the literary setting of *Dracula*. Approaching Aberdeen, the villages are scattered with sports cars, and the sky is busy with helicopters heading back and forth to the oil platforms. The landscape has become entirely tamed: fields, plantations, and golf courses. I feel myself yearning for the Highlands. The next morning, I start my walk at 5 a.m., below a starry sky. With miles upon miles of firm, straight beaches along this stretch of coast, I make good time, and by sunset, it's the same moon ahead, the same beach underfoot and the same lights of Aberdeen in the distance, but now 30 kilometres closer.

Opposite:

Boka Pegasus, a multi-purpose offshore vessel, Aberdeen Harbour

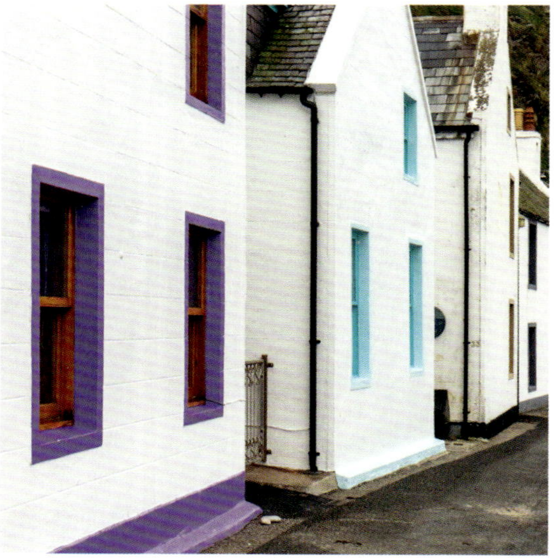
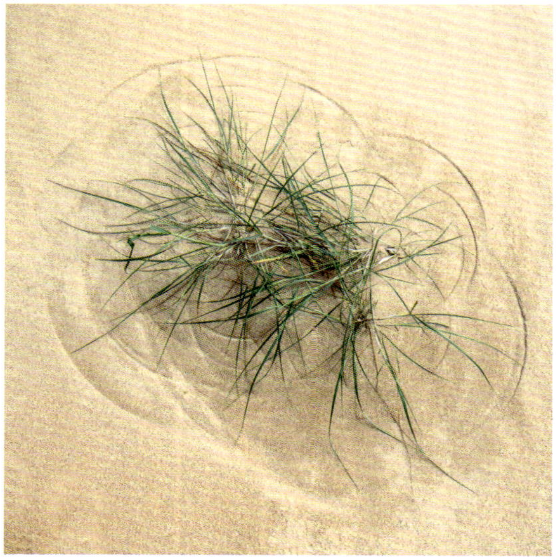
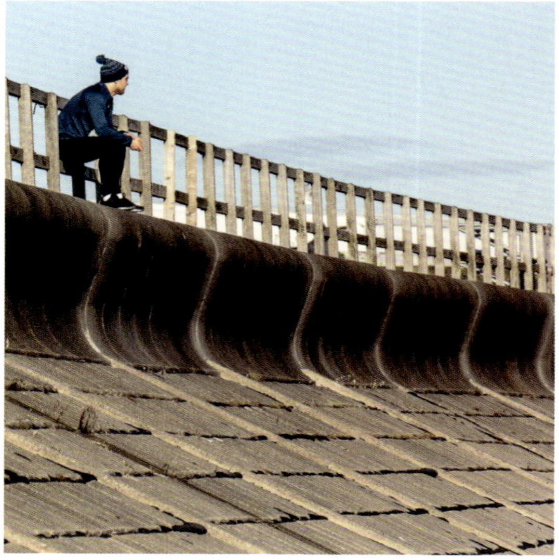
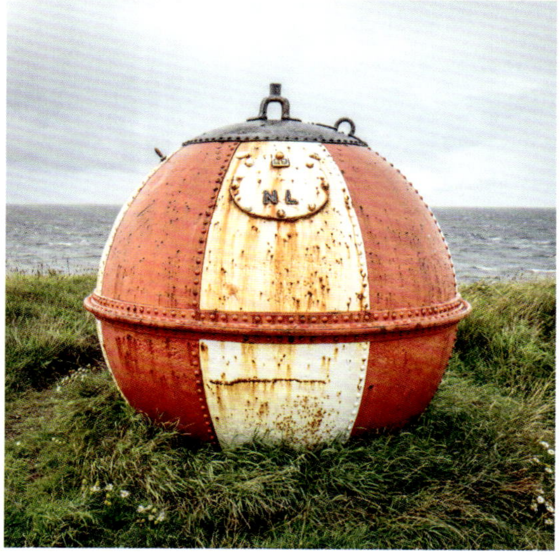
NL
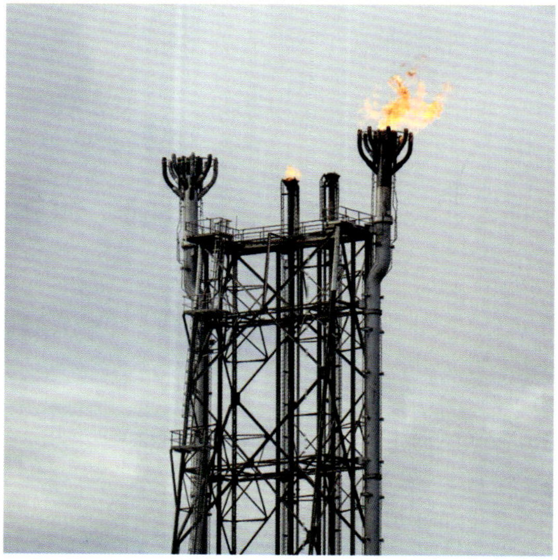
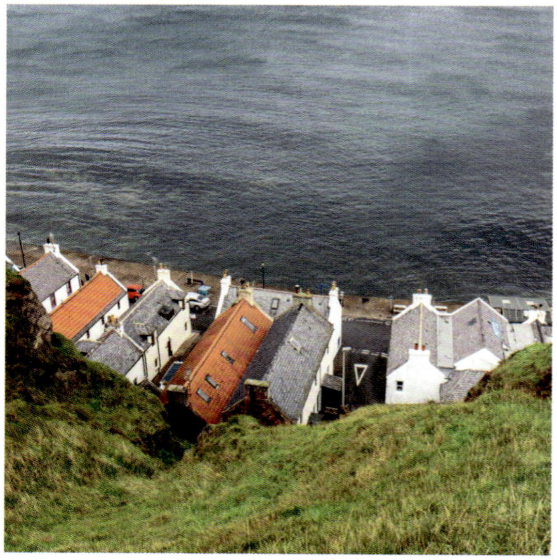
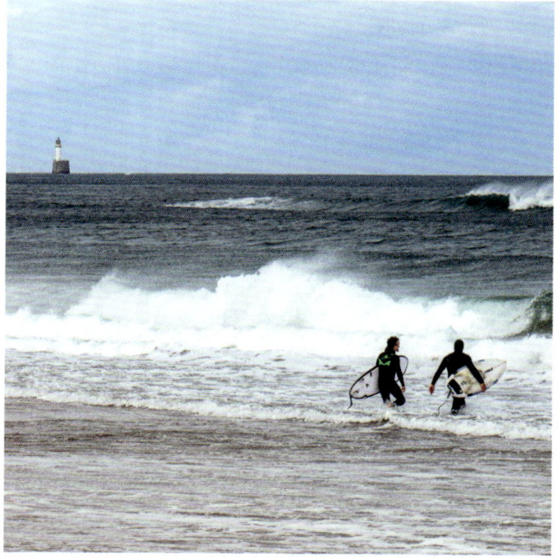
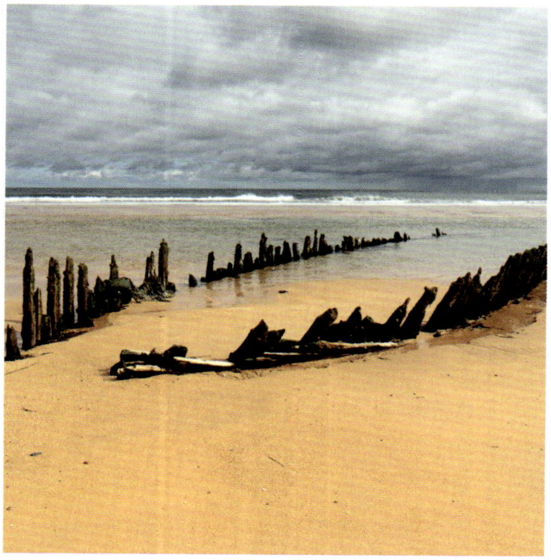
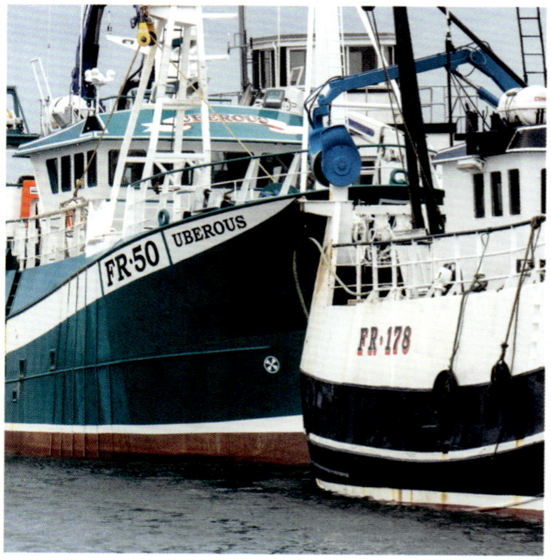
FR·50
UBEROUS
FR·178

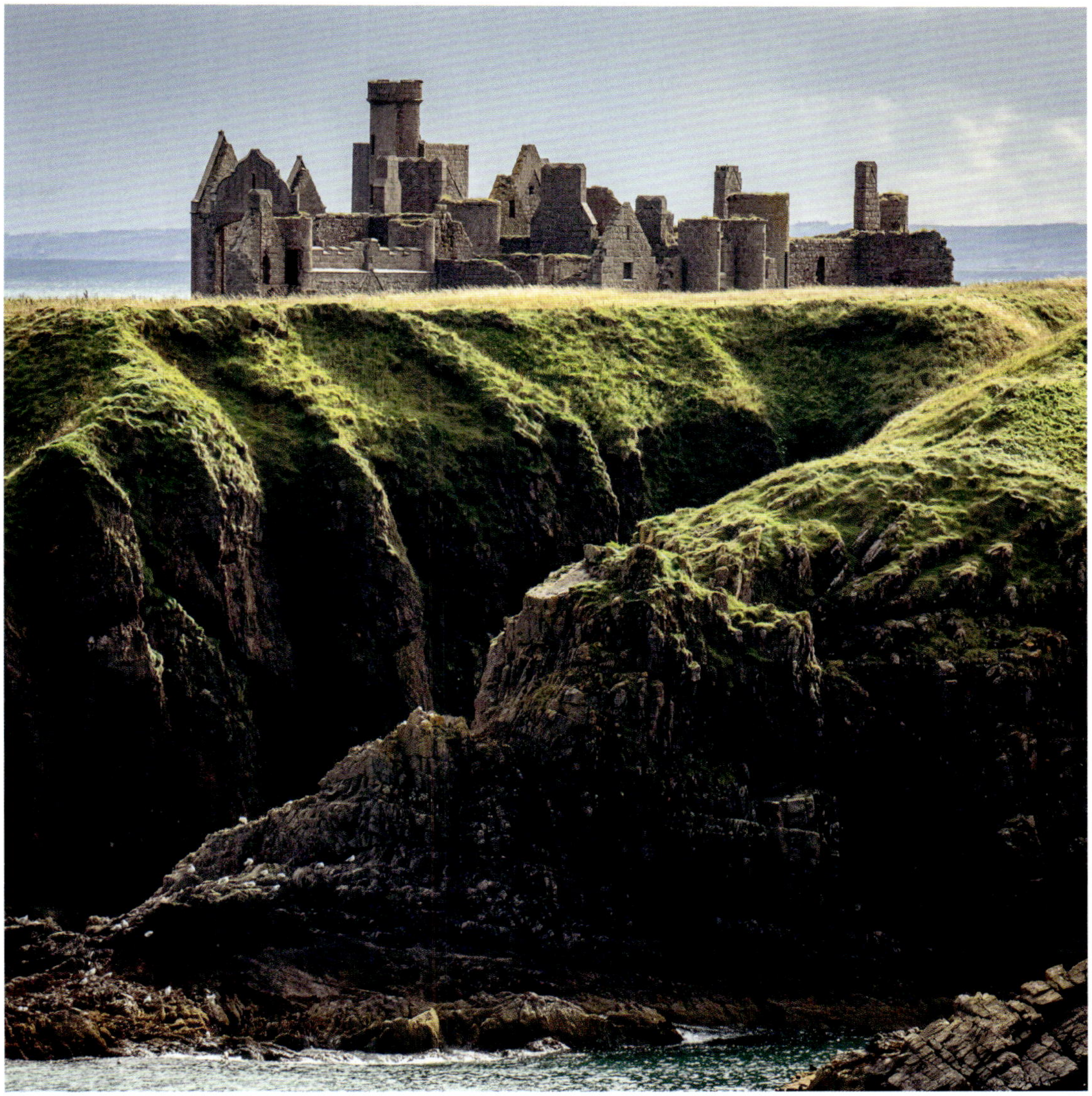

Opposite, from top left:

Pennan gables

Circumference: Rattray Head

Aberdeen esplanade

From centre left:

Chonky boi: Fraserburgh

St Fergus Gas Terminal, Rattray Head

A slice of Pennan

From bottom left:

Surfers by St Fergus Gas Terminal

Wreck of the *Excelsior*, a Norwegian barque (three-masted sailing ship) which ran aground in 1881 near Rattray Head

Trawlers *Uberous* and *Crystal River*, Fraserburgh

From top left:

Slains Castle is believed to be the inspiration for the setting of *Dracula* as Bram Stoker was a visitor there. Originally built in 1597, it was remodelled as a Scots baronial mansion in 1836

Cormorants near Rattray Head

Aberdeen Wind Farm

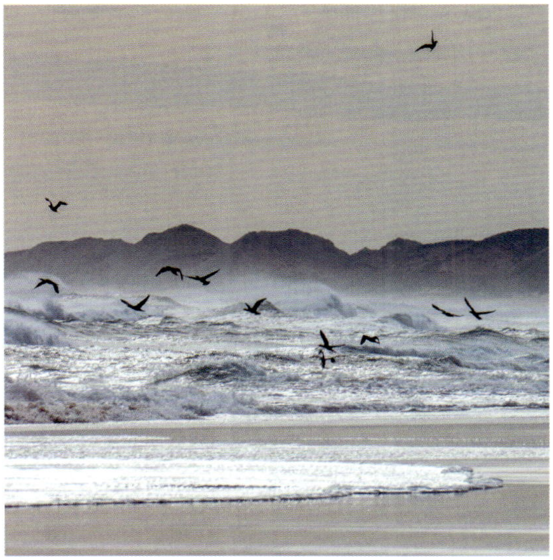

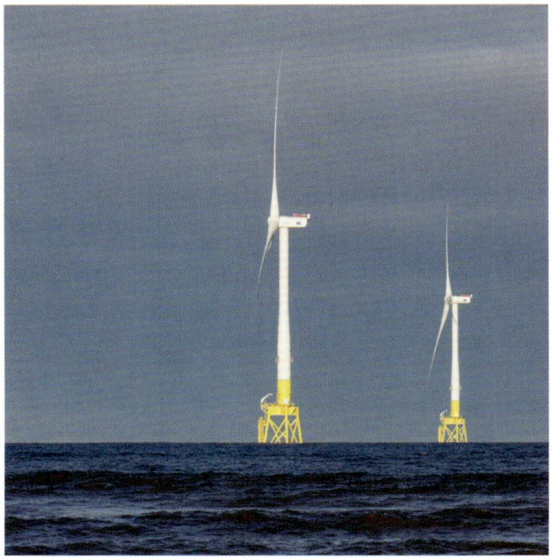

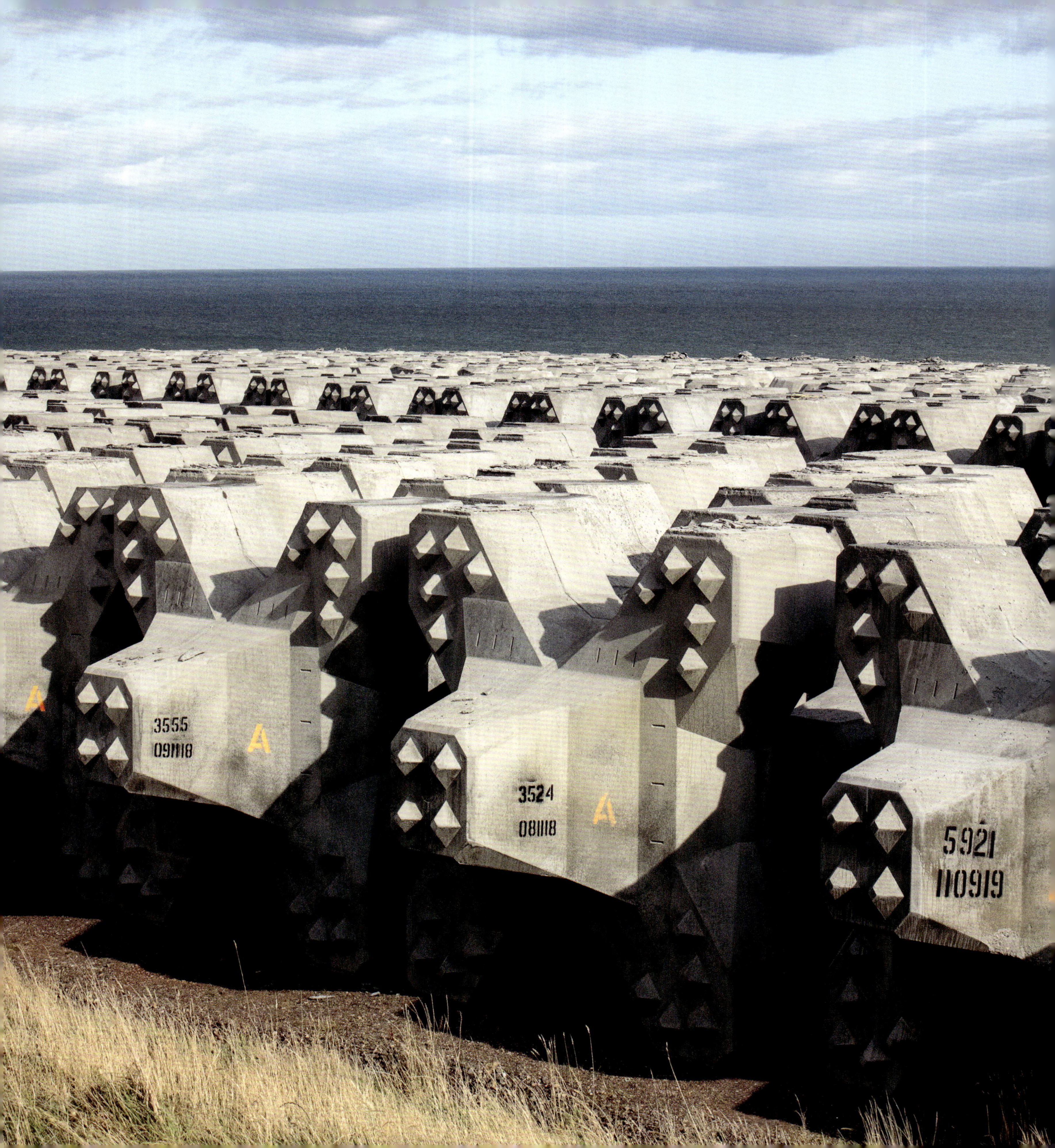
3555
09III8
A
3524
08III8
A
5921
110919
A

38 KINCARDINESHIRE

OCTOBER 2019

DAY 349–352 | 08,549–08,623KM | 74KM

As I head south along the cliffs away from Aberdeen, I walk past what appears to be a dormant robot army looming above me at twice my height. Serried ranks of menacingly anthropomorphic angular concrete blocks face the sea as if they've just emerged from the ocean. Not recognising what I'm seeing, I look up a local news story that explains they are accropodes – structures designed to resist the action of waves and act as armour for the breakwaters of Aberdeen's new South Harbour.

By the afternoon, despite being firmly within Alba, I pass a farm called England. The landscape here feels wild away from the fields, but the regular rattle of the train and rumble of the main road belie the isolation. Now that my journey is taking me south, I no longer see the sun setting over the sea on the west coast. Yet, as if in perfect compensation, the moon rises over the North Sea as soon as the sun sinks. At Stonehaven, the moon is so bright that the world appears monochrome, tinged with blue and resembling a Victorian oil painting. There's even enough light to use a fast shutter speed to freeze the moon shimmering on the waves while hand-holding the camera.

The following afternoon, Dunnottar Castle emerges ahead of me, spectacularly perched on a rock promontory and silhouetted against a velvety sea. This is where the Scottish crown jewels were hidden from Oliver Cromwell's invading army and I'm excited to explore. I follow a zigzag path down to the castle gate, where a formidable array of gun loops overlook the ticket office at the entrance, suggesting harsh consequences for those unwilling to pay the £10.50 entrance fee. The site is filled with tourists and coach tours; a happy class of American students pose below a saltire with the castle as a backdrop. Being around this many people is a little overwhelming – the crowded honeypots that punctuate the coast are always strange to experience after having spent so much time alone.

But it's a good chance to acclimatise to being sociable again, especially as the plan is to spend my last night in the home of a local architectural historian. I arrive outside Inverbervie just after nightfall and am quickly ushered into a homely living room with a hearth. Dinner is delicious and our conversation flows, but it's when I'm presented with the opportunity to visit a bunker that things really get interesting. An unassuming door in the living room is opened to reveal a lift shaft with industrial steps that descend into darkness. I'm ablaze with curiosity as I clamber down, following the historian first through a set of double doors and then a long corridor, illuminated with red light. He turns the corner and opens a pair of thick, steel blast doors, secured with eleven metal levers. I follow his lead and step inside. Immediately, I'm dumbstruck. I've never seen anything like this massive hidden complex. There are over a dozen rooms around a double-height control centre, some containing dusty telex machines, and a huge air-conditioning plant. But the most uncanny feature is the complete and unnatural absence of sound. When I ask, I'm told the bunker is a remnant of the Cold War era, one of many built along the east coast as part of an elaborate air-defence radar system designed to withstand attack from nuclear weapons. I'm soon keen to escape to the open air, leaving behind the subterranean stillness borne of a threat that never materialised, where the only sounds are one's paranoid imaginings.

Opposite:

Accropodes (unreinforced concrete structures to resist the action of waves) that act as armour for the breakwaters of Aberdeen's new South Harbour

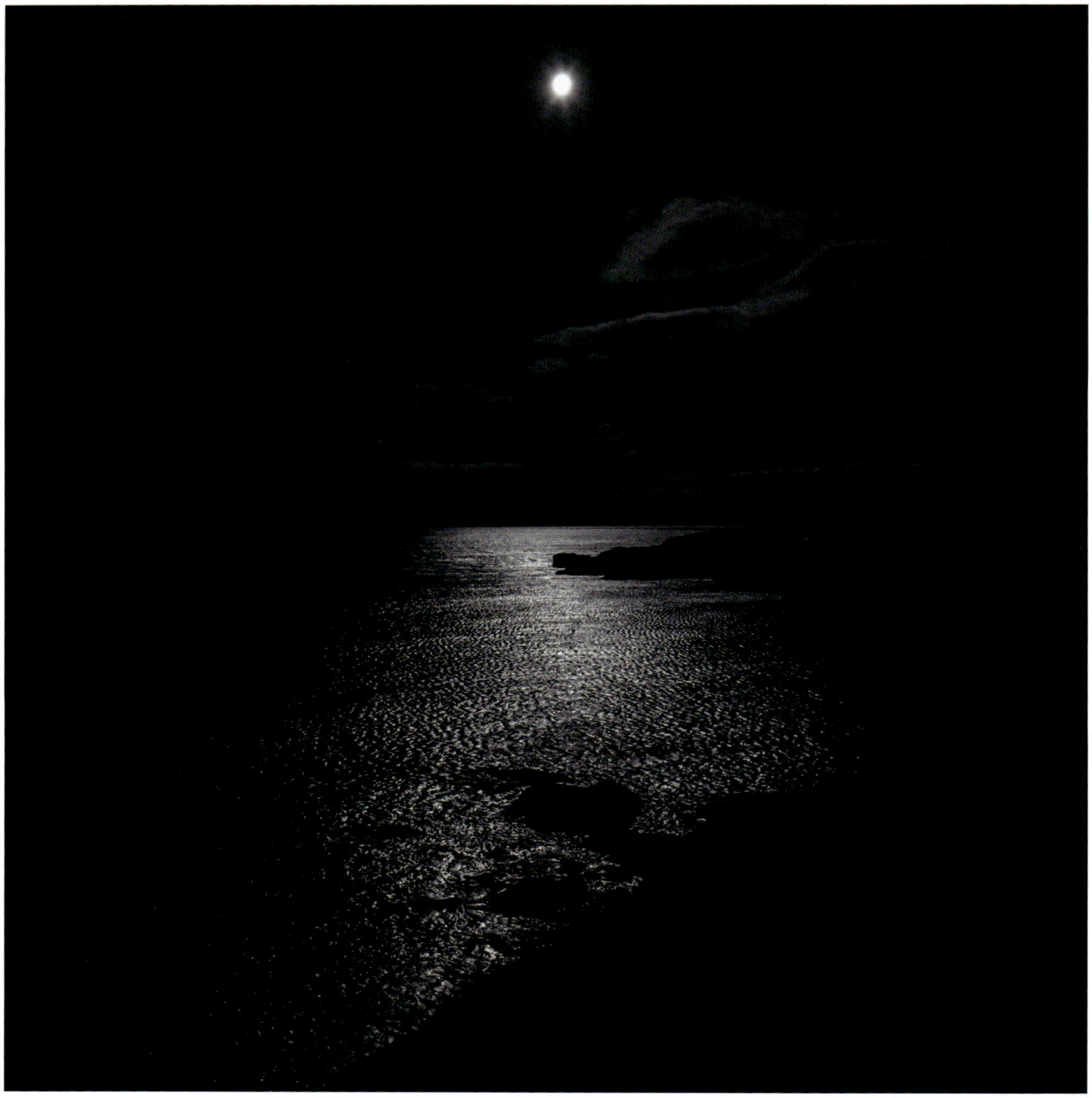

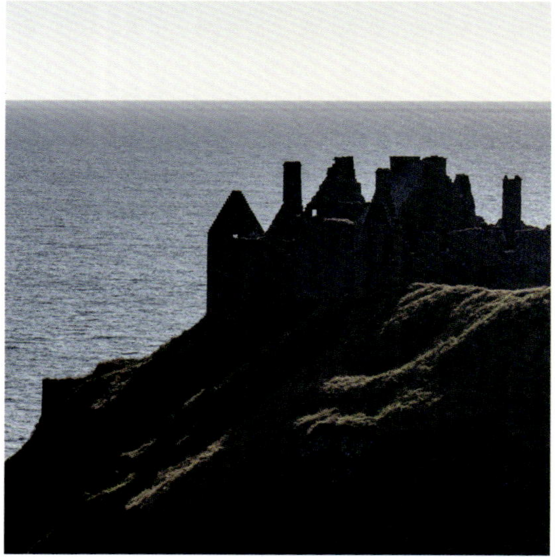

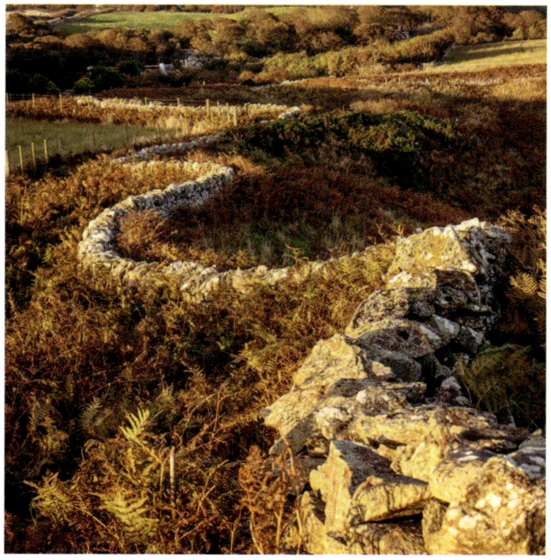

From top left:

Moonlit sea from Downie Point, Stonehaven

Approaching Dunnottar Castle

Autumn light on a drystone wall near Limpet Burn

Opposite, from top left:

Tunnel to the Cold War bunker at RAF Inverbervie Radar Station (now Bervie Brow Research Station)

Blast doors, RAF Inverbervie Radar Station

From bottom left:

PBX switchboard, Room 27, Comm Ops, RAF Inverbervie Radar Station

Room 27, Comm Ops, RAF Inverbervie Radar Station

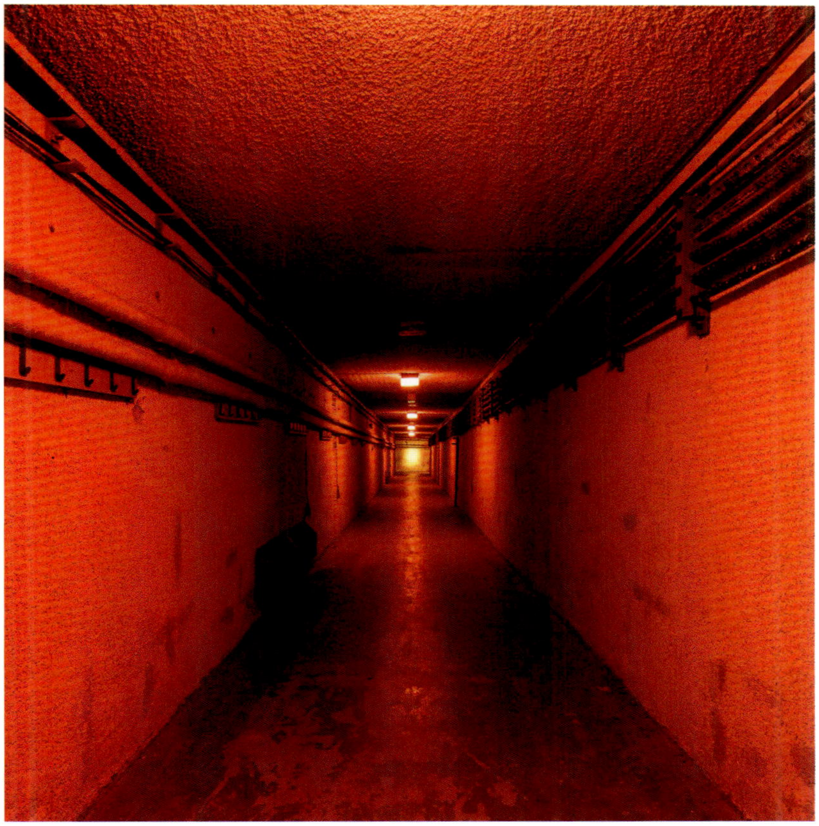

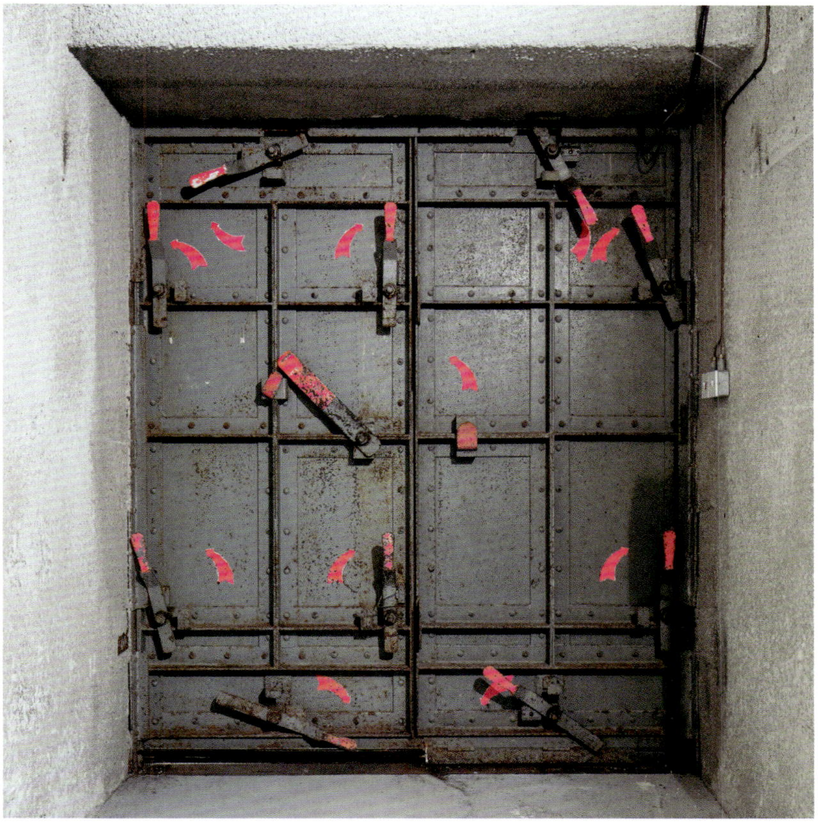

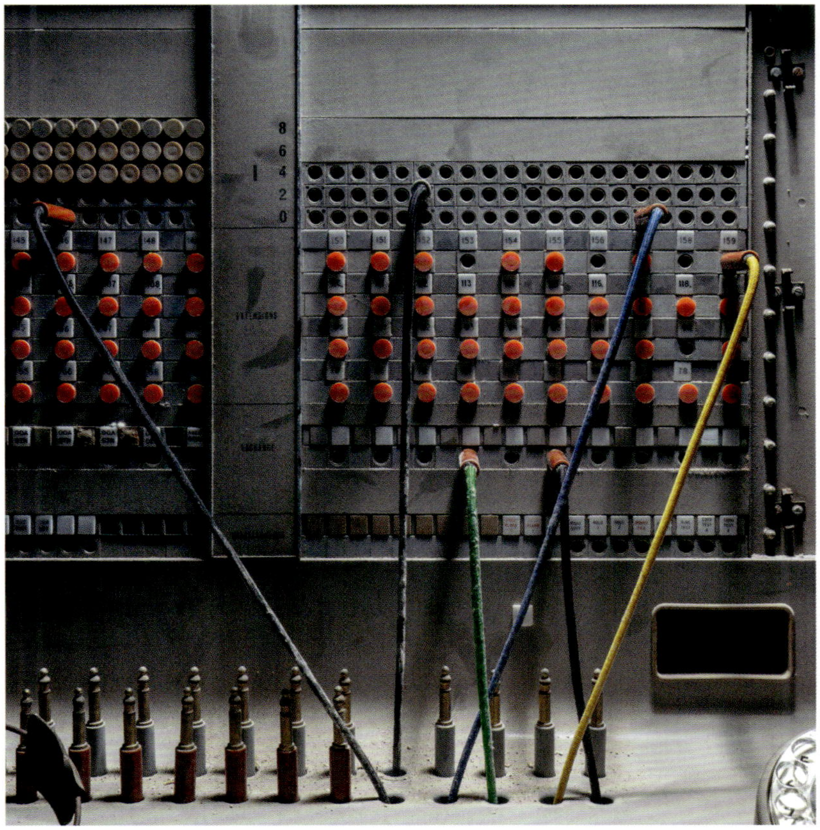

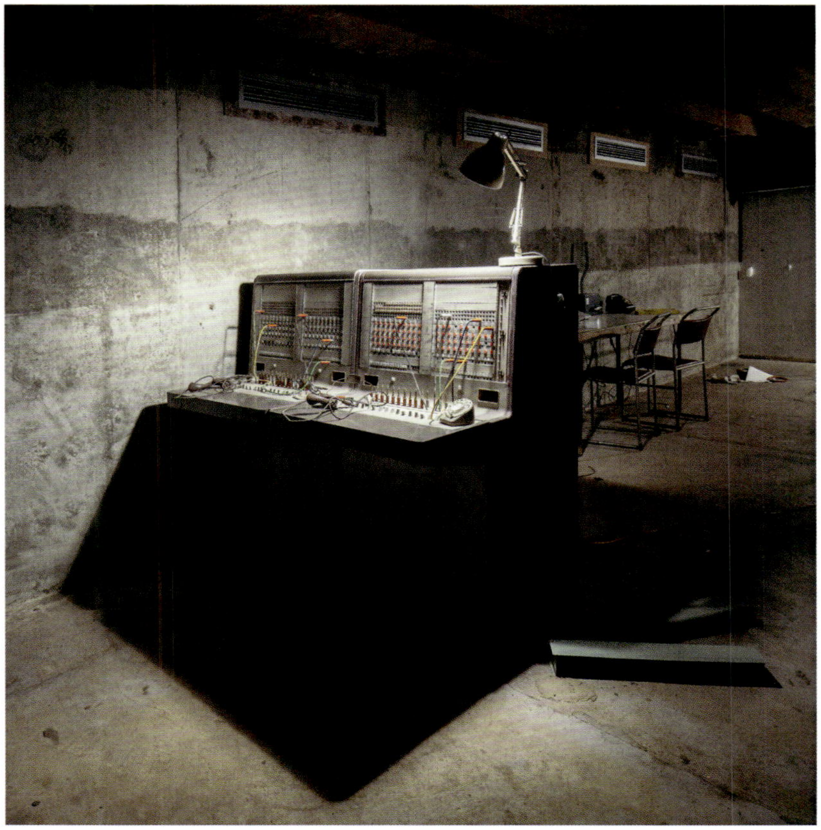

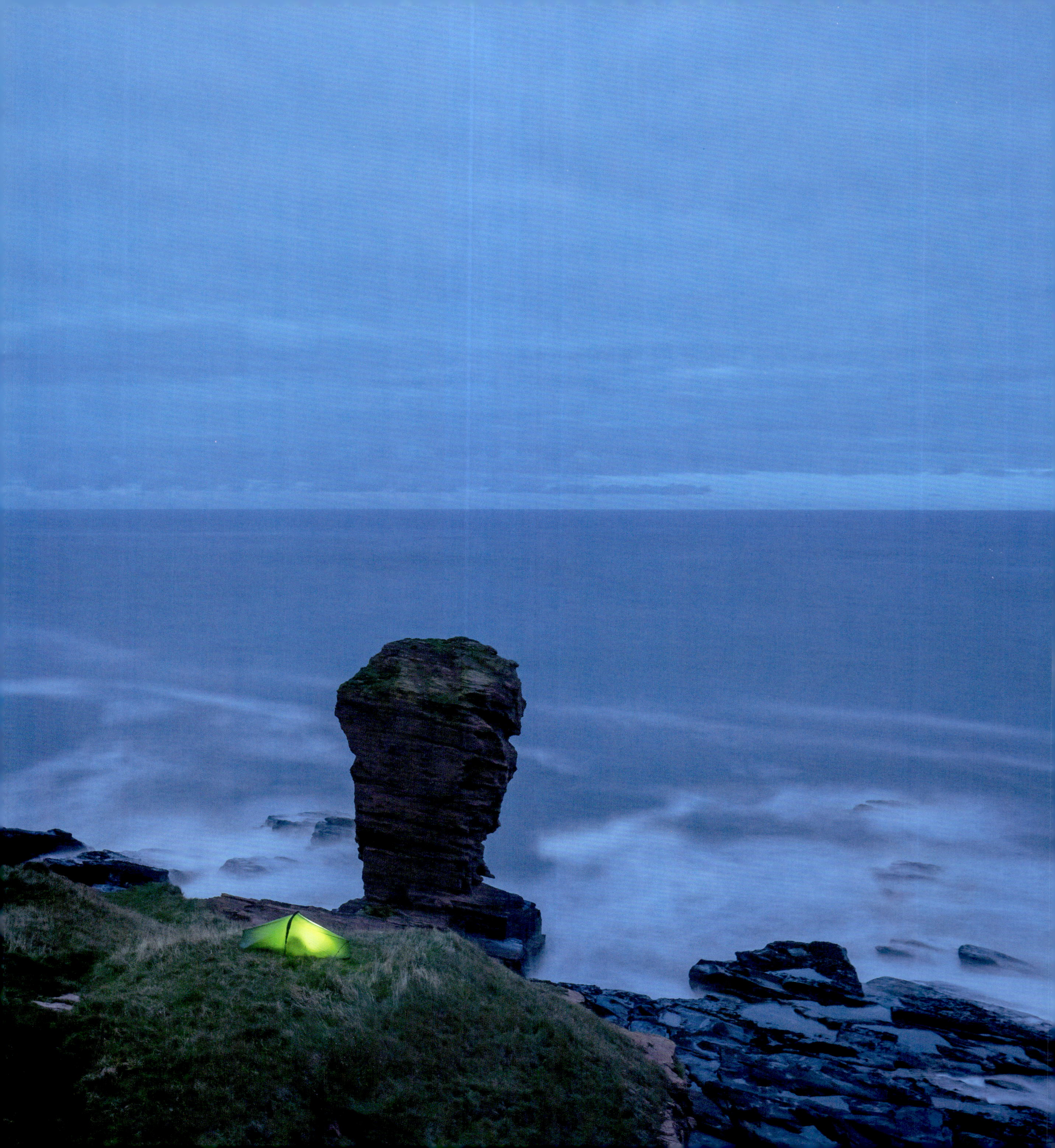

39 ANGUS

OCTOBER 2019

DAY 353–355 | 08,623–08,702 KM | 79 KM

As I leave Montrose and head towards the North Sea, Angus seems in no rush to reveal itself to me. At first, a railway bridge emerges hesitantly from the damp white void. Then, dozens of washing lines extending along the shore above my head, followed by a whitewashed daymark, invisible against the mist, that fails completely in its purpose. It's only when I reach the ocean that the fog evaporates to reveal a brilliant blue sky, Scurdie Ness Lighthouse and distant views south along the craggy coastline.

Colour slowly returns, as the day unfolds, with red sandstone cliffs that appear incredibly vivid after my achromatic start. The warm evening light casts a golden glow over the sandstone ruins of Red Castle, and at Lunan Bay the sun sets over the sea with the brightest of magentas.

The following day, I climb to the top of the sandstone cliffs of Red Head. As I focus my camera on the breathtaking sculptural drama of the promontory, a Land Rover, a mere speck in the vastness, daringly manoeuvres to the very edge. Its presence accentuates the epic scale of the geological formations unfolding before me. Unsurprisingly, the area's ancient inhabitants utilised Red Head's unassailable location to establish an Iron Age fort, protecting it with a single rampart and a broad ditch.

I spend the night camped next to the Deil's Heid (Devil's Head), a red rock resembling the profile of a demonic face that rises above the ocean. From the tent, I can see the signal from Bell Rock Lighthouse offshore and hear the waves booming below. A young man, silhouetted in the fading light, performs controlled press-ups on a distant clifftop before running off towards the horizon like the heroic opening of a boxing film.

My journey to Dundee is eased by a delightful stop in the town of Arbroath, where I'm eager to indulge in a local culinary speciality – the Arbroath smokie. The harbour is adorned with several establishments proudly advertising this delicacy, and I choose one with a free table overlooking the boats. As the smoked haddock is served, filleted on a large oval plate, I'm immediately captivated by the dish's aroma, texture and smoky flavour. It's a welcome change from the rehydrated meals I'm accustomed to in the tent.

The following day, I'm filled with anticipation as I set out to explore the sights of Dundee. My first stop is the impressive new V&A design museum, its cladding inspired by the strata of Scottish cliffs, and its overall form a nod to the city's shipbuilding past. Like many other visitors, I can't resist capturing the iconic diamond-shaped walkway between the two 'hulls', a structure that seems tailor-made for Instagram. At the Jute Museum, I'm immersed in local history, learning about the punishing work of men who carried 180-kilogram bags of jute on their backs on the docks in the 1970s, which puts my 20-kilogram backpack into perspective.

My happy day of Dundee tourism comes to a conclusion strolling the decks of the famed Antarctic research ship *Discovery*. The well-travelled vessel was built in Dundee before sailing on Scott and Shackleton's 1901–04 expedition that was the first to penetrate the then unknown interior of Antarctica. It survived two overwinterings frozen into the ice before sailing home. As I wander around, enthralled to be in direct contact with such a foundational piece of exploration history, I'm amused to discover that the 'medical comforts' carried on board the ship included 27 gallons of whisky, 27 gallons of brandy, 60 gallons of port wine, 36 gallons of sherry, 75 gallons of something called Real Turtle Soup and an unspecified quantity of champagne.

Opposite:

Dusk camp at Deil's Head

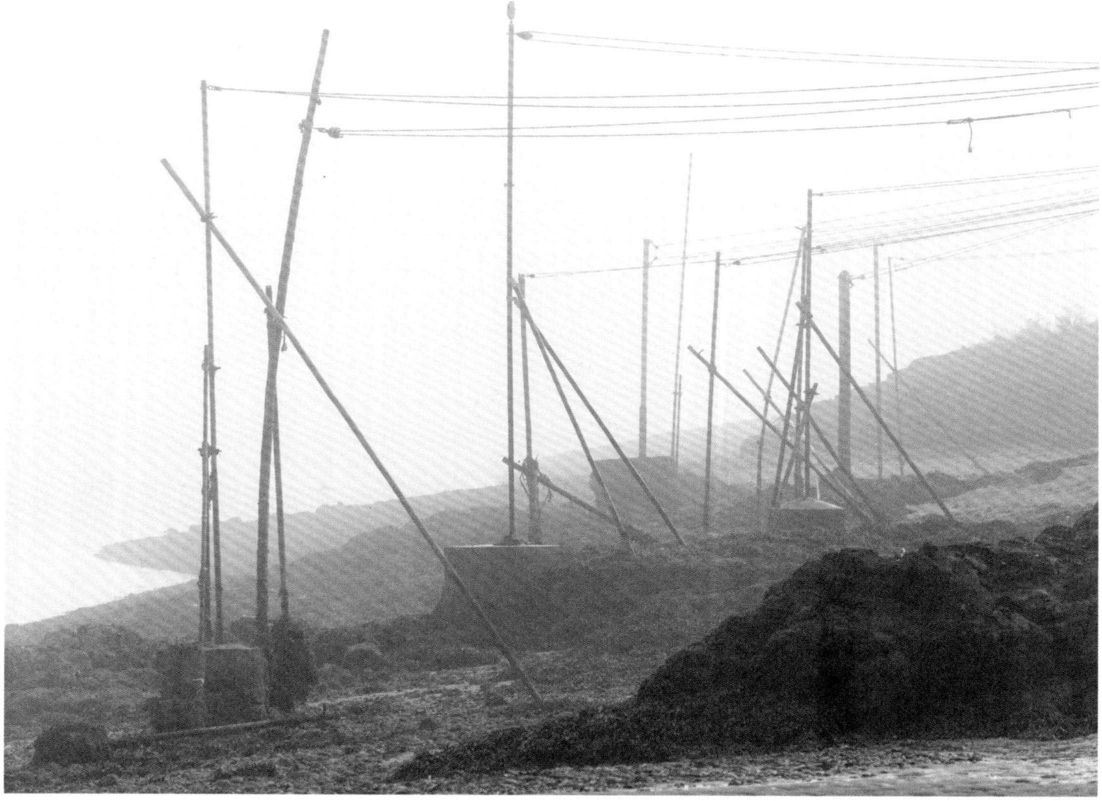

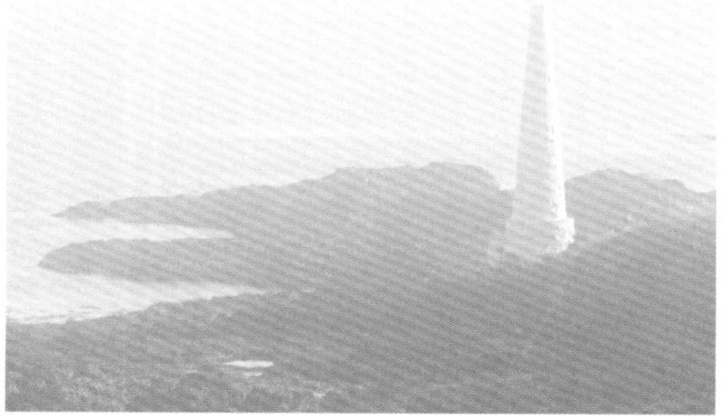

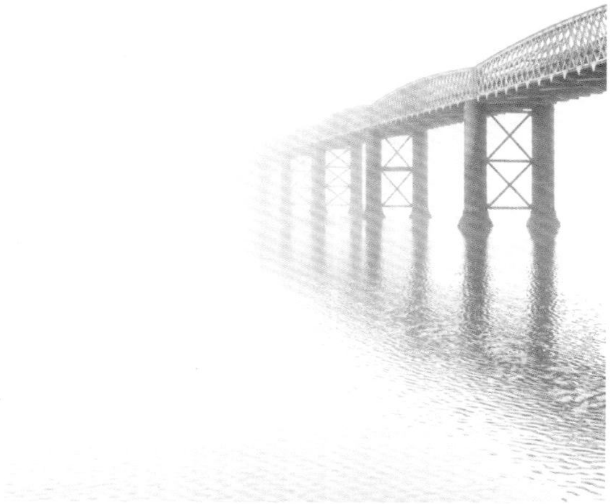

From top left:

Washing lines, Ferryden

Daymark by Scurdie Ness Lighthouse

South Esk Viaduct, Montrose

Opposite, from top left:

Red and blue at the V&A Dundee, designed by Kengo Kuma, 2018

Lunan Bay from Boddin Point

From bottom left:

Polytunnel arches, East Seaton

Creels, Arbroath Harbour

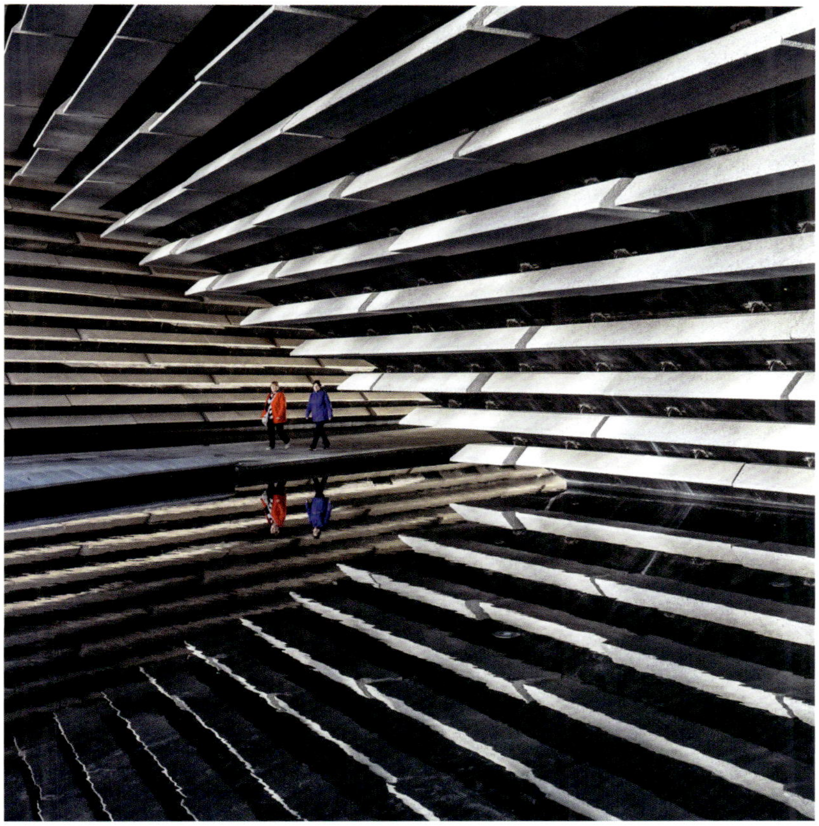
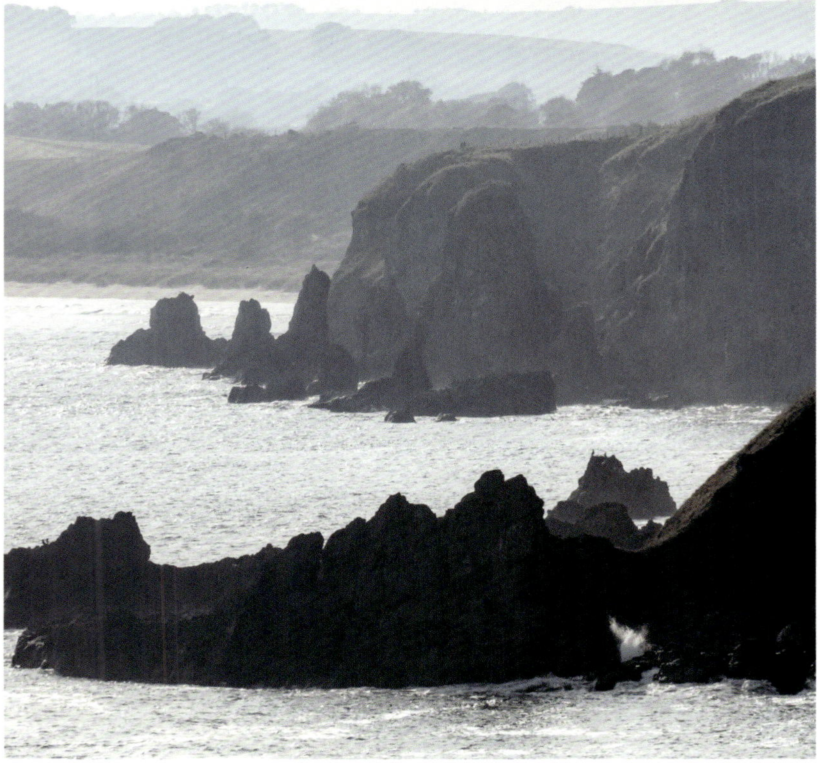
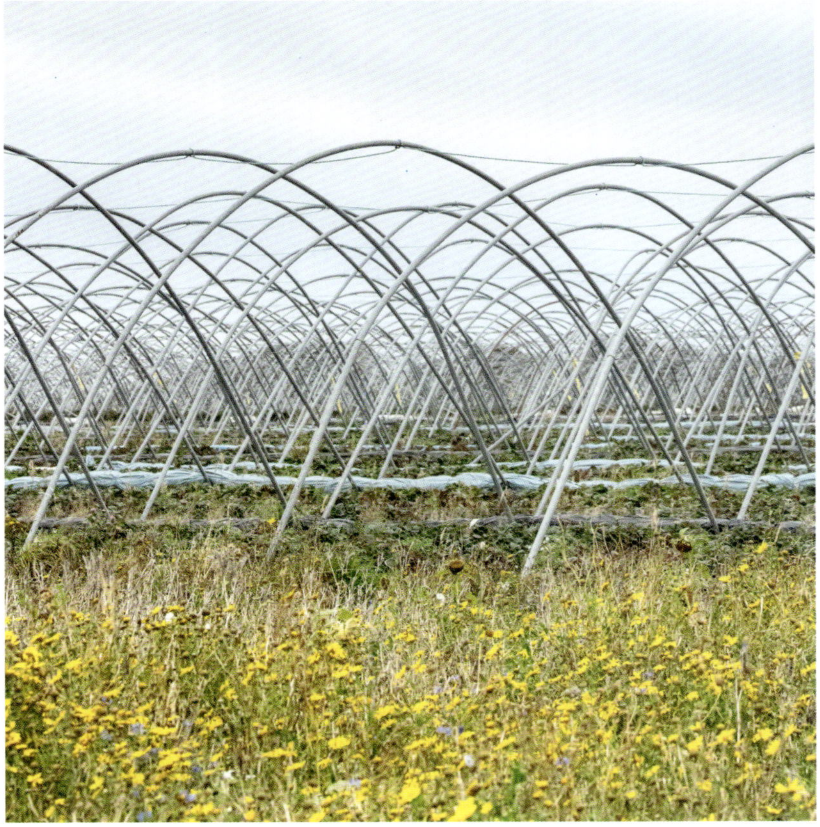
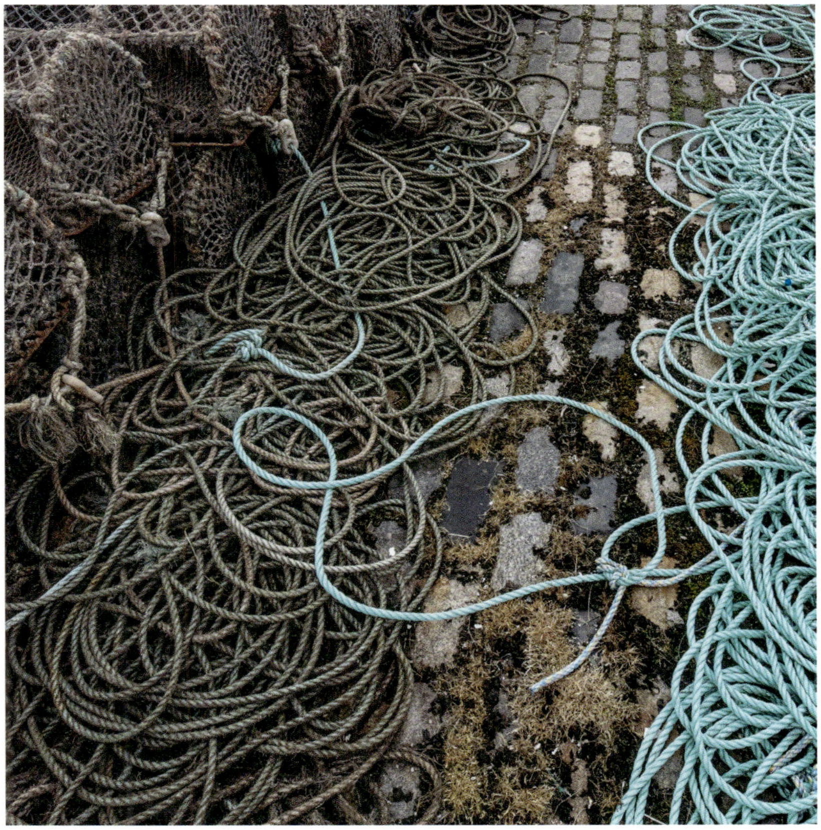

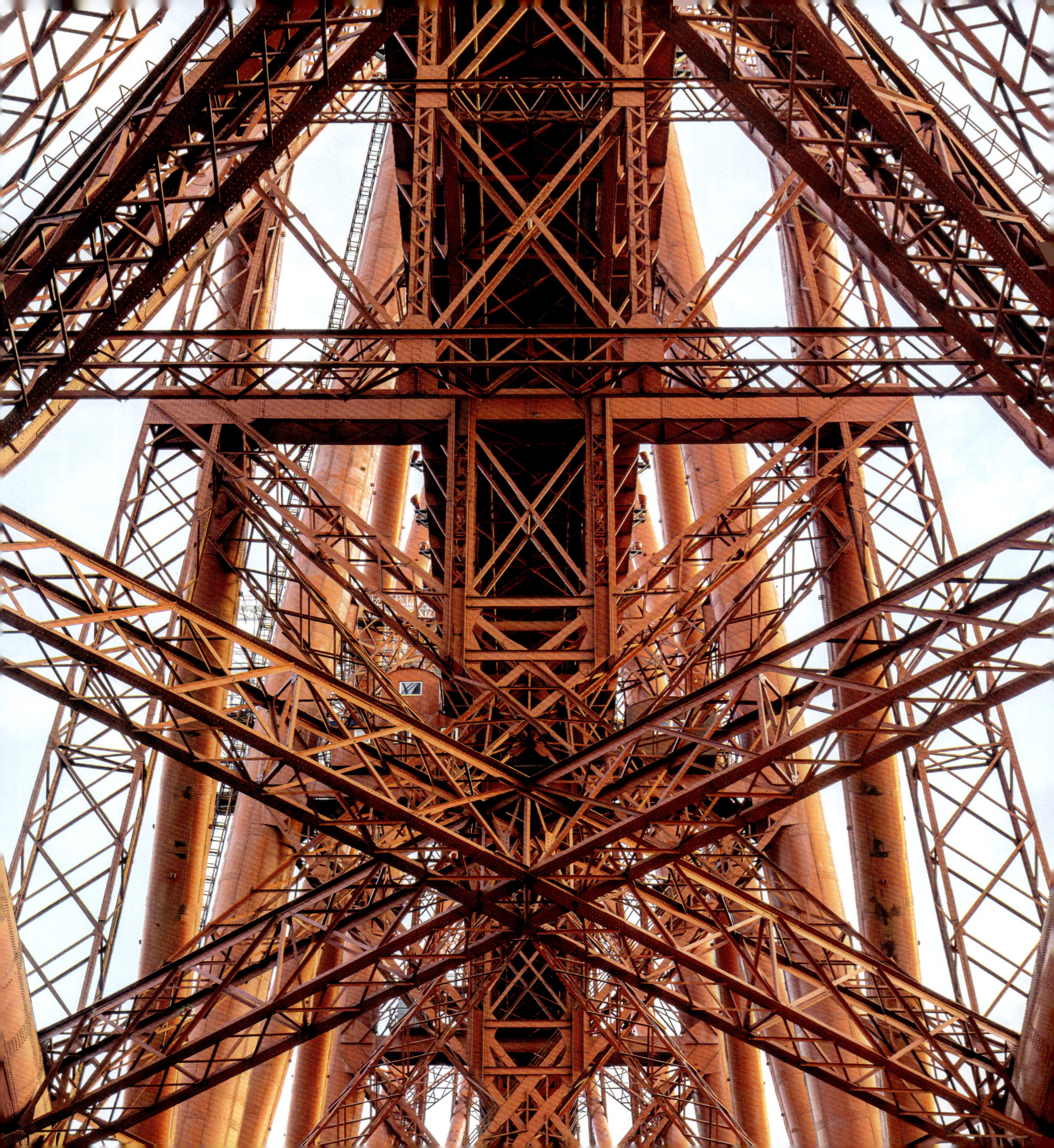

40 FIFE

OCTOBER 2019

DAY 356–361 | 08,702–08,855KM | 153KM

It takes a bracing 2-kilometre walk over the Tay Road Bridge to cross from Dundee into Fife. The goal today is to reach St Andrews via Tentsmuir Forest, and whenever I bring up my journey to anyone local, they gush over the forest. I soon understand why when I witness the intoxicating combination of Corsican and Scots pine growing on the rolling dunes, with some trails leading directly to sandy beaches and views of the North Sea. After an hour of walking amid the rustling of leaves, the gentle rhythm of waves and the melodic calls of birds, I feel as though I've absorbed the forest's tranquillity into my very being.

After waking from a deep sleep among the dunes, the first sign of life as I approach St Andrews is a young man being stripped by a gang of friends on the famous golf course. I turn the corner to see a woman, arms bound, being led along the street with a leash by a group dressed in angel wings and fluffy haloes. Bemused, I ask a passing student what's going on. 'Oh, it's Raisin Weekend. It's a small town here; we have to make our fun. Sometimes, pranks get repaid over the generations. It can get pretty complicated!' he adds with a chuckle. A cafe in the centre proudly advertises itself as the place *where Kate met Wills (for coffee)*. On the beach, a gaggle of female students with trilling Home Counties accents enact bizarre rituals for their friends on camera. One holds a cocktail aloft while standing up to her waist in the freezing ocean. I keep walking and witness a pair of American students enacting a drunken (and impressively word-perfect) rendition of *Romeo and Juliet* from street to balcony. And then, as suddenly as it disappeared, the windswept silence of the coast path returns.

On my third day of walking, I arrive at Anstruther and spot a soulful-looking man staring out at Bass Rock with his guitar lying next to him. I can't resist taking a photo, which in the square format, looks like an album cover. When I show it to him, he tells me he comes here to serenade the place where his wife's ashes are scattered, before adding, 'Aye, you got my bald spot nicely – very artistic!'

I carry on, smitten by the villages on the Fife coast – Crail, Cellardyke, Pittenweem and St Monans – where every settlement seems more beautiful than the last. But I must have crossed some invisible border when the burns I step over are no longer peaty golden brown. As I get closer to Edinburgh, the coastal settlements get larger and the distance between them smaller.

At Jonathan's Cave below the village of East Wemyss, I'm astonished to be able to make out Pictish rock engravings, which show a Viking longboat, possibly the oldest drawing of a ship in Scotland. I start to see some English attitudes slipping across the border with the return of the *Private* sign, a delightful absence throughout most of the Scottish countryside. At Burntisland, the Norse influence is now in the form of hygge rather than pillaging when I stop off at a Scandinavian-inspired cafe, 'Høme of the røasting project'.

Back on the trail, I get a surprise visit from an Alsatian, whose idea of a greeting is sinking its teeth into my derriere. 'Sorry, pal,' the owner mumbles, as if this sort of thing happens every day. When I tell this story later to an Edinburger, he replies with a twinkle in his eye, 'Aye, it takes a lang spoon tae sup with a Fifer.' Only in Scotland could a dog bite lead to such profound wisdom about the art of socialising.

On my sixth and final day in Fife, I make a big push from Kirkcaldy to reach the Forth Bridges before darkness. The effort pays off, and I cross the Forth Road Bridge as the sun sets. For four years and 362 days of walking, I've dreamt of crossing here with the iconic rail bridge at my side, and tonight I did. Tomorrow I'll arrive in Scotland's capital.

Opposite:

Under the Forth Bridge, North Queensferry

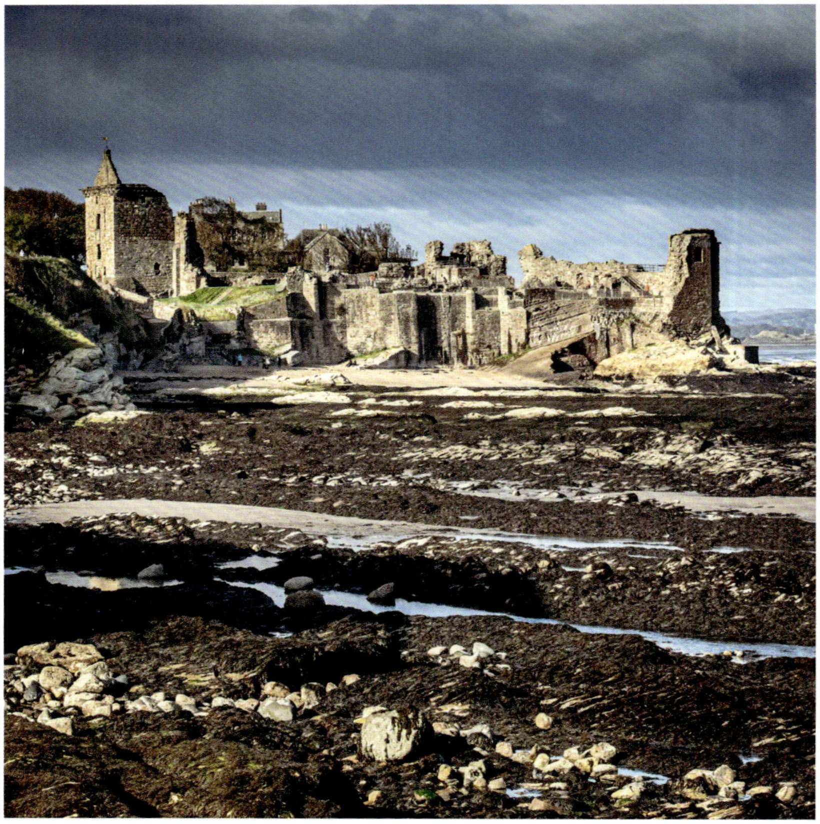

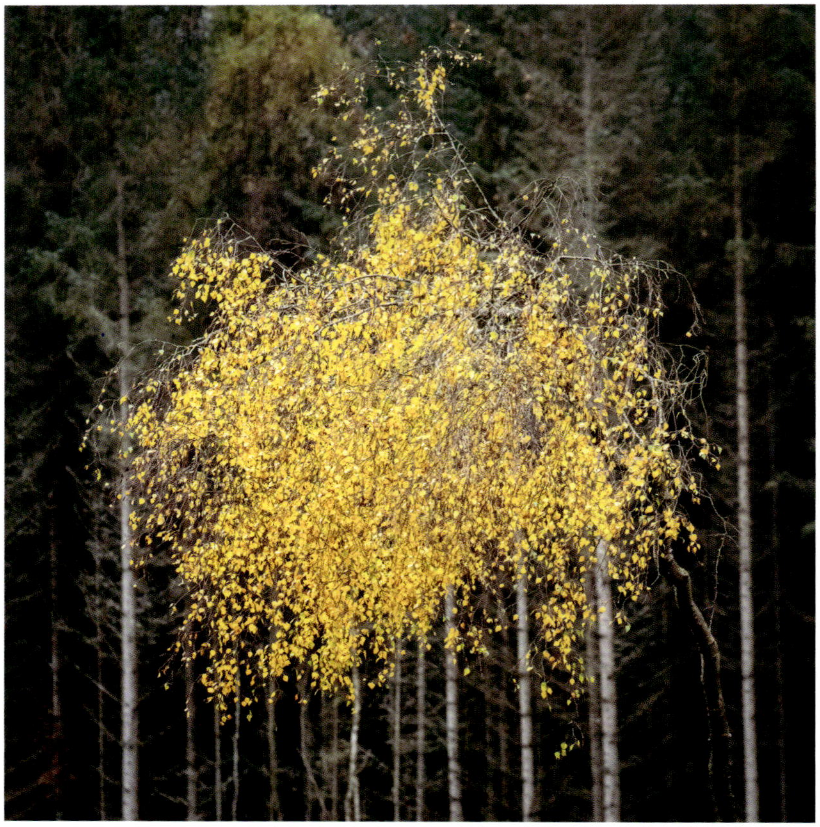

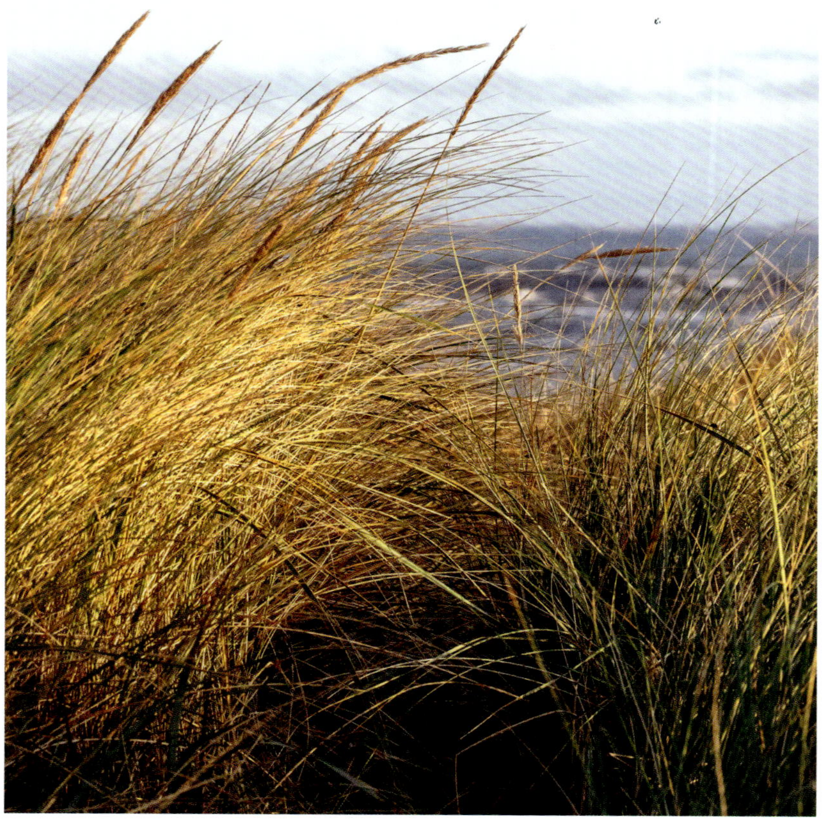

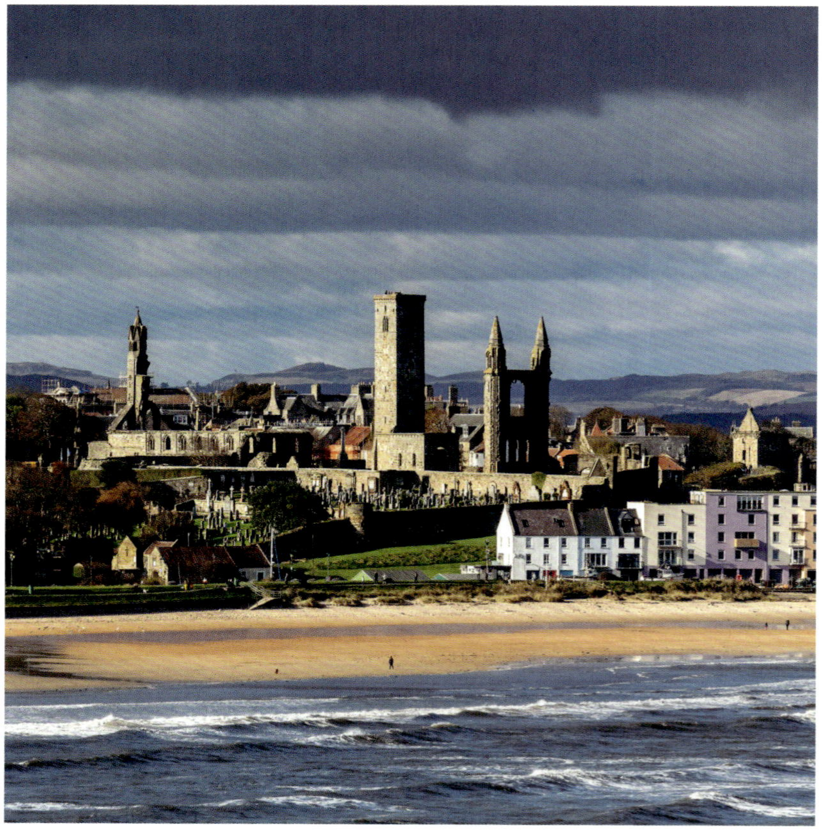

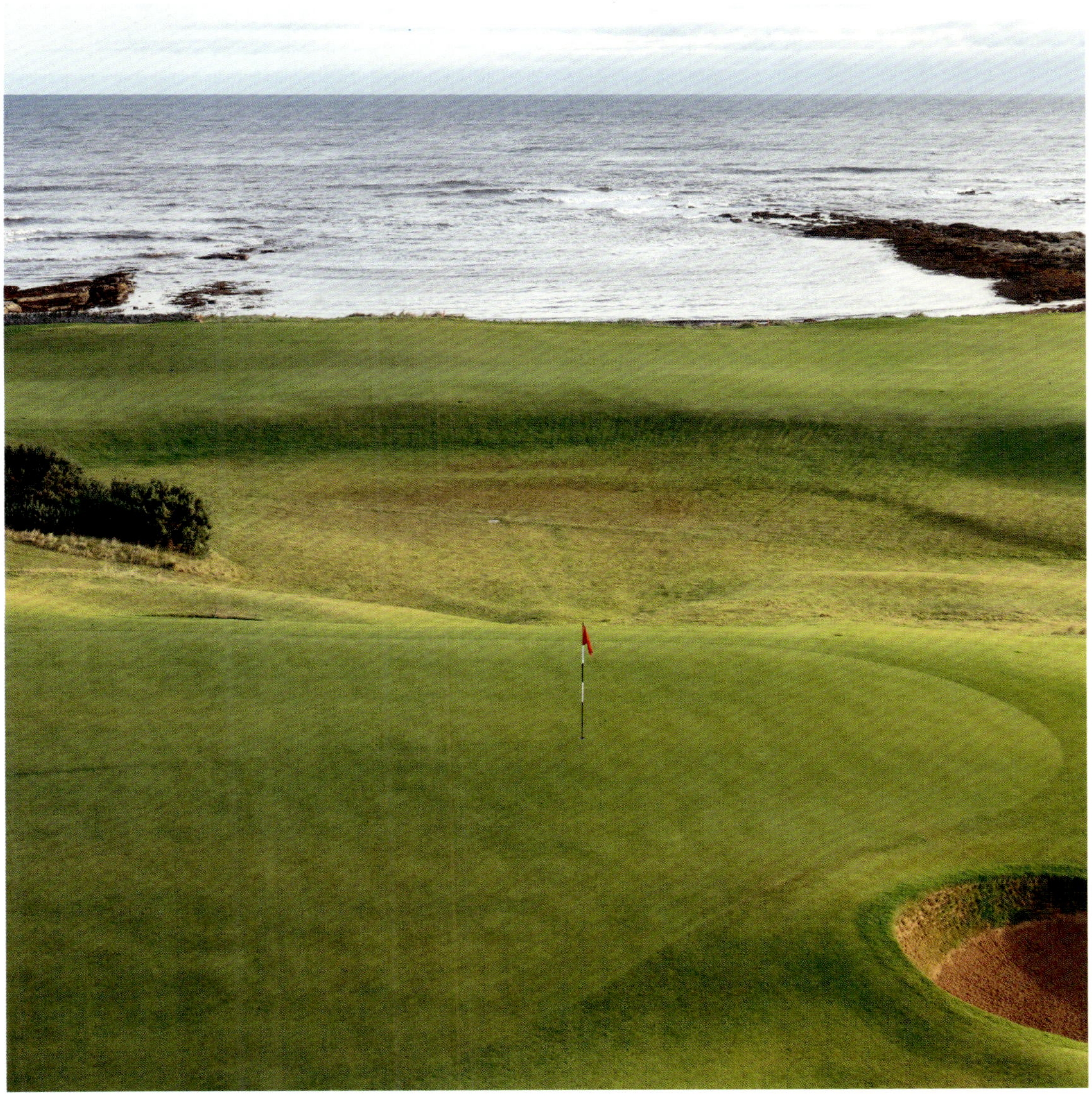

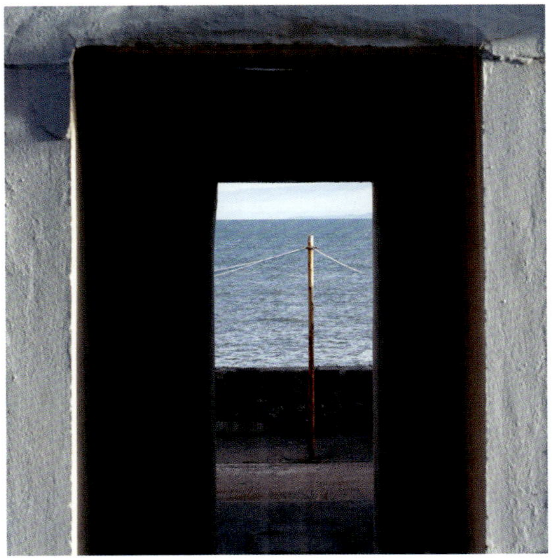

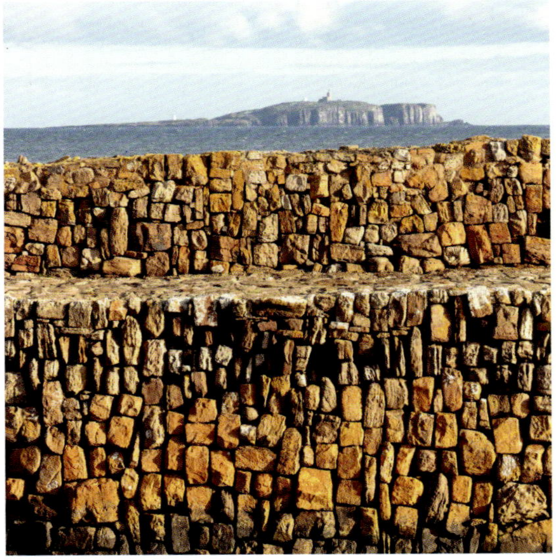

Opposite, from top left:

St Andrews Castle, built c.1200 and fell into ruin after the trials and tribulations of the Scottish Reformation by 1656

Tentsmuir Forest

From bottom left:

Dune grass by West Sands, St Andrews Bay

St Andrews Cathedral rises above East Sands after being abandoned in 1661, two years after it was destroyed in the Reformation

From top left:

Kingsbarns Golf Links

The Firth of Forth from George Street in Cellardyke

Cellardyke Harbour wall with the Isle of May

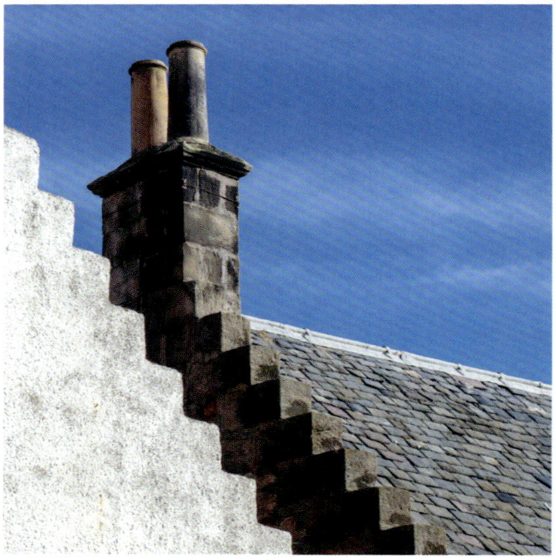

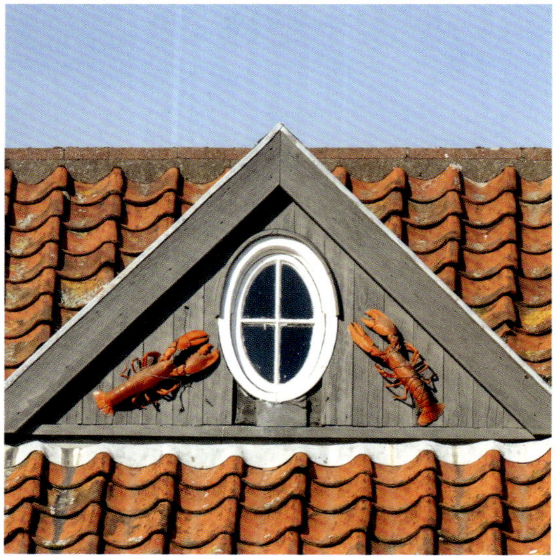

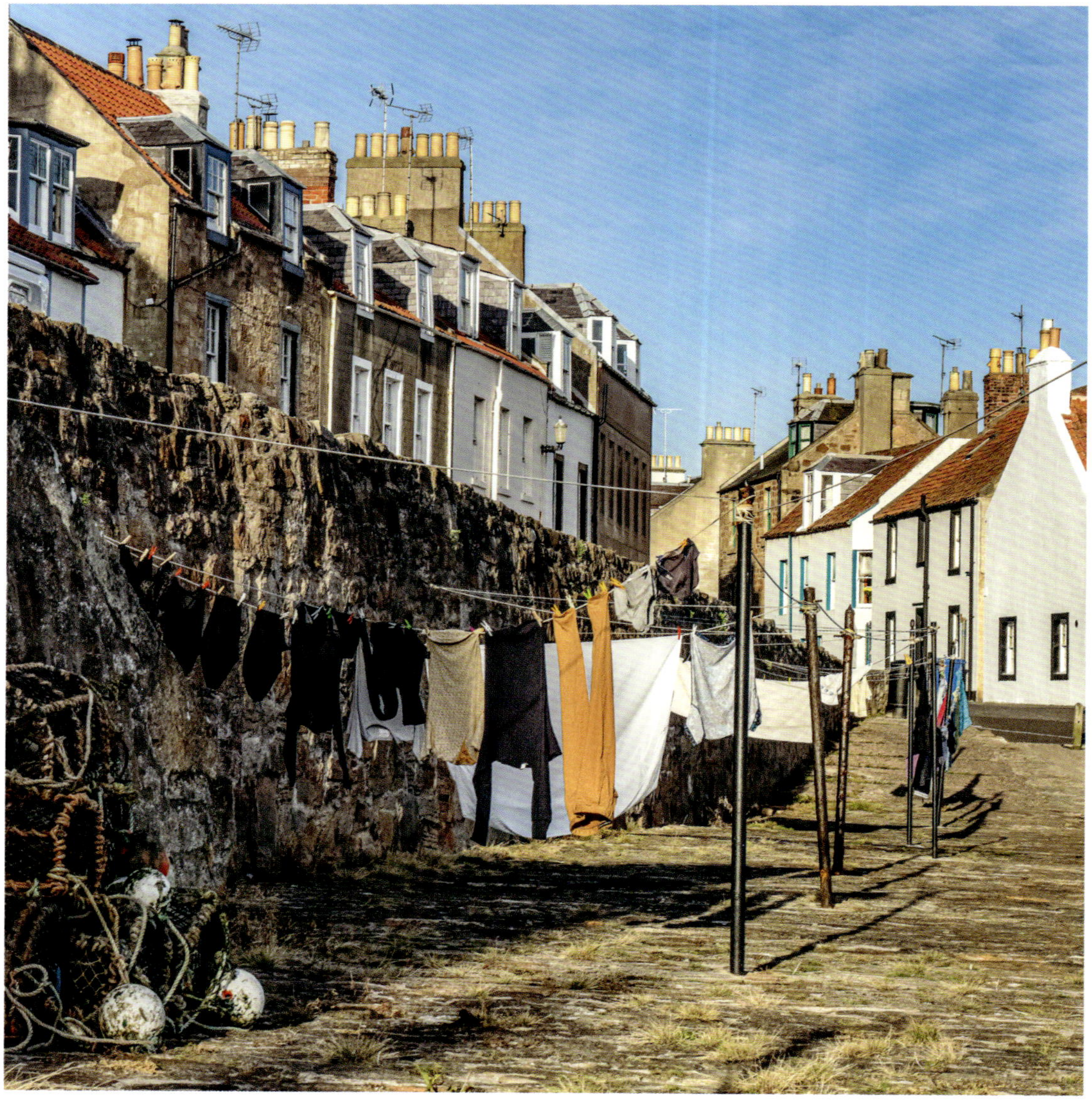

From top left:

Crow-stepped gables, Crail

Lobsters, Crail

Washing day, Cellardyke Harbour

Opposite, from top left:

St Monans Auld Kirk

The Ship Inn, Elie

From bottom left:

East Vows Beacon, Elie. Constructed in 1847 by Alan Stevenson, the cage was intended as a refuge for shipwrecked mariners

Fishers of men: St Monans Auld Kirk

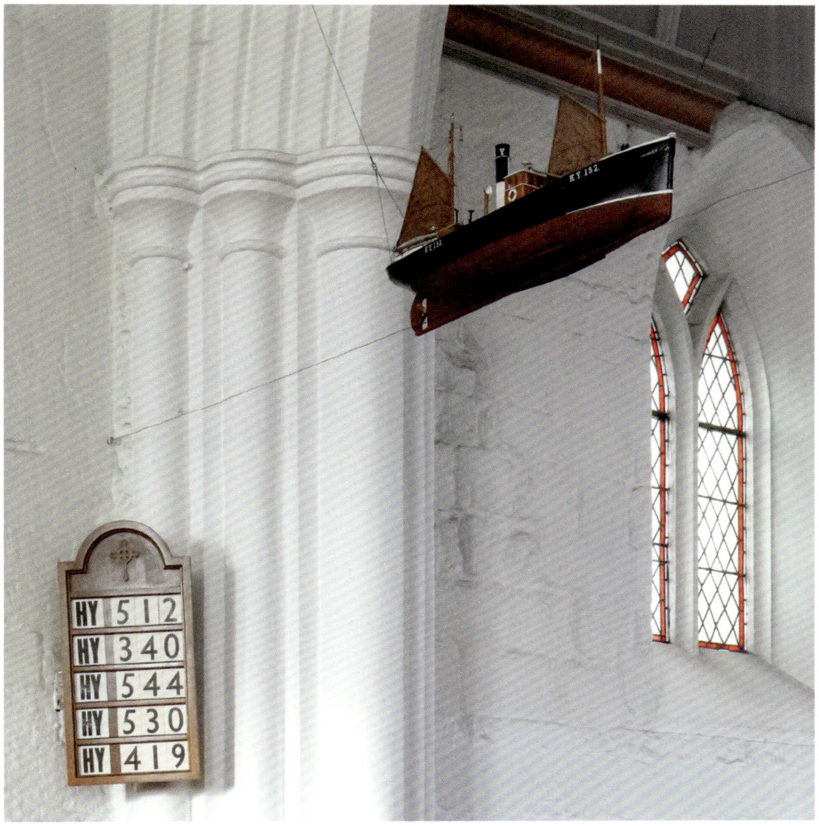
HY 512
HY 340
HY 544
HY 530
HY 419

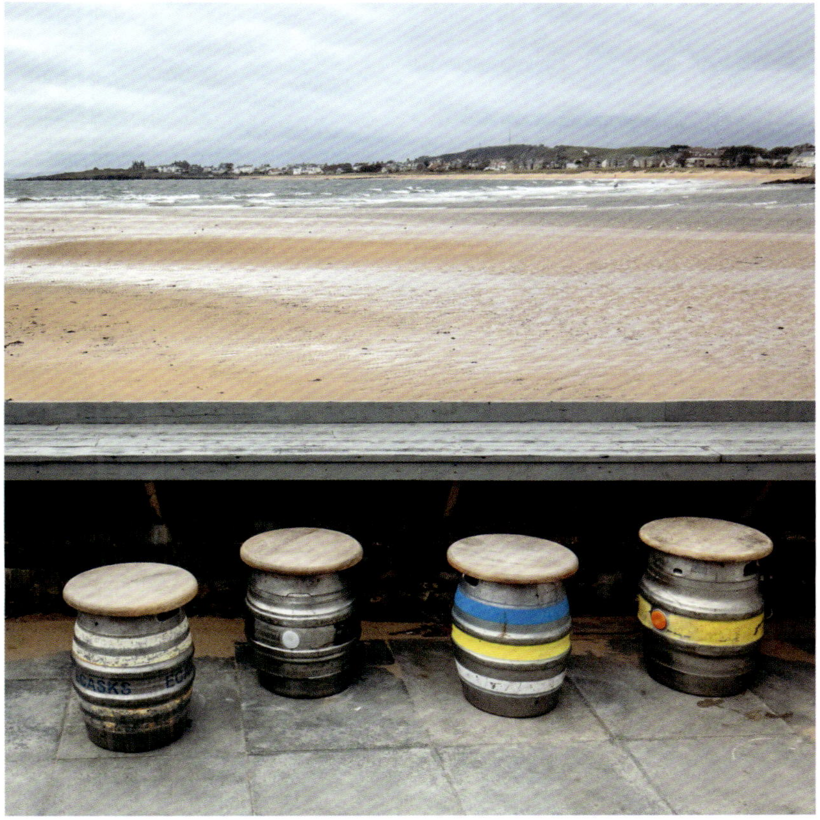

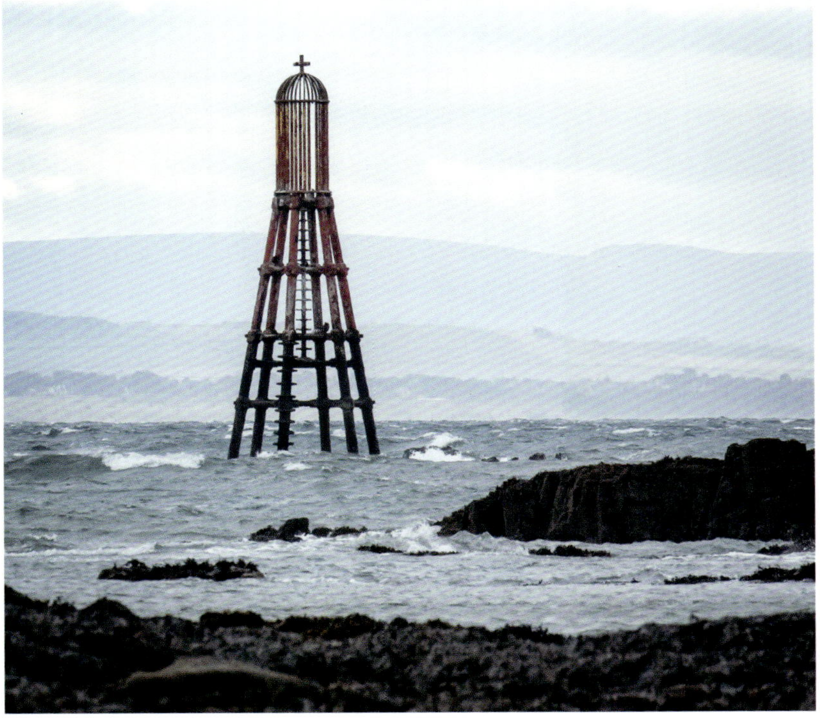

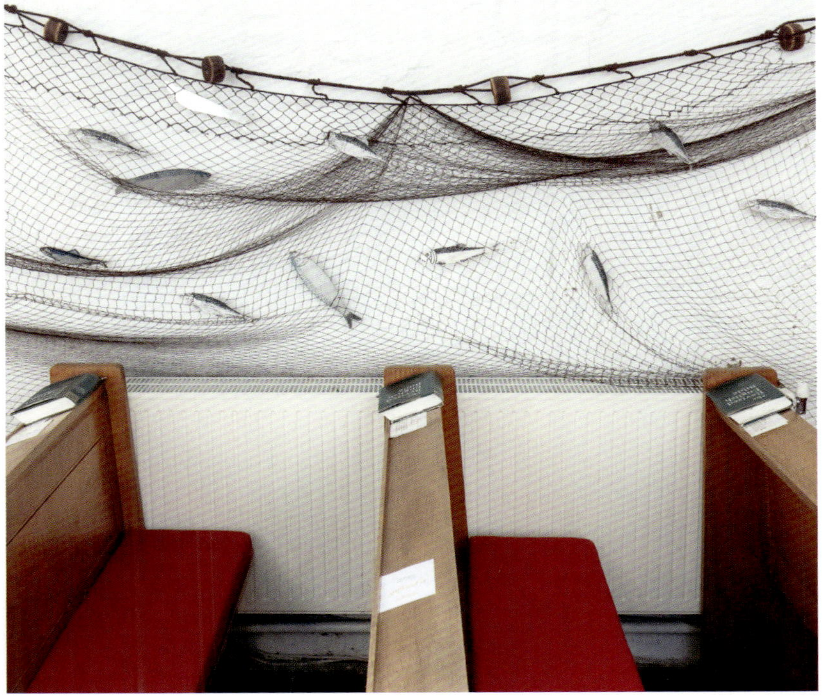

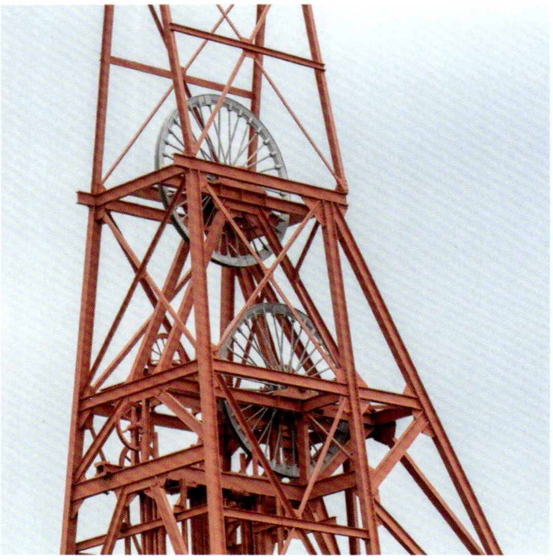

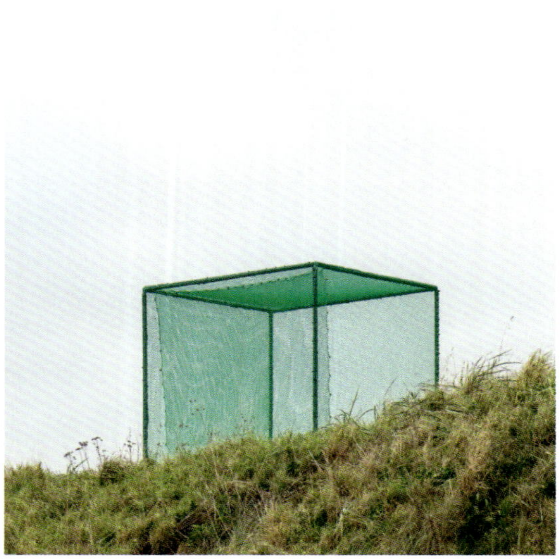

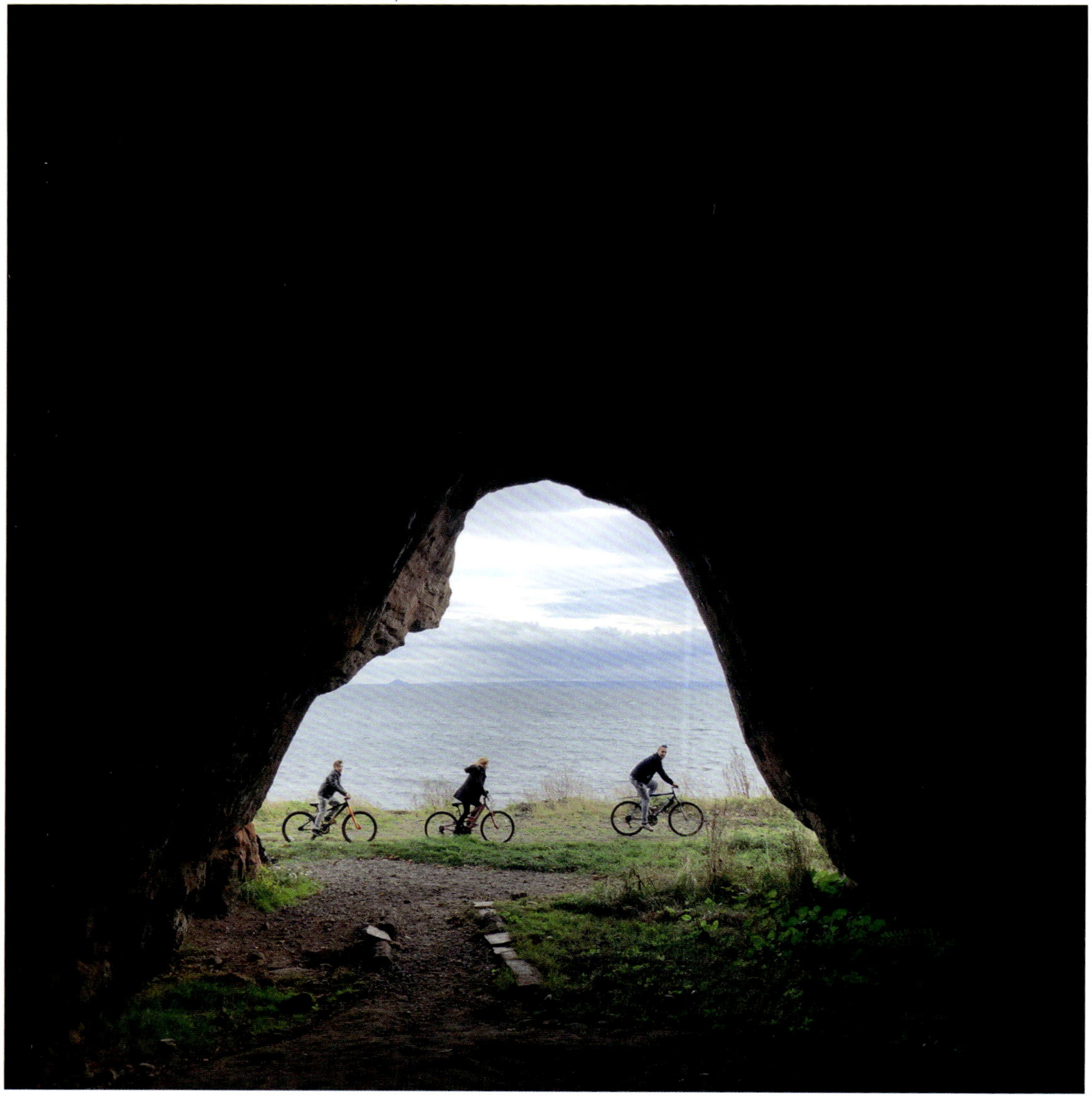

From top left:

Headframe at the former Frances Colliery, Dysart. Sunk *c.*1850 and closed in 1985, Frances worked under-sea coals from its clifftop location and was known locally as 'the Dubbie' because of its wet under-ground conditions. At its peak it employed 1,482

Lundin Links

Doo Cave, a rare example of a medieval cave dovecot. Doo, like the other Wemyss caves, also contains Pictish carvings

Opposite:

Criss-cross: Queensferry crossing at dusk

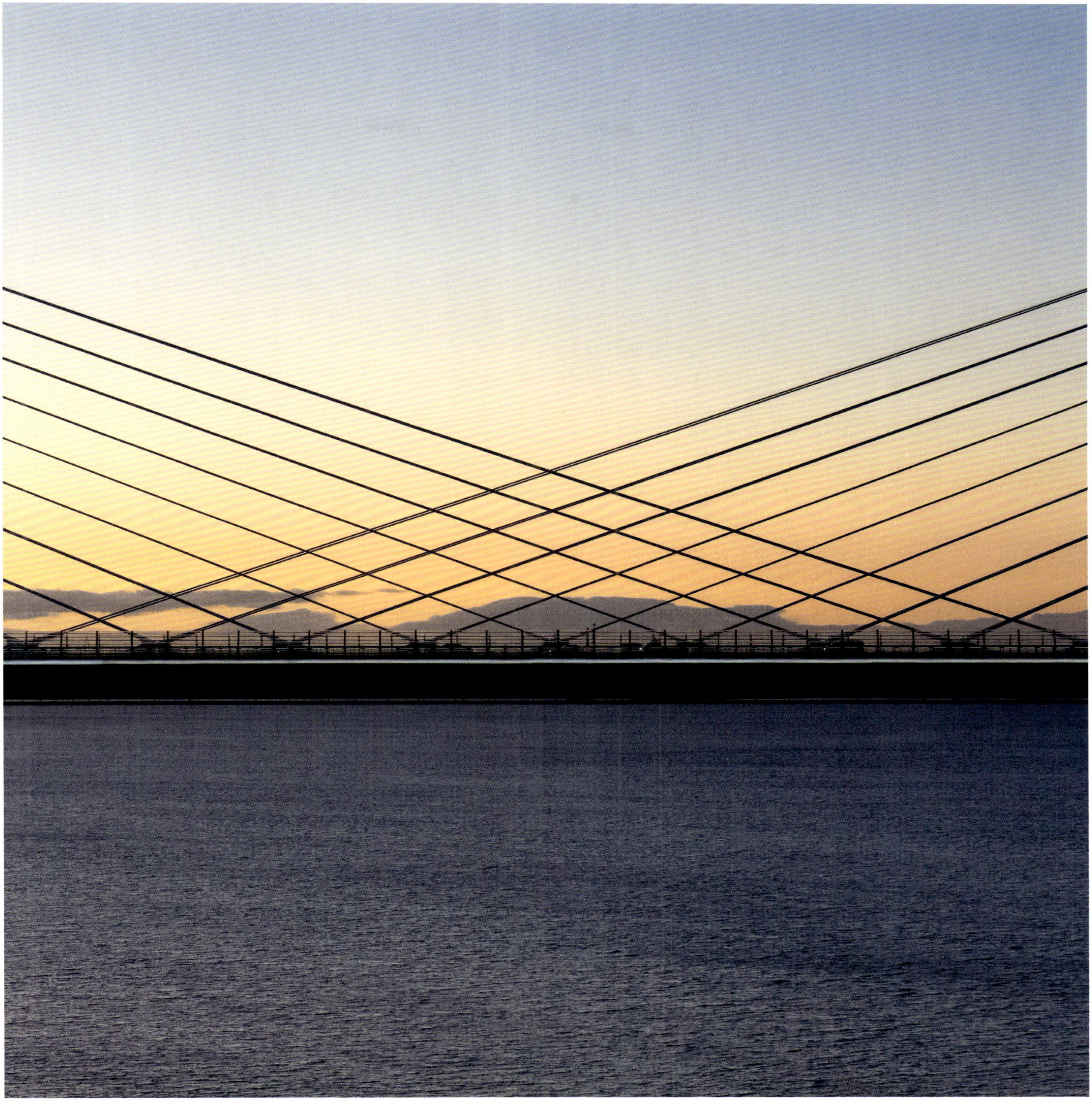

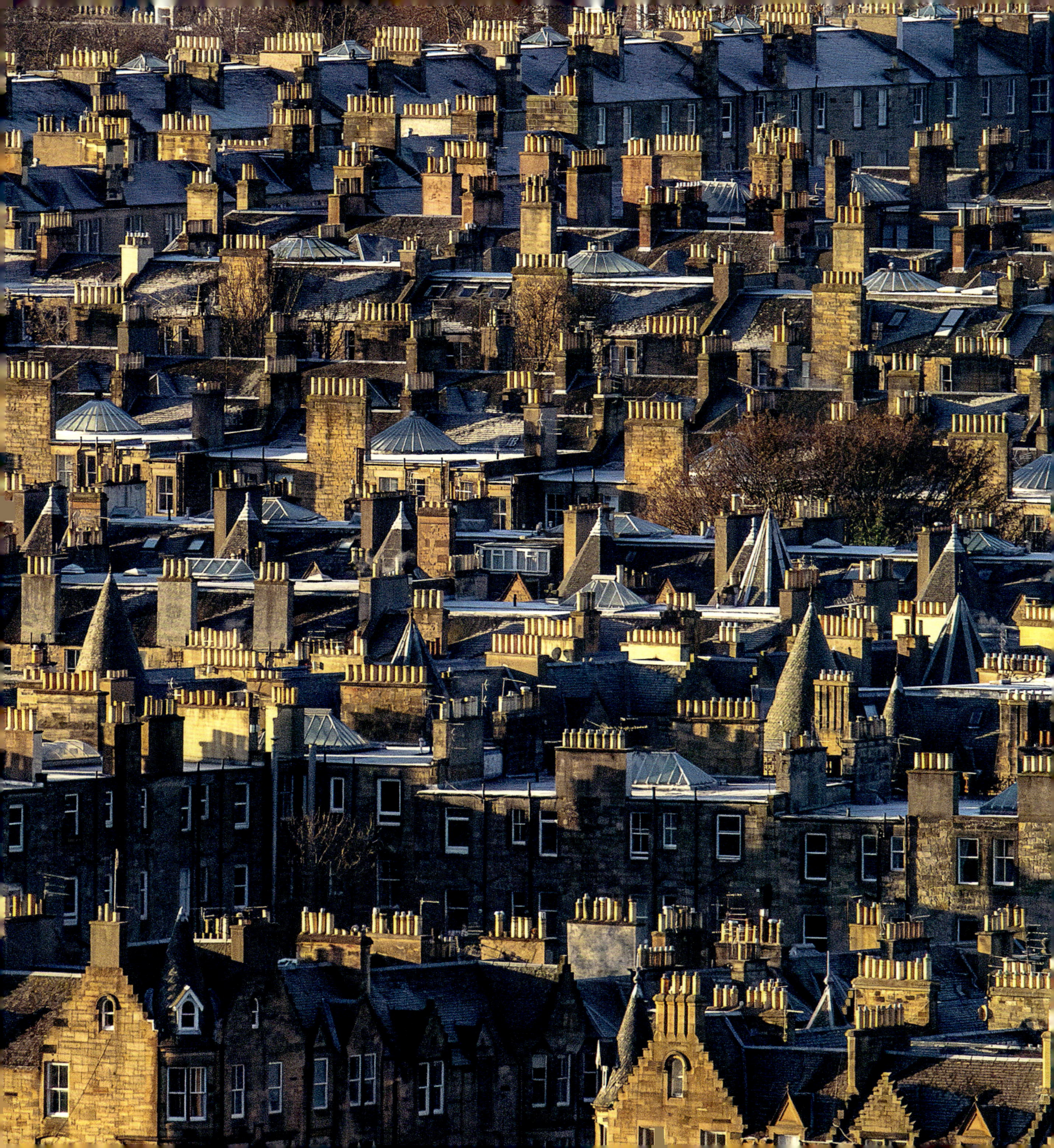

41 MIDLOTHIAN

DECEMBER 2019

DAY 362–363 | 08,855–08,891KM | 36KM

Months of walking past clearance villages and Highland crofts have created abiding memories of the Scottish landscape, so it comes as a jolt to pass the rarefied wealth and grandeur of the Dalmeny Estate with its vast manor house, manicured grounds and equine sculpture. It's an incongruous sight, standing as it does just a stone's throw away from the untamed beauty of the wooded banks of the River Almond. Opposite the mouth of the river, I spot Cramond Island, from where a line of 3-metre pointed concrete pyramids, Second World War fast boat defences, emerges from the shallow tidal water like a row of vicious teeth.

Being so close to Scotland's capital, the third and final capital city encountered on this journey, it is hard to focus on anything else as I continue to make my way along the Forth, past unspoiled and peaceful beaches. As I get nearer to Edinburgh, the houses become more spacious and Georgian architecture more prevalent before I share the central streets rammed with locals and other tourists alike. But, for me, arrival at my cheap, windowless B&B bedroom is heralded by a *No Food Allowed in this Kettle* label – surely the sign of a quality establishment!

Like Prague or Oxford, Edinburgh is so attractive that it's hard to take a photo with any authorship – but it's a joy to try in the four days I'm here before returning to the trail. The creative challenge comes when cities are designed with consideration: the views, silhouettes and spatial relationships have been so thoughtfully conceived all one can do with the camera is portray the ideas of others, either more or less powerfully.

I spend a few cold and luminous days exploring Edinburgh, catching the sunrise over the city from Arthur's Seat, the last kiss of light on Edinburgh Castle, a frosty morning on Blackford Hill and sunset at Calton Hill. The biggest surprise is the wild mountain feel of walking along the tops of Salisbury Crags, the remains of an underground magma intrusion. It's incredible that I can wander these lofty cliffs and, minutes later, be back in the heart of a metropolis.

I visit the National Museum of Scotland to admire the light-filled three-storey interior of the Grand Gallery, which was inspired by the airy elegance of the Crystal Palace. As daylight wanes, I ascend to the rooftop, greeted by vistas that stir the soul. Camera in hand, I frame the delicate filigree of St Giles's High Kirk's crown steeple against the fading light, and the radiant Golden Boy perched atop the University of Edinburgh's dome. Twilight is sudden at this time of year, so I don't have long to wait for a spine-tingling view of Edinburgh Castle, windows glowing against the lingering sunset. I leave the museum exhilarated; I've captured a week's worth of images in the last few hours.

I'm obsessed with photographing the serried ranks of beautiful chimney pots that gave the city its nickname, 'Auld Reekie', from the stinking smoke these thousands of chimneys once belched out. There's something slightly precious and pompous about the New Town, especially in comparison to the raw energy of Glasgow. There seem to be a lot of yoga establishments, and I get the feeling a lot of time is spent choosing just the right shade of paint to complement the airy Georgian architecture.

Close to Christmas, Princes Street is lit artfully, and I want to take a traffic-light-trail photo from Calton Hill. It seems every other photographer in Edinburgh has exactly the same idea. There's a small icy mound with just the right elevation for a compelling image. Comic scenes of slipping, swearing and tangles of human and tripod legs ensue.

Opposite:

Edinburgh chimneys

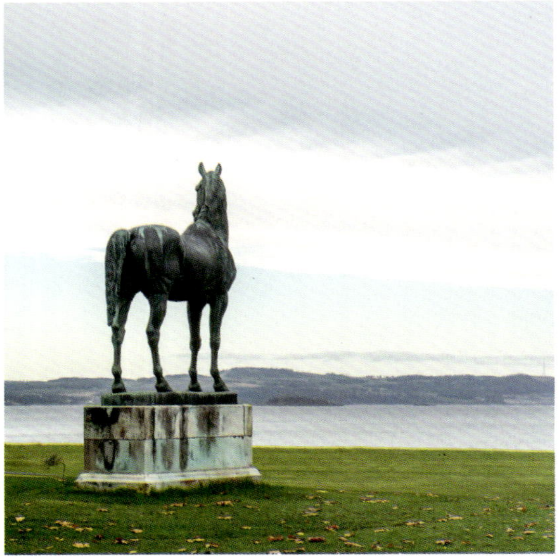

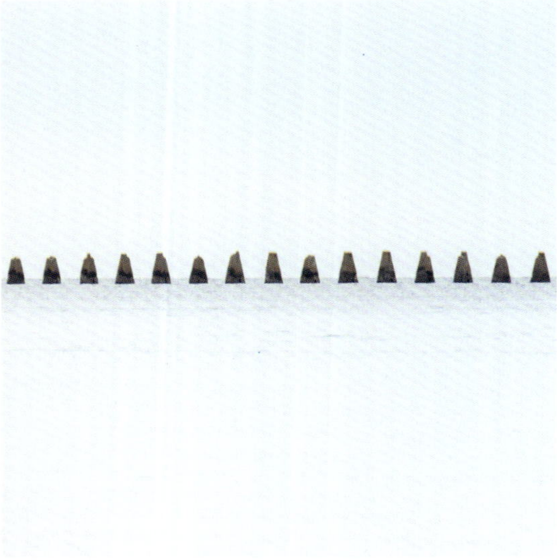

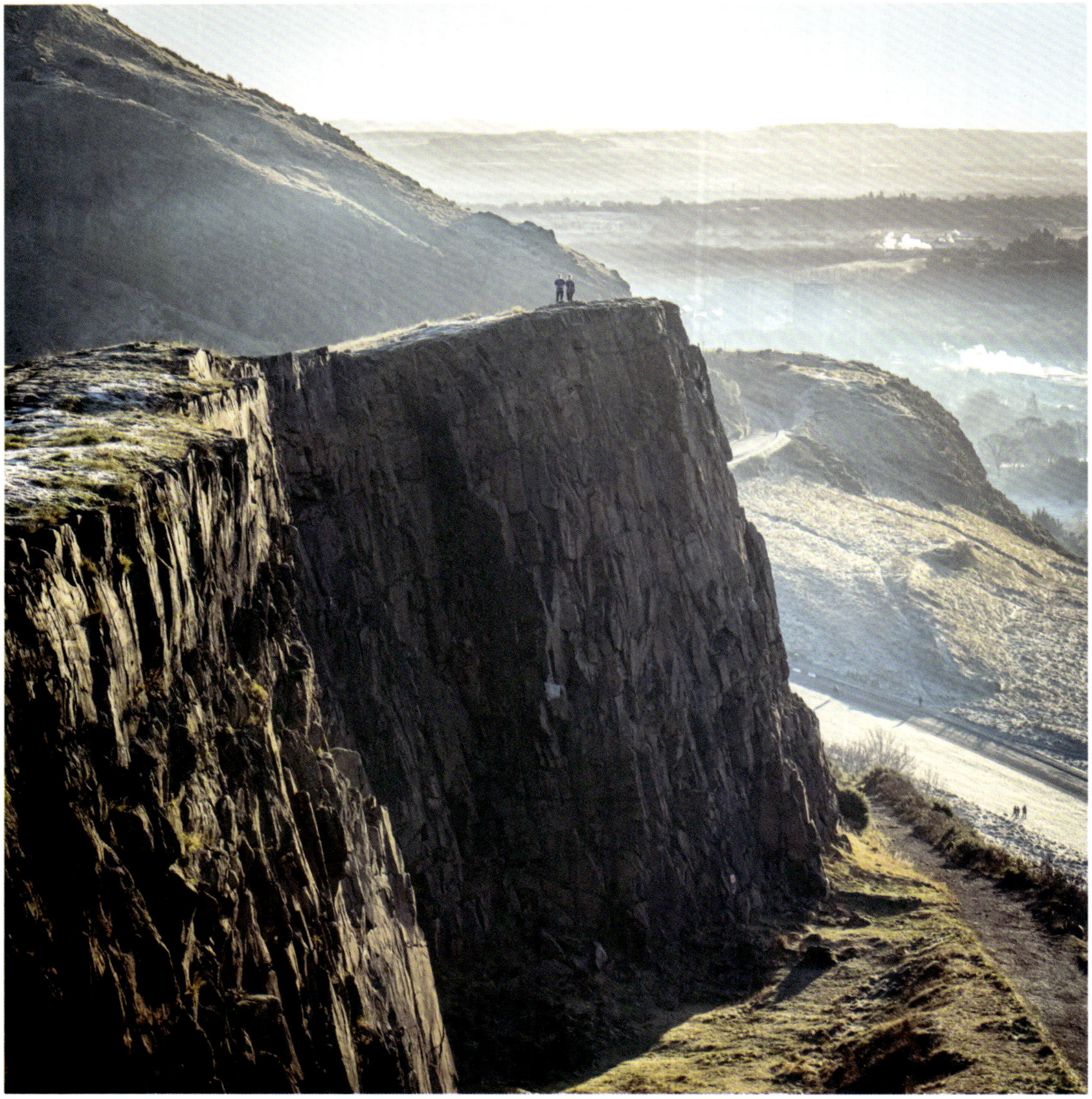

From top left:

King Tom, a bronze statue commemorating a favourite racehorse of the Earl of Rosebery, Dalmeny House

Second World War anti-boat pillars, Cramond Island causeway

Winter's morning at Salisbury Crags, Edinburgh

Opposite, from top left:

Edinburgh spires

Edinburgh Castle atop the rock

From bottom left:

Waiting for sunrise: Arthur's Seat, Edinburgh

Dugald Stewart Monument with laser, Calton Hill, Edinburgh

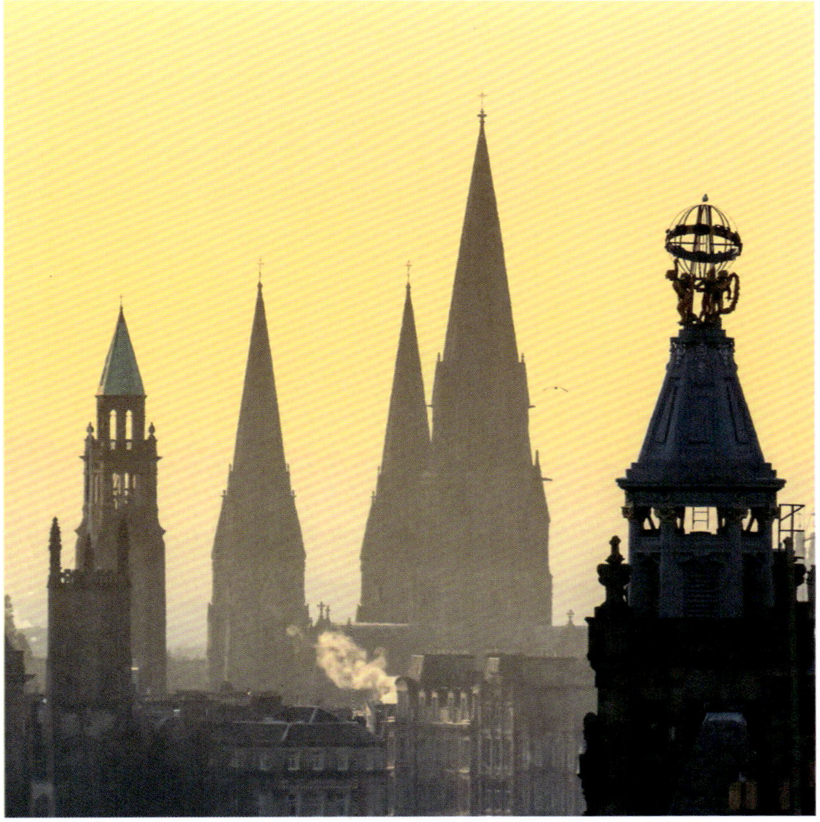

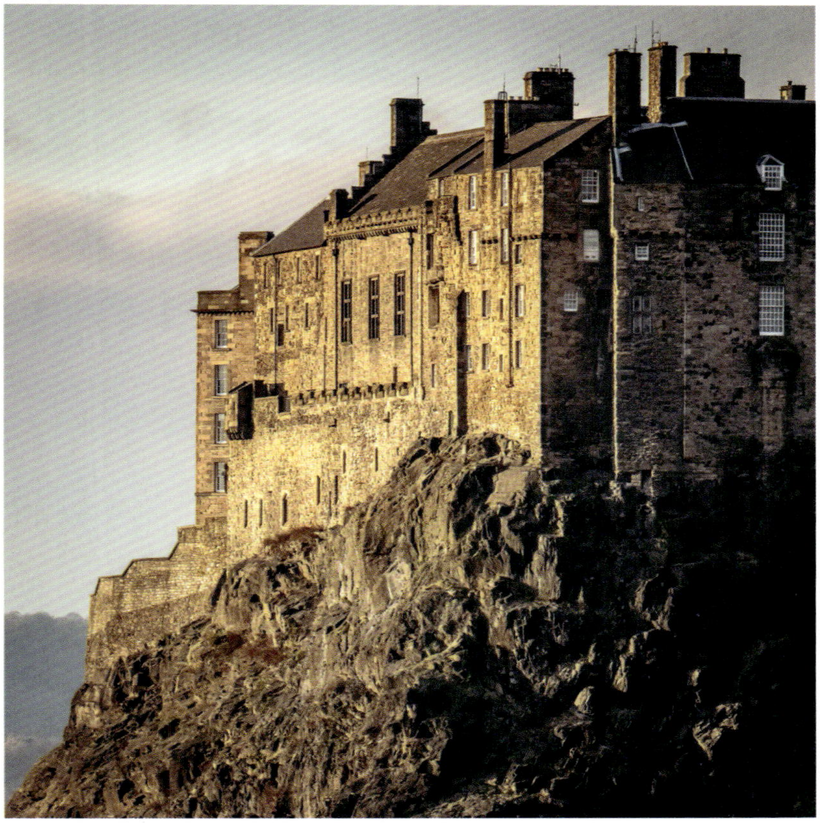

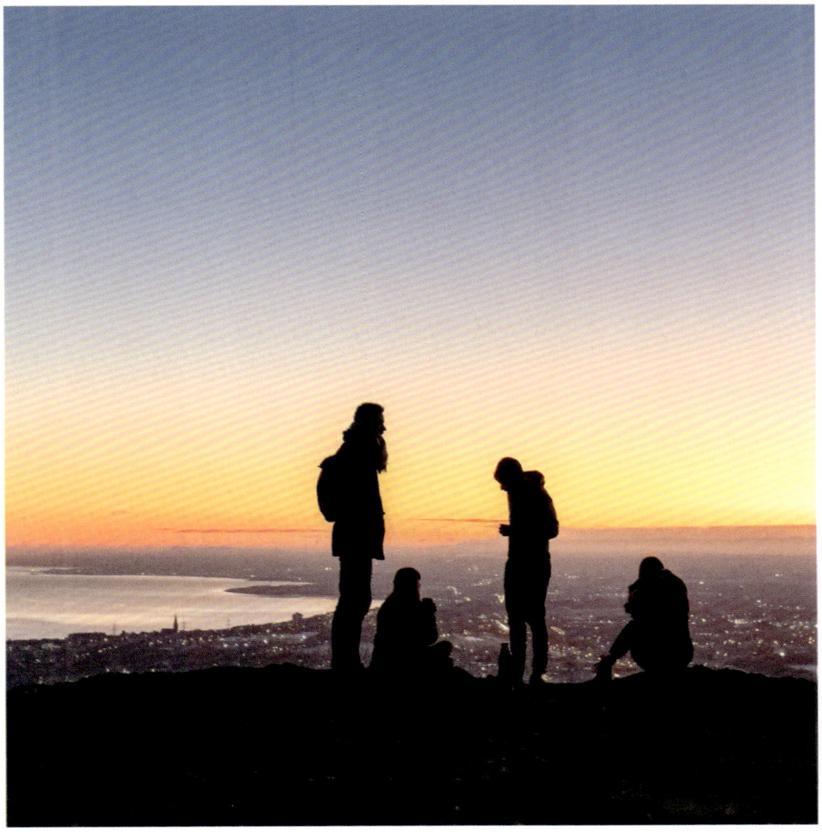

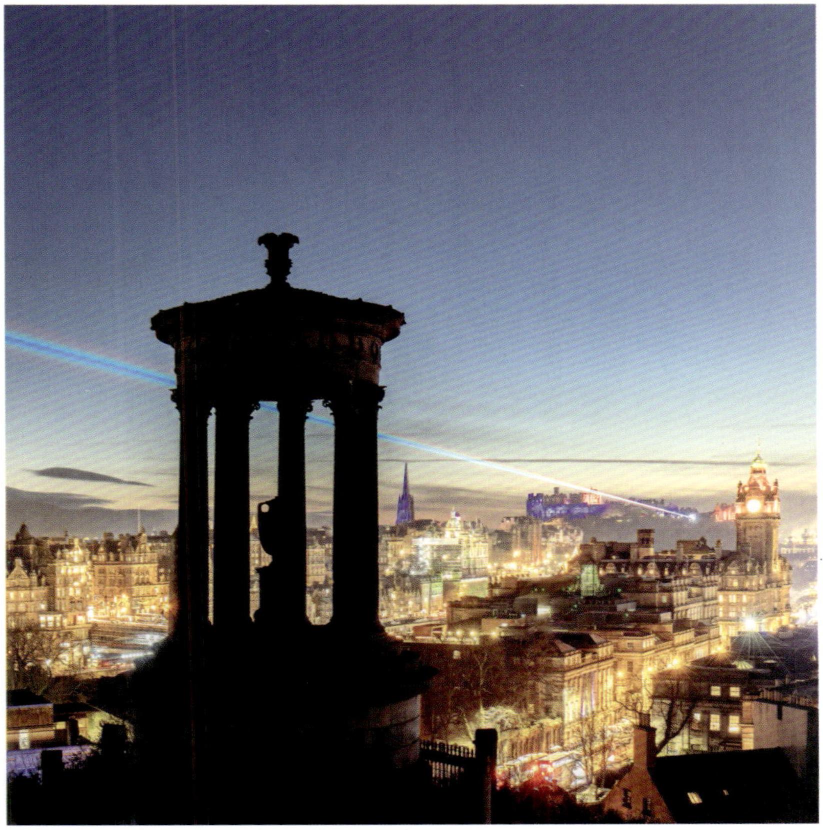

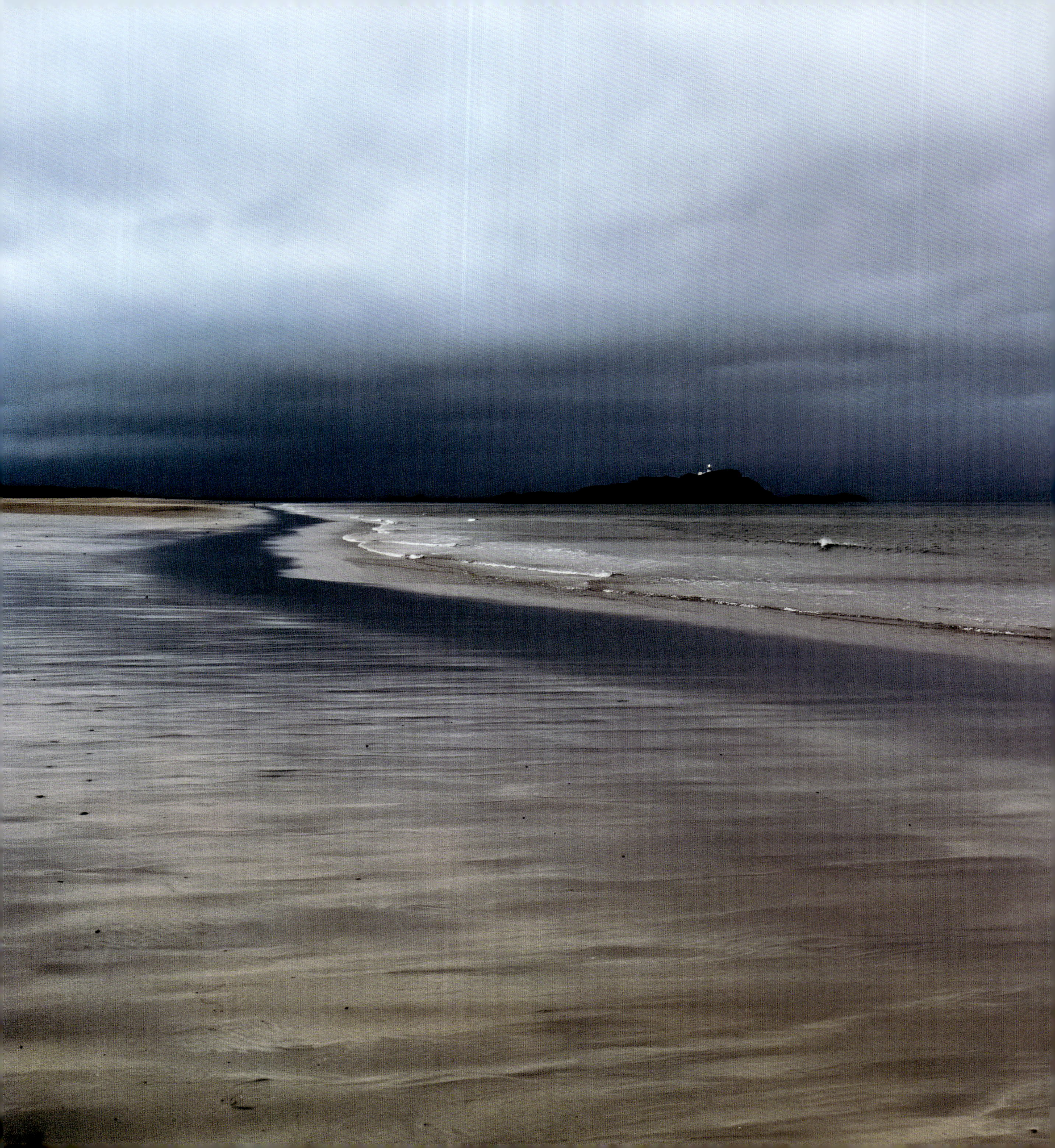

42 EAST LOTHIAN

DECEMBER 2019

DAY 364–367 | 08,891–08,971KM | 80KM

Beyond Musselburgh, beside the ever-expanding Firth of Forth, I'm following the John Muir Way for a few miles but not getting many John Muir vibes along the graffitied concrete sea wall. For a moment, there's a break in the winter squall, and I look behind me to see Portobello and Arthur's Seat lit up below a brooding sky. I can just make out the gleaming white trig point on the summit. A few hours later, after nightfall, while trying to find a path to Gullane Point, I manage to fall into an electric fence while trying to push the wires down with my sticks. I get three bolts before I untangle myself. The sparks are dramatic in the darkness and effective in keeping me awake.

The beach-lined coast towards North Berwick is a journey along rain-hardened sand, a canvas painted with a palette of muted earthy tones. The vibrant oranges of sea buckthorn berries and yellow-green of winter sea grass stand out, contrasting with a sky of tumultuous greys. This mood reaches its crescendo as I pass the tiny island of Fidra in the fading light. The beach, alive with a thin layer of wind-blown sand, blends the colours of the scene, transforming my photos as if nature has applied the oil paint filter. My attention is drawn to the only bright point: the island's pulsating lighthouse.

The following day, I come up close and personal with Bass Rock, which seems like Ailsa Craig's long-lost sister pushed apart forever by the mainland of Scotland. Like its sibling, the rock is a volcanic core that exerts a magnetic pull on my soul, and I can't look away while it's in view. The island seems to reflect the desires of whoever gazes upon it, as it has variously housed a hermitage, castle, chapel, prison and lighthouse.

The English border must be getting close because the castles are enormous, and their histories bloody. Tantallon Castle, located opposite Bass Rock on a rocky promontory above the waves, is especially dramatic, consisting of one immense curtain wall, with the other sides being protected by the cliffs. As I wander around the silent ruins, I learn that Tantallon was besieged by King James IV in 1491 and by his successor, James V, in 1528, when extensive damage was done. The long-suffering castle also saw action in the First Bishops' War in 1639 and again during Oliver Cromwell's invasion of Scotland in 1651, when it was once more severely damaged. I'm struck by the turbulent past of these now peaceful lands.

At Seacliff, within sight of Tantallon, I'm delighted by a tiny harbour carved out of the sandstone, the smallest in Britain. Measuring no more than 12 metres on its longest side, and with an entrance barely 2 metres across, this is a true one-person, one-boat harbour. It was built in 1890 by Andrew Laidley, the then owner of the Seacliff Estate, by using a steam engine and compressed air to cut the stone.

The golden winter light and fascinating locations are great for photography, but come at the expense of forward progress. With the short winter days, I'm less than halfway to Dunbar when it gets dark. But even knowing I am running behind, I can't resist stopping to photograph the Plough above Hedderwick Sands and Belhaven Bridge silhouetted against a starry night.

Not all nights are made for photography, though, and on my last one in East Lothian, a storm emerges. My strategy to weather it is to pitch in the lee of some cliffs and try to shut it out with a good dinner and fairy lights. I realise my plan works a little too well when I wake up in the morning with half the tent collapsed over me. Remarkably, I'd slept through the entire thing! As I fold up my sodden tent, I comprehend that Scotland's elemental essence will not taper off as it nears England but rather retain its drama until the very end.

Opposite:

Fidra from Broad Sands, North Berwick

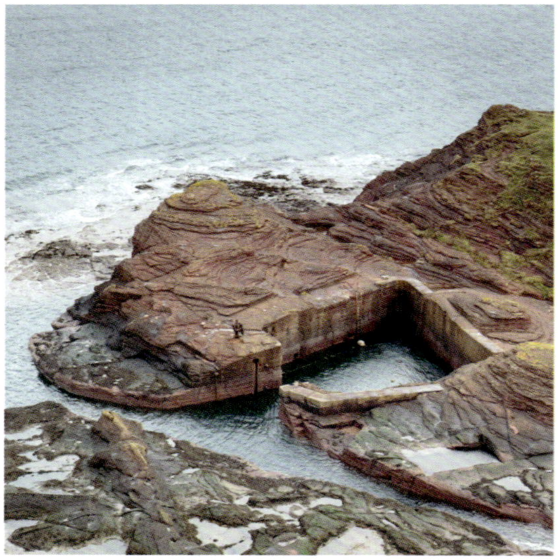
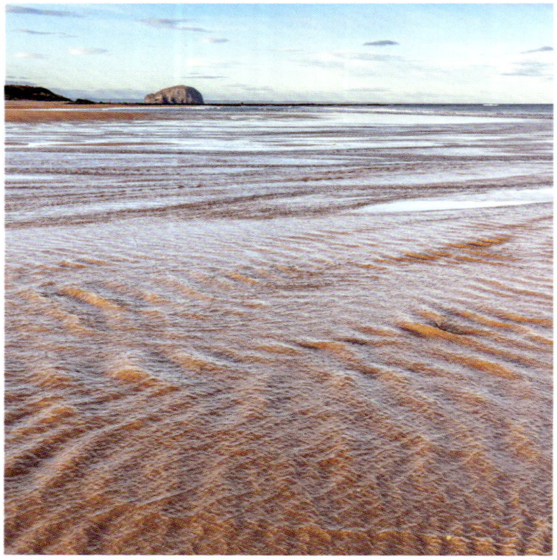
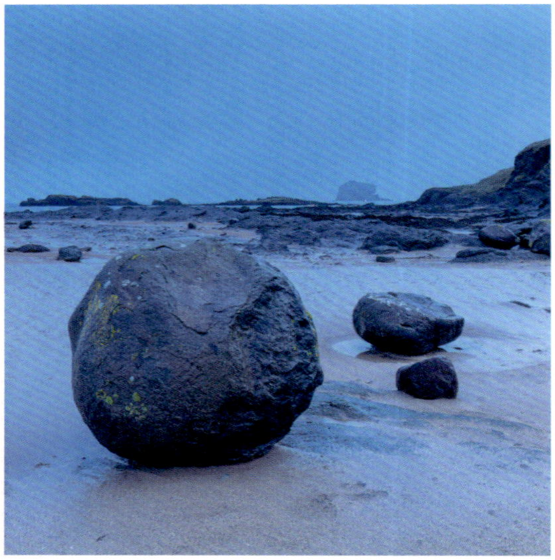
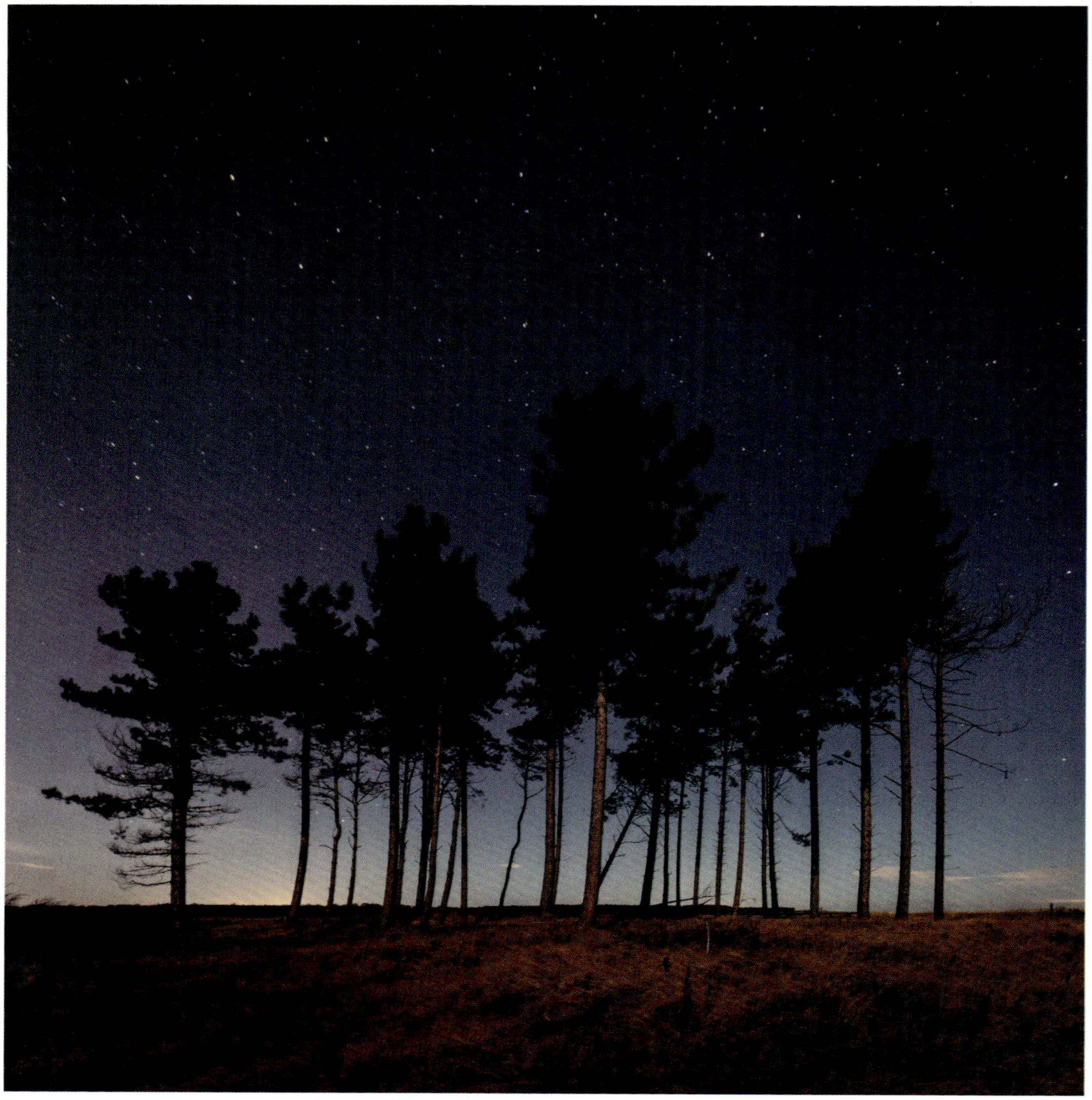
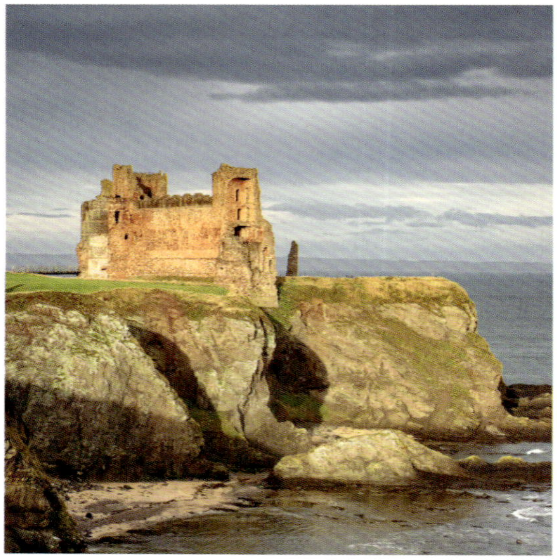
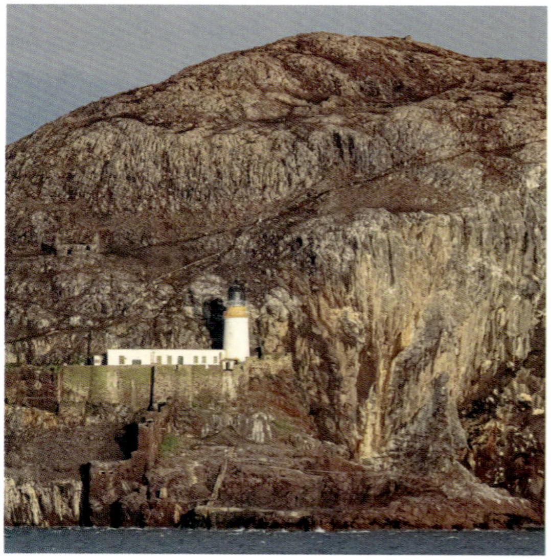

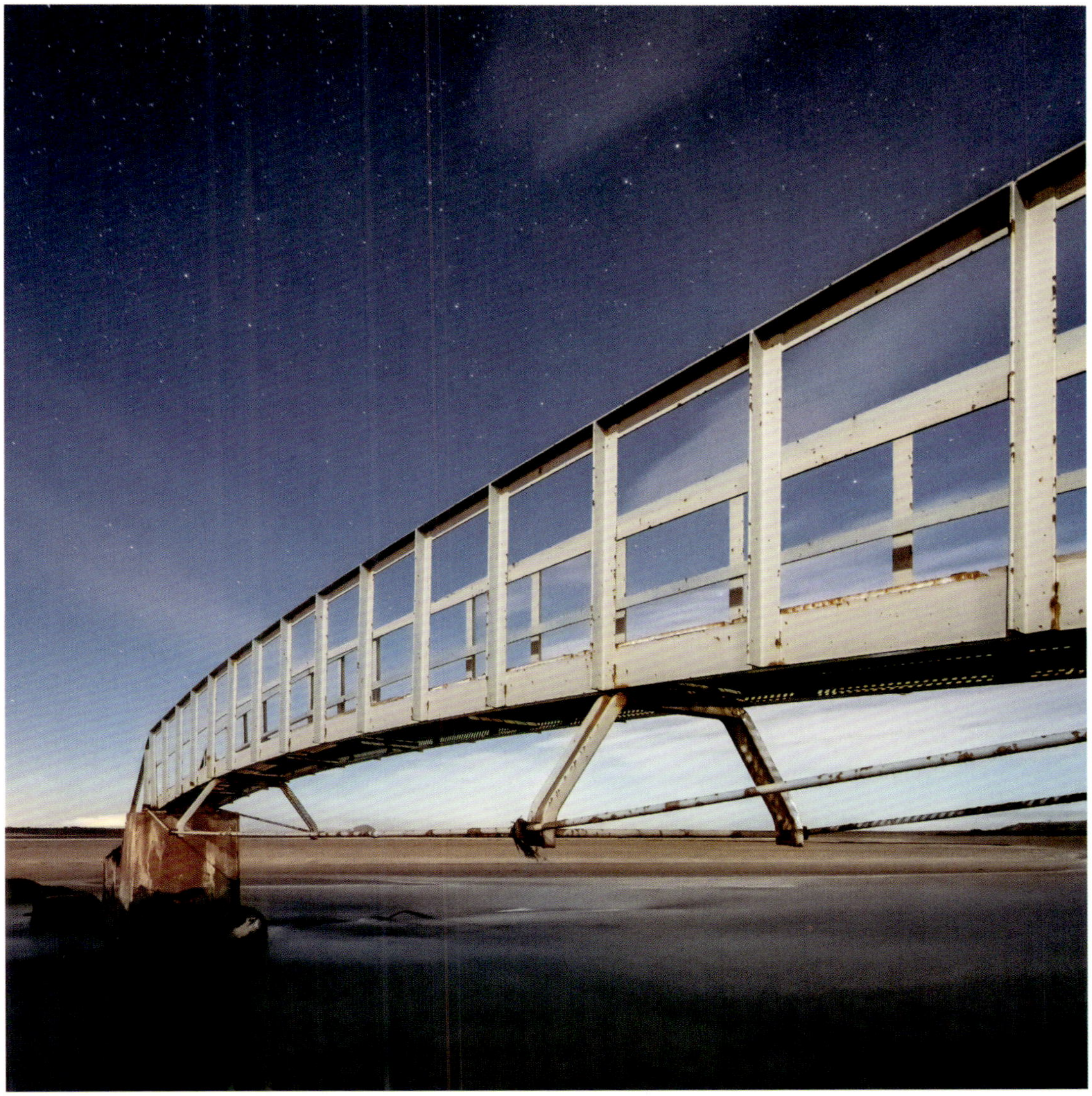

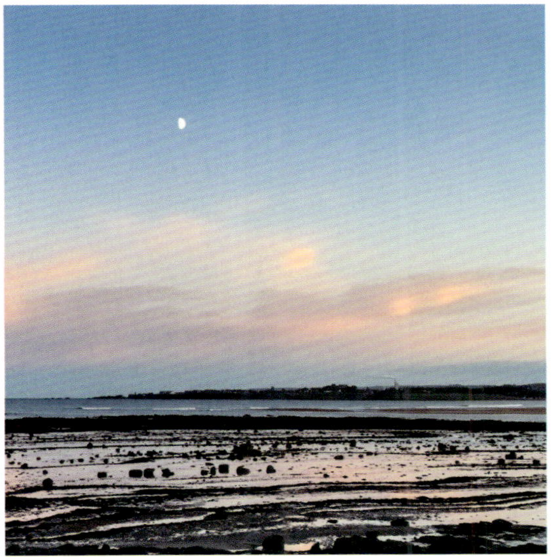

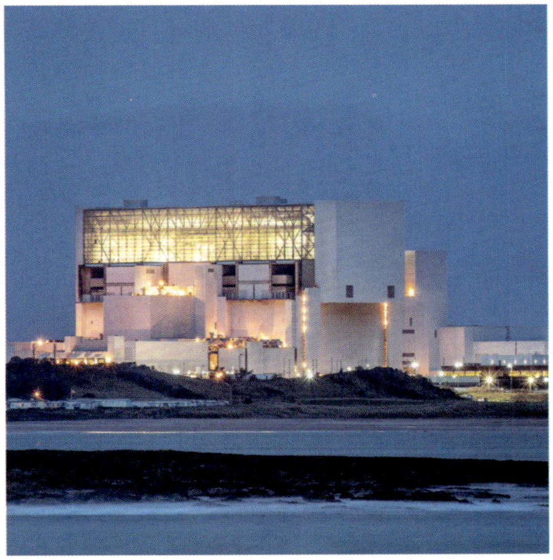

Clockwise from top left:

Seacliff, the UK's smallest harbour

Where the burn meets the sea with Bass Rock, Peffer Sands

Bass Rock at dawn from Milsey Bay, North Berwick

Tantallon Castle was built in 1350 and consists of one massive wall blocking off the headland

Bass Rock Lighthouse

By Hedderwick Sands

From top left:

Belhaven Bridge under a starry sky, Dunbar. Also known as the 'Bridge to Nowhere' as it sits like an island surrounded by an expanse of sea at high tide

Tyne Mouth and Dunbar

Torness nuclear power station at dusk

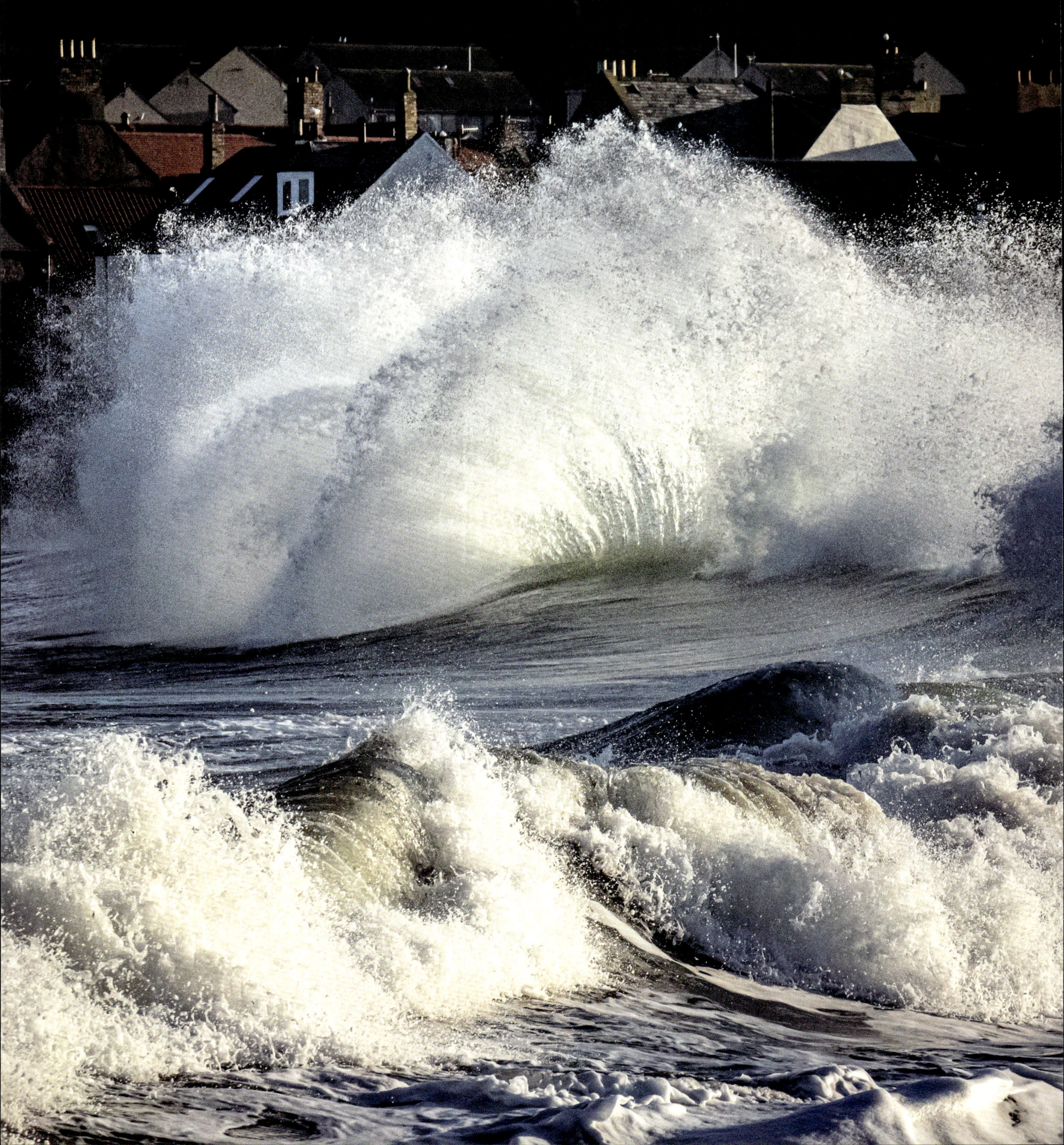

43 BERWICKSHIRE

DECEMBER 2019

DAY 368–369 | 08,971–09,013KM | 42KM

With two days to the English border, I wake to witness a fight taking place over the North Sea. The tail end of last night's storm clouds is going head-to-head with the rising sun until a truce is agreed in the form of a diffused peachy blush that wetly saturates the entire sky. Below the heavenly glow, my eyes trace the jutting headlands I'll be walking over in the day ahead. I notice that far beneath the nearest headland, two triangles catch the dawn light: the eaves of two cottages. Surprised to see any houses here and wanting to know more, I follow a track from the cliffs to discover a secret sheltered beach accessible by a small tunnel cut through the rocks. I relish the miraculously windless solitude of this hidden place, marked Cove Harbour on the map, where three bobbing fishing boats and the gentle lapping of waves are the only movement.

After retracing my steps, I walk the last couple of kilometres of the Southern Upland Way, a 344-kilometre coast-to-coast long-distance footpath. With Cove Harbour still within sight, I meet a dog walker on the path who tells me about a cafe in Pease Bay Holiday Park. I'm relieved to be able to sit down and get out of the elements – as is the only other wind-blown person in the restaurant, an intrepid Mexican man, cycling around Britain alone. We chat about last night's storm as dozens of stallholders busy themselves around us, setting up a Christmas fair.

Later that night, I spend four hours hiking in biting wind towards an almost full moon, punctuated by occasional seal calls emanating from the blackness. Under a clear, starry sky, huge sea cliffs catch the silvery light while the totemic white-painted Admiralty distance pole reflects my torchlight in front of Orion. My camp at St Abb's Head will be the last time I enjoy the Scottish access laws and pitch my tent where I choose.

On my last morning in Scotland, it feels like the wind is trying to push me back the way I've come as I struggle to walk in a straight line to St Abbs Lighthouse. When I reach the top of the headland, I'm forced to lie down to photograph the bubbling waves breaking over the rocks below. As I stagger towards the fishing village of St Abbs, it seems to be two seasons simultaneously: a summery, warm, hazy light above a wintery, boiling sea.

I reach Eyemouth by lunchtime, which is renowned for its massive waves during spring tide. The sidelight illuminates the central wave crests, contrasting with the dark houses beyond, making it especially spectacular – a shutter speed of 1/8,000 second is needed to freeze each of the thousands of atomised droplets of seawater. Walking away from Eyemouth as darkness descends, I couldn't have asked for a better last day in Scotland. It felt like a choreographed crescendo with the elements full of drama from dawn to dusk, starting with a storm-force wind and clear skies and ending with another moonlit night.

The final picture I take in Scotland is of the moon shimmering on the North Sea at Burnmouth Harbour just when the ultramarine of dusk fades into the black of night. After hours of night-hiking, my torch picks out a modest sign by the edge of a field that reads: *The English Border*. I feel like I'm slipping out of Scotland by the side door while everyone is asleep. I go through the gate and turn around to smile at the much larger *Welcome to Alba* sign before thanking it out loud for granting me safe passage. It's been 196 days of walking since I last saw a notice like this at Gretna Green in the west. The footpath ahead is hemmed in between a corridor of barbed wire. I'm in a different nation now.

Opposite:

Eyemouth breakers

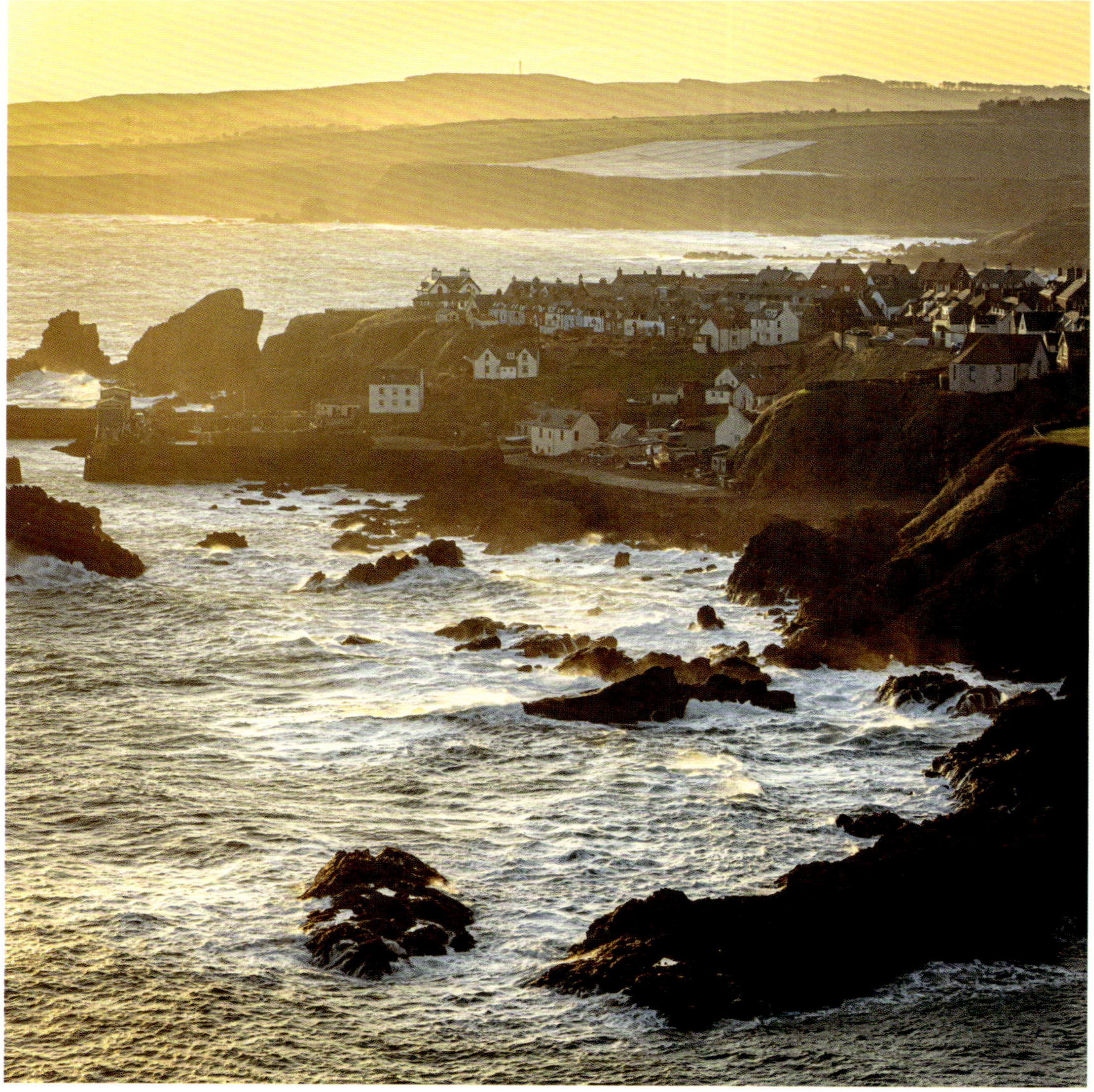

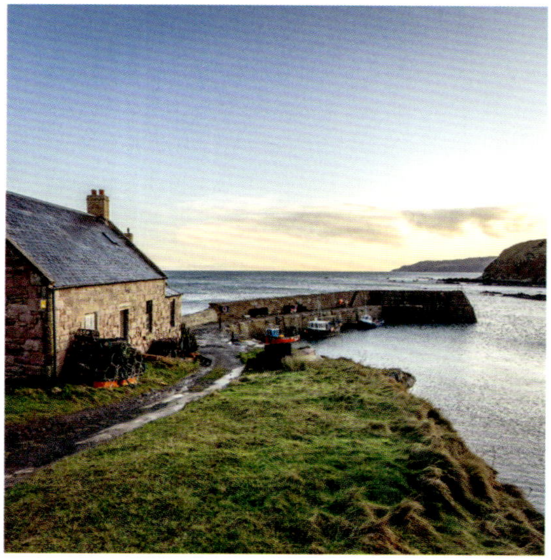

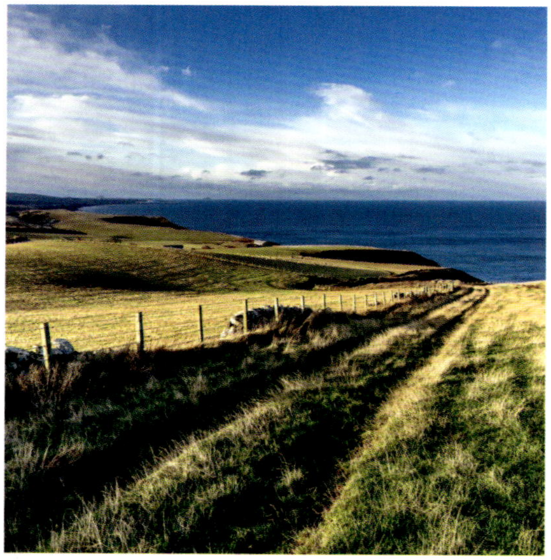

From top left:

A golden morning at St Abbs

Brightening up at Cove Harbour, Cockburnspath

Track from Red Heugh

Opposite, clockwise from top left:

Eyemouth Harbour

Rush: Coldingham Bay

St Abbs Independent Lifeboat Station

The last picture in Scotland: the moon with Burnmouth Harbour

Pease Bay Leisure Park, Cockburnspath

Creels and windows, St Abbs

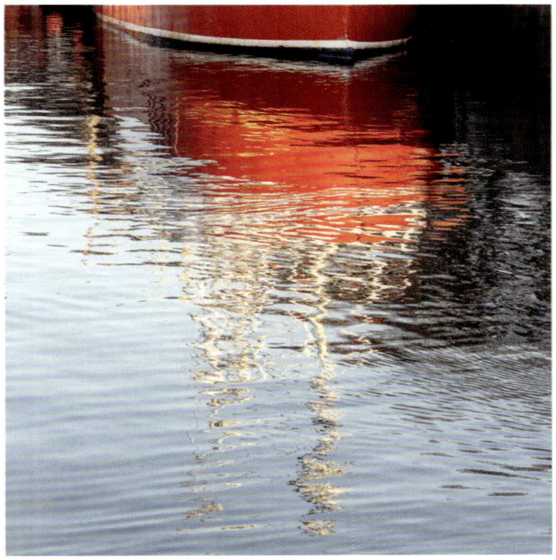

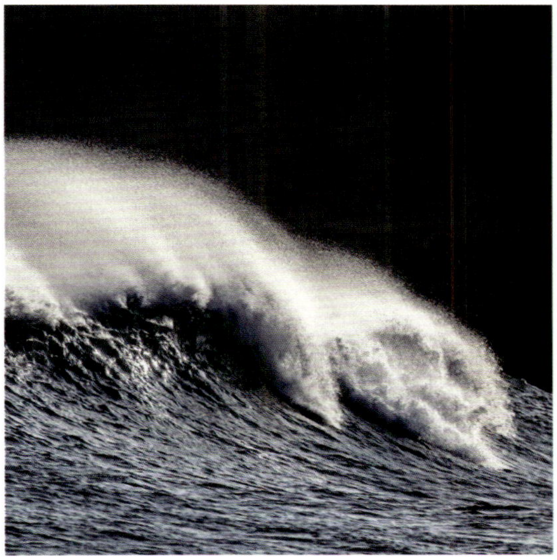

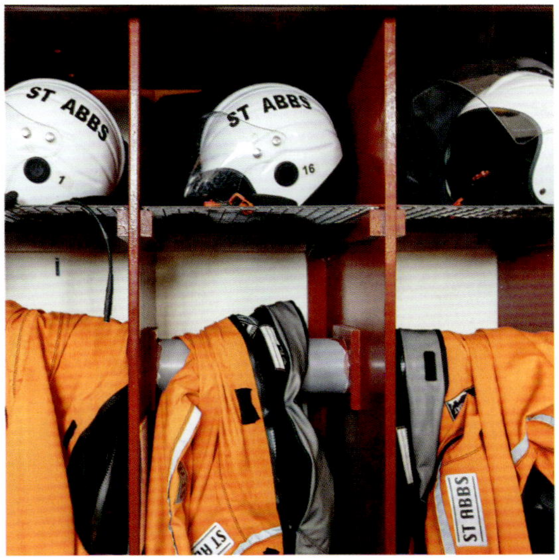
ST ABBS
ST ABBS
ST ABBS

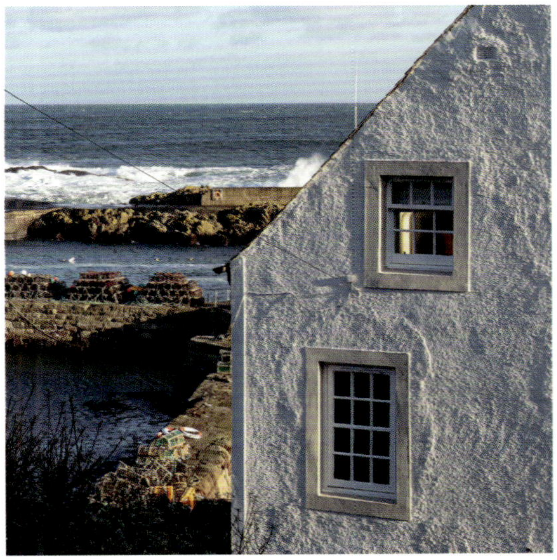

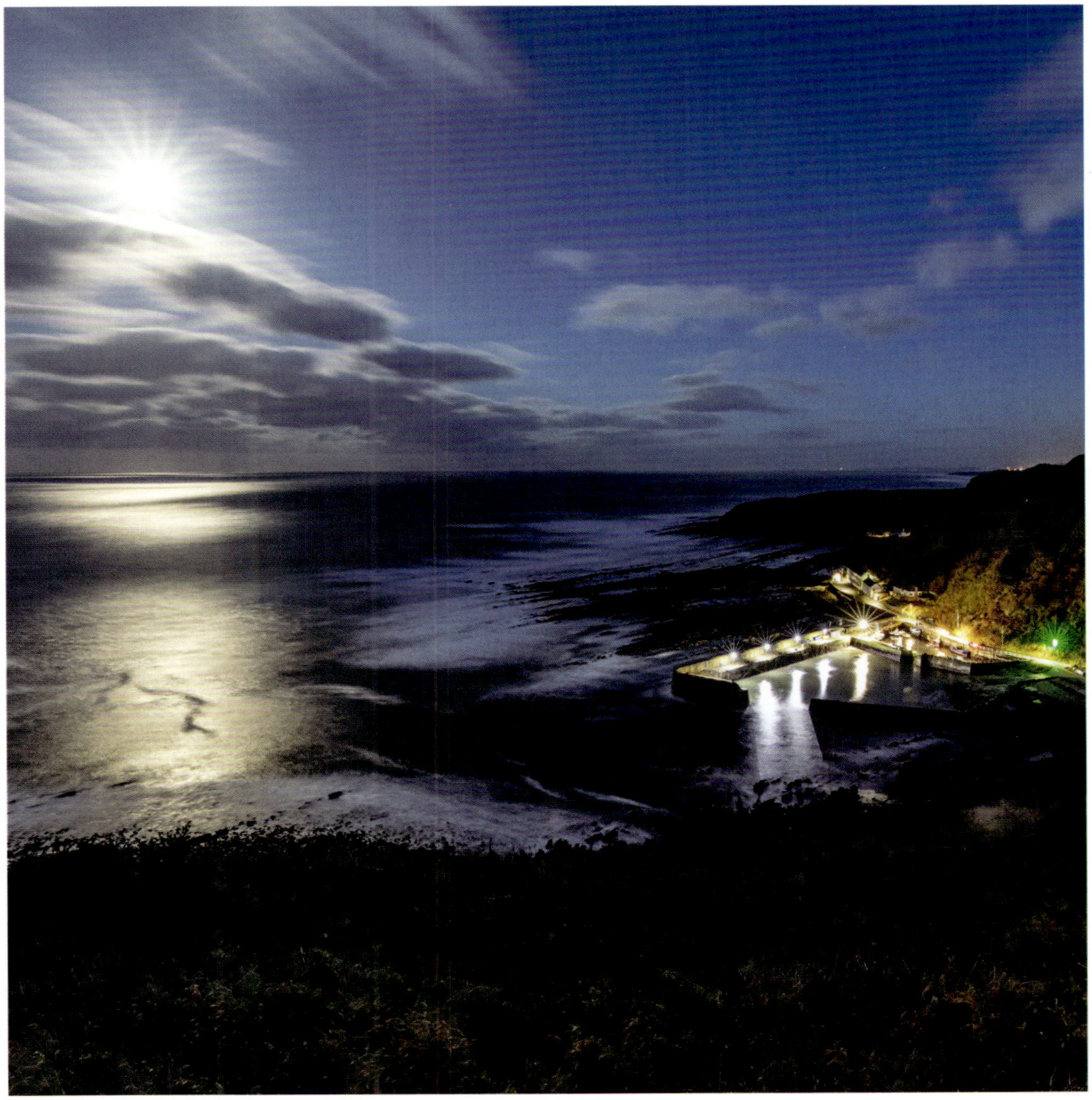

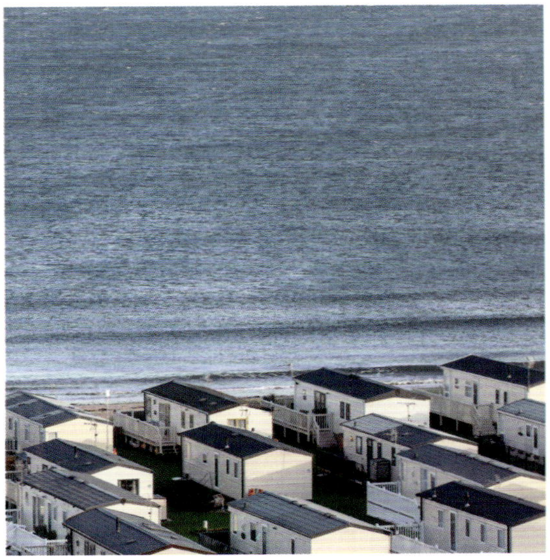

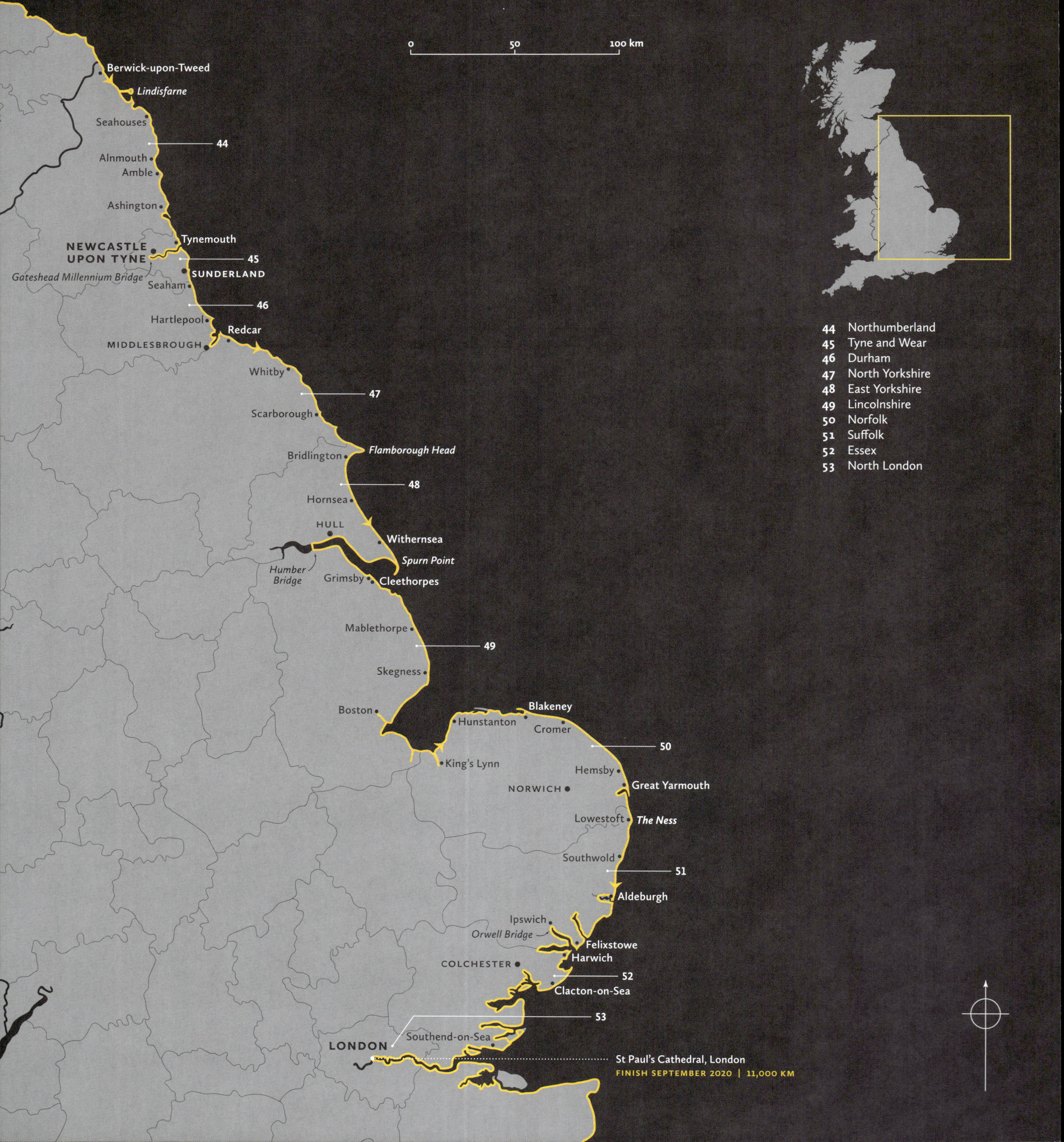
0
50
100 km
Berwick-upon-Tweed
Lindisfarne
Seahouses
44
Alnmouth
Amble
Ashington
Tynemouth
NEWCASTLE UPON TYNE
45
SUNDERLAND
Gateshead Millennium Bridge
Seaham
46
Hartlepool
Redcar
MIDDLESBROUGH
Whitby
47
Scarborough
Flamborough Head
Bridlington
48
Hornsea
HULL
Withernsea
Spurn Point
Humber Bridge
Grimsby
Cleethorpes
Mablethorpe
49
Skegness
Boston
Blakeney
Hunstanton
Cromer
50
King's Lynn
Hemsby
Great Yarmouth
NORWICH
Lowestoft
The Ness
Southwold
51
Aldeburgh
Ipswich
Orwell Bridge
Felixstowe
Harwich
COLCHESTER
52
Clacton-on-Sea
53
Southend-on-Sea
LONDON
St Paul's Cathedral, London
FINISH SEPTEMBER 2020 | 11,000 KM
44 Northumberland
45 Tyne and Wear
46 Durham
47 North Yorkshire
48 East Yorkshire
49 Lincolnshire
50 Norfolk
51 Suffolk
52 Essex
53 North London

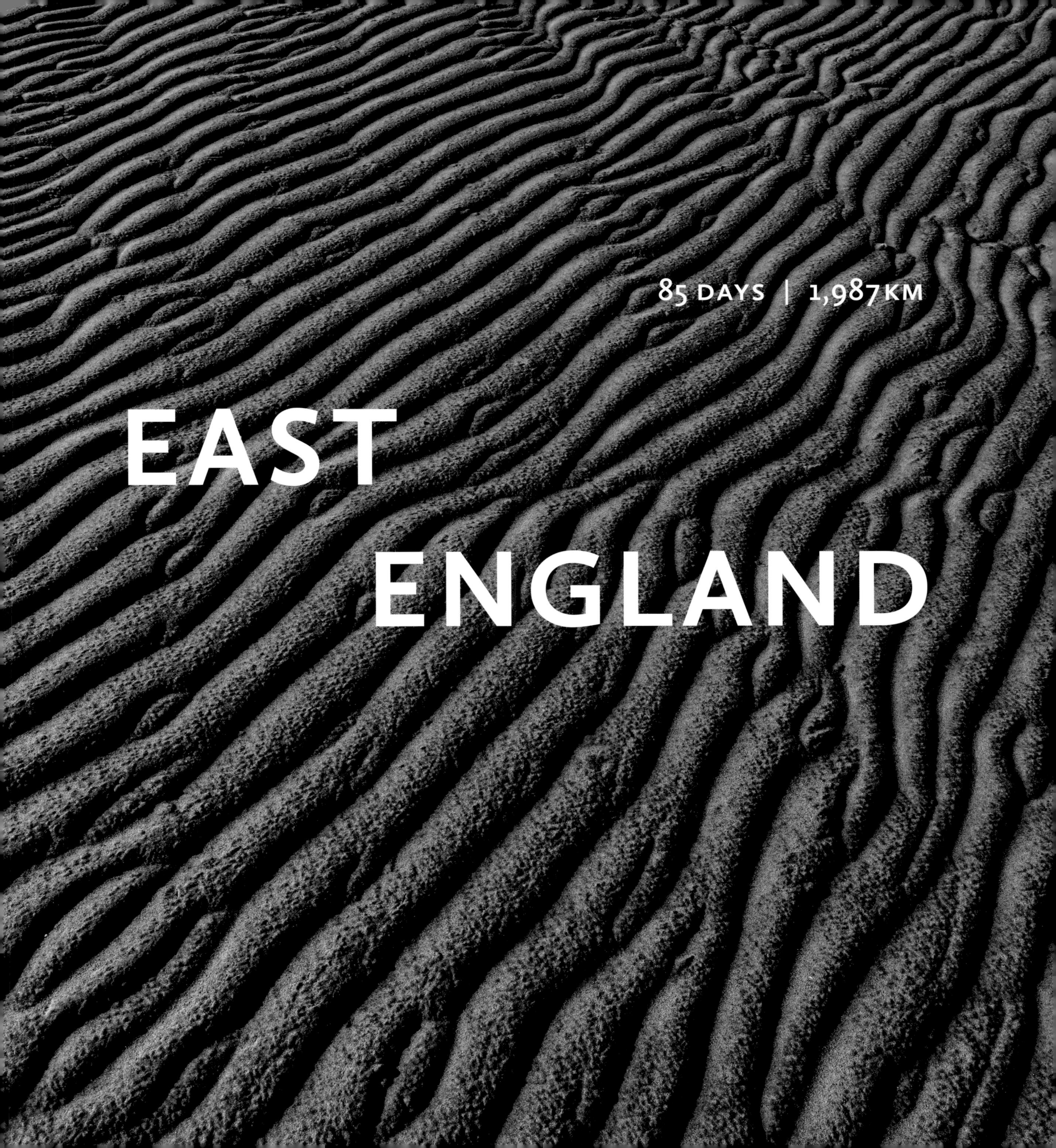

85 DAYS | 1,987KM

EAST ENGLAND

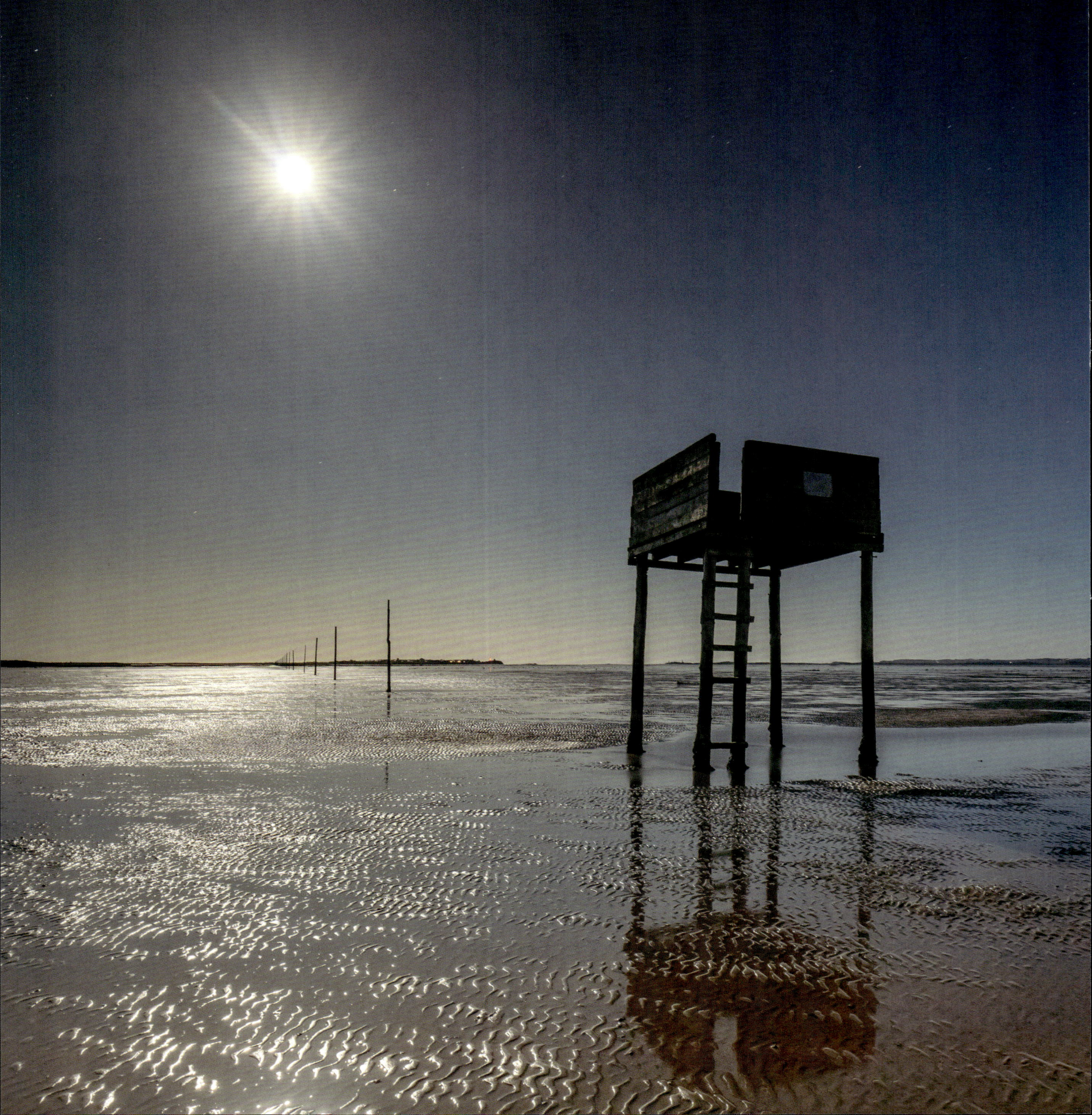

44 NORTHUMBERLAND

DECEMBER 2019

DAY 370–377 | 09,013–09,192 KM | 179 KM

Previous:

Fingerprint of the sea: Blakeney Point, Norfolk

Opposite:

Tidal refuge shelter on the Pilgrim's Way to the Holy Island of Lindisfarne, under a full moon. The first monastery to be built at Lindisfarne was founded by St Aidan in AD 635. After the death of St Cuthbert in AD 687, his tomb on Lindisfarne became a major pilgrimage destination, as were his relics, which were believed to possess miraculous powers

Private Land: No Public Access or Right of Way is my welcome back to the foibles of England when, with my boots still covered in the mud of Scotland, I take a shortcut through some unused scrubland in Berwick-upon-Tweed. After a couple of years of enjoying the freedom of Scottish land access, I'm surprised by how quickly I must return to the charade of English stealth-camping and following designated footpaths in Northumberland. Immediately, there's an infestation of authoritarian signage, and every fence is topped with barbed wire. Dog breeds here are small and comic rather than something that could take your arm off over the border. Walking through a manicured golf course, I pass a pair of sit-on mowers patrolling to and fro that seem like the English border guard hunting down escaped Scots.

My nostalgia for leaving Scotland is short-lived as the wonder of Holy Island, only one day's walk from the border, anchors me back to the present. Lindisfarne Castle, built on a high rock on the island, is visible for miles in this flat landscape. As I approach, I am reminded of the blood-splattered depiction of the first Viking raids on Lindisfarne Abbey, as portrayed in the *Vikings* TV series. But thoughts of slaughter eventually yield to spirituality as the full moon rises over the North Sea, illuminating my steps at low tide along the Pilgrim's Way, on ripples of sand for over 3 kilometres across the estuary. I stop midway along the dreamlike half-land, half-sea with my heart racing and work fast to set up my tripod and take photos of the tidal shelters and silhouetted marker posts that march towards Lindisfarne. I'm miles from the shore and all too aware of how dangerous it can be to get caught by a rising tide here.

On the coast path to Dunstanburgh Castle, the crisp winter light accents the wooden kissing gate, polished by many hands. At the castle entrance, I'm delighted to be told I can 'follow our lovely perimeter walk' and to 'enjoy your photographising'. As I wander around the impressive gatehouse and towers rising over the North Sea, I learn of the violent past these stones have witnessed, embroiled in the wars both of Scottish Independence and of the Roses. I'm always curious about what others make of the places I visit, so I am charmed to see the castle has received my favourite-ever Tripadvisor review: 'When I went last year, I had a sword fight with a very bored gift shop worker. She ran me out of the main gate with wooden toy weaponry. For that reason alone, I love this place.'

The coast starts to darken with the remains of the coal industry. I pass Lynemouth Power Station, where the former coal tips create black cliffs, and sea-coalers still collect coal from the beach in sacks to sell. After a sleepless night in a B&B with no heating in the room and a ukulele concert strumming away right below my bed, I hear the first proper Geordie accent when I chat to a bunch of rail workers who are balancing the tracks where they get twisted. 'We're waiting for a coal train, like. Won't be here for long, mind: nobody wants coal any more.' 'Can you understand us, like?' they ask with a grin. 'Aye, that's a canny job, like,' they reply when I tell them what I'm doing.

In Alnmouth, I enjoy a hearty soup and a meat pie with peas and gravy, the first square meal I've eaten in a while – and my first northern pie in the east. When the chef comes out of the kitchen to tell me that it's 'Not often we get an order for two main courses. A hungry gentleman!' I feel a glowing sense of pride.

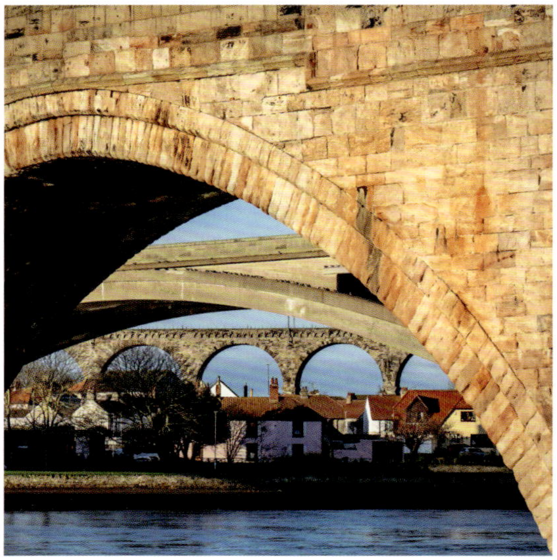

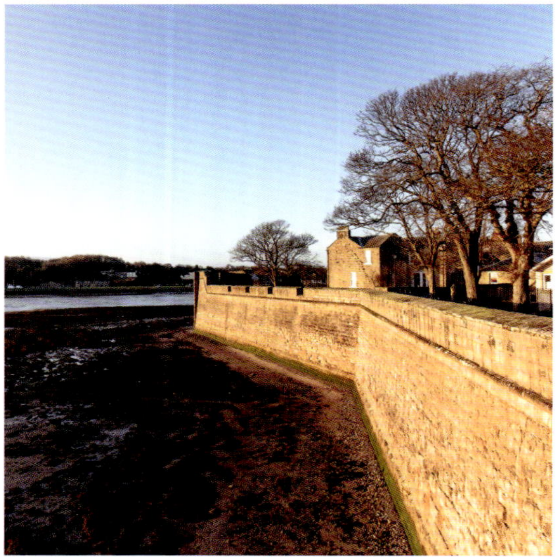

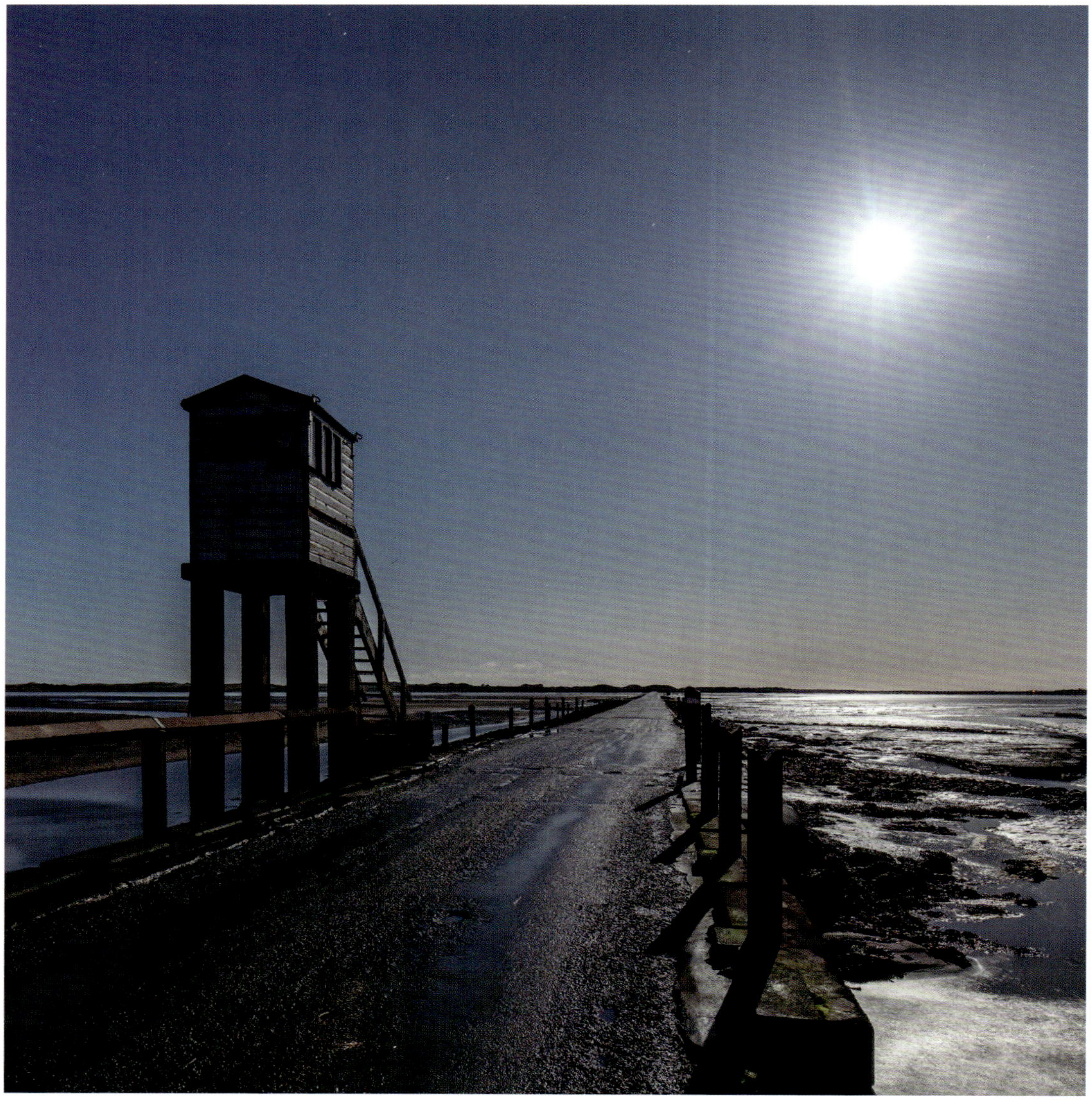

From top left:

The three bridges of Berwick-upon-Tweed

The Elizabethan town wall, Berwick-upon-Tweed

Tidal refuge shelter on the Holy Island causeway with a full moon

Opposite, from top left:

Britain's first daymark, built in 1810, Emmanuel Head, Lindisfarne

Castle Point Lime Kilns, Lindisfarne

From bottom left:

Moonlit markers, Pilgrim's Way to Lindisfarne

Boat shed, Lindisfarne

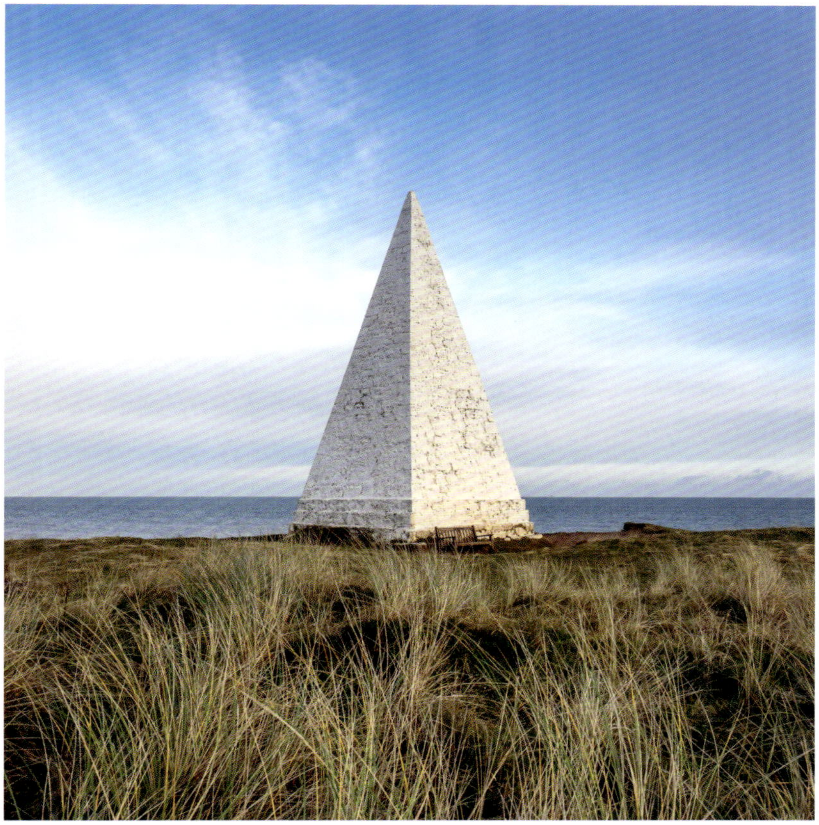
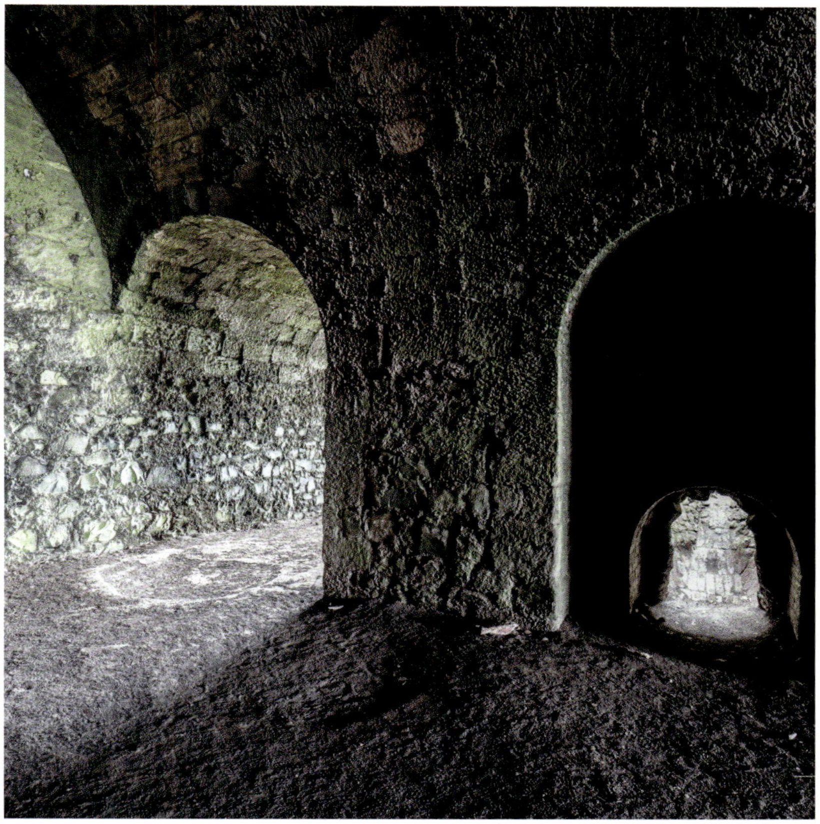
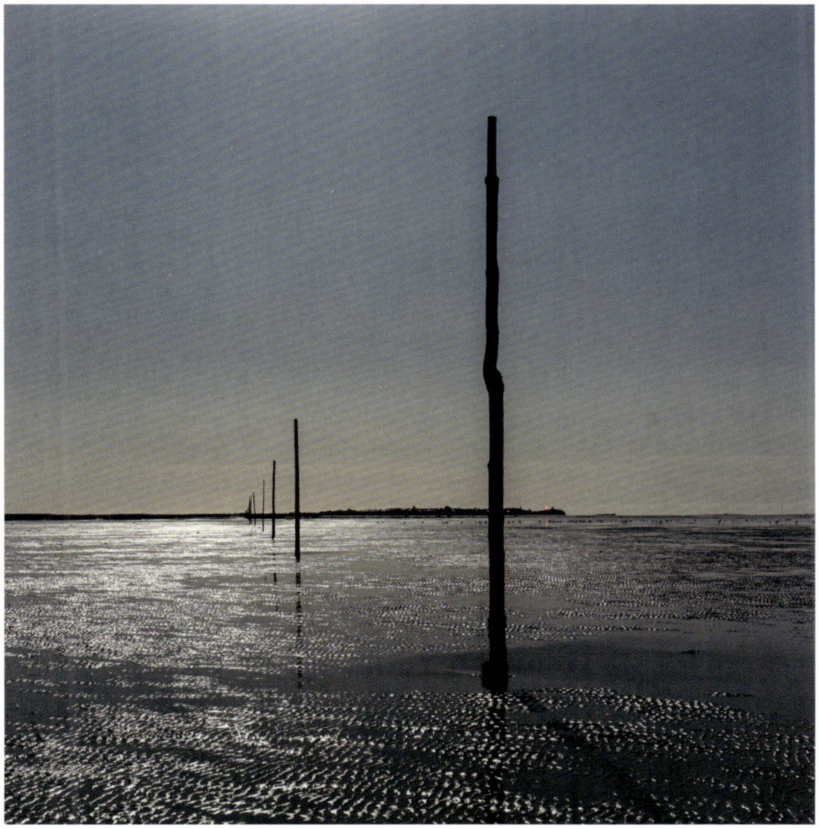
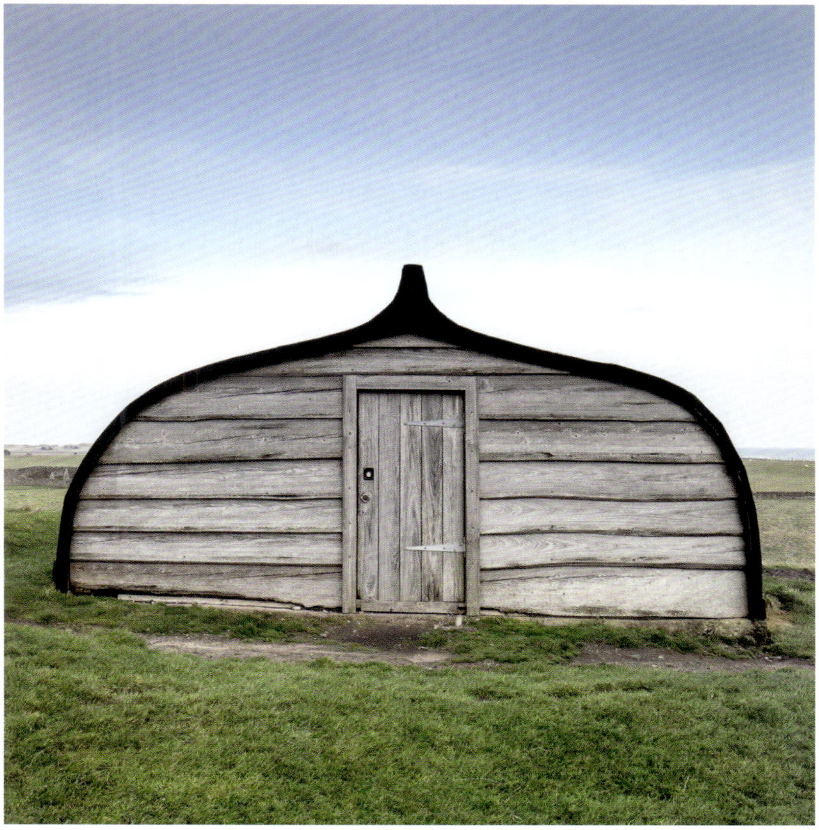

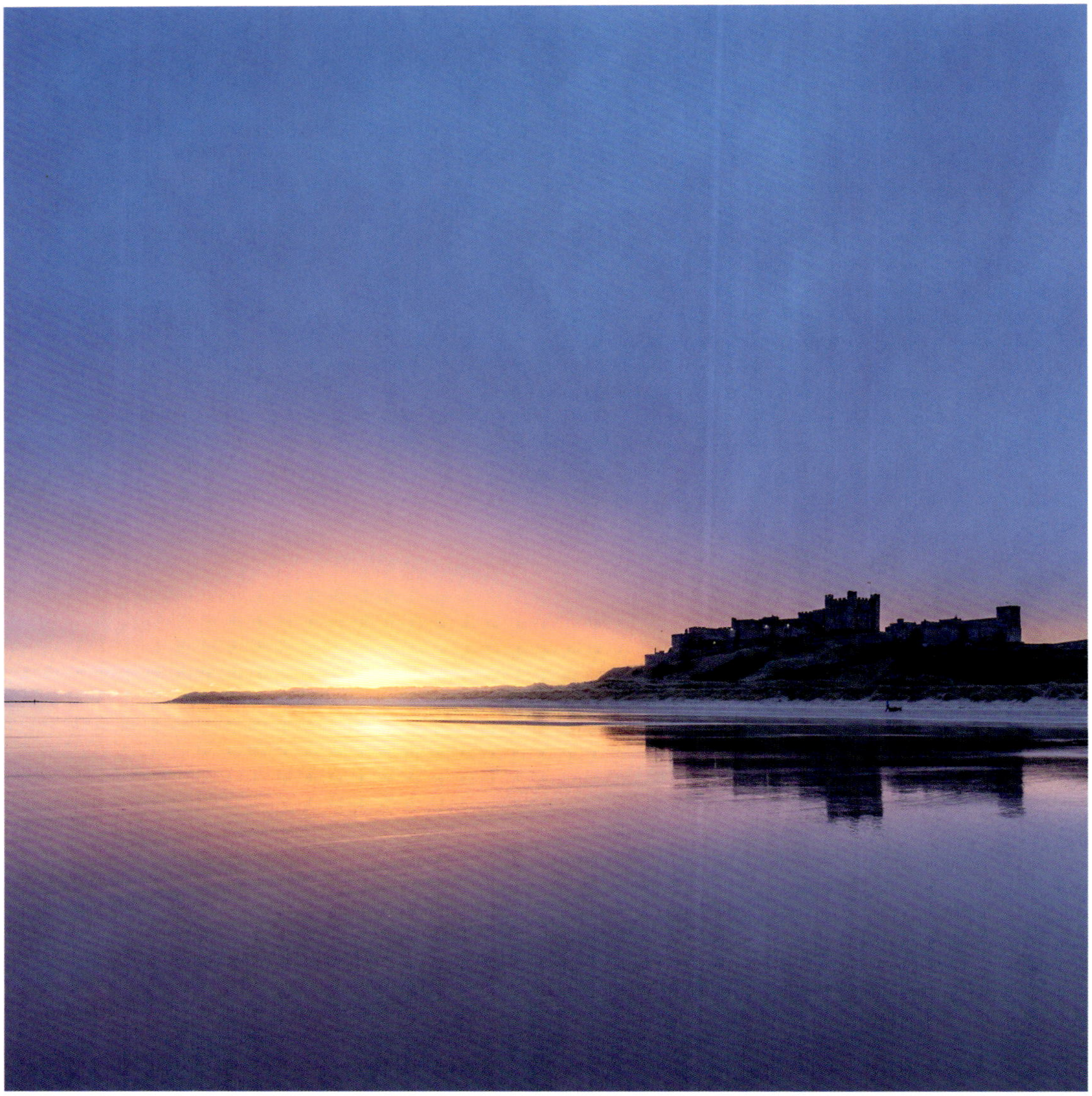

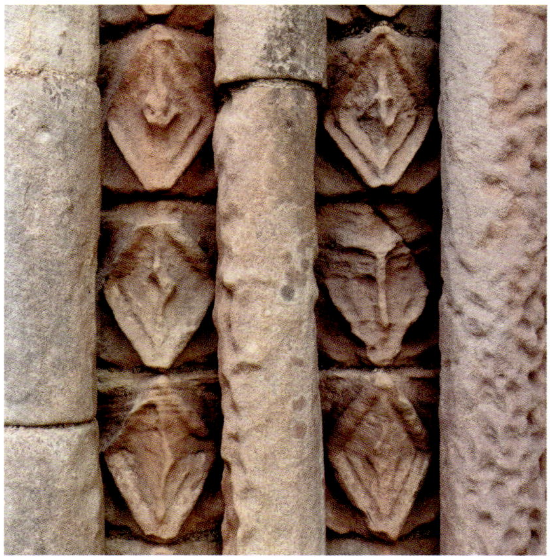

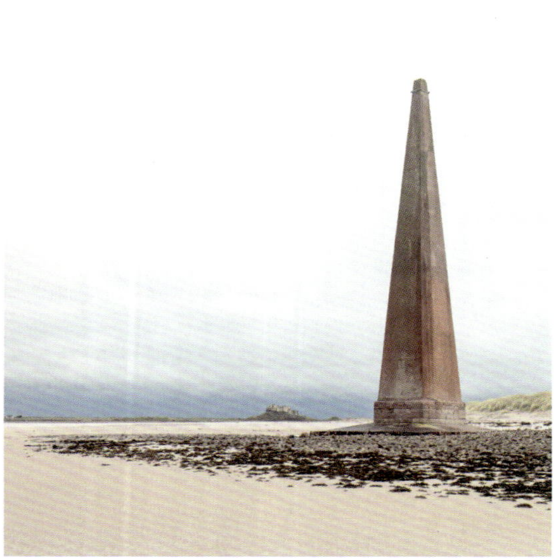

From top left:

Low tide and first light at Bamburgh Castle. The site was originally home to a Celtic Brittonic fort and is believed to have served as the capital of the Kingdom of Bernicia from around 420 until 547. Following several shifts in control between the Britons and Anglo-Saxons, the fort ultimately fell under Anglo-Saxon rule in 590. In 993, it was destroyed by Viking invaders. Later, the Normans built a new castle on the site, which now forms the core of the current structure

Lindisfarne Priory, built in 1150

Old Law Beacon, Guile Point

Opposite, clockwise from top left:

Funny-looking dogs: Druridge Bay

Warkworth Castle over-looking 800 years of traffic between England and Scotland

Shadow of Dunstanburgh Castle, a fourteenth-century fortification involved in the Despenser Wars, the Wars of Scottish Independence, the Wars of the Roses and the Second World War

Like a frozen wave: Greymare Rock is made up of a series of limestone beds twisted by heat and pressure that were caused during the formation of the Whin Sill on which the nearby Dunstanburgh Castle stands

Hand-smoothed gate near Dunstanburgh Castle

Beach hut at Embleton Bay

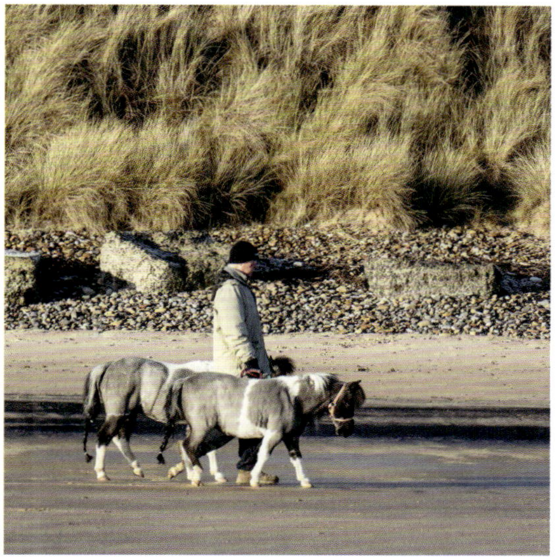

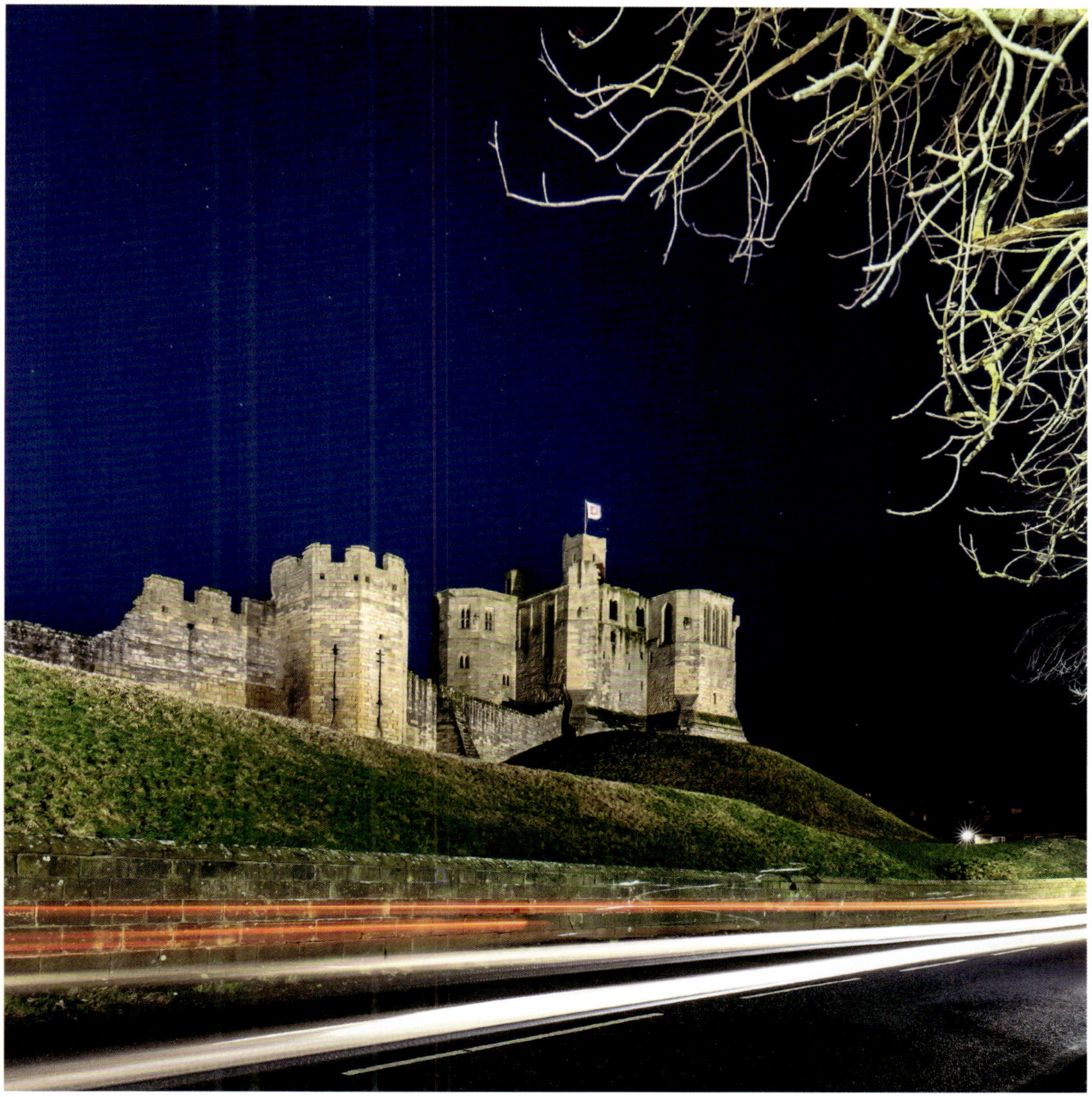

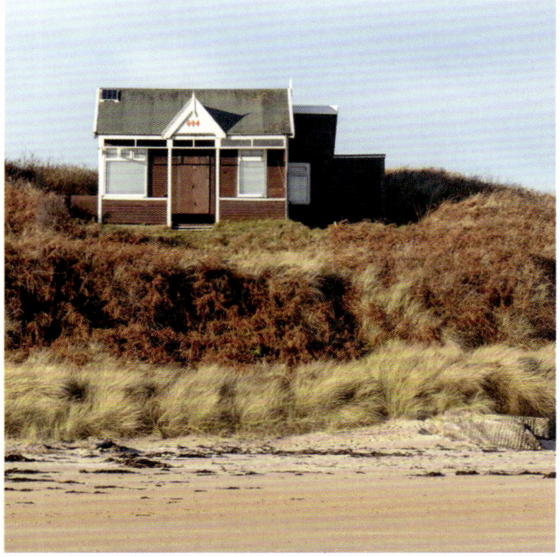

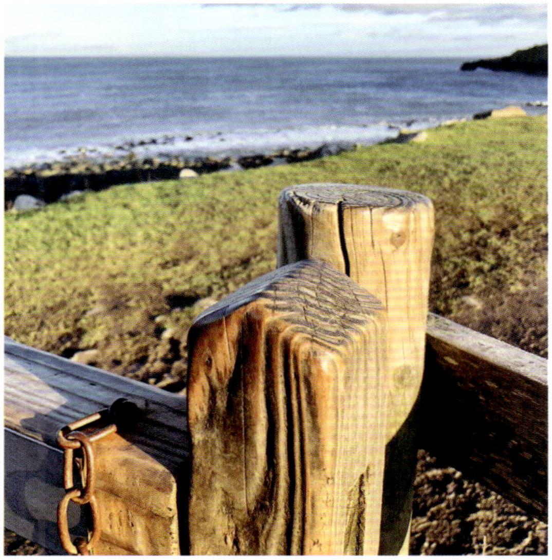

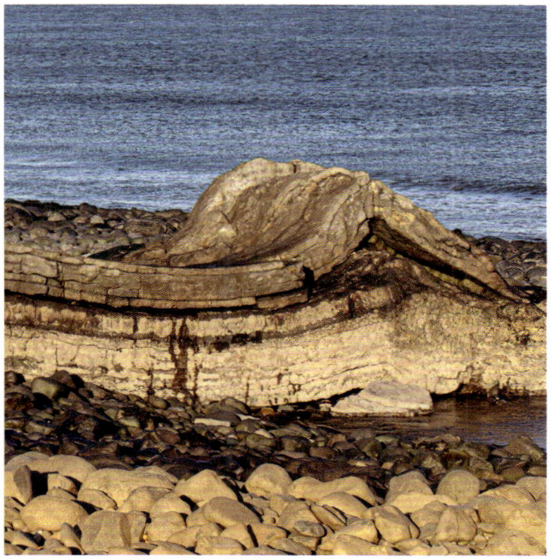

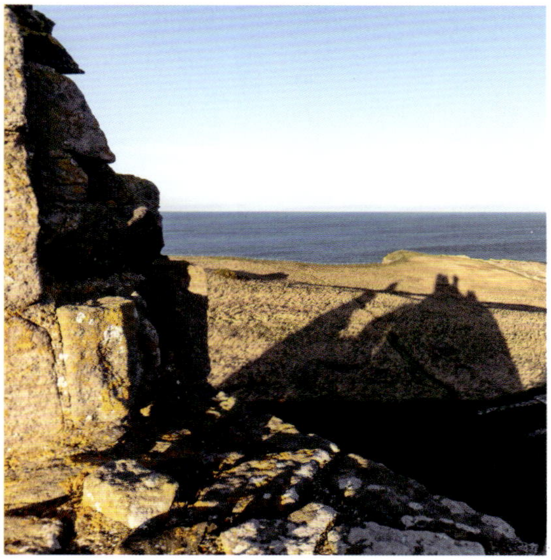

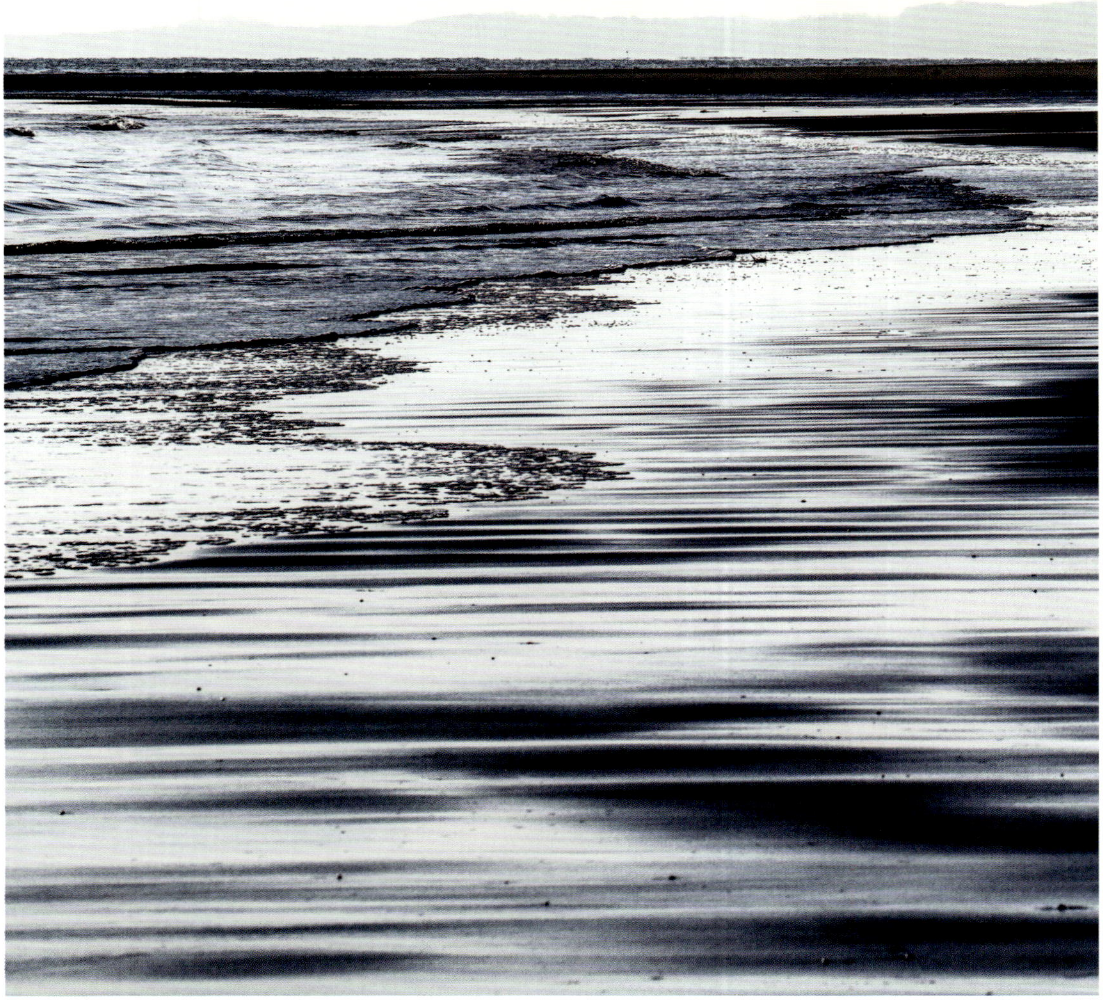

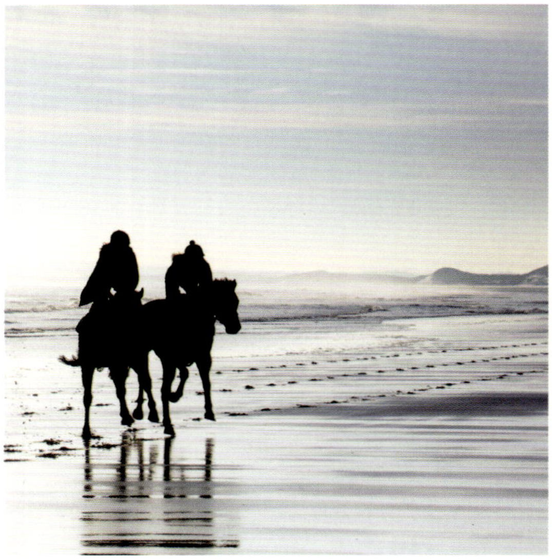

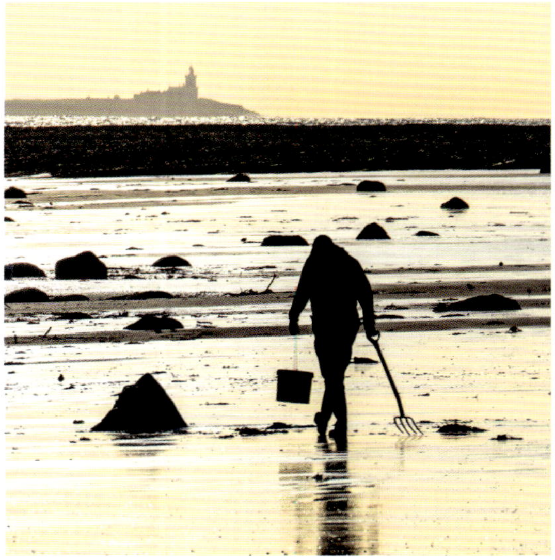

From top left:

Druridge Bay catching the morning light

Riders, Druridge Bay

Fork on the foreshore: Coquet Island Lighthouse from Boulmer

Opposite, from top left:

Amble at Amble

Heavy sky over Blyth Beach with black patches of sea-coal and pebbles. St Mary's Island is on the horizon

From bottom left:

Night-fishing by Lynemouth Power Station

Waiting for the throw below the alumina silos at North Blyth Harbour

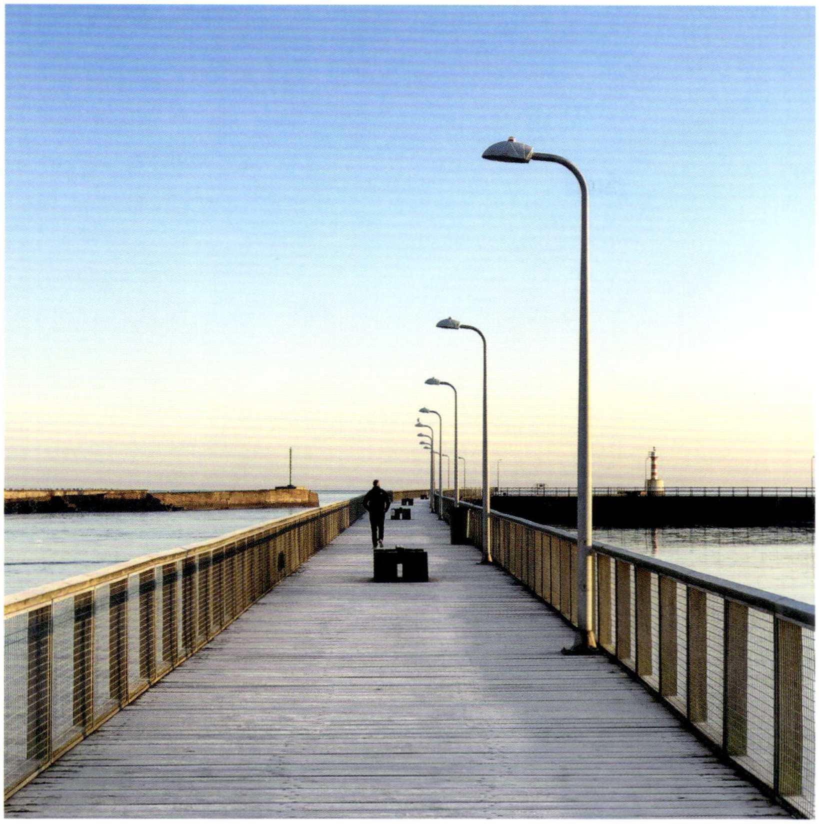

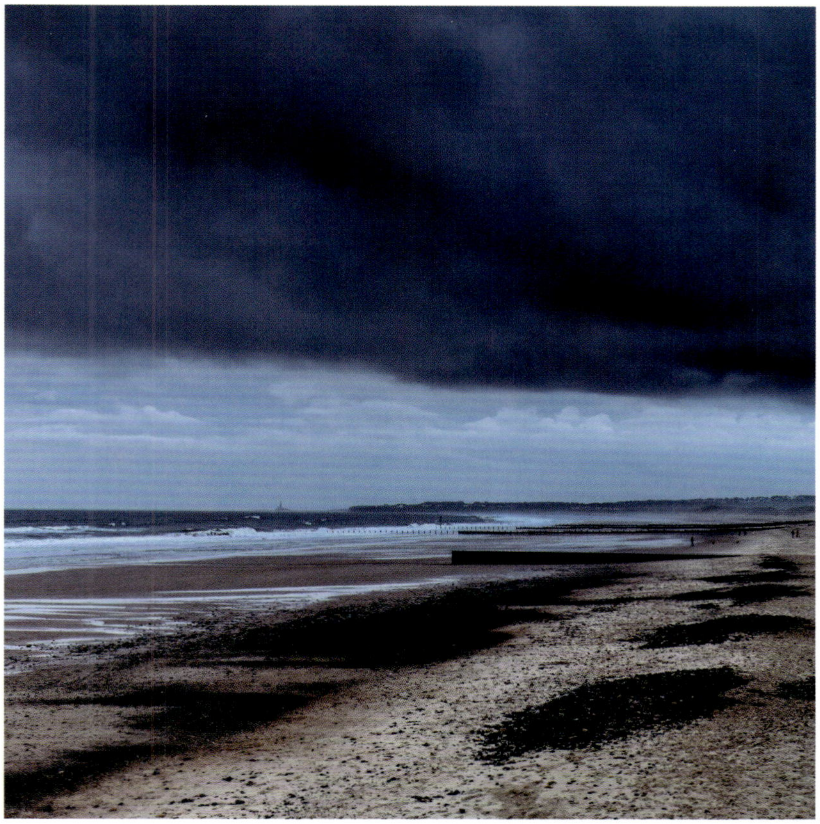

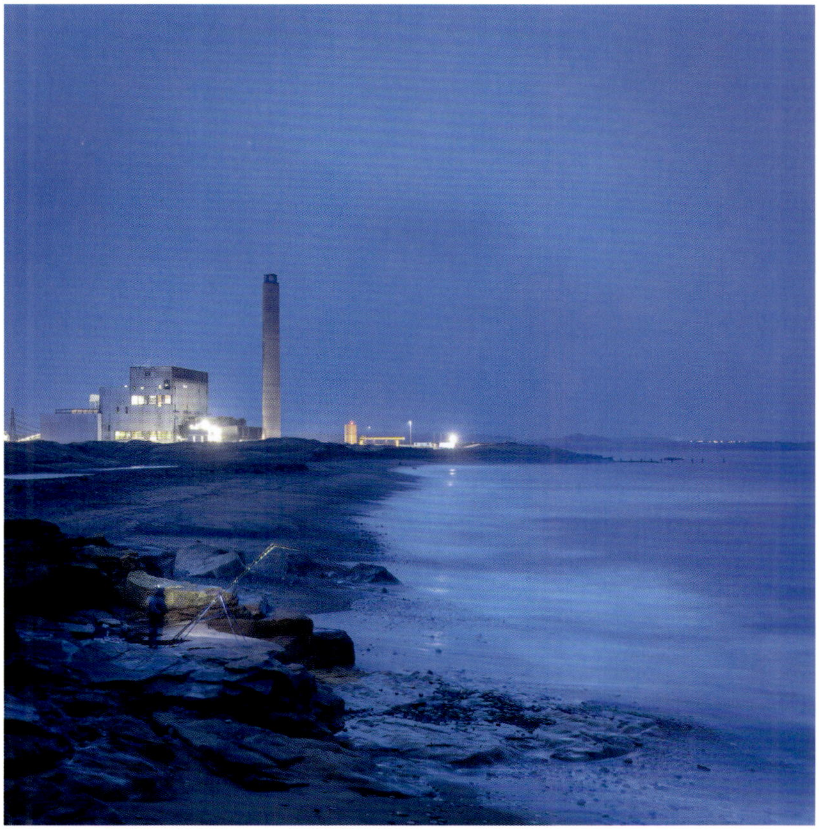

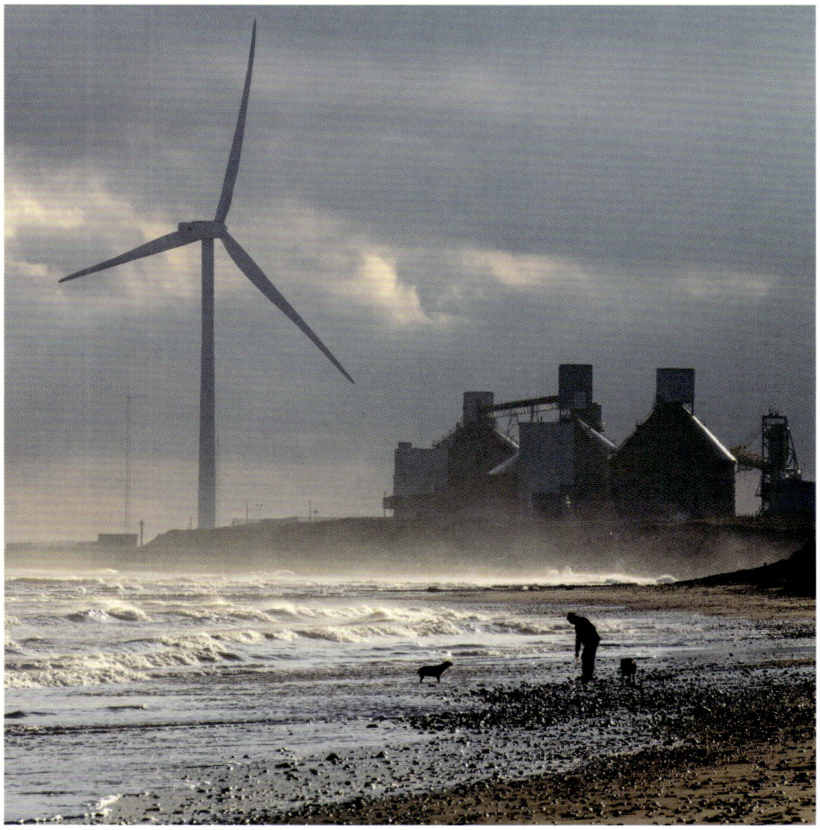

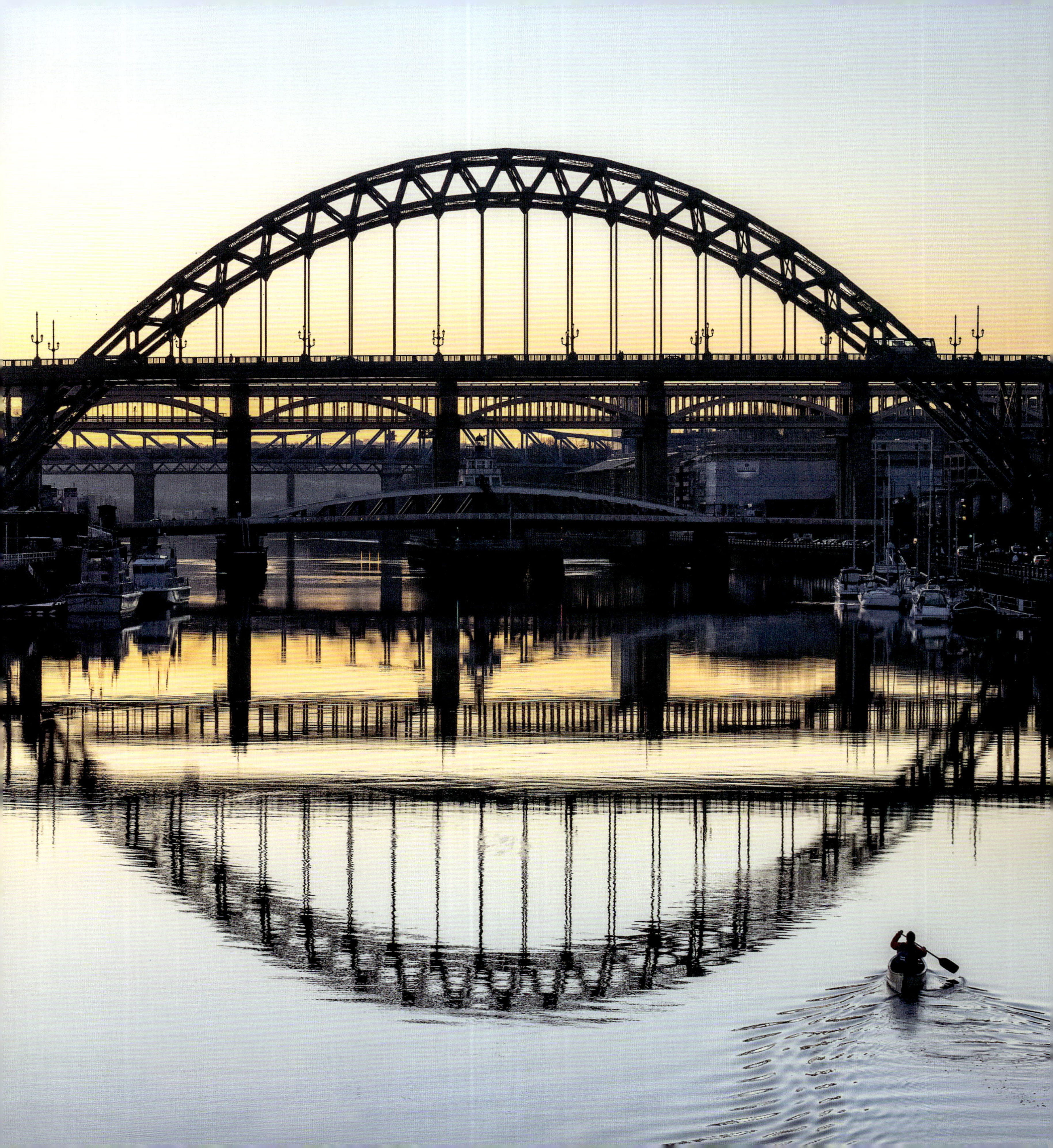

45 TYNE AND WEAR

DECEMBER 2019–JANUARY 2020
DAY 378–380 | 09,192–09,272 KM | 80 KM

At Tynemouth, I must turn my back on the sea for a while and follow the Tyne to Newcastle – just in time for the last Friday before Christmas. I pass the crudely truncated eastern end of Hadrian's Wall at Wallsend by the Swan Hunter shipyard, where its path is lost among a scattering of crisp packets. In Roman times, a pier extended from the wall's end into the Tyne, culminating in a temple. As I look at the map to trace the route of Hadrian's Wall across the north of England, I realise it was 206 days ago that I stood at the western edge of the monument near Carlisle.

Gigantic tubular steel structures at Wallsend tower incongruously above the houses at the end of residential streets. They're much larger than I'd imagined, so it takes me a while to recognise them as rows of wind turbine jackets – the trussed tripod legs that support turbines on the seabed – that I've often seen in the distance on offshore wind farms. As the jackets are fabricated in the former shipyards, the scene is a strange modern echo of the tankers that once hulked over the terraces of Wallsend.

Architectural studios, appealing bars and restaurants add to the feeling of energy on the approach to Newcastle along the Tyne. The city's centre is stunning with its overlapping layers of bridges crossing the Tyne and its muscular Chicago-like urbanism. On New Year's Eve, I'm certainly the only one wearing Gore-Tex and hiking boots. 'Are you all by yourself? Come and have a drink with us,' ask a group of revellers; when I tell them what I'm up to, we all hug, and they suggest I 'Come to Greggs and get a steak bake, that'll set you up.'

I leave my B&B at dawn the following day, emerging on to empty streets that make me think I'm the sole person in the city not nursing a hangover. The only people I pass are a handful of street cleaners sweeping up last night's broken bottles. As the sound of tinkling glass fades, the city rapidly discards its urbane charm, returning to its industrial roots past the Baltic. I pass Walker Quay, which once made the huge vessels of the past, including aircraft carriers HMS *Ark Royal* and HMS *Illustrious*, and now produces umbilical spools for the offshore industry.

At Jarrow, I come across an ancient bridge that used to lead to Jarrow Monastery, the home of the Venerable Bede, a character I've become interested in as his *Ecclesiastical History of the English People*, completed in AD 731, is one of the few written sources for understanding early English history. The bridge now leads to nowhere, cut off by industrial land, but I can hear the chant of a nearby footy pitch and referees' whistles. I'm soon passing through South Shields, where all the bars and restaurants seem to have bouncers outside. After 22 kilometres, I break free from the Tyne to return to the sea, where I'm forced to watch my step as fresh and impressive sinkholes punctuate the grassy cliffs near Souter Lighthouse.

I reach Sunderland the next day, a city once known as the largest place for shipbuilding in the world. As I walk along the banks of the former-heavily industrialised Wear, I encounter a patronising industrial-heritage sculpture topped with CCTV and a pleasantly sanitised university campus. It's a much shorter walk upriver to the first crossing of the Wear than the Tyne, yet the arched green Wearmouth Bridge and the Monkwearmouth Railway Bridge are no less impressive in their scale and design. Their riveted steel plates are a testament to the same skill, materials and technology that once propelled the ships from these shores. I pause to capture their magnificence in photographs, realising that these bridges are the true monuments to Sunderland's industrial past.

Opposite:

New Year's Eve paddler, the Tyne Bridge, designed by the engineering firm Mott, Hay and Anderson in 1928

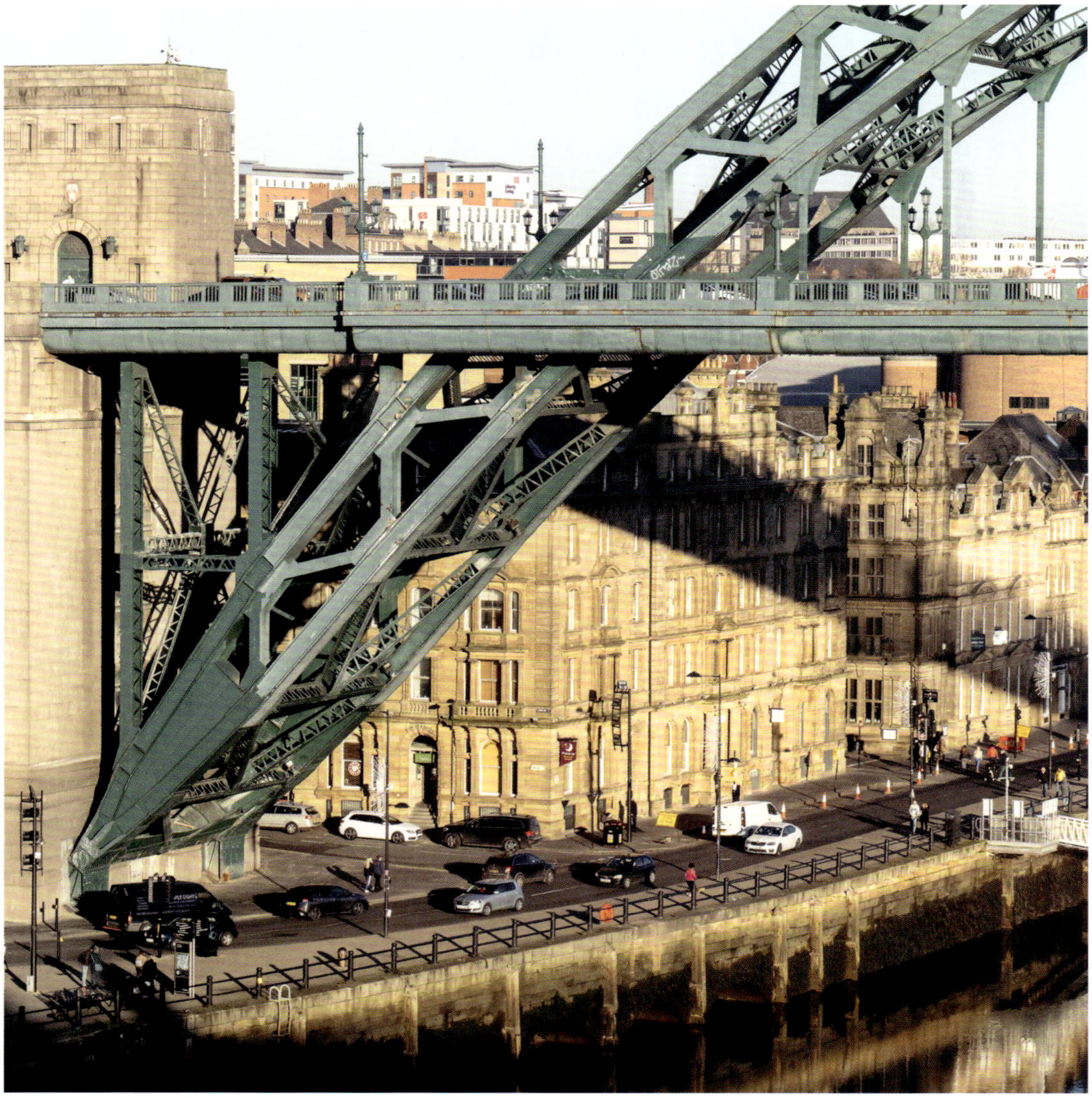

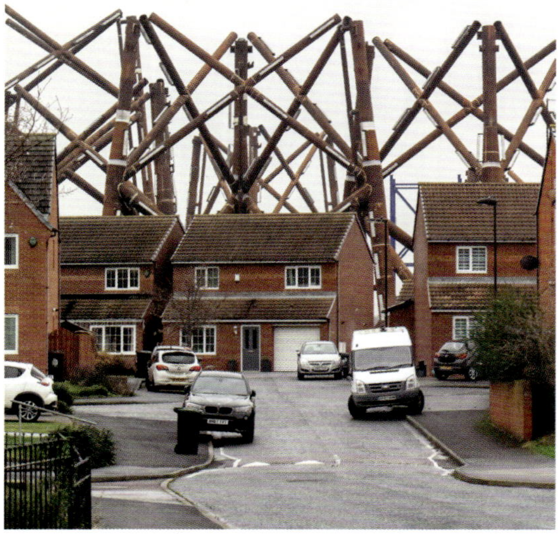

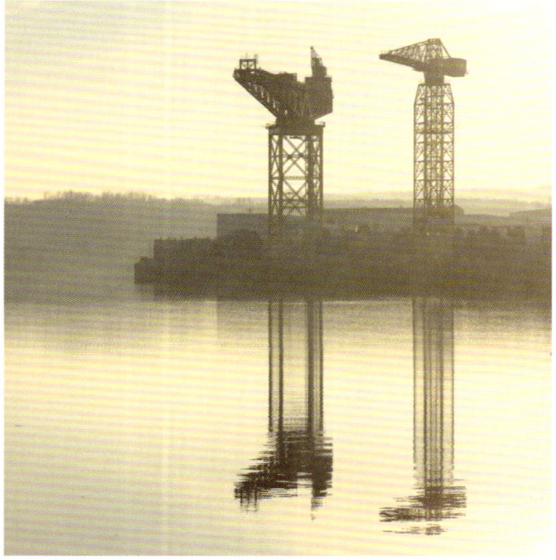

From top left:

The thrilling scale of the Tyne Bridge, Newcastle

Wind turbine jackets by the Tyne, Wallsend

Cranes of the long-gone Walker Naval Yard, Newcastle. Still being used by Bridon, manufacturers of industrial wire and fibre ropes

Opposite, from top left:

The hull of *Federal Asahi*, a bulk carrier, in the Port of Sunderland

Wearmouth Bridge, designed by Thomas Paine and opened in 1796, Sunderland

From bottom left:

Tyne crossings, Newcastle

By the Tyne from Hebburn: fabrication of the fifty-five wind turbine jackets for the Moray East Offshore Wind Farm, at the Hadrian Yard in Wallsend for Smulders

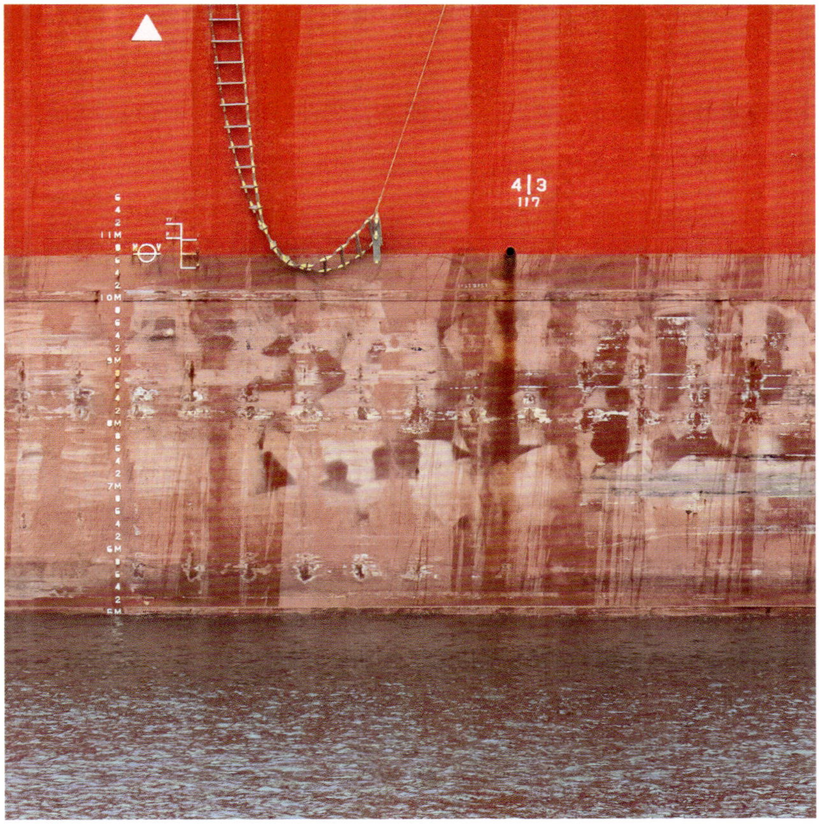

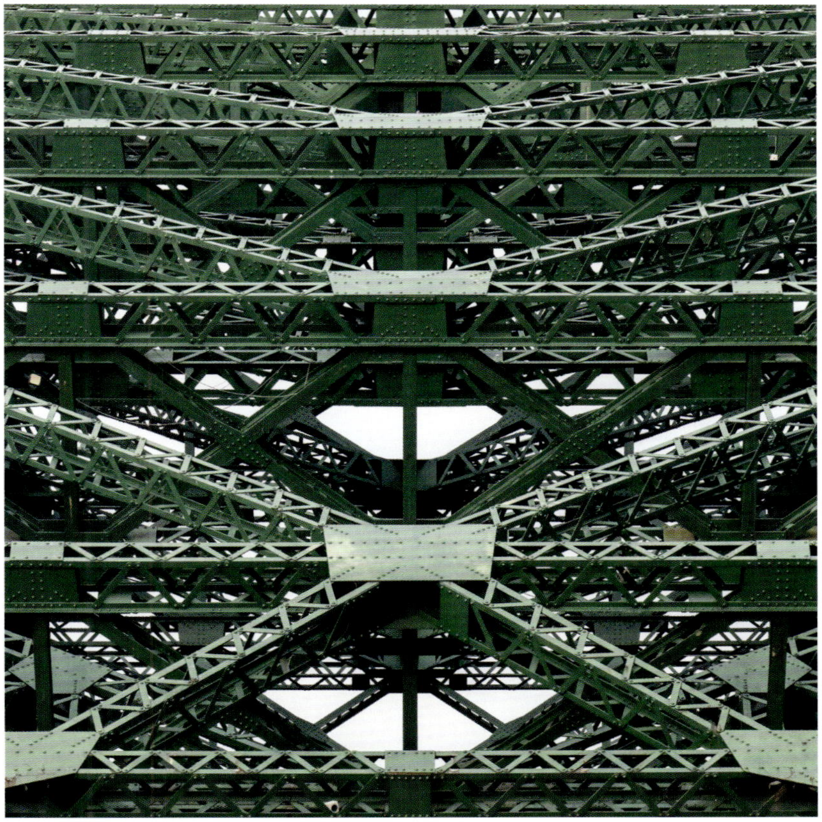

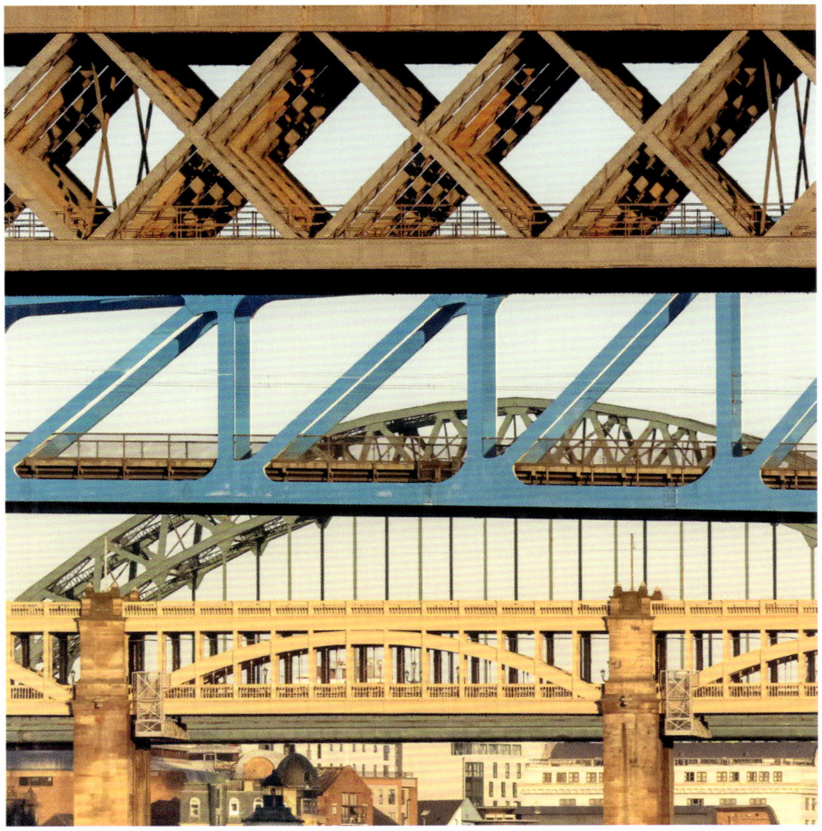

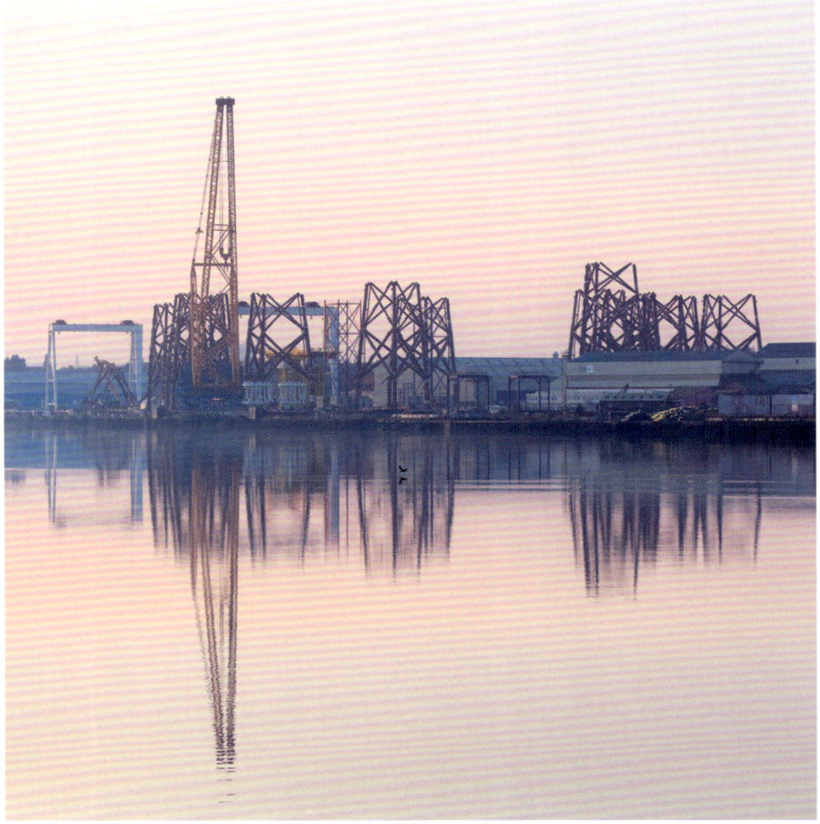

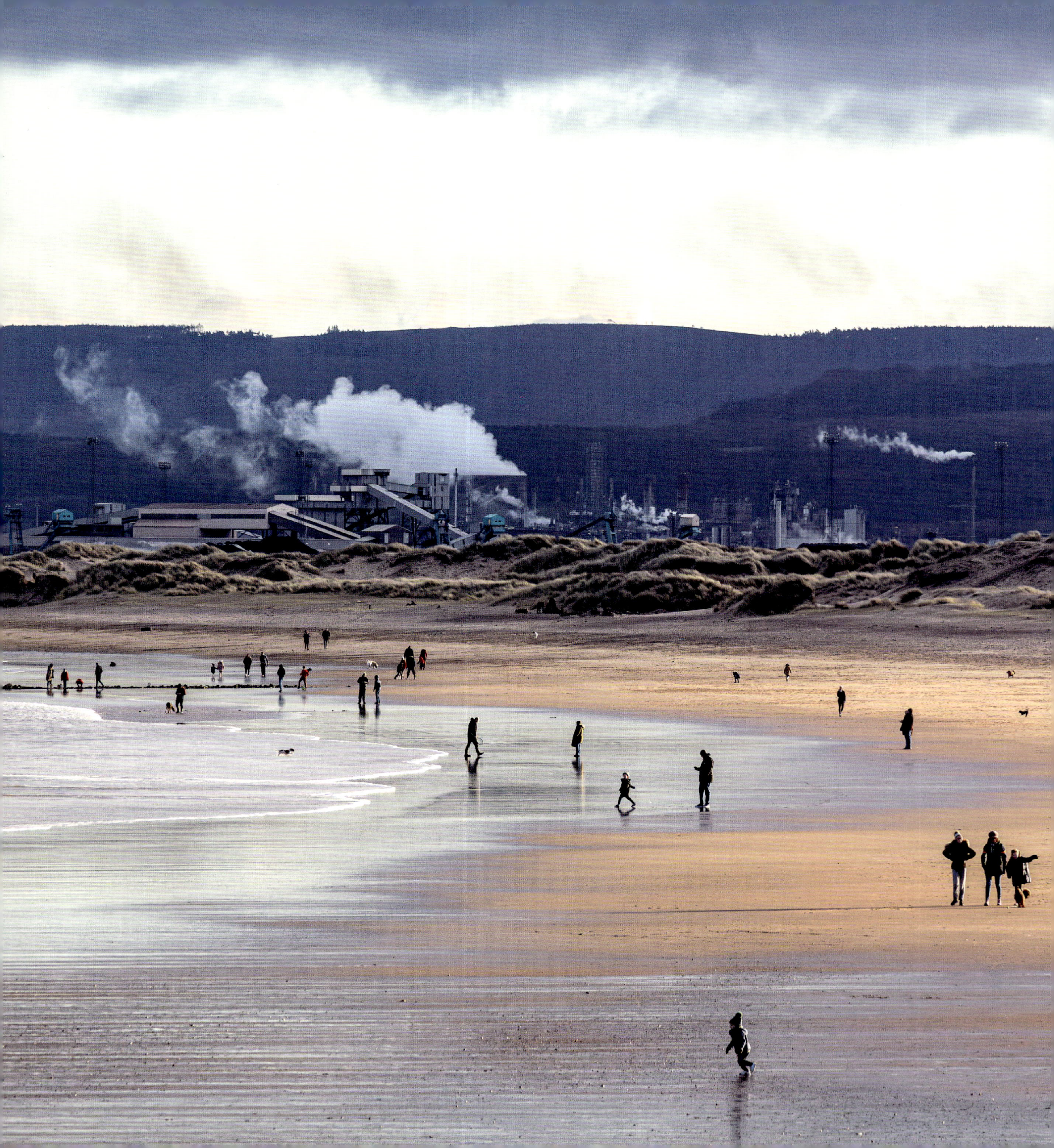

46 DURHAM

JANUARY 2020

DAY 381–383 | 09,272–09,338 KM | 66 KM

It's a spectacular morning on the Durham coast, where I'm camped below a magnesian limestone cliff shimmering in the sunlight. I follow what at first glance appears to be a natural geological feature but I soon realise must be a long shelf of lumpy concrete-like colliery spoil beside a beach whose sand is darkened by coal dust. Curious, I google how the beach used to look: mountains of black colliery waste once fanned out to sea, completely obliterating it. This dystopian scene served as the inhuman location in the movies *Get Carter* and *Alien 3*. Little remains now, thanks to the Turning the Tide regeneration project. Though in the evening, at Parton Rocks near Hartlepool, I walk across a small section of the shore that is composed entirely of waste from a former steelworks: a conglomeration of rusting slag, concrete blocks and brick.

In the morning, as I walk back on myself to loop around the headland at Hartlepool, the people I meet greet me with 'all right'. Yesterday's 'alreet' is a thing of the past, making me wonder if this coastline where Geordie 'wey ayes' meld into Yorkshire 'ey ups' has the most distinct accents to be heard within a single day's walk. These musings give way to hunger when I pass a butcher's and buy a perfect handmade pork pie straight from the oven. I munch it happily in the sun before picking up a fresh-baked vanilla cheesecake for £1. These simple pleasures make me feel a long way from the remote stretches of Scotland, where I needed to carry five days of food at a time.

At Seaton Sands, the beach is populated by dozens of black shadowless figures, fully dressed for winter with striding legs and a backdrop of smoking industrial chimneys like a living Lowry painting. The artist lived and made work nearby, so it seems not so much has changed in the last six decades. As I approach the River Tees, an acrid burning smell fills the air from the chemical works and leaves a tart metallic taste in the back of my mouth. I photograph a man chasing a husky in front of the steelworks. A moment later, he Facebook messages me to say hi – it turns out he knows me from Facebook's wild-camping group.

From the banks at the mouth of the Tees, a low rumble of container ships flows up and down the river. I'm excited to be photographing a fully synthetic landscape. In every direction, there's a forest of glistening chimneys, plumes of steam, towering flare stacks that occasionally erupt into flame; with such a clear visual parallel, it's easy to see how childhood memories of Teesside inspired Ridley Scott for the opening scene of *Blade Runner*. The real-life oil refinery appears like an unknown city with flare stacks like the sacred flame for an unknown god. I camp nearby to continue photographing this other-worldly scene into the night. From the tent, I hear the steady hum of the nuclear power station interrupted by the moaning of seals. Early the following day, I'm woken up by an unusually assertive 'Good morning' from outside. I unzip the tent to see two black-clad armed police officers standing over me, wanting to know what I'm doing. When I explain, they relax and wish me well, even letting me take a jovial photo of them standing guard over my tiny shelter.

Back on the road towards Billingham, I'm dwarfed below a gargantuan rusty oil platform, the 25,000-tonne Shell Brent Bravo, slowly being disassembled by giant machinery. The structure, while still recognisable, looks like it's been picked over by vultures, with ribbons of steel hanging off it like entrails. By the evening, it feels like I've been walking all day in a sci-fi world constructed for machines rather than humans, so on the outskirts of Middlesbrough, I am reassured by the silhouette of a person waiting at a bus stop below massive cooling towers billowing steam into the night sky.

Opposite:

After Lowry: Seaton Sands

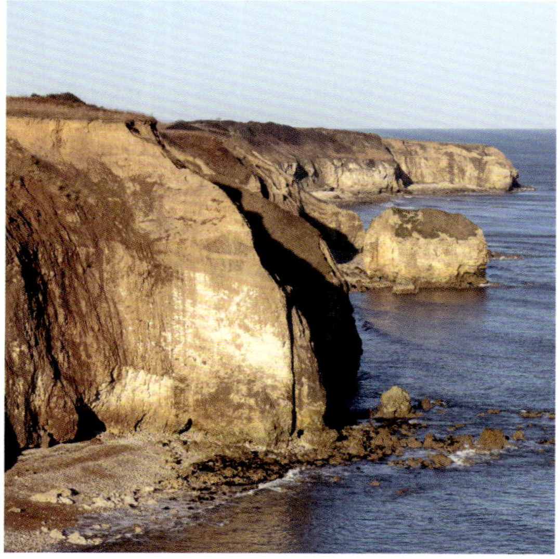
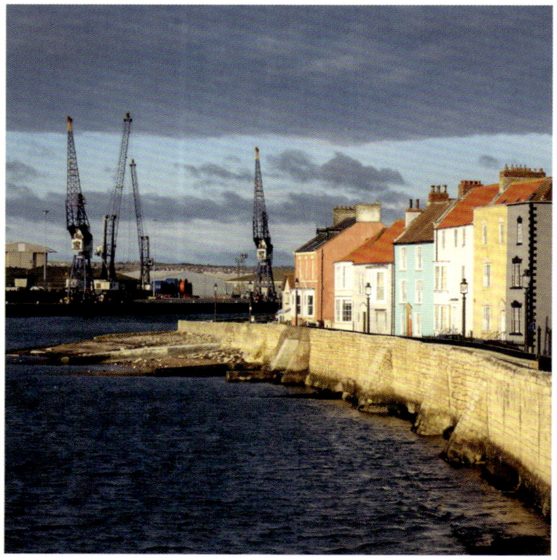
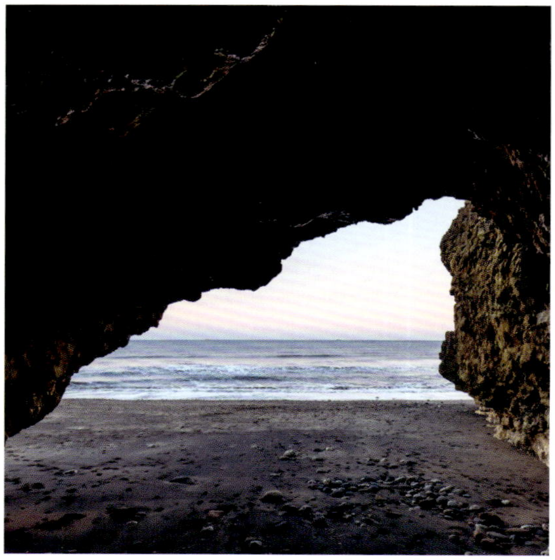
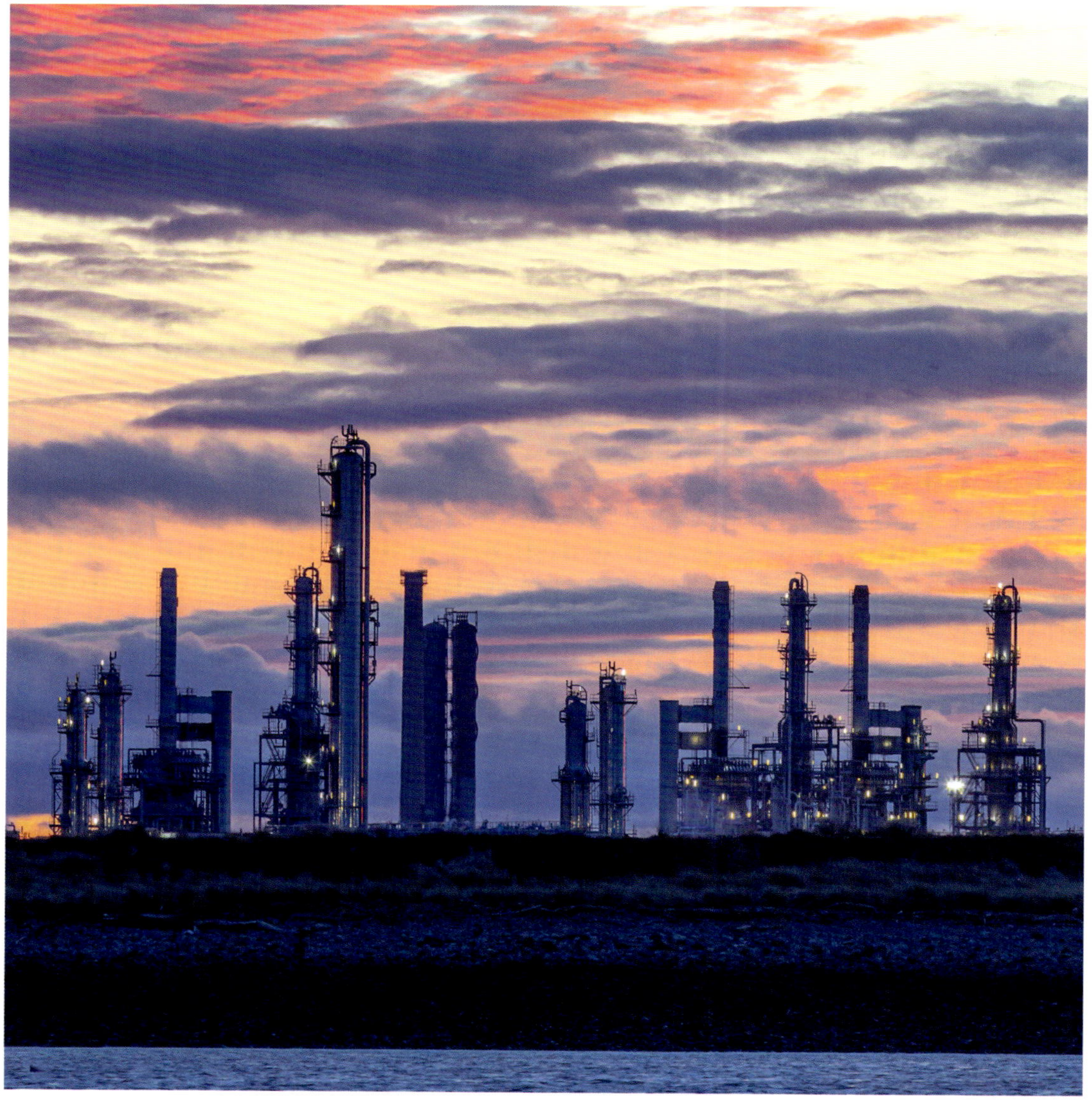
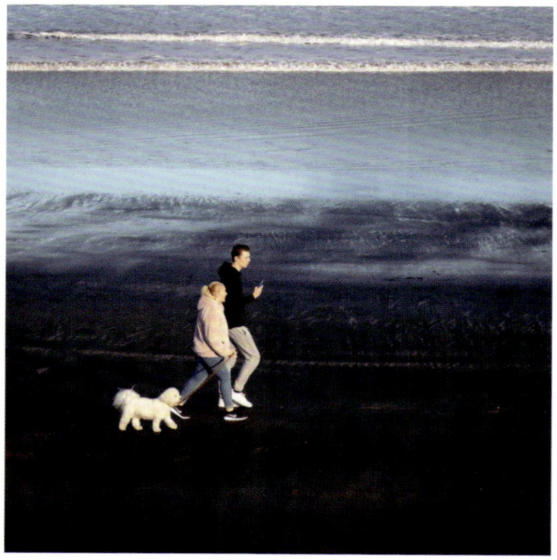
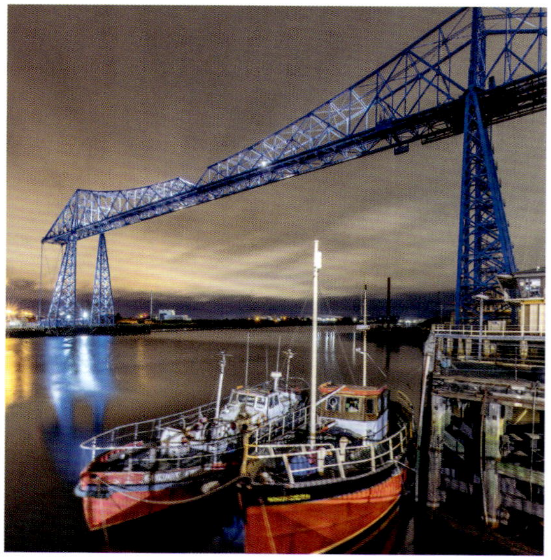

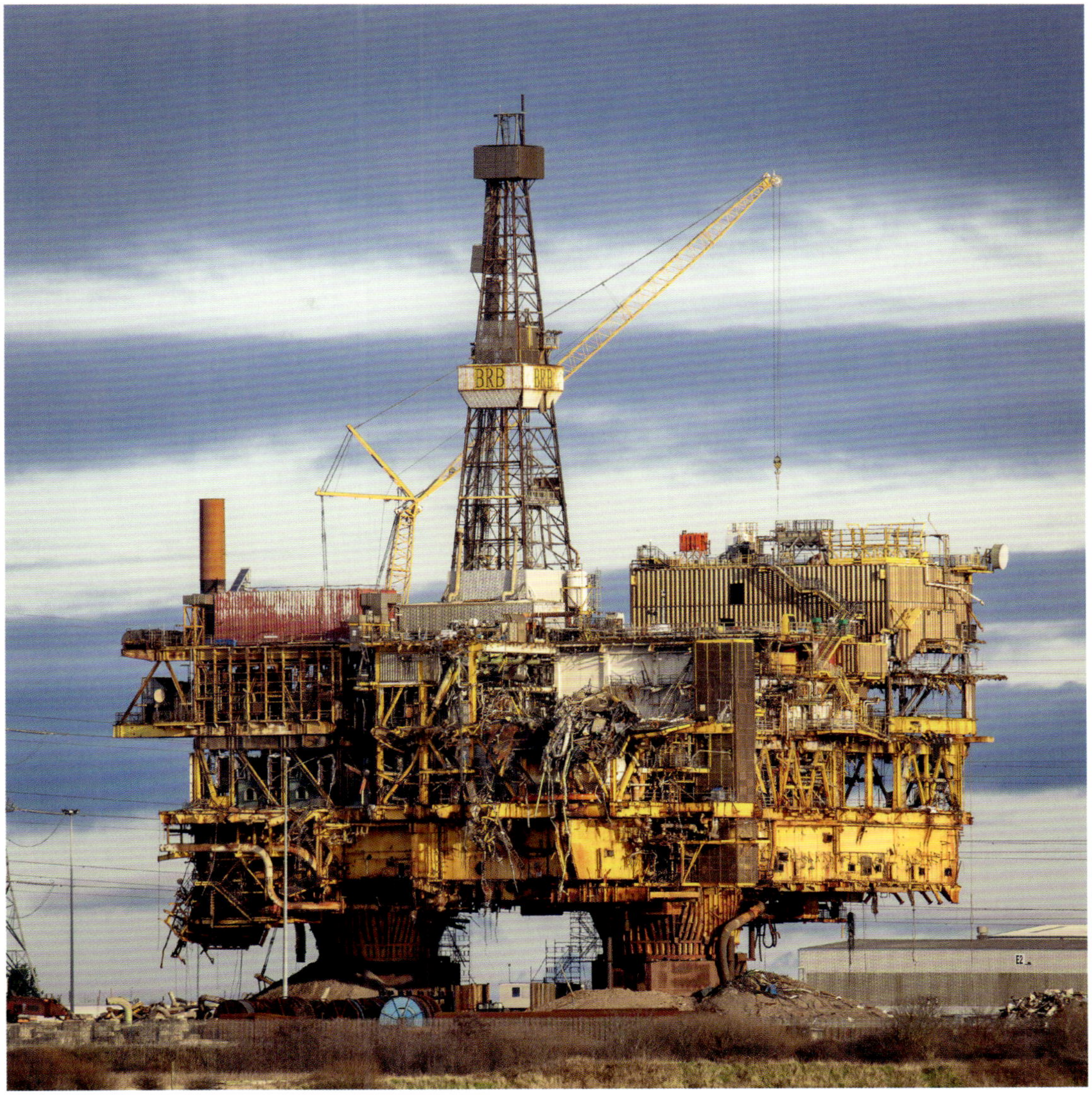

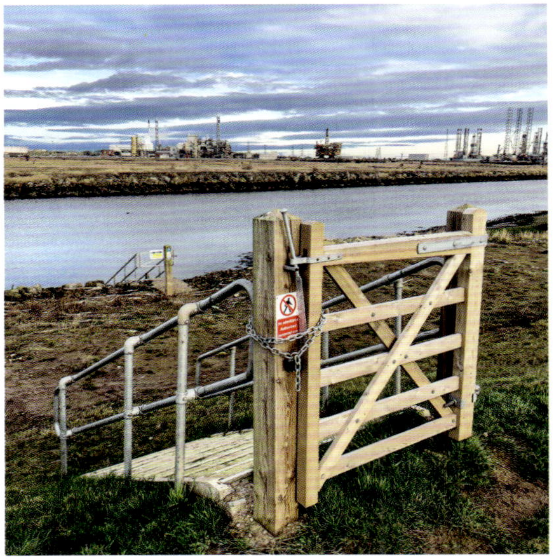

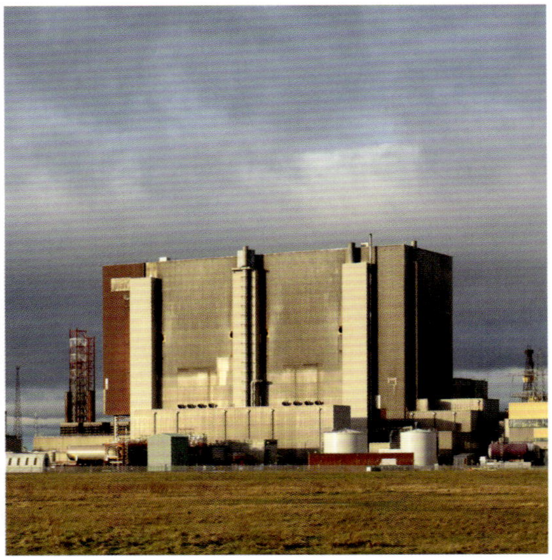

Opposite, clockwise from top left:

Magnesian limestone cliffs at Chourdon Point, Hawthorn Hive

Town wall, Headland, Hartlepool

Sea cave at Blackhall Rocks

Strolling on the coal-blackened beach at Seaton Carew

Middlesbrough Transporter Bridge at dusk (from the North Yorkshire side)

Teesside Oil Terminal, Seal Sands

From top left:

Decommissioning of the 25,000-tonne Shell Brent Bravo oil platform at Able Seaton Port

Only in England: Greatham Creek

Hartlepool nuclear power station

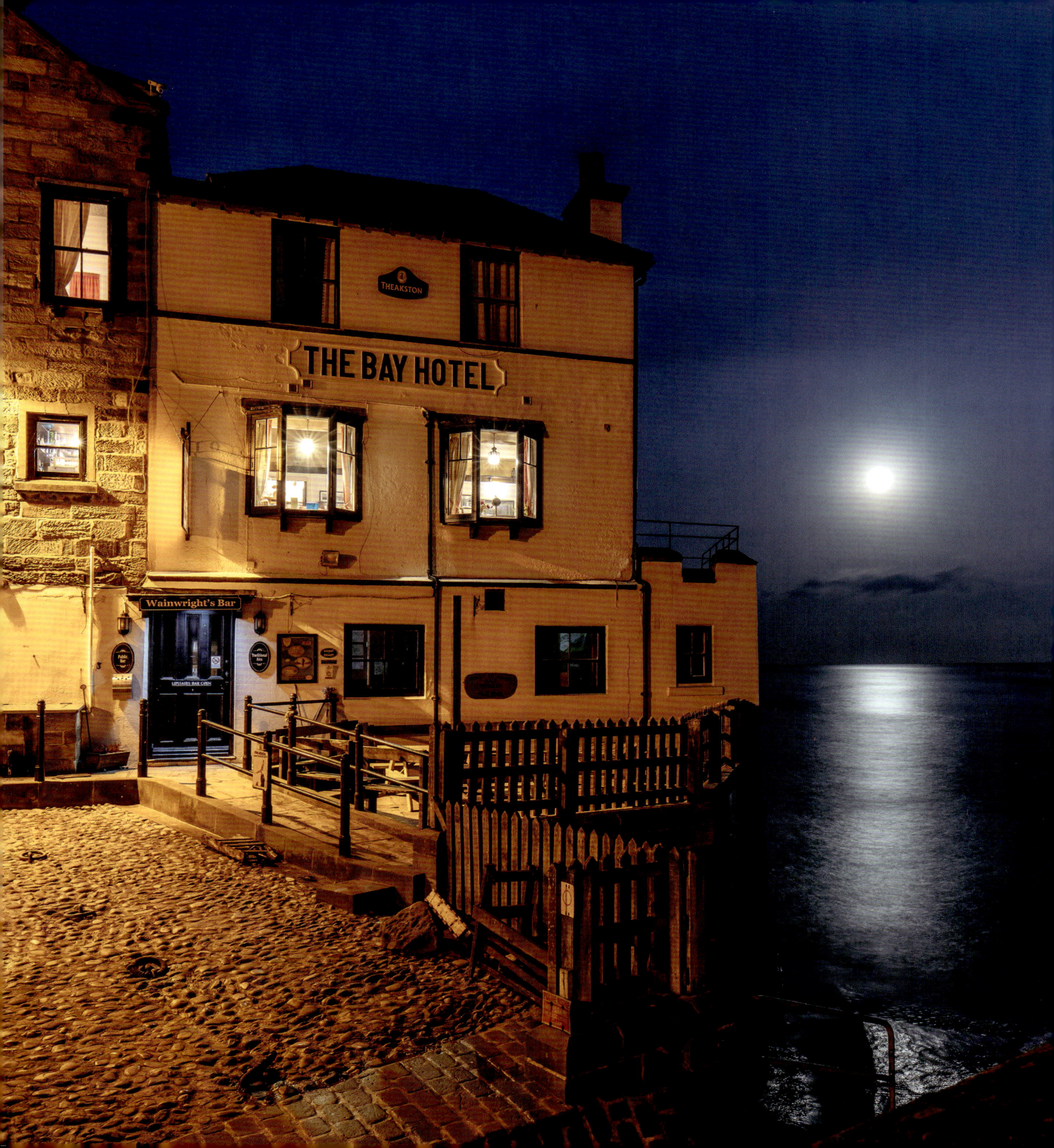
THEAKSTON
THE BAY HOTEL
Wainwright's Bar

47 NORTH YORKSHIRE

JANUARY 2020

DAY 384–389 | 09,338–09,488 KM | 150 KM

My journey through Yorkshire starts in Middlesbrough with an interview on BBC Radio Tees, after my tweets on the local area were picked up by a journalist who asked me to drop by. I leave my backpack outside the door of the broadcast studio to meet the friendly presenters of the *Breakfast* show, where we launch into a chat about my geographical confusion as to exactly where Teesside ends and Yorkshire begins and if the name Cleveland is ever used now, not to mention how Middlesbrough fits into this stew. The presenter's joshingly contradictory opinions soon make me understand that it's not just outsiders like me who are perplexed. However, they do tell me that 'You're just a small town in Yorkshire!' is a taunt that doesn't go down very well at Boro football matches.

Leaving Middlesbrough is a fascinatingly dystopian experience that involves walking along a narrow, fenced path past oil refineries, derelict steelworks and a very active container port. The notion that Britain imports far more goods than it exports seems tangible here. A continuous flow of empty flatbed trucks passes the silent Lackenby Steelworks towards the sea, returning from the port fully loaded. I follow gas pipelines for miles towards South Gare, where the rusting coke ovens and retired blast furnaces at Redcar Steelworks make me think of the work of Bernd and Hilla Becher. Photographing the steelworks is inspiring, and I'm particularly captivated by the Dorman Long coke ovens and the towering blast furnaces. I get a true sense of the vast scale of the dormant industry in Teesside from how tiny the demolition machinery looks against a landscape of flare stacks and gas cylinders. It seems like an entire way of life is being erased, and I can't help but think how traumatic it must be for the thousands who once worked here, watching their history being dismantled around them.

At Saltburn-by-the-Sea, the industry has faded away into the horizon. I'm back in romantic walking country, having joined the Cleveland Way, and am happy to be on clifftops again. The view inland is of a misty patchwork of rolling green fields while the coastal erosion is so rapid here that many paths marked on my map no longer exist. For a few days natural and architectural beauty alternate, culminating on an inky, rainy night when I descend into Whitby to a beautiful pealing of bells after twelve hours on the move. Jet-black jewellery shimmers lustrous in the windows, and the cobbled streets glisten in the wet.

As the light fades on my last night in North Yorkshire, the final miles of clifftop path to Scarborough look like an undulating dark green carpet running down to where the castle is silhouetted. There are hundreds of metres of ascent and descent, and my legs start burning in protest – it's butt and thigh night on the Cleveland Way! In the far distance, Flamborough Head Lighthouse pulses.

I wake up early the next day for dawn photography of Scarborough only to be graced by the moon. With the Grand Hotel and seafront as my subject, I place the tripod legs in the gently lapping waves. I start when I notice the heads of seals bobbing close to shore behind me, only to realise they are Scarborough's hardy wild swimmers emerging from the icy waves at first light. Their swimming caps gleam in the moonlight as they march past me, excitedly chatting with each other, goggles in hand.

After the rain, the Yorkshire coast path has a particularly slippery variety of mud, so I slither up and down the cliffs, grateful for my trekking poles. By the time I reach Filey, I've developed a carapace of God's Own Mud that gets more expansively plastered over my backpack, tripod, tent, clothes and sleeping mat with each passing day. Only my stove and camera remain free of the stuff. I suspect it will be up to my neck when I reach Hull.

Opposite:

Moonrise by the Bay Hotel, Robin Hood's Bay

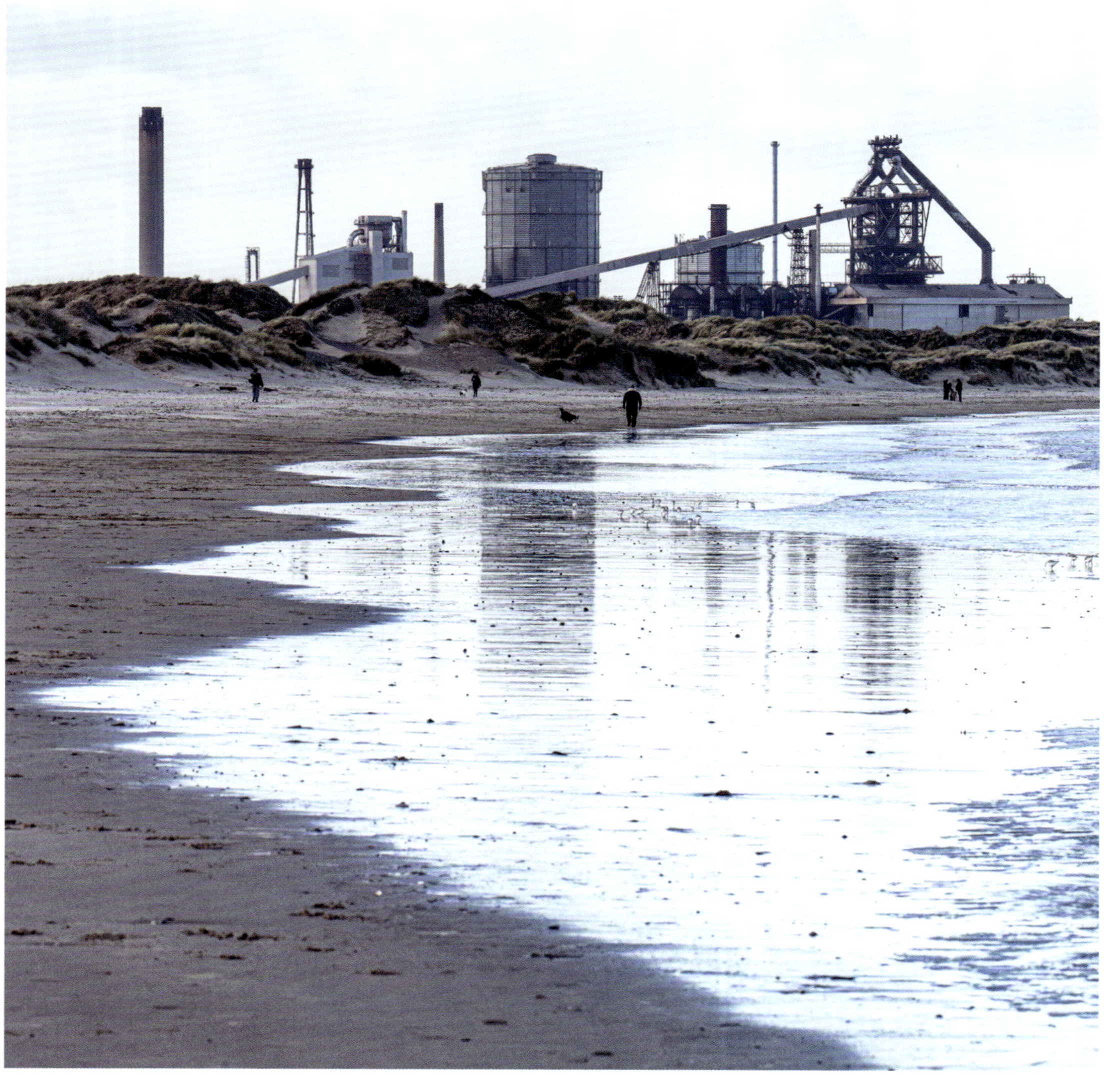

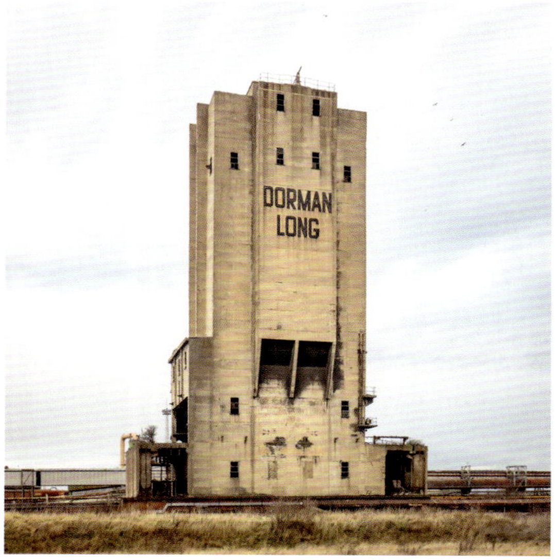

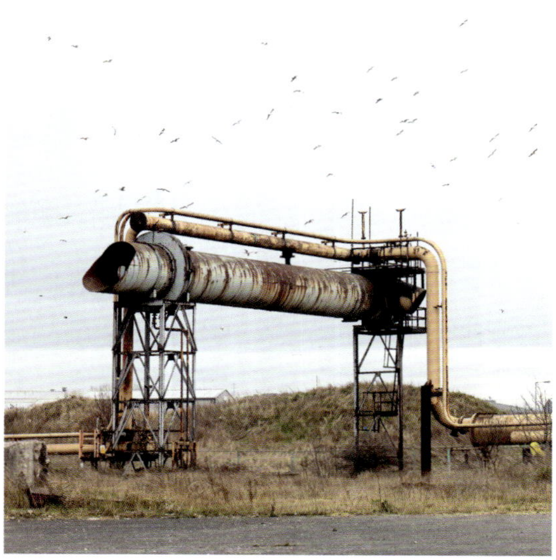

From top left:

Redcar Steelworks from Coatham Sands (closed 2015, all demolished 2021–23)

Dorman Long tower built in 1955–56, a coal bunker to supply the coking plant for steel production, a symbol of Teesside's industrial heritage and an early example of brutalist architecture. The unique and charismatic structure was demolished at 2 a.m. on 19 September 2021 despite Grade II listing

Truncated pipeline, Teesside

Opposite:

Redcar Steelworks blast furnace, the largest in the UK and the second largest in Europe (opened 1979, closed 2015, demolished 2021–23), and the fishing huts at South Gare

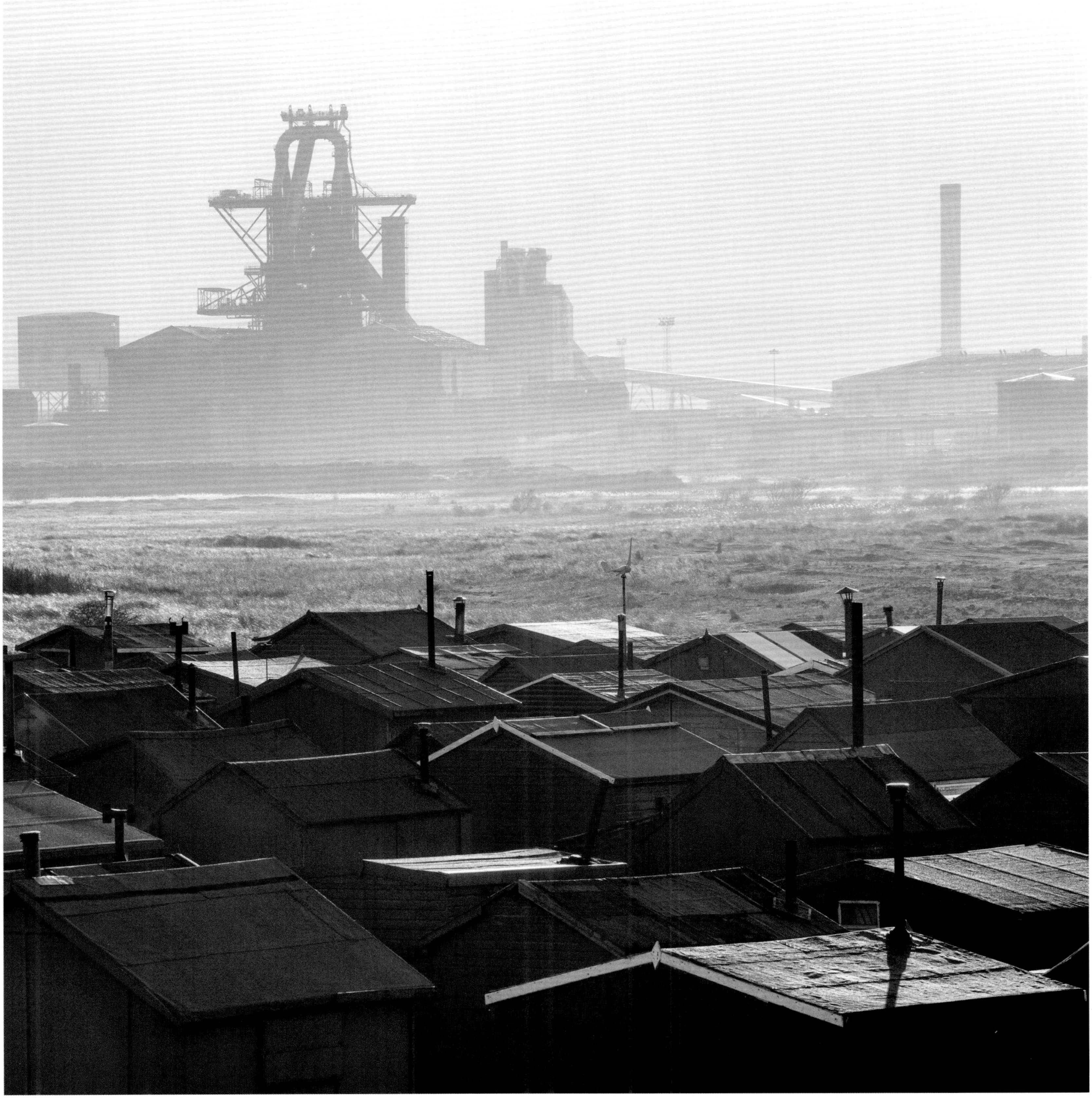

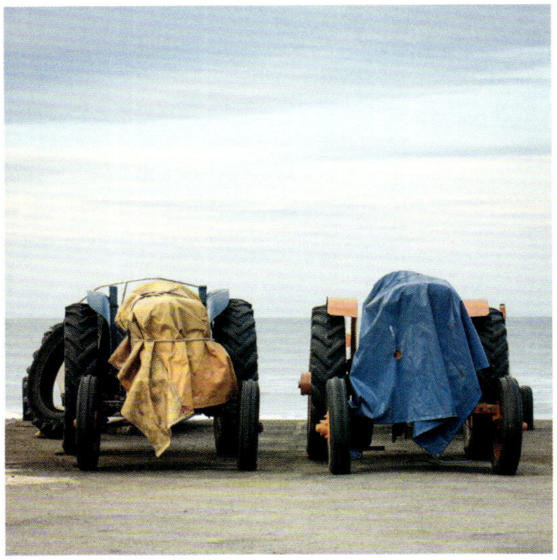

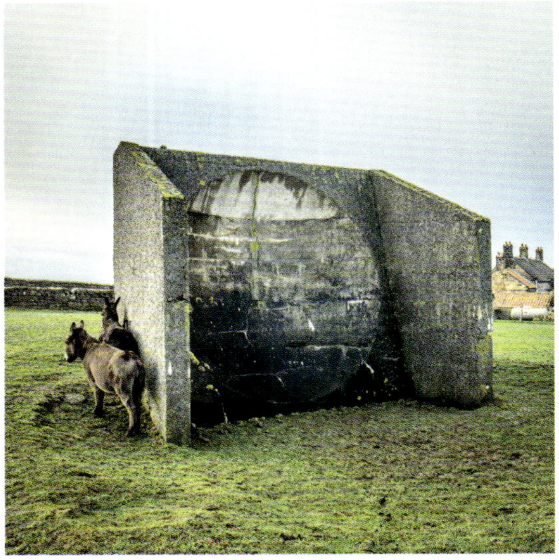

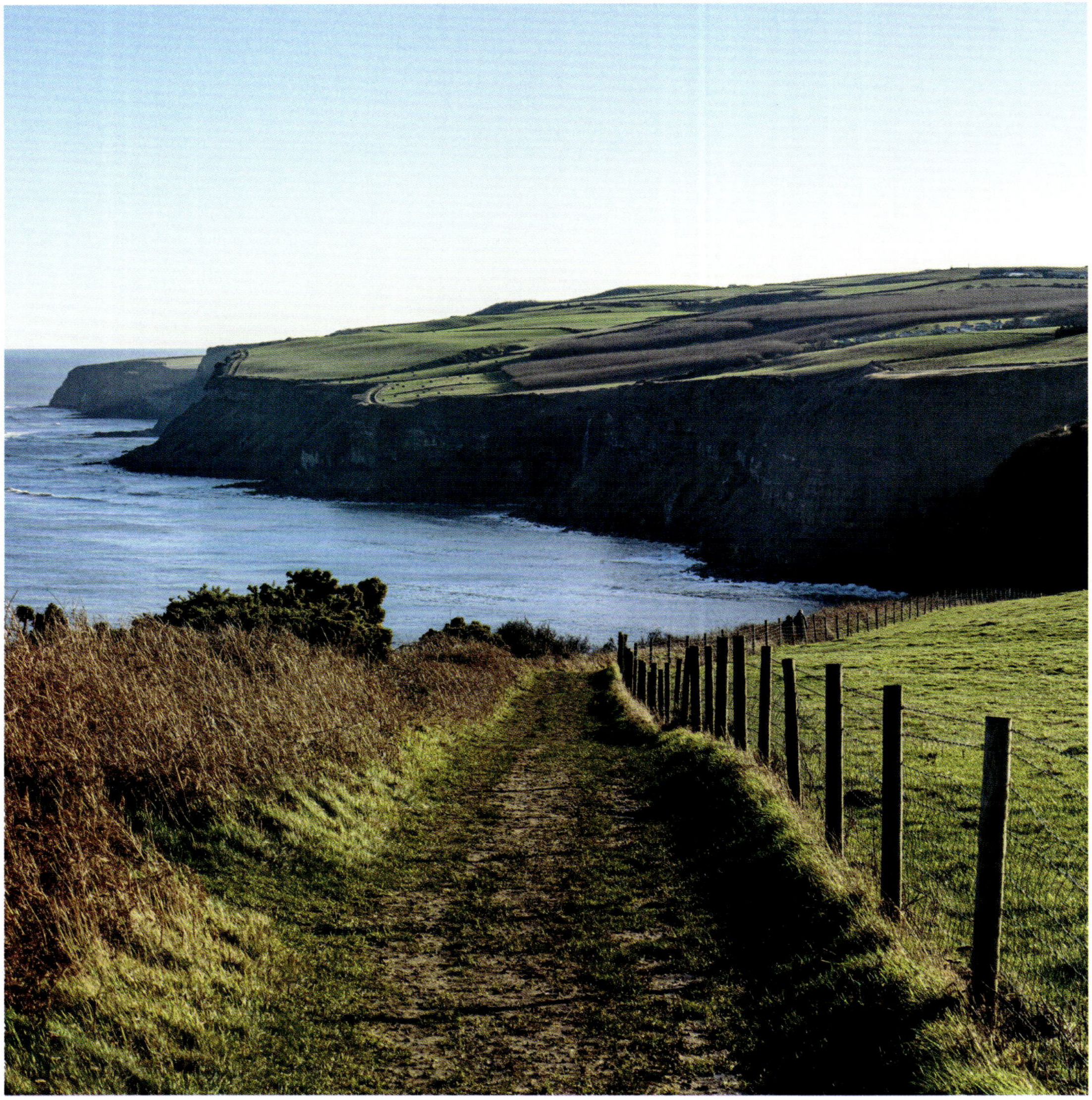

From top left:

Saltburn-by-the-Sea

Boulby Sound Mirror, built in 1916 during the First World War to provide early warning of Zeppelin attacks on the Skinningrove Iron Works. The farmer on whose land this lies told me that in the past there were two gates attached to form a pigsty!

The Cleveland Way coast path to Robin Hood's Bay from near Whitby

Opposite:

Staithes in mizzle

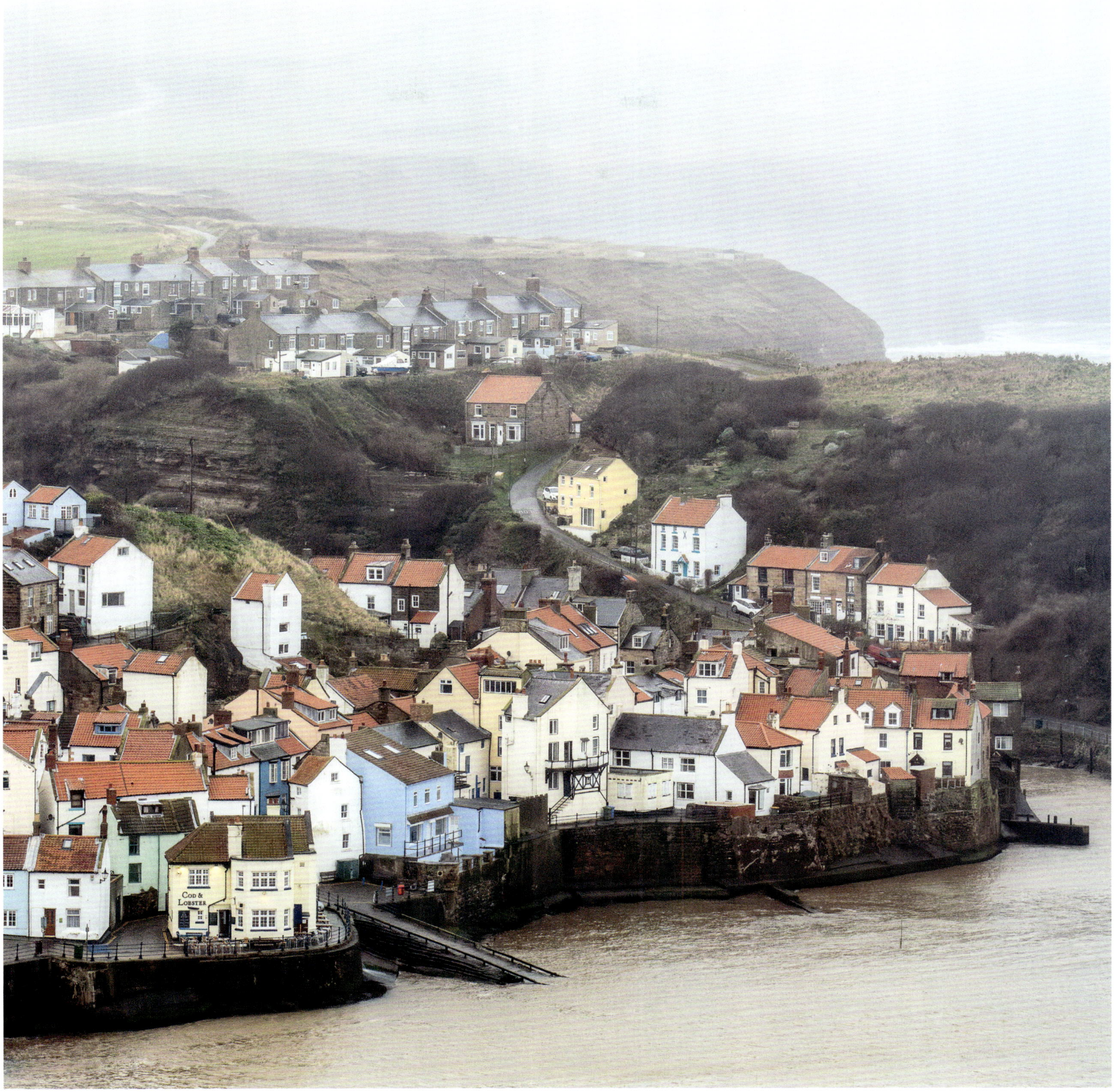
Cod &
Lobster

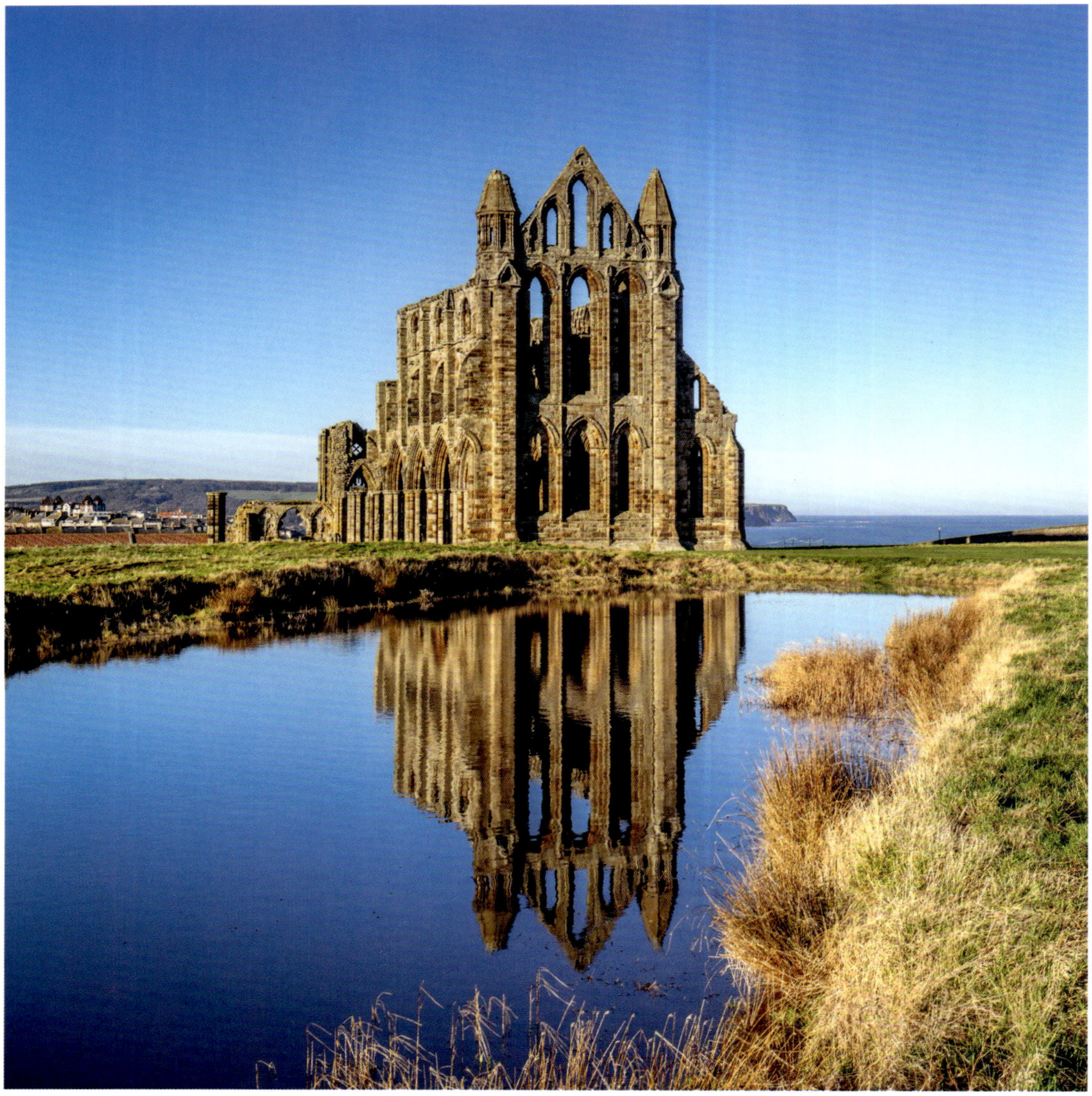

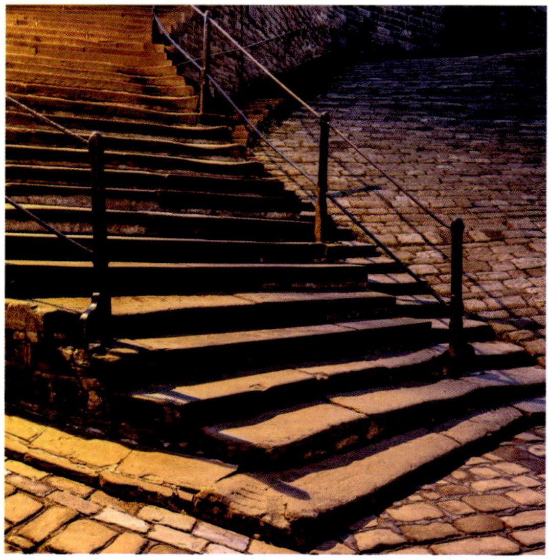

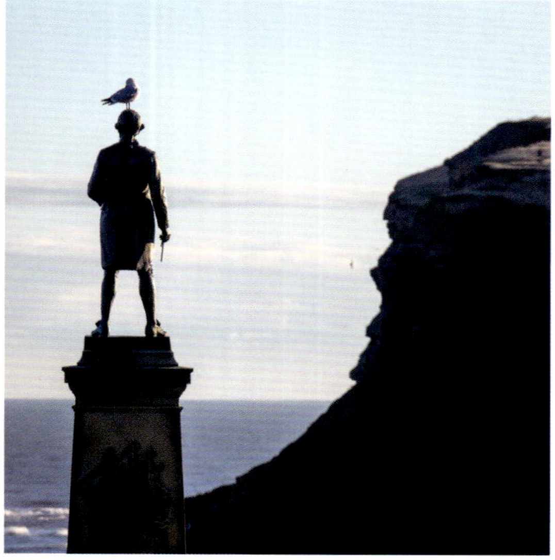

From top left:

Whitby Abbey, a seventh-century Christian monastery that later became a Benedictine abbey. In the thirteenth century, the monastery church was rebuilt in the Gothic style. The abbey and its possessions were confiscated by the Crown under Henry VIII during the Dissolution of the Monasteries between 1536 and 1545

The first record of the 199 steps in Whitby comes from 1340, but they're believed to be even older. They were originally made from wood with the stone replacement we see today dating from 1774. It is thought ascending them was a test of Christian faith. Bram Stoker's 1897 novel *Dracula* featured Count Dracula as a creature resembling a large dog which came ashore at the headland and ran up the steps to the graveyard of St Mary's Church in the shadow of the Whitby Abbey ruins

Captain Cook learned his craft in local vessels and two of the ships he used on his long and perilous voyages – *Resolution* and *Endeavour* – were built in Whitby

Opposite, clockwise from top left:

Rock shop, Scarborough

Snapped Second World War section post pillbox above Cayton Bay (demolished 2021)

Ocean Drive Crazy Golf, Filey

As the waves lapped gently over the legs of my tripod, I turned, surprised by the wet footsteps of swimmers emerging from the dark ocean behind me. Grand Hotel and Olympia Leisure, Scarborough

Dormer windows of the Grand Hotel, Scarborough

Telling it like it is: Cayton Bay

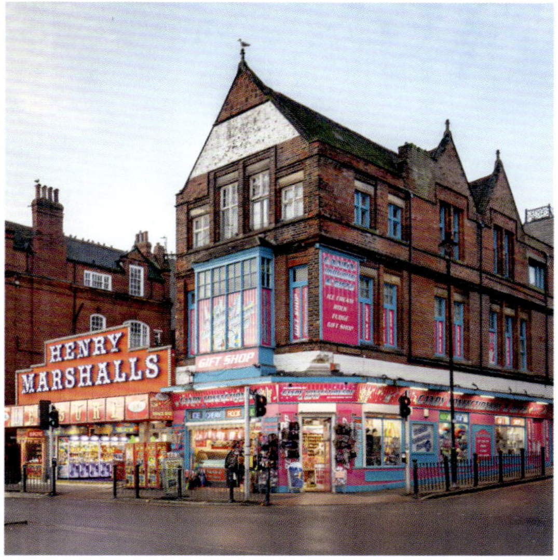
HENRY
MARSHALLS
GIFT SHOP

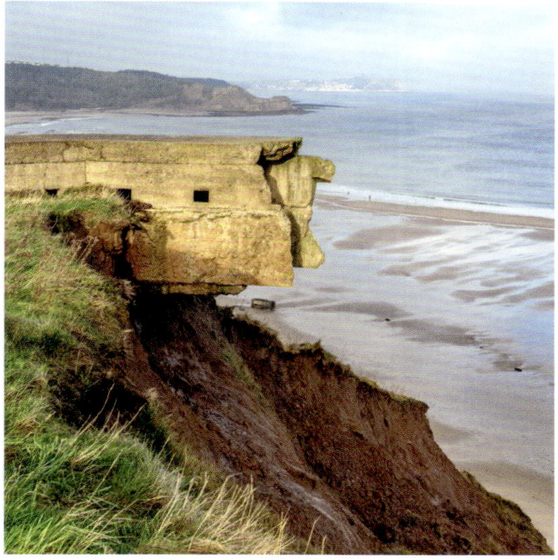

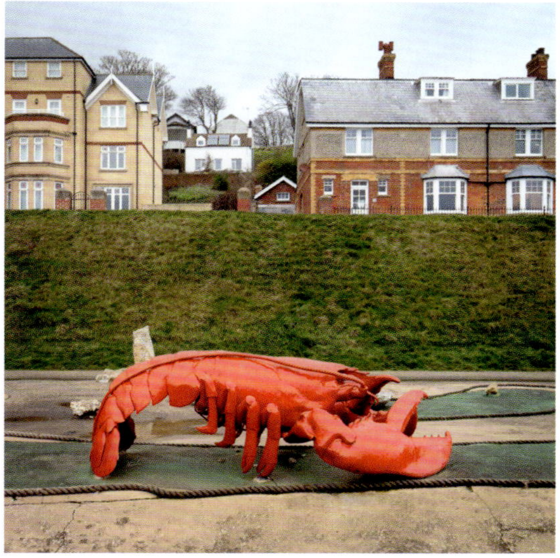

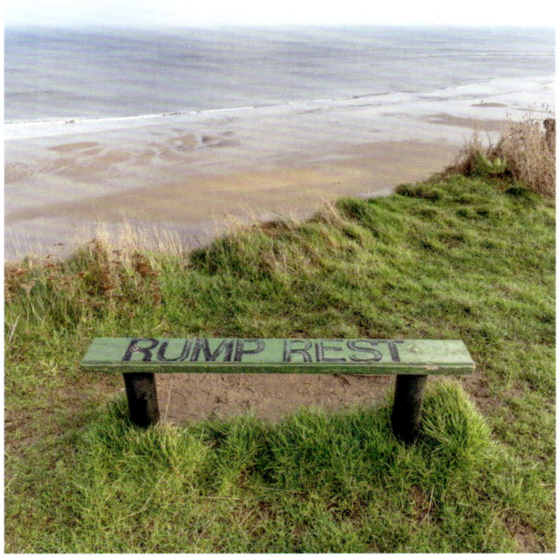
RUMP REST

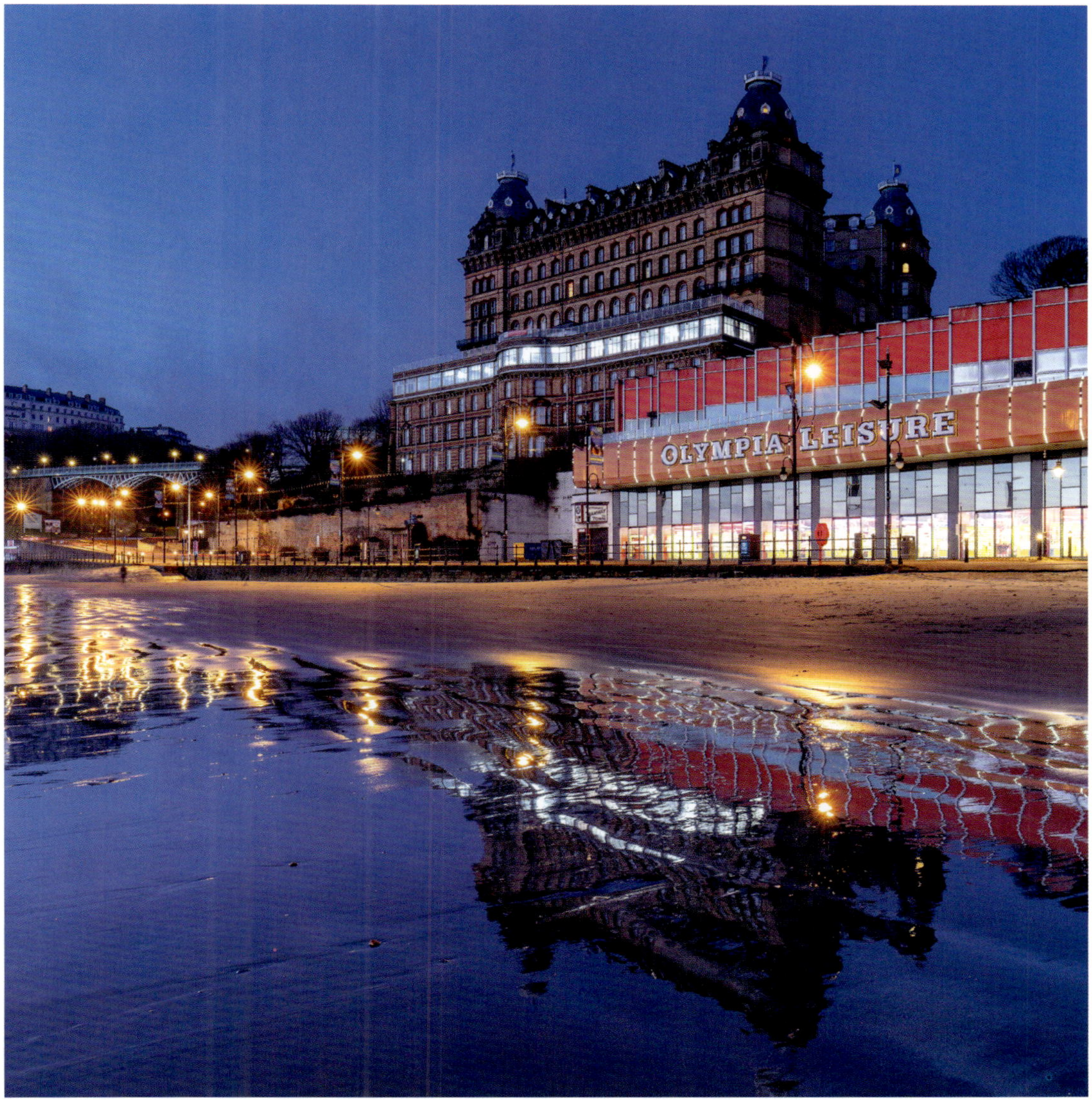
OLYMPIA LEISURE

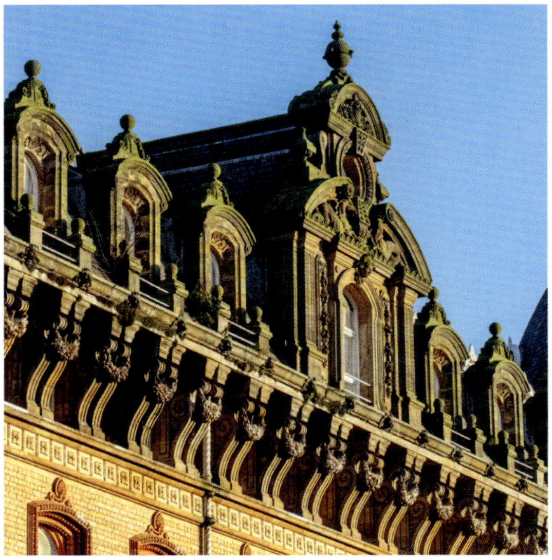

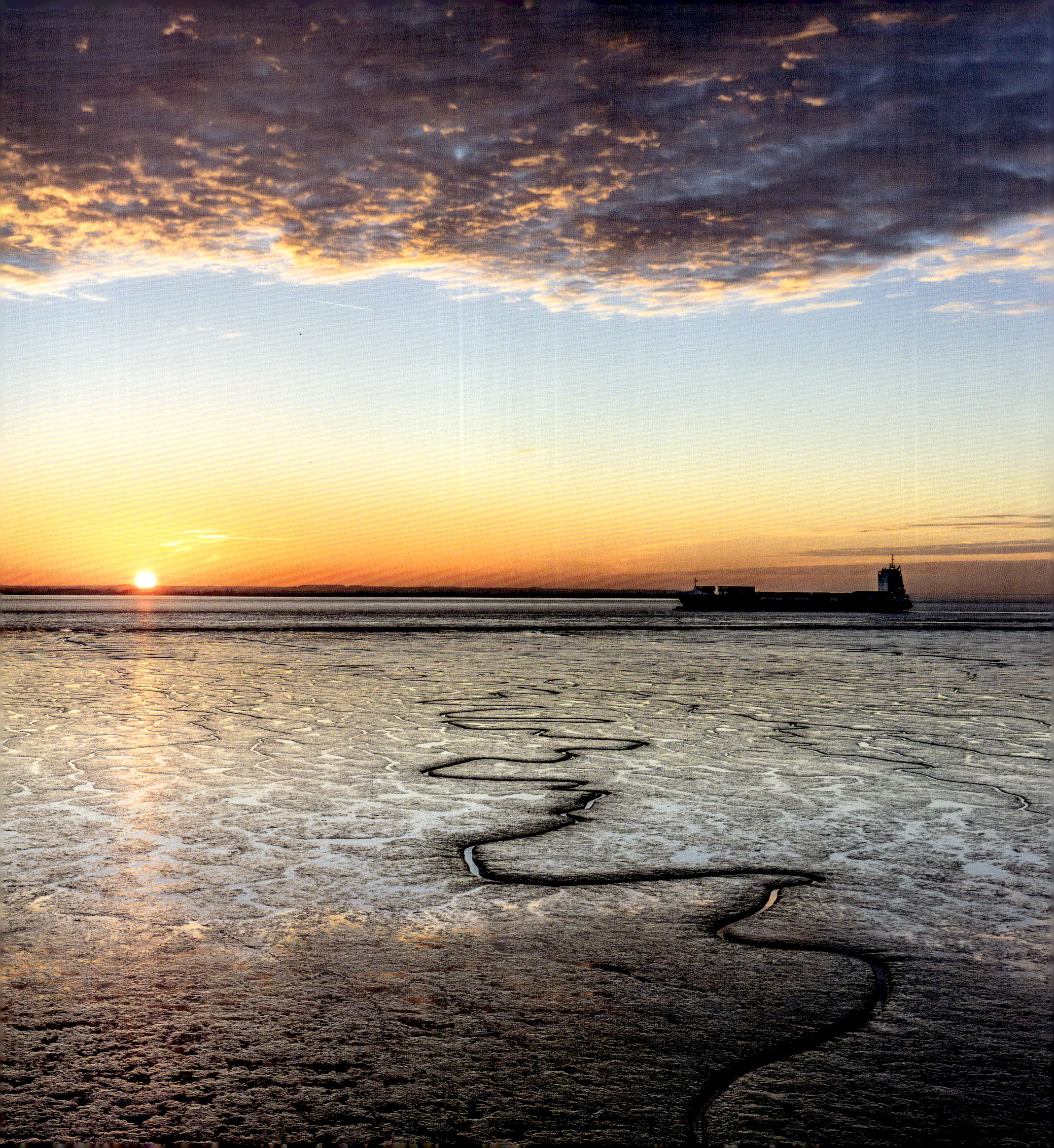

48 EAST YORKSHIRE

JANUARY–FEBRUARY 2020

DAY 390–396 | 09,488–09,651KM | 163KM

Usually, England's attempts at lousy weather are amusingly ineffectual compared to Scotland's, but not today. As Storm Brendan takes hold, the day becomes wetter and colder and by the time I reach the 120-metre chalk cliffs on the way to Flamborough, I'm struggling to walk against the wind-blown rain, let alone use my camera. I shelter in the lee of a winter-closed cafe, unable to move my fingers until I make a hot drink.

The next day, as the storm subsides, the cliffs taper down to flatness at Bridlington. As I make my way through the high street looking for food, a megaphone-wielding evangelist calls out in my direction, 'Going for a walk, then? But are you walking with God?' I leave the town on a flat beach curving away to the horizon; the sun is shining, the tide is low, and my stomach is full. It's a nice change of pace from the previous day's ordeal!

But the peace doesn't last for long. A few hours later, as I'm making good progress on firm sand along the 20 kilometres of uninterrupted cliff-lined beach towards Hornsea, I begin to notice the tide rising. I pull out my map only to realise that, though it shows plenty of tracks to get back up the cliff, in reality there aren't any steps or ramps. In desperation, I try climbing up, but my feet sink into the clay soil like wet concrete. I retreat, fearing that I'll get stuck or cause a landslip.

When the sea laps over my boots, I start to run. Further ahead, the map shows the cliff is 10 metres lower, which I hope will be less fragile or at least quicker to climb up. I sweep my torch around and spot a patch with the texture of garden soil and torn bits of turf. Gingerly, I clamber up it, trying not to disturb anything. Miraculously, the soil here is firmer, and I ascend steadily away from the waves. Relief washes over me when my hands reach the top lip, and I throw my backpack down, shaking uncontrollably in a dark, open field.

Once I come to my senses and stop swearing, I take my phone out. How the hell did I get myself into this situation? And why was the map not accurate? A quick google reveals that the cliffs along the Holderness Coast erode at the fastest pace in Europe, decreasing by 7 metres a year in places, with an average annual rate of 2 metres. I'm astonished to learn that 5 kilometres of land, including twenty-three towns and villages, have been lost since Roman times. The map I'd been relying on shows roads running off the cliff's edge towards these long-lost destinations.

The following day, I'm back to the torn edge of Holderness, where farmers plough their dwindling fields a wary distance from the cliff edge. I check every kilometre ahead with Google Earth's detailed satellite map to avoid making the same mistake. Soon, I'm below the melting cliffs again, which in parts appear as wet lava. Occasionally, globules of clay fall from a cliff, and as the clay turns red past Hornsea, so does the sea. On one section below the cliffs, there are sausages of clay, half dissolved, that give the squashy impression of walking on hundreds of dog turds.

It's a long, flat hike to Hull from Spurn Point on the embankments of the busy shipping channel that is the Humber. These winter days are short, but they are sunny and beautiful; a barn owl glides past me in daylight. On my last morning, I wake up to find the tent covered in a thick layer of frost and my boots frozen solid. Walking along with two ice cubes for feet puts me in a bit of a grump so I'm cheered when a Yorkshireman greets me on the path to Sunk Island with an upbeat 'Ey up!' I thought that only happened on TV!

Opposite:

Last light over the Humber at Paull

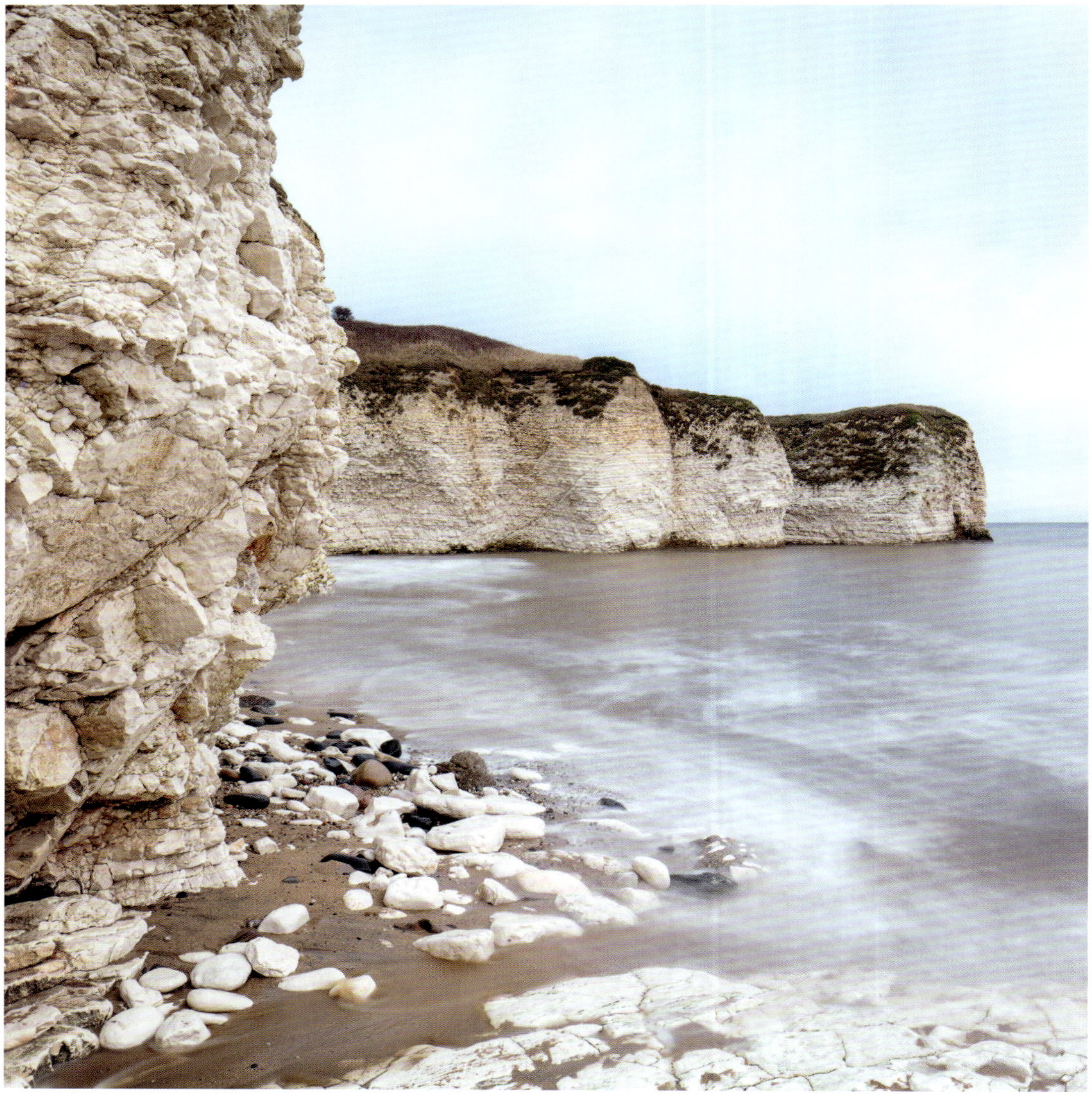

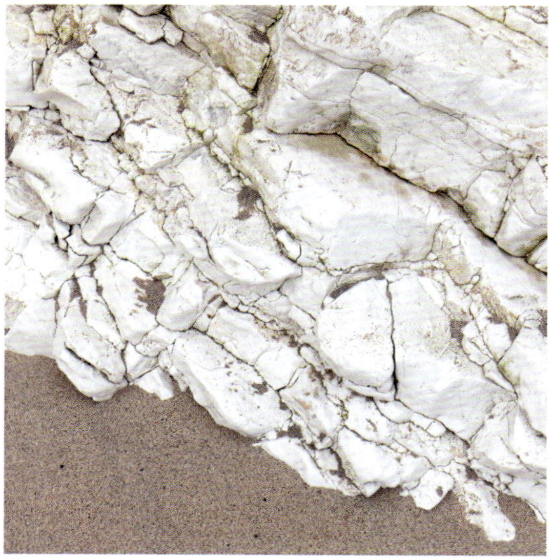

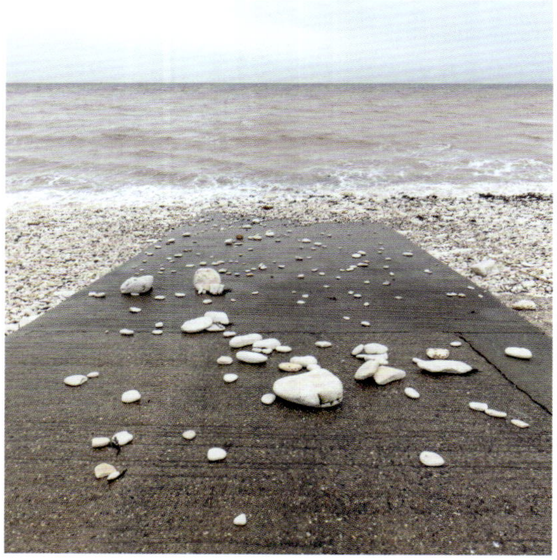

From top left:

High tide at Selwicks Bay, Flamborough Head

Underfoot, Selwicks Bay, Flamborough Head

Chalk pebbles on the slipway at Flamborough Lifeboat Station after Storm Brendan

Opposite, clockwise from top left:

In step: Bridlington

Jolly Roger, Holderness. Some 5 kilometres of land, including twenty-three towns and villages, have been lost since Roman times along the Holderness coast due to erosion

Road's end, Atwick, Holderness.The erosion is so fast in Holderness as strong prevailing winds create longshore drift that moves material south along the coastline, and the cliffs are made of soft boulder clay, which erodes rapidly when saturated

Winning the war, losing the land: Holderness

Static dynamic: Holderness

Bridlington

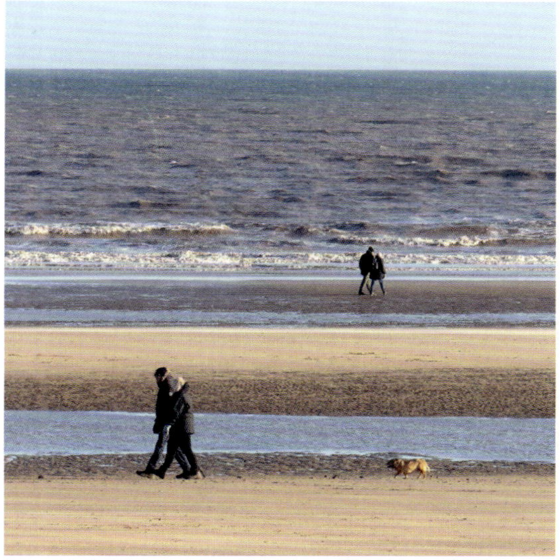
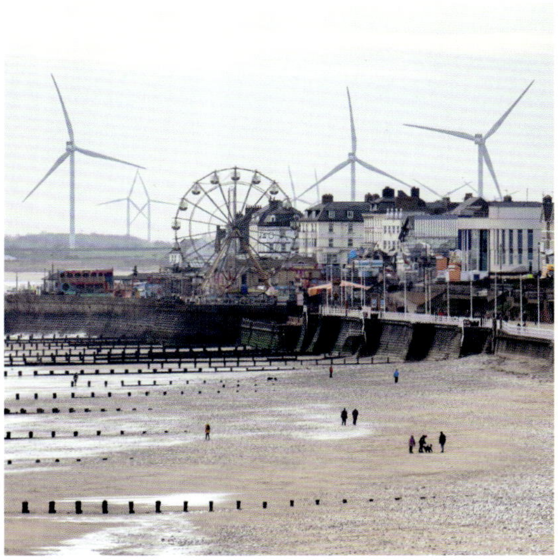
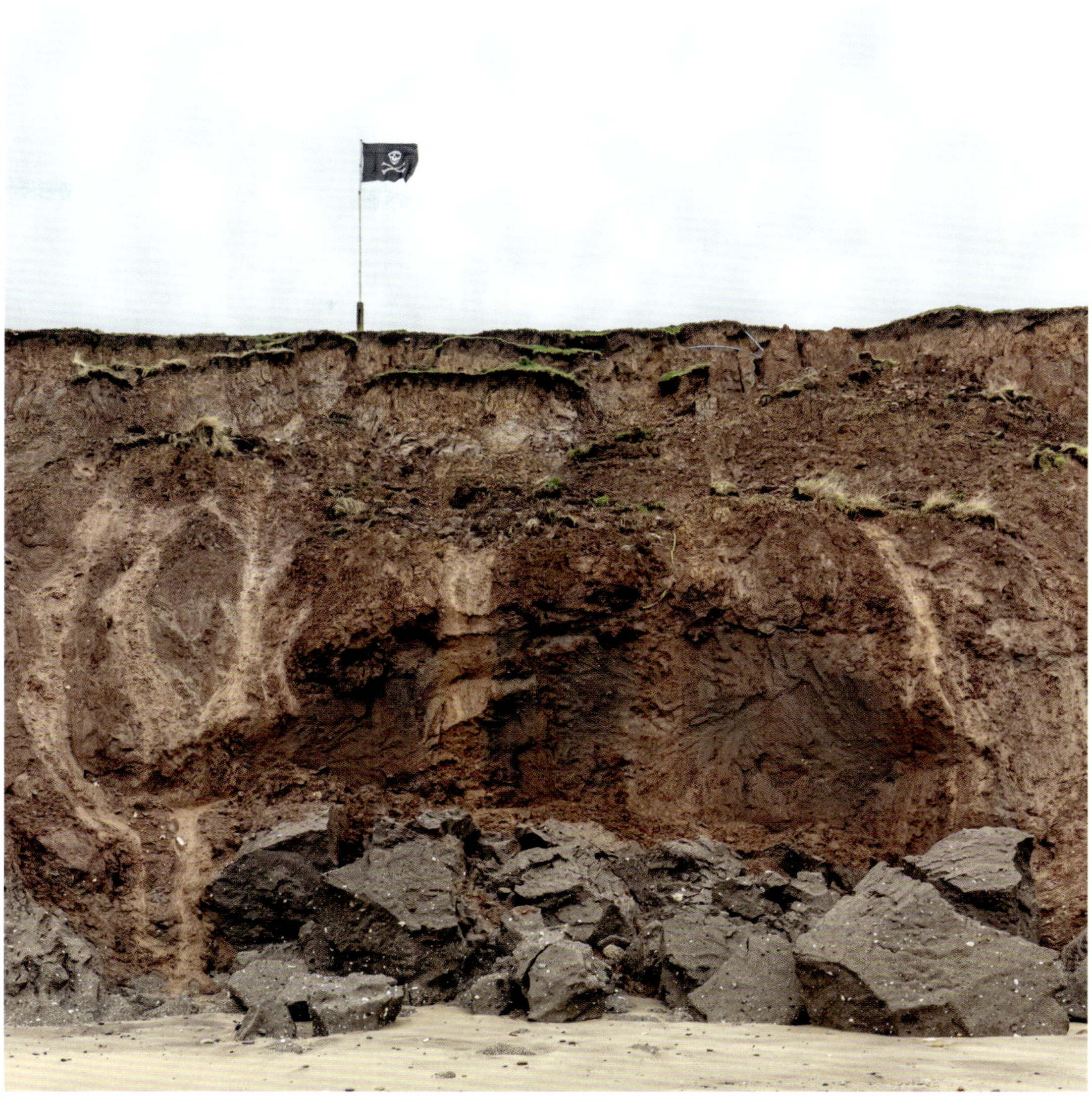
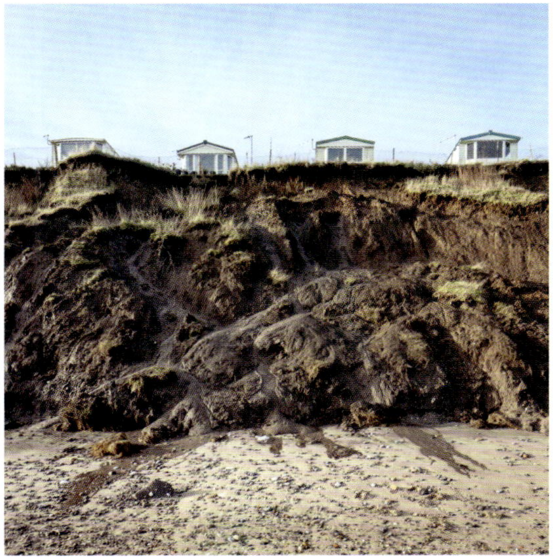
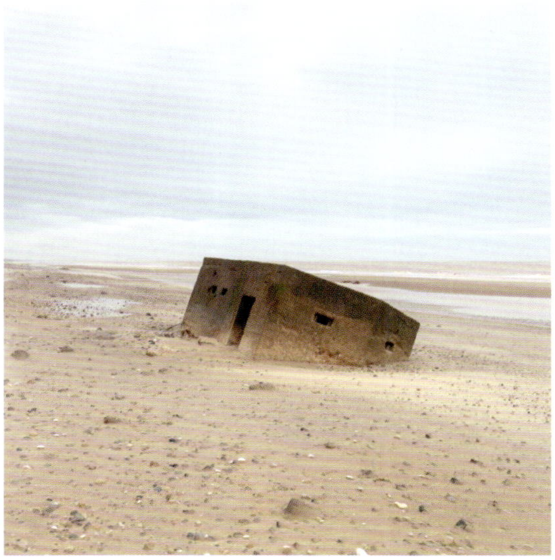
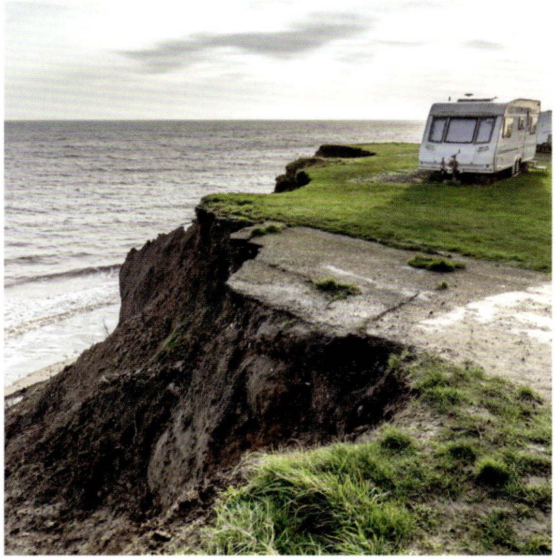

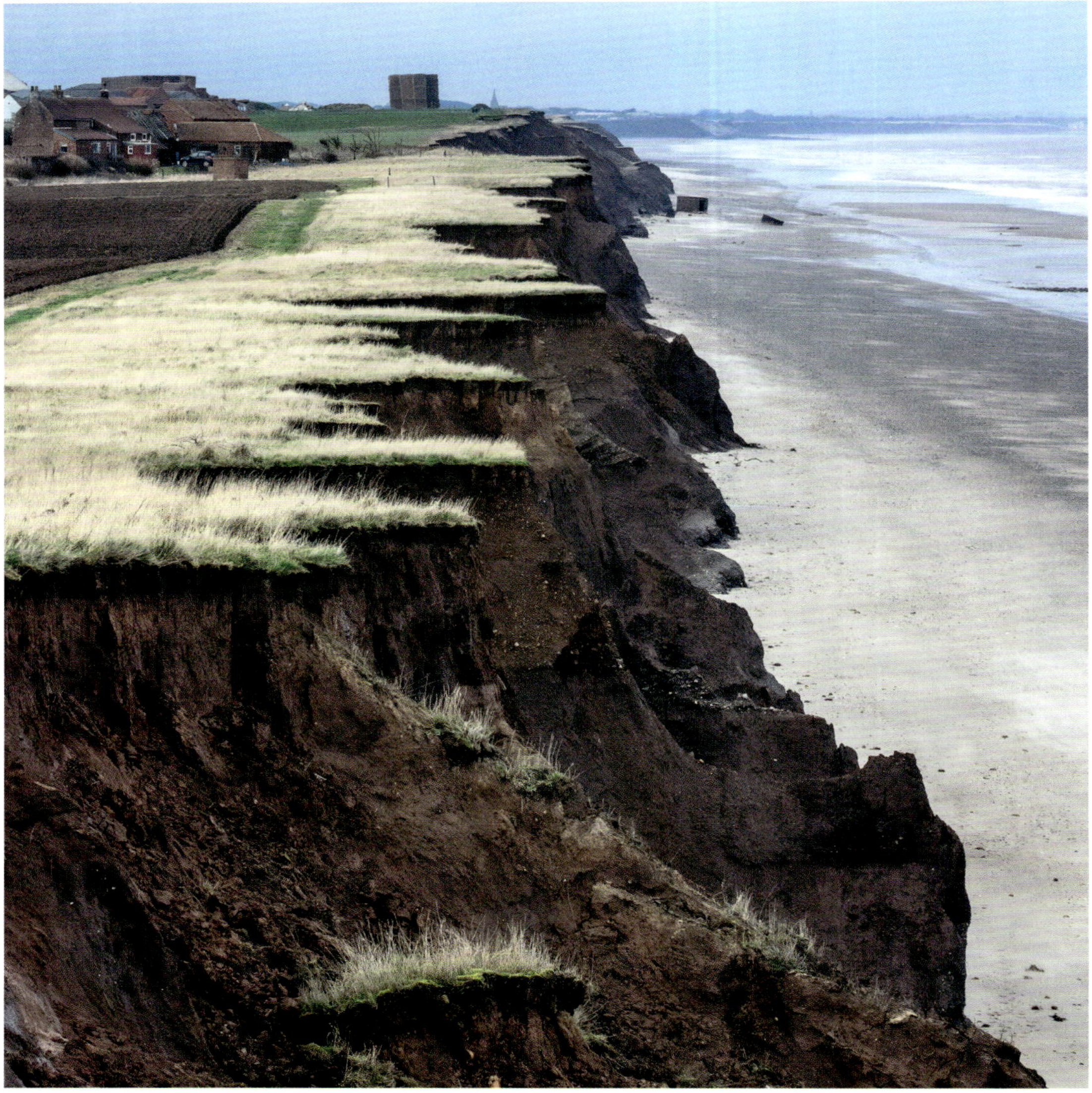

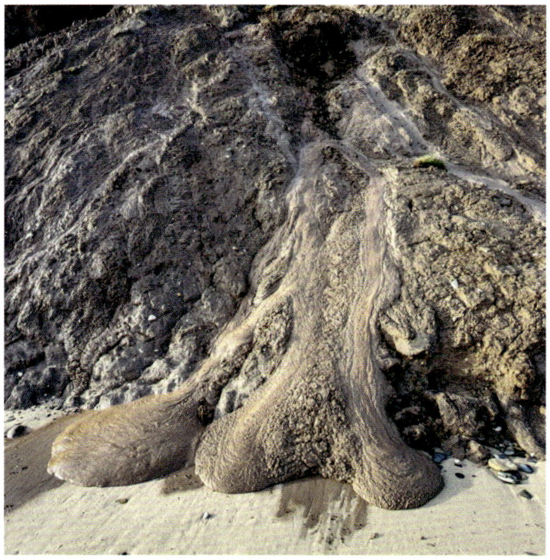

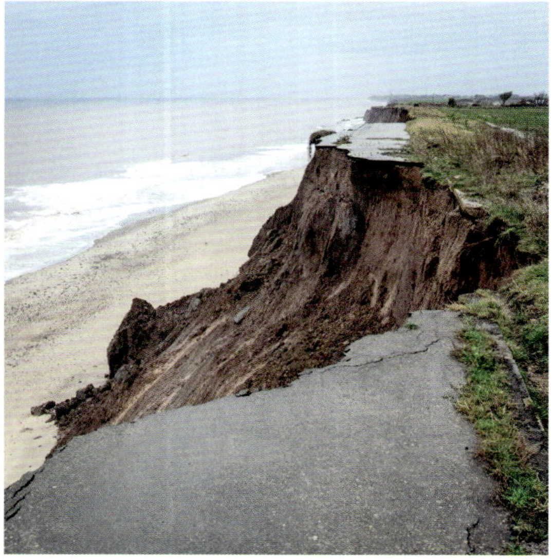

From top left:

The torn edge of Holderness: the coast here erodes at the fastest pace in Europe

Melting cliffs of Holderness

Seaside Lane, Tunstall, Holderness

Opposite, from top left:

Withernsea from Holmpton, Holderness

Last light over the Humber: Burstall Bank, Skeffling Clays

From bottom left:

Skeffling Clays by the Humber

Frosty camp at Hawkin's Point by the Humber

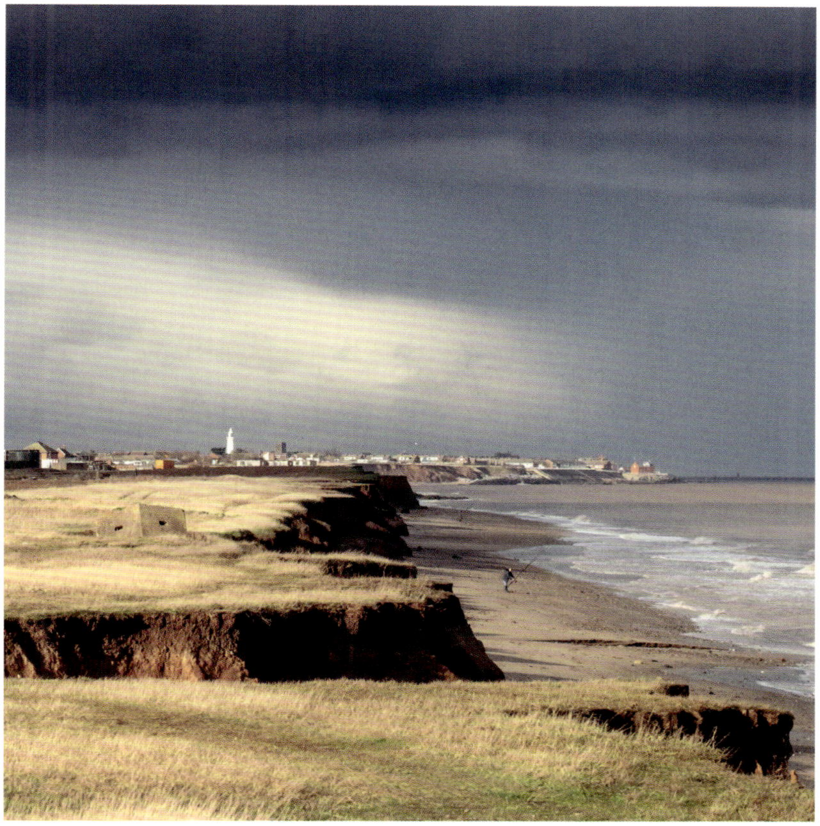

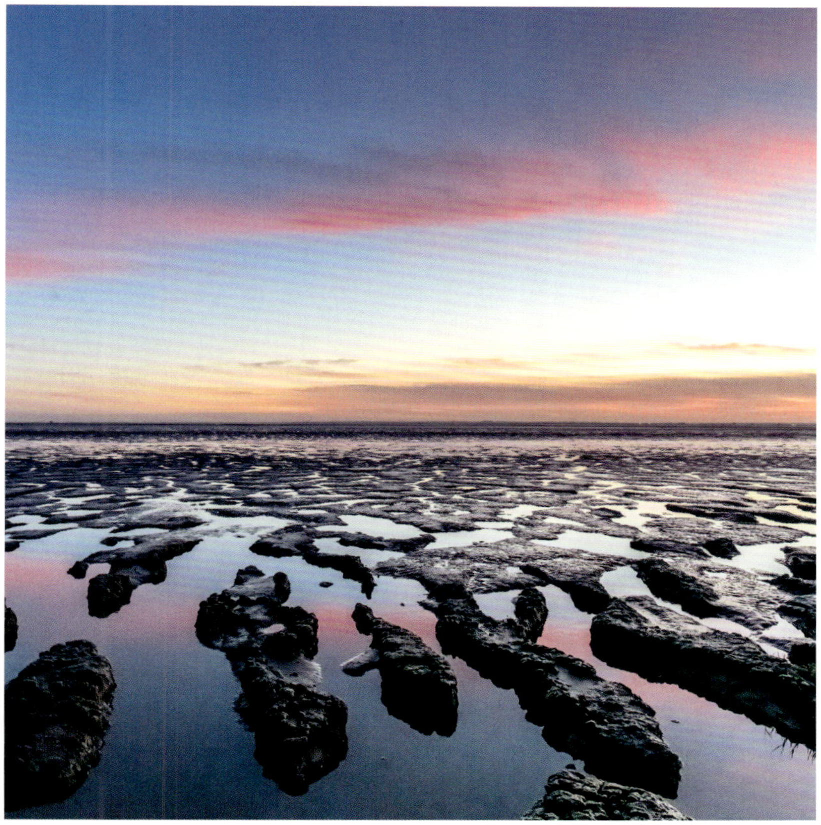

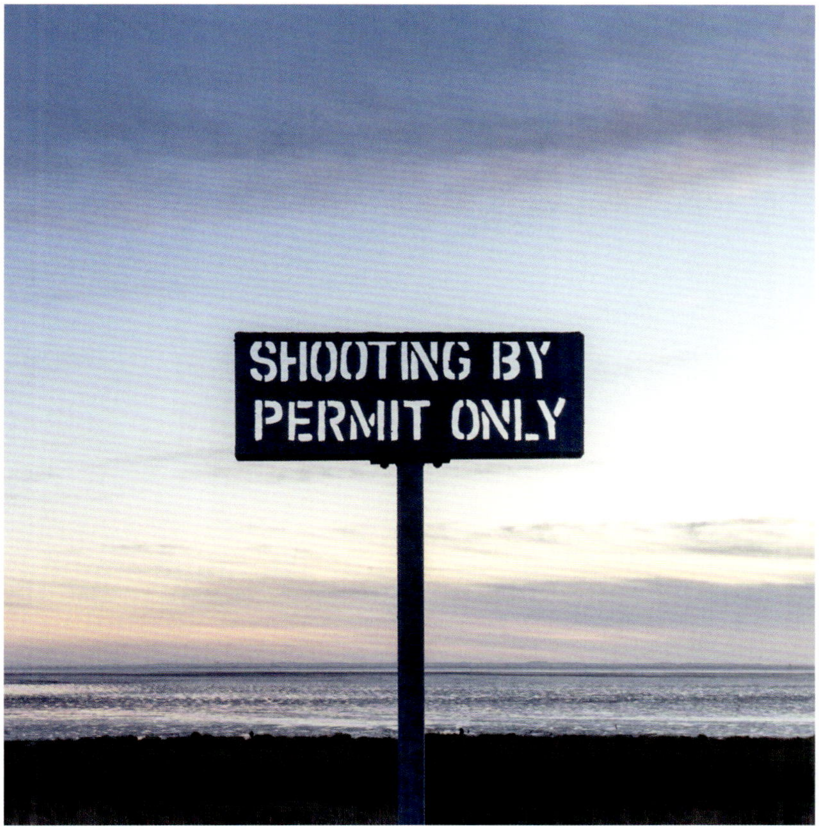
SHOOTING BY
PERMIT ONLY

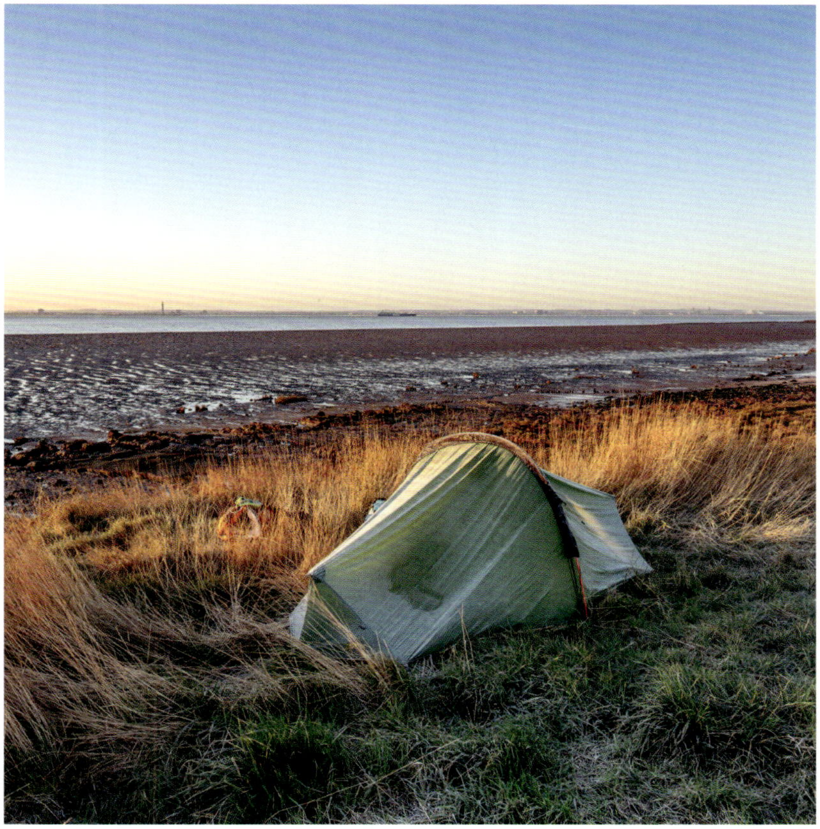

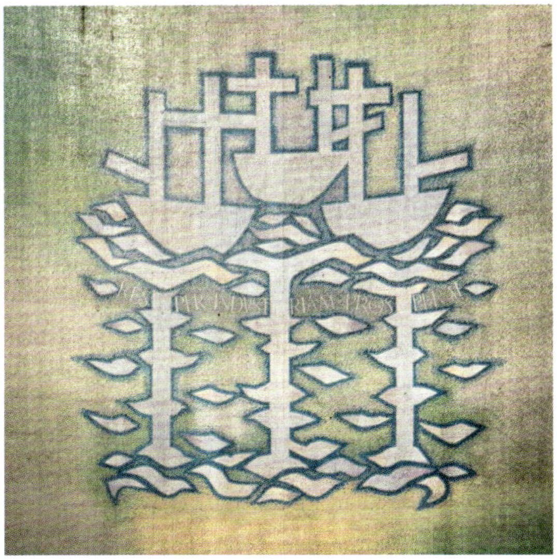

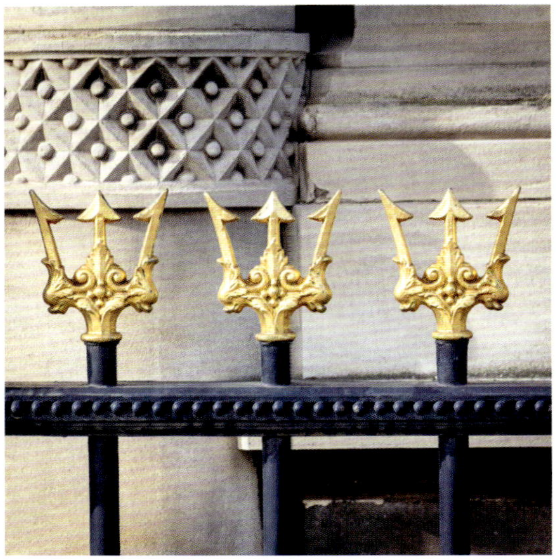

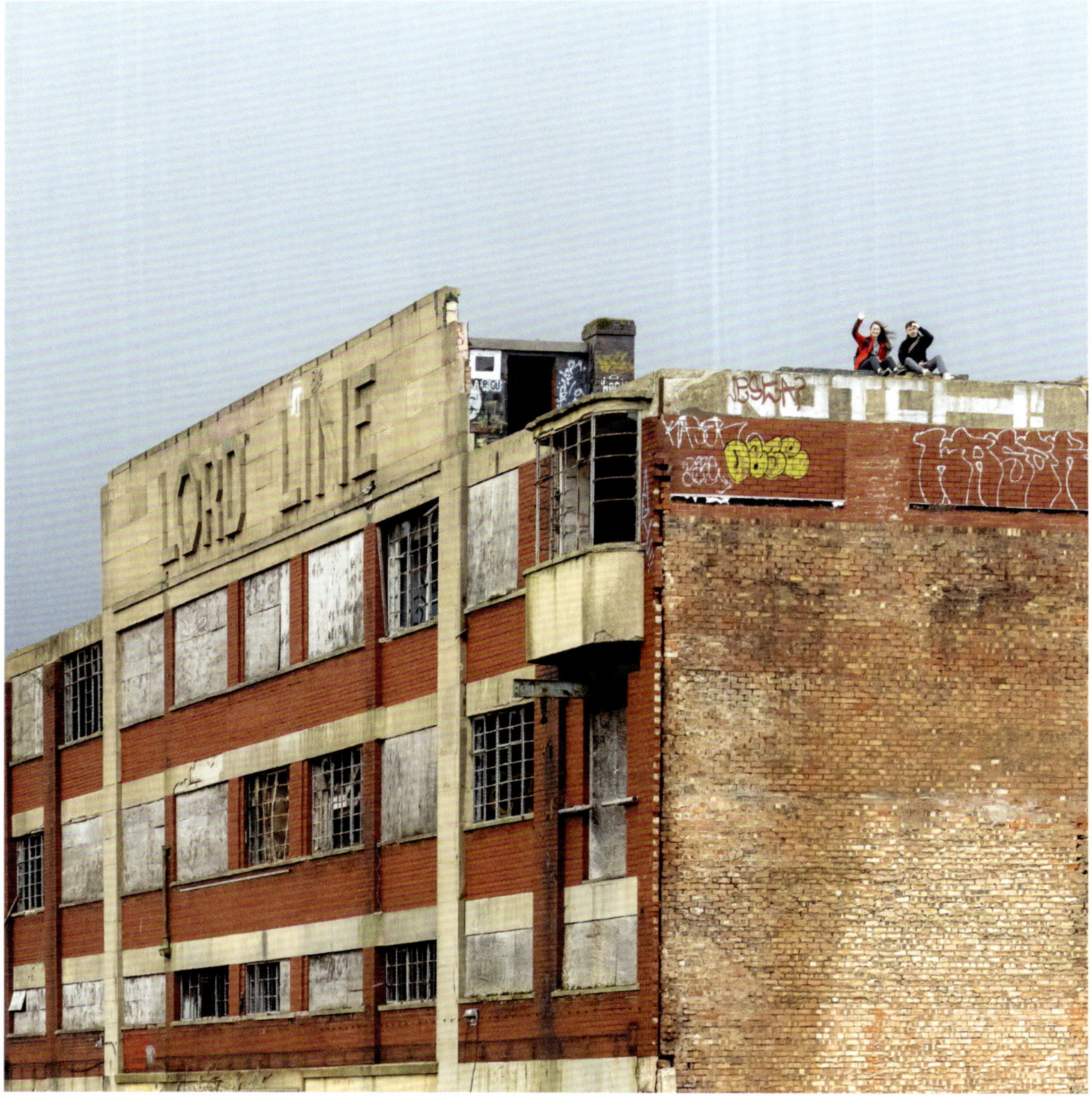

From top left:

Three Ships mosaic by Alan Boyson, 1963, in the centre of Hull

Trident railings outside the Hull Maritime Museum which opened in 1871 as Hull's Dock Offices

The Lord Line trawler company offices, built in 1949, once served as the home of the world's largest deep-water fishing fleet

Opposite:

Cottages on the Hessle foreshore below the Humber Bridge

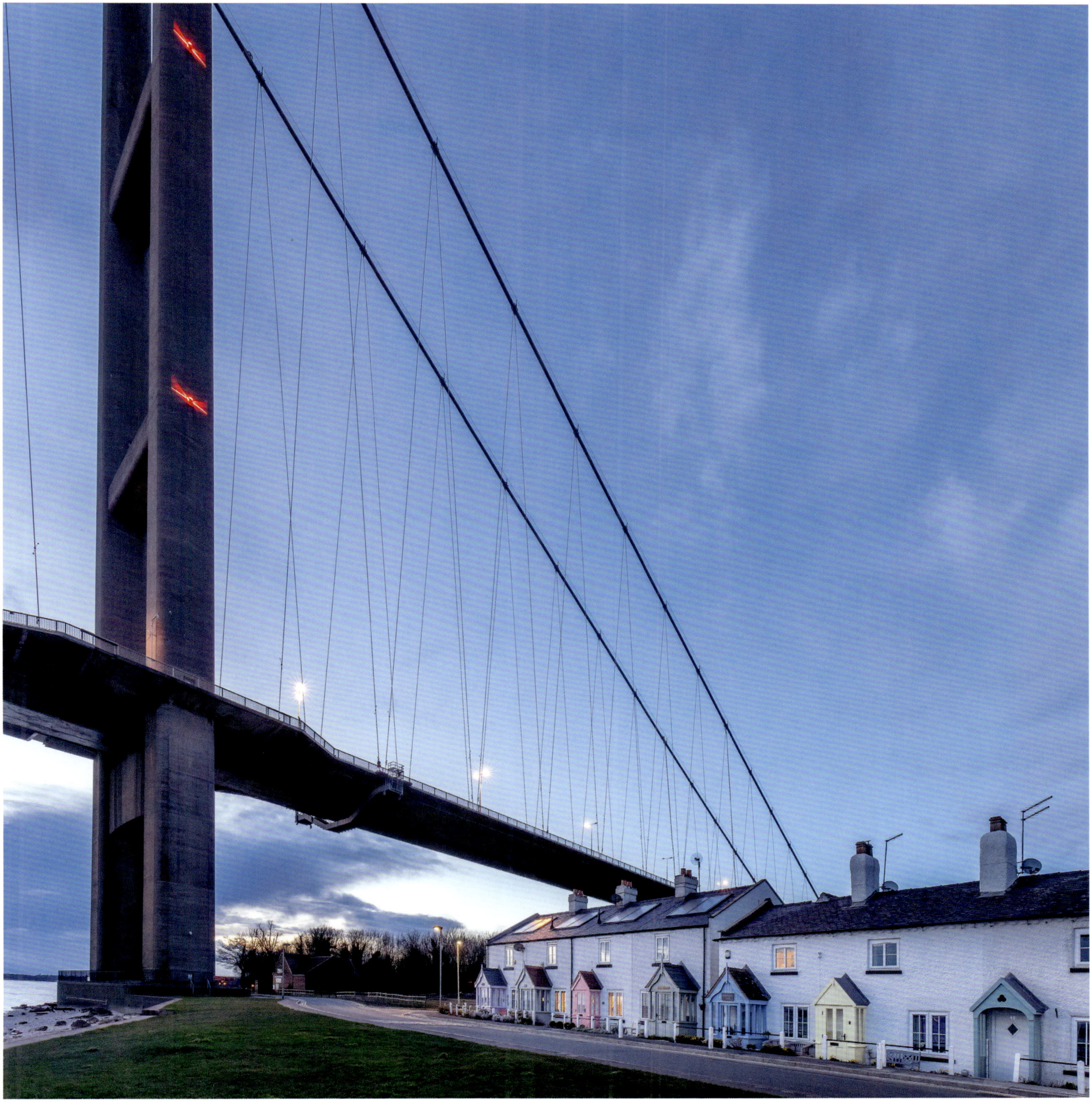

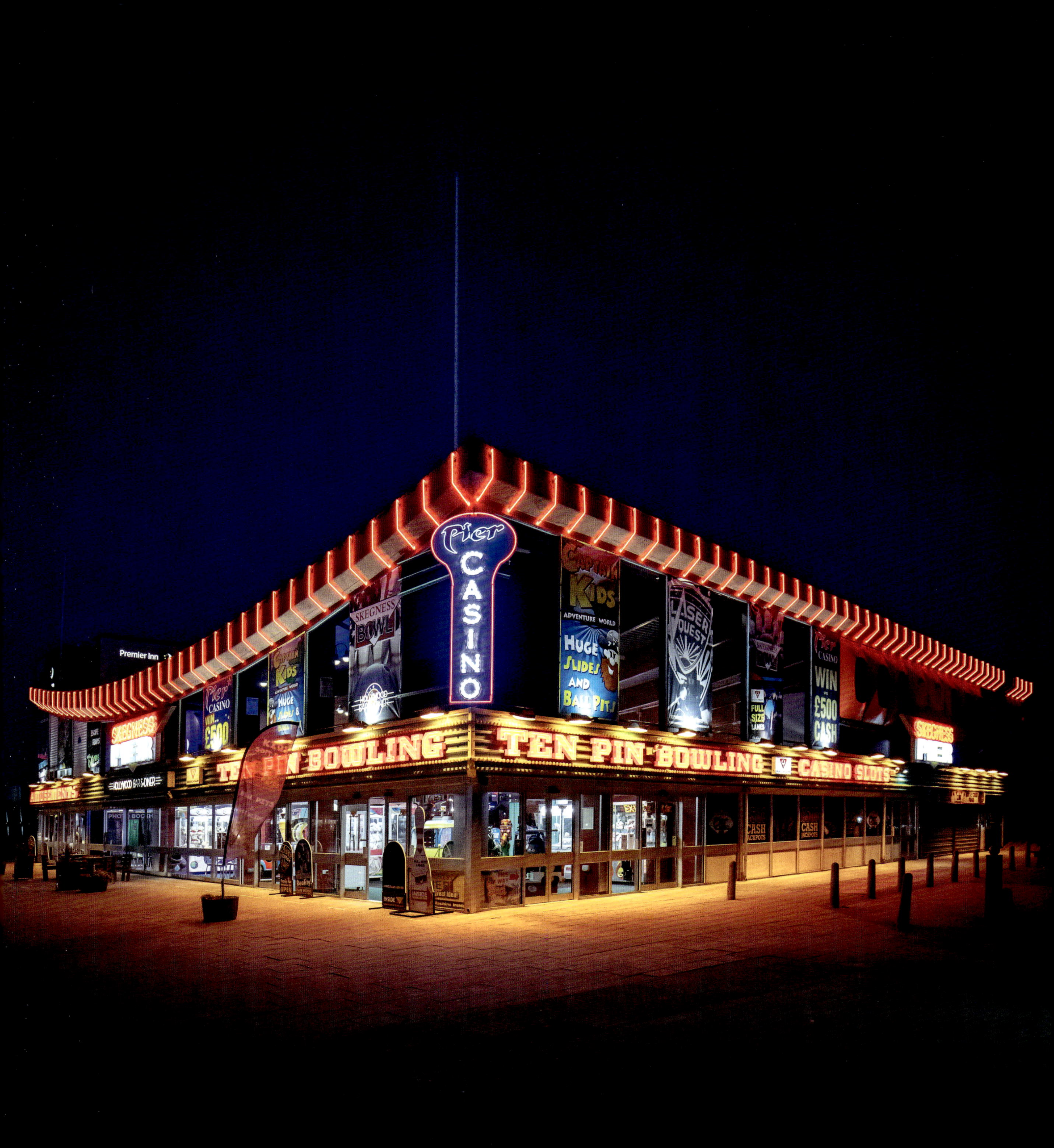

Premier Inn
Pier
CASINO
CAPTAIN KIDS
ADVENTURE WORLD
HUGE SLIDES AND BALL PITS
LASER QUEST
SKEGNESS BOWL
Pier CASINO WIN £500 CASH
SKEGNESS PIER
TEN PIN BOWLING
TEN PIN BOWLING
CASINO SLOTS
HOLLYWOOD BAR & DINER
CASH JACKPOTS

49 LINCOLNSHIRE

FEBRUARY–MARCH 2020

DAY 397–405 | 09,651–09,891KM | 240KM

The first day of walking in Lincolnshire starts below the Humber Bridge, alongside nodding reedbeds in golden sun and traditional tileries with their smoking square brick chimneys. Soon, modern industry dominates, creating many no-go areas for pedestrians as I detour around the ore terminal and oil refineries where the few public footpaths marked on the map certainly don't feel like it. Walkers are escorted on foot by hi-vis-clad security through the stream of trucks and containers at Humber Sea Terminal.

At Grimsby, I'm keen to walk around the Kasbah, the centre of the largest fishing fleet in the world in the mid-twentieth century. The unique dock architecture is in various states of dereliction, epitomised by the gigantic Grimsby Ice Factory. Once, its crushed-ice conveyors criss-crossed the road overhead, but they now lie cut down, rusting and forlorn on the ground. The docks themselves primarily seem to be parking for imported vehicles, with their wipers lifted, spreading out into the distance like a synthetic sea. A fisherman lifts his head from fixing a net on the deck of his trawler to shout over to me with a grin, 'If you've come to look for something to photograph, you've come to the wrong place!'

After a close encounter with quicksand past Cleethorpes and a day navigating flat marshes, I camp in the dunes at the edge of the Donna Nook Air Weapons Range, which is used for air-to-ground target practice by fast jets and helicopters. According to my map, the target area is an 18 × 2-kilometre expanse of sand revealed at low tide. The following day, as the tide is out and the warning flags are not flying, I walk into the freshly exposed sand towards mysterious objects on the horizon that I take to be targets.

When I get closer, I can see they are life-size scaffolding structures that resemble Middle Eastern pickup trucks, which evokes a scene from *Mad Max*, especially with the gale-force wind picking up the sand. The frames are covered in mesh to make them look solid from a distance. Up close, they are curiously delicate and feminine, in contrast to the bullet holes that puncture the supporting steel scaffolding poles, hinting at the violence that rains down from above.

On my 400th day walking, I cross the invisible line from the north into the south – though I can't imagine Lincolnshire folk identifying as southerners. The landscape by The Wash is uber-flat, all drainage ditches and sky, but there's a powerful abstraction to the scene that encourages a graphic approach to photography. The flatness makes the sky the main component of the landscape. In the distance, I see a hiker with a backpack from miles off. Not a common sight away from dog-walking areas. It turns out he's another around-the-coast-of-Britain walker heading in the opposite direction, and we share notes on the way we've each come.

Then, unexpectedly, coronavirus dominates the news. Italy and Denmark are in lockdown while the Cheltenham Festival, in my hometown, still goes ahead. Putting one foot in front of the other in this time of uncertainty is therapeutic. I cover 27 kilometres and find a sheltered spot by a reedbed for the night, silently unfolding the tent under piercing bright stars.

A pair of lighthouses at the mouth of the broad and fast-flowing River Nene stand as sentinels in the horizontal landscape. At dusk, multiple skeins of geese follow the Nene in both directions. I guess it's the ideal waymarker from the air. 'Are you going camping?' asks the friendly cashier in the Co-op in Sutton Bridge. 'People are buying weird stuff, stockpiling because of the virus.'

Opposite:

Skegness Pier

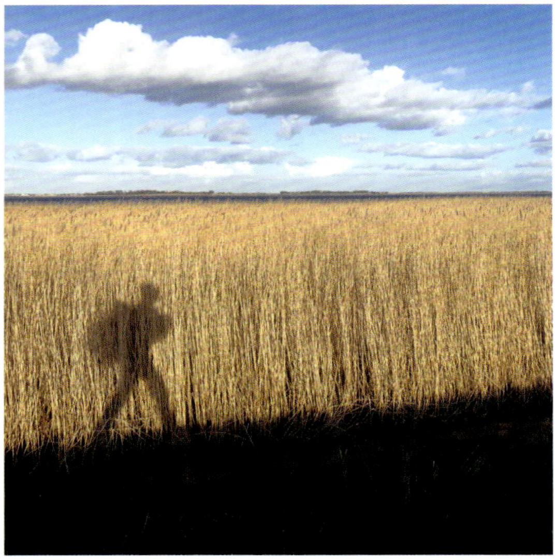

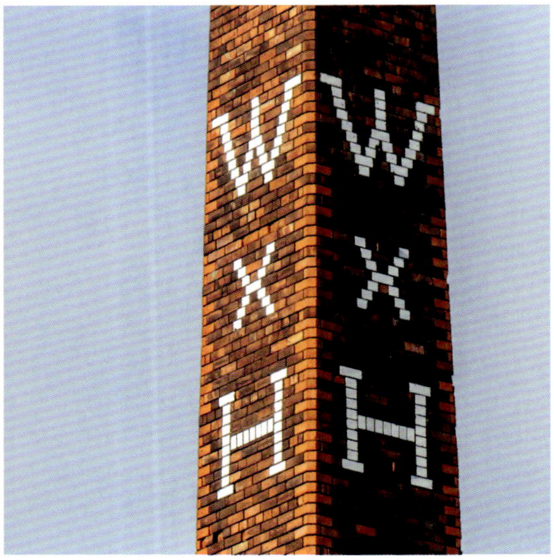
WXH
WXH

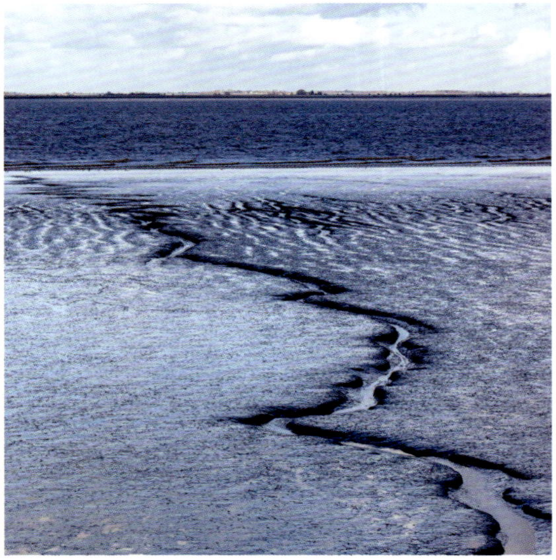

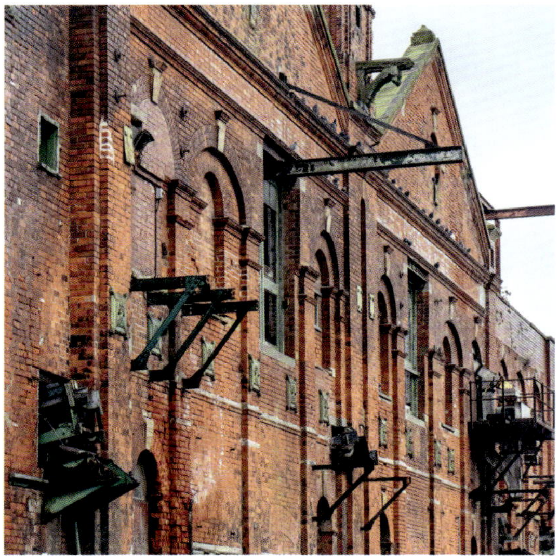

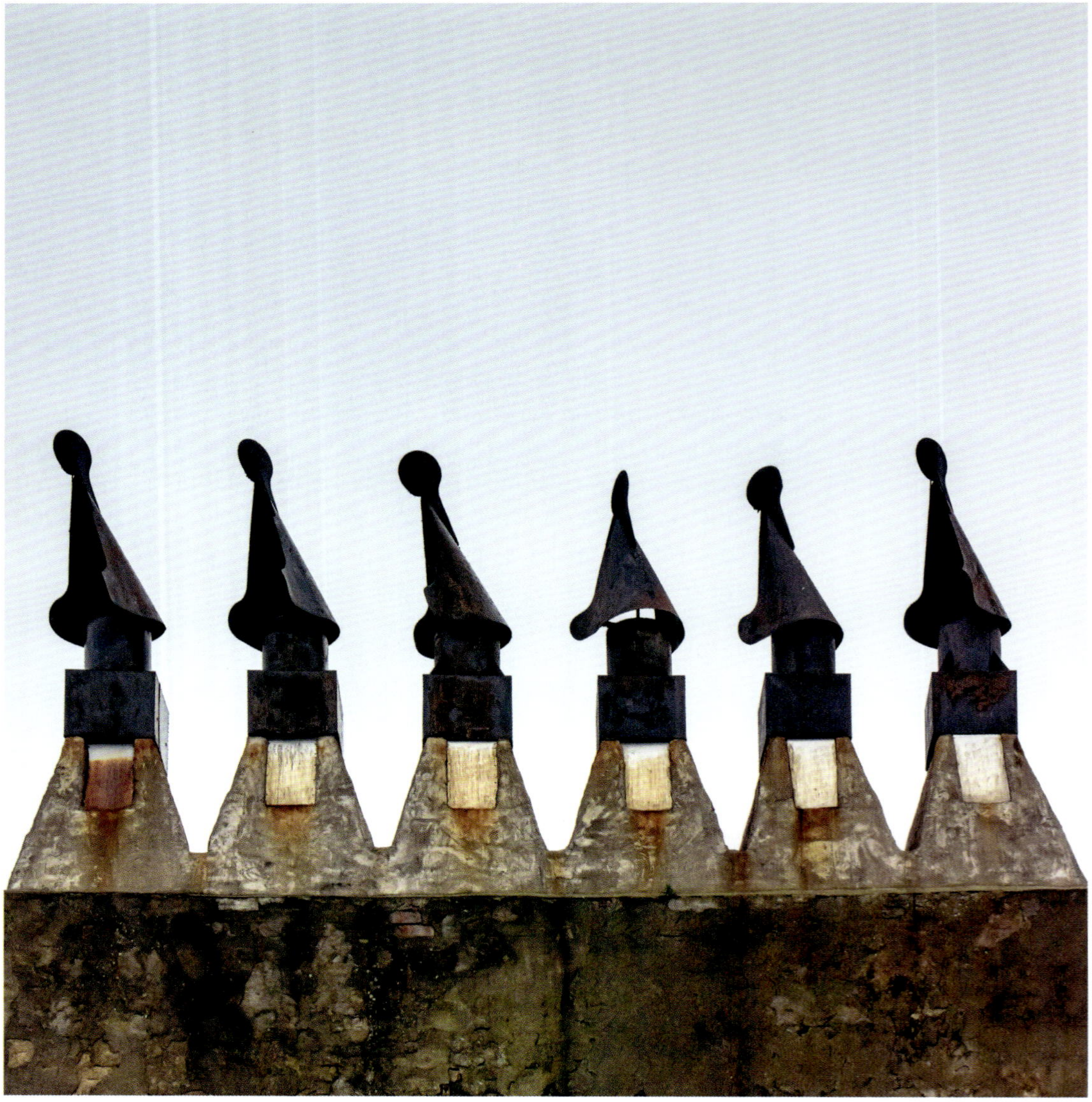

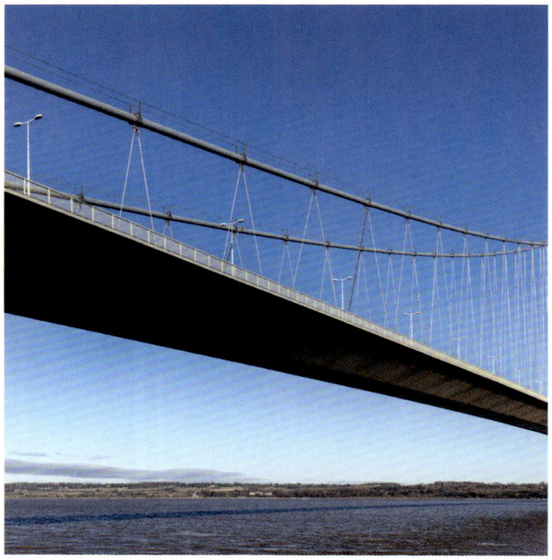

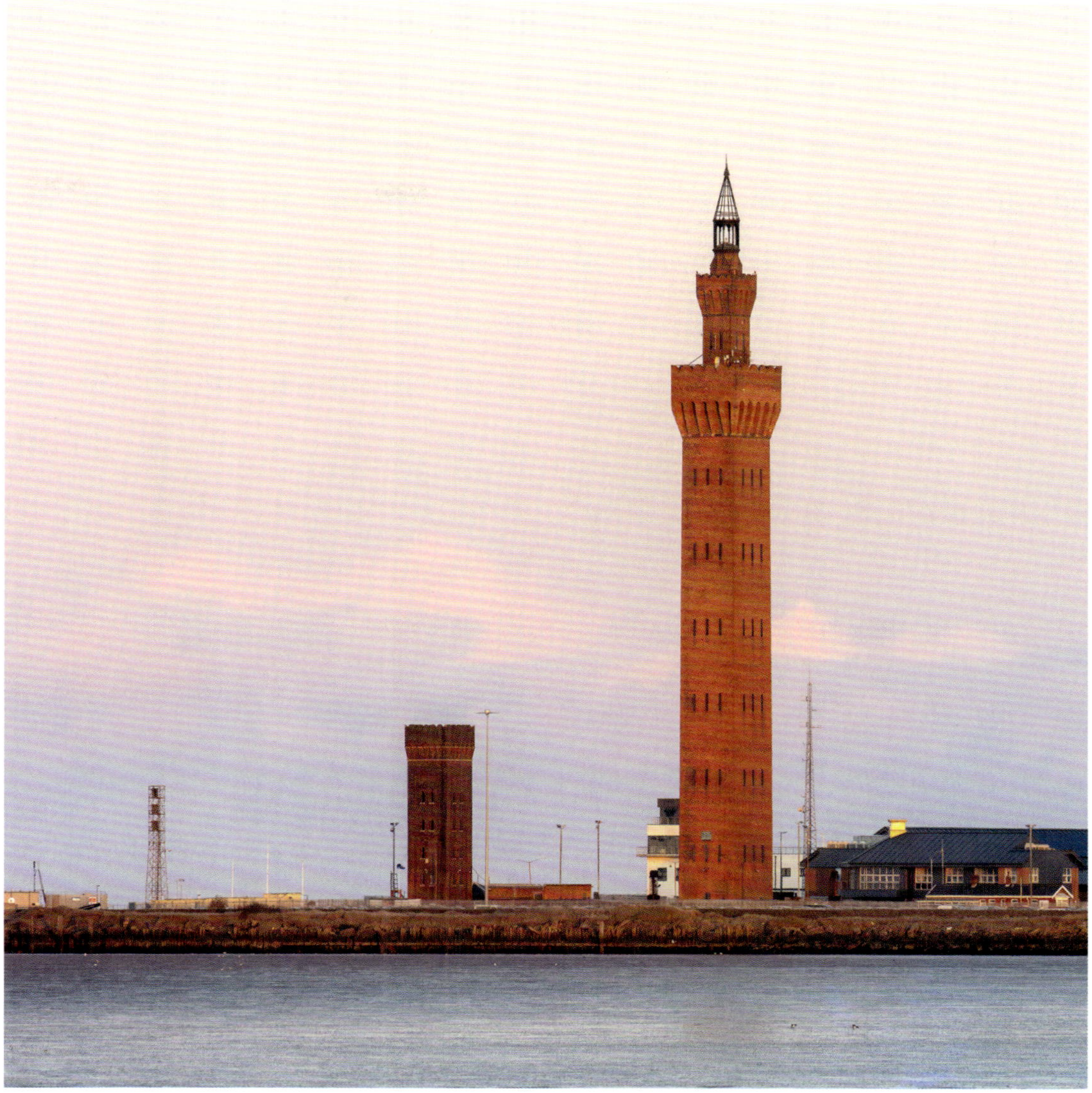

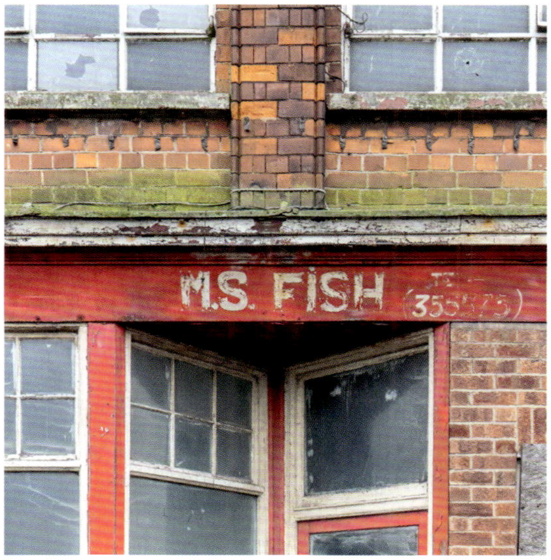

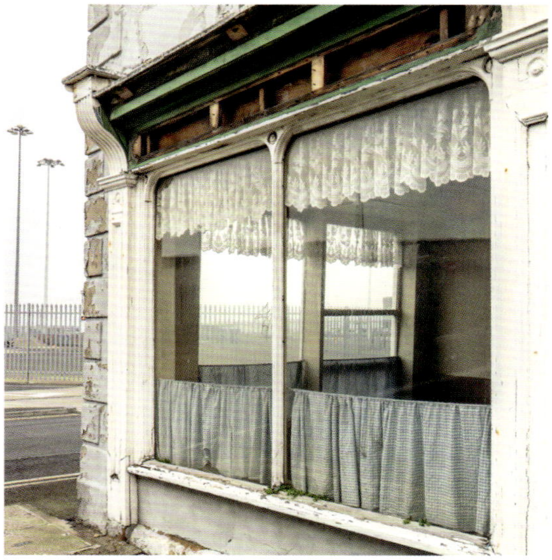

Opposite, clockwise from top left:

Walking along the reedbeds by the Humber

Wilkinson and Houghton Brick and Tile Works, Halton Marshes, closed 1939

The Humber near Grimsby

The distinctive chimney cowls at Alfred Enderby Smokehouse, Kasbah, Grimsby

Humber levitate: Barton Waterside

Facade of the Victorian Grimsby Ice Factory with remnants of the truncated ice conveyors

From top left:

Last light at Grimsby Dock Tower, designed in 1852 by James William Wild who based its appearance on the Torre del Mangia in Siena. It functioned as a hydraulic accumulator tower that was used to power the machinery of the Grimsby Docks until 1892

M.S. Fish, Fish Dock Road, Kasbah

Abandoned Solly's Cafe, on the corner of Hutton Road and Fish Dock Road, which was run by the Salsbury family for 150 years

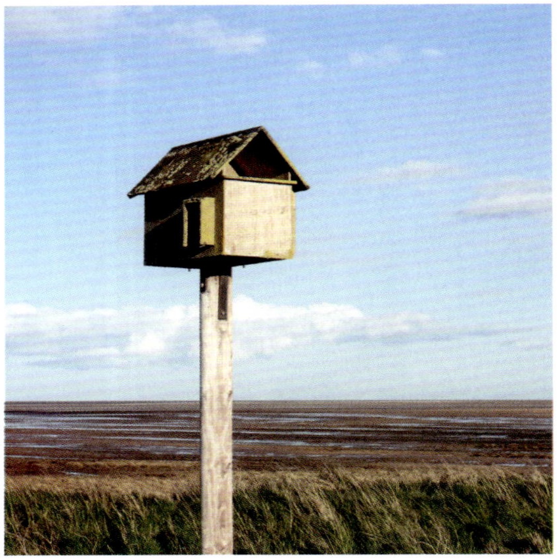

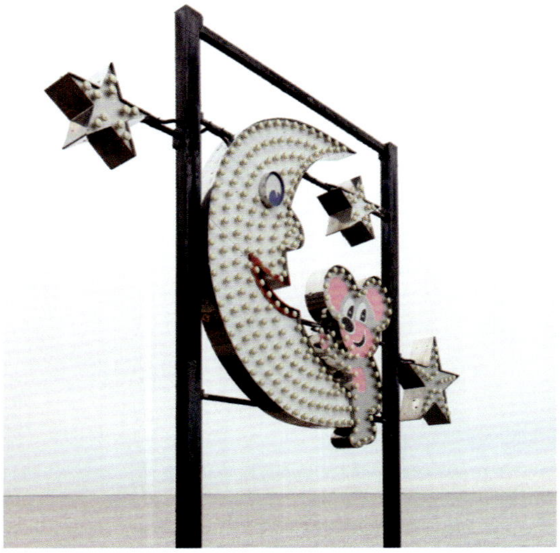

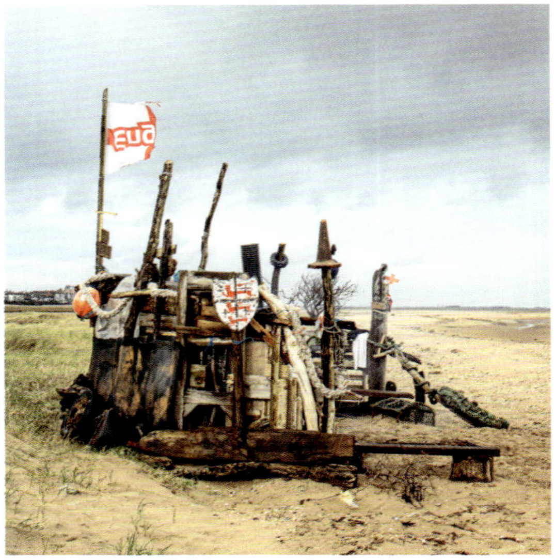

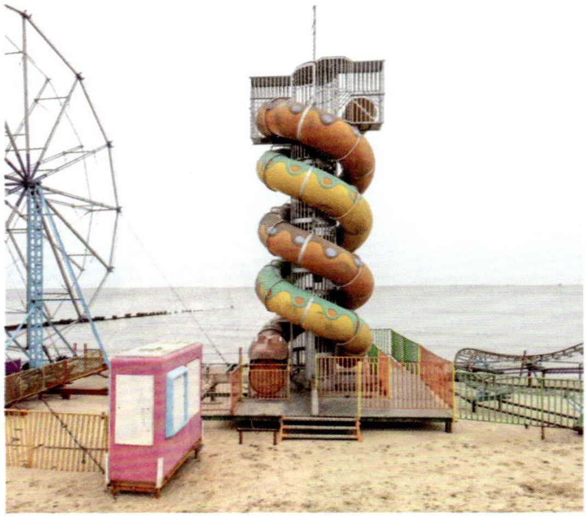

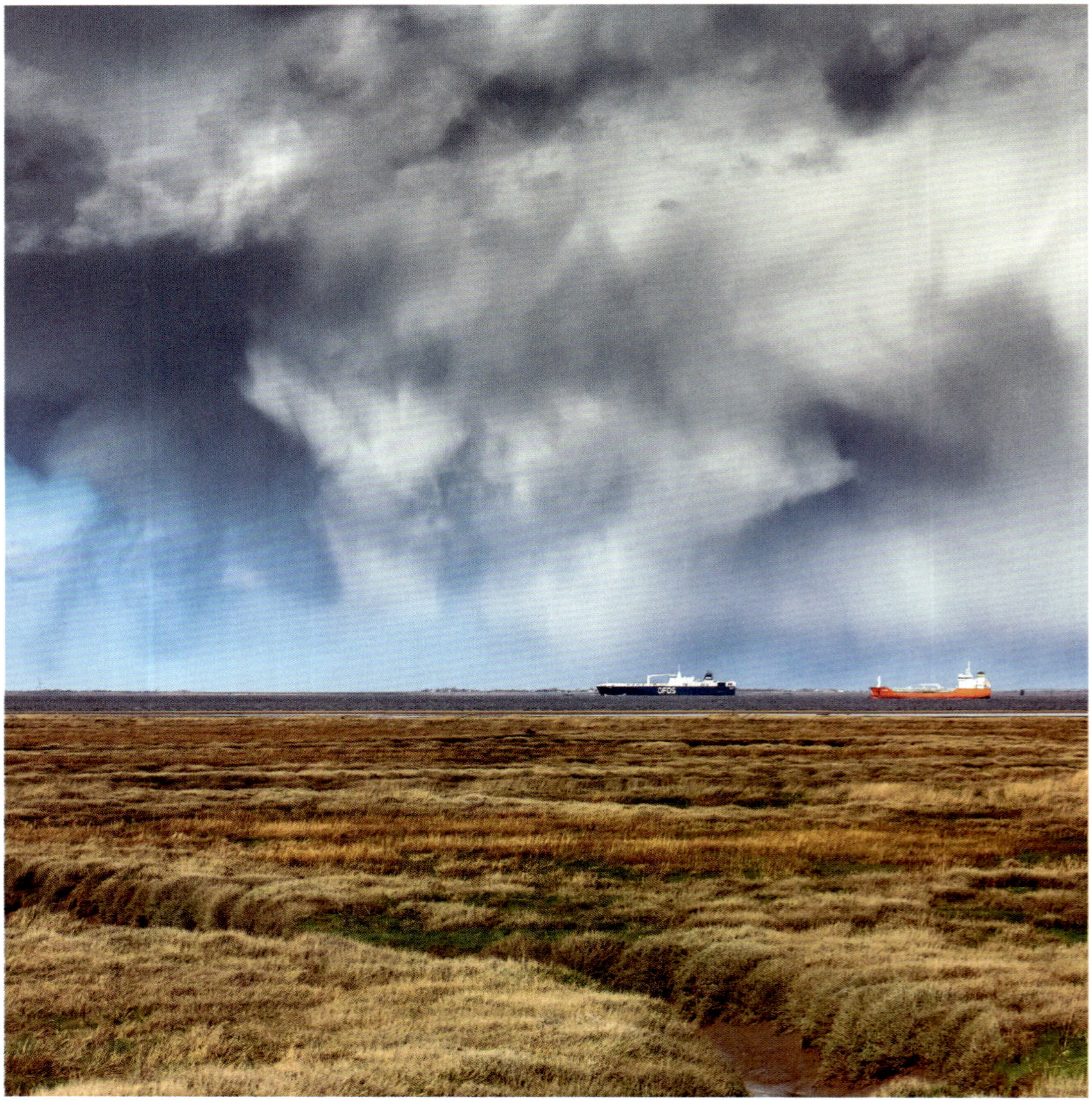

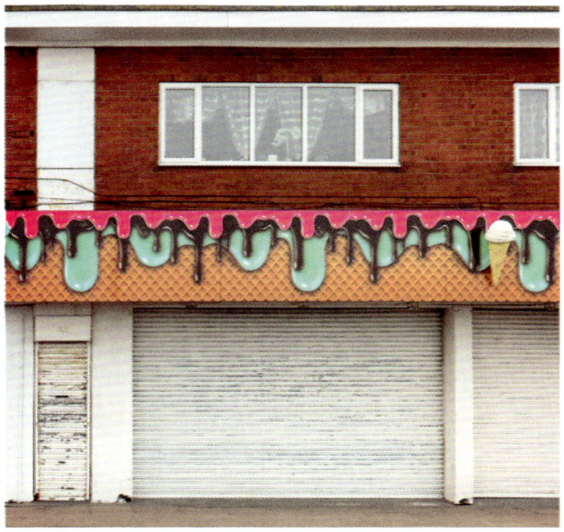

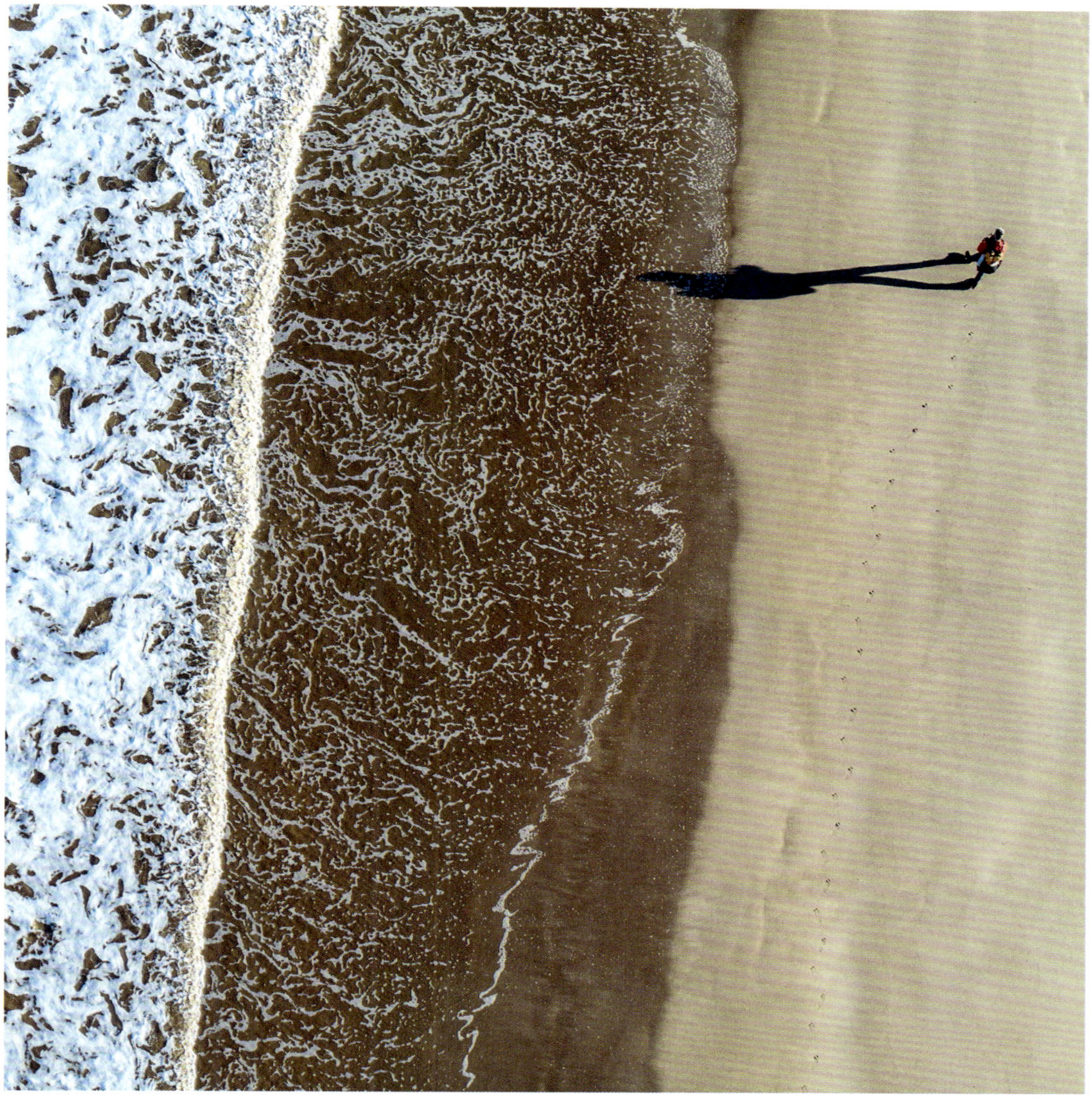

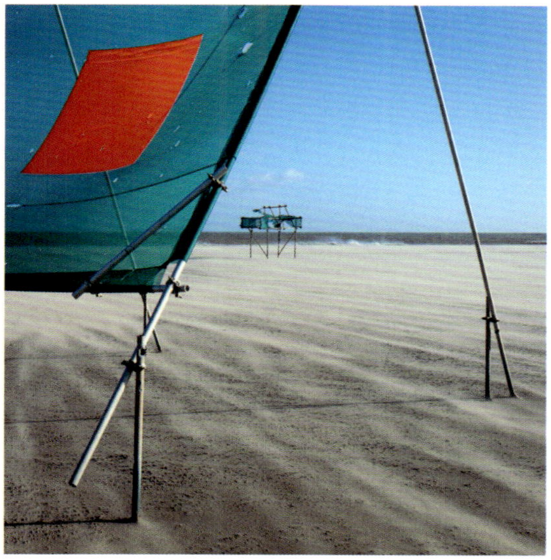

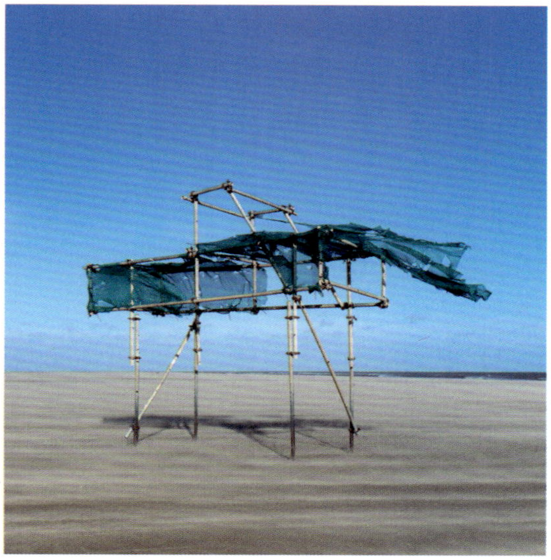

Opposite, clockwise from top left:

House of dreams: Tetney Marshes

Mouse in the moon, Cleethorpes

Buck Beck Beach Bench, Cleethorpes (destroyed by arson in 2023 and rebuilt by volunteers the next day)

Turbulent sky over the Humber, which is the UK's busiest trading estuary with 30–40,000 vessel movements per annum

Scoops Ice Cream Parlour, North Promenade, Cleethorpes

Helter-skelter, Cleethorpes Beach

From top left:

Drone selfie on Seathorne Beach towards Skegness

Targets at Donna Nook Bombing Range

Scaffolding and mesh pick-up truck target, Donna Nook Bombing Range

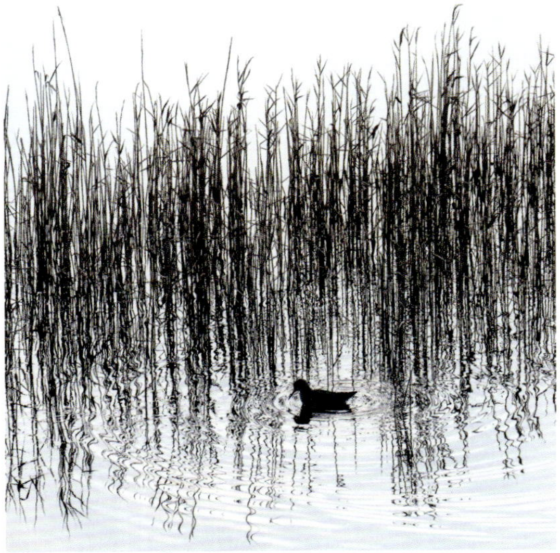

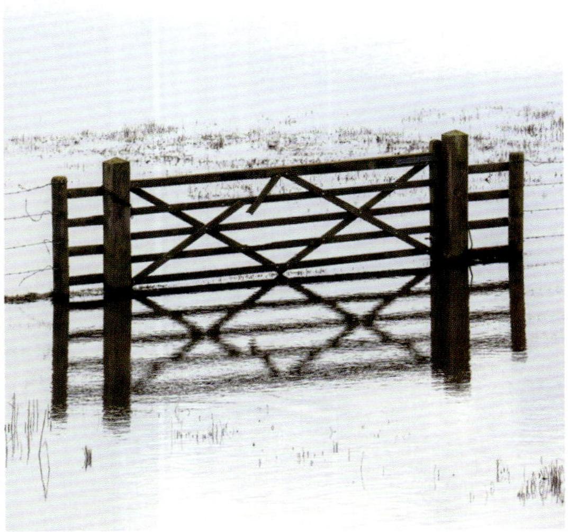

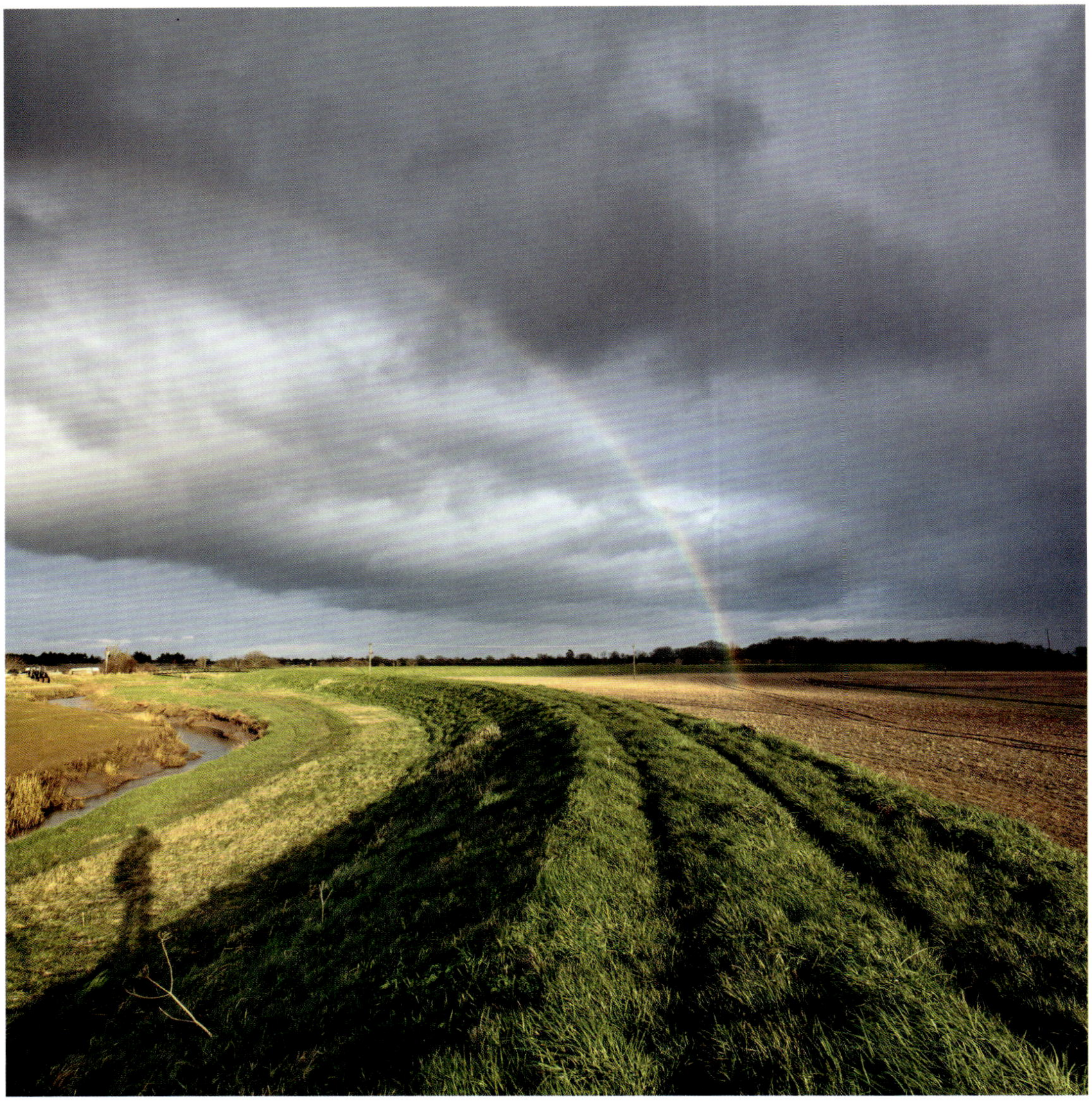

From top left:

A redshank in Lutton Leam

Floodland, Freiston

Sea wall by the Steeping River at Gibraltar

Opposite:

Last light by the River Nene

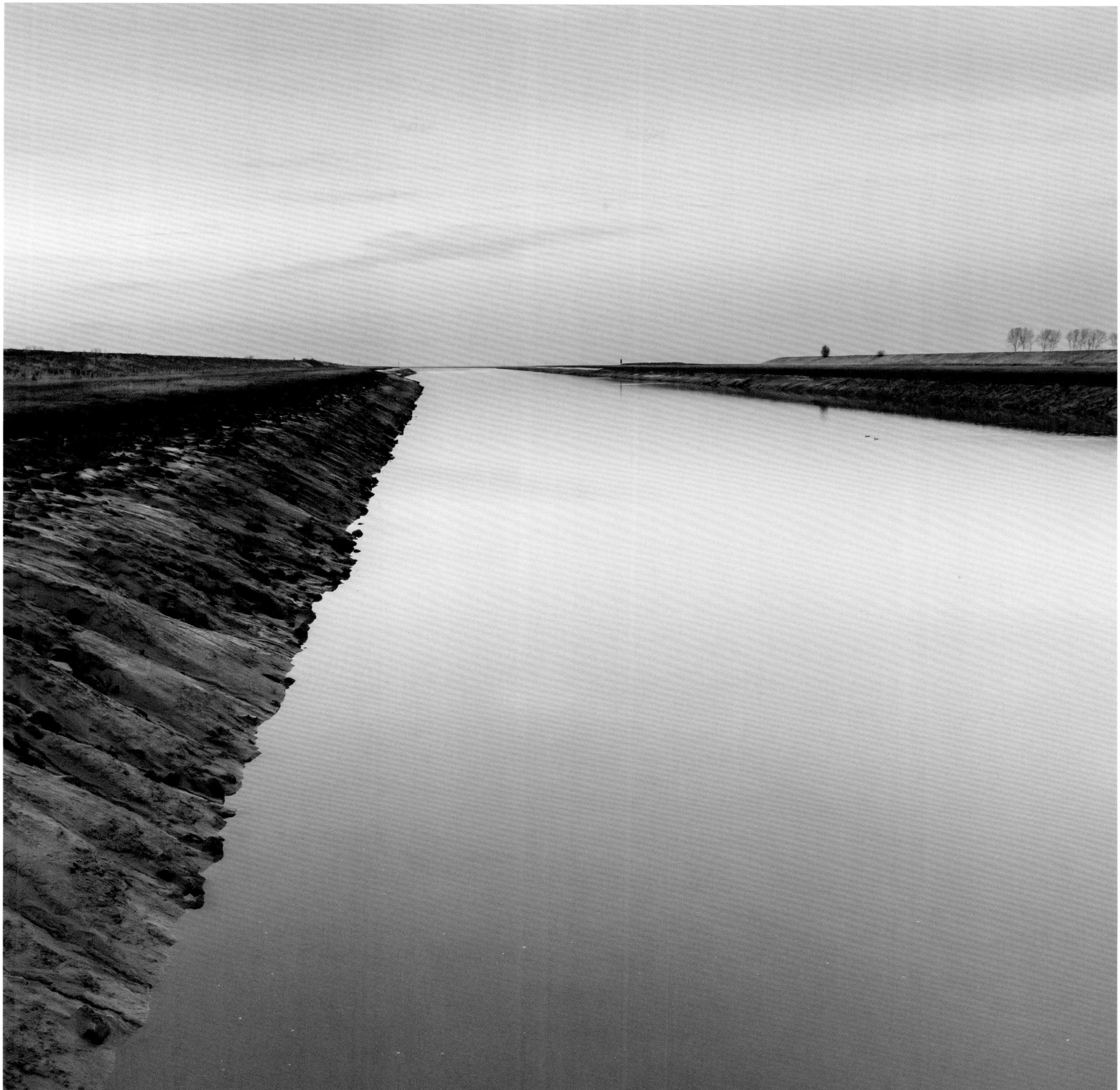

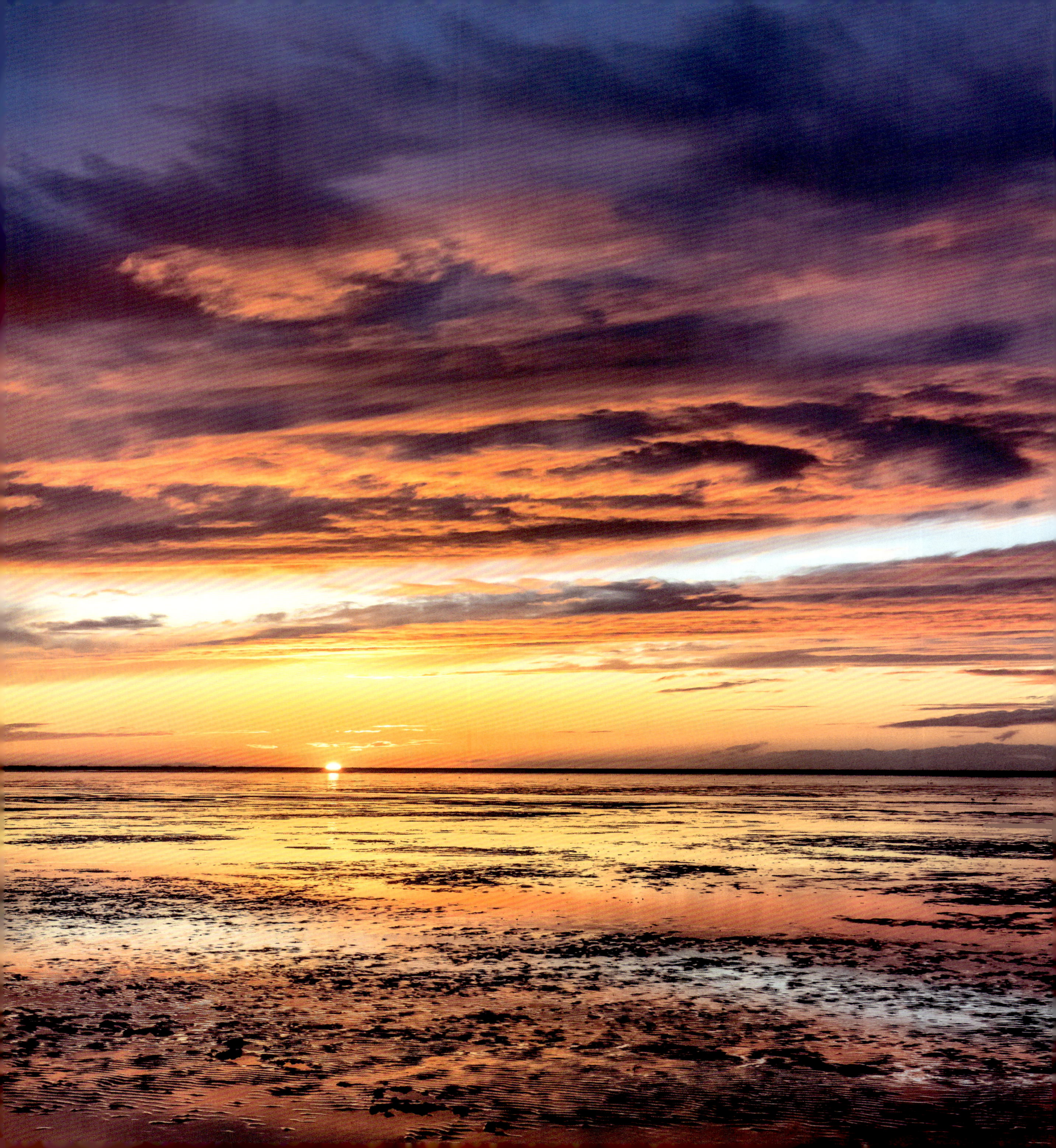

50 NORFOLK

MARCH–JULY 2020
DAY 406–417 | 09,891–10,119 KM | 228 KM

Opposite:

Snettisham sunset: the sun slips below the horizon beyond The Wash

On a stretch of nondescript sea wall beside The Wash near the River Nene I walk across the invisible border from Lincolnshire into Norfolk, my county of birth. I only lived in Norfolk for the first few years of my life, but I'd always imagined my love of wide-open spaces comes from spending time on the dune-lined beaches of Norfolk as a toddler. The excellently named River Great Ouse leads to King's Lynn, with its charming historic centre where the town hall is decorated with a flint checkerboard design – remarkable, as knapping flint into a square shape can't be easy.

It takes a day of walking from King's Lynn to reach Snettisham Beach, one of the only places on the east coast of England where you can see the sunset over the sea, and the shape of The Wash seems to enhance the focused quality of the light and the contrast of blues and reds. I stand stock-still on the beach with the camera pressed to my eye as the sun slides below the horizon; a fiery sunset lights up the sky, perfectly reflected in the calm sea below, before gradually transitioning to luminous pinks and lilacs.

It's mid-March, and the Covid-19 pandemic is sweeping across the world; many other European countries are in strict lockdown, but harsh restrictions in Britain have not yet been enforced. Solo-camping seems like an ideal way to remain socially distanced, so I carry on walking along the North Norfolk coast, starting each morning listening to terrifying news bulletins and then spending the remainder of the day letting the wind blow that news away. Most nights are spent nestled in my tent within the dunes, eating dehydrated food by the beach.

Maybe because people are hungry for a positive news story among all the doom and gloom, I start to get more enquiries for media interviews and I meet Mike Liggins and cameraman Shaun from BBC *Look East*. We greet with an awkward elbow bump instead of a handshake, and because of social distancing, it's the first conversation I've had in a while. Their TV report on my walk opens with 'Either the luckiest man in Britain or slightly unhinged'. When it becomes clear that a national lockdown is imminent, I accept the inevitable and decide to pause the journey and head for the nearest train station at Sheringham to go home. I'm unsure if it's the East Anglian wind or my emotional state making my eyes water as I pack up the tent for the last time in the foreseeable future.

Being forced to stop by something entirely out of my control is hard to accept after so many obstacles already overcome over the last five years. Six and a half hours on an empty train, and I'm home. The 'See it. Say it. Sorted' of the rail announcement seems like the fears of a different epoch now the next few months are defined by 'Stay at home. Protect the NHS. Save lives'. As I'm walking home from the train station, the lack of traffic on the roads is startling: a solitary jogger is the only movement on the street.

Seventeen weeks later, I return to Norfolk on the day lockdown is lifted, determined to complete the journey in a final two-month push. I'm not the only one to flock back to the coast, and the beaches around Cromer are alive with families enjoying the sun and freedom, which makes me alone, with boots and a backpack, feel decidedly out of place. In the evening, windbreaks are rolled up, blankets are shaken free of sand as day-trippers leave, and a new ecosystem of dog walkers emerges. I keep walking until the sun sets, when the only sign of humanity is the fleeting empire of discarded sandcastles.

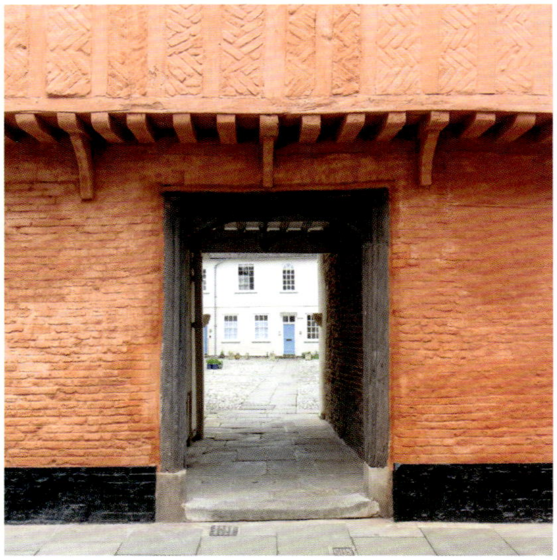

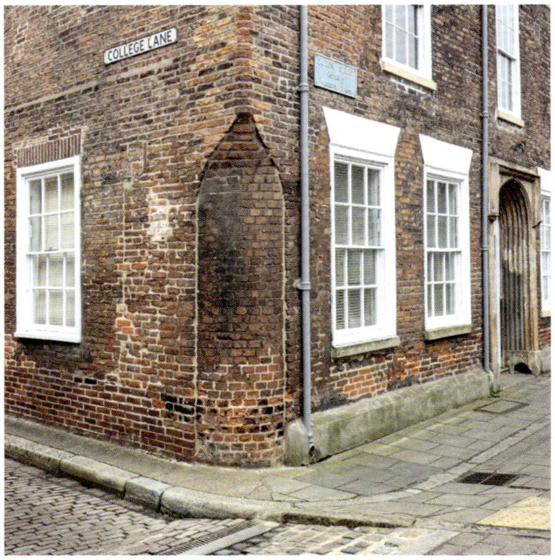

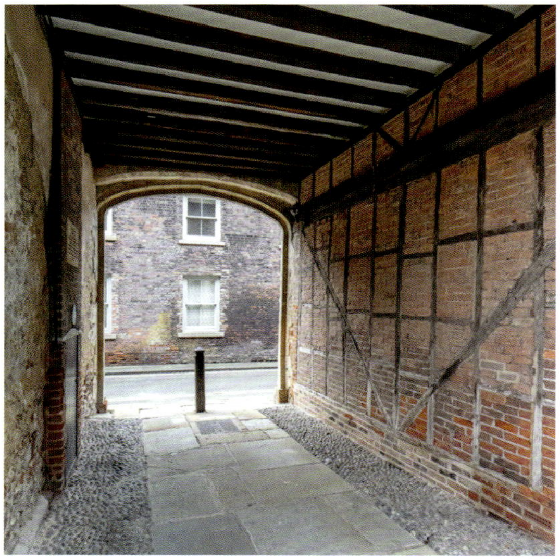

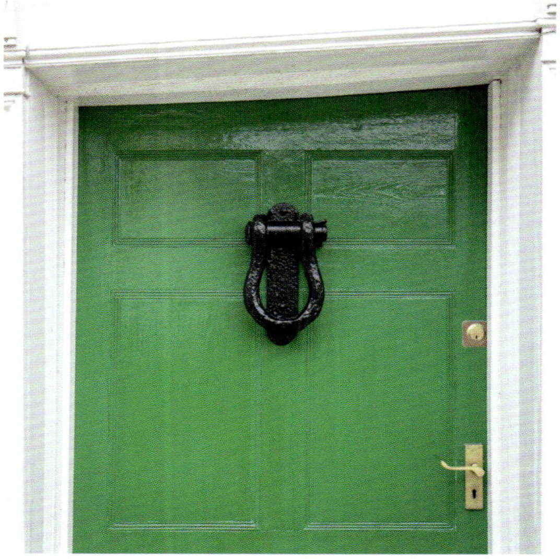

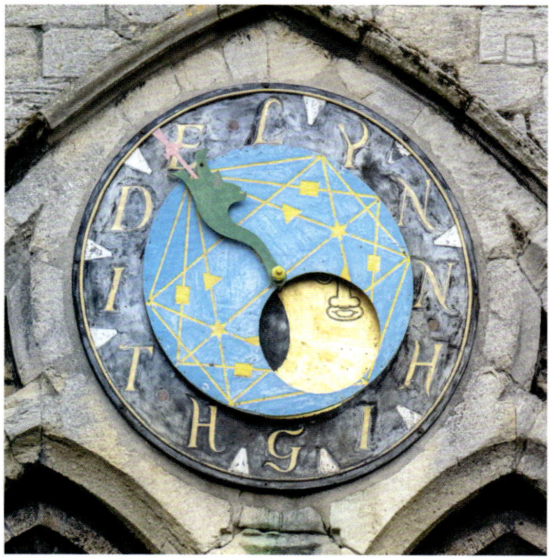

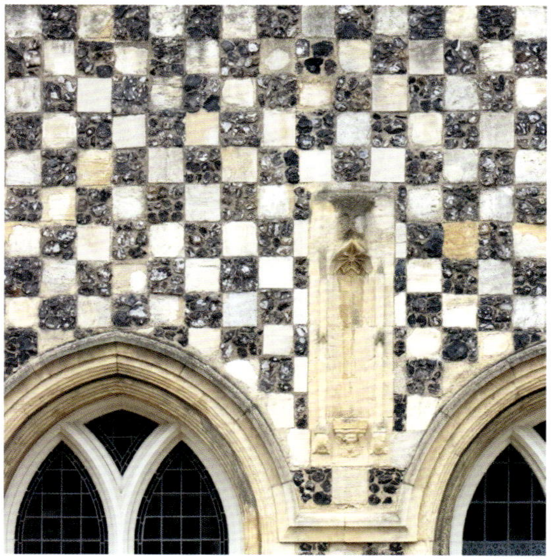

From top left:

Hampton Court, a merchant's courtyard house in King's Lynn, named after the seventeenth-century baker John Hampton. Built in the early fourteenth century and Grade I listed

The corner between College Lane and Queen Street, King's Lynn

From centre left:

The archway that led into King's Lynn Benedictine Priory in the fourteenth century. After the dissolution, the archway was blocked up and incorporated into a cottage. In 1972 Priory Lane Cottages were restored, including opening up the archway again

The Crown & Mitre, King's Lynn

From bottom left:

Tide clock at King's Lynn Minster. The letters in 'LYNN HIGH TIDE' are arranged on the even hours, two hours apart, starting with the 'L' at twelve o'clock, 'G' at midnight, and with dots and triangles for odd hours, thus a 24-hour dial. The dragon pointer of the clock completes a full rotation every twenty-nine and a half days. If the pointer indicated a high tide at 'H' (2 a.m.), then the opposite mark ('Y') would be almost the time (within twenty-five minutes) of the next high tide. A mechanism also controls the moon that revolves eccentrically behind a hole and indicates the lunar phases

Chequered knapped flint flushwork of King's Lynn Guildhall, 1428

Opposite, clockwise from top left:

Holme Beach shadows

Canon promo film crew, Sam Stronge, Tom Martin and Tim Mills, Holme Beach

Camp at Titchwell Marsh during Covid-19 social isolation

Marshworld: (wildfowler's house boat), Wootton

Shaun from BBC *Look East*

Thornham reedbeds

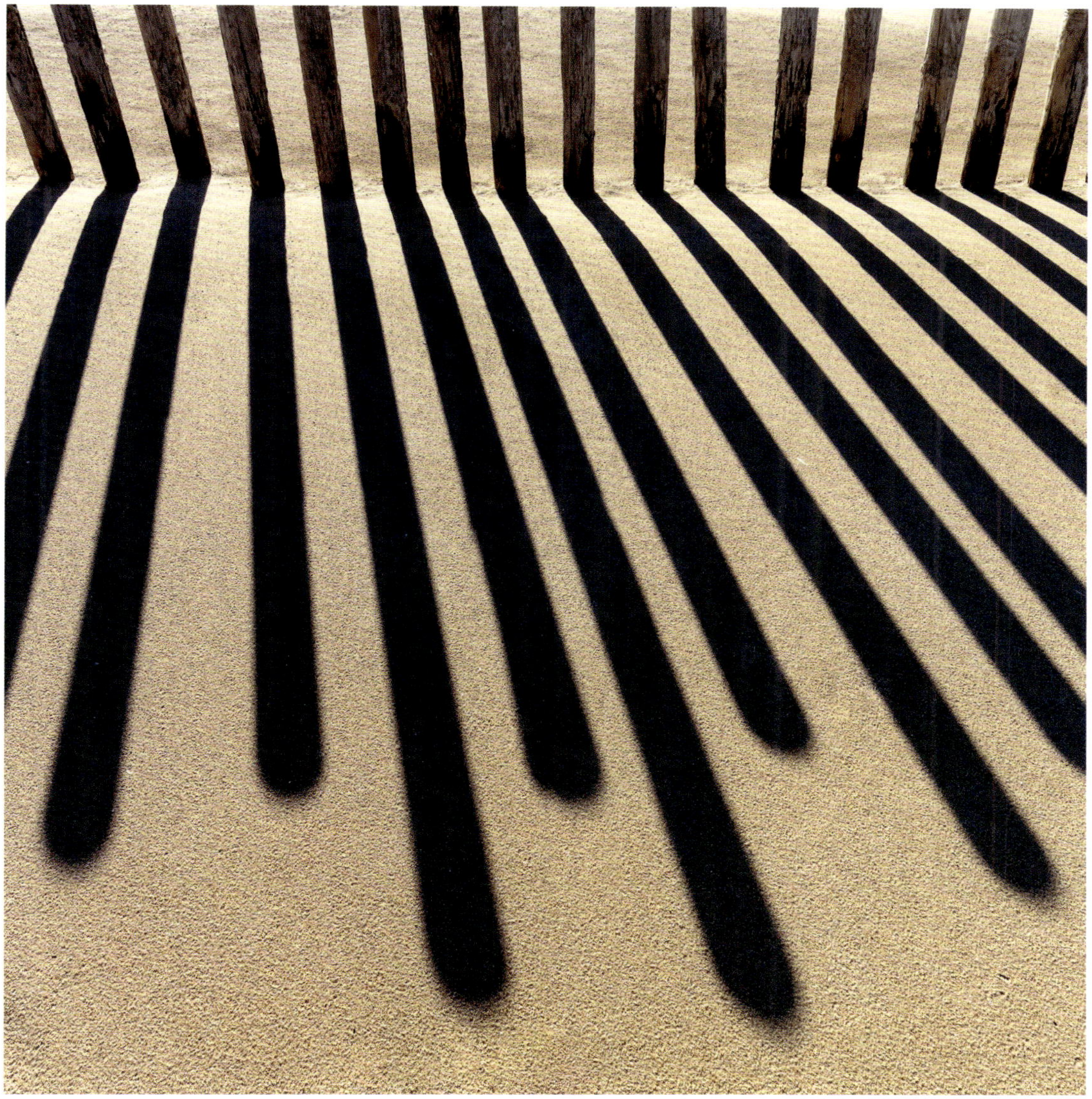

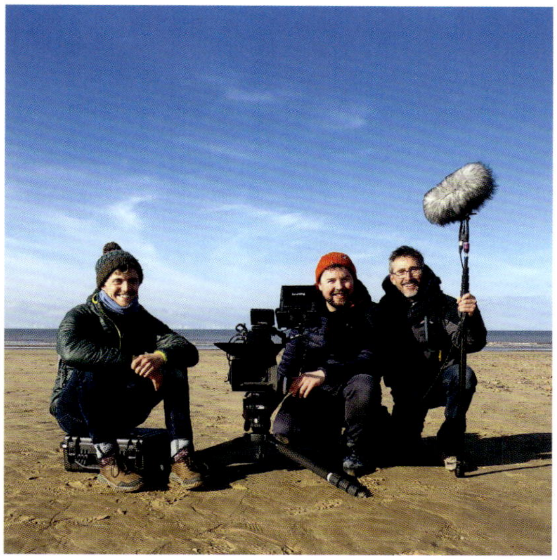

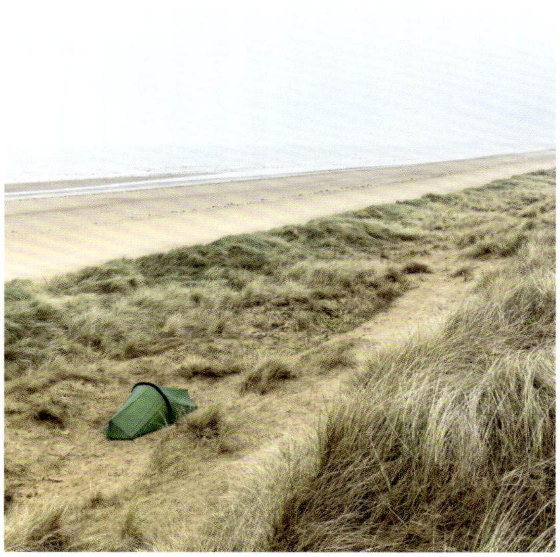

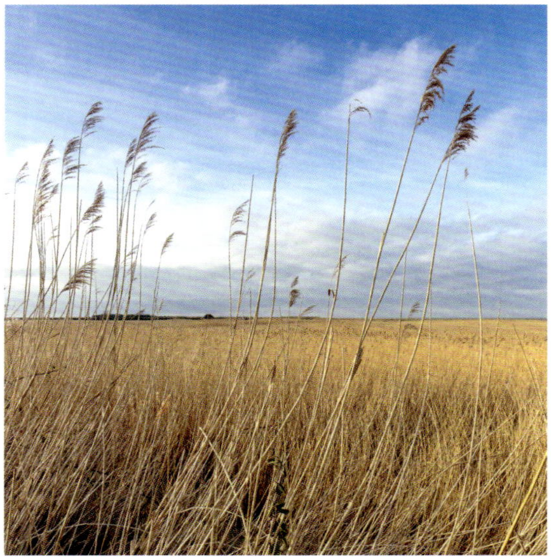

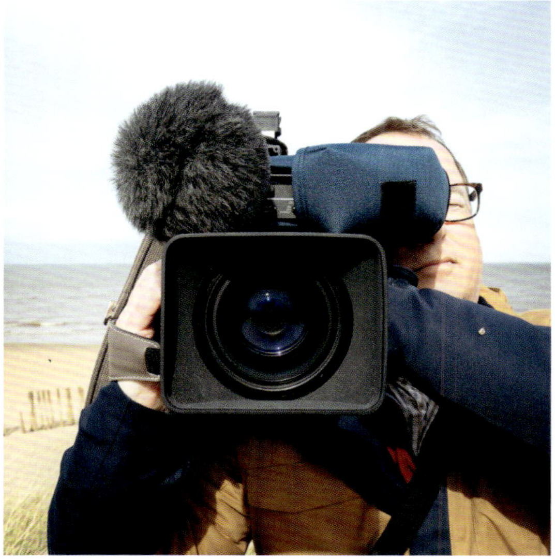

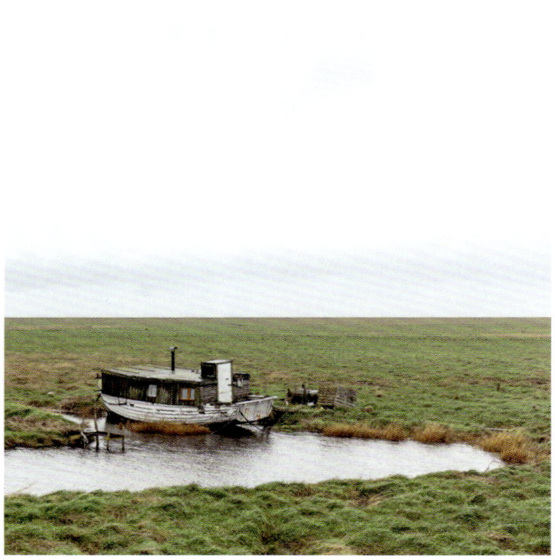

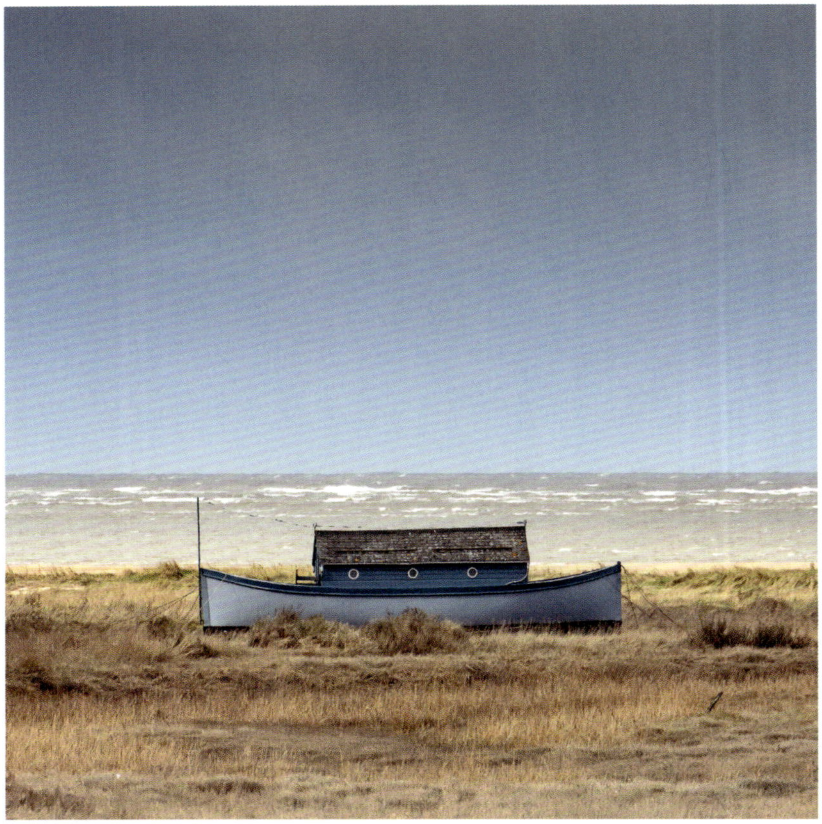

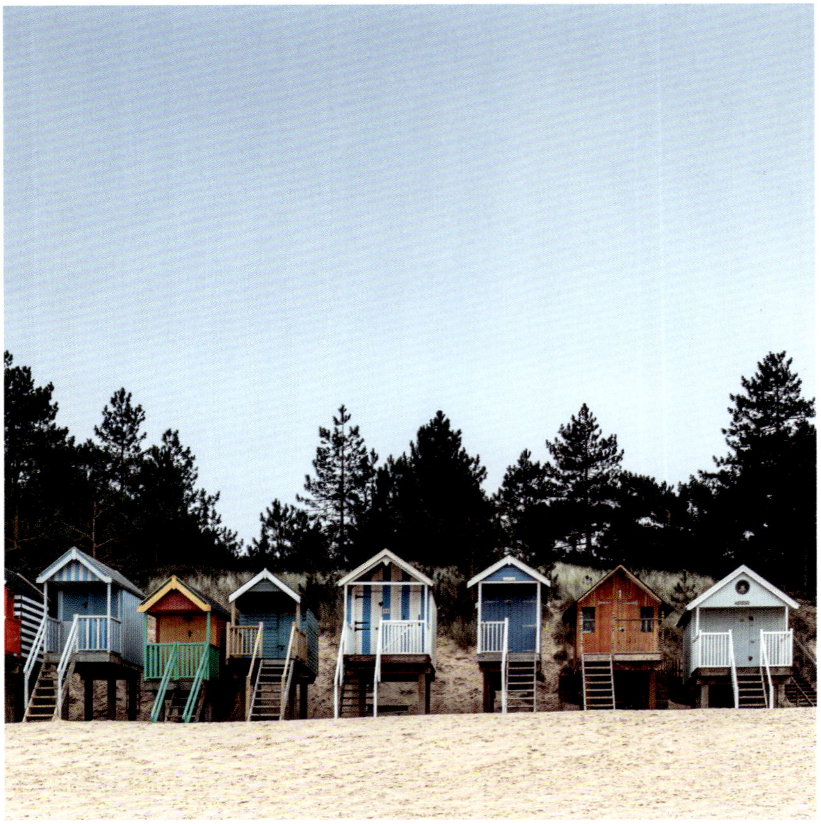

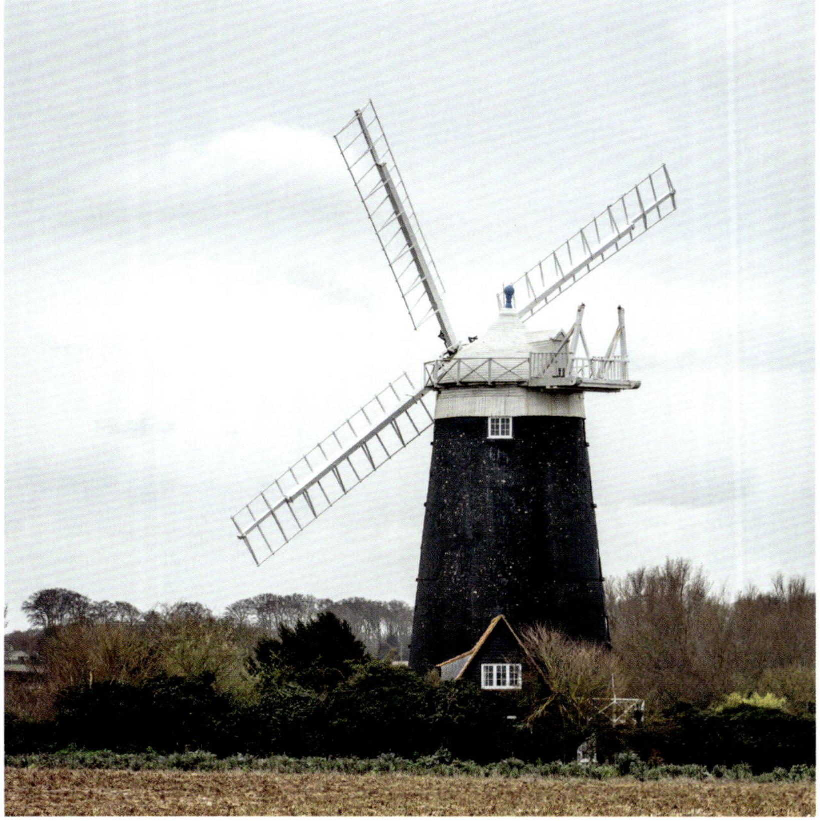

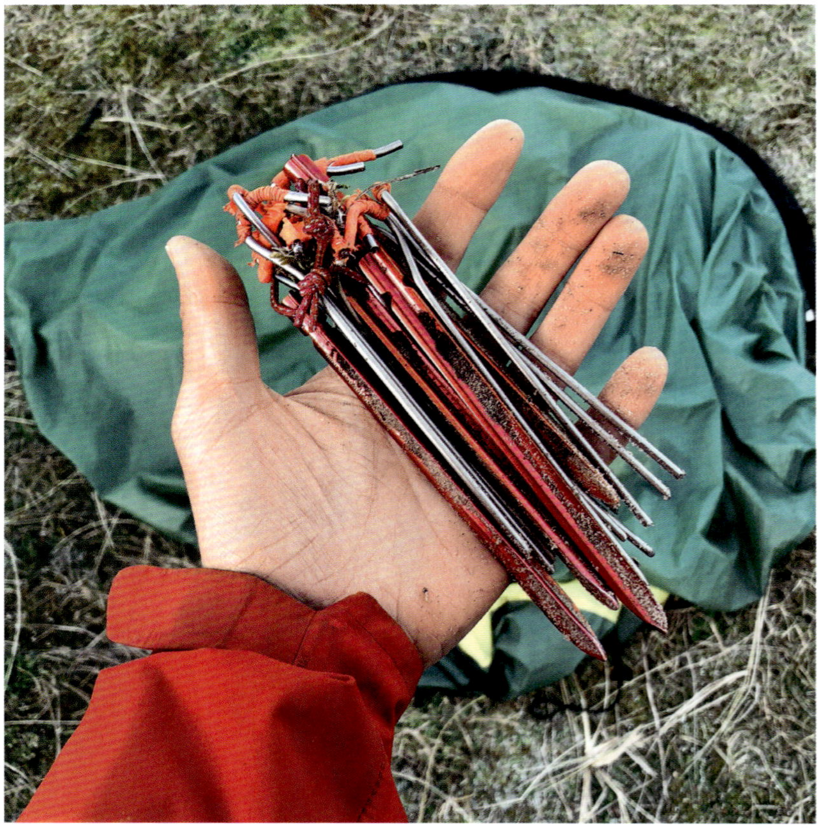

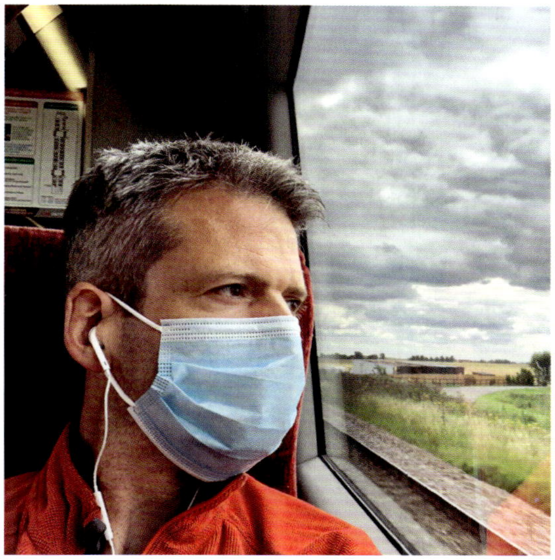

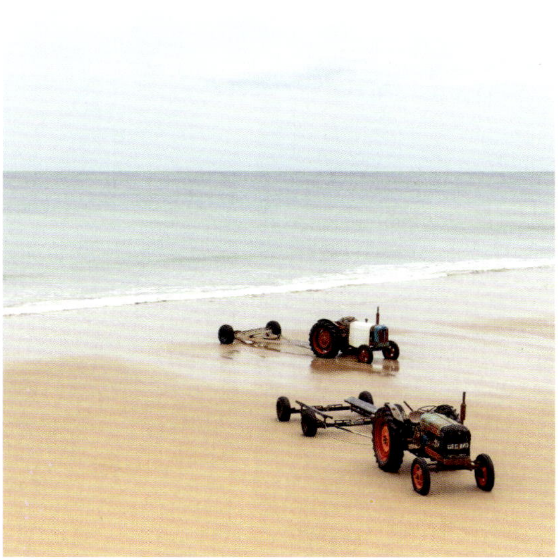

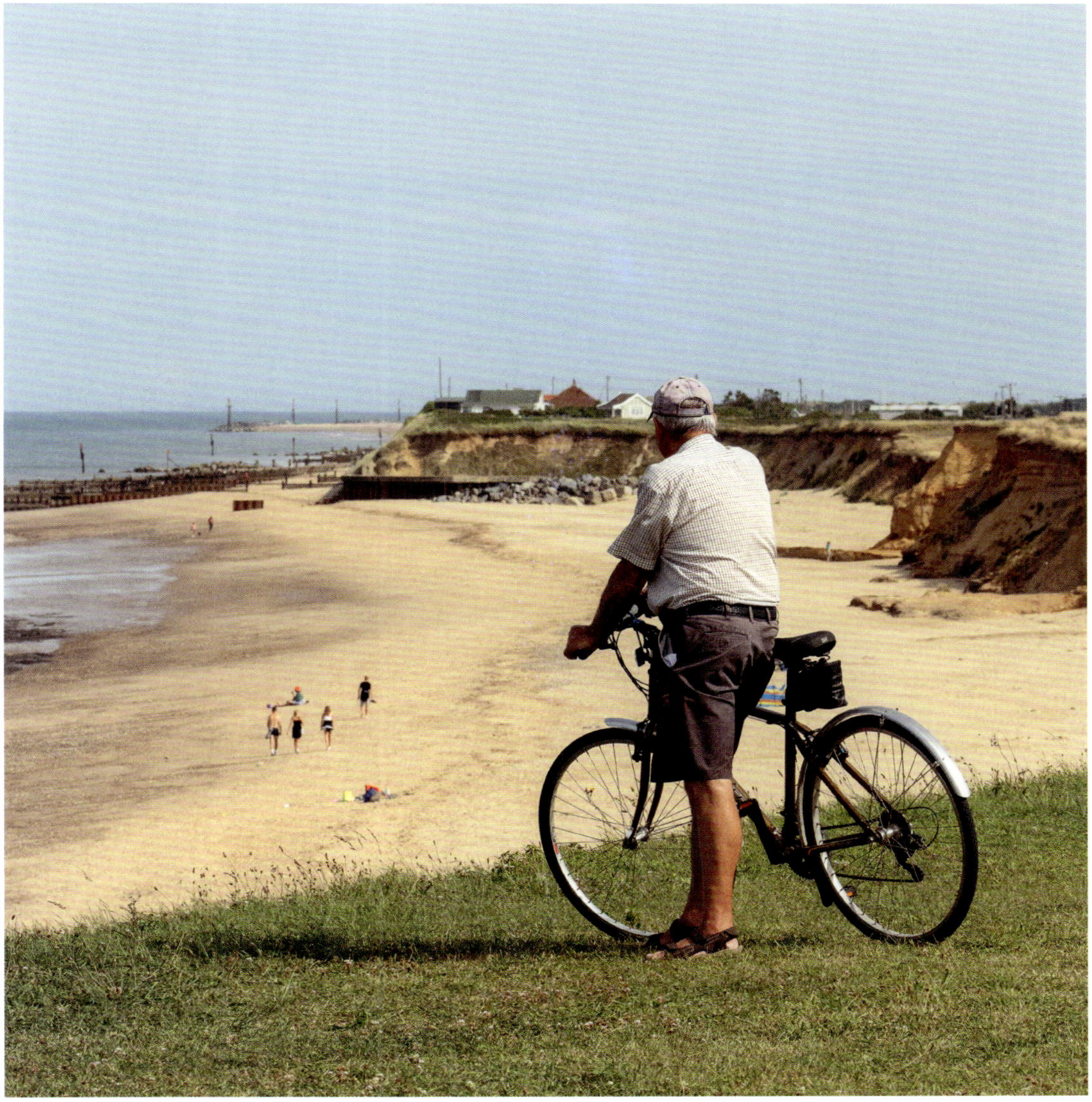

Opposite, from top left:

Ark: Morston Saltmarsh, Blakeney

Beach huts at Wells-next-the-Sea

From bottom left:

Burnham Overy Staithe Windmill, built in 1816 and now a holiday home

Packing up to head home after the Covid-19 national lockdown announcement halts the journey

From top left:

Returning to the coast after a seventeen-week hiatus for the first Covid-19 lockdown

Launched: Cromer

Happisburgh Beach

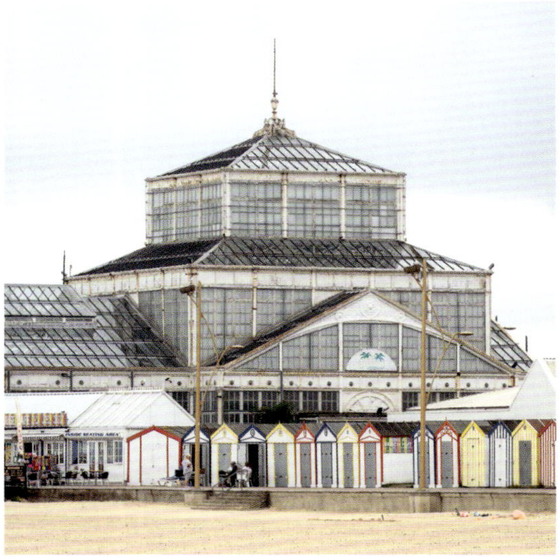

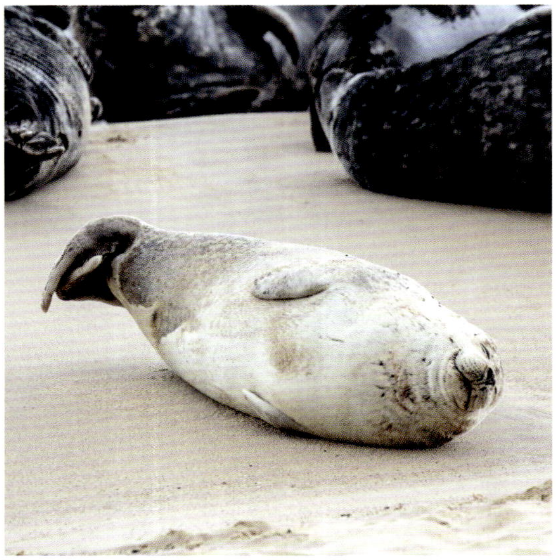

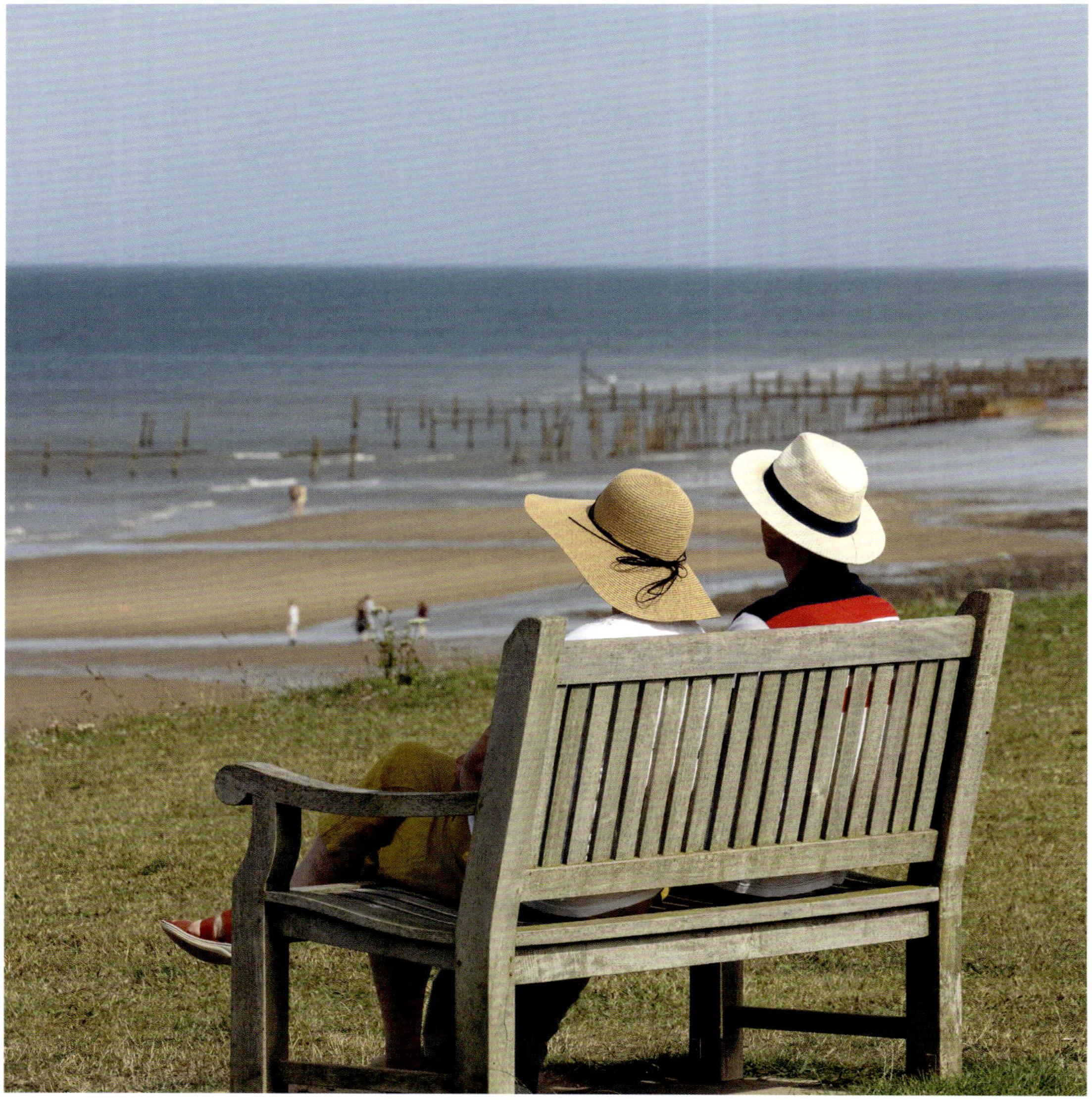

From top left:

The Victorian Winter Gardens, Great Yarmouth

Contentment: Horsey Gap seal colony

The couple: Happisburgh Beach

Opposite:

Drifting apart: Great Yarmouth Beach

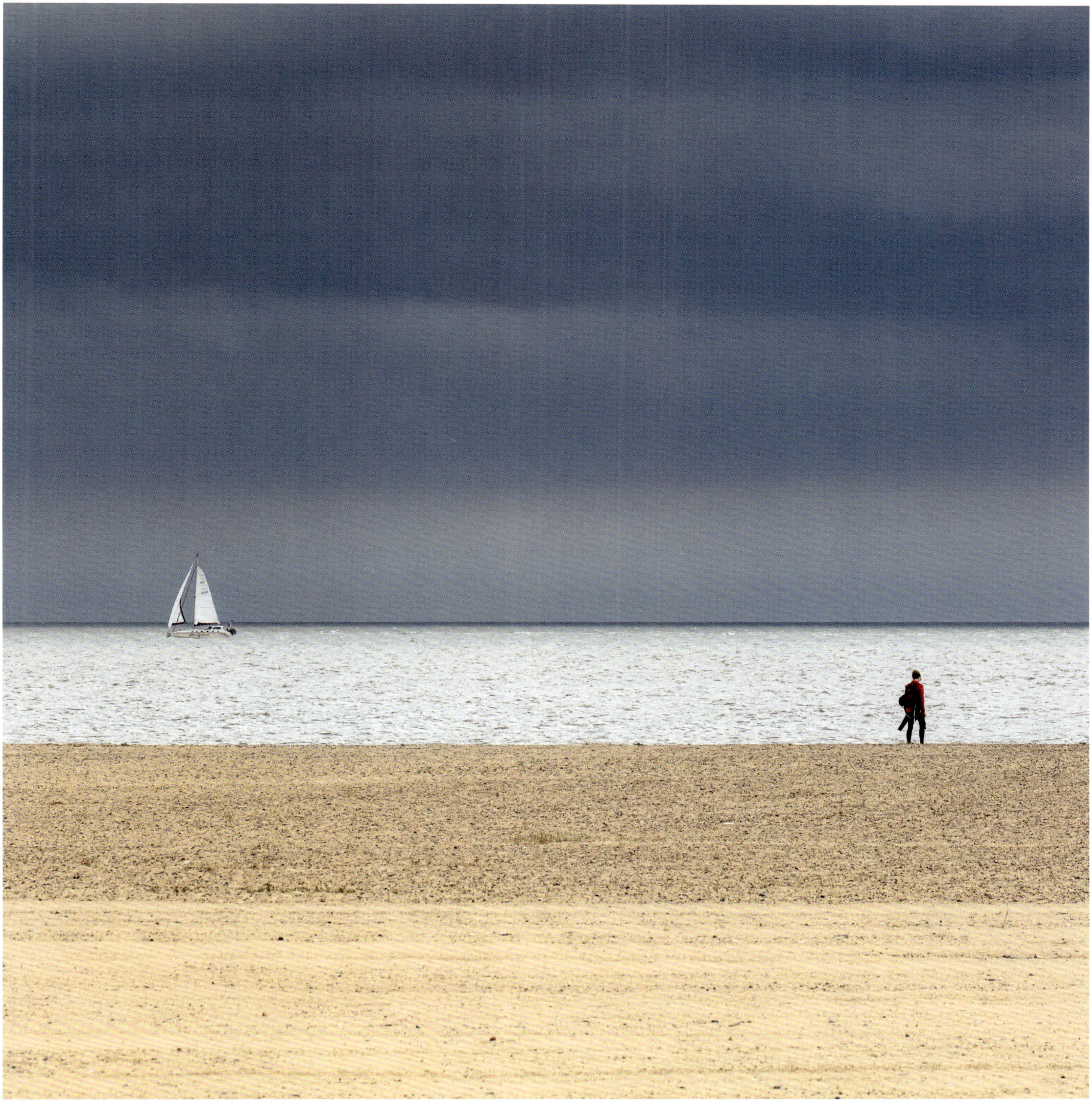

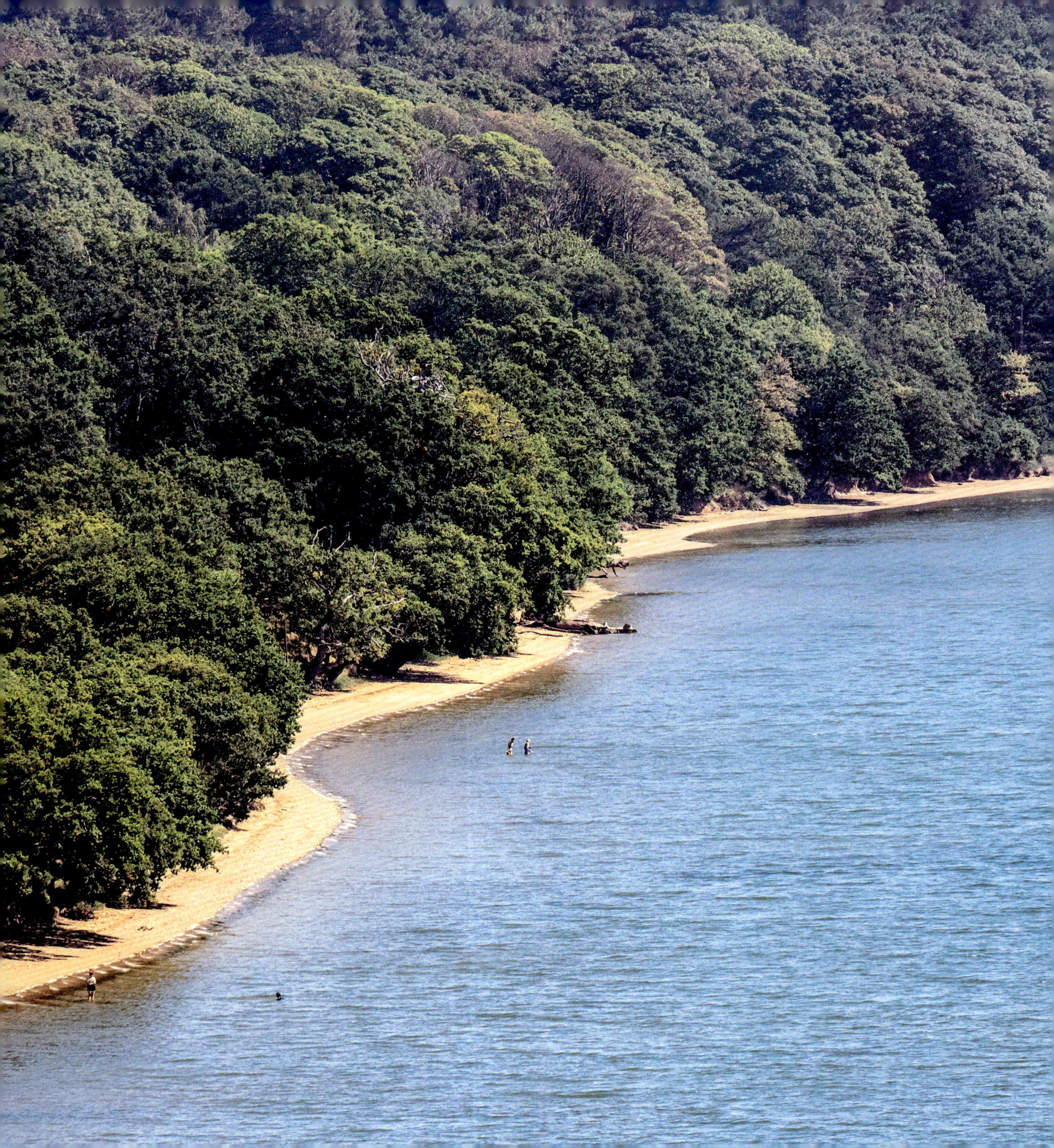

51 SUFFOLK

JULY–AUGUST 2020

DAY 418–429 | 10,119–10,374 KM | 255 KM

Opposite:

Bathers by the oak-lined shore of the River Orwell. Novelist Eric Arthur Blair gave himself the pen name George Orwell after the River Orwell in Suffolk, a location of which he was fond

It's an auspicious entry into Suffolk when I find a tenner at the edge of a barley field the moment I cross the border during an August heatwave. I soon reach Ness Point, at Lowestoft, the easternmost point of the British mainland and the fourth and final cardinal point of the journey. From there, I speed south along gorgeous shores lined with beach huts and past sandy, fast-eroding cliffs. A bulky dragonfly of blue and gold follows me as I pass Sizewell nuclear power station, whose dome resembles a large mosque from a distance, where the warm water from the outfall attracts fish and, in turn, gulls and fishermen.

At Aldeburgh, I see the first milestone to London: 60 miles, though it's more like 600 miles via my coastal route. Overheard conversations from tourists on the beach suggest a different locus too: 'It's well paid, but I don't know what the game plan is; I mean, you don't get equity.' I pass a beautiful brick house with ornamental chimneys and a thatched roof, an Ocado delivery, a Porsche and a Range Rover parked outside. Affluence is draped elegantly all around.

On the UK's third-hottest day on record, I pass the spit of Orford Ness on the mainland, which I'm frustrated to find is inaccessible to coast walkers. As night falls, I lie by the water, grateful for the respite from the heat, when I suddenly realise I'm not alone in the marsh as many of the yachts moored all around are occupied unlit. Peals of laughter and snippets of jovial conversation travel over the water, blending with the chatter of geese; it must have been a perfect day to be afloat. Before I retreat inside my tent, Orford Castle appears in the distance as a precise orange rectangle defined by the floodlights, while out to sea, the horizon blushes intermittently from forks of lightning.

Suffolk seems to have more *Keep Out. No Trespassing* signs than anywhere else in England. I continually need to cross private land to make progress, especially when following the rivers upstream flanked by grand estates that don't want to share their back yards. When I go up the River Butley, I find it fenced off with a *Please Turn Back* sign; my frustration finds voice in the handwritten 'miserable bugger' that someone has added to it.

After nine days of walking, I see the cranes of the UK's busiest container port at Felixstowe rise above the trees. When I get closer, the shipping containers tower above a boxed-in beach busy with sun-seekers like a multicoloured mosaic, and I'm reminded of Bill Bryson's comment in *Notes from a Small Island*: 'Nothing gives the English more pleasure, in a quiet but determined sort of way, than to do things oddly.' The path next to the Port of Felixstowe seems to be fenced off by the rail line – until I see a notice telling me that I need to call the signaller to unlock the gates across the tracks. When I'm through, there's a bench where I sit for a while, mesmerised by watching the loading and unloading of thousands of containers and feeling connected to the rest of the world.

On my last night in Suffolk, I camp by the shore of the River Orwell on a tiny platform of soil, barely bigger than the tent and just above the tide line, from where the unloading of containers in the distant port sounds like the rumble of thunder. The evening is so warm that I cook with my shirt off below shading oaks that hang generously over the riverbank, though I still feel like a fugitive encircled by *Keep Out* signs. Before turning in, I eagerly study the map for the day ahead: a loop around the Shotley Peninsula to Essex, with over five hundred kilometres of coastline, the last big county of the journey.

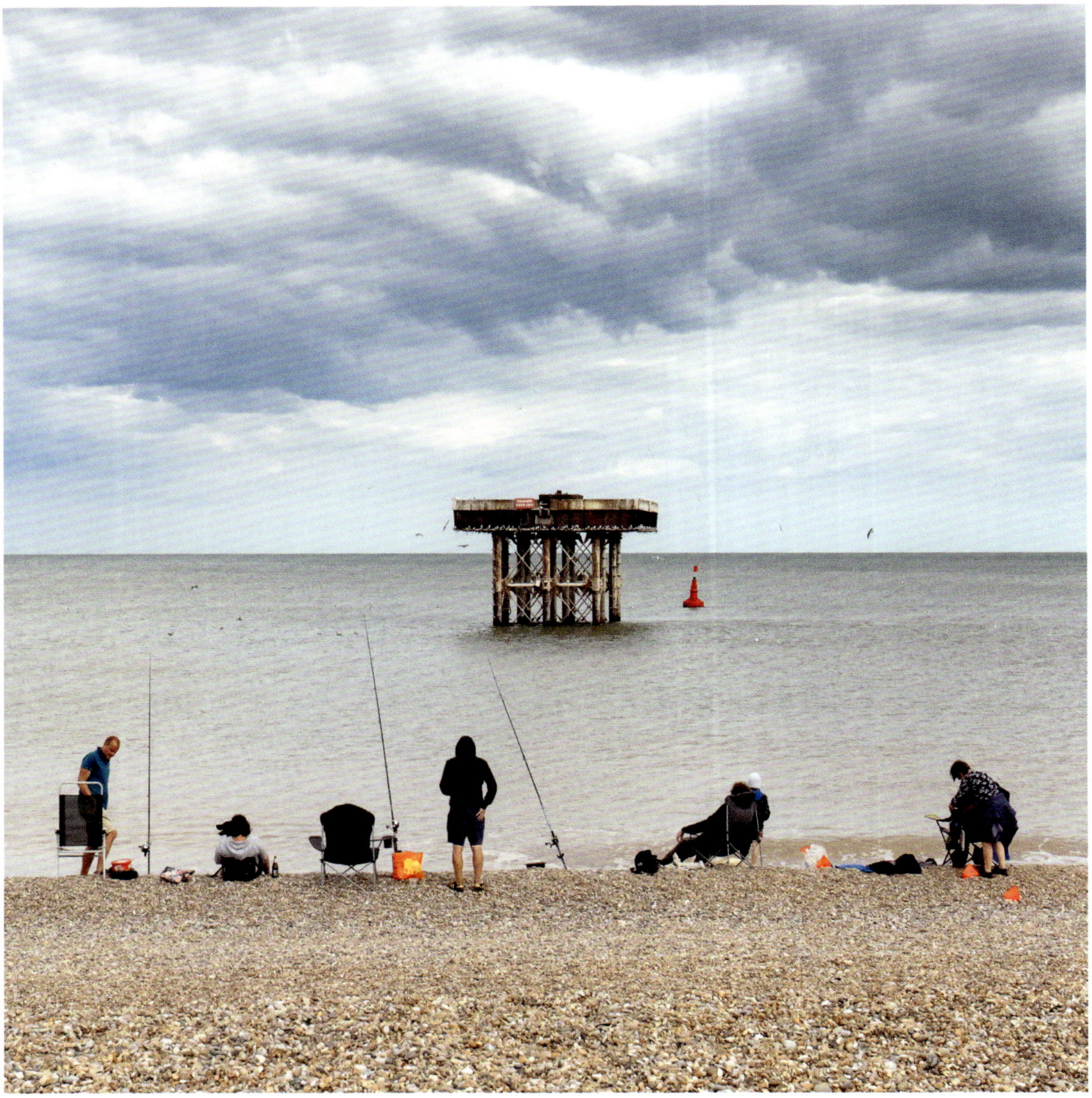

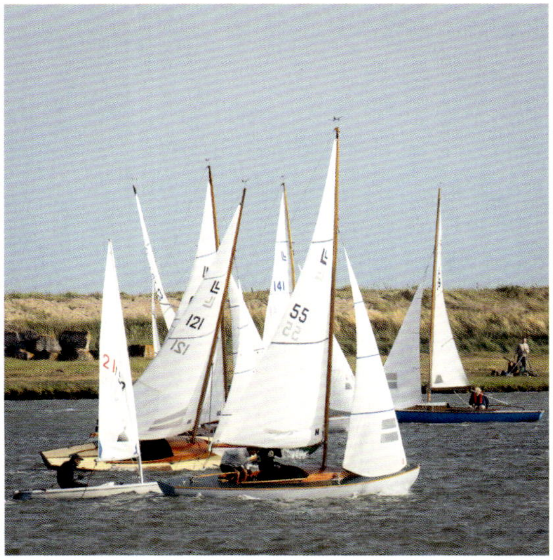

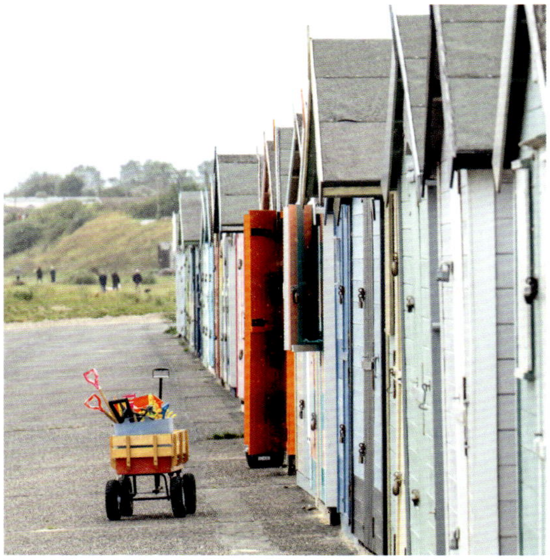

Opposite, from top left:

The first milestone for London, Aldeburgh

Sizewell B nuclear power station

Windbreak, Felixstowe Beach

From centre left:

Ornate brick chimneys, Iken

The House in the Clouds, a former water tower at Thorpeness built to take water from the nearby windmill in 1923. The design, hilariously, aimed to 'disguise' the tank and 'fit in' with Thorpeness's mock-Tudor and Jacobean houses. In 1979 the tank was removed to convert the building into a home

Pakefield Beach, Lowestoft

From bottom left:

Dune House, Thorpeness, designed by Jarmund/Vigsnæs Architects for Living Architecture in 2010

Moot Hall, Aldeburgh, built c.1520

Sea kale, Shingle Street

From top left:

Warm water from the Sizewell nuclear power station outfall attracts fish and, in turn, gulls and anglers

A flock of dinghies in the River Alde, Aldeburgh

Pakefield beach huts, Lowestoft

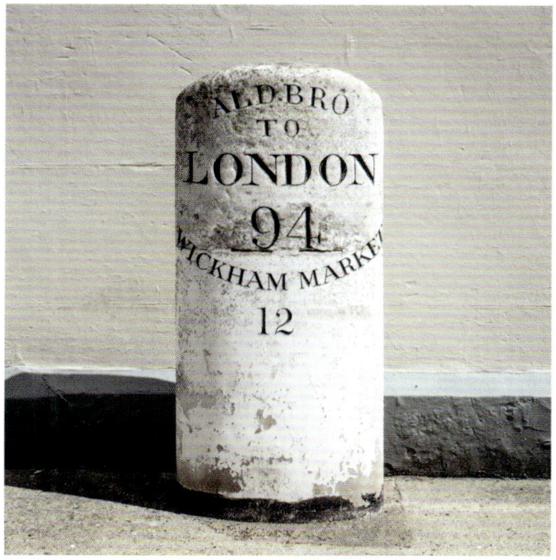
ALDBRO
TO
LONDON
94
ICKHAM MARKE
12

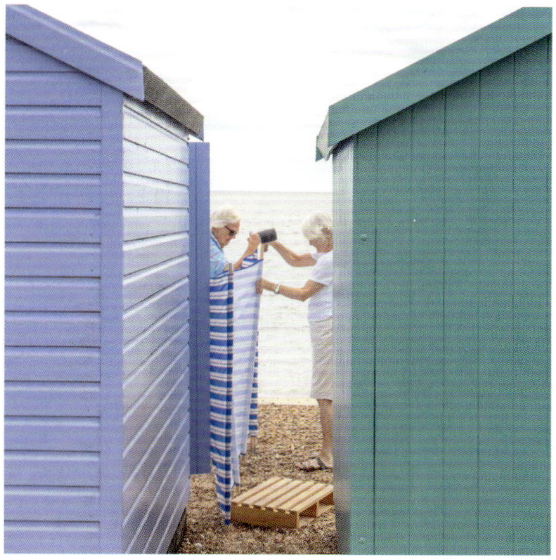

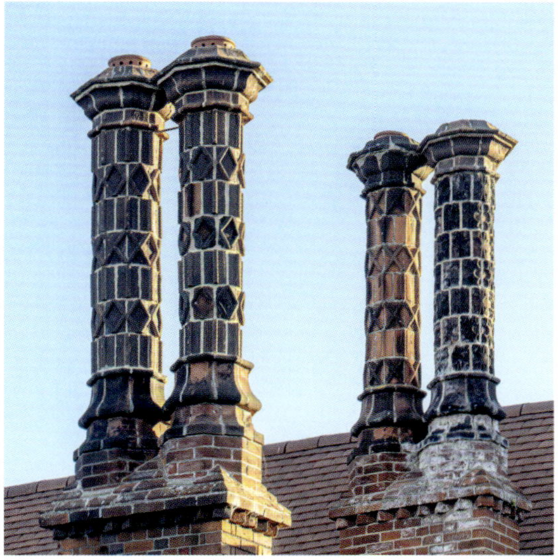

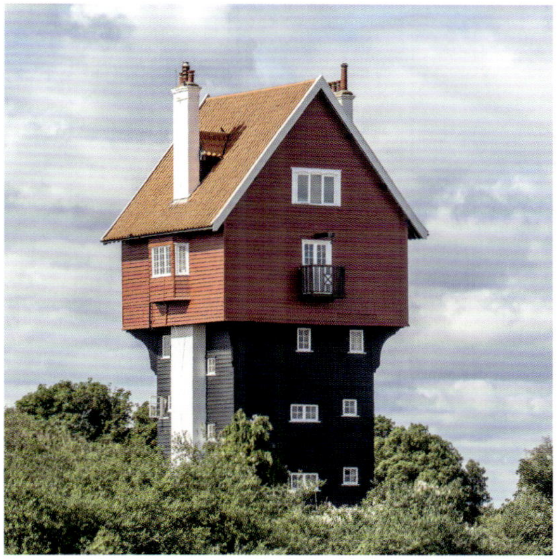

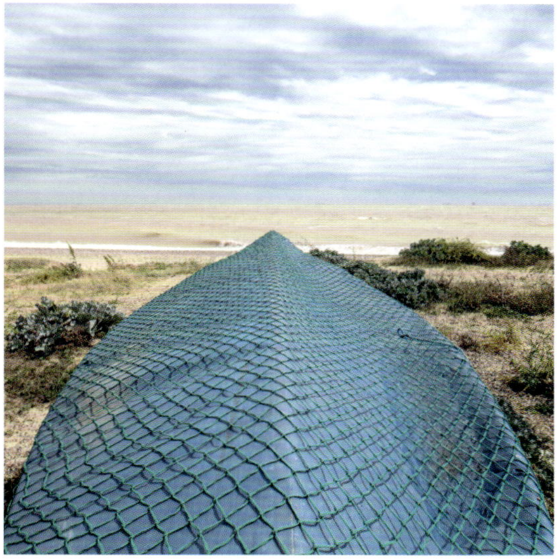

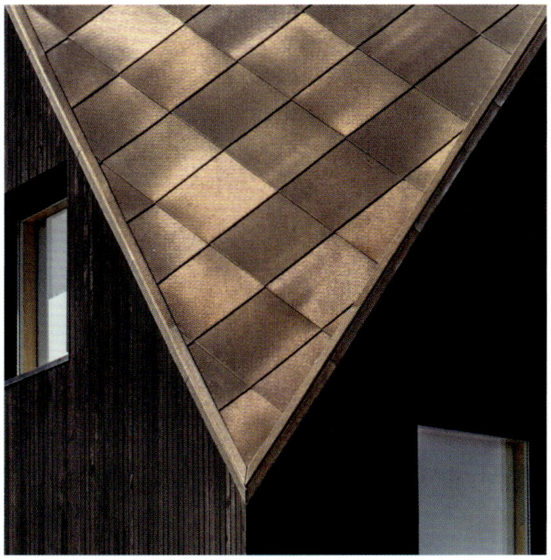

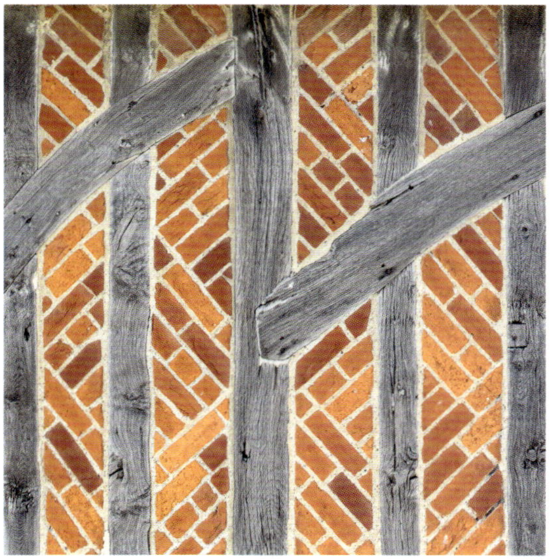

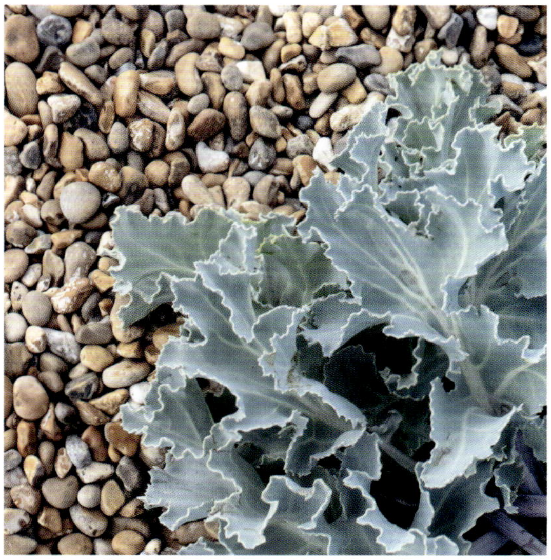

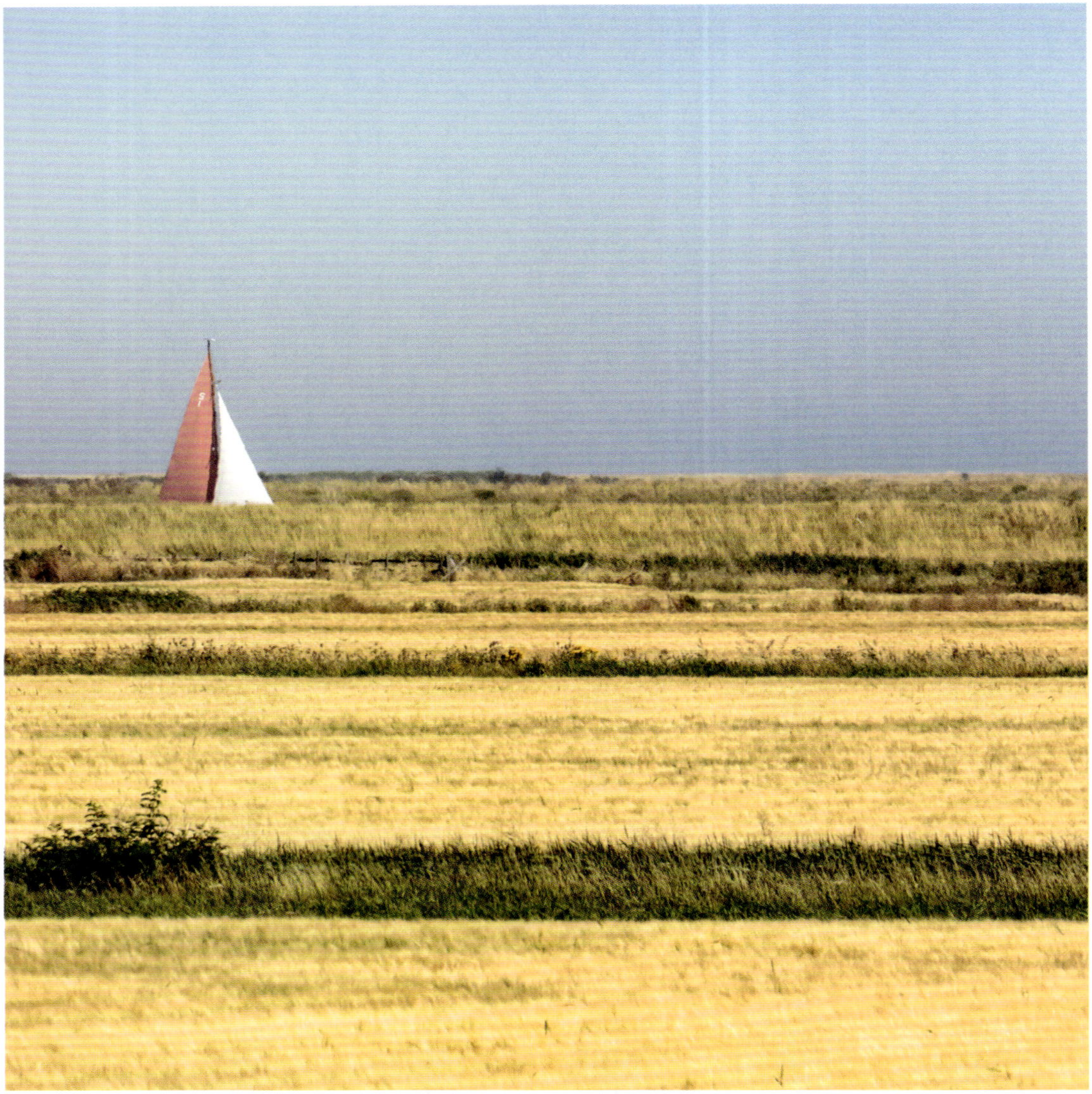

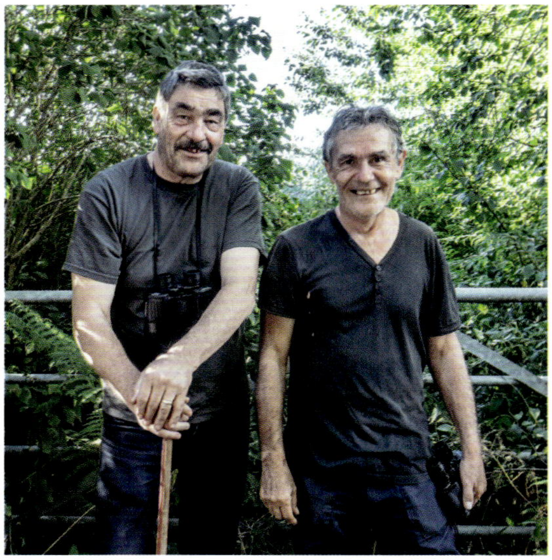

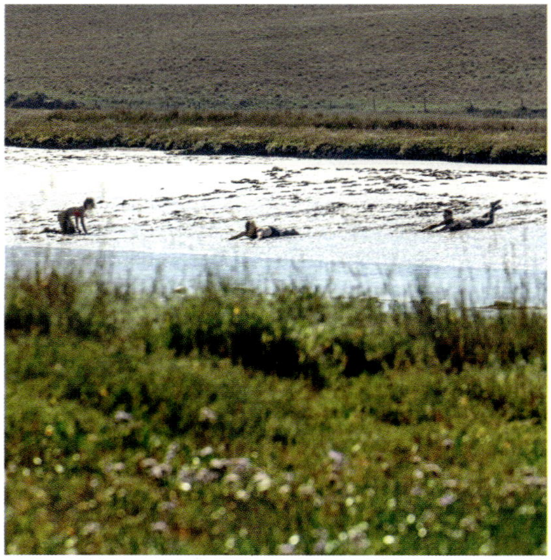

From top left:

Sailing past: Orford Ness

John and Mike – who met at school and now go birding together – at Iken Cliff by the River Alde: 'If anything, the National Trust has reduced biodiversity here by flooding the marshes; there used to be short-eared owls and terns'

Mud-sliding by the Butley River

Opposite, clockwise from top left:

Martello Tower Z (built 1810–12) with additional Second World War gun emplacement at Buckanay Farm. Martello Tower AA at Shingle Street beyond

Boyton Marshes Second World War tank range target control blockhouse

Scott and Margaret Millar, Sutton

The apogee of Englishness: Bawdsey Quay

Chalking the door, All Saints Church, Hemley. The first and last numbers refer to the current year. The letters 'CMB' come from the traditional names for the three kings: Caspar, Melchior and Balthazar. They also stand for the Latin sentence *Christus Mansionem Benedicat* which means 'May Christ bless this dwelling'

Woodbridge Tide Mill, whose waterwheel still turns and is capable of grinding wholemeal flour

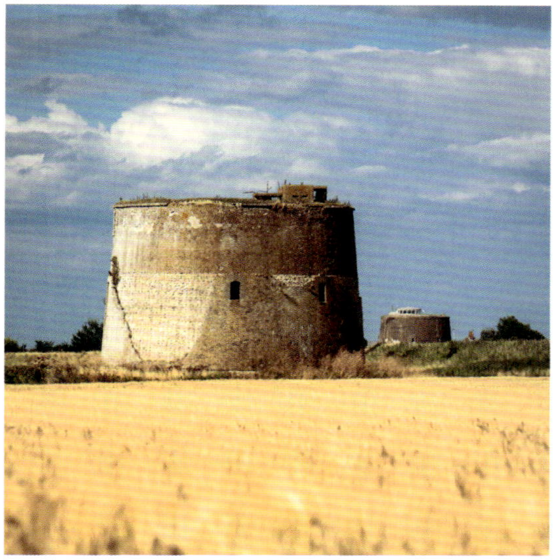

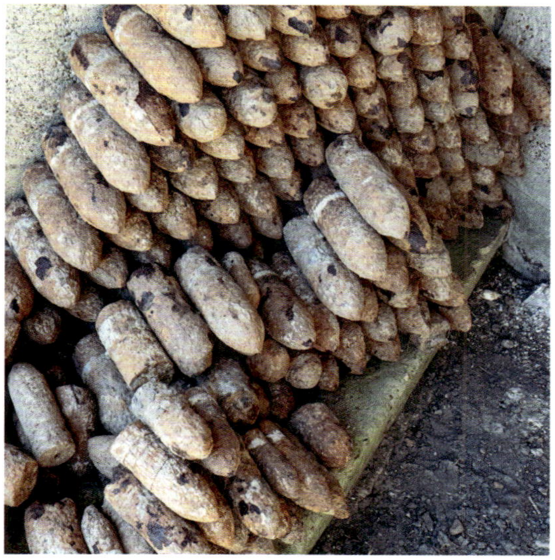

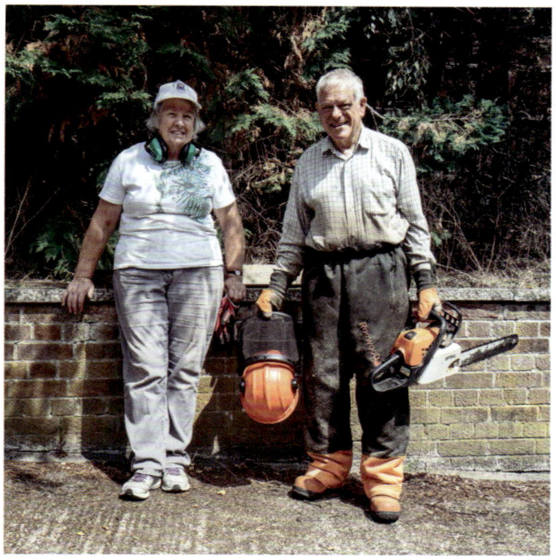

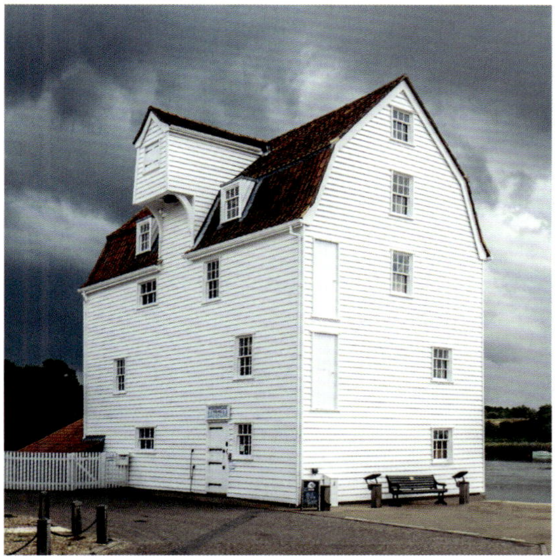

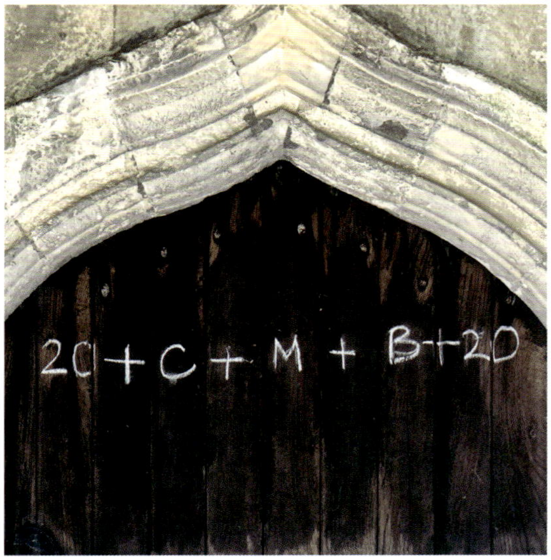

20+C+M+B+20

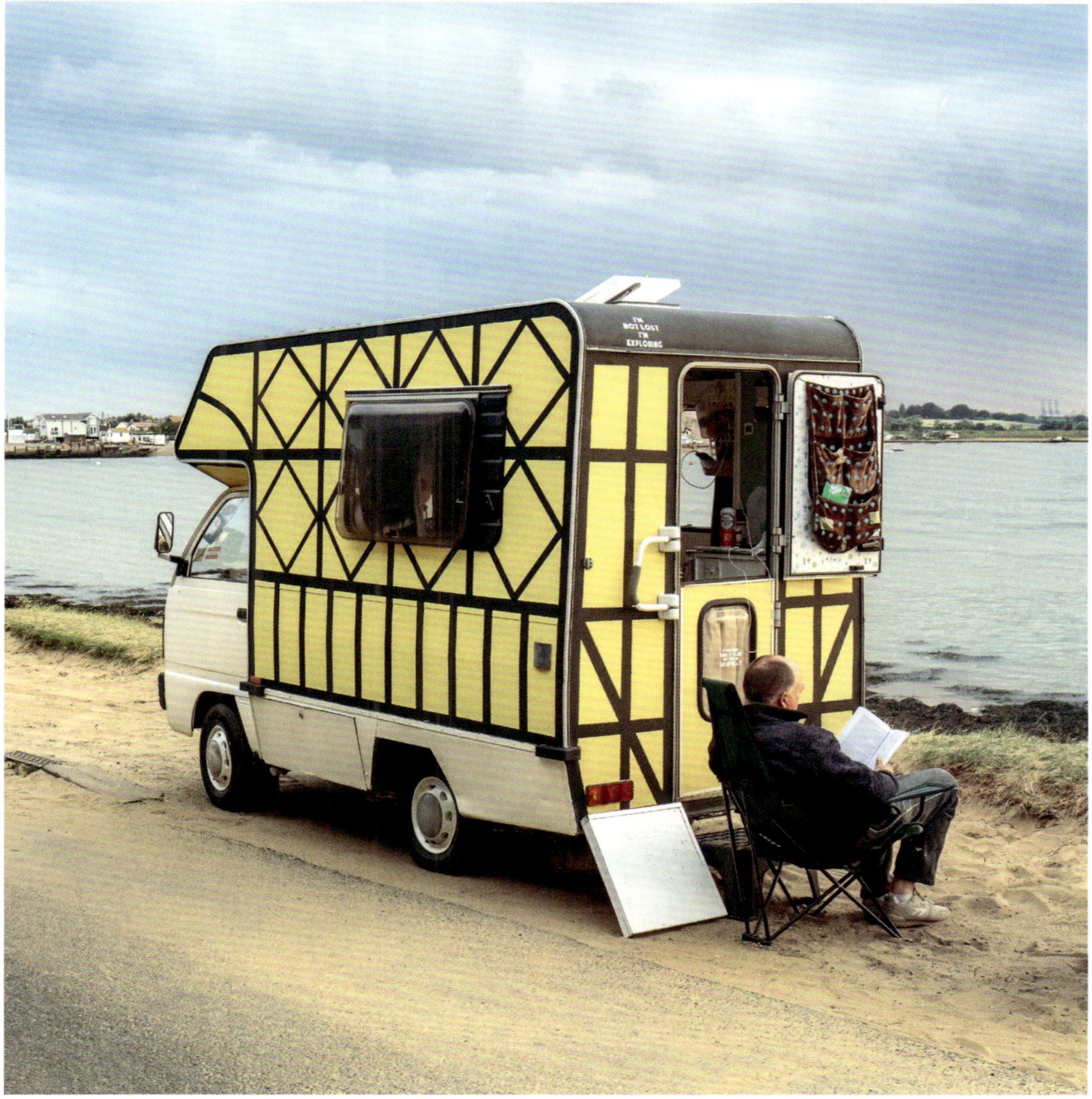

I'M
NOT LOST
I'M
EXPLORING

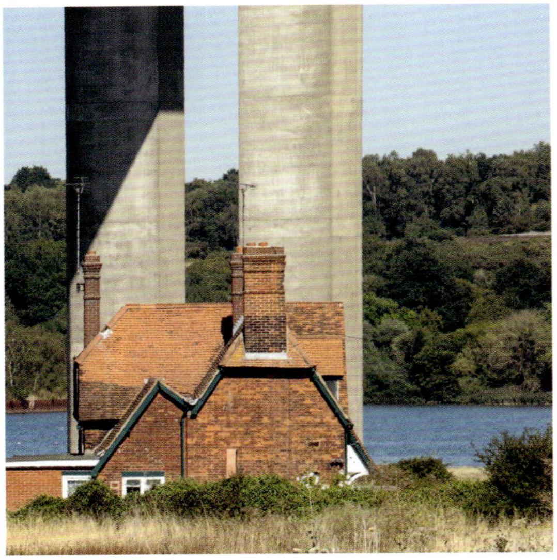

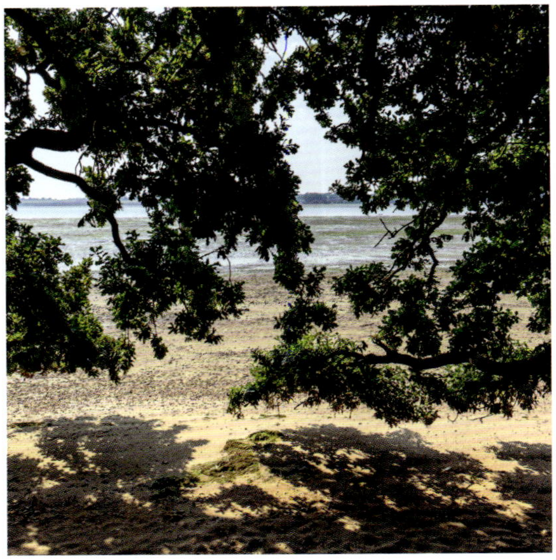

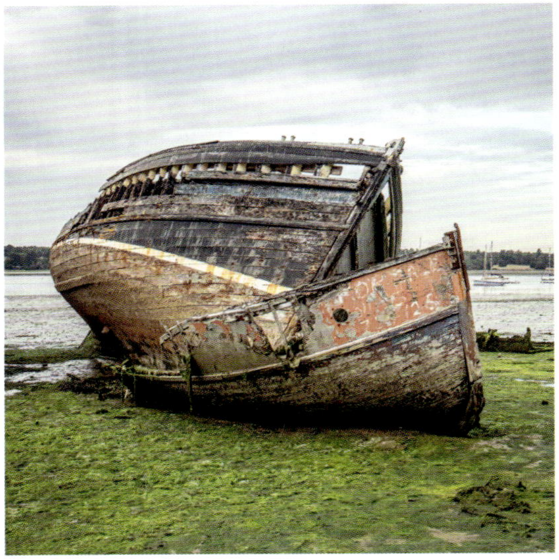

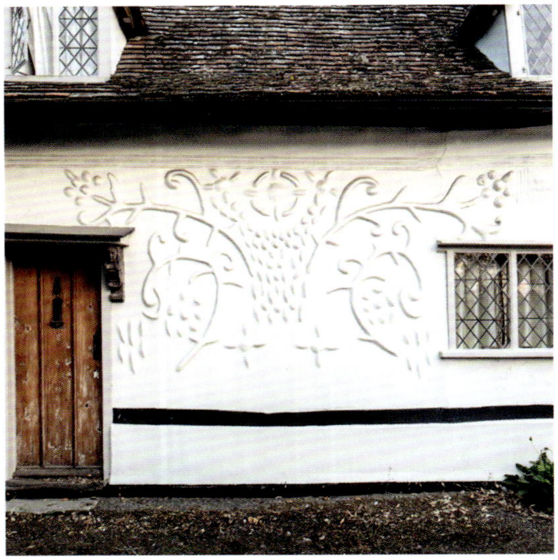

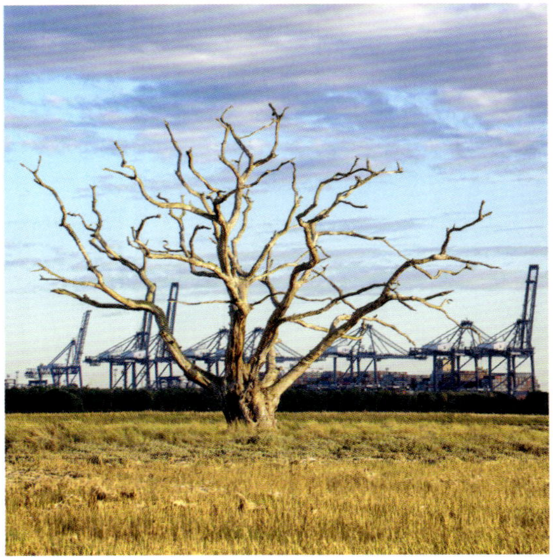

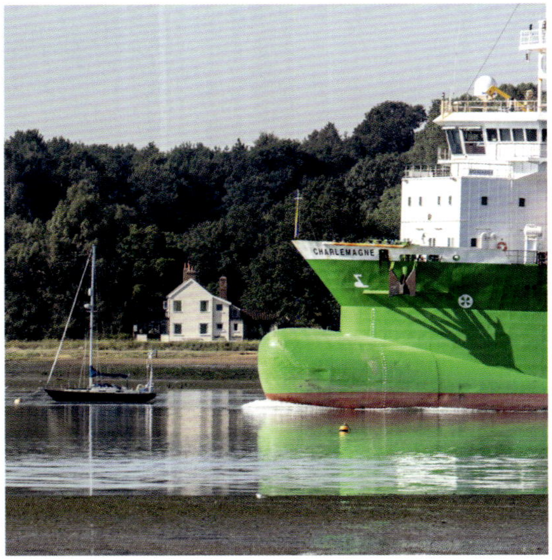

From top left:

Below the Orwell Bridge

Overhanging oaks at Seafield Bay by the Stour

From centre left:

Pin Mill wrecks

The first and most memorable example of pargeting (decorative plastering found in Suffolk and Essex) I saw on the early-seventeenth-century Ancient House in Stutton

From bottom left:

The Port of Felixstowe from Trimley Marshes

Charlemagne, a hopper dredger, by the Nacton shore of the River Orwell

Opposite:

Package holiday: Port of Felixstowe. The beaches were bustling due to Covid restrictions

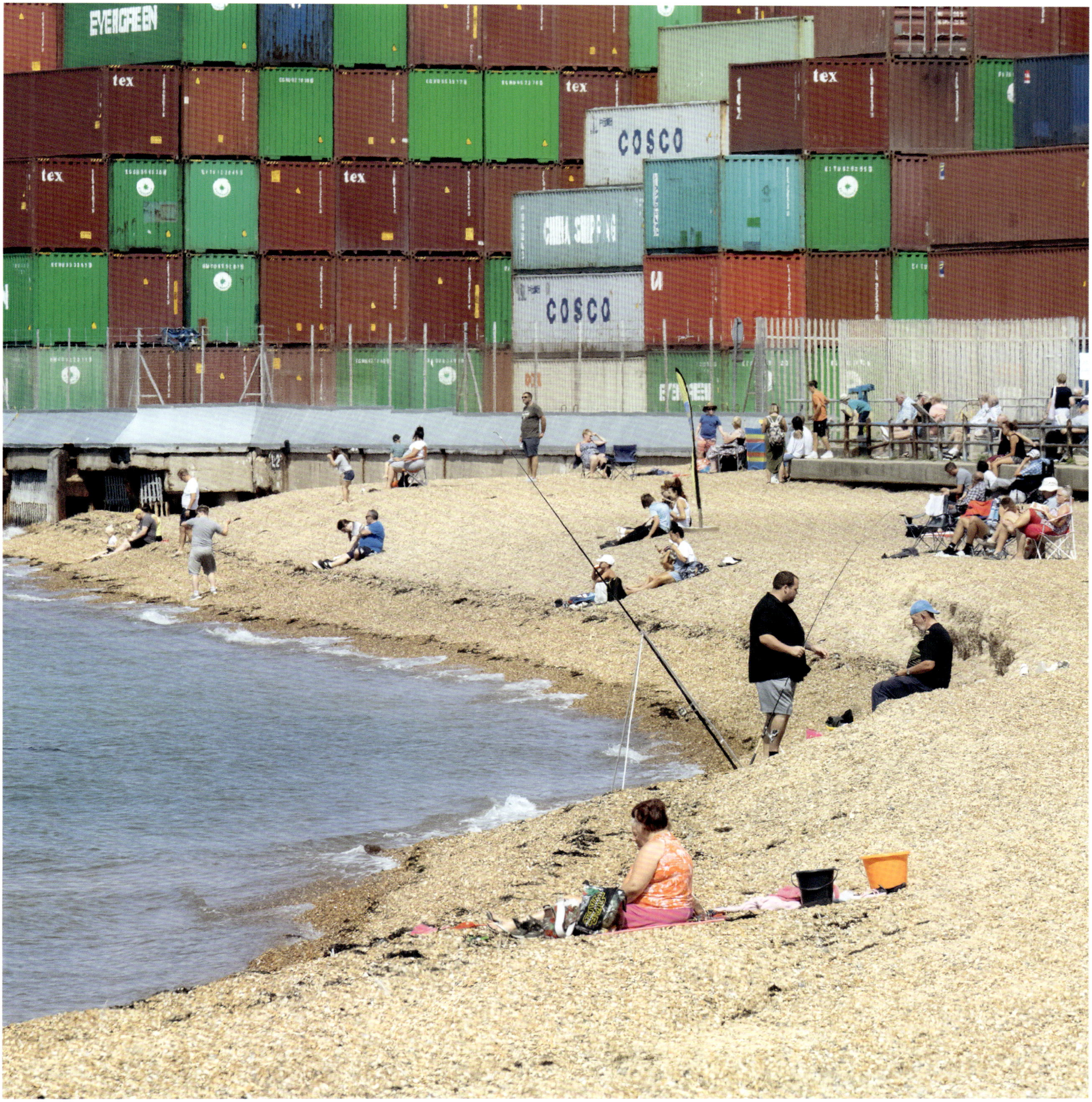
EVERGREEN
tex
tex
tex
tex
tex
COSCO
COSCO

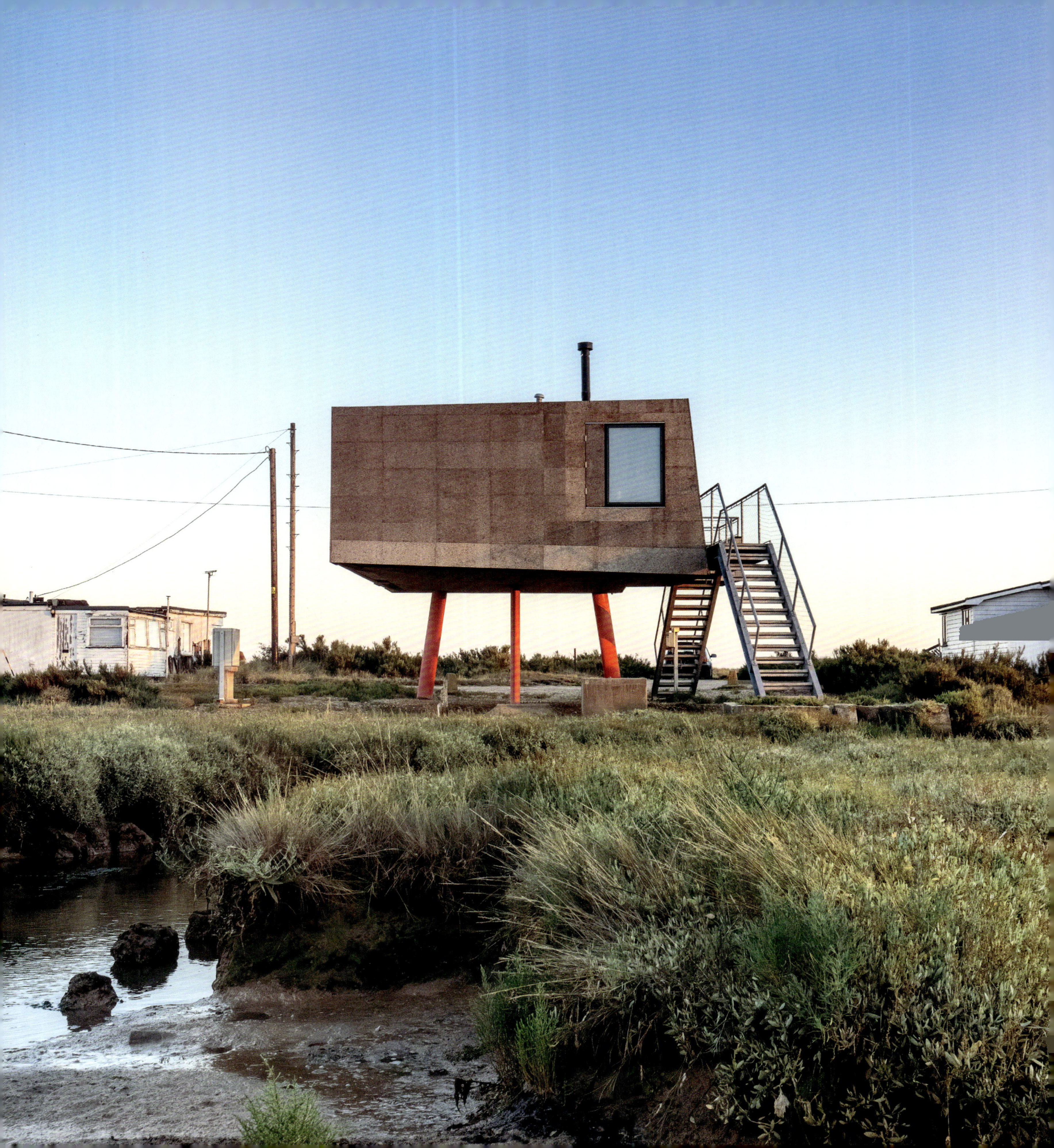

52 ESSEX

AUGUST–SEPTEMBER 2020

DAY 430–452 | 10,374–10,952 KM | 578 KM

Opposite:

Redshank studio, Lee-over-Sands, a cork-clad cabin raised above a tidal saltmarsh. Designed by architect Lisa Shell for artist Marcus Taylor in 2016

I cross the Stour into Essex, which has a walkable coastline of 578 kilometres. It's a place many I met in Suffolk called 'a world apart' and I'm immediately beguiled by the sudden differences. Here, it's 'babe' not 'darling', jet skis not yachts. Everyone makes direct eye contact, often accompanied by a witty comment, which reminds me of Scotland. I see girls dancing in the supermarket and lads launching themselves belly-first with shrieking abandon down the muddy banks of a creek. In Essex, life is grasped with both hands. This vitality seems to manifest in one of the first buildings I pass, A House for Essex, designed by FAT Architecture and Grayson Perry. It is an absolute joy with its sculptural ceramic tiles and finials.

After four days of sea-wall walking I reach Harwich before following the River Colne to Colchester, a town with many charms and an epic history. In Roman times, it was the capital of Britain (and Britain's first city) until it was razed to the ground by Queen Boudicca in AD 60 and the title was transferred to London. Passing by the weathered walls of Colchester Castle, I uncover its fascinating past. This edifice, constructed by the Normans, stands on the foundations of the Temple of Claudius. Once the most illustrious Roman building in Britain, the temple was a place of refuge during Boudicca's attack, which led to the slaughter of all within and its destruction.

I arrive on Mersea Island in the dark and tuck my tent out of the way. The following morning, I have a feudal awaking: as I'm lying on the ground in my tiny shelter, my body starts to vibrate from horse hooves close by me; a woman calls down imperiously from the saddle, 'I don't know why you are camping there.'

I loop around the island in a reverie of mesmerising Mersea cloud-watching before passing Cakehole Deli, a name undoubtedly synonymous with the highest art of gastronomy. Leaving Mersea Island, I have the unpleasant choice between a 12-kilometre trespass on sea walls or heading inland on fast, dangerous roads with no walkway. Today has not been fun; the flat landscape makes it hard to keep out of sight, I've been asked to leave someone's land already, so I wait under a wild rose bush for it to get dark enough to put the tent up without being noticed. It is starting to feel like an escape-and-evasion exercise.

As I plan to reach the finish line at St Paul's in a couple of weeks, I announce my end date and time on social media while trying to figure out how I can celebrate despite the virus restrictions, currently the 'rule of six'. With another lockdown imminent, I'm desperate to increase my daily mileage to finish before that happens. The stakes are raised further when *The One Show* calls to say they want to send a film crew, and a handful of other journalists call to say they will send photographers and reporters.

In the unsettling oddness of Dengie National Nature Reserve, I'm interviewed by Ray Clark for BBC Essex, who remembers when the marsh was a patchwork of dozens of farms (there are only three today) employing hundreds of workers. 'I had a proper Essex accent then, like from rural Suffolk, but I had to lose that as I wanted a career in radio. That would be different today.' At the far edge of Dengie stands a stark, modest chapel, St Peter-on-the-Wall, that was founded circa 654, making it one of the first still-standing Christian chapels in Britain. It was built over the ruined gate of the abandoned third-century Roman fort of Othona, reusing Roman stones and bricks in its construction, literally 'on the wall' of the original. A few hours later, a very different structure, the hexagonal, pyramid-topped Dengie Minefield Control Tower, looms out of the marsh. It's a reminder of how well the River Crouch was defended as a potential invasion route to London from 1941. I'm startled by a ground-shaking explosion from the secretive military site on Foulness Island. It must be hard to get used to if you live nearby. John Betjeman's comment that Essex has 'a stronger contrast of beauty and ugliness than any southern English county' is starting to ring true.

I receive some top-quality smart-arse commentary near Battlebridge when a market gardener, seeing me hesitate in locating the footpath between the fields, calls over, ''E don't know where 'e's going, but 'e's going there anyway.' Walking through South Woodham Ferrers on a Bank Holiday Monday morning is like *The Truman Show*; husbands trim hedges and wash cars outside immaculate homes, ready with a warm smile and a wave.

Even though I'm a few days from the finish in London, there is still one more major obstacle: the Broomway. This notorious 10-kilometre tidal route on the Essex foreshore connects the mainland to Foulness Island and has been called 'the most perilous byway in England'. It has probably claimed more than a hundred lives over the years, as the tide comes in faster than a person can run. Furthermore, the path (which is invisible on the ground) must be followed very precisely as on one side there is sinking mud and on the other unexploded ordnance; the air pressure and wind speed can dramatically affect the speed of the rising tide, and sea mist can suddenly blow in, removing all visual references.

Starting the Broomway alone at dawn on a falling tide, I set off with some trepidation from Wakering Stairs, probing ahead of me in the mud and sand with my poles. The only landmark after leaving the security of the shore is the Maypole, a navigation aid at the mouth of Havengore Creek. I follow the Broomway via GPS, double-checking with a compass bearing for 9 kilometres as it runs parallel and 500 metres from the shore. I notice that if I don't check the bearing and location regularly, my route curves towards the shore (and the sinking mud) as if I have a magnetic attraction to the land. The clouds are reflected in the wet surface like a mirror, giving the sensation of walking on water in a potent mixture of exhilaration and adrenaline.

The moment I touch land on Foulness, I'm intercepted by two burly security guards. They seem happy enough with my reasons and leave me to circumnavigate the militarised island. I pass pylons with hanging steel cages like giant medieval torture devices and buzzing warehouses surrounded by earth berms. The pub and shop are boarded up so I make lunch on the picnic bench outside, glad I brought my own water with me. After scurrying around the island, I wait on the slipway for four hours to let the tide fall enough to return. At Asplins Head slipway, I meet a farmer who used to be a guide on the Broomway.

He points offshore. 'The old boys call this the Black Ground, which is close to the shore from all the weed. If you start to sink, keep moving, and if you really sink, just roll over.' He looks out at the falling tide. 'You'll be away in an hour.' Sure enough, an hour later, I make my first sloshing steps through the water and back to the mainland. As I surreptitiously put up the tent a few hours later on an inactive firing range, I can't believe that the lights on the other side of the Thames Estuary are Kent and that I've already been there. Some days, life can slip through your fingers, but not this one.

I'm soon on Southend Pier, the longest pleasure pier in the world at 2.14 kilometres, which is long enough to have its own train, though I opt to stroll along on my final rest day. Nikolaus Pevsner was right when he said, 'Essex is not as popular a touring and sightseeing county as it deserves to be.'

Resilient Canvey Island is encircled by its concrete sea defences after the disastrous floods of 1953. Memorials to the 'Heroes of the Essex Delta' Canvey pub rock band Dr Feelgood are painted on the sea wall. On the edge of Canvey Island, a blush at sunset illuminates Southend after a grey day to the distant rumble of a huge container ship gliding up the Thames. It might be the friendliest place I've walked through down south, with repeated greetings of 'All right, mate'.

It's still rural, despite the proximity of London Gateway Port, and at Fobbing Marsh the only other human visible in the landscape is a jet skier roaring under Fobbing Horse Barrier. At dusk, truck stops by the gargantuan distribution centres are at capacity, all with black curtains drawn over the cab, and the sounds of TV in different languages coming from within. A Romanian truck driver prepares a tasty meal on a gas stove outside his cab and raises his head to say hello.

Tonight is the last time I'll pitch the tent, by the Thames near London Gateway, where I drift off to the clanking of containers being unloaded. In the morning, I'm packing away my peripatetic home for the last time. I feel tingles of contentment that unless I do something spectacularly stupid, the biggest obstacles should all be behind me: no more way-finding, sourcing water, trespassing and stealth-camping. Towards the QE2 Bridge, the concrete flood barrier by the Thames heading for the Dartford crossing is a dazzling, kilometres-long ribbon of street art. When I reach Purfleet, there's a pink sunset over the river, and I can make out the silhouette of Canary Wharf Tower ahead. London, the end of the journey, is within sight.

Opposite, from top left:

Mistley waterfront, Manningtree

A House for Essex, Wrabness, designed by FAT Architecture and Grayson Perry in 2015 for Living Architecture

From bottom left:

Dovecote at Home Farm, Ramsey

Jib of the Harwich treadmill crane

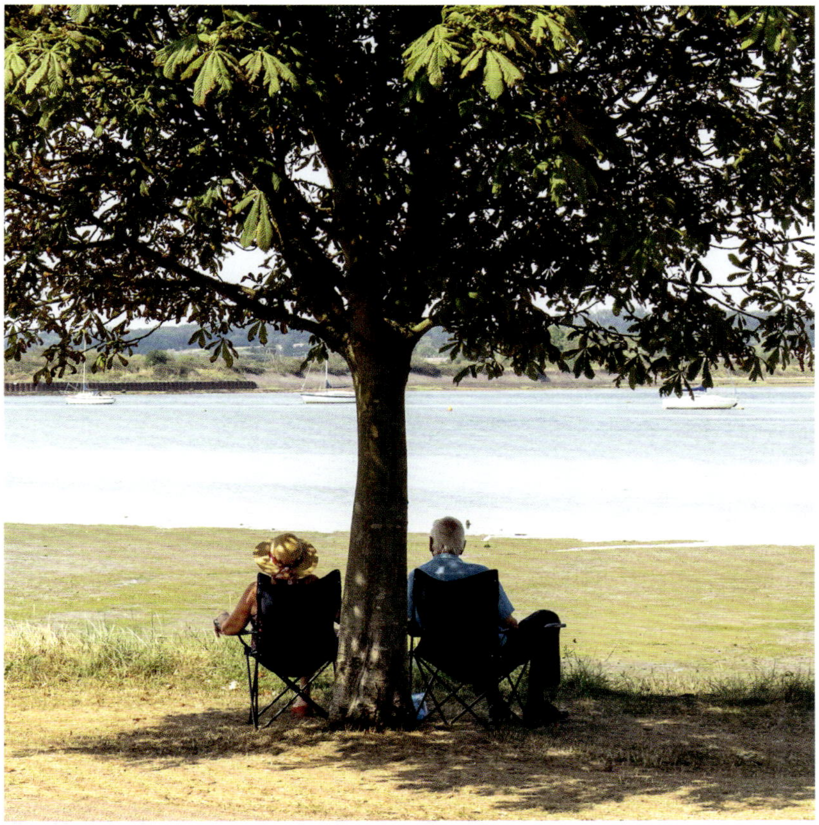

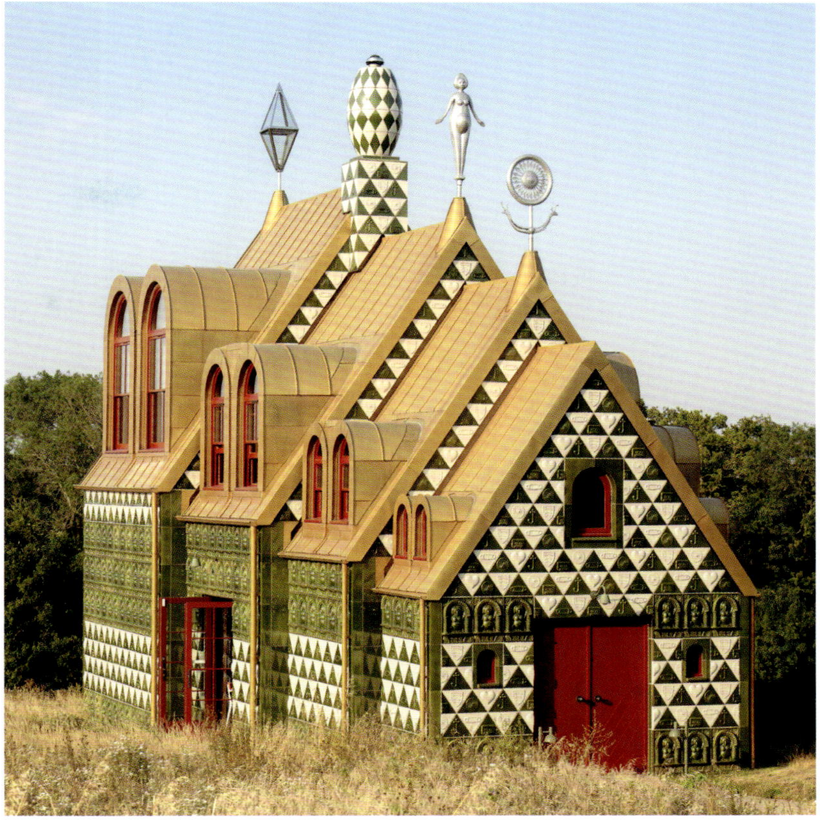

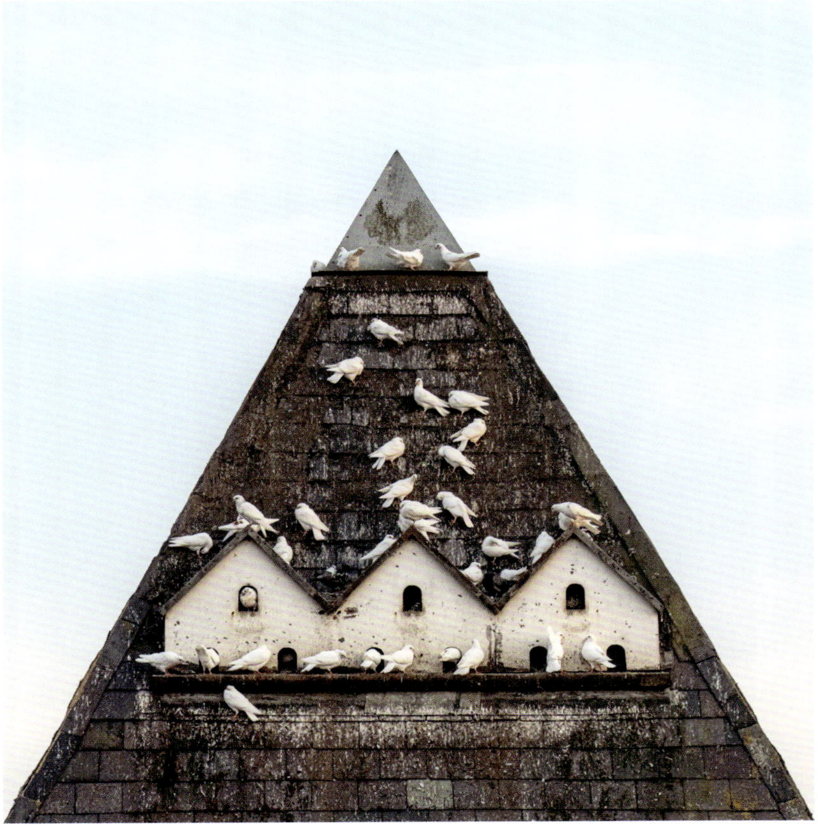

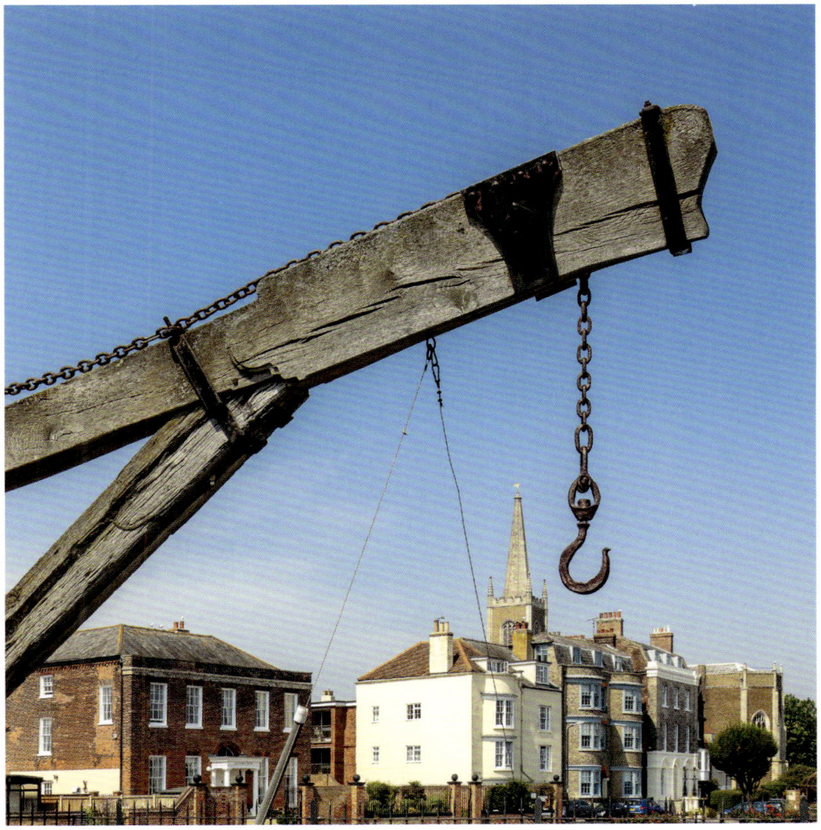

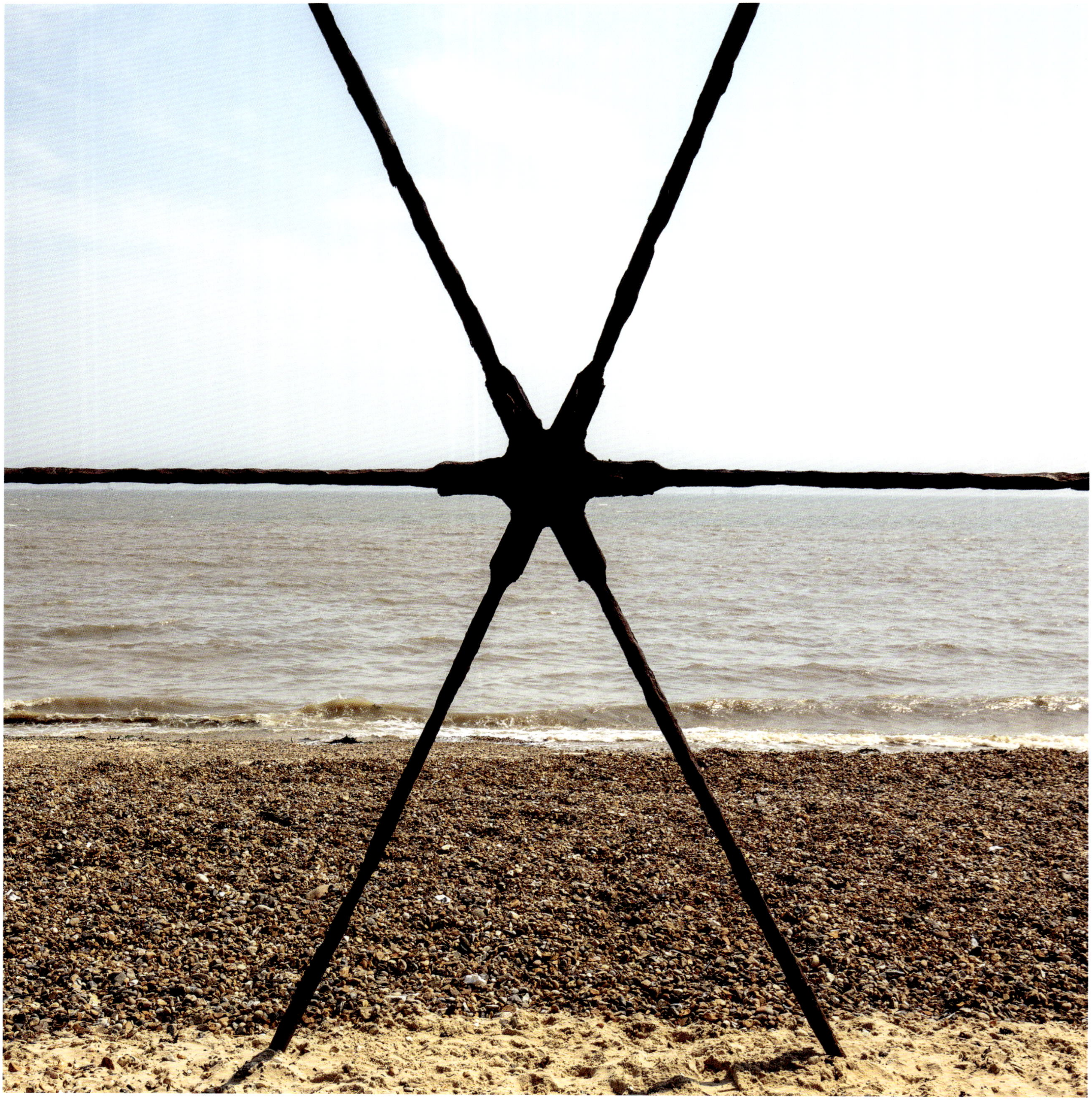

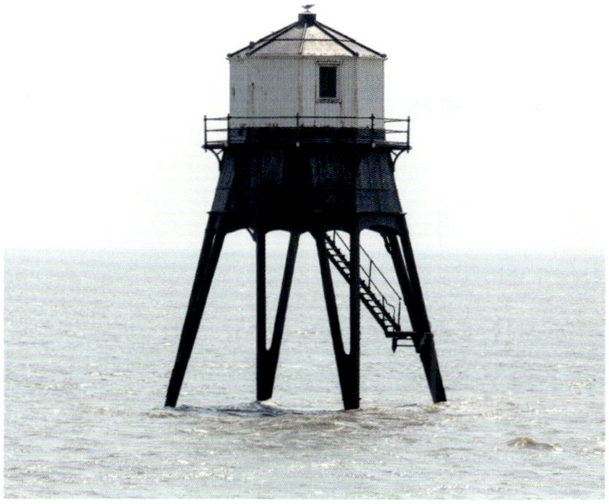

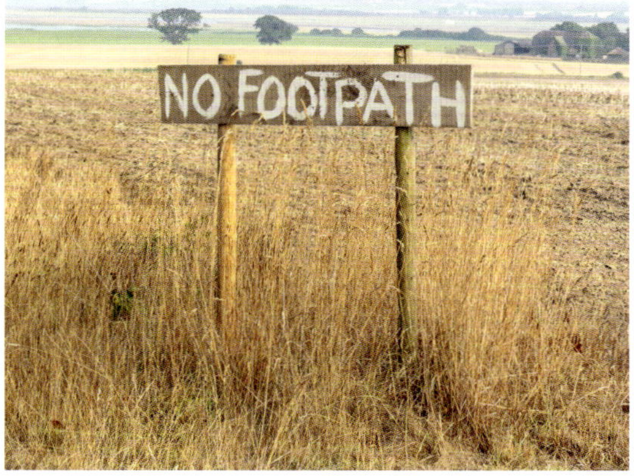

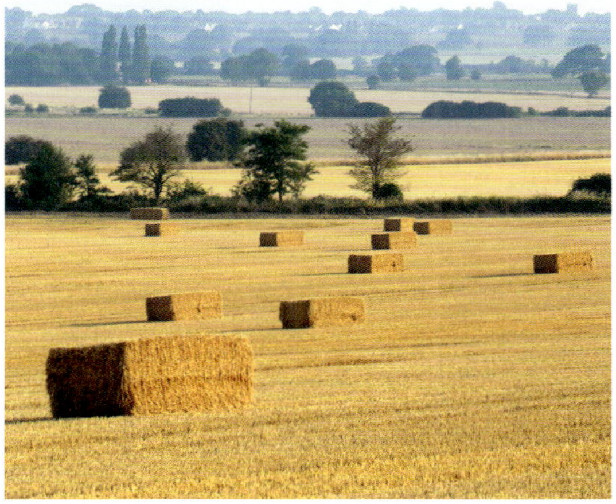

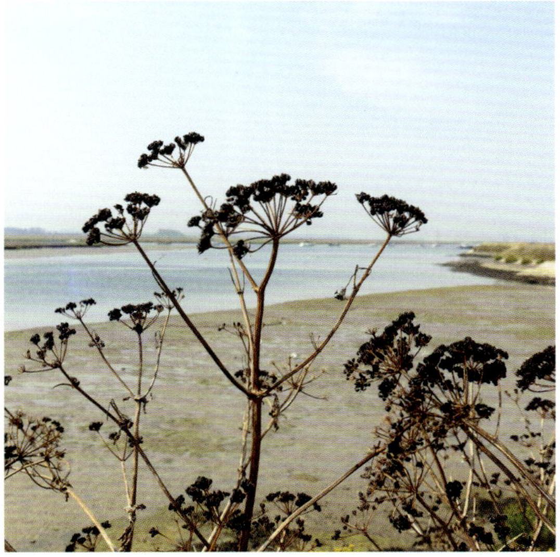

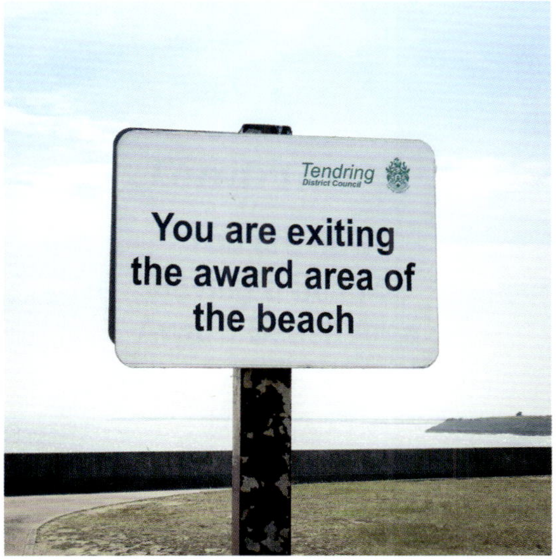

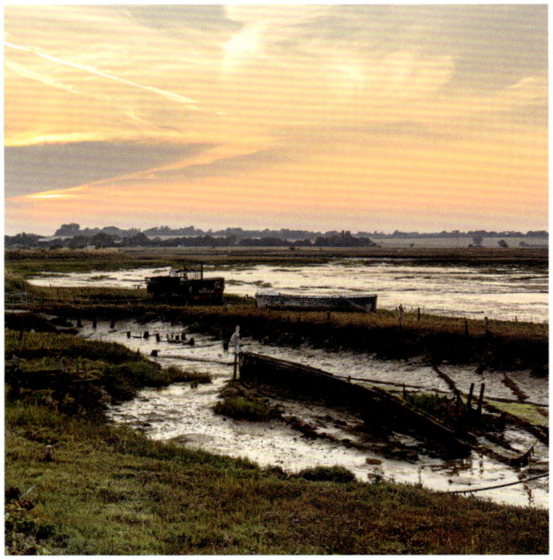

From top left:

Dovercourt Outer Lighthouse, Harwich

No footpath: Great Oakley

From centre left:

Bales, Beaumont

Walton Channel, Walton-on-the-Naze

From bottom left:

Expectation management: Harwich

Evening glow at Landermere Wharf

Opposite:

Segments: Dovercourt Inner Lighthouse, Harwich

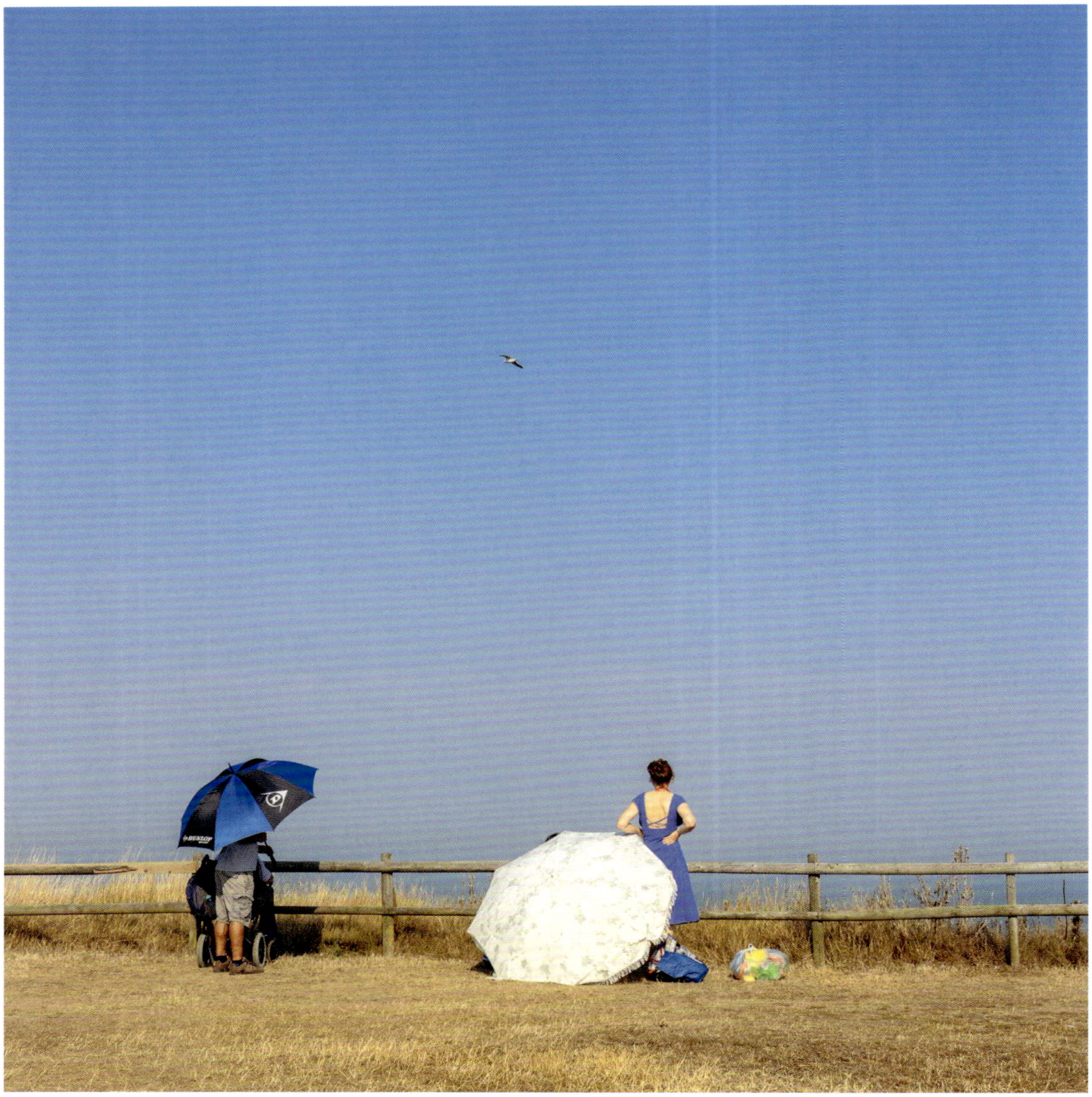

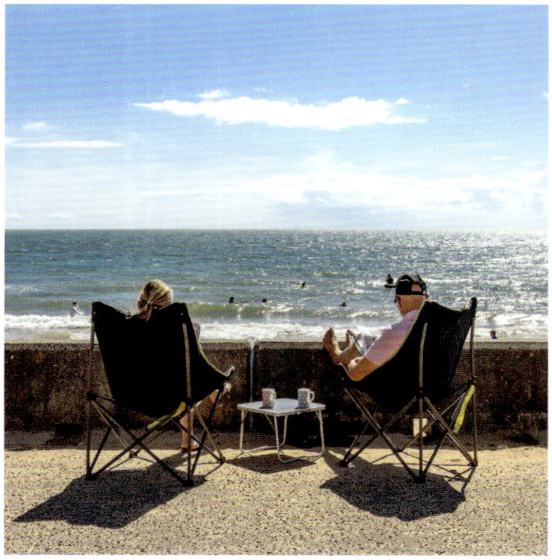

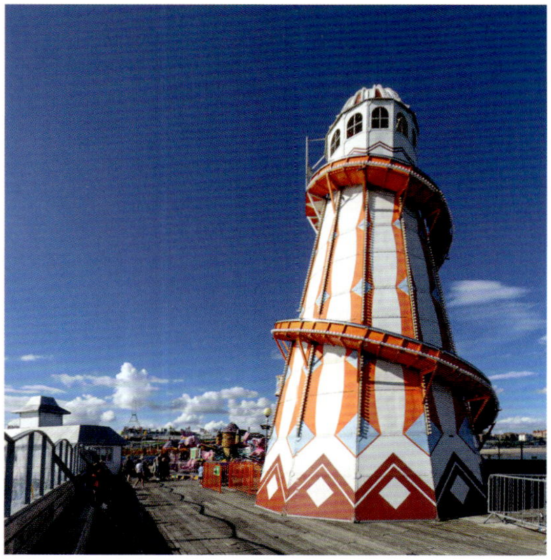

From top left:

Heatwave at the Naze, Walton-on-the-Naze

Teatime, Walton-on-the-Naze

Helter-skelter, Clacton Pier

Opposite, from top left:

Approaching Lee-over-Sands, St Osyth Marsh

Ten-foot-long whelk made of sand and marble mixed with resin by artist Michel de Bono, Point Clear

From bottom left:

Laundry day, St Osyth Creek

Last light at Beach Road, Lee-over-Sands

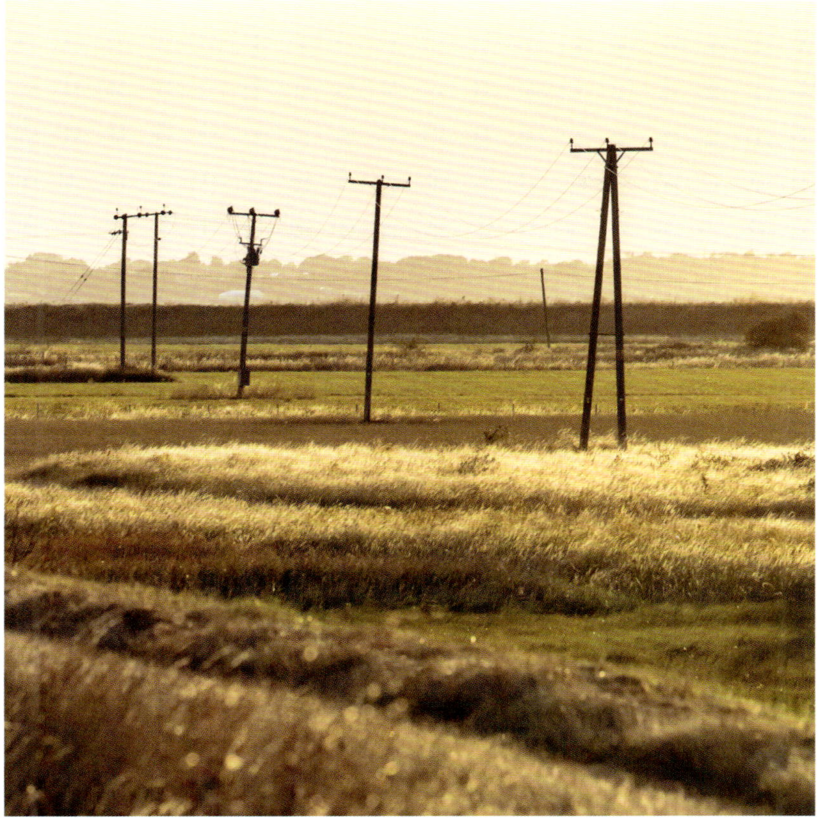

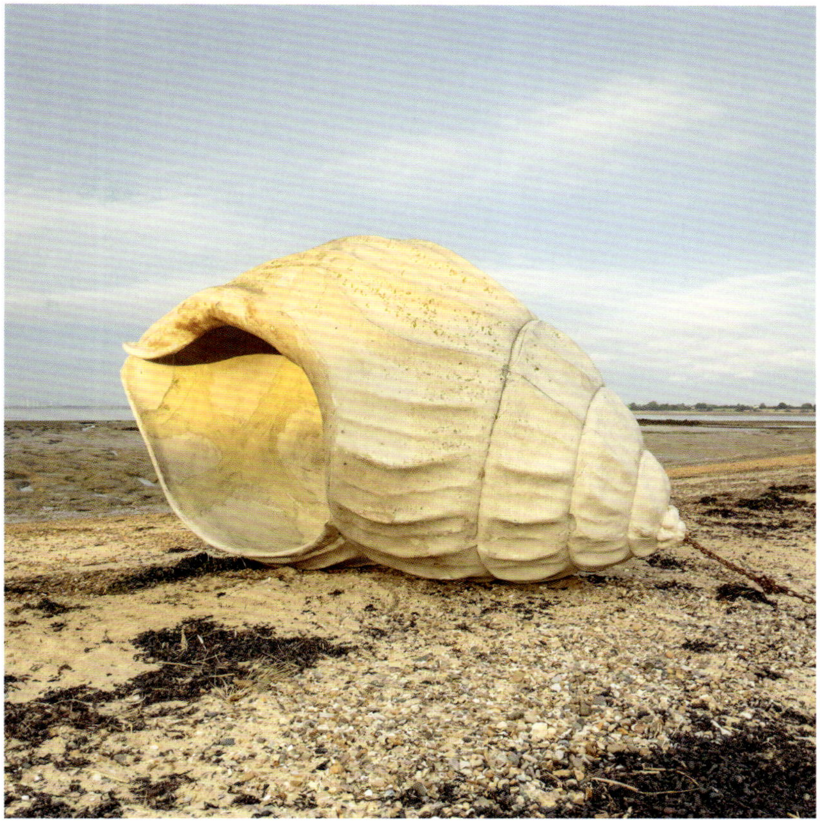

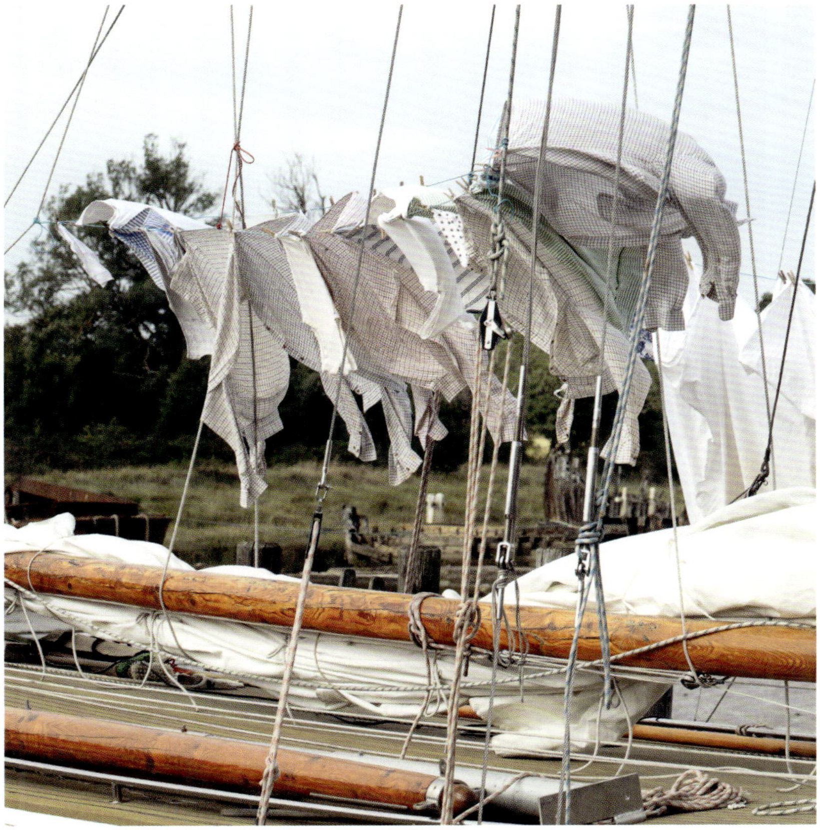

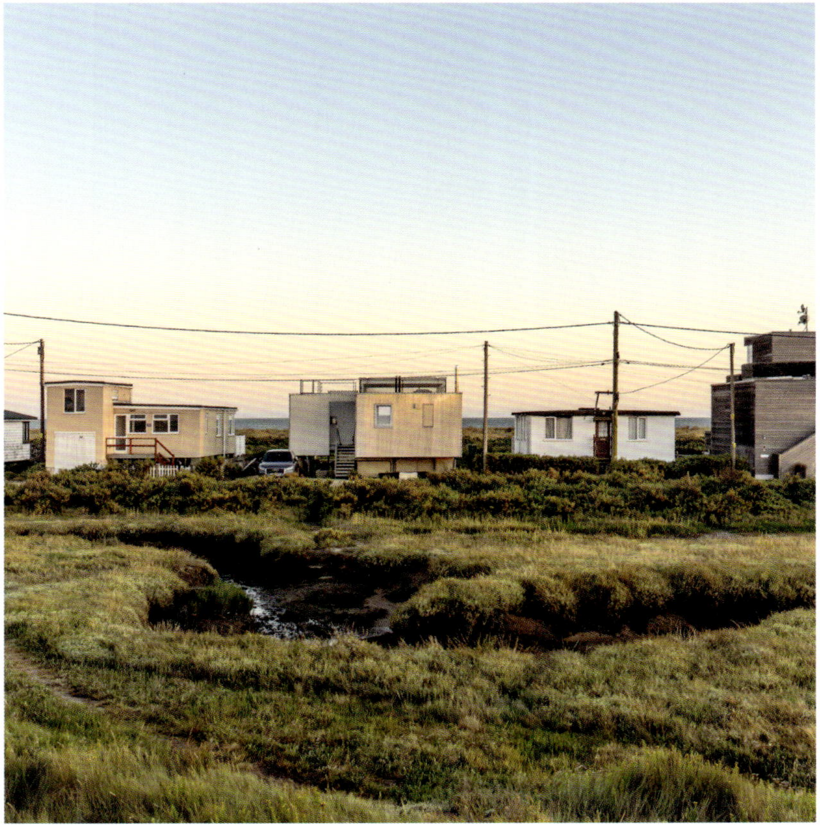

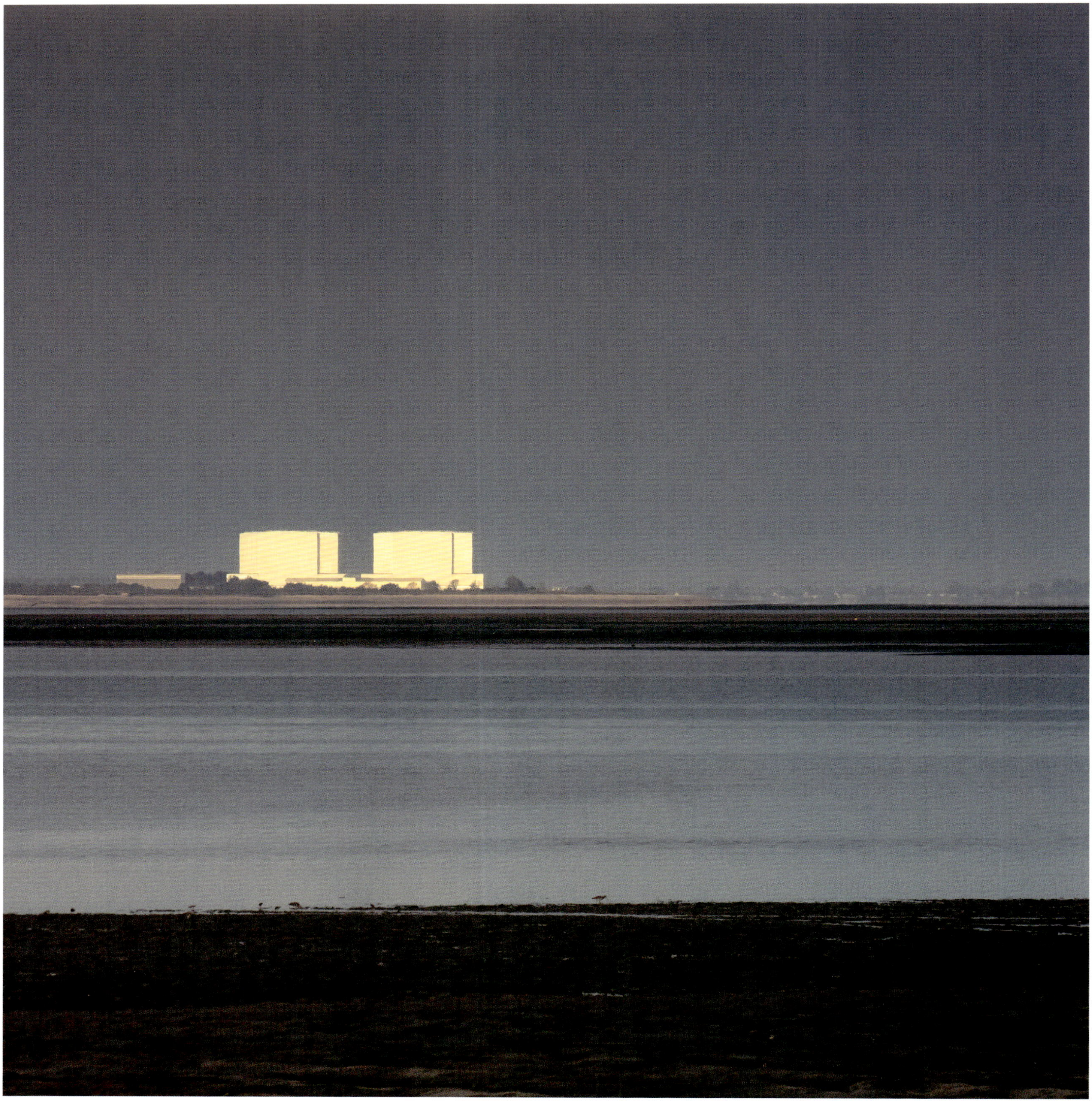

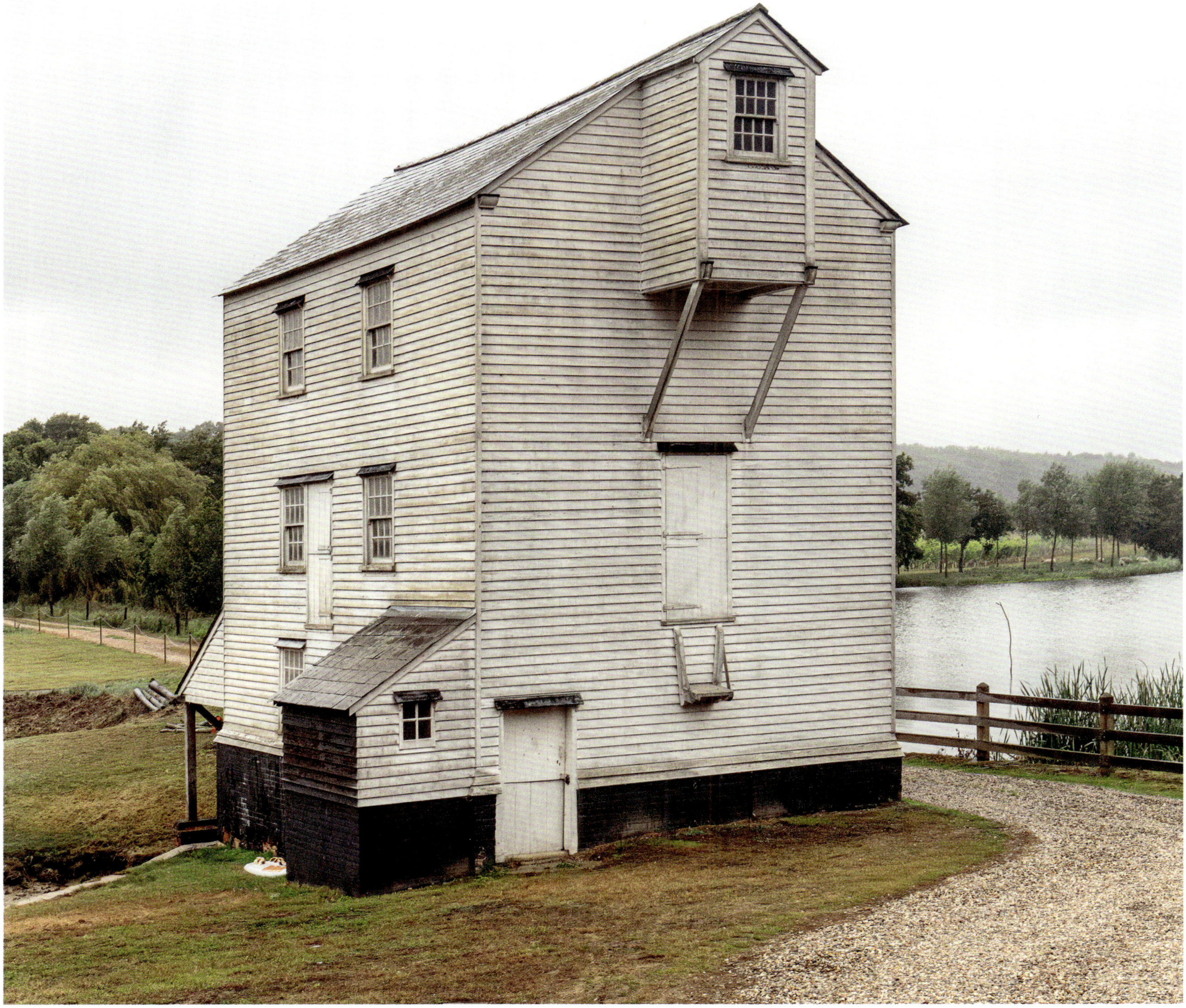

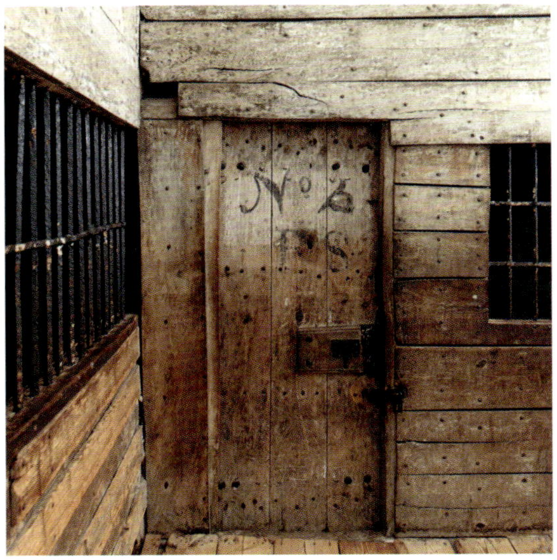

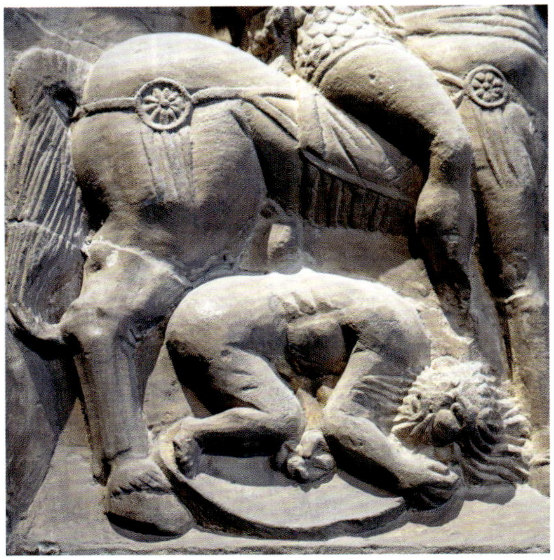

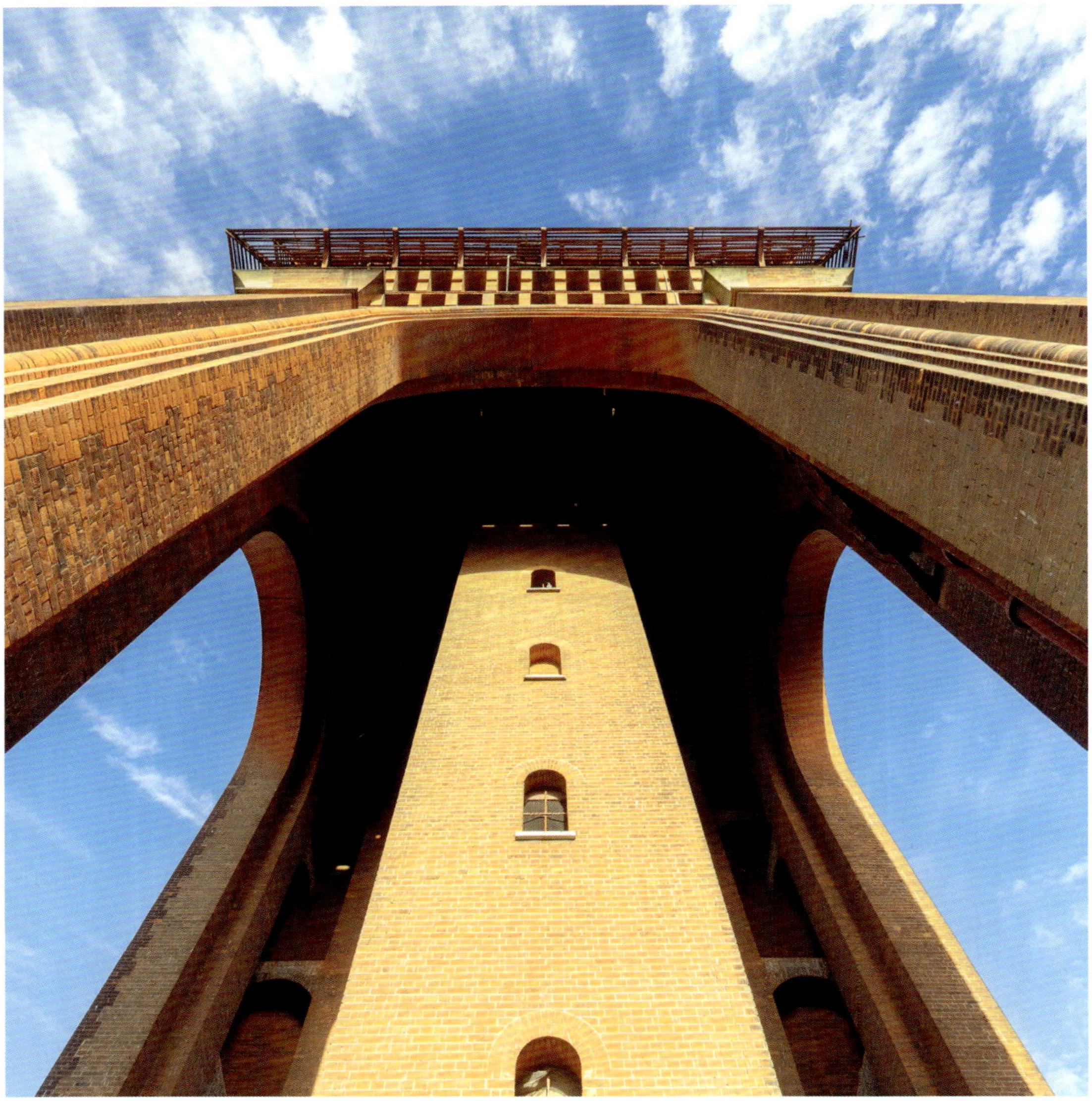

Opposite, clockwise from top left:

Bradwell Power Station

A squall over Dengie sea wall, Ray Sand

Surely the most ominous building in Britain: Dengie Minefield Control Tower controlled mines laid across the mouth of the River Crouch, which was well defended as a potential route of invasion to London in the Second World War

Magwitch trees by Tollesbury Fleet. The trees died as a consequence of flooding during the managed retreat of the sea walls. The opening shot of the 2011 BBC *Great Expectations* series was filmed here, showing escaped convict Abel Magwitch emerging from the marsh

The ambiguous edge of Essex: Dengie Flat

Modest beginnings: St Peter-on-the-Wall, Bradwell-on-Sea, was founded c.654 and was built over the ruined gate of the abandoned third-century Roman fort of Othona, reusing Roman stones and bricks in its construction. It is literally 'on the wall' of the Roman fort

Previous, from left to right:

Bradwell nuclear power station, decommissioned in 2002, from Point Clear

Thorrington Tide Mill at Alresford Creek. Built in 1831, its white-painted weatherboarding is typical of Essex mill buildings

From top left:

The prison cells under Colchester Castle, dating from 1727, complete with massive oak doors and iron-barred windows

A defeated and hirsute Briton cowering on the tombstone of Roman cavalryman Longinus who took part in the invasion of Britain and died in Colchester in AD 55

Jumbo Water Tower, by the Balkerne Gate in Colchester, is the largest remaining Victorian water tower in Britain. Built in 1882 by engineer Charles Clegg in the Romanesque Revival 'Campanile' style, it is 40 metres tall and contains 1.2 million red bricks

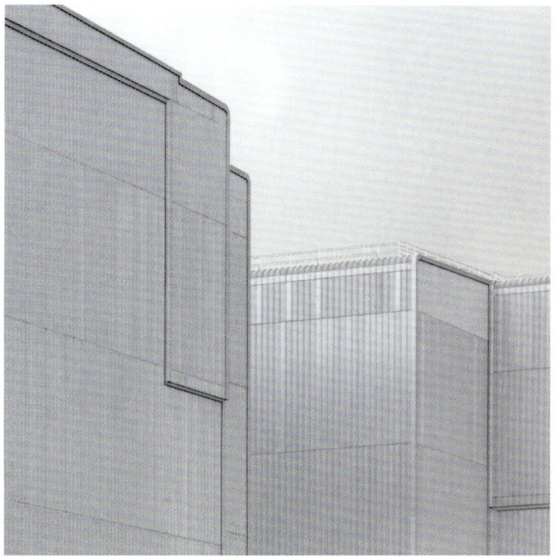
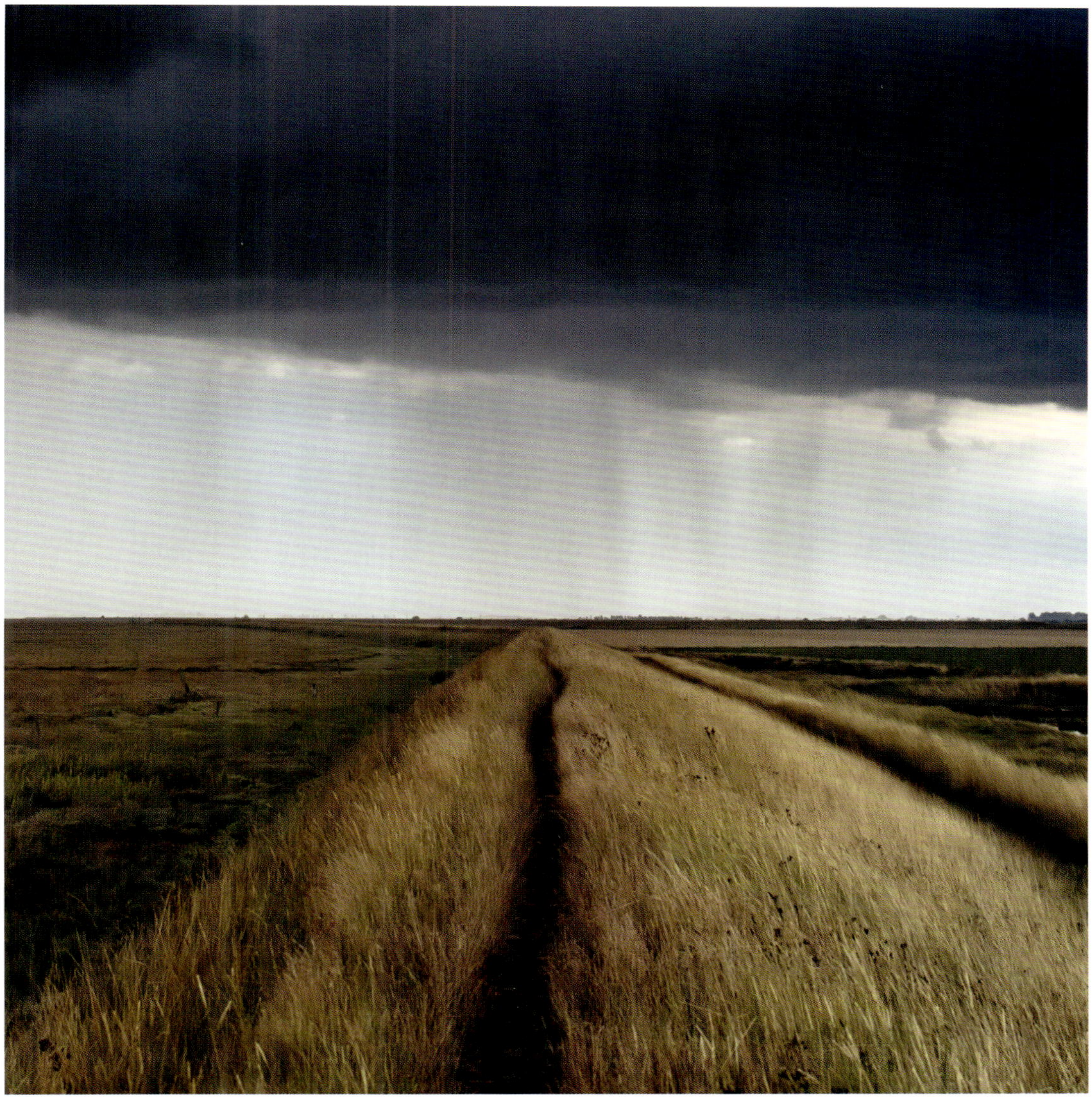
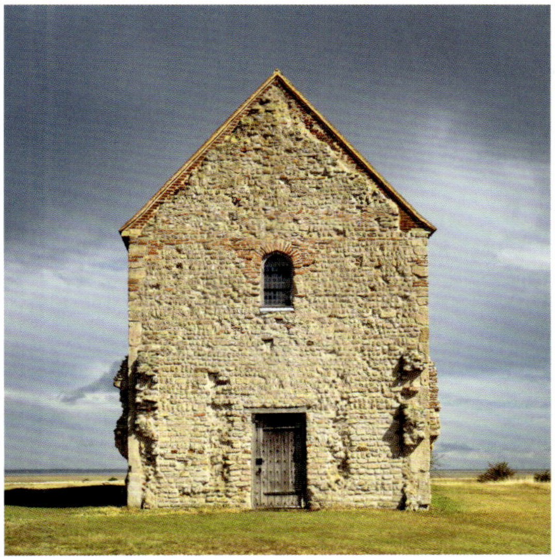
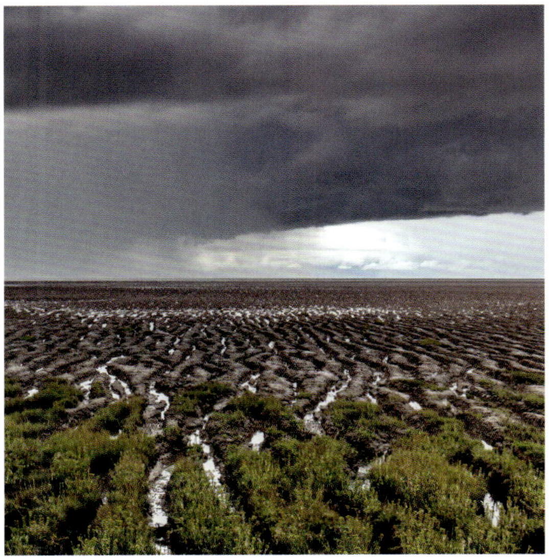
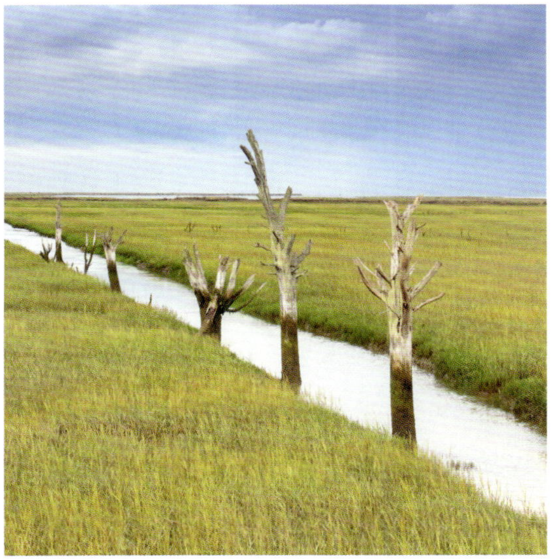
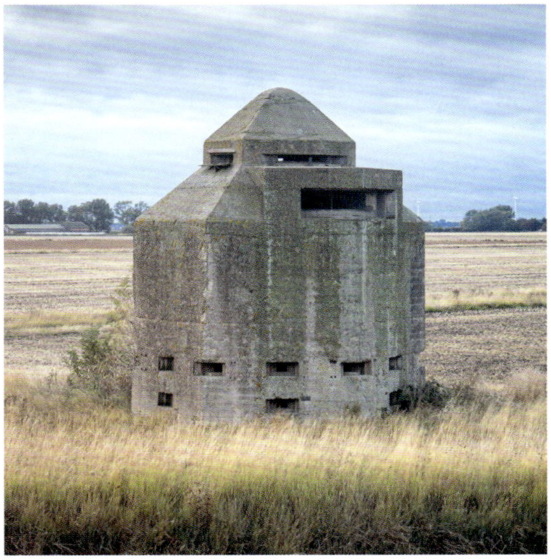

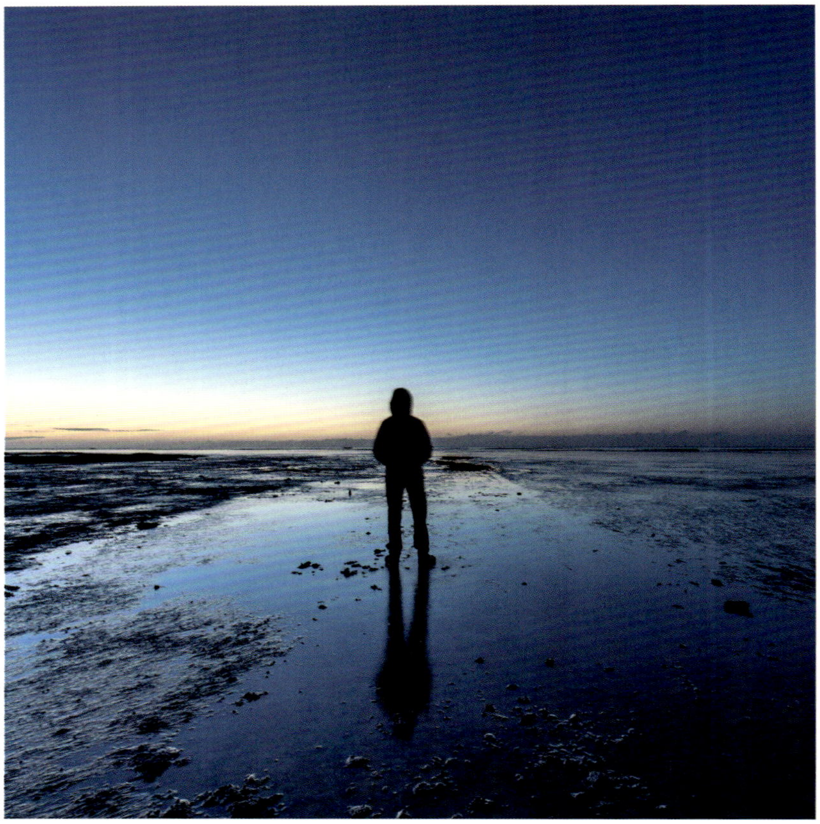

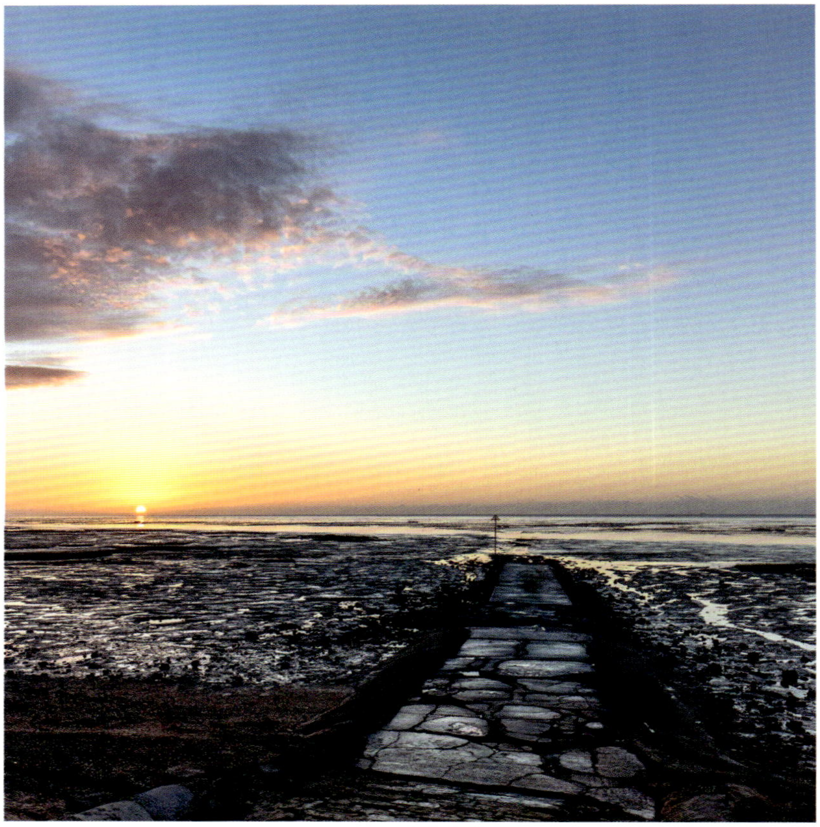

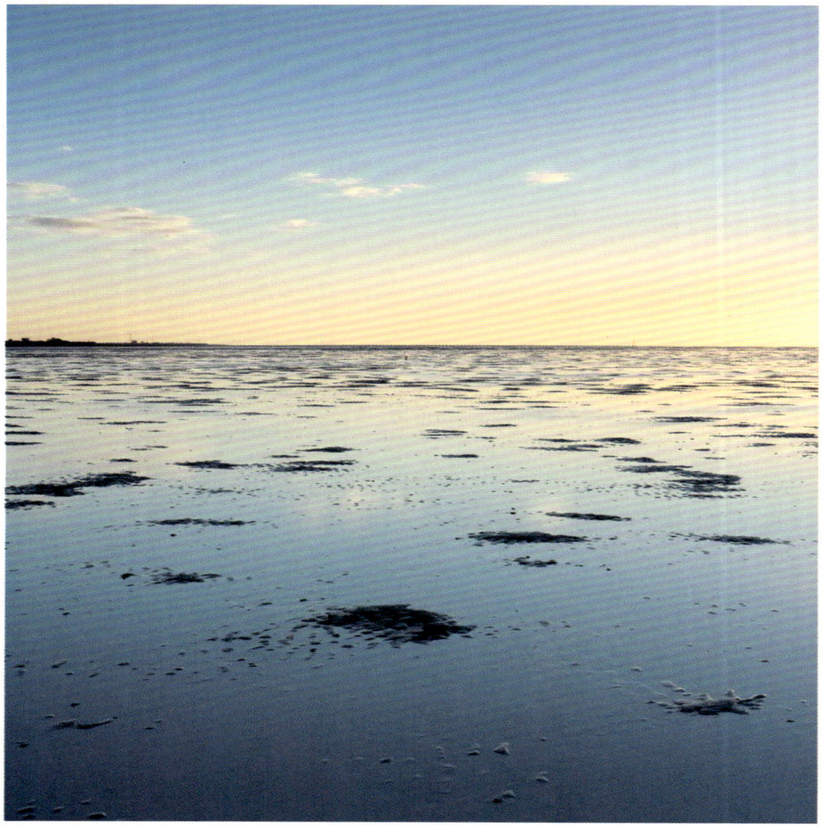

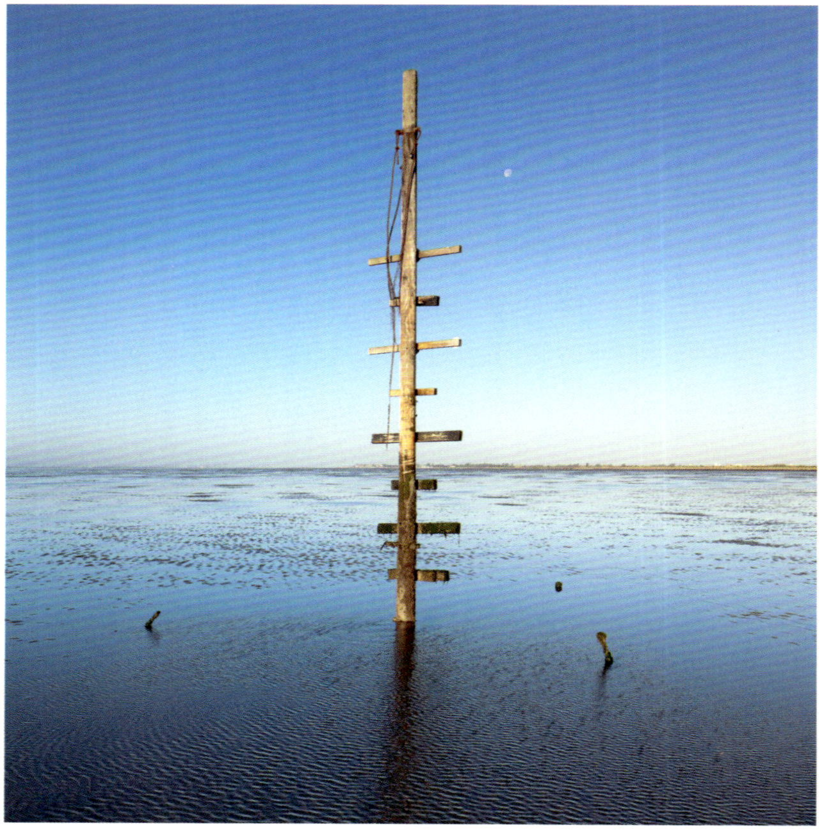

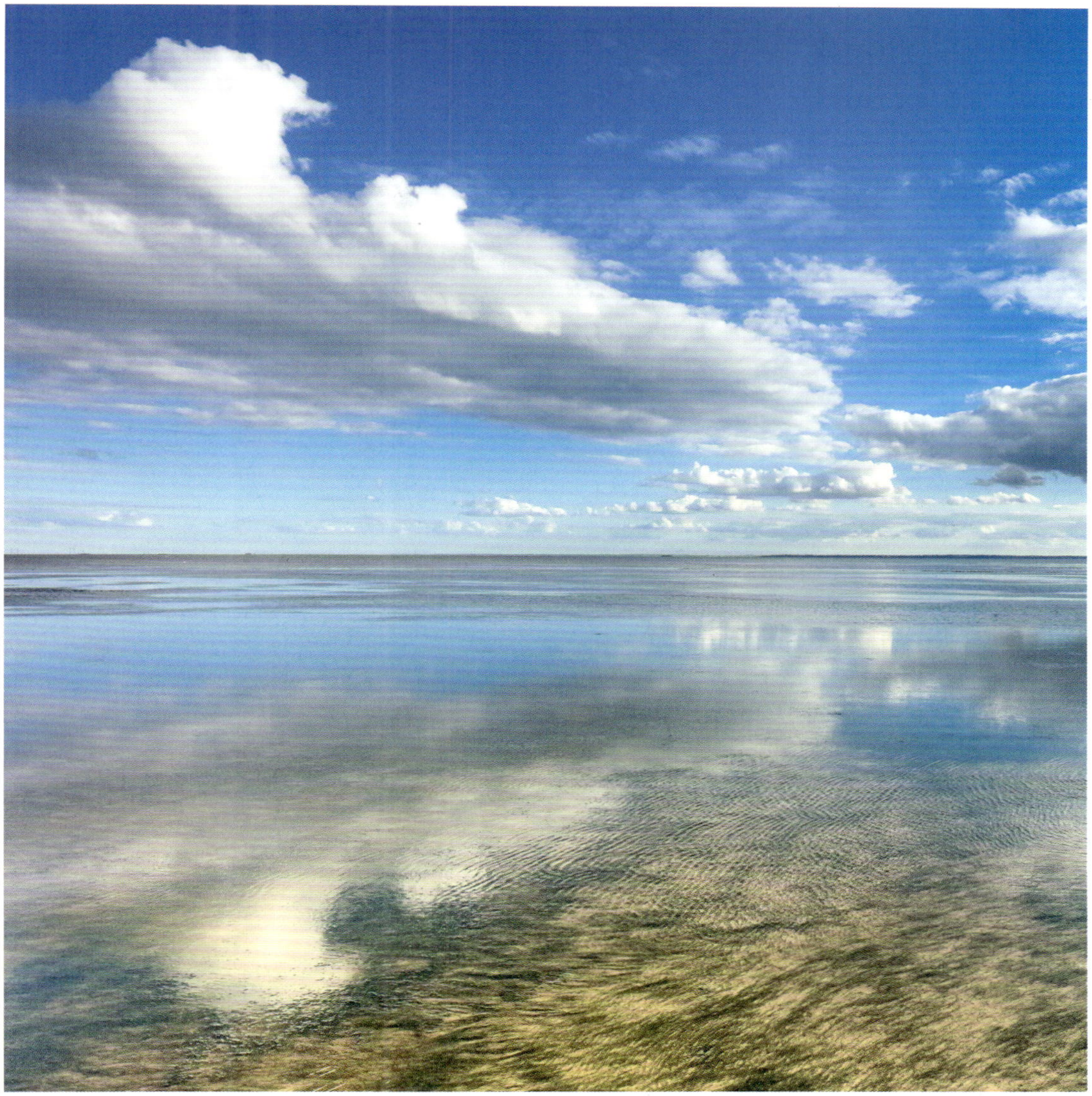

Opposite, from top left:

4.53 a.m.: waiting for the tide to fall a bit more before starting the Broomway at Wakering Stairs. Already hard to tell what is land and what is sea

5.23 a.m.: sunrise over the mouth of the Thames Estuary from Wakering Stairs

From bottom left:

5.51 a.m.: the Broomway

6.16 a.m.: the Maypole, the channel marker at the mouth of Havengore Creek on the Broomway

From top left:

5.39 p.m.: walking back to the mainland alone via the Broomway on a falling tide through the seagrass. Feeling a lot less anxiety having survived the much longer walk across in the morning

1.59 p.m.: the George and Dragon, abandoned in 2007, Churchend, Foulness Island

6.58 p.m.: the first mini island of solid ground near the mainland

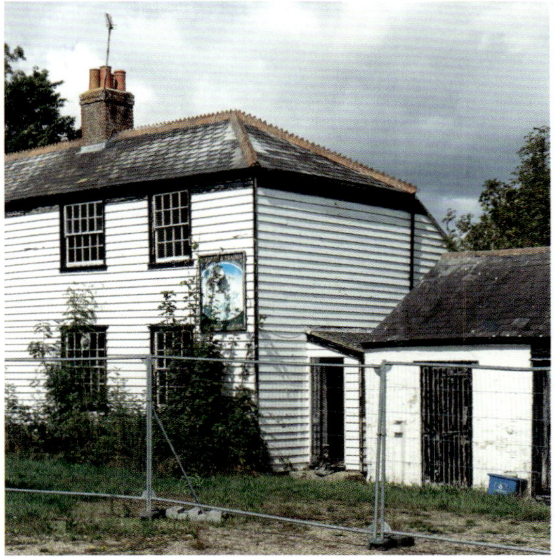

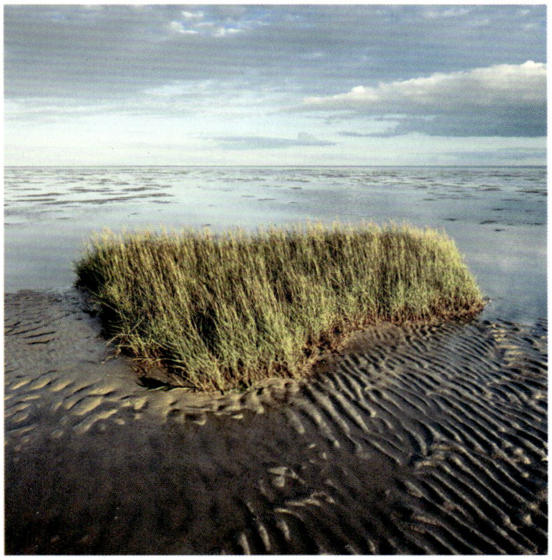

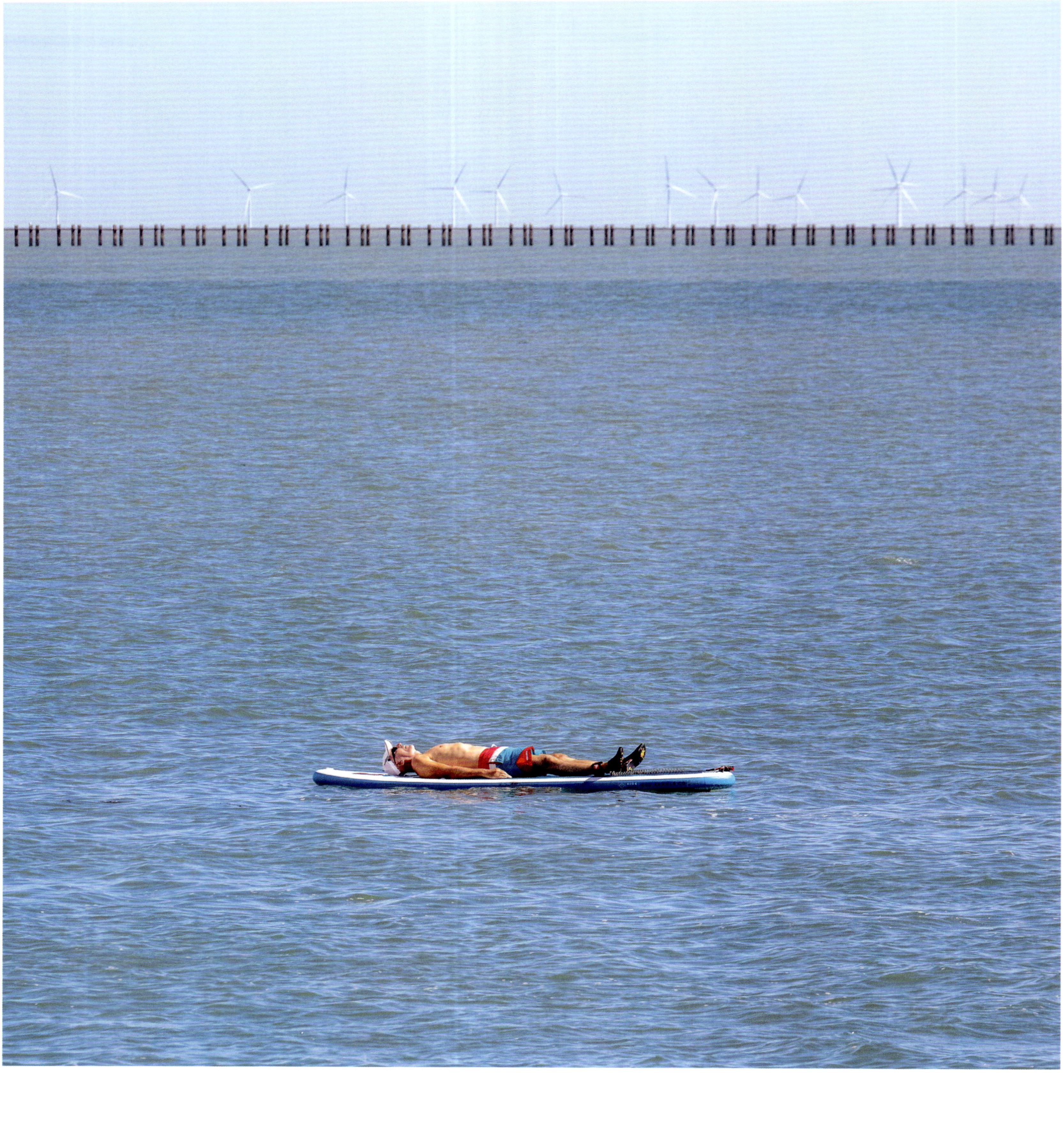

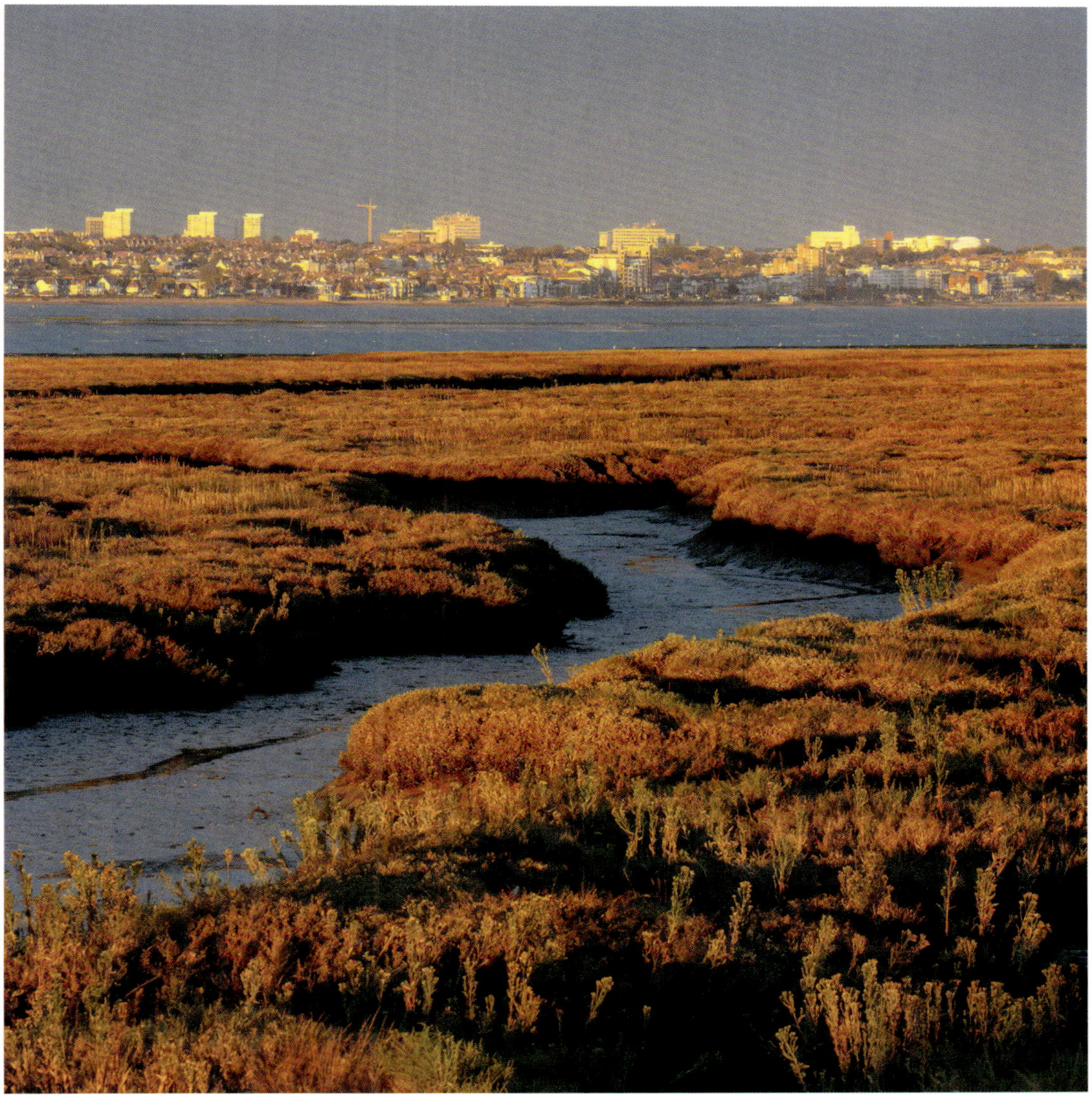

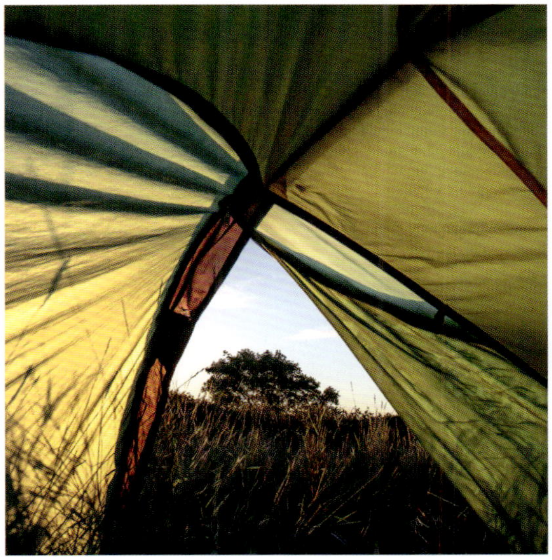

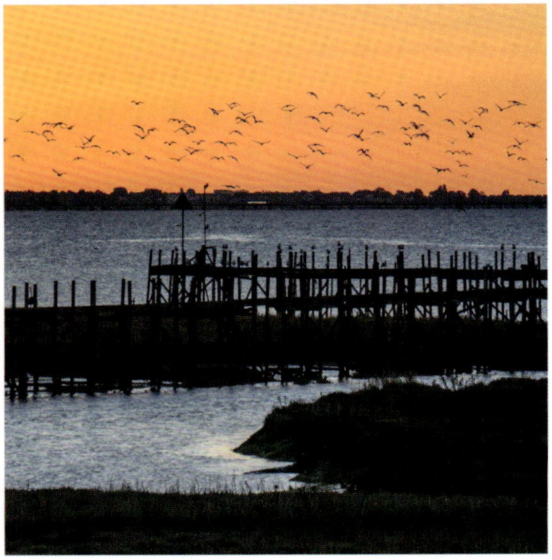

Opposite:

Flat out: floating below Shoeburyness Cold War anti-submarine boom and Kentish Flats Wind Farm

From top left:

Southend from Canvey Island in golden evening light

Canvey Island start

First light at Oyster Creek, Canvey Island

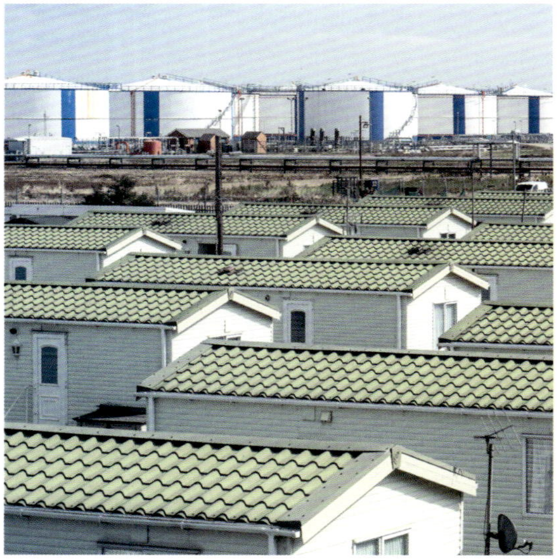

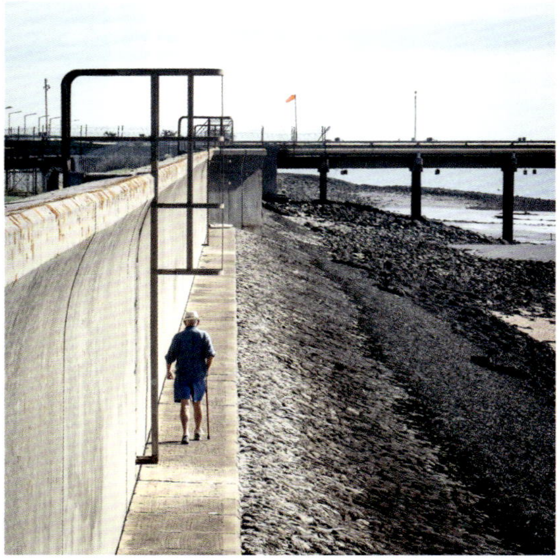

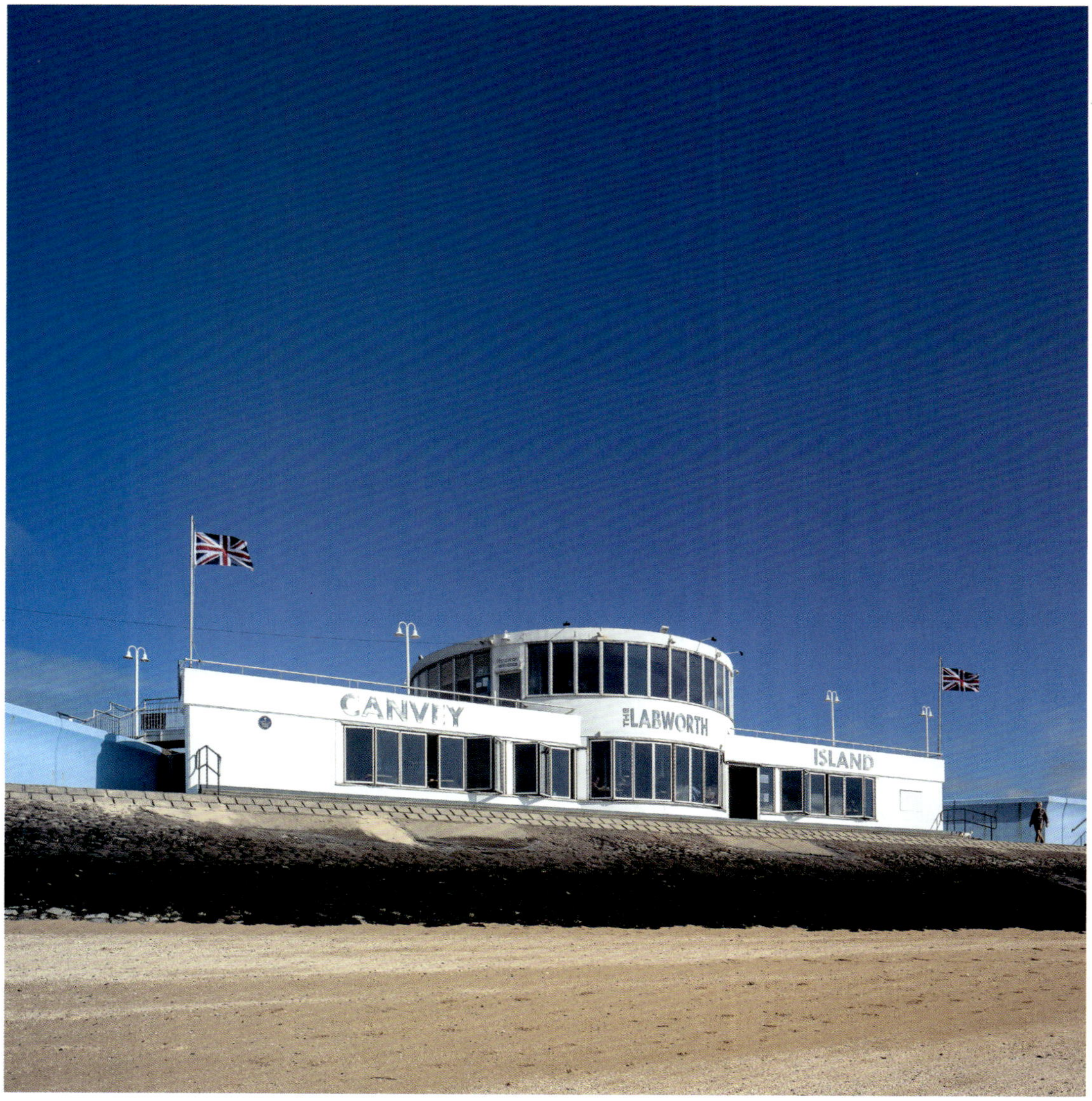

From top left:

Echoes of Oil City: Canvey Island

This older gentleman deftly hooked his stick on the sea-wall ladder before climbing down to walk back and forth along the Canvey Island waterfront

The early-twentieth-century Labworth Cafe, Canvey Island, designed by Ove Arup to resemble the bridge of the *Queen Mary*

Opposite, clockwise from top left:

Camp at Stanford-le-Hope Marshes near London Gateway Port, the last of the journey

Second World War radar tower disguised as a water tower near Coalhouse Fort on the Thames. It was used to detect enemy vessels and to guide Allied shipping through the minefield in the river

The unapologetic mass of Fobbing Horse movable flood barrier

Georgia's Diner, near London Gateway Port

The sole remaining spherical, high-pressure fuel tank on the former Coryton oil refinery site

Their unmissable first album redefines the Fobbing Marshes electro sound

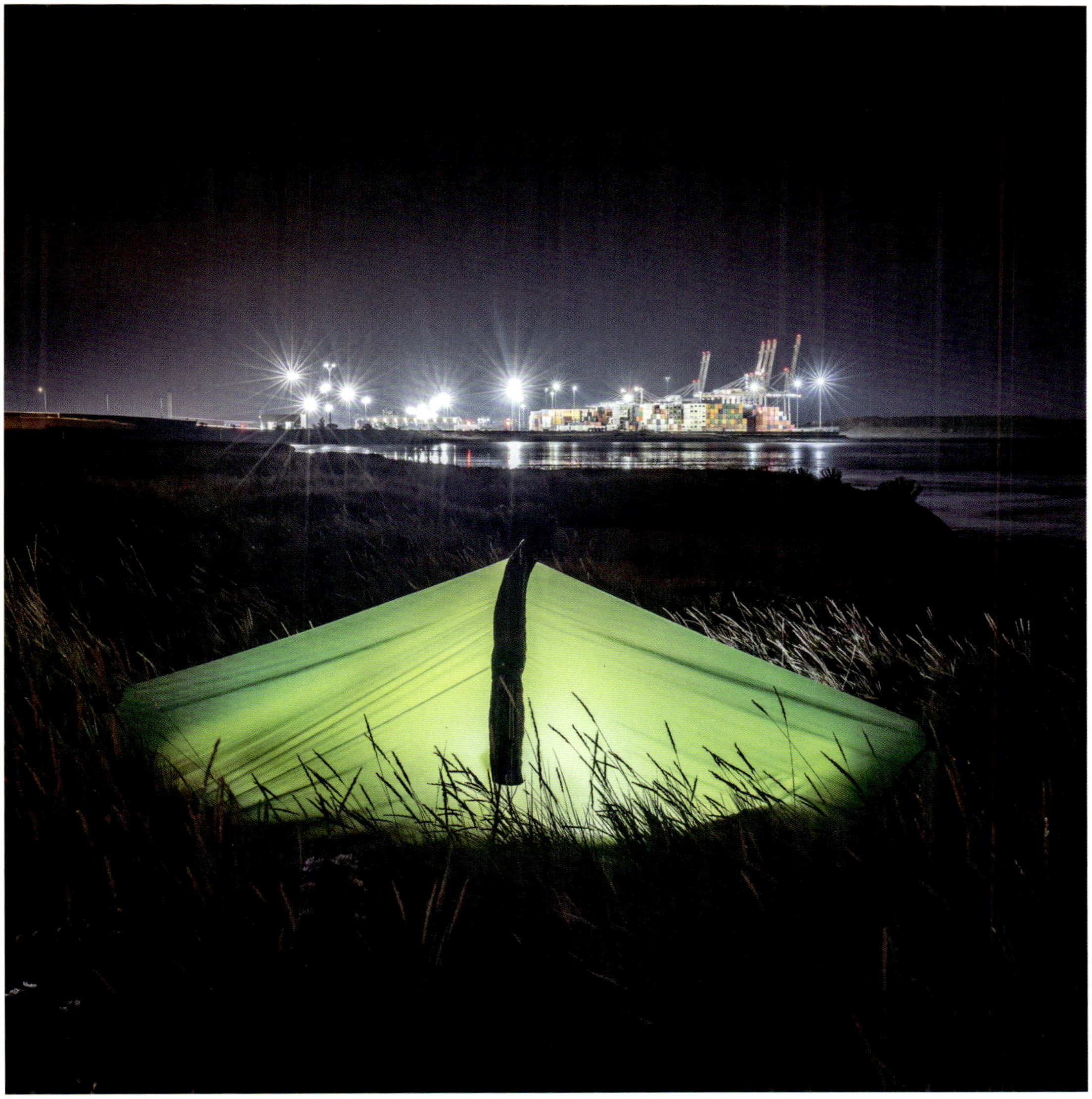

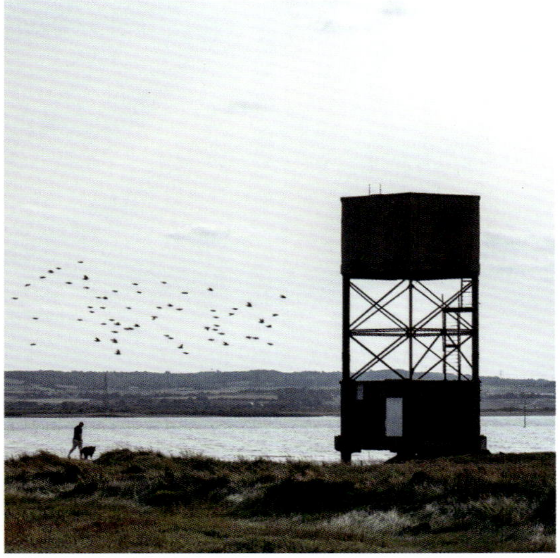

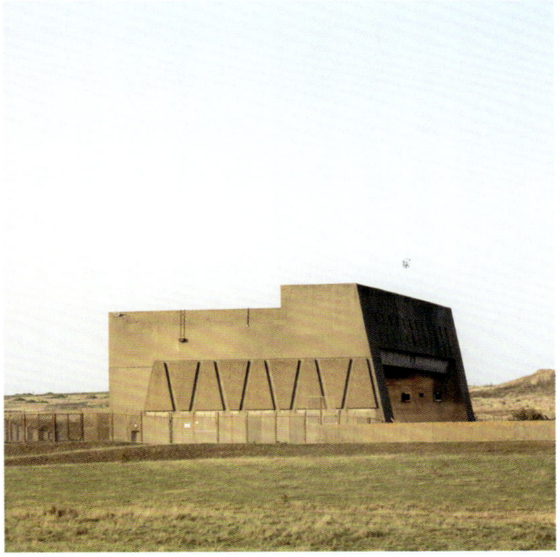

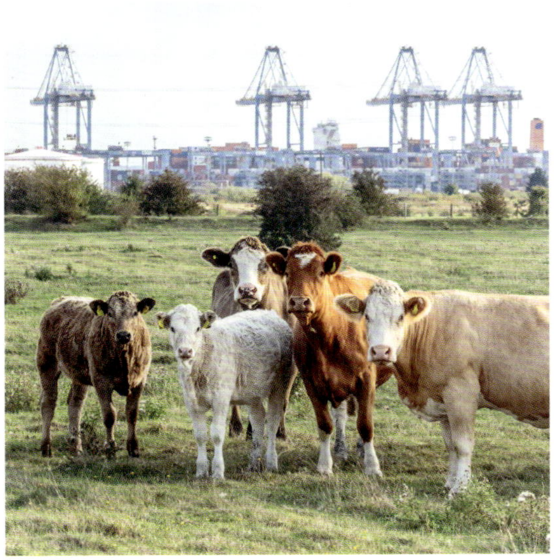

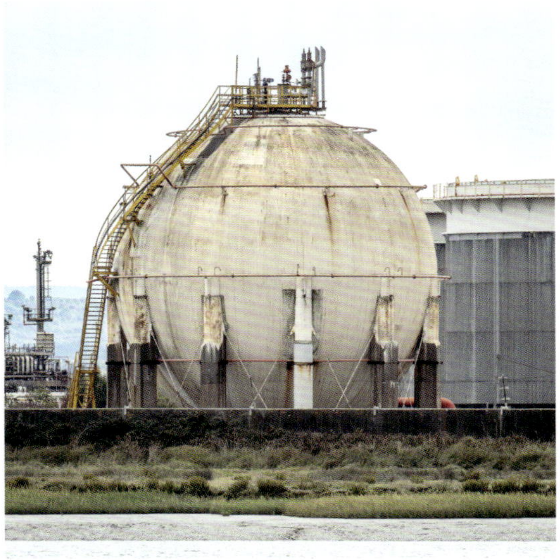

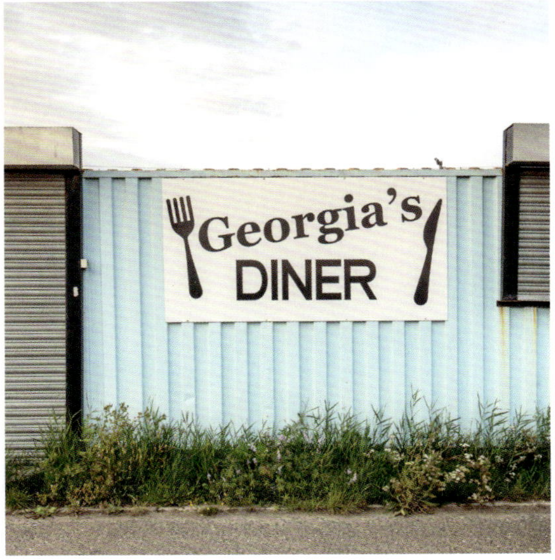
Georgia's
DINER

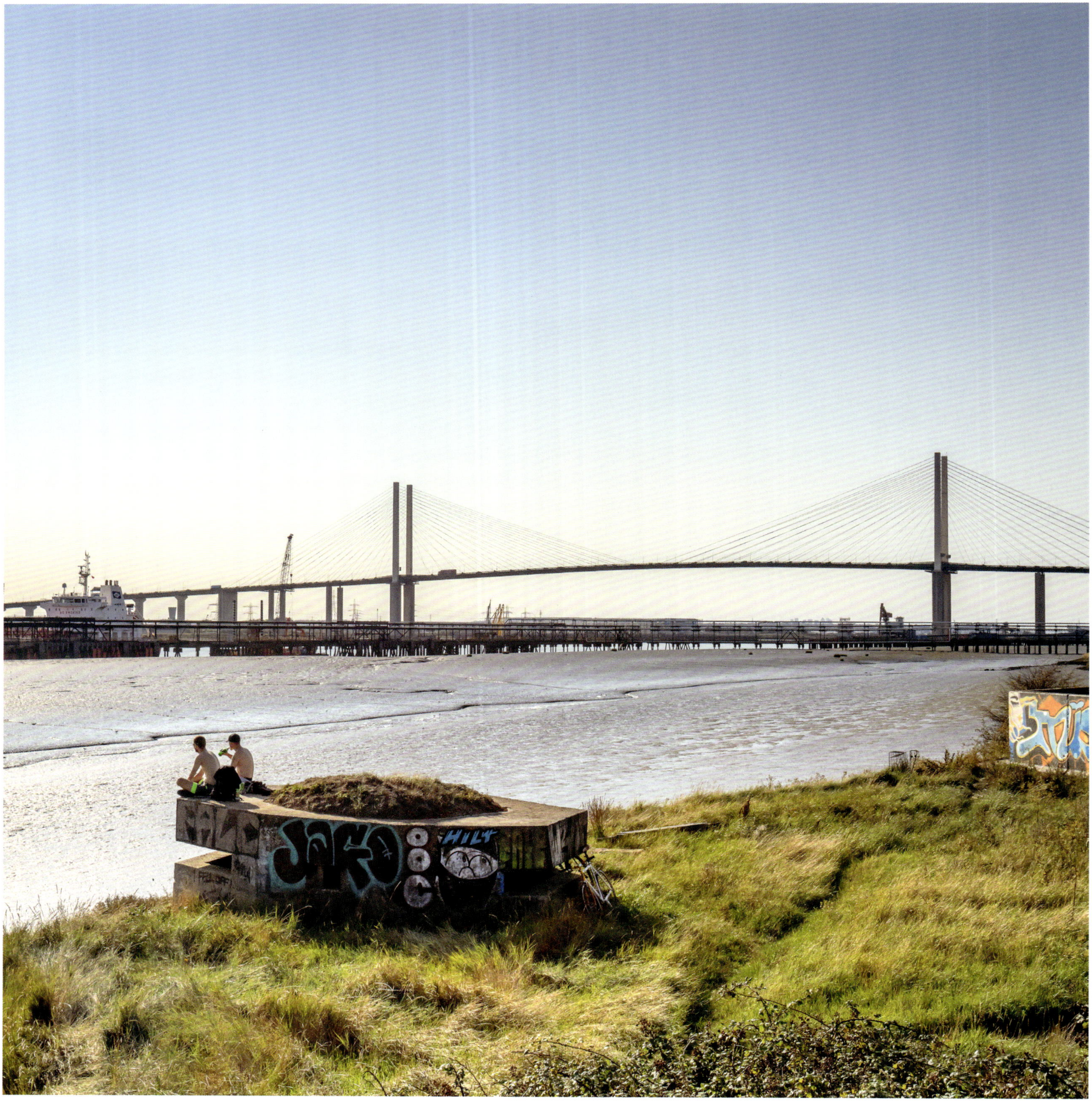

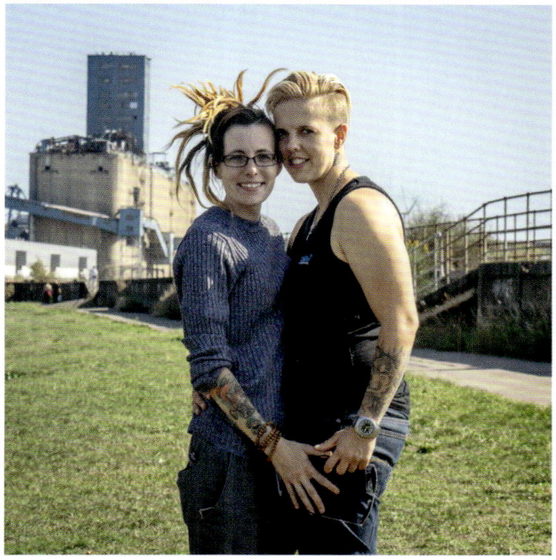

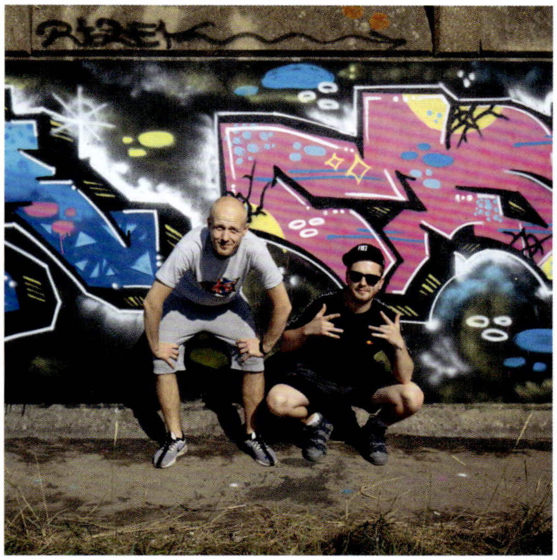

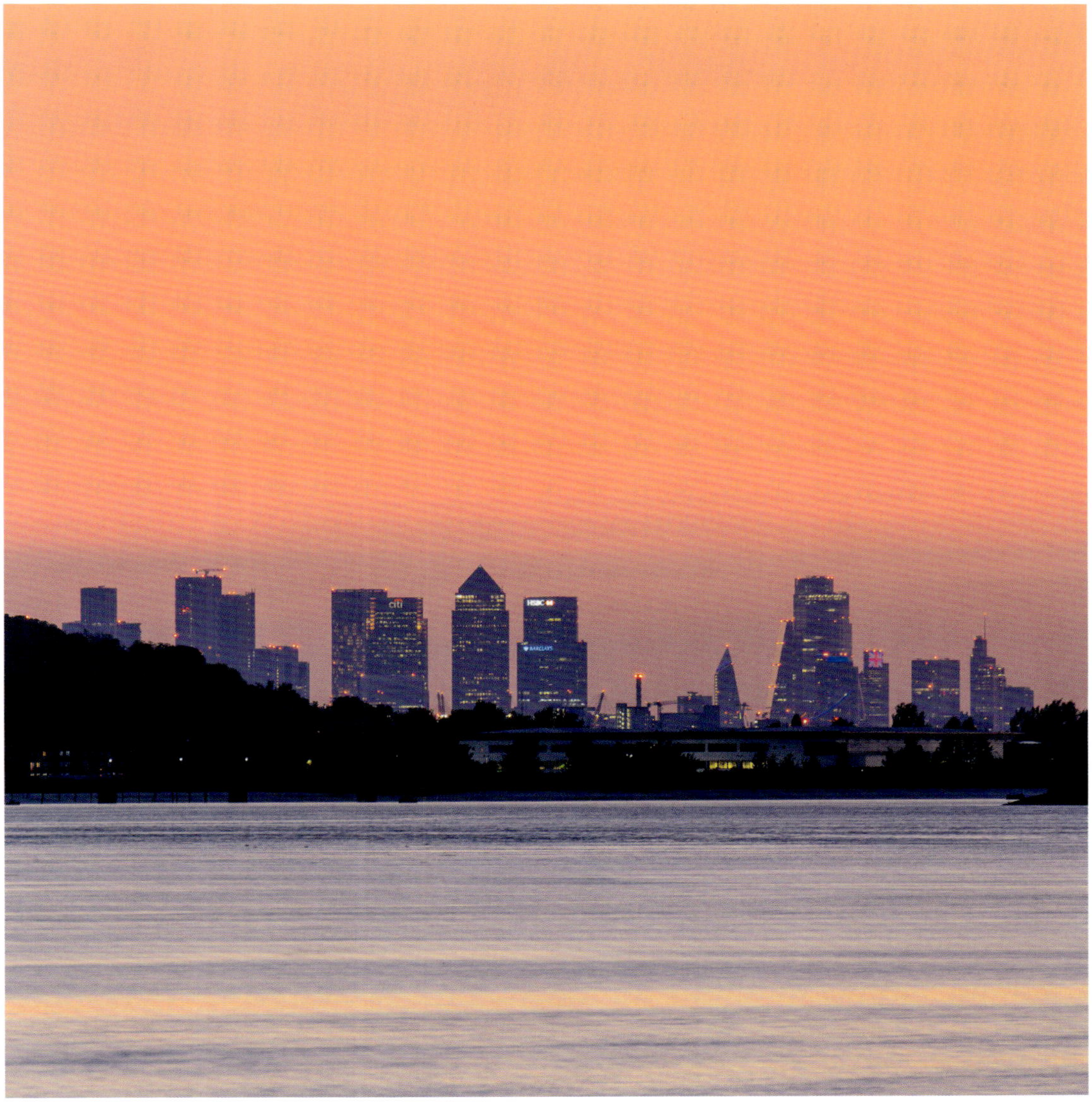

Opposite:

Pillbox beers by the QEII Bridge over the Thames, West Thurrock

From top left:

Rachael and Moni, Grays

Richard and Jakub with their sea-wall street art, Grays

The last image in Essex is a long-lens photo of Canary Wharf with the Thames, taken from Purfleet. London, which is two days away, is the end of the journey

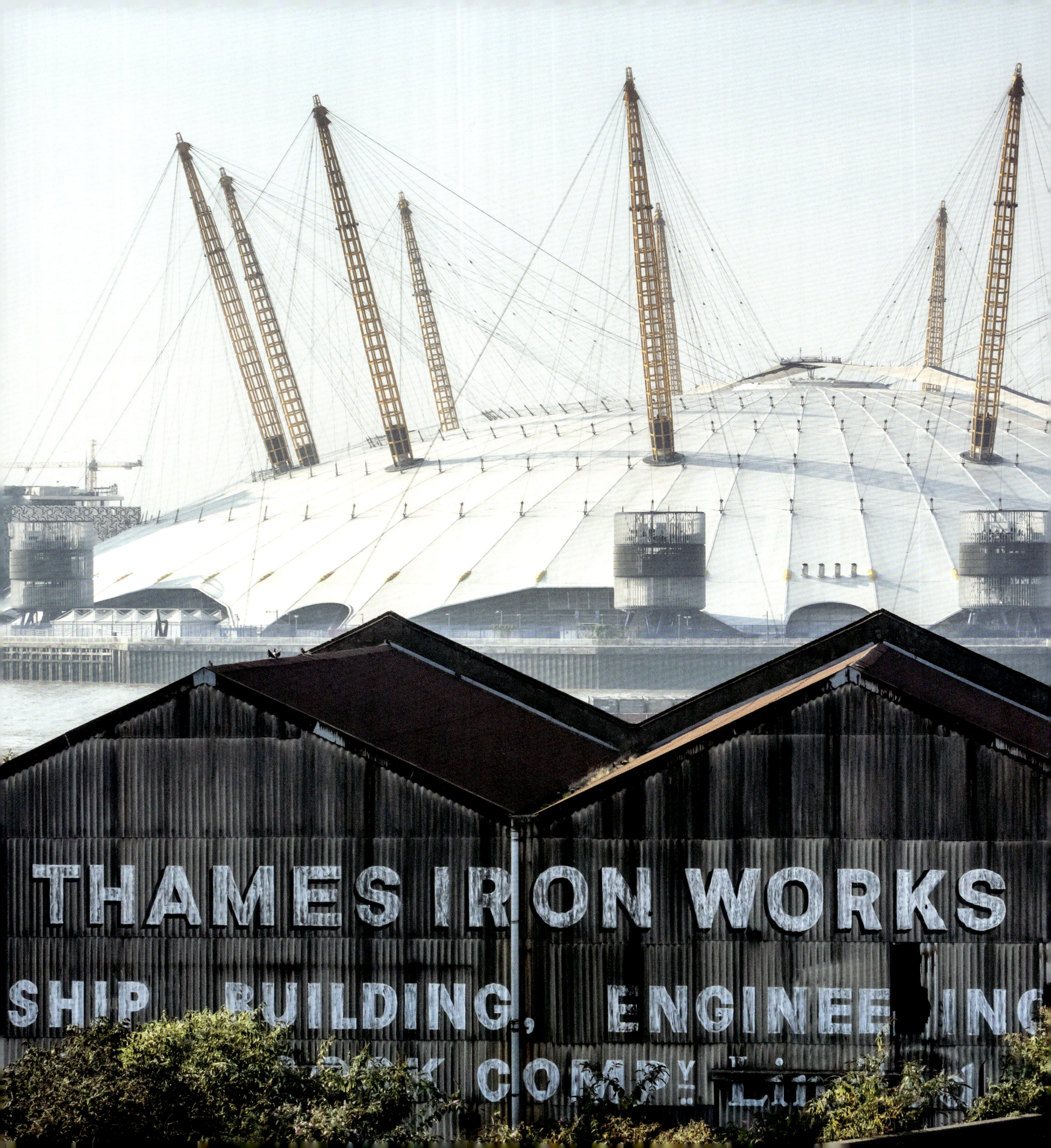
THAMES IRON WORKS
SHIP

53 NORTH LONDON

SEPTEMBER 2020

DAY 453–454 | 10,952–11,000 KM | 48 KM

Report Any Unsafe Acts announces a bold yellow sign marking the unofficial entry into London from Essex, where the Thames footpath winds past a busy landfill. At Rainham Marshes, I jump from deck to deck between a cluster of sixteen semi-submerged concrete barges built during the Second World War when steel was in short supply. I do my best to hug the banks of the Thames as it funnels towards the centre of London but need to detour inland around the melancholy flattened site of the Ford Motor Works at Dagenham, the giant guillotine-like Barking Creek Barrier and the vast Beckton Sewage Treatment Works.

Idling car engines and honking horns are ubiquitous as I walk past sluggish commuter traffic in 27-degree heat. Even here, so close to the capital, it is a third-rate feeling to be on foot, and I'm incredulous to see a *No Pedestrians* sign beside a road in North Woolwich. As night falls, I reach the Thames Flood Barrier, its stainless-steel cowls glistening above the swathes of brown-grey mud exposed at low tide. I extend my tripod for the last time to photograph this unique structure.

On the final morning of my walk, I wake early in a modern corporate hotel by London City Airport, where I announce on social media that I will be finishing at St Paul's Cathedral at 3 p.m. Too nervous to eat, I lace my boots and hoist my battered pack on to my back for the final stretch.

I'm soon reunited with the Thames, sharing the path with runners and dog walkers around the apartment-lined Isle of Dogs. Familiar landmarks like the O2 Arena and Greenwich Naval College pass by in the blink of an eye – I'd last walked past them five years ago on the other side of the river. As the skyscrapers of Canary Wharf come into view, nostalgia turns into excitement at the prospect of being reunited with my family. I wonder if any friends will show up, what with the tightening restrictions on public gatherings and another lockdown looking imminent.

It's a fleeting thought as my attention is soon taken up by the messages and calls I'm inundated with from journalists and producers who are keen to cover the last moments of my journey. Having spent the past five years tweeting and blogging photo updates daily to a tight-knit and engaged community, I'm no stranger to sharing my experiences, but it's nerve-wracking suddenly to receive so much interest. I do my best to field the calls and prepare myself for photos at the finish line. A media-ready wardrobe is one thing I'm not carrying, so I make do by rubbing the worst of the mud off my trousers and ensuring my single sun-bleached T-shirt is on the right way round.

It's not long before I see the familiar shape of Tower Bridge in the distance. As I get closer, I can't help but beam at the sight of twenty familiar figures, all wearing a *Perimeter* T-shirt with my face printed on it. No more anonymity, then! A film crew for the BBC *One Show* joins our merry band, interviewing me as we walk past the Tower of London.

All too soon, we are below the Millennium Bridge at Paul's Walk, and after ascending a few steps, I can see the first view of the end, the dome of the cathedral. It's a clear, sunny day, and as the clock strikes three, I walk up the steps of St Paul's into the arms of my wife, Mila, and the kids to the sound of applause. The church authorities graciously let me inside to the centre point, where I stand for a few moments below the dome in thanks, holding my family close. After five years and 11,000 kilometres, the circle is now complete.

Opposite:

Oxygen and iron: the Thames Ironworks and Shipbuilding Company, 1837–1912, was one of the early adopters of iron rather than wood. The company made the world's first all-iron warship, HMS *Warrior*, launched in 1860. However, this is faux placemaking signage, recently painted ghost signs adding industrial grittiness to the pricey apartment blocks now rising in this area. The real Thames Ironworks was on the other side of the River Lea

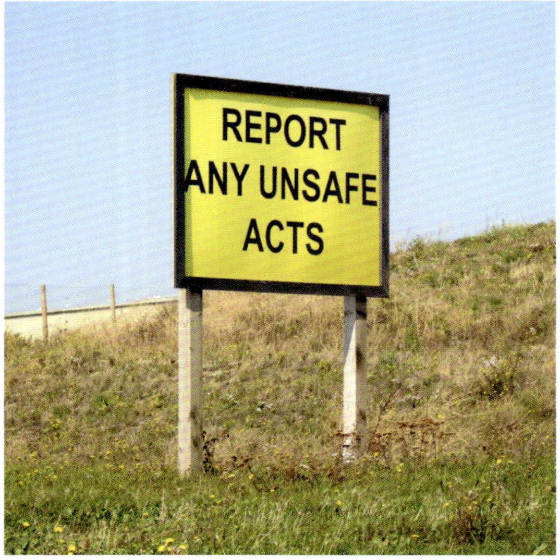
REPORT
ANY UNSAFE
ACTS

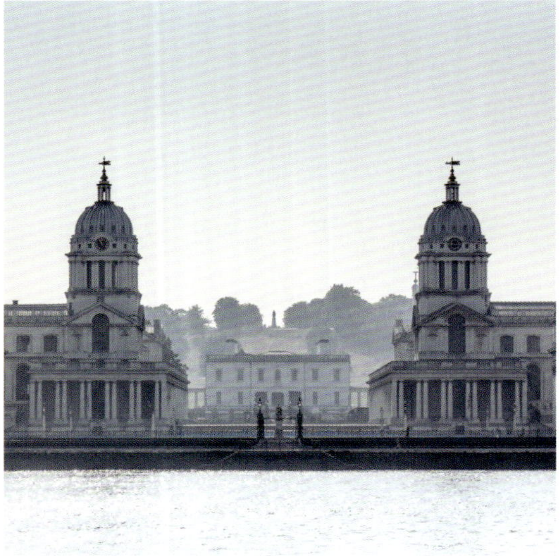

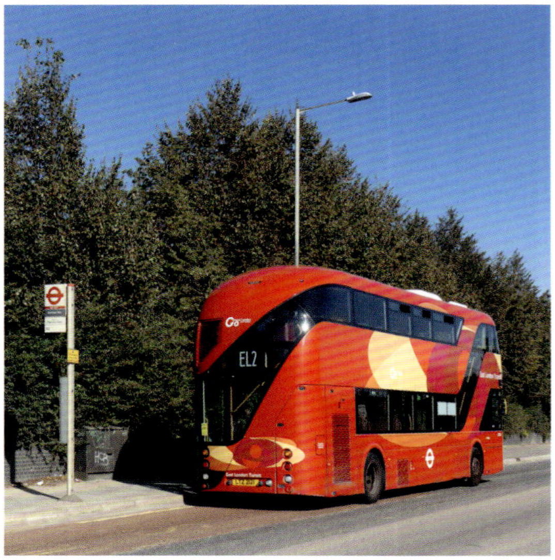
EL2

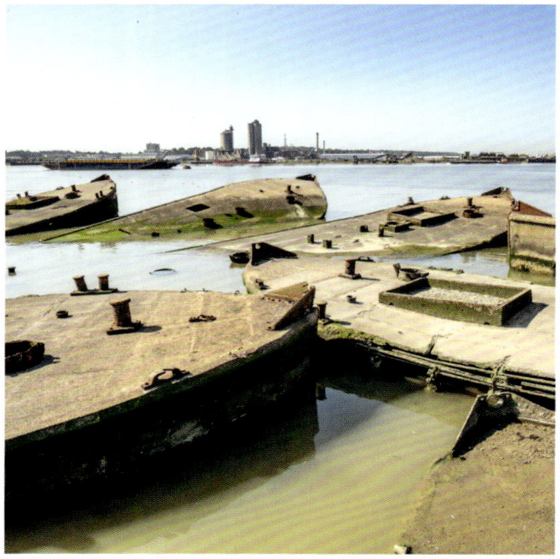

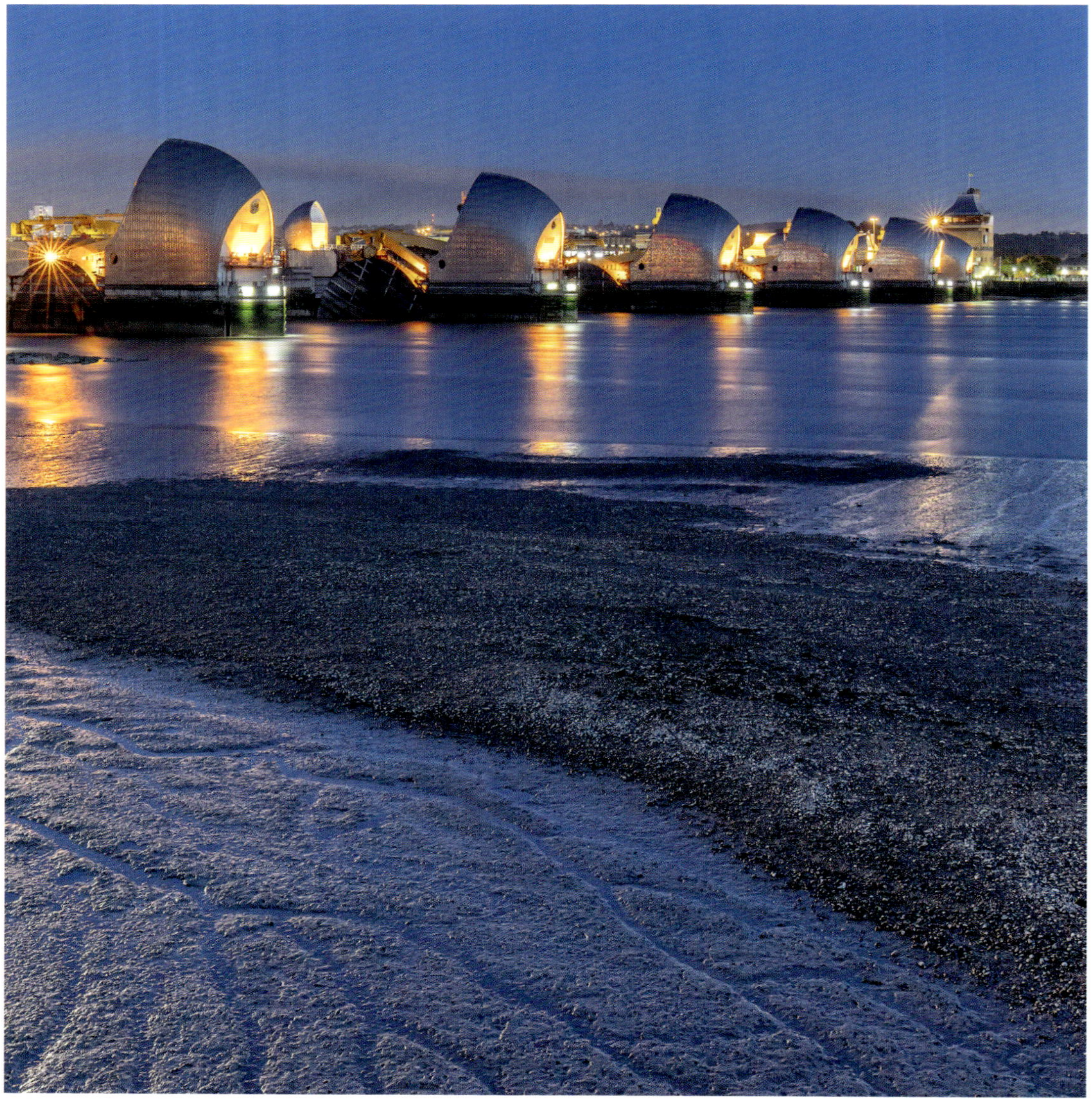

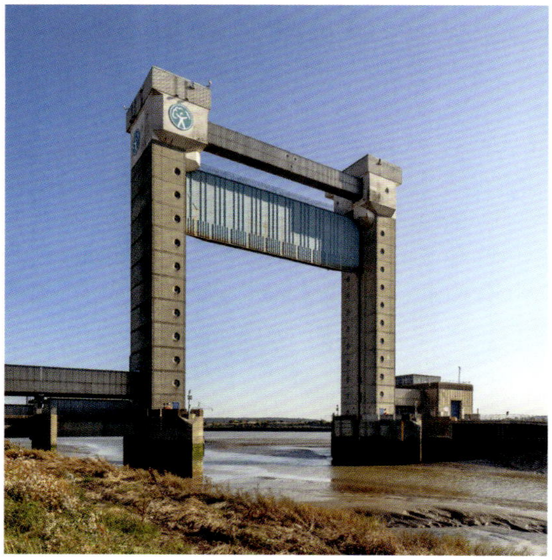

Opposite, clockwise from top left:

The first official notice to greet the pedestrian on walking from Essex into London via Rainham Marshes! Disappointingly, the sign is directed at truck drivers in Rainham Landfill Site

The Old Royal Naval College, Greenwich, designed by Christopher Wren and built between 1696 and 1712. In the centre sits the Palladian Queen's House by Inigo Jones, constructed from 1616 to 1635

It must be London: Dagenham

Low tide at the Thames Barrier. Built to protect the floodplain of most of Greater London, the barrier has been raised 221 times since it opened in 1984

Barking Creek Barrier is normally closed before, and opened after, the Thames Barrier, like all the subsidiary gates. The 40-metre towers allow boats to pass at high tide while the smaller barriers beside the whopper maintain the river flow during normal tides

Rainham Marsh Concrete Barges are ferro cement barges (FCBs), a 1941 design from Wates. Not a part of the Mulberry harbours, according to Second World War historian Stephen Fisher, but they conceivably went to Normandy as bulk fuel supply

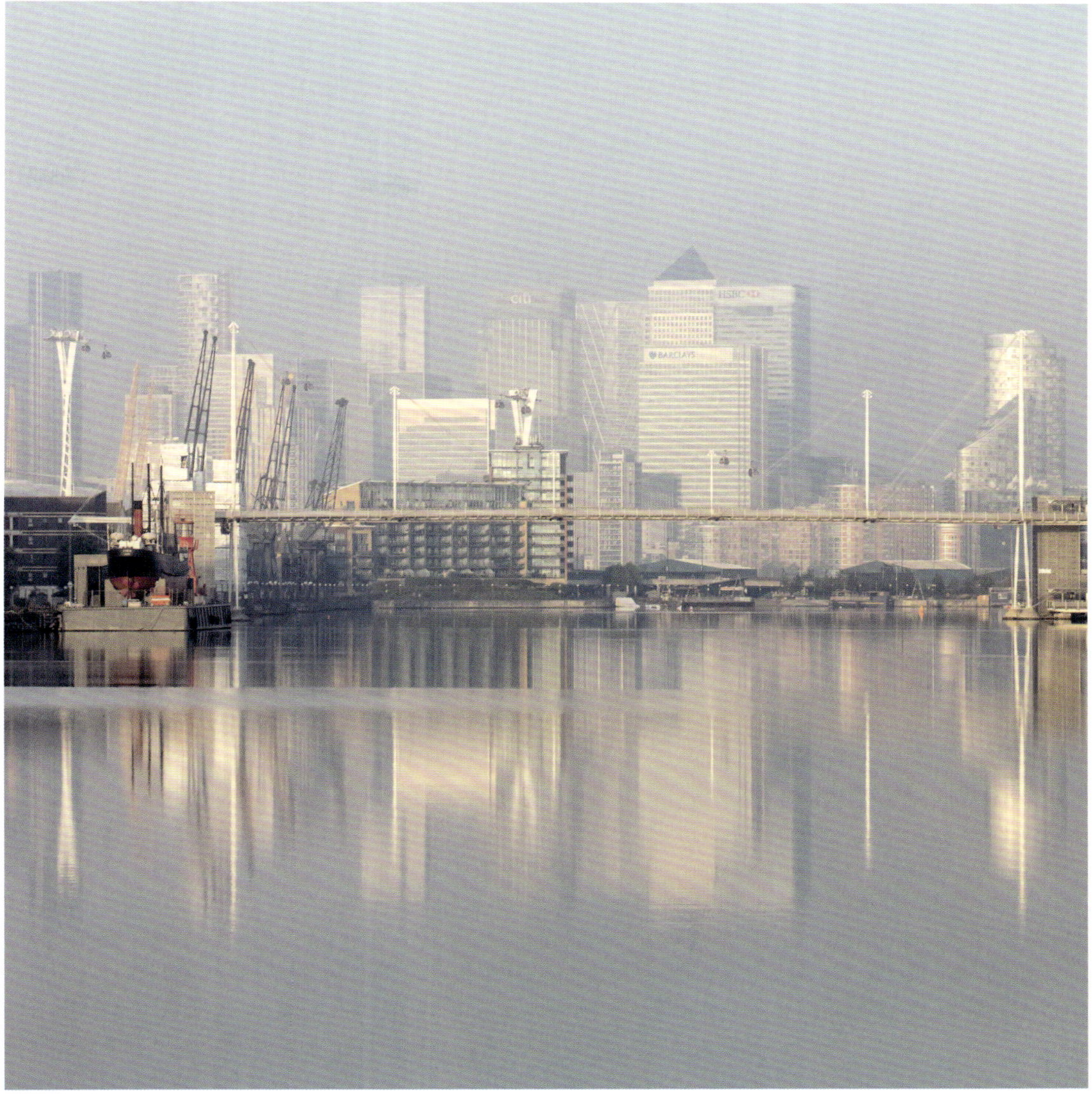

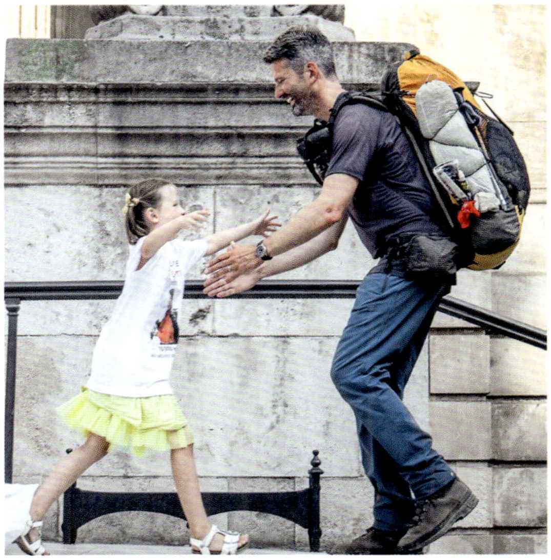

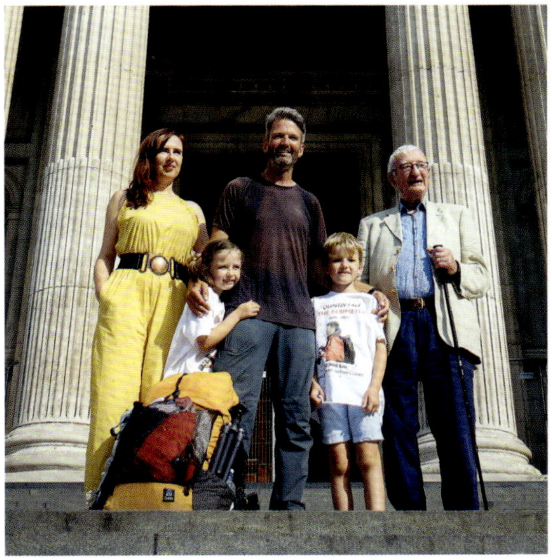

From top left:

Morning light at Canary Wharf from Royal Victoria Dock

The last steps: as the bell tolls 3 p.m., I'm reunited with my daughter, Viola, at the main entrance to St Paul's Cathedral

The circle is complete: with my family on the steps of St Paul's Cathedral

CONCLUSION

'In every outthrust headland, in every curving beach, in every grain of sand there is the story of the earth.'

– RACHEL CARSON

As a photographer, my greatest source of inspiration is the world around me. When I'm surrounded by nature, the reality of life often bursts through in unexpected ways. Walking alone outdoors, in particular, primes my senses to notice when subject, light and composition align to form something beautiful. One of my favourite photos in this book is of the cottage of Skiary by Loch Hourn. I'd seen isolated coastal houses before, but dwarfed as it was below the steep snowy mountains and shrouded in mist, it caught my eye and captured my imagination afresh. As I moved around the headland in a burst of activity, experimenting with various angles and framing, I knew from the tingle in my spine that I had taken a special photo.

Embarking on this journey, my goal was to document the diverse beauty of the British coastline and to share these moments of creative revelation. From the rugged cliffs of Sutherland to the expansive sands of Norfolk, each stretch of coast revealed its unique character and narrative. But this project was not without its trials. There were times when the physical demands seemed overwhelming, when the weather turned treacherous, or when solitude felt particularly acute. I spent hundreds of days walking the pathless coast of north-west Scotland, where the broken ground, a profusion of small cliffs, bogs and dense undergrowth frequently made progress impossible or dangerous. The most important lesson I learnt from this journey was to persist in my efforts and take one step at a time.

Through my photographs and stories, I hope to inspire a greater appreciation of and commitment to preserving the natural world. The landscapes I encountered are not just scenic vistas but vibrant ecosystems facing significant threats from climate change and human impact. Global warming has precipitated flooding that disproportionately impacts low-lying areas of the country and will speed up erosion in the soft coastlines of East Yorkshire. In the seemingly pristine Kyles of Bute, the strandline contained hidden pockets thick with layers of marine plastic pollution. Some progress has been made on both fronts – the numerous wind farms I saw along the coast were a heartening sign that action is being taken to reduce our carbon footprint. And beach clean-up teams around the country have been instrumental in keeping our shores free from the worst visible plastic. Still, more needs to be done to preserve our oceans and our coastline.

And more needs to be done to make the outdoors accessible. Having spent half of this hike in Scotland where the right to roam afforded me the freedom to explore, it saddens me that in England we have a right of access to only 8 per cent of the land and 3 per cent of the rivers. As the population increases, and evidence of the physical and mental health benefits from being outdoors mounts, it seems unsustainable and inequitable for open spaces, woods and riverbanks to remain private property, as they are in much of England and Wales.

Backpacking adventures continue to be a regular fixture in my life, and since completing *The Perimeter* in 2020, I've finished walking all sixteen National Trails. I'm over halfway through my current project, walking up the 442 mountains of England and Wales and camping on the summits when the weather permits. The road ahead is filled with possibilities, and I am eager to embark on new adventures with the insights and inspirations from this coastal odyssey.

The Perimeter is not just an end but a beginning. I hope this book inspires you to embark on your own adventure along our coast, and if you'd like to get in touch, I'd love to hear from you either on X or Instagram under @quintinlake.

See the entire archive of images from *The Perimeter* and buy prints at theperimeter.uk.

ACKNOWLEDGEMENTS

Creating *The Perimeter* has been a deeply rewarding journey that would not have been possible without the support and encouragement of many remarkable individuals and organisations. I am profoundly grateful to everyone who has contributed to making this book a reality.

First and foremost, thank you to my wife, Mila Fürstová, for the nine years of understanding and encouragement, both emotionally and practically, during my frequent absences that underpinned this project – I am forever grateful. You were the first to see the photographs and your creative insight into editing and resolving image selection dilemmas is steeped throughout the project. Thanks to my kids, Leo and Viola: the banner you made for the finish line is my most treasured possession. I hope that one day, you, too, will choose to visit many of the wonderful places in this book. Thanks to my parents, John and Susan, whose childhood walks and coastal holidays set in motion a way of seeing the world whose value only grows. Thanks to my friends who braved the ambiguous Covid restrictions to cheer me on for the last few steps.

I am immensely grateful to those of you who have purchased my prints. Your financial support made the practicalities of the trek possible. Thank you to Robert Greenfield and Paul Testa, who made unsolicited donations while I walked when things went wrong. Thanks to those of you who made donations on my website.

Thank you to the medical professionals who helped me get back to the trail after injury, particularly physiotherapist Stuart Fossella, who helped me diagnose and rehab after my split tendon and stress response. Thank you to the Broomfield Hospital Ophthalmology team for fast-tracking my blood test and meds for uveitis so I could finish the walk before the second Covid lockdown.

Thank you to Benedict Brain, editor of *Digital Camera* magazine, who asked me to write a monthly illustrated column on the perimeter over four years. The ensuing journal was the foundation of this book. I remain amazed and grateful for all the journalists, particularly those at the BBC, who covered the project during and after the walk; without the publicity, this project would not have reached the eyes of those who made this book possible.

To my Agent, Tom Killingbeck of A. M. Heath, your introductory phone call to me as I walked down Southend Pier near the end of the walk was the best possible outcome I could have wanted. Your encouragement and creative input throughout the process of making the book a reality have been invaluable. Thank you to my publishing director, Helen Conford, for having faith in this project, maintaining the spirit of its inception, and bringing together such an able team. To my editor, Vanessa Phan, who gamely helped me wrangle my streams of consciousness from journals into the potent vignettes we have ended up with. Not to mention sparing the reader from an illustrated anthology of foot complaints it might have been otherwise. Thank you, Clare Skeats, the graphic designer who created a layout of beauty and harmony despite being faced with curating a mountain of potential images for each chapter. It's been a joy to collaborate with you, and the book would not have been possible without you. Thank you to Nicky Barneby, who created the gorgeous maps.

To the countless individuals I met along the coastline, thank you for your warmth, hospitality, and willingness to share your stories. Each of you contributed to the rich tapestry of the expedition, and your kindness will not be forgotten. Special thanks to the local communities that welcomed me and shared the unique experiences of the regions they call home. Particular thanks to those who put me up, giving me a much-needed respite from the tent: Jan and Ingrid Frydenbø-Bruvoll, Mac Mackenney, Victoria Ratcliffe, Emily and John, Mat and Debbie, James and Di Morley, Nic Dafis and Phillipa, Hannah Engelkamp, Rob and Harriet Fraser, Jennie Dennett, Ann and John Lingard, Marianthi Lainas and Alistair, Esther and Warren, Joseph and Ellen, Tom McClean, Jeremy Fenton, Chris Scott and Lucy Ridout, Elisabeth Tonsberg and Angus, Vivien Scotson, Sue Court and Robert Coghill, Monica McMahon, Pat Escott, Donald Escott, Harry Willis Fleming, Simon Philips, Kate Guthrie, James Whitburn, Julian and Cari Hakes, Mark Whitby and Dawn and Andrew.

Thanks to those whose footsteps I follow, particularly to marathon walker John Merrill, whose book *Turn Right at Lands End* I purchased as a teenager, which sowed the seeds to make my own coast walk. Thanks also to my fellow coast walk bloggers, particularly Ruth Livingstone, whose blog proved invaluable.

A huge thank-you to my fellow photographers, long-distance backpackers and adventurers on X / Twitter who provided inspiration, advice and camaraderie along the way. Your shared experiences and wisdom online were incredibly valuable, and our conversations kept my spirits high during challenging times.

Lastly, to the readers of *The Perimeter*, thank you for embarking on this journey with me. Your interest and engagement bring this project full circle, making all the effort worthwhile. I hope this book inspires you to explore, appreciate and protect the wonders that surround us.

ABOUT THE AUTHOR

Quintin Lake is a multi-award-winning photographer specialising in landscape and architecture, with twenty-five years of experience. A fellow of the Royal Geographical Society and Royal Society of Arts, his work has been featured in leading publications such as *National Geographic Traveler*, the *Guardian* and *Der Spiegel*. Trained as an architect at London's Architectural Association, where he held a scholarship, his photography is deeply influenced by his interest in geometry and the built environment. Quintin has captured images from over seventy countries, including in Arctic Greenland and the Peruvian Amazon. In 2020, he was named The Great Outdoors' Outdoor Personality of the Year. He lives in Cheltenham with his family.

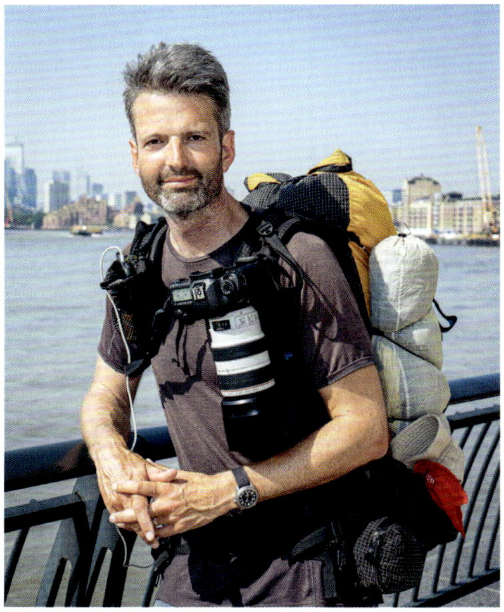

Endpapers:

A selection of camping spots made during 'The Perimeter' between March 2016 to September 2020, from Trevose Head in Cornwall to Stanford-le-Hope Marshes in Essex

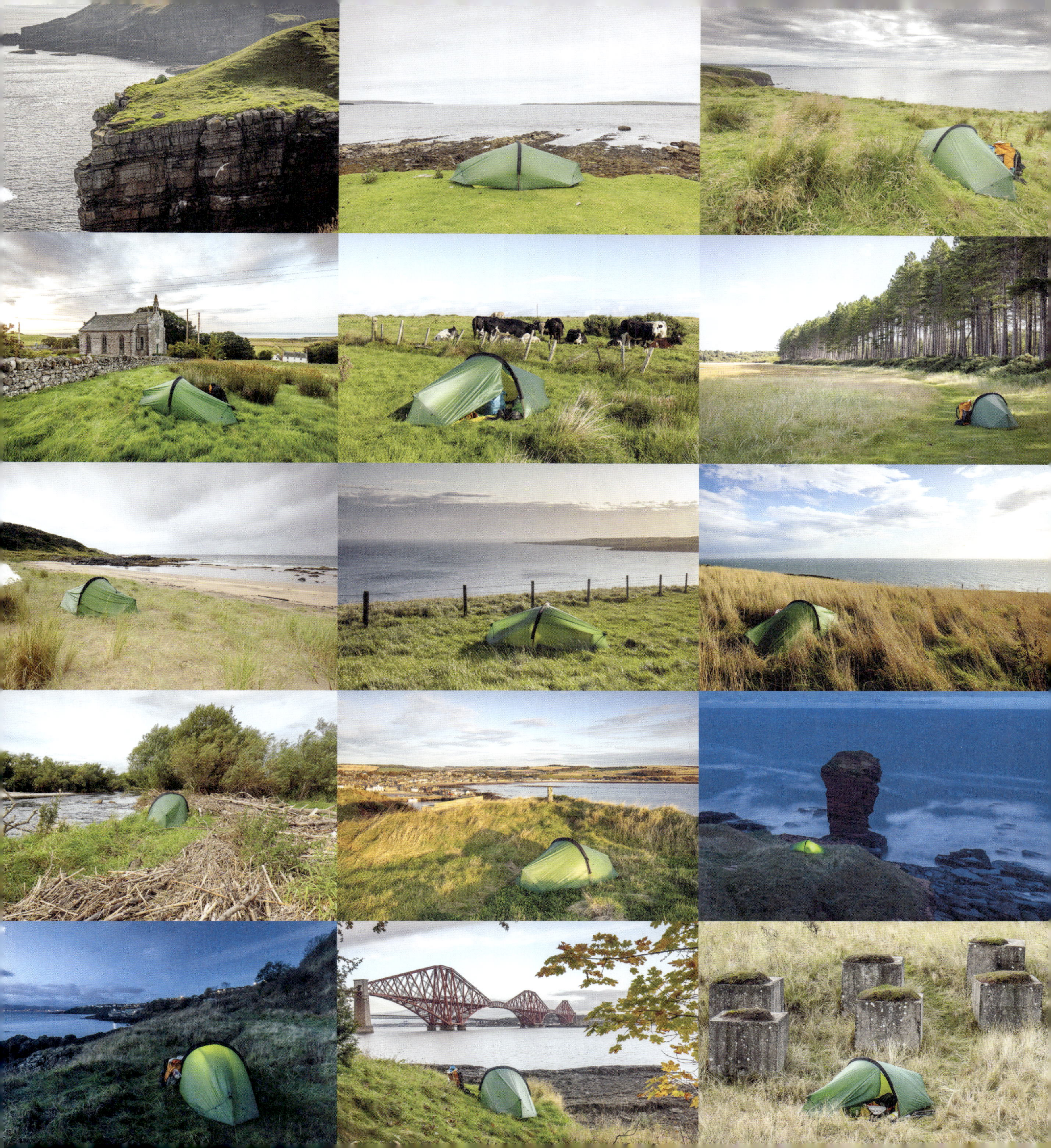

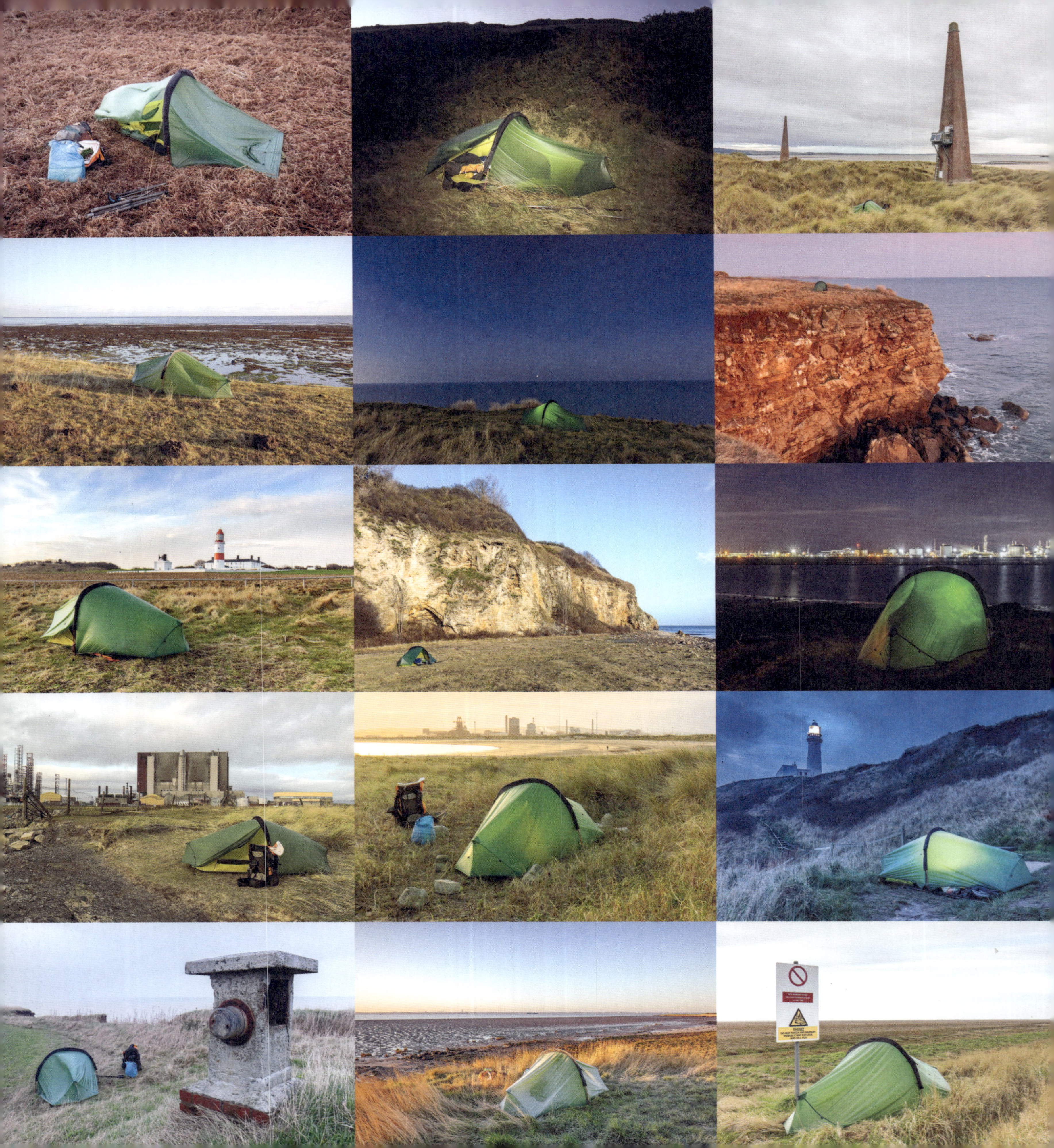